Mechanical Engineering

Rasheed Ahmed Khan
Ali Hasan
Ravinder Kumar Anand

ATLANTIC
PUBLISHERS & DISTRIBUTORS (P) LTD

Published by

ATLANTIC

PUBLISHERS & DISTRIBUTORS (P) LTD

7/22, Ansari Road, Darya Ganj,
New Delhi-110002
Phones : +91-11-23273880, 23275880, 23280451
Fax : +91-11-23285873
Web : www.atlanticbooks.com
E-mail : info@atlanticbooks.com

Branch Office
5, Nallathambi Street, Wallajah Road,
Chennai-600002
Phones : +91-44-64611085, 32413319
E-mail : chennai@atlanticbooks.com

Printed in India at Nice Printing Press, A-33/3A, Site-IV,
Industrial Area, Sahibabad, Ghaziabad, U.P.

Preface

Mechanical Engineering is an engineering discipline that involves the application of principles of Physics for analysis, design, manufacturing, and maintenance of mechanical systems. It requires a solid understanding of key concepts including mechanics, kinematics, thermodynamics and energy. Mechanical engineers use these principles in the design and analysis of manufacturing plants, industrial equipment and machinery, aircraft, heating & cooling systems, watercraft, motor vehicles, medical devices and more.

The book is divided into three parts. Part A provides fundamental concepts relating to Mechanical Engineering and definitions of various terms related to this field. Different laws of thermodynamics, viz. Zeroth Law, First Law and Second Law have been explained in detail giving suitable examples. The applications of these laws have been illustrated with diagrams and figures. The working of the internal combustion engine including two-stroke engine and four-stroke engine has also been explained.

Part B includes two-dimensional force systems and analyses. Explanation of basic concepts of force, mass, space and laws of motion is followed by analyses of Varignon's Theorem and Force-Couple systems. A number of theoretical questions on concurrent forces in a plane have been included. Several examples have been given to explain the concept of equilibrium. Different types of supports such as knife edge, roller, pin-joint, smooth, fixed or built-in have been illustrated with examples. When a solid body slides over a stationary body, force is exerted at the surface of contact. This force is called the force of friction and it always acts in the direction opposite to the motion. Exclusive chapters on friction and belt friction have been included to study different mechanisms of friction.

A beam is a structural member resting on supports to carry transverse, lateral or vertical loads to its axis. Various types of beams such as cantilever, simple, overhanging, rigidly fixed are widely used in construction. Trusses consist exclusively of straight members connected at joints located at the ends of each member. Like trusses frames are also designed to support loads and are stationary but they always contain at least one multi-force member. The tensile and compressive stresses act on planes which are normal to the line of action of the applied external forces. A shaft is a metal bar that joins parts of a machine or an engine together, establishing power and movement to be passed from one part to another. Part C concentrates on beams, trusses, frames, stresses and shafts. Centre of gravity is a point through which the whole weight of the body acts. The centre of gravity of a plane figure, where its entire area is concentrated, is known as centroid. Locating the centre of gravity of different types of bodies is of utmost importance because it will determine the designing of whole structure. Considering this, an exclusive chapter has been devoted to the study of centre of gravity explaining centroids of plane geometrical figures like triangle, circle, trapezium, cylinder, sphere, cone, rod, etc.

A rotating body about an axis in a reference frame resists any change in its rotational motion. Due to this property, the body is said to possess a moment of inertia. Calculating the moment of inertia in standard sections is necessary to engineer different mechanical functions. Hence, it forms a separate chapter of Part C.

It is a complete textbook for the students of Mechanical Engineering pursuing B.Tech in various engineering colleges and technical universities. All key concepts have been explained in a lucid manner and illustrated with figures wherever necessary. It is rich with examples, theoretical as well as numerical questions, simple solutions and diagrams. Additional theoretical questions and numerical problems have been included at the end of each chapter for self-attempt by the students to gain proficiency. B. Tech First Semester Examination, 2006-07 Mechanical Engineering paper has been included to give the students an understanding of what to expect in the examination. Bibliography has been provided to facilitate extensive reading on the subject. The students and teachers of Mechanical Engineering will find this book immensely useful.

Rasheed Ahmed Khan
Ali Hasan
Ravinder Kumar Anand

Contents

PART A

1

Fundamental Concepts and Definitions

1.1 Thermodynamics

Definition: Thermodynamics is a combination of two words—thermo and dynamics. Thermo means heat and dynamics means motion.

So thermodynamics is the science that deals with heat and work and the properties related to them. The science has 3"Es" namely energy, entropy and equilibrium. It is based on some basic laws known as zeroth, first, second and third law of thermodynamics. Thermodynamics is based on experimental results and observations of experience and there is no mathematical proof of these laws.

1.2 System, Surrounding and Universe

System: A thermodynamic system is a quantity of matter or a control volume upon which attention is focused.

Surrounding: Everything external to the system is called surrounding.

Universe: The combination of system and surrounding represents the universe.

1.3 Types of Thermodynamic Systems

Based on interaction of mass and energy, thermodynamic system may be divided into **three** categories.

a. *Open System:* The system which exchanges both mass and energy with the surrounding is called open system. Fig. 1.1 shows an open system.

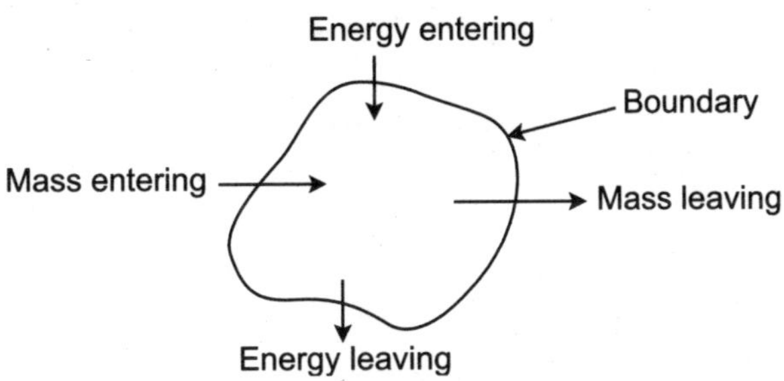

Fig. 1.1: Open System

Examples of Open System:

i. Boiler or Steam Generator: Boiler converts water into steam. Both mass and energy interaction takes place in this process.

ii. Car Engine: The engine draws the mixture of air and petrol and exhausts the spent-up gases to the atmosphere. Thus, both energy and mass interaction takes place.

b. *Closed System:* A closed system exchanges energy with the surrounding and there is no exchange of mass. Fig. 1.2 shows a closed system.

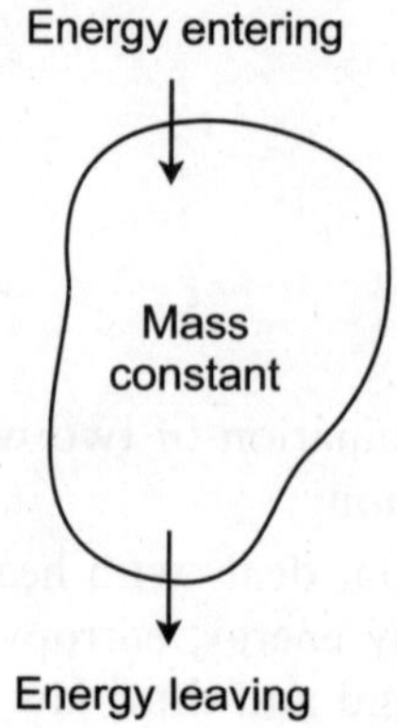

Fig. 1.2: Closed System

Examples of Closed System:

i. Battery in Motor Car: There is no exchange of mass in the battery. But energy is stored in the form of electricity and is supplied when required.

ii. Refrigerator: It converts electrical energy to cooling effect. But there is no exchange of mass.

iii. Bomb Calorimeter: A spark is caused by electrical energy. There is heat interaction across the boundary after combustion, but there is no mass transfer.

c. *Isolated System:* In isolated system neither mass nor energy exchange takes place between system and surrounding. Fig. 1.3 shows an isolated system.

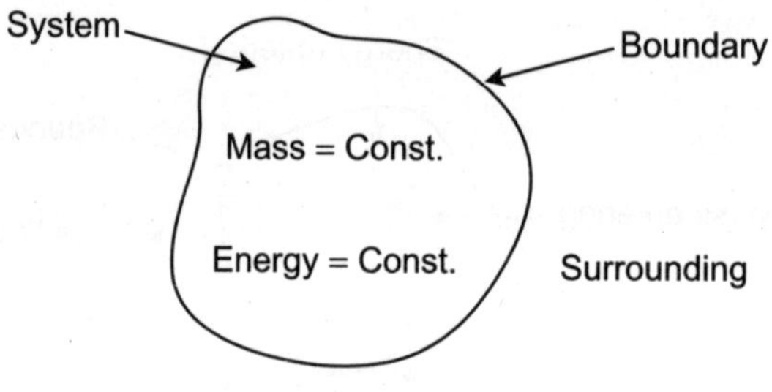

Fig. 1.3: Isolated System

Examples of Isolated System:

The fluid enclosed in perfectly insulated and perfectly closed vessels (such as flask) is the example of isolated system.

Based on phase, a system may be divided as:

a. Homogeneous System: Phase is a quantity of matter that is uniform in physical structure and chemical composition. So a homogeneous system has a single phase, i.e. solid, liquid or gas.

b. Heterogeneous System: It is a multiphase system e.g. mixture of ice and water, water and mercury, wet steam, etc.

1.4 Concept of Continuum

Matter consists of a large number of molecules which are in a state of random motion. They have intermolecular forces of attraction and repulsion. They are separated by a distance of the order of their mean free path.

So from a microscopic point of view, the matter is neither continuous nor homogeneous. However, these molecules have a large number. For example, 1 cm^3 of a gas contains 2.69×10^{11} molecules at S.T.P. At macroscopic level, because of such a large number of molecules in a small volume, the matter appears to be continuous. This is called concept of continuum.

This concept is only a convenient assumption, which loses its validity when the mean free path of the molecules approaches the order of magnitude of the dimensions of the vessel.

Let δV = Small volume of the system

δm = The corresponding mass

$\delta V'$ = The smallest volume for which the mass can be considered as continuous.

$$\text{Specific volume, } v = \lim_{\delta \to \delta V'} \frac{\delta V}{\delta m}$$

So, volumes smaller than this will lead to the recognition that mass is not evenly distributed in space. This is shown in Fig. 1.4, where for the limit of a zero volume the specific volume may be infinite (the volume does not contain any mass) or very small (the volume is part of a nucleus).

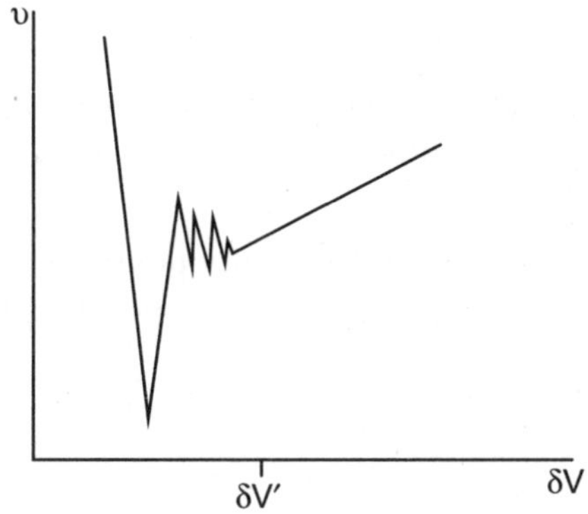

Fig. 1.4: The Continuum Limit for Specific Volume

1.5 Macroscopic and Microscopic Point of View

Thermodynamics has following two approaches:

1. Macroscopic approach (macro means big or total)
2. Microscopic approach (micro means small)

The difference between the two approaches is as follows:

Macroscopic Approach	*Microscopic Approach*
A certain quantity of matter is focused upon without taking into account the events occurring at molecular level.	The approach considers that system is made up of a very large number of discrete particles known as molecules.
The approach is concerned with gross or overall behaviour. This is known as classical approach of thermodynamics.	This approach is directly concerned with the structure of matter and is known as statistical approach.
The values of the properties of the system are their average values. These values can be easily measured. For example, temp., pressure, etc.	The properties which describe the molecule cannot be easily measured.
It needs only a few properties to describe the system.	Large number of variables are needed to describe the system. So the approach becomes complicated.

1.6 Density

Density is defined as mass per unit volume and it is a measure of working substance contained in a given volume.

$$\rho = \frac{m}{V} \qquad \ldots (1.1)$$

where, m = Mass of the substance
V = Volume of the substance

The units of density are kg/m^3 or Ns/m^4.

The relation is valid only when the substance fills the given volume without any blank space, i.e. the fluid is a continuum. For a non-homogeneous fluid, these relations give average specific weight and density.

To determine the absolute value of w and ρ at any point, the volume is regarded as tending to zero and the limit of corresponding ratio is calculated. So absolute values are

$$w = \underset{V \to 0}{\text{Lt}} \frac{w}{V} = \frac{dW}{dV} \qquad \ldots (1.2)$$

$$\rho = \underset{V \to 0}{\text{Lt}} \frac{m}{V} = \frac{dm}{dV} \qquad \ldots (1.3)$$

1.7 Specific Volume

Specific volume of a substance is defined as the volume per unit mass and is given by the symbol υ. It is an intensive property. The specific volume of a system in a given gravitational field may vary from point to point. For example, if we consider atmosphere as a system, its specific volume increases with increase in elevation. So the specific volume is defined at a point in a system.

It is given by the relation

$$\upsilon = \lim_{\delta V \to \delta V'} \frac{\delta V}{\delta m} \qquad \text{(1.4)}$$

where $\delta V'$ is the smallest volume for which the mass can be considered a continuum. δV is the small volume in a system having a mass of δm.

Example 1.1

A fan delivers 3 m^3 of air having a mass equal to 3.75 kg. Calculate (i) Specifi weight (ii) Density and (iii) Specific volume of the air being delivered.

Solution:

$$\text{Volume, } V = 3 \text{ m}^3$$

$$\text{Mass, } m = 3.75 \text{ kg}$$

i. $$\text{Specific wt} = \frac{\text{Weight}}{\text{Volume}} \text{ N/m}^3$$

$$= \frac{\text{Mass} \times \text{Acc}^n \text{ due to gravity}}{\text{Volume}} \text{ N/m}^3$$

$$= \frac{3.75 \times 9.81}{3} \text{ N/m}^3$$

$$= \mathbf{12.26} \text{ N/m}^3$$ **Ans.**

ii. $$\text{Density, } \rho = \frac{\text{Mass (m)}}{\text{Volume (V)}} \text{ kg/m}^3$$

$$= \frac{3.75}{3} \text{ kg/m}^3$$

$$= \mathbf{1.25 \text{ kg/m}^3}$$ **Ans.**

iii. $$\text{Specific volume, } \upsilon = \frac{\text{Volume (V)}}{\text{Mass (m)}} \text{ m}^3\text{/kg}$$

$$= \frac{3}{3.75} \text{ m}^3\text{/kg}$$

$$= \mathbf{0.8 \text{ m}^3\text{/kg}}$$ **Ans.**

1.8 Pressure

Pressure is defined as force per unit area. Pressure is exerted by liquids, vapours and gases. The instruments used for pressure measurement, generally indicate pressure as the difference between two pressures. Such devices show the pressure either above or below that of atmospheric pressure. When it is above the atmospheric pressure, it is termed as positive pressure or gauge pressure. When it is below the atmospheric pressure, then it is called negative or vacuum pressure. Mathematically,

i. Absolute Pressure = Atmospheric Pressure + Gauge Pressure

$$P_{abs} = P_{atm} + P_{gauge}$$

ii. Vacuum Pressure = Atmospheric Pressure – Absolute Pressure

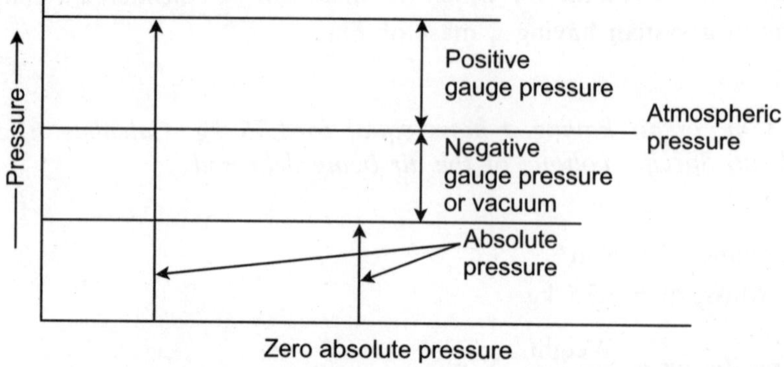

Fig. 1.5: Positive, Negative and Absolute Pressures

Units:

1 Pascal (Pa) = 1 N/m^2
1 kPa = 10^3 Pa
1 MPa = 10^6 Pa
1 bar = 10^5 N/m^2 = 10^5 Pa
1 atm = 1.01235 bar = 101325 Pa
= 760 mm of Hg
= 760 Torr

Types of Pressure Measuring Instruments: These may be classified as:

1. Manometer gauges:
   i. U-tube manometer
   ii. Cistern manometer
   iii. Micromanometer etc.
2. Pressure gauges:
   i. Bourdon tube pressure gauge
   ii. Diaphragm gauge
   iii. Vacuum gauge

Example 1.2

Manometer measures the pressure of a tank as 250 cm of mercury. For the density of mercury 13.6×10^3 kg/m³ and atmospheric pressure 101 KPa, calculate the tank pressure in MPa.

(UPTU IInd Sem. Exam., 2000-2001)

Solution:

Height of mercury, h = 250 cm = 2.5 m

Density, $\rho = 13.6 \times 10^3$ kg/m³

Acc^n due to gravity, g = 9.81 m/s²

$$
\begin{aligned}
\text{Gauge pressure, } P_{gauge} &= h\rho g \\
&= 2.5 \times 13.6 \times 10^3 \times 9.81 \ \text{N/m}^2 \\
&= 0.333 \times 10^6 \ \text{N/m}^2 \\
&= 0.333 \text{ MPa} \\
\text{Atmospheric pressure} &= 101 \text{ kPa} \\
&= 0.101 \text{ MPa} \\
\text{Absolute pressure} &= \text{Atmospheric pressure + gauge pressure} \\
&= 0.101 + 0.333 \\
&= \mathbf{0.434\ MPa}
\end{aligned}
$$

Ans.

Example 1.3

Convert the following readings of pressure to KPa assuming that the barometer reads 760 mm Hg.

a. 90 cm Hg gauge

b. 40 cm Hg vacuum

c. 1.2 m H_2O gauge

(U.P. Technical Sample Question Bank)

Solution:

a. 90 cm Hg gauge

$$
\begin{aligned}
P_{gauge} &= \rho g h \\
&= 13.6 \times 10^3 \times 9.81 \times 90/100 \\
&= 120 \times 10^3 \ \text{N/m}^2 \\
&= 120 \text{ kPa} \\
P_{atm} &= 76 \text{ cm of Hg} \\
&= \frac{76}{100} \times 13.6 \times 10^3 \times 9.81 \\
&= 101.39 \text{ kPa} \\
P_{abs} &= P_{gauge} + P_{atm} \\
&= 120 + 101.39 \\
&= \mathbf{221.39\ kPa}
\end{aligned}
$$

Ans.

b.
$$P_{gauge} = 40 \text{ cm Hg vacuum} = -40 \text{ cm vacuum gauge}$$
$$P_{atm} = 760 \text{ mm Hg} = 76 \text{ cm Hg}$$
$$P_{abs} = P_{gauge} + P_{atm}$$
$$= (-40 + 76) \text{ cm Hg}$$
$$= 36 \text{ cm Hg}$$
$$= \frac{36}{100} \times 13.6 \times 10^3 \times 9.81 \text{ N/m}^2$$
$$= 48.03 \times 10^3 \text{ N/m}^2$$
$$= \mathbf{48.03 \text{ kPa}}$$ **Ans.**

c. 1.2 m H_2O gauge
$$P_{gauge} = \rho gh$$
$$= 1000 \times 9.81 \times 1.2 \text{ N/m}^2$$
$$= 11.772 \times 10^3 \text{ N/m}^2$$
$$= 11.772 \text{ KPa}$$
$$P_{atm} = 101.39 \text{ KPa}$$
$$P_{abs} = P_{gauge} + P_{atm}$$
$$= 11.772 + 101.39$$
$$= \mathbf{113.162 \text{ kPa}}$$ **Ans.**

Example 1.4

Calculate the height of water equivalent to atmospheric pressure of 1 bar if the water is at 15°C. What is the height if water is replaced by mercury?

Solution:

$$\text{Pressure, } P = 1 \text{ bar} = 1 \times 10^5 \text{ N/m}^2$$
$$\text{Now } P = \rho gh$$
$$= 1000 \times 9.81 \times h$$
$$\therefore h = \frac{1 \times 10^5}{1000 \times 9.81} = \mathbf{0.749 \text{ m}}$$ **Ans.**

Example 1.5

The gas used in gas engine trial was tested. The pressure of gas supply is 10 cm of water column. Find absolute pressure of the gas if the barometeric pressure is 760 mm of Hg.

(U.P. Technical Sample Question Bank)

Solution:

$$\text{Height, } h = 10 \text{ cm} = 0.1 \text{ m}$$
$$\text{Gauge pressure, } P_{gauge} = \rho gh$$

$$= 1000 \times 9.81 \times 0.1$$
$$= 981 \text{ N/m}^2$$
$$P_{atm} = \rho gh$$
$$= 13.6 \times 10^3 \times 9.81 \times 0.76$$
$$= 101.39 \times 10^3 \text{ N/m}^2$$
$$P_{abs} = P_{gauge} + P_{atm}$$
$$= 981 + 101.39 \times 10^3$$
$$= 102.37 \times 10^3 \text{ N/m}^2$$
$$= \mathbf{102.39\ kPa}$$ **Ans.**

Example 1.6

The pressure of a gas in a pipeline is measured with a mercury manometer having one limb open. The difference in the level of two limbs is 562 mm. Calculate the gas pressure (absolute) in terms of bar. **(U.P. Technical Sample Question Bank)**

Solution:

Difference in pressure, $P_1 - P_2 = \rho gh$

$$= 13.640 \times 10^3 \times 9.81 \times 0.562$$
$$= 75.2 \times 10^3 \text{ N/m}^2$$
$$= 75.2 \text{ kPa}$$

Here P_2 = Atmospheric pressure (as one limb is open)

$$= 101.3 \text{ kPa}$$
$$P_1 = 101.3 + 75.2$$
$$= 176.5 \text{ kPa}$$
$$= \mathbf{1.765\ bar}$$ **Ans.**

Example 1.7

A manometer shows a vacuum of 260 mm Hg. What will be the value of this pressure in N/m² in the form of absolute pressure and what will be absolute pressure (N/m²), if the gauge pressure is 60 mm of Hg? Explain the difference between these two pressures.

(U.P. Technical Sample Question Bank)

Solution:

Pressure, $P = \rho gh$

$$= 13.6 \times 10^3 \times 9.81 \times \frac{260}{1000} \text{ (vacuum)}$$
$$= 34.688 \times 10^3 \text{ N/m}^2 \text{ (vacuum)}$$
$$P_{gauge} = -34.688 \times 10^3 \text{ N/m}^2$$

Absolute pressure $= \text{Atmospheric pressure} + \text{Gauge pressure}$

$$= 101.3 \times 10^3 - 34.688 \times 10^3$$

$$= \mathbf{66.61 \times 10^3 \;\; N/m^2} \qquad \textbf{Ans.}$$

Now given that

$$\text{Gauge pressure, } P_g = 260 \text{ mm Hg}$$

$$P_{atm} = 760 \text{ mm Hg}$$

$$P_{abs} = (260 + 760) \text{ mm Hg}$$

$$= 1020 \text{ mm Hg}$$

$$= \frac{1020}{1000} \times 13.6 \times 10^3 \times 9.81 \;\; N/m^2$$

$$= 135.988 \times 10^3 \;\; N/m^2$$

$$= \mathbf{135.988 \; kPa} \qquad \textbf{Ans.}$$

Example 1.8

A vacuum gauge fitted to a steam condenser indicates 700 mm of mercury when the barometer records 760 mm of mercury. Calculate the absolute pressure in the condenser in kg_f/cm^2, bar and kPa. **(U.P. Technical Sample Question Bank)**

Solution:

$$P_{vacuum} = \rho g h$$

$$= 13.6 \times 10^3 \times 9.81 \times \frac{700}{1000} \;\; N/m^2$$

$$= 93.39 \times 10^3 \;\; N/m^2$$

$$P_{gauge} = -93.39 \times 10^3 \;\; N/m^2$$

$$P_{atm} = 13.6 \times 10^3 \times 9.81 \times \frac{760}{1000} \;\; N/m^2$$

$$= 101.3 \times 10^3 \; N/m^2$$

$$P_{abs} = P_{atm} + P_{gauge}$$

$$= 101.3 \times 10^3 - 93.39 \times 10^3$$

$$= 7.91 \times 10^3 \;\; N/m^2$$

$$= \mathbf{7.91 \; kPa} \qquad \textbf{Ans.} \qquad [1 \text{ Pa} = 10^3 \;\; N/m^2]$$

$$= \frac{7.91 \times 10^3}{1 \times 10^5} \text{ bar} \qquad [1 \text{ bar} = 10^5 \;\; N/m^2]$$

$$= \mathbf{0.079 \; bar} \qquad \textbf{Ans.}$$

$$= \frac{7.91 \times 10^3}{9.81 \times 100 \times 100} \; kg_f/cm^2 \;\; \left[\text{As } 1N = 9.81 \; kg_f \text{ and } 1m^2 = 100 \times 100 \text{ cm}^2\right]$$

$$= \mathbf{8.053 \times 10^{-6} \; kg_f/cm^2} \qquad \textbf{Ans.}$$

1.9 Thermodynamic Equilibrium

A system is in thermodynamic equilibrium if the temperature and pressure at all points are same; there should be no velocity gradient; the chemical equilibrium is also necessary. For thermodynamic equilibrium, following three types of equilibrium states must be achieved:

i. *Mechanical Equilibrium*: There are no unbalanced forces within the system or between the surroundings. The pressure in the system is same at all points and does not change with time.

ii. *Chemical Equilibrium*: This is identified by equality of chemical potential. There is no chemical reaction in the system and chemical composition is same throughout the system and does not change with time.

iii. *Thermal Equilibrium (Equality of Temperature)*: The temperatures of the system does not change with the time and has same value at all points of the system.

If a system is in mechanical and thermal equilibrium but not in chemical equilibrium, then it is called in metastable equilibrium.

1.10 Property

A property of a system is the characteristic of the system which depends upon its state but not how the state has been reached. There are two types of properties:

1. Intensive Properties: These properties do not depend upon mass of the system. For example, temperature, pressure.
2. Extensive Properties: These properties depend on the mass of the system. For example, volume, energy, enthalpy and entropy.

1.10.1 Feature of a Property

i. Property can be measured. It describes a system, and helps to distinguish one system from another.

ii. It has a definite unique value when the system is in a particular state.

iii. It is dependent only on the state of the system; it does not depend on the path or route the system follows.

iv. Its differential is exact.

Since a thermodynamic property is a function of state of system, it is referred to as a point function or a state function.

1.10.2 Check for a Property

A given expression dp = Mdx + Ndy would be a thermodynamic property if its differential is exact, i.e. if

$$\left[\frac{\partial M}{\partial y}\right]_x = \left[\frac{\partial N}{\partial x}\right]_y \qquad (1.5)$$

Example 1.9

Discuss whether the following quantities represent the system properties or not.

(i) pdv *(ii) vdp* *(iii) pdv + vdp*

Solution:

We will have to check whether these functions are exactly differentiable or not.

i. pdv: p is a function of v. The integration $\int pdv$ can be determined only if relationship between p and v is known. Thus, pdv is not exect differential and hence not a property.

ii. vdp: As in case of pdv, vdp is also not an exact differential and hence not a property.

iii. pdv + vdp = d(pv). Its integration is pv. So it is exact differential and hence a property.

1.11 State

Definition: State is the condition of the system at an instant of time as described or measured by its properties.

OR

Each unique condition of a system is called a state. Properties have unique values at each state.

1.12 Path

Any operation in which one or more properties of the system change, is called change of state. The succession of states passed through during a change of state is called the path.

1.13 Process

When the path is completely specified, the change of state is called a process e.g. a constant pressure process. One very well known process in thermodynamics is quasi-static process.

1.13.1 Quasi-static Process

Consider a system of a gas contained in a cylinder. The gas is compressed by a piston which has small weights placed on it.

The upward force exerted by the gas just balances the weights on the piston. Let initial position (state) of the system be p_1, v_1, T_1. Now these weights are removed slowly so that unbalanced potential is infinitesimally small. The piston moves slowly upward and system can be considered close to state of equilibrium. Every state passed by the system will be an equilibrium state. The locus of series of such states is known as quasi-static process. Fig. 1.6 shows a quasi-static process.

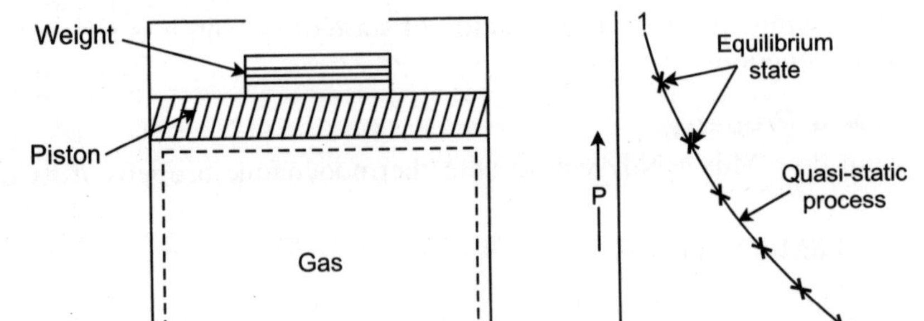

Fig. 1.6: Quasi-static Process

1.14 Reversible and Irreversible Process

1.14.1 Reversible Process

A process is said to be reversible if the system passes through a continuous series of equilibrium states. This is shown by a line drawn through the points representing the equilibrium states. Fig. 1.7 shows a reversible process 1–2. If the process is reversed, path 2–1 will be followed and system will gain its initial state.

Conditions for a process to be reversible:

i. There should be no friction.

ii. Heat exchange between the system and surrounding should be through infinitely small temperature differences.

iii. The process speed should be infinitely slow, i.e. process should be quasi-static.

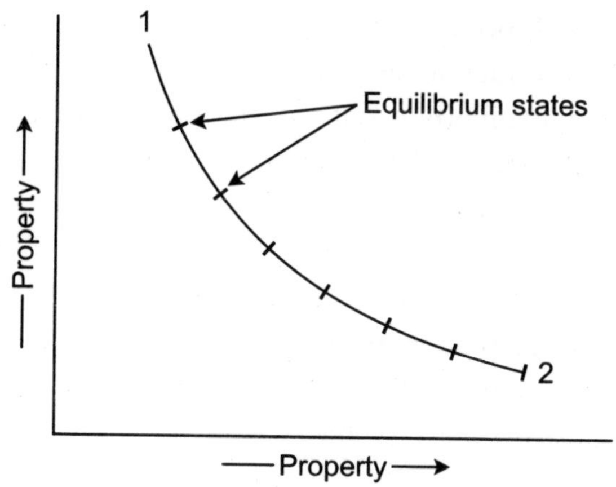

Fig. 1.7: Quasi-static and Reversible Process

Examples: Although no process is perfectly reversible, yet we can consider some processes to be nearly reversible.

i. Isothermal and frictionless adiabatic process.

ii. Elastic loading of a solid.

iii. Controlled expansion or compression.

iv. Electric circuit with zero resistance.

v. Restrained discharge of a battery.

1.14.2 Irreversible Process

The process is called to be irreversible if the system passes through a series of non-equilibrium states. When the process performed in the reverse direction, the original state of the system cannot be reached. Fig. 1.8 shows an irreversible process.

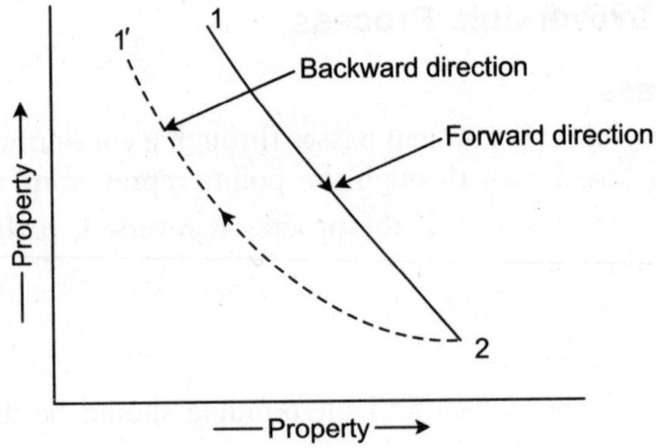

Fig. 1.8: Irreversible Process

Characteristics of Irreversible Process:

i. It cannot be reversed without some permanent changes in the surrounding.
ii. The system is never in equilibrium state at any point during the process.
iii. It can be performed in single direction only.
iv. The rate is not infinitely slow.

Examples: All natural processes are irreversible. Some are:

i. Free expansion and throttling process.
ii. Heat energy transfer with finite temperature differences.
iii. Electric circuit with resistance, inductance or capacitances.
iv. Inelastic or plastic deformation of solids.

1.15 Cyclic Process

When a system undergoes through a series of processes such that the final state is same as the initial state, the process is called cyclic process. The change in the value of property for a cyclic process is zero. Mathematically,

$\oint dP = 0$, where P is a property and symbol $\oint$ represents a cyclic integral.

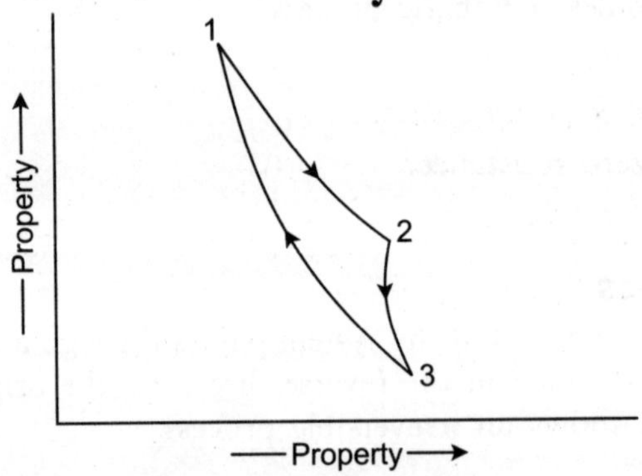

Fig. 1.9: Cyclic Process

1.16 Energy and Its Forms

Energy is defined as capacity to do work or capacity to produce a change from existing conditions. Units of energy are Joule, Kilo Joule, etc. The energy may be:

i. *Stored energy*: Energy contained within the system boundaries. Example are kinetic energy, internal energy, potential energy.

ii. *Energy in transit*: The energy which crosses the system boundaries is called energy in transit. For example, heat energy, electrical energy, mechanical energy.

Heat energy is expressed in Calori, Kilocalori.

Electrical energy is expressed in watt hr, Kilowatt-hour (kWh). 1 kWh = 3.6×10^6 J

Two common types of energy are:

a. *Kinetic Energy:* The energy due to motion is called Kinetic Energy.

Let m = Mass of system

dx = Distance moved by the system in the direction of applied force.

$$\text{Acceleration} = \frac{dV}{dt}$$

where dV is change in vel. in time dt.

$$\therefore \text{ Elementary work done} = \left(m\frac{dV}{dt}\right)dx$$

$$= mV\,dV \qquad \left[\because V = \frac{dx}{dt}\right]$$

$$\text{Total K.E. in the body} = \int_0^V mV\,dV$$

$$= m\frac{V^2}{2} \qquad \ldots\ldots\ldots (1.6)$$

Let intial vel. = 0

and final vel. = V

b. *Potential Energy*: It is the energy possessed by a system due to its position or elevation.

Let m = Mass of the system in kg

g = Acceleration due to gravity

h = Distance of the system above the ground

Then P.E. = mgh Joule .... (1.7)

if g = 9.81 m/s^2 and h is in meter.

Example 1.10

A system has a mass of 4 kg and it is moving at velocity of 50 m/s and height 100 m above the sea level. Determine its potential energy and kinetic energy relative to the earth.

Soluion:

$$\text{Mass, } m = 4 \text{ kg}$$
$$\text{Velocity, } V = 50 \text{ m/s}$$
$$\text{Height, } h = 100 \text{ m}$$

$$\text{i. Potential Energy, P.E.} = mgh = 4 \times 9.81 \times 100 \text{ J} = 39.24 \times 10^2 \text{ J} = 3.924 \times 10^3 \text{ J} = \mathbf{3.924 \text{ kJ}}$$

Ans.

$$\text{ii. Kinetic Energy, K.E.} = \frac{1}{2} mV^2 = \frac{1}{2} \times 4 \times (50)^2 = 5000 \text{ J} = 5 \text{ kJ}$$

Ans.

1.17 Work and Heat

1.17.1 Work

Work is defined as a force, F, acting through a displacement x, the displacement being in the direction of the force.

$$W = \int_1^2 F\,dx$$

here 1 and 2 represent initial and final states.

Thermodynamic definition of work—Work is done by a system if the sole effect on the surrounding (everything external to the system) is equivalent to the raising of a weight. Work done by a system is considered to be positive and work done on a system is considered to be negative. Work is denoted by a symbol W.

Units of work are Joule, Kilo Joule, etc. It is an inexact differential, so is written as W_{1-2}.

1.17.2 Heat

Heat is defined as the form of energy that is transferred across the boundary of the system at a given temperature to another system (or the surrounding) at a lower temperature by virtue of temperature difference between the two systems. That is, heat is transferred from the system at higher temperature to the system at the lower temperature and it occurs solely because of temperature differences between the two systems. Heat is an inexact differential and therefore any integration of the elemental quantity of heat which appears during a change from state 1 to state 2 must be written as

$$\int_1^2 \delta Q = Q_{1-2}$$

1.17.3 Comparison of Work and Heat

a. *Similarities*:
   i. Both are path functions and inexact differentials.
   ii. Both are boundary phenomenon, *i.e.* both are recognised at the boundaries of the system as they cross them.
   iii. Both are associated with a process, not a state. Unlike properties, work or heat has no meaning at a state.
   iv. Systems possess energy, but not work or heat.

b. *Differences*:
   i. In heat transfer, temperature difference is required which is not necessary during work done.
   ii. In a stable system there cannot be work transfer, however, there is no restriction for the transfer of heat.
   iii. In work transfer, the sole effect external to the system could be reduced to rise of a weight but in case of a heat transfer other effects are also observed.

1.18 Displacement Work: pdV

Consider a system formed by a gas contained in a piston cylinder arrangement. Let the piston moves outward through a small distance dx $(dx \to 0)$ during a small interval dt. Since piston moves through a small distance, the pressure p acting on the piston can be assumed to be constant. The infinitesimal work done by the system is

$$\begin{aligned} \delta W &= \text{Force} \times \text{Distance} \\ &= \text{Pressure} \times \text{Area} \times \text{Distance} \\ &= p\, Adx \\ &= pdV \qquad (1.8) \end{aligned}$$

here Adx represents infinitesimal volume dV swept by the piston.

The expansion of the gas can be represented on p–V diagram by 1–2. The shaded area represents the work done due to small movement of the piston. Total work done by the gas is

$$W = \int_1^2 pdV$$

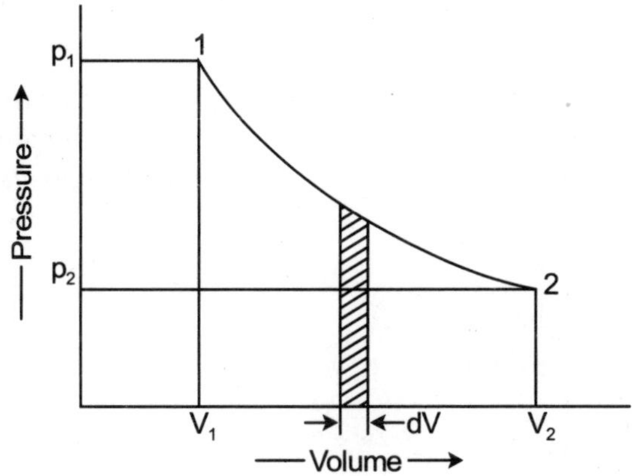

Fig. 1.10: Quasi-static pdV Work

The relation is valid only for quasi-static process.

For a non quasi-static process

$$W \neq \int pdV \quad \ldots\ldots (1.9)$$

Unstrained (free) expansion and paddle work are examples of the case of $W \neq pdV$.

1.19 Specific Heat and Heat Capacity

The heat received or rejected by a system during heating or cooling process in kJ is given by

$$Q = mc(t_2 - t_1) \quad \ldots\ldots (1.10)$$

where m = Mass of the substance (kg)

$t_2 - t_1$ = Difference in the temperature (°C or K)

c = Specific heat of the substance (kJ/kg K)

The specific heat may be defined as the quantity of heat transferred through a unit mass of the substance when there is a temperature difference of 1°C or 1 K.

The product ($m \times c$) is called heat capacity or water equivalent of the system.

The value of specific heat depends upon:

i. substance comprising the system.

ii. condition under which the change of state occurs.

iii. state of the system at the time of heat interaction.

The specific heat of liquids and solids varies with temperature. The specific heat for gases is expressed as at constant pressure (c_P) and at constant volume (c_V).

For air: c_P = 1.005 kJ/kg–deg

c_V = 0.718 kJ/kg–deg

The ratio c_p/c_V is called adiabatic constant (γ).

For air $\gamma = 1.4$.

The difference of c_P and c_V is equal to gas constant (R).

$$c_P - c_V = R$$

Example 1.11

A gas system having a piston cylinder arrangement, undergoes a change of state such that the product of pressure and volume remains constant. If the process begins at a pressure 300 kPa and a volume 0.015 m³ and proceeds until the pressure falls to half its initial value, determine the amount of work transfer.

Solution:

The path followed is such that

$$pV = \text{constant } C = p_1V_1 = p_2V_2$$

$$\text{or } p = \frac{C}{V}$$

$$\text{Work done } W_{1-2} = \int pdV$$

$$= \int_{V_1}^{V_2} p dV$$

$$= \frac{C}{V}\int_{V_1}^{V_2} dV$$

$$= C \log_e \frac{V_2}{V_1}$$

$$= p_1V_1 \log_e \frac{V_2}{V_1} = p_1V_1 \log_e \frac{p_1}{p_2}$$

$$= 300 \times 10^3 \times 0.015 \log_e (2) \text{ J}$$

$$= \mathbf{3119.16\ J}$$ **Ans.**

Example 1.12

Determine the work done by the air which enters into an evacuated vessel from atmosphere when the valve is opened. The atmosphere pressure is 1.013 bar and 1.0 m^3 of air at atmospheric condition enters into the vessel.

Solution:

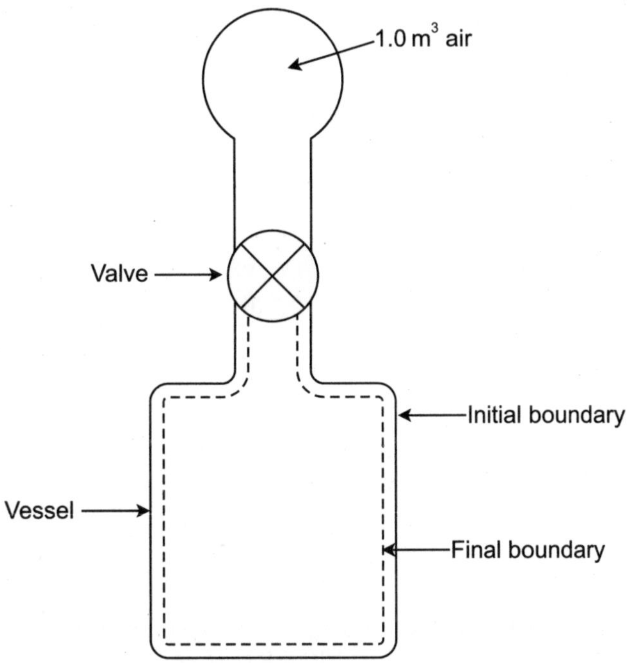

Fig. 1.11

Fig. 1.11 shows the initial and final conditions of the system. No work is done by the boundary in contact with the vessel as the boundary does not move. Work done by the external boundary at constant pressure

$$W = \int_{V_1}^{V_2} pdV = \int_{1.0}^{0} pdV$$
$$= p\ (0 - 1.0) = 1.013 \times 10^5\ (-1.0)$$
$$= -1.013 \times 10^5\ J$$
$$= \mathbf{-101.3\ kJ}$$

Ans.

Example 1.13

A gas having a volume of 0.05 m³ and pressure of 6.9 bar expands reversibly in a cylinder behind a piston according to law $pV^{1.2}$ = const. until the volume is 0.08 m³. Calculate the work done on the fluid.

Solution:

The relation between p and V is given by

$$pV^{1.2} = C = p_1V_1^{1.2} = p_2V_2^{1.2}$$

Work done
$$W = \int_{V_1}^{V_2} pdV$$
$$= \int_{V_1}^{V_2} C/V^{1.2}\ dV$$
$$= C\int_{V_1}^{V_2} V^{-1.2}\ dV$$
$$= C\left[\frac{V^{-1.2+1}}{-1.2+1}\right]_{0.05}^{0.08}$$
$$= p_1V_1^{1.2}\left[\frac{(0.08)^{-0.2} - (0.05)^{-0.2}}{-0.2}\right]$$
$$= 6.9 \times 10^5 \times (0.05)^{1.2} \times 0.8166$$
$$= 154.74\ \text{Joule}$$
$$= \mathbf{15.474\ kJ}$$

Ans.

Example 1.14

A gas contained in a piston cylinder arrangement expands from 0.75 m³ volume to 1.25 m³ whilst the pressure remains constant at 200 kPa. If the gaseous system receives 80 kJ work from a paddle wheel, determine the net work done by the system.

Solution:

Initial volume, $V_1 = 0.75\ m^3$

Final volume, $V_2 = 1.25\ m^3$

Pressure, $p = 200$ kPa

$= 200 \times 10^3$ N/m^2

Work done $= \int_{V_1}^{V_2} p dV = p(V_2 - V_1)$

$= 200 \times 10^3 [1.25 - 0.75]$ Joule

$= 100 \times 10^3$ J

$= 100$ kJ

Work received from paddle wheel $= 80$ kJ

Net work done by the system $= 100 - 80$

$= \mathbf{20\ kJ}$ **Ans.**

Example 1.15

The specific heat capacity of the system during a certain process is given by

$c_n = (0.4 + 0.004\ T)$ *kJ/kg °C*

If the mass of the gas is 6 kg and its temperature changes from 25°C to 125°C find:

i. Heat transferred *ii. Mean specific heat of the gas*

Solution:

Mass of the gas, $m = 6$ kg

Initial temperature, $T_1 = 25°C$

Final temperature, $T_2 = 125°C$

i. Heat transferred, $Q = \int m\, c_n\, dT$

$$= 6\int_{25}^{125} (0.4 + 0.004\ T)\, dT$$

$$= 6\left[0.4T + 0.004\frac{T^2}{2}\right]_{25}^{125}$$

$$= 6[0.4(125 - 25) + 0.002\ (125^2 - 25^2)]$$

$$= 6(40 + 30)$$

$$= \mathbf{420\ kJ}$$ **Ans.**

ii. Mean specific heat of the gas, c_n

$$= \frac{Q}{mdT}$$

$$= \frac{420}{6 \times (125 - 25)} = \mathbf{0.7\ kJ/kg\ °C}$$ **Ans.**

Example: 1.16

An ideal gas requires 1150 kJ/kg of heat to raise its temperature from 20°C to 100°C, when heated at constant pressure. When heat is supplied to the same gas at constant volume, the heat requirement is 825 kJ for the same temperature range. Determine specific heat and constant pressure, specific heat at constant volume and adiabatic component.

Solution:

i. Specific heat at constant pressure, c_P:

$$Q = mc_P\, dT$$

$$c_P = \frac{1150}{100-20} = \mathbf{14.375\ kJ/kg\ K}$$ **Ans.**

ii. Specific heat at constant volume, c_V:

$$Q = m\ c_v\ dT$$

$$c_V = \frac{825}{100-20} = 10.31\ kJ/kg\ K$$

iii. Adiabatic exponent, γ:

$$\gamma = c_P/c_V = \frac{14.375}{10.31}$$

$$= \mathbf{1.394}$$ **Ans.**

1.19 Enthalpy

It is defined as the sum of internal energy (μ) and product (pv)

$$\therefore h = \mu + pv$$

The enthalpy is a property because it is sum and product of properties.

Total enthalpy of mass m can be expressed as

$$H = U + pV \qquad \text{where } H = mh$$

For a perfect gas

$$u = c_V T$$

$$\text{and } pv = RT$$

$$\therefore h = c_V T + RT$$

$$= (c_V + R)\ T$$

$$h = c_P\, T$$

$$H = m\ c_P\, T$$

THEORETICAL QUESTIONS

1. Define thermodynamics. Explain statistical and classical approaches.
2. Explain thermodynamic system, surrounding and universe.
3. Define Closed, Open and Isolated Systems. Give one example of each.
4. Explain the term 'phase'. Differentiate between homogeneous and heterogeneous systems.
5. Discuss the concept of continuum. What is its importance in engineering thermodynamics?
6. Differentiate between macroscopic and microscopic approaches. Which approach is used in study of engineering thermodynamics?
7. Define: (i) Density (ii) Specific volume, using the concept of continuum.
8. Differentiate among absolute, gauge, atmospheric and vacuum pressure.
9. What do you understand by 'Thermodynamic Equilibrium'?
10. Define 'property'. Differentiate between extensive and intensive properties.
11. Explain the terms state, path, process and cycle.
12. Define a quasi-static process and state its characteristics.
13. What do you mean by a cyclic process?
14. Distinguish between reversible and irreversible processes.
15. Explain the different forms of energy.
16. Give thermodynamic definition of work. Discuss similarities and dissimilarities between work and heat.
17. Explain the term 'Enthalpy'.

NUMERICAL PROBLEMS

1. Convert the following readings of pressure to kPa assuming that barometer reads 760 mm of Hg.
   i. 180 cm of Hg
   ii. 4.35 m H_2O gauge
   iii. 130 cm Hg vacuum
2. An oil of specific gravity 0.8 is contained in a tube to a depth of 480 mm. Determine the gauge pressure at this depth in kN/m^2.

$$\left[\text{Hint : Specific gravity} = \frac{\text{Density of oil}}{\text{Density of water}}\right]$$

3. A vessel of cylindrical shape is 50 cm in diameter and 75 cm high. It contains 5 kg of gas. The pressure measured with manometer indicates 60 mm of Hg above atmosphere when barometer reads 760 mm of Hg.

   Determine:
   i. The absolute pressure of the gas in the vessel in bar.
   ii. Specific volume and density of the gas.

4. A U-tube manometer is connected to a gas pipe. The level of the liquid in the manometer arm open to the atmosphere is 190 mm lower than the level of liquid in the arm connected to the gas pipe. The liquid in the manometer has specific gravity of 0.8. Find the absolute pressure of the gas if the manometer reads 760 mm of Hg.

5. Estimate the mass of a piston that can be supported by a gas entrapped under the piston in a 200 mm diameter vertical cylinder when a manometer indicates a difference of 119 mm of Hg column for the gas pressure.

6. An artificial satellite of mass 800 kg is moving towards the moon. Make calculations for the kinetic and potential energies.
   i. relative to the earth when 50 km from launching and travelling at 2500 km/hr. Take earth's gravitational field equal to 7.9 m/s^2.
   ii. relative to the moon when travelling at the same speed.

7. A non-flow reversible process occurs for which pressure and volume are correlated by the expression p $(V^2 + 6/V)$, where p is in bar and V is in m^3. What amount of work will be done when volume changes from 1 m^3 to 4 m^3?

8. A spherical balloon of 1.4 m diameter contains a gas at 300 kPa and 300 K. The gas inside the balloon is heated until the pressure reaches 600 kPa. During the process of heating, the pressure of gas inside the balloon is proportional to the diameter of the balloon. Make calculations for the work done by the gas inside the balloon.

9. A fluid contained in a horizontal cylinder fitted with a frictionless leak-proof piston is continuously agitated by a stirrer passing through the cylinder cover. The diameter of the cylinder is 80 cm and the piston is held against the fluid due to atmospheric pressure equal to 100 kPa. The stirrer turns 8000 revolutions with an average torque of 1.5 Nm. If the piston slowly moves outwards by 60 cm, determine the net work transfer to the system.

10. A mild steel piece of 5 kg mass is heated to 145°C and dropped into an insulated vessel containing 30 kg of water at 30°C. Due to heat flow from the hot mild steel piece, the rise in the temperature of water is measured to be 3.5°C. Make calculations for the specific heat of mild steel.

11. 2 litres of water initially at 25°C is heated to a temperature of 80°C. What time will be required to achieve this objective if 0.5 kW electric heater is used for this purpose? There is no transfer of heat between the system and the surrounding.
    Take specific heat of water = 4.187 kJ/kg K.

2

Zeroth Law of Thermodynamics

2.1 Concept of Temperature

Temperature is defined as the degree of hotness or coldness of a body. It is the driving force causing the flow of heat. The heat always flows from a hot body to cold body. It determines whether a system is in thermal equilibrium or not. It is an intensive property.

The temperature is measured on

i. Centigrade Scale (°C)

ii. Fahrenheit Scale (°F)

iii. Kelvin Absolute Scale (K)

iv. Rankine Absolute Scale (°R)

The relations among different scales are given by the following formulae:

i. $C = 5/9\ (F - 32)$ .... (2.1)

ii. $K = C + 2.73.16$ .... (2.2)

iii. $R = F + 459.67$ .... (2.3)

2.2 Zeroth Law of Thermodynamics

When two bodies at different temperatures are brought in contact with each other, after some time their temperatures become equal and they are said to be in thermal equilibrium.

Zeroth law of thermodynamics states that "when a body 1 is in thermal equilibrium with a body 2, and also separately with a body 3, then 2 and 3 will be in thermal equilibrium with each other".

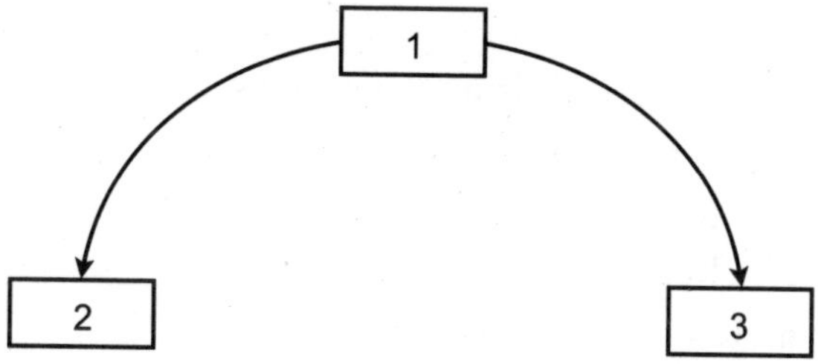

Fig. 2.1: Zeroth Law

Consider two bodies 1 and 2. Let T_1 and T_2 be their initial temperatures. When they are in thermal equilibrium, $T_1 = T_2$. Now consider two bodies 1 and 3. When they are in thermal equilibrium, then $T_1 = T_3$. So we can see $T_2 = T_3$. So body 2 is in thermal equilibrium with body 3.

Zeroth law is the basis for the measurement of a temperature of system. The thermometer acts as a third body and compares the unknown temperature of a system at a known reference temperature. This is called 'Zeroth law' because it was given after 1st law of thermodynamics. But as it was more basic in nature, so was named 'Zeroth law'.

Example 2.1

Estimate triple point of water in Fahrenheit, Rankine and Kelvin Scales.

(B. Tech. IInd Sem., July 2002)

Solution:

Triple point of water $= 0.01°C$

We know that

$$C = 5/9\ (F - 32)$$

where C = Value of temperature in °C

F = Value of temperature in °F

$$0.01 = 5/9\ (F - 32)$$

Temperature in Fahrenheit

$$F = \mathbf{32.018°F}$$ **Ans.**

Now

Temperature in Rankine

$$R = F + 459.67$$
$$= 32.018 + 459.67$$
$$= \mathbf{491.688°R}$$ **Ans.**

Temperature in Kelvin

$$K = C + 273.16$$
$$= 0.01 + 273.16$$
$$= \mathbf{273.17\ K}$$ **Ans.**

Example 2.2

At what temperature will the Kelvin Scale reading be double the Fahrenheit reading?

Solution:

Relation between Fahrenheit and Celsius is given by

$$C = 5/9\ (F - 32) \quad \text{(Eq. 1)}$$

where C = Reading in °C

and F = Reading in °F

Now reading in Kelvin, $K = C + 273.16$

$$\therefore \quad C = K - 273.16$$

Putting the value of C in Eq. 1 we get

$$K - 273 = 5/9\ (F - 32) \quad \text{.......... (Eq. 2)}$$

But we are given that Kelvin Scale reading is double the Fahrenheit reading

So $\qquad K = 2F$

We get from Eq. 2

$$2F - 273 = 5/9\ (F - 32)$$

$$2F - 273 = 5/9\ F - 160/9$$

$$\frac{13}{9}F = 255.22$$

$$F = \mathbf{176.69°F} \qquad \textbf{Ans.}$$

$$= \mathbf{353.38\ K} \qquad \textbf{Ans.}$$

Example 2.3

If the temperature of a human body is 99.2°F, determine the temperature in degree Celsius, Rankine (R) and Kelvin (K) scales.

Solution:

We know that

Temp. of Celsius, $C = 5/9\ (F - 32)$

$= 5/9\ (99.2 - 32)$

$= \mathbf{37.33°C}$ **Ans.**

Temp. in Rankine, $R = F + 459.67$

$= 99.2 + 459.67$

$= \mathbf{558.87°R}$ **Ans.**

Temp. in Kelvin, $K = C + 273.16$

$= 37.33 + 273.16$

$= \mathbf{310.49\ K}$ **Ans.**

THEORETICAL QUESTIONS

1. State the concept of temperature.
2. Define and explain the Zeroth law of thermodynamics. Why is it called 'Zeroth law'?
3. Establish a relation between Centigrade and Fahrenheit temperature scales.

NUMERICAL PROBLEMS

1. Two thermometers, one Centigrade and other Fahrenheit are immersed in a fluid. After the thermometers reach equilibrium with the fluid, it is noted that both the thermometers indicate the same numerical value. Find that identical numerical value shown by the thermometers. What would be the corresponding temperature of the fluid expressed in degrees Kelvin and degrees Rankine?
2. The temperature of a furnace is 900°C. Express this temperature on
   i. Rankine scale.
   ii. Kelvin scale.

3

First Law of Thermodynamics

3.1 First Law of Thermodynamics

It is a special case of law of conservation of energy and states that:

- Energy can neither be created nor destroyed, but it can be converted from one form to another.
- Total energy of an isolated system in all its forms remains constant.
- When a system undergoes a thermodynamic cycle then the net heat supplied to the system from the surrounding is equal to net work done by the system on its surroundings.

$$\oint dQ = \oint dW$$

where $\oint$ represents the sum for a complete cycle.

- No machine can produce work without corresponding expenditure of energy, *i.e.* it is impossible to construct a perpetual motion machine of first kind PMM1.

The first law of thermodynamics cannot be proved analytically, but experimental evidence has confirmed its validity.

Fig. 3.1 shows the experiment for checking first law of thermodynamics.

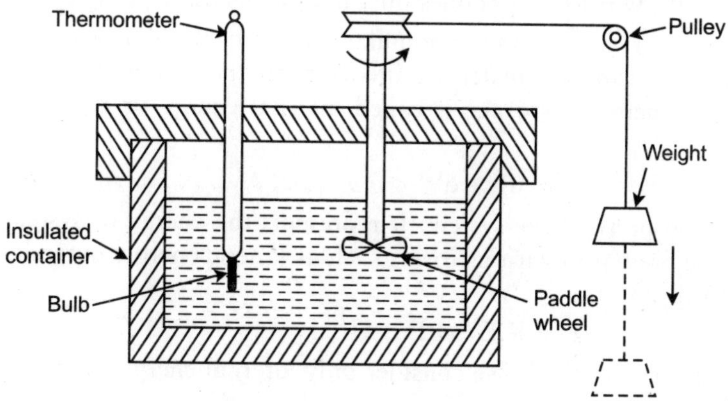

Fig. 3.1: Heat and Work

Consider a closed system which consists of a known mass of water contained in an adiabatically insulated vessel having a thermometer and a paddle wheel. The quantity of work can be measured by the fall of weight which drives the paddle wheel through a pulley. The corresponding rise in temperature is measured by the thermometer.

Let the system be returned to its initial state by transferring heat from the system, thus completing the cycle. When the amount of heat and work are compared we find that the two are always proportional.

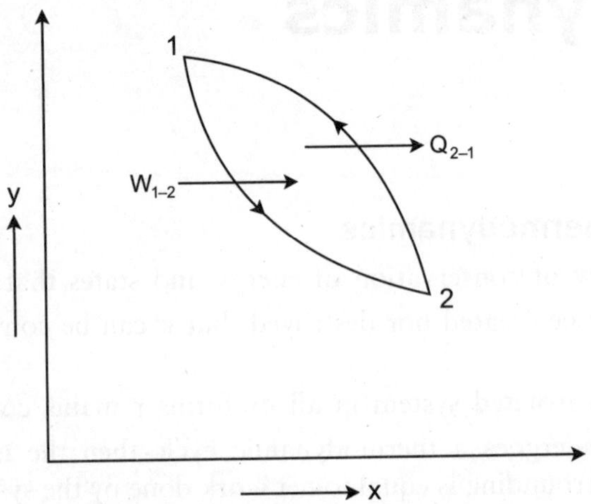

Fig. 3.2: Cycle with Adiabatic Work W_{1-2} Followed by Heat Transfer Q_{2-1}

The constant of proportionality is called the Joule's equivalent or the mechanical equivalent of heat. Thus, algebrically

$$\oint dW = J\oint dQ \qquad (3.1)$$

3.2 First Law for a Closed System Undergoing a Change of State

The expression $\oint dW = J\oint dQ$ applies only to systems undergoing cycles and the algebric sum of all energy transfers across system boundaries is zero. But if a system changes its state during which both heat and mass transfer are involved, the net energy transfer will be stored within the system. The energy in storage is called internal energy or energy of the system.

So

$$\delta Q = dE + \delta W \qquad (3.2)$$

Energy is a property of the system. It represents the energy of system in a given state. The energy might be present in various forms such as kinetic energy, potential enegy and molecular or internal energy.

$$E = K.E. + P.E. + U$$

For a closed system usually we consider only internal energy as other energies are negligible

$$\delta Q = dU + \delta W \qquad (3.3)$$

Example: 3.1

In a cyclic process, heat transfers are +34.7 kJ, –35.2 kJ, –13.56 kJ and + 31.5 kJ. What is the net work for this cyclic process?

Solution:

For a cyclic process

$$\oint dW = \oint dQ$$

$$\Sigma W = \Sigma Q$$

$$\therefore \text{Net Work} = (34.7) + (-35.2) + (-13.56) + (31.5)$$

$$= \mathbf{17.34\ kJ}$$ **Ans.**

Example: 3.2

A domestic refrigerator is loaded with food and the door closed. During a certain period the machine consumes 1/6 kWh of energy and the internal energy of the system drops by 8000 kJ. Find the net heat transferred in the system.

Solution:

Energy consumed = Net work done on the system

$$\delta W = -1/6 \text{ kWh}$$
$$= -1/6 \times 1000 \times 3600 \text{ J}$$
$$= -0.6 \times 10^6 \text{ J}$$
$$= -600 \text{ kJ}$$

Drop in internal energy $U_2 - U_1 = -8000$ kJ

According to 1st law of thermodynamics

$$\text{Heat transfer} \quad \delta Q = dU + \delta W$$
$$= U_2 - U_1 + \delta W$$
$$= -8000 - 600 = -8600 \text{ kJ}$$
$$= -8.6 \times 10^6 \text{ J}$$
$$= \mathbf{-8.6\ MJ}$$ **Ans.**

Example: 3.3

1.5 kg of liquid having a constant specific heat of 2.5 kJ/kg °C is stirred in a well insulated chamber causing temperature to rise by 15°C. Find:

i. Change in internal energy

ii. Work done for the process

Solution:

Mass, m = 3 kg

Specific heat, c = 2.5 kJ/kg °C

Temperature rise, ΔT = 15°C

Heat transferred, $\delta Q = mc\Delta T$ = Work done on the system

$= -3 \times 2.5 \times 15$

$\delta W = \mathbf{-112.5\ kJ}$ **Ans.**

As the chamber is insulated, so net heat transfer

$$\delta Q = 0$$

According to first law of thermodynamics

$$\delta Q = dU + \delta W$$

$$0 = dU + (-112.5)$$

$\therefore$ Change in internal energy $U_2 - U_1 = \mathbf{112.5\ kJ}$ **Ans.**

Example 3.4

A stationary mass of gas is compressed without friction from an initial state of 2 m^3 and 3×10^5 N/m^2 to a final state of 1 m^3 and 2×10^5 N/m^2, the pressure remaining the same. There is a transfer of 360 kJ of heat from the gas during the process. How much does the internal energy of the gas change?

Solution:

Pressure, $p = 2 \times 10^5$ N/m^2

Initial volume, $V_1 = 2$ m^3

Final volume, $V_2 = 1$ m^3

Work transfer, $\delta W = \int_{V_1}^{V_2} pdV$

$= p\ (V_2 - V_1)$

$= 3 \times 10^5\ (1 - 2)$

$= -3 \times 10^5$ J $= -300$ kJ

Heat transfer from the system

$$\delta Q = -360 \text{ kJ}$$

According to first law of thermodynamics

$$\delta Q = dU + \delta W$$

$$-360 = dU + (-300)$$

$$dU = -360 + 300$$

Change in internal energy = **–60 kJ** **Ans.**

Example 3.5

A system is composed of a stone having a mass of 10 kg and a bucket containing 100 kg of water. Initially the stone and water are at the same temperature, the stone then falls into the water. The stone is 10 m above the water level initially. Determine ΔU, ΔKE, ΔPE, ΔQ and ΔW for the following cases:

i. At the instant the stone is about to enter the water.

ii. Just after the stone comes to rest in the bucket.

Solution:

Mass of stone = 10 kg

Mass of water in the tank = 100 kg

Height of stone above water level = 10 m

Applying the 1st law of thermodynamics

$$\Delta Q = (U_2 - U_1) + m\left(\frac{C_2^2 - C_1^2}{2}\right) + mg(Z_2 - Z_1) + \Delta W$$

$$= \Delta U + \Delta KE + \Delta PE + \Delta W$$

Here Q = Heat leaving the boundary

i. When the stone is about to enter the water, $\Delta Q = 0, \Delta W = 0, \Delta U = 0$

$$\because \quad -\Delta KE = \Delta PE = mg\ (Z_2 - Z_1)$$

$$= 10 \times 9.81\ (0 - 10)$$

$$= -981 \text{ J}$$

$$\Delta KE = 981 \text{ J}$$

and $\Delta PE =$ **−981 J** **Ans.**

ii. When the stone dips into the tank and comes to rest

$\Delta Q = 0, \Delta W = 0, \Delta KE = 0$

So

$$0 = \Delta U + 0 + \Delta PE + 0$$

$$\Delta U = -\Delta PE$$

$$= -(-981) \text{ J}$$

= **981 J** **Ans.**

Example 3.6

A storage battery, having a terminal potential of 6 volts, draws a current of 4 amperes for 2 hours. If the stored energy in the battery increases by 350 kJ, evaluate the heat interaction across the boundary enveloping the storage battery.

Solution:

Work done in 2 hours= VIT

$$= \frac{6 \times 4 \times 2}{1000} \text{ kWh}$$

$$= \frac{6 \times 4 \times 2}{10\not{0}\not{0}} \times 36\not{0}\not{0}$$

$$= 172.8 \text{ kJ}$$

This is a positive work as the current flows out of the battery. Further, the battery forms a closed system and then from the non-flow energy equation

$$\delta Q = \delta W + dU$$
$$= 172.8 + (-350)$$
$$= -177.2 \text{ kJ}$$

Example 3.7

When a system is taken from state a to state c in Fig. 3.3 along path adc 175 kJ of heat flows into the system, and the system does 64 kJ of work:

i. *How much will be the heat that flows into the system along path abc if the work done is 21 kJ?*

ii. *When the system is returned from c to a along the curved path, work done on the system is 42 kJ. Does the system absorb or liberate heat and how much of heat is absorbed or liberated?*

iii. *If $U_a = 0$ and $U_b = 84$ kJ, find the heat absorbed in the process ab and bc.*

Solution:

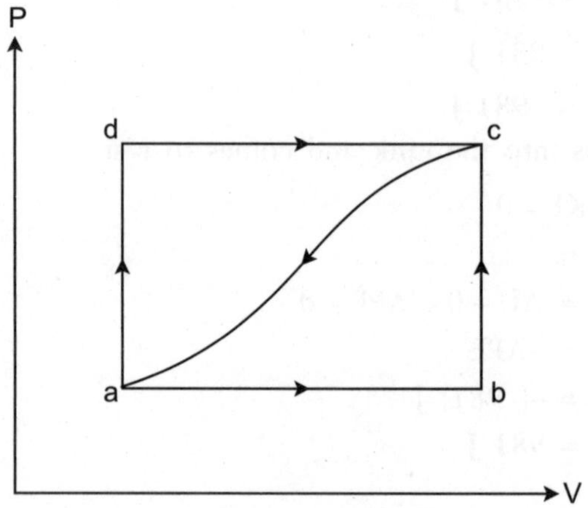

Fig. 3.3

$$Q_{a\text{-}d\text{-}c} = 175 \text{ kJ}$$
$$W_{a\text{-}d\text{-}c} = 64 \text{ kJ}$$

We have,

$$Q_{a\text{-}d\text{-}c} = (U_c - U_a) + W_{a\text{-}d\text{-}c}$$
$$175 = (U_c - U_a) + 64$$
$$U_c - U_a = \mathbf{111 \text{ kJ}}$$ **Ans.**

i.
$$Q_{a\text{-}b\text{-}c} = (U_c - U_a) + W_{a\text{-}b\text{-}c}$$
$$= 111 + 21$$
$$= \mathbf{132 \text{ kJ}}$$ **Ans.**

ii. $Q_{c-a} = (U_a - U_c) + W_{c-a}$

$= -111 + (-42) = \mathbf{-153\ kJ}$ **Ans.**

The system liberates 153 kJ

iii. $W_{a-b-c} = W_{a-b} + W_{b-c}$

$= W_{a-c} = 21$ kJ

[$\because W_{b-c} = 0$, since volume does not change.]

$\therefore$ $Q_{a-b} = (U_b - U_a) + W_{a-b}$

$= (84 - 0) + 21$

$= \mathbf{105\ kJ}$ **Ans.**

Now $Q_{a-b-c} = 132\ \text{kJ} = Q_{a-b} + Q_{b-c}$

$Q_{b-c} = 132 - Q_{a-b}$

$= 132 - 105$

$= \mathbf{27\ kJ}$ **Ans.**

Example 3.8

A system undergoes a thermodynamic cycle comprising of constant volume, constant pressure and adiabatic processes in that order. During the constant volume process 85 kJ of heat is supplied to the system. It is followed by the constant pressure process when the system rejects 90 kJ of heat and 20 kJ of work is done on it. Determine the amount of work and its direction during the adiabatic process when the system is brought to its original state.

(UPTU 1st Sem., 2003-04 Examination)

Solution:

	Process	Work done (kJ)	Heat supplied (kJ)
1.	Const. volume	0	+ 85 kJ
2.	Const. pressure	– 20 kJ	– 90 kJ
3.	Adiabatic	+x	0
	Sum (Σ)	x – 20	–5

For a cyclic process

$$\Sigma W = \Sigma Q$$

$$x - 20 = -5$$

Work done during adiabatic process

$$x = 15 \text{ kJ}$$

It is a positive quantity, therefore work is done by the system.

Example 3.9

A closed system undergoes a thermodynamic cycle consisting of four separate and distinct processes. The heat and work transferred in each process are as tabulated below:

Process	*Heat transfer (kJ/sec)*	*Work transfer (kJ/sec)*
1–2	*0*	*–4500*
2–3	*10000*	*0*
3–4	*–1000*	*10000*
4–1	*–4000*	*–500*

Show that the data is consistent with the first law of thermodynamics. Also, calculate the net work done, the thermal efficiency of the cycle and change in internal energy for each process.

Solution:

For a cyclic process

$$\Sigma Q = \Sigma W$$

$$\Sigma Q = 0 + 10000 - 1000 - 4000 = 5000 \text{ kJ/sec}$$

$$\Sigma W = -4500 + 0 + 10000 - 500 = 5000 \text{ kJ/sec}$$

Since $\Sigma Q = \Sigma W$, the data is in accordance with the first law.

Work done for the cycle = **5000 kJ/sec** **Ans.**

It is positive, so work is done by the system.

$$\text{Thermal efficiency} = \frac{\text{Work output}}{\text{Heat input}} = \frac{5000}{10000} = 0.5 \text{ or } 50\%$$

[Heat input = 10000 because only positive quantity for heat is in process 2–3]

Change in internal energy for each process is gvien by

Process	dQ	dW	dU = dQ – dW (kJ/sec)
1–2	0	– 4500	4500
2–3	10000	0	10000
3–4	– 1000	10000	– 11000
4–1	– 4000	– 500	– 3500

For a complete cycle

$$\Sigma dU = 4500 + 10000 - 11000 - 3500 = 0$$

We see that for the complete cycle, the total change in internal energy is zero. This is so because in a cyclic process, the system returns to the initial state and internal energy depends only on the state point and is independent of path.

3.3 Non-Flow Processes

The basic thermodynamic processes are:

3.3.1 Constant Volume or Isochoric Process

During this process both pressure and temperature change. The pressure and temperature increase with supply of heat.

Let p_1 and p_2 = Initial and Final Pressures

and T_1 and T_2 = Initial and Final Temperatures

Then $$\frac{p_1}{p_2} = \frac{T_1}{T_2} \quad \text{[for const. volume V]}$$

Since there is no change is volume. So mechanical work $\int pdV = 0$

Now change in internal energy

$$dU = mc_V(T_2 - T_1)$$

or $$du = c_V(T_2 - T_1)$$

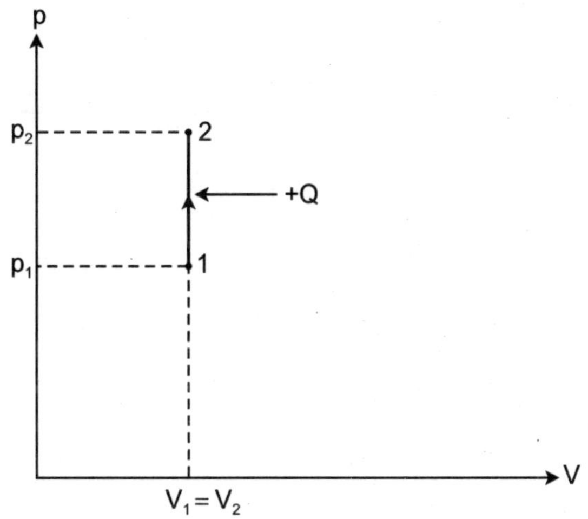

Fig. 3.4: Isochoric Process

Now $$\delta q = du + 0$$
$$= c_V(T_2 - T_1) \quad \text{(3.4)}$$

here c_V = Specific heat at constant volume.

c_V can be defined as change in specific internal energy with change in temperature when the process is carried out at constant volume.

3.3.2 Constant Pressure (Isobaric Process)

During this process, both volume and temperature change. Volume and temperature increase with absorption of heat and decrease with rejection of heat.

For initial state $p_1V_1 = mRT_1$

For final state $p_2V_2 = mRT_2$

So $$\frac{p_1}{p_2} = \frac{T_1}{T_2}$$

Mechanical work $W_{1-2} = \int_1^2 pdV = p(V_2 - V_1)$

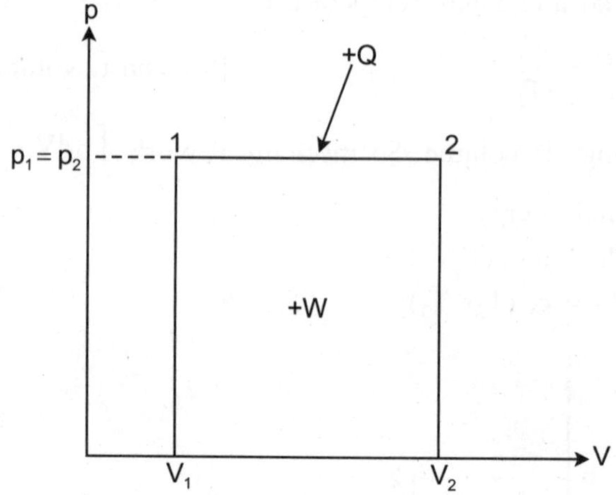

Fig. 3.5: Isobaric Process

For non-flow processes

$$\begin{aligned} Q_{1-2} &= p(V_2 - V_1) + (U_2 - U_1) \\ &= (U_2 + p_2V_2) - (U_1 + p_1V_1) \\ &= H_2 - H_1 \\ &= mc_p(T_2 - T_1) \quad \ldots\ldots (3.6) \end{aligned}$$

For unit mass

$$\delta q = dh = c_p dT \quad \ldots\ldots (3.7)$$

$$c_p = \frac{dh}{dt} \quad \ldots\ldots (3.8)$$

So c_p may be defined as the rate of change of specific enthalpy with change in temperature when the process is carried out at constant pressure.

3.3.3 Relaton between c_p and c_v

Let a unit mass of ideal gas undergoes a constant volume process and constant pressure process separately. Let T_1 and T_2 are initial and final temperatures respectively.

At constant volume process:

$$q_{1-2} = c_V(T_2 - T_1)$$

and $$w_{1-2} = 0$$

So $$du = c_V(T_2 - T_1)$$

At constant pressure process

$$q_{1-2} = c_P(T_2 - T_1)$$

and $$w_{1-2} = p(v_2 - v_1)$$

So $$du = c_P(T_2 - T_1) - p(v_2 - v_1) \quad \ldots (3.9)$$

For an ideal gas $u = f(T)$. Since both the processes have been carried out through the same temperature range, the change in internal energy would be same for both cases

$$\therefore \quad c_V(T_2 - T_1) = c_P(T_2 - T_1) - p(v_2 - v_1)$$

Now $$pv_1 = RT_1$$

and $$pv_2 = RT_2$$

$$c_V(T_2 - T_1) = c_P(T_2 - T_1) - R(T_2 - T_1)$$

$$c_V = c_P - R$$

$$c_P - c_V = R \quad \ldots (3.10)$$

IInd Method: For an ideal gas

$$pv = RT$$

$$c_V = \frac{du}{dT}$$

$$c_V = \frac{dh}{dT}$$

Now enthalpy, $$h = u + pv$$

$$= u + RT$$

$$\frac{dh}{dT} = \frac{du}{dT} + R$$

$$c_P = c_V + R$$

$$c_P - c_V = R$$

c_P is greater than c_V because heat supplied at constant pressure is utilised in doing external work and increasing the internal energy.

$$\frac{c_P}{c_V} = \gamma = \text{Adiabatic index}$$

$$\therefore \quad c_V = \frac{R}{\gamma - 1} \quad \ldots (3.11)$$

$$c_P = \frac{R\gamma}{\gamma - 1} \quad \ldots (3.12)$$

3.3.4 Isothermal (Constant Temperature Process)

In this process, both pressure and volume change.

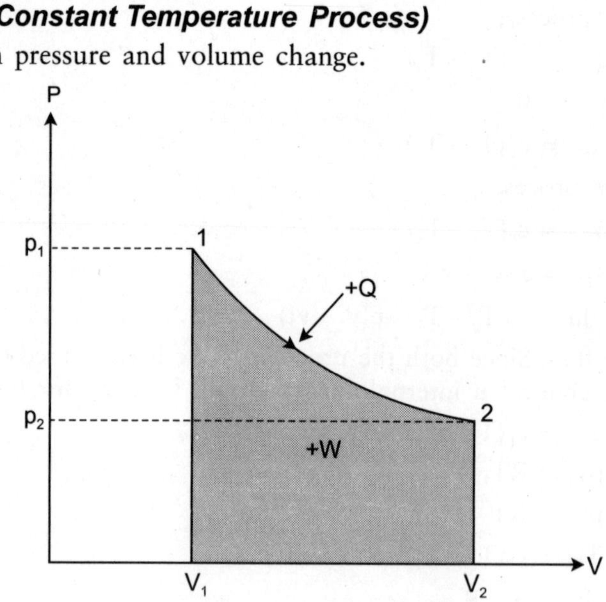

Fig. 3.6: Isothermal Process

For initial state, $p_1V_1 = mRT_1$

For final state, $p_2V_2 = mRT_2$

Dividing 2nd eqn. by eqn. 1st

$$\frac{p_2V_2}{p_1V_1} = \frac{mRT_2}{mRT_1}$$

$$\frac{p_2V_2}{p_1V_1} = 1 \qquad [\because T_1 = T_2]$$

$$p_1V_1 = p_2V_2 = pV = \text{Constant } C$$

Work done, $$W_{1-2} = \int_1^2 p\,dV$$

$$= \int_1^2 \frac{C}{V} dV$$

$$= C \ln\frac{V_2}{V_1}$$

$$= p_1V_1 \ln\frac{V_2}{V_1}$$

$$= p_1V_1 \ln\frac{p_1}{p_2} \qquad \ldots\ldots (3.13)$$

Internal energy, $dU = mc_V(T_2 - T_1)$

$= 0$ [As $T_1 = T_2$]

$$Q_{1-2} = W_{1-2} + (U_2 - U_1)$$

$$= W_{1-2}$$

3.3.5 Adiabatic Process

When heat exchange between the system and the surrounding is zero, the process is adiabatic process.

Consider a unit mass of gas. From 1st law

$$dq = \delta W + du$$

$$= pdV + c_VdT$$

For adiabatic process $dq = 0$

$$\therefore \quad 0 = pdV + c_VdT \quad \dots\dots (3.14)$$

Gas equation is given by

$$pV = RT$$

Differentiating

$$pdV + Vdp = RdT$$

$$dT = \frac{pdV + Vdp}{R} \quad \dots\dots (3.15)$$

Substituting the value of dT in Eqn. (3.14)

$$pdV + c_V\left(\frac{pdV + Vdp}{R}\right) = 0$$

$$pRdV + c_V(pdV + Vdp) = 0$$

$$p(c_P - c_V)dV + c_V(pdV + Vdp) = 0$$

$$pc_PdV + V\,c_V\,dp = 0$$

Dividing both sides by c_V pV we get

$$\frac{c_P}{c_V}\frac{dV}{V} + \frac{1}{p}dp = 0$$

$$\gamma\frac{dV}{V} + \frac{dp}{p} = 0$$

$$\gamma \log_e V + \log_e p = \log_e \text{ constant}$$

$$pV^\gamma = e^{\text{constant}} = \text{Constant} \quad \dots\dots (3.16)$$

Work done, $W_{1-2} = \int_1^2 pdV$

$$= C\int_1^2 \frac{dV}{V^\gamma}$$

$$= \frac{C}{1-\gamma}\left(V_2^{1-\gamma} - V_1^{1-\gamma}\right) \quad \ldots\ldots (3.17)$$

Now $\quad C = p_1V_1^\gamma = p_2V_2^\gamma$

Putting the value of C, we get

$$W_{1-2} = \frac{p_2V_2 - p_1V_1}{1-\gamma} = \frac{p_1V_1 - p_2V_2}{\gamma-1}$$

Since

$\delta Q = 0$ for adiabatic process

$$\delta W + dU = 0$$

$$dU = -\left(\frac{p_1V_1 - p_2V_2}{\gamma - 1}\right)$$

$$U_1 - U_2 = \frac{p_1V_1 - p_2V_2}{\gamma - 1} \quad \ldots\ldots (3.18)$$

From $\quad p_1V_1^\gamma = p_2V_2^\gamma$

and $\quad \frac{p_1V_1}{T_1} = \frac{p_2V_2}{T_2}$

We have

$$\frac{T_2}{T_1} = \left(\frac{p_2}{p_1}\right)^{\frac{\gamma-1}{\gamma}} = \left(\frac{V_1}{V_2}\right)^{\gamma-1} \quad \ldots\ldots (3.19)$$

3.3.6 Polytropic Process

The governing equation for this process is

$$pV^n = C$$

Work done during a polytropic process is given by

$$W_{1-2} = \int_1^2 pdV$$

$$= \int_1^2 \frac{C}{V^n}\,dV$$

$$= C\left[\frac{V^{-n+1}}{-n+1}\right]_{V_1}^{V_2}$$

$$= p_1V_1^n \text{ or } p_2V_2^n \frac{\left[V_2^{-n+1} - V_1^{-n+1}\right]}{-n+1}$$

$$= \frac{p_2V_2 - p_1V_1}{1-n}$$

$$= \frac{p_1V_1 - p_2V_2}{n-1} \quad \text{.......... (3.20)}$$

$$= \frac{mR(T_1 - T_2)}{n-1} \quad \text{.......... (3.21)}$$

For unit mass $W_{1-2} = \dfrac{R(T_1 - T_2)}{n-1}$ .... (3.22)

Change in internal energy

$$U_2 - U_1 = m\ c_V(T_2 - T_1) \quad \text{.......... (3.23)}$$

or $u_2 - u_1 = c_V(T_2 - T_1)$

Heat interaction

$$q_{1-2} = w_{1-2} + (u_2 - u_1)$$

$$= \frac{p_1v_1 - p_2v_2}{n-1} + c_V(T_2 - T_1)$$

$$= \frac{pv_1 - p_2v_2}{n-1} + \frac{R}{\gamma - 1}(T_2 - T_1)$$

$$= \frac{p_1v_1 - p_2v_2}{n-1} + \frac{(p_2v_2 - p_1v_1)}{\gamma - 1}$$

$$= \frac{\gamma - n}{n-1} \times \frac{p_1v_1 - p_2v_2}{n-1} \quad \text{.......... (3.24)}$$

$$= \frac{\gamma - n}{n-1} \times \text{Polytropic work done}$$

Polytropic specific heat c_n

$$q_{1-2} = \frac{p_1v_1 - p_2v_2}{n-1} + c_V(T_2 - T_1)$$

$$= \frac{R(T_1 - T_2)}{n-1} + c_V(T_2 - T_1)$$

$$= \frac{(c_p - c_v)(T_1 - T_2)}{n-1} + c_V(T_2 - T_1)$$

$$= (T_2 - T_1)\left[c_V + \frac{(-1)}{n-1}(c_P - c_V)\right]$$

$$= \frac{c_P - nc_V}{1-n}(T_2 - T_1)$$

$$= c_n\ (T_2 - T_1) \quad \ldots\ldots (3.25)$$

Substituting the value $c_p/c_V = \gamma$

$$c_n = \frac{\gamma - n}{1 - n} c_V$$

$$= -\left(\frac{\gamma - n}{n - 1}\right) c_V \quad \ldots\ldots (3.26)$$

c_n is negative when $(\gamma - n)/(n - 1)$ is positive, i.e. when $\gamma > n > 1$

$$q_{1-2} = \frac{\gamma - n}{1 - n} c_V (T_2 - T_1)$$

$$= \frac{\gamma - n}{n - 1} c_V (T_1 - T_2)$$

$$= \frac{\gamma - n}{n - 1} \times \frac{R}{(\gamma - 1)} (T_1 - T_2)$$

$$= \left(\frac{\gamma - n}{\gamma - 1}\right) \frac{R(T_1 - T_2)}{n - 1}$$

$$= \left(\frac{\gamma - n}{\gamma - 1}\right)\left(\frac{p_1 v_1 - p_2 v_2}{n - 1}\right)$$

$$q_{1-2} = \left(\frac{\gamma - n}{\gamma - 1}\right) w_{1-2} \quad \ldots\ldots (3.27)$$

In a polytropic process, the index n depends only on the heat and work quantities during the process. The various processes considered earlier are special cases of polytropic processes for a perfect gas. For example:

i. If $n = 0$, $pV^n = C$ becomes $p = C$ which indicates a isobaric process.

ii. If $n = 1$, then $pV = C$

   which represents an isothermal process.

iii. If $n = \gamma$, then we have $pV^\gamma = C$ which represents an adiabatic process.

iv. When nth root is taken

   $p^{\frac{1}{n}} V = C^{\frac{1}{n}} = C^1$

   where C^1 is another constant.

   Now if $n = \infty$, then $p^{\frac{1}{n}} = p^{\frac{1}{\infty}} = p^0 = 1$

   $pV^n \rightarrow V = C$

   which indicates a constant volume process.

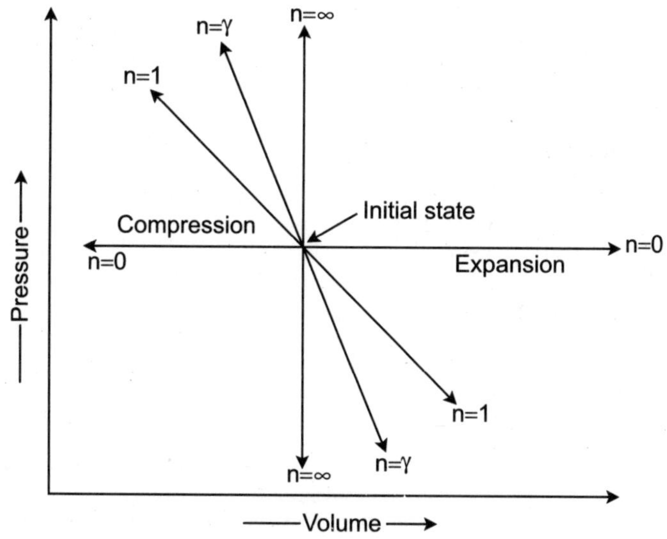

Fig. 3.7

Differentiating the eqn. $pV^n = C$

we get

$$V^n\,dp + pnV^{n-1}\,dV = 0$$

$$\frac{dp}{dV} = -n\frac{p}{V}$$

The slope of the curve thus increases in the negative direction with increase of exponent n.

Polytropic Index n:

Polytropic equation is given by

$pV^n = C$ or $p_1V_1^n = p_2V_2^n$

Taking log on both sides

$$\ln p_1 + n\ln V_1 = \ln p_2 + n\ln V_2$$

or $$n(\ln V_1 - \ln V_2) = \ln p_2 - \ln p_1$$

$$n = \frac{\ln(p_2/p_1)}{\ln(v_1/v_2)} \qquad (3.28)$$

Now $\dfrac{p_2}{p_1} = \left(\dfrac{V_1}{V_2}\right)^n$ and $\dfrac{p_2}{p_1} = \dfrac{V_1}{V_2}\times\dfrac{T_2}{T_1}$

Equating the two values of p_2/p_1

$$\frac{T_2}{T_1} = \frac{(V_1/V_2)^n}{(V_1/V_2)} = (V_1/V_2)^{n-1}$$

Again $\dfrac{V_1}{V_2} = \left(\dfrac{p_2}{p_1}\right)^{\frac{1}{n}}$ and $\dfrac{V_1}{V_2} = \left(\dfrac{p_2}{p_1}\right)\left(\dfrac{T_1}{T_2}\right)$

Equating the two values of $\dfrac{V_1}{V_2}$

$$\left(\frac{p_1}{p_2}\right)^{\frac{1}{n}} = \left(\frac{p_2}{p_1}\right) \times \left(\frac{T_1}{T_2}\right)$$

$$\therefore \frac{T_2}{T_1} = \frac{\dfrac{p_2}{p_1}}{\left(\dfrac{p_2}{p_1}\right)^{\frac{1}{n}}} = \left(\frac{p_2}{p_1}\right)^{1-\frac{1}{n}}$$

$$= \left(\frac{p_2}{p_1}\right)^{\frac{n-1}{n}} \qquad \text{......} \qquad (3.29)$$

Example 3.10

5 m^3 of air at 2 bar, 27°C is compressed upto 6 bar pressure following $pV^{1.3}$ = const. It is subsequently expanded adiabatically to 2 bar. Considering the two processes to be reversible, determine the net work. Also plot the processes on T-S diagram. **(UPTU Dec., 2002)**

Solution:

Initial volume $V_1 = 5 \text{ m}^3$

Initial pressure $p_1 = 2 \text{ bar} = 2 \times 10^5 \text{ N/m}^2$

Initial Temperature $T_1 = 27°C = 27 + 273 = 300 \text{ K}$

After polytropic process

$p_2 = 6 \text{ bar} = 6 \times 10^5 \text{ N/m}^2$

After adiabatic process

$p_3 = 2 \text{ bar} = 2 \times 10^5 \text{ N/m}^2$

The process on T–S diagram is shown in Fig. 3.8.

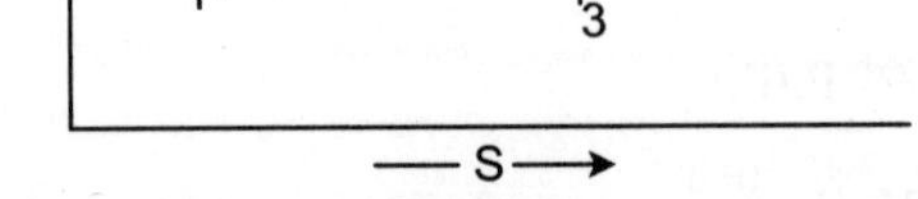

Fig. 3.8

Polytropic index $n = 1.3$

Adiabatic exponent for air $\gamma = 1.4$

Now

$$p_1V_1 = mRT_1$$

$$m = \frac{p_1V_1}{RT_1}$$

$$= \frac{2 \times 10^5 \times 5}{287 \times 300}$$

$$= 11.6 \text{ kg}$$

For polytropic process 1–2

$$p_1V_1^n = p_2V_2^n$$

$$2 \times 10^5 \times 5^{1.3} = 6 \times 10^5 \times V_2^{1.3}$$

$$V_2 = 2.1476 \text{ m}^3$$

Work done for process 1–2

$$W_{1-2} = \frac{p_1V_1 - p_2V_2}{n-1}$$

$$= \frac{2 \times 10^5 \times 5 - 6 \times 10^5 \times 2.1476}{1.3 - 1}$$

$$= -9.62 \times 10^5 \text{ N-m}$$

This work done is negative because of compression process.

Now, for adiabatic process 2–3

$$p_3V_3^\gamma = p_2V_2^\gamma$$

$$2 \times 10^5 \times V_3^{1.4} = 6 \times 10^5 \times (2.1476)^{1.4}$$

$$V_3 = 4.7 \text{ m}^3$$

Work done during adiabatic process 2–3

$$W_{2-3} = \frac{p_2V_2 - p_3V_3}{\gamma - 1}$$

$$= \frac{6 \times 10^5 \times 2.1476 - 2 \times 10^5 \times 4.7}{0.4}$$

$$= 8.714 \times 10^5 \text{ N-m}$$

Net work $1\text{–}3 = (-9.62 + 8.714) \times 10^5$

$$= -0.906 \times 10^5 \text{ N-m}$$

$= -90.6$ kJ work is done on the system.

Example 3.11

10 kg of air at an absolute pressure of 1.5 bar and 360 K is compressed at constant temperature until it reduces to ¼th of original value. Make calculations for initial and final parameters, work performed and heat transfer.

Solution:

Mass of air, $m = 10$ kg

Pressure, $p_1 = 1.5$ bar

Temperature, $T_1 = 360$ K

Final volume, $V_2 = \frac{1}{4} V_1$

For isothermal process

$$p_1V_1 = p_2V_2$$

$$1.5 \times 10^5 V_1 = p_2 \times \frac{1}{4} V_1$$

$$p_2 = 1.5 \times 10^5 \times 4$$

$$= 6 \times 10^5 \text{ N/m}^2$$

$$= \mathbf{6\ bar}$$ **Ans.**

Initial volume

$$V_1 = \frac{mRT}{p_1}$$

$$= \frac{10 \times 287 \times 360}{1.5 \times 10^5}$$

$$= \mathbf{6.88\ m^3}$$ **Ans.**

Final volume, $V_2 = V_1/4 = \mathbf{1.722\ m^3}$ **Ans.**

Final pressure, $p_2 = \frac{mRT}{V_2}$

$$= \frac{10 \times 287 \times 360}{1.722}$$

$$= \mathbf{6\ bar}$$ **Ans.**

Work done, $W = p_1 V_1 \ln\left(\frac{V_2}{V_1}\right)$

$$= 1.5 \times 10^5 \times 6.88 \ln(1/4)$$

$$= -14.31 \times 10^5 \text{ J}$$

$$= \mathbf{-1431\ kJ}$$ **Ans.**

Heat transfer

$$Q_{1-2} = (U_2 - U_1) + W_{1-2}$$
$$= 0 + (-1431) \qquad \text{[Change in internal energy at const. temp = 0]}$$
$$= \mathbf{-1431\ kJ}$$

Ans.

Example 3.12

0.2 m^3 of air at 4 bar and 130°C is contained in a system. A reversible adiabatic expansion takes place till the pressure falls to 1.02 bar. The gas is then heated at constant pressure till enthalpy increases by 72.5 kJ. Calculate:

i. *The work done.*
ii. *The index of expansion if the above processes are replaced by a single reversible polytropic process giving the same work between the same initial and final states.*

Take $c_P = 1$ *kJ/kg K*
$c_V = 0.714$ *kJ/kg K*

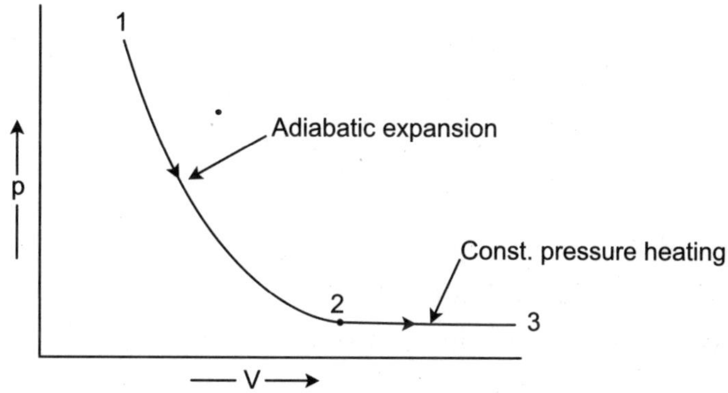

Fig. 3.9

Solution:

Initial conditions at state 1

$$V_1 = 0.2 \text{ m}^3$$
$$p_1 = 4 \text{ bar} = 4 \times 10^5 \text{ N/m}^2$$
$$T_1 = 130 + 273 = 403 \text{ K}$$

Conditions after adiabatic expansion (at state 2)

$$p_2 = 1.02 \text{ bar}$$
$$= 1.02 \times 10^5 \text{ N/m}^2$$

Increase in enthalpy during const. pressure process 2–3 = 72.5 kJ

i. Work done:

For process 1–2: Reversible adiabatic process

$$p_1 V_1^{\gamma} = p_2 V_2^{\gamma}$$

$$V_2 = V_1\left(\frac{p_1}{p_2}\right)^{\frac{1}{\gamma}}$$

$$\gamma = \frac{c_P}{c_V} = \frac{1}{0.714} = 1.4$$

$$\therefore \quad V_2 = 0.2\left(\frac{4\times10^5}{1.02\times10^5}\right)^{\frac{1}{1.4}}$$

$$= 0.53 \text{ m}^3$$

Also

$$\frac{T_2}{T_1} = \left(\frac{p_2}{p_1}\right)^{\frac{\gamma-1}{\gamma}}$$

$$T_2 = 403\left(\frac{1.02\times10^5}{4\times10^5}\right)^{\frac{1.4-1}{1.4}}$$

$$= 272.7 \text{ K}$$

Mass of gas,

$$m = \frac{p_1V_1}{RT_1} = \frac{4\times10^5\times0.2}{286\times403}$$

$$= 0.694 \text{ kg}$$

where

$$R = c_P - c_V = (1\text{–}0.714) \text{ kJ/kg K}$$

$$= 286 \text{ J/kg K}$$

Process 2–3 (const. prassure process)

$$Q_{2-3} = mc_P\,(T_3 - T_2)$$

$$72.5\times10^3 = 0.694\times1\,(T_3 - 272.7)$$

$$T_3 = 377 \text{ K}$$

Now

$$\frac{V_2}{T_2} = \frac{V_3}{T_3}$$

$$V_3 = T_3\left(\frac{V_2}{T_2}\right) = \frac{0.53\times377}{272.7} = 0.732 \text{ m}^3$$

Work done by the path 1–2–3

$$W_{1-2-3} = W_{1-2} + W_{2-3}$$

$$= \frac{p_1V_1 - p_2V_2}{\gamma-1} + p_2(V_3 - V_2)$$

$$= \frac{4\times10^5\times0.2 - 1.02\times10^5\times0.53}{1.4-1} + 1.02\times10^5(0.732-0.53)$$

$$= \mathbf{85454 \text{ N-m or J}}$$ **Ans.**

ii. Index of expansion n:

$$\text{Work done during 1–3 } W_{1-3} = \frac{p_1V_1 - p_3V_3}{n-1}$$

$$85454 = \frac{4 \times 10^5 \times 0.2 - 1.02 \times 10^5 \times 0.732}{n-1}$$

$$= \frac{5336}{n-1}$$

$$n = \mathbf{1.062}$$ **Ans.**

Example 3.13

A cycle comprised of three processes a polytropic compression (n = 1.5) from 143.5 kPa and 27°C followed by constant pressure and constant volume processes. The heat rejected is 143 kJ/kg and the substance is air. Determine

i. Pressure, temperature and specific volume around the cycle.

ii. Net work per kg.

iii. Heat added per kg.

Solution:

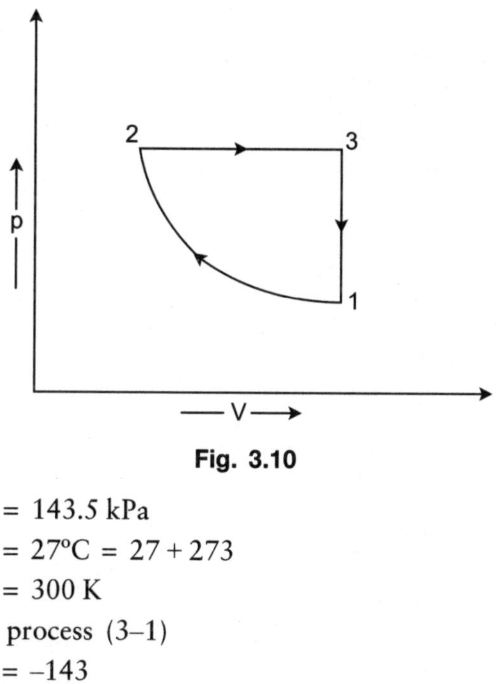

Fig. 3.10

$$p_1 = 143.5 \text{ kPa}$$
$$T_1 = 27°C = 27 + 273$$
$$= 300 \text{ K}$$

For a constant volume process (3–1)

$$c_V(T_1 - T_3) = -143$$
$$0.711\ (300 - T_3) = -143$$
$$T_3 = 501.125 \text{ K}$$

$$\text{Specific volume,} \quad v_1 = \frac{RT_1}{p_1}$$

$$= \frac{1 \times 0.287 \times 300}{143.5}$$

$$= 0.6 \text{ m}^3/\text{kg}$$

$$v_3 = v_1 = 0.6 \text{ m}^3/\text{kg}$$

$$\frac{p_1 v_1}{T_1} = \frac{p_2 v_2}{T_2}$$

$$p_3 = \left(\frac{p_1 v_1}{T_1}\right) T_3$$

$$= \frac{143.5 \times 0.6 \times 501.125}{300 \times 0.6}$$

$$= 239.7 \text{ kPa}$$

$$p_2 = p_3 = 239.7 \text{ kPa}$$

$$T_2 = T_1 \left(\frac{p_2}{p_1}\right)^{\frac{n-1}{n}}$$

$$= 300\left(\frac{329.7}{143.5}\right)^{\frac{1.5-1}{1.5}}$$

$$= 355.95 \text{ K}$$

Work done/kg, $$w_{1\text{-}2} = \frac{p_1 v_1 - p_2 v_2}{n-1} = \frac{R(T_1 - T_2)}{n-1}$$

$$= -32.11 \text{ kJ/kg}$$

Process 2–3: Contant pressure process

$$w_{2\text{-}3} = p(v_3 - v_2)$$

$$= R(T_3 - T_2)$$

$$= 0.287\ (501.125 - 355.95)$$

$$= 41.66 \text{ kJ/kg}$$

Process 3–1: Constant volume process

$$w_{1\text{-}3} = 0$$

$$\text{Net work} = -32.11 + 41.66 + 0$$

$$= 9.555 \text{ kJ/kg}$$

Heat added/kg

Process 1–2

$$q_{1\text{-}2} = \left(\frac{\gamma - n}{\gamma - 1}\right) \text{work}$$

$$= \left(\frac{1.4 - 1.5}{1.4 - 1}\right) \times (-32.11)$$

$$= 6.422 \text{ kJ/kg}$$

Process 2–3: Constant pressure process

$$q_{2-3} = \text{Heat added}$$

$$= mc_P (T_3 - T_2)$$

$$= 1 \times 1.005(501.125 - 355.95) = 145.90 \text{ kJ/kg}$$

Process 3–1: Constant volume process

$$q_{1-3} = -143 \text{ kJ/kg}$$

Net heat added $= 6.422 + 145.93 - 143 = 9.35$ kJ/kg

3.4 First Law Applied to Flow Processes

Continuity Equation:

Consider an ideal fluid flowing in a tube.

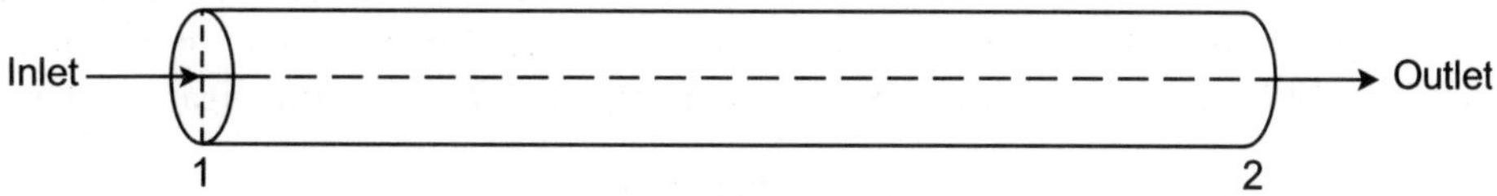

Fig. 3.11: First Law Applied to Flow Processes

Let characteristics at inlet and outlet are (Fig. 3.11)

Area : A and (A + dA)

Density : ρ and (ρ + dρ)

Velocity : V and (V + dV)

The mass flow at inlet in time dt = ρAVdt

The mass flow at outlet in time dt = (ρ + dρ)(A + dA)(V + dV)dt

The accumulated mass between inlet and outlet

$$dm = \rho AVdt - (\rho + d\rho)(A + dA)(V + dV)dt$$

or

$$\frac{dm}{dt} = -(AVd\rho + \rho VdA + \rho AdV) \quad (3.30)$$

For a steady flow mass remains constant with time.

$\therefore AVd\rho + \rho VdA + \rho AdV = 0$

Dividing throughout by ρAV, we get

$$\frac{d\rho}{\rho} + \frac{dA}{A} + \frac{dV}{V} = 0 \quad (3.31)$$

or

$$d(\rho AV) = 0$$

$$\rho AV = \text{Constant} \quad (3.32)$$

This equation is called continuity equation and represents the mass conservation

Mass flow rate for two sections 1 and 2

$$\dot{m} = \rho_1 A_1 V_1 = \rho_2 A_2 V_2$$

or
$$\dot{m} = \frac{A_1 V_1}{v_1} = \frac{A_2 V_2}{v_2}$$

because specific volume $v = \frac{1}{\rho}$

3.5 Flow Process and Control Volume

Flow Process: A flow process forms an open system which allows the working fluid to enter and leaves from the surface of the system. It also allows energy interactions in the form of heat and work, internal energy, potential energy and kinetic energy.

Control Surface and Control Volume: The imaginary envelope which is supposed to exist around the piece of equipment is called control surface and the space thus bounded is called control volume. The control surface is fixed in position and does not change its shape or orientation during the flow process. The concept of control volume relates energy interactions with average change of state of fluid from entrance to exit section. This concept is used in devices such as engines, turbines, pumps and compressors, boilers and heat exchanges, etc.

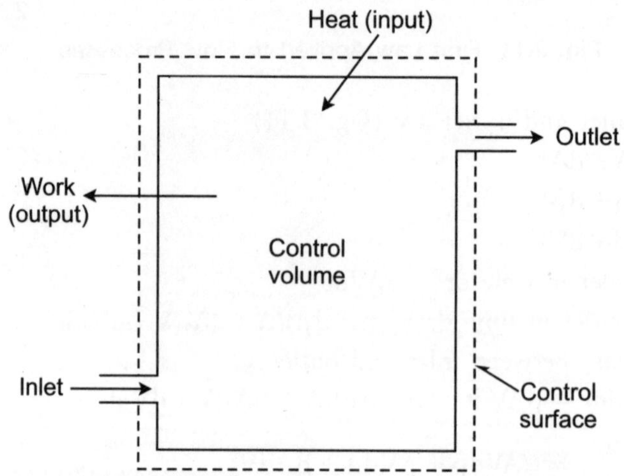

Fig. 3.12: Flow Process and Control Volume

3.6 Flow Work or Flow Energy

The amount of work required to displace a certain quantity of fluid from its position against the existing pressure is called flow work or flow energy.

Let A = Area of cross-section of a channel through which a unit mass of fluid passes. Let p and F are the pressure and force at the entrance

$\therefore$ $F = pA$

Let l = Distance through which fluid mass is displaced

Work done = Force × Distance

$= pA \times l$

$= pAl$ .... (3.34)

where Al represents the volume of fluid about to enter the control volume.

$\therefore$ Flow work per unit mass = pv

Thus, flow work is the product of pressure and specific volume of the flowing fluid. The work is supplied to the system when mass enters and to the surrounding when the mass leaves the system.

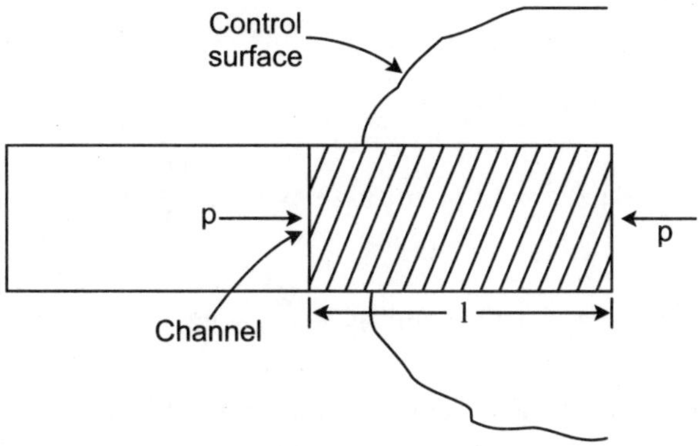

Fig. 3.13: Flow Work

3.7 Steady and Unsteady Flow

Steady Flow Process: When fluid parameters (velocity, pressure, temperature, etc.) do not change with time, the process is called steady flow process.

Unsteady Flow Process: When conditions vary with respect to time, the process is called unsteady flow process.

Characteristics of steady flow process:

i. The mass inflow and outflow in control volume is same.
ii. The fluid is uniform in state, i.e. properties do not change with position.
iii. Heat and work interactions are at constant rate.
iv. There is no change in chemical composition of the fluid in control volume.

3.8 Steady Flow Energy Equation

Consider a fluid entering a system at 1 and leaving the system at 2.

Let V_1, p_1, v_1 and u_1 be the velocity, pressure, specific volume and internal energy at the entrance.

Let V_2, p_2, v_2 and u_2 be the corresponding properties at the exit.

Let q and w be the heat and work interaction in control surface.

According to law of conservation of energy

Total energy at entrance = Total energy at exit

Now, Total energy = Internal energy + Kinetic energy + Potential energy + Flow work + Heat or Mechanical work

$$\text{Total energy at entrance} = m_1\left(u_1 + p_1v_1 + \frac{V_1^2}{2} + gz_1\right) + Q \quad \ldots\ldots\ldots\ldots (3.35)$$

$$\text{Total energy at exit} = m_2\left(u_2 + p_2v_2 + \frac{V_2^2}{2} + gz_2\right) + W \quad \ldots\ldots\ldots\ldots (3.36)$$

Assuming mass to be constant, we have

$$m_1 = m_2 = m$$

$$\therefore \quad m\left(u_1 + p_1v_1 + \frac{V_1^2}{2} + gz_1\right) + Q = m\left(u_2 + p_2v_2 + \frac{V_2^2}{2} + gz_2\right) + W$$

$$m\left(h_1 + \frac{V_1^2}{2} + gz_1\right) + Q = m\left(h_2 + \frac{V_2^2}{2} + gz_2\right) + W$$

This equation is called steady flow energy equation (SFEE).

i. On unit mass basis, dividing the equation by m we have

$$u_1 + p_1v_1 + \frac{V_1^2}{2} + gz_1 + q_{1-2} = u_2 + p_2v_2 + \frac{V_2^2}{2} + gz_2 + w$$

$$h_1 + \frac{V_1^2}{2} + gz_1 + q_{1-2} = h_2 + \frac{V_2^2}{2} + gz_2 + w$$

All the terms in this equation have units J/kg or kJ/kg.

ii. On unit time basis, the equation is

$$\frac{dm}{dt}\left(h_1 + \frac{V_1^2}{2} + gz_1\right) + \frac{dQ}{dt} = \frac{dm}{dt}\left(h_2 + \frac{V_2^2}{2} + gz_2\right) + \frac{dW}{dt}$$

where $\frac{dm}{dt}$ = Rate of fluid flow across the surface in kg/sec.

$\frac{dQ}{dt}$ = Rate of heat transfer across the control surface in J/s.

$\frac{dW}{dt}$ = Rate of work transfer across the control surface in J/s.

When there are a number of streams entering and leaving the control surface, the SFEE can be written as

$$\frac{dQ}{dt} - \frac{dW}{dt} = \sum_{outlet} \frac{dm}{dt}\left(h + \frac{V^2}{2} + gz\right) - \sum_{inlet} \frac{dm}{dt}\left(h + \frac{V^2}{2} + gz\right) \quad \ldots\ldots (3.37)$$

SFEE on unit mass is more suitable when only a single stream of fluid enters and leaves the control volume. When more than one streams are there, analysis should be done by SFEE on unit time basis.

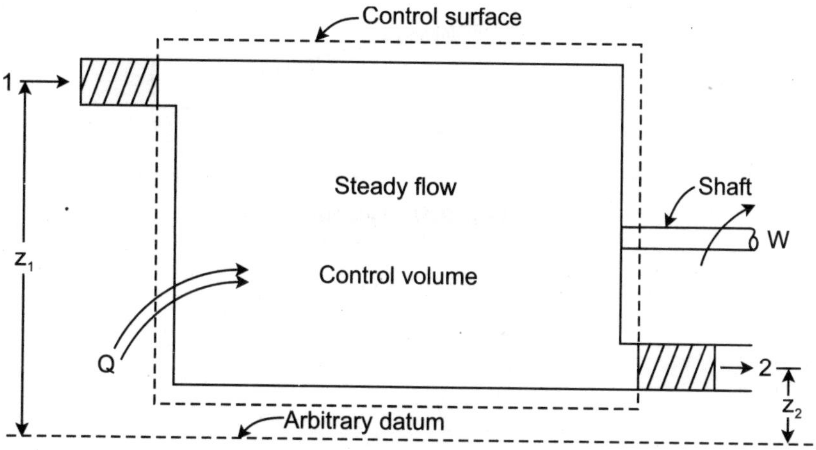

Fig. 3.14: First Law Analysis of Steady Flow

3.9 Applications of Steady Flow Energy Equation

SFEE equation is applied to flow processes in engines, turbines, boilers, condensers, pumps, compressors nozzles and diffusers.

a. Nozzle and Diffuser

A nozzle is used for increasing the velocity of fluid at the expense of its pressure drop. The enthalpy of fluid decreases. In a nozzle flow

i. Mechanical work, W = 0

ii. Heat interaction, Q = 0

iii. Entry and exit are at same level, i.e. $z_1 = z_2$

So SFEE becomes

$$\frac{V_2^2 - V_1^2}{2} = h_1 - h_2 \quad \ldots\ldots (3.38)$$

∴ Increase in kinetic energy = Decrease in enthalpy

From continuity equation

$$m = \frac{A_1V_1}{v_1} = \frac{A_2V_2}{v_2}$$

$$V_1^2 = \left(\frac{A_2 v_1}{A_1 v_2}\right)^2 V_2^2$$

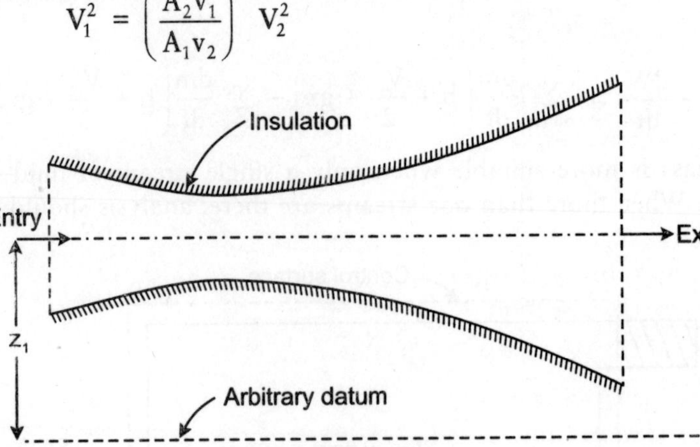

Fig. 3.15: Nozzle

Putting this value of V_1^2 in equation (3.38)

$$V_2^2 - \left(\frac{A_2 v_1}{A_1 v_2}\right)^2 V_2^2 = 2\,(h_1 - h_2)$$

$$V_2^2\left[1 - \left(\frac{A_2 v_1}{A_1 v_2}\right)^2\right] = 2\,(h_1 - h_2)$$

$$V_2 = \left(\frac{1}{1 - \left(\frac{A_2 v_1}{A_1 v_2}\right)^2}\right)^{\frac{1}{2}} \sqrt{2(h_1 - h_2)} \quad \ldots\ldots\ldots\ldots (3.39)$$

When the inlet velocity, $V_1 = 0$

$$V_2 = \sqrt{2(h_1 - h_2)} \quad \ldots\ldots\ldots\ldots (3.40)$$

If working fluid is a perfect gas, then

$$pv = RT$$

$$h = c_p T$$

and

$$\frac{T_2}{T_1} = \left(\frac{p_2}{p_1}\right)^{\frac{\gamma-1}{\gamma}}$$

$$\frac{V_2^2 - V_1^2}{2} = \text{Change in K.E.} = h_1 - h_2$$

$$= c_p(T_1 - T_2)$$

$$= c_p T_1 \left[1 - \frac{T_2}{T_1}\right]$$

$$= c_p T_1 \left[1 - \left(\frac{p_2}{p_1}\right)^{\frac{\gamma-1}{\gamma}}\right] \quad \ldots\ldots\ldots (3.41)$$

A diffuser is a passage of varying cross-section. It is used for reducing the velocity of a fluid. When the velocity is subsonic, the cross-section is diverging. When the velocity is supersonic, the cross-section is converging.

b. Boiler

Boiler is used for generation of steam. Thermal energy released by burning of fuel is used for converting the water into steam.

A boiler has following features:

i. There is no mechanical work produced W = 0

ii. There is no change in kinetic energy

$$\frac{V_1^2 - V_2^2}{2} = 0$$

iii. Inlet and exit are at same level

$$z_1 = z_2$$

So SFEE reduces to

$$mh_1 + Q = mh_2$$

$$Q = m(h_2 - h_1) \quad \ldots\ldots\ldots (3.42)$$

So heat energy supplied to the system increases the enthalpy of the system.

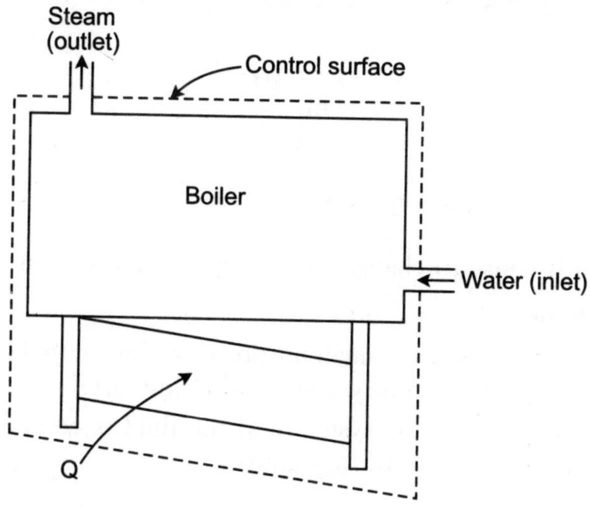

Fig. 3.16: Boiler

c. *Steam or Gas Turbine*

A turbine is used to produce work from a steam fluid expanding from high pressure to low pressure.

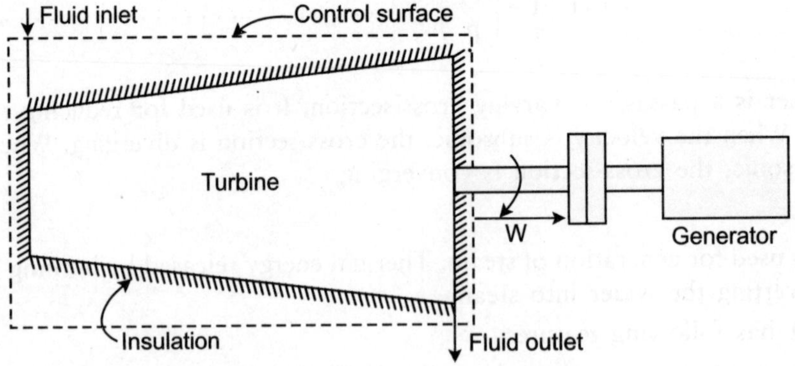

Fig. 3.17: Steam or Gas Turbine

The features of flow through steam or gas turbine are:

i. Negligible velocity change in the flow, i.e. $V_1 = V_2$

ii. Negligible potential energy change $z_1 = z_2$

iii. No heat transfer as the walls are insulated, i.e.

$$Q = 0$$

SFEE is given as

$$m\left(h_1 + \frac{V_1^2}{2} + gz_1\right) + \cancel{Q}^0 = m\left(h_2 + \frac{V_2^2}{2} + gz_2\right) + W$$

$$m(h_1 - h_2) = m\left(\frac{\cancel{V_2^2}}{2} - \frac{\cancel{V_1^2}}{2} + \cancel{gz_2} - \cancel{gz_1}\right) + W$$

$$m(h_1 - h_2) = W \quad \text{(3.43)}$$

So work done is equal to change in enthalpy of the system.

d. *Rotary Compressor*

Rotary compressor is used for medium pressure rise (upto 10 bar) and large flow rate (50 m^3/s). The features of rotary compressor flow are:

i. Shaft work is done on the system and the fluid is compressed, W is negative.

ii. Potential energy changes are negligible

$$z_1 = z_2$$

iii. Heat is lost from the surrounding, Q is negative.

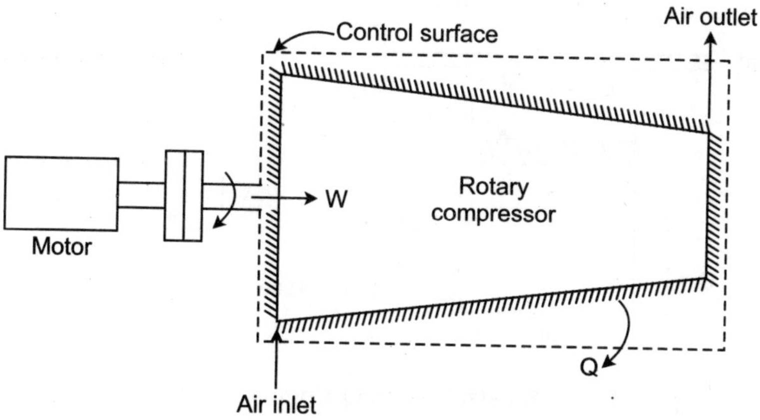

Fig. 3.18: Rotary Compressor

SFEE reduces to

$$m\left(h_1 + \frac{V_1^2}{2}\right) - Q = m\left(h_2 + \frac{V_2^2}{2}\right) - W$$

or
$$W = m\left(h_2 + \frac{V_2^2}{2}\right) - m\left(h_1 + \frac{V_1^2}{2}\right) + Q \quad \text{.................. (3.44)}$$

If velocity change is neglected and process is adiabatic ($Q = 0$)

$$W = m(h_2 - h_1) \quad \text{.................................. (3.45)}$$

Since $h_2 > h_1$, W is negative.

e. Reciprocating Compressor

It is used for increasing the pressure of a fluid with the help of piston-cylinder mechanism. It sucks the fluid, compresses it and then delivers it to a receiver.

It is used for compressing small volume (maximum 5 m^3/s) of fluid to high pressure (as high as 100 bar).

The features of steady flow compression are:

i. Potential and kinetic changes are negligible.

ii. The work done is on the system, so W is negative.

iii. The heat is lost from the system, so Q is negative.

Now steady flow energy equation becomes

$$\dot{m}\left(h_1 + \cancel{\frac{V_1^2}{2}} + \cancel{z_1}\right) - Q = m\left(h_2 + \cancel{\frac{V_2^2}{2}} + \cancel{z_2}\right) - W$$

$$mh_1 - Q = mh_2 - W$$

or
$$W = Q + m(h_2 - h_1) \quad \text{........................ (3.46)}$$

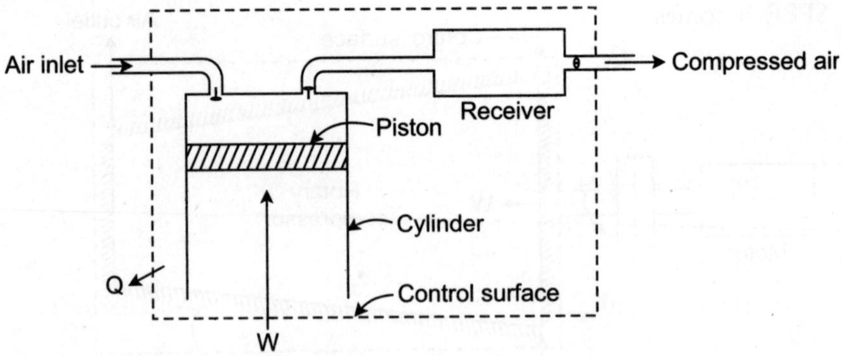

Fig. 3.19: Reciprocating Compressor

f. Centrifugal Water Pump

A centrifugal pump converts the mechanical energy of a motor or an engine to the potential energy of a liquid.

It is used for pumping the liquid from lower level to higher level.

The features of the process are:

i. There is no heat transfer, so Q = 0.

ii. The work is done on the system, so W is negative.

iii. The temperature remains constant, so there is no change in internal energy, i.e. du = 0.

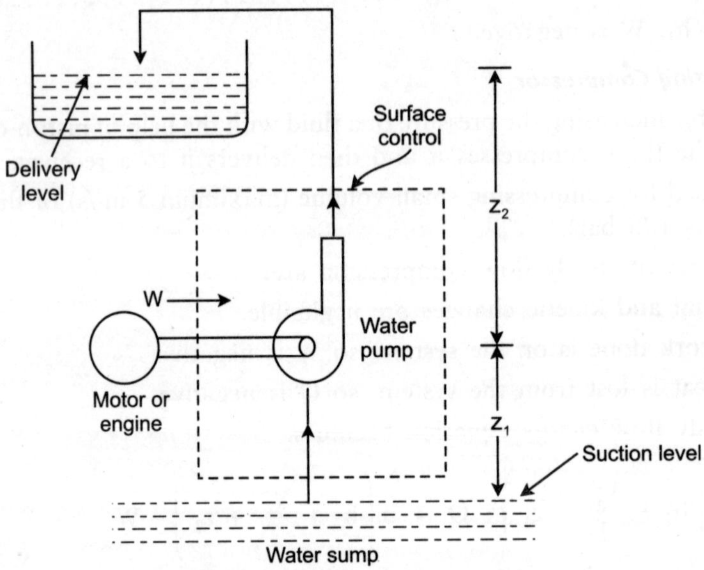

Fig. 3.20: Centrifugal Water Pump

The SFEE becomes

$$m\left(\cancel{u_1} + p_1v_1 + \frac{V_1^2}{2} + gz_1\right) + \cancel{Q}^0 = m\left(\cancel{u_2} + p_2v_2 + \frac{V_2^2}{2} + gz_2\right) + \underset{(-ve)}{W}$$

$$m\left(p_1v_1 + \frac{V_1^2}{2} + gz_1\right) = m\left(p_2v_2 + \frac{V_2^2}{2} + gz_2\right) - W \quad \ldots\ldots\ldots\ldots\ldots \quad (3.47)$$

g. *Hydraulic Turbine*

It converts the potential and the kinetic energy of water into usable mechanical energy. The features are:

i. There is no heat transfer, $Q = 0$.

ii. Temperature remains constant, $du = 0$.

iii. Work is done by the system, W is positive.

The SFEE becomes

$$m\left(p_1v_1 + \frac{V_1^2}{2} + gz_1\right) = m\left(p_2v_2 + \frac{V_2^2}{2} + gz_2\right) + W \quad \ldots\ldots\ldots\ldots\ldots\ldots\ldots \quad (3.48)$$

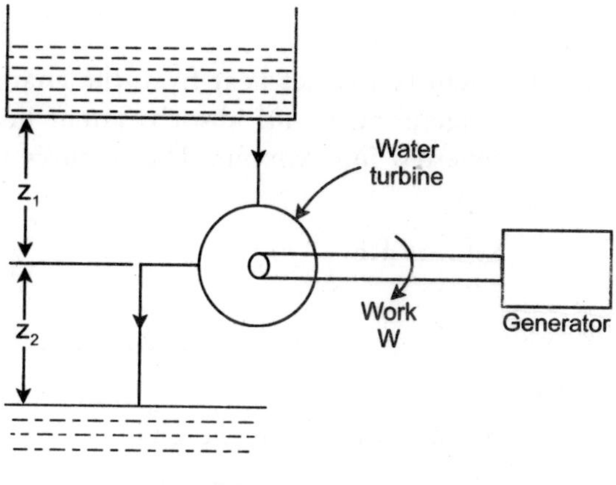

Fig. 3.21: Water Turbine

h. *Heat Exchanger (Condenser)*

Heat exchanger is used to transfer the heat from one fluid to other. A steam condenser is a heat exchanger in which steam passes its heat to water flowing through the tubes. The flow has following characteristics:

i. There is no mechanical work, $W = 0$.

ii. There is no change in potential or kinetic energy.

iii. There is no heat exchange with the surrounding, $Q = 0$.

From energy equation we can write

$$m_s\,(h_1 - h_2) = m_w(h_4 - h_3) \quad \ldots\ldots\ldots\ldots\ldots\ldots\ldots\ldots\ldots\ldots \quad (3.49)$$

where m_s and m_w = Mass flow of steam and water respectively.

h_1 and h_2 = Enthalpy at entrance and exit of the steam.

h_3 and h_4 = Enthalpy at entrance and exit of water.

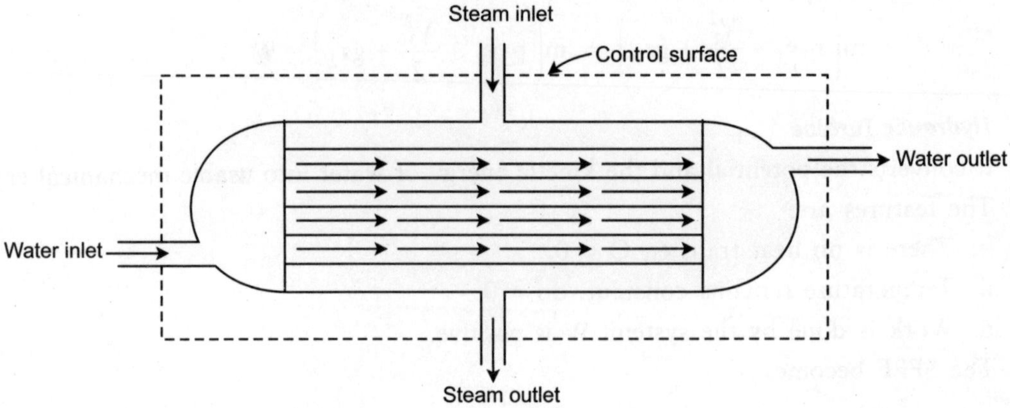

Fig. 3.22: Heat Exchanger (Condenser)

i. Evaporator

It is used in refrigeration system to extract heat from the chamber which is to be kept at low temperature. The refrigerating liquid absorbs latent heat from the chamber at constant pressure and is converted into vapour. The features of the flow are:

i. Work done is zero, W = 0.

ii. There is no change in K.E. or P.E.

The SFEE becomes

$$mh_1 + Q = mh_2 \quad \ldots\ldots\ldots\ldots \quad (3.50)$$

$$Q = m(h_2 - h_1)$$

Q is taken positive because heat flows from the chamber to the evaporator.

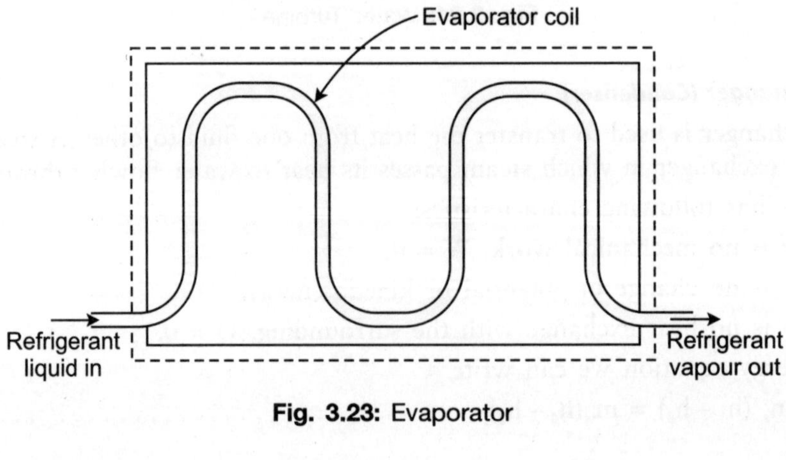

Fig. 3.23: Evaporator

Example 3.14

In an isentropic flow through nozzle, air flows at the rate of 700 kg/hr. At inlet to the nozzle, pressure is 2 MPa and temperature is 127°C. The exit pressure is 0.5 MPa. If initial air velocity is 300 m/s, determine

i. exit velocity of air, and

ii. inlet and exit area of the nozzle.

Solution:

$$\text{Mass flow rate, } \frac{dm}{dt} = 700 \text{ kg/hr} = \frac{700}{3600} \text{ kg/sec} = \frac{7}{36} \text{ kg/sec.}$$

Inlet conditions

$$p_1 = 2 \text{ MPa} = 2 \times 10^6 \text{ N/m}^2$$

$$T_1 = 127 + 273 = 400 \text{ K}$$

$$V_1 = 300 \text{ m/s}$$

Exit conditions

$$p_2 = 0.5 \text{ MPa} = 0.5 \times 10^6 \text{ N/m}^2$$

$$\frac{T_2}{T_1} = \left(\frac{p_2}{p_1}\right)^{\frac{\gamma-1}{\gamma}}$$

$$R_{air} = 287 \text{ J/kg K}$$

$$v_1 = \frac{RT_1}{p_1} = \frac{287 \times 400}{2 \times 10^6}$$

$$= 0.0574 \text{ m}^3\text{/kg}$$

Now

$$\frac{dm}{dt} = \frac{A_1 V_1}{v_1}$$

$$\frac{7}{36} = \frac{A_1 \times 300}{0.0574}$$

Inlet area $\mathbf{A_1 = 3.72 \times 10^{-5}\ m^2}$ **Ans.**

$$c_P = 1000 \text{ J/kg K}$$

$$c_V = 713 \text{ J/kg K}$$

$$\text{Adiabatic constant, } \gamma = \frac{c_P}{c_V} = \frac{1000}{713} = 1.4$$

$$\text{Exit temperature, } T_2 = T_1\left(\frac{p_2}{p_1}\right)^{\frac{\gamma-1}{\gamma}}$$

$$= 400(0.25)^{\frac{1.4-1}{1.4}}$$

$$= 269.18 \text{ K}$$

Specific volume, $v_2 = \dfrac{RT_2}{p_2}$

$$= \frac{287 \times 269.18}{0.5 \times 10^6}$$

$$= 0.155 \text{ m}^3\text{/kg}$$

Exit area, $A_2 = \dfrac{dm}{dt} \times \dfrac{v_2}{V_2}$

$$= \frac{7}{36} \times \frac{0.155}{V_2}$$

Applying SFEE

$$h_1 + \frac{V_1^2}{2} = h_2 + \frac{V_2^2}{2}$$

Exit velocity, $V_2 = \sqrt{2}\left[c_P(T_1 - T_2) + \dfrac{V_1^2}{2}\right]^{\frac{1}{2}}$

$$= \sqrt{2}\left[1000(400 - 269.18) + \frac{(300)^2}{2}\right]^{\frac{1}{2}}$$

$$= \mathbf{592.9 \text{ m/s}}$$ **Ans.**

Exit area, $A_2 = \dfrac{7 \times 0.155}{36 \times 592.9} = \mathbf{5.083 \times 10^{-5} \text{ m}^2}$ **Ans.**

Example 3.15

Water enters a boiler with enthalpy 100 kJ/kg and gets vaporised into steam with enthalpy 2825 kJ/kg. Apply steady flow energy equation to the boiler, make appropriate assumptions and work out the heat transferred per kg of steam generated.

Solution:

SFEE for a boiler is

$$Q = m(h_2 - h_1)$$

$$q = h_2 - h_1$$

$$= 2825 - 100$$

$$= \mathbf{2725 \text{ kJ/kg}}$$ **Ans.**

Example 3.16

A steady flow of water at enthalpy 250 kJ/kg enters a section of the heating plant of a building in which there are no pumps. The water leaves the section at enthalpy 200 kJ/kg. The exit pipe is 25 m above the inlet pipe. Find the net heat transferred.

Solution:

$$h_1 = 250 \text{ kJ/kg}$$
$$h_2 = 200 \text{ kJ/kg}$$
$$z_1 = 0 \text{ meter}$$
$$z_2 = 25 \text{ m}$$

The SFEE is given as

$$h_1 + gz_1 + q = h_2 + gz_2 + w$$
$$q = (h_2 - h_1) + g(z_2 - z_1) + w$$
$$= (200 - 250) \times 10^3 + 9.81(25 - 0) + 0$$
$$= (-50 \times 10^3 + 245.25) \text{ J/kg}$$
$$= (-50 + 0.245) \text{ kJ/kg}$$
$$= \mathbf{-49.755 \text{ kJ/kg}}$$ **Ans.**

This is negative because heat is transferred from the water.

Example 3.17

A steam turbine operating under steady flow conditions receives 3600 kg of steam per hour. The steam enters the turbine at velocity of 80 m/s, an elevation of 10 m and specific enthalpy of 3276 kJ/kg. It leaves the turbine at a velocity of 150 m/s, an elevation of 3 m and a specific enthalpy of 2465 kJ/kg. Heat losses from the turbine to the surrounding amount to 36 MJ/hour. Estimate the power output of the turbine. **(UPTU 2001-02)**

Solution:

Mass flow rate, $\frac{dm}{dt} = 3600$ kg/hour

$$= \frac{3600}{3600} \text{ kg/sec} = 1 \text{ kg/sec}$$

Inlet velocity, $V_1 = 80$ m/s

Inlet elevation, $z_1 = 10$ m

Inlet enthalpy, $h_1 = 3276$ kJ/kg

Exit velocity, $V_2 = 150$ m/s

Exit elevation, $z_1 = 3$ m

Exit enthalpy, $h_1 = 2465$ kJ/kg

$$\text{Heat lost from the surrounding, } Q = \frac{-36\times10^6}{3600} \text{ J/sec}$$

$$= -1\times10^4 \text{ J/sec}$$

The SFEE is given by

$$\frac{dm}{dt}\left[h_1 + \frac{V_1^2}{2} + gz_1\right] + Q = \frac{dm}{dt}\left[h_2 + \frac{V_2^2}{2} + gz_2\right] + W$$

$$1\left[3276\times10^3 + \frac{(80)^2}{2} + (9.81\times10)\right] + \left(-1\times10^4\right) = 1\left[2645\times10^3 + \frac{(150)^2}{2} + (9.81\times3)\right] + W$$

$$\text{Work done } W = +613018 \text{ J/sec.}$$

$$= \mathbf{+613.018\ kW}$$ **Ans.**

Work done is positive because it is done by the system.

Example 3.18

A gas turbine receives 60 kg/min of fuel-air mixture at 4 MPa pressure, 1320 K temperature with a velocity of 200 m/s. At exit the mixture has 0.1 MPa pressure and 100 m/s velocity. The turbine is well insulated and the flow process can be assumed adiabatic. Evaluate the power output of the turbine. Neglect changes in elevation and take c_P = 1.05 kJ/kg K, γ = 1.4 and R = 300 J/kg K.

Solution:

$$\text{Mass flow rate, } \frac{dm}{dt} = 60 \text{ kg/min}$$

$$= 1 \text{ kg/sec}$$

$p_1 = 4 \times 10^6$ N/m^2

T_1 = 1320 K

V_1 = 200 m/s

$h_1 = c_P T_1$

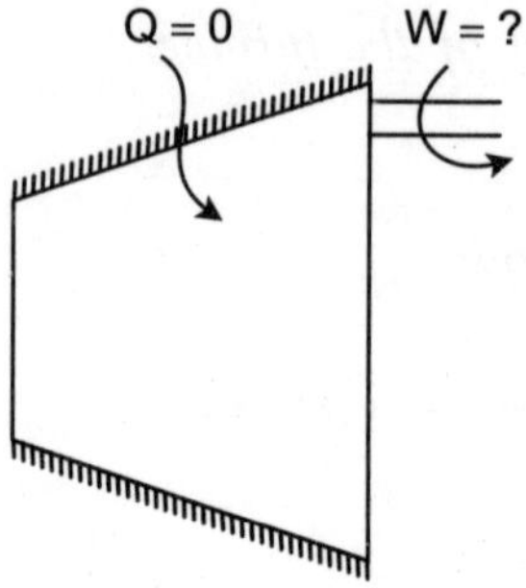

$p_2 = 0.1\times10^6$ N/m^2

V_2 = 100 m/s

$$h_2 = c_P T_2 = c_P T_1\left[\frac{p_2}{p_1}\right]^{\frac{\gamma-1}{\gamma}}$$

$$= c_P\times1320\left[\frac{1}{40}\right]^{\frac{0.4}{1.4}}$$

$$= c_P\times460$$

Applying SFEE equation

$$\frac{dm}{dt}\left[h_1 + \frac{V_1^2}{2} + \cancel{gz_1}\right] + \cancel{Q}^0 = \frac{dm}{dt}\left[h_2 + \frac{V_2^2}{2} + \cancel{gz_2}\right] + W$$

$$1\left[c_P(T_1 - T_2) + \frac{V_1^2 - V_2^2}{2}\right] = W$$

$$W = 1.05\times10^3(1320-460) + \frac{(200)^2-(100)^2}{2}$$

$$= \mathbf{918000\ J/s = 918\ kW} \qquad \textbf{Ans.}$$

Example 3.19

The gas leaving the turbine jet engine flows steadily into the jet pipe with enthalpy 960 kJ/kg and velocity 250 m/s relate to the pipe. The exit from the pipe is at enthalpy 860 kJ/kg and the exhaust is in line with intake. Neglecting the heat loss from the system, determine the relative velocity of gas leaving the pipe.

Solution:

$$h_1 = 960\ \text{kJ/kg}$$
$$V_1 = 250\ \text{m/s}$$
$$h_2 = 860\ \text{kJ/kg}$$
$$V_2 = ?$$

Applying SFEE

$$h_1 + \frac{V_1^2}{2} + \cancel{q}^0 = h_2 + \frac{V_2^2}{2} + \cancel{w}^0$$

$$V_2 = \sqrt{2(h_1-h_2) + V_1^2}$$

$$= \sqrt{2(960-860)\times10^3 + (250)^2}$$

$$= \sqrt{200\times10^3 + 62500}$$

$$= \mathbf{512.35\ m/s} \qquad \textbf{Ans.}$$

Example 3.20

An air compressor compresses atmospheric air at 0.1 MPa and 27°C by ten times of inlet pressure. During compression the heat loss to surrounding is estimated to be 5% of the compression work. Air enters compressor with velocity of 40 m/s and leaves with 100 m/s. Inlet and exit cross-section areas are 100 cm² and 20 cm² respectively. Estimate the temperature of air at exit from compressor and power input to compressor. **(UPTU 2nd Sem., 2001-02)**

Solution:

At compressor inlet

$$p_1 = 0.1\ \text{MPa} = 0.1\times10^6\ \text{N/m}^2 = 10^5\ \text{N/m}^2 = 100\ \text{kN/m}^2$$

$$T_1 = 27+273 = 300\ \text{K}$$

$$p_1v_1 = RT_1$$

$$v_1 = \frac{RT_1}{p_1} = \frac{0.287\times300}{100} = 0.861\ \text{m}^3/\text{kg}$$

$$\frac{dm}{dt} = \frac{A_1V_1}{v_1}$$

$$= \frac{100 \times 10^{-4} \times 40}{0.861}$$

$$= 0.464576 \text{ kg/sec}$$

$$v_2 = \frac{A_2V_2}{\left(\frac{dm}{dt}\right)} = \frac{20\times10^{-4}\times100}{0.464576} = 0.4305 \text{ m}^3\text{/kg}$$

Exit temperature, $T_2 = \frac{p_2v_2}{R} = \frac{1000 \times 0.4305}{0.287} = 1500 \text{ K}$

$$= 1500 - 273 = 1227°\text{C}$$

Applying steady state equation

$$Q_{1-2} - W_{1-2} = \frac{dm}{dt}\left[c_P(T_2 - T_1) + \frac{V_2^2 - V_1^2}{2\times10^3}\right]$$

$$Q_{1-2} = 0.05\ W_{1-2}$$

Q_{1-2} and W_{1-2} both are negative.

$$\therefore \quad - Q_{1-2} - W_{1-2} = 0.4305\left[1.05(1500-300) + \frac{100^2 - 40^2}{2\times10^3}\right]$$

$$-0.05\ W_{1-2} + W_{1-2} = 0.4305[1.05\times1200 + 42]$$

$$0.95\ W_{1-2} = 560.511$$

$$W_{1-2} = \mathbf{590\ kW}$$

Ans.

Example 3.21

A centrifugal compressor delivers 15 kg of air per minute. The inlet and outlet conditions are:

At inlet:

Velocity = 5 m/s, enthalpy = 5 kJ/kg

Heat loss to cooling water is 756 kJ/minute

At outlet:

Velocity = 7.5 m/s, enthalpy = 173 kJ/kg

Find:

i. The power of motor required to derive the compressor.

ii. Ratio of inlet pipe diameter to outlet pipe diameter when specific volumes of air at inlet and outlet are 0.5 m³/kg and 0.15 m³/kg respectively. Inlet and outlet lines are at the same level. **[UPTU 1st Semester, 2002-03]**

Solution:

i.

$$V_1 = 5 \text{ m/s} \qquad V_2 = 7.5 \text{ m/s}$$

$$h_1 = 5 \times 10^3 \text{ J/kg} \qquad h_2 = 173\times10^3 \text{ J/kg}$$

$$Q = -756 \times 10^3 \text{ J/min} \qquad \frac{dm}{dt} = 15 \text{ kg/min}$$

$$= \frac{-756}{60}\times10^3 \text{ J/sec} \qquad = \frac{1}{4} \text{ kg/sec}$$

$$\frac{dm}{dt}\left[h_1 + \frac{V_1^2}{2} + gz_1\right] + Q = \frac{dm}{dt}\left[h_2 + \frac{V_2^2}{2} + gz_2\right] + W$$

$$W = \frac{dm}{dt}\left[(h_1 - h_2) + \frac{V_1^2 - V_2^2}{2}\right] + Q$$

$$= \frac{1}{4}\left[(5-173)\times10^3 + \frac{(5)^2-(7.5)^2}{2}\right] - \frac{756\times10^3}{60}$$

$$= \frac{1}{4}[-168 - 15.625] - 12.6\times10^3$$

$$= \mathbf{-12645.9 \text{ J/sec.}}$$ **Ans.**

ii.

$$\frac{dm}{dt} = \frac{A_1V_1}{v_1} = \frac{A_2V_2}{v_2}$$

$$\frac{A_1}{A_2} = \frac{V_2}{V_1} \times \frac{v_1}{v_2}$$

$$= \frac{7.5}{5} \times \frac{0.5}{0.15}$$

$$= 5$$

$$\frac{d_1}{d_2} = \sqrt{5}$$

$$= \mathbf{2.236}$$ **Ans.**

Example 3.22

A centrifugal water pump delivers 2750 kg of water per minute from initial pressure of 0.8 bar absolute to a final pressure of 2.8 bar absolute. The suction is 2 m below and the delivery is 5 m above the centre of pump. If the suction and delivery pipes are of 15 cm and 10 cm diameter respectively, make calculations for the power required to run the pump.

Solution:

Here there is no change in internal energy and no heat interaction. The steady flow energy equation is given by

$$p_1v_1 + \frac{V_1^2}{2} + gz_1 = p_2v_2 + \frac{V_2^2}{2} + gz_2 + w$$

$$\frac{p_1}{\rho_1} + \frac{V_1^2}{2} + gz_1 = \frac{p_2}{\rho_2} + \frac{V_2^2}{2} + gz_2 + w$$

From continuity consideration

$$\frac{dm}{dt} = \frac{A_1V_1}{v_1} = \frac{A_2V_2}{v_2}$$

$$= \rho_1A_1V_1 = \rho_2A_2V_2$$

Density of water, $\rho = \rho_1 = \rho_2 = 1000$ kg/m^3

$$\frac{2750}{60} = 1000 \times \frac{\pi}{4}(1.15)^2 \times V_1$$

$$V_1 = 2.59 \text{ m/s}$$

$$V_2 = 5.84 \text{ m/s}$$

Taking suction level as datum for elevation head $z_1 = 0$, $z_2 = 2+5 = 7$ m

$$w = \frac{p_1 - p_2}{\rho} + \frac{V_1^2 - V_2^2}{2} + g(z_1 - z_2)$$

$$= \frac{(0.8 - 2.8) \times 10^5}{1000} + \frac{(2.59)^2 - (5.84)^2}{2} + 9.81(0 - 7)$$

$$= -200 - 13.70 - 68.67$$

$$= -282.37 \text{ J/kg}$$

The negative sign indicates that work is absorbed by the pump. The power required to derive the pump will be

$$\frac{dm}{dt} \times w = \frac{2750}{60} \times 282.37$$

$$= 12942 \text{ J/sec}$$

$$= \mathbf{12.942 \text{ kW}}$$

Ans.

Example 3.23

Carbon dioxide passing through a heat exchanger at a rate of 120 kg/hr is cooled down from 800°C to 50°C. Write the steady flow energy equation. Assuming that the changes in pressure, kinetic energy and potential energy and flow work interaction are negligible, determine the rate of heat removal. (Take c_P = 1.08 kJ/kg K) **[UPTU 1st Sem. (CO) 2003]**

Solution:

Mass flow rate, $\frac{dm}{dt} = 120 \text{ kg/hr} = \frac{120}{3600} \text{ kg/sec}$

Initial temperature, $T_1 = 800°C = 800 + 273 = 1073 \text{ K}$

Final temperature, $T_2 = 50°C = 50 + 273 = 323 \text{ K}$

Change in pressure energy = 0

Change in kinetic energy = 0

Change in potential energy = 0

Flow work interaction, W = 0

Rate of heat removal, Q = ?

$$\frac{dm}{dt}\left[c_P(T_1 - T_2)\right] + Q = W^0$$

$$\frac{120}{3600}\left[1.08 \times 10^3 (800 - 50)\right] + Q = 0$$

$$Q = -27000 \text{ J/sec}$$

$$= \mathbf{-27 \ kW}$$

Ans.

Example 3.24

Refrigerant Freon-12 enters the condenser of a refrigeration plant with enthalpy 224 kJ/kg at 15°C and leaves with enthalpy 64.85 kJ/kg at 20°C. Make calculations for the mass flow rate of cooling water for unit mass of refrigerant.

Solution:

$$h_1 = 224 \text{ kJ/kg} = 224 \times 10^3 \text{ J/kg}$$

$$h_2 = 64.85 \text{ kJ/kg} = 64.85 \times 10^3 \text{ J/kg}$$

$$T_1 = 15°C = 15 + 273 = 288 \text{ K}$$

$$T_2 = 20 + 273 = 293 \text{ K}$$

Heat lost by refrigerant = Heat gained by water

$$m_r(h_1 - h_2) = m_w\, c(T_1 - T_2)$$

$$m_w = \frac{m_r(h_1 - h_2)}{c(T_1 - T_2)}$$

$$= \frac{1(224 - 64.85) \times 10^3}{4.2(15 - 20) \times 10^3}$$

$$= \mathbf{7.6 \ kg}$$

Ans.

Example 3.25

0.5 kg/sec of fluid flows in a steady state process. The properties of fluid at entrance are measured as p_1 = 1.4 bar, density 2.5 kg/m³, u_1 = 920 kJ/kg while at exit the properties are p_2 = 5.6 bar, density = 5 kg/m³ and u_2 = 720 kJ/kg. The velocity at entrance is 20 m/s while at exit it is 180 m/s. It rejects 50 kW of heat and rises through 60 m during the flow. Find the change of enthalpy and the rate of work done.

Solution:

$$\frac{dm}{dt} = 0.5 \text{ kg/sec}$$

$$p_1 = 1.4 \times 10^5 \text{ N/m}^2 \qquad p_2 = 5.6 \times 10^5 \text{ N/m}^2$$

$$v_1 = \frac{1}{2.5} \text{ m}^3\text{/kg} \qquad v_2 = \frac{1}{5} \text{ m}^3\text{/kg}$$

$$u_1 = 920 \times 10^3 \text{ J/kg} \qquad u_2 = 720 \times 10^3 \text{ J/kg}$$

$$V_1 = 200 \text{ m/s} \qquad V_2 = 180 \text{ m/s}$$

$$z_1 = 0 \qquad z_2 = 60 \text{ m}$$

$$Q = -50 \text{ kW}$$

Change in enthalpy = $h_1 - h_2$ = ?

Work done W = ?

Change in enthalpy

$$h_1 - h_2 = (u_1 + p_1v_1) - (u_2 + p_2v_2)$$

$$= (u_1 - u_2) + (p_1v_1 - p_2v_2)$$

$$= (920 - 720) \times 10^3 + \left(1.4 \times 10^5 \times \frac{1}{2.5} - 5.6 \times 10^5 \times \frac{1}{5}\right)$$

$$= 144 \times 10^3 \text{ J/kg} = \mathbf{144 \text{ kJ/kg}}$$ **Ans.**

Applying SFEE

$$\frac{dm}{dt}\left[h_1 + \frac{V_1^2}{2} + gz_1\right] + Q = \frac{dm}{dt}\left[h_2 + \frac{V_2^2}{2} + gz_2\right] + W$$

$$W = \frac{dm}{dt}\left[(h_1 - h_2) + \frac{V_1^2 - V_2^2}{2} + g(z_1 - z_2)\right] + Q$$

$$= 0.5\left[144\times10^3 + \frac{(200)^2 - (180)^2}{2} + 9.81(0-60)\right] - 52\times10^3$$

$$= 21605.7 \text{ J/sec}$$

$$= \mathbf{21.6 \text{ kW}}$$ **Ans.**

Example 3.26

Air at a temperature of 20°C passes through a heat exchanger at a velocity of 40 m/s where its temperature is raised to 820°C. It then enters a turbine with same velocity of 40 m/s and expands till the temperature falls to 620°C. On leaving the turbine, the air is taken at a velocity of 55 m/s to a nozzle where it expands until the temperature has fallen to 520°C. If the air flow rate is 2.5 kg/sec calculate:

i. Rate of heat transfer to the air in the heat exchanger.

ii. The power output from the turbine assuming no heat loss.

iii. The velocity at exit from the nozzle, assuming no heat loss.

Take the enthalpy of air as $h = c_P T$ where c_P is the specific heat equal to 1.005 kJ/kg °C and T is the temperature.

Solution:

Let entry at heat exchanger, turbine and nozzle be 1, 2 and 3 respectively.

Then, as per given conditions:

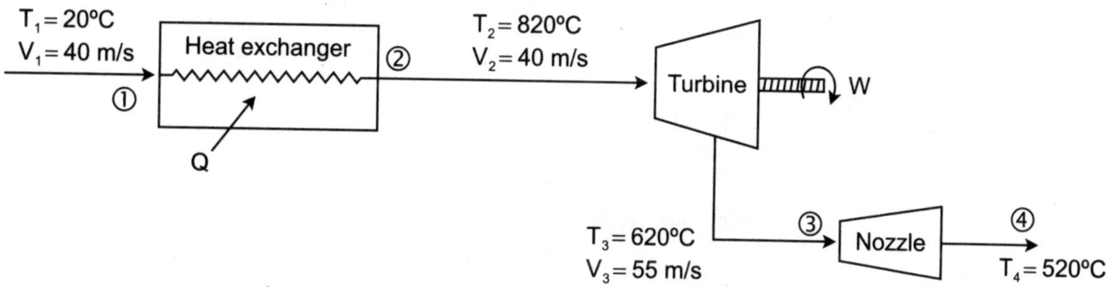

Mass flow rate, $\frac{dm}{dt} = 2.5$ kg/sec

i. Heat exchanger: Applying SFEE

$$\frac{dm}{dt}\left[h_1 + \frac{V_1^2}{2} + gz_1\right] + Q = \frac{dm}{dt}\left[h_2 + \frac{V_2^2}{2} + gz_2\right] + W_{1-2}$$

Here $z_1 = z_2$, $V_1 = V_2 = 40$ m/s, $W_{1-2} = 0$

$$\therefore \quad Q_{1-2} = \frac{dm}{dt}[(h_2 - h_1)] = \frac{dm}{dt}c_P(T_2 - T_1)$$

$$= 2.5 \times 1.005 \times 10^3(820 - 20)$$

$$= 2010 \times 10^3 \text{ J/sec} = \mathbf{2010\ kW}$$ **Ans.**

ii. Turbine:

Power output of turbine

Again applying SFEE

$$\frac{dm}{dt}\left[h_2 + \frac{V_2^2}{2}\right] = \frac{dm}{dt}\left[h_3 + \frac{V_3^2}{2}\right] + W_{2-3}$$

$$W_{2-3} = \frac{dm}{dt}\left[(h_2 - h_3) + \frac{V_2^2 - V_3^2}{2}\right]$$

$$= 2.5\left[c_P (T_2 - T_3) + \frac{V_2^2 - V_3^2}{2}\right]$$

$$= 2.5\left[1.005\times10^3 (820-620) + \frac{(40)^2 - (55)^2}{2}\right]$$

$$= 504.3\times10^3 \text{ J/sec}$$

$$= \mathbf{504.3 \text{ kW}}$$ **Ans.**

iii. Nozzle:

Velocity at exit from the nozzle:

Energy equation for nozzle gives

$$h_3 + \frac{V_3^2}{2} = h_4 + \frac{V_4^2}{2}$$

$$\frac{V_4^2}{2} = c_P (T_3 - T_4) + \frac{V_3^2}{2}$$

$$= 1.005\times10^3 (620 - 520) + \frac{(55)^2}{2}$$

$$= 102012.5$$

$$V_4 = 319.4 \text{ m/sec}$$

Velocity at exit from the nozzle = **319.4 m/s** **Ans.**

THEORETICAL QUESTIONS

1. What is the essence of first law of thermodynamics? Write down expressions for first law applied to a (i) cycle and (ii) process.
2. What is the mechanical equivalent of heat? Write down its value when heat is expressed in kJ and work is expressed in N-m.
3. What do you mean by 'Perpetual Motion Machine of First Kind (PMM1)?
4. How enthalpy is related to internal energy?
5. Define internal energy. Is it a function of state or a process?
6. Prove that the rate of change of heat interchange per unit change of volume when gas is compressed or expanded is given by $\frac{\gamma-n}{\gamma-1}\times\frac{pdv}{J}$.
7. Prove that polytropic work

$$w = \frac{p_1v_1-p_2v_2}{n-1}$$

   where the terms have their usual meanings.
8. Show that when an ideal gas is compressed in a piston-cylinder arrangement according to the polytropic law pV^n = constant, the
   i. heat rejected : increase in internal energy: Work done

   $$::(\gamma-n):(n-1):(\gamma-1)$$

   ii. $c_n = c_V\frac{\gamma-n}{n-1}$

   where c_n and c_V are polytropic and constant volume specific heats respectively.
9. Write down the general energy equation for steady flow system and then apply it to
   i. Steam nozzle or diffuser
   ii. Steam or gas turbine
   iii. Rotary air compressor
   iv. Reciprocating air compressor
   v. Centrifugal water pump
   vi. Boiler or steam generator
   vii. Heat exchanger
10. Explain the concept of flow work.
11. How control volume is different from a system?

NUMERICAL PROBLEMS

1. In a vessel 10 kg of oxygen is heated in a reversible, constant volume process so that the pressure of oxygen is increased two times that of the initial value. The initial temperature is 25°C. Calculate
   i. The final temperature.
   ii. The change in the internal energy.
   iii. The heat transfer.
2. A system comprising of a pure substance undergoes a process in which the internal energy decreases by 40 kJ. The heat transfer to the system is 20 kJ.
   i. Determine the magnitude and direction of work done.
   ii. If in undergoing a different process between the same end states the work done had been zero, what would be the magnitude and direction of heat transfer.
3. In a non-flow reversible process, the pressure and volume are related by

   $p = V^2 + \frac{10}{V}$ where p is in bar and V is in m^3.

   During a process, the volume changes from 0.5 m^3 to 1.5 m^3. The heat added during the process is 1000 kJ. Determine the change in internal energy.
4. A closed system of constant volume experiences a temperature rise of 20°C when a certain process occurs. The heat transferred in the process of 15 kJ. The specific heat at constant volume for the pure substance comprising the system is 1.0 kJ/kg °C, the system contains 2 kg of the substance. Determine the change in internal energy and work done.
5. The internal energy of a certain substance is given by the following equation:

   $u = pv + 80$

   where u is given in kJ/kg, p is in kPa and v in m^3/kg.

   A system composed of 3 kg of this substance expands from an initial pressure of 500 kPa and a volume of 0.20 m^3 to a final pressure 10 kPa in which pressure and volume are related by

   $pv^{1.4} = \text{Constant}$

   i. If the expansion is quasi-static, find Q, ΔU and W for the process.
   ii. In another process the same system expands according to same pressure-volume relationship as in part (i) and from the same initial state to the same final state (i) but the heat transfer in this case is 30 kJ. Find the work transfer for this process.
   iii. Explain the difference in work transfer in parts (i) and (ii).
6. A fluid is contained in a cylinder by a spring loaded frictionless piston so that the pressure in the fluid is linear function of volume ($p = a + bV$). The internal energy of the fluid is given by the following equation

   $U = 35 + 3.0\ pV$

where U is in kJ, p in kPa and V in cubic meter. If the fluid changes from an initial state of 190 kPa, 0.03 m^3 to a find state of 400 kPa, 0.06 m^3, with no work other than that done on the piston, find the direction and magnitude of the work and heat transfer.

7. In a certain steam plant, the turbine develops 1000 kW. The heat supplied to the steam in the boiler is 3000 kJ/kg, the heat received by the system from cooling water in the condenser is 2400 kJ/kg and the feed pump work required to pump the condensate back into the boiler is 5 kW. Calculate the steam flow round the cycle in kg/sec.
8. A closed system undergoes a reversible process at a constant pressure of 3.0 bar and its volume changes from 0.15 m^3 to 0.05 m^3. 25 kJ of heat is rejected by the system during the process. Determine the change in internal energy of the system.
9. 1 kg of nitrogen (molecular wt. 28) is compressed reversibly and isothermally from 1.05 bar, 20°C to 4.2 bar. Calculate the work done and heat flow during the process. Assume the nitrogen to be a perfect gas.
10. Oxygen (molecular wt. 32) is compressed reversibly and polytropically in a cylinder from 1.05 bar, 25°C to 4.2 bar in such a way that 1/3rd of the work input is rejected as heat to the cylinder walls. Calculate the final temperature of the oxygen. Take $c_V = 0.649$ kJ/kg K.
11. Prove that for an adiabatic process

$$T^{a_2}\, e^{\left(bT + (c/2)T^2\right)} v^{(a_1 - a_2)} = \text{constant}$$

where

$$c_P = a_1 + bT + cT^2$$

$$c_V = a_2 + bT + cT^2$$

12. A certain amount of gas at 300°C expands from 0.0361 m^3 according to law pv^n = constant. The initial pressure is 14 bar and the final pressure is 1 bar. The value of specific heat at constant volume is 0.18 at 300°C and at this temperature the value of $\gamma = 1.39$. The specific heat at constant pressure and constant volume are given by

$$c_P = a + 0.00012T$$

$$c_V = b + 0.00012T$$

Find the

(a) final temperature (b) work done (c) change in internal energy

(d) heat transfer (e) polytrophic specific heat

13. A cylinder contains 2.5 m^3 of gas at 1×10^5 N/m^2 and 100°C. The gas is compressed to a volume of 0.625 m^3, the final pressure being 6×10^5 N/m^2. Determine:
    i. The mass of gas
    ii. The value of index 'n' for compression
    iii. The increase in internal energy of gas
    iv. The heat received or rejected by the gas during compression

    ($\gamma = 1.4$, R = 294.2 Nm/kg °C)

FIRST LAW APPLIED TO FLOW PROCESSES

14. Steam enters a nozzle at a pressure of 7 bar and 20°C (i.e. initial enthalpy 2850 kJ/kg) and leaves at a pressure of 1.5 bar. The initial velocity of steam at the entrance is 40 m/s and exit velocity from the nozzle is 1400 m/sec. The heat loss from the nozzle is 1100 kJ/hr. Determine the final enthalpy of steam and nozzle area if the specific volume 1.24 m^3/kg.
15. An adiabatic diffuser is employed to reduce the velocity of steam of air from 238 m/s to 50.4 m/s. The inlet pressure is 1.02 bar and inlet temperature is 390°C. Determine the final pressure and the required outlet area if the mass flow rate is 5.83 kg/sec.
16. In a boiler, water enters with an enthalpy of 160 kJ/kg and steam leaves with enthalpy of 2925 kJ/kg. Find the heat transferred per kg of steam. The change is kinetic energy and potential energy may be neglected.
17. The boiler used in a paper factory is fed with 1,50,000 kg/hr of water having an enthalpy of 836 kJ/kg. The steam leaves the boiler for utilisation at an enthalpy of 3345 kJ/kg. The amount of coal burnt having calorific value as 30900 kJ/kg is 15000 kg/hr. For the combustion process, 13 kg of air is supplied per kg of coal in the boiler at an enthalpy of 293 kJ/kg. Calculate the energy that is not accounted for per kg of coal if the changes in kinetic energy and potential energy are negligible.
18. A metal extrudes slowly through a die under a pressure of 2000 bar. The density of the material 94000 kg/m^3 and its specific heat is 0.21 kJ/kg. The metal may be assumed as incompressible material. Calculate the rise in temperature of the metal if there is no cooling of the metal during extruding process.
19. In a gas turbine, the mass flow rate of gas through the turbine is 17 kg/sec. The power developed by the turbine is 1000 kW. The enthalpies of gases at inlet and outlet are 1200 kJ/kg and 360 kJ/kg respectively, the velocity of gas at the inlet and outlet are 60 m/s and 150 m/s respectively. Calculate the rate at which heat is rejected from the turbine. Calculate also the area of inlet pipe if specific volume of gas at inlet is 0.5 m^3/kg.
20. The mass flow of air through a reciprocating compressor is 0.4 kg/sec. The air enters at 6 m/s with pressure of 1 bar and specific volume of 0.85 m^3/kg and leaves at 4.5 m/s with a pressure of 6.9 bar and specific volume of 0.16 m^3/kg. The internal energy of air leaving the compressor is 80 kJ/kg greater than that of air entering. Cooling water of cylinder jacket absorbs heat at the rate of 59 kW. Determine the power required to drive the compressor and the inlet and outlet pipe cross-section area.
21. An air stream of 2 kg/min with a velocity of 20 m/s and temperature 30°C is mixed with another air stream of 4 kg/min with velocity 30 m/s and temperature 40°C. 20 kJ/kg of mixture of heat is lost to the surrounding during the mixing. Draw the system with control volume and find the temperature of stream mixture leaving the system. Take $h = c_p T$ where c_p = 1040 kJ/kg.

4

Second Law of Thermodynamics

4.1 Limitations of First Law of Thermodynamics and Introduction to Second Law

The energy can flow from a system in the form of heat or work. The first law sets no limit to the amount of total energy of a system which can be caused to flow out as work. The second law sets the limit for energy flow. This states that heat will flow naturally from one energy reservoir to another at a lower temperature, but not in opposite direction without assistance. This is important because a heat engine operates between two energy reservoirs at different temperatures.

Further, the first law establishes equivalence between the quantity of heat used and the mechanical work but does not specify the conditions under which the conversion of heat into work is possible, neither the direction in which heat transfer can take place. Answers to these questions have been given by the second law of thermodynamics.

4.2 Thermal Reservoir

A thermal reservoir is that part of environment which can exchange heat with a system. Thermal reservoir has sufficiently large heat capacity and its temperature is not affected by the quantity of heat transferred to or from it. A thermal reservoir has a constant temperature. The change in temperature because of heat addition or rejection is so small that processes within it are quasi-static. High temperature reservoir which supplies heat is known as heat source. Examples of source are boiler furnace, combustion chamber and a nuclear reactor, etc. Low temperature reservoir which rejects the heat is called the heat sink. Examples of sink are atmosphere, ocean and river.

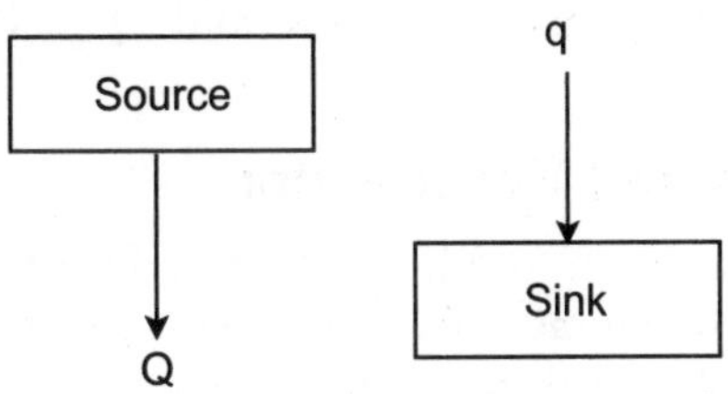

Fig. 4.1: Source and Sink

4.3 Heat Engine and Thermal Efficiency

A heat engine produces work from heat while operating in a cyclic process. Both heat and work interactions take place across the boundary of this cyclically operating device.

A heat engine has following features:

i. It receives heat Q_1 from a high temperature source at T_1.
ii. It partially converts the received heat into mechanical work W.
iii. It rejects the remaining heat Q_2 to a low temperature sink at T_2.
iv. It is a cyclic process and working substance flows through the engine.

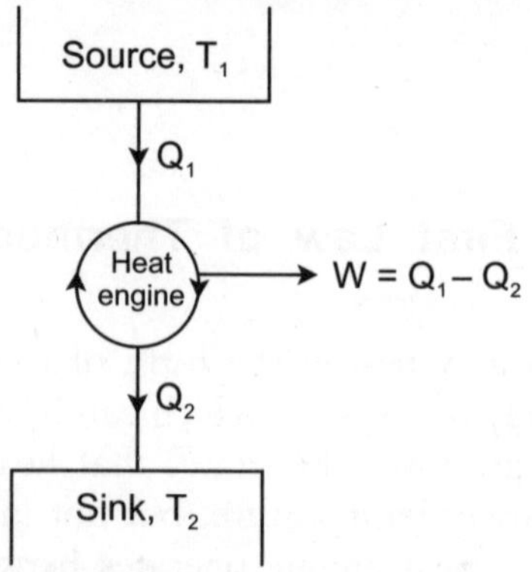

Fig. 4.2: Heat Engine

We know that efficiency of machine is the ratio of output to the input.

So, thermal efficiency of a heat engine

$$\eta_{th} = \frac{\text{Net work output}}{\text{Total heat supplied}}$$

$$= \frac{Q_1 - Q_2}{Q_1}$$

$$= 1 - \frac{Q_2}{Q_1} \quad \ldots\ldots (4.1)$$

So, thermal efficiency of a heat engine operating between two thermal reservoirs is always less than unity. Thermal efficiency can be increased by reducing the heat rejected Q_2 while keeping the heat supplied Q_1 constant.

Thermal efficiency can be unity when $Q_1 \to \infty$ and $Q_2 = 0$ which is not possible in real practice.

4.4 COP of Heat Pump and Refrigerator

Refrigerators and heat pumps are reversed heat engines. These operate in backward direction. The direction of heat and work interactions are opposite to that of a heat engine, i.e. work input and heat output. These devices transfer heat from a body at low temperature to a body at high temperature.

When the desired purpose is to remove the heat from a cooled body, it is called a refrigerator. It operates between the temperature of surrounding and a temperature below that of surrounding.

The heat pump is used to supply heat to a body which is already at a high temperature than its surrounding. So it operates between the temperature of surrounding and temperature above that of surrounding. Heat pump is used to keep the rooms warm in the winter.

The performance of a refrigerator and heat pump is expressed in terms of co-efficient of performance (COP).

$$COP = \frac{\text{Desired effect}}{\text{Work input}}$$

In a refrigerator, the desired effect is the amount of heat extracted Q_2

$$\therefore \quad (COP)_{ref} = \frac{Q_2}{W}$$

But $W = Q_1 - Q_2$

$$\therefore \quad (COP)_{ref} = \frac{Q_2}{Q_1 - Q_2} \quad \text{.......... (4.2)}$$

In a heat pump, the desired effect is the amount of heat supplied, Q_1

$$\therefore \quad (COP)_{H.P.} = \frac{Q_1}{W} = \frac{Q_1}{Q_1 - Q_2} \quad \text{.......... (4.3)}$$

$$= 1 + \frac{Q_2}{Q_1 - Q_2} = 1 + (COP)_{ref} \quad \text{.......... (4.4)}$$

So, COP of a heat pump is higher than COP of a refrigerator by unity when they are operating between same temperatures.

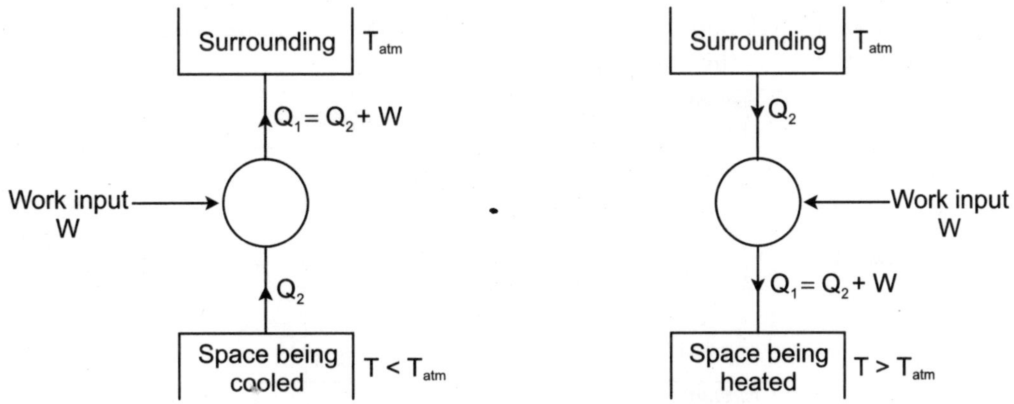

Fig. 4.3: Refrigerator and Heat Pump

4.5 Statements of Second Law

4.5.1 Kelvin-Plank Statement

According to this statement, 'It is impossible to construct an engine that operates in a cycle and produces no effect other than work output and exchange of heat with a single reservoir'.

So an engine cannot be developed that receives Q_1 amount of heat from a source and converts it into an equivalent amount of work, *i.e.* $W = Q_1$. The thermal efficiency of such an engine η_{th} or 100%. So according to the above statement no heat engine can have 100% thermal efficiency.

So for continuous power output from a heat engine, it is necessary that some part of the supplied heat is rejected to a sink at low temperature.

This amount is Q_2. So $W = Q_1 - Q_2$

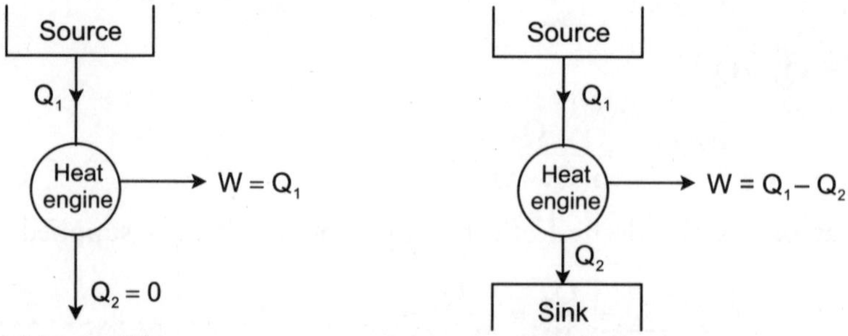

(a) Impossible (b) Possible

Fig. 4.4: Kelvin-Plank Statement

4.5.2 Clausius Statement

The statement says, "It is impossible to construct a device that operates in a cycle and produces no effect other than the transfer of heat from a system at low temperature to another system at high temperature."

It implies that heat itself cannot flow from a cooler body to a hotter body. Fig. 4.5 shows schematic representation of the statement

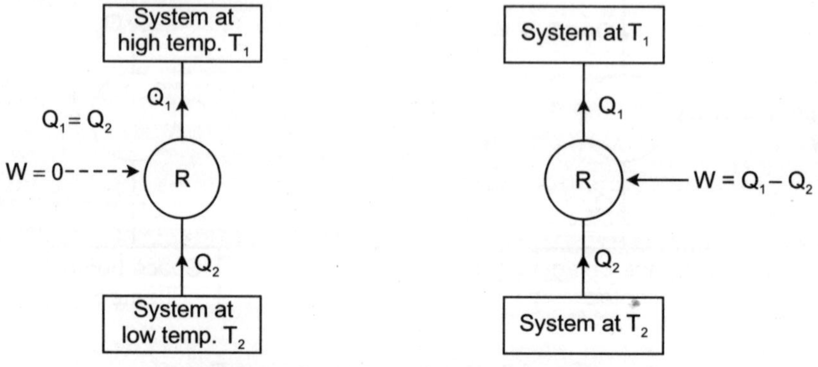

(a) Impossible (b) Possible

Fig. 4.5: Clausius Statement

In Fig. 4.5(a), we see that $Q_1 = Q_2$ or $W = 0$.

So $COP = Q_2/0 = \infty$ which is not possible.

The only alternative to transfer heat from a body at low temperature to a body at high temperature is that some external work must be applied to the machine.

4.5.3 Equivalence of Kelvin-Plank and Clausius Statements

The two statements are complimentary to each other. Violation of one leads to violation of other. Fig. 4.6 shows a refrigerator R that operates in a cycle and transfers heat from a low temperature reservoir (at temperature T_2) to a high temperature reservoir (at temperature T_1) without any external work. This is the violation of the Clausius statement. There is also a heat engine E that operates in a cycle. This engine takes Q_1 amount of heat from high temperature reservoir, delivers $(Q_1 - Q_2)$ amount of work to the surrounding and rejects the remaining Q_2 amount of heat to the low temperature reservoir. This engine operates in conformity with the Kelvin-Plank statement.

When this refrigerator and heat engine are coupled together, the composite system constitutes a device that receives $(Q_1 - Q_2)$ amount of heat from a high temperature reservoir and converts it completely into an equivalent amount of works, $W = (Q_1 - Q_2)$ without rejecting any heat to low temperature reservoir. This composite system violates the Kelvin-Plank statement.

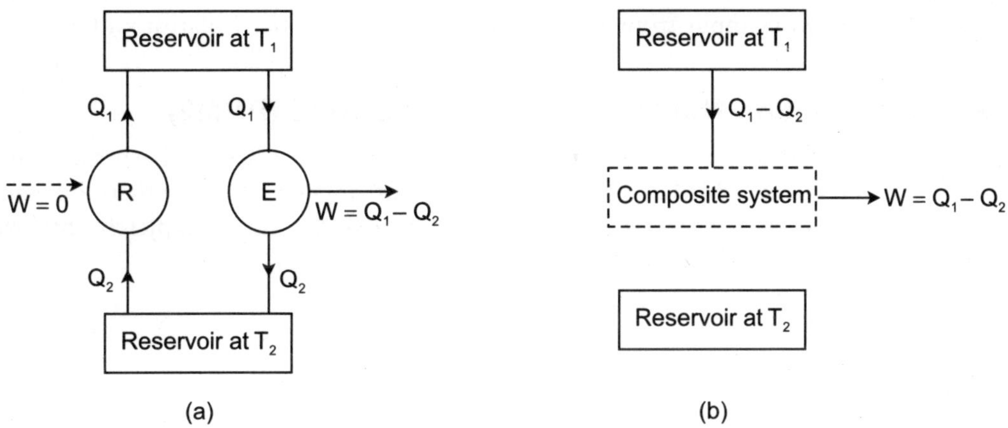

Fig. 4.6: Violation of Clausius statement leads to violation of Kelvin-Plank statement

Violation of Kelvin-Plank statement leads to violation of Clausius statement. Fig. 4.6 shows an engine E which operates from a single heat reservoir at temperature T_1. It receives Q_1 amount of heat from this reservoir and converts it completely into an equivalent amount of work, $W = Q_1$ without rejecting any heat to the low temperature reservoir at T_2. This is the violation of Kelvin-Plank statement. In Fig. 4.7(a) a refrigerator R is shown alongwith it, which extracts Q_2 amount of heat from low temperature reservoir, does Q_1 amount of work on it and supplies $(Q_1 + Q_2)$ amount of heat to the high temperature reservoir. The refrigerator operates in conformity with the Clausius statement.

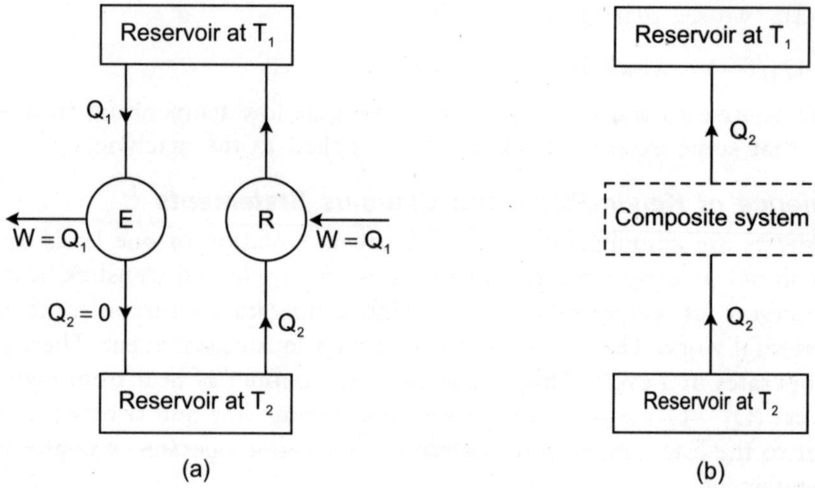

Fig. 4.7: Violation of Kelvin-Plank Statement Leads to Violation of Clausius Statement

Fig. 4.7 (b) shows a composite system in which output of heat engine is used to derive the refrigerator. So this device transfers heat from a low temperature reservoir to a high temperature reservoir without any work input from an external agency. This is the violation of the Clausius statement.

4.6 Perpetual Motion Machine of the Second Kind (PMM2)

A machine which violates the second law of thermodynamics is called Perpetual Motion Machine of the Second Kind (PMM2). This machine does not violate first law of thermodynamics. It absorbs heat from a single thermal reservoir and converts the heat completely into work. The efficiency of such a machine is 100%.

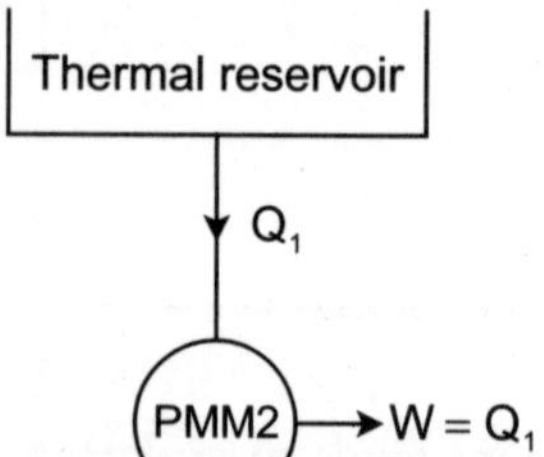

Fig. 4.8: Perpetual Motion Machine of the Second Kind (PMM2)

4.7 Carnot Cycle

It is a reversible hypothetical cycle. For a piston-cylinder arrangement, the cycle consists of following four successive processes.

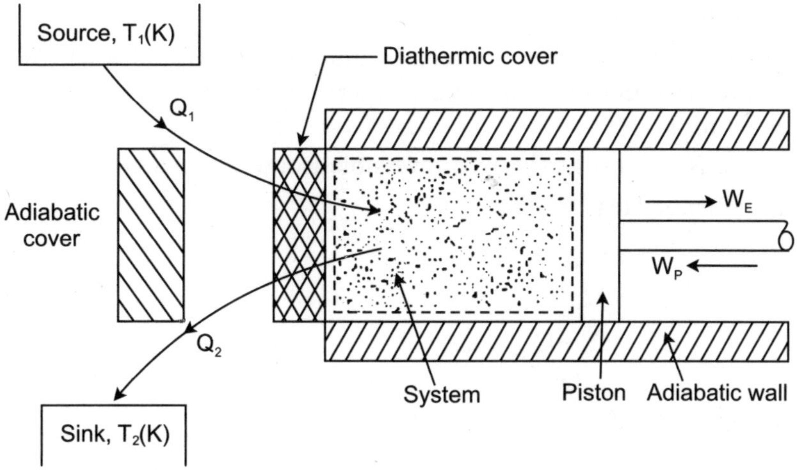

Fig. 4.9: Carnot Heat Engine

a. *Reversible Isothermal Process*

Heat, Q_1, enters the systems at T_1 reversibly from a constant temperature source at T_1 when the cylinder cover is in contact with the diathermic cover. The internal energy of the system increases.

b. *Reversible Adiabatic Process*

Diathermic cover is replaced by the adiabatic cover. The work, W_E, is done by the system adiabatically and reversibly at the expense of its internal energy and the temperature of system decreases from T_1 to T_2.

c. *Reversible Isothermal Process*

Again, adiabatic cover is replaced by diathermic cover and heat, Q_2, leaves the system at T_2 to a constant temperature sink at T_2 reversibly and the internal energy of the system further decreases.

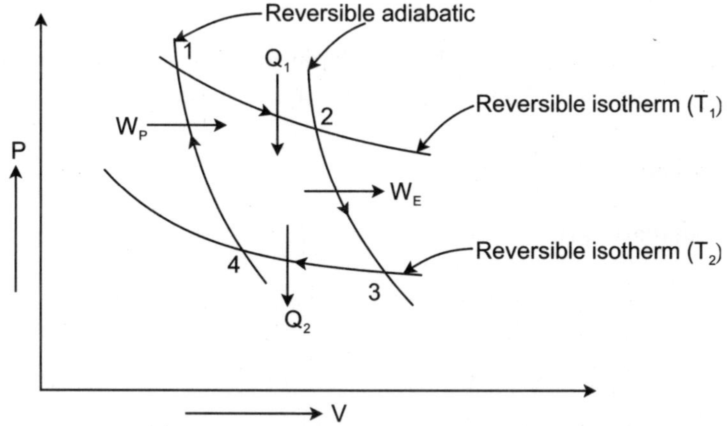

Fig. 4.10: Carnot Cycle

d. Reversible Adiabatic Process

Now, diathermic cover is again replaced by adiabatic cover and work, W_P, is done upon the system reversibly and adiabatically and internal energy of the increases and temperature rises from T_2 to T_1.

So a Carnot cycle is constituted by two reversible isotherms and two reversible adiabatics. Efficiency of a Carnot Heat Engine:

$$\eta_{H.E.} = \frac{W_{net}}{Q_1}$$

$$= \frac{Q_1 - Q_2}{Q_1}$$

Heat supplied during isothermal process 1–2

$$|Q_1| = W_{1-2} = p_1 V_1 \log_e \frac{V_2}{V_1} = mRT_1 \log_e \frac{V_2}{V_1}$$

Heat rejected during isothermal process 3–4

$$|Q_2| = W_{3-4} = p_3 V_3 \log_e \left|\frac{V_4}{V_3}\right|$$

$$= mRT_2 \log_e V_3/V_4 \qquad \text{(4.5)}$$

$$\eta_{H.E.} = \frac{mRT_1 \log_e \frac{V_2}{V_1} - mRT_2 \log_e \frac{V_3}{V_4}}{mRT_1 \log_e \frac{V_2}{V_1}}$$

$$= 1 - \frac{T_2 \log_e \frac{V_3}{V_4}}{T_1 \log_e \frac{V_2}{V_1}} \qquad \text{(4.6)}$$

For an ideal gas undergoing reversible adiabatic process, the temperature and volume are related by $TV^{\gamma-1}$ = constant. Therefore, for adiabatic process 2–3.

$$T_1 V_2^{\gamma-1} = T_2 V_3^{\gamma-1} \text{ or } \frac{T_1}{T_2} = \left(\frac{V_3}{V_2}\right)^{\gamma-1}$$

Similarly for adiabatic process 4–1

$$\frac{T_1}{T_2} = \left(\frac{V_4}{V_1}\right)^{\gamma-1}$$

$$\therefore \quad \frac{V_3}{V_2} = \frac{V_4}{V_1} \text{ or } \frac{V_3}{V_4} = \frac{V_2}{V_1}$$

$$\therefore \qquad \eta = 1-\frac{T_2}{T_1} = \frac{T_1-T_2}{T_1} \qquad \text{.......} \qquad (4.7)$$

4.8 Thermodynamic Temperature

The efficiency of a heat engine operating between two reservoirs is given by

$$\therefore \qquad \eta_{th} = \frac{Q_1-Q_2}{Q_1} = 1-\frac{Q_2}{Q_1}$$

The temperature of reservoir remains uniform and fixed irrespective of heat transfer. This means that reservoir has only one property defining its state and the heat transfer. This means that reservoir has only one property defining its state and the heat transfer from a reservoir is some function of that property, temperature. Thus, $Q = \phi(K)$ where K is the temperature of reservoir.

$$\frac{Q_1}{Q_2} = \frac{\phi(K_1)}{\phi(K_2)} \text{ becomes } \frac{\phi_1}{\phi_2} = \frac{T_1}{T_2}$$

where T_1 and T_2 are thermodynamic temperatures of the reservoirs.

The SI unit of thermodynamic temperature is Kelvin (K). The relation between triple point of water and 1 K is

$$1 \text{ K} = \frac{1}{273.16} \text{ temperature of 'Triple point of water'.}$$

4.9 Clausius Inequality

The efficiency of a reversible heat engine operating within the temperature limits T_1 and T_2 is given by

$$\eta = \frac{Q_1-Q_2}{Q_1} = \frac{T_1-T_2}{T_1} = 1-\frac{T_2}{T_1}$$

$$\frac{Q_1}{T_1} = \frac{Q_2}{T_2}$$

With positive sign for heat absorption and negative sign for heat rejection

$$\frac{Q_1}{T_1} - \left(\frac{-Q_2}{T_2}\right) = 0$$

$$\frac{Q_1}{T_1} + \frac{Q_2}{T_2} = 0 \qquad \text{.......} \qquad (4.8)$$

or

$$\sum\frac{Q}{T} = 0 \text{ for a reversible engine.}$$

The efficiency of a irreversible engine is lower than that of reversible engine operating within the same temperature limit

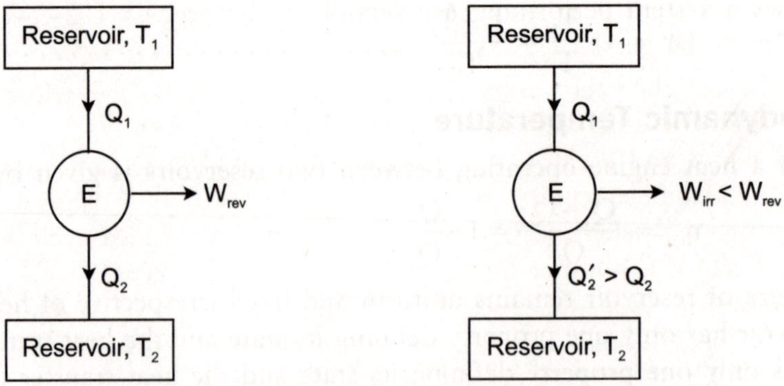

Fig. 4.11: Reversible and Irreversible Heat Engine

Therefore,

$$\frac{Q_1 - Q'_2}{Q_1} < \frac{T_1 - T_2}{T_1}$$

or $$1 - \frac{Q'_2}{Q_1} < 1 - \frac{T_2}{T_1}$$

or $$\frac{Q_1}{T_1} < \frac{Q'_2}{T_2}$$

Taking the sign convention for heat engine into account, we may write

$$\frac{Q_1}{T_1} - \frac{(-Q'_2)}{T_2} < 0$$

and $$\frac{Q_1}{T_1} + \frac{Q_2}{T_2} < 0 \qquad (4.9)$$

$$\sum \frac{Q}{T} < 0 \text{ for an irreversible engine.}$$

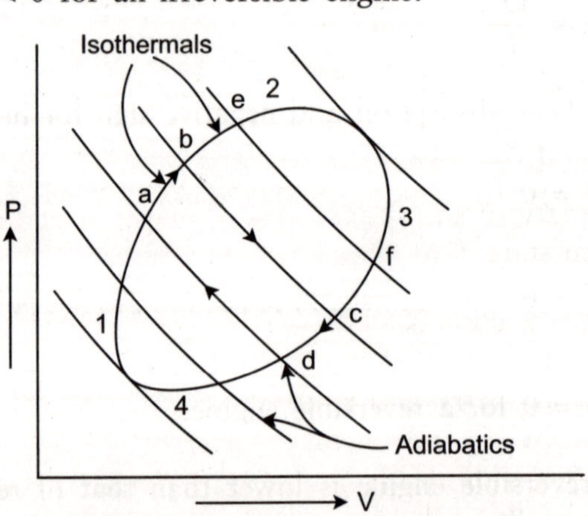

Fig. 4.12: Clausius Inequality

Fig. 4.12 shows a system performing a reversible cyclic process 1–2–3–4 drawn on p–V diagram. Let the cycle be cut by adiabatic lines similar to ad, bc, ef, etc.

The elementary cycle abcd then consists of two adiabatics da and bc and two elementary paths ab and cd. Since the adiabatics lie close to each other, the distance ab tends to be zero and so temperature at a and b can be imagined to be equal. Similarly points c and d are at the same temperature. The elementary paths ab and cd then conform to isothermal conditions and cycle abcd becomes an elementary Carnot cycle. Thus, the given cycle 1–2–3–4 may be considered to be made of a number of Carnot cycles.

So the total work from reversible cycle is the sum of work generated by individual cycles.

$$\sum \frac{Q_i}{T_i} = 0 \qquad \text{or} \qquad \left(\frac{\delta Q}{T}\right)_R = 0 \qquad (4.10)$$

Subscript R refers to reversible cycle. The equation is called Clausius theorem and it states that "The algebric sum of the ratio $\frac{\delta Q}{T}$, i.e. the heat interaction to the absolute temperature for a reversible heat engine is zero."

For an irreversible cycle

$$\sum \frac{Q_i}{T_i} < 0 \qquad \text{or} \qquad \oint_I \frac{\delta Q}{T} < 0 \qquad (4.11)$$

Here I refers to irreversible cycle. This equation is called Clausius inequality and states that "The algebric sum of ratio $\frac{\delta Q}{T}$, i.e. heat interaction to the absolute temperature for an irreversible heat engine is less than zero."

We can combine the two equations as

$$\oint \frac{\delta Q}{T} \leq 0 \quad \text{for an engine}$$

or

$$\oint \frac{\delta Q}{T} + I = 0 \qquad (4.12)$$

where I = Irreversibility

4.10 Entropy

Clausius theorem states that $\oint \frac{\delta Q}{T}$ for a reversible process is zero. It means that $\frac{\delta Q}{T}$ is a point function and hence a property of the system. The property is called entropy and is denoted by S. Entropy change from state 1 to state 2 during a reversible process

$$\int_1^2 \left(\frac{\delta Q}{T}\right)_{rev} = \int_1^2 dS = S_2 - S_1$$

Entropy is an extensive property and depends on the mass of the system. Its units are kJ/K. Specific entropy (entropy per unit mass) is denoted by s and its units are kJ/kg K. The entropy of a system increases with absorption of heat and decreases with heat rejection. For a reversible adiabatic process $\delta Q = 0$ and so will be the entropy change $(dS = 0)$.

Thus, entropy remains constant during a reversible adiabatic process. The process is called isentropic process. However, an isentropic process need not be an adiabatic process.

Entropy is a measure of degree of randomness or disorderness of molecules in a system.

4.11 Entropy is a Point Function

Consider a system from state 1 to state 2 by a reversible path A. The system may come back to initial state by following path B or C. The paths A and B together form a reversible cycle and so paths A and C. So according to Clausius statement

$$\int_1^2 \left(\frac{\delta Q}{T}\right)_A + \int_2^1 \left(\frac{\delta Q}{T}\right)_B = 0$$

Also $$\int_1^2 \left(\frac{\delta Q}{T}\right)_A + \int_2^1 \left(\frac{\delta Q}{T}\right)_C = 0$$

The above expression indicates that

$$\int_2^1 \left(\frac{\delta Q}{T}\right)_B = \int_2^1 \left(\frac{\delta Q}{T}\right)_C$$

So the integral of $\left(\frac{\delta Q}{T}\right)_{rev}$ is independent of path and depends only on end states. So $\left(\frac{\delta Q}{T}\right)_{rev}$ is an exact differential and hence a property of the system.

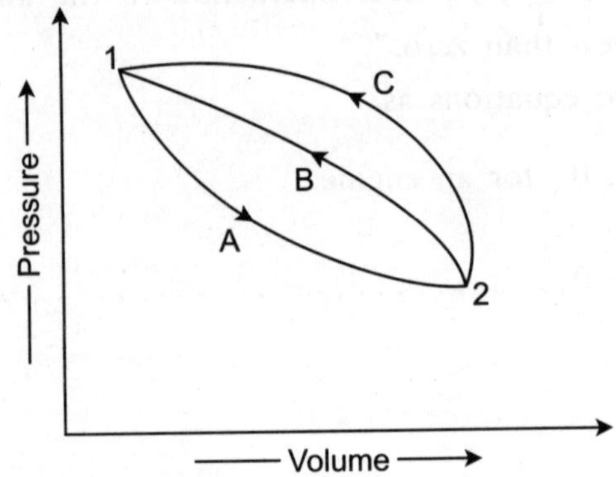

Fig. 4.13: Entropy a Point Function

4.12 Entropy Change for a Process

Consider a system that changes states from 1 to 2 through a reversible process A. Let the system comes back to initial state 1 by an irreversible process B.

The paths A and B together form an irreversible cycle. Applying Clausius inequality to the cycle, we have

$$\oint \frac{\delta Q}{T} = \int_1^2 \left(\frac{\delta Q}{T}\right)_A + \int_2^1 \left(\frac{\delta Q}{T}\right)_B < 0$$

As path A is reversible, so

$$\int_1^2 \left(\frac{\delta Q}{T}\right)_A = \int_1^2 (dS)_A$$

$$\therefore \int_1^2 (dS)_A + \int_2^1 \left(\frac{\delta Q}{T}\right)_B < 0$$

Now for a reversible path, limits of integration can be reversed with a negative sign

So $$\int_1^2 (dS)_A = -\int_2^1 (dS)_A$$

Then, we have

$$-\int_2^1 (dS)_A + \int_2^1 \left(\frac{\delta Q}{T}\right)_B < 0$$

or $$dS > \left(\frac{\delta Q}{T}\right)_{irrev}$$

Thus, entropy change for an irreversible process is

$$dS > \left(\frac{\delta Q}{T}\right)_{irrev}$$

Hence, in general

$$dS \geq \frac{\delta Q}{T}$$

or $$S_2 - S_1 \geq \int_1^2 \frac{\delta Q}{T}$$

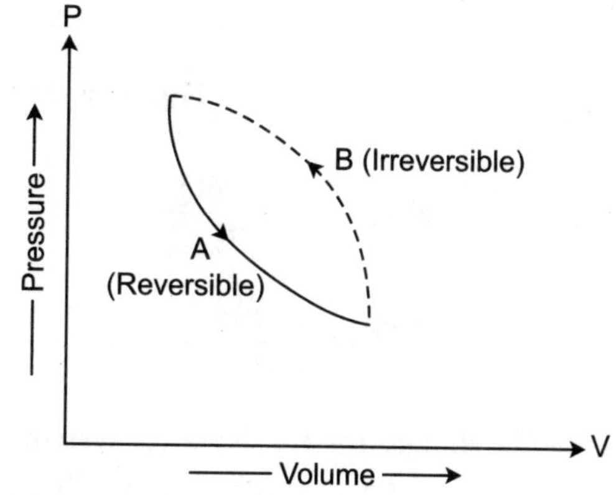

Fig. 4.14

The equality sign is for a reversible process and inequality sign for an irreversible process. So entropy increases for an irreversible process and remains conserved for a reversible process.

For an adiabatic process, $\delta Q = 0$

So $dS \geq 0$

This means that entropy change is zero for a reversible adiabatic process and greater than zero for an irreversible adiabatic process.

4.13 Entropy Principle

"Entropy of an isolated system either increases or remains constant."

For an isolated system, $\delta Q = 0$

So $dS \geq 0$

For a reversible process

$dS = 0$ or $S = \text{constant}$

For an irreversible process

$dS > 0$ or entropy increases.

Thus, entropy of an isolated system never decreases. Either it increases or remains constant. This is called principle of entropy increase.

An isolated system is generated when the system and surrounding are closed in a single boundary.

Consider an isolated system consisting of a system and its surrounding. If $T_{System} > T_{Surr}$, there is an irreversible heat transfer from the system to the surrounding.

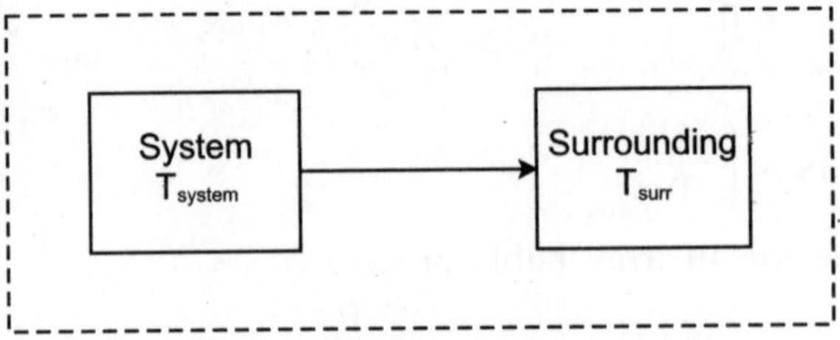

Fig. 4.15: Entropy Principle

$$(dS)_{system} = -\frac{\delta Q}{T_{system}}$$

$$(dS)_{surr} = \frac{\delta Q}{T_{surr}}$$

So entropy change for the isolated system

$$(dS)_{iso} = (dS)_{system} + (dS)_{surr}$$

$$= \delta Q\left[\frac{1}{T_{surr}} - \frac{1}{T_{system}}\right] > 0$$

Thus, the entropy of an isolated system increases if it undergoes an irreversible process. When $T_{system} = T_{surr}$, the process becomes reversible and entropy becomes constant.

So $dS \geq 0$ for an isolated system

4.13.1 T–S Plot

For a reversible process 1–2

$$Q_{rev} = \int_1^2 T\,dS$$

So area under the curve on T – S co-ordinates represents the quantity of heat interaction. Fig. 4.16 shows T–S plots for different processes

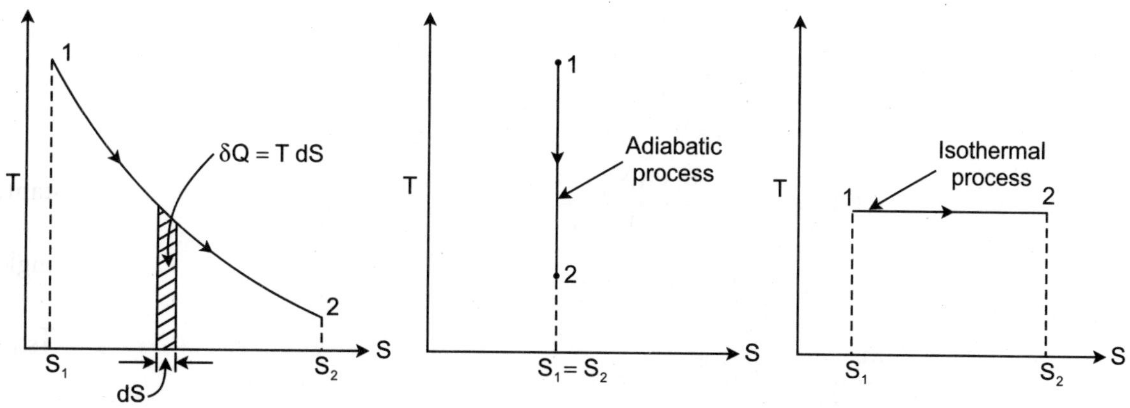

Fig. 4.16: T–S Plots

Example 4.1

Heat pump is used for heating the premises in winter and cooling the same during summer such that temperature inside remain 25°C. Heat transfer across the water and roof is found 2 MJ/hour/degree temperature difference between interior and exterior. Determine the minimum power required for operating the pump in winter when outside temperature is 1°C and also give the maximum temperature in summer for which the device shall be capable of maintaining the premises at desired temperature for same power output. [UPTU July, 2002]

Solution:

Heat pump in winter:

$$T_1 = 25 + 273 = 298 \text{ K}$$

$$T_2 = 1 + 273 = 274 \text{ K}$$

$$Q_1 = \frac{2\times10^3}{3600}(298 - 274)$$

$$= 13.33 \text{ kJ/sec}$$

$$\text{COP} = \frac{T_1}{T_1 - T_2} = \frac{298}{298-274} = 12.4$$

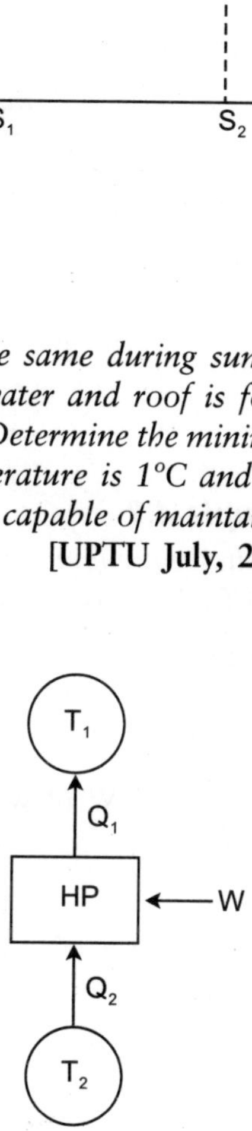

Fig. 4.17

But $\text{COP} = \frac{Q_1}{W}$

$\therefore$ Power input, $W = \frac{Q_1}{\text{COP}} = \frac{13.33}{12.4} = 1.075 \text{ kW}$

Air conditioner in summer

$$\text{COP} = \frac{T_2}{T_1 - T_2} = \frac{298}{T_1 - 298}$$

$$Q_2 = \frac{2 \times 10^3}{3600}(T_1 - T_2)$$

$$W = 1.075 \text{ kW}$$

$$COP = \frac{Q_2}{W} = \frac{0.5168\,(T_1 - T_2)}{1.075}$$

$$= \frac{0.5168}{1.075}(T_1 - 298)$$

$$\frac{298}{T_1 - 298} = \frac{0.5168}{1.075}(T_1 - 298)$$

$$T_1 - 298 = \sqrt{\frac{298 \times 1.075}{0.5168}}$$

$$= 24.897$$

$$T_1 = 322.897 \text{ K}$$

$$= 49.9°C$$ **Ans.**

Example 4.2

A cyclic heat engine operates between a source temperature of 800°C and a sink temperature of 30°C. What is the least rate of heat rejection per kW net output of the engine?

Solution:

$$T_1 = 800 + 273 = 1073 \text{ K}$$

$$T_2 = 25 + 273 = 298 \text{ K}$$

$$Q_2/\text{kW of work} = ?$$

Work, $$W = 1 \text{ kW}$$

$$1 - \frac{Q_2}{Q_1} = 1 - \frac{T_2}{T_1}$$

$$= 1 - \frac{298}{1073}$$

$$\frac{W}{Q_1} = 0.722$$

$$\frac{Q_1}{W} = 1.384$$

$$\frac{Q_1}{Q_2} = \frac{T_1}{T_2}$$

$$Q_2 = Q_1\left(\frac{T_2}{T_1}\right) = 1.384\left(\frac{298}{1073}\right)$$

$$= \mathbf{0.3845\ kW} \qquad \textbf{Ans.}$$

Example 4.3

A domestic food freezer maintains a temperature of –15°C. The ambient air temperature is 30°C. If heat leaks into the freezer at continuous rate of 1.95 kJ/sec, what is the least power necessary to pump this heat out continuously?

Solution:

$$T_1 = 30 + 273 = 303\ K$$

$$T_2 = -15 + 273 = 258\ K$$

Now,

$$COP = \frac{T_2}{T_1 - T_2} = \frac{258}{303-258} = \frac{258}{45} = 5.73$$

In terms of heat interaction

$$COP = \frac{Q_2}{Q_1 - Q_2} = \frac{Q_2}{W}$$

$$W = \frac{Q_2}{COP} = \frac{1.95}{5.73}$$

$$= \mathbf{0.3403\ kW} \qquad \textbf{Ans.}$$

Example 4.4

A reversible heat engine operates between two reservoirs at temperatures of 600°C and 40°C. The engine drives a reversible refrigerator which operates between reservoirs at temperature of 40°C and –20°C. The heat transfer to the heat engine is 2000 kJ and net work output for the combined engine and refrigerator is 360 kJ. (i) Calculate the heat transfer to the refrigerator and the net heat transfer to the reservoir at 40°C. (ii) Reconsider (i) given that the efficiency of the heat engine and the COP of the refrigerator are 40% and 45% of their maximum possible values respectively.

Solution:

$$T_1 = 600 + 273 = 873\ K$$

$$T_2 = 40 + 273 = 313\ K$$

$$T_3 = 40 + 273 = 313\ K$$

$$T_4 = -20 + 273 = 253\ K$$

Heat transfer to heat engine, $Q_1 = 2000$ kJ

The net work output of combined engine refrigerator plant,

$$W = W_1 - W_2 = 360\ kJ$$

i. Maximum efficiency of heat engine cycle is given by

$$\eta_{max} = 1 - \frac{T_2}{T_1} = 1 - \frac{313}{873} = 0.641$$

Again, $$\frac{W_1}{Q_1} = 0.641$$

$$\therefore \quad W_1 = 0.641 \times 2000 = 1282.93 \text{ kJ}$$

$$(COP)_{max} = \frac{T_4}{T_3 - T_4} = \frac{253}{313-253} = 4.216$$

Also $$COP = \frac{Q_4}{W_2} = 4.216$$

$$W = W_1 - W_2 = 360 \text{ kJ}$$

$$W_2 = W_1 - W = 1282.93 - 360 = 922.93 \text{ kJ}$$

$$Q_4 = 4.216 \times 922.93 = 3891.07 \text{ kJ}$$

$$Q_3 = Q_4 + W_2 = 3891.07 + 922.93 = 4814 \text{ kJ}$$

$$Q_2 = Q_1 + W_1 = (2000 - 1282.93) \text{ kJ} = 717.07 \text{ kJ}$$

Heat rejected to 40°C reservoir $= Q_2 + Q_3$
$= 717.07 + 4814$
$= 5531.07$ kJ

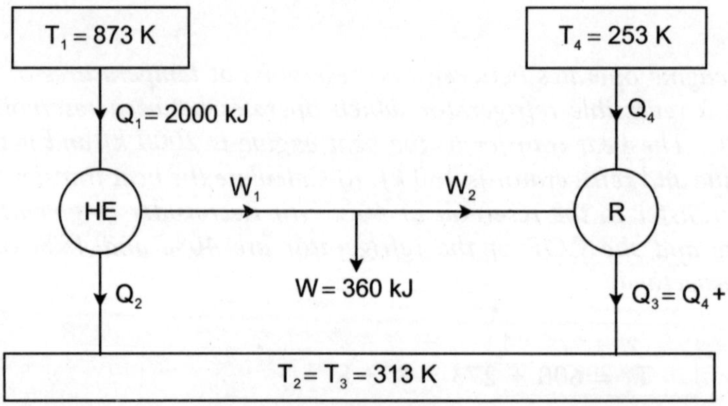

Fig. 4.18

ii. Efficiency of actual heat engine cycle

$$\eta = 0.4\,\eta_{max} = 0.4 \times 0.641 = 0.2564$$

$$W_1 = \eta \times Q_1 = 0.2564 \times 2000 = 512.8 \text{ kJ}$$

$$W_2 = 512.8 - 360 = 152.8 \text{ kJ}$$

COP of actual refrigerator cycle

$$= Q_4/W_2 = 0.45 \times 4.216 = 1.8972$$

$$Q_4 = 1.8972 \times 152.8 = 289.89 \text{ kJ}$$

$$Q_3 = 289.89 + 152.8 = 442.69 \text{ kJ}$$

$$Q_2 = 2000 - 512.8 = 1487.2 \text{ kJ}$$

Heat rejected to 40°C reservoir

$$= Q_3 + Q_2$$

$$= 442.69 + 1487.2$$

$$= \mathbf{1929.89 \text{ kJ}}$$ **Ans.**

Example 4.5

An ice plant working on a reversed Carnot cycle heat pump produces 15 tonnes of ice per day. The ice is formed from water at 0°C and the formed ice is maintained at 0°C. The heat is rejected to the atmosphere at 25°C. The heat pump used to run the ice plant is coupled to a Carnot engine which absorbs heat from a source which is maintained at 220°C by burning liquid fuel of 44560 kJ/kg calorific value and rejects the heat to the atmosphere. Determine:

i. Power developed by the engine.

ii. Fuel consumed per hour.

Take enthalpy of fusion of ice = 334.5 kJ/kg

Solution:

i.

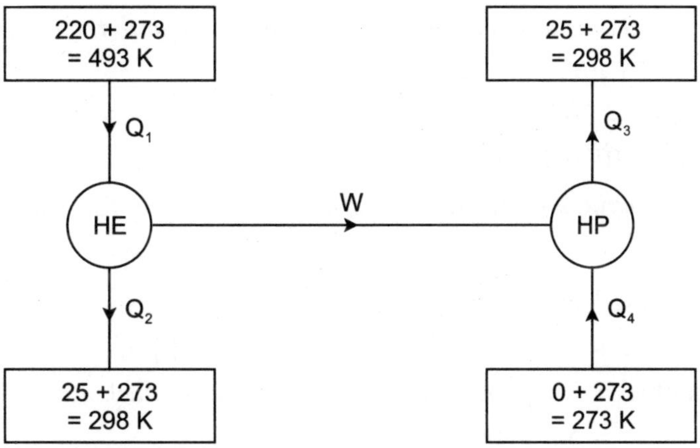

Fig. 4.19

The amount of heat removed by the heat pump

$$Q_4 = \frac{15 \times 1000 \times 334.5}{24 \times 60} = 3484.4 \text{ kJ/min}$$

$$(COP)_{H.P.} = \frac{Q_4}{W} = \frac{273}{298-273}$$

$$W = 3484.4 \times \frac{25}{273} = 319.08 \text{ kJ/min}$$

This work must be developed by Carnot engine

∴ Power developed by the engine

$$= \frac{319.08}{60} = 5.3 \text{ kJ/sec} = \mathbf{5.3 \text{ kW}}$$ **Ans.**

ii. Efficiency of Carnot engine

$$\eta = \frac{W}{Q_1} = 1 - \frac{298}{493} = 0.396$$

$$Q_1 = \frac{W}{0.396} = \frac{5.3}{0.396} = 13.38 \text{ kJ/sec}$$

$$Q_1 \text{ per hour} = 13.38 \times 60 \times 60 = 48168 \text{ kJ}$$

$$\text{Quantity of fuel consumed per hr} = \frac{48168}{44560}$$

$$= \mathbf{1.081 \text{ kg/hr}}$$ **Ans.**

Example 4.6

An engine manufacturer claims to have developed a heat engine with the following specifications:

Power developed = 75 kW; Fuel burnt = 5 kJ/hr

Heating value of fuel = 75000 kJ/kg

Temperature limits = 1000 K and 500 K

Is the claim of the manufacturer true or false? Give reasons for your answer.

Solution:

For the engine proposed by the manufacturer

$$\text{Work done} = 75 \text{ kW} = 75 \times 3600 = 27 \times 10^4 \text{ kJ/hr}$$

$$\text{Heat supplied} = \text{Mass of fuel} \times \text{Heating value of fuel}$$

$$= 5 \times 75000$$

$$= 37.5 \times 10^4 \text{ kJ/hr}$$

$$\text{Thermal efficiency, } \eta_{th} = \frac{\text{Work done}}{\text{Heat supplied}}$$

$$= \frac{27 \times 10^4}{37.5 \times 10^4} = 0.72 \quad \text{or} \quad 72\%$$

Thermal efficiency of a reversible engine working between the same temperature limits

$$\eta_{rev} = \frac{T_1 - T_2}{T_1} = \frac{1000 - 500}{1000} = 0.5$$

Since the manufacturer's claim of efficiency is greater than the efficiency of a reversible engine, the claim is false and engine needs to be redesigned.

Example 4.7

An engine working on Carnot cycle absorbs Q_1 units of heat from a source at T_1 and rejects Q_2 units of heat to a sink at T_2. Because of imperfect heat transfer, the maximum (ϕ_1) and minimum (ϕ_2) absolute temperatures attained during the cycle are given by

$$\phi_1 = T_1 - KQ_1 \quad \text{and} \quad \phi_2 = T_2 + KQ_2$$

where K is a constant. Show that efficiency of the plant is given by

$$\eta = 1 - \frac{T_2}{T_1 - 2KQ_1}$$

Solution:

Carnot cycle efficiency

$$\eta = \frac{Q_1 - Q_2}{Q_1} = \frac{\phi_1 - \phi_2}{\phi_1}; \quad \frac{Q_2}{Q_1} = \frac{\phi_2}{\phi_1}$$

From the given relations

$$\frac{\phi_2 - T_2}{T_1 - \phi_1} = \frac{Q_2}{Q_1}$$

$$\therefore \qquad \phi_2 = \frac{T_2\phi_1}{2\phi_1 - T_1} = \frac{T_2\phi_1}{2(T_1 - KQ_1) - T_1} = \frac{T_2\phi_1}{T_1 - 2KQ_1}$$

Substituting this value of ϕ_2 in the expression for thermal efficiency

$$\eta = \frac{\phi_1 \left(\dfrac{T_2\phi_1}{T_1 - 2KQ_1} \right)}{\phi_1}$$

$$= 1 - \frac{T_2}{T_1 - 2KQ_1} \quad \text{which is the required expression.}$$

Example 4.8

a. *Which is more effective way to increase the efficiency of a Carnot heat engine: to increase the source temperature T_1 while the sink temperature T_2 is held constant or to decrease the sink temperature by the same amount while the source temperature is held constant.*
b. *How the result would be affected in case of a Carnot Heat Pump?*

Solution:

a. Let η_1 be the efficiency when the source temperature is increased by dT while the sink temperature is held constant. Then,

$$\eta_1 = \frac{T_1 - T_2}{T_1} = \frac{(T_1 + dT) - T_2}{T_1 + dT}$$

$$\eta_2 = \frac{T_1 - T_2}{T_1} = \frac{T_1 - (T_2 - dT)}{T_1}$$

$$= \frac{(T_1 + dT) - T_2}{T_1}$$

From the above two equations, we see that numerators are constant and denominator in first equation is more by an amount dT.

$\therefore \quad \eta_2 > \eta_1$

Hence, a decrease in the sink temperature while the source temperature is held constant is more effective in increasing the efficiency of a Carnot heat engine.

b. Let $(COP)_1$ be the co-efficient of performance of heat pump when the temperature of a high temperature reservoir is increased by dT while the low temperature reservoir is held at constant temperature and $(COP)_2$ be the co-efficient of performance if the temperature of the low temperature reservoir is decreased by dT while the high temperature reservoir is held at constant temperature.

Then

$$(COP)_1 = \frac{T_1}{T_1 - T_2} = \frac{T_1 + dT}{(T_1 + dT) - T_2}$$

$$(COP)_2 = \frac{T_1}{T_1 - T_2} = \frac{T_1}{T_1 - (T_2 - dT)}$$

$$= \frac{T_1}{(T_1 + dT) - T_2}$$

we see that $(COP)_1 > (COP)_2$

Thus, increasing the temperature of high temperature reservoir while keeping the temperature of low temperature reservoir is more effective.

Example 4.9

A reversible heat engine in outer space operates between a high temperature reservoir T_1 and radiating panel at T_2. The radiation heat transfer from the panel is proportional to its area and fourth power of its absolute temperature. Show that for a given work output and value of T_1, the area of panel will be minimum when $T_2/T_1 = 3/4$. Also find the corresponding minimum area.

Solution:

For a reversible heat engine,

$$\eta = \frac{W}{Q_1} = \frac{Q_1 - Q_2}{Q_1}$$

$$= \frac{T_1 - T_2}{T_1}$$

So $$\frac{Q_1}{T_1} = \frac{Q_2}{T_2}$$

$$\frac{W}{T_1 - T_2} = \frac{Q_1}{T_1} = \frac{Q_2}{T_2} = \frac{KAT_2^4}{T_2}$$

or $$A = \frac{W}{KT_2^3 (T_1 - T_2)}$$

where K is a constant.

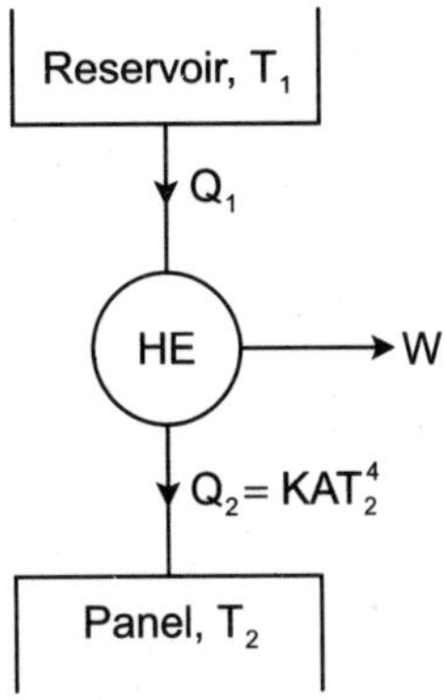

Fig. 4.20

For a given value of W and T_1, A is minimum when $T_2^3 (T_1 - T_2)$ is maximum. Differentiating it w.r.t. T_2 and putting the derivative equal to zero we get,

$$\frac{d}{dT_2}\left(T_2^3 T_1 - T_2^4\right) = 0$$

or $$3T_2^2 T_1 - 4T_2^3 = 0$$

That gives $$\frac{T_2}{T_1} = \frac{3}{4}$$

$\therefore$ $$A_{min} = \frac{W}{K(0.75\,T_1)^3 (T_1 - 0.75\,T_1)}$$

$$= 9.48\,\frac{W}{KT_1^4}$$ **Ans.**

Example 4.10

Fig. 4.21 shows a system that undergoes a reversible cycle during which it exchanges heat with three thermal reservoirs

Show that

$$\frac{Q_1}{\frac{1}{T_2} - \frac{1}{T_3}} = \frac{Q_2}{\frac{1}{T_3} - \frac{1}{T_1}} = \frac{Q_3}{\frac{1}{T_1} - \frac{1}{T_2}}$$

regardless of actual process involved.

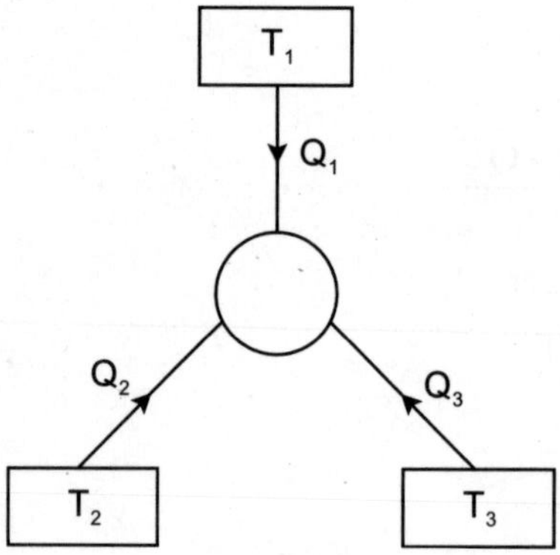

Fig. 4.21

Solution:

From the figure we see that

$$Q_1 = -(Q_2 + Q_3) \quad \ldots\ldots \text{(i)}$$

$$Q_1 + Q_2 + Q_3 = 0 \quad \ldots\ldots \text{(ii)}$$

Since it is a cyclic process, Clausius theorem gives

$$\frac{Q_1}{T_1} + \frac{Q_2}{T_2} + \frac{Q_3}{T_3} = 0 \quad \ldots\ldots \text{(iii)}$$

Substituting the value $Q_3 = -(Q_1 + Q_2)$, we get

$$\frac{Q_1}{T_1} + \frac{Q_2}{T_2} - \frac{(Q_3 + Q_2)}{T_3} = 0$$

$$Q_1\left(\frac{1}{T_1} - \frac{1}{T_3}\right) = Q_2\left(\frac{1}{T_3} - \frac{1}{T_2}\right) \quad \ldots\ldots \text{(iv)}$$

$$\frac{Q_1}{\frac{1}{T_2} - \frac{1}{T_3}} = \frac{Q_2}{\frac{1}{T_3} - \frac{1}{T_1}} \quad \ldots\ldots \text{(iv)}$$

Now substituting value $Q_2 = -(Q_1 + Q_3)$ in equation (iii)

we have

$$\frac{Q_1}{T_1} - \frac{(Q_1 + Q_3)}{T_2} + \frac{Q_3}{T_3} = 0$$

$$Q_1\left(\frac{1}{T_1} - \frac{1}{T_2}\right) = Q_3\left(\frac{1}{T_2} - \frac{1}{T_3}\right)$$

$$\frac{Q_1}{\frac{1}{T_2} - \frac{1}{T_3}} = \frac{Q_3}{\frac{1}{T_1} - \frac{1}{T_2}} \quad \ldots\ldots \text{(vi)}$$

From equations (v) and (vi)

$$\frac{Q_1}{\frac{1}{T_2}-\frac{1}{T_3}} = \frac{Q_2}{\frac{1}{T_3}-\frac{1}{T_1}} = \frac{Q_3}{\frac{1}{T_1}-\frac{1}{T_2}}$$

which is the required expression.

Example 4.11

A Carnot engine E_1 operates between temperatures T_1 and T_2 rejects its waste heat at its sink temperature T_2 to Carnot engine E_2 which operates between temperature limits T_2 and T_3. Set up an expression relating the thermal efficiency of engineS E_1 and E_2 to that of Carnot engine E_3 operating directly between temperatures T_1 and T_3.

Solution:

From Fig. 4.22 we see that

$$\eta_1 = \frac{T_1 - T_2}{T_1} = 1 - \frac{T_2}{T_1}$$

$$1-\eta_1 = \frac{T_2}{T_1}$$

Similarly,

$$1-\eta_2 = \frac{T_3}{T_2}$$

$$\therefore \quad (1-\eta_1)(1-\eta_2) = \frac{T_3}{T_1}$$

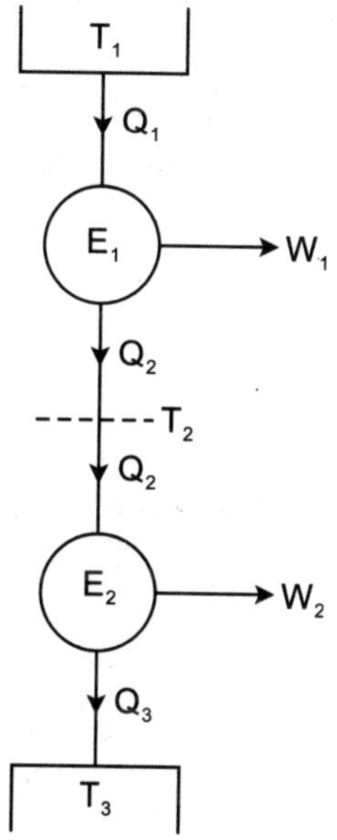

Fig. 4.22

For a Carnot engine operating between temp. T_1 and T_3

$$\eta_3 = \frac{T_1 - T_3}{T_1} = 1 - \frac{T_3}{T_1}$$

$$1-\eta_3 = \frac{T_3}{T_1}$$

So from two equations

$$1-\eta_3 = (1-\eta_1)(1-\eta_2)$$

$$= 1-\eta_2-\eta_1+\eta_1\,\eta_2$$

$$\eta_3 = \eta_1+\eta_2-\eta_1\,\eta_2$$

Entropy

Example 4.12

A closed system undergoes the internally reversible process from temperature $T_1 = 200$ K, $S_1 = 1$ kJ/K to temperature $T_2 = 600$ K and $S_2 = 3$ kJ/K. What would be the heat interaction during the process if variation is assumed to be linear?

Solution:

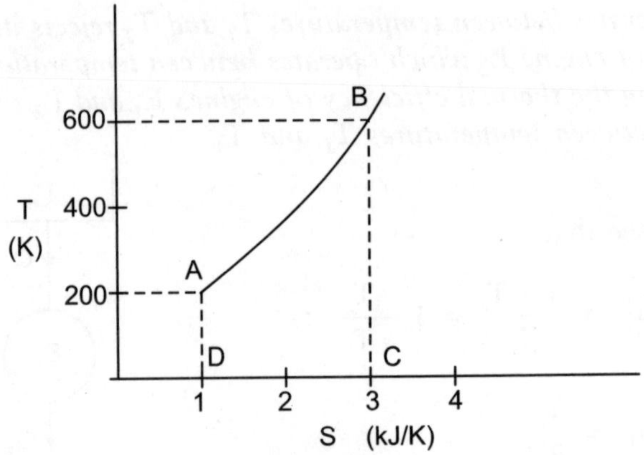

Fig. 4.23

$$\text{Heat flow} = \text{Area under AB}$$
$$= \frac{1}{2}(\text{AD} + \text{BC}) \times \text{DC}$$
$$= \frac{1}{2}(200 + 600) \times 2$$
$$= \mathbf{800\ kJ}$$

Ans.

Example 4.13

A fluid transfers 2000 kJ of heat to the environment at 300 K. If the entropy change of the fluid is –5.67 kJ/K, determine the overall entropy change and comment on the nature of process whether possible, reversible, irreversible.

Solution:

$$(dS)_{system} = -5 \text{ kJ/K}$$
$$(dS)_{surrounding} = \frac{\delta Q}{T} = \frac{2000}{300} = 6.667 \text{ kJ/K}$$
$$(dS)_{overall} = (dS)_{system} + (dS)_{surrounding}$$
$$= -5.67 + 6.67$$
$$= 1.0 \text{ kJ/K}$$

We know that for a reversible process dS = 0 and for an irreversible process, dS > 0. So process is possible and irreversible.

Example 4.14

An electric motor of 3 kW is subjected to a braking test for one hour. The heat generated by frictional forces in the process gets dissipated to the surroundings at 300 K. Determine the resulting increase in entropy.

Solution:

$$\text{Power} = 3 \text{ kW}$$

$$\text{Heat energy in one hour} = 3 \times 3600 = 10800 \text{ kJ}$$

$$\text{Temperature, T} = 300 \text{ K}$$

Increase in entropy, $dS = \frac{\delta Q}{T} = \frac{10800}{300} = \mathbf{36\ kJ/K}$ **Ans.**

Example 4.15

A gear box receives 755 kW power and delivers 750 kW power when operating in a steady state at 325 K. If the surroundings are at 280 K, determine the rate of entropy growth in the gear box and the surroundings.

Solution:

$$\text{Rate of increase in energy} = 755 - 750 = 5 \text{ kW} = 5 \text{ kJ/sec} = 300 \text{ kJ/min}$$

Temperature, $T_{system} = 325$ K

Increase in entropy of the system

$$(dS)_{system} = \frac{\delta Q}{T} = \frac{300}{325} = 0.923 \text{ kJ/K} - \text{min}$$

Increase in entropy of the surrounding

$$(dS)_{surrounding} = \frac{300}{280}$$

$$= \mathbf{1.0714\ kJ/K - min}$$ **Ans.**

Example 4.16

a. *One kg of water at 273 K is brought into contact with a heat reservoir at 373 K. When the water has reached 373 K, find the entropy change of water, of heat reservoir and of universe.*

b. *If the water is heated from 273 K to 373 K by first bringing it in contact with a reservoir at 323 K and then with a reservoir at 373 K, what will the entropy change of the universe be?*

c. *Explain how water might be heated from 273 K to 373 K with almost no change in the entropy of the universe?*

Solution:

a. Water is being heated through a finite temperature difference. The entropy of water would increase and that of reservoir would decrease so that the net entropy change of water (system) and the reservoir together will be positive definite, water is being heated irreversibly and to find the entropy change of water, we have to assume a reversible path between the end states which are at equilibrium.

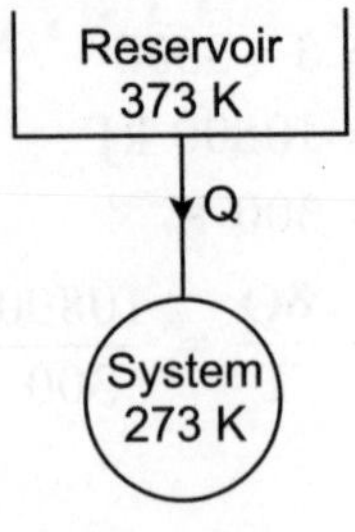

Fig. 4.24

$$(\Delta S)_{water} = \int \frac{dQ}{T} = \int_{T_1}^{T_2} \frac{mcdT}{T} = mc \ln \frac{T_2}{T_1}$$

$$= 1 \times 4.187 \times \ln \frac{373}{273} = 1.305 \text{ kJ/K}$$

The reservoir temperature remains constant irrespective of the amount of heat withdrawn from it.

Amount of heat absorbed by the system from the reservoir

$$Q = 1 \times 4.187 \times (373 - 273) = 418.7 \text{ kJ}$$

Entropy change of the reservoir

$$(\Delta S)_{res} = -\frac{Q}{T} = \frac{-418.7}{373} = -1.122 \text{ kJ/K}$$

∴ Entropy change of the universe

$$(\Delta S)_{universe} = (\Delta S)_{system} + (\Delta S)_{res}$$

$$= 1.305 \quad 1.122$$

$$= 0.183 \text{ kJ/K}$$

Ans.

b. Water is being heated in two stages, first from 273 K to 323 K by bringing it in contact with a reservoir at 323 K and then from 323 to 373 K by bringing it in contact of a second reservoir at 373 K.

$$(\Delta S)_{water} = \int_{273}^{323} \frac{mcdT}{T} + \int_{323}^{373} \frac{mcdT}{T}$$

$$= 4.187\left(\ln \frac{323}{273} + \ln \frac{373}{323}\right)$$

$$= 1.305 \text{ kJ/K}$$

$$(\Delta S)_{res-I} = -\frac{1 \times 4.187 \times (323 - 273)}{323} = -0.647 \text{ kJ/K}$$

$$(\Delta S)_{res-II} = -\frac{1 \times 4.187 \times (373 - 323)}{373} = -0.56 \text{ kJ/K}$$

$$(\Delta S)_{universe} = (\Delta S)_{water} + (\Delta S)_{res-I} + (\Delta S)_{res-II}$$

$$= 1.305 - 0.647 - 0.56$$

$$= \mathbf{0.098 \text{ kJ/K}}$$ **Ans.**

c. The entropy change of the universe would be less and less, if the water is heated in more and more stages, by bringing the water in contact successively with more and more heat reservoirs, each succeeding reservoir being at a higher temperature than the preceding one.

When water is heated in infinite steps, by bringing it in contact with an infinite number of reservoirs in succession so that at any instant the temperature difference between the water and the reservoir in contact is infinitesimally small, then the net entropy change of the universe would be zero and water would be reversibly heated.

Example 4.17

m_1 kg of water at T_1 is isobarically and adiabatically mixed with m_2 kg of water at T_2 ($T_1 > T_2$). Show that for equal masses of water, the entropy change of the mixture is given by

$$(dS)_{universe} = 2mc_p \log_e \left[\frac{T_1 + T_2}{2\sqrt{T_1 T_2}} \right]$$

and prove that the change is necessarily positive.

Solution:

Let T_f be the final temperature of the mixture.

Then from principle of energy conservation,

Heat lost by m_1 kg of water = Heat gained by m_2 kg of water

$$m_1 c_P (T_1 - T_f) = m_2 c_P (T_f - T_2)$$

$$T_f = \frac{m_1 T_1 + m_2 T_2}{m_1 + m_2}$$

Change in entropy of m_1 kg of water, whose temperature decreases from T_1 to T_f

$$(dS)_1 = m_1 c_P \log_e \frac{T_f}{T_1} = m_1 c_P \log_e \frac{m_1 T_1 + m_2 T_2}{(m_1 + m_2) T_1}$$

Change in entropy of m_2 kg of water whose temperature increases from T_2 to T_f

$$(dS)_2 = m_2 c_P \log_e \frac{T_f}{T_2} = m_2 c_P \log_e \frac{m_1 T_1 + m_2 T_2}{(m_1 + m_2) T_2}$$

∴ Change in entropy of universe

$$(dS)_{universe} = (dS)_1 + (dS)_2$$

$$= m_1 c_p \log_e \frac{m_1 T_1 + m_2 T_2}{(m_1 + m_2) T_1} + m_2 c_p \log_e \frac{m_1 T_1 + m_2 T_2}{(m_1 + m_2) T_2}$$

If $m_1 = m_2 = m$, then

$$(dS)_{universe} = mc_p \log_e \frac{T_1 + T_2}{2T_1} + mc_p \log_e \frac{T_1 + T_2}{2T_2}$$

$$= mc_p \left[\log_e \frac{T_1 + T_2}{2T_1} + \log_e \frac{T_1 + T_2}{2T_2} \right]$$

$$= mc_p \left[\log_e \frac{(T_1 + T_2)^2}{4T_1 T_2} \right]$$

$$= mc_p \log_e \left(\frac{(T_1 + T_2)}{2\sqrt{T_1 T_2}} \right)^2$$

$$= 2mc_p \log_e \frac{T_1 + T_2}{2\sqrt{T_1 T_2}}$$

Now $\frac{T_1 + T_2}{2}$ = Arithmetic mean of T_1 and T_2

$\sqrt{T_1 T_2}$ = Geometric mean of T_1 and T_2

So, $\frac{T_1 + T_2}{2\sqrt{T_1 T_2}}$ is always positive.

So, $(dS)_{universe}$ is always positive. Hence, entropy of the universe always increases.

Example 4.18

A heat engine operates between two thermal reservoirs; source at temperature T_1 and sink at temperature T_2. If the source and sink are of mass m and specific heat c, set up the following expression for the maximum work output possible.

$$W_{max} = mc\left(\sqrt{T_1} - \sqrt{T_2}\right)^2$$

Solution:

For the maximum work output or maximum efficiency, the heat engine must be reversible and for a reversible cycle engine, Clausius equation gives $\oint \frac{\delta Q}{T} = 0$. This means that entropy change for a reversible cycle is zero.

Let T_m be the common temperature when the working of a engine stops. Then,

$$(dS)_{source} + (dS)_{sink} = 0$$

$$mc \log_e \frac{T_m}{T_1} + mc \log_e \frac{T_m}{T_2} = 0$$

$$mc\left[\log_e \frac{T_m}{T_1} + \log_e \frac{T_m}{T_2}\right] = 0$$

$$mc \log_e \frac{T_m^2}{T_1 T_2} = 0 = \log_e 1$$

$$T_m^2 = T_1 T_2$$

or

$$T_m = \sqrt{T_1 T_2}$$

Now, work done= Heat supplied – Heat rejected

$$= mc(T_1 - T_m) - mc(T_m - T_2)$$

$$= mc(T_1 + T_2 - 2T_m)$$

$$= mc(T_1 + T_2 - 2\sqrt{T_1 T_2})$$

Example 4.19

A heat pump operates between two identical systems, both being at temperature T_1 to start with. Due to operation of pump, one of the system gets cooled down to temperature T_2. Show that this operation of pump, the minimum work required by the heat pump is

$$W_{min} = c\left[\frac{T_1^2}{T_2} + T_2 - 2T_1\right]$$

where c is the specific heat of two identical systems.

Solution:

For the minimum work input, the pump is to operate on a reversed cycle for which

$$\oint \frac{\delta Q}{T} = 0$$

This implies that net entropy change for the two systems is zero.

$$(dS)_{system\ I} + (dS)_{system\ II} = 0$$

Let T_f = Final temperature of high temperature system

Then,

$$c \log_e \frac{T_f}{T_1} + c \log_e \frac{T_2}{T_1} = 0$$

or

$$\log_e\left[\frac{T_f}{T_1} \times \frac{T_2}{T_1}\right] = 0 = \log_e 1$$

$$\therefore \qquad T_f = \frac{T_1^2}{T_2}$$

From the principle of energy conservation

$$\oint dW = \oint dQ$$

$\therefore$ Work input = Heat rejected at high temperature – Heat absorbed at low temperature

$$= c\int_{T_1}^{T_f} dT - \int_{T_2}^{T_1} = c\left[T_f + T_2 - 2T_1\right]$$

Substituting the value of $T_f = \dfrac{T_1^2}{T_2}$, we get

$$\text{Minimum work input, } W_{min} = c\left[\frac{T_1^2}{T_2} + T_2 - 2T_1\right] \qquad \textbf{Ans.}$$

THEORETICAL QUESTIONS

1. What are the limitations of first law of thermodynamics?
2. What is a heat reservoir? Define in terms of heat source and heat sink.
3. What is a heat engine? Define thermal efficiency of a heat engine.
4. What is a heat pump? How is it different from a refrigerator?
5. Show that COP of a heat pump is greater than COP of a refrigerator by unity.
6. State the Kelvin-Plank and Clausius statements of second law of thermodynamics. Establish the equivalence between them.
7. What is perpetual motion machine of second kind? Why is it impossible to construct such a machine in actual practice?
8. Derive an expression for efficiency of a Carnot cycle.
9. Comment on the validity of the statement: All reversible engines operating between the same two thermal reservoirs have the same efficiency.
10. What do you mean by Clausius inequality?
11. Show that whenever a system executes a complete cyclic process $\oint \frac{\delta Q}{T}$ is less than zero or in the limit is equal to zero. Hence, prove that entropy is a property of the system.
12. Comment on the statement: "The entropy of the universe tends to be maximum".

NUMERICAL PROBLEMS

1. A heat engine develops 10 kW power when receiving heat at the rate of 2200 kJ/min. Evaluate the corresponding rate of heat rejection from the engine and its thermal efficiency.
2. A machine operating as a heat pump extracts heat from the surrounding atmosphere, is driven by a 80 kW motor and supplies 2×10^5 kJ/hr heat to a house needed for its heating in the winter. Find co-efficient of performance for the heat pump. How this COP will be affected if the objective of the same machine is to cool the house in summer requiring 2×10^5 kJ/hr of heat rejection?
3. A heat engine working on Carnot cycle converts one-fifth of the heat input into work. When the temperature of the sink is reduced by 82°C, the efficiency gets doubled. Make calculations for the temperature of the source and sink.
4. A domestic food refrigerator maintains a temperature of –10°C. The ambient air temperature is 35°C. If the heat leaks into the freezer at the continuous rate of 2 kJ/sec, determine the least power necessary to pump this heat out continuously.
5. A perfect reversed heat engine is used for making ice at –5°C from water available at 20°C. The temperature of freezing mixture is –10°C. Calculate the quantity of ice formed per kWH.

   For ice: sp heat 2.1 kJ/kg K and latent heat = 335 kJ/kg
6. A heat engine is used to drive a heat pump. The heat transfer from the heat engine and from the heat pump are used to heat the water circulating through the radiators of

a building. The efficiency of the heat engine is 29% and the COP of the heat pump is 4. Evaluate the ratio of heat transfer to the circulating water to the transfer to the heat engine.

7. Two reversible heat engines A and B are arranged is series. A rejecting heat directly to B. Engine A receives 220 kJ at a temperature of 421°C from a hot source while engine B is in communication with a cold sink at a temperature of 4.4°C. If the work output of A is twice that of B, find (a) the intermediate temperature between A and B, (b) the efficiency of each engine and (c) heat rejected to the cold sink.
8. Two Carnot heat pumps A and B are arranged in series. Express COP of the composite system.
9. Three Carnot engines A, B and C working between temperatures of 2000 K and 800 K are in a series combination. The work produced by these engines are in the ratio of 5:4:3. Make calculations for temperature of intermediate reservoirs.
10. A reversible engine operates between temperatures T_1 and T ($T_1 > T$). The energy rejected by the engine is received by a second reversible engine at the same temperature T. The second engine rejects the heat at T_2 ($T_2 < T$). Prove that (a) $T = \dfrac{T_1 + T_2}{2}$ if the engine produced same work output and (b) $T = \sqrt{T_1 T_2}$ if the engine developed the work at same efficiency.

Entropy

11. Heat flows from a hot reservoir at 800 K to another reservoir at 200 K. If the entropy change of the overall process is 4.25 kJ/K, make calculations for the heat flowing out of the high temperature reservoir.
12. A lump of steel of mass 18 kg at 1000 K is dropped in 180 kg of oil at 300 K. Make calculations for the entropy change of steel, the oil and the universe. Take specific heat of steel and oil as 0.5 kJ/kg K and 3.5 kJ/kg K respectively.
13. Air in a cylinder is compressed reversibly and isothermally from 90 kPa, 25°C to 270 kPa. The initial volume is 0.162 m^3. Determine the work input, the heat transfer, the entropy change of the air being compressed.
14. Air at 15°C and 1.1 bar occupies 0.02 m^3. The air is heated at constant volume until the pressure is 4.4 bar and then cooled at constant pressure back to the original temperature. Calculate the net heat flow. Sketch the process on T–S diagram.
15. A heat engine is supplied with 278 kJ/sec of heat at constant fixed temperature of 283°C and the heat rejection takes place at 5°C. The following results were reported (i) 208 kJ/sec, (ii) 139 kJ/sec and (iii) 70 kJ/sec. All heats were rejected. Classify the cycles in terms of reversible, irreversible and impossible.

5

Properties of Steam

5.1 Some Terms Associated with Steam

5.1.1 Pure Substance and Phase

A pure substance consists of only single species with characteristic feature of being homogeneous and invariable composition irrespective of phase.

The three conditions of a pure substance namely solid, liquid and vapour (or gas) are know as phases.

5.1.2 Vapourisation, Evaporation and Boiling

Vaporisation involves change from the liquid phase to vapour phase. Water vapours are obtained by evaporation and steam boiling.

Evaporation is the process of vapour generation only from the surface of a liquid.

Boiling refers to the process of vapour formation that takes place in the whole mass of the body.

5.1.3 Saturation Temperature and Saturation Pressure

The temperature at which boiling takes place is called saturation temperature. It depends on physical properties of the liquid and pressure.

The pressure at a specific temperature, at which liquid boils or is in equilibrium with its own vapour, is called saturation pressure. Saturation temperature of water is 100°C and the corresponding saturation pressure is 1.01325 bar. Saturation pressure is also called vapour pressure.

5.1.4 Saturated and Superheated Steam

When the molecules escaping from the liquid become equal to the molecules returning to it, the saturated steam has a maximum density. The liquid at its boiling point at a specified pressure is called a saturated liquid. Saturated steam may be dry or wet. Dryness fraction of steam is expressed as

$$x = \frac{\text{Mass of dry saturated vapour}}{\text{Mass of mixture}}$$

$$= \frac{m_g}{m} = \frac{m_g}{m_f + m_g} \quad \ldots\ldots (5.1)$$

where m_g = Mass of dry saturated steam

and m_f = Mass of water vapour

The dryness fraction expressed in % form is called 'quality' of steam.

Superheated steam has a temperature higher than its saturation temperature. The state of a superheated steam is described by its pressure p and temperature t_{sup}.

Degree of superheat = $t_{sup} - t_s$ .... (5.2)

5.1.5 Sensible Heat (h_f), Latent Heat (h_{fg}) and Total Heat or Enthalpy (h)

Sensible heat (h_f) of water is defined as the quantity of heat absorbed by 1 kg of water when it is heated from 0°C (freezing point) to boiling point. It is also called total heat or enthalpy of water.

Latent heat or hidden heat (h_{fg}) is the amount of heat required to convert the water at a given temperature and pressure into the steam. Its value varies with pressure.

Total heat or enthalpy of wet steam (h) is defined as the quantity of heat required to convert 1 kg of water at 0°C into wet steam at constant pressure.

It is the sum of sensible heat and latent heat

$$h = h_f + x\,h_{fg} \quad \ldots\ldots (5.3)$$

where x = Dryness fraction

For dry and saturated steam, x = 1

5.1.6 Volume of Wet and Dry Steam

Let x = Dryness fraction of steam

So, 1 kg of steam contains x kg of dry steam and (1 – x) kg of water. Let v_f and v_g be the volume of 1 kg of water and 1 kg of dry steam respectively.

Then Volume of 1 kg wet steam = Volume of x kg of dry steam + Volume of (1 – x) kg of wet steam

$$= xv_g + (1 - x)v_f$$

$$= xv_g + v_f - xv_f$$

$$= v_f + x(v_g - v_f)$$

$$= v_f + xv_{fg} \quad \ldots\ldots (5.4)$$

$$= v_f + xv_{fg} + v_{fg} - v_{fg}$$

$$= (v_f + v_{fg}) - (1 - x)v_{fg}$$

$$= v_g - (1 - x)v_{fg} \quad \ldots\ldots (5.5)$$

5.1.7 Volume of Superheated Steam

Superheated steam behaves like an ideal gas, so its volume can be found in the same way as gases.

Let v_g = Specific volume of dry steam at pressure p

T_s = Saturation temperature in K

T_{sup} = Temperature of superheated steam in K

v_{sup} = Specific volume of superheated steam at pressure p

Then

$$\frac{pv_g}{T_s} = \frac{pv_{sup}}{T_{sup}}$$

$$v_{sup} = \frac{v_g T_{sup}}{T_s} \quad \text{.......} \quad (5.6)$$

5.2 Thermodynamic Properties of Steam and Steam Tables

There are six basic thermodynamic properties of a fluid. These are pressure (p), specific volume (v), temperature (T), internal energy (u), enthalpy (h) and entropy (s).

The values of these properties are determined theoretically or experimentally and are tabulated in the form of tables which are known as 'Steam Tables'.

Following properties of steam are tabulated in the form of table:

p = Absolute pressure in bar of kPa

T_s = Saturation temperature (°C)

h_f = Enthalpy of saturated liquid (kJ/kg)

h_{fg} = Enthalpy or latent heat of vapourisation

h_g = Enthalpy of saturated vapour (kJ/kg)

S_f = Entropy of saturated liquid (kJ/kg K)

S_{fg} = Entropy of vapourisation (kJ/kg K)

S_g = Entropy of saturated vapour (steam) in kJ/kg K

v_f = Specific volume of saturated liquid (m^3/kg)

v_g = Specific volume of saturated vapour (steam) in m^3/kg

Now

$$h_{fg} = h_g - h_f$$

$$S_{fg} = S_g - S_f$$

$$v_{fg} = v_g - v_f$$

$$u = h - pv$$

These properties at different pressure are tabulated in the form of tables known as steam tables.

5.2.1 External Work during Evaporation

When water is evaporated to form saturated steam, its volume increases from v_f to v_g at a constant pressure and thus external work is done.

The energy for this work is obtained during the absorption of latent heat. This work is called external work of evaporation and given by $p(v_g - v_f)$.

At a low pressure v_f is very small and hence neglected.

So, work of evaporation is pv_g.

In case of wet steam it is x pv_g, where x is dryness fraction.

5.2.2 Internal Latent Heat

A certain amount of latent heat supplied to water during the evaporation process is utilised in expanding the volume and thus producing external work. The latent heat of steam minus the external work is called the latent heat.

$$\text{Internal latent heat} = h_{fg} - pv_g \quad \text{(5.7)}$$

5.2.3 Internal Energy of Steam

It is the actual energy stored in the steam. The total heat of steam is sum of sensible heat, internal latent heat and external work of evaporation. Work of evaporation is not stored in the steam as it is utilised in the doing external work. Hence, internal energy of steam can be found by subtracting work of evaporation from the total heat.

$$\therefore \quad u = h - \frac{pv_g}{J} \quad \text{(5.8)}$$

In case of wet steam with dryness fraction x

$$u = h - \frac{pxv_g}{J} \quad \text{(5.9)}$$

For a superheated steam with specific volume v_{sup}

$$h_{sup} = h_f + h_{fg} + c_{Ps}\,(T_{sup} - T_s) \quad \text{(5.10)}$$

$$u = h_{sup} - \frac{pv_{sup}}{J} \quad \text{(5.11)}$$

5.2.4 Entropy of Water (s_f)

Let 1 kg of water be heated from temperature T_1 and T_2 at constant pressure. Entropy change is then given by

$$ds = \frac{\delta Q}{T} = c_P \frac{dT}{T}$$

$$s_2 - s_1 = c_P \log_e \frac{T_2}{T_1} \quad \text{(5.12)}$$

If $\quad T_1 = 0°C = 273$ K

and $\quad s_1 = 0$

Then

$$s_f = c_P \log_e \frac{T}{273} \quad \text{(5.13)}$$

where s_f is the entropy of water at any temperature T above freezing point of water. If heating of water continues upto saturation temperature T_s, then

$$s_f = c_P \log_e \frac{T_s}{273} \quad \text{(5.14)}$$

5.2.5 Entropy of Evaporation

The change in entropy $$ds = \frac{\delta Q}{T}$$

or $$s_2 - s_1 = \frac{Q}{T}$$ where Q is the heat absorbed.

When the water is evaporated to steam completely the heat absorbed is the latent heat and this heat goes into water without showing any rise of temperature.

$$Q = h_{fg}$$

$$s_{evaporation} = \frac{h_{fg}}{T_s} \quad \ldots\ldots (5.15)$$

For a wet steam with dryness fraction x, the evaporation will be partial and heat absorbed will be xh_{fg} per kg of steam. The change in entropy will be $\frac{xh_{fg}}{T_s}$.

5.2.6 Entropy of Wet Steam

The total entropy of wet steam is the sum of entropy of water (s_f) and entropy of evaporation (s_{fg})

So, $$s_{wet} = s_f + \frac{xh_{fg}}{T_s} \quad \ldots\ldots (5.16)$$

5.2.7 Entropy of Superheated Steam

Let 1 kg of dry saturated steam at T_s (saturation temperature of steam) be heated T_{sup}. If the specific heat at constant pressure is c_{Ps}, then change of entropy during the superheating at constant pressure p

$$= c_{Ps} \log_e\left(\frac{T_{sup}}{T_s}\right) \quad \ldots\ldots (5.17)$$

Total entropy of superheated steam above the freezing point of water s_{sup} = entropy of dry saturated steam + change of entropy during superheating

$$= s_f + \frac{h_{fg}}{T_s} + c_{Ps} \log_e\left(\frac{T_{sup}}{T_s}\right)$$

$$= s_g + c_{Ps} \log_e\left(\frac{T_{sup}}{T_s}\right) \quad \ldots\ldots (5.18)$$

5.3 Temperature Entropy (T–s) Diagram

Some salient features of T–s diagram are:

i. The specific entropy is plotted along x-axis and temperature is plotted along y-axis.

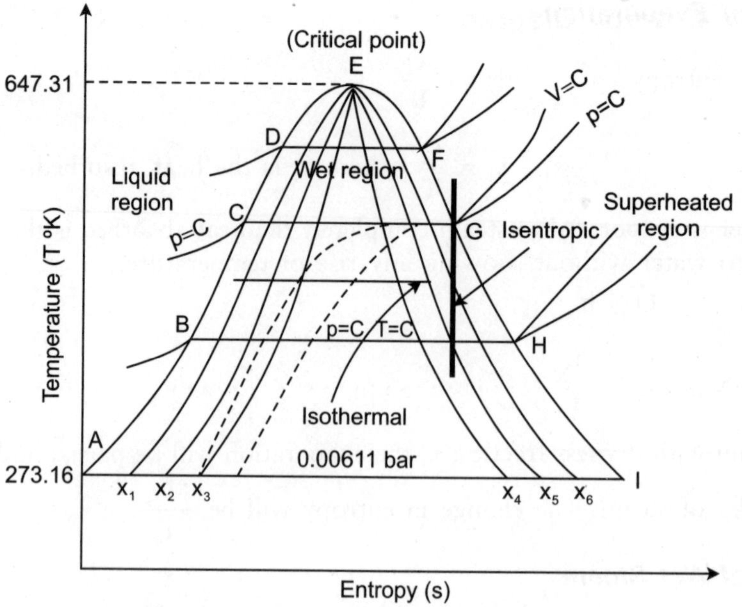

Fig. 5.1: Temperature – Entropy Diagram

ii. The liquid boundary line starts at y-axis at a temperature of 273.16 K; this is so because entropy of liquid at the triple point is equal to zero.

iii. The boundary curves and saturated vapour line divide the diagram into three parts. These are liquid region, wet vapour region and superheated region.

iv. The boundary curves meet at a point which is the critical point of water. The pressure at critical point is 221.2 bar and temperature is 647.31 K.

v. The constant pressure lines are parallel to constant temperature lines in the wet region. These lines are curved in the superheated region.

vi. The wet region contains constant dryness fraction plots and constant volume lines.

vii. The constant volume lines are steeper than constant pressure lines in the superheated zone.

viii. The slopes of constant pressure lines in the liquid, wet and superheated region are

$$\left(\frac{\partial T}{\partial s}\right)_v = \frac{T}{c_V} \quad \text{.......} \quad (5.19)$$

$$\left(\frac{\partial T}{\partial s}\right)_v = \frac{T}{c_P} \quad \text{.......} \quad (5.20)$$

ix. The area between the line of a reversible process and the abscissa represents the quantity of heat added to 1 kg of working medium and is equal to $q = \int T ds$.

x. An isothermal process plots as horizontal line and a reversible adiabatic process is represented by a vertical line.

5.4 Enthalpy–Entropy Diagram

Dr. Mollier plotted total heat against entropy and the diagram is used more widely than T–s diagram because work done can be scaled from the diagram directly as a length, whereas on T–s diagram it is represented by an area. Some salient features of this diagram are:

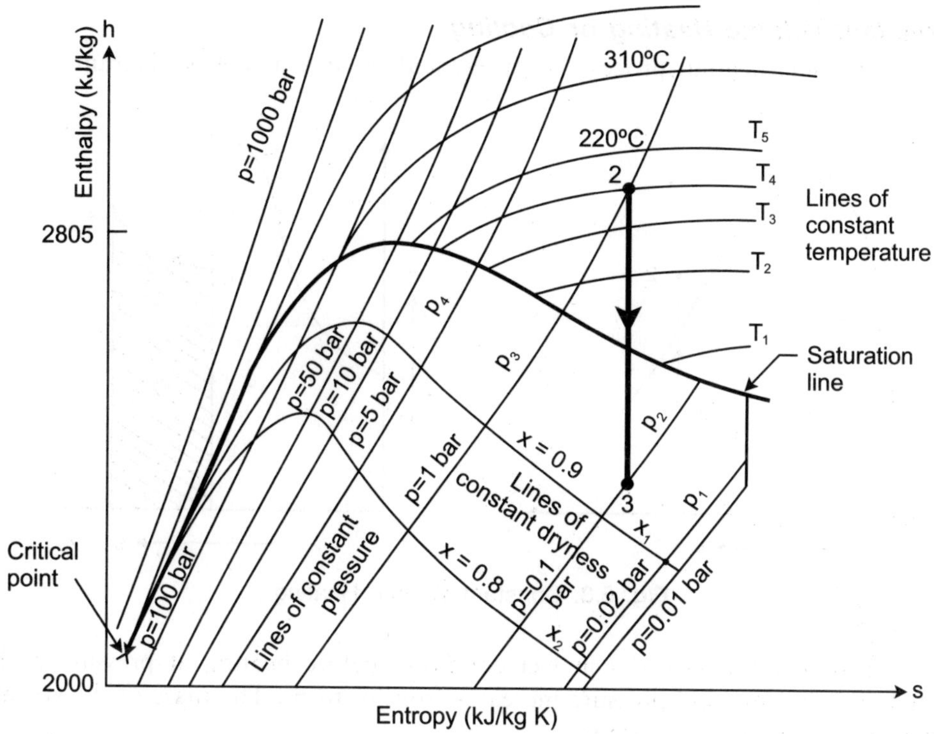

Fig. 5.2: Enthalpy–Entropy Chart

i. Lines of constant pressure are shown by p_1, p_2, etc. and lines of constant temperature are shown by T_1, T_2, etc.

ii. Any two independent properties which appear on the chart are sufficient to define the state.

iii. In the superheated region, pressure and temperature can define the state (e.g. p_3 and T_4 define the state 2, and h_2 can be read off).

iv. A line of constant entropy between two states 2 and 3 defines the properties at all points during an isentropic process between two states.

5.5 Thermodynamics Processes Involving Steam

The basic equations derived from first and second law of thermodynamics can also be used for vapours. The equations for work done, heat added, enthalpy and internal energy changes for gases can also be applied for vapours with suitable modifications.

The basic energy equations for the non-flow and flow processes are also valid for vapours

$$dq = du + pdv \text{ for non-flow processes}$$

$$dq = dh - vdp \text{ for flow processes}$$

Different non-flow processes are:

5.5.1 Constant Volume Heating or Cooling

The constant volume heating process is represented on p–v and T–s diagram as shown in Fig. 5.3.

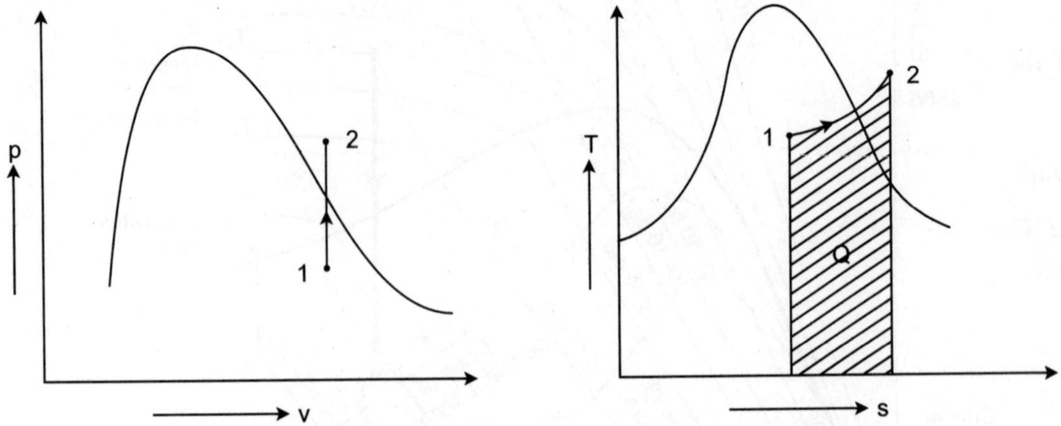

Fig. 5.3: Constant Volume Heating

It is assumed that the steam is in wet condition before heating at pressure p_1 becomes superheated after heating and pressure increases from p_1 to p_2. The mass of the steam during the heating process remains constant

$$m = \frac{V}{x_1 v_{s_1}} = \frac{V}{v_{sup_2}}$$

$$\therefore \quad v_{sup_2} = v_{s_2}\frac{T_{sup_2}}{T_{s_2}} = x_1 v_{s_1}$$

$$\therefore \quad \frac{T_{sup_2}}{T_{s_2}} = \frac{x_1 v_{s_1}}{v_{s_2}} \quad \text{(5.21)}$$

T_{s_2} and v_{s_2} will be known from steam tables corresponding to pressure p_2 and T_{s_2} can be calculated by using the above equation. Once the final condition is known, the change in all other properties can be easily obtained.

If the condition of steam remains wet after cooling then the final dryness fraction can be obtained by the equation

$$\frac{V}{x v_{s_1}} = \frac{V}{x_2 v_{s_2}};\ x_2 = \frac{x_1 v_{s_1}}{v_{s_2}}$$

v_{s_2} can be known from table at p_2.

Applying the first law of thermodynamics

$$q = \Delta u + \int_1^2 pdv = \Delta u \qquad \text{as} \int_1^2 pdv = 0$$

$$= u_2 - u_1 = \left[h_2 - p_2\left(x_2 v_{sup_2}\right)\right] - \left[h_1 - p_1\left(x_1 v_{s_1}\right)\right] \ldots\ldots\ldots \quad (5.22)$$

If the steam condition remains wet after heating, then

$$q = u_2 - u_1 = \left[h_2 - p_2\left(x_2 v_{s_2}\right)\right] - \left[h_1 - p_1\left(x_1 v_{s_1}\right)\right] \ldots\ldots\ldots\ldots \quad (5.23)$$

During cooling, the same equations are used except that the suffixes 1 and 2 are interchanged.

5.5.2 Constant Pressure Heating or Cooling

Constant pressure heating process is represented on p–v and T–s diagram as below:

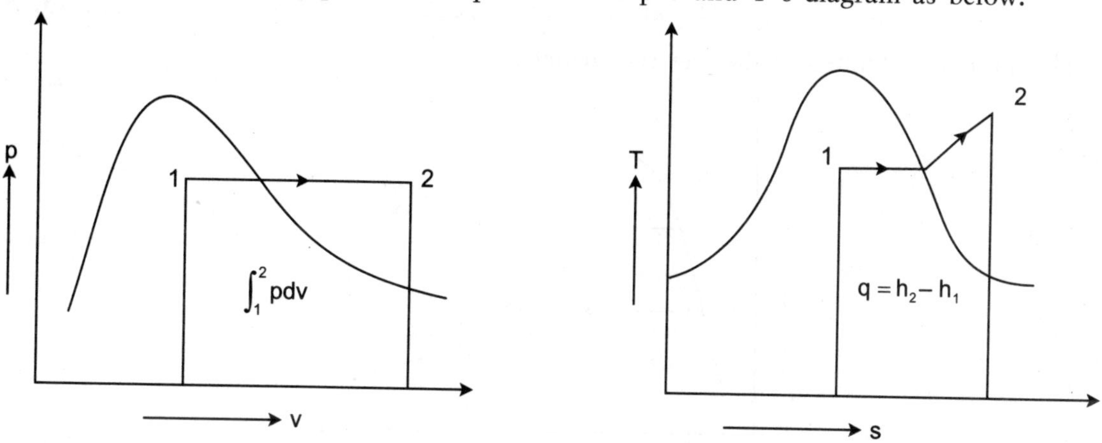

Fig. 5.4: Constant Pressure Heating

Applying the first law energy equation to the constant pressure heating non-flow process.

$$\begin{aligned} q &= \Delta u + \int_1^2 pdv \\ &= (u_2 - u_1) + p(v_2 - v_1) \\ &= (u_2 - pv_2) - (u_1 - pv_1) \\ &= h_2 - h_1 \end{aligned}$$

If the initial condition of steam is wet and final condition is superheated, then

$$\begin{aligned} q &= (u_2 + pv_{sup_2}) - (u_1 + px_1 v_{s_1}) \\ &= h_2 - h_1 \end{aligned}$$

Here h_1 and h_2 are actual enthalpies of steam per kg before heating and after heating.

The heat added during the constant pressure process is equal to the change in enthalpy of steam during the process.

The work done is given by

$$w = p\left(v_{sup_2} - x_1 v_{s_1}\right) \quad \ldots\ldots (5.24)$$

When the steam is wet before heating and becomes superheated after heating.

5.5.3 Constant Temperature or Isothermal Expansion

In wet region, isothermal process is also an isobaric process. Once the steam becomes superheated, the process is converted into hyperbolic process (pv = c). Fig. 5.5 shows wet steam heated at constant temperature till it becomes dry saturated. During this region, heat transfer q is given by

$$q = h_2 - h_1 \quad \text{and} \quad w = p_1\left(v_{s_2} - x v_{s_1}\right)$$

$$v_{s_2} = v_{s_1} \text{ as pressure remains constant}$$

$$\therefore \quad w = p_1 v_{s_1}(1 - x) \quad \ldots\ldots (5.25)$$

This process is limited to the wet region only.

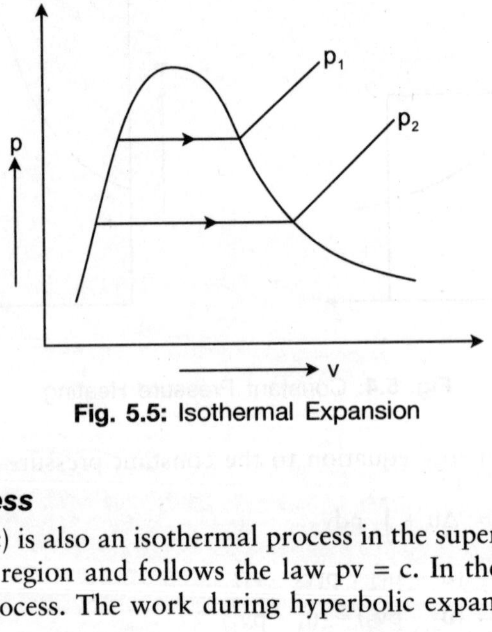

Fig. 5.5: Isothermal Expansion

5.5.4 Hyperbolic Process

Hyperbolic process (pv = c) is also an isothermal process in the superheated region as the steam behaves like a gas in this region and follows the law pv = c. In the wet region, pv = c is not a constant temperature process. The work during hyperbolic expansion in non-flow system is given by

$$w = \int_1^2 p\,dv = \int_1^2 \frac{c}{v}\,dv = c \log_e\left(\frac{v_2}{v_1}\right)$$

where v_1 and v_2 are specific volumes before and after expansion.

From first law

$$q = \Delta u + \int_1^2 pdv = (u_2 - u_1) + p_1v_1 \log_e\left(\frac{v_2}{v_1}\right)$$

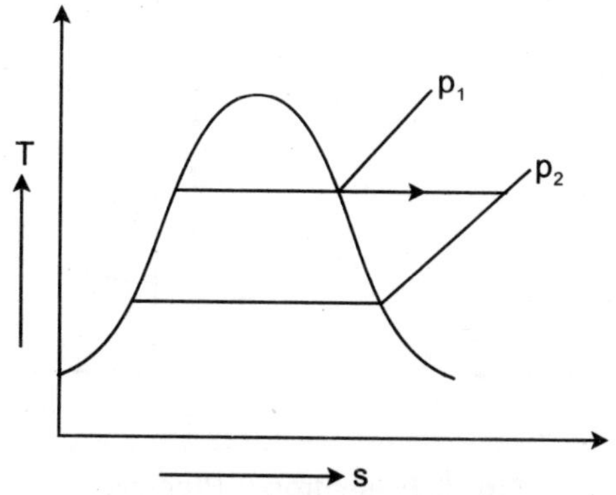

Fig. 5.6: Hyperbolic Process

$$q = (h_2 - p_2v_2) - (h_1 - p_1v_1) + p_1v_1\log_e\left(\frac{v_2}{v_1}\right)$$

As $$p_2v_2 = p_1v_1$$

$$q = (h_2 - h_1) + p_1v_1 \log_e\left(\frac{v_2}{v_1}\right) \quad \ldots\ldots\ldots\ldots\ldots\ldots\ldots \quad (5.26)$$

5.5.5 Reversible Adiabatic or Isentropic Process

It is represented by a vertical line on T–s and h–s diagrams as shown in Fig. 5.7.

Considering the process is non-flow reversible adiabatic and applying the first law

$$q = \Delta u + \int_1^2 pdv = (u_2 - u_1) + w$$

As $$q = 0 \text{ for adiabatic process}$$

$\therefore$ $$w = u_2 - u_1$$

For a steady flow reversible adiabatic process

$$h_1 + q = h_2 + w \qquad \text{or} \qquad w = h_1 - h_2$$

The values of h_1 and h_2 can be read directly from the chart

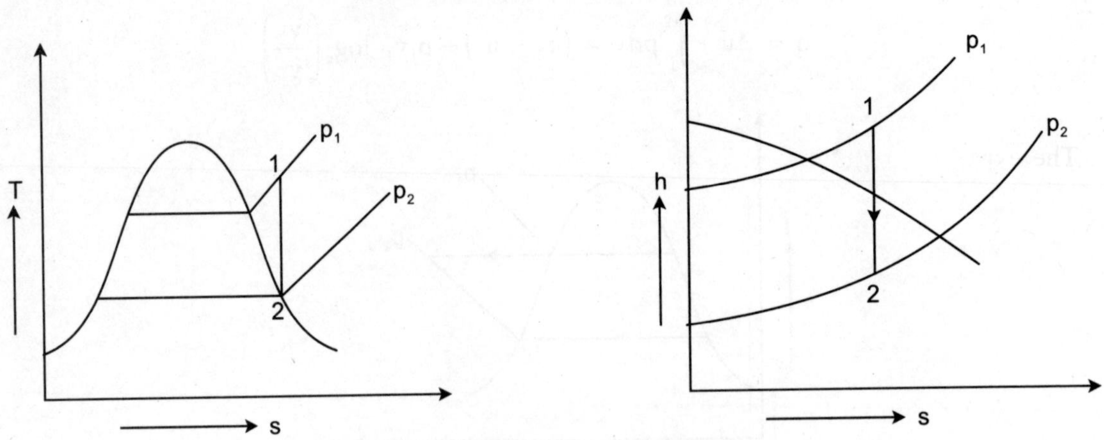

Fig. 5.7: Isentropic Process

If we are to use steam tables only, then

As $$s_1 = s_2$$

From the specification of p_1 and x_1 or p_1 and T_1, s_1 can be found.

From the specification of p_1, s_{f_2}, s_{fg_2}, s_{g_2} can be found. Using $s_1 = s_{f_2} + x_2\, s_{fg_2}$, x_2 can be found. If $x_2 > 1$, then the final condition is in the superheated regions, then

$$s_1 = s_{g_2} + c_{Ps} \log_e\left(\frac{T_{sup}}{T_{s_2}}\right) \quad \text{......} \quad (5.27)$$

T_{sup} is the only unknown and can be calculated.

From p_2 and T_{sup}, h_2, u_2 or any other property at end condition can be calculated.

5.5.6 Polytropic Process

The work done during a polytropic process ($pv^n = c$) is given by

$$w = \frac{p_1 v_1 - p_2 v_2}{n-1} \text{ Nm/kg}$$

Apply first law

$$q = \Delta u + w = (u_2 - u_1) + \frac{p_1 v_1 - p_2 v_2}{n-1}$$

$$= (h_2 - p_2 v_2) - (h_1 - p_1 v_1) + \frac{p_1 v_1 - p_2 v_2}{n-1}$$

$$= (h_2 - h_1) + (p_1v_1 - p_2v_2) + \left(1 + \frac{1}{n-1}\right)$$

$$= (h_2 - h_1) + \left(\frac{n}{n-1}\right)(p_1v_1 - p_2v_2) \quad \text{.....................} \quad (5.28)$$

The expansion of non-flow process following the law $pv^n = c$ is shown in Fig. 5.8.

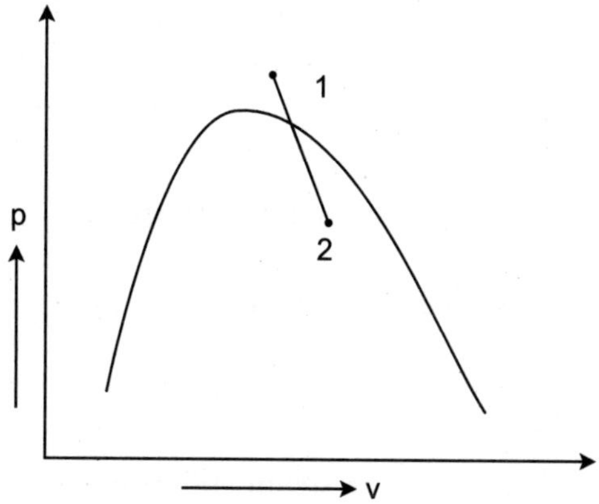

Fig. 5.8: Polytropic Process

In adiabatic process $q = 0$ and if $\Delta s \neq 0$, then the process behaves like an adiabatic process and not isentropic. So for such a process with steam

$$w = -\Delta u = u_1 - u_2$$

The approximate value of n for adiabatic compression of steam are

$$n = 1.13 \text{ for wet steam}$$

and $$n = 1.3 \text{ for superheated steam}$$

If both initial and final conditions are in the wet region, then

$$p_1 (x_1 v_1)^n = p_2 (x_2 v_2)^n$$

If end conditions are in superheated region, then

$$p_1 (x_1 v_1)^n = p_2 v_2^n$$

$$\therefore \quad v_2 = v_{s_2} \times \frac{T_{sup}}{T_{s_2}}, \; T_{sup} \text{ is calculated}$$

Knowing T_2 and T_{sup}, all properties at end conditions can be calculated.

5.5.7 Throttling Process

It is a constant enthalpy process and it is represented on T–s and h–s diagrams as shown in Fig. 5.9.

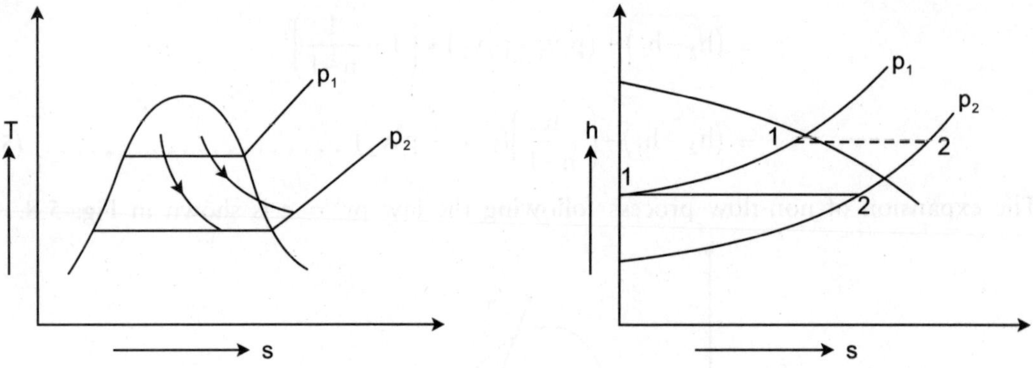

Fig. 5.9: Throttling Process

As the total enthalpy remains constant during throttling

$$\therefore \qquad h_1 = h_2$$

$$\therefore \qquad h_{f_1} + x h_{fg_1} = h_{f_2} + x_2 h_{fg_2}$$

The above equation is applied when the steam still remains in wet region as shown by the process 1–2 by full line.

If the steam becomes superheated after throttling as shown by dotted line 1–2, then

$$h_{f_1} + x h_{fg_1} = h_{f_2} + h_{fg_2} + c_{Ps}\left(T_{sup_2} - T_{s_2}\right)$$

$$= h_g + c_{Ps}\left(T_{sup_2} - T_{s_2}\right)$$

During throttling, the pressure always falls

$$\therefore \qquad p_2 < p_1$$

$$\therefore \qquad h_{f_1} > h_{f_2} \text{ and } h_{fg_1} < h_{fg_2}$$

If the sensible heat difference $\left(h_{f_1} - h_{f_2}\right) = h_1$ is greater than $\left(h_{fg_2} - h_{fg_1}\right) = h_2$, then the heat $(h_1 - h_2)$ is utilised to dry-out the steam to even superheat which depends on initial condition of steam (x_1) and final pressure after throttling.

5.6 Rankine Cycle

Rankine cycle is a modified Carnot cycle. It is a theoretical cycle on which the steam turbine (or engine) works. It is also a reversible cycle. It differs from Carnot cycle in the following respects:

i. The condensation process is allowed to complete. The exhaust steam from the turbine is completely condensed. At the end of condensation, the working fluid is completely in liquid form.

ii. The pressure of liquid water can be easily raised to the boiler pressure by employing a small sized pump.

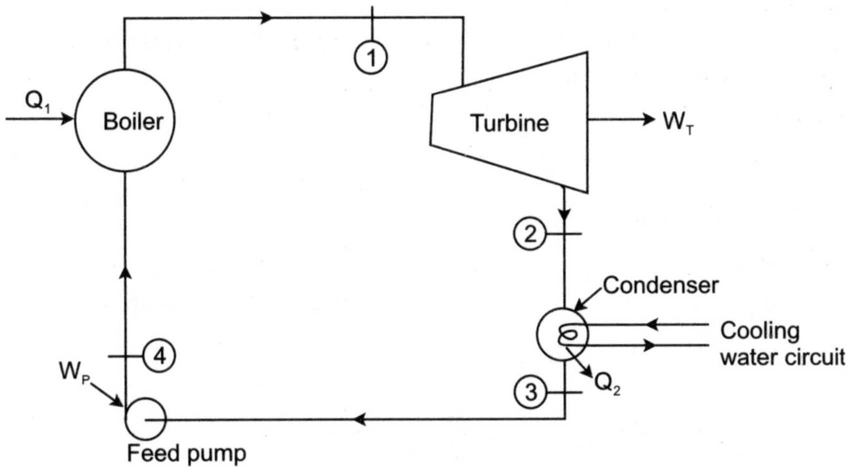

Fig. 5.10: Rankine Cycle

Rankine cycle comprises of the following processes:

i. Reversible adiabatic expansion in turbine or steam engine (Process 1–2)

ii. Constant pressure transfer of heat in the condenser (Process 2–3)

iii. Reversible adiabatic pumping process in the feed pump (Process 3–4)

iv. Constant pressure transfer of heat in the boiler (Process 4–1)

Fig. 5.11 shows Rankine cycle on p–v, T–s and h–s diagrams.

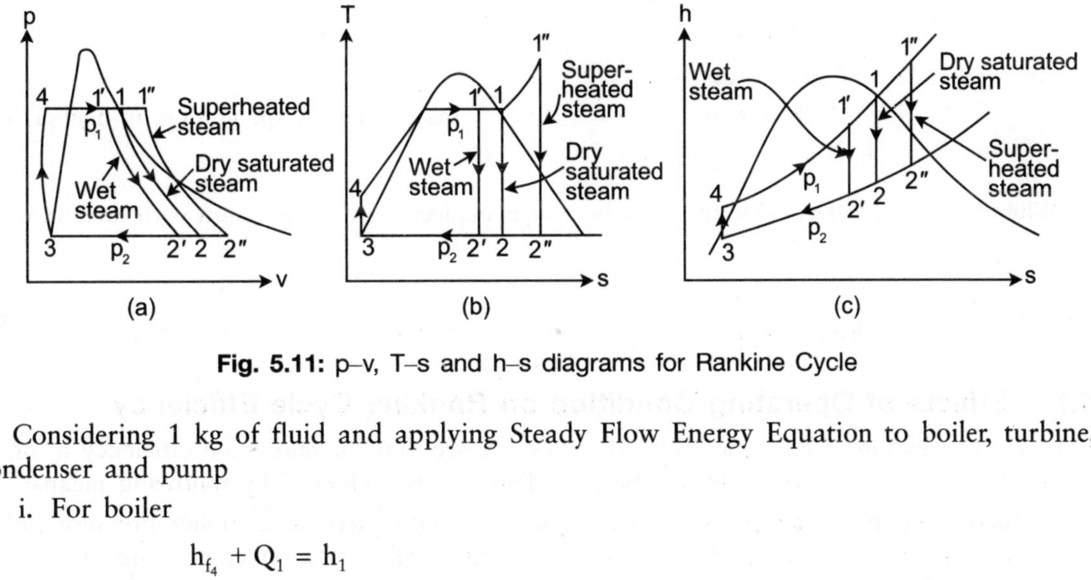

Fig. 5.11: p–v, T–s and h–s diagrams for Rankine Cycle

Considering 1 kg of fluid and applying Steady Flow Energy Equation to boiler, turbine, condenser and pump

i. For boiler

$$h_{f_4} + Q_1 = h_1$$

$$Q_1 = h_1 - h_{f_4}$$

ii. For turbine

$$h_1 = W_T + h_2 \qquad \text{where } W_T = \text{Turbine work}$$

$$\therefore \quad W_T = h_1 - h_2$$

iii. For condenser

$$h_2 = Q_2 + h_{f_3}$$

$$Q_2 = h_2 - h_{f_3}$$

iv. For feed pump

$$h_{f_3} + W_P = h_{f_4} \qquad \text{where } W_P = \text{Pump work}$$

$$\therefore \quad W_P = h_{f_4} - h_{f_3}$$

Efficiency of Rankine cycle $\eta_{Rankine} = \dfrac{W_{net}}{Q_1}$

$$= \frac{W_T - W_p}{Q_1}$$

$$= \frac{(h_1 - h_2) - (h_{f_4} - h_{f_3})}{(h_1 - h_{f_4})} \quad \ldots\ldots\ldots\ldots\ldots\ldots\ldots (5.29)$$

The feed pump handles liquid water which is incompressible which means with the increase in pressure its density or specific volume undergoes a little change. Using relations for reversible adiabatic process expansion, we get

$$Tds = dh - vdp$$

as $\quad ds = 0$

$$\therefore \quad dh = vdp$$

$$\Delta h = v\Delta p \qquad \text{(as change in sp. volume is negligible)}$$

$$h_{f_4} - h_{f_3} = v_3(p_1 - p_2)$$

When boiler pressure is low, the term $h_{f_4} - h_{f_3}$ is neglected in comparision with turbine work W_T

$$\therefore \quad \eta_{Rankine} = \frac{h_1 - h_2}{h_1 - h_{f_4}} \quad \ldots\ldots\ldots\ldots\ldots\ldots\ldots\ldots\ldots\ldots\ldots\ldots\ldots (5.30)$$

5.7 Effects of Operating Condition on Rankine Cycle Efficiency

From the expression of Rankine cycle efficiency, we see that for maximum efficiency h_1 or T_1 should be more and h_2 or T_2 should be less. This can be achieved by following means:

i. Increasing the boiler pressure: The cycle rises with increase in boiler pressure (other factors remaining same). It reaches its maximum value at a boiler pressure of 166 bar [Fig. 5.12(a)].

ii. Superheating: Rankine efficiency may be increased if the steam is superheated before allowing it to expand. Superheated steam also increases the blade life because of absence of erosion from high velocity water particles that are suspended in wet vapour [Fig. 5.12(b)].

iii. Reduced condenser pressure: The thermal efficiency can be improved by reducing the condenser pressure (which in turn reduces the heat rejecting temperature) especially in high vacuums. But it is obtained with increased cost of condensation apparatus [Fig. 5.12(c)].

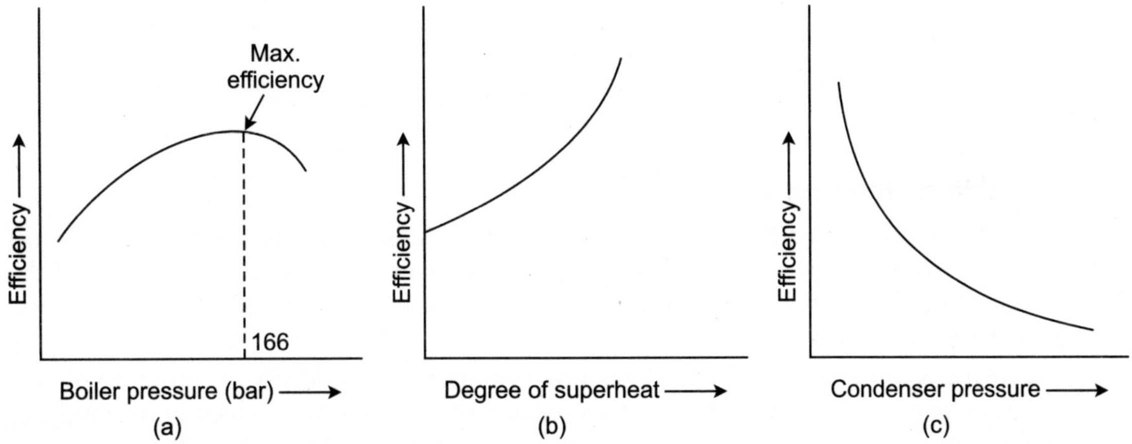

Fig. 5.12: Effect of Operating Conditions on Thermal Efficiency of the Rankine Cycle

iv. Regenerative feed heating: The average temperature at which heat is added to working fluid can be increased by preheating the feed water before it enters the boiler. For this purpose, part of steam is withdrawn or extracted at some intermediate stage during expansion in the turbine. The rest of the steam expands in the turbine to the condenser pressure.

v. By reheating the steam: In a reheat cycle, the expansion of steam is carried out in two or more stages. After partial expansion to an intermediate pressure in the high pressure turbine, the steam is withdrawn and reheated to the original temperature at constant pressure. Steam is then returned to the low pressure turbine and further expanded to the condenser pressure. The reheat cycle reduces the moisture content at the low pressure turbine exhaust. It also increases the output, though at the cost of additional consumption of heat required for reheating the steam (Fig. 5.13).

Improved efficiency of the cycle is

$$\eta = \frac{(h_1 - h_2) + (h_3 - h_4) - (h_6 - h_5)}{(h_1 - h_6) + (h_3 - h_2)} \quad \ldots\ldots\ldots\ldots \quad (5.31)$$

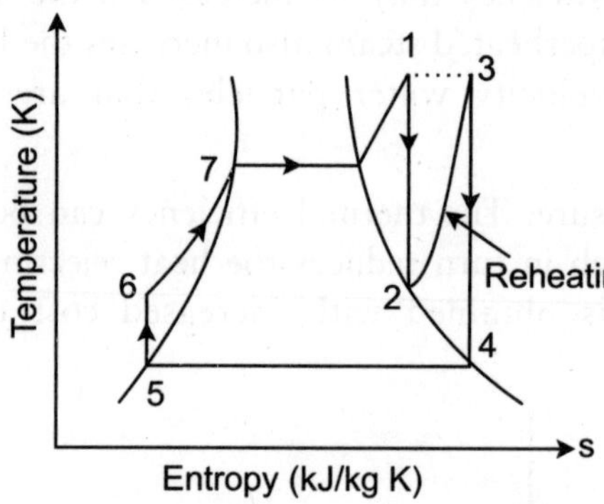

Fig. 5.13: Reheat Cycle

5.8 Modified Rankine Cycle

Fig. 5.14 shows the modified Rankine cycle on p–v and T–s diagrams (neglecting pump work) respectively. It will be noted that p–v diagram is very narrow at the toe, i.e. point 2 and the work obtained near 2 is very small. In fact this work is too inadequate to overcome friction (due to reciprocating parts etc.).

So, adiabatic is terminated at 2′. The pressure drop decreases suddenly at constant volume. This operation is represented by line 2–3. This reduces the stroke length which in turn reduces the cylinder dimensions. So, small cylinders can be used at the expense of small loss of work (area 2–3–2′).

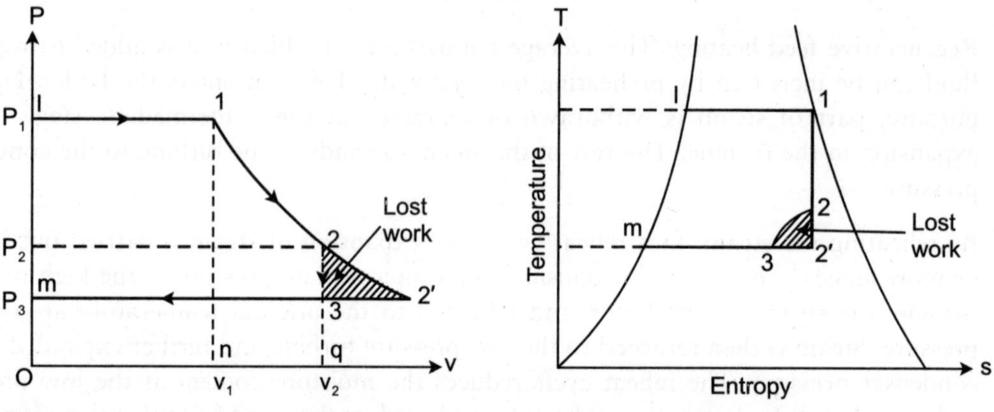

Fig. 5.14: p–v and T–s Diagram for Modified Rankine Cycle

Work done/kg of steam

$$= \text{Area l–1–2–3–m}$$

$$= \text{Area 0–l–1–n}' + \text{Area 1–2–q–n} - \text{Area 0–m–3–q}$$

$$= p_1v_1 + (u_1 - u_2) - p_3v_2 \quad \text{.......... (5.32)}$$

Heat supplied = $h_1 - h_{f_3}$

$$\text{Modified Rankine efficiency} = \frac{\text{Work done}}{\text{Heat supplied}}$$

$$= \frac{p_1v_1 + (u_1 - u_2) - p_3v_2}{h_1 - h_{f_3}} \quad \text{................. (5.33)}$$

Example 5.1

Calculate the enthalpy of 1 kg of steam at a pressure of 0.8 MPa and dryness fraction of 0.8. How much heat would be required to raise 2 kg of this steam from water at 20°C.

Solution:

$$p = 0.8 \text{ MPa}; \ x = 0.8$$

Enthalpy of 1 kg of steam

From steam tables, corresponding to a pressure of 0.8 MPa, we find that

$$h_f = 720.9 \text{ kJ/kg and } h_{fg} = 2046.5 \text{ kJ/kg}$$

We know that enthalpy of 1 kg of wet steam

$$h = h_f + x\ h_{fg}$$

$$= 720.9 + 0.8 \times 2046.5$$

$$= \mathbf{2358.1\ kJ} \quad \textbf{Ans.}$$

Heat required to raise 2 kg of this steam from water at 20°C.

Heat already in water = $4.2 \times 20 = 84$ kJ

Heat required per kg of steam

$$= 2358.1 - 84 = 2274.1 \text{ kJ}$$

∴ Heat required for 2 kg of steam

$$= 2 \times 2274.1 = 4548.2 \text{ kJ}$$

Example 5.2

A sample of superheated steam exists at 8 bar and a temperature 280°C. Using steam table, find the enthalpy, specific volume and entropy of this sample on per kg basic.

[UPTU Dec., 2003]

Solution:

From superheated steam tables,

p(bar)	*t(°C)*	*h*	*v*	*s*
8	250	2950	0.2931	7.0385
	300	2797.2	0.3241	7.2328
	280 = (250 + 30) (°C)	2858.32 kJ/kg	0.3117 m^3/kg	7.1546 kJ/kg K

Example 5.3

5 kg of steam at 5 bar and 200°C is expanded adiabatically to 0.1 bar, show the process on skeleton mollier chart and find the amount of work done. **[UPTU Dec., 2003]**

Solution:

Mass $m = 5$ kg

Initial pressure $p_1 = 5$ bar

Initial temperature $T_1 = 200°C$

From superheated steam tables

$$h_1 = 2855.4 \text{ kJ/kg}$$

$$s_1 = 7.0592 \text{ kJ/kg}$$

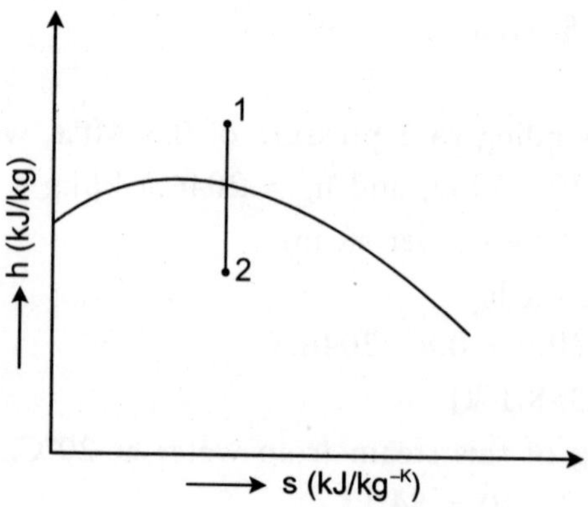

Fig. 5.15: Mollier Diagram

For isentropic process 1–2

$$s_1 = s_2 = s_{f_2} + x_2 \, s_{fg_2}$$

For a pressure of 0.1 bar, from saturated steam tables

$$s_{f_2} = 0.6493 \text{ kJ/kg K}$$

$$h_{f_2} = 191.83 \text{ kJ/kg K}$$

$$s_{fg_2} = 7.5009 \text{ kJ/kg K}$$

$$h_{fg_2} = 2392.8 \text{ kJ/kg K}$$

$$x_2 = \frac{s_2 - s_{f_2}}{s_{fg_2}} = \frac{7.0592 - 0.6493}{7.5009}$$

$$= 0.85455$$

$$\therefore \quad h_2 = h_{f_2} + x_2 h_{fg_2} = 191.83 + 0.85455\ (2392.8)$$

$$= 2236.597 \text{ kJ/kg}$$

Work done $= m(h_1 - h_2) = 5(2815.7 - 2236.517)$

$= \mathbf{3094\ kJ}$ **Ans.**

Example 5.4

In a steam power plant, the steam at 0.1 bar and 0.95 dry enters the condenser and leaves as saturated liquid at 0.1 bar and 45°C. Cooling water enters the condenser in separate steam at 20°C and leaves at 35°C without any loss of its pressure and no phase change. Neglecting the heat interaction between the condenser and the surroundings and changes in K.E. and P.E., determine the ratio of mass flow rate of cooling water to condensing steam.

[UPTU 2002-03]

Solution:

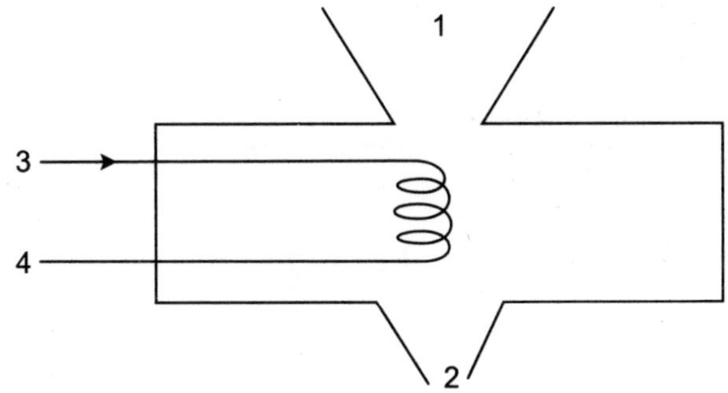

Fig. 5.16

$$h_1 = h_{f_1} + x h_{fg_1} \text{ (at 0.1 bar)}$$
$$= 191.8 + 0.95 \times 2392.9$$
$$= 2464 \text{ kJ/kg}$$
$$h_2 = h_{f_2} = 188.4 \text{ kJ/kg (at 45°C)}$$
$$\dot{m}_s(h - h_2) = \dot{m}_w\, c_{pw}\, (35-20)$$
$$\frac{\dot{m}_w}{\dot{m}_s} = \frac{h_1 - h_2}{4.186 \times 15} = \frac{2465 - 188.4}{4.186 \times 15}$$
$$= \mathbf{36.26}$$ **Ans.**

Example 5.5

5 kg of steam is condensed in a condenser following reversible constant pressure process from 0.75 bar and 150°C. At the end of the process, the steam gets completely condensed. Determine the heat recovered from steam and change in entropy. Also sketch the process on T–s diagram and shade the area representing. [UPTU July, 2002]

Solution:

Let points 1 and 2 represent the initial and final state of condensation process.

From steam table state 1 is superheated steam as saturation temperature at 0.75 bar is

$$\frac{91.42 + 92.14}{2} = 91.78°C$$

From steam table, by interpolation

$$h_1 = \frac{2778.6 + 2777.8}{2} = 2778.2 \text{ kJ/kg}$$

$$s_1 = \frac{7.783 + 7.720}{2} = 7.7515 \text{ kJ/kg K}$$

Point 2 is the saturation liquid at 0.75 bar

$$h_2 = h_{f_2} = \frac{382.9 + 385.9}{2} = 384.4 \text{ kJ/kg}$$

$$s_2 = s_{f_2} = \frac{1.209 + 1.217}{2} = 1.213 \text{ kJ/kg K}$$

Heat removed

$$\begin{aligned} Q_{1-2} &= m(h_1 - h_2) \\ &= 5(2778.2 - 384.4) \\ &= 11969 \text{ kJ} \end{aligned}$$

Change in entropy

$$\begin{aligned} s_1 - s_2 &= m(s_1 - s_2) \\ &= 5(7.7515 - 1.213) \\ &= 32.6925 \text{ kJ/kg} \end{aligned}$$

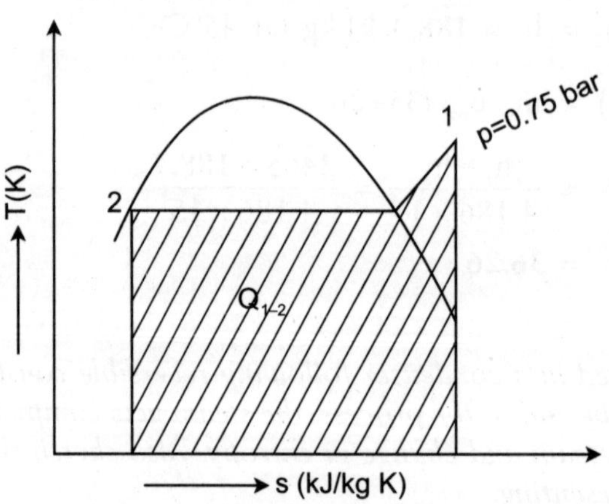

Fig. 5.17

Example 5.6

A vessel having a capacity of 0.05 m^3 contains a mixture of saturated water and saturated steam at a temperature of 245°C. The mass of liquid present is 10 kg. Find the

i. Pressure, ii. Mass, iii. Specific volume, iv. Specific enthalpy, v. Specific entropy and vi. Specific internal energy.

Solution:

From steam tables at 245°C temp.

$$p_{sat} = 36.5 \text{ bar}, v_f = 0.001239 \text{ m}^3/\text{kg}, v_g = 0.0546 \text{ m}^3/\text{kg}$$
$$h_f = 1061.4 \text{ kJ/kg}, h_{fg} = 1740.2 \text{ kJ/kg}$$
$$s_f = 2.7474 \text{ kJ/kg K}, s_{fg} = 3.3585 \text{ kJ/kg K}$$

i. Pressure = **36.5 bar** **Ans.**

ii. Mass of mixture, m:

Volume of liquid, $V_f = m_f v_f$

$= 10 \times 0.001239 \text{ m}^3$

$= 0.01239 \text{ m}^3$

Volume of vapour, $V_g = 0.05 - 0.01239$

$= 0.03761 \text{ m}^3$

Mass of vapour, $m_g = V_g/v_g = \dfrac{0.03761}{0.0546} = 0.688 \text{ kg}$

Total mass of mixture

$m = m_f + m_g = 10 + 0.688$

$= \mathbf{10.688 \text{ kg}}$ **Ans.**

iii. Specific volume, v:

Dryness fraction, $x = \dfrac{m_g}{m_g + m_f} = \dfrac{0.688}{0.688 + 10} = 0.064$

$v = v_f + x\, v_{fg}$

$= 0.001239 + 0.064(0.0546 - 0.001239)$

$= \mathbf{0.004654 \text{ m}^3/\text{kg}}$ **Ans.**

iv. Specific enthalpy, h:

$h = h_f + x\, h_{fg}$

$= 1061.4 + 0.064 \times 1740.2$

$= \mathbf{1172.77 \text{ kJ/kg}}$ **Ans.**

v. The specific entropy, s:

$s = s_f + x\, s_{fg}$

$= 2.7474 + 0.064 \times 3.3585$

$= \mathbf{2.9623 \text{ kJ/kg K}}$ **Ans.**

vi. Specific internal energy

$$u = h - pv$$

$$= 1172.77 - \frac{36.5 \times 10^5 \times 0.004654}{1000}$$

$$= \mathbf{1155.78\ kJ/kg}$$ **Ans.**

Example 5.7

Steam initially at 3 bar, 250°C is cooled at constant volume.

a. *At what temperature will the steam become saturated vapour?*
b. *What is the quality at 80°C?*
c. *What is the heat transferred per kg of steam in cooling from 250°C to 80°C?*

Solution:

a. At $p = 3$ bar

$$t_{sat} = 133.55°C$$

Since $t > t_{sat}$, the state would be in superheated region.

From table of properties of superheated steam at 3 bar, 250°C

$$v = 0.7964\ m^3/kg$$

$$h = 2967.6\ kJ/kg$$

$$v_1 = v_3 = v_2 = 0.7964\ m^3/kg$$

Now from table

when $v_g = 0.8919$ $t_{sat} = 120°C$

when $v_g = 0.7706$ $t_{sat} = 125°C$

So, for $v_g = 0.7964$ we have

$t_{sat} = 123.9°C$ (by linear interpolation)

b. At 80°C

$$v_f = 0.001029\ m^3/kg,\ v_g = 3.407\ m^3/kg$$

$$h_f = 334.91\ kJ/kg,\ h_{fg} = 2308.8\ kJ/kg$$

$$p_{sat} = 47.39\ kPa$$

$$v_1 = v_2 = 0.7964\ m^3/kg$$

$$0.7964 = v_f + x_2 v_{fg} \text{ at } 80°C$$

$$= 0.001029 + x_2\ (3.407 - 0.001029)$$

$$x_2 = \mathbf{0.234}$$ **Ans.**

c. $h_2 = 334.91 + 0.234 \times 2308.8 = 875.9$ kJ/kg

From first law of thermodynamics

$$dQ = du + pdv$$

$$(dQ)_v = du$$

$$Q_{1-2} = (u_2 - u_1) = (h_2 - p_2 v_2) - (h_1 - p_1 v_1)$$
$$= (h_2 - h_1) + v(p_1 - p_2)$$
$$= (875.9 - 2967.6) + 0.7964\ (300 - 47.39)$$
$$= \mathbf{-1890.2\ kJ/kg}$$

Ans.

Example 5.8

A boiler is supplied with feed water at a temperature of 45°C. The water is converted into steam at a pressure of 0.55 MPa and a temperature of 188°C. Determine the quantity of heat supplied per kg of steam. Assume suitable data.

Solution:

$$t_w = 45°C;\ p = 0.55\ MPa;\ t_{sup} = 188°C$$

From steam tables, corresponding to a pressure of 0.55 MPa, we have

$$h_f = 655.8\ kJ/kg$$
$$h_{fg} = 2095.9\ kJ/kg$$
$$t_{sat} = 155.5°C$$

Since given temperature 188°C > t_{sat} (155°C)

∴ Steam produced is superheated.

Let c_p for superheated steam is 2.1 kJ/kg K

So, enthalpy or total heat of superheated steam

$$h_{sup} = h_f + h_{fg} + c_p\ (t_{sup} - t)$$
$$= 655.8 + 2095.9 + 2.1(188 - 155.5)$$
$$= 2820\ kJ/kg$$

Since the water is supplied at 45°C, therefore heat already present in the feed water

$$= 4.2 \times 45 = 189\ kJ$$

∴ Heat actually required $= 2820 - 189$

$$= \mathbf{2631\ kJ/kg}$$

Ans.

Example 5.9

One kg of steam with initial parameters of 1.2 MPa pressure and 0.95 dryness fraction is made to undergo isothermal expansion to 0.1 MPa pressure. Use Mollier diagram to determine the quantity of heat received, the work performed, and the change in internal energy of steam.

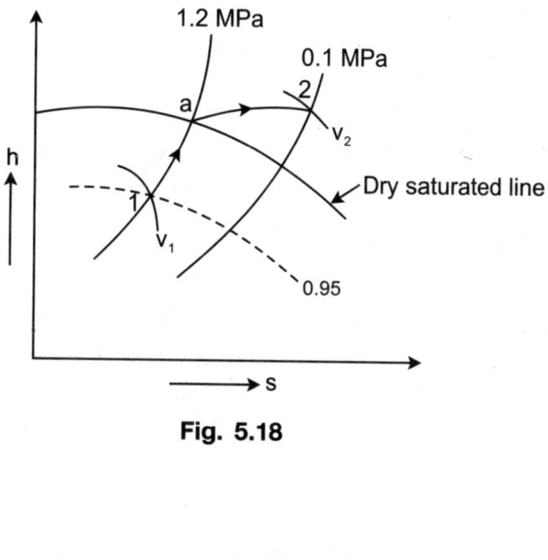

Fig. 5.18

Solution:

i. Point 1 is located at the intersection of 1.2 MPa and 0.95 dryness fraction.

ii. Move along the isothermal line 1–a–2 upto intersection with the given pressure $p_2 = 0.1$ MPa. It is to be noted that in the wet region the constant temperature line coincides with the pressure line.

iii. Project the initial state point 1 and final state 2 onto the axis of ordinates and onto the axis of abscissa.

The following values are then read from the chart:

$h_1 = 2685$ kJ/kg; $v_1 = 0.16$ m^3/kg; $s_1 = 6.35$ kJ/kg K

$h_2 = 2835$ kJ/kg; $v_2 = 2.1$ m^3/kg; $s_2 = 7.75$ kJ/kg K

and $t_1 = t_2 = 180°C = 453$ K

$$u_1 = h_1 - p_1v_1$$

$$= 2685 - \frac{1.2 \times 10^6 \times 0.16}{10^3} = 2493 \text{ kJ/kg}$$

$$h_2 = u_2 + p_2v_2$$

$$u_2 = h_2 - p_2v_2$$

$$= 2835 - \frac{0.1 \times 10^6 \times 2.1}{10^3} = 2625 \text{ kJ/kg}$$

Change in internal energy, $du = 2625 - 2493$

$= 132$ kJ/kg

Quantity of the heat received, $q = T(s_2 - s_1)$

$= 453(7.75 - 6.35) = 634.2$ kJ/kg

From first law of thermodynamics

Work performed, $w = q - du = 634.2 - 132 =$ **502.2 kJ/kg** **Ans.**

Example 5.10

Two boilers A and B delivering steam in equal proportions to a common main, both at a pressure of 14 bar. Boiler A has a superheater and boiler B is without superheater. The temperature of steam supplied by boiler A is 300°C. The temperature of resulting mixture of steam in the steam main is 235°C. Estimate the quality of steam supplied by the boiler without superheater, i.e. (B). **[M.U. Summer, 1991 (revised)]**

Solution:

The temperature in the main 235°C is greater than the saturation temperature 195°C at 14 bar so the steam in the main is also superheated.

Total enthalpy before mixing = Total enthalpy after mixing

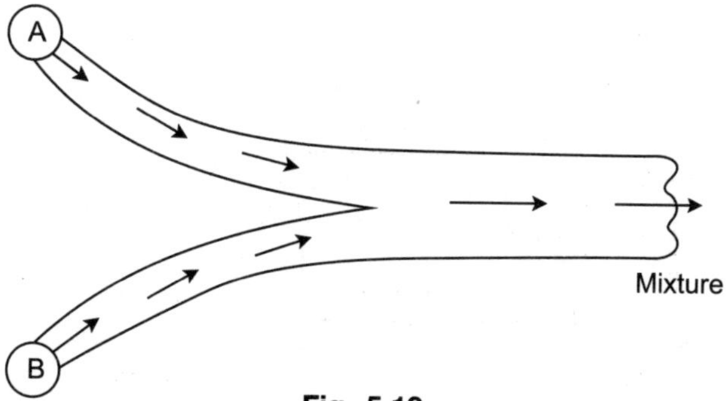

Fig. 5.19

Assuming the dryness fraction of steam supplied by the boiler B is x_b, we can write

$$m_a\left[h_{f_a} + h_{fg_a} + c_{ps}\left(T_{sup_a} - T_{g_a}\right)\right] + m_b\left[h_{f_b} + x_b h_{fg_b}\right]$$
$$= \left(m_a + m_b\right)\left[h_f + h_{fg} + c_{ps}\left(T_{sup} - T_g\right)\right]$$

As $\quad m_a = m_b$

and pressure in both boilers is same, i.e. 14 bar

$$h_{f_a} = h_{f_b} = h_f$$

and $\quad h_{f_a} = h_{f_b} = h_{fg}$

and $\quad T_{ga} = T_g$

$$\therefore \left[h_{fg} + c_{ps}\left(T_{sup_a} - T_g\right)\right] + \left[x_b h_{fg}\right] = 2 \times \left[h_{fg} + c_{ps}\left(T_{sup} - T_g\right)\right]$$

Now substituting the values from steam table as

$$1957.7 + 2.25(300 - 195) + x_b \times 1957.7 = 2[1957.7 + 2.25(235 - 195)]$$

$$\therefore \quad 1957.7 + 236.25 + 1957.7\, x_b = 4095.4$$

$$x_b = \frac{1901.45}{1957.7} = \mathbf{0.9713}$$ **Ans.**

Example 5.11

In a Rankine cycle, the steam at inlet to turbine is saturated at pressure of 3.5 MPa and the exhaust pressure is 20 kPa. Determine:

i. The pump work, *ii. The turbine work,* *iii. The Rankine efficiency,*
iv. The condenser heat flow and *v. The dryness at the end of expansion.*
Flow rate is 9.5 kg/sec.

Solution:

At inlet of turbine, conditions are

$$p_1 = 3.5 \text{ MPa}, x = 1$$

Exhaust pressure, $p_2 = 20$ kPa

Mass flow rate $= 9.5$ kg/sec

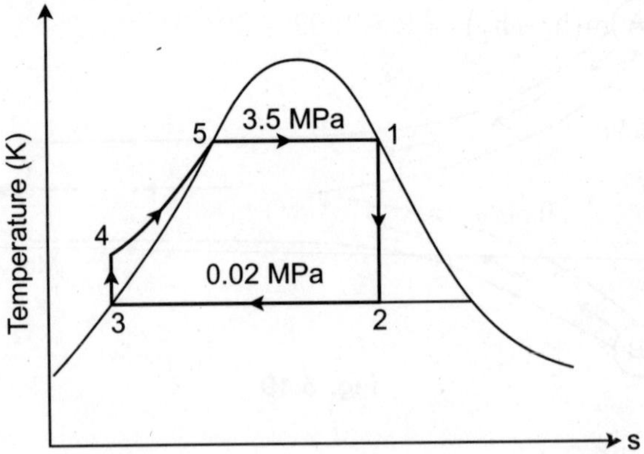

Fig. 5.20

From steam table

At 3.5 MPa $h_1 = h_{g_1} = 2802$ kJ/kg

$s_{g_1} = 6.1228$ kJ/kg K

At 0.02 MPa $h_f = 251.5$ kJ/kg, $h_{fg} = 2358.4$ kJ/kg

$v_f = 0.001017$ m^3/kg

$s_f = 0.8321$ kJ/kg K

$s_{fg} = 7.0773$ kJ/kg K

i. *The pump work:*

$$\text{Pump work} = (p_4 - p_3)v_f$$
$$= (3.5 - 0.02) \times 10^6 \times 0.001017$$
$$= 3.54 \text{ kJ/kg}$$

But $\quad$ Pump work $= h_{f_4} - h_{f_3}$

$\therefore \quad 3.54 = h_{f_4} - h_{f_3}$

$$h_{f_4} = 3.54 + 251.5 = 255.04 \text{ kJ/kg}$$

Power required for the pump $= 3.54 \times 9.5$

$= \mathbf{33.63\ kW}$ **Ans.**

ii. *The turbine work:*

$$s_1 = s_2 = s_{f_2} + x_2\, s_{fg_2}$$
$$6.1228 = 0.8321 + x_2 \times 7.0773$$
$$x_2 = \frac{6.1228 - 0.8321}{7.0773} = 0.747$$

$\therefore \quad h_2 = h_{f_2} + x_2\, h_{fg_2} = 251.5 + 0.747 \times 2358.4$

$= 2013$ kJ/kg

Turbine work = $\dot{m}(h_1 - h_2)$ = 9.5(2802 – 2013)

= **7495.5 kW** **Ans.**

iii. *Rankine efficiency:*

$$\eta_{Rankine} = \frac{h_1 - h_2}{h_1 - h_{f_2}}$$

$$= \frac{2802 - 2013}{2802 - 251.5} = \frac{789}{2550.5}$$

= **0.3093 or 30.93%** **Ans.**

iv. *Condenser heat flow:*

The condenser heat flow = $\dot{m}(h_2 - hf_3)$

= 9.5(2013 – 251.5)

= **16734.25 kW** **Ans.**

v. *Dryness fraction at the end of expansion:*

x_2 = 0.747

= **74.7%** **Ans.**

Example 5.12

The following data refer to a simple power plant:

Sl. No.	*Location*	*Pressure*	*Quality/Temp.*	*Velocity (m/s)*
1.	*Inlet to turbine*	*6.0 MPa*	*380°C*	–
2.	*Exit from turbine And inlet to condenser*	*10 kPa*	*0.9*	*200 m/s*
3.	*Exit from condenser and inlet to pump*	*9 kPa*	*Sat. liquid*	–
4.	*Exit from pump and inlet to boiler*	*7.0 MPa*	–	–
5.	*Exit from boiler*	*6.5 MPa*	*400°C*	–

Calculate:

i. *Power output of the turbine.*
ii. *Heat transfer per hour in the boiler and condenser separately.*
iii. *Mass of cooling water circulated per hour in the condenser. Take inlet and exit temperature of cooling water in condenser as 20°C and 30°C respectively.*
iv. *Diameter of the pipe connecting turbine with condenser.*

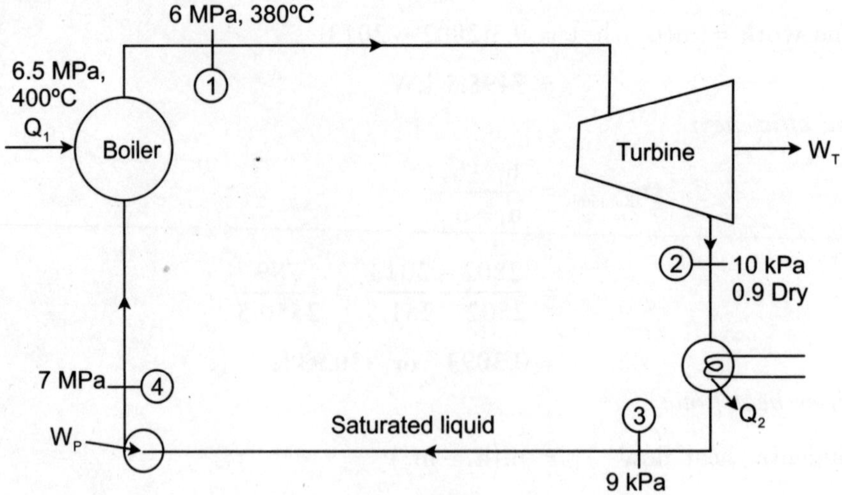

Fig. 5.21

Solution:

i. *Power output of the turbine, P:*

From steam table

at 60 bar, 380°C

$$h_1 = 3123.5 \text{ kJ/kg}$$

and at 0.1 bar,

$$h_{f_2} = 191.8 \text{ kJ/kg}$$

$$h_{fg_2} = 2392.8 \text{ kJ/kg}$$

$$x_2 = 0.9 \text{ (Given)}$$

$$\therefore \quad h_2 = h_{f_2} + x_2 h_{fg_2}$$

$$= 191.8 + 0.9 \times 2392.8$$

$$= 2345.3 \text{ kJ/kg}$$

Power output of the turbine $= m_s(h_1 - h_2)$ kW

$$= \frac{10000}{3600}(3123.5 - 2345.3)$$

$$= \mathbf{2162 \text{ kW}}$$ **Ans.**

ii. *Heat transfer per hour in the boiler and condenser:*

At 70 bar: $h_{f_4} = 1267.4$ kJ/kg

At 65 bar, 400°C: $h_a = \dfrac{3177.2 \text{ (at 60 bar)} + 3158.1 \text{(at 70 bar)}}{2}$

$$= 3167.6 \text{ kJ/kg}$$

Heat transfer per hour in the boiler

$$Q_1 = 10000\left(h_a - h_{f_4}\right)\ \text{kJ/h}$$
$$= 10000(3167.6 - 1267.4)$$
$$= \mathbf{1.9 \times 10^7\ kJ/h}$$ **Ans.**

At 0.09 bar, $h_{f_3} = 183.3$ kJ/kg

Heat transfer per hour in the condenser

$$Q_2 = 10000\left(h_a - h_{f_3}\right)$$
$$= 10000(2345.3 - 183.3)$$
$$= \mathbf{2.16 \times 10^7\ kJ/h}$$ **Ans.**

iii. *Mass of cooling water ciculated per hour in the condenser, m_w:*

Heat lost by the steam = Heat gained by the cooling water

$$Q_2 = m_w\ c_{pw}\ (t_2 - t_1)$$
$$2.16 \times 10^7 = m_w \times 4.18\ (30 - 20)$$
$$m_w = \frac{2.16 \times 10^7}{4.18(30 - 20)} = \mathbf{0.0516 \times 10^7\ kJ/h}$$ **Ans.**

iv. *Diameter of the pipe connecting turbine with condenser, d:*

$$\frac{\pi}{4} d^2 \times c = m_s\ x_2\ v_{g2}$$

where

c = Vel. of steam = 200 m/s (given)

m_s = Mass flow rate of steam in kg/sec

x_2 = Dryness fraction at 2′

v_{g_2} = Specific volume at 0.1 bar = 14.67 m^3/kg

Substituting the values, we get

$$\frac{\pi}{4} d^2 \times 200 = \frac{10000}{3600}(0.9)(14.67)$$
$$\mathbf{d = 0.483\ m = 483\ mm}$$ **Ans.**

Example 5.13

A vessel contains 1 kg of steam which contains 1/3rd liquid and 2/3rd vapour by volume. The temperature of the steam is 151.86°C. Find the quality, specific volume and specific enthalpy of the mixture.

Solution:

The pressure in the vessel must be the pressure corresponding to saturation temperature of 151.86°C that is 5 bar

As per the given condition

$$\frac{V_f}{V_g} = \frac{\frac{1}{3}}{\frac{2}{3}} = \frac{1}{2} = \frac{m_f v_f}{m_g v_g}$$

$$\therefore \qquad \frac{m_f \times 0.00109}{m_g \times 0.375} = \frac{1}{2}$$

$$\frac{m_f}{m_g} = 172.5$$

The quality of steam is $$x = \frac{m_g}{m_f + m_g} = \frac{1}{\frac{m_f}{m_g}+1} = \frac{1}{173.5}$$

$$= \mathbf{0.0576} \qquad \textbf{Ans.}$$

The specific volume of the mixture is $v_m = (1 - x)v_f + xv_g$

Taking v_f and v_g from steam table at 5 bar pressure

$$v_m = 0.99624 \times 0.00109 + 0.00576 \times 0.375$$
$$= 0.003245 \text{ m}^3\text{/kg}$$

The enthalpy of mixture is $$h_m = (1 - x)h_f + xh_g$$
$$= (1 - 0.00576) \times 640.23 + (0.00576) \times 2108.5$$
$$= \mathbf{650.5 \text{ kJ/kg}} \qquad \textbf{Ans.}$$

Example 5.14

If 1 kg of steam at a pressure of 0.4 MPa and 10% wet expands isentropically in a cylinder to a pressure of 0.1 MPa. Find work done on the piston. Then find the work done using the steam tables and by using the value of n.

Solution:

At 0.4 MPa

$$h_{f_1} = 605 \text{ kJ/kg}$$
$$h_{fg_1} = 2134 \text{ kJ/kg}$$
$$v_{g_1} = 0.4706 \text{ m}^3\text{/kg}$$
$$s_{f_1} = 1.776 \text{ kJ/kg K}$$
$$t_1 = 142.92°\text{C} = 415.92 \text{ K}$$

At 0.1 MPa from steam table

$$h_{f_2} = 417 \text{ kJ/kg}$$
$$h_{fg_2} = 2258 \text{ kJ/kg}$$
$$s_{f_2} = 1.303 \text{ kJ/kg K}$$

$$v_{g_2} = 1.725 \text{ m}^3/\text{kg}$$

$$t_2 = 99.1°\text{C}$$

As process is isentropic

$$\therefore \quad s_{f_1} + \frac{x_2 h_{fg_1}}{T_1} = s_{f_2} + \frac{x_2 h_{fg_2}}{T_2}$$

$$1.776 + \frac{0.9 \times 2134}{415.92} = 1.303 + \frac{x_2 \times 2258}{372.1}$$

$$6.3937 = 1.303 + 6.068\ x_2$$

$$x_2 = 0.84$$

as $$\frac{p_1}{p_2} = \left(\frac{v_2}{v_1}\right)^n$$

$$n = \frac{\log\left(\frac{p_1}{p_2}\right)}{\log\left(\frac{v_2}{v_1}\right)} = \frac{\log\left(\frac{p_1}{p_2}\right)}{\log\left(\frac{x_2 v_{g2}}{x_1 v_{g1}}\right)}$$

$$= \frac{\log\left(\frac{4}{1}\right)}{\log\left(\frac{0.838 \times 1.725}{0.90 \times 0.4206}\right)}$$

$$= \frac{\log(4)}{\log(3.413)}$$

$$= 1.13$$

$$h_1 = h_{f_1} + x_1 h_{fg_1} = 605 + 0.9 \times 2134 = 2525.6 \text{ kJ/kg}$$

$$h_2 = h_{f_2} + x_2 h_{fg_2} = 417 + (0.84)(2258) = 2313.72$$

$$u_1 = h_1 - 100 \times p_1 x_1 v_{g_1} = 2525.6 - 100 \times 4 \times 0.9 \times 0.4706$$

$$= 2356.18$$

$$u_2 = h_2 - 100 \times p_2 x_2 v_{g_2} = 2313.72 - 100 \times 1 \times 0.84 \times 1.725$$

$$= 2168.8 \text{ kJ/kg}$$

$\therefore$ Work done by steam table,

$$w = u_1 - u_2 = 2356.18 - 2168.8 = 187.38 \text{ kJ/kg}$$

Work done on piston by using value of n

$$= 100\left(p_1 x_1 v_{g_1} - p_2 x_2 v_{g_2}\right)$$

$$= \frac{100(4 \times 0.9 \times 0.4706 - 1 \times 0.84 \times 1.725)}{1.13 - 1}$$

$$= \mathbf{188.5846 \text{ kJ/kg}}$$ **Ans.**

Example 5.15

Steam at a pressure of 1.5 MPa and 300°C is delivered to the throttle of an engine. The steam expands to 0.2 MPa when release occurs. The steam exhaust takes place at 1.1 bar. A performance test gives the result of the specific steam consumption of 12.8 kg/kWh and a mechanical efficiency of 80%. Determine

i. Modified Rankine engine work per kg.
ii. Modified Rankine engine efficiency.
iii. Indicated and brake work per kg.
iv. Brake thermal efficiency.
v. Relative efficiency.

Solution:

From steam tables:

1. At 15 bar and 300°C

$$h_1 = 3037.6 \text{ kJ/kg}$$
$$v_1 = 0.169 \text{ m}^3\text{/kg}$$
$$s_1 = 6.918 \text{ kJ/kg K}$$

2. At 2 bar

$$t_{s_2} = 120.2°\text{C}$$
$$h_{f_2} = 504.7 \text{ kJ/kg}$$
$$h_{fg_2} = 2201.6 \text{ kJ/kg}$$
$$s_{f_2} = 1.5301 \text{ kJ/kg K}$$
$$s_{fg_2} = 5.5967 \text{ kJ/kg K}$$
$$v_{f_2} = 0.00106 \text{ m}^3\text{/kg}$$
$$v_{g_2} = 0.885 \text{ m}^3\text{/kg}$$

3. At 1.1 bar

$$t_{s_3} = 102.3°\text{C}$$
$$h_{f_3} = 428.8 \text{ kJ/kg}$$
$$h_{fg_3} = 2250.8 \text{ kJ/kg}$$
$$s_{f_3} = 1.333 \text{ kJ/kg K}$$
$$s_{fg_3} = 5.9947 \text{ kJ/kg K}$$
$$v_{f_3} = 0.001 \text{ m}^3\text{/kg}$$
$$v_{g_3} = 1.549 \text{ m}^3\text{/kg}$$

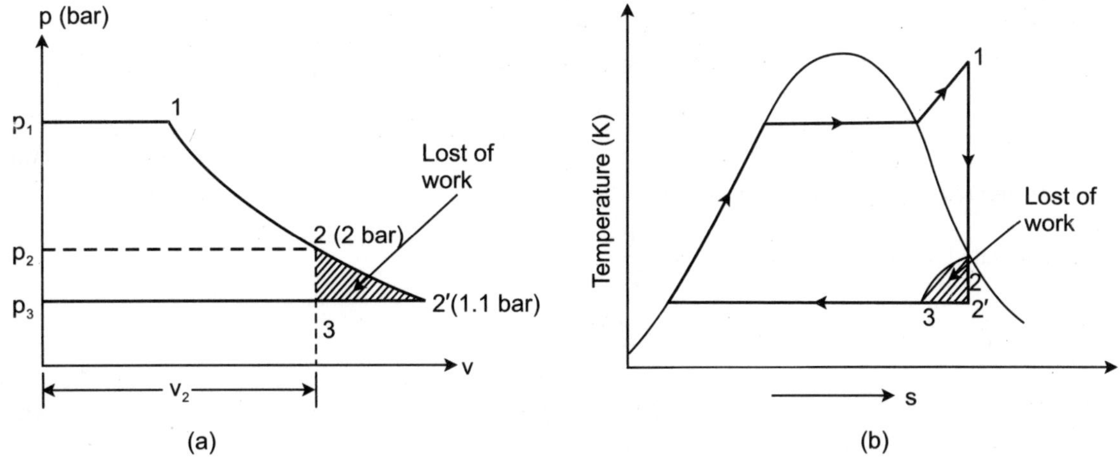

Fig. 5.22: p–v and T–s

During isentropic expansion 1–2

$$s_1 = s_2$$

$$6.918 = s_{f_2} + x_2 s_{fg_2}$$

$$= 1.5301 + x_2(5.5967)$$

$$x_2 = 0.96$$

Similarly,

$$h_2 = h_{f_2} + x_2 h_{fg_2}$$

$$= 504.7 + (0.96)(2201.6)$$

$$= 2618.2 \text{ kJ/kg}$$

$$v_2 = x_2 v_{g_2} + (1 - x_2) v_{f_2}$$

$$= (0.96)(0.885) + (1 - 0.96)(0.00106)$$

$$= 0.849 \text{ m}^3\text{/kg}$$

i. *Ideal work:*

Modified Rankine engine work/kg

$$w = (h_1 - h_2) + (p_2 - p_3)\, v_2$$

$$= (3037.6 - 2618.2) + (2 - 1.1) \times 10^5 \times \frac{0.849}{1000}$$

$$= 419.4 + 76.41$$

$$= \mathbf{495.8 \text{ kJ/kg}}$$ **Ans.**

ii. Rankine engines efficiency:

$$\eta_{\text{Rankine}} = \frac{\text{Work done}}{\text{Heat supplied}}$$

$$= \frac{495.8}{h_1 - h_{f_3}} = \frac{495.8}{3037.6 - 428.8}$$

$= 0.19$

$= \mathbf{19\%}$ **Ans.**

iii. *Indicated and brake work per kg*

Indicated work/kg, $w_{indicated} = \frac{I.P.}{m}$

$$= \frac{1 \times 3600}{12.8}$$

$= \mathbf{281.25\ kJ/kg}$ **Ans.**

Brake work/kg, $w_{brake} = \frac{B.P.}{m}$

$$= \frac{\eta_{mech.} \times I.P.}{m}$$

$$= \frac{0.8 \times 1 \times 3600}{12.8}$$

$= \mathbf{225\ kJ/kg}$ **Ans.**

iv. *Brake thermal efficiency*

$$\eta_{brake\ th} = \frac{w_{brake}}{h_1 - h_{f_3}} = \frac{225}{3037.6 - 428.8}$$

$= 0.086$

$= \mathbf{8.6\%}$ **Ans.**

v. *Relative efficiency*

$$= \frac{w_{indicated}/(h_1 - h_{f_3})}{w/(h_1 - h_{f_3})}$$

$$= \frac{w_{indicated}}{w} = \frac{281.25}{495.8} = \mathbf{0.567 \text{ or } 56.7\%}$$ **Ans.**

Relative efficiency on the basis of brake work

$$= \frac{w_{brake}/(h_1 - h_{f_3})}{w/(h_1 - h_{f_3})} = \frac{w_{brake}}{w}$$

$$= \frac{225}{495.8}$$

$= \mathbf{0.4538 \text{ or } 45.38\%}$ **Ans.**

THEORETICAL QUESTIONS

1. Explain the following terms relating to steam:
   i. Sensible heat of water
   ii. Latent heat of steam
   iii. Dryness fraction of steam
   iv. Enthalpy of wet steam and
   v. Superheated steam
2. What do you mean by following
   i. Internal latent heat
   ii. Internal energy of steam
   iii. External work of evaporation
   iv. Entropy of evaporation
   v. Entropy of wet steam
   vi. Entropy of superheated steam
3. Define the terms saturated temperature and saturated pressure.
4. Write a short note on Mollier chart.
5. Describe the different operations of Rankine cycle. Derive an expression for its efficiency.
6. What are different methods for increasing the thermal efficiency of a Rankine cycle ?

NUMERICAL PROBLEMS

1. Find specific volume, dryness fraction and internal energy of a steam at 7 bar and enthalpy 3000 kJ/kg.
2. Determine the state of steam at
   i. p = 10 bar and v = 0.19 m^3/kg
   ii. p = 12 bar and t = 210°C
3. Steam at 1 MPa and 200°C is cooled till it becomes dry saturated and then throttled to 1 Mpa pressure. Find
   i. Change in enthalpy and heat transferred in each process.
   ii. The quality of steam at the end of throttling process.
4. Wet steam at 15 bar is throttled to 1 bar.
   The temperature after throttling is found to be 120°C. Find the quality of wet steam.
5. Find the internal energy of 1 kg of steam at 1.4 MPa under the following conditions
   i. When the steam is 0.85 dry
   ii. When the steam is dry and saturated
   iii. When the temperature of steam is 300°C.
   Take c_{ps} = 2.25 kJ/kg K
6. A vessel of spherical shape having a capacity of 0.8 m^3 contains steam at 1 MPa and 0.95 dryness. Steam is blown off until the pressure drops to 0.5 MPa. The valve is then

closed and the steam is allowed to cool until the pressure falls to 0.4 MPa. Assuming that the enthalpy of steam in the vessel remains constant during blowing off period, determine:

i. The mass of steam blown off
ii. The dryness fraction of steam in the vessel after cooling and
iii. The heat lost by steam per kg during cooling

7. Wet steam at 2 MPa pressure and 0.9 dryness fraction is heated reversibly at constant pressure to a temperature of 300°C. Make calculations for the work done, heat supplied and change in the internal energy and entropy. Represent the process on T–s diagram and indicate there upon the area which represents the heat interaction.

8. One-tenth per cent of 1 m^3 capacity closed vessel is occupied by water and remaining by steam in thermal equilibrium with water at 10 bar pressure. This vessel is heated by external means.

   The pressure at the end of heating is 1.2 MPa. After heating, 25% mass is blown-off from the vessel.

   Determine

   i. Quality of steam at the beginning
   ii. Degree of superheat at the end of heating process
   iii. Heat supplied by external means
   iv. Final mass of steam in the vessel.

9. Steam at an absolute pressure of 10 bar and 250°C expands isentropically in a steam turbine till the pressure drops to 1 bar. Estimate the quality of steam leaving the turbine work developed per kg of steam. If the actual drop is 90% of isentropic drop and steam flow rate through the turbine is 500 kg/min, determine the power developed by the turbine. Use Mollier chart.

10. Steam supplied to a steam turbine is at 30 bar and 400°C and expands in the turbine isentropically till its pressure falls to 5 kPa. Determine the condition of steam at the end of expansion and fall in enthalpy per kg of steam.

11. A steam power plant works between 40 bar and 0.05 bar. If the steam supplied is dry saturated and the cycle of operation is Rankine, find

    i. Cycle efficiency
    ii. Specific steam consumption

12. In a Rankine cycle, the steam at inlet to turbine is saturated at a pressure of 31 bar and the exhaust pressures is 0.5 bar. Determine:

    i. Pump work
    ii. Rankine efficiency
    iii. Turbine work
    iv. Condenser heat flow
    v. Dryness at the end of expansion

    Assume flow rate of 10 kg/sec.

6

Internal Combustion Engine

6.1 Heat Engine

Any machine which derives heat energy from the combustion of fuel and converts part of this energy into mechanical work is known as heat engine.

6.1.1 Heat Engines are Mainly Divided in Two Groups

i. *External Combustion Engine (E.C. Engine)*: In this case, combustion of fuel takes place outside the cylinder as in case of a steam engine. Other examples are hot air engines, steam turbines and closed cycle gas turbines, etc. These engines generally find application in locomotives, ships, electric power generation, etc.

ii. *Internal Combustion Engine*: The combustion of fuel in presence of air takes place inside the cylinder and products of combustion directly act on piston to develop the power.

6.1.2 Advantages of External Combustion Engine Over Internal Combustion Engine

i. Starting torque is high.

ii. Cheaper fuels can be used in external combustion engines.

iii. External combustion engines have more flexibility in arrangement.

iv. No external equipment or device is required for starting as in case of IC engines.

6.1.3 Advantages of Reciprocating IC Engines Over EC Engines

i. Overall efficiency is high.

ii. Mechanical simplicity is more.

iii. Initial cost is low.

iv. They can be easily started from cold conditions.

v. They have less weight/power ratio.

vi. They are compact and require less space.

6.2 Classification of IC Engines

The internal combustion engines are classified according to:

1. *Cycle of operation*:
   a. Two stroke engines: There is one power stroke for one revolution of crankshaft.
   b. Four stroke engines: There is one power stroke for two revolutions of crankshaft.
2. *Cycle of combustion*:
   a. Otto cycle: Combustion at constant volume.
   b. Diesel cycle: Combustion at constant pressure.
   c. Dual cycle: Combustion partly at constant volume and partly at constant pressure.
3. *Arrangement of cylinders*:
   a. Inline engine
   b. V-type engine
   c. Opposed piston engine
   d. Radial engine
   e. Rotary engine
4. *The fuel used*:
   a. Petrol engine
   b. Diesel engine
   c. Gas engine
5. *The method of ignition*:
   a. Spark Ignition (S.I.) engine
   b. Compression Ignition (C.I.) engine
6. *The method of cooling*:
   a. Air-cooled engine
   b. Water-cooled engine
7. *The speed of engine*:
   a. High speed engine
   b. Medium speed engine
   c. Low speed engine
8. *The method of governing*:
   a. Quantity governing
   b. Quality governing
   c. Hit and miss governing
9. *Use of engine*:
   a. Stationary engine
   b. Automobile engine
   c. Marine engine

d. Aero engine

e. Locomotive engine

6.3 Different Parts of an IC Engine

a. *Parts common to both petrol and diesel engine*:

1. Cylinder
2. Cylinder head
3. Piston
4. Piston ring
5. Gudgeon pin
6. Connecting rod
7. Crankshaft
8. Crank
9. Crank case
10. Engine bearing
11. Flywheel
12. Governor
13. Valves and operating mechanisms

b. *Parts only in petrol engine*:

1. Spark plug
2. Carburettor

c. *Parts only in diesel engine*:

1. Fuel pump
2. Injector

The purpose of different part is described as follows

1. *Cylinder*: It is the main body of the engine in which piston reciprocates. It has to withstand high pressure (about 7 MPa) and temperature (about 2200°C) because it is in direct contact with the products of combustion. So, its material should be such that it can retain strength at high temperature, should be good conductor of heat and should resist to rapid wear and tear due to reciprocating parts. Generally the ordinary cast iron is used, but in case of heavy duty engines, alloy steels are used. Sometimes, when engine blocks are heavy and for easy maintenance, sleeves or liners are inserted into the cylinder which can be replaced when worn out. Liners are generally made of Nickel Chrome iron.
2. *Cylinder head*: One end of the cylinder is closed by cylinder head. It houses the inlet and exhaust valves through which the charge is taken inside the cylinder and burned gases are exhausted to the atmosphere from the cylinder. Cylinder head is usually cast as one piece and bolted to the top of the cylinder. A copper and asbestos gaskets are provided between the cylinder and the cylinder head to obtain a gas-tight joint. The cylinder head is usually made of cast iron or aluminium.
3. *Piston*: It is fitted to each cylinder as a face to receive gas pressure and transmit the thrust to the connecting rod. The pistons are usually made of cast iron, cast steel and aluminium alloys. The aluminium alloy has the advantage of higher thermal conductivity and light weight. Piston is the heart of the engine.
4. *Piston rings*: These are housed in the circumferential grooves provided on the outer surface of the piston. It gives gas-tight fittings between the piston and the cylinder and prevents the leakage of high pressure gases. These are made of special grade cast iron. This material retains its elastic properties at very high temperatures. The upper piston rings are called compression rings and lower rings are called oil rings.

5. *Gudgeon pin*: These are hardened steel pins fitted through the piston bosses and small and bushes or eyes to allow the connecting rods to swivel. These are press fit in the piston bosses. These can be removed by dipping the piston in hot oil or hot water. The pin is made hollow for lightness since it is a reciprocating part.
6. *Connecting rod*: The connecting rod transmits the piston load to the crank, causing latter to turn, thus converting the reciprocating motion of the piston into rotary motion of the crankshaft. It is usually a steel forging of circular, rectangular, I, T or H section and is highly polished for increased endurance strength. Its small end forms a hinge and pin joint with the piston and big end is connected to the crank by crank pin. It has a passage for transfer for lubricating oil from the big end bearing to small end bearing.

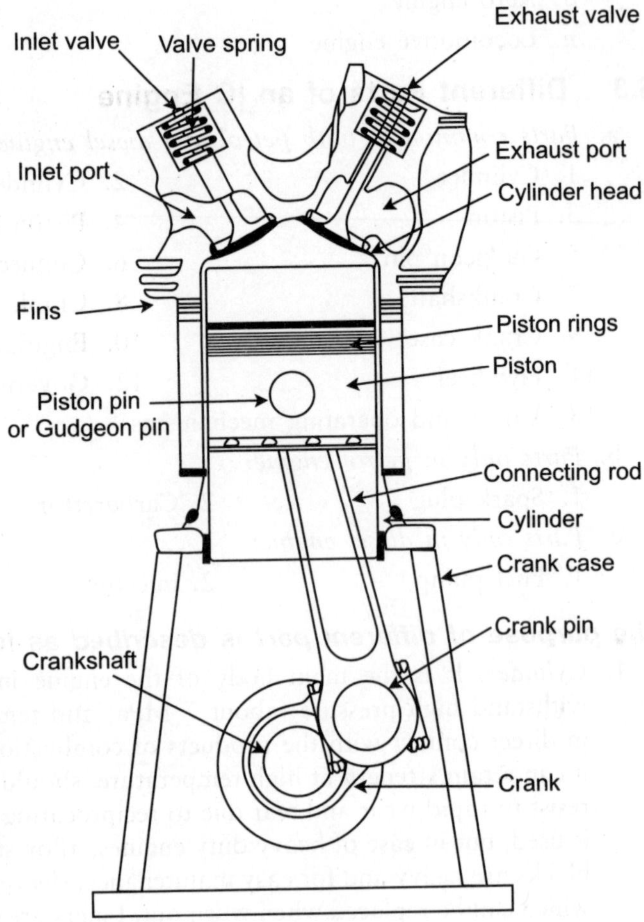

Fig. 6.1: IC Engine

7. *Crank*: The piston moves in a cylinder with a reciprocating motion. This motion is converted into rotary motion. For this, a crank and connecting rod are used. The connecting rod connects the piston to the crank.
8. *Crankshaft*: The crankshaft receives the efforts supplied by the pistons to the connecting rods via its cranks.

   Crankshaft is usually a steel forging. It is supported in a main bearing and has a heavy wheel called flywheel. The crankshaft is the backbone of the engine.
9. *Engine Bearings*: The bearings are used to reduce the friction and allow the parts to move easily. In IC engine, there are many bearings. The crankshaft is supported by bearing. The connecting rod end is attached to the crankpin on the crank of the crankshaft by a bearing. The piston pin also rides in a bearing. These bearings are lubricated with oil to make the relative motion easier.

10. *Crankcase*: The main body of the engine to which the cylinders are attached and which contains the crankshaft and crankshaft bearing is called crankcase. This member also holds other parts in alignment and resists the explosion and inertia forces. It also protects the parts from dirt etc. and serves as a part of lubricating system.
11. *Flywheel*: A flywheel on the crankshaft performs the following functions:
    i. Brings the mechanisms out of dead centres.
    ii. Stores energy required to rotate the shaft during preparatory strokes.
    iii. Makes crankshaft rotation more uniform.
    iv. Helps in starting the engine.
12. *Governor*: It is a device used for regulating automatically output of a machine by regulating the supply of a working fluid. When the speed decreases due to increase in load, the supply valve is opened by mechanism operated by the governor and the engine therefore speeds up again to its original speed. If the speed increases due to a decrease of load, the governor mechanism closes the supply valve sufficiently to slow the engine to its original speed.

6.4 Parts Used Only in Petrol Engine

1. *Spark plug*: It is used to conduct the high potential from the ignition system into the combustion chamber. It provides the proper gap across which spark is produced by applying high voltage, to ignite the combustion chamber.
2. *Carburettor*: The function of a carburettor is to atomise and meter the liquid fuel and mix it with the air as it enters the induction system of the engine, maintaining under all conditions of operation fuel-air proportions appropriate to those conditions.

   All modern carburettors are based upon Bernoulli's theorem

   $$C^2 = 2gh \qquad (6.1)$$

   where C = velocity in m/sec

   h = Head causing the flow in m of height column
3. *Fuel pump (for petrol engine)*: This is used for supply of fuel to the carburettor. Due to rotation of the crankshaft the cam pushes the lever in the upward direction. One end of the lever is hinged while the other end pulls the diaphragm rod with the diaphragm.

   So, the diaphragm comes in the downward direction against the compression of the spring and thus vacuum is produced in the pump chamber from the glass bowl through the strainer and inlet valve. The impurities deposite at the bottom of glass bowl. On the return stroke, the spring pushes the diaphragm in the upward direction forcing the fuel from the pump chamber into carburettor through the outlet valve.

6.5 Terms Related to IC Engines

1. *Bore*: The inside diameter of the cylinder is called bore.
2. *Stroke*: The maximum distance travelled by the piston in the cylinder in one direction is known as stroke and it is equal to twice the radius of the crank.
3. *Top Dead Centre (TDC)*: The topmost position of the piston towards cover end side of the cylinder is called "Top Dead Centre" position.

4. *Bottom Dead Centre (BDC)*: The extreme position of the piston at the bottom of the cylinder is called "Bottom Dead Centre" position.
5. *Clearance Volume*: The volume contained in the cylinder above the top of the piston when the piston is at TDC is called the clearance volume and is denoted by v_c.
6. *Piston Displacement or Swept Volume*: The volume swept through by the piston in moving between TDC and BDC is defined as the piston displacement or swept volume. It is denoted by v_s. So cylinder volume is $(v_s + v_c)$.
7. *Compression Ratio*: The ratio of the volume when the piston is at BDC to the volume when piston is at TDC is called compression ratio and it is denoted by r_c.

$$r_c = \frac{v_1}{v_2} = \frac{v_s + v_c}{v_c} \quad \ldots \ldots \ldots \ldots \ldots \ldots \ldots \ldots \ldots \ldots \quad (6.2)$$

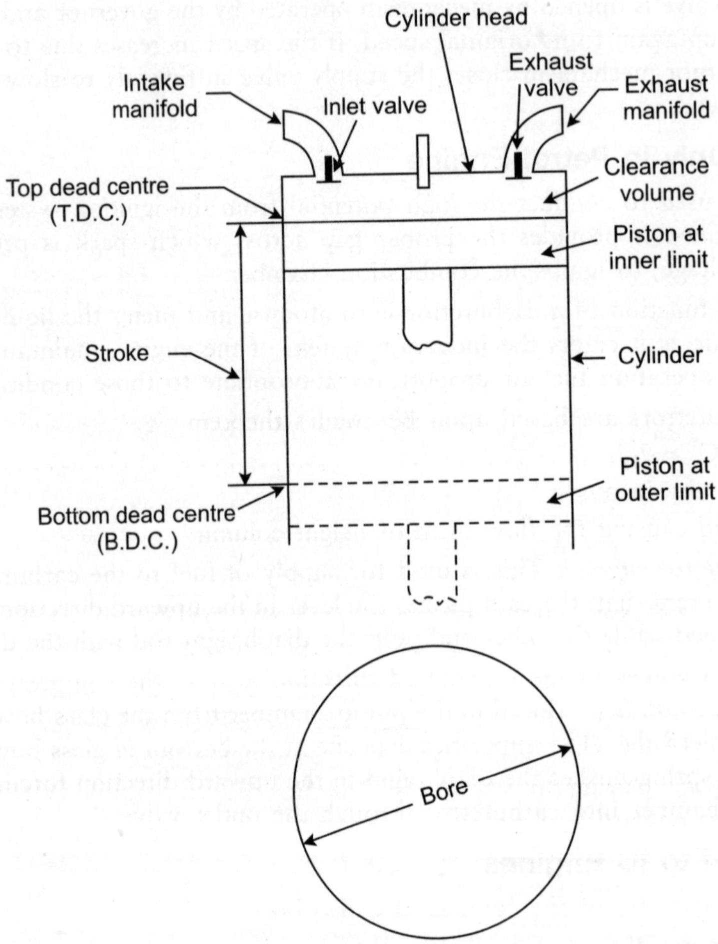

Fig. 6.2: Terms Related to IC Engine

6.6 Four-Stroke Cycle Engines

Four-stroke Otto (Petrol) Engine

The working cycle of the engine is completed in 4-strokes or 2 revolutions of crank and petrol is used as fuel.

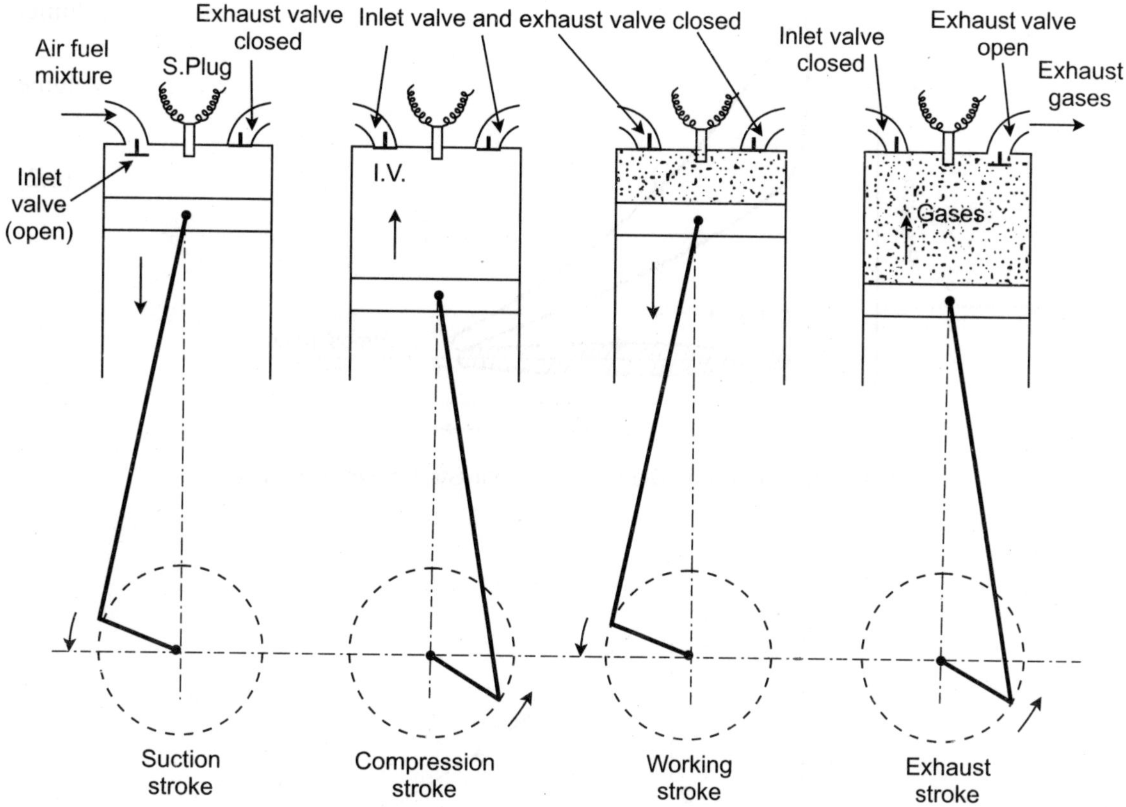

Fig. 6.3: Four-Stroke Otto Cycle Engine

i. *Suction Stroke*: During this stroke the piston move from top dead centre (TDC) to bottom dead centre (BDC). The inlet valve opens and proportionate fuel air mixture is sucked in the cylinder. The exhaust valve remains closed throughout the operation.

ii. *Compression Stroke*: During this stroke both valves (inlet and exhaust) are closed and the piston moves upward and compresses the charge enclosed in the cylinder. The pressure and the temperature of the mixture increases continuously during this process. Just before the end of this stroke the operating-plug initiates a spark plug which ignites the mixture and combustion takes place at constant volume.

iii. *Power or Expansion Stroke*: The increased pressure of the mixture exerts a large force and pushes the piston down. During the expansion stroke, both valves remain closed. The high pressure and high temperature gases push the piston downward and gas pressure gradually decreases. During this stroke piston moves from TDC to BDC. This stroke is known as power stroke, as work is done during this stroke. The exhaust valve opens as the piston reaches BDC piston and pressure falls suddenly to atmospheric pressure at constant volume.

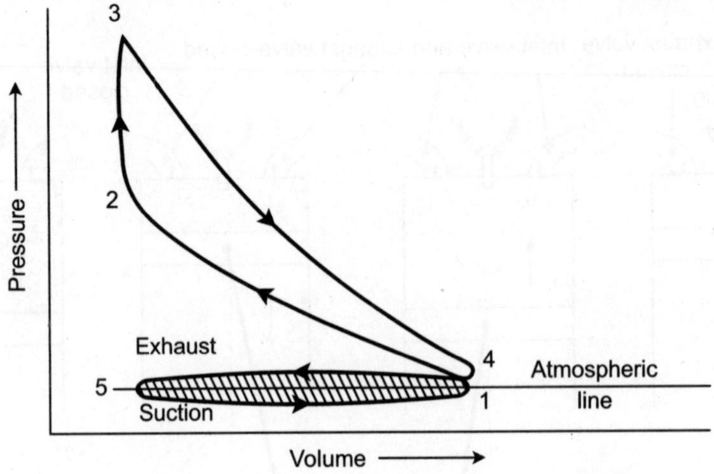

Fig. 6.4: Actual p-v Diagram for Four-Stroke Petrol Engine

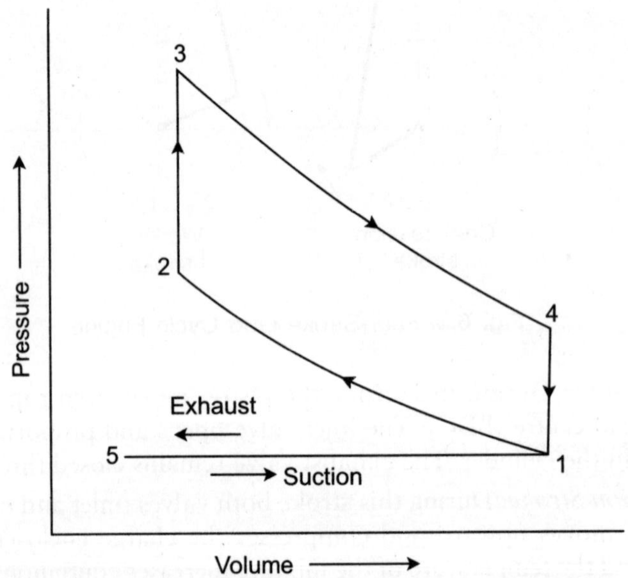

Fig. 6.5: Theoretical p-v Diagram for Four-Stroke Petrol Engine

iv *Exhaust Stroke*: During the upward motion of the piston, the exhaust valve is open and inlet valve is closed. The piston moves up in the cylinder pushing out the burnt gases through the exhaust valve. As the piston reaches the TDC, again the inlet valve opens and fresh charge is taken in during next downward movement of the piston and the cycle is repeated.

Fig. 6.4 shows actual indicator diagram. It is found that line 5–1 is below the atmospheric pressure line. This is due to the fact that due to restricted area of the inlet passage, the entering air-fuel mixture cannot cope with the speed of the piston. The exhaust line 4–5 is slightly above the atmospheric pressure line. This is due to restricted exhaust passages which do not allow the exhaust gases to leave the engine-cylinder quickly.

The loop which has area 4–5–1 is called negative loop. It gives the pumping loss due to admission of fuel-air mixture and removal of exhaust gases. The area 1–2–3–4 is the total or gross negative work from the area 1–2–3–4, i.e. gross work.

6.7 Four-Stroke Diesel Engine

1. *Suction Stroke*: As the piston moves from TDC to BDC, the inlet valve opens and air at atmospheric pressure is drawn inside the engine cylinder. The exhaust valve remains closed.
2. *Compression Stroke*: The drawn air is compressed to high pressure and temperature (35 bar and 600°C respectively) as the piston moves from BDC to TDC. Both inlet and exhaust valves remain closed.

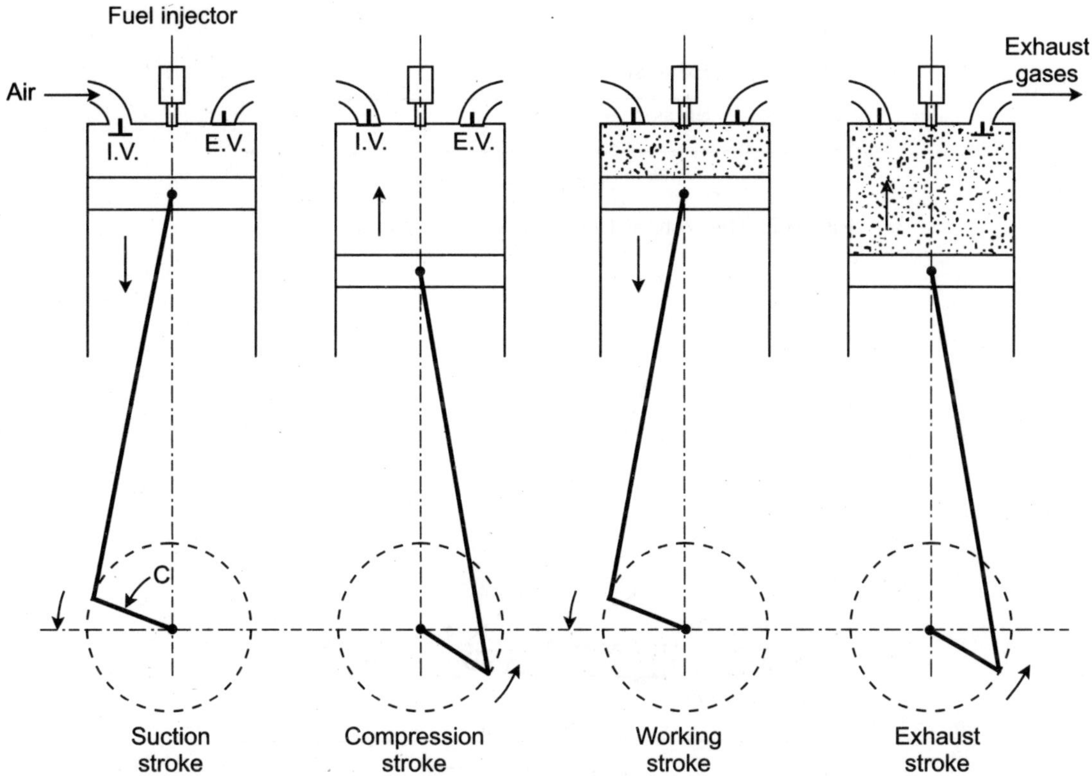

Fig. 6.6: Four-Stroke Diesel Engine Cycle

3. *Expansion or Working Stroke:* During this stroke, the inlet and exhaust valves are closed and fuel valve opens just before the beginning of the third stroke.
   The supply of the fuel is continued at constant pressure as long as fuel valve is open. The high pressure and high temperature gases push the piston down even after the fuel valve is closed. The exhaust valve opens when the piston reaches BDC.
4. *Exhaust Stroke*: During this stroke, the inlet and fuel valves remain closed and exhaust valve remains open. The piston moves up in the cylinder and pushes out the burnt gases. The piston reaches the TDC completing the exhaust and is ready for next cycle.

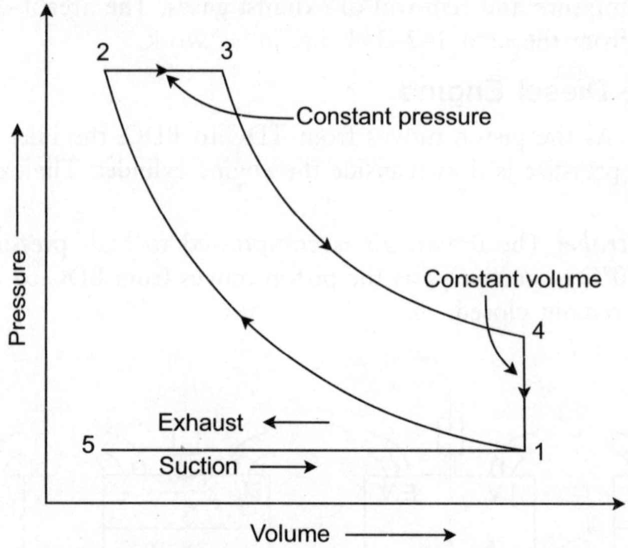

Fig. 6.7: Theoretical Diagram for Four-Stroke Engine

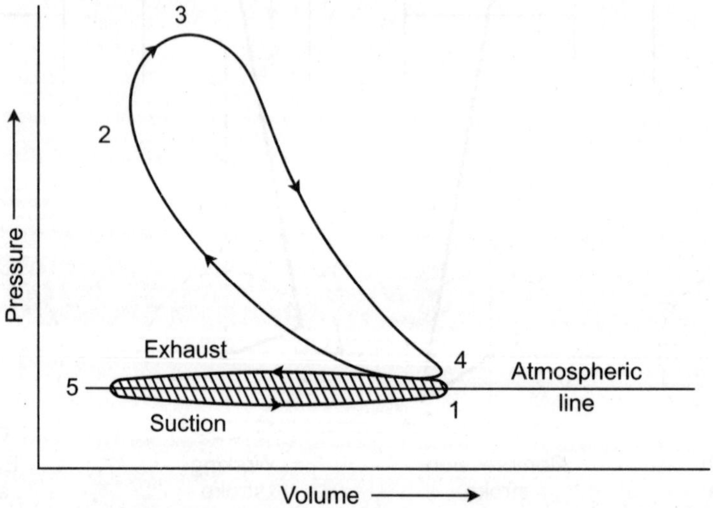

Fig. 6.8: Actual p-v Diagram for Four-Stroke Diesel Engine

6.8 Two-Stroke Engines

In this engine, suction and exhaust strokes are eliminated. Here instead of valves, ports are used. The exhaust gases are driven out from the engine cylinder by the fresh charge of fuel entering the cylinder nearly at the end of working stroke.

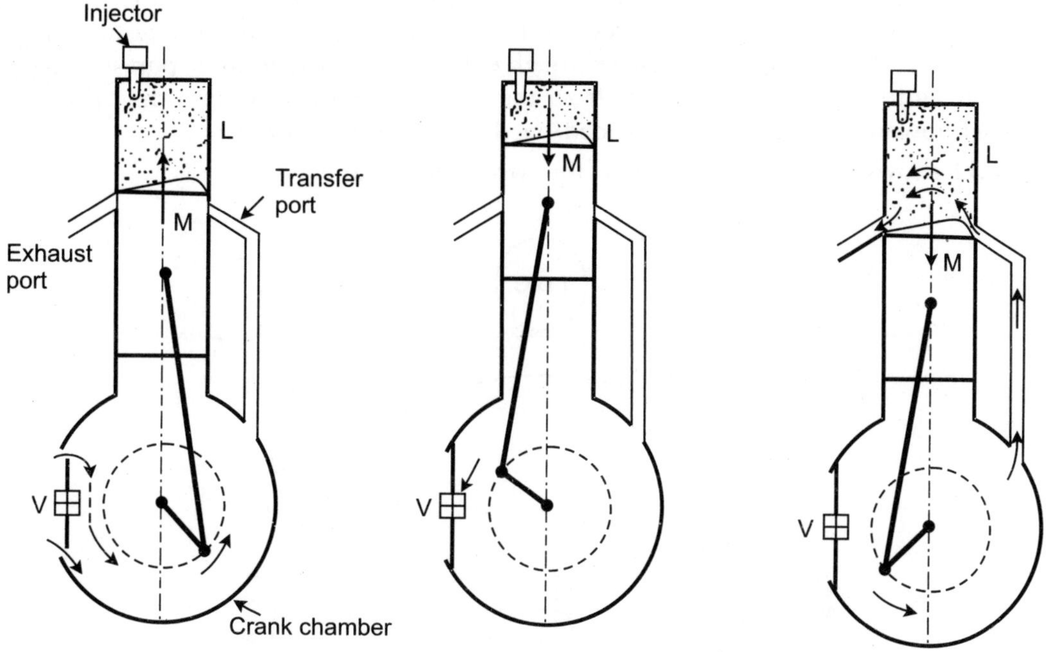

Fig. 6.9: Two-Stroke Engine

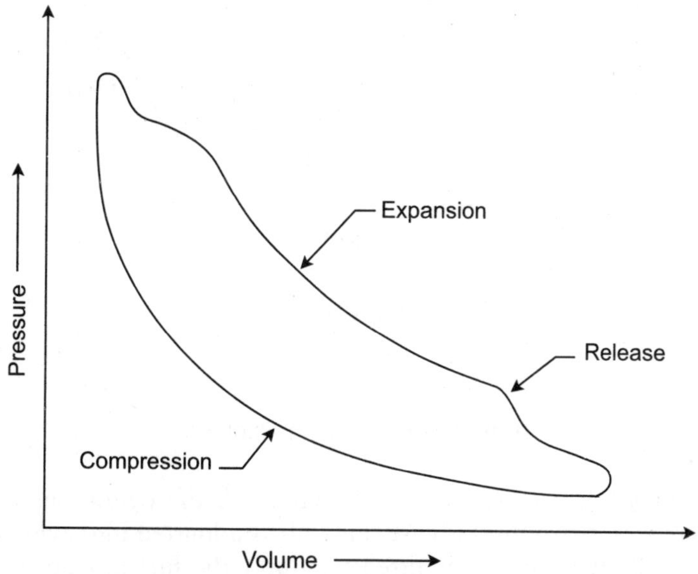

Fig. 6.10: p-v Diagram for Two-Stroke Cycle Engine

Fig. 6.9 shows a two stroke petrol engine. The cylinder is connected to a closed crank chamber. During the upward stroke of the piston, the gases in the cylinder are compressed and at the same time fresh air and petrol mixture enters the crank chamber through the valve. When the piston moves upwards and is compressing an explosive charge which has previously been supplied to the cylinder. Ignition takes place at the end of the stroke. The piston then travels downwards due to expansion of the gases and near the end of the stroke the piston uncovers the exhaust port. The burnt gases escape through exhaust port. The transfer port is uncovered immediately and the compressed charge from the crank chamber flows into the cylinder and is deflected upwards by the hump provided on the head of the piston.

Fig. 6.11 shows valve timing diagram for two-stroke engine.

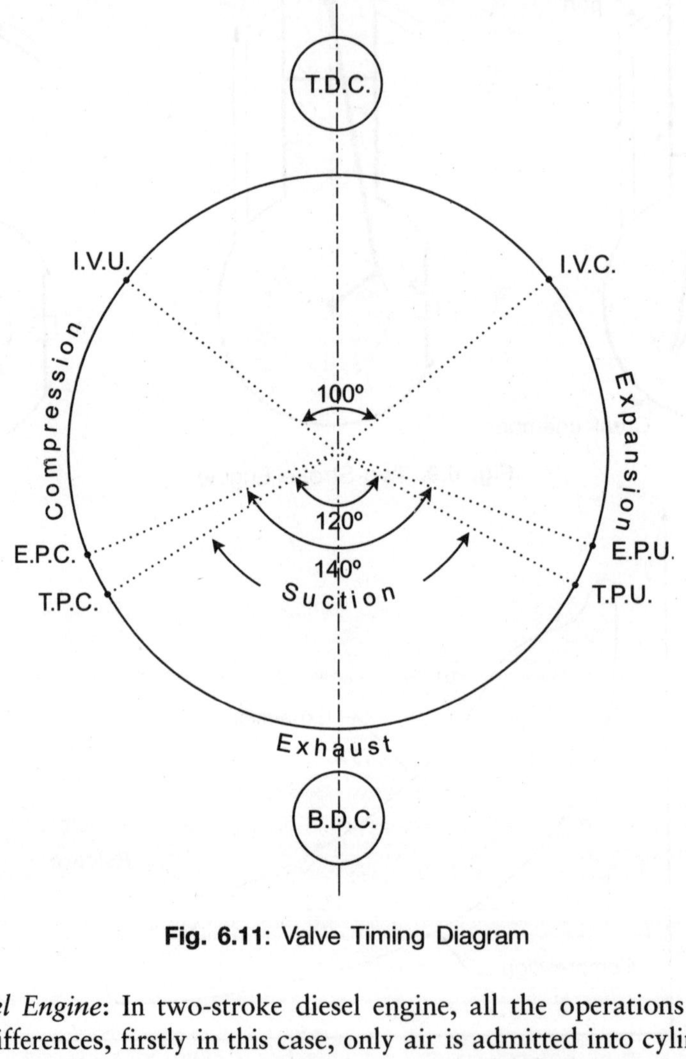

Fig. 6.11: Valve Timing Diagram

Two-Stroke Diesel Engine: In two-stroke diesel engine, all the operations are same as in SI engine with the differences, firstly in this case, only air is admitted into cylinder instead of air-fuel mixture and secondly fuel injector is fitted to supply the fuel instead of a sparking plug.

6.9 Comparison of Four-Stroke and Two-Stroke Engines

S. No.	*Aspect*	*4-Stroke Engine*	*2-Stroke Engine*
1.	Cycle completion	The cycle is completed in 4-strokes of the piston or two revolutions of the crankshaft. So one power stroke is obtained in two revolutions of the crankshaft.	The cycle is completed in 2-strokes of the piston or in one revolution of the crankshaft. So there is one power stroke for each revolution.
2.	Power produced for same size of engine	Power produced is less as compared to 2-stroke engine.	Because of one power stroke for each revolution, power produced is more as compared to 4-stroke engine.
3.	Size of flywheel	Heavier flywheel is required.	Lighter flywheel is required as turning-moment is uniform.
4.	Valves or ports	It contains valve and valve mechanism.	It does not contain valves. It contains ports in place of valves.
5.	Wear and tear	Less wear and tear.	More wear and tear.
6.	Cooling and lubrication	Less requirement.	More requirement.
7.	Initial cost	High	Low
8.	Volumetric efficiency	More	Less
9.	Thermal and part load efficiency	Better efficiencies.	Lesser efficiencies.
10.	Applications	Used where efficiency is more important e.g. cars, buses, tractors, aeroplanes, power generators, etc.	Used where low cost, light weight and small size are important e.g. scooters, motorcycles and ships.

6.10 Advantages and Disadvantages of Two-Stroke Engine over Four-Stroke Engine

Advantages

1. The actual power developed by two-stroke engine is about 1.7 to 1.8 times the power developed by four-stroke engine for same dimension and speed.
2. It provides mechanical simplicity as valves, rocker arms, push rods, cam and camshafts are not required. The friction loss is also less, so it gives higher mechanical efficiency.
3. It can be easily started as compared to four-stroke engine.
4. Initial cost and wt/H.P. is less.

Disadvantages

1. Thermodynamic efficiency is less as compared to four-stroke engine.
2. It requires greater amount of cooling as compared to four-stroke engine.
3. Because of high operating temperature, lubricating oil consumption is high.
4. Sudden release of burnt gases makes the exhaust more noisy.
5. The scavenging is not complete in high speed engines as very short time is available.
6. The turning moment of two-stroke engine is more non-uniform compared with four-stroke engine.

6.11 Comparison of Spark Ignition (SI) and Compression Ignition (CI) Engines

S. No.	*Aspect*	*S.I. Engines*	*C.I. Engines*
1.	Thermodynamic cycle	Otto cycle	Diesel cycle for slow speed and dual cycle for high speed engines.
2.	Fuel	Petrol	Diesel
3.	Air-fuel ratio	10 : 1 to 20 : 1	18 : 1 to 100 : 1
4.	Compression ratio	Upto 11; most common 7 to 9, limited by anti-knock quality of fuel.	12 to 24; most common 15 to 18, limited by thermal and mechanical stresses.
5.	Combustion	Spark plug is used.	Injector is used.
6.	Fuel supply	By carburettor – cheap method.	By injector – expansive method.
7.	Power control	Quantity Governing – by throttle.	Quality governing – by rack.
8.	Operating pressure i. Compression ii. Maximum	 7 to 15 bar 45 to 60 bar	 30 to 50 bar 60 to 120 bar
9.	Operating speed	High speed : 2000 to 6000 r.p.m.	Low – 400 r.p.m. Medium – 400 to 1200 r.p.m. High – 1200 to 3500 r.p.m.
10.	Calorific value of fuel	44 MJ/kg	42 MJ/kg
11.	Running cost	High	Low
12.	Maintenance cost	Less	More
13.	Thermal efficiency	Upto 25%	Upto 40%
14.	2-stroke operation	Less suitable	More suitable
15.	Used for high power	No	Yes
16.	Applications	Mopeds, scooters, cars, motorcycles, aircrafts, etc.	Buses, trucks, tractors, locomotives, power generating sets.

6.12 Otto-cycle or Constant Volume Air Cycle

This cycle was discovered by a German scientist Dr. A.N. Otto. The cycle is applied for working of petrol and gas engines. The cycle consists of two reversible adiabatic and two constant volume processes.

Fig. 6.12 shows the theoretical p–v diagram and theoretical T–s diagram of this cycle respectively.

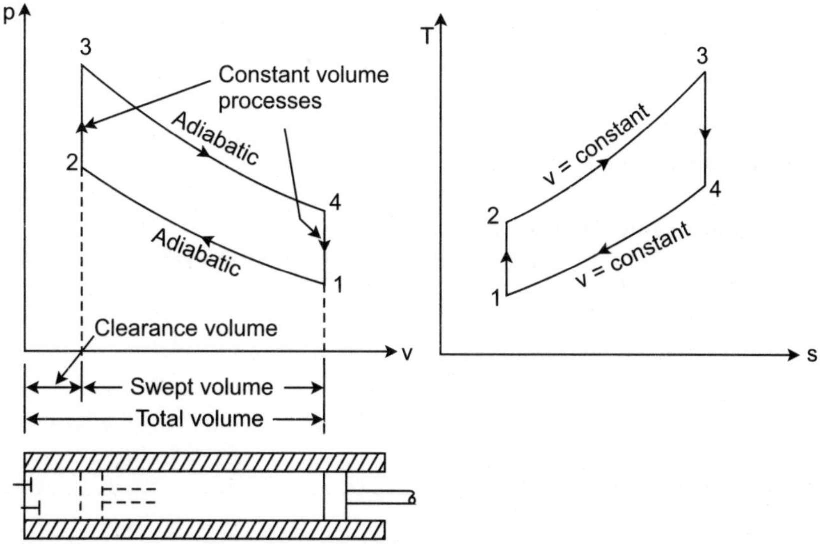

Fig. 6.12: Otto Cycle

The point 1 shows that cylinder is full of air with volume v_1, pressure p_1 and absolute temperature T_1.

Line 1–2 shows the adiabatic compression. p_1, v_1 and T_1 change to p_2, v_2 and T_2 respectively.

Line 2–3 represents the supply of heat to the air at constant volume so that p_2 and T_2 change to p_3 and T_3 (v_2 remaining constant).

Line 3–4 represents the adiabatic expansion of the air. During expansion p_3, v_3 and T_3 change to a final value of p_4, v_4 and T_4 respectively.

Line 4–1 shows the rejection of heat by air at constant volume till original state (point 1) reaches.

Consider 1 kg of working substance (Air)

Heat supplied at constant volume $= c_v(T_3 - T_2)$

Heat rejected at constant volume $= c_v(T_4 - T_1)$

$$\text{Work done} = \text{Heat supplied} - \text{Heat rejected}$$

$$= c_v(T_3 - T_2) - c_v(T_4 - T_1)$$

$$\text{Efficiency} = \frac{\text{Work done}}{\text{Heat supplied}}$$

$$= \frac{c_v(T_3 - T_2) - c_v(T_4 - T_1)}{c_v(T_3 - T_2)}$$

$$= 1 - \frac{(T_4 - T_1)}{T_3 - T_2} \quad \ldots\ldots\ldots\ldots\ldots\ldots \quad (6.3)$$

Let r_c = Compression ratio = $\frac{v_1}{v_2}$

and expansion ration $r_e = r_c = \frac{v_4}{v_3}$

These two ratios are same in this cycle.

As
$$\frac{T_2}{T_1} = \left(\frac{v_1}{v_2}\right)^{\gamma-1}$$

$$T_2 = T_1\left(\frac{v_1}{v_2}\right)^{\gamma-1}$$

$$= T_1(r)^{\gamma-1} \quad \ldots\ldots\ldots\ldots\ldots\ldots \quad (6.4)$$

Similarly

$$\frac{T_3}{T_4} = \left(\frac{v_4}{v_3}\right)^{\gamma-1}$$

$$T_3 = T_4(r)^{\gamma-1}$$

Putting these values of T_2 and T_3 in the Eq. (6.3) for efficiency

$$\eta_{Otto} = 1 - \frac{T_4 - T_1}{T_4(r)^{\gamma-1} - T_1(r)^{\gamma-1}}$$

$$= 1 - \frac{T_4 - T_1}{r^{\gamma-1}(T_4 - T_1)}$$

$$= 1 - \frac{1}{(r)^{\gamma-1}} \quad \ldots\ldots\ldots\ldots\ldots\ldots \quad (6.5)$$

This is known as air standard efficiency of Otto cycle.

Net work done per kg in the Otto cycle may be expressed as

$$W = \left(\frac{p_3v_3 - p_4v_4}{\gamma - 1} - \frac{p_2v_2 - p_1v_1}{\gamma - 1}\right) \quad \ldots\ldots\ldots\ldots\ldots\ldots \quad (6.6)$$

but $$\frac{p_3}{p_4} = r^{\gamma} = \frac{p_2}{p_1}$$

∴ $$\frac{p_3}{p_2} = \frac{p_4}{p_1} = r_p$$

where r_p = Pressure ratio

$$v_1 = rv_2 \text{ and } v_4 = rv_3$$

$$W = \frac{1}{\gamma-1}\left[p_4v_4\left(\frac{p_3v_3}{p_4v_4} - 1\right) - p_1v_1\left(\frac{p_2v_2}{p_1v_1} - 1\right)\right]$$

$$= \frac{1}{\gamma-1}\left[p_4v_4\left(\frac{p_3}{p_4r} - 1\right) - p_1v_1\left(\frac{p_2}{p_1r} - 1\right)\right]$$

$$= \frac{v_1}{\gamma-1}\left[p_4\left(r^{\gamma-1} - 1\right) - p_1\left(r^{\gamma-1} - 1\right)\right]$$

$$= \frac{v_1}{\gamma-1}\left[\left(r^{\gamma-1} - 1\right)\left(p_4 - p_1\right)\right]$$

$$= \frac{p_1v_1}{\gamma-1}\left[\left(r^{\gamma-1} - 1\right)\left(r_p - 1\right)\right] \quad \ldots\ldots\ldots\ldots \quad (6.7)$$

Mean effective pressure

$$p_m = \left[\left(\frac{p_3v_3 - p_4v_4}{\gamma-1}\right) - \left(\frac{p_2v_2 - p_1v_1}{\gamma-1}\right)\right] \Big/ \left(v_1 - v_2\right)$$

$$= \frac{\left[\frac{p_1v_1}{\gamma-1}\left(r^{\gamma-1} - 1\right)\left(r_p - 1\right)\right]}{\left(v_1 - v_2\right)}$$

$$= \frac{\frac{p_1v_1}{\gamma-1}\left[\left(r^{\gamma-1} - 1\right)\left(r_p - 1\right)\right]}{\left(v_1 - \frac{v_1}{r}\right)}$$

$$= \frac{\frac{p_1v_1}{\gamma-1}\left[\left(r^{\gamma-1} - 1\right)\left(r_p - 1\right)\right]}{v_1\left(\frac{r-1}{r}\right)}$$

$$p_m = \frac{p_1 r\left[\left(r^{\gamma-1}-1\right)\left(r_p-1\right)\right]}{(\gamma-1)(r-1)} \quad \ldots\ldots\ldots\ldots\ldots\ldots\ldots\ldots (6.8)$$

6.13 Constant Pressure or Diesel Cycle

The cycle was introduced by Dr. R. Diesel in 1897. It differs from Otto cycle in that heat is supplied at constant pressure instead of at constant volume. Fig. 6.13 shows p–v and T–s diagrams.

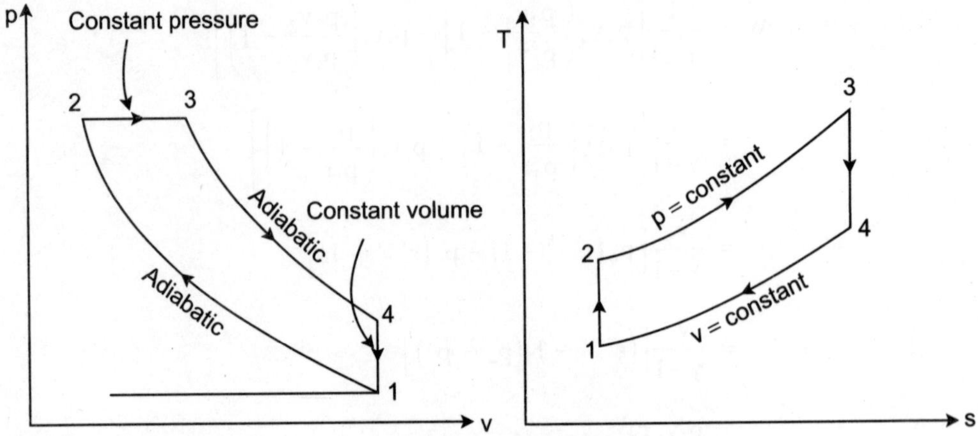

Fig. 6.13: Diesel Cycle

The cycle has four processes:

i. 1–2 Adiabatic compression
ii. 2–3 Heat supplied at constant pressure
iii. 3–4 Adiabatic expansion
iv. 4–1 Heat rejection at constant volume

Let p_1, v_1 and T_1 be the corresponding pressure, volume and temperature at point 1. The piston then compresses the air adiabatically (i.e. $pv^{\gamma} = c$) till the values become p_2, v_2 and T_2 respectively at point 2. Now heat is supplied at constant pressure. Let volume and temperature increases to v_3 and T_3 respectively during this process. The point 3 is called point of cut-off. The air then expands adiabatically to the conditions p_4, v_4 and T_4 respectively. This is corresponding to point 4. The system returns to its initial state (i.e. point 1) by rejecting heat to the cold body at constant volume.

Considering 1 kg of working substance (air)

Heat supplied at constant pressure = $c_p(T_3 - T_2)$

Heat rejected at constant volume = $c_v(T_4 - T_1)$

$$\text{Work done} = \text{Heat supplied} - \text{Heat rejected}$$

$$= c_p(T_3 - T_2) - c_v(T_4 - T_1)$$

$$\text{Efficiency } \eta_{diesel} = \frac{\text{Work done}}{\text{Heat supplied}}$$

$$= \frac{c_p(T_3 - T_2) - c_v(T_4 - T_1)}{c_p(T_3 - T_2)}$$

$$= 1 - \frac{(T_4 - T_1)}{\gamma(T_3 - T_2)} \quad \left[\text{Putting } \frac{c_v}{c_p} = \frac{1}{\gamma}\right] \quad \ldots\ldots\ldots\ldots\ldots\ldots \text{(6.9)}$$

Compression ratio, $r = \dfrac{v_1}{v_2}$

and cut off ratio, $\rho = \dfrac{v_3}{v_2}$, i.e. $\dfrac{\text{Volume at cut off}}{\text{Clearance volume}}$

Now, during adiabatic compression 1–2,

$$\frac{T_2}{T_1} = \left(\frac{v_1}{v_2}\right)^{\gamma-1} = (r)^{\gamma-1}$$

or $\qquad T_2 = T_1 \, (r)^{\gamma-1}$

During constant pressure process 2–3,

$$\frac{T_3}{T_2} = \frac{v_3}{v_2} = \rho$$

$$T_3 = \rho T_2 = \rho T_1 (r)^{\gamma-1}$$

During adiabatic expansion 3–4,

$$\frac{T_3}{T_4} = \left(\frac{v_4}{v_3}\right)^{\gamma-1} = \left(\frac{r}{\rho}\right)^{\gamma-1} \qquad \left[\because \frac{v_4}{v_3} = \frac{v_1}{v_3} = \frac{v_1}{v_2} \times \frac{v_2}{v_3} = \frac{r}{\rho}\right]$$

$$T_4 = \frac{T_3}{\left(\frac{r}{\rho}\right)^{\gamma-1}} = \frac{\rho T_1 (r)^{\gamma-1}}{\left(\frac{r}{\rho}\right)^{\gamma-1}}$$

$$= T_1 \rho^{\gamma}$$

By putting the volues of T_2, T_3 and T_4 in the Eq. (6.9) for efficiency

$$\eta_{diesel} = 1 - \frac{\left(T_1 \rho^\gamma - T_1\right)}{\gamma\left(\rho T_1 r^{\gamma-1} - T_1 (r)^{\gamma-1}\right)}$$

$$= 1 - \frac{\left(\rho^\gamma - 1\right)}{\gamma (r)^{\gamma-1} (\rho - 1)}$$

$$= 1 - \frac{1}{\gamma (r)^{\gamma-1}} \left[\frac{\rho^\gamma - 1}{\rho - 1}\right] \qquad (6.10)$$

We see that $\rho > 1$, hence $\frac{1}{\gamma}\left(\frac{\rho^{\gamma-1}}{\rho-1}\right) > 1$

$$\eta_{diesel} < \eta_{Otto}$$

for a fixed value of compression ratio (r).

Net work for Diesel Cycle

$$W = p_2\left(v_3 - v_2\right) + \frac{p_3 v_3 - p_4 v_4}{\gamma - 1} - \frac{p_2 v_2 - p_1 v_1}{\gamma - 1}$$

$$\left[\begin{array}{ll} \because \frac{v_3}{v_2} = \rho & \therefore v_3 = \rho v_2 \\ \text{and } \frac{v_1}{v_2} = r & v_1 = r v_2 \\ \text{but } v_4 = v_1 = r v_2 & \end{array}\right]$$

$$W = p_2 v_2 (\rho - 1) + \frac{p_3 \rho v_2 - p_4\, r v_2}{\gamma - 1} - \frac{p_2 v_2 - p_1 r v_2}{\gamma - 1}$$

$$= \frac{v_2\left[p_2(\rho - 1)(\gamma - 1) + p_3 \rho - p_4 r - (p_2 - p_1 r)\right]}{\gamma - 1}$$

$$= \frac{v_2\left[p_2(\rho - 1)(\gamma - 1) + p_3\left(\rho - \frac{p_4 r}{p_3}\right) - p_2\left(1 - \frac{p_1 r}{p_2}\right)\right]}{\gamma - 1}$$

$$= \frac{p_2 v_2 \left[(\rho - 1)(\gamma - 1) + \rho - \rho^{\gamma} r^{1-\gamma} - \left(1 - r^{1-\gamma}\right)\right]}{\gamma - 1}$$

$$\left[\because \frac{p_4}{p_3} = \left(\frac{v_3}{v_4}\right)^{\gamma} = \left(\frac{\rho}{r}\right)^{\gamma} = \rho^{\gamma} r^{-\gamma}\right]$$

$$= \frac{p_1 v_1 r^{\gamma-1}\left[(\rho - 1)(\gamma - 1) + \rho - \rho^{\gamma} r^{1-\gamma} - \left(1 - r^{1-\gamma}\right)\right]}{(\gamma - 1)}$$

$$\left[\because \frac{p_2}{p_1} = \left(\frac{v_1}{v_2}\right)^{\gamma} \quad \text{or} \quad p_2 = p_1 r^{\gamma} \text{ and } \frac{v_1}{v_2} = r \text{ or } v_2 = v_1 r^{-1}\right]$$

$$W = \frac{p_1 v_1 r^{\gamma-1}\left[\gamma(\rho - 1) - r^{1-\gamma}\left(\rho^{\gamma} - 1\right)\right]}{\gamma - 1} \quad \ldots\ldots\ldots\ldots\ldots\ldots \quad (6.11)$$

Mean effective pressure, p_m, is given by

$$p_m = \frac{p_1 v_1 r^{\gamma-1}}{(\gamma - 1) v_1 \left(\frac{r-1}{r}\right)}\left[\gamma(\rho - 1) - r^{1-\gamma}\left(\rho^{\gamma} - 1\right)\right]$$

$$= \frac{p_1 r^{\gamma}}{(\gamma - 1)(r - 1)}\left[\gamma(\rho - 1) - r^{1-\gamma}\left(\rho^{\gamma} - 1\right)\right] \quad \ldots\ldots\ldots\ldots\ldots\ldots \quad (6.12)$$

6.14 Comparison of Otto, Diesel and Dual Cycles

The performance of these cycles is measured in terms of their efficiency, η, with the following variable factors:

i. Compression ratio
ii. Maximum pressure
iii. Heat supplied
iv. Heat rejected
v. Net work

i. η *vs.* C.R.

Fig. 6.14 shows efficiencies of Otto, Diesel and Dual Cycles at various compression ratios with a fixed cut-off ratio for Diesel and Dual cycles. We see that efficiency increases with increase in C.R.

For a given compression ratio

$$\eta_{Otto} > \eta_{Dual} > \eta_{Diesel}$$

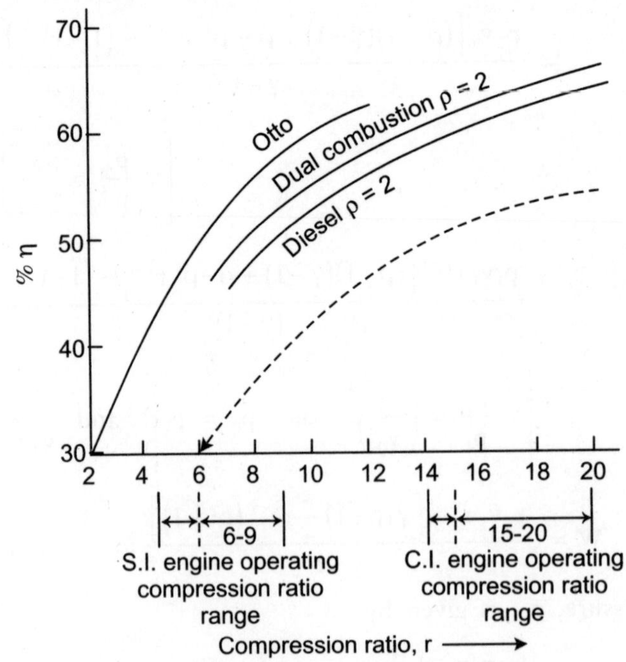

Fig. 6.14: Comparison of Efficiency at Various Compression Ratio

ii. Efficiency for same C.R. and same heat input

Fig. 6.15 shows comparison of η for same C.R. and same heat input

$$\text{We know that } \eta = 1 - \frac{\text{Heat rejected}}{\text{Heat supplied}}$$

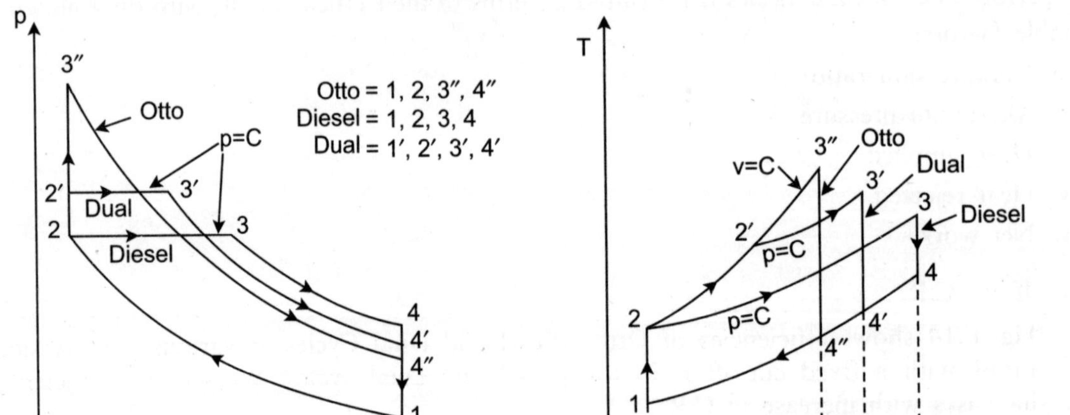

Fig. 6.15: (a) p–v Diagram (b) T–s Diagram

iii. For constant maximum pressure and heat supplied

Fig. 6.16 shows the Otto and Diesel cycles on p–v and T–s diagrams for constant maximum pressure and heat input respectively.

- For the maximum pressure the points 3 and 3′ must lie on a constant pressure line.
- On T–s diagram the heat rejected from the Diesel cycle is represented by the area under the line 4 to 1 and this area is less than the Otto cycle area under 4′ to 1′, hence Diesel cycle is more efficient than Otto cycle for the condition of maximum pressure and heat supplied.

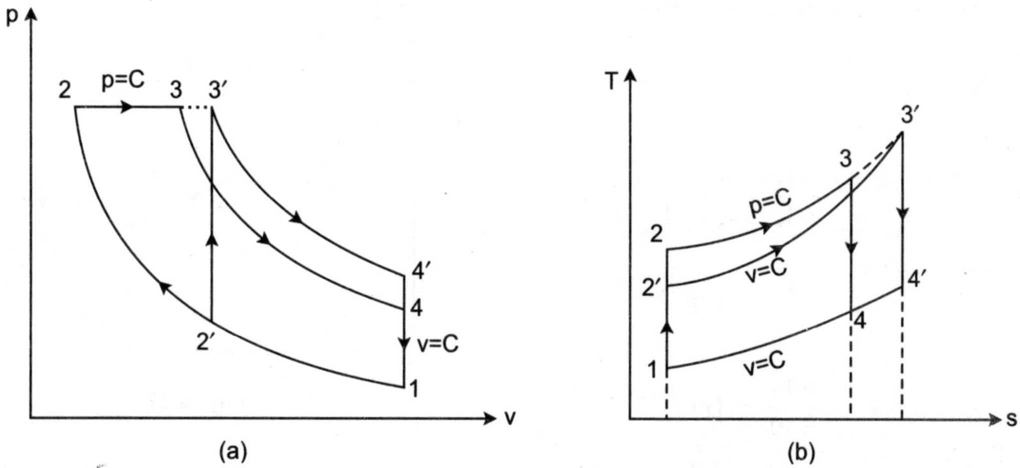

Fig. 6.16: (a) p–v Diagram (b) T–s Diagram

SOLVED EXAMPLES

Example 6.1

An engine working on Otto cycle has temperature of 330 K and 600 K at the beginning and end of compression stroke. Determine the compression ratio and air standard efficiency.

Solution:

Here $T_1 = 330$ K

$T_2 = 600$ K

Process 1–2 is an isentropic process

So

$$T_1 v_1^{\gamma-1} = T_2 v_2^{\gamma-1}$$

$$\frac{T_2}{T_1} = \left(\frac{v_1}{v_2}\right)^{\gamma-1}$$

$$\frac{T_2}{T_1} = (r)^{\gamma-1}$$

$$\frac{600}{330} = (r)^{0.4}$$

$$r = \mathbf{4.457}$$ **Ans.**

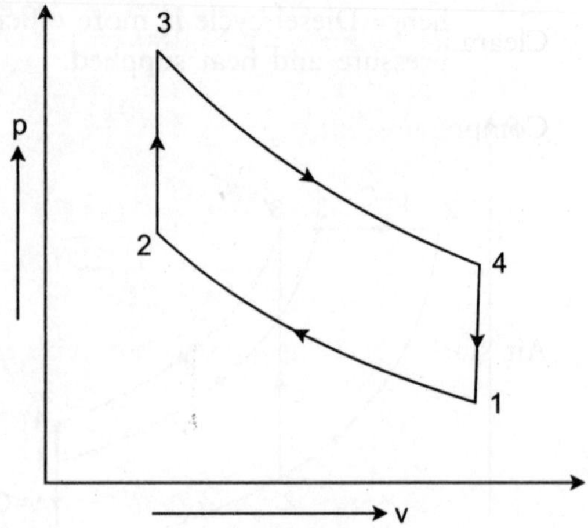

Fig. 6.17

Air standard efficiency

$$\eta = 1 - \frac{1}{(r)^{\gamma-1}}$$

$$= 1 - \frac{1}{(4.457)^{0.4}}$$

$$= 0.45$$

$$= \mathbf{45\%}$$ **Ans.**

Example 6.2

An engine working on Otto cycle has

Cylinder bore = *13.7 cm*

Stroke length = *13.0 cm*

Clearance volume = *280 cm³*

Calculate the air standard efficiency of the engine.

Solution:

Swept volume, $v_s = \frac{\pi}{4} d^2 l$

$$= \frac{\pi}{4}(13.7)^2(13)$$

$$= 1915.4 \text{ cm}^3$$

Clearance volume, $v_c = 280 \text{ cm}^3$

Compression ratio, $r = 1 + \frac{v_s}{v_c}$

$$= 1 + \frac{1915.4}{280}$$

$$= 7.84$$

Air standard efficiency of Otto cycle is given by

$$\eta = 1 - \frac{1}{r^{\gamma-1}} = 1 - \frac{1}{(7.84)^{1.4-1}}$$

$$= 0.562$$

$$= \mathbf{56.2\%}$$ **Ans.**

Example 6.3

Compare the change in efficiency of an Otto cycle when compression ratio changes from 4 to 5. Take $\gamma = 1.4$ for air.

Solution:

Efficiency of Otto cycle

$$\eta_{Otto} = 1 - \frac{1}{r^{\gamma-1}}$$

$$\eta_1 = 1 - \frac{1}{r_1^{\gamma-1}} = 1 - \frac{1}{(4)^{0.4}}$$

$$= 1 - 0.575$$

$$= 0.425 \quad \text{or} \quad 42.5\%$$

$$\eta_2 = 1 - \frac{1}{r_2^{\gamma-1}} = 1 - \frac{1}{(5)^{0.4}} = 1 - 0.5253 = 0.4747$$

$$= 47.47\%$$

Hence percentage change in efficiency $= \frac{0.4747 - 0.425}{0.425} \times 100$

$$= \mathbf{11.69\%}$$ **Ans.**

Example 6.4

Show that, for the maximum work to be done per kg of air in Otto cycle between given upper and lower limits of absolute temperature T_3 and T_1 respectively, the ratio of compression should have the value

$$\left(\frac{T_3}{T_1}\right)^{1.25} \quad \text{when } \gamma = 1.4$$

Solution:

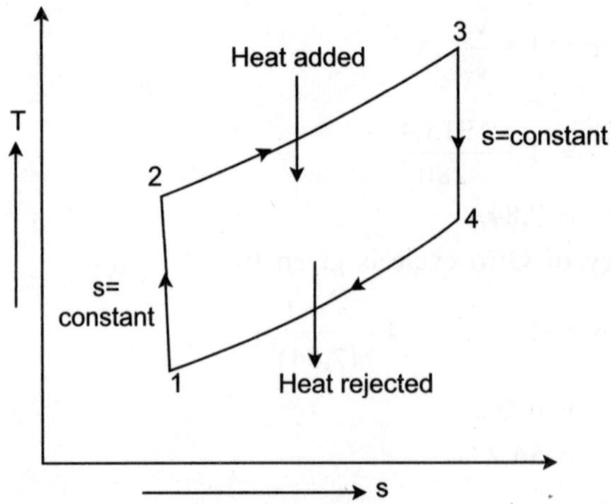

Fig. 6.18

Work done per cycle = Heat added – Heat rejected

$$w = c_v\,(T_3 - T_2) - c_v(T_4 - T_1)\ \text{kJ/kg}$$

From isentropic compression process 1–2

$$T_2 = T_1\,(r)^{\gamma-1} \qquad \text{where } r_1 = \frac{v_1}{v_2} = \frac{v_4}{v_3}$$

From isentropic expansion process 3–4

$$T_4 = T_3\left(\frac{1}{r}\right)^{\gamma-1}$$

$$w = c_v\left[T_2 - T_1\,r^{\gamma-1} - T_3\left(\frac{1}{r}\right)^{\gamma-1} - T_1\right]$$

To obtain maximum work, differentiating w.r.t. r and putting equal to zero.

$$\frac{dw}{dr} = 0$$

$$c_v\left[T_2 - T_1\,r^{\gamma-1} - T_3\left(\frac{1}{r}\right)^{\gamma-1} - T_1\right] = 0$$

$$\frac{T_1}{T_3} = r^{2-2\gamma}$$

$$\frac{T_3}{T_1} = r^{2\gamma-2}$$

$$= r^{2.8-2} \quad = r^{0.8}$$

$$r = \left(\frac{T_3}{T_1}\right)^{1.25}$$ **Ans.**

Example 6.5

An engine 20 cm bore and 30 cm stroke works on Otto cycle. The clearance volume is 1600 cm^3*. The initial pressure and temperature are 1 bar and 60°C. If the maximum pressure is limited to 24 bar, find the following:*

a. Air standard efficiency of the cycle

b. The mean effective pressure of the cycle

Assume ideal conditions.

Solution:

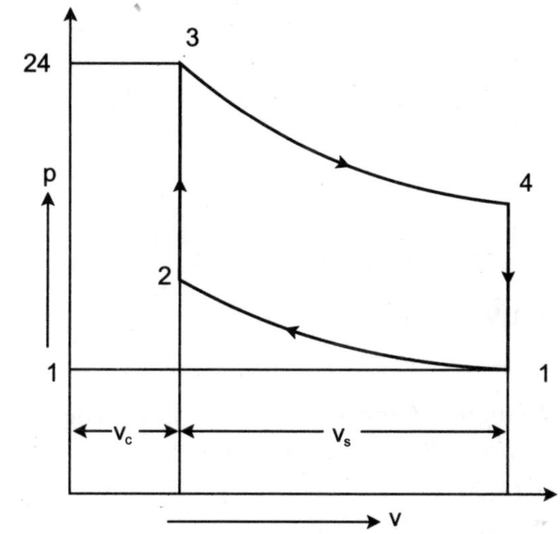

Fig. 6.19

$$v_s = \frac{\pi}{4} d^2 L = \frac{\pi}{4} \times (20)^2 \times 30 = 9420 \text{ cm}^3$$

Compression ratio, $$r = \frac{v_s + v_c}{v_c} = 1 + \frac{v_s}{v_c} = 1 + \frac{9420}{1600} = 7$$

The air standard efficiency

$$\eta_{air} = 1 - \frac{1}{(r)^{\gamma-1}}$$

$$= 1 - \frac{1}{(7)^{1.4-1}}$$

$$= 0.5408$$

$$= 54.08\%$$

For the isentropic process 1–2

$$p_2 = p_1\left(\frac{v_1}{v_2}\right)^{\gamma-1}$$

$$= 1(r)^{\gamma}$$

$$= (7)^{1.4} = \mathbf{15.245\ bar}$$ **Ans.**

Explosion ratio, $\alpha = \frac{p_B}{p_2} = \frac{24}{15.245} = 1.574$

Mean effective pressure,

$$p_m = p_1 r \frac{(\alpha-1)}{(\gamma-1)}\left[\frac{r^{\gamma-1}-1}{r-1}\right]$$

$$= 1 \times 7 \times \frac{(1.577-1)}{(1.4-1)}\left[\frac{(7)^{0.4}-1}{7-1}\right]$$

$$= \mathbf{1.972\ bar}$$ **Ans.**

Example 6.6

Calculate the diameter and length of the stroke of a diesel engine working on four-stroke constant pressure cycle from the following given data

I.P. = 18.75 kW

r.p.m. = 220

Compression Ratio = 14

Fuel cut-off = 1/20th of the stroke

Index of expansion = 1.3

Index of compression = 1.35

L/d = 1.5

Assume the pressure and temperature of air at the inlet are 1 bar and 40°C respectively.

Solution:

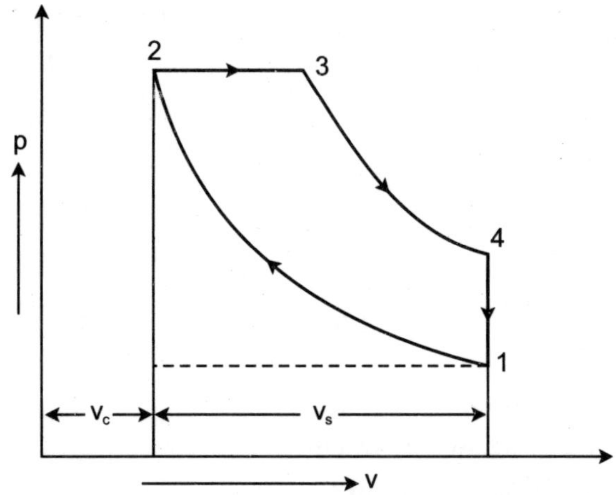

Fig. 6.20

$$r = \frac{v_s + v_c}{v_c} = 1 + \frac{v_s}{v_c}$$

$$v_s = (r-1)v_c$$

$$p_2 = p_1 r^n$$

$$= 1(14)^{1.35} \quad = 35 \text{ bar}$$

$$p_2 = p_3$$

$$p_3 v_3^{1.3} = p_4 v_4^{1.3}$$

$$p_4 = p_3\left(\frac{v_3}{v_4}\right)^{1.3}$$

Now $$v_3 = v_c + \frac{v_s}{20}$$

$$= v_c + \frac{(r-1)v_c}{20}$$

and $$v_4 = v_c + v_s$$

So $$p_4 = 35\left[\frac{1 + \frac{1}{20}(14-1)}{1+13}\right]^{1.3} = 35\left[\frac{1.65}{14}\right]^{1.3} = \mathbf{2.18 \text{ bar}}$$ **Ans.**

$$p_m = \frac{1}{v_s}\left[p_2(v_3 - v_2) + \frac{p_3 v_3 - p_4 v_4}{n_1 - 1} - \frac{p_2 v_2 - p_1 v_1}{n_2 - 1}\right]$$

$$v_1 = r v_c, \quad v_2 = v_c$$

$$v_3 = 1.65 \ v_c$$

$$v_4 = v_1 = 14 \ v_c$$

$$p_m = \frac{1}{(r-1)v_c}\left[35(1.5\ v_c - v_c) + \frac{35\times1.65v_c - 2.18\times14v_c}{1.3-1} - \frac{35\times v_c - 1\times14v_c}{1.35-1}\right]$$

$$= 3.7 \text{ bar}$$

$$\text{I.P.} = \frac{100\times p_m LAN}{1}$$

$$30 = \frac{3.7\times\frac{\pi}{4}d^2\times\frac{1.5d}{100}\times\frac{220}{2\times60}}{1}$$

$$d^3 = 0.0306$$

$$d = 0.32 \text{ m} = 32 \text{ cm}$$

$$L = 1.5d = \mathbf{48\ cm}$$ **Ans.**

Example 6.7

An oil engine with 20 cm diameter 30 cm stroke works on theoretical Diesel cycle. The initial pressure and temperature of the air used are 1 bar and 30°C. The cut-off is 10% of the stroke. Find the following:

1. *Pressure and temperature at all salient points*
2. *Theoretical air standard efficiency*
3. *Mean effective pressure*
4. *Power developed by the engine if the working cycles per minute are 400.*

Assume the compression ratio is 16 and working fluid is air.

Take all ideal conditions.

Solution:

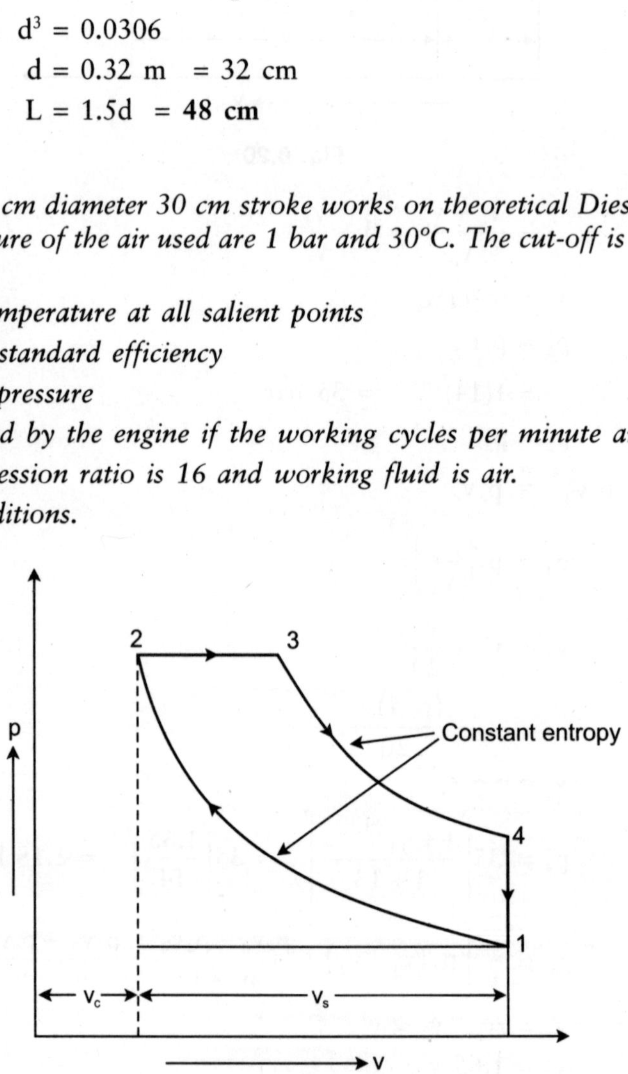

Fig. 6.21

Given

$$p_1 = 1 \text{ bar}$$

$$T_1 = 30°C = 30 + 273 = 303 \text{ K}$$

$$r = 16$$

$$v_s = \frac{\pi}{4} d^2 L = \frac{\pi}{4}(20)^2 \times 10^{-4} \times 30 \times 10^{-2} = 9.42 \times 10^{-3} \text{ m}^3$$

$$v_c = \frac{v_s}{r - 1}$$

$$v_1 = v_s + v_c = v_s + \frac{v_s}{r-1} = \frac{r}{r-1} \times v_s$$

$$= \frac{16}{15} \times 9.42 \times 10^{-3} = 10 \times 10^{-3} \text{ m}^3$$

The mass of the air in the cylinder

$$m = \frac{p_1 v_1}{RT_1} = \frac{1 \times 10^5 \times 10 \times 10^{-3}}{287 \times 303} = 0.115 \text{ kg/cycle}$$

1. For the isentropic process 1–2

(a)
$$p_2 = p_1 r^{\gamma} = 1 \times (16)^{1.4} = 48.5 \text{ bar}$$

$$T_2 = T_1 \, (r)^{\gamma - 1} = 303 \times (16)^{0.4} = 920 \text{ K}$$

$$v_2 = v_c = \frac{v_s}{r - 1} = \frac{9.42 \times 10^{-3}}{15}$$

$$= 0.628 \times 10^{-3} \text{ m}^3$$

(b)
$$p_3 = p_2 = 48.5 \text{ bar}$$

$$v_3 = \rho v_2$$

where $\rho = 1 + K\,(r - 1)$

$$= 1 + \frac{10}{100}(16 - 1) = 2.5$$

$\therefore$
$$v_3 = 2.5 \times 0.628 \times 10^{-3} = 1.57 \times 10^{-3} \text{ m}^3$$

For the constant pressure process 2–3

$$\frac{v_3}{T_3} = \frac{v_2}{T_2}$$

$$T_3 = T_2 \frac{v_3}{v_2} = T_2 \rho = 920 \times 2.5$$

$$= 2300 \text{ K}$$

(c) $$r_e = \frac{r}{\rho} = \frac{16}{2.5} = 6.4$$

For isentropic process 3–4

$$p_4 = \frac{p_3}{(r_e)^\gamma} = \frac{48.5}{(6.4)^{1.4}} = 3.6 \text{ bar}$$

$$T_4 = \frac{T_1}{(r_e)^{\gamma-1}} = \frac{2300}{(6.4)^{0.4}} = 1095 \text{ K}$$

$$v_4 = v_1 = 10\times10^{-3} \text{ m}^3$$

Air standard efficiency

$$\eta_{\text{Diesel}} = 1 - \frac{1}{(r)^{\gamma-1}}\left[\frac{\rho^\gamma - 1}{\rho - 1} \times \frac{1}{\gamma}\right]$$

$$= 1 - \frac{1}{(16)^{0.4}}\left[\frac{(2.5)^{1.4} - 1}{2.5 - 1} \times \frac{1}{1.4}\right]$$

$$= 0.59 = 59\%$$

4. The mean effective pressure of the cycle is given by

$$p_m = \frac{1}{v_s}\left[p_2(v_3 - v_2) + \frac{p_3v_3 - p_4v_4}{\gamma - 1} - \frac{p_2v_2 - p_1v_1}{\gamma - 1}\right]$$

$$v_1 = v_4 = rv_c$$

$$v_2 = v_c$$

$$v_3 = \rho v_c$$

$$v_s = (r-1)v_c$$

$$p_m = \frac{1}{(r-1)v_c}\left[p_2(\rho v_c - v_c) + \frac{p_3\rho v_c - p_4 r v_c}{\gamma - 1} - \frac{p_2 v_c - p_1 r v_c}{\gamma - 1}\right]$$

$$= \frac{1}{(r-1)}\left[p_2(\rho - 1) + \frac{p_3\rho - p_4 r}{\gamma - 1} - \frac{p_2 - p_1 r}{\gamma - 1}\right]$$

$$= \frac{1}{(16-1)}\left[48.5(2.5-1) + \frac{(48.5)(2.5) - (3.6\times16)}{1.4-1} - \frac{48.5 - (1)(16)}{1.4-1}\right]$$

$$= \mathbf{10 \text{ bar}}$$ **Ans.**

The work done per cycle

$$W = p_m\, v_s = \frac{10\times10^5 \times 9.42\times10^{-3}}{1000}$$

$$= 9.42 \text{ kJ/cycle}$$

$$\text{Power} = (\text{Work done/cycle}) \times (\text{No. of cycles/sec})$$

$$= 9.42 \times \frac{400}{60}$$

$$= \mathbf{62.8\ kW}$$

Ans.

Example 6.8

The following information is available about an engine working on diesel cycle

Maximum cycle temperature = 1890 K

Heat supplied = 860 kJ/kg

Ambient conditions = 1 bar, 300 K

Determine compression ratio, cut-off ratio, maximum pressure and air standard efficiency.

Solution:

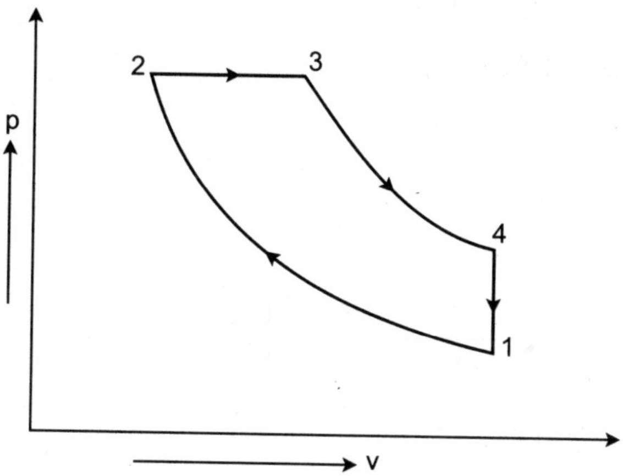

Fig. 6.22

$$p_1 = 1000 \text{ kPa}$$

$$T_1 = 300 \text{ K}$$

$$Q = 860 \text{ kJ/kg}$$

$$T_3 = 1890 \text{ K}$$

$$p_1 v_1 = RT_1$$

$$100\ v_1 = 0.287 \times 300$$

$$v_1 = 0.861 \text{ m}^3$$

$$Q = c_p (T_3 - T_2)$$

$$860 = 1.005 (1890 - T_2)$$

$$T_2 = 1034.3 \text{ K}$$

For isentropic process 1–2

$$T_1 v_1^{\gamma-1} = T_2 v_2^{\gamma-1}$$

$$\left(\frac{v_1}{v_2}\right)^{\gamma-1} = \frac{T_2}{T_1} = \frac{1034.3}{300} = 3.447$$

$$\frac{v_1}{v_2} = (3.447)^{\frac{1}{0.4}}$$

Compression ratio, $r = \frac{v_1}{v_2} = \mathbf{22}$ **Ans.**

For constant pressure process 2–3

$$\frac{p_2 v_2}{T_2} = \frac{p_3 v_3}{T_3}$$

$$p_2 = p_3$$

$$\therefore \quad \frac{v_2}{T_2} = \frac{v_3}{T_3}$$

$$\frac{v_3}{v_2} = \frac{T_3}{T_2} = \frac{1890}{1034.3} = 1.827$$

$\therefore$ Cut-off ratio, $\rho = \mathbf{1.827}$ **Ans.**

Air standard efficiency

$$\eta = 1 - \frac{1}{(r)^{\gamma-1}}\left[\frac{\rho^{\gamma} - 1}{\gamma(\rho - 1)}\right]$$

$$= 1 - \frac{1}{(22)^{0.4}}\left[\frac{(1.8)^{1.4} - 1}{1.4(1.8 - 1)}\right]$$

$$= 0.667$$

$$= 66.7\%$$

Maximum pressure

$$p_3 = p_2$$

$$p_1 v_1^{\gamma} = p_2 v_2^{\gamma}$$

$$p_2 = p_1\left(\frac{v_1}{v_2}\right)^{\gamma}$$

$$= 1(22)^{1.4}$$

$$= \mathbf{75.75\ bar}$$ **Ans.**

Example 6.9

A car has a four-stroke cylinder in line diesel engine with compression ratio 20 : 1 and expansion ratio 10 : 1. Calculate

a. Cut-off ratio b. air standard efficiency.

Solution:

a. Cut-off ratio, $\rho = \frac{v_3}{v_2} = \frac{v_3}{v_4} \times \frac{v_1}{v_2}$ as $v_1 = v_4$

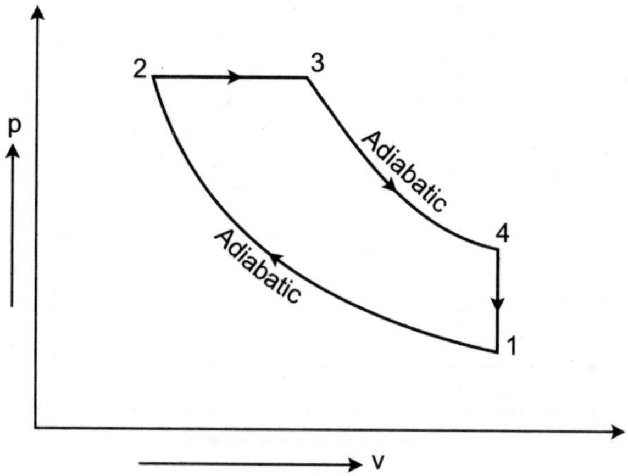

Fig. 6.23

$$\text{Compression ratio, } r = \frac{v_1}{v_2} = 20$$

and $$\text{Expansion ratio, } \frac{v_4}{v_3} = 10$$

$$\text{Cut-off ratio} = \frac{20}{10} = 2$$ **Ans.**

b. Air standard efficiency of Diesel cycle

$$\eta = 1 - \frac{1}{\gamma (r)^{\gamma - 1}} \left[\frac{\rho^{\gamma} - 1}{\rho - 1} \right]$$

$$= 1 - \frac{1}{(20)^{0.4}} \left[\frac{\left(2^{1.4} - 1\right)}{1.4(2-1)} \right]$$

$$= 0.646 \quad \text{or} \quad 64.67\%$$ **Ans.**

Example 6.10

A Diesel engine working on Diesel cycle takes in air at pressure 0.1 MPa and temperature 30°C. The pressure at the end of compression is 3.0 MPa and the cut-off is 6% of the stroke. Calculate (a) the compression ratio, (b) the percentage clearance, (c) the heat supplied, (d) the heat rejected, (e) the thermal efficiency and (f) mean effective pressure.

Solution:

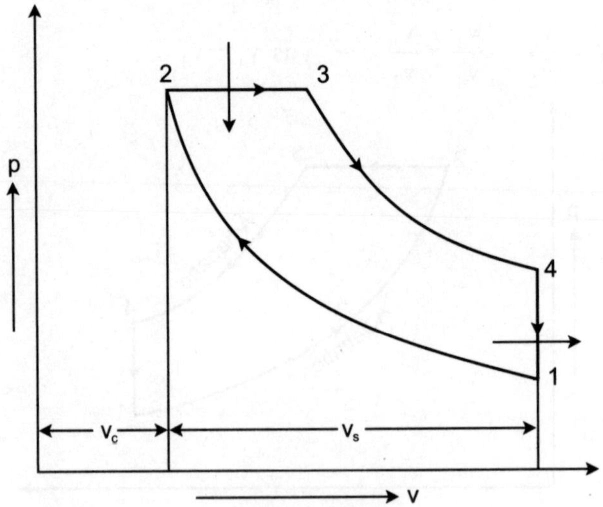

Fig. 6.24

Let 1 kg of air is there

a. Compression ratio,

$$r = \frac{v_1}{v_2} = \left(\frac{p_2}{p_1}\right)^{\frac{1}{\gamma}} = \left(\frac{3.0}{0.1}\right)^{\frac{1}{1.4}} = \mathbf{11.352} \qquad \textbf{Ans.}$$

b. Clearance volume,

$$v_c = v_2$$

Percentage clearance

$$\frac{v_2}{v_s} \times 100 = \frac{v_2}{v_1 - v_2} = \frac{100}{r-1}$$

$$= \frac{100}{10.352} = \mathbf{9.659\%} \qquad \textbf{Ans.}$$

c. $$\frac{T_2}{T_1} = \left(\frac{v_1}{v_2}\right)^{\gamma-1} = (11.352)^{0.4}$$

$$= 2.6425$$

$$T_2 = (273 + 30) \times 2.6425$$

$$= 800.67 \text{ K}$$

$$v_3 - v_2 = 0.06\ v_s$$

but $$v_2 = \frac{v_s}{r-1} = \frac{v_s}{10.352} = 0.09659\ v_s$$

$$v_3 = 0.09659\ v_s + 0.06\ v_s = 0.1565\ v_s$$

and $$\frac{v_3}{v_2} = \rho = \frac{0.1565}{0.09659} = 1.6202$$

From constant pressure heat addition process 2–3

$$T_3 = T_2\frac{v_3}{v_2} = 800.67 \times 1.6202 = 1297.24\ K$$

$$\text{Heat added} = c_p(T_3 - T_2) = 1.005(1297.24 - 800.67)$$

$$= 499.05\ kJ/kg$$

From isentropic process 3–4

$$\frac{T_4}{T_3} = \left(\frac{v_3}{v_4}\right)^{\gamma-1} = \left(\frac{v_3}{v_1}\right)^{0.4}$$

$$= \left(\frac{0.1565\ v_s}{11.352 \times 0.09659\ v_s}\right)^{0.4}$$

$$T_4 = 1297(0.1425)^{0.4}$$

$$= \mathbf{595.92\ K}$$ **Ans.**

d. $$\text{Heat rejected} = c_v\ (T_4 - T_1)$$

$$= 0.718(595.42 - 303)$$

$$= \mathbf{209.95\ kJ/kg}$$ **Ans.**

e. $$\eta_{Diesel} = 1 - \frac{1}{\gamma r^{\gamma-1}}\left[\frac{\rho^{\gamma}-1}{\rho-1}\right]$$

$$= 1 - \frac{1}{1.4(11.352)^{1.4-1}}\left[\frac{(1.6292)^{1.4}-1}{1.6292-1}\right]$$

$$= \mathbf{0.5793 = 57.93\%}$$ **Ans.**

f. Mean effective pressure

$$p_m = p_1 r\left[\frac{\gamma r^{\gamma-1}(\rho-1) - (\rho^{\gamma}-1)}{(r-1)(\gamma-1)}\right]$$

$$= 1 \times 11.352 \left[\frac{1.4 \times (11.352)^{0.4} (1.6202 - 1) - \left(1.6202^{1.4} - 1\right)}{(11.352 - 1)(1.4 - 1)} \right]$$

$$= \mathbf{3.644 \text{ bar}} \qquad \textbf{Ans.}$$

Example 6.11

For the same compression ratio, show that the efficiency of Otto cycle is greater than that of Diesel cycle.

Solution:

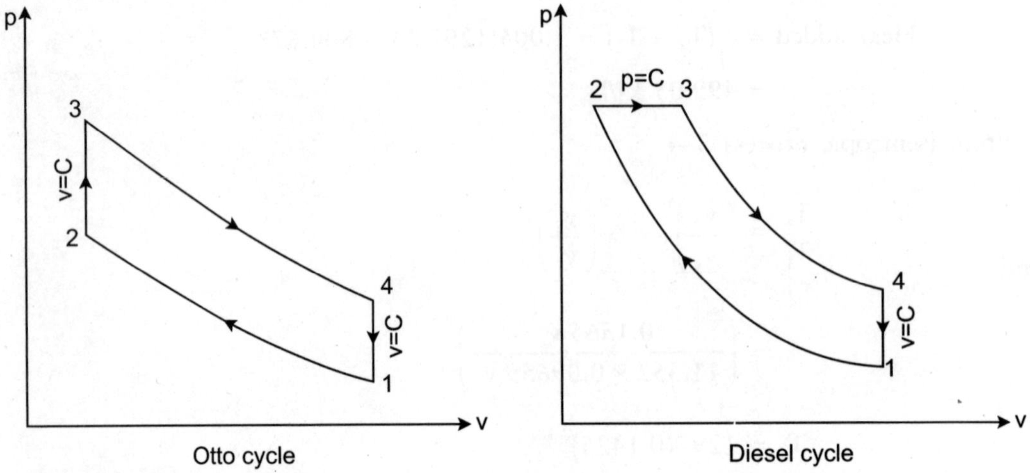

Fig. 6.25

We know that

$$\eta_{Otto} = 1 - \frac{1}{(r)^{\gamma - 1}}$$

$$\eta_{Diesel} = 1 - \frac{1}{(r)^{\gamma - 1}} \frac{1}{\gamma} \left[\frac{\rho^{\gamma} - 1}{\rho - 1} \right]$$

As the compression ratio is same

$$\frac{V_1}{V_2} = \frac{V_1'}{V_2'} = r$$

If $\quad \dfrac{V_4'}{V_3'} = r_1$ then cut-off ratio

$$\rho = \frac{V_3'}{V_2'} = \frac{r}{r_1}$$

Putting the value of ρ in η_{Diesel}, we get

$$\eta_{Diesel} = 1 - \frac{1}{(r)^{\gamma-1}} \times \frac{1}{\gamma}\left[\frac{\left(\frac{r}{r_1}\right)^{\gamma} - 1}{\left(\frac{r}{r_1}\right) - 1}\right]$$

From the above equation, we observe

$$\frac{r}{r_1} > 1$$

Let $\quad r_1 = r - \delta \quad$ where δ is a small quantity.

Then

$$\frac{r}{r_1} = \frac{r}{r-\delta} = \frac{r}{r\left(1-\frac{\delta}{r}\right)}$$

$$= \left(1-\frac{\delta}{r}\right)^{-1} = 1 + \frac{\delta}{r} + \frac{\delta^2}{r^2} + \frac{\delta^3}{r^3} \cdots$$

and

$$\left(\frac{r}{r_1}\right)^{\gamma} = \frac{r^{\gamma}}{r^{\gamma}\left(1-\frac{\delta}{r}\right)^{\gamma}} = \left(1-\frac{\delta}{r}\right)^{-\gamma}$$

$$= 1 + \frac{\gamma\delta}{r} + \frac{\gamma(\gamma+1)}{2}\cdot\frac{\delta^2}{r^2} + \ldots..$$

$$\eta_{Diesel} = 1 - \frac{1}{(r)^{\gamma-1}} \times \frac{1}{\gamma}\left[\frac{\frac{\gamma\delta}{r} + \frac{\gamma(\gamma+1)}{21}\cdot\frac{\delta^2}{r^2} + \ldots..}{\frac{\delta}{r} + \frac{\delta^2}{r^2} + \ldots..}\right]$$

$$= 1 - \frac{1}{(r)^{\gamma-1}}\left[\frac{\frac{\delta}{r} + \frac{\gamma+1}{2}\cdot\frac{\delta^2}{r^2} + \ldots..}{\frac{\delta}{r} + \frac{\delta^2}{r^2} + \ldots..}\right]$$

The ratio inside the bracket is greater than 1 since the co-efficient terms δ^2/r^2 is greater than 1 in the numerator. It means that something more is subtracted in case of diesel cycle than in Otto cycle.

Hence for same compression ratio

$$\eta_{Otto} > \eta_{Diesel}$$

THEORETICAL QUESTIONS

1. Differentiate between internal and external combustion engines.
2. List the various advantages of I.C. engines over external combustion (steam) engines.
3. On what basis I.C. engines are classified?
4. Write short notes on
   i. Piston rings ii. Spark plug iii. Crank and crankshaft
   iv. Camshaft and value mechanism v. Flywheel
5. How does a two-stroke engine differ from a four-stroke engine?
6. Mention the advantages and disadvantages of two-stroke engines when compared with four-stroke engines.
7. Define the following terms in relation to reciprocating engine
   i. Dead centre ii. Stroke iii. Piston speed iv. Compression ratio
8. Derive an expression for the air standard efficiency and mean effective pressure of an Otto cycle. State the assumptions made.
9. Derive an expression for the air standard efficiency of the Diesel cycle in terms of the compression ratio, cut-off ratio and the adiabatic index. Proceed to show that the efficiency of this cycle is less than that of Otto cycle for the same compression ratio. Why in actual practice a diesel engine preferred for some applications?
10. What is cut-off ratio? How does it affect the air standard efficiency of a diesel cycle?

NUMERICAL PROBLEMS

1. In an air-standard Otto cycle the compression ratio is 10, the compression begins at 300 K, 1 bar and the maximum temperature of the cycle is 1300 K. Determine (a) heat supplied per kg of air, (b) the work done per kg of air, (c) the maximum pressure of the cycle and (d) the thermal efficiency.
2. At the beginning of compression in an air standard Otto cycle cylinder the temperature is 300 K, the pressure is 1.0 bar and volume is 0.000707 m^3. At the end of compression the pressure is 10.55 bar. The heat supplied to the cycle is 1.5 kJ. Calculate (a) the compression ratio, (b) the net work per cycle and (c) the mean effective pressure.
3. An engine working on Otto cycle has a compression ratio of 7 : 1. If the specific heat at constant volume decreases by 1 per cent, determine the corresponding percentage change in thermal efficiency.
4. The compression curve on the pressure-volume diagram of a gas engine working on Otto cycle follows the polytropic law $pv^{1.3} = c$. At two points on the curve at 1/4th stroke and 3/4th stroke, the pressures are measured to be 1.4 bar and 3.6 bar. Determine the compression ratio of the engine. Proceed to calculate the gas consumption per kW hour if relative efficiency is 0.4 and gas has calorific value of 18850 kJ/m^3.
5. An engine working on Diesel cycle has air intake conditions of 1 bar and 300 K and it operates through compression ratio 16. After the fuel has burnt, the temperature reached at 1700°C. Make calculations for air standard efficiency and the net work output per cycle.

6. An engine working on Diesel cycle has a compression ratio of 14 and expansion ratio of 7. If the air at suction has a temperature of 300 K, calculate the efficiency and work output.
7. The stroke and cylinder diameter of a compression ignition are 250 mm and 150 mm respectively. If the clearance volume is 4×10^{-4} m^3 and fuel injection takes place at constant pressure for 5 per cent of the stroke, determine the efficiency of the engine. Assume the engine working on the Diesel cycle.
8. An engine with 200 mm cylinder diameter and 300 mm stroke works on theoretical Diesel cycle. The initial pressure and temperature of air used are 1 bar and 27°C. The cut-off is 7% of the stroke.

Determine:

i. Pressure and temperature at all salient points.
ii. Theoretical air standard efficiency.
iii. Mean effective pressure.
iv. Power of the engine, if working cycle per minute are 380.

PART B

7

Two Dimensional Force Systems and Analysis

7.1 Basic Concepts

Knowledge of certain concepts and definitions are necessary for the study of Engineering Mechanics and Strength of Materials.

7.2 Force

A force has a tendency to move a body in the direction of its action. The action of a force is measured by its magnitude, direction of its action and its point of application on the body. Force is a vector quantity. The unit of force is the Newton (N).

7.3 Mass

It is a measure of inertia of a body, which is its resistance to a change of state (rest or motion). It can be measured as the quantity of matter in a body. The unit of mass is kilogram (kg).

7.4 Space

Space is the geometric region occupied by bodies whose positions are described by linear and angular measurements, relative to a co-ordinate system.

7.5 Particle

A body of negligible dimensions is called a particle.

7.6 Rigid Body

A rigid body means the body does not deform or the distance between any two points of the body does not change under the action of an applied external load.

7.7 Scalars and Vectors

Scalars quantities are those with which a magnitude alone is associated, e.g. time, volume, density, speed, energy and mass, etc.

Vector quantities possess direction as well as magnitude, e.g. displacement, velocity, acceleration, force, moment, momentum, etc.

7.8 Laws of Motion

Sir Isaac Newton was the first to state the basic laws governing the motion of a body.

These laws are:

LAW I:

A body remains at rest or continues to move in a straight line with a uniform velocity if there is no external force acting on it.

LAW II:

The acceleration of a particle is proportional to the resultant force acting on it and is in the direction of this force.

This law forms the basis for most of the analysis in dynamics.

$$a \propto F$$

or $$a(\text{Mass}) = F$$

$\Rightarrow$ $$\mathbf{F = ma}$$

where:

a—resulting acceleration (m/s^2)
m—mass of the body (kg)

then $$F = kg\frac{m}{s^2} \text{ or N.}$$

LAW III:

The forces of action and reaction between interacting bodies are equal in magnitude, opposite in direction and collinear.

They always occur in pairs of equal and opposite forces. Thus, the downward force by paper weight on the table is accompanied by an upward force of equal magnitude exerted on the paper weight by the table.

7.9 Units

Quantity	*Dimensional Symbol*	*S.I. Units*	*Symbol*
Mass	M	kilogram	kg
Length	L	meter	m
Time	T	Second	s
Force	F	Newton	N

7.10 Law of Gravitation

This law was also formulated by Newton. This law is expressed by the equation

$$F = G\frac{m_1 m_2}{r^2}$$

where,

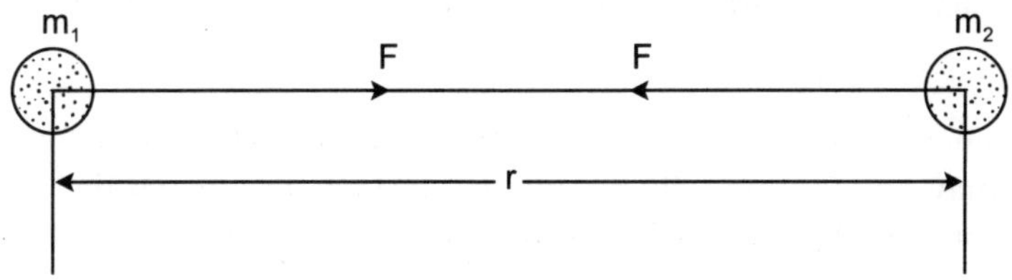

Fig. 7.1

F = Mutual force of attraction between two particles.

G = Constant of gravitation = 6.673×10^{-11} m^3/kgs^2.

m_1, m_2 = The masses of the two particles.

r = The distance between the centres of the particles.

7.11 Method of Solving Problems in Mechanical Engineering

Each solution should follow a logical sequence of steps from hypothesis to conclusion as

1. Given data
2. Desired data
3. Necessary sketches/diagrams
4. Calculations
5. Results and conclusion

In addition, we should observe reasonableness of numerical magnitudes, accuracy and dimensional homogeneity of the terms. All work should be neat and orderly. Many problems which at first may seem difficult and complicated become clear and straight forward when begun in a logical and disciplined way.

7.12 Principle of Transmissibility of a Force

It states that the state of equilibrium or the state of motion of rigid body will remain unchanged if the point of application of a force acting on the rigid body is transmitted to act at any other point along its line of action.

A force F acting on a rigid body at point A, having the line of action ab, can be replaced by the same force F but acting at point B lies along the line of action ab of the force. (Fig. 7.2).

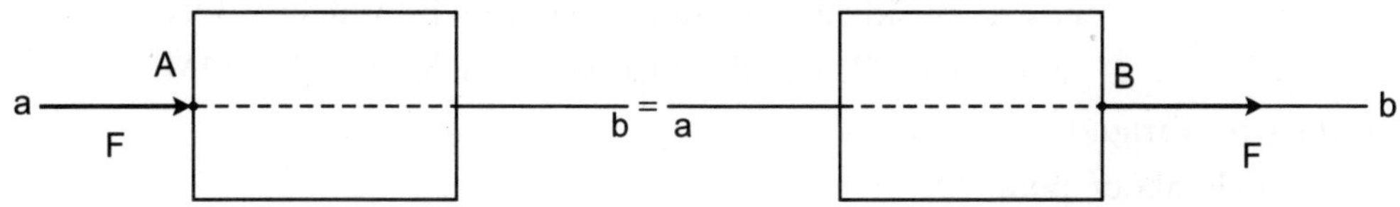

Fig. 7.2

In other words, the force F acting at point A can be transmitted to act at any other point B along its line of action without changing its effect on the rigid body equilibrium.

7.13 Moment

A force has a tendency to move or rotate a body in the direction of its application or about an axis. This axis may be any line which neither intersects nor is parallel to the line of action of the force. This rotational tendency is known as the moment of force (M). Moment is also referred to as torque.

$$M = F.d$$

where,

F = Force

d = Moment arm or perpendicular distance from the axis to the line of action of force.

7.14 Varignon's Theorem

It states that the moment of a force about any point is equal to the sum of moments of the components of the force about the same point.

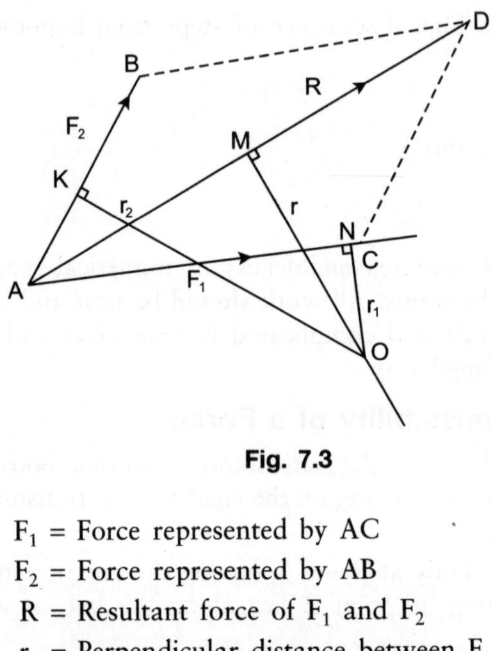

Fig. 7.3

F_1 = Force represented by AC

F_2 = Force represented by AB

R = Resultant force of F_1 and F_2

r_1 = Perpendicular distance between F_1 and O = ON

r_2 = Perpendicular distance between F_2 and O = OK

r = Perpendicular distance between R and O = OM

According to Varignon's theorem,

Moment of R about point O

= Moment of F_1 about O + Moment of force F_2 about O

$$\Rightarrow \quad R \cdot r = F_1 \cdot r_1 + F_2 \cdot r_2$$

Proof of Varignon's Theorem:

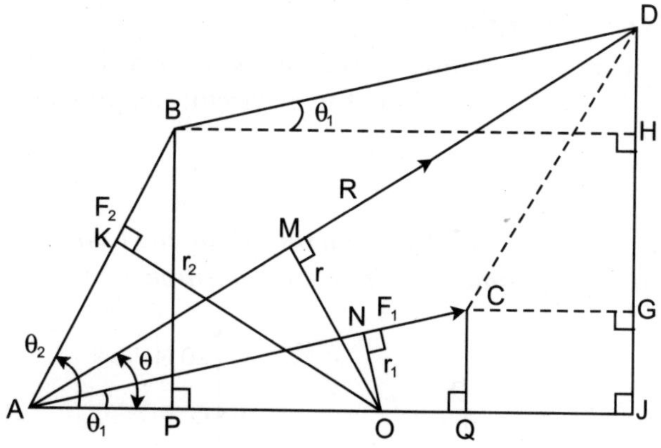

Fig. 7.4

$\angle OAC = \theta_1$	$ON = r_1$
$\angle OAD = \theta$	$OM = r$
$\angle OAB = \theta_2$	$OK = r_2$

$$\overrightarrow{AC} = F_1$$
$$\overrightarrow{AD} = R$$
$$\overrightarrow{AB} = F_2$$

To Prove: $\quad R \cdot r = F_1 \cdot r_1 + F_2 r_2$

Proof:

Moment of R about O

$= R \times$ perpendicular distance between R and O

$= R \times r$

$= R \times AO \sin\theta$

$= R \sin\theta \times AO$

$= DJ \times AO$

$= (DH + HJ) \times AO$

$= (BD \sin\theta_1 + BP) \times AO$

$= (F_1 \sin\theta_1 + AB \sin\theta_2) \times AO$

$= (F_1 \sin\theta_1 + F_2 \sin\theta_2) \times AO$

$= F_1 \cdot AO \sin\theta_1 + F_2 \cdot AO \sin\theta_2$

$= F_1 \cdot r_1 + F_2 \cdot r_2$

= Moment of F_1 about O + Moment of F_2 about O

$$\sin\theta = \frac{DJ}{AD}$$

$$\sin\theta = \frac{DJ}{R}$$

Hence,

$$R \times r = F_1 r_1 + F_2 r_2 \qquad \textit{Proved}$$

The principle of moments or Varignon's principle is not restricted to only two concurrent forces but is also applicable to any coplanar force system, i.e. concurrent or non-concurrent or parallel force system.

Example 7.1

Four forces of magnitudes 10, 20, 30 and 40 N acting along the four sides of a square as shown in Fig. 7.5. Determine the magnitude, direction and position of resultant force.

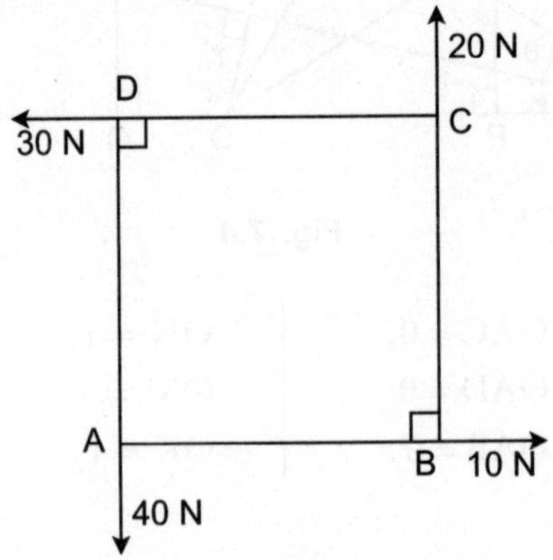

Fig. 7.5

Solution:

$F_1 = 10$ N

$F_2 = 20$ N

$F_3 = 30$ N

$F_4 = 40$ N

Let AB = BC = CD = DA = a

The net force in horizontal direction

$$\sum F_x = 10 - 30 = -20 \text{ N.}$$

The net force in vertical direction

$$\sum F_y = 20 - 40 = -20 \text{ N.}$$

The Resultant

$$R = \sqrt{(\Sigma F_x)^2 + (\Sigma F_y)^2}$$

$$= \sqrt{(-20)^2 + (-20)^2} \qquad = 20\sqrt{2} \text{ N} \qquad \textbf{Ans.}$$

The direction of resultant R with horizontal axis

$$\tan\theta = \frac{\Sigma F_y}{\Sigma F_x} = \frac{-20}{-20} = 1$$

$$\theta = 45^\circ$$

or $\theta = 180 + 45 = \mathbf{225^\circ}$ **Ans.**

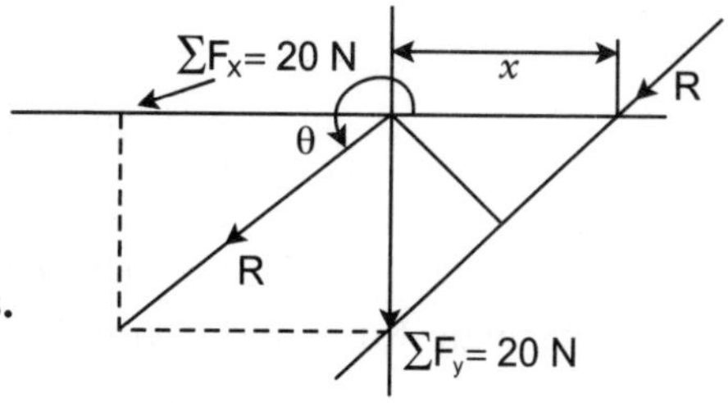

Fig. 7.6

As per Varignon's theorem; $R \times r = F_1 \times r + F_2 \times r_2$.

Taking moment about point A

$$R \times x = 20a + 30a$$

$$x = \frac{50a}{20\sqrt{2}} = \frac{5a}{2\sqrt{2}}$$ **Ans.**

Example 7.2

A system of parallel forces is acting on a rigid bar as shown in Fig. 7.7. Reduce this system to:

i. a single force

ii. a single force and a couple at A.

iii. a single force and a couple at B.

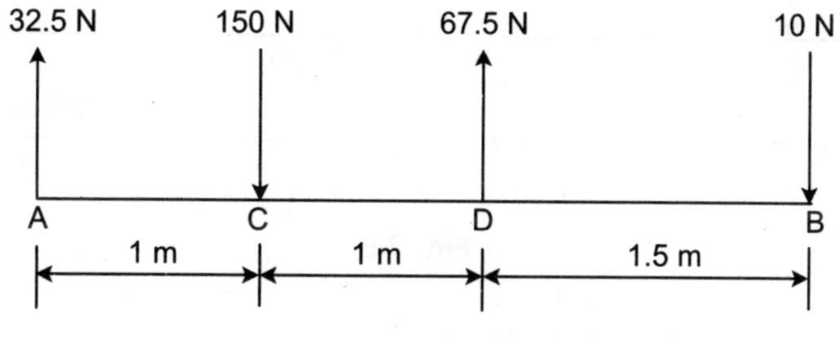

Fig. 7.7

Solution:

i. Single force system:

Resultant, $R = 32.5 - 150 + 67.5 - 10$

$= -60$ N

$\mathbf{R = 60\ N\ (\downarrow)}$ **Ans.**

Let x = distance of resultant (R) from A towards B

Using Varignon's theorem:

$R \times x$ = Algebraic sum of all moments of all forces

$= 32.5\times0 + 150\times1(\circlearrowright) + 67.5\times2(\circlearrowleft) + 10\times3.5(\circlearrowright)$

$$= 0 + 150(\circlearrowright) + 135.0(\circlearrowleft) + 35(\circlearrowright)$$

$$= 150 + 35 - 135 = 50(\circlearrowright) \text{ N.m}$$

$$x = \frac{50}{60} = \frac{5}{6} \text{m}$$

$$x = \mathbf{0.833 \text{ m or } 833 \text{ mm}}$$ **Ans.**

ii. A single force and a couple at A:

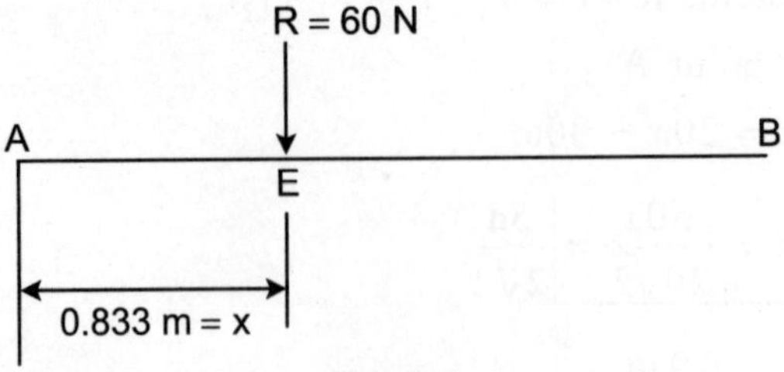

Fig. 7.8

The resultant force R acting at point E can be replaced by an equal force applied at point A in the same direction together with a couple.

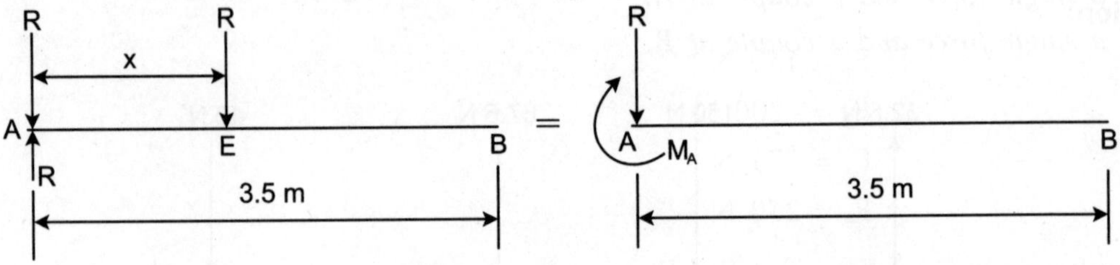

Fig. 7.9

$\therefore$ Force acting at A = R = **60 N(↓)** **Ans.**

Couple at A = M_A = R × x = 60 × 0.833 = **49.98 N.m**$(\circlearrowright)$ **Ans.**

iii. A single force and a couple at B.

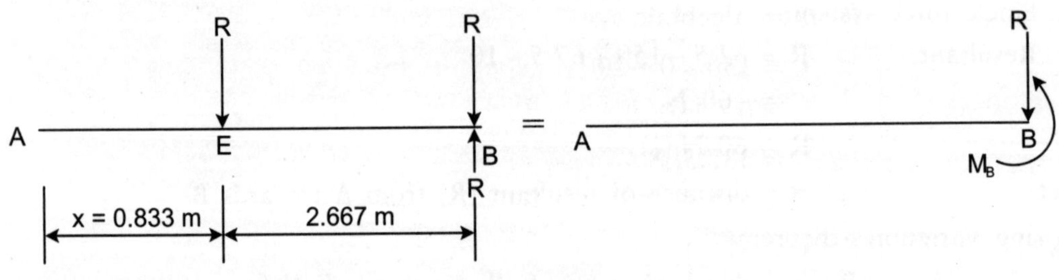

Fig. 7.10

$\therefore$ Force at B = R = **60 N (↓)** **Ans.**

Couple at B = R × (3.5 – 0.833) = 60 × 2.667 (↺)

M_B = **160 N.m (↺)** **Ans.**

Example 7.3

Four parallel forces of magnitudes 150 N, 200 N, 75 N and 250 N are shown in Fig. 7.11. Find the magnitude of the resultant and distance of the resultant from point A.

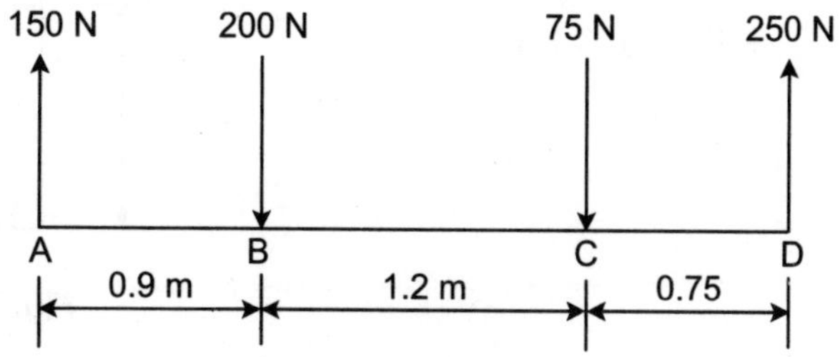

Fig. 7.11

Solution:

F_1 = 150 N	Sign Convention
F_2 = –200 N	Force ↑ ⇒ +ve
F_3 = –75 N	Force ↓ ⇒ –ve
F_4 = 250 N	

Resultant $\Sigma F_y = F_1 + F_2 + F_3 + F_4$

$= 150 - 200 - 75 + 250$

$= 400 - 275 = 125$ N (↑)

$\therefore$ Resultant, R = **125 N (↑)** **Ans.**

Using Varignon's theorem:

R × x = Algebraic sum of all moments

= 150 × 0 + 200 × (0.9)(↻) + 75 × 2.1(↻) + 250 × 2.85(↺)

= 0 + 180(↻) + 157.5(↻) + 712.5(↺)

= 337.5(↻) + 712.5(↺)

= 712.5 – 337.5

⇒ 125 × x = 375(↺)

$$x = \frac{375}{125} = \textbf{3 m from A}$$ **Ans.**

7.15 Couple

The moment produced by two equal, opposite and parallel, non-colinear forces is known as couple.

$$
\begin{aligned}
M_O &= F(a+d)(\circlearrowleft) + F \times a(\circlearrowright) \\
&= F(a+d) - F \cdot a \\
&= F \cdot d\ (\circlearrowleft)
\end{aligned}
$$

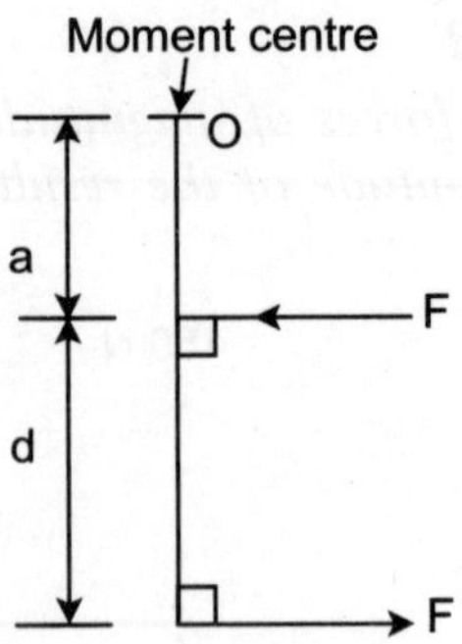

Fig. 7.12

7.16 Force-Couple Systems

The tendency of a force is to pull or push and to rotate the body. The representation of this double effect is shown in Fig. 7.13 by replacing a given force by an equal parallel force and a couple to compensate for the change in the moment of the force.

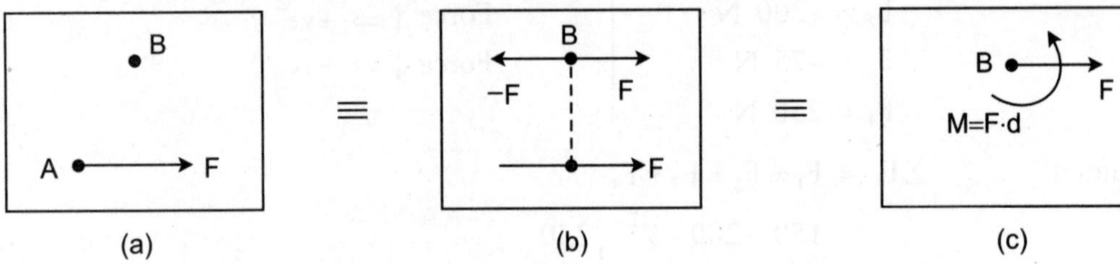

Fig. 7.13

A given force F acting at point A is replaced by an equal force F at point B and the counter-clockwise couple, $M = F \cdot d$.

Original force at A and equal and opposite one at B constitute the couple $M = F \cdot d$. Thus, we have replaced the original force at A by the same force acting at a different point B and a couple without changing the external effects of the original force on the body. Such combination of force and couple is known as a force-couple system.

Example 7.4

A rigid body is subjected to a couple consisting of the two 50 N forces. Replace this couple by an equivalent couple consisting of the two forces P and –P, each of which has a magnitude of 400 N. Find the proper angle θ.

All dimensions are in mm

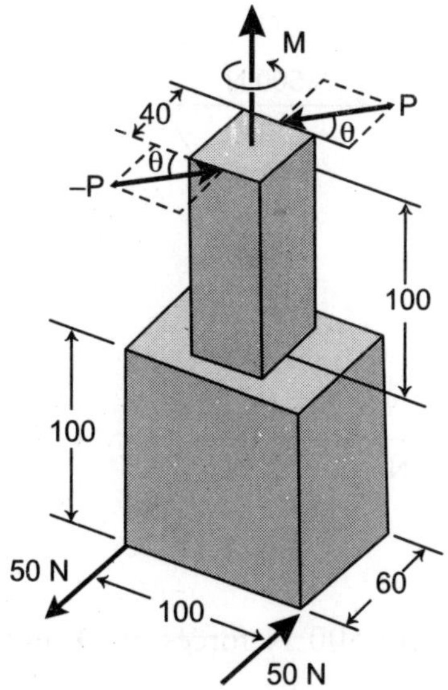

Fig. 7.14

Solution:

The given couple is anti-clockwise.

$$M_1 = F{\cdot}d = 50 \times 100(\circlearrowleft) \text{ N.mm}$$

The force P and –P will produce a counter clockwise couple.

$$M_2 = F{\cdot}d = 400 \cos\theta \times 40(\circlearrowleft) \text{ N.mm}$$

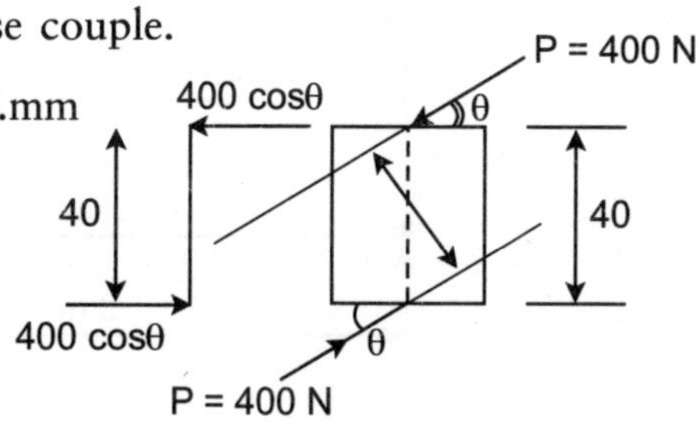

Fig. 7.15

Equate M_1 and M_2

$$400 \cos\theta \times 40 = 50 \times 100$$

$$\theta = 71.79° \quad \textbf{Ans.}$$

Example 7.5

Replace the horizontal 500 N force acting on the lever by an equivalent system consisting of a force at O and a couple.

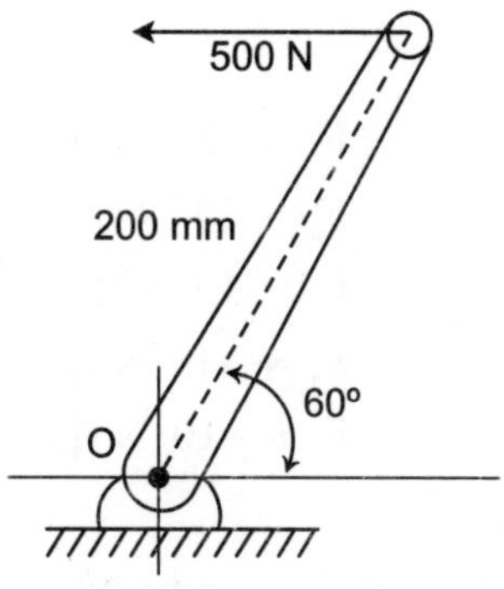

Fig. 7.16

Solution:

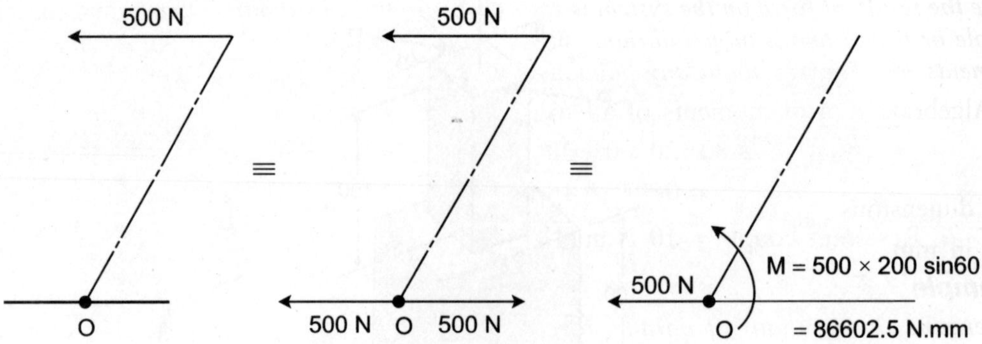

Fig. 7.17

We apply two equal and opposite 500 N forces at O and identify the counter clockwise couple

$$M_1 = F{\cdot}d = 500 \times 200 \sin 60 = 86602.5 \text{ N.mm}$$

Example 7.6

Five forces are acting on a body as shown in Fig. 7.18. Determine the resultant.

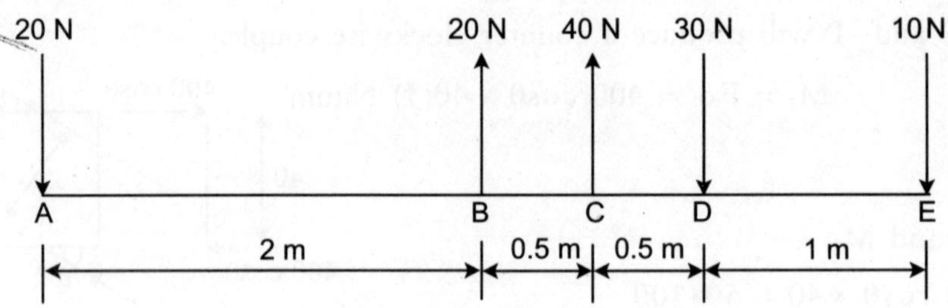

Fig. 7.18

Solution:

$F_1 = -20$ N (↓)	R = ?
$F_2 = 20$ N (↑)	m = ?
$F_3 = 40$ N (↑)	
$F_4 = -30$ N (↓)	
$F_5 = -10$ N (↓)	

Resultant

$$R = \Sigma F_y = -20 + 20 + 40 - 30 - 10 = 0$$ **Ans.**

Note:

Since the resultant force on the system is zero, there are two possibilities. The system has a resultant couple or the system is in equilibrium. To distinguish between these two possibilities, take sum of moments of all forces about any point. Let us take the moments about point A.

Algebraic sum of moments of all forces about A

$$= 20 \times 0 + 20 \times 2 + 40 \times 2.5 - 30 \times 3 - 10 \times 4$$
$$= 0 + 40 + 100 - 90 - 40 = 140 - 130 = 10 \text{ N.m}$$

∴ Resultant couple = **10 N.m (↺)** **Ans.**

Example 7.7

Determine the resultant of parallel forces shown in Fig. 7.19.

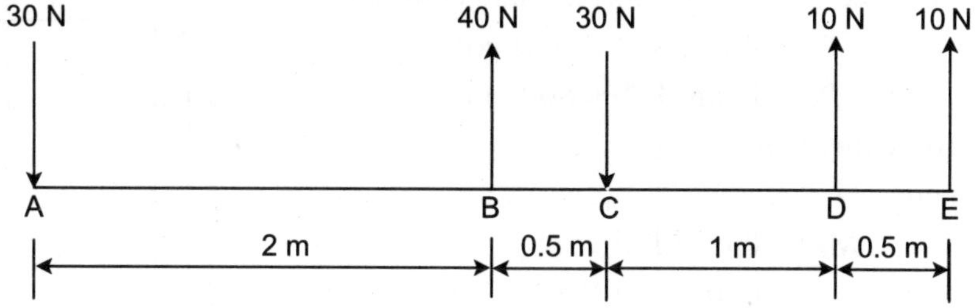

Fig. 7.19

Solution:

$$F_1 = -30 \text{ N}, F_2 = 40 \text{ N}, F_3 = -30 \text{ N}, F_4 = 10 \text{ N}, F_5 = 10 \text{ N}$$

Resultant

$$R = \Sigma F_y = -30 + 40 - 30 + 10 + 10 = \mathbf{0}$$ **Ans.**

$$M_A = 30 \times 0 + 40 \times 2(↺) - 30 \times 2.5 + 10 \times 3.5 + 10 \times 4$$
$$= 0 + 80 - 75 + 35 + 40$$
$$= 155 - 75 = 80 \text{ N.m}$$
$$M_A = 80 \text{ N.m } (↺)$$

∴ Resultant couple at A = **80 N.m (↺)** **Ans.**

Example 7.8

Determine the magnitude of the moment about the base point O of the 600 N force.

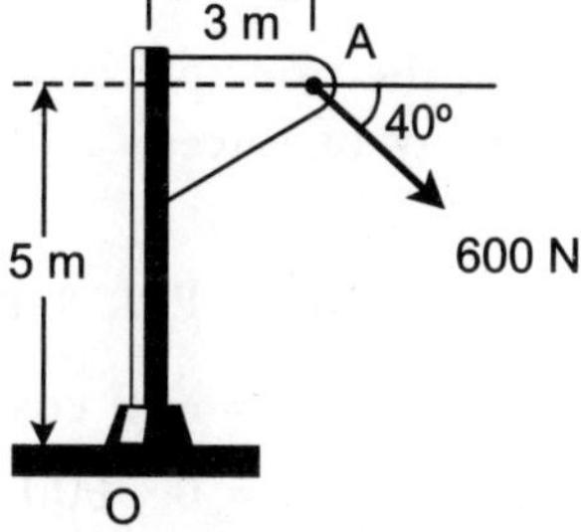

Fig. 7.20

Solution:

$$P = 600 \text{ N}$$
$$M_O = ?$$

Method 1:

$$d = \text{moment arm}$$
$$= 5 \cos 40° + 3 \cos 50°$$
$$= 5.758585$$

$\therefore$ $$M_O = F{\cdot}d$$
$$= 600 \times 5.76 \text{ N.m}$$
$$= \mathbf{3455.15 \text{ N.m}} \text{ (↻)} \quad \textbf{Ans.}$$

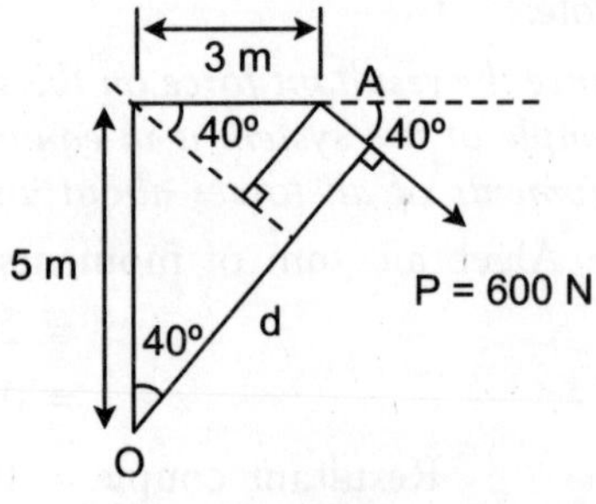

Fig. 7.21

Method 2:

Replace the force at A by its rectangular components

$$P_1 = P \cos 40° = 600 \cos 40°$$
$$P_2 = P \sin 40° = 600 \sin 40°$$

By Varignon's theorem:

Net moments

$$M_O = P_1 d_1 + P_2 d_2$$
$$= 600 \cos 40° \times 5 + 600 \sin 40° \times 3$$
$$= \mathbf{3455.15 \text{ N.m}} \text{ (↻)} \quad \textbf{Ans.}$$

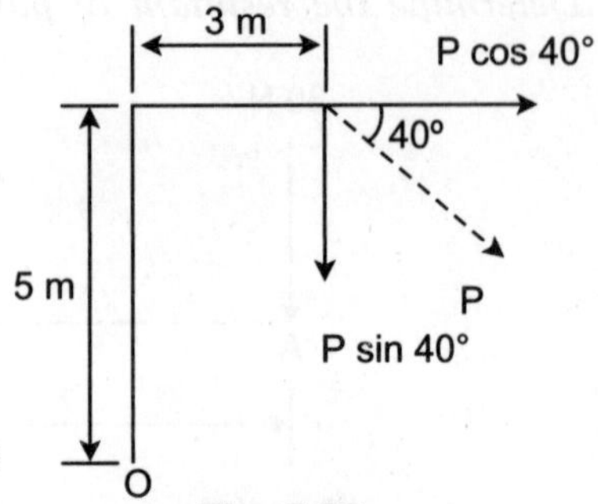

Fig. 7.22

Method 3:

By using principle of transmissibility:

$$M_O = P_1 d_1 + P_2 d_2$$
$$= 600 \cos 40° \times OB + 600 \sin 40° \times 0$$
$$= 600 \cos 40° \times (5 + 3 \tan 40°) + 0$$
$$= \mathbf{3455.15 \text{ N.m}} \text{ (↻)} \quad \textbf{Ans.}$$

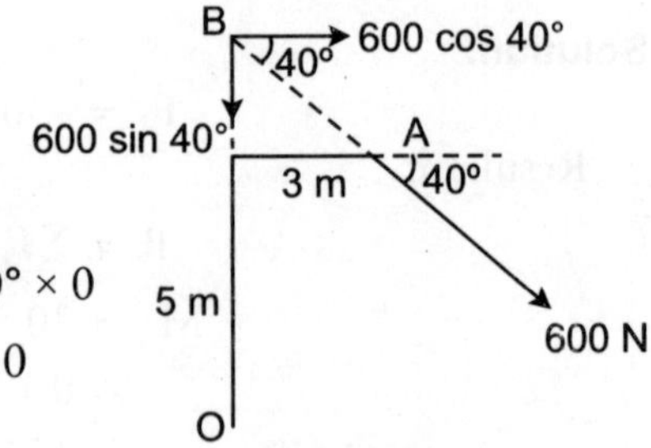

Fig. 7.23

Method 4:

Again using the principle of transmissibility of forces

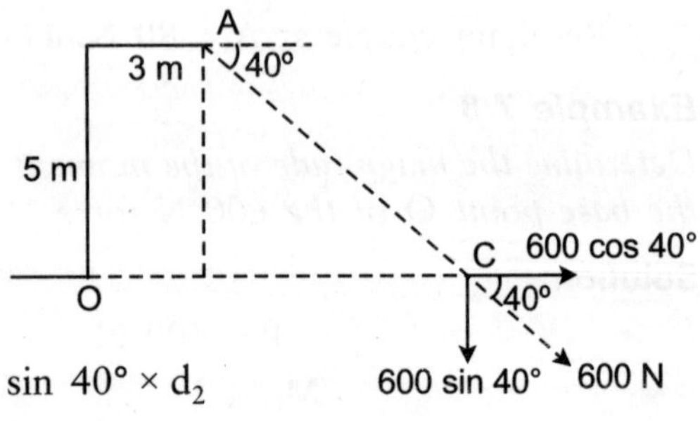

$$M_O = P_1 d_1 + P_2 d_2$$
$$= 600 \cos 40° \times 0 + 600 \sin 40° \times d_2$$
$$= 0 + 600 \sin 40° \times (3 + 5 \cot 40°)$$
$$= \mathbf{3455.15 \text{ N.m}} \text{ (↻)} \quad \textbf{Ans.}$$

Fig. 7.24

8

Concurrent Forces in a Plane

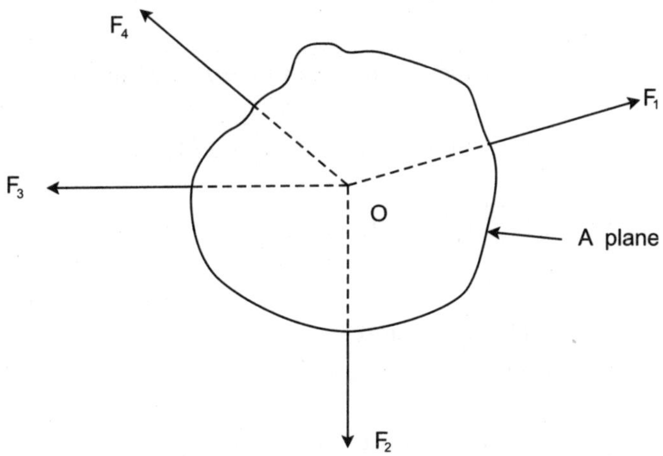

Fig. 8.1: Concurrent Coplanar Forces

8.1 Resultant of Concurrent Coplanar Forces

8.1.1 Parallelogram Law

If two forces acting at a point are represented in magnitude and direction by the adjacent sides of a parallelogram then the diagonal passing through their point of intersection represents the resultant in both magnitude and direction.

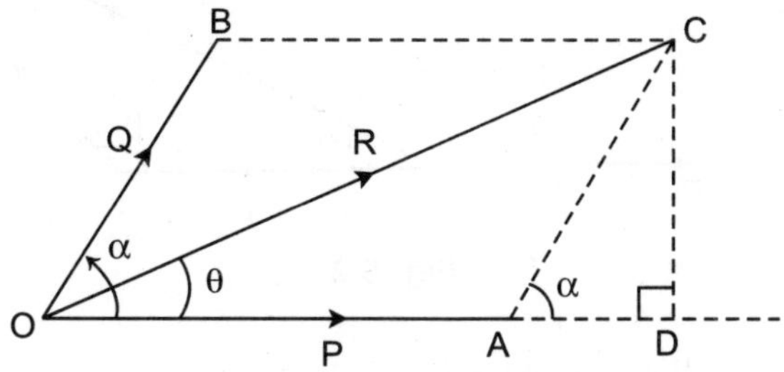

Fig. 8.2

$$\vec{R} = \vec{P} + \vec{Q} = \vec{Q} + \vec{P}$$

Also P and Q are two concurrent forces. α is the angle between P and Q. Then Resultant

$$R = \sqrt{(OD)^2 + (CD)^2}$$

$$= \sqrt{(OA + AD)^2 + (CD)^2}$$

$$= \sqrt{(P + AC\cos\alpha)^2 + (AC\sin\alpha)^2}$$

$$= \sqrt{(P + Q\cos\alpha)^2 + (Q\sin\alpha)^2}$$

$$= \sqrt{P^2 + Q^2\cos^2\alpha + 2PQ\cos\alpha + Q^2\sin^2\alpha}$$

$$= \sqrt{P^2 + Q^2\left(\cos^2\alpha + \sin^2\alpha\right) + 2PQ\cos\alpha}$$

$$R = \sqrt{P^2 + Q^2 + 2PQ\cos\alpha}$$

Direction of R;

$$\tan\theta = \frac{CD}{OD} = \frac{Q\sin\alpha}{P + Q\cos\alpha}$$

$$\therefore \qquad \theta = \tan^{-1}\left(\frac{Q\sin\alpha}{P + Q\cos\alpha}\right)$$

8.1.2 Law of Triangle of Forces

If two forces acting at a point are represented by the two sides of a triangle taken in order, then their resultant is represented by the third side taken in an opposite order.

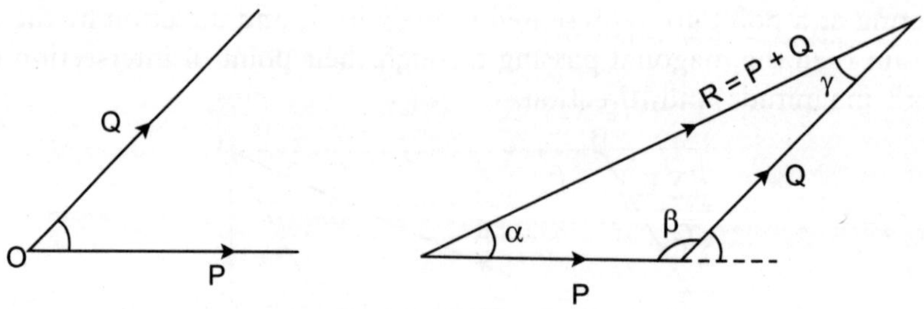

Fig. 8.3

$$\vec{R} = \vec{P} + \vec{Q} = \vec{Q} + \vec{P}$$

The magnitude of the resultant R can be found out graphically by measuring the length of vector R of the force triangle.

Also

$$R^2 = P^2 + Q^2 + 2PQ\cos(180 - \beta)$$
$$R^2 = P^2 + Q^2 - 2PQ\cos\beta$$

For finding remaining angle, we may use the sines rule as

$$\frac{P}{\sin\gamma} = \frac{Q}{\sin\alpha} = \frac{R}{\sin\beta}$$

8.2 Resultant of More Than Two Forces

8.2.1 Analytical Method

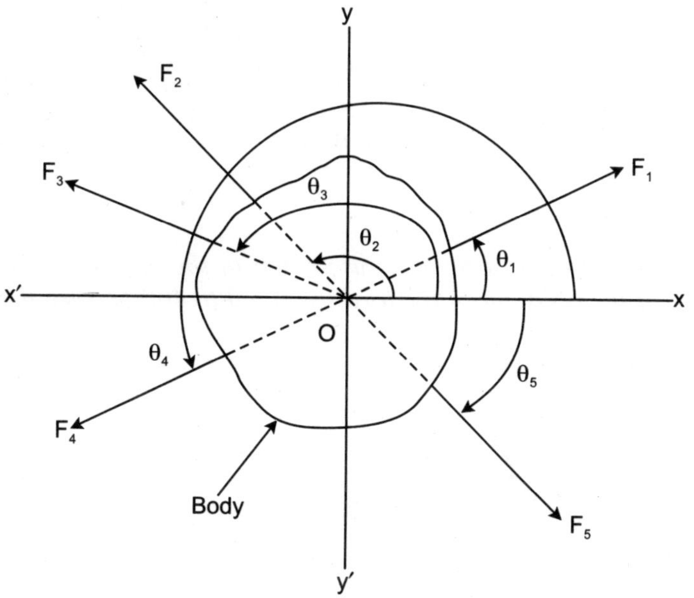

Fig. 8.4

$$\Sigma F_x = F_1\cos\theta_1 + F_2\cos\theta_2 + F_3\cos\theta_3 + F_4\cos\theta_4 - F_5\cos\theta_5$$
$$\Sigma F_y = F_1\sin\theta_1 + F_2\sin\theta_2 + F_3\sin\theta_3 + F_4\sin\theta_4 - F_5\sin\theta_5$$
$$R = \sqrt{(\Sigma F_x)^2 + (\Sigma F_y)^2}$$
$$\tan\theta = \frac{\Sigma F_y}{\Sigma F_x}$$

θ = Inclination of resultant (R) with x-axis in anticlockwise direction.

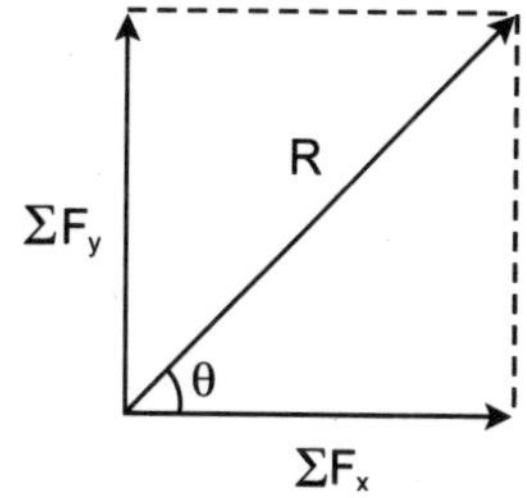

8.2.2 Polygon Law

If a number of concurrent coplanar forces are acting at a point such that they can be represented in magnitude and direction by the sides of a polygon taken in an order, their resultant is represented in both magnitude and direction by the closing side of the polygon taken in the opposite order.

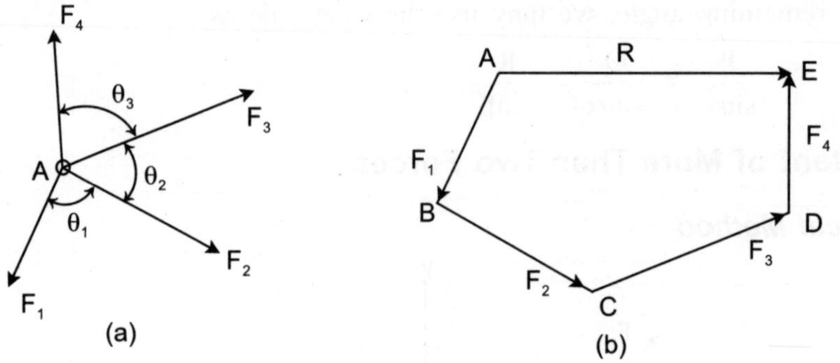

Fig. 8.5

Example 8.1

Two forces P and Q are acting at a point O as shown in the Fig. 8.6. The force P = 240 N and force Q = 200 N. If the resultant of the forces is equal to 400 N, then determine the values of angles α, β and γ.

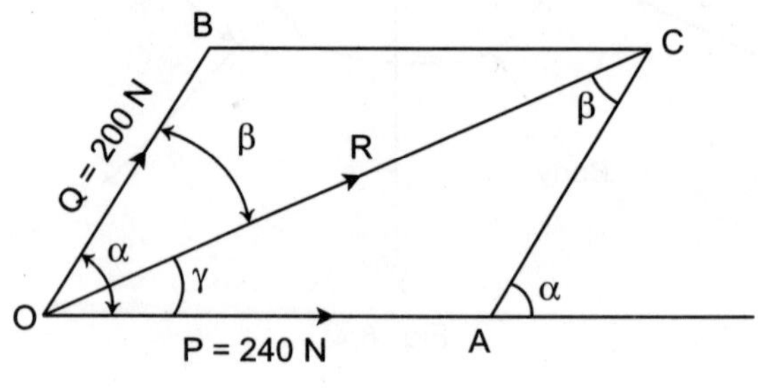

Fig. 8.6

Solution:

$$P = 240 \text{ N}$$
$$Q = 200 \text{ N}$$
$$R = 400 \text{ N}$$
$$\alpha = ?$$
$$\beta = ?$$
$$\gamma = ?$$

We know that

$$R = \sqrt{P^2 + Q^2 + 2PQ\cos\alpha}$$

$$\Rightarrow \quad 400^2 = (240)^2 + (200)^2 + 2 \times 240 \times 200 \times \cos\alpha$$

$$\Rightarrow \quad \cos\alpha = 0.65$$

$$\alpha = \mathbf{49.4^\circ}$$ **Ans.**

Now, using sine formulae for ΔOAC.

$$\frac{P}{\sin\beta} = \frac{Q}{\sin\gamma} = \frac{R}{\sin(180-\alpha)}$$

$$\therefore \quad \sin\beta = \frac{P\sin(180-\alpha)}{R} = \frac{240\sin(180-49.4)}{400} = 0.455$$

$$\therefore \quad \beta = \mathbf{27.1^\circ}$$ **Ans.**

and

$$\sin\gamma = \frac{Q\sin(180-\alpha)}{R} = \frac{200\sin(180-49.4)}{400} = 0.38$$

$$\gamma = \mathbf{22.2^\circ}$$ **Ans.**

Example 8.2

The forces F_1, F_2 and F_3 act at a point A of the bracket as shown in the Fig. 8.7. Determine the x and y scalar components of the three forces.

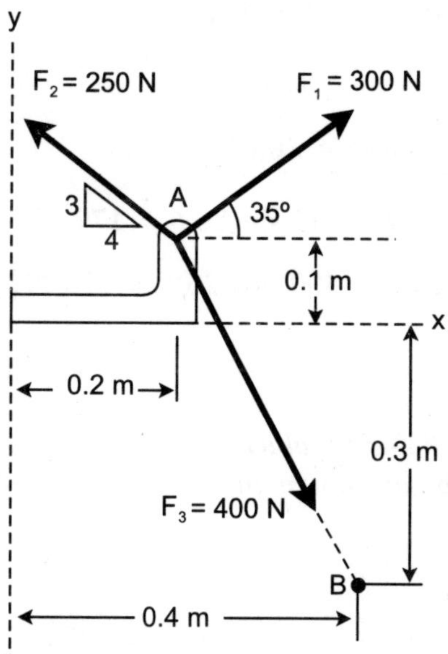

Fig. 8.7

Solution:

Scalar components of F_1

$$F_{1_x} = F_1 \cos 35 = 300 \cos 35$$
$$= \mathbf{245.8\ N} \qquad \textbf{Ans.}$$
$$F_{1_y} = F_1 \sin 35 = 300 \sin 35$$
$$= \mathbf{172\ N} \qquad \textbf{Ans.}$$

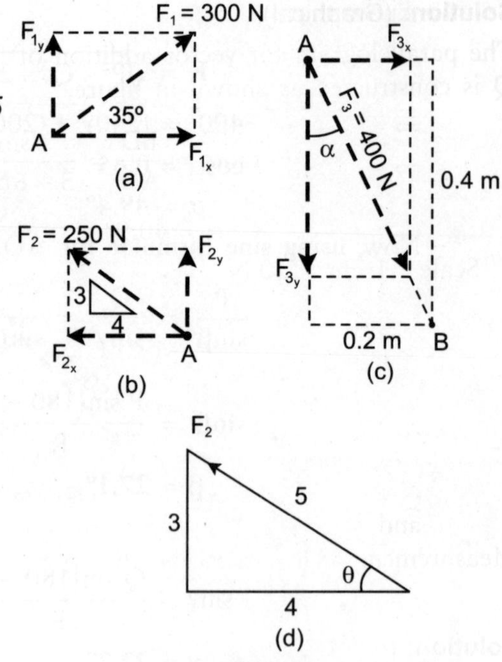

Fig. 8.8

Scalar components of F_2

$$\tan\theta = \frac{3}{4}$$

$$\therefore \quad F_{2_x} = F_2 \cos\theta(\leftarrow)$$
$$= 250 \times \frac{4}{5} = \mathbf{200\ N}\ (\leftarrow) \qquad \textbf{Ans.}$$
$$F_{2_y} = F_2 \sin\theta$$
$$= 250 \times \frac{3}{5} = \mathbf{150\ N}\ (\leftarrow) \qquad \textbf{Ans.}$$

Scalar components of F_3

$$\tan\alpha = \frac{0.2}{0.4} \Rightarrow \alpha = 26.6^\circ$$

$$\therefore \quad F_{3_x} = F_3 \sin\alpha = 400 \sin 26.6 = \mathbf{179\ N} \qquad \textbf{Ans.}$$
$$F_{3_y} = F_3 \cos\alpha = 400 \cos 26.6 = \mathbf{358\ N}(\downarrow) \qquad \textbf{Ans.}$$

Example 8.3

Find the resultant of two forces P and Q which act on the fixed structure at B, as shown in Fig. 8.9.

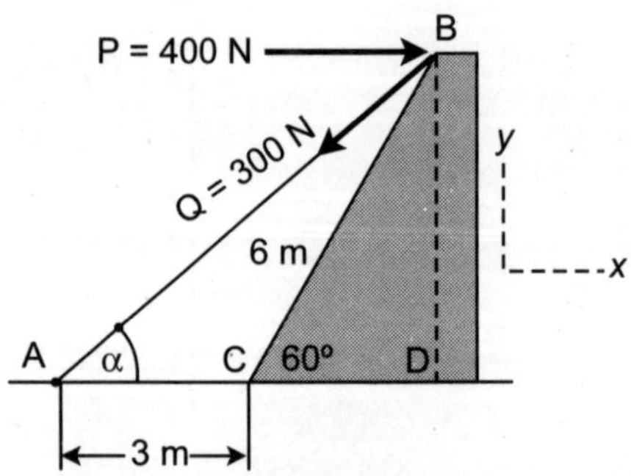

Fig. 8.9

Solution: (Graphical)

The parallelogram for vector addition of forces P and Q is constructed as shown in figure.

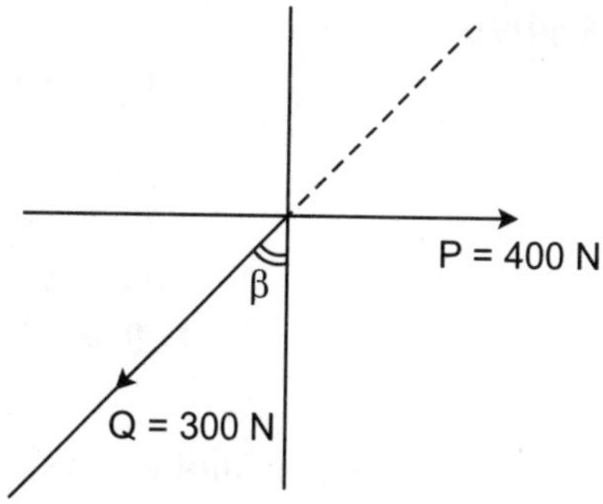

$$\tan\alpha = \frac{BD}{AD} = \frac{6\sin 60}{3 + 6\cos 60} = 0.866$$

$$\alpha = 40.9^\circ$$

Scale : 1 cm = 50 N

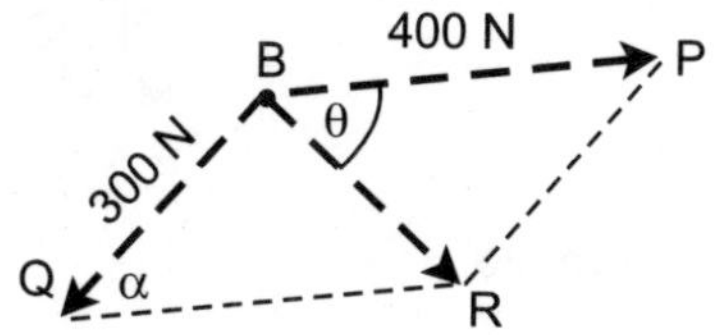

Fig. Vector Parallelogram

Measurement of length R and direction Q of the resultant force R are as:

$$R = 262 \text{ N}, \ \theta = 49^\circ$$

Solution: (Algebraic)

$$\Sigma F_x = 400 - 300 \sin 49.1 = 173.2 \text{ N} \ (\because \beta = 90 - \alpha = 90 - 40.9 = 49.1^\circ)$$

$$\Sigma F_y = -300 \cos 49.1 = -196.4 \text{ N}$$

$$\therefore \quad R = \sqrt{(\Sigma F_x)^2 + (\Sigma F_y)^2} = \sqrt{(173.2)^2 + (196.4)^2} = \mathbf{261.9\ N} \quad \textbf{Ans.}$$

$$Q = \tan^{-1}\left(\frac{\Sigma F_y}{\Sigma F_x}\right) = \tan^{-1}\left(\frac{196.4}{173.2}\right) = \mathbf{-48.6^\circ} \quad \textbf{Ans.}$$

Example 8.4

The resultant of 4 forces which are acting at a point as shown in Fig. 8.10, is along y-axis. Find the magnitude and direction of force F_2. The resultant is 72 kN.

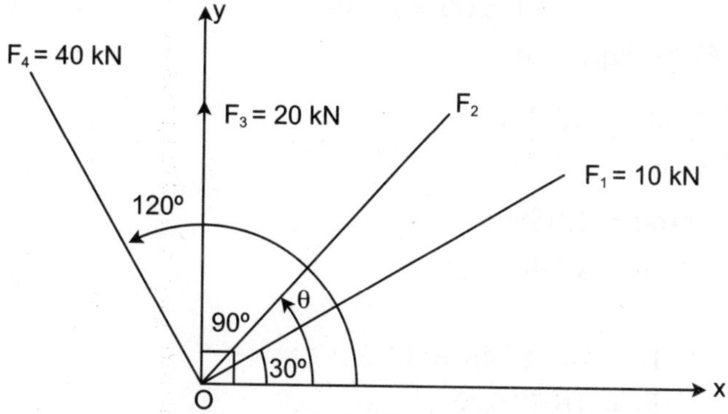

Fig. 8.10

Solution:

$F_1 = 10$ kN	$\theta_1 = 30°$
$F_2 = ?$	$\theta_2 = \theta$
$F_3 = 20$ kN	$\theta_3 = 90°$
$F_4 = 40$ kN	$\theta_4 = 120°$
$R = 72$ kN	

$\because$ Resultant is along y axis,

$$\theta = 90°$$

or $$\tan\theta = \frac{\Sigma F_y}{\Sigma F_x} = \tan 90$$

It means $$\Sigma F_x = 0 \quad \text{.......... (8.1)}$$

and $$\Sigma F_y = R \quad \text{.......... (8.2)}$$

From Eq. (8.1)

$$\Sigma F_x = 0 \Rightarrow F_1 \cos\theta_1 + F_2 \cos\theta_2 + F_3 \cos\theta_3 + F_4 \cos\theta_4 = 0$$

$$\Rightarrow 10 \cos 30 + F_2 \cos\theta + 20 \cos 90 + 40 \cos 120 = 0$$

$$\Rightarrow 5\sqrt{3} + F_2 \cos\theta + 0 + 40 \times \left(-\frac{1}{2}\right) = 0$$

$$\Rightarrow F_2 \cos\theta = 11.34 \quad \text{.......... (8.3)}$$

From Eq. (8.2)

$$\Sigma F_y = R \Rightarrow F_1 \sin\theta_1 + F_2 \sin\theta_2 + F_3 \sin\theta_3 + F_4 \sin\theta_4 = R$$

$$\Rightarrow 10 \sin 30 + F_2 \sin\theta + 20 \sin 90 + 40 \sin 120 = 72$$

$$\Rightarrow 5 + F_2 \sin\theta + 20 + 20\sqrt{3} = 72$$

$$\Rightarrow 25 + F_2 \sin\theta + 20\sqrt{3} = 72$$

$$\Rightarrow F_2 \sin\theta = 12.36 \quad \text{.......... (8.4)}$$

Dividing Eq. (8.4) by Eq. (8.3)

$$\frac{F_2 \sin\theta}{F_2 \cos\theta} = \frac{12.36}{11.34}$$

$\Rightarrow$ $$\tan\theta = \mathbf{1.0899°} \quad \textbf{Ans.}$$

$$\theta = \mathbf{47.46°} \quad \textbf{Ans.}$$

From Eq. (8.4)

$$F_2 = \sin 47.46 = 12.36$$

$$F_2 = \mathbf{16.77\ kN} \quad \textbf{Ans.}$$

Example 8.5

Determine the magnitude of a horizontal force P applied at the centre C of a roller of weight 1000 N and radius 15 cm, which will be necessary to pull it over a 3 cm curb.

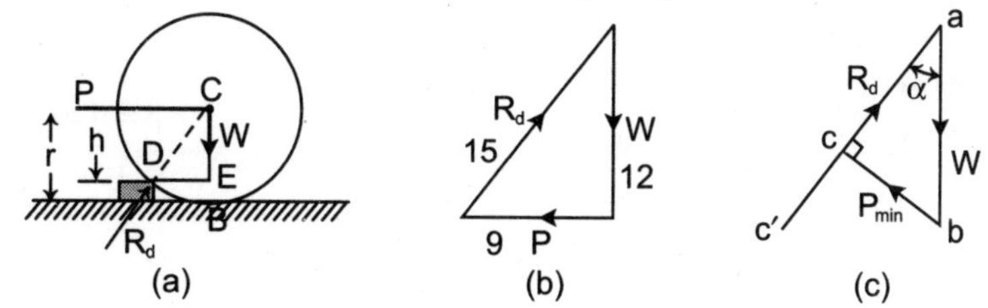

Fig. 8.11

Solution:

$$W = 1000\ N \qquad r = 15\ cm$$
$$P = ? \qquad BE = 3\ cm$$

When P is just sufficient to cause motion of the roller to impend, then there will be no reaction between roller and horizontal plane at B. Since, P and W intersect at the centric of the cylinder, the reaction R_d must pass through this same point as the forces are concurrent.

The triangle of forces will be similar to ΔCED, from which

$$\frac{P}{W} = \frac{DE}{CE} = \frac{9}{12} = \frac{3}{4}$$

$$\therefore \quad P = \frac{3}{4} \times 1000 = \mathbf{750\ N} \qquad \textbf{Ans.}$$

and

$$\frac{R_d}{W} = \frac{15}{12} = \frac{5}{4}$$

$$\therefore \quad R_d = 1000 \times \frac{5}{4} = \mathbf{1250\ N} \qquad \textbf{Ans.}$$

Example 8.6

A weight of 3 kN is supported by two chains AC and BC as shown in Fig. 8.12. Determine the tension in each chain.

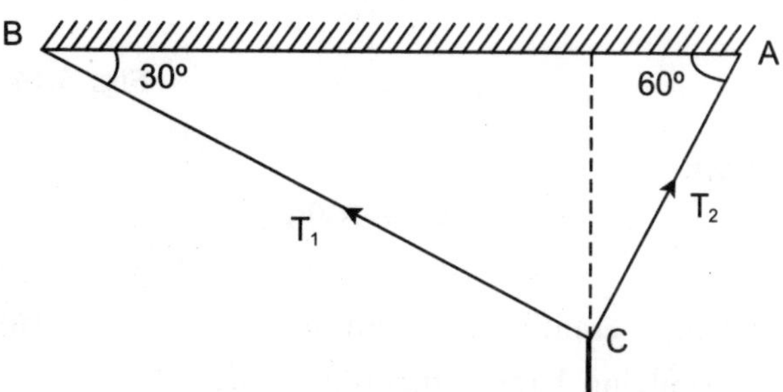

Fig. 8.12

Solution:

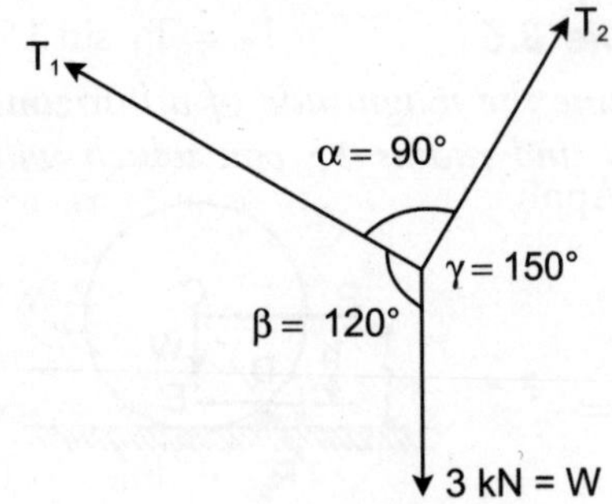

Fig. 8.13

$$W = 3 \text{ kN} = 3000 \text{ N}$$
$$T_1 = ?$$
$$T_2 = ?$$

Using Lame's theorem

$$\frac{T_1}{\sin\gamma} = \frac{T_2}{\sin\beta} = \frac{W}{\sin\alpha}$$

$$\Rightarrow \quad \frac{T_1}{\sin 150°} = \frac{T_2}{\sin 120°} = \frac{3000}{\sin 90°}$$

$$\therefore \quad T_1 = 3000 \sin 150 = \mathbf{1500\ N}$$ **Ans.**

$$T_2 = 3000 \sin 120 = \mathbf{2598\ N}$$ **Ans.**

Example 8.7

A string ABCDE has weights W_1 and W_2 attached to it at B and C and passes round a smooth peg at D carrying a weight of 1000 N at the free end E. If in a state of equilibrium BC is horizontal, AB and CD make angles of 150° and 120° respectively with BC, find:

i. the tensions in portions AB, BC, CD and DE of the string.

ii. the value of weights W_1 and W_2.

iii. the pressure on the peg D.

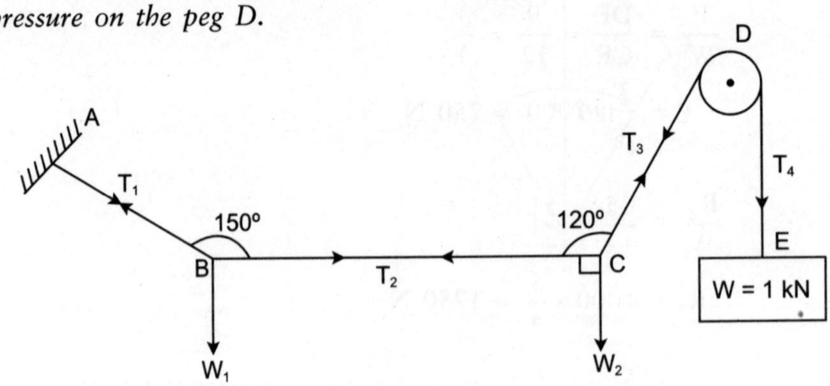

Fig. 8.14

Solution:

$$W = 1000 \text{ N}$$
$$T_1 = ?;\ T_2 = ?;\ T_3 = ?;\ T_4 = ?$$

i. Under equilibrium condition. $T_3 = T_4 = 1000$ N

Applying Lame's theorem at C.

$$\frac{T_2}{\sin 150°} = \frac{T_3}{\sin 90°} = \frac{W_2}{\sin 120°}$$

$$T_2 = T_3 \sin 150° = 1000 \sin 150° = 500 \text{ N}$$

$$W_2 = 1000 \sin 120 = \mathbf{866 \text{ N}}$$ **Ans.**

ii. Applying Lame's theorem at point B.

$$\frac{T_1}{\sin 90°} = \frac{T_2}{\sin 120°} = \frac{W_1}{\sin 150°}$$

$$\Rightarrow \quad T_1 = 500 \sin 90°/\sin 120° = 577.4 \text{ N}$$

$$W_2 = 500 \sin 150°/\sin 120° = \mathbf{288.6 \text{ N}}$$ **Ans.**

iii. Pressure at D = $T_3 \sin 60° + 1000 = \mathbf{1866 \text{ N}}$ **Ans.**

Example 8.8

Find the resultant of forces 3, $\sqrt{3}$, 6, $\sqrt{3}$ and 2 N that act an angular point of a rectangular hexagon towards the other angular points takes in order.

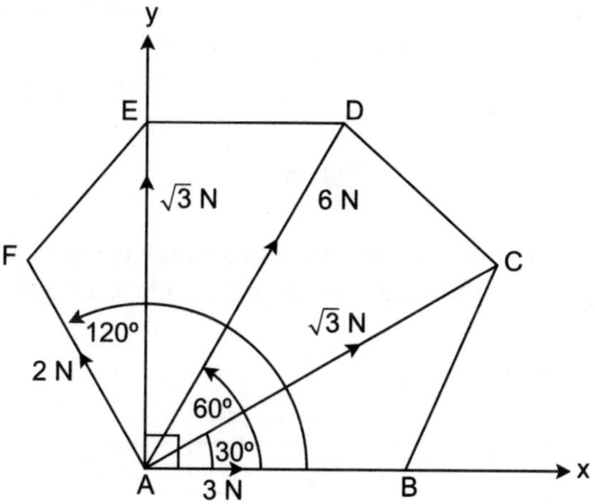

Fig. 8.15

Resolving all the forces along x axis and y axis.

Solution:

$$\Sigma F_x = 3 + \sqrt{3} \cos 30° + 6 \cos 60° + \sqrt{3} \cos 90° + 2 \cos 120° = 6.5 \text{ N}$$

$$\Sigma F_y = \sqrt{3} \sin 30° + 6 \sin 60° + \sqrt{3} \sin 90° + 2 \sin 120° = 9.53 \text{ N}$$

$$R = \sqrt{(\Sigma F_x)^2 + (\Sigma F_y)^2} = \sqrt{(6.5)^2 + (9.53)^2} = \mathbf{11.53 \text{ N}}$$ **Ans.**

$$\theta = \tan^{-1}\left(\frac{\Sigma F_y}{\Sigma F_x}\right) = \tan^{-1}\left(\frac{9.53}{6.5}\right) = \mathbf{55.7°}$$ **Ans.**

THEORETICAL & NUMERICAL QUESTIONS

1. Define matter, particle and body. How does a rigid body differ from an elastic body?
2. State Newton's Law of Motion.
3. Two rods and one cable are attached to the support at O. If the two of the forces are as shown, determine the magnitude F and direction Q of the third force so that the resultant of the three forces is vertically downward with a magnitude of 6 kN.

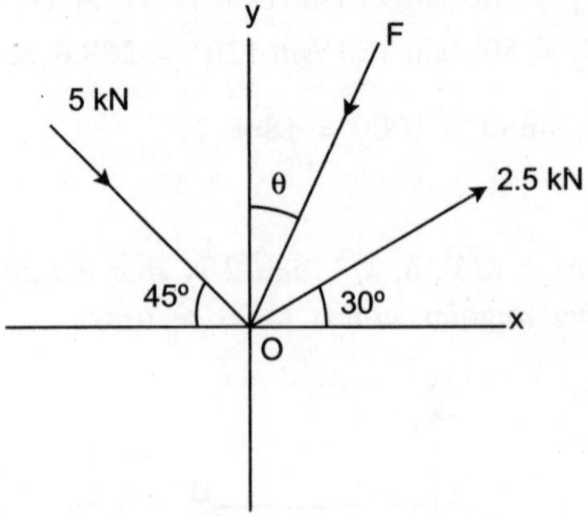

Fig. 8.16

4. Determine the equivalent force-couple system at the centre C for each of the three cases of forces being applied to the edges of a square plate of side a.

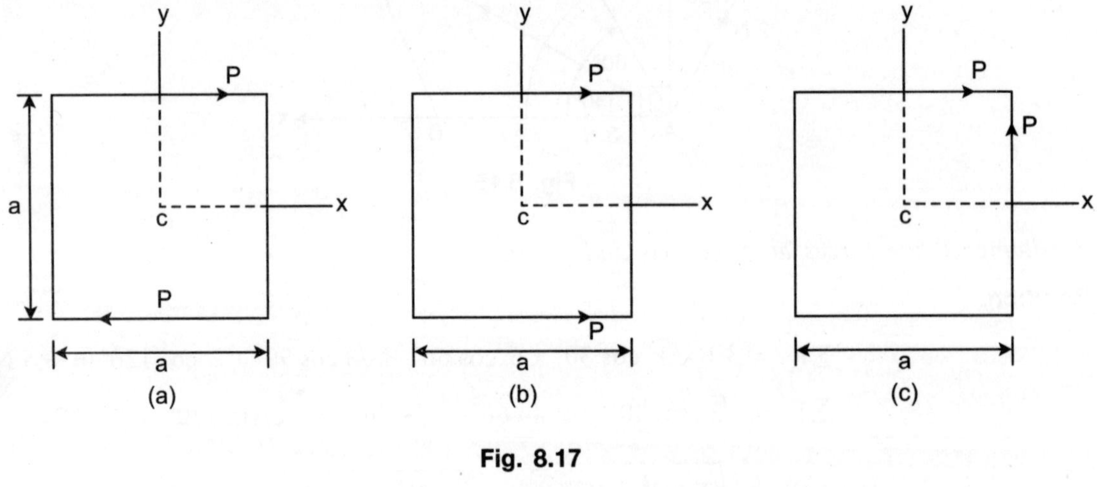

Fig. 8.17

5. A flanged steel cantilever beam with riveted bracket is subjected to the couple and two forces are shown. Replace the two forces and couple by an equivalent couple M and resultant force R at A.

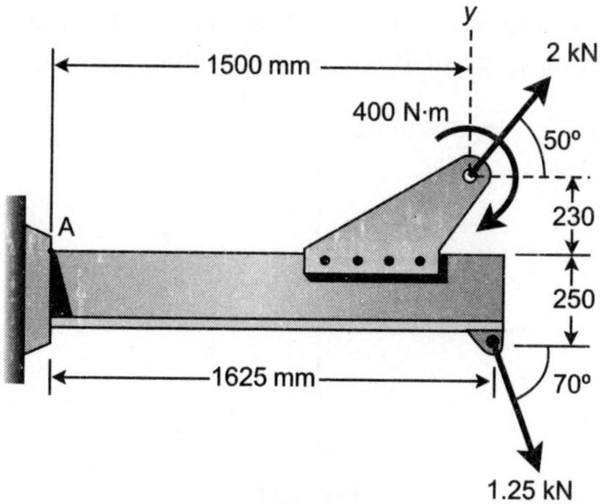

Fig. 8.18

6. Determine height h above the base B at which the resultant of the three forces acts. (h = 1500 mm)

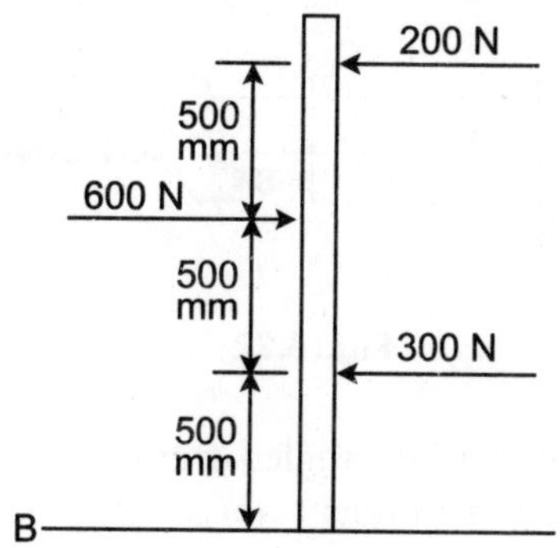

Fig. 8.19

7. Determine and locate the resultant R of the two forces and one couple acting on the I-beam. [3 kN↓, x = 2.67 m]

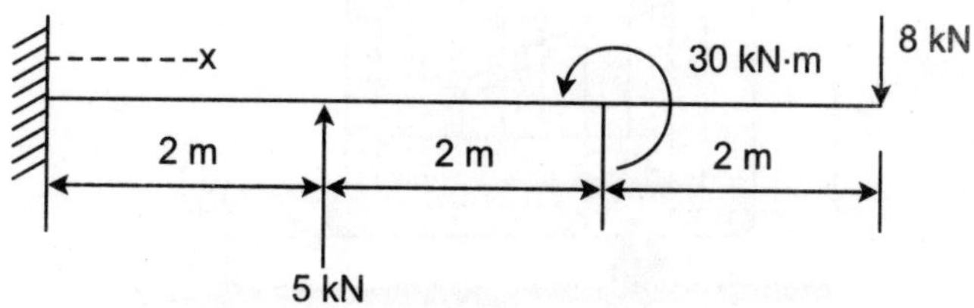

Fig. 8.20

8. The 30 kN force F is applied at a point A. Calculate the moment of F about point O. Specify the x-cordinate of point B on the x-axis about which the moment of F is zero.

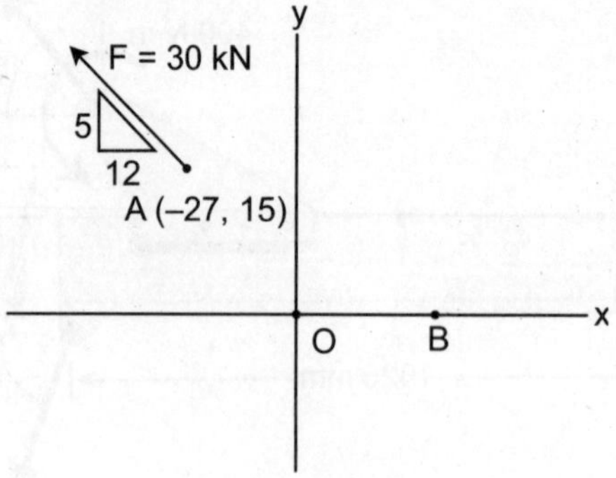

Fig. 8.21

9. Calculate the moment of the 250 N force on the handle of the monkey wrench about the centre of the bolt.

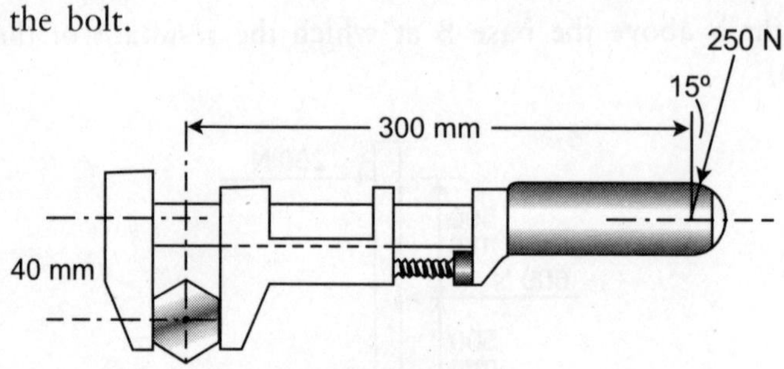

Fig. 8.22

10. A wooden crate is resting on a right angled frame that is pivoted at O and supported at A. The force P must supply a moment about O of 1.5 kN·m in order to reduce the support force at A to zero.

Find F.

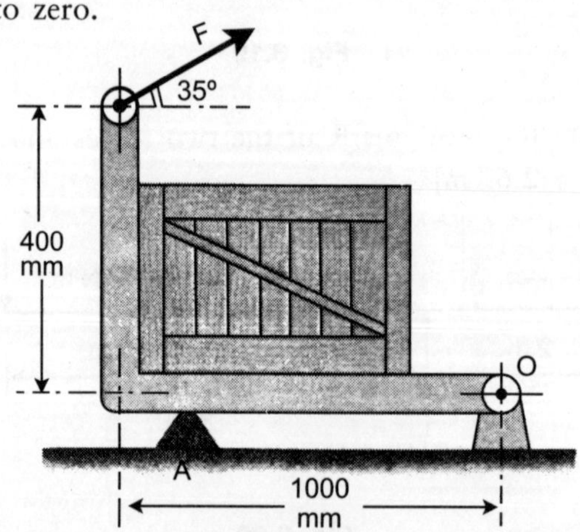

Fig. 8.23

11. Determine the moment about point A caused by the 200 kN tension in the hoisting cable of the tractor crane.

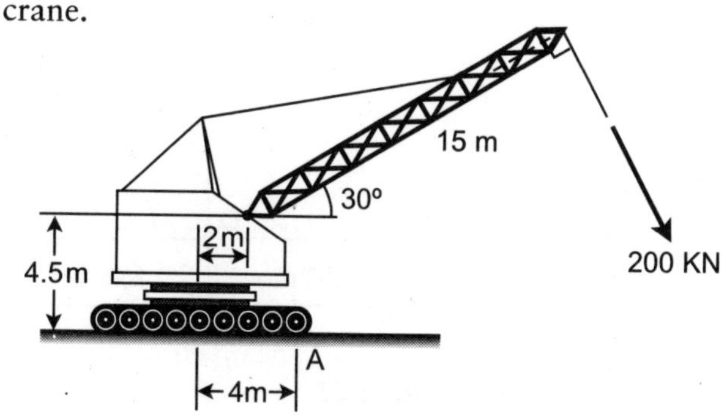

Fig. 8.24

12. In raising the flagpole from the position shown, the tension T in the cable must supply a moment about O of 8.2 kN·m. Determine T.

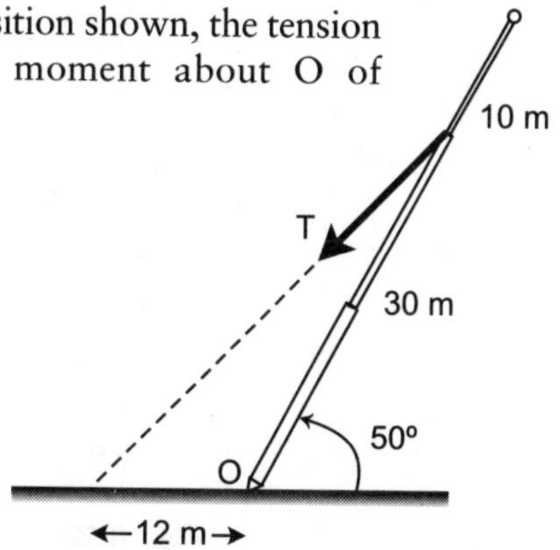

Fig. 8.25

13. The uniform work platform, which has a mass per unit length of 30 kg/m, is simply supported by cross rods A and B. The 80 kg construction worker starts from point B and walks to the right. At what locations, the combined moment of the weights of the man and platform about point B be zero.

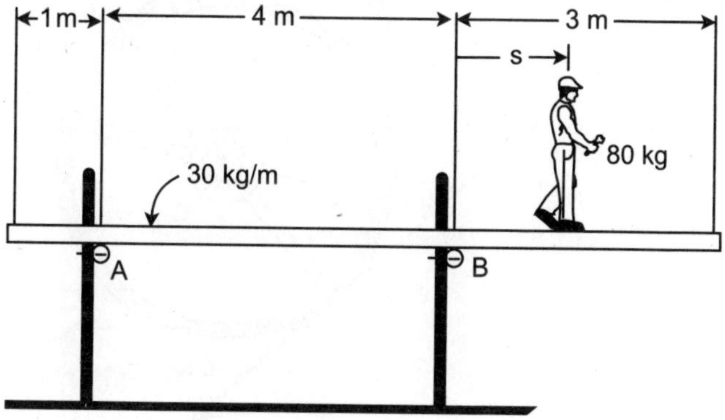

Fig. 8.26

14. Calculate the combined moment of the two 600 N forces about point O and about point A.

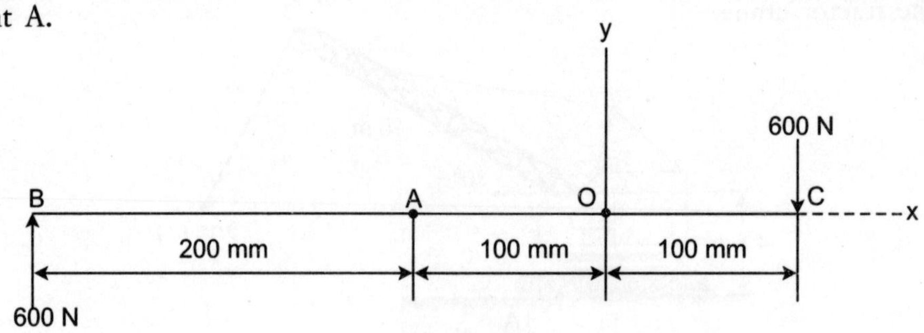

Fig. 8.27

15. Replace the 12 kN force acting at a point A by a force couple system at point O, at point B.

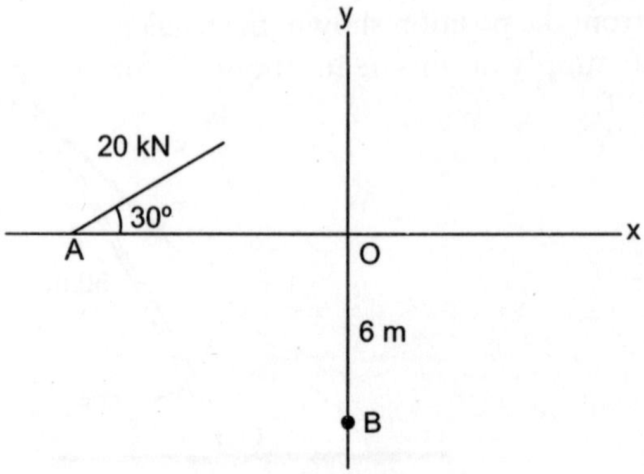

Fig. 8.28

16. When making a left turn, a driver exerts two forces on a steering wheel. Find moment associated with these forces.

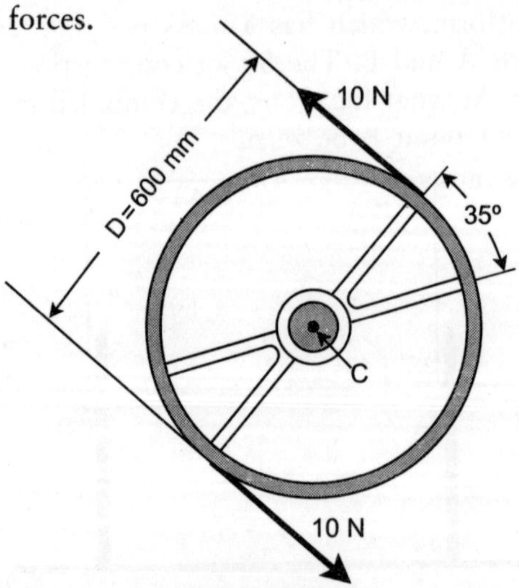

Fig. 8.29

17. In the design of the lifting hook the action of the applied force P at the critical section of the hook is a direct pull at B and a couple. If the magnitude of the couple is 6000 N·m, determine magnitude of F.

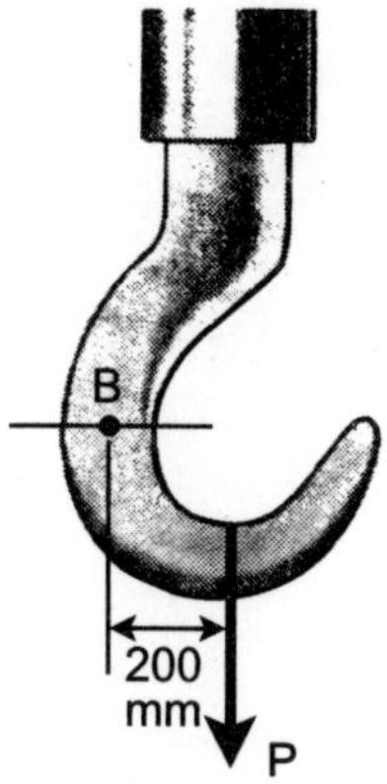

Fig. 8.30

18. Different loads are acting on a beam as shown. Determine the resultant of the loads.

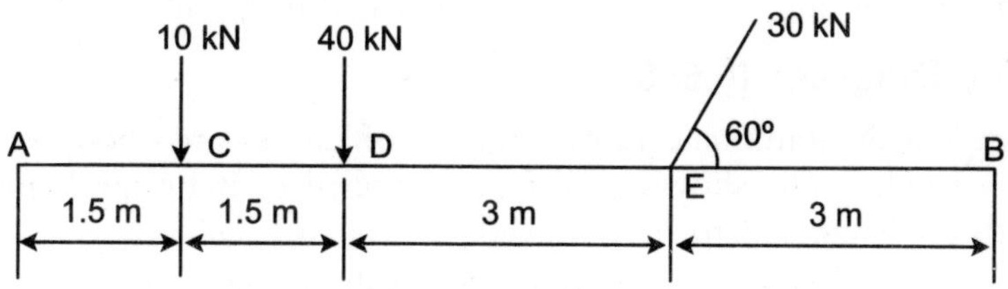

Fig. 8.31

9 Equilibrium

9.1 Introduction

When a body is in equilibrium, the resultant force R and resultant couple M are both zero and we have the equations

$$\Sigma F = 0 \quad \text{(9.1)}$$

$$\Sigma M = 0 \quad \text{(9.2)}$$

These requirements are both necessary and sufficient for equilibrium.

9.2 Free Body Diagram (F.B.D.)

Free body diagram is a diagrammatic representation of the isolated body or combination of bodies treated as a single body, showing all forces applied to it by mechanical contact with other bodies which are imagined to be removed.

The F.B.D. is the most important single step in the solution of problems in solid mechanics.

Table 9.1

Type of contact and force origin		*Action on Body to be isolated*
1. Smooth surfaces	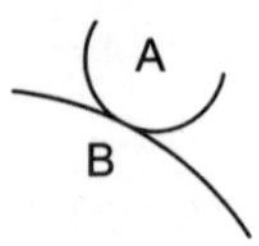	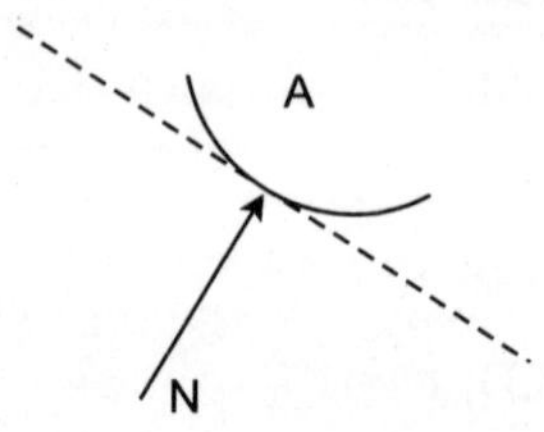
2. Rough surfaces	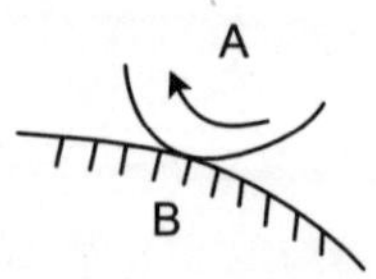	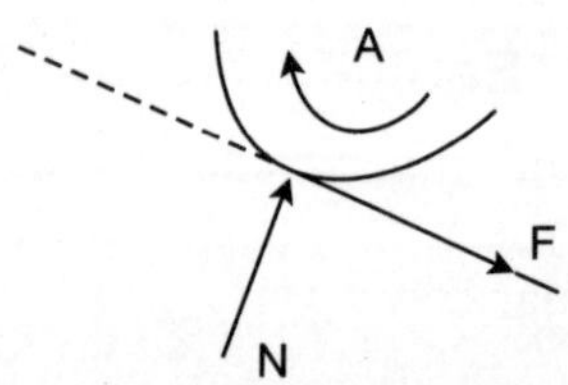

Type of contact and force origin		*Action on body to be isolated*
3. Roller support	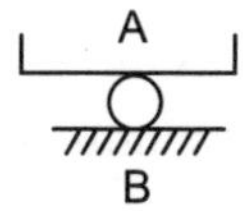	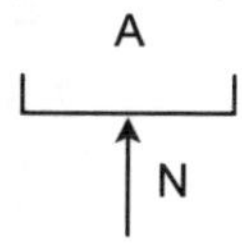
4. Pin or Hinge connection	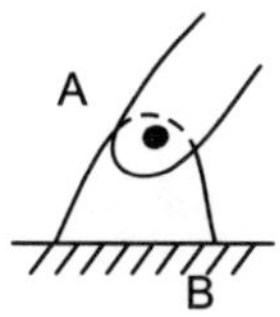	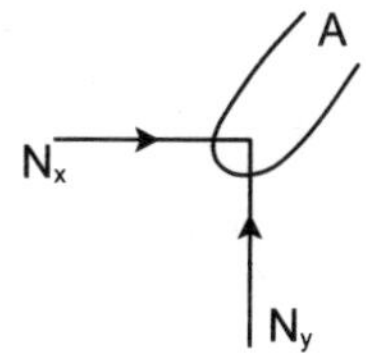
5. Built in or fixed support		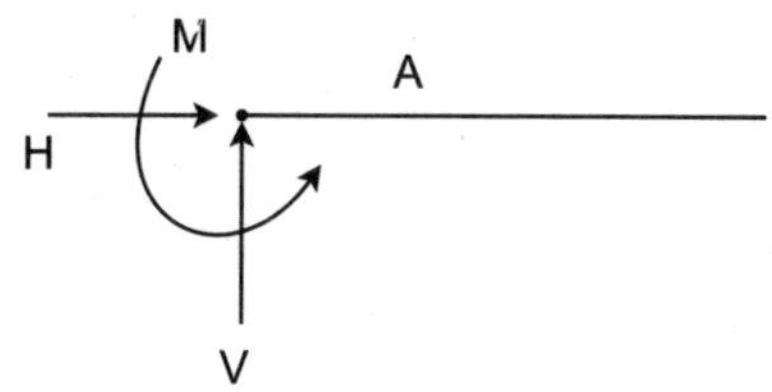

9.3 Construction of F.B.D.

Main steps are:

1. A clear decision is made concerning which body or combination of bodies is to be isolated.
2. The body chosen is isolated by a diagram which represents its complete external boundary. This is an important task. We should always be certain that we have completely isolated the body before proceeding to the next step.
3. All forces which act on the isolated body as applied by the removed contacting or attracting bodies are next represented in their proper positions on the diagram of the isolated body.
4. The choice of coordinate axes should be indicated correctly on the diagram.

F.B.D. serves the purpose of focussing accurate attention on the action of the external forces. When all the above four steps are completed, a correct F.B.D. will result.

9.4 Equilibrium Conditions

In equilibrium condition, the resultant of all forces acting on a body is zero. In other words, a body is in equilibrium if all forces and moments applied to it are in balance. It may be written in scalar form as

$$\Sigma F_x = 0 \quad \text{.......} \quad (9.3a)$$

$$\Sigma F_y = 0 \quad \text{.......} \quad (9.3b)$$

$$\Sigma M_o = 0 \quad \text{.......} \quad (9.3c)$$

Where ΣF_x = Sum of all horizontal forces

ΣF_y = Sum of all vertical forces

ΣM_o = Sum of all moments

These are the necessary and sufficient conditions of equilibrium.

Example 9.1

Determine the magnitude of the forces F_2 and F_4, which along with the other three forces shown in Fig. 9.1.

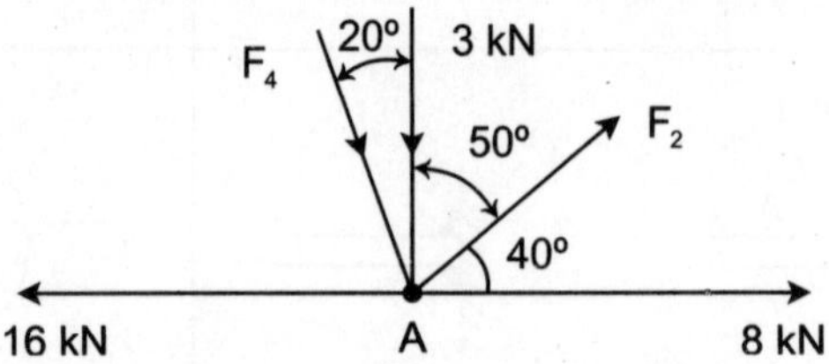

Fig. 9.1

Solution:

$F_1 = 8$ kN

$F_2 = ?$

$F_3 = 3$ kN

$F_4 = ?$

$F_5 = 16$ kN

$\theta_1 = 0$

$\theta_2 = 40°$

$\theta_3 = 270°$

$\theta_4 = 290°$

$\theta_5 = 180°$

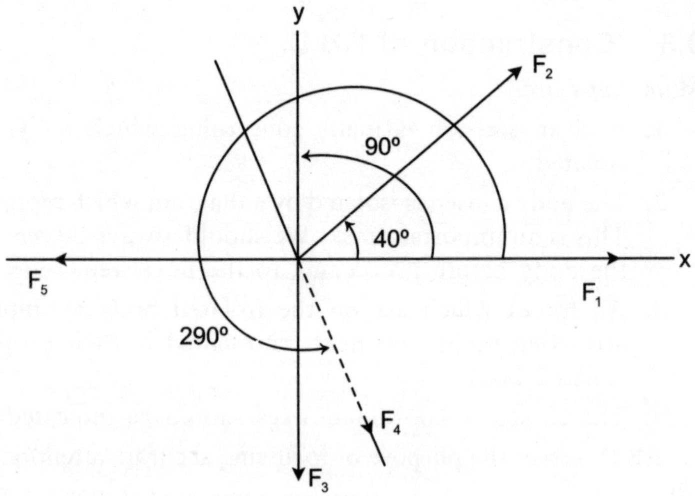

Fig. 9.2

Now, for equilibrium

$$\Sigma F_x = 0$$

$$\Rightarrow F_1 \cos\theta_1 + F_2 \cos\theta_2 + F_3 \cos\theta_3 + F_4 \cos\theta_4 + F_5 \cos\theta_5 = 0$$

$$\Rightarrow 8 \cos 0 + F_2 \cos 40 + 3 \cos 270 + F_4 \cos 290 + 16 \cos 180 = 0$$

$$\Rightarrow 8 \times 1 + F_2 \times 0.766 + 3 \times 0 + F_4 \times 0.342 + 16 \times (-1) = 0$$

$$\Rightarrow \; 8 + 0.766F_2 + 0 + 0.342F_4 - 16 = 0$$

$$\Rightarrow \; 8 + 0.766F_2 + 0.342F_4 - 16 = 0$$

$$\Rightarrow \; 0.766F_2 + 0.342F_4 = 8 \quad \ldots\ldots (9.4)$$

Now

$$\Sigma F_y = 0$$

$$\Rightarrow \; F_1 \sin\theta_1 + F_2 \sin\theta_2 + F_3 \sin\theta_3 + F_4 \sin\theta_4 + F_5 \sin\theta_5 = 0$$

$$\Rightarrow \; 8 \sin 0 + F_2 \sin 40 + 3 \sin 270 + F_4 \sin 290 + 16 \sin 180 = 0$$

$$\Rightarrow \; 8 \times 0 + F_2 \times 0.643 + 3 \times (-1) + F_4 \times (-0.94) + 16 \times 0 = 0$$

$$\Rightarrow \; 0 + 0.643F_2 - 3 - 0.94F_4 + 0 = 0$$

$$\Rightarrow \; 0.643F_2 - 0.94F_4 = 3 \quad \ldots\ldots (9.5)$$

From Eq. (9.4),

$$F_2 = \left(\frac{8 - 0.342\,F_4}{0.766}\right) \quad \ldots\ldots (9.6)$$

From Eq. (9.4),

$$F_2 = \left(\frac{3 + 0.94\,F_4}{0.643}\right) \quad \ldots\ldots (9.7)$$

Equating Eqs. (9.6) and (9.7)

$$\frac{8 - 0.342F_4}{0.766} = \frac{3 + 0.94F_4}{0.643}$$

$$\Rightarrow \; 5.144 - 0.22F_4 = 2.30 + 0.72F_4$$

$$\Rightarrow \; 0.72F_4 + 0.22F_4 = 5.14 - 2.30$$

$$\Rightarrow \; F_4 = \frac{2.84}{0.94} = 3.02 \text{ kN}$$

$$\therefore \; \mathbf{F_4 = 3.02 \text{ kN}}$$ **Ans.**

Now, from Eq. (9.6)

$$F_2 = \frac{8 - 0.342F_4}{0.766}$$

$$= \frac{8 - 0.342 \times 3.02}{0.766}$$

$$\mathbf{F_2 = 9.09 \text{ kN}}$$ **Ans.**

Example 9.2

Three parallel forces F_1, F_2 and F_3 are acting on a body as shown in Fig. 9.3 and the body is in equilibrium. If force F_1 = 300 N, F_3 = 1200 N and distance between F_1 and F_2 is 1 m, then determine the magnitude of force F_2 and the distance of F_2 from force F_3.

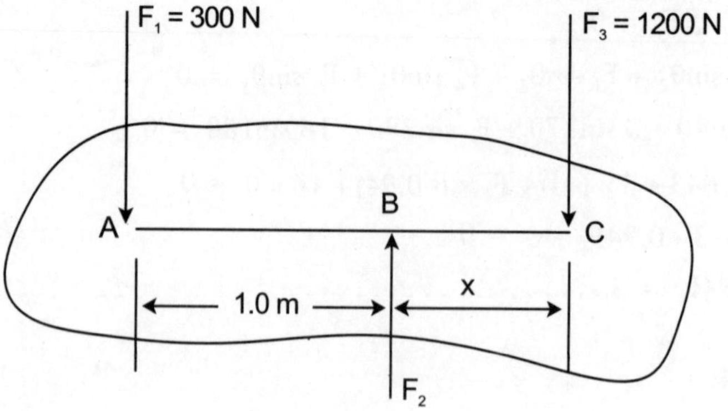

Fig. 9.3

Solution:

F_1 = 300 N, F_2 = ?, F_3 = 1200 N, AB = 1.0 m, BC = ?

For equilibrium of the body,

$$\Sigma F_x = 0 \Rightarrow \text{No force in horizontal direction.}$$

$$\Sigma F_y = 0 \Rightarrow F_1 + F_3 = F_2$$

$$\Rightarrow 300 + 1200 = F_2$$

$$\Rightarrow F_2 = \mathbf{1500\ N}$$ **Ans.**

Also, for equilibrium,

$$\Sigma M = 0 \Rightarrow \Sigma M_A = 0$$

$$\Rightarrow F_3 \times AC\ (\circlearrowright) + F_2 \times AB (\circlearrowleft) = 0$$

$$\Rightarrow F_3 \times (1 + x) = F_2 \times 1$$

$$\Rightarrow 1 + x = \frac{1500}{1200}$$

$$\Rightarrow x = \frac{5}{4} - 1$$

$$x = \mathbf{0.25\ m}$$ **Ans.**

Example 9.3

Calculate the magnitude T of the tension in the cable and the force on the pin at A for the jib crane shown. The beam AB is 6.0 m I-beam with a mass of 90 kg per meter of length.

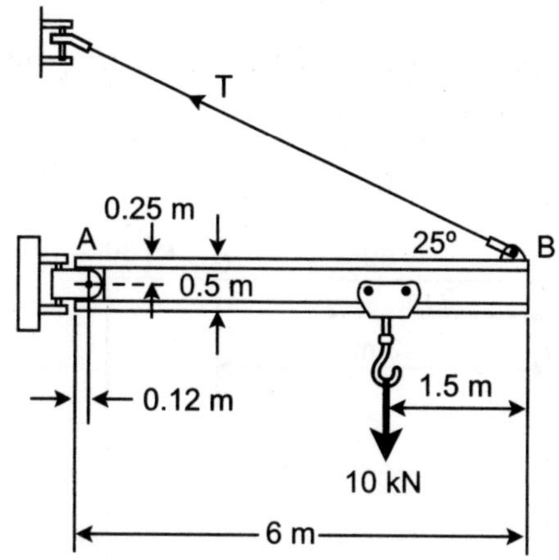

Fig. 9.4

Solution:

$$T = ?,\ R_A = ?$$

The weight of beam is

$$W = 90 \times 6 \times 9.81 \text{ N}$$
$$= 5297.4 \text{ N}$$
$$= 5.3 \text{ kN}$$

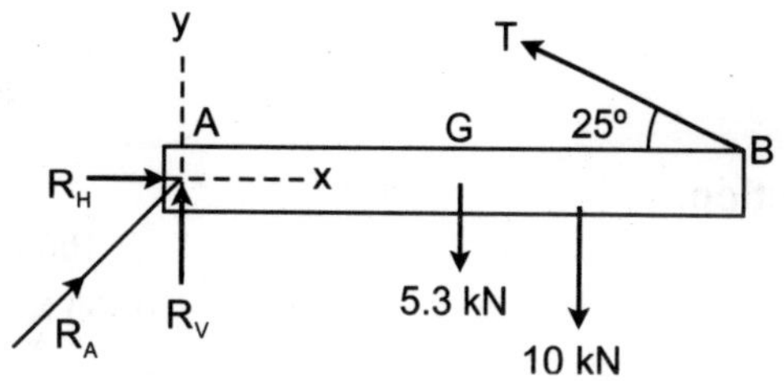

Fig. 9.5

For equilibrium;

$$\Sigma M_A = 0 \Rightarrow T\cos 25 \times 0.25(\circlearrowleft) + T\sin 25 \times (6 - 0.12)(\circlearrowleft) + 10 \times (6 - 1.5 - 0.12)(\circlearrowright) + 5.3 \times (3 - 0.12)(\circlearrowright)$$

$$\Rightarrow 0.249T + 2.485T = 43.8 + 15.264$$

$$\Rightarrow 2.734T = 59.064$$

$$T = \mathbf{21.6\ kN}$$ **Ans.**

Now

$$\Sigma F_x = 0 \Rightarrow R_H = T\cos 25$$

$$\therefore \quad R_H = 21.6\cos 25 = 19.58 \text{ kN}$$

$$\Sigma F_y = 0 \Rightarrow R_V = T\sin 25 = 5.3 + 10$$

$$\therefore \quad R_V = 15.3 - 9.13 = 6.17 \text{ kN}$$

$$\therefore \quad R_A = \sqrt{(R_H)^2 + (R_V)^2}$$

$$= \sqrt{(19.58)^2 + (6.17)^2}$$

$$R_A = 20.53 \text{ kN}$$ **Ans.**

Example 9.4

Figure (below) shows the Co-planar System of forces acting on a flat plate. Find resultant vertical and horizontal intercepts of the resultant.

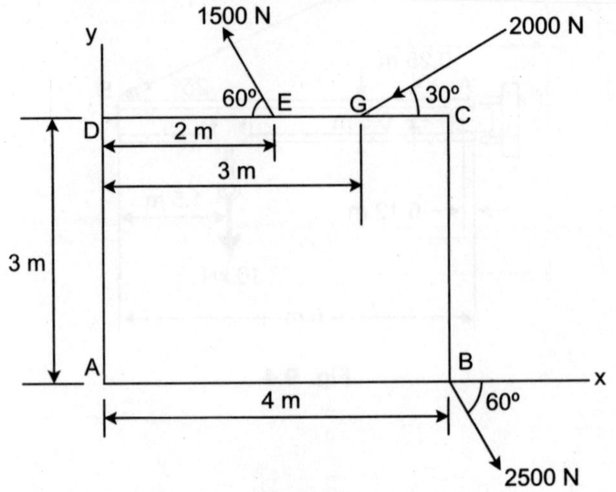

Fig. 9.6

Solution:

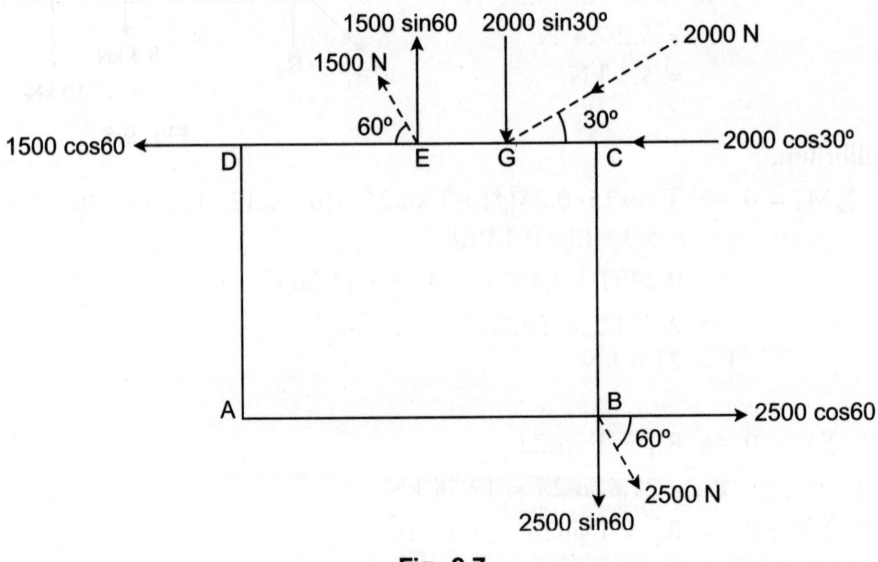

Fig. 9.7

Resultant, R = ?

Intercepts on x-axis and y-axis = ?

All the forces acting at points B, G and E are resolved in horizontal and vertical components as shown in Fig. 9.8.

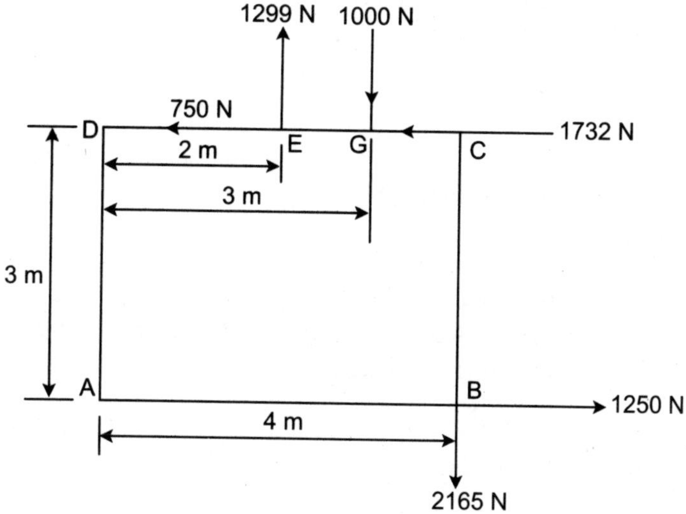

Fig. 9.8

Now

Net force along x-axis

$$\Sigma F_x = 1250 - 1732 - 750 = -1232 \text{ N } (\leftarrow)$$

and $$\Sigma F_y = -2165 - 1000 + 1299 = -1866 \text{ N } (\downarrow)$$

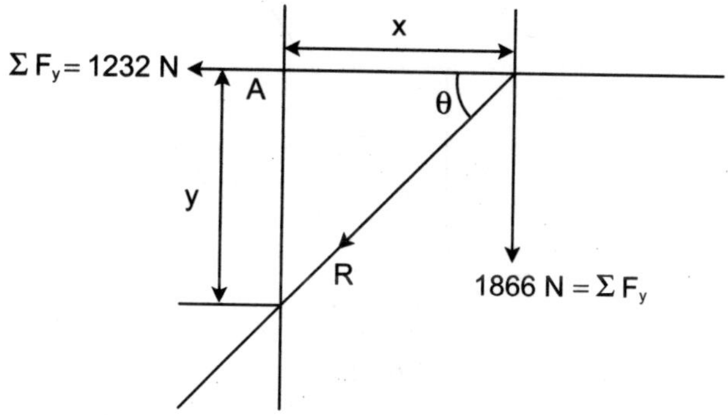

Fig. 9.9

Resultant Force,

$$R = \sqrt{(\Sigma F_x)^2 + (\Sigma F_y)^2}$$

$$= \sqrt{(1232)^2 + (1866)^2} = 2236 \text{ N}$$

$$\mathbf{R = 2236 \text{ N}}$$ **Ans.**

Angle made by resultant R with x-axis is given by

$$\tan\theta = \frac{\Sigma F_y}{\Sigma F_x} = \frac{1866}{1232}$$

$$\theta = 56.7^\circ$$

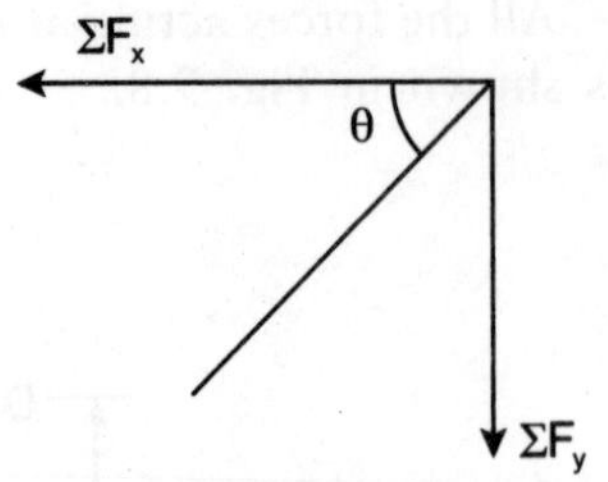

Fig. 9.10

Net moment about point A (see Fig. 9.8)

$$\Sigma M_A = 0$$

$$\Rightarrow 2165 \times 4(\circlearrowright) + 1732 \times 3(\circlearrowleft) + 1000 \times 3(\circlearrowright) + 1299 \times 2(\circlearrowleft) + 750 \times 3(\circlearrowleft)$$

$$= 2165 \times 4(\circlearrowright) + 3000(\circlearrowright) + 1732 \times 3(\circlearrowleft) + 1299 \times 2(\circlearrowleft) + 750 \times 3(\circlearrowleft)$$

$$= 11660(\circlearrowright) + 10044(\circlearrowleft)$$

$$= 1616(\circlearrowright)$$

$$\Sigma M_A = 1616 \text{ N·m (Clockwise)}$$

It means that the body has a tendency to rotate in clockwise direction. Therefore, the resultant must pass towards right of point A, making an angle of 56.7° with x-axis as shown in Fig. 9.11.

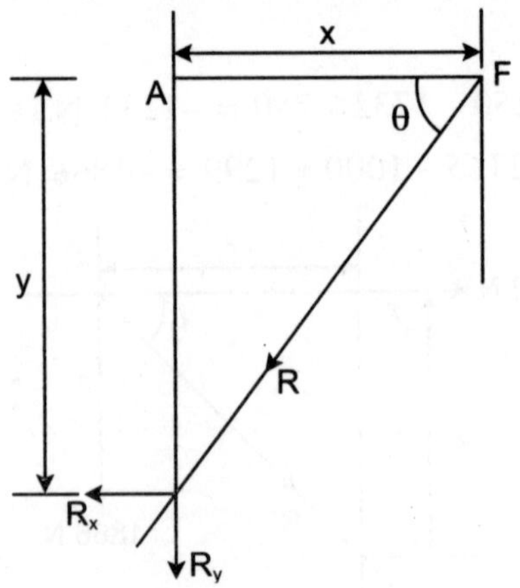

Fig. 9.11

Intercepts of resultant on x-axis and y-axis are x and y.

Using Varignon's theorem:

Taking moment about point 'A'

$$R_x \cdot y = \text{Sum of all moments}$$

$$R\cos\theta \cdot y = 1616$$

$$1866 \times \cos 56.7 \times y = 1616$$

$$y = \mathbf{1.58 \text{ m} \quad below\ A}$$ **Ans.**

Taking moment about F,

$$R_y \cdot x = 1616$$

$$1866 \times \sin 56.7 \times x = 1616$$

$$x = \mathbf{1.03\ m\ \ right\ of\ A}$$ **Ans.**

Example 9.5

A circular roller of weight 200 N and radius 20 cm, hangs by a tie rod AB = 40 cm and rests against a smooth vertical wall at C as shown in Fig. 9.12. Determine (a) The force F in the tie rod and (b) The reaction at point C.

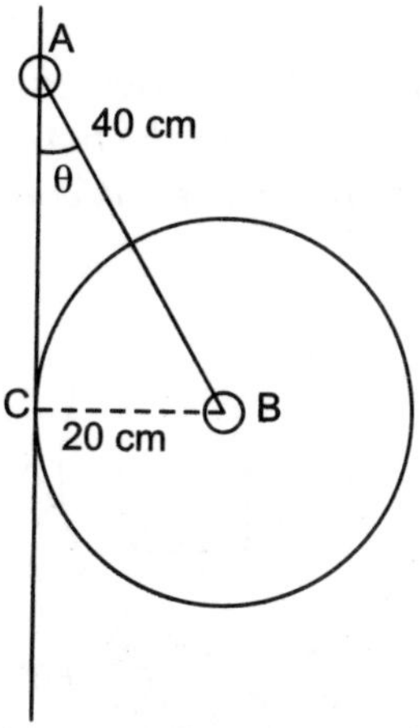

Fig. 9.12

Solution:

$$W = 200\ N$$
$$BC = r = 20\ cm$$
$$AB = 40\ cm$$
$$F = ?$$
$$R_C = ?$$

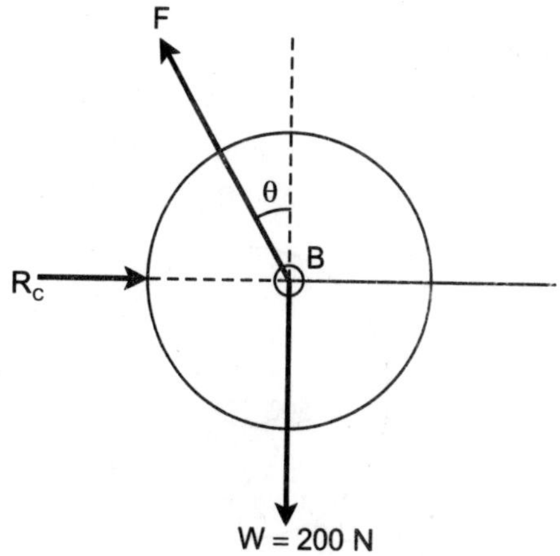

Fig. 9.13

Now

$$\sin\theta = \frac{BC}{AB} = \frac{20}{40}$$

$$\theta = 30^\circ$$

For equilibrium

$$\Sigma F_x \Rightarrow 0 \Rightarrow R_C = F\sin\theta \quad \text{(9.8)}$$

$$\Sigma F_y = 0 \Rightarrow F\cos\theta = W = 200 \quad \text{(9.9)}$$

From Eq. (9.7)

$$F = \frac{200}{\cos 30} = 231 \text{ N}$$

$$\therefore \quad F = \mathbf{231\ N} \qquad \textbf{Ans.}$$

From Eq. (9.6)

$$R_C = F \sin\theta$$
$$= 231 \sin 30$$
$$\therefore \quad R_C = \mathbf{115.5\ N} \qquad \textbf{Ans.}$$

Example 9.6

A ball of weight 220 N rests in a right angled groove, as shown in Fig. 9.14. The sides of the groove are inclined to an angle of 30° and 60° to the horizontal. If all the surfaces are smooth, then determine reaction, R_A and R_C at the points of contact.

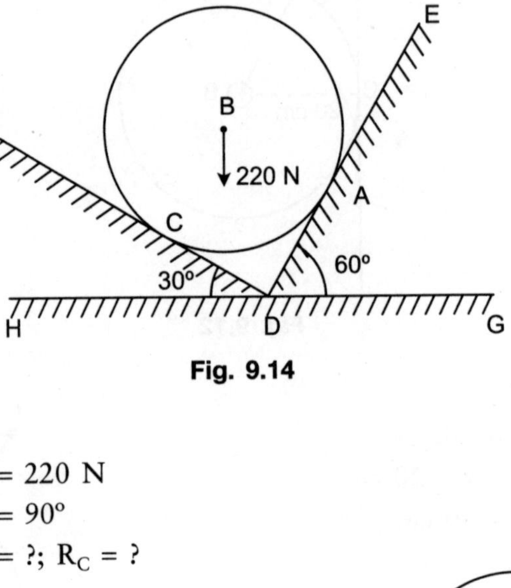

Fig. 9.14

Solution:

$$W = 220 \text{ N}$$
$$\text{Groove angle} = 90°$$
$$R_A = ?;\ R_C = ?$$

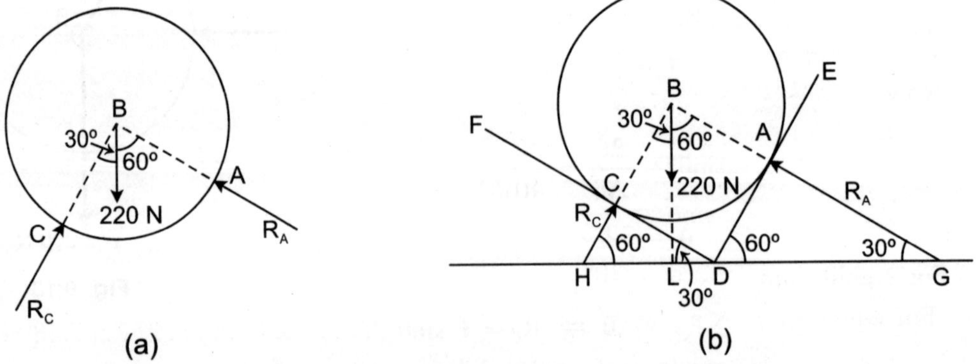

Fig. 9.15: F.B.D. of Ball

For equilibrium:

$$\Sigma F_x = 0 \Rightarrow R_C \cos 60 - R_A \cos 30 = 0$$

$$\Rightarrow R_C = 1.732\ R_A$$

$$\Sigma F_y = 0 \Rightarrow R_C \sin 60 + R_A \sin 30 = 220$$

$$= 1.732\ R_A \sin 60 + R_A \sin 30 = 220$$

$$= R_A(1.732 \sin 60 + \sin 30) = 220$$

$$R_A = \mathbf{110\ N}$$

and $R_C = \mathbf{190.5\ N}$ **Ans.**

Example 9.7

A circular roller of radius 100 mm and weight 200 N rests on a smooth horizontal surface and is held in position by an inclined bar AB of 200 mm as shown in Fig. 9.16. A horizontal force of 300 N is acting at B. Find tension (or force) in the bar AB and reaction at C.

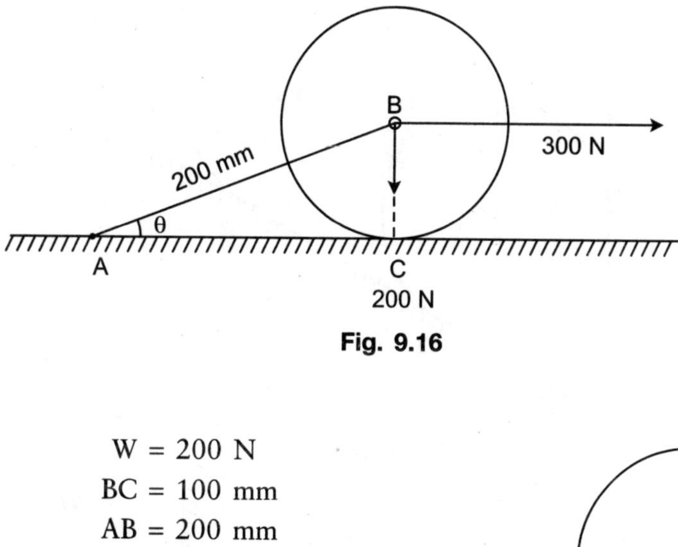

Fig. 9.16

Solution:

$W = 200$ N

$BC = 100$ mm

$AB = 200$ mm

Horizontal force at

$B = 300$ N

$F = ?$

$R_C = ?$

$$\sin\theta = \frac{BC}{AB} = \frac{100}{200} = 0.5$$

$$\theta = 30°$$

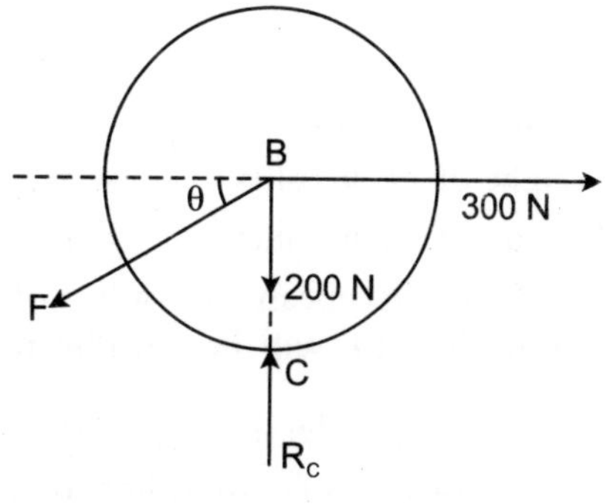

Fig. 9.17: F.B.D. of Roller

For equilibrium,

$$\Sigma F_x = 0 \Rightarrow F \cos\theta = 300 \quad \ldots\ldots (9.10)$$

$$\therefore \qquad F = \frac{300}{\text{Cos}\theta} = \frac{300}{\text{Cos}30} = 346.4 \text{ N}$$

$$F = \mathbf{346.4\ N} \qquad \textbf{Ans.}$$

$$F_y = 0 \Rightarrow R_C = 200 + F\sin\theta$$

$$= 200 + 346.4 \sin 30$$

$$R_C = \mathbf{373.2\ N} \qquad \textbf{Ans}$$

Example 9.8

Two identical rollers A and B, each of weight W, are supported by an inclined plane and a vertical wall as shown in Fig. 9.18. Assume all surfaces to be smooth. Draw free body diagram of:

(a) roller A, (b) roller B, (c) roller A and B taken together.

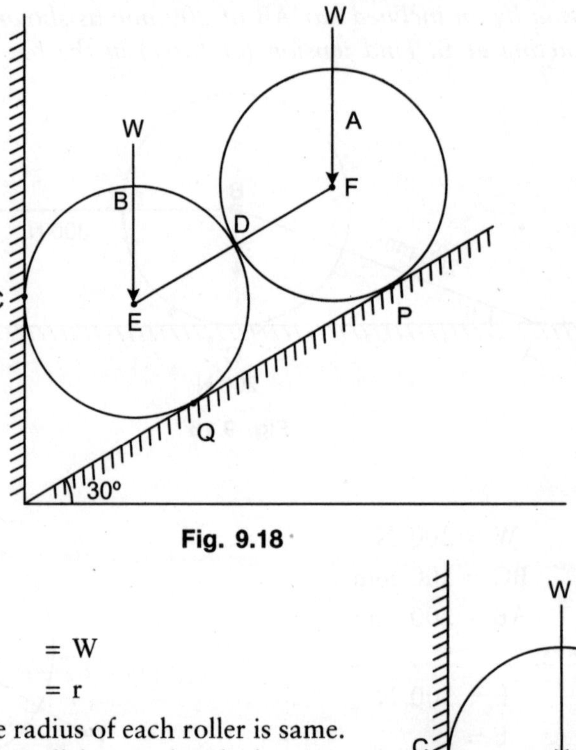

Fig. 9.18

Solution:

Weight of each roller = W
Radius of each roller = r

Identical roller means the radius of each roller is same. Therefore, line EF will be parallel to inclined plane.

(a) F.B.D. of roller B (Fig. 9.19)

To draw F.B.D. of roller B, isolate the roller B completely and find the forces acting on roller B. The roller B, has points of contacts at Q, C and D. The forces acting on the roller B will be

i. Weight of roller W.

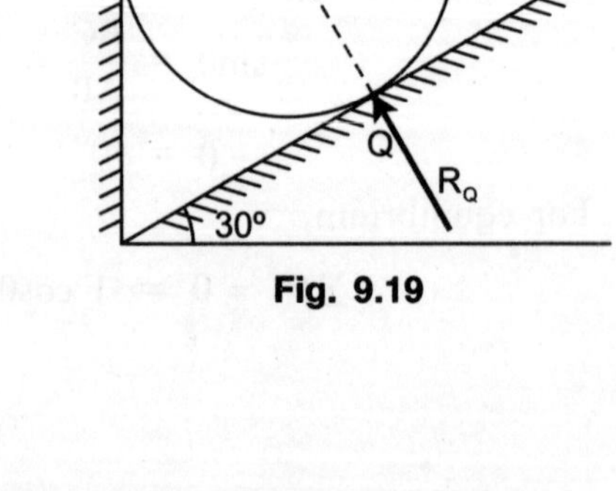

Fig. 9.19

ii. Reaction R_Q at point Q.
iii. Reaction R_C at point C.
iv. Reaction R_D at point D.

(b) F.B.D. of roller A (Fig. 9.20)
The forces acting on roller A are
i. Weight W.
ii. Reaction R_P at point P.
iii. Reaction R_D at point D.
R_P and R_D will pass through centre of roller A.

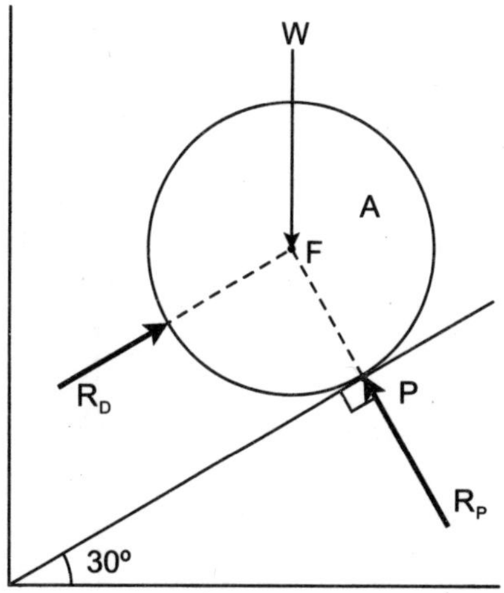

Fig. 9.20

(c) F.B.D. of rollers A and B taken together (Fig. 9.21):
The forces acting are
i. Weight W on each roller.
ii. Reaction R_P at point P.
iii. Reaction R_Q at point Q.
iv. Reaction R_C at point C.
In this case, there will be no reaction at point D.

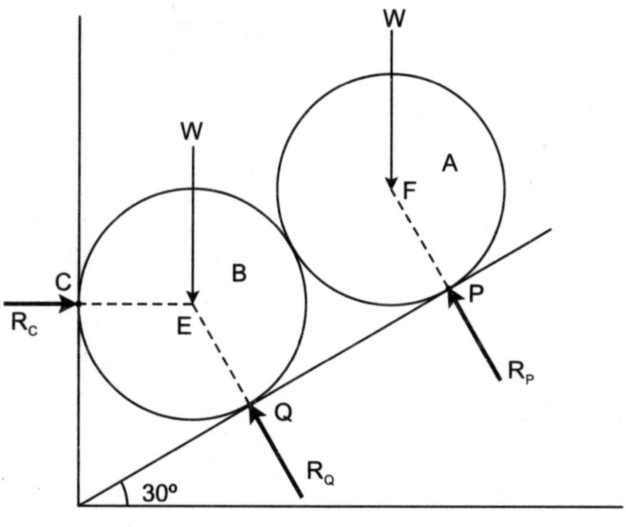

Fig. 9.21

Example 9.9

Two identical rollers, each of weight W= 2000 N, are supported by an inclined plane and a vertical wall as shown in Fig. 9.22. Find the reactions at the points of supports A, B and C. Assume all the surfaces to be smooth.

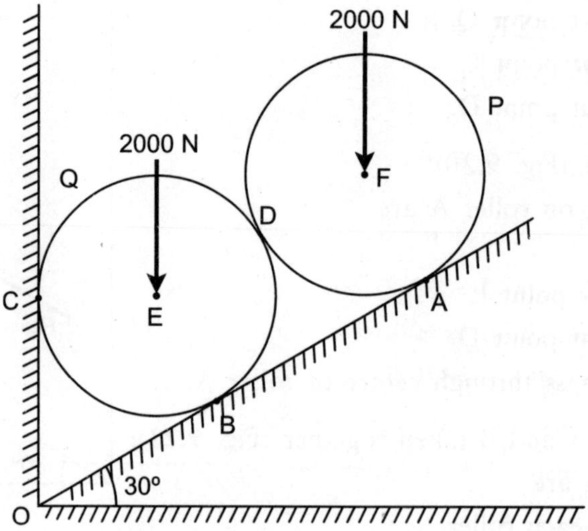

Fig. 9.22

Solution:

$R_A = ?$

$R_B = ?$

$R_C = ?$

Weight of each roller

$W = 2000$ N

Radius of each roller is same

Line $EF \parallel AB$.

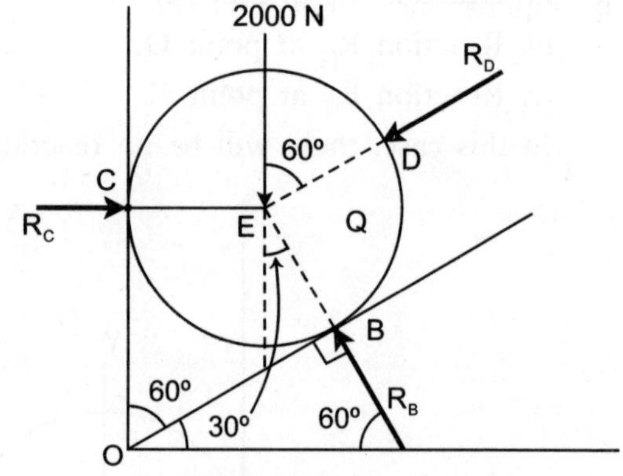

Fig. 9.23: F.B.D. of Roller Q

a. Equilibrium of roller P (Fig. 9.24):
   There are three loads acting on roller P.
   i. $W = 2000$ N
   ii. $R_D = ?$
   iii. $R_A = ?$

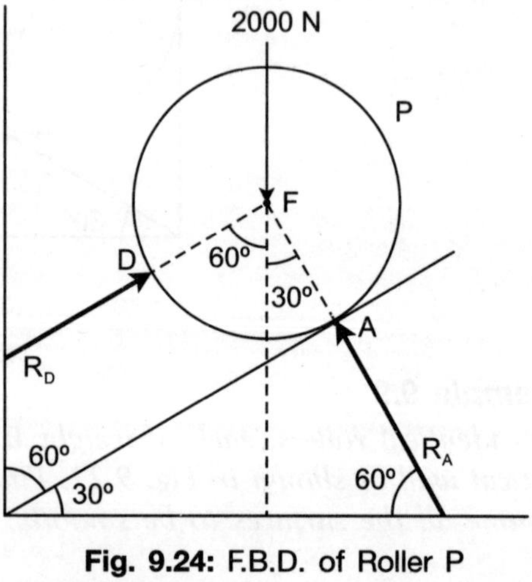

Fig. 9.24: F.B.D. of Roller P

$$\Sigma F_x = 0$$

$$\Rightarrow \quad R_D \cos 30 = R_A \cos 60$$

$$\therefore \quad R_D = R_A \frac{\cos 60}{\cos 30} = 0.577\ R_A$$

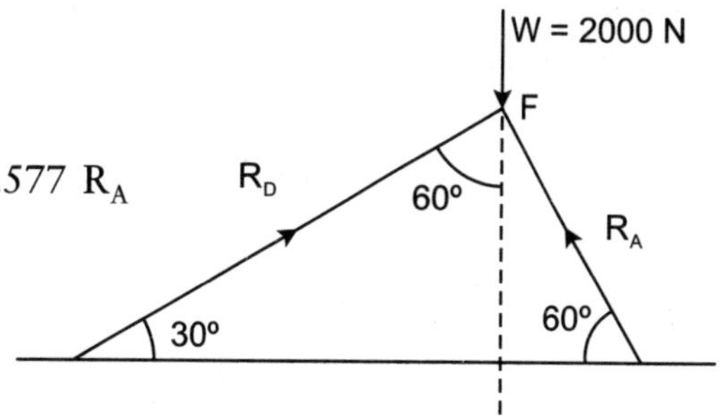

Fig. 9.25

$$\Sigma F_y = 0$$

$$\Rightarrow \quad R_D \sin 30 + R_A \sin 60 = 2000$$

$$0.577\ R_A \sin 30 + R_A \sin 60 = 2000$$

$$R_A\ (0.577\ \sin 30 + \sin 60) = 2000$$

$$R_A = \frac{2000}{1.154} = \mathbf{1732.3\ N}$$ **Ans.**

$$R_D = 0.577\ R_A = \mathbf{999.5\ N}$$ **Ans.**

b. Equilibrium of roller Q (Fig. 9.23):

i. W = 2000 N
ii. R_D = 999.5 N
iii. R_B = ?
iv. R_C = ?

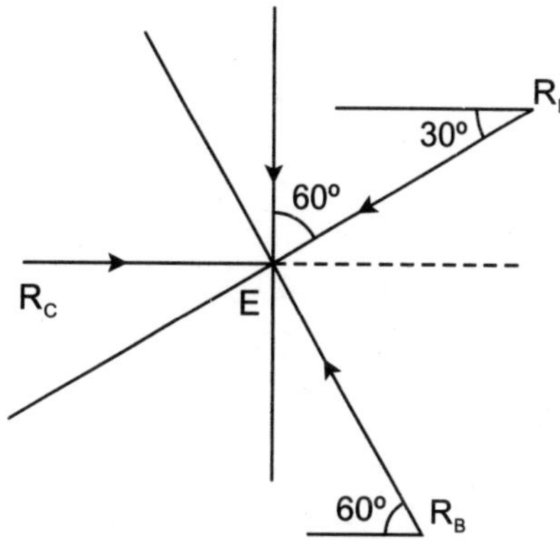

Fig. 9.26

$$\Sigma F_x = 0$$

$$\Rightarrow \quad R_B \cos 60 + R_D \cos 30 = R_C$$

$$(0.5\ R_B + 865.6) = R_C$$

$$\therefore \quad R_B \cos 60 + 999.5 \cos 30 = R_C$$

or

$$R_C = 0.5\ R_B + 865.6 \qquad (9.11)$$

Now

$$\Sigma F_y = 0$$

$$\Rightarrow \quad R_B \sin 60 = W + R_D \sin 30$$

$$\Rightarrow \quad R_B \sin 60 = 2000 + 999.5 \sin 30$$

$$R_B = \frac{2499.75}{\sin 60} = 2886.5\ N$$

$$R_B = \mathbf{2886.5\ N}$$ **Ans.**

From Eq. (9.11)

$$R_C = 0.55\ R_B + 865.6$$

$$= 0.5 \times 2886.5 + 865.6$$

$$R_C = \mathbf{2308.8\ N}$$ **Ans.**

Example 9.10

Two spheres, each of weight 500 N and of radius 250 mm rest in a horizontal channel of width 900 mm as shown in Fig. 9.27. Find reactions on the points of contacts.

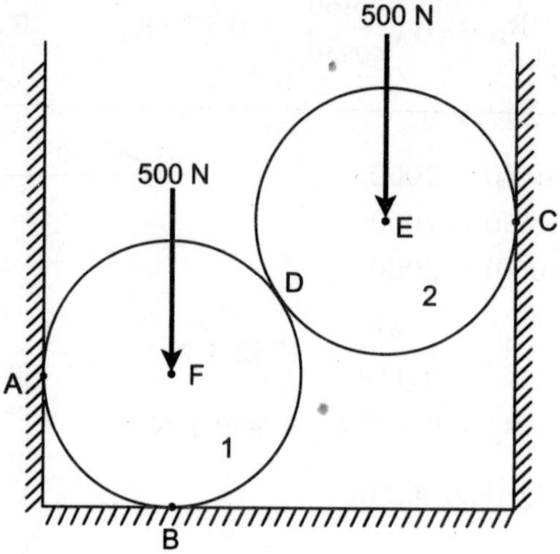

Fig. 9.27

Solution:

$$W = 500 \text{ N}$$
$$R = 250 \text{ mm}$$
$$R_A = ?$$
$$R_B = ?$$
$$R_C = ?$$
$$R_D = ?$$
$$AF = BF = FD = DE = 250 \text{ mm}$$

Now width of horizontal channel = 900 mm

$$EF = 250 + 250 = 500 \text{ mm}$$
$$FG = 400 \text{ mm}$$
$$EG = EF^2 - FG^2$$
$$= \sqrt{500^2 - 400^2} = 300 \text{ mm}$$

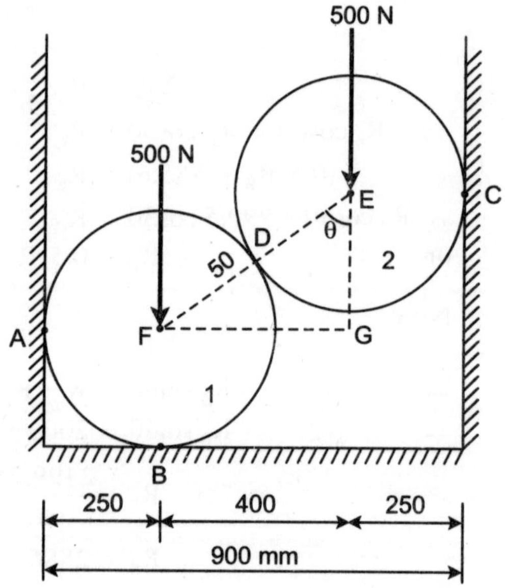

Fig. 9.28

$$\cos\theta = \frac{EG}{EF} = \frac{300}{500} = \frac{3}{5}$$

and $$\sin\theta = \frac{4}{5}$$

i. Equilibrium of Sphere 2 (Fig. 9.29)

$$\Sigma F_x = 0$$

$$\Rightarrow \quad R_D \sin\theta = R_C \quad \ldots\ldots\ldots\ldots \quad (9.12)$$

$$\Sigma F_y = 0$$

$$\Rightarrow \quad R_D \cos\theta = 500$$

$$R_D = \frac{500}{3/5} = 833.3 \text{ N}$$

$$R_D = \mathbf{833.3 \text{ N}} \qquad \textbf{Ans.}$$

From Eq. (9.12),

$$R_C = R_D \operatorname{Sin}\theta$$

$$R_C = 833.3 \times \frac{4}{5} = \mathbf{666.7 \text{ N}} \qquad \textbf{Ans.}$$

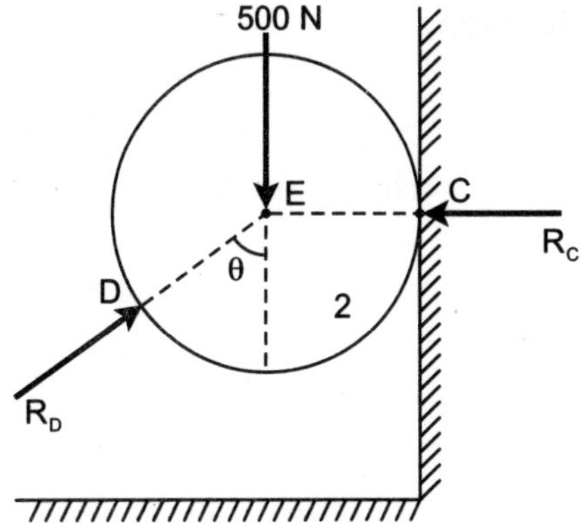

Fig. 9.29

ii. Equilibrium of Sphere 1 (Fig. 9.30)

$$\Sigma F_x = 0$$

$$R_A = R_D \sin\theta$$

$$= 833.3 \times \frac{4}{5}$$

$$= \mathbf{666.7 \text{ N}} \qquad \textbf{Ans.}$$

$$\Sigma F_y = 0$$

$$R_B = W + R_D \cos\theta$$

$$= 500 + 833.3 \times \frac{3}{5}$$

$$= \mathbf{1000 \text{ N}} \qquad \textbf{Ans.}$$

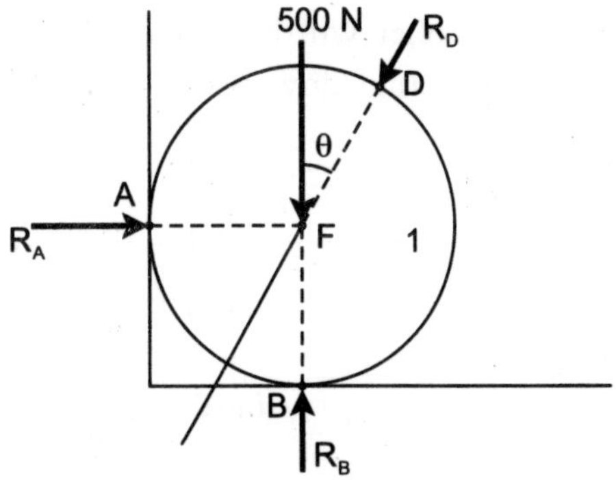

Fig. 9.30

Example 9.11

A roller of radius 500 mm, weighing 2000 N is to be pulled over a rectangular block of height 250 mm as shown in Fig. 9.31, by a horizontal force applied at the end of a string wound round the circumference of the roller. Find the magnitude of horizontal force which will just turn the roller over the corner of the rectangular block. Also determine the magnitude and direction of reactions at A and B. All surfaces may be taken as smooth.

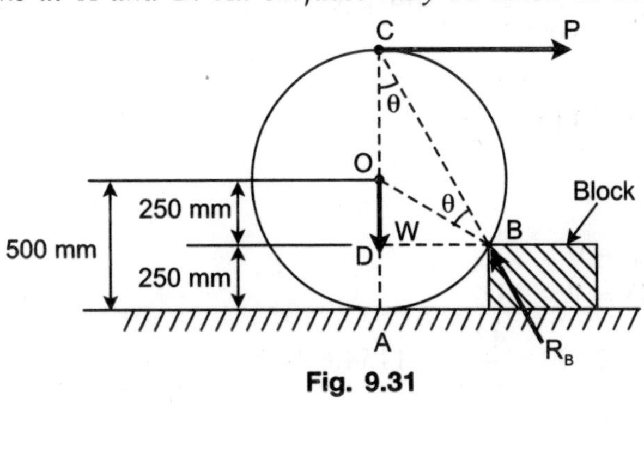

Fig. 9.31

Solution:

$$R = 500 \text{ mm}$$
$$W = 2000 \text{ N}$$
$$\text{Height of Block} = 250 \text{ mm}$$
$$P = ?$$
$$R_A = ?$$
$$R_B = ?$$

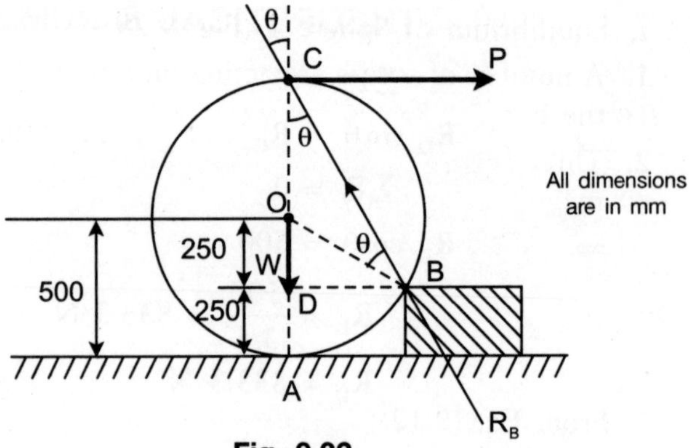

Fig. 9.32

When the roller will just turn over the corner of the rectangular block, the roller leaves point A and $R_A = 0$.

Now roller will be in equilibrium under the following loads.

i. W acting downward = 2000 N

ii. P

iii. R_B

$$OD = OA - AD = 500 - 250 = 250 \text{ mm}$$

$$BD = \sqrt{BO^2 - OD^2} = \sqrt{500^2 - 250^2} = 433 \text{ mm}$$

$$\tan\theta = \frac{BD}{CD} = \frac{433}{750} = 0.577$$

$$\theta = 30^\circ$$

Now

$$\Sigma F_x = 0$$

$$P = R_B \sin\theta$$

$\Rightarrow$ $$P = R_B \sin 30 = 0.5 \, R_B \quad \text{......} \quad (9.13)$$

$$\Sigma F_y = 0$$

$\Rightarrow$ $$R_B \cos\theta = W = 2000 \text{ N}$$

$$R_B = \frac{2000}{\cos 30} = \mathbf{2309.4 \text{ N}}$$ **Ans.**

From Eq. (9.13)

$$P = \mathbf{1154.7 \text{ N}}$$ **Ans.**

Alternative Method:

For just equilibrium

$$\Sigma M_B = 0$$

$\therefore$ $$P \times CD = W \times BD$$

$$P = 2000 \times \frac{433}{750} = 1154.6 \text{ N}$$

THEORETICAL & NUMERICAL QUESTIONS

1. A number of forces are acting on a body. What are the conditions of equilibrium so that the body is in equilibrium?
2. Three forces P_1, P_2 and P_3 are acting on a body and the body is in equilibrium. If the magnitude of force P_3 is 350 N, find magnitudes of forces P_1 and P_2.

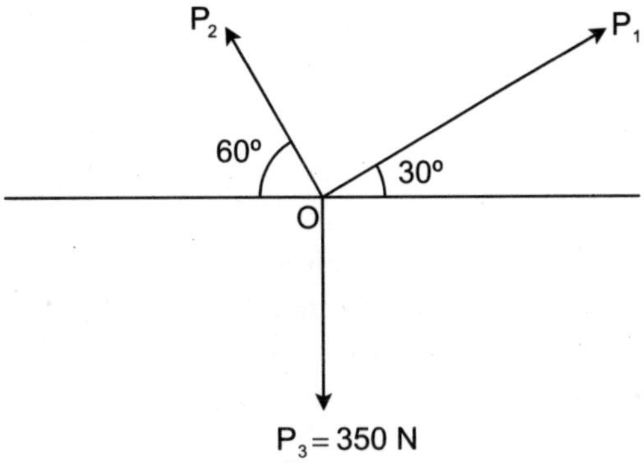

Fig. 9.33

3. Three forces of magnitudes P, 200 N and 300 N are acting at a point O. Determine magnitude and direction of the force P.

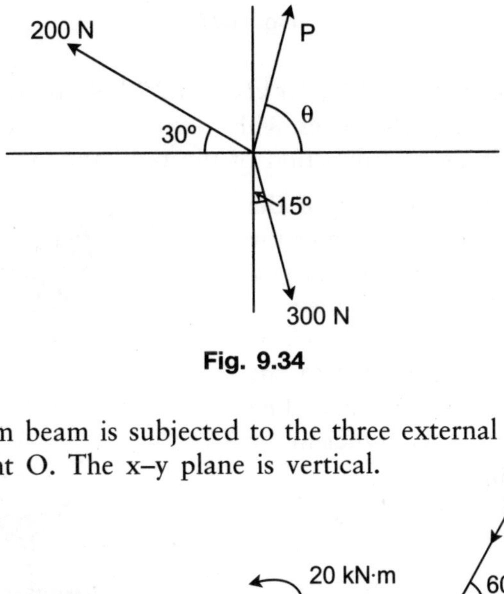

Fig. 9.34

4. The 400 kg uniform beam is subjected to the three external loads. Calculate reactions at the support point O. The x–y plane is vertical.

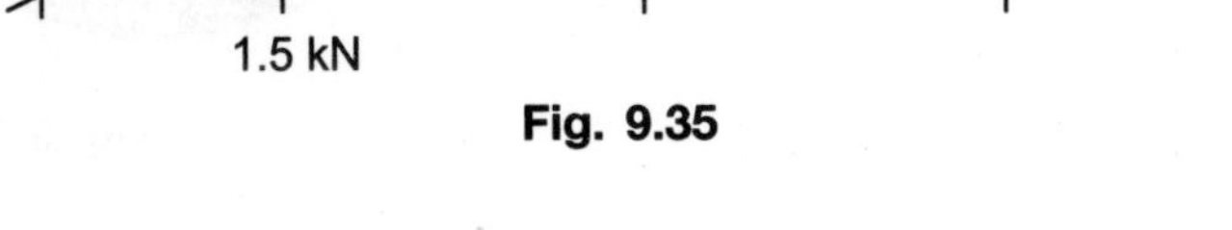

Fig. 9.35

5. Cable AB passes over the small ideal pulley C without a change in its tension. What length of the cable is required for static equilibrium in the position shown? What is the tension T in cable CD?

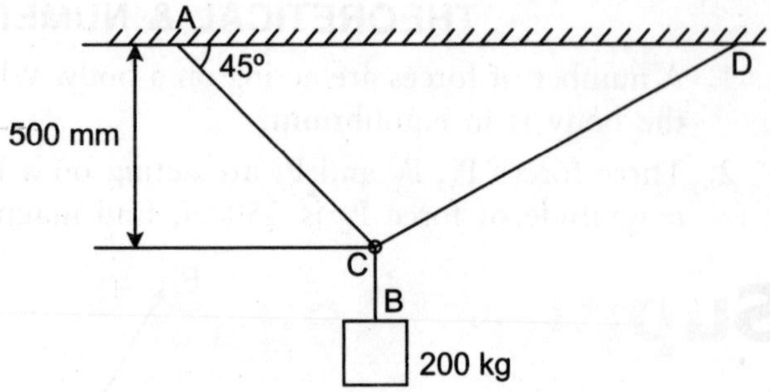

Fig. 9.36

6. Three parallel forces P_1, P_2 and P_3 are acting on a body and the body is in equilibrium. If F_1 = 200 N, and F_3 = 1 kN and distance between F_1 and F_2 is 2 m, then calculate the magnitude of force F_2 and distance of F_3 from force F_2.

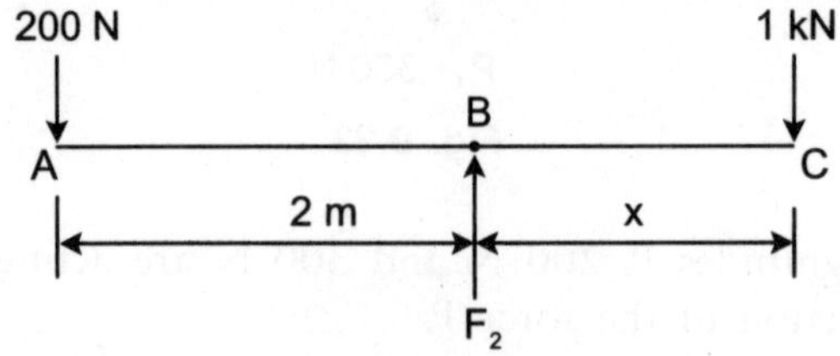

Fig. 9.37

7. Three forces of magnitude 50 kN, 20 kN and 25 kN are acting at a point. The angles made by 50, 20 and 25 kN forces with x-axis are 60°, 120° and 240° respectively. Calculate the magnitude and direction of the resultant force.

8. A block placed under the head of the claw hammer as shown to facilitates the extraction of the nail. If the 200 N pull on the handle is required to pull the nail, calculate the tension T in the nail and the magnitude F of the force exerted by the hammer head on the block. The contacting surface at A is sufficient by rough to prevent slipping.

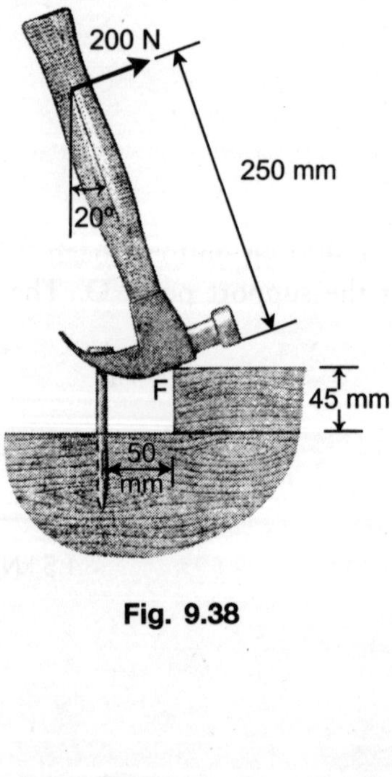

Fig. 9.38

10

Support Reactions

10.1 Introduction

When a number of forces are acting on a member and the member is supported on another member, then the second member exerts a force known as reaction on the first member at the points of contacts, so that the first member or body is in equilibrium. The second member is known as support and the force, exerted by the second member on the first member, is known as support reactions.

10.2 Types of Supports

Main supports are as follows:

i. Simple supports or Knife-edge supports.
ii. Roller support.
iii. Pin-joint (or hinged) support.
iv. Smooth surface support.
v. Fixed support or built in support.

i. *Simple Support or Knife-edge support*

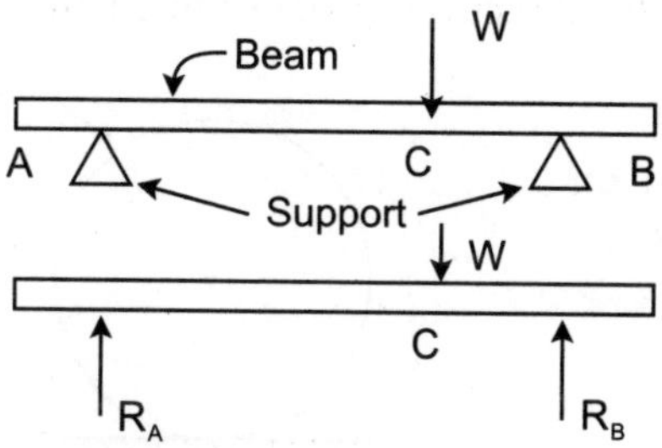

Fig. 10.1: F.B.D. of Beam

The reactions at A and B in case of Knife-edge support will be normal to the surface of the beam.

ii. *Roller Support*

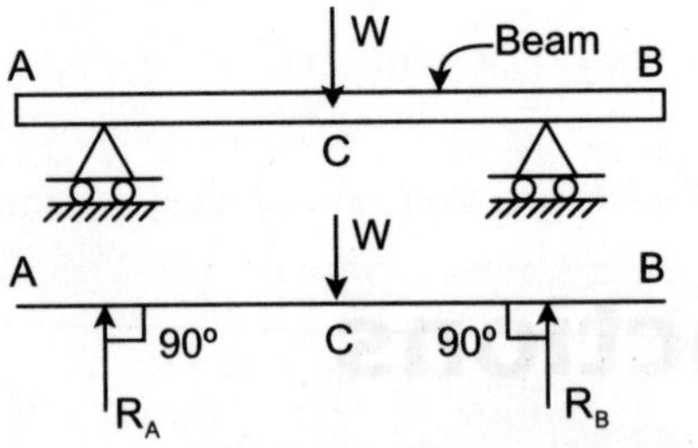

Fig. 10.2: F.B.D. of Beam

The word 'roller' means a solid roller or cylinder on which the supported body rests. The entire reaction can only be perpendicular to the supporting surface, with its line of action passing through the centre of the roller.

iii. *Pin Joint (or Hinged) Support*

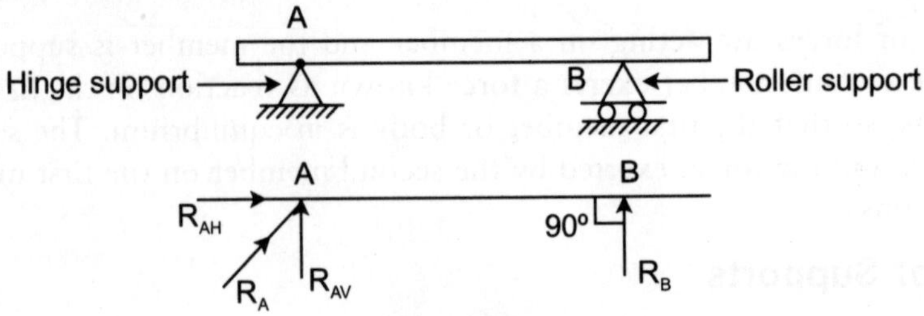

Fig. 10.3

The reaction at the hinged end has two components, i.e. horizontal and vertical components. If the load is vertical, then the reaction will also be vertical and horizontal component will be zero, but if the load is inclined then the reaction at the hinged end will also be inclined.

The hinge is supposed to be frictionless or ideally lubricated with the result that no turning moment can be transmitted from the pin to the beam or *vice-versa*. This type of support therefore develops only of force whose line of action always pass through the centre of the hinge. Its direction is determined by the conditions of equilibrium.

iv. *Smooth Surface Support*

There will be no friction on smooth surface supports.

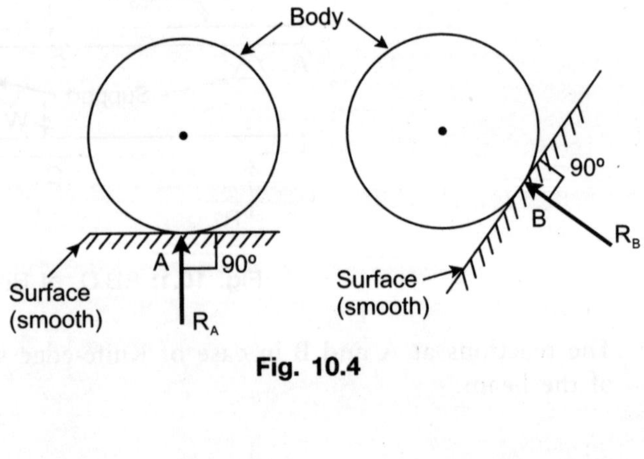

Fig. 10.4

The reaction will always act normal to the support.

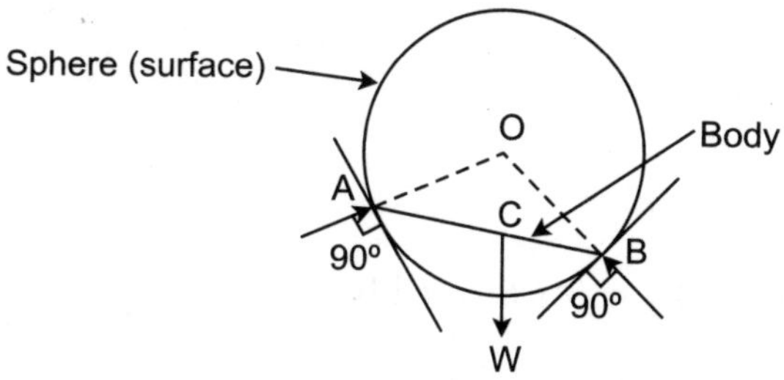

Fig. 10.5

In Fig. 10.5, a rod AB resting inside a sphere, whose surfaces are smooth. Here, the rod is a body and sphere is a surface. The reactions at the ends of the rod will be normal to the sphere surface at A and B. The normal at any point on the surface of the sphere will always pass through the centre of the sphere.

v. *Fixed or Built in Support*

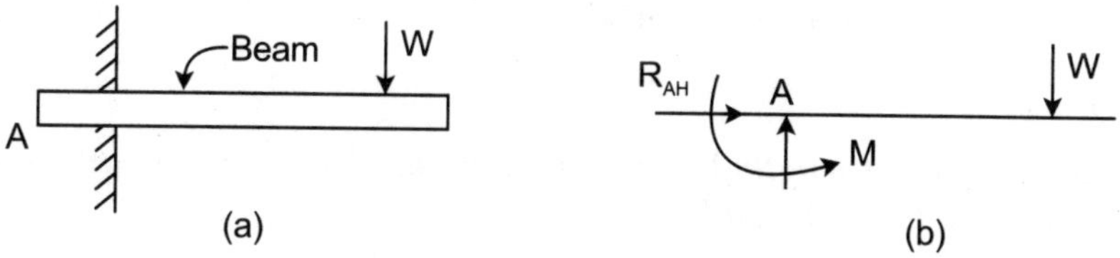

Fig. 10.6: F.B.D. of Beam

The body to be supported has a portion of it firmly built in into the support, e.g. an end of a beam may be taken well inside a thick wall and firmly embeded into it using concrete or mortar or some such hardening material.

Example 10.1

A simply supported beam of span 9 m carries point loads of 3 kN and 6 kN at a distance of 3 m and 6 m from the left end. Find reactions at ends.

Solution:

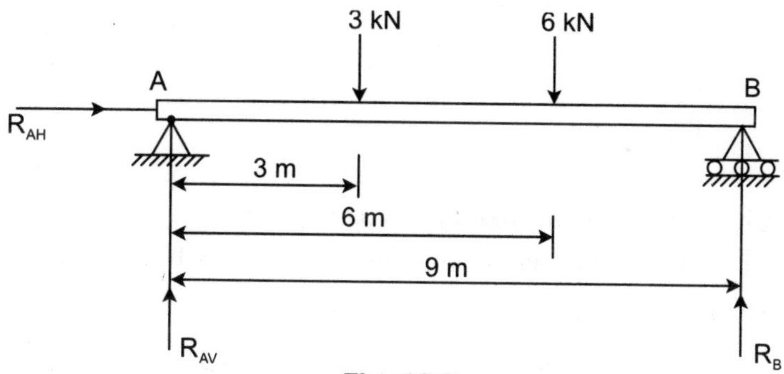

Fig. 10.7

$$AB = 9 \text{ m}$$
$$R_A = ?$$
$$R_B = ?$$

For equilibrium

$$\Sigma F_x = 0 \Rightarrow R_{AH} = 0$$

$$\Sigma F_y = 0 \Rightarrow R_{AV} + R_B = 3 + 6 = 9 \text{ kN} \quad \text{.........................} \quad (10.1)$$

$$\Sigma M_A = 0 \Rightarrow R_B \times 9 = 6 \times 6 + 3 \times 3$$

$$\Rightarrow R_B = \frac{36 + 9}{9} = \frac{45}{9} = 5 \text{ kN}$$ **Ans.**

and $$R_B = 9 - 5 = 4 \text{ kN}$$

From Eq. (10.1), $$R_A = \sqrt{(R_{AV})^2 + (R_{AH})^2}$$

$$= \sqrt{4^2 + 0} = 4 \text{ kN}$$ **Ans.**

Example 10.2

A simply supported beam of length 10 m carries the u.d.l. and two point loads as shown in Fig. 10.8. Calculate reactions R_A and R_B.

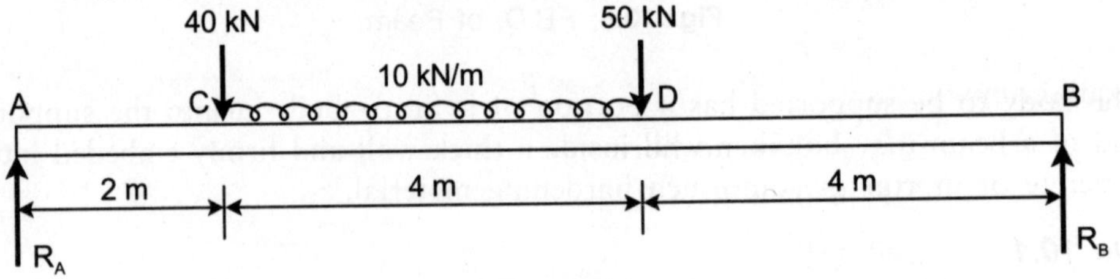

Fig. 10.8

Solution:

$$AB = 10 \text{ m}$$
$$R_A = ?$$
$$R_B = ?$$

For equilibrium

$$\Sigma F_x = 0 \Rightarrow \text{no horizontal force is given.}$$

$$\Sigma F_y = 0 \Rightarrow R_A + R_B = 40 + 50 + 4 \times 10 = 130 \quad \text{................} \quad (10.2)$$

$$\Sigma M_A = 0$$

$$\Rightarrow R_B \times 10 = 50 \times 60 + 40 \times 2 + 10 \times 4 \times \left(2 + \frac{4}{2}\right)$$

$$\Rightarrow 10\ R_B = 300 + 80 + 40 \times 4$$
$$R_B = 30 + 8 + 16 = 30 + 24$$
$$R_B = \mathbf{54\ kN}$$ **Ans.**

From Eq. (10.2), $R_A = 130 - 54$

$\therefore$ $R_A = \mathbf{76\ kN}$ **Ans.**

Example 10.3

A beam of span 8 m, overhanging at both sides, is leaded as shown in Fig. 10.9. Calculate reactions at both the ends.

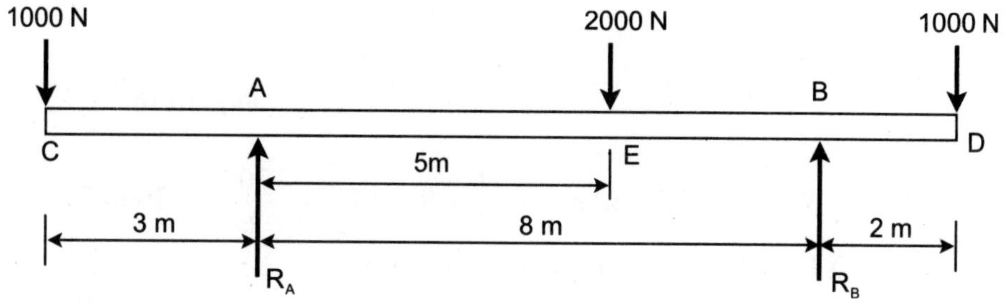

Fig. 10.9

Solution:

$$R_A = ?$$
$$R_B = ?$$

For equilibrium

$$\Sigma F_x = 0 \Rightarrow \text{no horizontal force is given.}$$
$$\Sigma F_y = 0 \Rightarrow R_A + R_B = 1000 + 2000 + 1000 = 4000\ \text{N} \quad \ldots\ldots\ (10.3)$$
$$\Sigma M = 0$$

Taking moment about point A;

Sum of clockwise moments = Sum of anticlockwise moments

$$\Sigma M_A = 0$$
$$\Rightarrow 2000 \times 5 + 1000 \times (8 + 2)$$
$$= R_B \times 8 + 1000 \times 3$$
$$\Rightarrow 10000 + 10000 = 8\ R_B + 3000$$
$$\Rightarrow 8\ R_B = 20000 - 3000$$
$$8\ R_B = 17000\ \text{N}$$

From (10.3), $\therefore$ $R_B = \mathbf{2125\ N}$ **Ans.**

$R_A = 4000 - 2125 = \mathbf{1875\ N}$ **Ans.**

Example 10.4

A simply supported beam of span 9 m carries a uniformly varying load form zero at one end and 800 N/m at other end. Calculate reactions at the supports.

Solution:

$R_A = ?$

$R_B = ?$

$W = 800$ N/m

$l = 9$ m

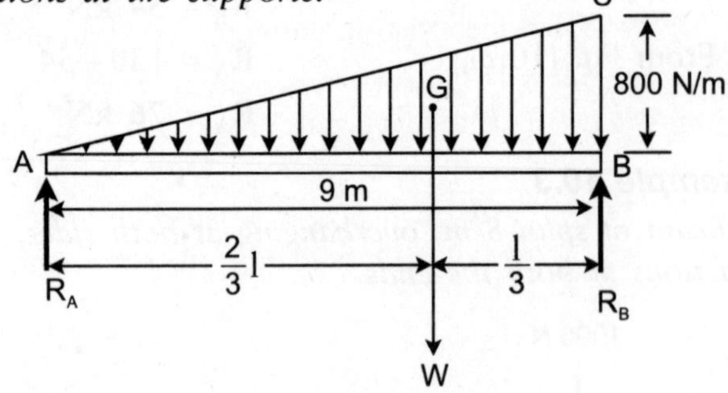

Fig. 10.10

Total load

$$W = \text{Area of } \Delta ABC = \frac{1}{2} \times 9 \times 800 = \frac{7200}{2} = 3600 \text{ N}$$

$$\Sigma F_y = 0 \Rightarrow R_A + R_B = W = 3600 \text{ N} \quad \ldots\ldots\ldots\ldots \quad (10.4)$$

$$\Sigma M_A = 0$$

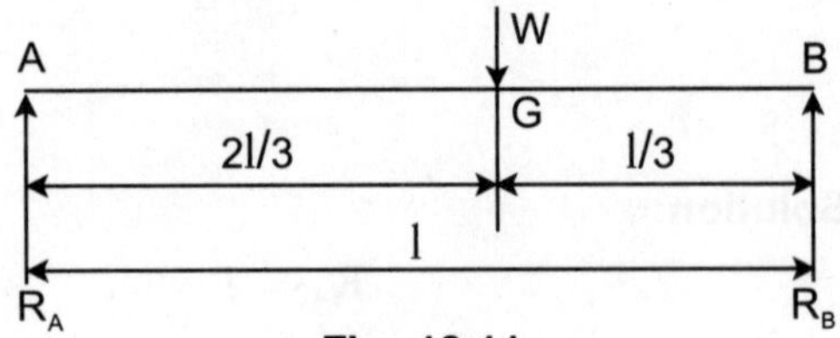

Fig. 10.11

$$\Rightarrow R_B \times 9 = W \times \frac{2}{3} l$$

$$\Rightarrow \quad R_B = \frac{3600}{9} \times \frac{2}{3} \times 9$$

$$R_B = \frac{7200}{3} = \mathbf{2400 \text{ N}} \quad \ldots\ldots\ldots\ldots \quad \textbf{Ans.}$$

From Eq. (10.4),

$$R_A = 3600 - 2400 = \mathbf{1200 \text{ N}} \quad \ldots\ldots\ldots\ldots \quad \textbf{Ans.}$$

Example 10.5

A beam is loaded as shown in Fig. 10.12. Determine the reactions at A and B.

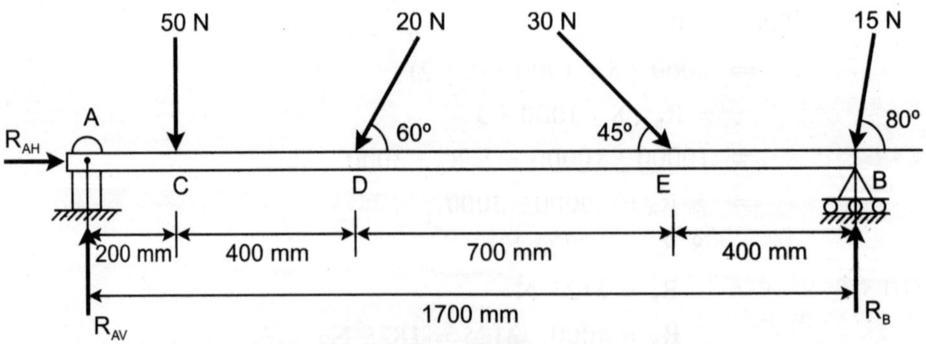

Fig. 10.12

Solution:

$$R_A = ?$$
$$R_B = ?$$
$$R_A = \sqrt{(R_{AV})^2 + (R_{AH})^2}$$

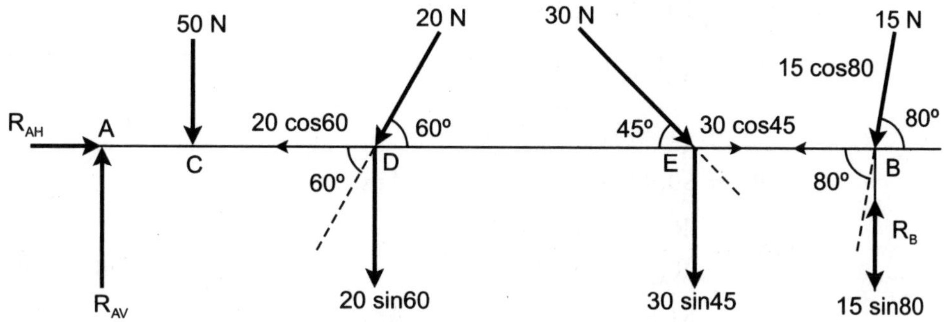

Fig. 10.13

Inclined loads are resolved in horizontal and vertical components at points D, E and B. For equilibrium

$$\Sigma F_x = 0$$
$$\Rightarrow R_{AH} - 20\cos 60 + 30\cos 45 - 15\cos 80 = 0$$
$$\Rightarrow R_{AH} - 20 \times \frac{1}{2} - 30 \times \frac{1}{\sqrt{2}} + 15\cos 80$$
$$= 10 - 21.21 + 2.6$$
$$= 12.6 - 21.21$$
$$= -8.61 \text{ N}$$
$$R_{AH} = -8.61 \text{ N}$$

Negative (–ve) sign indicates that the direction of R_{AH} is in opposite to that assumed.

$$\therefore \quad R_{AH} = -8.61 \text{ N} (\leftarrow)$$

Now

$$\Sigma F_y = 0$$
$$\Rightarrow R_{AV} - 50 - 20\sin 60 - 30\sin 45 - 15\sin 80 + R_B = 0$$
$$\Rightarrow R_{AV} = 50 + 20 \times \frac{\sqrt{3}}{2} + 30 \times \frac{1}{\sqrt{2}} + 15\sin 80 - R_B$$
$$= 50 + 17.32 + 21.21 + 14.77 - R_B$$
$$R_{AV} = 10.33 - R_B \quad \text{......} \quad (10.5)$$

Now

$$\Sigma M_A = 0$$

$$R_B \times 1700 = 50 \times 200 + 20 \sin 60 \times 600 + 30 \sin 45 \times 1300 + 15 \sin 80 \times 1700$$

$$R_{RB} = \mathbf{42.98\ N} \qquad \textbf{Ans.}$$

From Eq. (10.5);

$$R_{AV} = 103.3 - 42.98 = 60.32 \text{ N}$$

and

$$R_A = \sqrt{(R_{AV})^2 + (R_{AH})^2}$$

$$= \sqrt{(60.32)^2 + (8.61)^2}$$

$$R_A = \mathbf{60.92\ N} \qquad \textbf{Ans.}$$

$$\tan\theta = \frac{R_{AV}}{R_{AH}} = \frac{60.32}{8.61} = 7.006$$

$$\theta = \mathbf{81.8^\circ} \qquad \textbf{Ans.}$$

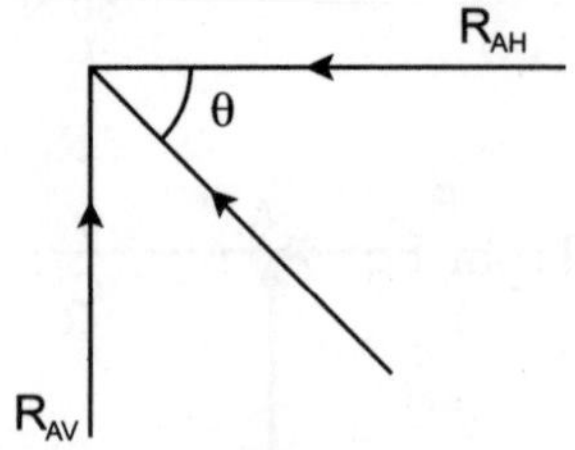

Fig. 10.14

Example 10.6

A simply supported beam AB of 7000 mm span is subjected to (a) 5000 N.m clockwise couple at 2 m from A. (b) 8 kN.m anticlockwise couple at 5 m from A. (c) a triangular load with zero intensity at 2 m from A increasing to 4 kN per m at a point 5 m from A. Determine reactions at A and B.

Solution:

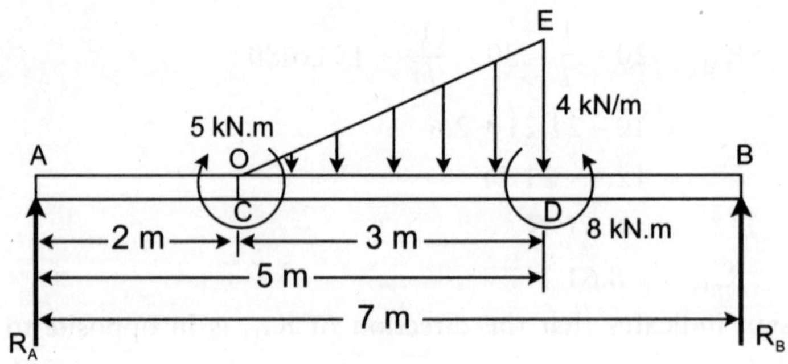

Fig. 10.15

$$R_A = ?$$

$$R_B = ?$$

Total load on beam acting downward

$$W = \frac{3 \times 4}{2} = 6 \text{ kN}$$

For equilibrium

$\Sigma F_x = 0 \Rightarrow$ no horizontal force is given.

$\Sigma F_y = 0 \Rightarrow R_A + R_B = W = 6$ kN .... (10.6)

$$\Sigma M_A = 0$$

$$\Rightarrow R_B \times 7 + 8 = 5 + W \times \left(2 + \frac{2}{3} \times 3\right)$$

$$7\,R_B + 8 = 5 + 6 \times (2 + 2)$$

$$R_B = \left(\frac{5 + 24 - 8}{7}\right)$$

$$R_B = \frac{21}{7}\text{ kN} \qquad \textbf{Ans.}$$

From Eq. (10.6);

$$R_A = 6 - R_B$$

$$= 6 - \frac{21}{7} = \frac{42 - 21}{7}$$

$$= \frac{21}{7}\text{ kN} \qquad \textbf{Ans.}$$

10.3 Structures Made up of Articulated or Jointed Beams

If two or more beams are joined with the help of pinned joints, then such beams are called jointed beams. The joints are considered frictionless.

The main property of these pinned joints is that they can transmit only a force and cannot transmit a moment.

Example 10.7

An articulated beam has supports A, B, C and D and internal hinge connections at E and F. The structure carries loads as shown in Fig. 10.16. Calculate the reactions at the supports and the forces transmitted through the hinges E and F.

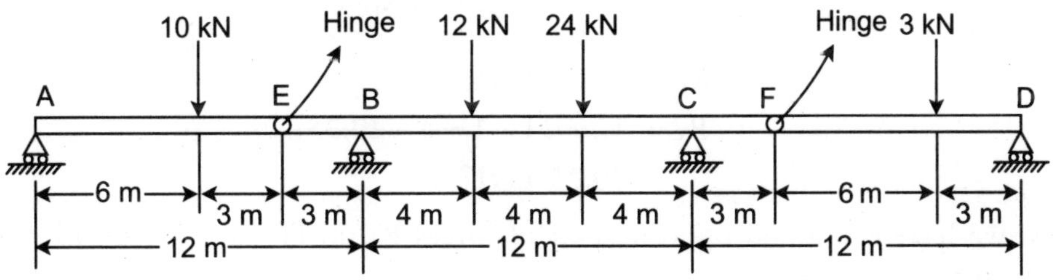

Fig. 10.16

Solution:

R_A = ?, R_B = ?, R_C = ?, R_D = ?, R_E = ?, R_F = ?

The structure consists of three beams AE, EF and FD. Each of these three beams is statistically determinate and in equilibrium under the action of forces on it. Since the pin connections at E and F are frictionless, no moment can be transmitted through them.

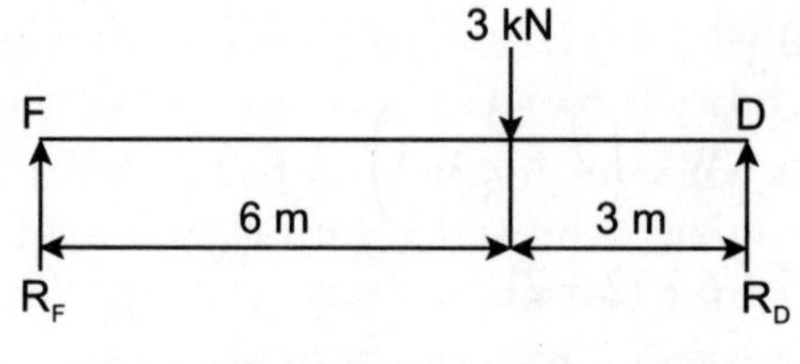

Fig. 10.17: F.B.D. of Beam FD

For equilibrium

$$\Sigma M_F = 0 \Rightarrow R_D \times 9 = 3 \times 6$$

$$\Rightarrow R_D = \mathbf{2\ kN}\ (\uparrow) \qquad \textbf{Ans.}$$

and $$R_F = \mathbf{1\ kN}\ (\uparrow) \qquad \textbf{Ans.}$$

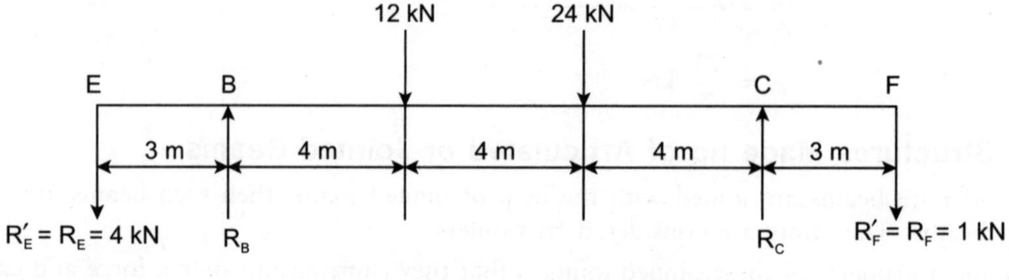

Fig. 10.18: F.B.D. of Beam EF

For equilibrium

$$\Sigma M_B = 0 \Rightarrow R_C \times 12 = 1 \times 15 + 24 \times 8 + 12 \times 4 - 4 \times 3$$

$$= 15 + 192 + 48 - 12$$

∴ $$R_C = \frac{243}{12} = 20.55\ \text{kN}$$

∴ $$R_C = \mathbf{20.25\ kN}\ (\uparrow) \qquad \textbf{Ans.}$$

and $$R_B = 12 + 24 + 1 + 4 - 20.25$$

$$= \mathbf{20.75\ kN}\ (\uparrow) \qquad \textbf{Ans.}$$

Similarly, we have equal and opposite pair of forces R_F on FD and R'_F on EF transmitted through pin there.

Now

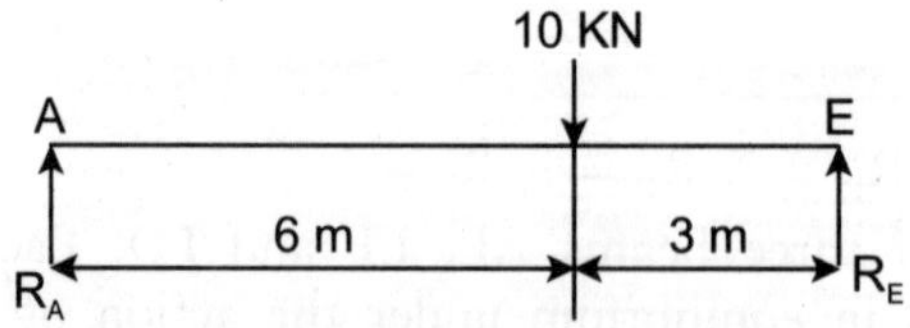

Fig. 10.19: F.B.D. of Beam EA

For equilibrium

$$\Sigma M_A = 0 \Rightarrow R_E \times 9 = 6 \times 10$$

$$\Rightarrow \quad R_E = \mathbf{6.7\ kN}(\uparrow) \qquad \textbf{Ans.}$$

and $$R_A = 10 - 6.7 = \mathbf{3.3\ kN}(\uparrow) \qquad \textbf{Ans.}$$

Example 10.8

The reactive effort, F on an automobile is acting at a height of 100 mm from the ground. The wheel base is 300 mm as shown in Fig. 10.20. Weight of automobile is 5 tonn. Determine reactions at each wheel.

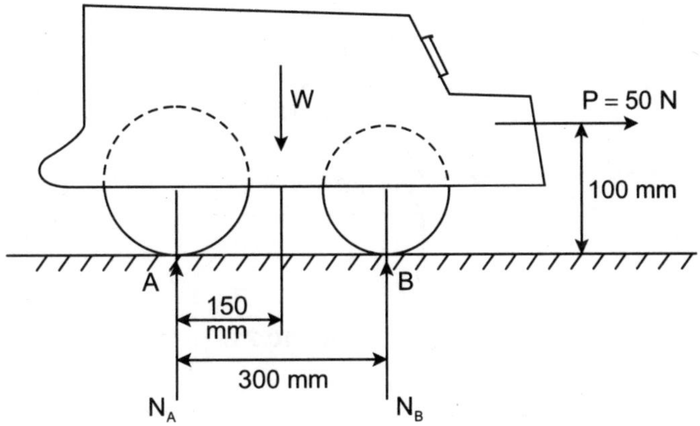

Fig. 10.20

Solution:

$$\Sigma M_A = 0$$

$$\Rightarrow N_B \times 300 - W \times 150 - P \times 100 = 0$$

$$N_B = 5 \times 1000 \times 9.81 + 50 \times 100$$

$$N_B = 49050 + 5000 = \frac{54050}{300} = 163.5 \text{ N}$$

$$\Sigma F_y = 0$$

$$\Rightarrow N_A + N_B = W$$

$$N_A = 5 \times 1000 \times 9.81 - 163.5 = 48886.5 \text{ N}$$

Now

there are two rear wheels and two front wheels.

$\therefore$ Reactions on each front wheel $= N'_B = \dfrac{N_B}{2} = 81.75$ N

and reactions on each rear wheel $= N'_A = \dfrac{N_A}{2} = \mathbf{24.4\ kN}$ **Ans.**

Example 10.9

Two men support a weightless wooden beam AB with a weight of 2 kN hanging from the beam as shown Fig. 10.21. Find the load shared by the each man.

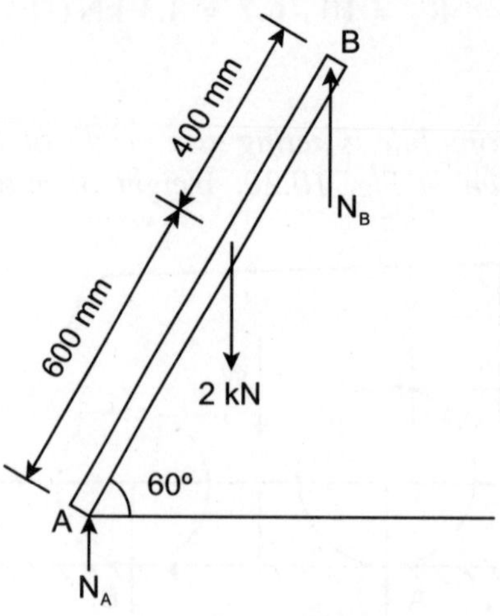

Fig. 10.21

Solution:

$$N_A = ?$$
$$N_B = ?$$
$$W = 2\text{ kN} = 2000\text{ N}$$

For equilibrium

$$\Sigma F_y = 0 \Rightarrow N_A + N_B = 2\text{ kN}$$
$$\Sigma M_A = 0 \Rightarrow N_B \times 1000\cos 60 = 2000 \times 600\cos 60$$
$$N_B = \frac{2000 \times 600}{1000} = \mathbf{1200\text{ N}} \qquad \textbf{Ans.}$$
$$N_A = 2000 - 1200 = \mathbf{800\text{ N}} \qquad \textbf{Ans.}$$

Example 10.10

Three beams AB, BC and CD are hinged at their ends and loaded and supported as shown in Fig. 10.22. Determine the reactions at the points A, E, F and D.

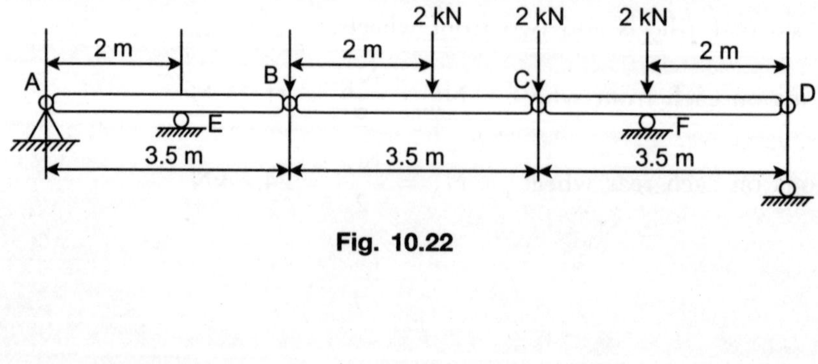

Fig. 10.22

Solution:

Considering the F.B.D. of beam CD.

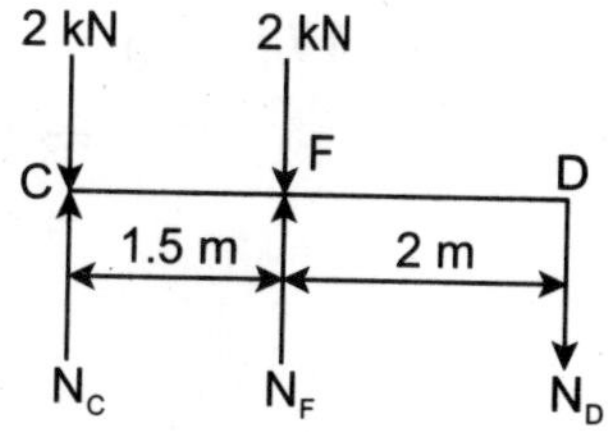

Fig. 10.23: F.B.D. of Beam CD

$$\Sigma M_C = 0$$

$$\Rightarrow 2000 \times 1.5 + N_D \times 3.5 = N_F \times 1.5$$

$$\Rightarrow 1.5\ N_F - 3.5\ N_D = 3000$$

or

$$N_F - 2.33\ N_D = 2000 \quad \ldots\ldots \quad (10.7)$$

Considering the F.B.D. of combined beams BC and CD (Fig. 10.24)

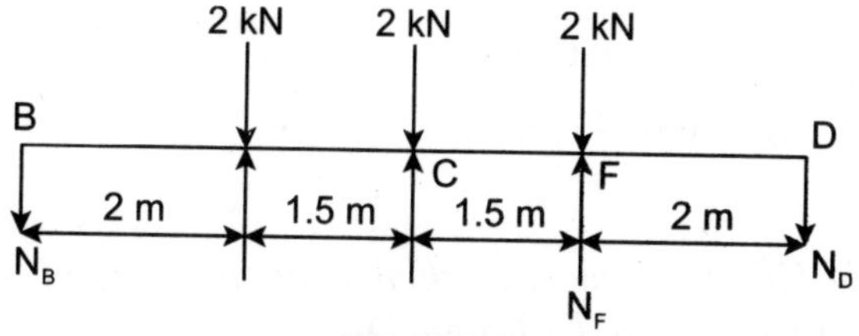

Fig. 10.24

$$\Sigma M_B = 0$$

$$\Rightarrow N_D \times 7 + 2000 \times 5 + 2000 \times 3.5 + 2000 \times 2 = N_F \times 5$$

$$\Rightarrow 5\ N_F = 7\ N_D + 10 \times 10^3 + 7 \times 10^3 + 4 \times 10^3$$

$$5\ N_F = 7\ N_D + 21 \times 10^3$$

$$\Rightarrow N_F = 1.4\ N_D + 4.2 \times 10^3 \quad \ldots\ldots\ldots\ldots \quad (10.8)$$

From Eqs. (10.7) and (10.8),

$$1.4\ N_D + 4.2 \times 10^3 - 2.33\ N_D = 2000$$

$$0.93\ N_D = 4200 - 2000$$

$$N_D = \mathbf{2365.6\ N\ (\uparrow)}$$ **Ans.**

and

$$N_F = \mathbf{7511.8\ N\ (\uparrow)}$$ **Ans.**

Now

Considering the F.B.D. of beams AB, BC and CD as a whole (Fig. 10.25)

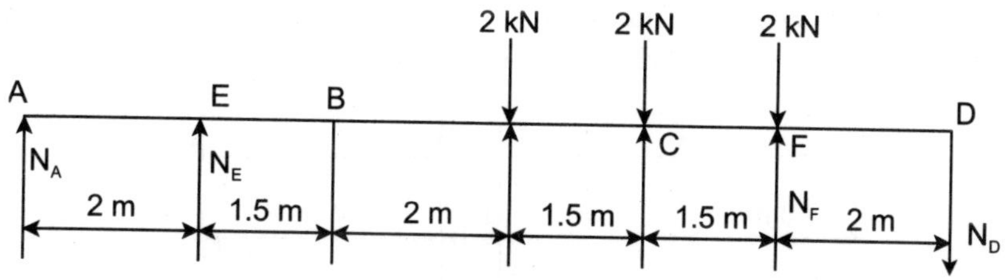

Fig. 10.25

$$\Sigma F_y = 0$$

$$\Rightarrow N_A + N_E + N_F = 2000 + 2000 + 2000 + N_D$$

$$\Rightarrow N_A + N_E = 6000 + 2365.6 - 7511.8 = 853.8$$

$$\Rightarrow N_A + N_E = 853.8 \quad \ldots\ldots\ldots\ldots \quad (10.9)$$

$\Sigma M_A = 0$

$$\Rightarrow N_E \times 2 + N_F \times 8.5 = 2000 \times 5.5 + 2000 \times 7 + 2000 \times 8.5 + N_D \times 10.5$$

$$\Rightarrow N_E \times 2 = 11 \times 10^3 + 14 \times 10^3 + 17 \times 10^3 + 2365.6 \times 10.5 - 7511.8 \times 8.5$$

$$= 42 \times 10^3 + 24838.8 - 63850.3$$

$$= 42 \times 10^3 - 39011.5 = 2988.5$$

$\therefore \quad N_E = \mathbf{1494.25\ N\ (\uparrow)}$ **Ans.**

From Eq. (10.9),

$$N_A = -640.45 \text{ N}$$

or $\quad N_A = \mathbf{640.45\ N\ (\downarrow)}$ **Ans.**

Example 10.11

Three beams AB, BC and CD are hinged at their ends and loaded and supported as shown in Fig. 10.26. Determine reactions at E, F and D.

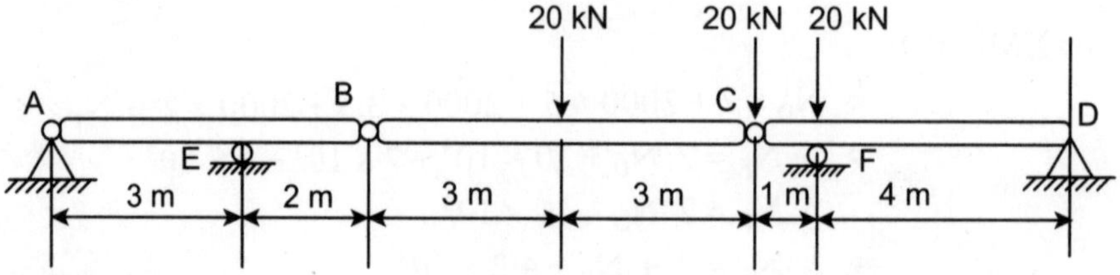

Fig. 10.26

Solution:

Considering equilibrium of beam CD (Fig. 10.27)

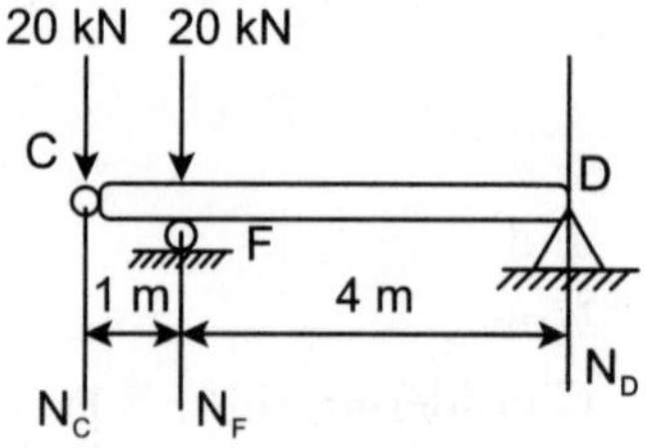

Fig. 10.27

$\Sigma M_C = 0$

$$\Rightarrow N_D \times 5 = 2000 \times 1 - N_F \times 1$$

$$5\ N_D + N_F = 2000 \ldots\ldots \quad (10.10)$$

Equilibrium of beam BCD (Fig. 10.28):

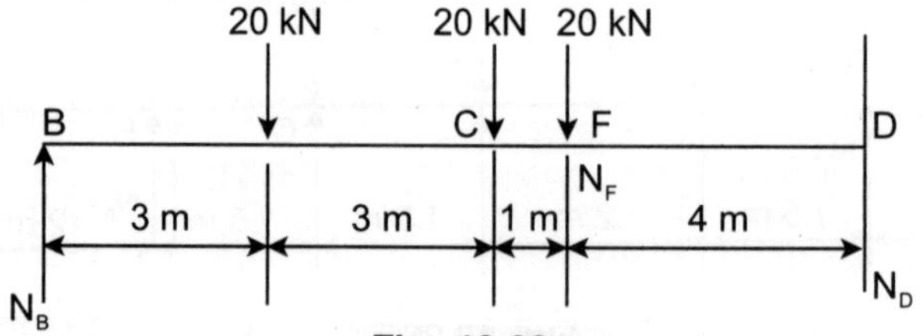

Fig. 10.28

$\Sigma M_B = 0$

$$\Rightarrow N_D \times 11 + N_F \times 7 = 2000 \times 3 + 2000 \times 6 + 2000 \times 7$$

$$\Rightarrow 11\ N_D + 7\ N_F = 2000 \times 16$$

$$\Rightarrow \quad N_D + 0.64\ N_F = 2909.9 \ldots\ldots\ldots\ldots\ldots\ldots\ldots \quad (10.11)$$

From Eqs. (10.10) and (10.11),

$$N_F = \mathbf{5702.5\ N\ (\uparrow)} \qquad \textbf{Ans.}$$

$$N_A = -740.5 = \mathbf{740.5\ N\ (\downarrow)} \qquad \textbf{Ans.}$$

Equilibrium of beam ABCD as a whole.

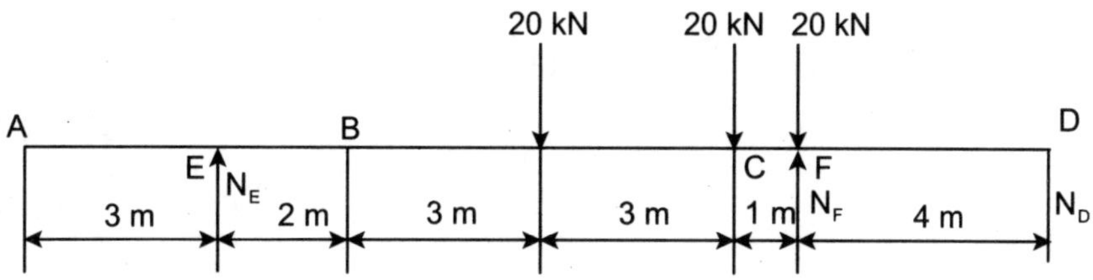

Fig. 10.29

$$\Sigma M_A = 0$$

$$\Rightarrow N_D \times 16 + N_F \times 12 + N_E \times 3$$

$$= 2000\,(8 + 11 + 12)$$

$$\Rightarrow -740.5 \times 16 + 5702.5 \times 12 + N_E \times 3 = 62000$$

$$\Rightarrow 3\,N_E = 62000 + 11848 - 68430$$

$$\therefore \quad N_E = \mathbf{5418\ N\ (\uparrow)} \qquad \textbf{Ans.}$$

Hence,

$$\left.\begin{aligned} N_E &= \mathbf{5418\ N\ (\uparrow)} \\ N_F &= \mathbf{5702.5\ N\ (\uparrow)} \\ N_D &= \mathbf{740.5\ N\ (\downarrow)} \end{aligned}\right] \qquad \textbf{Ans.}$$

Example 10.12

A man weighing 900 N stands on the middle run of a 30 N ladder resting on a smooth floor and against a wall, the ladder is prevented from slipping by a string OD. Find tension in the string and reactions at A and B a shown in Fig. 10.30.

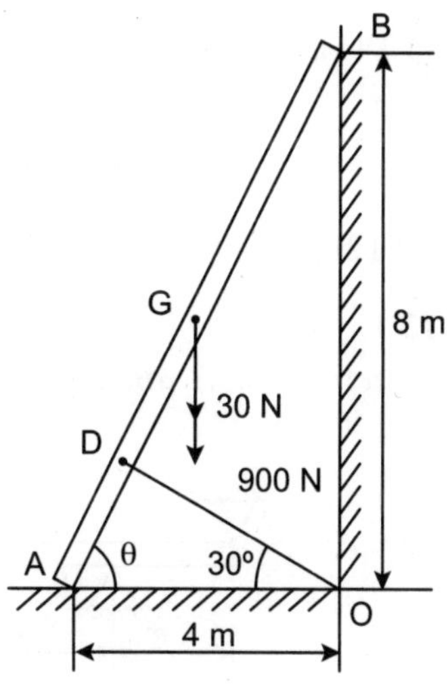

Fig. 10.30

Solution:

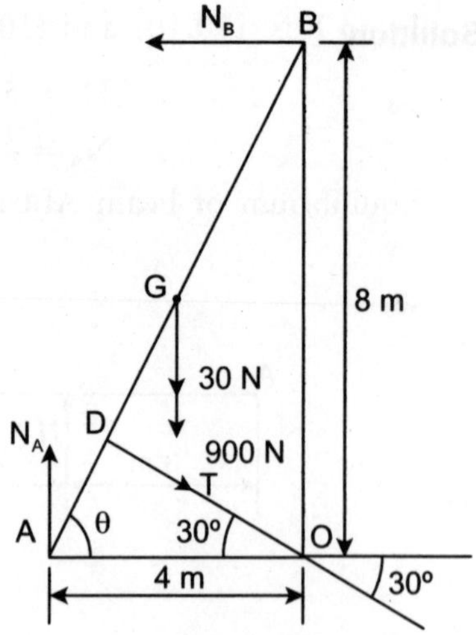

Fig. 10.31

$$W_l = 30 \text{ N}, W_m = 900 \text{ N}$$
$$T = ?$$
$$R_A = ?$$
$$R_B = ?$$
$$\theta = \tan^{-1}\left(\frac{8}{4}\right) = 63.43^\circ$$

For equilibrium

$$\Sigma F_x = 0$$
$$\Rightarrow \quad N_B = T\cos 30 \ldots \quad (10.12)$$
$$\Sigma F_y = 0$$
$$\Rightarrow \quad N_A = (900 + 30) + T\sin 30 \quad \ldots\ldots (10.13)$$
$$\Sigma M_0 = 0$$
$$\Rightarrow N_A \times 4 = (900 + 30) \times 2 + N_B \times 8$$
$$\Rightarrow 4\ N_A = 930 \times 2 + 8\ N_B$$
$$\Rightarrow \quad N_A = 465 + 2\ N_B \quad \ldots\ldots (10.14)$$

From Eq. (10.12), $T = \dfrac{N_B}{\cos 30}$, substituting in Eq. (10.13)

$$N_A = 930 + \frac{N_B}{\cos 30} \times \sin 30$$
$$N_A - 0.577\ N_B = 930 \quad \ldots\ldots (10.15)$$

From Eqs. (10.14) and (10.15),

$$\left.\begin{aligned} N_A &= \mathbf{1118.5\ N} \\ N_B &= \mathbf{326.8\ N} \end{aligned}\right]$$ **Ans.**

From Eq. (10.12), $T = \mathbf{377.4\ N}$ **Ans.**

Example 10.13

Determine the reactions at A and B on the lever as shown in the Fig. 10.32

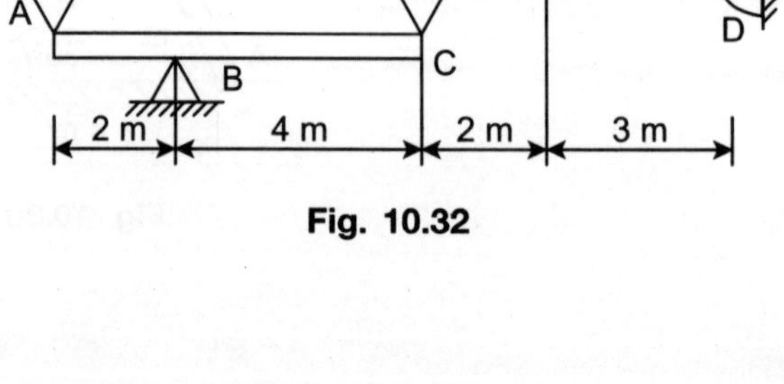

Fig. 10.32

Solution:

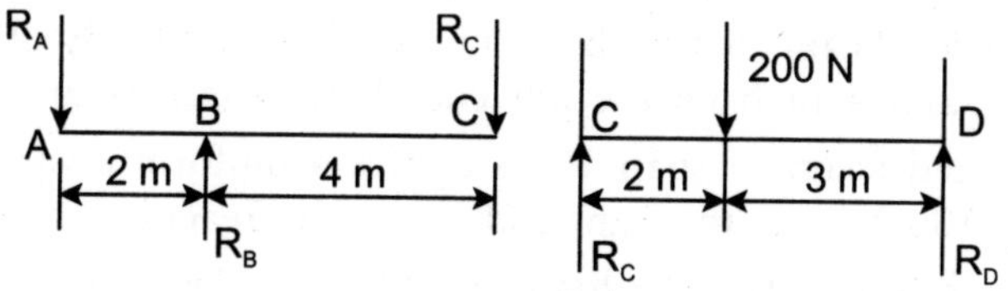

Fig. 10.33

$$R_A = ?$$

$$R_B = ?$$

$$\Sigma M_C = 0 \Rightarrow R_D \times 5 = 200 \times 2$$

$$\Rightarrow R_D = 80 \text{ N}$$

$$\Sigma F_y = 0 \Rightarrow R_C + R_D = 200$$

$$\Rightarrow R_C = 200 - 80 = 120 \text{ N}$$

$$\Sigma M_A = 0 \Rightarrow R_B \times 2 = R_C \times 6$$

$$\Rightarrow R_B = \frac{120 \times 6}{2} = 360 \text{ N}$$

$$\Sigma F_y = 0 \Rightarrow R_A + R_C = R_B$$

$$R_A = 360 - 120 = 240 \text{ N}$$

$$\therefore \quad \mathbf{R_A = 240\ N}, \quad \mathbf{R_B = 360\ N}$$

Ans.

NUMERICAL QUESTIONS

1. A simply supported beam of length 10 m carries point loads of 4 kN and 8 kN at a distance of 2 m and 4 m from the left end. Find reactions at both the ends.
2. A simply supported beam of span 10 m carries a uniformly varying load from zero at the left end to 1500 N/m at the right end. Calculate reactions at both the ends of beam.
3. An overhanging beam carries the loads as shown in Fig. 10.34. Calculate reactions at both the ends.

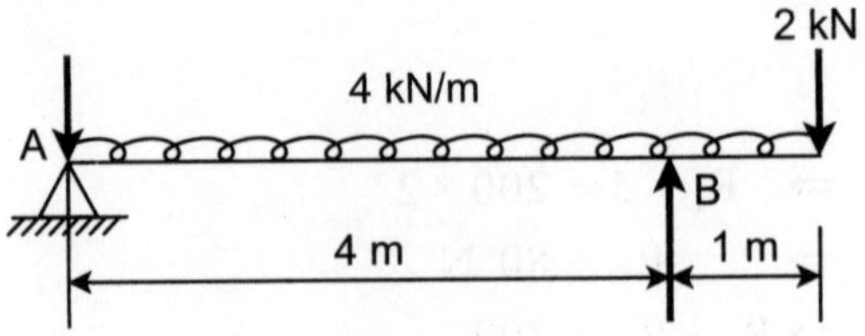

Fig. 10.34

4. A beam is load as shown in Fig. 10.35. Calculate reactions at both ends.

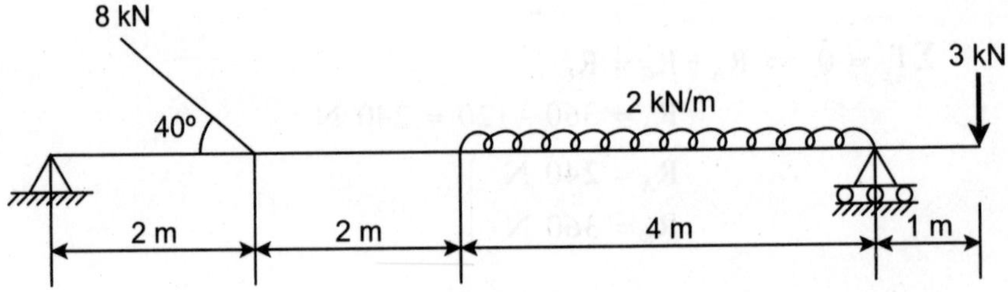

Fig. 10.35

5. A beam is loaded as shown in Fig. 10.26. Calculate reactions at both ends.

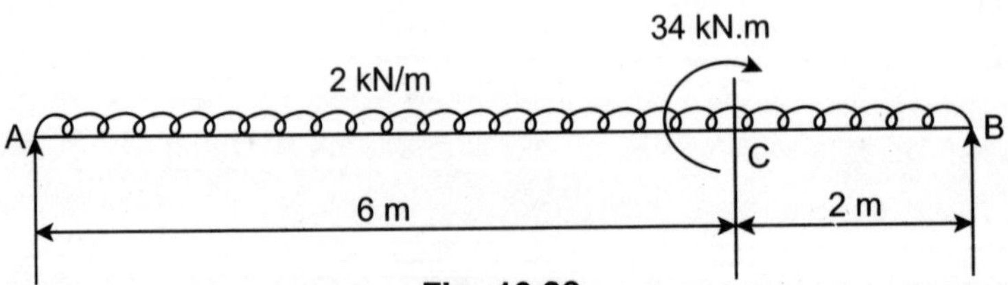

Fig. 10.36

6. A simply supported beam AB is subjected to a distributed load increasing from 1000 N/m to 4000 N/m from end A to end B. The span AB = 6 m. Determine the support reactions [R_B = 9000 N, R_A = 6000 N].

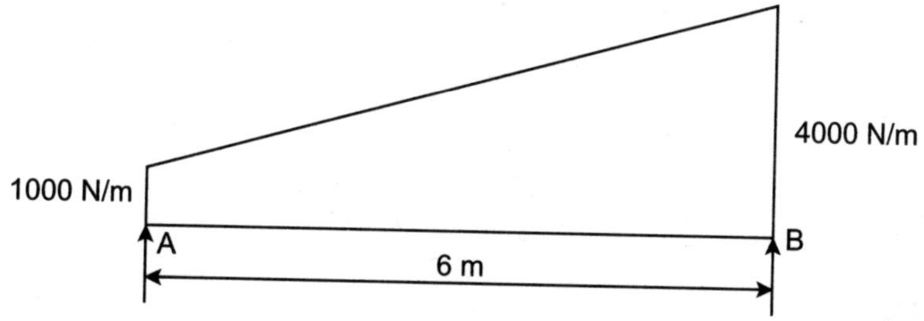

Fig. 10.37

7. Find the maximum weight that can be lifted by crane weighing 100 kN without tipping over wheel B. Calculate the corresponding reactions at the supports C and D.

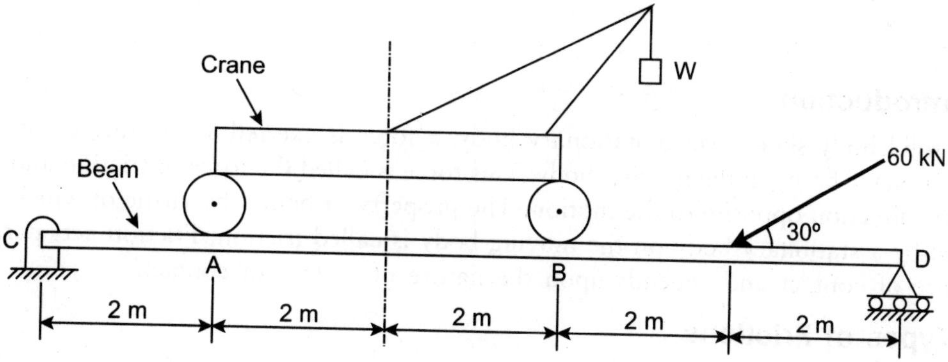

Fig. 10.38

11

Friction

11.1 Introduction

When a solid body slides over a stationary body, a force is exerted at the surface of contact by the stationary body on the moving body. This force is called the force of friction and always acts in the direction opposite to the motion. The property of bodies by virtue of which a force is exerted by a stationary body on the moving body is called friction. Friction acts parallel to the surface of contact and depends upon the nature of surface of contact.

11.2 Types of Frictions

1. Dry friction
2. Fluid friction
3. Internal friction

Dry friction exists between two un-lubricated surfaces contact under a condition of sliding or tendency to slide.

A friction force is always tangential to the surface of contact. The direction of force always opposes the motion. Dry friction is also called coulomb friction.

11.3 Notations Used

W = Weight of body/member (N)

N = Normal reaction (N)

P = External effort applied (N)

μ = Coefficient of friction

θ = Inclination of plane with horizontal

α = Angle between inclined plane and line of action of effort P or Helix angle

ϕ = Angle of friction

p = pitch of the screw thread

11.4 Mechanism of Dry Friction

The friction is mainly due to roughness of surfaces of the bodies in contact. Friction force always acts in a direction opposite to that in which the body has a tendency to move over the surface of another body. Friction is a self adjusting force.

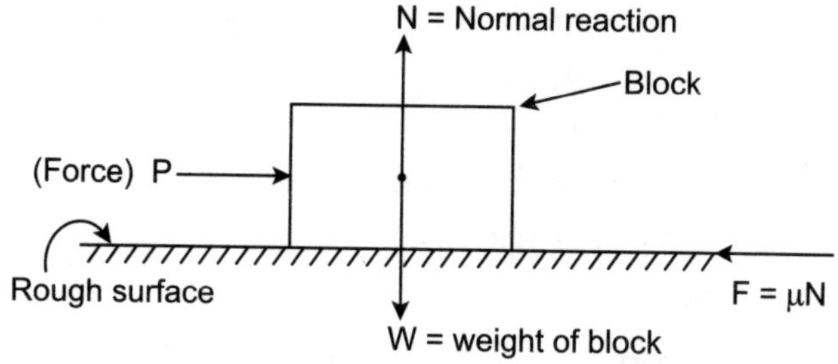

Fig. 11.1

Initially, the block remains stationary, it means that apart from the normal reaction N equating W, an equal and opposite force of friction 'F' must be developed at the same time along the contact surface to neutralise the applied force P. As P is increased, F too increases, exactly equal to P in magnitudes at all times, since the block keeps to its position of rest.

If at any time

$$F < P$$

The block will move to the right under the action of resultant force (P – F) and in limiting position, $F_s = P$.

But this situation does not continue indefinitely and as P increases, a time comes when F attained F_s (limiting static friction), does not increase further. This is the stage of impending motion. Any further slightest increase in P, sets the block in motion. As soon as the block starts moving, the applied force P is reduced and yet the block kept in motion.

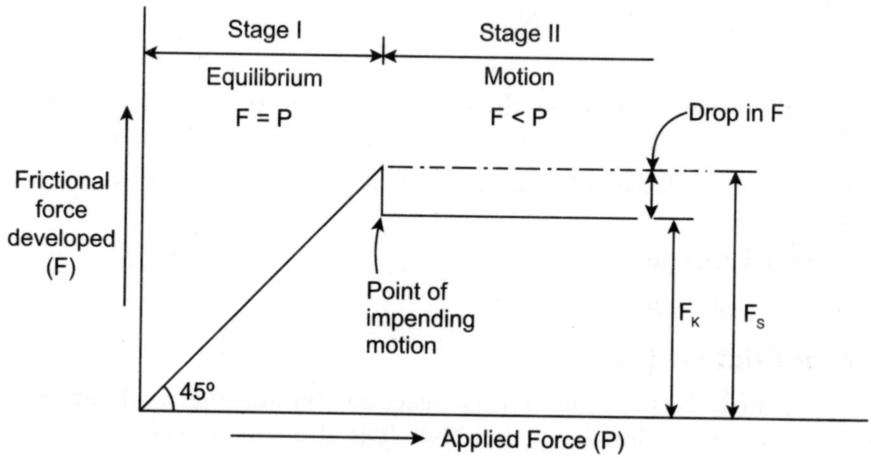

Fig. 11.2: Mechanism of Dry Friction

11.5 Laws of Dry Friction or Coulomb Friction

1. F is independent with the magnitude of area of contact between two bodies.
2. F always act in a direction opposite to the direction of slippage.
3. $F_k < F_s$, i.e.
   Kinetic force of friction < Static force of friction
4. $F_s \alpha N$ or $F_s = \mu_s N$ .... (11.1)
   $F_k \alpha N$ or $F_k = \mu_k N$ .... (11.2)
   where $\mu_s/\mu_k \rightarrow$ Coefficient of static/Kinetic friction
   $N \rightarrow$ Normal reaction
   $\mu_s > \mu_k$

11.6 Coefficient of Friction

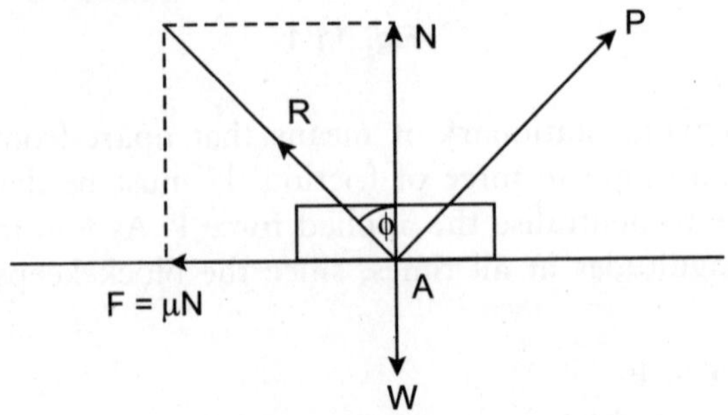

Fig. 11.3

It may be defined as the ratio of limiting force of friction (F) to the normal reaction (N) between two bodies. It is denoted by symbol μ. Thus,

$$\mu = \frac{F_{limiting}}{N} = \frac{F}{N} \quad \text{.................................... (11.3)}$$

or

$$F = F_{lim} = \mu N$$

In most cases, the value of μ is less than one. There are two value of μ. When there is limiting equilibrium, the coefficient of friction is called static coefficient of friction (μ_s).

When the bodies are in relative motion, the coefficient of friction is called kinetic coefficient of friction (μ_k).

From laws of solid friction

$$\mu_s > \mu_k$$

11.7 Angle of Friction (φ)

It is defined as the angle between the normal reaction (N) and the resultant (R) of limiting force of friction (μN) and normal reaction (N). It is denoted by symbol φ. In Fig. 11.3, A body is resting on horizontal surface, P is a force which tends to move the body. Limiting force of friction F = μN is developed. Then angle of friction (ϕ) is the angle between N and R.

Mathematically,

$$\tan\phi = \frac{F}{N} = \frac{\mu N}{N} = \mu$$

$$\therefore \quad \mu = \tan\phi \quad \ldots\ldots (11.4)$$

i.e. the tangent of angle of friction is equal to the coefficient of friction.

11.8 Cone of Fiction

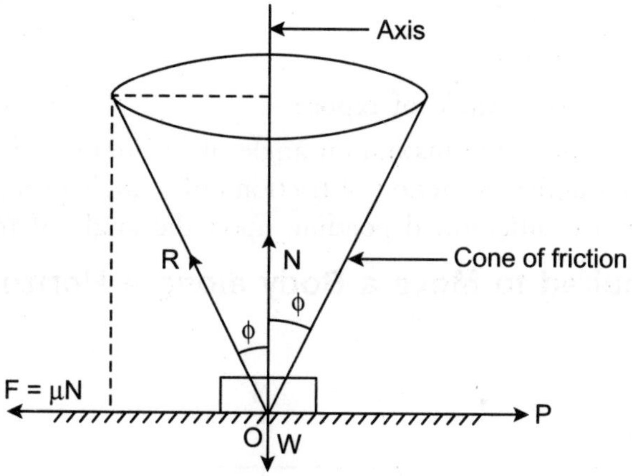

Fig. 11.4

When F and N meet at point O, then R is the resultant, which makes an angle ϕ with N. Thus, O is the vertex of a cone whose axis is N and semi-vertical angle is ϕ, then such a right circular cone is called as cone of friction. This right circular cone of friction is generated by changing the force P gradually through 360° and resultant R generates a right circular cone.

11.9 Angle of Repose

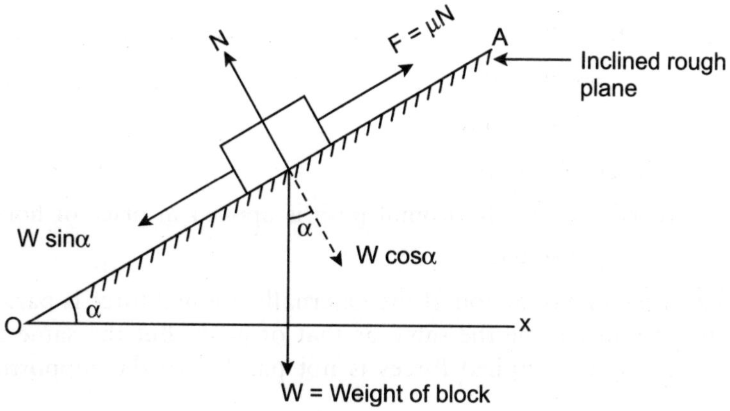

Fig. 11.5

If the angle of inclination, α, is increased gradually, such that the body is just on the point of sliding. The forces keeping the body in equilibrium are: W, N and F (or μN).

For equilibrium:

$$N = W\cos\alpha \quad \text{(11.5)}$$

and
$$\mu N = W\sin\alpha \quad \text{(11.6)}$$

$$\Rightarrow \quad \mu = \tan\alpha \quad \text{[Divide Eq. (11.6) by Eq. (11.5)]}$$

$$\text{But} \quad \mu = \tan\phi$$

$$\Rightarrow \quad \phi = \alpha$$

$$\therefore \quad \phi = \alpha$$

or Angle of friction = Angle of repose

Hence, angle of repose is the maximum angle of inclination of the plane at which a body remains in equilibrium under the action of friction only. Angle of repose for different materials, i.e. coal, wheat, etc. are different, depending upon the angle of friction.

11.10 Force Required to Move a Body along a Horizontal Plane

Case (a) Fig. 11.6

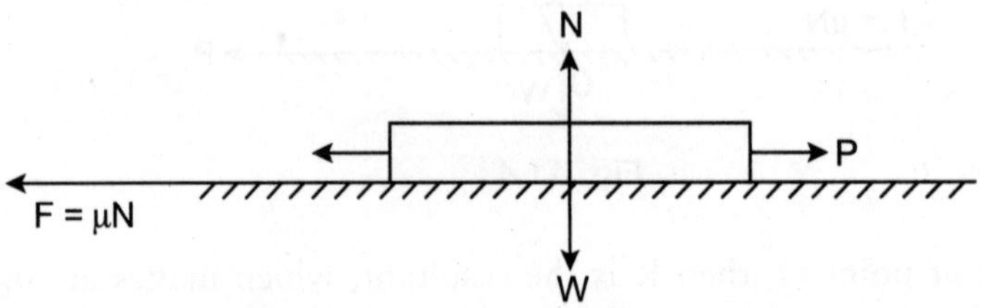

Fig. 11.6

For equilibrium

$$\Sigma F_y = 0 \Rightarrow N = W \quad \text{(11.7)}$$

$$\Sigma F_x = 0 \Rightarrow P = F \quad \text{(11.8)}$$

$$\Rightarrow P = \mu N \quad \text{(11.9)}$$

$$\Rightarrow P = \mu W$$

where μ = coefficient of friction.

Note: It can be proved that if a horizontal push is applied in place of horizontal pull then also

$$P = \mu W$$

It means that if the line of action of the externally applied force is parallel to the supporting plane, the value of pull will be the same as that of push. But the same is not true if the line of action of the externally applied forces is not parallel to the supporting plane.

Case (b) Fig. 11.7

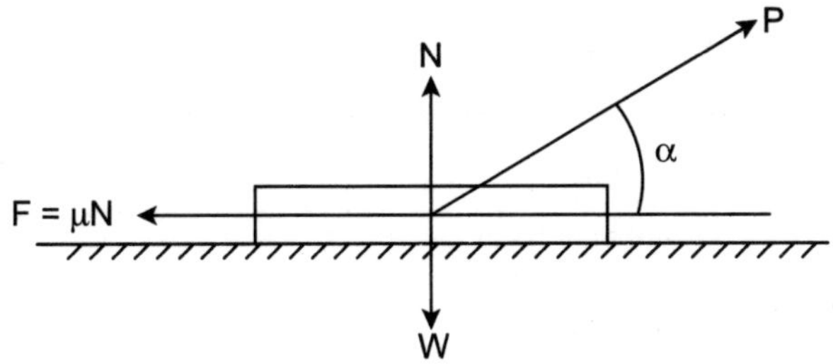

Fig. 11.7

α = Angle made by the line of action of pull P with the horizontal.

For equilibrium of the body:

$$\Sigma F_x = 0 \Rightarrow P\cos\alpha = F = \mu N \qquad (11.10)$$

$$\Sigma F_y = 0 \Rightarrow N + P\sin\alpha = W \qquad (11.11)$$

From Eqs. (11.10) and (11.11),

$$P\cos\alpha = \mu(W - P\sin\alpha)$$

$$\Rightarrow \quad P\cos\alpha = \mu W - \mu P\sin\alpha$$

$$\Rightarrow \quad P(\cos\alpha + \mu\sin\alpha) = \mu W$$

$$\Rightarrow \quad P = \frac{\mu W}{\cos\alpha + \mu\sin\alpha} \qquad (11.12)$$

But $\mu = \tan\phi$

where ϕ = friction angle

From Eq. (11.12),

$$P = \frac{W\tan\phi}{\cos\alpha + \tan\phi\sin\alpha}$$

$$= \frac{W\sin\phi/\cos\phi}{\cos\alpha + \dfrac{\sin\phi}{\cos\phi}\cdot\sin\alpha}$$

or
$$P = \frac{W\sin\phi}{\cos\alpha\cos\phi + \sin\alpha\sin\phi}$$

$$P = \frac{W\sin\phi}{\cos(\alpha - \phi)} \qquad (11.13)$$

For P to be least, $\cos(\alpha - \phi) = 1$

or $\alpha = \phi$

and $P_{least} = W s$ .... (11.14)

Note: We can show that if force P is push in place of pull then Eq. (11.13) will become as

$$P = \frac{W \sin\phi}{\cos(\alpha + \phi)} \quad \text{.............................} \quad (11.15)$$

and

$$P_{least} = W \sin\phi$$

which is same as given by Eq. (11.14).

11.11 Force Required to Move a Body along an Inclined Plane

Pull required to move a body up an inclined plane

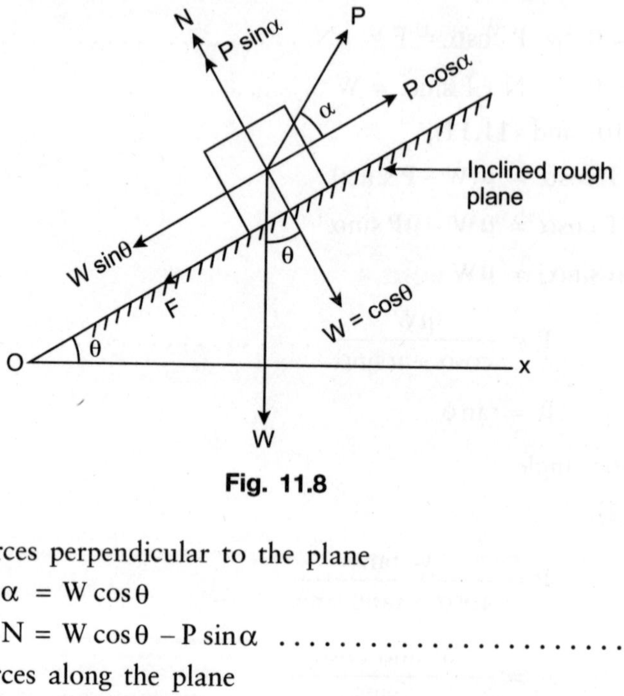

Fig. 11.8

Resolving all the forces perpendicular to the plane

$$N + P \sin\alpha = W \cos\theta$$

$$\Rightarrow \quad N = W \cos\theta - P \sin\alpha \quad \text{.............................} \quad (11.16)$$

Resolving all the forces along the plane

$$P \cos\alpha = F + W \sin\theta$$

$$\Rightarrow \quad P \cos\alpha = \mu N + W \sin\theta \quad \text{.............................} \quad (11.17)$$

Substituting the value of N from Eq. (11.16) into Eq. (11.17)

$$P \cos\alpha = \mu(W \cos\theta - P \sin\alpha) + W \sin\theta$$

or

$$P \cos\alpha = \mu W \cos\theta - \mu P \sin\alpha + W \sin\theta$$

or

$$P \cos\alpha + \mu P \sin\alpha = \mu W \cos\theta + W \sin\theta$$

$$\Rightarrow \qquad P = \frac{W(\sin\theta + \mu\cos\theta)}{(\cos\alpha + \mu\sin\alpha)} \qquad \ldots\ldots (11.18)$$

But $\mu = \tan\phi$

$$\therefore \qquad P = W\left(\frac{\sin\theta + \tan\phi\cos\theta}{\cos\alpha + \tan\phi\sin\alpha}\right)$$

$$= \frac{W(\text{Sin}\theta\,\text{Cos}\phi + \text{Cos}\theta\,\text{Sin}\phi)}{(\text{Cos}\alpha\,\text{Cos}\phi + \text{Sin}\alpha\,\text{Sin}\phi)}$$

$$P = \frac{W\sin(\theta + \phi)}{\cos(\alpha - \phi)} \qquad \ldots\ldots (11.19)$$

If P is acting along the inclined plane then $\alpha = 0$ and

$$P = \frac{W\sin(\theta + \phi)}{\cos(-\phi)} = \frac{W\sin(\theta + \phi)}{\cos\phi} \qquad \ldots\ldots (11.20)$$

For least pull, $\cos(\alpha - \theta) = 1 \Rightarrow \alpha = \phi$

$\therefore$ From Eq. (11.19),

$$P_{least} = W\sin(\theta + \phi) \qquad \ldots\ldots (11.21)$$

11.12 Inclined Pull (P) to Prevent a Body from Sliding Down an Inclined Plane

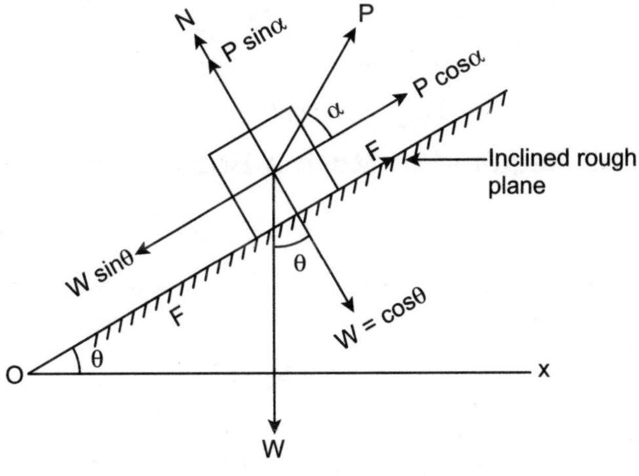

Fig. 11.9

In this case, since the body has a tendency to slide down the inclined plane, the limiting force of friction F will act upward along the inclined plane.

For equilibrium:

Resolving all the forces perpendicular to the plane

$$N + P\sin\alpha = W\cos\theta$$

$$\Rightarrow \quad N = W\cos\theta - P\sin\alpha \quad \ldots\ldots (11.22)$$

Resolving all the forces along the plane

$$P\cos\alpha + F = W\sin\theta$$

$$P\cos\alpha + \mu N = W\sin\theta \quad \ldots\ldots (11.23)$$

$$\Rightarrow \quad P\cos\alpha + \mu(W\cos\theta - P\sin\alpha) = W\sin\theta$$

$$\Rightarrow \quad P(\cos\alpha - \mu\sin\alpha) = W(\sin\theta - \mu\cos\theta)$$

$$\Rightarrow \quad P = W\left(\frac{\sin\theta - \mu\cos\theta}{\cos\alpha - \mu\sin\alpha}\right) \quad \ldots\ldots (11.24)$$

or

$$= \frac{W(\sin\theta - \tan\phi\cos\theta)}{\cos\alpha - \tan\phi\sin\alpha}$$

$$= \frac{W(\sin\theta\cos\phi - \cos\theta\sin\phi)}{\cos\alpha\cos\phi - \sin\alpha\sin\phi}$$

$$\therefore \quad P = \frac{W\sin(\theta - \phi)}{\cos(\alpha + \phi)} \quad \ldots\ldots (11.25)$$

When $\alpha = 0$, P becomes parallel to inclined plane and then

$$P = \frac{W\sin(\theta - \phi)}{\cos\phi} \quad \ldots\ldots (11.26)$$

For P_{least} from Eq. (11.25), $\cos(\alpha + \phi) = 1$

$$P_{least} = W\sin(\theta - \phi) \quad \ldots\ldots (11.27)$$

11.13 Inclined Pull Required to Move a Body Down an Inclined Plane

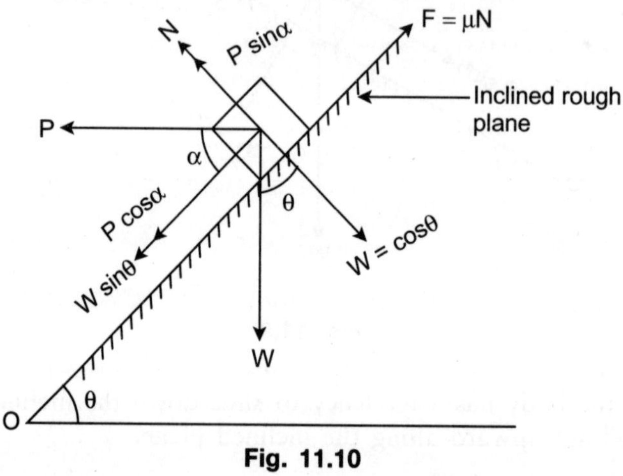

Fig. 11.10

For equilibrium

Resolving all forces perpendicular to the plane

$$N + P\sin\alpha = W\cos\theta$$

or $$N = W\cos\theta - P\sin\alpha \quad \ldots\ldots (11.28)$$

Resolving all forces along the plane

$$P\cos\alpha + W\sin\theta = F$$

or $$P\cos\alpha = \mu N - W\sin\theta \quad \ldots\ldots (11.29)$$

or $$P\cos\alpha = \mu(W\cos\theta - P\sin\alpha) - W\sin\theta$$

or $$P\cos\alpha = \mu W\cos\theta - \mu P\sin\alpha - W\sin\theta$$

or $$P(\cos\alpha + \mu\sin\alpha) = W(\mu\cos\theta - \sin\theta)$$

or $$P = \frac{W(\mu\cos\theta - \sin\theta)}{(\cos\alpha + \mu\sin\alpha)}$$

or $$P = \frac{W(\tan\phi\cos\theta - \sin\theta)}{(\cos\alpha + \tan\phi\sin\alpha)} = \frac{W(\sin\phi\cos\theta - \sin\theta\cos\phi)}{(\cos\alpha\cos\phi + \sin\phi\sin\alpha)}$$

or $$P = \frac{W\sin(\phi - \theta)}{\cos(\alpha - \phi)} \quad \ldots\ldots (11.30)$$

and when $\alpha = 0$, P becomes parallel to the plane and is given by

$$P = \frac{W\sin(\phi - \theta)}{\cos(-\phi)} = \frac{W\sin(\phi - \theta)}{\cos\phi} \quad \ldots\ldots (11.31)$$

and $$P_{least} = W\sin(\phi - \theta) \quad \ldots\ldots (11.32)$$

Example 11.1

A wooden block of weight 60 N rests on a horizontal plane. Determine the force required to just (i) Pull it and (ii) Push it. Coefficient of friction is 0.35 between mating surfaces. Comment on the result.

Solution:

Case I: When the applied force is parallel to plane

$W = 60$ N

$P = ?$

$\mu = 0.35$

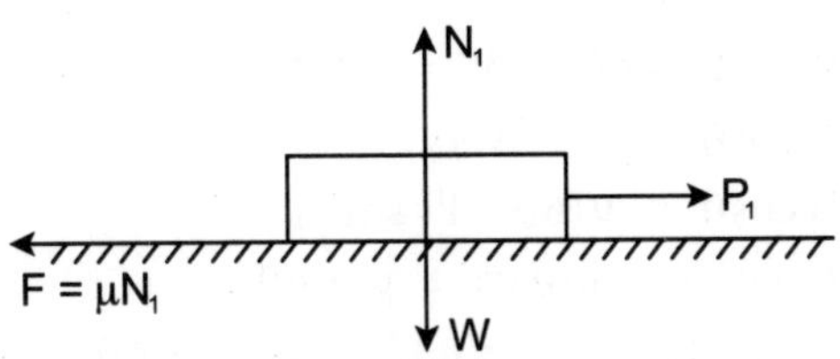

Fig. 11.11

(a) Pull P_1 = ?

For equilibrium

$$\Sigma F_y = 0 \Rightarrow N_1 = W = 60 \text{ N} \quad \ldots\ldots (11.33)$$

$$\Sigma F_x = 0 \Rightarrow P_1 = F = \mu N_1 = 0.35 \times 60 = 21 \text{ N}$$

$$\therefore \quad P_1 = 21 \text{ N}$$

(b) Push P_2 = ?

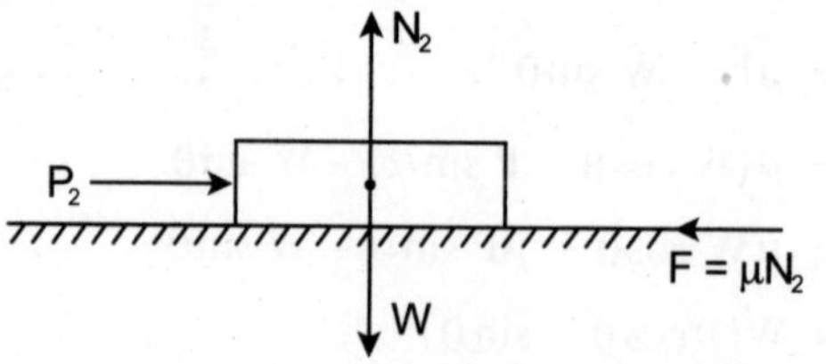

Fig. 11.12

For equilibrium

$$\Sigma F_y = 0 \Rightarrow N_2 = W = 60 \text{ N}$$

$$\Sigma F_x = 0 \Rightarrow P_2 = \mu N_2$$

$$= 0.35 \times 60 = 21 \text{ N}$$

$$\therefore \quad P_2 = 21 \text{ N}$$

Note: The value of pull and push is same if applied load is parallel to the horizontal plane.

Case II: When the applied load is not parallel to the horizontal plane.

Let the line of action of applied load makes on angle of 30° to the horizontal plane.

(a) Pull P_3 = ?

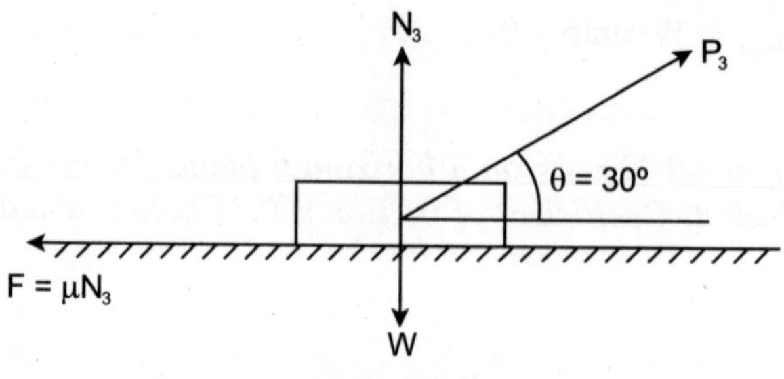

Fig. 11.13

For equilibrium

$$\Sigma F_y = 0 \Rightarrow N_3 + P_3 \sin\theta = W = 60 \text{ N} \quad \ldots\ldots (11.34)$$

$$\Sigma F_x = 0 \Rightarrow P_3 \cos\theta = F = \mu N_3 \quad \ldots\ldots (11.35)$$

$$\Rightarrow P_3 \cos\theta = \mu(60 - P_3 \sin\theta)$$

$$\Rightarrow P_3 (\cos\theta + \sin\theta\, \mu) = \mu \times 60$$

$$\Rightarrow P_3 (\cos 30 + 0.35 \sin 30) = 0.35 \times 60$$

$$\Rightarrow P_3 = \mathbf{20.17 \text{ N}}$$ **Ans.**

(b) Push P_4 = ?

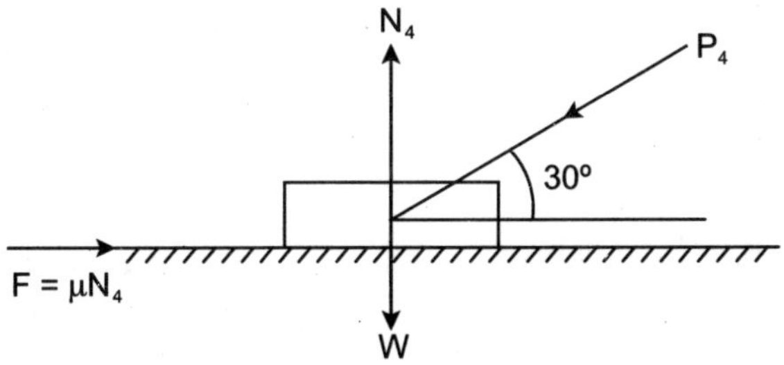

Fig. 11.14

For equilibrium

$$\Sigma F_y = 0 \Rightarrow N_4 = 60 + P_4 \sin 30$$

$$\Sigma F_x = 0 \Rightarrow P\cos 30 = \mu N_4 = \mu(60 + P_4 \sin 30)$$

$$\Rightarrow P(\cos 30 - \mu \sin 30) = 0.35 \times 60$$

$$\Rightarrow P = \mathbf{30.4\ N}$$ **Ans.**

Comments

1. If force is parallel to horizontal plane then Pull = Push.
2. If force is at an angle with plane then Pull < Push.

Example 11.2

Two blocks A and B of weight 8 kN and 4 kN respectively are in equilibrium position as shown in Fig. 11.15. The coefficient of friction between two blocks as well as between block and floor is 0.2. Calculate P required to move the block A.

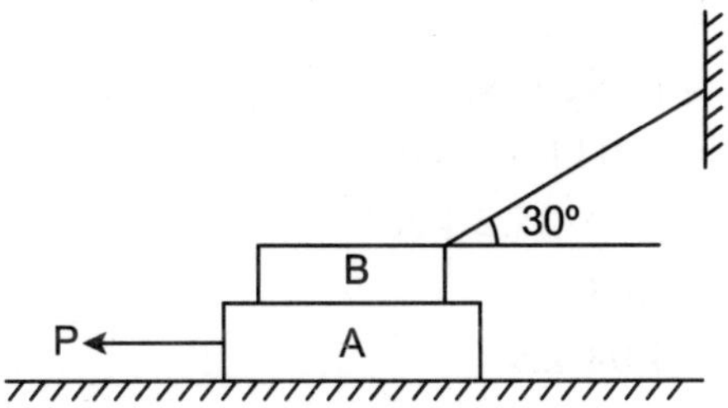

Fig. 11.15

Solution:

$W_A = 8$ kN

$W_B = 4$ kN

$\mu = 0.2$

P = ?

For Block B

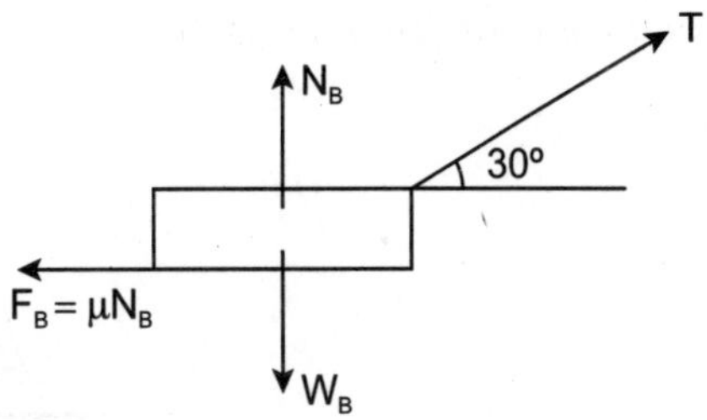

Fig. 11.16: F.B.D. of Block B

$$\Sigma F_y = 0$$

$$\Rightarrow \quad N_B + T\sin\theta = W_B$$

$$\Rightarrow \quad N_B = 4 - T\sin 30$$

$$N_B = \left(4 - \frac{T}{2}\right) \quad \ldots\ldots\ (11.36)$$

$$\Sigma F_x = 0$$

$$\Rightarrow \quad T\cos\theta = F_B = \mu N_B$$

$$\Rightarrow \quad T\cos 30 = 0.2 \times \left(4 - \frac{T}{2}\right)$$

$$T\frac{\sqrt{3}}{2} = 0.8 - \frac{0.2T}{2}$$

$$T\frac{\sqrt{3}}{2} + 0.1T = 0.8$$

$$T\left(\frac{\sqrt{3}}{2} + 0.1\right) = 0.8 \Rightarrow T = 0.828 \text{ kN}$$

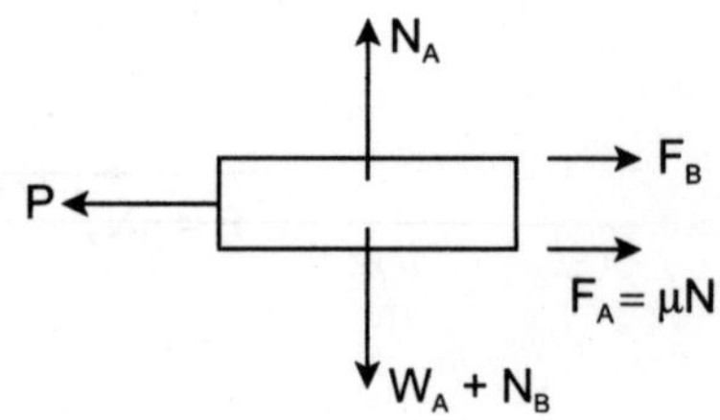

Fig. 11.17: F.B.D. of Block A

$$\therefore \quad N_B = 4 - \frac{T}{2} = 4 - 0.414 = 3.585 \text{ kN}$$

and $$F_B = \mu N_B = 0.2 \times 3.585 = 0.717 \text{ kN}$$

Now

Equilibrium of Block A

$$\Sigma F_y = 0 \Rightarrow N_A = W_A + N_B = 8 + 3.585 = 11.6 \text{ kN}$$

$$\Sigma F_x = 0 \Rightarrow P = F_A + F_B$$

$$= \mu(N_A + N_B)$$

$$= 0.2(11.6 + 3.6)$$

$$= 0.2 \times 25.2 \text{ kN}$$

$$= 3.04$$

$$P = 3.04 \text{ kN}$$

Ans.

Example 11.3

Find the maximum angle θ with the horizontal before the block of mass m begins to slip. The coefficient of frictions is μ.

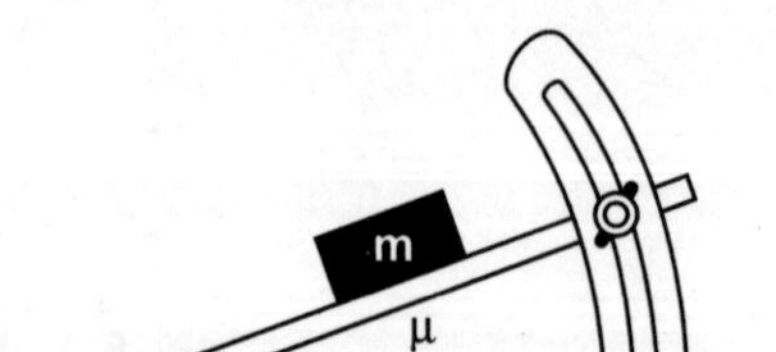

Fig. 11.18

Solution:

$\theta = ?$

$\mu = \mu$

$W = mg$

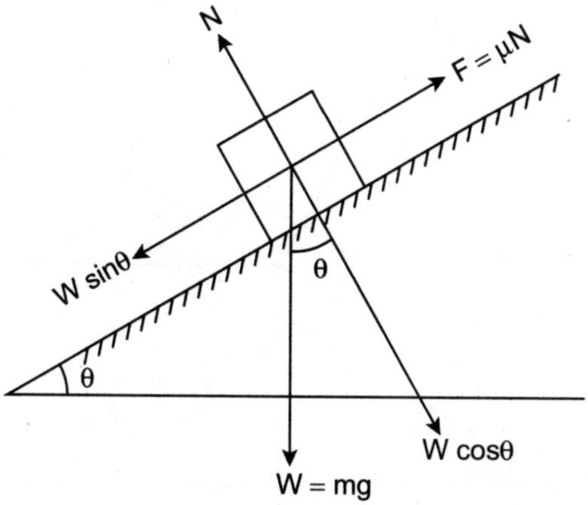

Fig. 11.19

The friction force acts in a direction to oppose the slipping which would occur if no friction is there.

For equilibrium of block

$$\Sigma F\,(\perp \text{ to plane}) = 0$$

$$\Rightarrow \quad N = W\cos\theta \qquad (11.37)$$

$$\Sigma F\,(\parallel \text{ to plane}) = 0$$

$$F = W\sin\theta$$

$$\Rightarrow \quad \mu N = W\sin\theta \qquad (11.38)$$

or $\quad \mu W\cos\theta = W\sin\theta$

or $\quad \tan\theta = \mu$

or $\quad \theta = \tan^{-1}(\mu)$ **Ans.**

Example 11.4

A block rests on an inclined plane as shown in the figure. The block is tied up by a horizontal string which has a tension of 20 N. The block weight is 50 N, determine

(a) Frictional force on the block

(b) Normal reaction of the inclined plane

(c) The coefficient of friction between the contacting surfaces.

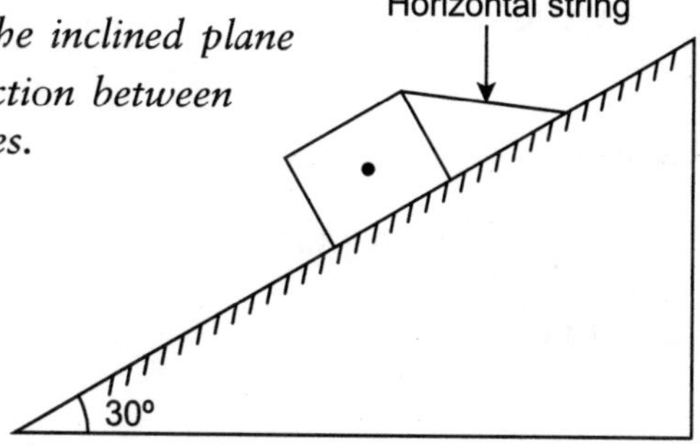

Fig. 11.20

Solution:

T = 20 N

W = 50 N

F = ?

N = ?

μ = ?

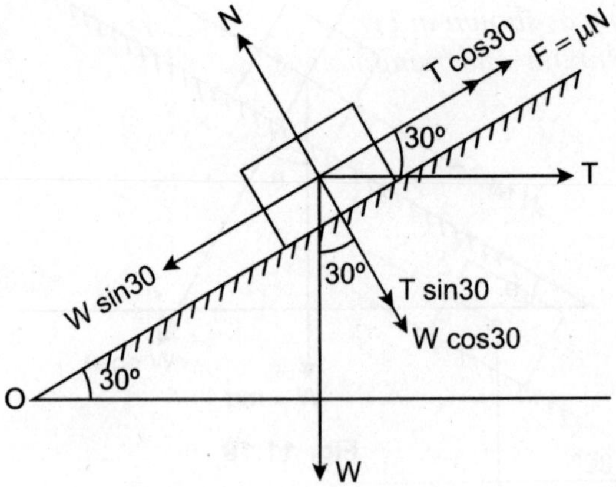

Fig. 11.21

For limiting condition

(a) Resolving all the forces perpendicular to the plane

$$N = W\cos 30 + T\sin 30 = 50\frac{\sqrt{3}}{2} + 20 \times \frac{1}{2} = 53.3 \text{ N} \quad \ldots\ldots (11.39)$$

Resolving all the forces along the plane

$$F + T\cos 30 = W\sin 30 \quad \ldots\ldots (11.40)$$

$$F = 50 \times \frac{1}{2} - 20 \times \frac{\sqrt{3}}{2}$$

$$= 25 - 10\sqrt{3}$$

$$= \mathbf{7.68\ N}$$ **Ans.**

(b) N = ?

From Eq. (11.39),

$$N = \mathbf{53.3\ N}$$ **Ans.**

(c) μ = ?

$$F = \mu N$$

$$\therefore \quad \mu = \frac{F}{N} = \frac{7.68}{53.3} = 0.144$$

$$\therefore \quad \mu = \mathbf{0.144}$$ **Ans.**

Example 11.5

A block of weight $W_1 = 100$ N rest on an inclined plane and weight W_2 is attached to the first weight W_1 through a string as shown in Fig. 11.22. If coefficient of friction is 0.2 between block and plane, find the maximum and minimum values of W_2 for equilibrium condition.

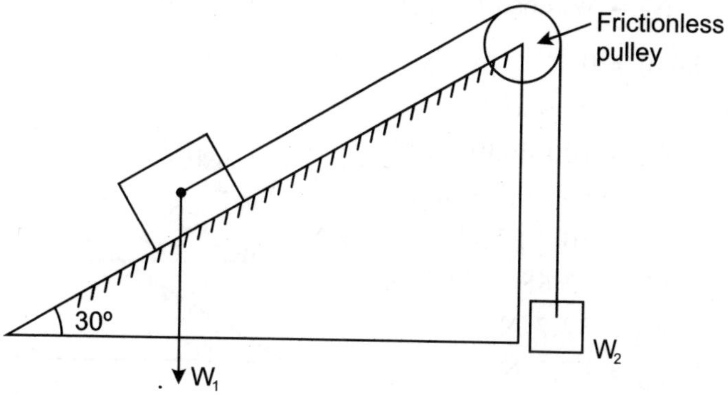

Fig. 11.22

Solution:

$W_1 = 100$ N

$W_2 = ?$

$\mu = 0.2$

There will be two cases.

(a) When the block is about to slide up the plane.

(b) When the block is about to slide down the plane.

Case (a): When the block is about to slide up the plane

For equilibrium condition

ΣF (perpendicular to plane) = 0

$$N_1 = W_1 \cos 30 = 100\frac{\sqrt{3}}{2}$$

or $$N_1 = 86.6 \text{ N} \quad \ldots\ldots\ldots (11.41)$$

$$\Sigma F \text{ (along the plane)} = 0$$

$$W_2 = F_1 + W_1 \sin 30$$
$$= \mu N_1 + 100 \sin 30$$
$$= 0.2 \times 86.6 + 50$$
$$= 67.3 \text{ N}$$

$\therefore$ $$W_2 = 67.3 \text{ N}$$

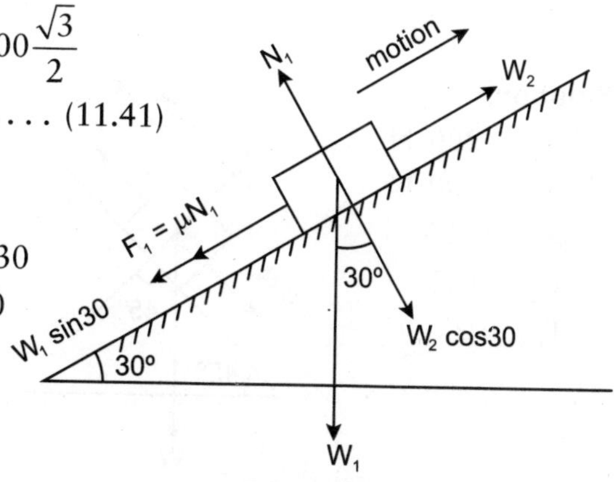

Fig. 11.23

Case (b): When the block is about to slide down the plane

For equilibrium condition

$$\Sigma F(\perp \text{ to plane}) = 0$$

$$\Rightarrow \quad N_2 = W_1 \cos 30 = 100\frac{\sqrt{3}}{2} = 50\sqrt{3} = 86.6 \text{ N} \quad \ldots\ldots\ldots\ldots \quad (11.42)$$

$$\Sigma F(\parallel \text{ to plane}) = 0$$

$$\Rightarrow \quad W_2 + F_2 = W_1 \sin 30$$

$$\Rightarrow \quad W_2 = 100 \sin 30 - \mu N_2$$

$$= 50 - 0.2 \times 86.6$$

$$= 50 \times 17.32 = 32.68 \text{ N}$$

$$W_2 = 32.68 = 32.7 \text{ N}$$

$$W_2 = \mathbf{32.7\ N}$$

$$\therefore \quad W_{2\,max} = 67.3 \text{ N}$$

$$W_{2\,min} = 32.7 \text{ N} \qquad \textbf{Ans.}$$

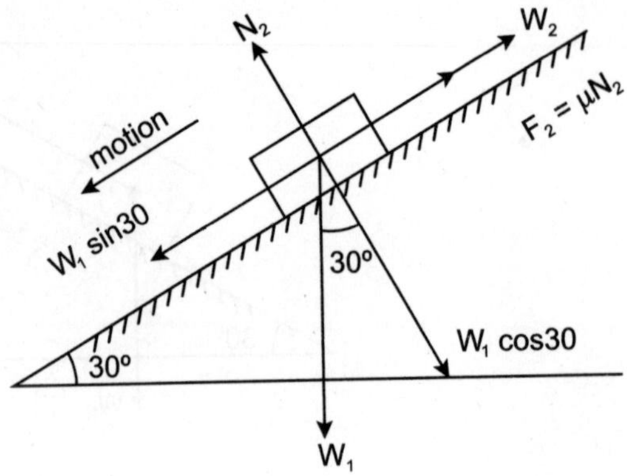

Fig. 11.24

Example 11.6

Two blocks of weight 200 N and 500 N are connected by a cord as shown in Fig. 11.25. Calculate the maximum tension in the chord limiting conditions of both the blocks.

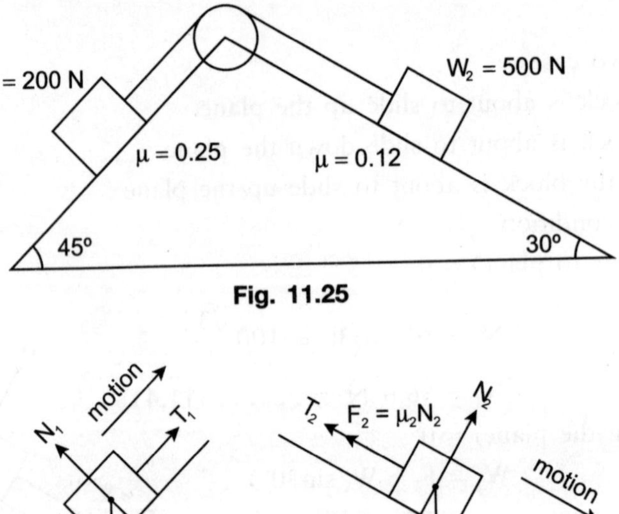

Fig. 11.25

Solution:

$W_1 = 200$ N

$W_2 = 500$ N

$\mu_1 = 0.25$

$\mu_2 = 0.12$

$T_{max} = ?$

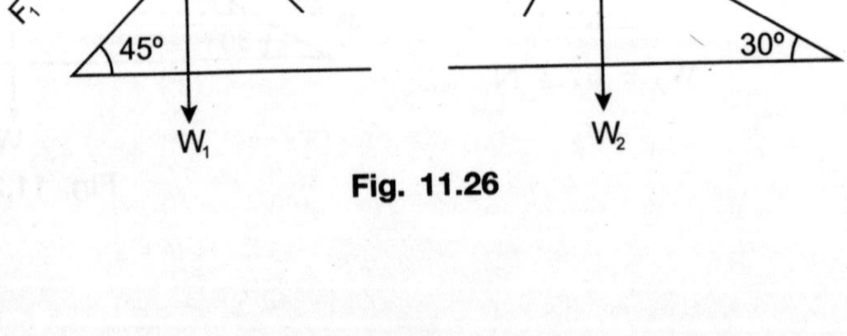

Fig. 11.26

For equilibrium block W_1

Resolving all forces perpendicular to planes

$$N_1 = W_1 \cos 45 = 200 \cos 45 = 141.42 \text{ N} \quad \ldots\ldots \quad (11.43)$$

Resolving all forces along the plane:

$$T_1 = F_1 + W_1 \sin 30 \quad \ldots\ldots \quad (11.44)$$

$$= \mu_1 N_1 + \frac{W_1}{2} = 0.25 \times 141.42 + \frac{200}{2}$$

$$T_1 = \mathbf{135.4 \text{ N}}$$

For equilibrium of block W_2

Resolving all the forces $\perp$ and $\parallel$ to the plane

$$N_2 = W_2 \cos 30$$

$$N_2 = 500\frac{\sqrt{3}}{2} = 433 \text{ N} \quad \ldots\ldots \quad (11.45)$$

and

$$T_2 + F_2 = W_2 \sin 30$$

$$T_2 = W_2 \sin 30 - \mu_2 N_2$$

$$= 500 \times \frac{1}{2} - 0.2 \times 433 = 250 - 86.6$$

$$T_2 = \mathbf{163.4 \text{ N}}$$

$\therefore \quad T_{max} = T_2 = \mathbf{163.4 \text{ N}}$ **Ans.**

Example 11.7

Two blocks A and B are placed as shown in Fig. 11.27. Calculate force P required to make the lower block A and the tension in the cable coefficient of friction for all contact surfaces is 0.3.

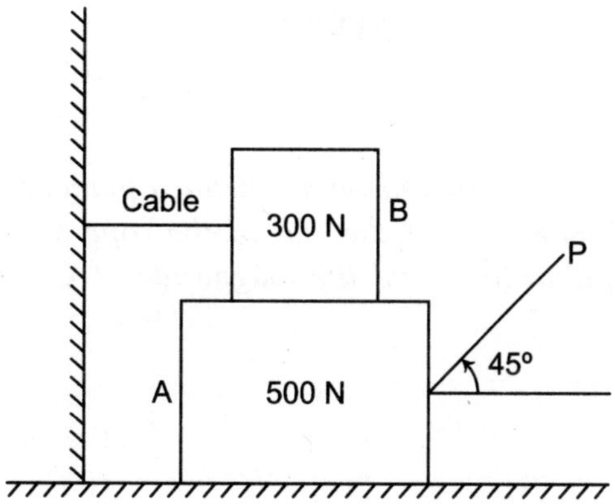

Fig. 11.27

Solution:

$W_A = 500$ N

$W_B = 300$ N

P = ?

$\mu = 0.3$

Equilibrium of block B

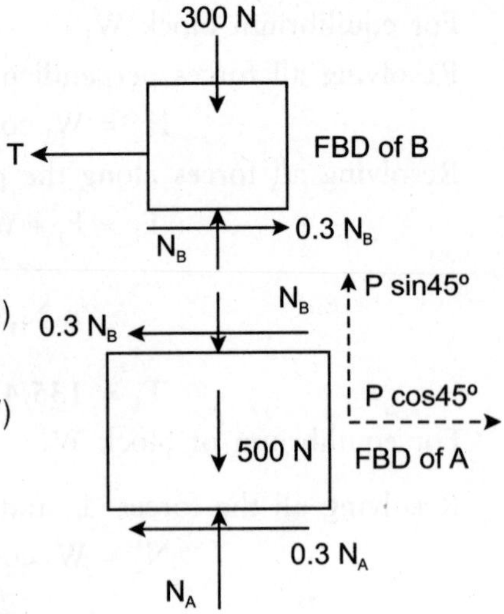

Fig. 11.28

$$\Sigma F_y = 0 \Rightarrow N_B = W_B = 300 \quad \text{(11.46)}$$

$$\Sigma F_x = 0 \Rightarrow T = \mu N_B = 0.3 \times 300$$

$$\Rightarrow T = 90 \text{ N} \quad \text{(11.47)}$$

Equilibrium of block A

$$\Sigma F_x = 0 \Rightarrow P\cos\theta = F_B + F_A$$

$$\Rightarrow P\cos\theta = 0.3\ N_B + 0.3\ N_A$$

$$P\cos\theta = 90 + 0.3\ N_A \quad \text{(11.48)}$$

$$\Sigma F_y = 0 \Rightarrow N_A + P\sin\theta = N_B + W_A$$

or $$P\sin\theta = N_B + W_A - N_A$$

or $$P\sin\theta = 300 + 500 - N_A$$

or $$P\sin\theta = 800 - N_A \quad \text{(11.49)}$$

Substitute the value of N_A from Eq. (11.48) into (11.49)

$$P\sin\theta = 800 - \left(\frac{P\cos\theta - 90}{0.3}\right)$$

$$= 800 \times 0.3 - P\cos\theta + 90$$

$\therefore$ $$P\sin\theta + P\cos\theta = 240 + 90$$

$$P = \left(\frac{330}{\sin 45 + \cos 45}\right)$$

$$= \mathbf{233.3\ N}$$ **Ans.**

Example 11.8

A cylinder of mass 'm', radius 'r' is placed on an inclined plane, the angle of inclination is θ. A rope is wound on the cylinder and at the end of the rope a weight Q is suspended. Due to load Q, cylinder is in equilibrium. Find the magnitude of Q and coefficient of friction at contact point A.

Solution:

Q = ?

μ = ?

W = mg

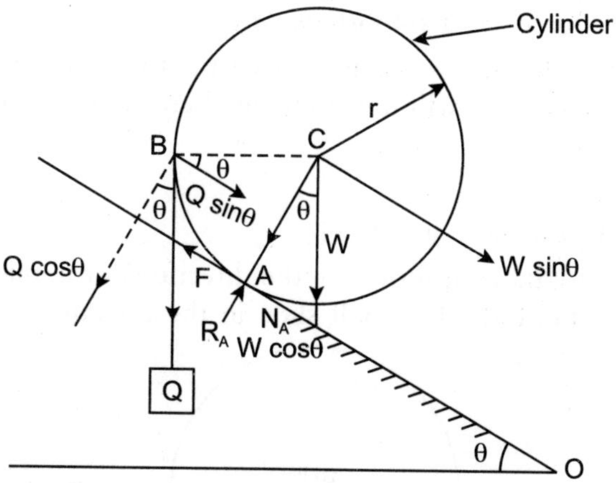

Fig. 11.29

Under the action of Q, the cylinder is in equilibrium. Resolving all the forces perpendicular and parallel to inclined plane.

$$N_A = W\cos\theta + Q\cos\theta \quad \text{(11.50)}$$

$$F = Q\sin\theta + W\sin\theta$$

or

$$\mu N_A = Q\sin\theta + W\sin\theta \quad \text{(11.51)}$$

$$\mu W\cos\theta + \mu Q\cos\theta = Q\sin\theta + W\sin\theta$$

$$\Rightarrow \quad (\mu W + \mu Q)\cos\theta = (Q + W)\sin\theta \quad \text{(11.52)}$$

$$\Rightarrow \quad \tan\theta = \frac{\mu(W+Q)}{(W+Q)} = \mu$$

$$\Rightarrow \quad \tan\theta = \mu \quad \text{or} \quad \mu = \tan\theta$$ **Ans.**

Taking moment about the centre of cylinder

$$Q \cdot r = F \cdot r$$

$$\therefore \quad Q = F = \mu N_A$$

$$\Rightarrow \quad Q = \tan\theta(N_A)$$

$$Q = (Q + W)\sin\theta \quad \text{[from Eq. (11.51)]}$$

$$\Rightarrow \quad Q(1 - \sin\theta) = W\sin\theta$$

$$\therefore \quad Q = \frac{W\sin\theta}{1 - \sin\theta}$$ **Ans.**

11.14 Friction in Wheels

There are mainly two types of wheels:

a. Wheels pulled by a force applied at the axle.
b. Wheels driven by the engine of an automobile.

a. *Wheels pulled by a force on a smooth surface*

A wheel is pulled by a force P over a perfectly smooth surface with coefficient of friction $\mu = 0$. In this case, the wheel will not rotate as there is no turning moment at the centre of the wheel because

$$N = W$$

and $$F = 0 \quad \text{as} \quad \mu = 0$$

The wheel will not rotate as it moves in the directions of applied force P. The diameter AB remains horizontal and wheel will slide in the direction of P without rotation.

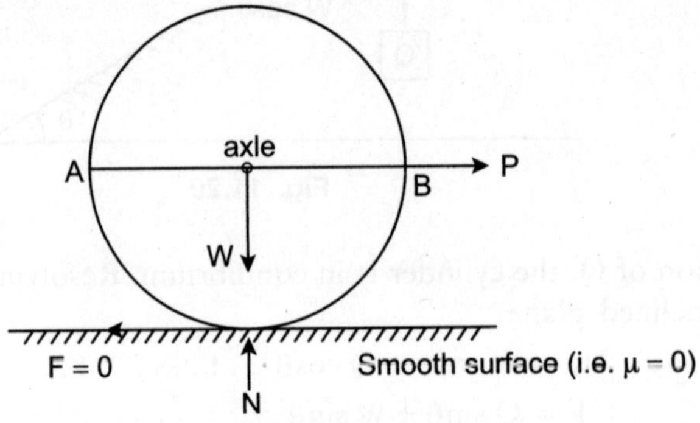

Fig. 11.30

b. *Wheels being pulled by a force on a rough surface*

The wheel is pulled in the direction of P on a rough horizontal plane.

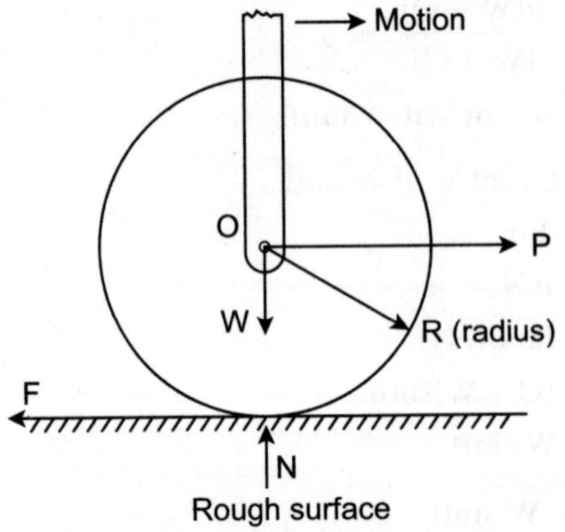

Fig. 11.31

Let μ = coefficient of friction between wheel and ground

$$F = \mu N$$

$N \rightarrow$ Normal reaction

and $$N = W$$

$\therefore$ $$F = \mu W$$

Turning moment at the centre of the wheel

$$T = F \cdot R = \mu WR$$

The wheel rotates in the clockwise direction and moves towards right. There are two conditions

i. if wheel moves without slip then $F < \mu N$.

ii. wheels slide then $F = \mu N$.

11.15 Driving and Driven Wheels of a Vehicle

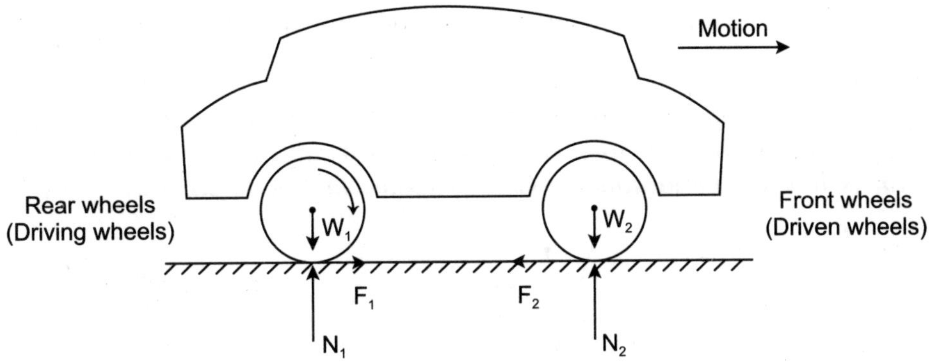

Fig. 11.32

For a rear wheel drive:

The vehicle moves towards right under the action of a driving torque (T), the torque provided by the engine through the propeller shaft to the driving wheels (*i.e.* rear wheels). The vehicle is moving towards right.

Note:

1. *Engine torque (T) tends to rotate the wheels (driving wheels) clockwise, if*

   (i) the road is perfectly smooth (i.e. $\mu = 0$), *the wheels will simply rotate clockwise about their axis, while the axle remains stationary and vehicle does not move towards right and vehicle becomes motionless. This phenomenon may be seen when a car is started on a slushy ground. But generally, the road is rough and frictional force F_1 acts on the outer surface of the wheel.*

   Frictional torque

   $$T_F = F_1 \times r$$

   where r = *radius of wheel*

   F_1 = *Frictional force*

   F_1 opposes the sliding motion of wheel. Due to clockwise motion, wheel will tend to slip towards left and force of friction on wheels will be towards right. So, the frictional force (F_1) on the driving wheel is responsible for producing motion of vehicle.

2. *Now, the driven wheels (Front wheels) are not driven by the engine but are pulled by the vehicle as the vehicle is propelled by the engine through the driving wheels. Friction on driven*

wheels (Front wheels in the present case) will be towards left and provides the clockwise rotation to the front wheels. Therefore, F_2 on front wheel tend to oppose the motion of the vehicle but provides clockwise turning moment ($F_2 \times r$) on the front wheels. Normally, $F_1 > F_2$.

11.15.1 Conclusion on Friction in Wheels

(a) On a smooth surface, driving wheels will rotate but vehicle will not move.

(b) Frictional torque on driving wheels is overcome by engine torque.

(c) Friction on driven wheels provide moving torque for the vehicle.

(d) Friction on driving wheels provides driving force for the vehicle.

Example 11.9

The coefficient of static and kinetic friction between tyre and road are 0.6 and 0.5 respectively. Find the maximum value of inclination (θ), so that the car can climb at a uniform speed. Total weight of car is W kN. The location of C.G. is shown in Fig. 11.33.

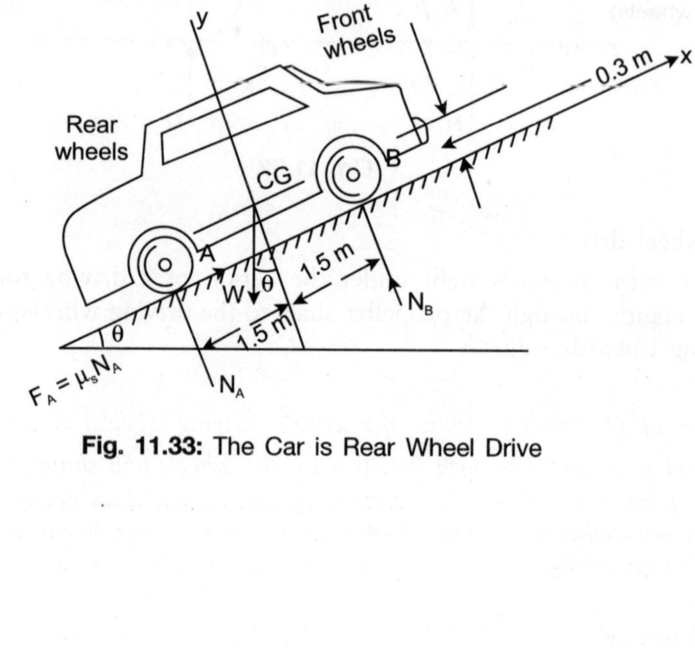

Fig. 11.33: The Car is Rear Wheel Drive

Solution:

$\mu_s = 0.6$

$\mu_k = 0.5$

$\theta = ?$

W = Weight of Car

i. Let at point of contact, driving wheels do not spin, the relative velocity between road and tyre at point of contact A is zero. For equilibrium:

$$\Sigma F_y = 0 \Rightarrow N_A + N_B = W\cos\theta \quad \text{.......... (11.53)}$$

$$\Sigma F_x = 0 \Rightarrow W\sin\theta = F = \mu_s N_A = 0.6\ N_A \quad \text{.......... (11.54)}$$

$$\Rightarrow N_A = \frac{W\sin\theta}{0.6} \quad \text{.......... (11.55)}$$

and $$N_B = W\cos\theta - N_A$$

$$N_B = \left(W\cos\theta - \frac{W\sin\theta}{0.6}\right) \quad \ldots\ldots\ldots\ldots\ldots\ldots \quad (11.56)$$

$$\Sigma M_A = 0 \Rightarrow N_B \times 3 = W\cos\theta \times 1.5 - W\sin\theta \times 0.3$$

$$\Rightarrow 3\ N_B = (\cos\theta \times 1.5 - \sin\theta \times 0.3)W \quad \ldots\ldots\ldots\ldots \quad (11.57)$$

Using Eqs. (11.56) and (11.57), we can determine the value of θ in terms of W.

ii. Let driving wheels are spinning then μ_k is used.

$$\Sigma F_x = 0 \Rightarrow W\sin\theta = \mu_k N_A$$

$$\Rightarrow W\sin\theta = 0.5\ N_A \Rightarrow N_A = \sin\theta \times 2\ W$$

$$\Sigma F_y = 0 \Rightarrow N_A + N_B = W\cos\theta \Rightarrow N_B = W\cos\theta - 2\ W\sin\theta \quad \ldots\ldots \quad (11.58)$$

$$\Sigma M_A = 0 \Rightarrow 3\ N_B = W\cos\theta \times 1.5 - W\sin\theta \times 0.3 \quad \ldots\ldots\ldots\ldots \quad (11.59)$$

Using Eqs. (11.58) and (11.59), we can find the value of θ.

Example 11.10

A four wheel drive car as shown in Fig. 11.30 has a weight of 200 N with passengers. The roadway is inclined at an angle θ with the horizontal. If the coefficient of static friction between the types and roads is 0.25, calculate maximum value of θ, so that the car can climb.

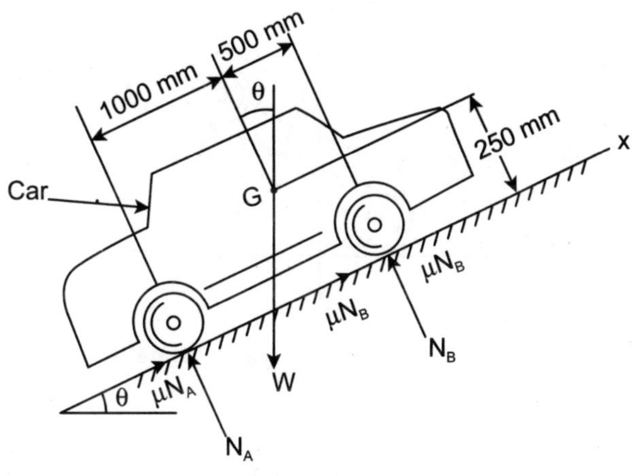

Fig. 11.34

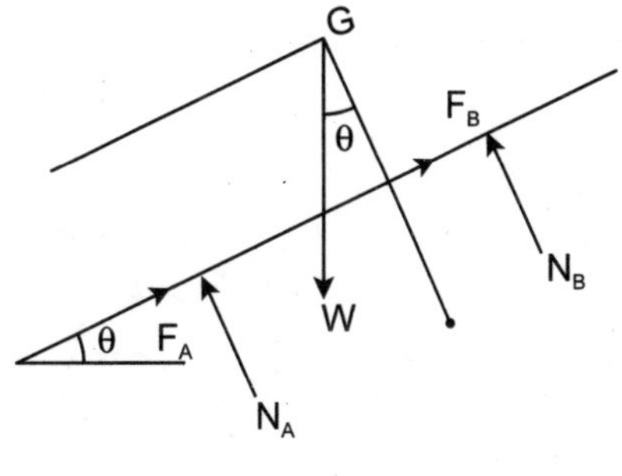

Fig. 11.35

Solution:

$W = mg = 200$ N

$\theta = ?$

$\mu = 0.25$

For equilibrium

$$\Sigma F_y = 0 \Rightarrow N_A + N_B = W\cos\theta \quad .. \quad (11.60)$$

$$\Sigma F_x = 0 \Rightarrow F_A + F_B = W\sin\theta$$

$$\Rightarrow F_A + F_B = 200\sin\theta \quad \ldots\ldots\ldots\ldots\ldots\ldots \quad (11.61)$$

$$\Rightarrow \mu N_A + \mu N_B = 200 \sin\theta \text{ or } N_A + N_B = \frac{200}{0.25}\sin\theta$$

or $$\Rightarrow N_A + N_B = 800 \sin\theta \quad \ldots\ldots (11.62)$$

From Eqs. (11.60) and (11.62),

$$W\cos\theta = 800\sin\theta$$

$$\frac{200}{800} = \tan\theta$$

$$\Rightarrow \theta = \mathbf{14.03^o}$$ **Ans.**

Note: In four wheel drive, all the wheels are independent to rotate and direction of friction will be as shown in Fig. 11.35. But in case of rear wheel drive, friction acts only on the rear wheels.

Example 11.11

A rear wheel drive car of weight 200 N is shown in Fig. 11.36, the road is inclined at an angle θ with the horizontal. If the coefficient of friction between the tyres and the road is 0.25, what is maximum inclination θ that the car can climb?

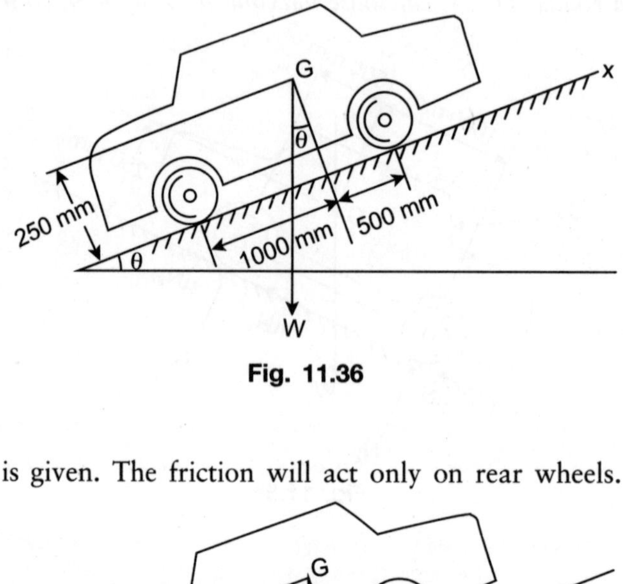

Fig. 11.36

Solution:

Rear wheel drive is given. The friction will act only on rear wheels.

W = 200 N

θ = ?

μ = 0.25

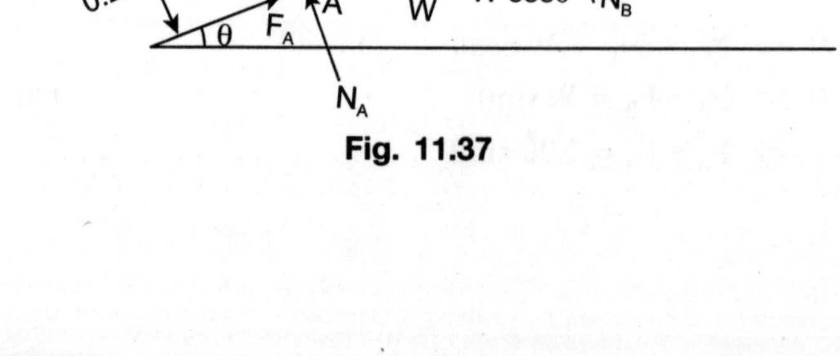

Fig. 11.37

For equilibrium

$$\Sigma F_y = 0 \Rightarrow N_A + N_B = W\cos\theta \quad \text{.......... (11.63)}$$

$$\Sigma F_x = 0 \Rightarrow F_A = W\sin\theta \quad \text{.......... (11.64)}$$

$$\Rightarrow \mu N_A = W\sin\theta$$

$$\Rightarrow 0.25 \times N_A = 200\sin\theta$$

$$\Rightarrow N_A = 800\sin\theta \quad \text{.......... (11.65)}$$

and $$\Rightarrow N_B = 200\cos\theta - N_A = (200\cos\theta - 800\sin\theta)$$

$$\Sigma M_A = 0 \Rightarrow N_B \times 1.5 + W\sin\theta \times 0.25 = W\cos\theta \times 1$$

$$\Rightarrow 1.5\ N_B + 50\sin\theta = 200\cos\theta$$

$$\Rightarrow 1.5\ (200\cos\theta - 800\sin\theta) + 50\sin\theta = 200\cos\theta$$

$$\Rightarrow 300\cos\theta - 1200\sin\theta + 50\sin\theta = 200\cos\theta$$

$$\therefore \quad 100\cos\theta = 1150\sin\theta$$

$$\Rightarrow \tan\theta = \left(\frac{100}{1150}\right)$$

$$\therefore \quad \theta = 5^\circ$$ **Ans.**

11.16 Equilibrium of a Ladder

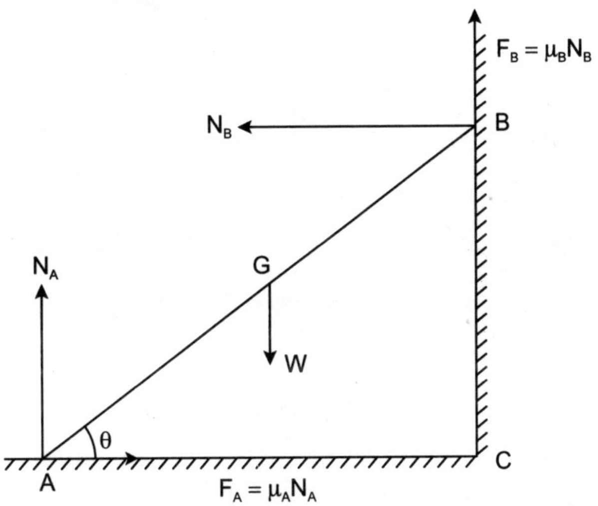

Fig. 11.38

For equilibrium of ladder

$$\Sigma F_y = 0 \Rightarrow N_A + F_B = W$$

$$\Rightarrow N_A = W - \mu_B N_B \quad \text{.......... (11.66)}$$

$$\Sigma F_x = 0 \Rightarrow N_B = F_A = \mu_A N_A \quad \text{.......... (11.67)}$$

$$\Sigma M_A = 0 \Rightarrow W \times AG\cos\theta = N_B \times BC + F_B \times AC$$

$$\Rightarrow W \times \frac{AB}{2}\cos\theta = N_B \times AB\sin\theta + F_B \times AB\cos\theta$$

$$\Rightarrow \frac{W}{2}\cos\theta = N_B \times \sin\theta + \mu_B N_B \cos\theta$$

$$\Rightarrow N_B = \frac{W\cos\theta}{2(\sin\theta + \mu_B\cos\theta)} \quad \ldots\ldots\ldots\ldots (11.68)$$

From Eqs. (11.66), (11.67) and (11.68), the unknown quantity can be determined.

Example 11.12

A uniform ladder of 10 m and weigh 30 N is placed against a smooth vertical wall with its lower end 8 m away from the wall. If the ladder is just to slip, determine

(a) The coefficient of friction between ladder and floor.

(b) The frictional force acting on the ladder at the point of contact between ladder and floor.

Solution:

$l = AC = 10$ m

$W = 30$ N

For smooth wall, $\mu = 0$

$AB = 8$ m

$\mu_f = ?$

$F_A = ?$

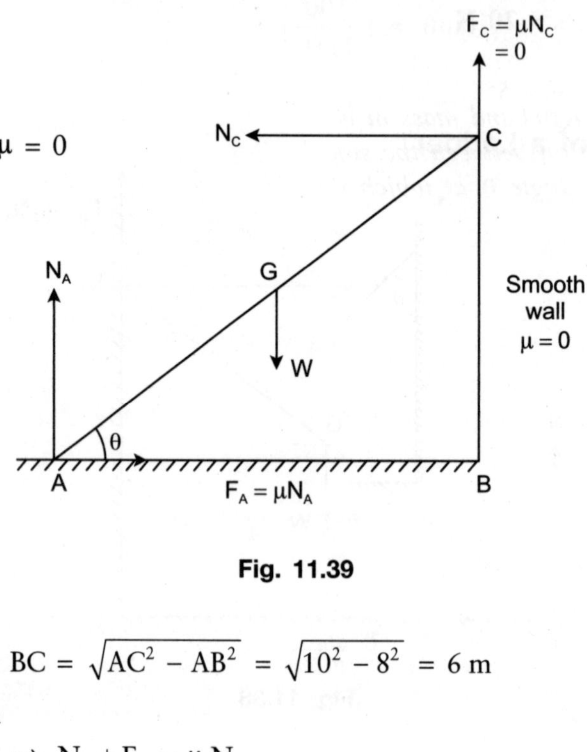

Fig. 11.39

Now $\quad BC = \sqrt{AC^2 - AB^2} = \sqrt{10^2 - 8^2} = 6$ m

(a) For equilibrium

$$\Sigma F_x = 0 \Rightarrow N_C + F_A = \mu_f N_A \quad \ldots\ldots\ldots\ldots (11.69)$$

$$\Sigma F_y = 0 \Rightarrow N_A + F_C = W$$

$$\Rightarrow N_A + 0 = W$$

$$\Rightarrow N_A = 30 \text{ N} \quad \ldots\ldots\ldots\ldots (11.70)$$

From Eq. (11.69), $N_C = 30\mu_f \quad \ldots\ldots\ldots\ldots (11.71)$

Taking moment about point A

$$W \times AG\cos\theta = N_C \times AC\sin\theta$$

$$W \times \frac{AC}{2}\cos\theta = N_C \times AC \times \sin\theta$$

or $$30 \times \frac{1}{2} \times \frac{AB}{AC} = 30\mu_f \times \frac{BC}{AC}$$

or $$15 \times \frac{8}{10} = 30 \times \mu_f \times \frac{6}{10}$$

or $$12 = 18\mu_f$$

$\Rightarrow$ $$\mu_f = \frac{12}{18} = \frac{2}{3} = 0.667$$ **Ans.**

(b) Frictional force between ladder and floor

$$F_A = \mu_f N_A = 0.667 \times 30$$
$$= 20 \text{ N}$$ **Ans.**

Example 11.13

The uniform pole of length l and mass m is leaned against the vertical wall as shown. If the coefficient of static friction between the supporting surfaces and the ends of the pole is 0.2, calculate the maximum angle θ at which the pole may be placed before it start to slip.

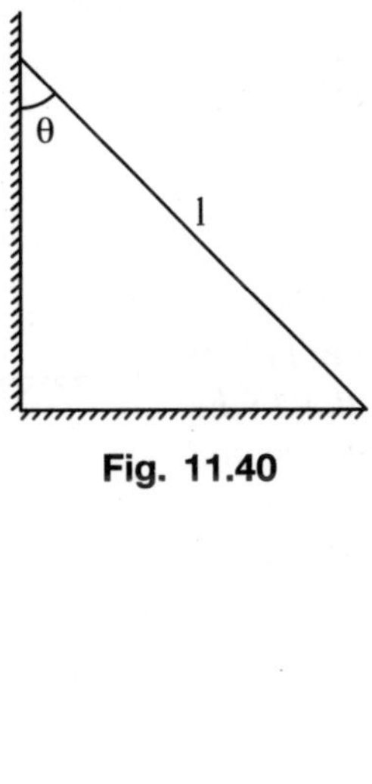

Fig. 11.40

Solution:

$AC = l$

$W = m.g$

$\mu = 0.20$

$\theta = ?$

For equilibrium

$$\Sigma F_x = 0 \Rightarrow N_C = F_A = \mu N_A \; \ldots\ldots\ (11.72)$$

$$\Sigma F_y = 0 \Rightarrow N_A + \mu N_C = W$$

$$\Rightarrow N_A + \mu{\cdot}\mu N_A = W$$

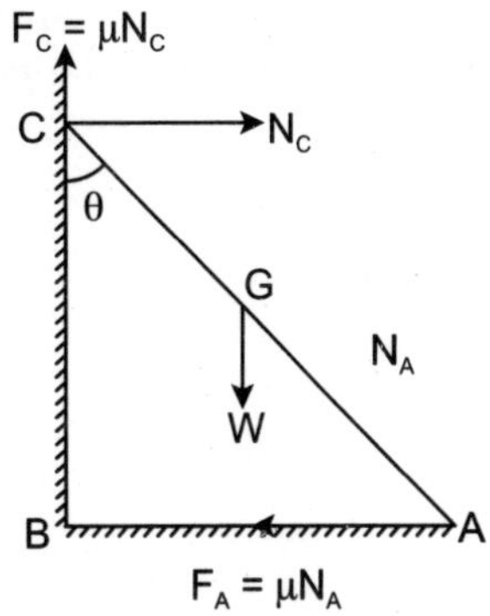

Fig. 11.41

$$\Rightarrow N_A(1 + \mu^2) = W$$

$$\Rightarrow N_A(1 + 0.2^2) = W$$

$$N_A = 0.96\ W \quad \ldots \quad (11.73)$$

$$\Sigma M_A = 0 \Rightarrow W \times AG \sin\theta = \mu N_C \times AC \sin\theta + N_C \times AC \cos\theta$$

$$\Rightarrow W \times \frac{AC}{2} = 0.2\ N_C \cdot AC + N_C \cdot \text{Cot}\theta \cdot AC$$

$$\Rightarrow \frac{W}{2} = 0.2\ N_C + N_C \cdot \text{Cot}\theta$$

$$\Rightarrow \frac{W}{2} = N_C(\text{Cot}\theta + 0.2)$$

$$\Rightarrow \frac{W}{2} = \mu N_A \cdot (\text{Cot}\theta + 0.2)$$

$$\Rightarrow \frac{W}{2} = \mu \times 0.96\ W(\text{Cot}\theta + 0.2)$$

$$\Rightarrow \frac{1}{2} = 0.2 \times 0.96(\text{Cot}\theta + 0.2)$$

$$\Rightarrow \text{Cot}\theta + 0.2 = 2.604$$

$$\Rightarrow \text{Cot}\theta = 2.604 - 0.2 = 2.404$$

$$\Rightarrow \tan\theta = \frac{1}{2.404} = 0.416$$

$$\Rightarrow \theta = 22.6^\circ$$

Ans.

Example 11.14

Calculate the distance x to which the 90 kg painter can climb without causing the 4 m ladder to slip at its lower end A. The top of the 15 kg ladder has a small roller and at the ground the coefficient of static friction is 0.25. The mass centre of the painter is directly above his feet.

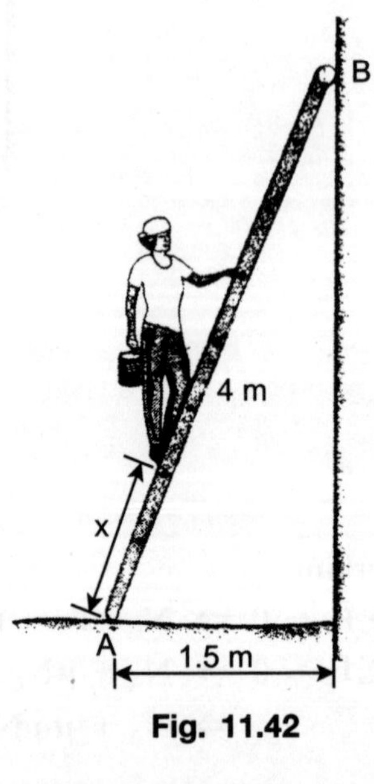

Fig. 11.42

Solution:

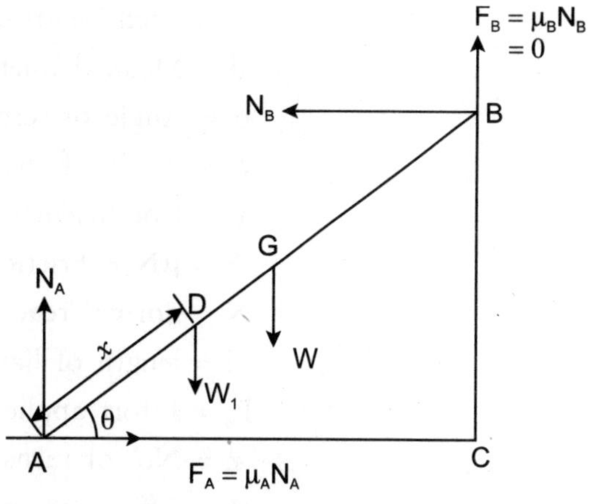

Fig. 11.43

$$x = ?$$
$$W_1 = 90 \text{ kg}$$
$$l = AB = 4 \text{ m}$$
$$W = 15 \text{ kg}$$
$$\mu = 0.25$$
$$AC = 1.5 \text{ m}$$

$$\therefore \quad \cos\theta = \frac{AC}{AB} = \frac{1.5}{4}$$

$$\Rightarrow \quad \theta = 68^\circ$$

At roller, there will be no friction, $F_B = 0$

$$AG = \frac{AB}{2} = \frac{4}{2} = 2 \text{ m}$$
$$AD = x = ?$$

Resolving all forces

$$\Sigma F_y = 0 \Rightarrow N_A + F_B = W_1 + W$$
$$\Rightarrow N_A + 0 = 90 + 15$$
$$\Rightarrow N_A = 105 \text{ kg} \quad \ldots (11.74)$$
$$\Sigma F_x = 0 \Rightarrow N_B = F_A = \mu N_A$$
$$\Rightarrow N_B = 0.25 \times 105 = 26.25 \text{ kg} \quad \ldots (11.75)$$
$$\Sigma M_A = 0 \Rightarrow W_1 \times AD\cos\theta + W \times AG\cos\theta = N_B \times AB\sin\theta$$
$$\Rightarrow 90 \times x \times \cos\theta = 26.25 \times AB\sin\theta - 15 \times \frac{AB}{2}\cos\theta$$
$$\Rightarrow x = \frac{AB}{90}\left(26.25\tan\theta - \frac{15}{2}\right)$$
$$\Rightarrow x = \frac{4}{90}(26.25\tan 68 - 7.5)$$
$$\Rightarrow x = 2.55 \text{ m}$$

$$\therefore \quad x = 2.55 \text{ m}$$ **Ans.**

11.17 Screw Jack Friction

Screws are used for fastenings and for transmitting power or motion. The friction developed in the threads determines the action of the screw. For transmitting power or motion the square threads are more efficient than the v-thread.

A screw jack is a device used for lifting or lowering heavy loads with the help of small effort.

Let W = Weight to be lifted

P = Effort applied at the end of the handle

p = Pitch (lead) of the screw

d = Mean diameter of screw

α = Angle of screw or helix angle

ϕ = Angle of friction

μ = Coefficient of friction

F = μN = Frictional force

N = normal reaction

l = length of handle

P_0 = Effort applied at the circumference of the screw

n = No. of turns

η = Efficiency of the jack

M·A = Mechanical advantage

V·R = Velocity ratio

The load to be lifted is placed on the head of the screw. At the end of the handle, an effort P is applied in the horizontal direction to lift the load W. The screw jack works on the same principle on which an inclined plane works.

When the handle is rotated through one complete turn of a screw thread the vertical distance moved by load in one turn is equal to p and circumferential distance will be πd.

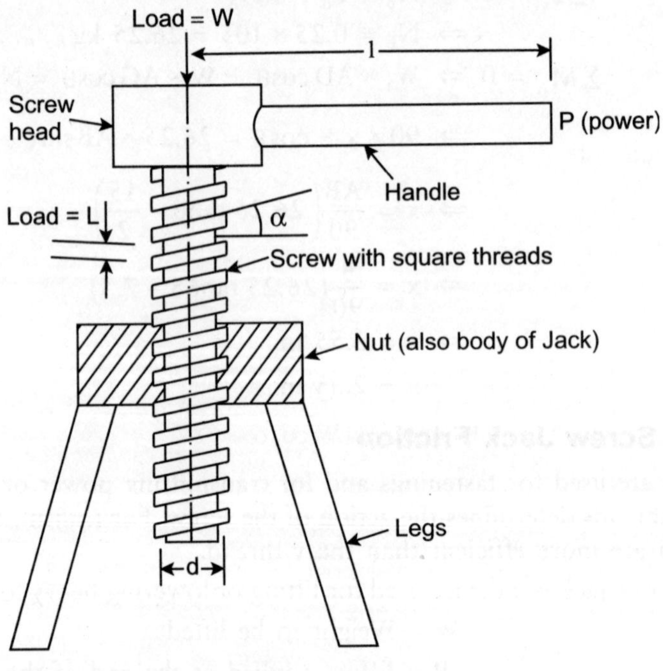

Fig. 11.44: Simple Screw Jack

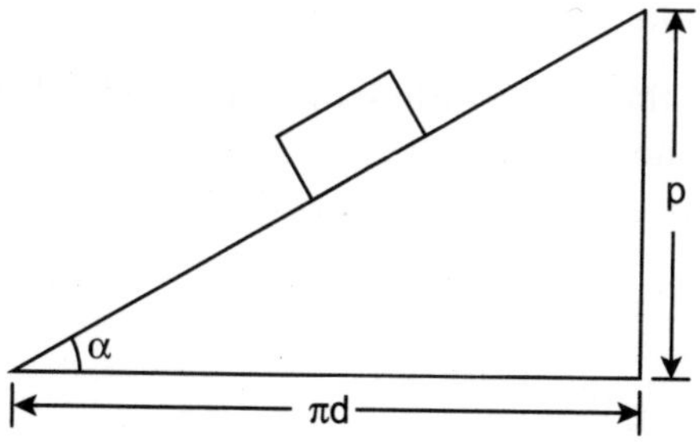

Fig. 11.45: Development of a Screw Thread

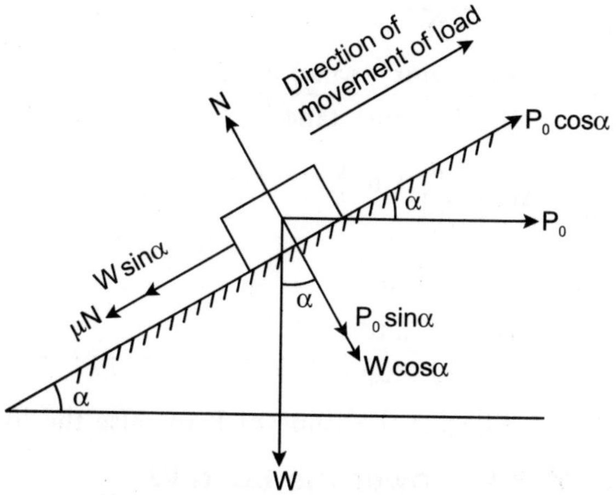

Fig. 11.46: Forces Acting on Body Placed on Jack

For equilibrium

Resolving all forces along the plane

$$W \sin\alpha + \mu N = P_0 \cos\alpha \quad \ldots\ldots \quad (11.76)$$

Resolving forces normal to inclined plane

$$N = W \cos\alpha + P_0 \sin\alpha \quad \ldots\ldots \quad (11.77)$$

Substituting the value of N from Eq. (11.77) in Eq. (11.76)

$$W \sin\alpha + \mu(W \cos\alpha + P_0 \sin\alpha) = P_0 \cos\alpha$$

or
$$W \sin\alpha + \mu W \cos\alpha + \mu P_0 \sin\alpha = P_0 \cos\alpha$$

But
$$\mu = \tan\phi$$

$\therefore$
$$W \sin\alpha + W \tan\phi \cos\alpha + P_0 \tan\phi \sin\alpha = P_0 \cos\alpha$$

or
$$W \sin\alpha \cos\phi + W \sin\phi \cos\alpha + P_0 \sin\phi \sin\alpha = P_0 \cos\phi \cos\alpha$$

or
$$W(\sin\alpha \cos\phi + \sin\phi \cos\alpha) = P_0 (\cos\alpha \cos\phi - \sin\alpha \sin\phi)$$

or
$$W[\sin(\alpha + \phi)] = P_0 \cos\alpha(\alpha + \phi)$$

or
$$P_0 = W \tan(\alpha + \phi) \quad \ldots\ldots \quad (11.78)$$

Now

P_0 is the effort applied at the mean radius of screw jack. But in actual practice, the effort is applied at the end of the handle.

Taking moment about the axis of the screw.

$$P_0 \times \frac{d}{2} = P \times l$$

$$\Rightarrow \quad P = \frac{P_0 \cdot d}{2l}$$

$$P = \frac{Wd\tan(\alpha + \phi)}{2l} \quad \ldots\ldots\ldots\ldots\ldots\ldots\ldots\ldots\ldots \quad (11.79)$$

or $$P = \frac{Wd}{2l}\left(\frac{\tan\alpha + \tan\phi)}{1 - \tan\alpha \cdot \tan\phi}\right)$$

or $$P = \frac{Wd}{2l}\left(\frac{\frac{p}{\pi d} + \mu}{1 - \frac{p}{\pi d}\mu}\right)$$

or $$P = \frac{Wd}{2l}\left(\frac{p + \mu\pi d}{\pi d - \mu p}\right) \quad \ldots\ldots\ldots\ldots\ldots\ldots\ldots\ldots\ldots \quad (11.80)$$

Equations (11.79) and (11.80) give the value of P to raise the load W.

11.18 Determination of P to Lower the Load W

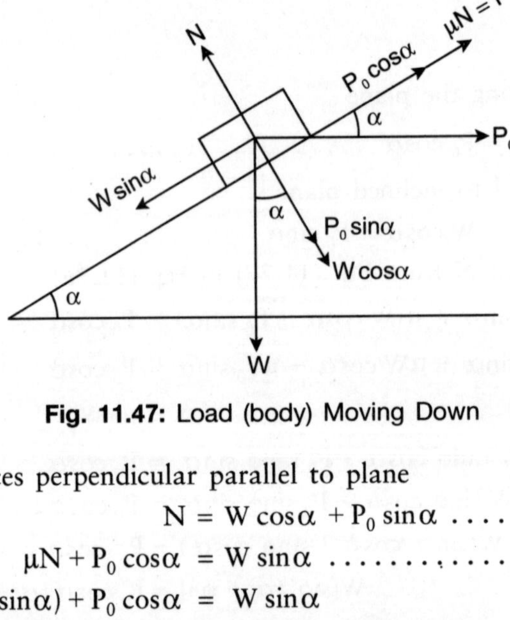

Fig. 11.47: Load (body) Moving Down

Resolving all the forces perpendicular parallel to plane

$$N = W\cos\alpha + P_0\sin\alpha \quad \ldots\ldots\ldots\ldots\ldots\ldots \quad (11.81)$$

$$\mu N + P_0\cos\alpha = W\sin\alpha \quad \ldots\ldots\ldots\ldots\ldots\ldots \quad (11.82)$$

or $$\mu(W\cos\alpha + P_0\sin\alpha) + P_0\cos\alpha = W\sin\alpha$$

or $$-\mu W\cos\alpha + W\sin\alpha = P_0\cos\alpha + \mu P_0\sin\alpha$$

or $$W(\sin\alpha - \tan\phi \cos\alpha) = P_0(\cos\alpha + \tan\phi \sin\alpha)$$

or $$W(\sin\alpha \cos\phi - \sin\phi \cos\alpha) = P_0(\cos\alpha \cos\phi + \sin\alpha \sin\phi)$$

or $$W[\sin(\alpha - \phi)] = P_0 \cos(\alpha - \phi)$$

or $$P_0 = W \tan(\alpha - \phi) \quad \text{......} \quad (11.83)$$

Taking moment about axis of the screw

$$P_0 \times \frac{d}{2} = P \times l$$

$\Rightarrow$ $$P = \frac{Wd}{2l}\tan(\alpha + \phi) \quad \text{......} \quad (11.84)$$

or $$P = \frac{Wd}{2l}\left(\frac{\mu\pi d - p}{\pi d + \mu p}\right) \quad \text{......} \quad (11.85)$$

11.19 Efficiency of a Screw Jack for Raising a Load W

$$P_{actual} = \frac{Wd}{2l}\tan(\alpha + \phi)$$

$$P_{ideal} = \frac{Wd}{2l}\tan\alpha \qquad (\because \text{ for ideal case, no friction exists})$$

$$\eta = \frac{P_{ideal}}{P_{actual}} = \frac{\tan\alpha}{\tan(\alpha + \phi)}$$

$\therefore$ $$\eta = \frac{\tan\alpha}{\tan(\alpha + \phi)} \quad \text{......} \quad (11.86)$$

$$\eta = \frac{\sin\alpha\cos(\alpha + \phi)}{\cos\alpha\sin(\alpha + \phi)}$$

or $$1 - \eta = \frac{\cos\alpha\sin(\alpha + \phi) - \sin\alpha\cos(\alpha + \phi)}{\cos\alpha\sin(\alpha + \phi)}$$

$$= \frac{\sin(\alpha + \phi - \alpha)}{\cos\alpha\sin(\alpha + \phi)} = \frac{\sin\phi}{\cos\alpha\sin(\alpha + \phi)}$$

$$= \frac{2\sin\phi}{2\cos\alpha\sin(\alpha + \phi)}$$

$$1 - \eta = \frac{2\sin\phi}{\sin(2\alpha + \phi) + \sin\phi}$$

For η_{max}, $(1 - \eta)$ should be minimum and $[\sin(2\alpha + \phi) + \sin\phi]$ should be maximum.

But ϕ = Constant

Therefore

$\text{Sin}(2\alpha + \phi)$ is maximum and it is possible if

$$2\alpha + \phi = 90^o \Rightarrow \alpha = \left[45 - \frac{\phi}{2}\right]$$

$$\alpha = 45 - \frac{\phi}{2}$$

From Eq. (11.86)

$$\eta_{max} = \frac{\tan\left(45 - \frac{\phi}{2}\right)}{\tan\left(45 + \frac{\phi}{2}\right)} = \frac{\dfrac{\tan 45 - \tan\frac{\phi}{2}}{1 + \tan 45 \tan\frac{\phi}{2}}}{\dfrac{\tan 45 + \tan\frac{\phi}{2}}{1 \tan 45 \cdot \tan\frac{\phi}{2}}}$$

$$= \frac{\dfrac{1 - \tan\frac{\phi}{2}}{1 + \tan\frac{\phi}{2}}}{\dfrac{1 + \tan\frac{\phi}{2}}{1 - \tan\frac{\phi}{2}}} = \frac{\left(1 - \tan\frac{\phi}{2}\right)^2}{\left(1 + \tan\frac{\phi}{2}\right)^2}$$

$$= \frac{\left(1 - \dfrac{\sin\frac{\phi}{2}}{\cos\frac{\phi}{2}}\right)^2}{\left(1 + \dfrac{\sin\frac{\phi}{2}}{\cos\frac{\phi}{2}}\right)} = \frac{\left(\cos\frac{\phi}{2} - \sin\frac{\phi}{2}\right)^2}{\left(\cos\frac{\phi}{2} + \sin\frac{\phi}{2}\right)^2}$$

$$= \frac{1 - 2\sin\frac{\phi}{2}\cos\frac{\phi}{2}}{1 + 2\sin\frac{\phi}{2}\cos\frac{\phi}{2}} = \frac{1 - \sin\phi}{1 + \sin\phi}$$

$$\therefore \quad \eta_{max} = \frac{1 - \sin\phi}{1 + \sin\phi} \qquad (11.87)$$

If η of a screw jack is less than 50% then the jack is self locking machine.

Also, in case of self locking, $\phi > \alpha$.

Example 11.15

A screw jack has square threads, the outer diameter of screw is 60 mm and two threads in 1 cm. The coefficient of friction at the screw threads is 0.05. The load to be lifted is 3 kN. Find the force required at the end of the handle of length 500 mm to lift the load. Determine also efficiency of the machine and state whether the machine is self locking. If yes then find the torque necessary to lower the load. If not, find the torque, which must be applied to keep the load from descending.

Solution:

Screw jack with squire threads.

$$do = 6 \text{ cm} = 60 \text{ mm}$$

2 threads in 1 cm

$$\mu = 0.05$$
$$W = 3 \text{ kN}$$
$$P = ?$$
$$l = 500 \text{ mm}$$
$$\eta = ?$$

Now

$$\text{Pitch of screw } p = \frac{1 \text{ cm}}{\text{No. of threads in 1 cm}} = \frac{1}{2} = 0.5 \text{ cm}$$

$\therefore$ $p = 5$ mm

From Fig. 11.49, we see

$$do = di + 2 \times (p/2)$$
$$= di + p$$

or $do = di + p$

$$60 = di + 5$$

$\Rightarrow$ $di = 60 - 5 = 55$ mm

Mean diameter of screw

$$d = \frac{di + do}{2} = \frac{55 + 60}{2} = 57.5 \text{ mm}$$

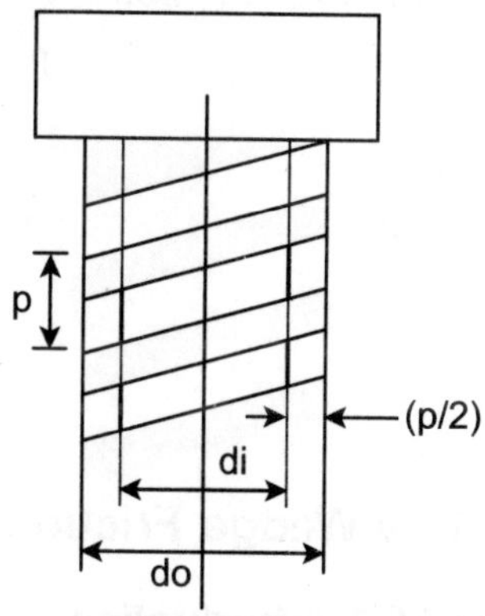

Fig. 11.48

We know that

$$P = \frac{W \cdot d}{2l} \tan(\alpha + \phi)$$

$$\tan\alpha = \frac{p}{\pi d} = \frac{5}{\pi \times 57.5} = 0.0276$$

$$\alpha = \tan^{-1}(0.0276) = 1.58°$$
$$\phi = \tan^{-1}(\mu) = \tan^{-1}(0.05) = 2.86°$$

$$\therefore \quad P = \frac{W \cdot d}{2l}\tan(\alpha + \phi)$$

$$= \frac{3 \times 57.5}{2 \times 500}\tan(1.58 + 2.86)$$

$$= 0.134 \text{ kN}$$

$$P = \mathbf{134\ N} \qquad \textbf{Ans.}$$

$$\text{Efficiency } \eta = \frac{\tan\alpha}{\tan(\alpha + \phi)} = \frac{\tan(1.58)}{\tan(1.58 + 2.86)} = 0.3552$$

$$\therefore \quad \eta = \mathbf{35.5\%} \qquad \textbf{Ans.}$$

since the efficiency of the screw jack is less than 50%. Therefore, the jack or machine is self locking.

Now

Torque necessary to lower the load.

$$T = P \times l = \frac{Wd}{2l}\tan(\alpha - \phi) \cdot l$$

$$= \frac{3 \times 57.5}{2 \times 500}\tan(2.86 - 1.58) \times 500$$

$$= \mathbf{1.927\ kN\ mm} \qquad \textbf{Ans.}$$

Alternate method

$$P' = W\tan(\alpha - \phi)$$

$$= 3\ \text{Tan}(2.86 - 1.58) = 0.067 \text{ kN}$$

and

$$T = P' \times \frac{d}{2}$$

$$= 0.067 \times \frac{57.5}{2}$$

$$= \mathbf{1.927\ kN\ mm} \qquad \textbf{Ans.}$$

11.20 Wedge Friction

11.20.1 Introduction

A wedge is a piece of metal or wood in the shape of a prism whose section is usually triangular or trapezoidal. It is the simplest and most useful machine and is used to produce small adjustments in position of a body. Wedges are largely dependent on friction. Generally, a wedge is used for lifting or lowering heavy loads, for tightening fits or keys, for shafts by applying a small force. When lifting loads, the wedge is placed below the load and a horizontal force (P) is applied. The wedge moves towards left and the load moves upward and there is a sliding motion at all contact surfaces. The wedge remains in position after being forced under the load due to the friction existing between the surfaces in contact.

The problems related to wedge friction can be solved by drawing F.B.D. of loads and wedge. The weight of wedge is generally neglected.

α = Wedge angle

P = Horizontal force

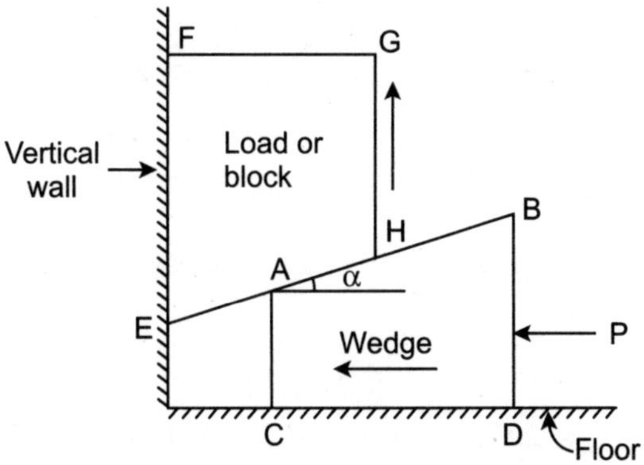

Fig. 11.49: Wedge-load System

Example 11.16

Calculate the force P required to start the movement of the wedge of negligible weight. The wedge angle is 10° and the load to be shifted is 1800 N. The coefficient of friction for all the surfaces is 0.3.

Solution:

$$W = 1800 \text{ N}$$
$$\theta = 10^\circ$$
$$\mu = \mu_1 = \mu_2 = \mu_3 = 0.3$$
$$P = ?$$

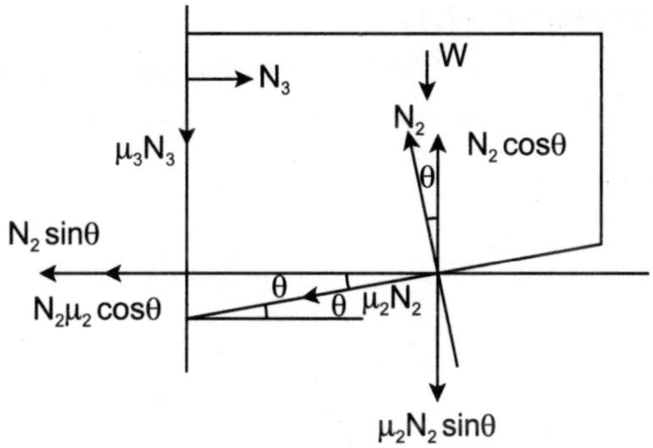

Fig. 11.50: F.B.D. of Block

Equilibrium of Block

$$\Sigma F_x = 0$$

$$\Rightarrow N_3 = N_2 \sin\theta + \mu_2 N_2 \cos\theta$$

$$N_3 = N_2 (\sin 10 + 0.3 \cos 10)$$

$$= 0.469 \ N_2 \quad \ldots\ldots (11.88)$$

$$\Sigma F_y = 0 \Rightarrow N_2 \cos\theta = W + \mu_3 N_3 + \mu_2 N_2 \sin\theta$$

$$\therefore \quad N_2 \cos\theta = 1800 + 0.3 \times 0.469 \ N_2 + 0.3 \times N_2 \sin 10 \quad \ldots\ldots (11.89)$$

$$N_2(\cos 10 - 0.3 \times 0.469 - 0.3 \times \sin 10) = 1800$$

$$N_2 = \frac{1800}{0.7920133} = 2272.7 \text{ N} \quad \ldots\ldots (11.90)$$

$$\therefore \quad N_3 = 2272.7 \times 0.469 = 1065.9 \text{ N} \quad \ldots\ldots (11.91)$$

Equilibrium of Wedge

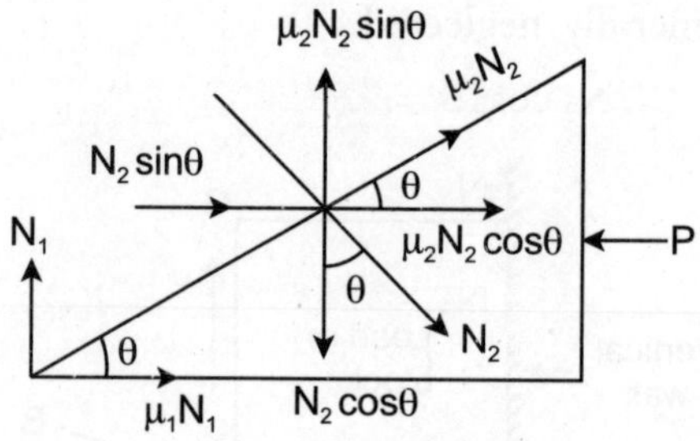

Fig. 11.51: F.B.D. of Wedge

$$\Sigma F_y = 0$$

$$\Rightarrow N_1 = N_2 \cos\theta - \mu_2 N_2 \sin\theta$$

or

$$N_1 = 2272.7(\cos 10 - 0.3 \times \sin 10) = 2119.8 \text{ N}$$

$$\Sigma F_x = 0$$

$$P = \mu_1 N_1 + N_2 \sin\theta + \mu_2 N_2 \cos\theta$$

$$= 2119.8 \times 0.3 + 2272.7(\sin 10 + 0.3 \times \cos 10)$$

$$= 635.9 + 1066.1 = 1702 \text{ N}$$

P = 1702 N **Ans.**

Example 11.17

A weight of 2500 N is to be raised by means of a 10° wedge. The coefficient of friction for all contact surfaces is 0.3. Calculate the horizontal force P on the wedge just to move it.

Solution:

W = 2500 N

θ = 10°

μ = 0.3

P = ?

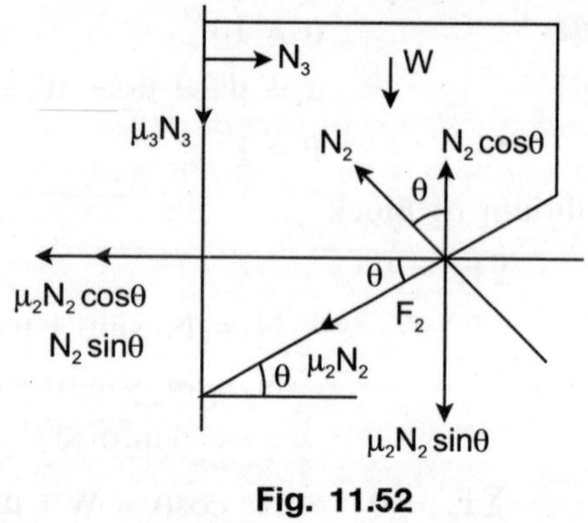

Fig. 11.52

Equilibrium of Block

$$\Sigma F_x = 0 \Rightarrow \quad N_3 = \mu_2 N_2 \cos\theta + N_2 \sin\theta \quad \ldots\ldots\ldots\ldots\ldots\ldots \quad (11.92)$$

$$= N_2(0.3 \cos 10 + \sin 10) = 0.469 \ N_2$$

$$\Sigma F_y = 0 \Rightarrow \quad N_2 \cos\theta = W + \mu_3 N_3 + \mu_2 N_2 \sin\theta \ldots\ldots\ldots\ldots\ldots\ldots \quad (11.93)$$

$$= W + \mu_3(0.469 \ N_2) + \mu_2 N_2 \sin\theta$$

$$= 2500 + 0.3(0.469\ N_2) + 0.3\ N_2 \sin 10$$
$$= 2500 + 0.14072\ N_2 + 0.05209\ N_2$$
$$N_2 \cos 10 = 2500 + 0.19282\ N_2$$
$$N_2 = \frac{2500}{(\text{Cos}10 - 0.19282)} = 3156.6\ \text{N}$$
$$\therefore \quad N_3 = 0.469 \times 3156.6 = 1480.4\ \text{N}$$

Equilibrium of Wedge

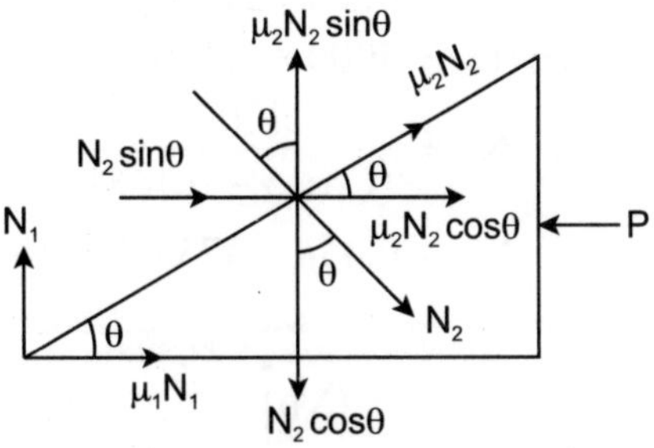

Fig. 11.53

$$\Sigma F_y = 0 \Rightarrow N_1 = N_2\cos\theta - \mu_2 N_2 \sin\theta$$
$$= 3156.6(\cos 10 - 0.3 \times \sin 10) = 2944.2\ \text{N}$$
$$\Sigma F_x = 0 \Rightarrow \quad P = N_2 \sin\theta + \mu_2 N_2 \cos\theta + \mu_1 N_1$$
$$= 3156.6(\sin 10 - 0.3 \times \cos 10) + 0.3 \times 2944.2$$
$$P = \mathbf{2364\ N}$$

Ans.

Example 11.18

A weight of 3000 N is to be raised by means of a 15° wedge. The weight of wedge is 500 N and coefficient of friction for all the contact surfaces may be assumed as 0.2. Determine the least horizontal for P on the wedge to just move it in the direction of its application.

Solution:

$W = 3000$ N

$\theta = 15^\circ$

$W_1 = 500$ N

$\mu = 0.2$

$P = ?$

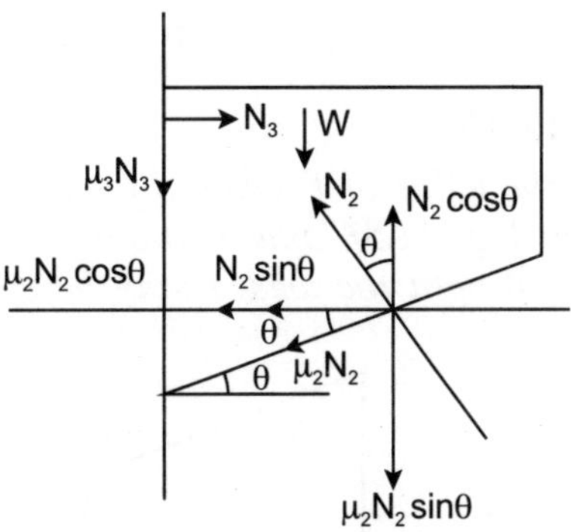

Fig. 11.54

Equilibrium of Block

$$\Sigma F_x = 0$$

$$\Rightarrow \quad N_3 = N_2 \sin\theta + \mu_2 N_2 \cos\theta \quad \ldots\ldots\ldots\ldots\ldots\ldots \quad (11.94)$$

$$= N_2 (\sin 15 + 0.2 \cos 15)$$

$$N_3 = 0.452\ N_2$$

$$\Sigma F_y = 0 \Rightarrow \quad N_2 \cos\theta = W + \mu_3 N_3 + \mu_2 N_2 \sin\theta \quad \ldots\ldots\ldots\ldots\ldots\ldots \quad (11.95)$$

$$N_2 \cos 15 = 3000 + 0.2 \times 0.452\ N_2 + 0.3 \times N_2 \sin 15$$

$$= 3000 + N_2(0.2 \times 0.452 + 0.3 \sin 15)$$

$$N_2 \cos 15 = 3000 + 0.168\ N_2$$

$$\therefore \quad N_2 = \frac{3000}{(\text{Cos}15 - 0.168)} = 3759.7 \text{ N}$$

$$N_3 = 0.456 \times 3759.7 = 1699.4 \text{ N}$$

Equilibrium of Wedge

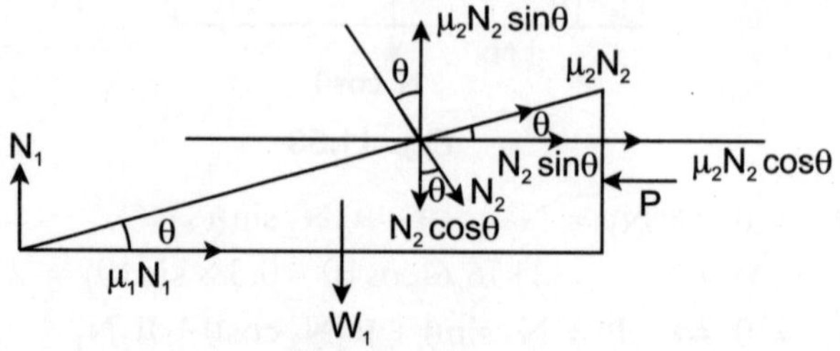

Fig. 11.55

$$\Sigma F_y = 0 \Rightarrow N_1 = W_1 + N_2 \cos\theta - \mu_2 N_2 \sin\theta$$

$$= 500 + 3759.7(\cos 15 - 0.2 \times \sin 15)$$

$$N_1 = 3937 \text{ N}$$

$$\Sigma F_x = 0 \Rightarrow \quad P = \mu_1 N_1 + \mu_2 N_2 \cos\theta + N_2 \sin\theta$$

$$= 0.2 \times 3937 + 3739.7(0.2 \times \cos 15 + \sin 15)$$

$$= 787.4 + 1690.4 = 2477.8 \text{ N}$$

$$P = 2477.8 \text{ N}$$

Ans.

Example 11.19

Determine the value of P when a weight of 200 kN is to be raised by means of two wedges as shown in Fig. 11.56 and is about to move upwards. The coefficient of friction is 0.3 for all surfaces. Weight the wedge may be considered as negligible.

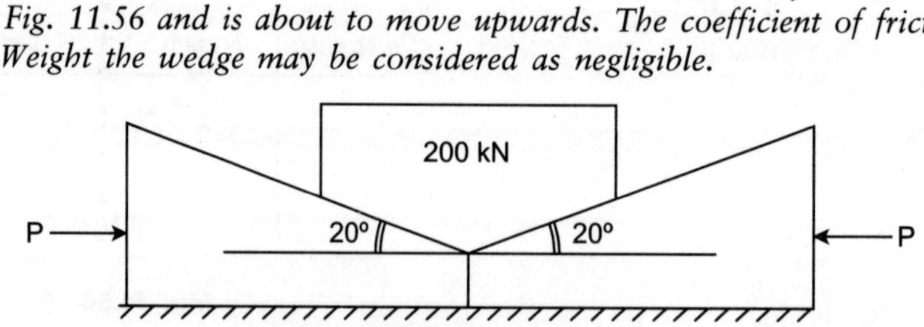

Fig. 11.56

Solution:

$$W = 200 \text{ kN}$$
$$P = ?$$
$$\mu = 0.3$$
$$\tan\theta = \mu$$
$$\alpha = 20^\circ$$

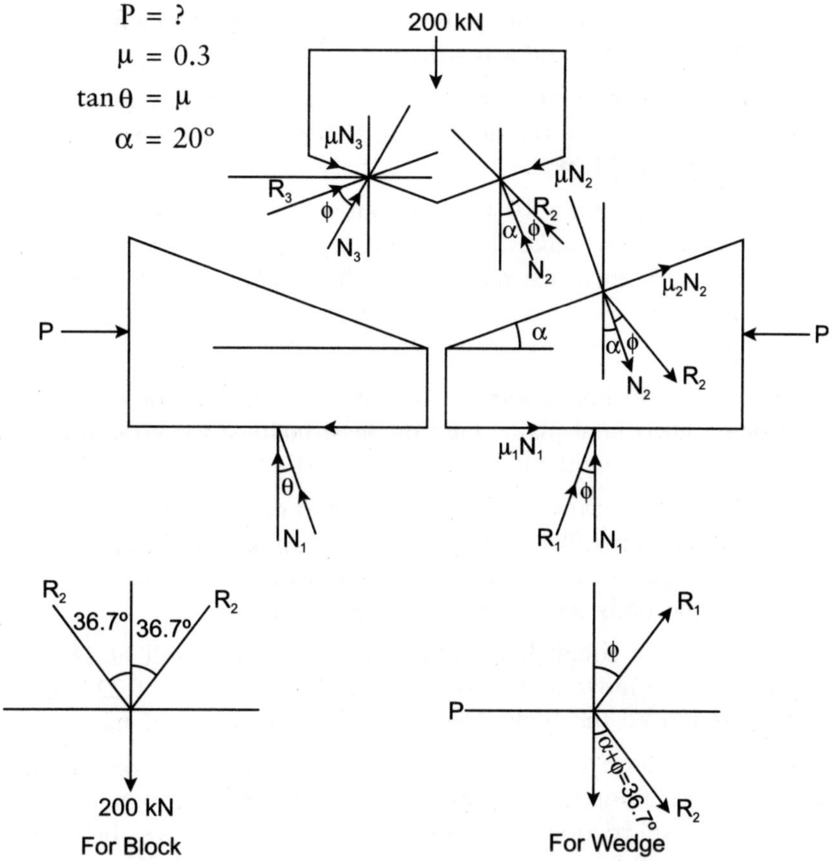

Fig. 11.57

For Block

$$\frac{R_2}{\sin 143.3} = \frac{200}{\sin 73.4}$$

$$R_2 = \frac{200 \sin 143.3}{\sin 73.4} = 124.8 \text{ N}$$

For Wedge

$$\frac{P}{\sin[180-(36.7+16.7)]} = \frac{R_2}{\sin(90+16.7)}$$

$\therefore$
$$P = 124\frac{\sin 126.6}{\sin 106.7}$$

$$P = \mathbf{103.9 \text{ N}}$$ **Ans.**

THEORETICAL AND NUMERICAL QUESTIONS

1. A body weight 800 N rests on a horizontal plane. Find the magnitude of the force required to move the body along the plane if the force is inclined upward at an angle of 50° to the horizontal. Take $\mu = 0.25$.
2. A block of stone resting on a horizontal plane can be just moved by a pulling force inclined upward at 40° to the horizontal. If $\mu = 0.5$, find the ratio of the pulling force to the weight of the block.
3. A block of stone weighing 10 kN rests on a horizontal floor. A man pulls the block through a string which makes an angle α with the horizontal. Calculate α for which the force necessary to move the block will be minimum. Find also minimum force. Take $\mu = \dfrac{1}{\sqrt{3}}$.
4. A body weighing 30 kN requires a horizontally applied force of 7.28 kN to draw it slowly along a horizontal plane. Find the least inclined force required to draw the body along the same horizontal plane.
5. An effort of 300 N is required just to move certain body up an inclined plane of angle 15°, the force acting parallel to the plane. If the angle of inclination of the plane is made 20°, the effort required, again applied parallel to the plane, is found to be 330 N. Find the weight of the body and coefficient of friction.
6. A body resting on a rough horizontal plane required a pull of 18 kN inclined at 30° to the plane just to move it. It was also found that a push of 22 kN inclined at 30° to the plane just moved the body. Determine the coefficient of friction.
7. A block A is placed on another named B which in turn rests on a third one C, kept on a rough horizontal floor, the weights of blocks are 400 N, 250 N and 200 N respectively. The coefficients of friction at various contact surfaces are: between A and B, 0.3, between B and C, 0.2 and between C and the floor, 0.15. The top block is subjected to a horizontal force P as shown in Fig. 11.58.

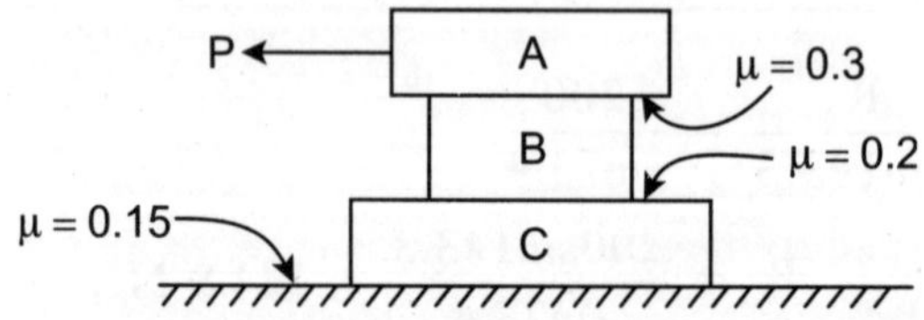

Fig. 11.58

(i) At impending motion, which blocks will tend to move. Also calculate the value of P at this stage.

(ii) If the last two values of the coefficient of friction are interchanged, calculate the new value of P at impending motion.

8. A body of weight 80 N is placed on a rough horizontal plane. To just move the body on the horizontal plane, a push of 20 N inclined at 20° to the horizontal plane is required. Find the coefficient of friction.
9. A block weighing 3 kN, overlying a 10° wedge on a horizontal floor and leaning against a vertical wall, is to be raised by applying a horizontal force to the wedge. Assuming the coefficient of friction between all the surfaces in contact to be 0.35. Determine the minimum horizontal force to be applied to raise the block.
10. A block weighing 2000 N is to be raised by means of a 15° wedge, weighing 800 N. Assuming the coefficient of friction between all contact surfaces to be 0.2, determine what minimum horizontal force P should be applied to raise the block.
11. A block of stone on a horizontal plane can be moved slowly along the plane by a horizontal force of 20 kN. A force of 9 kN inclined at 30° to the horizontal direction will suffice to draw the block along the same plane. Determine coefficient of friction and the weight of the block of stone.
12. Two blocks A and B which are interconnected by a weightless rod, weight 600 N and 800 N respectively. They are placed on a rough inclined plane whose angle with the horizontal is θ, A being down the slope from B. If the values of coefficient of friction under A and B are 0.15 and 0.4 respectively, find the value of θ at which motion of the system will impend. What will be the force in the bar under this condition? What will be the situation if the position of A and B are interchanged? Assume that the ends of the bars are connected to the blocks by frictionless hinges.

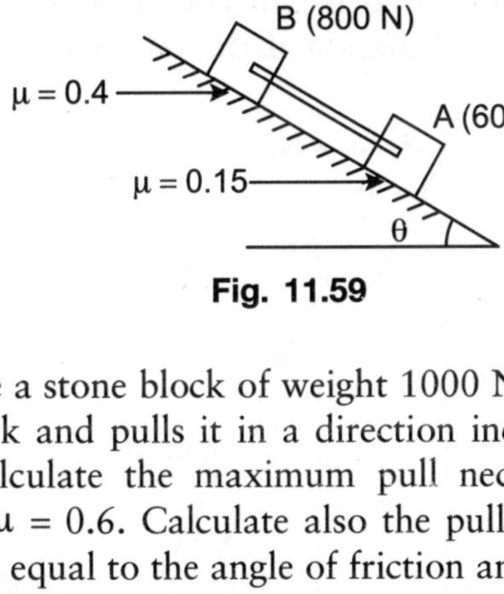

Fig. 11.59

13. A man wishing to slide a stone block of weight 1000 N over a horizontal concrete floor, ties a rope to the block and pulls it in a direction inclined upward at an angle of 30° to the horizontal. Calculate the maximum pull necessary to slide the block if the coefficient of friction $\mu = 0.6$. Calculate also the pull required if the inclination of the rope with horizontal is equal to the angle of friction and prove that this is the least force required to slide the block.
14. Determine the distance s to which the 80 kg painter can climb without causing the 4 m ladder to slip at its lower end A. The top of the 15 kg ladder has a small roller and at the ground the coefficient of static friction is 0.25. The mass center of the painter is directly above her feet.
15. The uniform 7 m pole has a mass of 180 kg and is supported as shown in Fig. 11.60. Calculate the force P required to move the pole if the coefficient of static friction for each contact position is 0.4.

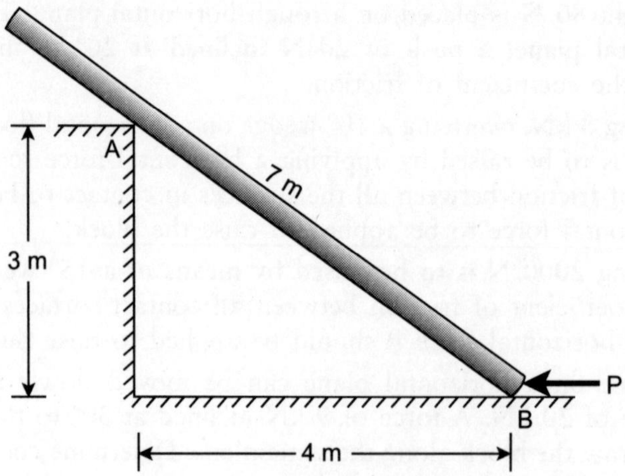

Fig. 11.60

16. A body of weight 10 kN is resting on a horizontal plane and can be just moved by a force of 5 kN applied horizontally. Find the coefficient of friction and the direction and magnitude of the resultant reaction.
17. Weight of 14 m long bar as shown in Fig. 11.61 is 600 N and it may be considered to be concentrated at a point 6 m from the bottom. It rests against a smooth vertical wall at A and a rough horizontal floor at B. The coefficient of static friction between the bar and floor is 1/3. Check by calculation if the bar would stand in the 60° position as shown.

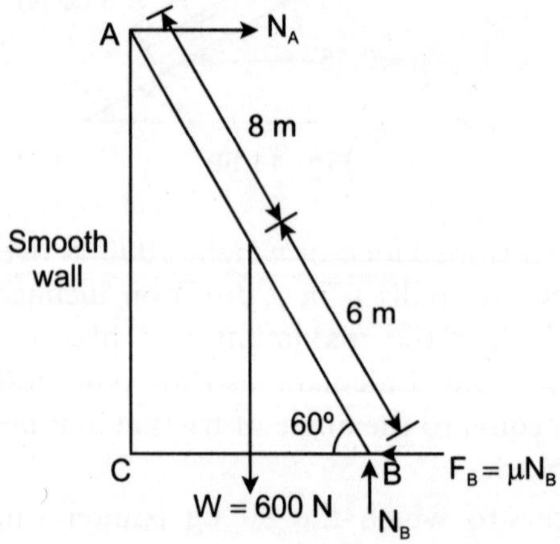

Fig. 11.61

18. A uniform ladder of 7 m rests against a vertical wall. The angle between ladder and floor is 45°, coefficient of friction between the ladder and the wall is 0.4 and between ladder and floor is 0.5. If a man, weight is one half of the ladder, ascends it, find distance at which the ladder slips.

19. A screw jack has a square threads of 75 mm mean diameter and 15 mm pitch. The load on the jack revolves with the screw. The coefficient of friction at the screw threads 0.05. Find (i) tangent force to be applied to the jack at a handle of 300 mm length. So as to lift a load of 5 kN, (2) whether the jack is self locking or not. If it is self locking, find the torque necessary to lower the load. If not, find the torque which must be applied to keep the load from descending.

20. The spindle of a screw jack has single start square threads of 50 mm root diameter and 8 mm pitch. The jack supports a load of 600 N on its head and that revolves with the screw. The coefficient of friction at the screw threads is 0.1. Calculate:

    (i) The effort to be applied at the end of the hand of 500 mm length to raise the load.

    (ii) Work done in lifting the load through 100 mm.

    (iii) Efficiency of the screw.

    (iv) Ratio of effort required to raise and lower the load.

12

Belt Friction

12.1 Flexible Belt Drives

Belts and ropes are generally used to transmit power from one shaft to another and are known as non-positive drives because of possibility of slip occurring between belt and the pulley.

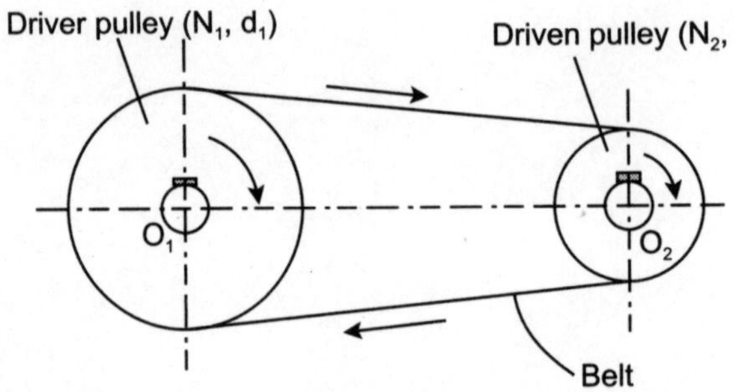

Fig. 12.1

N and d are r.p.m. and diameter of pulley respectively.

Length of belt that runs over pulley A per minute= $\pi N_1 d_1$

Length of belt that runs over pulley B per minute= $\pi N_2 d_2$

If there is no slip,

$$\pi N_1 d_1 = \pi N_2 d_2$$

$$\Rightarrow \quad \frac{N_2}{N_1} = \frac{d_1}{d_2} \qquad (12.1)$$

12.2 Types of Belt Drives

1. Open belt drives
2. Cross belt drives

12.2.1 Open Belt Drives: Length of the Belt

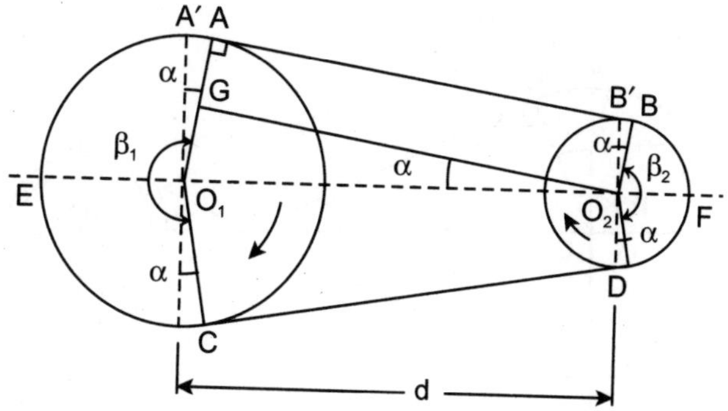

Fig. 12.2

$$\angle O_1AB = \angle O_2BA = 90^\circ$$

$$O_2G \parallel AB$$

Let $\angle GO_2O_1 = \alpha$ radians

Then $\angle A'O_1A = \angle B'O_2B = \alpha$

$$AB = GO_2$$

β_1, β_2 are angle of lap at driver and driven pulleys respectively.

∴ Length of Belt

$$l = 2(\text{Arc EA} + AB + \text{Arc BF}) \quad \ldots\ldots\ldots\ldots (12.2)$$

$$\text{Arc EA} = \left(\frac{\pi}{2} + \alpha\right) r_1$$

$$\text{Arc BF} = \left(\frac{\pi}{2} - \alpha\right) r_2$$

$$AB = GO_2 = \sqrt{d^2 - (r_1 - r_2)^2} = d\left[1 - \left(\frac{r_1 - r_2}{d}\right)^2\right]^{\frac{1}{2}}$$

$$= d\left[1 - \frac{1}{2}\left(\frac{r_1 - r_2}{d}\right)^2\right] \quad \text{(Using Binomial theorem)}$$

$$= d - \frac{(r_1 - r_2)^2}{2d} \text{ and } \sin\alpha = \alpha = \left(\frac{r_1 - r_2}{d}\right)$$

∴ From Eq. (12.2),

$$l = \pi(r_1 + r_2) + 2d + \frac{(r_1 - r_2)^2}{d} \quad \ldots\ldots\ldots\ldots (12.3)$$

12.2.2 Cross Belt Drive: Length of the Belt

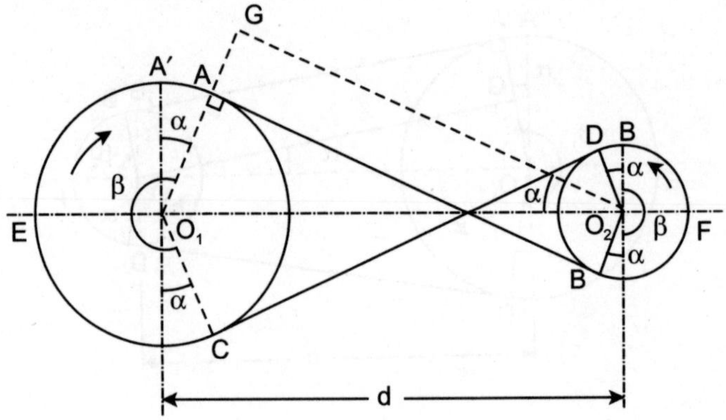

Fig. 12.3

Using the same procedure of open belt drive, we can find the length of belt in this case also, which is given as:

$$l = \pi (r_1 + r_2) + 2d + \frac{(r_1 + r_2)^2}{d}$$

12.3 Ratio of Tension

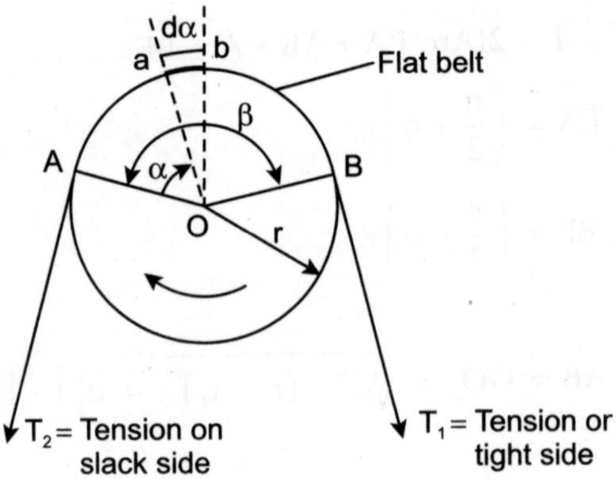

Fig. 12.4

Considering the smaller pulley of radius r

Let

β = The angle of contact or lap subtended by the portion of the belt AB in contact with the pulley.

Considering the F.B.D. of element ab, if μ = Coefficient of friction between pulley and belt.

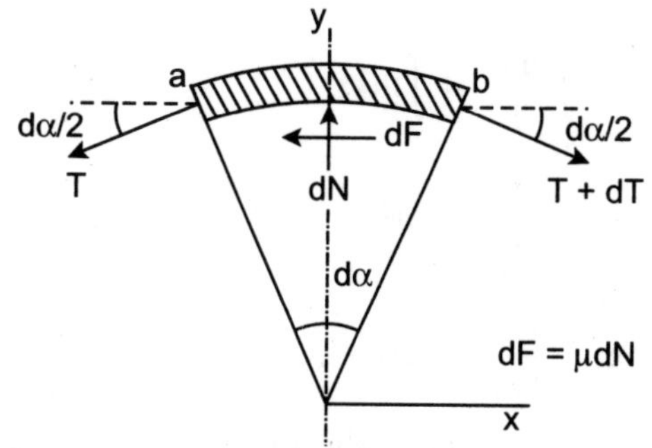

Fig. 12.5

Normal reaction = dN

Friction force dF = μdN

where, μ = coefficient of friction between the pulley and the belt

For equilibrium

$$\Sigma F_x = 0 \Rightarrow T\cos\frac{d\alpha}{2} + dF - (T + dT)\cos\frac{d\alpha}{2} = 0 \quad \text{(12.4)}$$

$$\Sigma F_y = 0 \Rightarrow dN - T\sin\frac{d\alpha}{2} - (T + dT)\sin\frac{d\alpha}{2} = 0 \quad \text{(12.5)}$$

As angle $d\alpha$ is very small, substitute,

$$\cos\frac{d\alpha}{2} \approx 1,\ \sin\frac{d\alpha}{2} \approx \frac{d\alpha}{2}$$

and $dF = \mu dN$ in the above equations

$$T + \mu dN - (T + dT) = 0$$

or

$$dT - \mu dN = 0 \quad \text{(12.6)}$$

and

$$dN - T\frac{d\alpha}{2} - (T + dT)\frac{d\alpha}{2} = 0$$

or

$$dN - T\,d\alpha = 0$$

Neglect $\left(dT\frac{d\alpha}{2}\right)$, being small in magnitude eliminating dN

$$dT = \mu T d\alpha$$

$$\frac{dT}{T} = \mu d\alpha \quad \text{(12.7)}$$

Integrating the above expression for the entire length AB of the belt in contact with the pulley using conditions.

At A, $\alpha = 0$ and $T = T_2$

At B, $\alpha = \beta$ and $T = T_1$

$$\int_{T_2}^{T_1} \frac{dT}{T} = \int_0^{\beta} \mu d\alpha$$

$$\Rightarrow \qquad \frac{T_1}{T_2} = e^{\mu\beta} \qquad \ldots\ldots (12.8)$$

or
$$2.3 \log_{10}\left(\frac{T_1}{T_2}\right) = \mu\beta \qquad \ldots\ldots (12.9)$$

The value of e = 2.718 can be used for the numerical calculations.

These results are valid for flat belt drive. In case of 'V' belt drive, the following equation may be used

$$\frac{T_1}{T_2} = e^{\mu\beta \cos\alpha} \qquad \ldots\ldots (12.10)$$

where α = Semi-grove angle

12.4 Centrifugal Tension (T_c)

Considering a small element of the belt subtending an angle $d\alpha$ at the pulley centre.

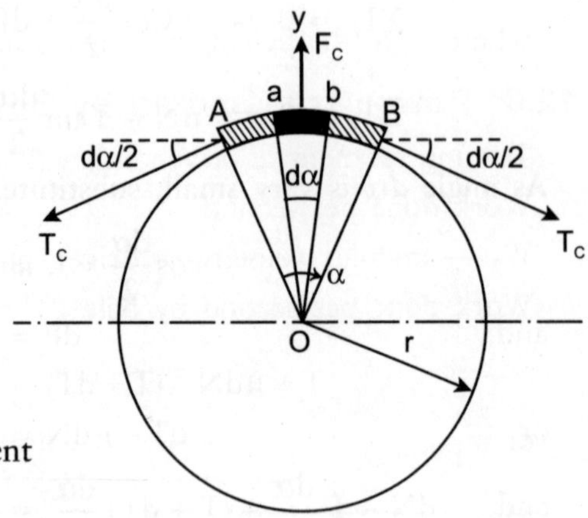

Fig. 12.6

Let

m = mass of belt per unit length

v = linear velocity of the belt

F_c = centrifugal force on ab

$= \text{mass of the element} \times \frac{v^2}{r}$

$= \text{mass per unit length} \times \frac{v^2}{r} \times \text{length of element}$

$$F_c = m\, r d\alpha \frac{v^2}{r} = mv^2 d\alpha$$

For equilibrium

$$\Sigma F_x = 0 \Rightarrow T_c \cos\frac{d\alpha}{2} - T_c \cos\frac{d\alpha}{2} = 0 \qquad \ldots\ldots (12.11)$$

$$\Sigma F_y = 0 \Rightarrow F_c - 2T_c \sin\frac{d\alpha}{2} = 0 \qquad \ldots\ldots (12.12)$$

For very small angle $d\alpha$, $\sin\frac{d\alpha}{2} = \frac{d\alpha}{2}$

Substituting value of $F_c = mv^2 d\alpha$ in Eq. (12.12)

$$mv^2 d\alpha - 2T_c \frac{d\alpha}{2} = 0$$

or $$mv^2 - T_c = 0$$

$\therefore$ $$T_c = mv^2 \quad \text{(12.13)}$$

Tension on the slack side = $T_1 - T_c$

12.5 Initial Tension in the Belt (T_0)

When the pulley is stationary, the tension in the belt on tight side as well as slack side are equal and is known as initial tension. Initial tension is necessary to grip pulley.

Increase in length of belt on tight side = $\alpha\,(T_1 - T_0)$

Decrease in length of the belt on slack side = $\alpha\,(T_0 - T_2)$

Now

Increase in length on tight side = decrease in length on slack side

$$\alpha\,(T_1 - T_0) = \alpha\,(T_0 - T_2)$$

$$T_1 - T_0 = T_0 - T_2$$

$\Rightarrow$ $$T_0 = \left(\frac{T_1 + T_2}{2}\right) \quad \text{(12.14)}$$

where α is coefficient of increase in belt length per unit force.

12.6 Power Transmitted by Belts

Turning moment at driven pulley B = $(T_1 - T_2)\,r_2$ N.m

Work done per second = $(T_1 - T_2)\,r_2 w_2$ watt.

$W_2 \rightarrow$ angular velocity of driven pulley B,

Work done per second by belt = $(T_1 - T_2)v$ watt.

$\therefore$ $$P = (T_1 - T_2)v \text{ watt.} \quad \text{(12.15)}$$

or $$P = T_1\left(1 - \frac{1}{K}\right)v \quad \text{(12.16)} \qquad \text{Let } K = \frac{T_1}{T_2}$$

Maximum permissible tension in the belt material

$$T_m = T_1 + T_c$$

$$T_c = \frac{w}{g}v^2$$

$$T_1 = T_m - T_c$$

From Eq. (12.16)

$$P = (T_m - T_c)\left(1 - \frac{1}{K}\right)v = \left(T_m - \frac{wv^2}{g}\right)\left(1 - \frac{1}{K}\right)v$$

For maximum power transmission

$$\frac{dP}{dV} = 0 \Rightarrow \left(T_m - \frac{wv^2}{g}\right)\left(1 - \frac{1}{K}\right)v = 0$$

$\Rightarrow$ $$T_m = 3T_c$$

or
$$T_c = \frac{T_m}{3} \qquad (12.17)$$

The power transmitted is maximum when the centrifugal tension in the belt is one-third the maximum permissible tension T_m in the belt.

and
$$\Rightarrow \qquad P_{max} = \frac{2}{3}T_m\left(1 - \frac{1}{K}\right)v \text{ watts.} \qquad (12.18)$$

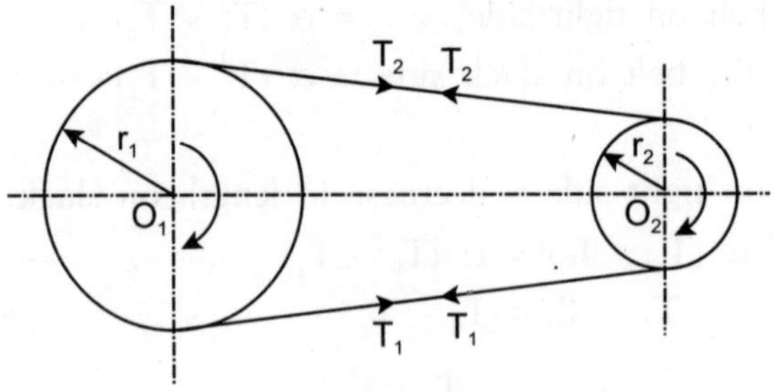

Fig. 12.7

Example 12.1

A belt supports the 200 kg load is passed over a fixed circular drum and subjected to a force P to maintain equilibrium. The coefficient of static friction μ between the cable and the fixed drum is 0.30. (a) For α = 0, determine the maximum and minimum values which P may have in order not to raise or lower the load. (b) For P = 600 N, determine the minimum value which the angle α may have before the load begins to slip.

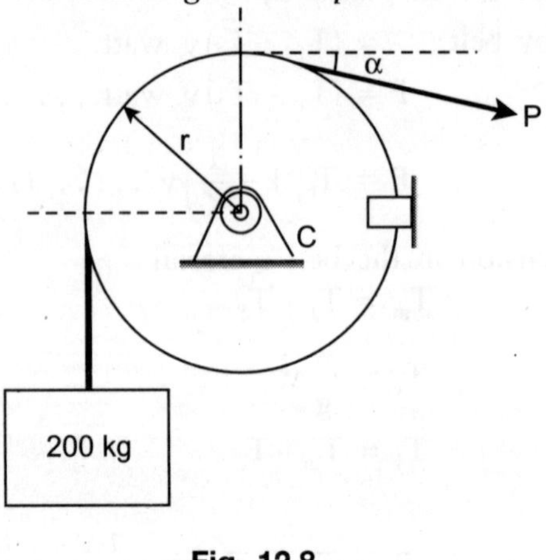

Fig. 12.8

Solution:

Case a $\alpha = 0$

$P_{max} = ?$

$P_{min} = ?$

$\mu = 0.3$

We know that

$$\frac{T_1}{T_2} = e^{\mu\beta} \quad \text{.................} \quad (12.19)$$

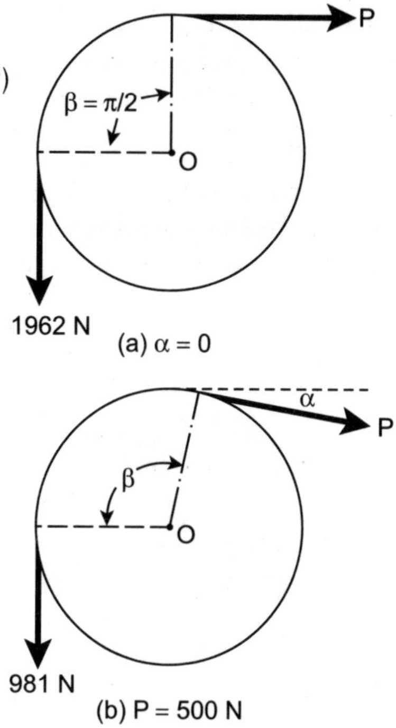

Fig. 12.9

When $\alpha = 0, \ \beta = \frac{\pi}{2}$ radians

$$\therefore \quad T_1 = P_{max}$$

$$T_2 = P_{min}$$

For equilibrium condition,

$$\frac{P_{min}}{1962} = e^{0.3 \times \frac{\pi}{2}}$$

$$\therefore \quad P_{min} = 1224.8 \text{ N}$$

From Eq. (12.19),

$$\frac{T_1}{T_2} = \frac{P_{max}}{P_{min}} = e^{\mu\beta} = e^{0.3 \times \frac{\pi}{2}}$$

$$\therefore \quad P_{max} = 2 \times 981 \times (2.718)^{0.3 \times \left(\frac{\pi}{2}\right)}$$

$$= 981 \times 1.602 \times 2$$

$$= 1571.46 \times 2 = 1572 \text{ N} \times 2$$

$$= \mathbf{3144 \text{ N}}$$

Ans.

Case b

$$\alpha = ?$$

$$T_2 = P_{min} = 600 \text{ N}$$

$$T_1 = P_{max} = 2 \times 981 \text{ N} = 1962 \text{ N}$$

$$\frac{T_1}{T_2} = e^{\mu\beta}$$

$$\Rightarrow \quad \left(\frac{981 \times 2}{600}\right) = (2.718)^{0.3\,\beta}$$

$$3.27 = (2.718)^{0.3\,\beta}$$

$$\log(3.27) = 0.3\beta \, \log(2.718)$$

$$0.5145 = 0.3\beta \times 0.4342$$

$$\therefore \quad \beta = 3.95 \text{ rad} = 226.3°, \ \alpha = \beta - \frac{\pi}{2}$$

$$= 226.3 - 90 = \mathbf{136.3°}$$

Ans.

Note: β must be expressed in radians.

Example 12.2

A belt supports two weights 2000 N and W_2 as shown in Fig. 12.10. Find minimum weight W_2 to keep 2000 N in equilibrium. Assume that the pulley is locked and μ = 0.25.

Solution:

The tensions in the belt are T_1 and T_2. Since the weight W_2 just checks the tendency of weight W_1 to move down, tension on the side of W_1 is larger.

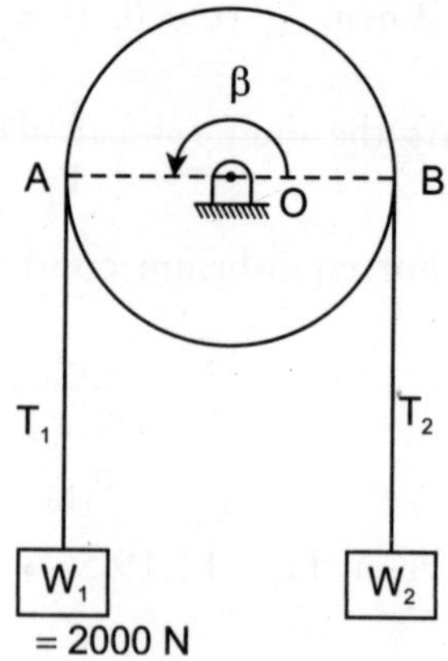

Fig. 12.10

That is, $T_1 > T_2$

$$\mu = 0.25,\ \beta = \pi,$$

$$W_1 = 2000 \text{ N}$$

Using $\dfrac{T_1}{T_2} = e^{\mu\beta}$

$$= 2.718^{\pi(0.25)}$$

$$\frac{T_1}{T_2} = 0.193$$

But $T_1 = W_1 = 2000$ N

$$T_2 = 2000 \times \frac{1}{2.193}$$

$$T_2 = 456 \times 2 = 912 \text{ N}$$

But $W_1 = T_2 = \mathbf{912\ N}$ **Ans.**

Example 12.3

Determine the power transmitted by a cross belt drive connecting two pulleys of 40 cm and 20 cm diameters which are 1.95 m apart. The maximum permissible tension in the belt is 1 kN, coefficient of friction is 0.25 and the speed of larger pulley is 100 r.p.m.

Solution:

$$\mu = 0.25,\quad r_1 = \frac{40}{2}\text{cm} = 20 \text{ cm} = 0.2 \text{ m}$$

$$r_2 = \frac{20}{2}\text{cm} = 0.1 \text{ m},\ P = ?$$

Let us calculate the angle of lap.

For cross-drive, angle of lap for both the pulleys is the same.

$$\beta = 180 + 2\theta$$

where $\theta = \sin^{-1}\left(\dfrac{r_1 + r_2}{d}\right) = \sin^{-1}\left(\dfrac{0.2 + 0.10}{1.95}\right)$

or $\theta = 8.9°$

$$\beta = 180° + 2(8.9) = 197.8°$$

$$\beta = 197.8 \times \frac{\pi}{180} = 3.45 \text{ radians}$$

$$T_{max} = T_1 + T_c = T_1 = 1 \text{ kN} = 1000 \text{ N}$$

$$\frac{T_1}{T_2} = e^{\mu\beta} = e^{0.25 \times 197.8}$$

(As the data for calculating T_c is not given so we assume $T_c = 0$)

$$\frac{T_1}{T_2} = 2.718^{(0.25 \times 197.8)}$$

$$\frac{T_1}{T_2} = 2.97, \; T_1 = 1000 \text{ N}$$

$$T_1 = \frac{1000}{2.97} = 336.7 \text{ N}$$

$$\text{Power} = (T_1 - T_2)v$$

Velocity of the belt $\quad v = \omega r = \dfrac{2\pi N}{60} \times r$

The values of N and r must be of the some pulley. Speed of larger pulley is 100 r.p.m.

$\therefore \quad v = \dfrac{2\pi N r}{60} = \dfrac{2\pi \times 100}{60} \times 0.2 = 2.1 \text{ m/sec}$

$\therefore$ Power

$$P = (T_1 - T_2)v$$

$$= (1000 - 336.7) \times 2.1 = 1392.9 \text{ watt.}$$

$$= \mathbf{1.39\ kW}$$ **Ans.**

Example 12.4

Determine minimum tension in the rope required to support a cylinder of 1000 kg. When the rope passes: (a) Once over the rod, (b) Two times over the rod. Take $\mu_s = 0.2$.

Solution:

$$T_1 = 1000 \text{ kg} = 1000 \times 9.81 \text{ N} = 9810 \text{ N}$$

$$\mu_s = \mu = 0.2$$

(a) When rope passes once over the rod

Angle of lap $\quad \beta = 180° = \pi$ rad

$$T_2 = ?$$

Using $\quad \dfrac{T_1}{T_2} = e^{\mu\beta}$

$$T_1 = T_2 \; e^{\mu\beta}$$

or $\quad T_1 = 9810/(2.718)^{0.2 \times \pi} = 5233.8$ N

or $\quad T_1 = \mathbf{5.2\ kN}$ **Ans.**

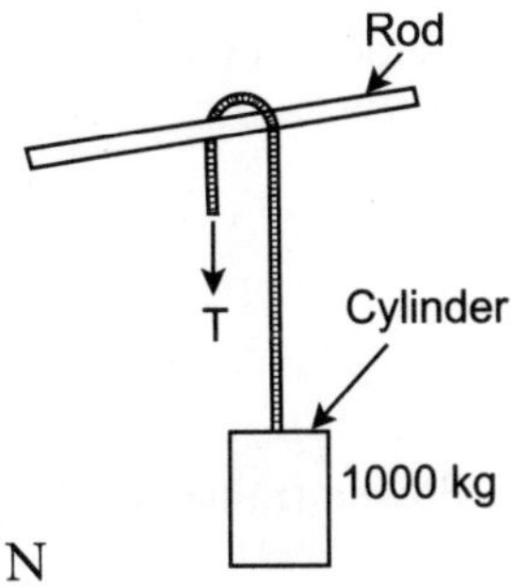

Fig. 12.11

(b) Rope passage twice over the rod

$$\beta = 1\tfrac{1}{2} \text{ turn}$$
$$= 360 + 180$$
$$= 540^\circ = 3\pi \text{ rad}$$

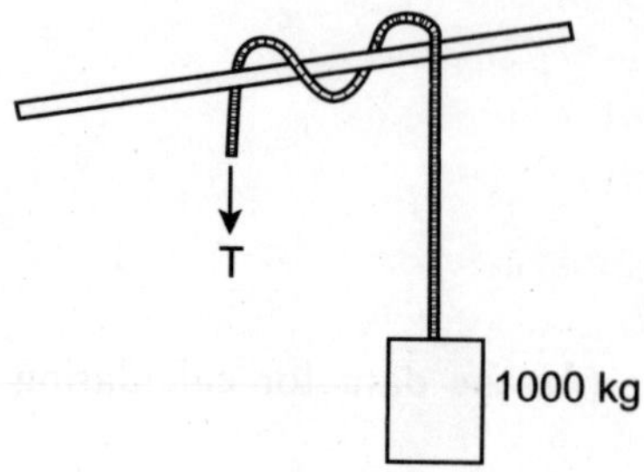

Fig. 12.12

Using $$\frac{T_1}{T_2} = e^{\mu\theta}$$

$\Rightarrow$ $$\frac{T_1}{T_2} = e^{\mu\theta} = (2.718)^{0.2 \times 3\pi}$$

$\Rightarrow$ $$T_2 = \frac{9810}{6.58} = 1489.8 \text{ N}$$

$$T_2 = \mathbf{1.49 \text{ kN}}$$ **Ans.**

Example 12.5

A belt drives a pulley of 300 mm diameter such that ratio of tensions in the tight side and slack side is 1.5. If the maximum tension in the belt is not to exceed 240 kN, find the safe power transmitted by the pulley at a speed of 100 r.p.m.

Solution:

$$d = 300 \text{ mm}$$
$$\frac{T_1}{T_2} = 1.5$$
$$T_1 = 240 \text{ kN}$$
$$P = ?$$
$$N = 100 \text{ r.p.m.}$$

Now

$$\frac{T_1}{T_2} = 1.5 \Rightarrow T_2 = \frac{T_1}{1.5}$$

$\therefore$ $$T_2 = \frac{240}{1.5} = 160 \text{ kN}$$

Velocity of belt

$$v = \frac{\pi N d}{60} \text{ m/sec}$$
$$= \frac{\pi \times 100 \times 0.30}{60}$$
$$= 1.57 \text{ m/sec}$$

Power transmitted by belt

$$P = (T_1 - T_2)v = (240 - 160) \times 1.57$$

$\therefore$ $$= \mathbf{125.6 \text{ kW}}$$ **Ans.**

Example 12.6

Find power transmitted by belt (cross-type drive connecting two pulleys of 500 mm and 250 mm diameter which are 2 m apart. The maximum permissible tension in the belt is 1 kN. Take μ = 0.25 and speed of larger pulley is 100 rpm.

Solution:

Cross belt drive (Refer Fig. 12.3)

$$d_1 = 500 \text{ mm}$$
$$d_2 = 250 \text{ mm}$$
$$d = 2 \text{ m}$$
$$T_{max} = T_1 = 1 \text{ kN}$$
$$\mu = 0.25$$
$$N = 100 \text{ r.p.m.}$$
$$r_1 = 250 \text{ mm}$$
$$r_2 = 125 \text{ mm}$$

$$\sin\theta = \frac{r_1 + r_2}{d} = \frac{0.250 + 0.125}{2} = 0.1875$$

$$\theta = 10.8° = 10.8° \times \frac{\pi}{180} = 0.188 \text{ rad}$$

$$\beta = 180 + 2\theta$$
$$= 180 + 10.8° = 190.8° = 3.33 \text{ rad}$$

Now

$$\frac{T_1}{T_2} = e^{\mu\beta}$$

$$\Rightarrow \quad \frac{1}{T_2} = (2.718)^{0.25 \times 3.33}$$

$$\Rightarrow \quad T_2 = 0.414 \text{ kN}$$

Velocity of belt

$$v = \frac{\pi N d}{60} \text{m/sec} = \frac{\pi N_1 d_1}{60} = \frac{\pi N_2 d_2}{60}$$

$$= \frac{\pi \times 100 \times 0.50}{60} = 2.62 \text{ m/sec}$$

Power transmitted

$$P = (T_1 - T_2)v$$
$$= (1 - 0.44) \times 2.62 \text{ kW}$$
$$= \mathbf{1.46 \text{ kW}}$$

Ans.

Example 12.7

A pulley is driven by a flat belt drive, running at a speed of 400 m/min. The angle of lap is at 160° and the coefficient of friction between the belt and pulley material is 0.3. If the maximum allowable tension in the belt is 800 N, calculate the net driving tension and power transmitted by the belt. Neglect the centrifugal tension.

Solution:

$$N = 400 \text{ m/min}$$

$$\beta = 160° = 160° \times \frac{\pi}{180} = 2.79 \text{ rad}$$

$$\mu = 0.3$$

$$T_m = T_1 + T_c = T_1 = 800 \text{ N}$$

$$(T_1 - T_2) = ?$$

$$P = ?$$

Now

$$\frac{T_1}{T_2} = e^{\mu\beta}$$

$$\Rightarrow \quad \frac{800}{T_2} = e^{0.3 \times 2.79}$$

$$\Rightarrow \quad T_2 = \frac{800}{(2.718)^{0.3 \times 2.79}} = 346.4 \text{ N}$$

Net driving tension

$$= (T_1 - T_2) = (800 - 346.4) \text{ N}$$

$$= 453.6 \text{ N}$$

Power transmitted

$$P = (T_1 - T_2)v = 453.6 \times \frac{400}{60} = 3023.7 \text{ watt.}$$

$$= \mathbf{3.024\ kW}$$

Ans.

NUMERICAL QUESTIONS

1. A belt supports two weights W_1 and W_2 over a pulley as shown. If W_1 = 1000 N, find minimum weight W_2 to keep W_1 in equilibrium. Assume that the pulley is locked and take μ = 0.25.

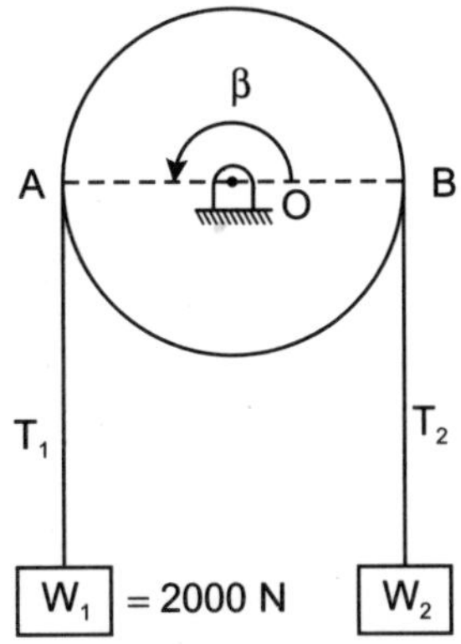

Fig. 12.13

2. Find the number of ropes required to transmit 100 kW. The maximum permissible tension in the rope 1500 N, velocity of rope is 10 m/sec and weight of the rope is 4 N/m. Assume the angle of contact as 180° and pulley groove angle as 60°.
3. A belt is running over a pulley of 1.5 m diameter at 350 r.p.m. The angle of contact is 120° and the coefficient of friction is 0.30. If the maximum tension in the belt is 400 N, find the power transmitted by the belt.
4. The maximum allowable tension in a V-belt groove angle 45°, is 1500 N. The angle of lap is 180° and coefficient friction between the belt and material of pulley is 0.3. If the belt is running at 2 m/sec, find net driving tension and power transmitted by the pulley.
5. In a flat belt, the maximum tension is 1160 N and the angle of lap is 160°. The coefficient of friction between the belt and pulley is 0.2. Diameter of pulley is 900 mm and it runs at 540 r.p.m. Find the power transmitted at this speed. Neglect the effect of centrifugal tension.
6. A rope drive is used for transmitting power through a pulley of 1.2 m diameter. The angle of lap is 180° and groove angle is 45°. Maximum allowable tension in rope is 1200 N and coefficient of friction between rope and groove is 0.3. Find torque provided by the rope on the pulley.

NUMERICAL QUESTIONS

1. A belt supports two weights W_1 and W_2 over a pulley as shown. If W_1 = 1000 N, find minimum weight W_2 to keep W_1 in equilibrium. Assume that the pulley is locked and take μ = 0.25.

Fig. 12.13

2. Find the number of ropes required to transmit 100 kW. The maximum permissible tension in the rope 1500 N, velocity of rope is 10 m/sec and weight of the rope is 4 N/m. Assume the angle of contact as 180° and pulley groove angle as 60°.
3. A belt is running over a pulley of 1.5 m diameter at 250 r.p.m. The angle of contact is 120° and the coefficient of friction is 0.30. If the maximum tension in the belt is 700 N, find the power transmitted by the belt.
4. The maximum allowable tension in a V-belt groove angle 45°, is 1500 N. The angle of lap is 180° and coefficient friction between the belt and material of pulley is 0.3. If the belt is running at 2 m/sec, find net driving tension and power transmitted by the pulley.
5. In a flat belt, the maximum tension is 1500 N and the angle of lap is 160°. The coefficient of friction between the belt and pulley is 0.2. Diameter of pulley is 500 mm and it runs at 560 r.p.m. Find the power transmitted at this speed. Neglect the effect of centrifugal tension.
6. A rope drive is used for transmitting power through a pulley of 1.2 m diameter. The angle of lap is 180° and groove angle is 45°. Maximum allowable tension in rope is 1200 N and coefficient of friction between rope and groove is 0.3. Find torque provided by the rope on the pulley.

PART C

13

Shear Force and Bending Moment in Beams

13.1 Beam

Beam is a structural member resting on supports to carry transverse, lateral or vertical loads to its axis. Beams are placed horizontally. The magnitude of external load which a beam may carry depends upon various factors like distance between supports, overhanging length from supports, type of loading, types of supports, cross-section and elasticity of beam.

13.2 Types of Beams

1. Cantilever beam: shown in Fig. 13.1.
2. Simply supported beam: shown in Fig. 13.2.
3. Simply supported overhanging beam: shown in Fig. 13.3.
4. Rigidly fixed or built in beam: shown in Fig. 13.4.
5. Continuous beam: shown in Fig. 13.5.

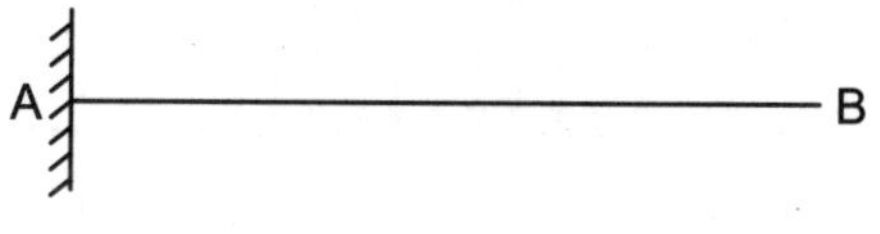

Fig. 13.1: Cantilever Beam

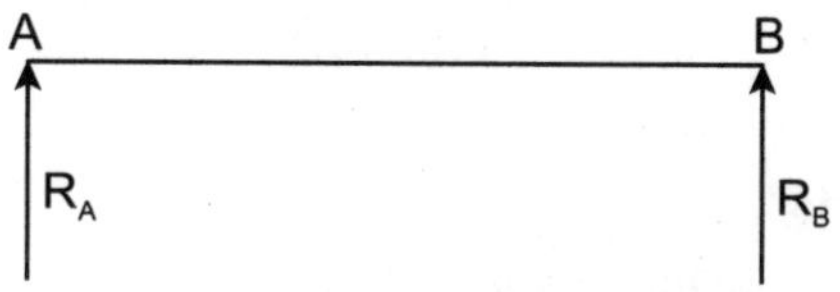

Fig. 13.2: Simply Supported Beam

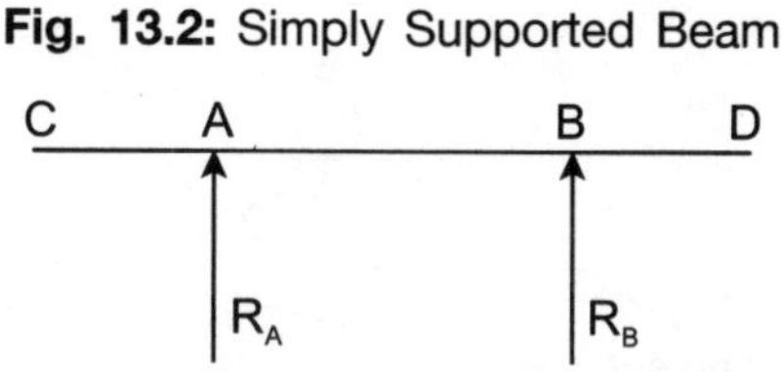

Fig. 13.3: Simply Supported Overhanging Beam

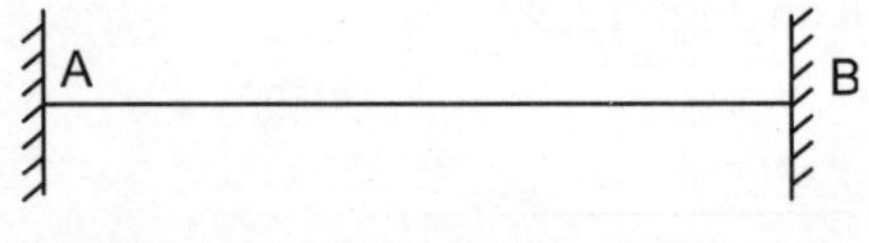

Fig. 13.4: Rigidly Fixed or Built in Beam

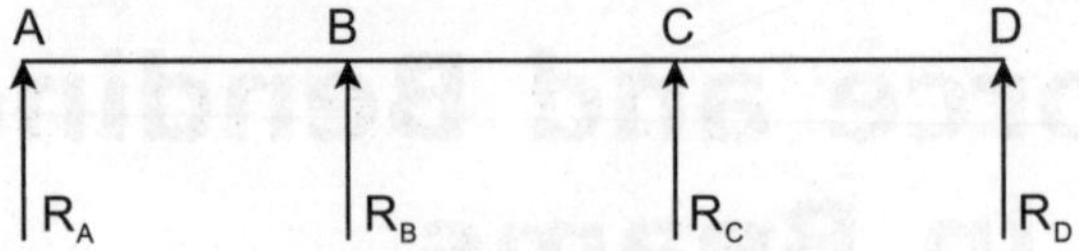

Fig. 13.5: Continuous Beam

13.3 Types of Loads

1. Point loads or concentrated load.
2. Uniformly distributed load (U.D.L.).
3. Gradually varying load (G.V.L.).
4. Non-uniformly varyig load.

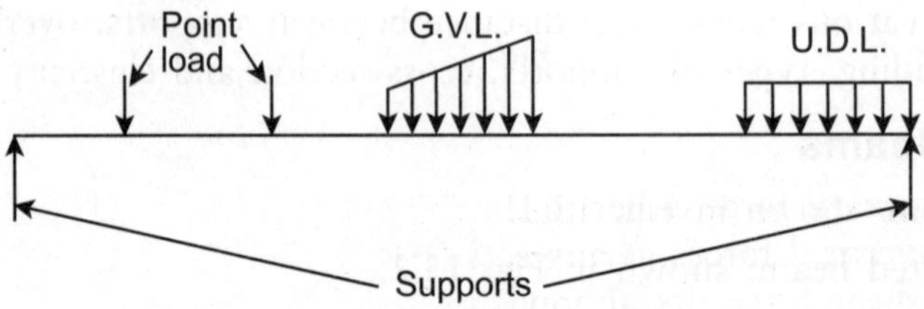

Fig. 13.6

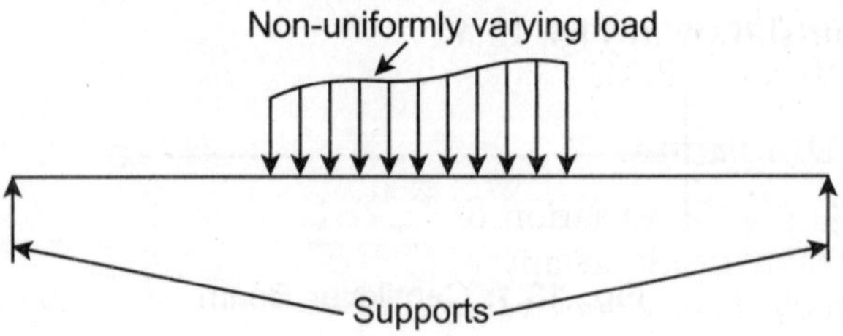

Fig. 13.7

13.4 Types of Supports

1. Roller supports: shown in Fig. 13.8.

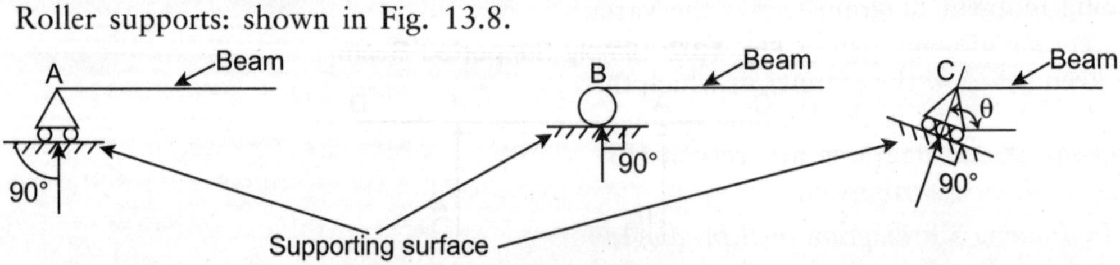

Fig. 13.8

2. Fixed supports: shown in Fig. 13.9.

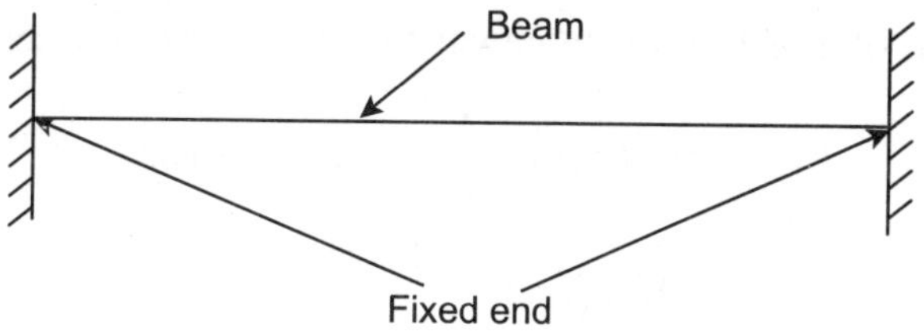

Fig. 13.9

3. Hinged or Pinned supports: shown in Fig. 13.10.

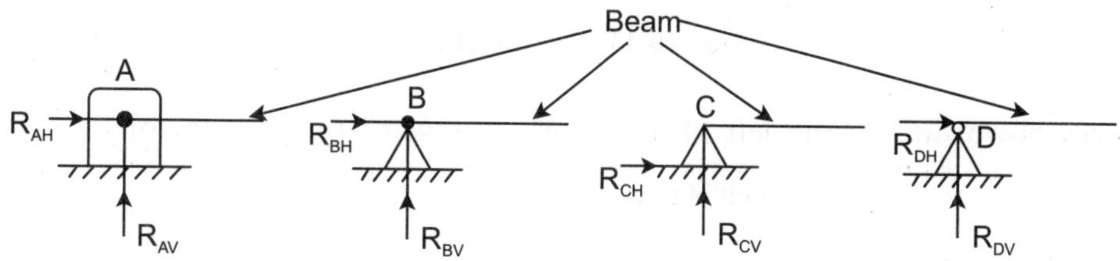

Fig. 13.10

13.5 Shear Force

It is the unbalanced vertical force either to the right or left of the section. In other words, the algebraic sum of the vertical forces at any section of a beam either to the right or left of the section is known as shear force. Its abbreviated form is S.F.

13.6 Bending Moment

It is the algebraic sum of the moments of all the forces acting either to right or left of the section. Its abbreviated form is B.M.

13.7 Shear Force Diagrams

A shear force diagram shows the variation of shear force along the length of the beam. Shear force can be calculated numerically at any particular section. But sometimes, we are keen to know the manner, in which these values vary, along the length of the beam. This can be done by plotting the shear force as ordinate and the position of the cross section as abscissa. These diagrams are very useful as they provide complete information about shear force distribution.

13.8 Bending Moment Diagrams

A bending moment diagram shows the variation of bending moment along the length of the beam. Bending moment can be calculated numerically at any particular section. But sometimes, we are keen to know the manner in which these values vary along the length of the beam. They can be done by plotting the bending moment as ordinate and the position of the cross section as abscissa. These diagrams are very useful as they provide complete information about of bending moment distribution.

Note: In drawing S.F. diagram or B.M. diagram, all positive values are plotted above the base line and negative values below the base line.

13.9 S.F. Sign Convention

Forces upward to the left of a section or downward to the right of the section are taken positive S.F.

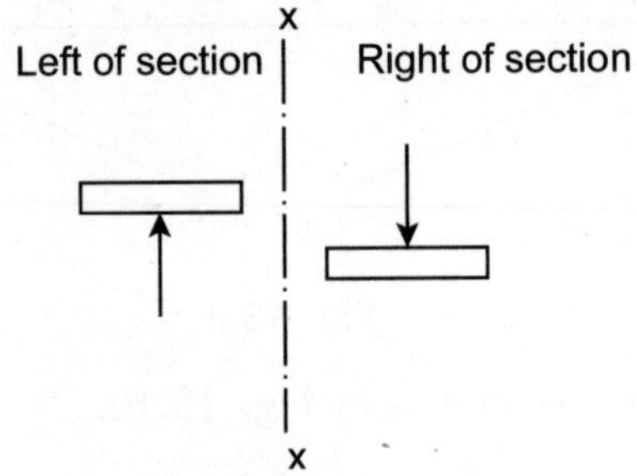

Fig. 13.11: S.F. Positive

And forces downward to the left of a section or upward to the right of the section are negative S.F.

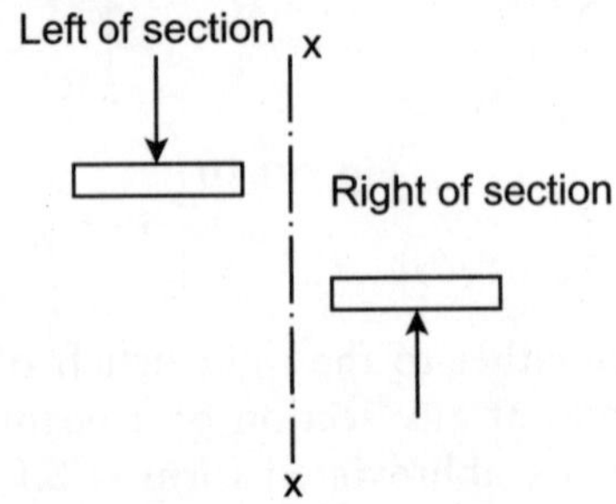

Fig. 13.12: S.F. Negative

Therefore, if someone uses right of the section only then sign convention will be as

$$\text{For right of the section} \quad \begin{matrix} \uparrow & \downarrow \\ -\text{ve} & +\text{ve} \\ \text{SF} & \text{SF} \end{matrix}$$

Similarly if any one considers left of the section then sign convention for S.F. will be as

$$\text{For left of the section} \quad \begin{matrix} \downarrow & \uparrow \\ -\text{ve} & +\text{ve} \\ \text{SF} & \text{SF} \end{matrix}$$

In addition to shear, every section of beam will be subjected to bending, i.e. to a resultant B.M. which is the net effect of the moments of each of individual loads.

13.10 B.M. Sign Convention

Clockwise moments to left and counter clockwise to the right are considered positive as shown in Fig. 13.13(a).

Similarly clockwise moments to the right and counter clockwise to the left are considered negative as shown in Fig. 13.13(b).

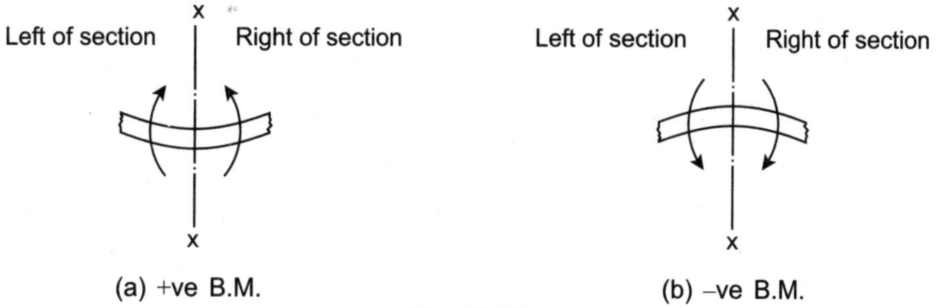

Fig. 13.13

13.11 Procedure for Drawing S.F. and B.M. Diagrams

For determinate beams:

1. Find the reactions of the support by taking moments round the hinged or pinned support.
2. Starting from one end, calculate the S.F. at all the sailent points. Draw the beam to some scale, show the loading on it and draw the S.F. diagram just below it.
3. Take some section at distance x from one end and find the moment of all the force on one side of the section (generally right hand side). This gives M_x. Now change the section x and find M_{x_1} at all sailent points. It gives the enough points to draw the B.M. diagram. Some points, like points of maximum +ve and –ve B.M. and points of contraflexure (where +ve B.M. changes to –ve or *vice versa*) are to be precisely known and should be calculated carefully.
4. Draw the B.M. diagram to some scale or at least proportional, just below the S.F. diagram. Points of zero S.F. should coincide with maximum or minimum B.M. The equation of B.M. should be formed at a section x to guess the shape of the B.M. and S.F. diagrams, from the loading diagram.

13.12 S.F. and B.M. Diagrams for Simply Supported Beam with a Point Load at its Mid-point

1. *Reactions calculation*

$$R_A + R_B = W \quad \ldots\ldots (13.1)$$

$$\Sigma M_A = 0$$

$$\Rightarrow \quad R_B \times l = W \times \frac{l}{2}$$

$$\Rightarrow \quad R_B = \frac{W}{2}$$

and

$$R_A = \frac{W}{2}$$

2. *S.F.D.: For right section* $\underset{-\text{ve}}{\uparrow}\ \underset{+\text{ve}}{\downarrow}$

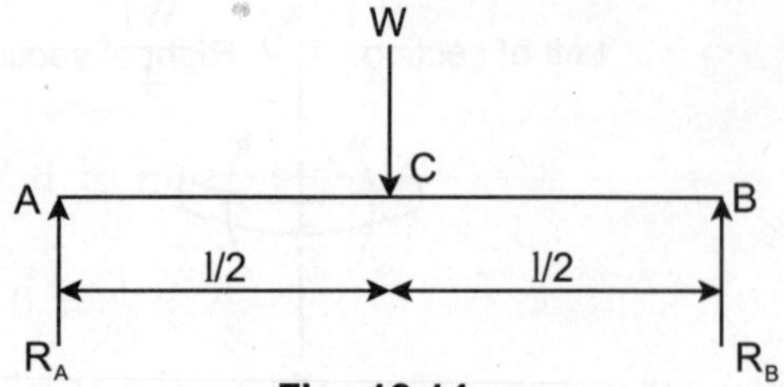

Fig. 13.14

F_{Br} = Algebraic sum of S.F. just the right of point B = 0

F_B = Algebraic sum of S.F. to the right of section including point B,

$$= 0 - R_B = -\frac{W}{2}$$

Similarly,

F_{Cr} = Algebraic sum of S.F. just the right point C

$$= -\frac{W}{2} = -\frac{W}{2}$$

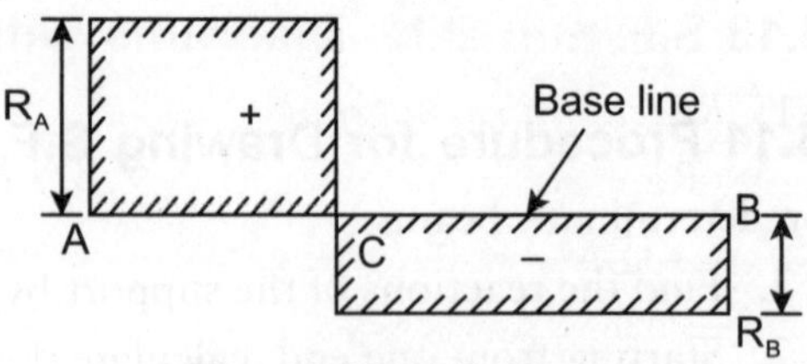

Fig. 13.15: S.F. Diagram

F_C = Algebraic sum of S.F. to the right section including point C

$$= -\frac{W}{2} + W = +\frac{W}{2}$$

Similarly,

F_{Ar} = Algebraic sum of S.F. just the right of point A

$$= +\frac{W}{2}$$

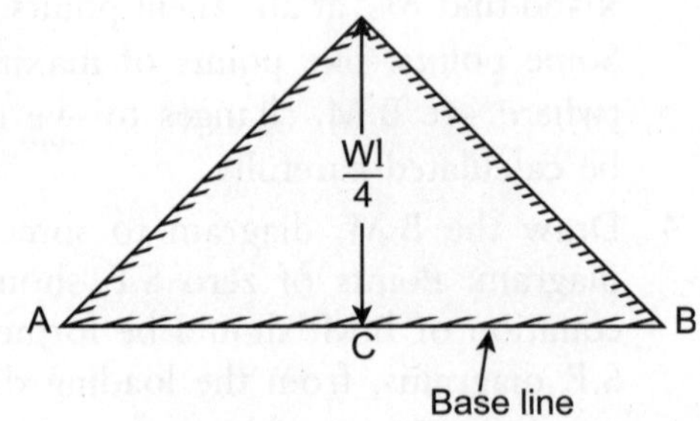

Fig. 13.16: B.M. Diagram

F_A = Algebraic sum of S.F. to the right section including point A

$$= \frac{W}{2} - \frac{W}{2} = 0$$

3. *B.M.D.: For right section* $\underset{+\text{ve}}{\curvearrowleft}\ \underset{-\text{ve}}{\curvearrowright}$

M_{Br} = Algebraic sum of B.M. just the right of point B = 0

M_B = Algebraic sum of B.M. of the right section including moment at point B = 0

M_{Cr} = Algebraic sum of B.M. just the right of point C

$$= +R_B \times \frac{l}{2} = \frac{W}{2} \times \frac{l}{2} = \frac{Wl}{4}$$

M_C = Algebraic sum of B.M. of the right section including moment at point C

$$= \frac{Wl}{4} + 0 = \frac{Wl}{4}$$

M_{Ar} = Algebraic sum of B.M. just the right of point A = $R_B \times l - W \times \frac{l}{2}$

$$= \frac{W}{2} \times l - W \times \frac{l}{2} = 0$$

M_A = Algebraic sum of B.M. of the right section including moment at point A = 0 + 0 = 0

13.13 S.F. and B.M. Diagrams with a Point Load not a Mix Span

1. *Reactions calculation*

$$R_A + R_B = W \ldots\ldots\ldots\ldots\ldots \quad (13.2)$$

$$\Sigma M_A = 0$$

$$\Rightarrow R_B \times l = W \times a$$

$$\Rightarrow R_B = \left(\frac{Wa}{l}\right)$$

and $R_A = \left(\frac{Wb}{l}\right)$

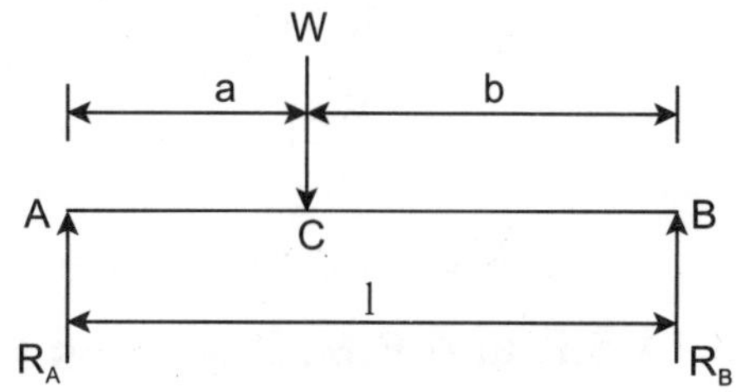

Fig. 13.17

2. *S.F.D.: For right of section* $\underset{-ve}{\uparrow}$ $\underset{+ve}{\downarrow}$

$$F_{Br} = 0$$

$$F_B = -R_B = -\left(\frac{Wa}{l}\right)$$

$$F_{Cr} = \frac{-Wa}{l}$$

$$F_C = \frac{-Wa}{l} + W$$

$$= \frac{-Wa + Wl}{l}$$

$$= \frac{-Wa + W(a+b)}{l}$$

$$= \frac{-Wa + Wa + Wb}{l}$$

$$= \frac{Wb}{l}$$

$$F_{Ar} = \frac{Wb}{l}$$

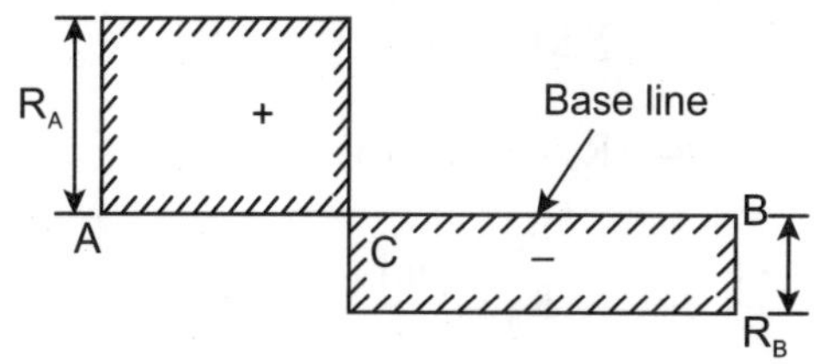

Fig. 13.18: S.F. Diagram

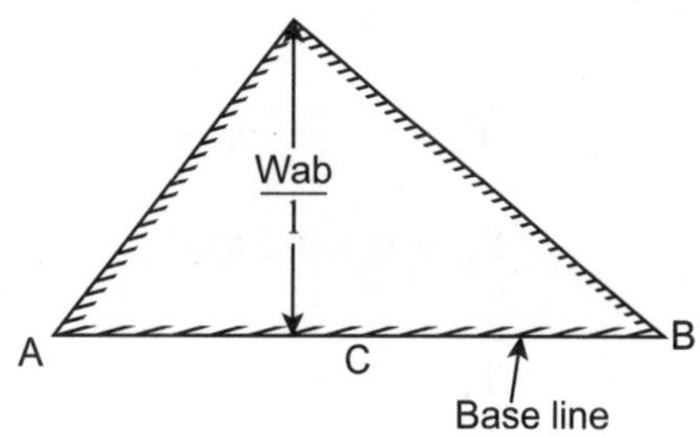

Fig. 13.19: B.M. Diagram

$$F_A = \frac{Wb}{l} - \frac{Wb}{l} = 0$$

3. *B.M.D.: For right of the section* $\circlearrowleft$ +ve $\circlearrowright$ –ve

$$M_{Br} = 0$$

$$M_B = 0$$

$$M_{Cr} = +R_B \cdot b = \frac{Wab}{l} = \frac{Wab}{l}$$

$$M_C = \frac{Wab}{l}$$

$$M_{Ar} = R_B \times l - W \cdot a$$

$$= \frac{Wa}{l} l - W \cdot a = 0$$

$$M_A = R_B \times l - W \cdot a = 0$$

13.14 S.F. and B.M. Diagrams for Simply Supported Beam with U.D.L. at the Whole Span

1. *Reactions calculation*

$$R_A + R_B = \omega l \quad \ldots\ldots\ldots\ldots\ldots \quad (13.3)$$

$$\Sigma M_A = 0$$

$$\Rightarrow R_B \times l = \omega l \times \frac{l}{2}$$

$$\Rightarrow \quad R_B = \frac{\omega l}{2}$$

$$\therefore \quad R_A = \frac{\omega l}{2}$$

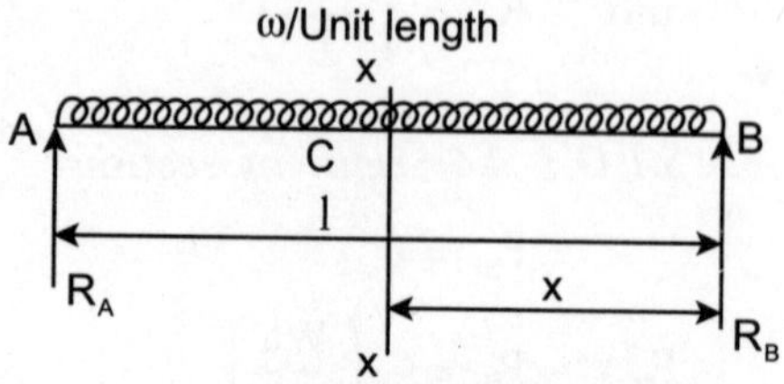

Fig. 13.20

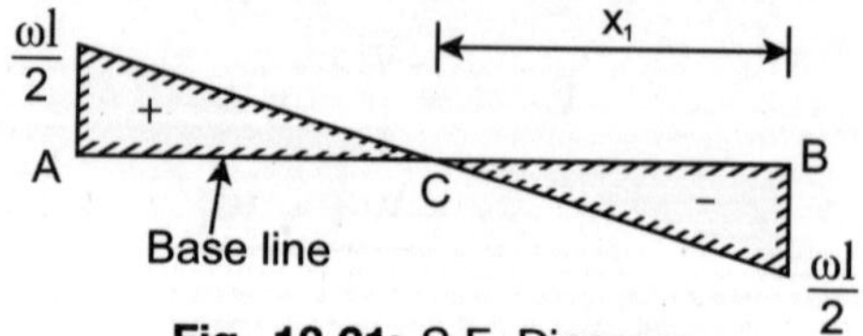

Fig. 13.21: S.F. Diagram

2. *S.F.D.: For right of the section* ↑ –ve ↓ +ve

$$F_x = \frac{-\omega l}{2} + \omega \cdot x$$

$$F_{Br} = 0 + 0 = 0$$

$$F_B = \frac{-\omega l}{2}$$

$$F_{Ar} = \frac{-\omega l}{2} + \omega l = +\frac{\omega l}{2}$$

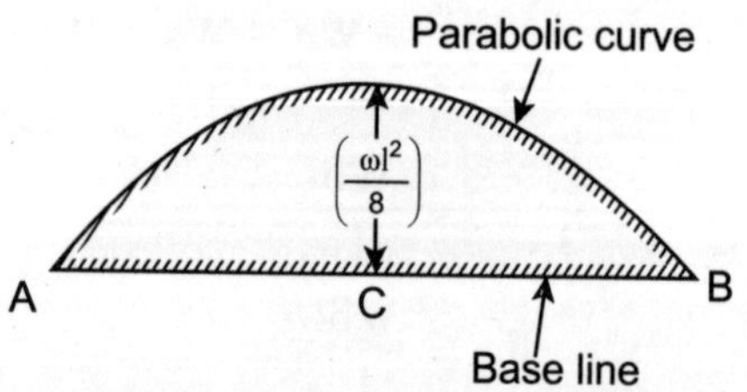

Fig. 13.22: B.M. Diagram

$$= \frac{+\omega l}{2}$$

$$F_A = \frac{\omega l}{2} - \frac{\omega l}{2} = 0$$

3. *B.M.D.: For right of the section* $\overset{\curvearrowleft}{+ve}$ $\overset{\curvearrowright}{-ve}$

$$M_x = R_B \cdot x - \omega x \cdot \frac{x}{2}$$

$$M_B = 0$$

$$M_A = \frac{\omega l}{2} \times l - \omega l \times \frac{l}{2} = 0$$

Now $F_C = \frac{-\omega l}{2} + \omega x_1 = 0 \Rightarrow x_1 = \frac{l}{2}$

$$M_C = R_B \cdot x_1 - \omega x_1 \cdot \frac{x_1}{2}$$

$$= \frac{\omega l}{2} \cdot \frac{l}{2} - \frac{\omega}{2} \cdot \left(\frac{l}{2}\right)^2 = \frac{\omega l^2}{4} - \frac{\omega l^2}{8} = \frac{\omega l^2}{8}$$

$$M_C = \frac{\omega l^2}{8} = \left(\frac{\omega l^2}{8}\right)$$

Note: 1. *When calculating B.M., it is assumed that a u.d.l. can be replaced by a concentrated load of equal value acting at the middle of its spread.*

2. *The point C of the symmetry is marked clearly, the B.M. is maximum when the S.F. is zero.*

Example 13.1

A simply supported beam 6 m long is subjected to two point loads of 4 kN and 6 kN each at a distance of 2 m and 4 m from left end. Draw S.F. and B.M. diagrams.

Solution:

1. *Reactions calculation*

$$R_A + R_B = 4 + 6 = 10 \quad \text{(13.4)}$$

$$\Sigma M_A = 0$$

$$\Rightarrow R_B \times 6 = 6 \times 4 + 4 \times 2$$

$$\Rightarrow R_B = \frac{24 + 8}{6} = 5.3 \text{ kN}$$

and $R_A = 4.7$ kN

2. *S.F.D.: For right of the section* $\underset{-ve}{\uparrow}$ $\underset{+ve}{\downarrow}$

$$F_{Br} = 0$$
$$F_B = -R_B = -5.3 \text{ kN}$$
$$F_{Dr} = -5.3 \text{ kN}$$
$$F_D = -5.3 + 6 = +0.7 \text{ kN}$$
$$F_{Cr} = +0.7 \text{ kN}$$
$$F_C = +0.7 + 4 = 4.7 \text{ kN}$$
$$F_{Ar} = 4.7 \text{ kN}$$
$$F_A = 4.7 - 4.7 = 0$$

Note: All the resultant S.F. are from the base line.

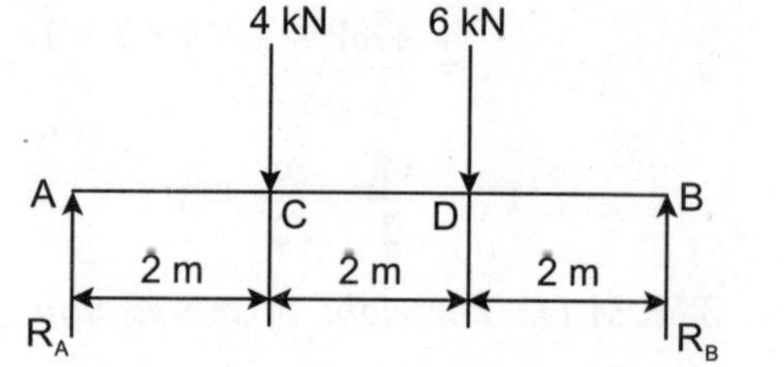

Fig. 13.23

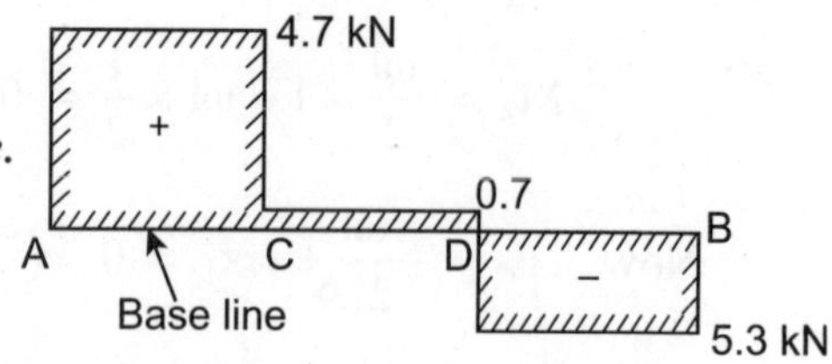

Fig. 13.24: S.F. Diagram

3. *B.M.D.: For right of the section* +ve −ve

$$M_{Br} = 0$$
$$M_B = 0$$
$$M_{Dr} = R_B \times 2 = 5.3 \times 2 = 10.6 \text{ kN.m}$$
$$M_D = 10.6 \text{ kN.m } (\because \text{ no additional moment is given at point D})$$
$$M_{Cr} = R_B \times 4 - 6 \times 2 = 5.3 \times 4 - 6 \times 2$$
$$= 9.2 \text{ kN.m}$$
$$M_C = 9.2 \text{ kN.m } (\because \text{ no additional moment is given at point C})$$
$$M_{Ar} = R_B \times 6 - 6 \times 4 - 4 \times 2$$
$$= 5.3 \times 6 - 6 \times 4 - 4 \times 2$$
$$= 5.333 \times 6 - 24 - 8$$
$$= 31.98 - 32$$
$$= 32 - 32 = 0$$

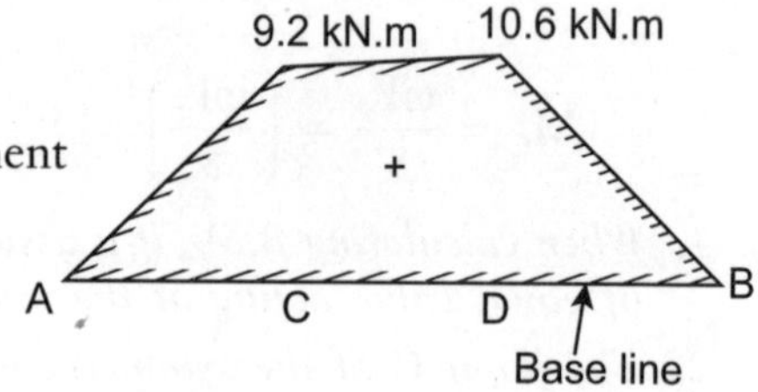

Fig. 13.25: B.M. Diagram

Example 13.2

A 6 m span simply supported beam is loaded as shown in Fig. 13.26. Draw S.F.D. and B.M.D.

Solution:

1. *Reactions calculation*

$$R_A + R_B = 4 \times 2 + 2 \times 2$$
$$R_A + R_B = 8 + 4 = 12 \quad \text{.......} \quad (13.5)$$
$$\Sigma M_A = 0$$
$$\Rightarrow R_B \times 6 = 2 \times 2 \times \left(4 + \frac{2}{2}\right) + 4 \times 2 \times \left(\frac{2}{2}\right)$$

$$= 2 \times 2 \times 5 + 4 \times 2 \times 1$$
$$= 20 + 8$$

or $\quad 6\ R_B = 28$

$$R_B = 4.66 \text{ t}$$
$$R_A = 7.34 \text{ t}$$

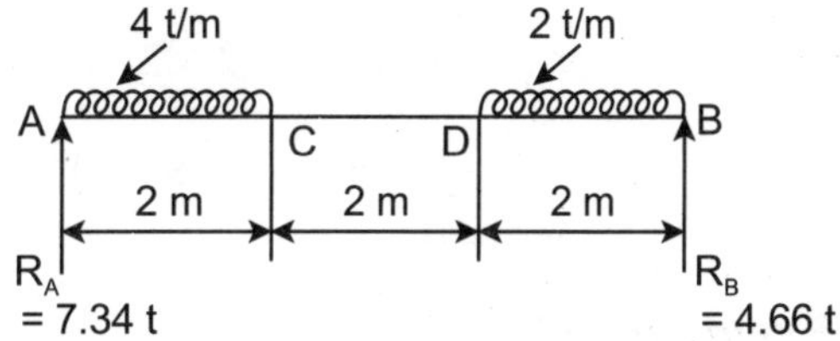

Fig. 13.26

2. *S.F.D.: For right of the section* $\underset{-\text{ve}}{\uparrow}\quad\underset{+\text{ve}}{\downarrow}$

$$F_{Br} = 0$$
$$F_B = -R_B = -4.66$$
$$F_{Dr} = -4.66 + 2 \times 2 = -0.66$$
$$F_D = -0.66 \text{ t}$$
$$F_{Cr} = -0.66 \text{ t}$$
$$F_C = -0.66 \text{ t}$$
$$F_{Ar} = -0.66 + 4 \times 2 = 7.34 \text{ t}$$
$$F_A = 7.34 - 7.34 \text{ t} = 0$$

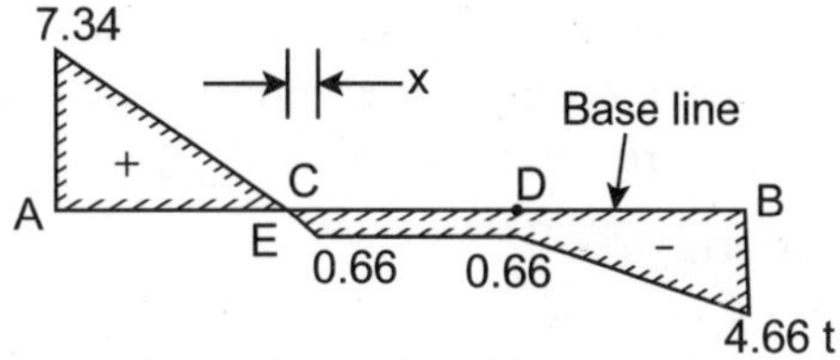

Fig. 13.27: S.F. Diagram (t)

3. *B.M.D.: At point E, S.F. = 0.*

So we will locate the point E also.

For this

$$F_E = 0$$
$$\Rightarrow \quad -R_B + 2 \times 2 + 4 \times x = 0$$
$$\Rightarrow \quad -4.66 + 4 + 4x = 0$$
$$\Rightarrow \quad x = 0.165 \text{ m}$$

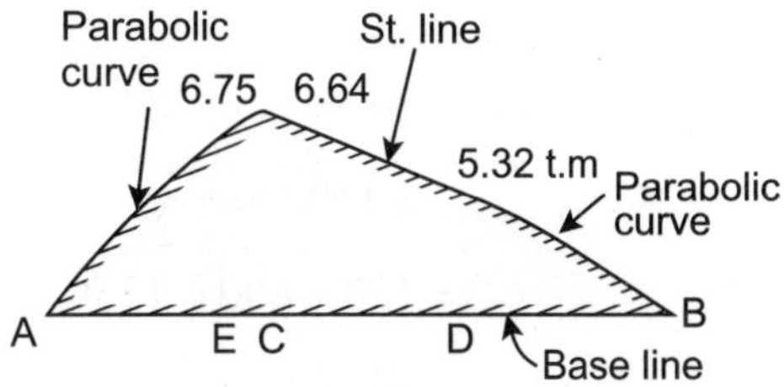

Fig. 13.28: B.M. Diagram (t.m)

Now, calculation of B.M.: For right of the section $\underset{+\text{ve}}{\circlearrowright}\ \underset{-\text{ve}}{\circlearrowleft}$

$$M_{Br} = 0$$
$$M_B = 0$$

$$M_{Dr} = +R_B \times 2 - 2 \times \frac{2}{2} \times 2$$
$$= 4.66 \times 2 - 2 \times 2 = 5.32 \text{ t.m.}$$
$$M_D = 5.32 \text{ t.m.}$$

$$M_{Cr} = R_B \times 4 - 2 \times \left(2 + \frac{2}{2}\right) \times 2$$
$$= 4.66 \times 4 - 2 \times 3 \times 2 = 18.64 - 12 = 6.64 \text{ t.m.}$$
$$M_C = 6.64 \text{ t.m.}$$

$$M_{Er} = R_B \times (4 + x) - 2 \times 2 \times \left(x + 2 + \frac{2}{2}\right)$$
$$= 4.66 \times (4 + 0.165) - 4\,(0.165 + 3) = 6.7489$$
$$M_E = 6.7489 = 6.75 \text{ t.m.}$$

$$M_{Ar} = 4.66 \times 6 - 2 \times 2 \times \left(4 + \frac{2}{2}\right) - 4 \times 2 \times \left(\frac{2}{2}\right)$$

$$= 27.96 - 20 - 8 = 0$$

$$M_A = 0$$

Example 13.3

A beam 6 m long is supported simply at the ends and carries a U.D.L. of 150 N/m (including its own weight) and three point loads of 100 N, 200 N and 300 N acting respectively at the left quarter point, centre point and right quarter point. Draw S.F. and B.M. diagrams and determine the maximum B.M.

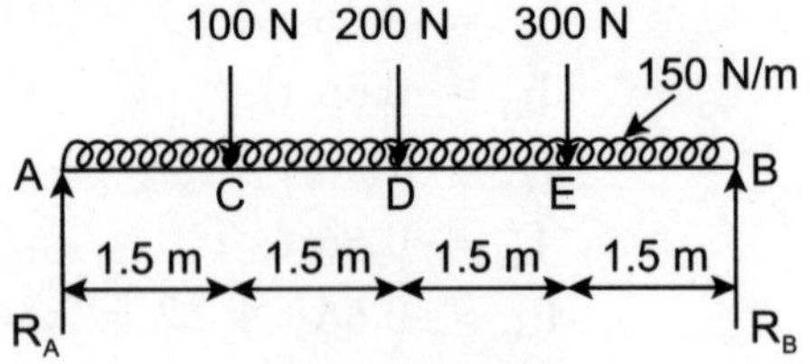

Fig. 13.29

Solution:

1. *Reactions*

$$R_A + R_B = 100 + 200 + 300 + 150 \times 6$$

$$\text{or } R_A + R_B = 1500 \text{ N} \quad \ldots\ldots\ldots\ldots\ldots \quad (13.6)$$

$$\Sigma M_A = 0$$

$$R_B \times 6 = 100 \times 1.5 + 200 \times 3 + 300 \times 4.5 + 150 \times 6 \times \frac{6}{2}$$

$$= 150 + 600 + 1350 + 2700$$

$$R_B = \frac{4800}{6} = 800 \text{ N} \ldots\ldots \quad (13.7)$$

$$R_A = 1500 - 800 = 700 \text{ N}$$

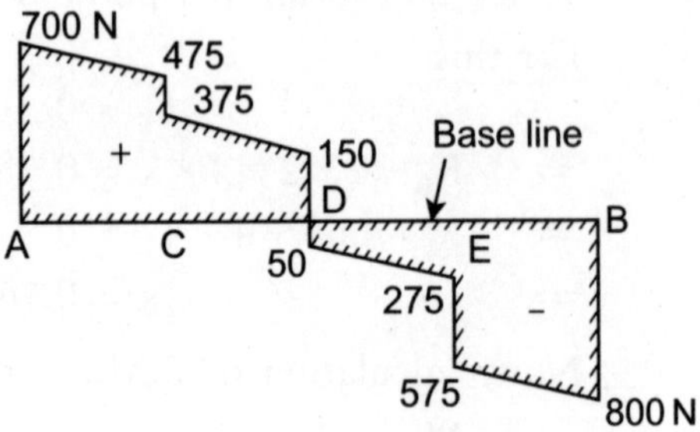

Fig. 13.30: S.F. Diagram (N)

2. *S.F.D.: For right of the section* $\underset{-ve}{\uparrow}$ $\underset{+ve}{\downarrow}$

$$F_{Br} = 0$$

$$F_B = -R_B = -800 \text{ N}$$

$$F_{Er} = -800 + 150 \times 1.5 = -575 \text{ N}$$

$$F_E = -575 + 300 = -275 \text{ N}$$

$$F_{Dr} = -275 + 150 \times 1.5 = -50 \text{ N}$$

$$F_D = -50 + 200 = +150 \text{ N}$$

$$F_{Cr} = 150 + 150 \times 1.5 = 375 \text{ N}$$

$$F_C = 375 + 100 = 475 \text{ N}$$

$$F_{Ar} = 475 + 150 \times 1.5 = 700 \text{ N}$$

$$F_A = 700 - 700 = 0$$

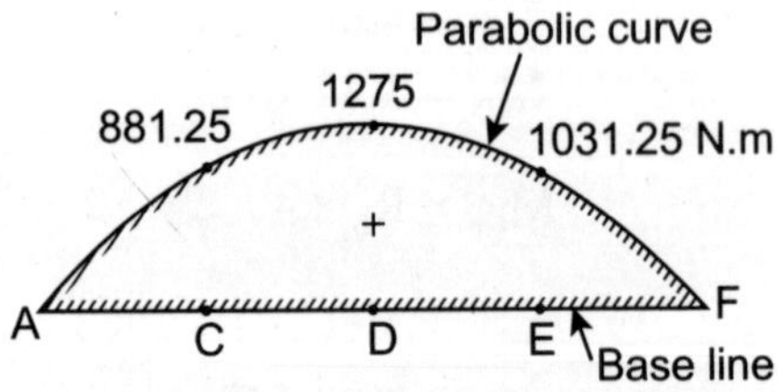

Fig. 13.31: B.M. Diagram (N.m)

3. *B.M.D.: For right of the section* $\underset{+ve}{\curvearrowleft}$ $\underset{-ve}{\curvearrowright}$

$$M_{Br} = 0$$

$$M_B = 0$$

$$M_{Er} = +R_B \times 1.5 - 150 \times 1.5 \times \frac{1.5}{2} = 800 \times 1.5 - 75 \times 1.5^2$$

$$= 1031.25 \text{ N.m.}$$

$$M_E = 1031.25 \text{ N.m.}$$

$$M_{Dr} = 800 \times 3 - 300 \times 1.5 - 150 \times 3 \times \frac{3}{2}$$

$$= 2400 - 450 - 675 = 1275 \text{ N.m.}$$

$$M_D = 1275 \text{ N.m.}$$

$$M_{Cr} = 800 \times 4.5 - 300 \times 3 - 200 \times 1.5 - 150 \times 4.5 \times \frac{4.5}{2}$$

$$= 3600 - 900 - 300 - 1518.75$$

$$= 3600 - 2718.75 = 881.25 \text{ N.m.}$$

$$M_C = 881.25 \text{ N.m.}$$

$$M_{Ar} = 800 \times 6 - 300 \times 4.5 - 200 \times 3 - 100 \times 1.5 - 150 \times 6 \times \frac{6}{2}$$

$$= 4800 - 1350 - 600 - 150 - 2700 = 0$$

$$M_A = 0$$

Max. B.M. = M_D = **1275 N.m** **Ans.**

13.15 A Cantilever Beam with a Point Load at the Free End

1. *Reactions*

   For right section, no need for reactions.

2. *S.F.D.: For right of the section* $\underset{-\text{ve}}{\uparrow}$ $\underset{+\text{ve}}{\downarrow}$

$$F_{Br} = 0$$
$$F_B = +W$$
$$F_x = +W$$
$$F_{Cr} = +W$$
$$F_C = +W$$
$$F_{Ar} = +W$$
$$F_A = W$$

3. *B.M.D.: For right section* $\underset{+\text{ve}}{\circlearrowright}$ $\underset{-\text{ve}}{\circlearrowleft}$

$$M_{Br} = 0$$
$$M_B = 0$$
$$M_x = -W \cdot x$$
$$M_{Ar} = -W \cdot l$$
$$M_A = -Wl$$

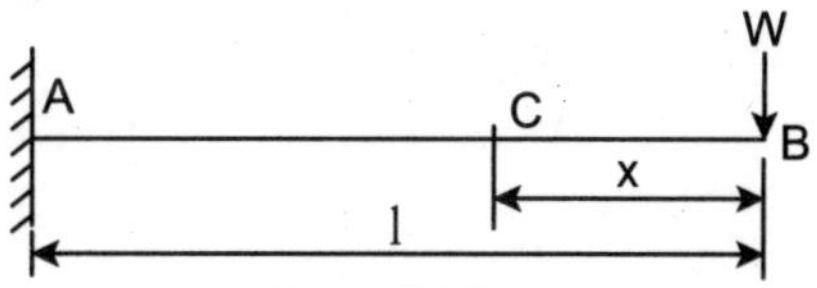

Fig. 13.32

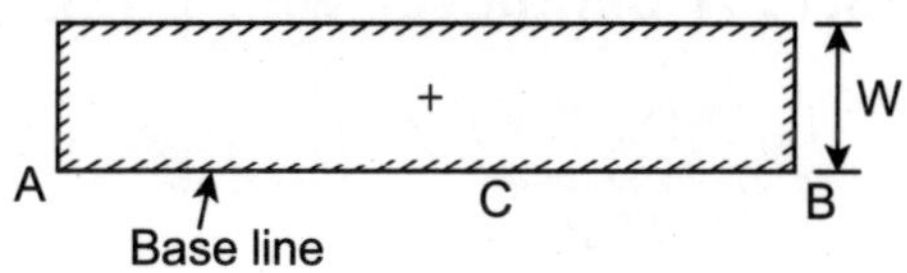

Fig. 13.33: S.F. Diagram

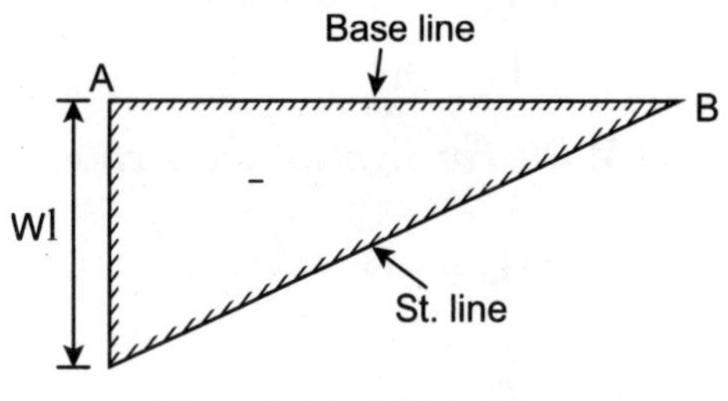

Fig. 13.34: B.M. Diagram

Example 13.4

A cantilever beam of length 1.5 m carries the point loads as shown in Fig. 13.35. Draw S.F. and B.M. diagrams.

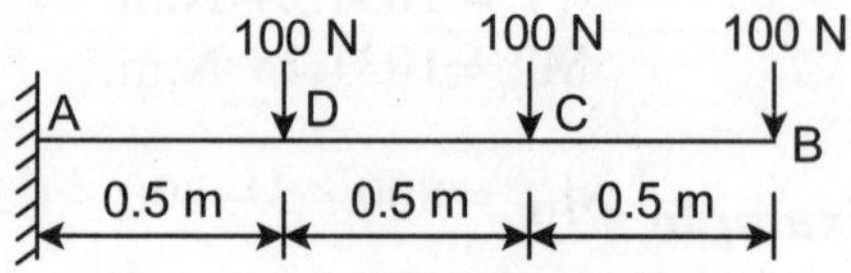

Fig. 13.35

Solution:

1. *S.F.D.: For right of the section* $\underset{-ve}{\uparrow}$ $\underset{+ve}{\downarrow}$

$$F_{Br} = 0$$
$$F_B = 100 \text{ N}$$
$$F_{Cr} = 100 \text{ N}$$
$$F_C = 100 + 100 = 200 \text{ N}$$
$$F_{Dr} = 200 \text{ N}$$
$$F_D = 200 + 100 = 300 \text{ N}$$
$$F_{Ar} = 300 \text{ N}$$
$$F_A = 0$$

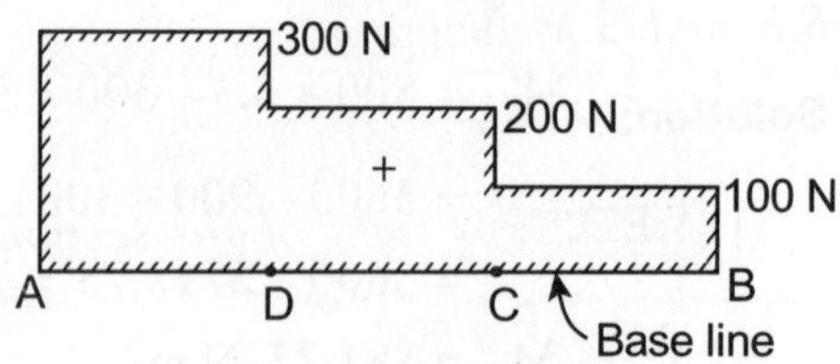

Fig. 13.36: S.F. Diagram (N)

2. *B.M.D.: For right of the section* $\underset{+ve}{\curvearrowright}$ $\underset{-ve}{\curvearrowleft}$

$$M_{Br} = 0$$
$$M_B = 0$$
$$M_{Cr} = 100 \times 0.5 = 50 \text{ N.m}$$
$$F_C = 50 \text{ N.m}$$
$$F_{Dr} = 100 \times 1 + 100 \times 0.5 = 150 \text{ N.m}$$
$$F_D = 150 \text{ N.m}$$
$$F_{Ar} = 100 \times 1.5 + 100 \times 1 + 100 \times 0.5$$
$$= 150 \times 100 \times 50 = 300 \text{ N.m}$$
$$F_A = 0$$

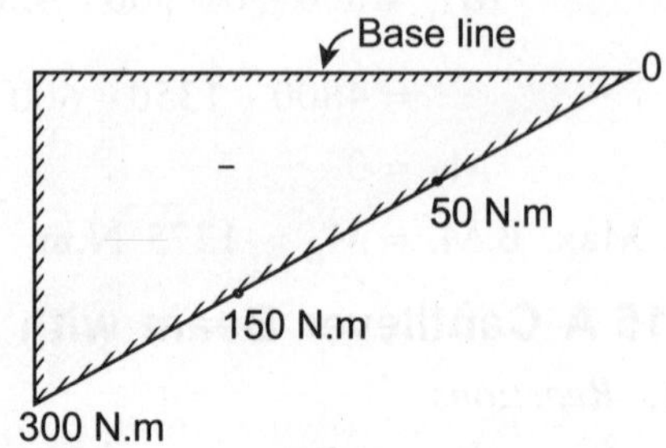

Fig. 13.37: B.M. Diagram (N.m)

13.16 A Cantilever with U.D.L. on Whole Span

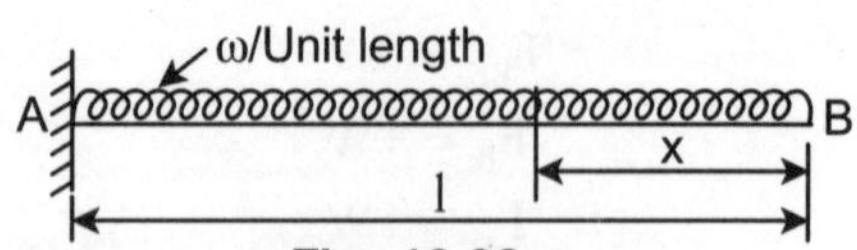

Fig. 13.38

1. *S.F.D.: For right of the section* $\underset{-ve}{\uparrow}$ $\underset{+ve}{\downarrow}$

$$F_{Br} = 0$$
$$F_B = 0$$
$$F_x = \omega x \rightarrow \text{equation of St. line}$$
$$F_A = \omega \cdot l$$

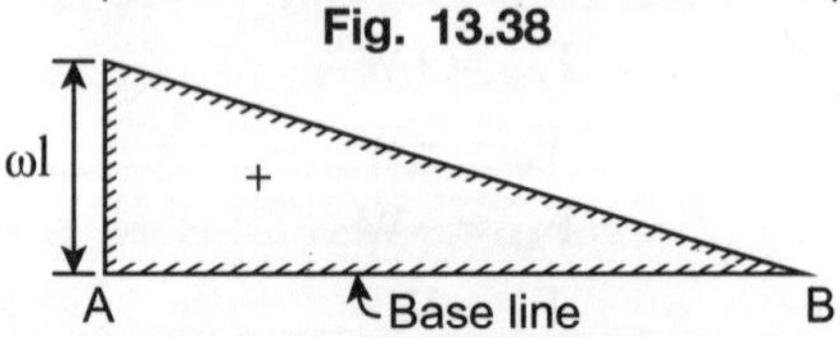

Fig. 13.39: S.F. Diagram

2. *B.M.D.: For right of the section* $\underset{+ve}{\curvearrowright}$ $\underset{-ve}{\curvearrowleft}$

$$M_x = -\omega x \times \frac{x}{2}$$
$$= -\frac{\omega x^2}{2} \rightarrow \text{equation of parabolic curve}$$

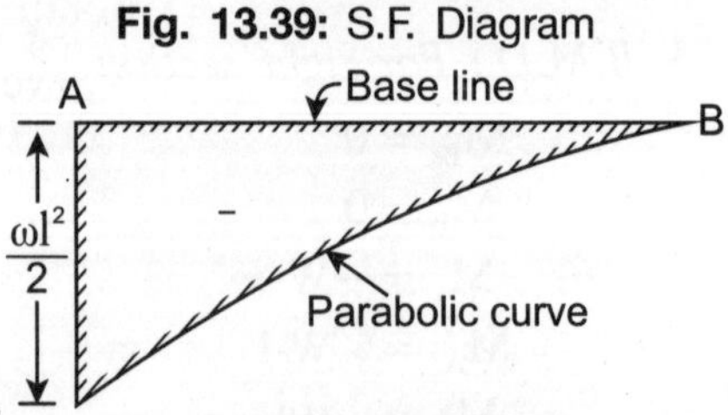

Fig. 13.40: B.M. Diagram

$$M_{Br} = 0$$
$$M_B = 0$$
$$M_A = -\frac{\omega \cdot l^2}{2}$$

Example 13.5

A cantilever 1.5 m long is loaded with a U.D.L. of 1 kN/m over a length of 1.25 m from the free end. It also carries a point load of 2 kN at a distance of 0.25 m from the free end. Draw S.F. and B.M diagrams.

Solution:

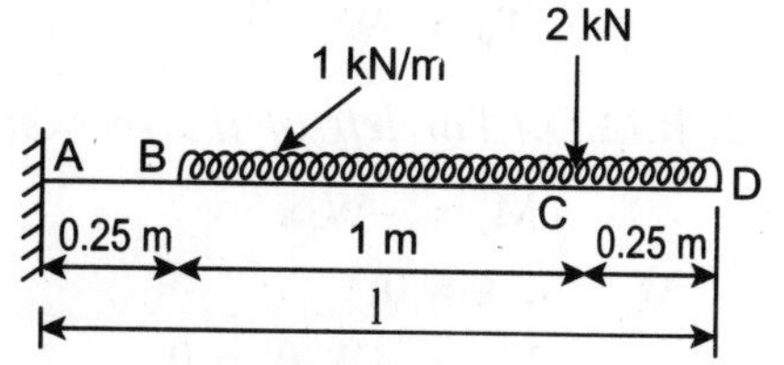

Fig. 13.41

1. *S.F.D.: For right of the section* $\underset{-ve}{\uparrow}$ $\underset{+ve}{\downarrow}$

$$F_{Dr} = 0$$
$$F_D = 0$$
$$F_{Cr} = +\omega \cdot x = 1 \times 0.25 = 0.25 \text{ kN}$$
$$F_C = 0.25 + 2 = 2.25 \text{ kN}$$
$$F_{Br} = 2.25 + 1 \times 1 = 3.25 \text{ kN}$$
$$F_B = 3.25 + 0 = 3.25 \text{ kN}$$
$$F_{Ar} = 3.25 \text{ kN}$$
$$F_A = 0$$

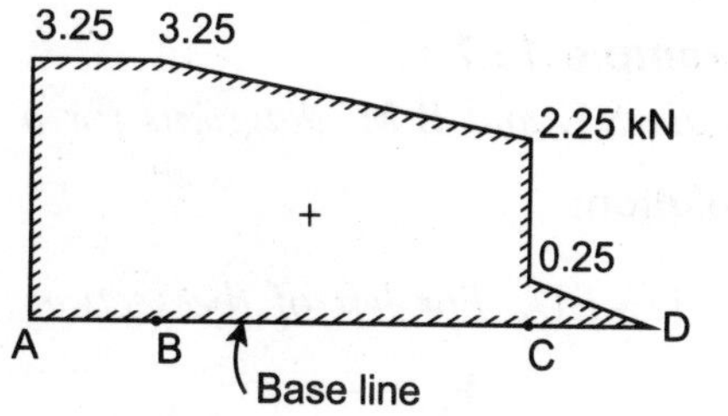

Fig. 13.42: S.F. Diagram

2. *B.M.D.: For right of the section* +ve −ve

$$M_{Dr} = 0$$
$$M_D = 0$$
$$M_{Cr} = +\omega x \frac{x}{2} = -1 \times 0.25 \times \frac{0.25}{2}$$
$$= -0.03125 \text{ kN.m.}$$
$$M_C = -0.03125 \text{ kN.m.}$$
$$M_{Br} = -1 \times 1.25 \times \frac{1.25}{2} - 2 \times 1$$
$$= -2.78125 \text{ kN.m.}$$
$$M_{Ar} = -1 \times 1.25 \times \left(0.25 + \frac{0.25}{2}\right) - 2 \times 1.25$$
$$= -3.59375 \text{ kN.m.}$$
$$M_A = 0$$

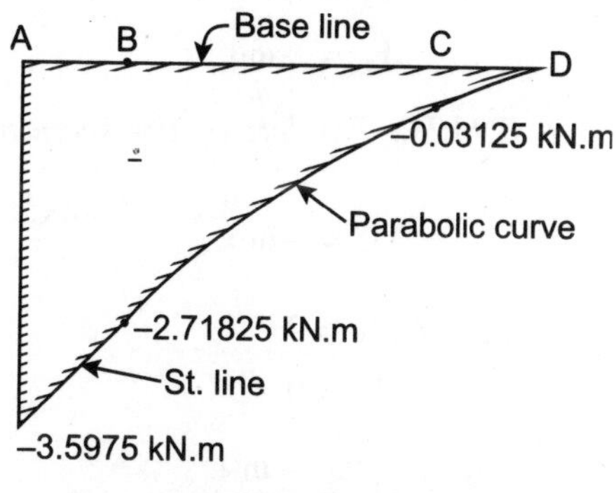

Fig. 13.43: B.M. Diagram

Example 13.6

Draw S.F. and B.M. diagrams for a cantilever with a concentrated load at the free end.

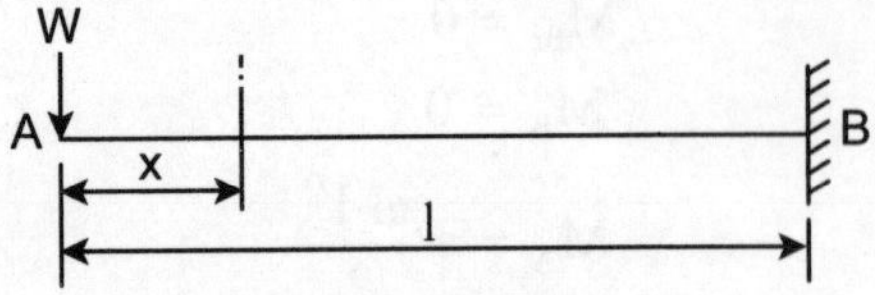

Fig. 13.44

Solution:

1. *S.F.D.: For left of the section* $\underset{-\text{ve}}{\uparrow}$ $\underset{+\text{ve}}{\downarrow}$

$$F_A = -W$$
$$F_x = -W$$
$$F_B = -W$$

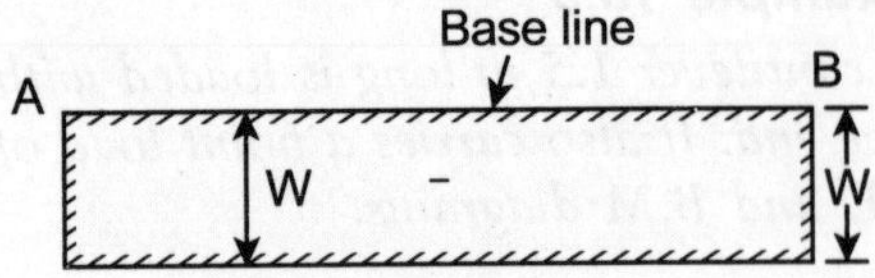

Fig. 13.45: S.F. Diagram

2. *B.M.D.: For left of the section* +ve –ve

$$M_x = -W \cdot x$$

At A, x = 0

$$M_A = -W \cdot 0 = 0$$
$$M_B = -W \cdot l$$

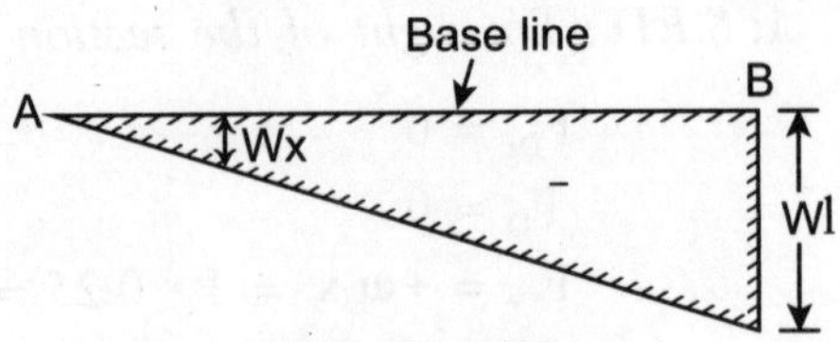

Fig. 13.46: B.M. Diagram

Example 13.7

Draw S.F. and B.M. diagrams for a cantilever beam with a U.D.L. at its entire span.

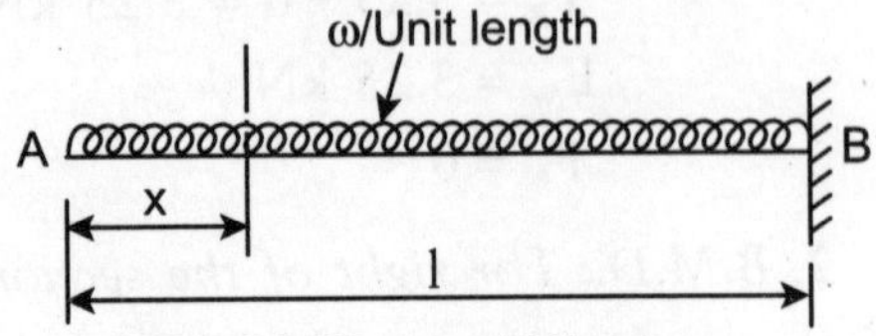

Fig. 13.47: Load Diagram

Solution:

1. *S.F.D.: For left of the section* $\underset{-\text{ve}}{\uparrow}$ $\underset{+\text{ve}}{\downarrow}$

$$F_x = -\omega \cdot x$$

At A, x = 0

$$\therefore \quad F_A = 0$$
$$F_B = -\omega \cdot l$$

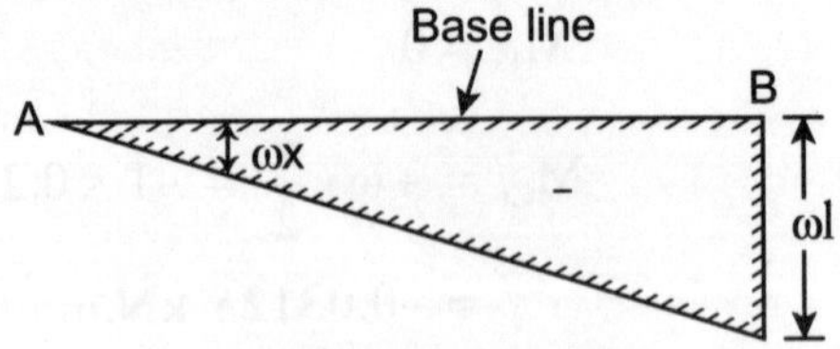

Fig. 13.48: S.F. Diagram

2. *B.M.D.: For left of the section* +ve –ve

$$M_x = -\omega \cdot x \frac{x}{2} = \frac{-\omega x^2}{2}$$

At A, x = 0

$$M_A = 0$$

$$M_B = \frac{-\omega \cdot l^2}{2}$$

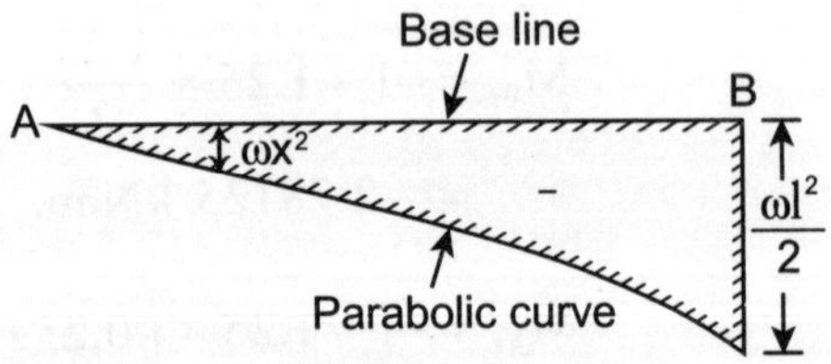

Fig. 13.49: B.M. Diagram

13.17 Simply Supported Over Hanging Beams

If the end portion of a beam is extended beyond the support, such beam is known as over hanging beam.

Over hanging beam = Simply supported beam + Cantilever beam(s)

13.18 Point of Contraflexure

It is the point where B.M. is zero after changing its sign from +ve to –ve or *vice-versa.* We know that B.M. in a cantilever is negative (–ve) whereas in case of simply supported beam, the B.M. is positive (+ve). Hence, at a point, the B.M. is zero after changing its sign from positive (+ve) to negative (–ve) or *vice-versa.* Such a point where B.M. changes its sign is known as point of contraflexure.

There may be more than one point of contraflexure and it is also possible that no point of contraflexure exist in the B.M. diagram of over hanging beams.

Example 13.8

Draw S.F. and B.M. diagrams for the beam shown in Fig. 13.50.

Solution:

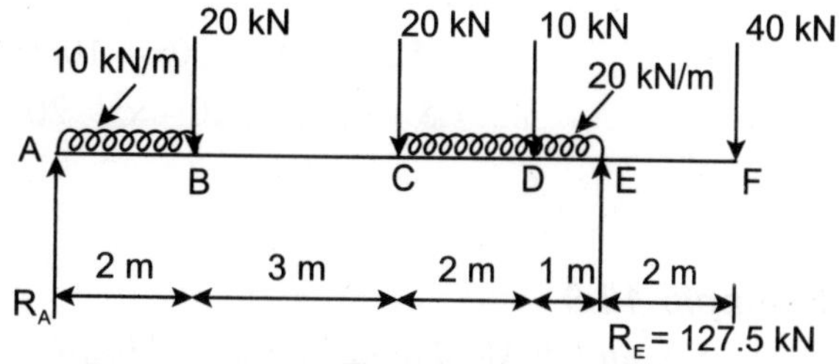

Fig. 13.50

1. *Reactions*

$$R_A + R_E = 20 + 20 + 10 + 40 + 10 \times 2 + 20 \times 3 = 170 \text{ kN}$$

$$\Sigma M_A = 0$$

$$R_E \times 8 = 40 \times 10 + 10 \times 7 + 20 \times 5 + 20 \times 2 + 20 \times 3 \times \left(5 + \frac{3}{2}\right) + 10 \times 2 \times \frac{2}{2}$$

$$= 1020 \text{ kN}$$

$$R_E = 127.5 \text{ kN}$$

$$R_A = 42.5 \text{ kN}$$

2. *S.F.D.* $\uparrow$ –ve $\downarrow$ +ve

$$F_F = +40 \text{ kN}$$

$$F_E = 40 - 127.5 = -87.5 \text{ kN}$$

$$F_{Dr} = -87.5 + 20 \times 1 = -67.5 \text{ kN}$$

$$F_D = -67.5 + 10 = -57.5 \text{ kN}$$

$$F_{Cr} = -57.5 + 40 = -17.5 \text{ kN}$$

$$F_C = -17.5 + 20 = 2.5 \text{ kN}$$

$$F_B = 2.5 + 20 = 22.5 \text{ kN}$$

$$F_{Ar} = 22.5 + 20 = 42.5 \text{ kN}$$

$$F_A = 0$$

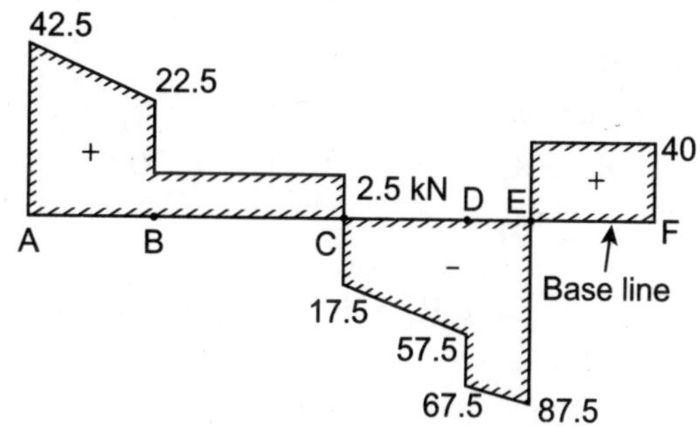

Fig. 13.51: S.F. Diagram (kN)

3. *B.M.D.* ↻ +ve ↺ –ve

$$M_F = 0$$

$$M_A = 0$$

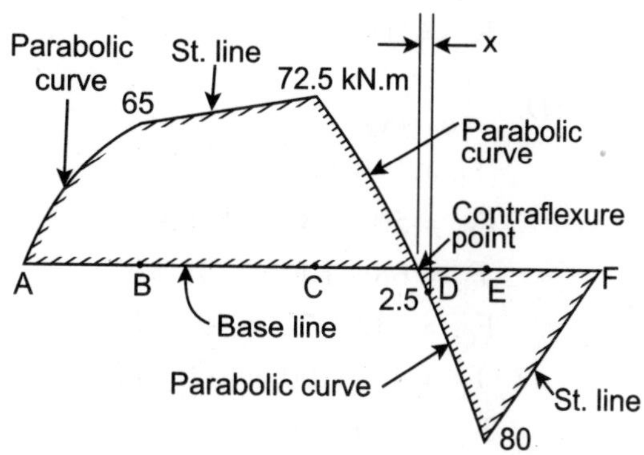

Fig. 13.52: B.M. Diagram (kN.m)

$$M_E = -40 \times 2 = -80 \text{ kN.m}$$

$$M_D = -40 \times 3 + 127.5 \times 1 - 20 \times 1 \times \frac{1}{2} = -2.5 \text{ kN.m}$$

$$M_C = -40 \times 5 - 10 \times 2 + 127.5 \times 3 - 20 \times 3 \times \frac{3}{2} = 72.5 \text{ kN.m}$$

$$M_B = -40 \times 8 - 10 \times 5 + 127.5 \times 6 - 20 \times 3 \times \left(3 + \frac{3}{2}\right) - 20 \times 3 = 65 \text{ kN.m}$$

Point of Contraflexure: Let point of contraflexure is at a distance x from point D

$$M_x = 0$$

$$-40 \times (3 + x) - 10 \times x - 20 \times \frac{(1 + x)^2}{2} + 127.5 \times (1 + x) = 0$$

$$\Rightarrow \quad -120 - 40x - 10x - 10(1 + x^2 + 2x) + 127.5 + 127.5x = 0$$

$$7.5 + 77.5x - 10 - x^2 - 20 = 0 \Rightarrow -22.5 + 77.5x - x^2 = 0$$

$$x^2 - 77.5x + 22.5 = 0$$

$$x = 0.29 \text{ m} \qquad \textbf{Ans.}$$

Example 13.9

Draw S.F. and B.M. diagrams for the beam loaded as shown in Fig. 13.53.

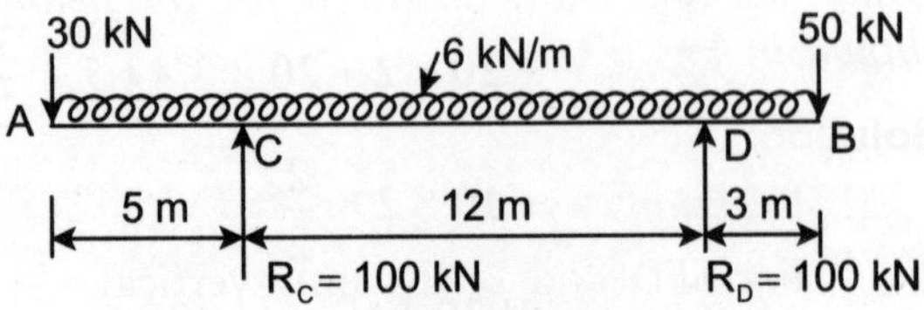

Fig. 13.53

Solution:

1. *Reactions*

$$R_C + R_D = 30 + 50 + 120 = 200$$

$$\Sigma M_C = 0$$

$$= R_D \times 12 + 30 \times 5 + 6 \times 5 \times \frac{5}{2}$$

$$= 50 \times 15 + 6 \times 15 \times \frac{15}{2}$$

$$R_D = 100$$

$$R_C = 100$$

2. *S.F.D.* $\uparrow$ −ve $\downarrow$ +ve

$$F_B = +50 \text{ t}$$

$$F_{Dr} = 50 + 18 = 68 \text{ kN}$$

$$F_D = 68 - 100 = -32 \text{ kN}$$

$$F_{Cr} = -32 + 72 = 40 \text{ kN}$$

$$F_C = 40 - 100 = -60 \text{ kN}$$

$$F_{Ar} = -60 + 30 = -30 \text{ kN}$$

$$F_A = -30 + 30 = 0$$

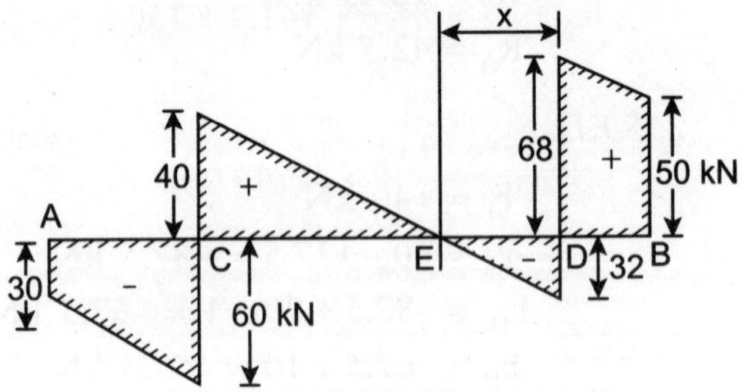

Fig. 13.54: B.M. Diagram (kN)

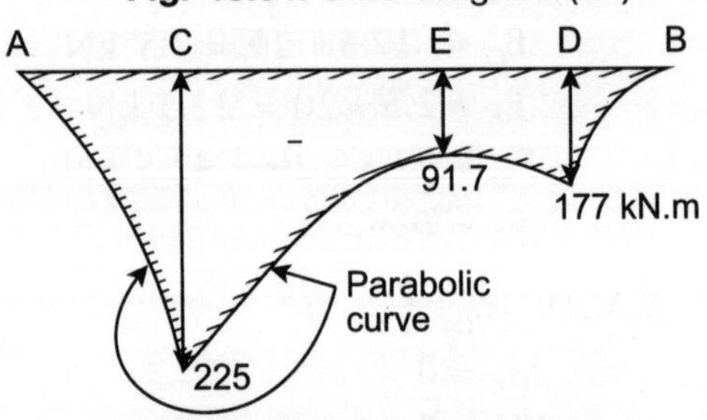

Fig. 13.55: B.M. Diagram (kN.m)

3. *For B.M.D.* $\overset{\curvearrowleft}{+ve}$ $\overset{\curvearrowright}{-ve}$

$$M_A = M_B = 0$$

$$M_D = -50 \times 3 - 6 \times \frac{3^2}{2} = -177 \text{ kN.m}$$

$$M_C = -50 \times 15 - 6 \times \frac{15^2}{2} + 100 \times 12$$

$$= -225 \text{ kN.m}$$

$$F_x = F_E = 0$$

$$= 50 + 6(3 + x) - 100 = 0$$

$$x = 5.33 \text{ m}$$

$$\therefore \quad M_x = M_E = -50 \times 8.33 - 6 \times \frac{8.33^2}{2} + 100 \times 5.33$$

$$= -91.7 \text{ kN.m.}$$

Example 13.10

Draw S.F. and B.M. diagrams for the beam shown in Fig. 13.56.

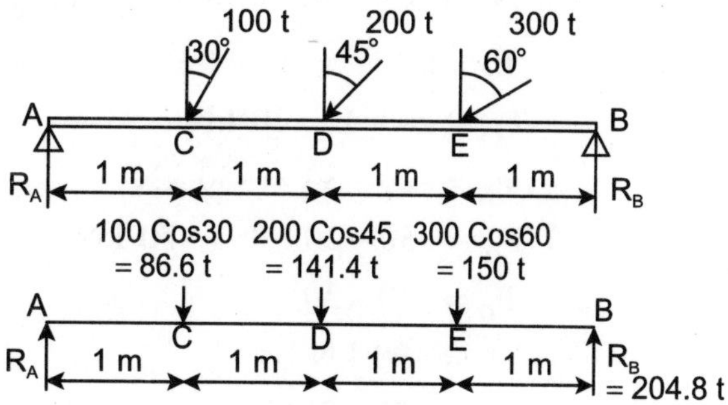

Fig. 13.56

Solution:

1. *Reactions*

For SFD and BMD, only vertical forces are considered.

$$\therefore R_A + R_B = 86.6 + 141.4 + 150$$

$$= 378 \text{ t}$$

$$\Sigma M_A = 0$$

$$R_B \times 4 = 150 \times 3 + 141.4 \times 2 + 86.6 \times 1$$

$$R_B = 204.8 \text{ t}$$

2. *S.F.D.* $\underset{-ve}{\uparrow}$ $\underset{+ve}{\downarrow}$

$$F_B = -204.8 \text{ t}$$

$$F_E = -204.8 + 150$$

$$= -54.8 \text{ t}$$

$$F_D = -54.8 + 141.4$$

$$= +86.6 \text{ t}$$

$$F_C = 86.6 + 86.6$$

$$= 173.2 \text{ t}$$

$$F_A = 0$$

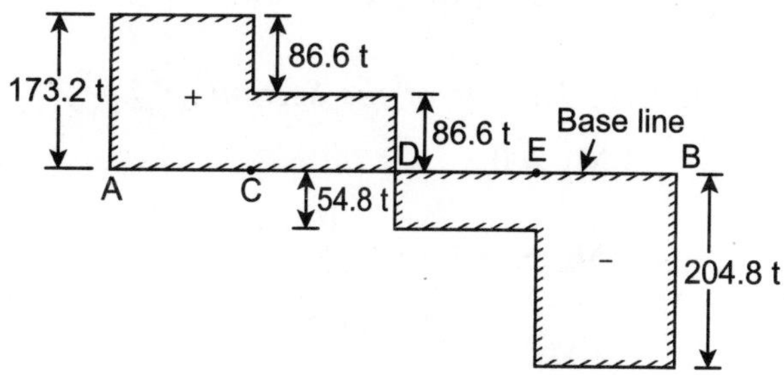

Fig. 13.57: S.F. Diagram (t)

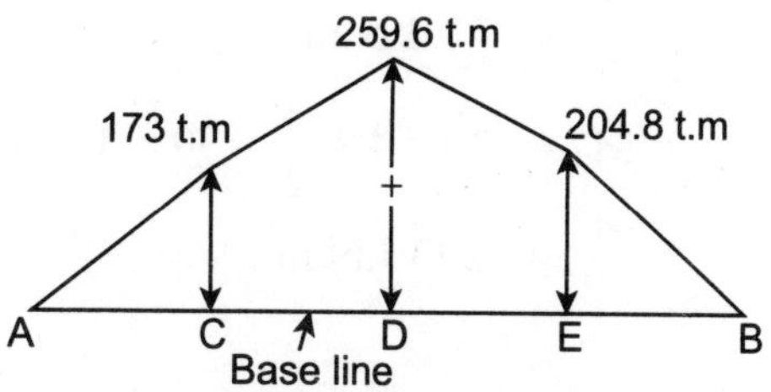

Fig. 13.58: B.M. Diagram (t.m)

3. *For B.M.D.* ↺ +ve ↻ −ve

$M_A = 0$

$M_B = 0$

$M_E = 204.8 \times 1 = 204.8$ t.m

$M_D = 204.8 \times 2 - 150 = 259.6$ t.m

$M_C = 204.8 \times 3 - 150 \times 2 - 141.4 \times 1$

$= 173$ t.m

Example 13.11

Draw S.F. and B.M. diagrams for a cantilever beam loaded as shown in Fig. 13.59.

Solution:

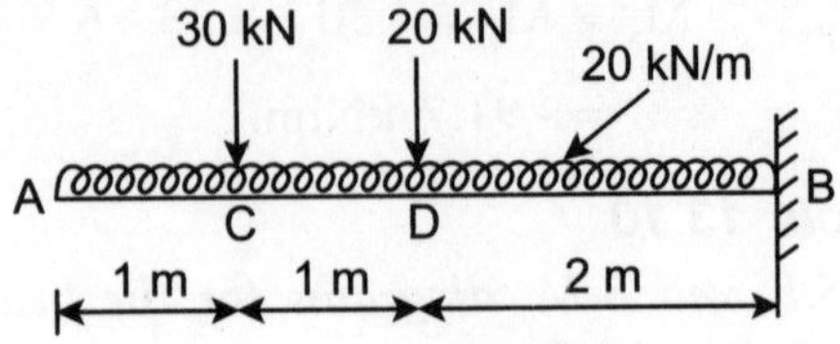

Fig. 13.59

1. *S.F.D.: For left of the section* ↓ −ve ↑ +ve

$F_A = 0$

$F_{Cl} = 20 \times 1 = 20$ kN

$F_C = -20 - 30 = -50$ kN

$F_{Dl} = -50 - 20 \times 1 = -70$ kN

$F_D = -70 - 20$

$= -90$ kN

$F_B = -90 - 20 \times 2$

$= -130$ kN

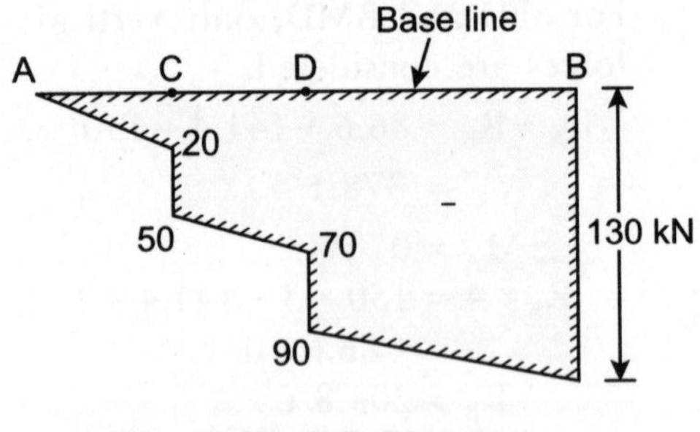

Fig. 13.60: S.F. Diagram

2. *B.M.D.: For left of the Section* ↻ +ve ↺ −ve

$M_A = 0$

$M_C = -20 \times 1 \times \frac{1}{2}$

$= -10$ kN.m

$M_D = -20 \times 2 \times \frac{2}{2} - 30 \times 1$

$= -70$ kN.m

$M_B = -20 \times 4 \times \frac{4}{2} - 30 \times 3 - 20 \times 2$

$= -290$ kN.m

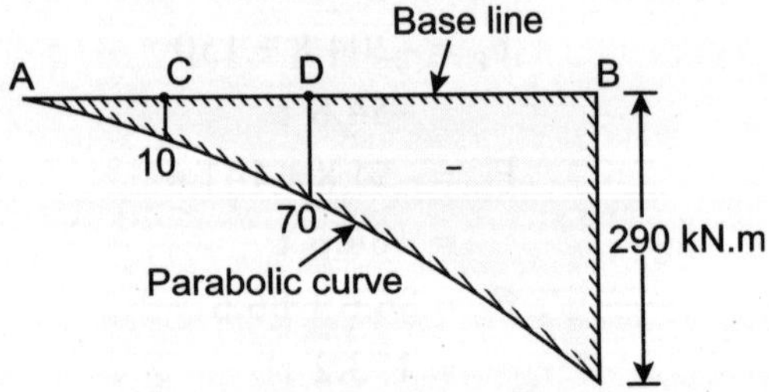

Fig. 13.61: B.M. Diagram

Example 13.12

Draw S.F. and B.M. diagrams for the beam loaded as shown in Fig. 13.62.

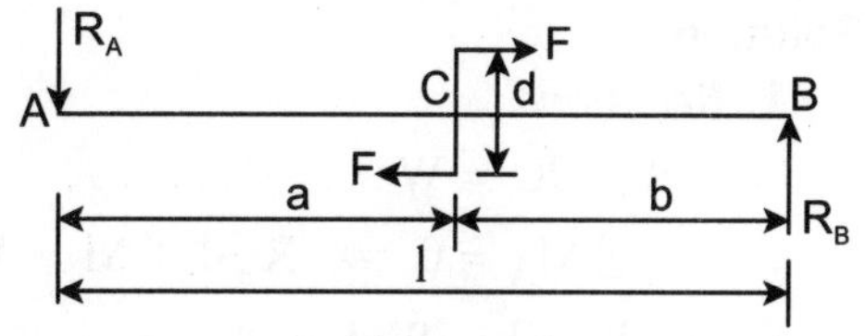

Fig. 13.62

Solution:

1. *Reactions*

$$R_B - R_A = 0 \quad \ldots\ldots\ldots\ldots\ldots \quad (13.8)$$

$$\Sigma M_A = 0$$

$$\Rightarrow \; R_B \times l = M = F{\cdot}d$$

$$\therefore \quad R_B = R_A = \frac{F{\cdot}d}{l} \quad \ldots\ldots\ldots \quad (13.9)$$

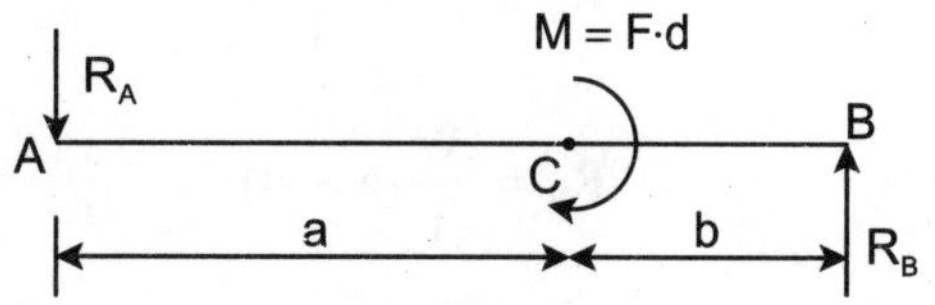

Fig. 13.63

2. *S.F.D.: For right of the section* $\underset{-ve}{\uparrow} \;\; \underset{+ve}{\downarrow}$

$$F_{Br} = 0$$

$$F_B = -R_B = \frac{-F{\cdot}d}{l}$$

$$F_C = \frac{-F{\cdot}d}{l}$$

$$F_{Ar} = \frac{-F{\cdot}d}{l}$$

$$F_A = \frac{-F{\cdot}d}{l} + \frac{F{\cdot}d}{l} = 0$$

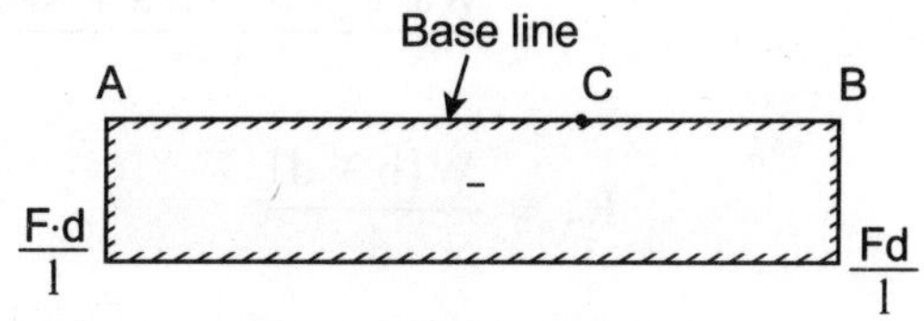

Fig. 13.64: S.F. Diagram

3. *B.M.D.: For right of the section* $\underset{+ve}{\circlearrowleft} \;\; \underset{-ve}{\circlearrowright}$

$$M_{Br} = 0$$

$$M_B = 0$$

$$M_{Cr} = +R_B{\cdot}b = \frac{F{\cdot}d}{l}{\cdot}b$$

$$M_C = \frac{F{\cdot}db}{l} - F{\cdot}d = F{\cdot}d\frac{\left[b-(a+b)\right]}{l}$$

$$= -\frac{F{\cdot}d{\cdot}a}{l}$$

$$M_{Ar} = R_B{\cdot}l - M = \frac{F{\cdot}d}{l}{\cdot}l - F{\cdot}d = 0$$

$$M_A = 0$$

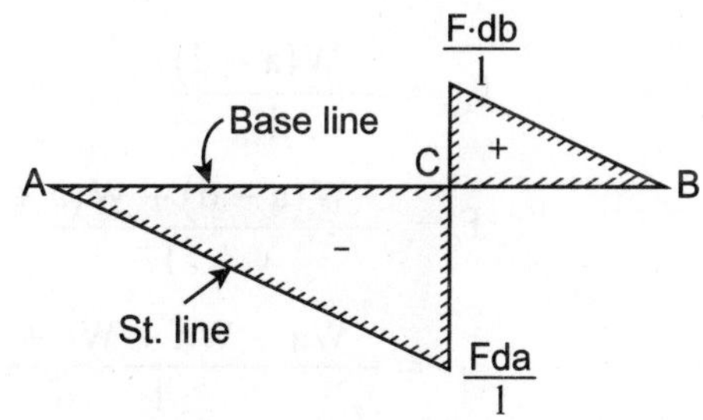

Fig. 13.65: B.M. Diagram

Example 13.13

Draw S.F. and B.M. diagrams for the beam loaded as shown in the Fig. 13.66.

Solution:

1. *Reactions*

$$R_A + R_b = W \dots\dots\dots\dots\dots \quad (13.10)$$

$$\Sigma M_A = 0 \Rightarrow R_B \cdot l + M = W \times a$$

$$\Rightarrow R_B \times l = W{\cdot}d = W \times a$$

$$R_B = \left(\frac{Wa - Wd}{l}\right)$$

$$R_B = \frac{W}{l}(a - d)$$

$$R_A = W - \frac{W}{l}(a - d) = \frac{W(a + b) - W(a - d)}{l}$$

$$= \frac{Wa + Wb - Wa + Wd}{l}$$

$$R_A = \frac{W(b + d)}{l}$$

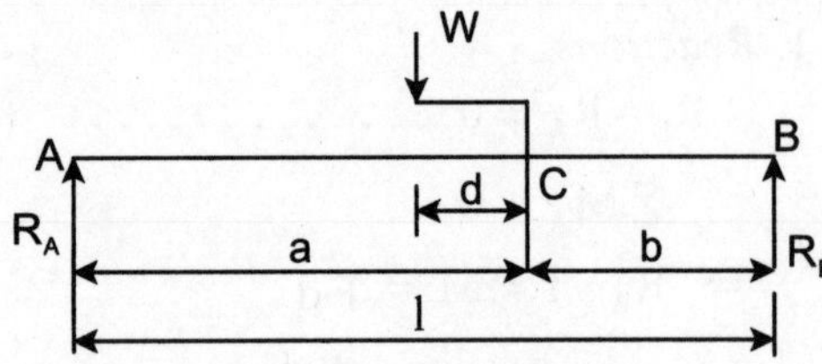

Fig. 13.66

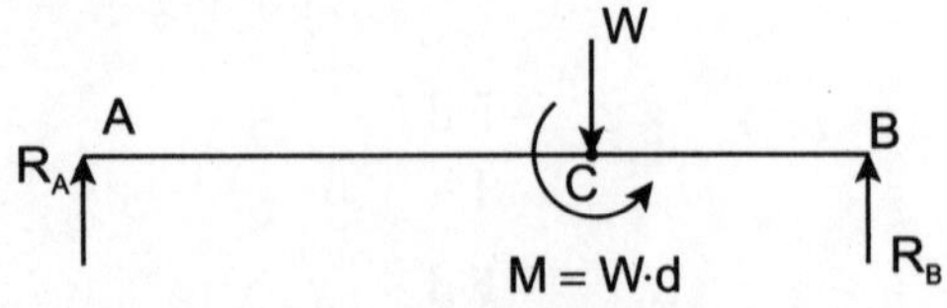

Fig. 13.67

2. *S.F.D.: For right of the section* $\underset{-ve}{\uparrow} \quad \underset{+ve}{\downarrow}$

$$F_{Br} = 0$$

$$F_B = -R_B = \frac{-W(a - d)}{l}$$

$$F_{Cr} = \frac{-W(a - d)}{l}$$

$$F_C = \frac{-W(a - d) + W(a + b)}{l}$$

$$= \frac{-Wa + Wd + Wa + Wb}{l}$$

$$= \frac{W(b + d)}{l}$$

$$F_{Ar} = \frac{W(b + d)}{l}$$

$$F_A = \frac{W(b + d)}{l} - R_A$$

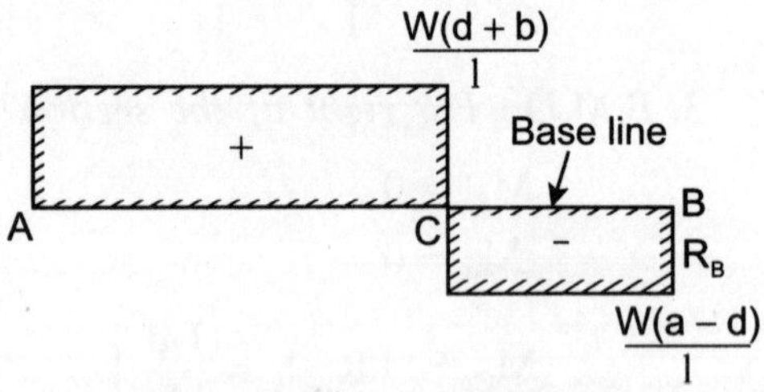

Fig. 13.68: S.F. Diagram

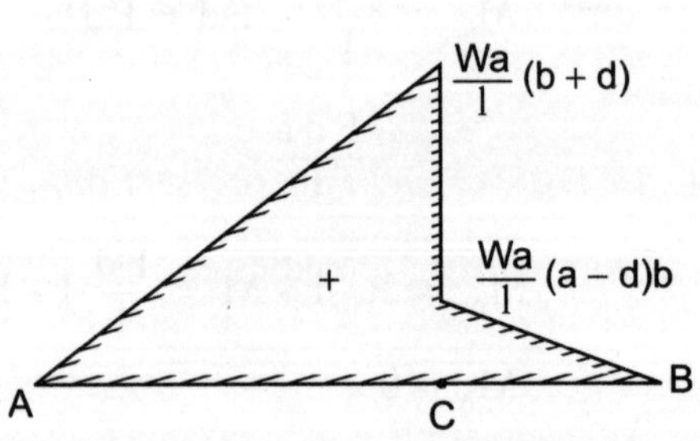

Fig. 13.69: B.M. Diagram

$$= \frac{W(d+b)}{l} - \frac{W(d+b)}{l} = 0$$

3. *B.M.D.: For right of the section* $\underset{+ve}{\curvearrowleft}$ $\underset{-ve}{\curvearrowright}$

$$M_{Br} = 0$$

$$M_B = 0$$

$$M_{Cr} = R_B \times b = \frac{W(a-d)}{l} \cdot b$$

$$M_C = \frac{W(a-d)b}{l} + M$$

$$= \frac{W(a-d)b}{l} + W \cdot d$$

$$= \frac{Wab - Wbd + Wda + Wdb}{l}$$

$$= \frac{Wa(b+d)}{l}$$

$$M_{Ar} = R_B \times l + M - W \times a$$

$$= \frac{W}{l}(a-d)(a+b) + W \cdot d - Wa$$

$$= \frac{W(a-d)(a+b) + Wd(a+b) - Wa(a+b)}{l}$$

$$= \frac{W}{l}\left[a^2 + ab - ad - bd + ad + bd - a^2 - ab\right]$$

$$= \frac{W}{l} \times 0 = 0$$

and $M_A = 0$

Example 13.14

Draw S.F. and B.M. diagrams for a cantilever beam with gradually varying load from zero to ω per unit length on the whole span.

Solution:

1. *S.F.D.: For right of the section* $\underset{-ve}{\uparrow}$ $\underset{+ve}{\downarrow}$

From similar triangles

$$\frac{AC}{AB} = \frac{DE}{BE} \Rightarrow \frac{\omega}{l} = \frac{DE}{x}$$

or $$DE = \left(\omega \cdot \frac{x}{l}\right)$$

$$F_x = F_E = \frac{1}{2} \times DE \times BE = \frac{1}{2}\frac{\omega x}{l}\cdot x$$

$$= \frac{1}{2l}\omega x^2$$

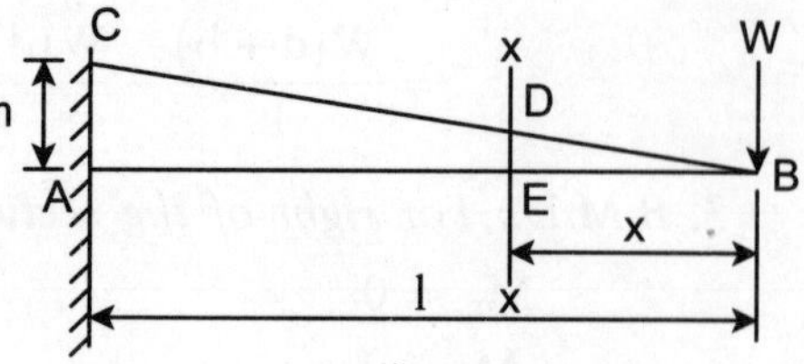

Fig. 13.70

$$\therefore \quad F_x = \frac{1}{2l}\omega x^2 \quad \text{shows parabolic curve}$$

$$\therefore \quad F_{Br} = 0$$

$$F_B = 0$$

$$F_{Cr} = \frac{1}{2l}\omega x^2$$

$$F_C = \frac{1}{2l}\omega x^2$$

$$F_{Ar} = \frac{1}{2l}\omega l^2 = \frac{\omega l}{2}$$

$$F_A = 0$$

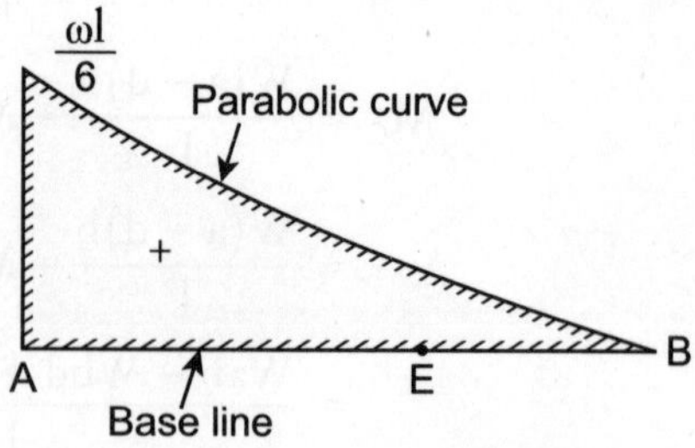

Fig. 13.71: S.F. Diagram

2. *B.M.D.: For right of the section* +ve –ve

$$M_{Br} = 0$$

$$M_B = 0$$

$$M_x = -Fx\cdot\frac{x}{3} = -\frac{\omega x^2}{2l}\cdot\frac{x}{3} = -\frac{\omega x^3}{6l}$$

$$M_x = -\frac{\omega x^3}{6l} \quad \text{shows a cubic curve}$$

$$M_{Ar} = -\frac{\omega l^3}{6l} = -\frac{\omega l^2}{6l}$$

$$M_A = 0$$

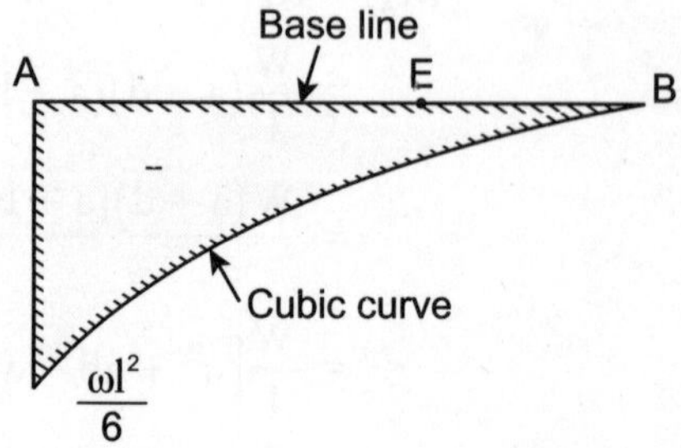

Fig. 13.72: B.M. Diagram

Example 13.15

Draw S.F. and B.M. diagrams for a simply supported beam having gradually varying load as shown in the Fig. 13.73.

Solution:

1. *Reactions*

$$R_A + R_B = \frac{\omega l}{2} \quad \ldots\ldots\ldots\ldots\ldots\ldots \quad (13.11)$$

$$\Sigma M_A = 0$$

$$\Rightarrow R_B \times l = \frac{\omega l}{2} \times \frac{l}{3}$$

$$R_B = \frac{\omega l}{6} \quad \ldots\ldots\ldots\ldots \quad (13.12)$$

$$R_A = \frac{\omega l}{2} - \frac{\omega l}{6} = \frac{2\omega l}{6}$$

$$= \frac{\omega l}{3}$$

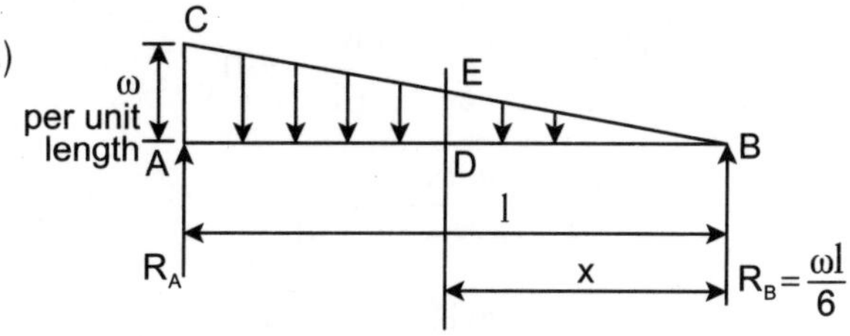

Fig. 13.73

2. *S.F.D.: For right of the section* $\underset{-ve}{\uparrow}$ $\underset{+ve}{\downarrow}$

$$DE = \left(\frac{\omega x}{l}\right)$$

$$F_x = F_D = \left(\frac{DE \times x}{2} - \frac{\omega l}{6}\right) \quad .. \quad (13.13)$$

$$\therefore \quad F_{Br} = 0$$

$$F_B = -\frac{\omega l}{6}$$

$$F_{Dr} = F_x = \left(\frac{\omega x^2}{2l} - \frac{\omega l}{6}\right)$$

$$F_D = \left(\frac{\omega x^2}{2l} - \frac{\omega l}{6}\right)$$

$$F_{Ar} = \frac{\omega l}{2} - \frac{\omega l}{6} = \left(\frac{2\omega l}{6}\right)$$

$$F_A = 0$$

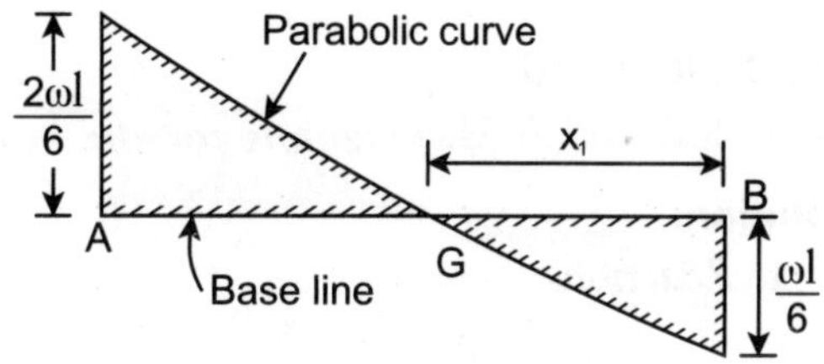

Fig. 13.74: S.F. Diagram

Now

$$F_{x_1} = F_G = 0 = \frac{\omega x_1}{l} \times \frac{x_1}{2} - \frac{\omega l}{6}$$

$$\Rightarrow \quad x_1 = \frac{l}{\sqrt{3}}$$

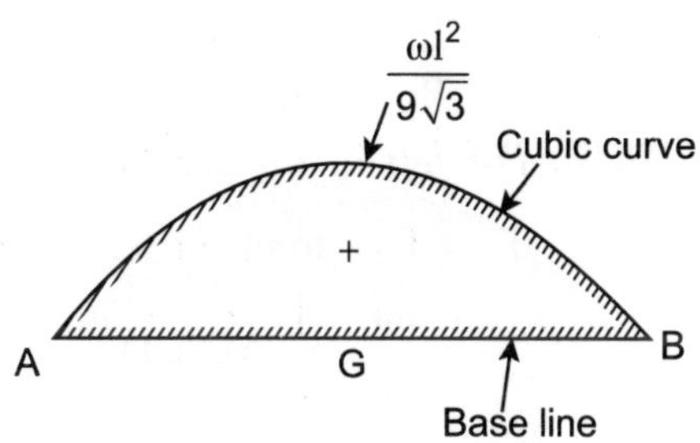

Fig. 13.75: B.M. Diagram

3. *B.M.D.: For right of the section* $\underset{+ve}{\circlearrowleft}$ $\underset{-ve}{\circlearrowright}$

$$M_x = R_B \times x - \frac{\omega x}{2l} \cdot x \cdot \frac{x}{3}$$

$$= \frac{\omega l x}{6} - \frac{\omega x^3}{6l} \quad \ldots\ldots\ldots\ldots\ldots\ldots\ldots\ldots \quad (13.14)$$

$$M_{Br} = 0$$

$$M_B = 0$$

$$M_{A(x=l)} = \frac{\omega l^2}{6} - \frac{\omega x^2}{6l} = 0$$

$$M_{x_1} = \frac{\omega \cdot l x_1}{6} - \frac{\omega x_1^3}{6l}$$

$$= \frac{\omega \cdot l}{6}\left(\frac{l}{\sqrt{3}}\right) - \frac{\omega}{6l}\left(\frac{l}{\sqrt{3}}\right)^3$$

$$= \frac{\omega l^2}{9\sqrt{3}}$$

Note: Different values of S.F. and B.M. should be calculated at intervals of 0.5 m or 1 m as per equations (13.13) and (13.14) and then plot the diagram.

Example 13.16

Draw S.F. and B.M. diagrams for the beam loaded as shown in Fig. 13.76.

Solution:

1. *Reactions*

$$\Sigma M_A = 0$$

$$R_B \cdot l = \frac{\omega l}{2} \cdot \left(\frac{2l}{3}\right)$$

$$R_B = \left(\frac{\omega l}{3}\right)$$

$$R_A = \frac{\omega l}{6}$$

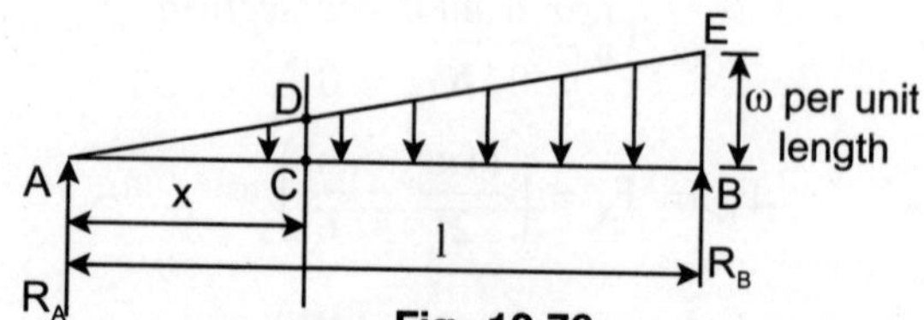

Fig. 13.76

2. *S.F.D.: For left of the section* $\underset{+ve}{\uparrow}$ $\underset{-ve}{\downarrow}$

$$F_x = R_A - \text{load on length AC.}$$

$$= \frac{\omega l}{6} - \frac{1}{2} \cdot AC \cdot CD$$

$$\frac{\omega}{CD} = \frac{l}{x}$$

$$CD = \left(\frac{\omega}{l}\right) \cdot x$$

$$\therefore \quad F_x = \frac{\omega l}{6} - \frac{1}{2} \cdot x \cdot \frac{\omega x}{l}$$

$$F_x = \left(\frac{\omega l}{6} - \frac{\omega x^2}{2l}\right) \quad \ldots. \quad (13.15)$$

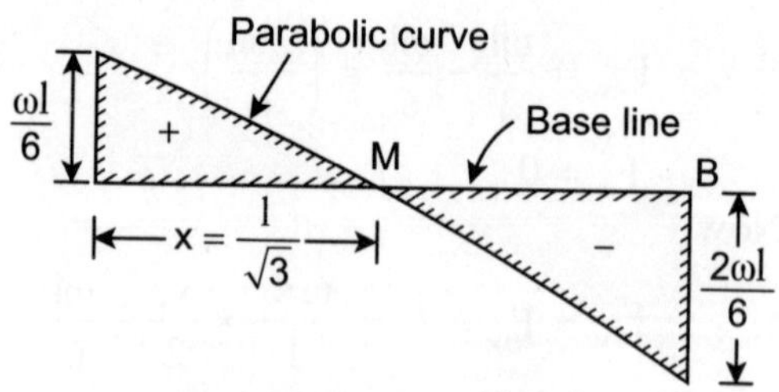

Fig. 13.77: S.F. Diagram

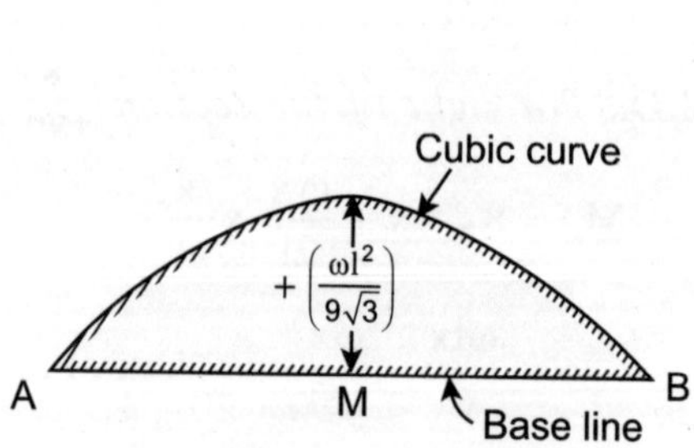

Fig. 13.78: B.M. Diagram

$$\therefore \quad F_A = \frac{\omega l}{6}$$

$$F_B = \frac{\omega l}{6} - \frac{\omega}{2\not{l}} \cdot l \cdot \not{l}$$

$$= \frac{\omega l}{6} - \frac{\omega l}{2} = \frac{\omega l - 3\omega l}{6} = \left(\frac{-2\omega l}{6}\right)$$

S.F. changes according to parablolic law. To find the position of point M.

$$F_x = 0$$

$$\therefore \quad \frac{\omega l}{6} - \frac{\omega x^2}{2l} = 0$$

$$x = \frac{l}{\sqrt{3}} = 0.577\ l$$

3. *B.M.D.: For left of the section* $\overset{\curvearrowright}{+ve}$ $\overset{\curvearrowleft}{-ve}$

$$M_A = 0,\ M_B = 0$$

$$M_x = R_B \times x - \text{load on length AC} \cdot \frac{x}{3}$$

$$M_x = \frac{\omega l}{6} \cdot x - \frac{\omega x^3}{6l}$$

at $\quad x = \frac{l}{\sqrt{3}}$

$$M_M = \frac{\omega l}{6} \cdot \frac{l}{\sqrt{3}} - \frac{\omega}{6l} \cdot \left(\frac{l}{\sqrt{3}}\right)^3$$

$$= \frac{\omega l^2}{9\sqrt{3}}$$

Example 13.17

Draw S.F. and B.M. diagrams for the beam shown in Fig. 13.79.

Solution:

1. *Reactions*

$$\Sigma M_A = 0$$

$$R_B \times 4 = 20 \times 3 + 30 + 20 \times 1.5 \times \frac{1.5}{2}$$

$$R_B = 28.125\ \text{t}$$

$$\therefore \quad R_A = 21.88\ \text{t}$$

2. *S.F.D.: Let sign convention for R.H. section is as* $\uparrow$ +ve $\downarrow$ −ve

$F_{Br} = 0$

$F_B = +R_B = 28.125$ t

$F_{Cr} = 28.125$ t

$F_C = 28.125 - 20 = 8.125$ t

$F_{Er} = 8.125$ t

$F_E = 8.125$ t

$F_{Ar} = 8.125 - 20 \times 1.5 = -21.88$ t

$F_A = 0$

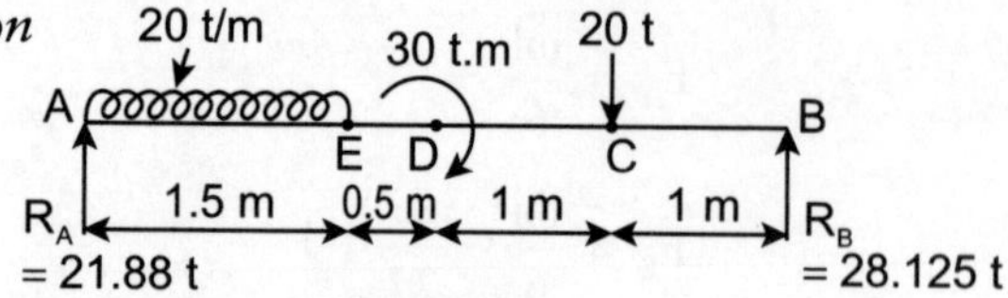

Fig. 13.79

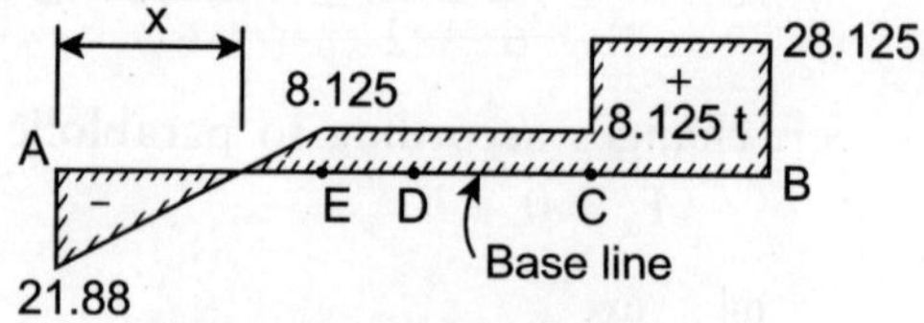

Fig. 13.80: S.F. Diagram

3. *B.M.D.: Let* ↻ +ve ↺ −ve

$M_A = 0, \; M_B = 0$

$M_{Cr} = 28.125 \times 1 = 28.125$ t

$M_C = 28.125$ t.m

$M_{Dr} = 28.125 \times 2 - 20 \times 1 = 36.25$ t.m

$M_D = 36.25 - 30 = 6.25$ t.m

$$M_E\,(\text{left}) = 21.88 \times 1.5 - 20 \times 1.5 \times \frac{1.5}{2}$$

$= 10.32$ t.m

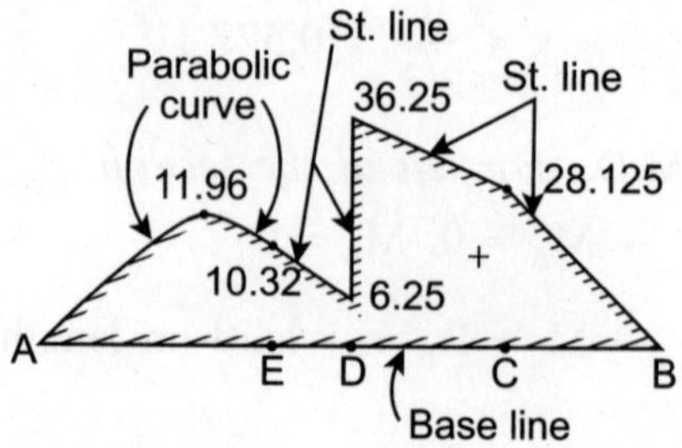

Fig. 13.81: B.M. Diagram

$F_x = -R_A + 20 \times x = 0$ (Considering LHS) $\left[\begin{matrix}\downarrow & \uparrow \\ +\text{ve} & -\text{ve}\end{matrix}\right]$

$20x = 21.88$

$x = 1.094$ m

$$M_x = +R_A \times x - 20 \times x \times \frac{x}{2}$$

$= 21.88 \times 1.094 - 10 \times (1.094)^2$

$= 11.96$ t.m

Example 13.18

Draw S.F. and B.M. diagrams for the beam as shown in Fig. 13.82.

Solution:

1. *Reactions*

$\Sigma M_A = 0$

$R_B \times 20 = 7.5 \times 10 \times (10 + 5)$

$+ 120 \times 5 - 417.5 + 282.5$

$= 1307.5 + 282.5 = 1590$

$R_B = 79.5$ kN
$R_A = 115.5$ kN

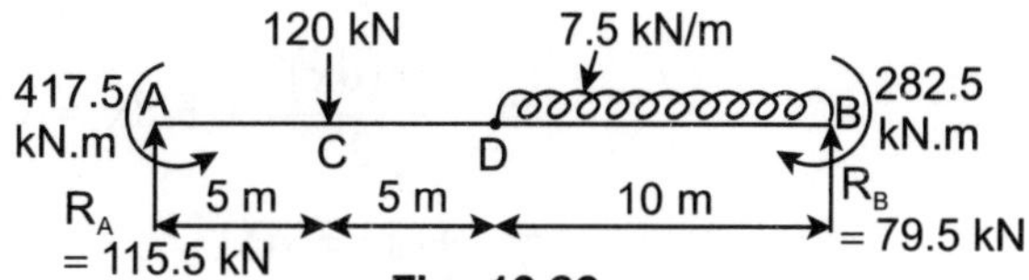

Fig. 13.82

2. *S.F.D.: Let for right of the section, sign convention is as* $\underset{+ve}{\uparrow}$ $\underset{-ve}{\downarrow}$

$$F_B = 79.5 \text{ kN}$$
$$F_D = 79.5 - 7.5 \times 10 = 4.5 \text{ kN}$$
$$F_C = 4.5 - 120$$
$$= -115.5 \text{ kN}$$

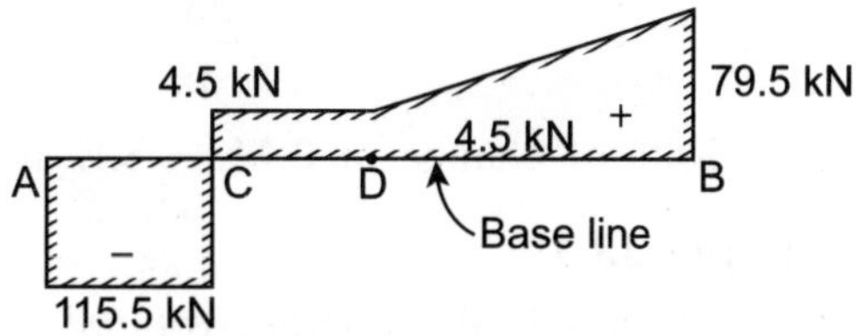

Fig. 13.83: S.F. Diagram

3. *B.M.D.: Let* $\underset{-ve}{\curvearrowright}$ $\underset{+ve}{\curvearrowleft}$

$$M_B = -282.5 \text{ kN.m}$$
$$M_D = -282.5 - 7.5 \times 10 \times 5 + 79.5 \times 10$$
$$= -282.5 - 375 + 795$$
$$= 137.5 \text{ kN.m}$$
$$M_C\,(\text{left}) = 115.5 \times 5 - 417.5$$
$$= 160 \text{ kN.m}$$
$$M_A = -417.5 \text{ kN.m}$$

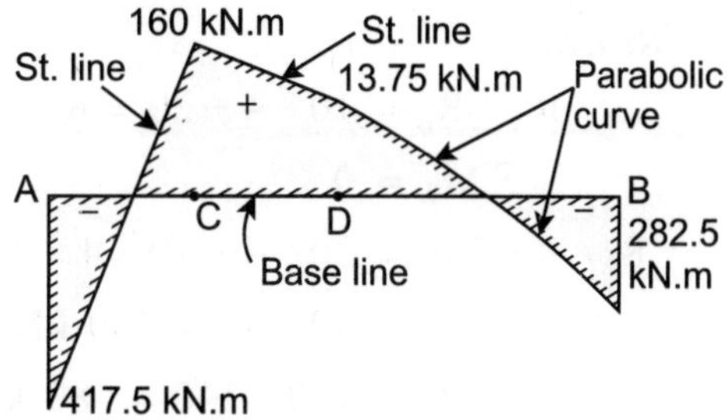

Fig. 13.84: B.M. Diagram

13.19 Relation between Load, Shear Force and Bending Moment

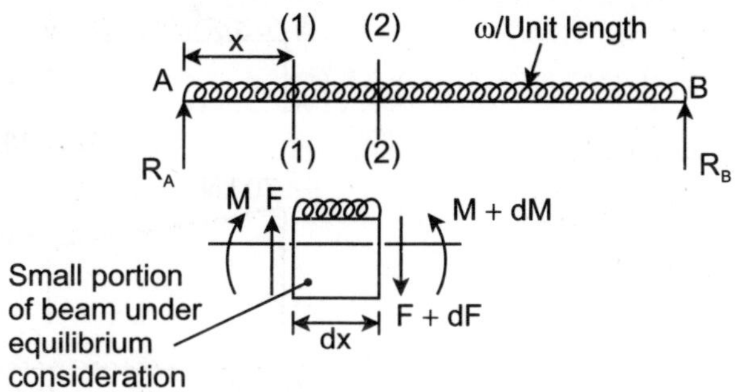

Fig. 13.85

For equilibrium of small portion of beam

$$\Sigma F_y = 0 \Rightarrow F - (F + dF) - \omega \cdot dx = 0$$
$$\Rightarrow -dF = \omega dx$$
$$\Rightarrow \left(\frac{dF}{dx}\right) = -\omega \qquad (13.16)$$

i.e. Rate of change of shear force = ω = rate of loading

$$\Sigma M_{(2)-(2)} = 0 \Rightarrow M + F \cdot dx - \omega \cdot dx \cdot \frac{dx}{2} = M + dM$$

$$\Rightarrow \frac{-\omega(dx)^2}{2} + F \cdot dx = dM, \text{ neglecting higher powers of small quantity.}$$

$$\Rightarrow F \cdot dx = dM$$

i.e. $$\Rightarrow F = \frac{dM}{dx} \quad \ldots\ldots (13.17)$$

i.e. Rate of change of B.M. = S.F. at the section.

Example 13.19

Draw S.F. and B.M. diagrams for the beam shown in Fig. 13.86.

Solution:

1. *Reactions*

$$R_A + R_B = 10 \times 4 + 20 = 60 \text{ kN}$$

$$\Sigma M_A = 0$$

$$R_B \times 8 + 240 = 20 \times 4 + 10 \times 4 \times 2$$

$$8R_B + 240 = 80 + 80 = 160 \text{ kN.m}$$

$$8R_B = 160 - 240 = -80 \text{ kN.m}$$

$$R_B = -10 \text{ kN}$$

$$R_A = 60 + 10 = 70 \text{ kN}$$

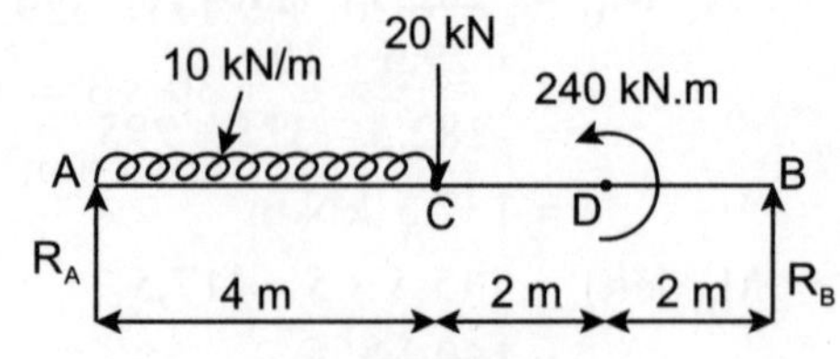

Fig. 13.86

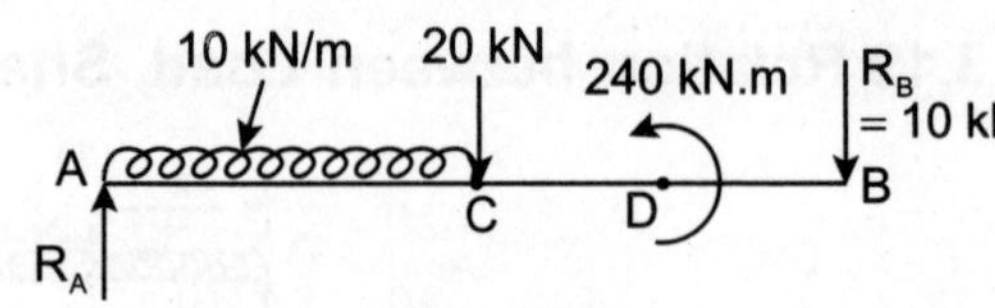

Fig. 13.87

2. *S.F.D.* $\underset{+ve}{\downarrow}$ $\underset{-ve}{\uparrow}$

$$F_B = +R_B = 10 \text{ kN}$$

$$F_C = 10 + 20 = 30 \text{ kN}$$

$$F_A = 30 + 10 \times 4 = 70 \text{ kN}$$

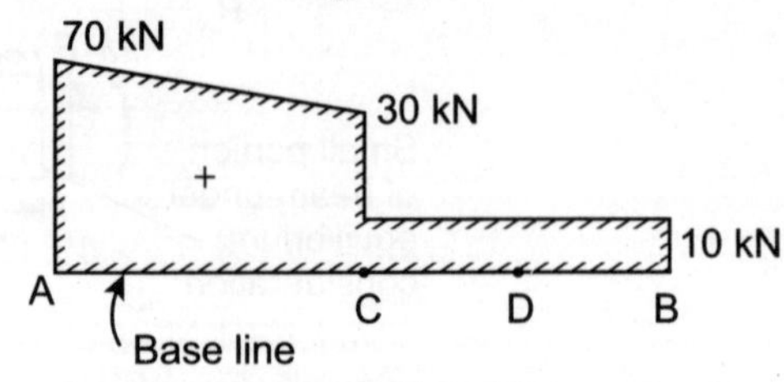

Fig. 13.88: S.F. Diagram

3. *B.M.D.* $\underset{-ve}{\curvearrowleft}$ $\underset{+ve}{\curvearrowright}$

$$M_B = 0$$

$$M_D = -10 \times 2$$

$$= -20 \text{ kN.m}$$

B.M. at point D along with couple

240 kN.m (↺) = −20 + 240 = 220 kN.m

$$M_C = -10 \times 4 + 240$$

$$= 200 \text{ kN.m}$$

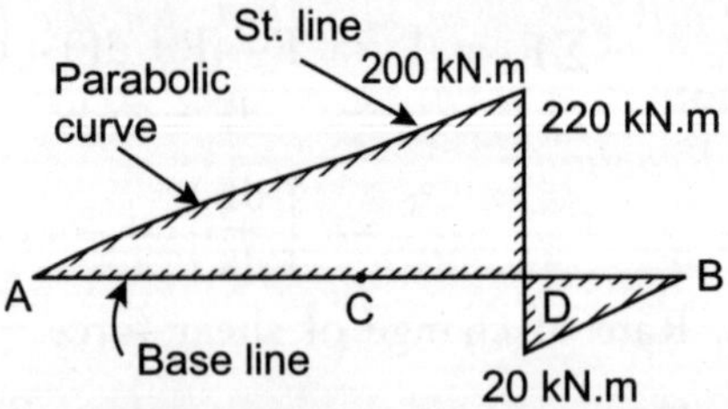

Fig. 13.89: B.M. Diagram

Example 13.20

Draw S.F. and B.M. diagrams for the beam shown in Fig. 13.90.

Solution:

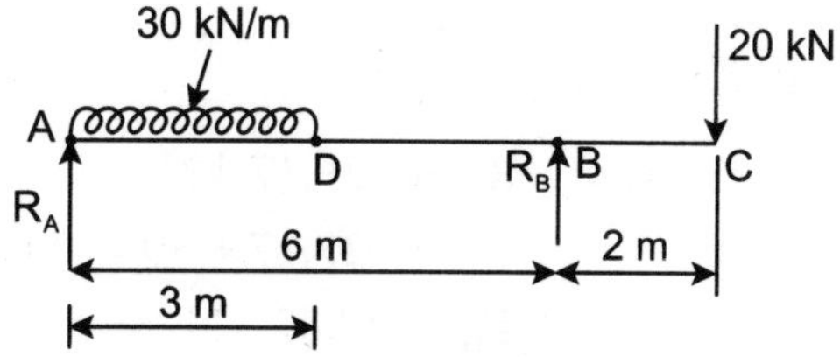

Fig. 13.90

1. *Reactions*

$$\Sigma M_A = 0$$

$$R_B \times 6 = 20 \times 8 + 30 \times 3 \times \frac{3}{2}$$

$$R_B = 49.17 \text{ kN}$$

2. *S.F.D.* $\underset{+ve}{\downarrow}$ $\underset{-ve}{\uparrow}$

$$F_C = +20 \text{ kN}$$

$$F_B = +20 - 49.17 = -29.17 \text{ kN}$$

$$F_A = -29.17 + 30 \times 3 = +60.83 \text{ kN}$$

I = point of inflection

$$F_x = 0$$

$$\Rightarrow 20 - 49.17 + 30 \cdot x = 0$$

$$x = 0.97 \text{ m}$$

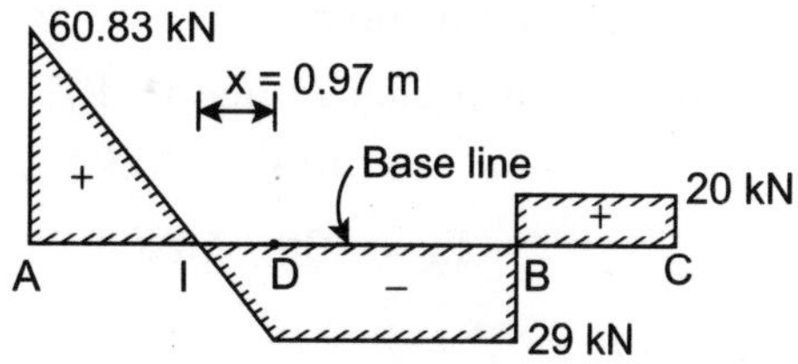

Fig. 13.91: S.F. Diagram

3. *B.M.D.* $\underset{-ve}{\curvearrowleft}$ $\underset{+ve}{\curvearrowright}$

$$M_C = 0$$

$$M_B = -20 \times 2 = -40 \text{ kN.m}$$

$$M_D = -20 \times 5 + 49.17 \times 3$$

$$= +47.51 \text{ kN.m}$$

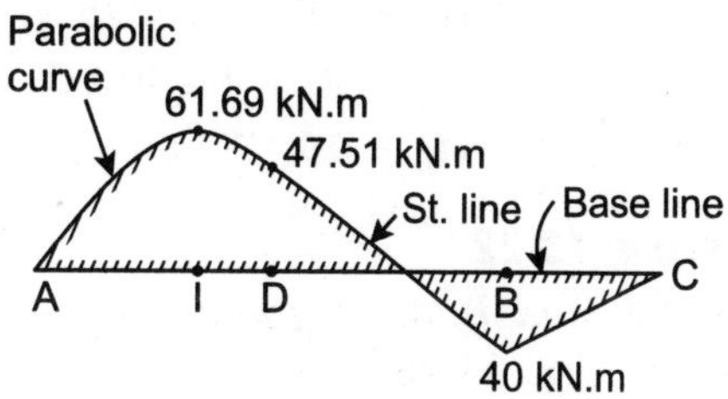

Fig. 13.92: B.M. Diagram

$$M_I = -20 \times 5.97 + R_B \times 3.97 - 30 \times 0.97 \times \frac{0.97}{2}$$

$$= -20 \times 5.97 + 49.17 \times 3.97 - \frac{30}{2} \times (0.97)^2$$

$$= 61.69 \text{ kN.m}$$

Example 13.21

Draw S.F. and B.M. diagrams for the beam shown in Fig. 13.93.

Solution:

1. *Reactions*

$$R_B + R_C = 50 + 10 \times 5 = 100$$

$$\Sigma M_C = 0$$

$$50 \times 2 + 10 \times 5 \times \left(\frac{5}{2} + 4\right) = R_B \times 6$$

$$R_B = 70.83 \text{ kN}$$

$$R_C = 100 - 70.83 = 29.17 \text{ kN}$$

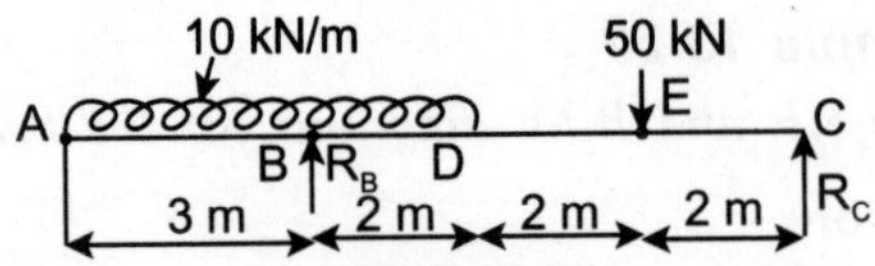

Fig. 13.93

2. *S.F.D.* $\underset{+ve}{\downarrow}$ $\underset{-ve}{\uparrow}$

$$F_C = -R_C = -29.17 \text{ kN}$$

$$F_E = -29.17 + 50 = 20.83 \text{ kN}$$

$$F_D = 20.83 \text{ kN}$$

$$F_B = 20.83 + 10 \times 2 = 40.83 \text{ kN}$$

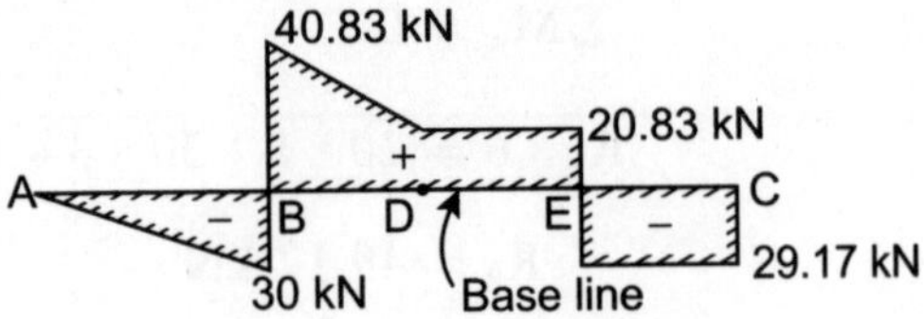

Fig. 13.94: S.F. Diagram

Shear load at point B due to reaction (↑)

or (Sudden change due to R_B) $= 40.83 - R_B$

$$= 40.83 - 70.83 = -30 \text{ kN}$$

$$F_A = -30 + 10 \times 3 = -30 + 30 = 0$$

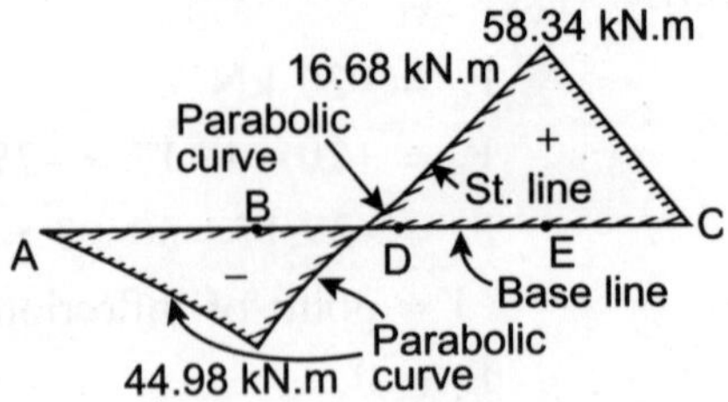

Fig. 13.95: B.M. Diagram

3. *B.M.D.* $\underset{-ve}{\curvearrowleft}$ $\underset{+ve}{\curvearrowright}$

$$M_C = 0$$

$$M_E = +R_C \times 2 = 29.17 \times 2 = 58.34 \text{ kN.m}$$

$$M_D = R_C \times 4 - 50 \times 2 = 29.17 \times 4 - 100 = 16.68 \text{ kN.m}$$

$$M_B = 29.17 \times 6 - 50 \times 4 - 10 \times 2 \times 1 = -44.98 \text{ kN.m}$$

Example 13.22

Draw S.F. and B.M. diagrams for the beam shown in Fig. 13.96.

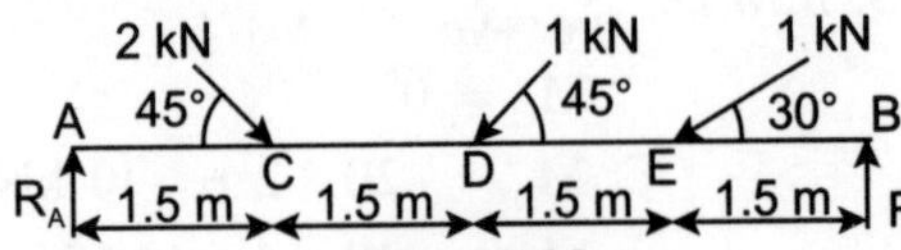

Fig. 13.96

Solution:

Resolve the forces along x-axis and y-axis.

1. Only vertical load will be taken into account for S.F.D. and B.M.D.

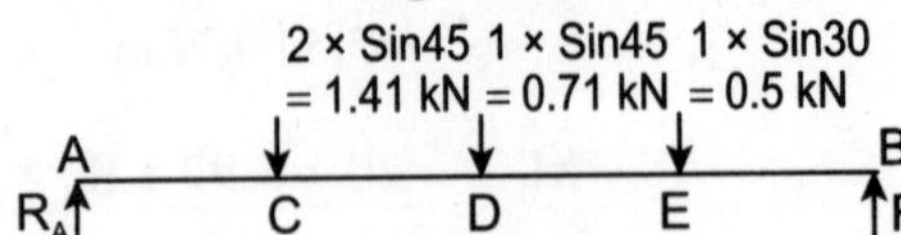

Fig. 13.97

$$R_A + R_B = 2 \text{ Sin}45 + \text{Sin}45 + \text{Sin}30$$

$$= 2.62 \text{ kN}$$

Taking moment about point A

$$R_B \times 6 = 1 \times \text{Sin}30 \times 4.5 + 1 \times \text{Sin}45 \times 3 + 2 \text{ Sin}45 \times 1.5$$

$$= 6.492$$

$$R_B = 1.08 \text{ kN}$$

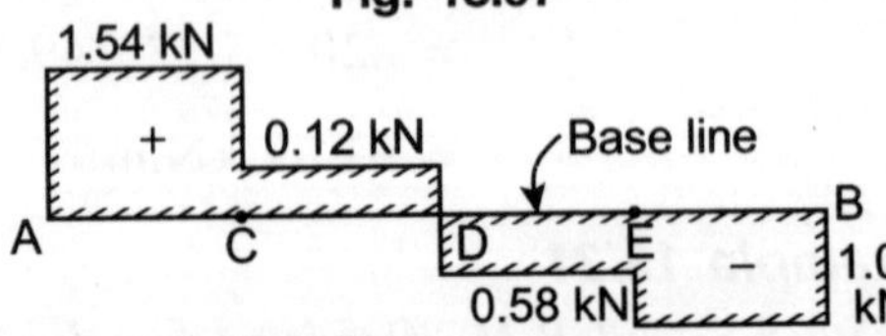

Fig. 13.98: S.F. Diagram

2. *S.F.D.* $\underset{+ve}{\downarrow}$ $\underset{-ve}{\uparrow}$

$$F_C = -R_B = -1.08 \text{ kN}$$

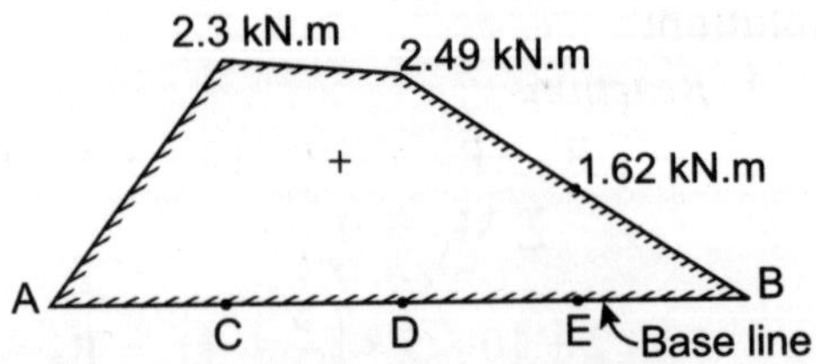

Fig. 13.99: B.M. Diagram

$$F_E = -1.08 + 0.5 = -0.58 \text{ kN}$$

$$F_D = -0.58 + \frac{1.41}{2} = +0.123 \text{ kN}$$

$$F_C = 0.123 + 1.41 = 1.53 \text{ kN}$$

3. *B.M.D.* ↲ ↱ −ve +ve

$$M_B = 0$$

$$M_E = R_B \times 1.5 = +1.08 \times 1.5$$
$$= 1.62 \text{ kN.m}$$

$$M_D = 1.08 \times 3 - 0.5 \times 1.5$$
$$= 2.49 \text{ kN.m}$$

$$M_C = 1.08 \times 4.5 - 0.5 \times 3 - 0.71 \times 1.5$$
$$= 2.295 \text{ kN.m}$$

$$M_A = 1.08 \times 6 - 0.5 \times 4.5 - 0.71 \times 3 - 1.41 \times 1.5 = 0$$

Example 13.23

Draw S.F. and B.M. diagrams for the beam shown in Fig. 13.100.

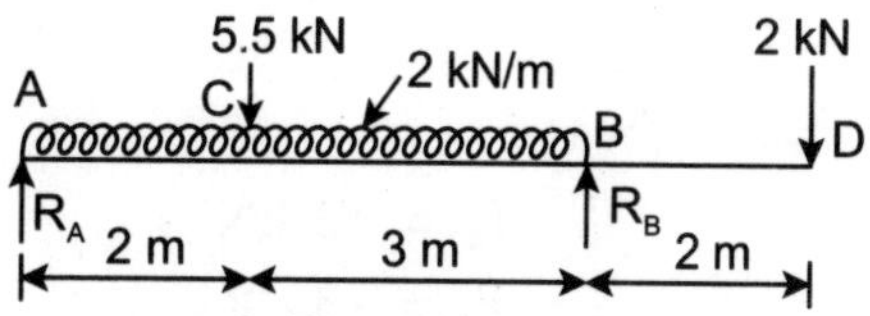

Fig. 13.100

Solution:

1. Taking moment about point A

$$R_B \times 5 = 5.5 \times 2 + 2 \times 7 + 2 \times 5 \times (2.5)$$
$$= 11 + 14 + 25$$

$$R_B = \frac{50}{5} = 10 \text{ kN}$$

2. *S.F.D.* ↓ ↑ +ve −ve

$$F_D = +2 \text{ kN}$$

$$F_B = +2 - R_B = +2 - 10$$
$$= -8 \text{ kN}$$

$$F_{Cr} = -8 + 2 \times 3 = -8 + 6$$
$$= -2 \text{ kN}$$

$$F_C = F_{\text{on C}} = -2 + 5.5 = 3.5 \text{ kN}$$

$$F_A = 3.5 + 2 \times 2 = 7.5 \text{ kN}$$

3. *B.M.D.* ↲ ↱ −ve +ve

$$M_D = 0$$

$$M_B = -2 \times 2 = -4 \text{ kN.m}$$

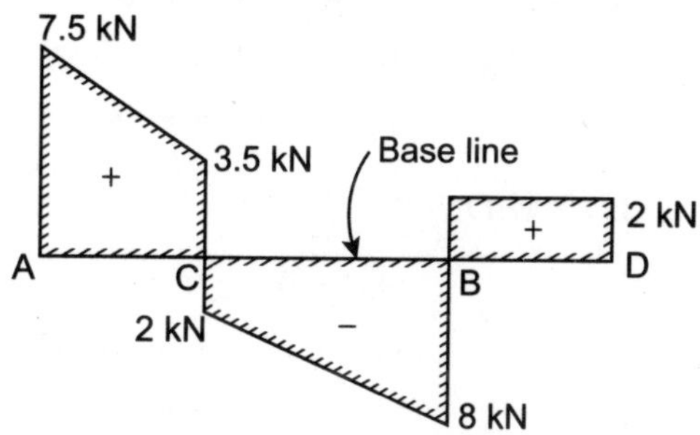

Fig. 13.101: S.F. Diagram

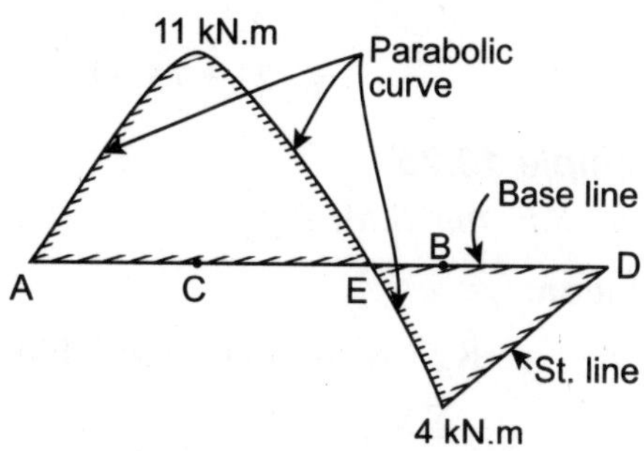

Fig. 13.102: B.M. Diagram

$$M_C = -2 \times 5 + 10 \times 3 - 2 \times 3 \times \frac{3}{2}$$
$$= -10 + 30 - 9$$
$$= 11 \text{ kN.m}$$

Example 13.24

Draw S.F. and B.M. diagrams for the beam shown in Fig. 13.103.

Solution:

1. $R_A + R_B = 3 + 3 = 6 \text{ kN}$

$$\Sigma M_B = 0$$
$$R_A \times 3 + 3 \times 2 = 3 \times 5$$
$$R_A = \frac{15 - 6}{3} = 3 \text{ kN}$$
$$\therefore \quad R_B = R_A = 3 \text{ kN}$$

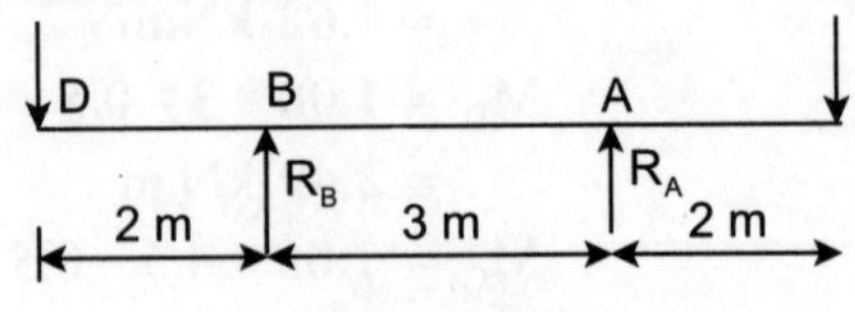

Fig. 13.103

2. S.F.D. $\downarrow$ +ve $\uparrow$ −ve

$$F_C = +3 \text{ kN}$$
$$F_A = +3 - R_A$$
$$= +3 - 3 = 0$$
$$F_B = -R_B = -3 \text{ kN}$$
$$F_D = -3 + 3 = 0$$

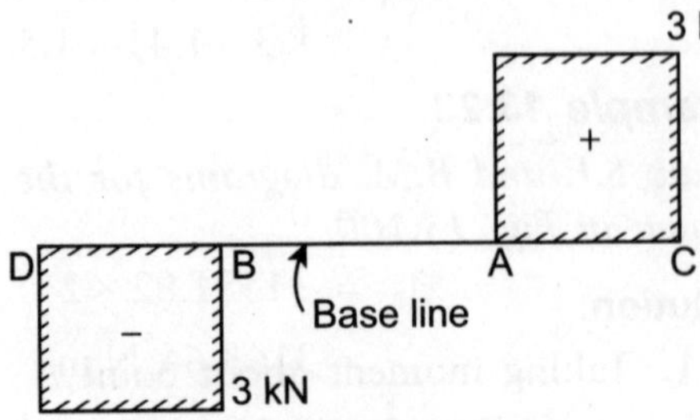

Fig. 13.104: S.F. Diagram

3. B.M.D. −ve +ve

$$M_C = 0$$
$$M_A = -3 \times 2 = -6 \text{ kN.m}$$
$$M_B = -3 \times 5 + 3 \times 3 = -15 + 9$$
$$= -6 \text{ kN.m}$$
$$M_D = -3 \times 7 + 3 \times 5 + 3 \times 2$$
$$= -21 + 15 + 6 = 0$$

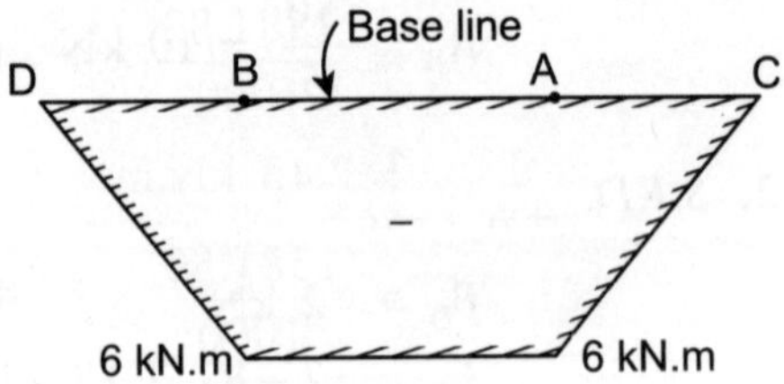

Fig. 13.105: B.M. Diagram

Example 13.25

Draw S.F. and B.M. diagrams for the beam shown in Fig. 13.106.

Solution:

1. $R_A + R_B = 800 \times 3 = 2400 \text{ N}$ .... (13.18)

$$\Sigma M_A = 0$$

$$R_B \times 11 = 4.2 \times 1000 + 800 \times 3 \times \left(4 + \frac{3}{2}\right)$$

$$R_B = 1581.82 \text{ N}$$

$$R_A = 818.18 \text{ N}$$

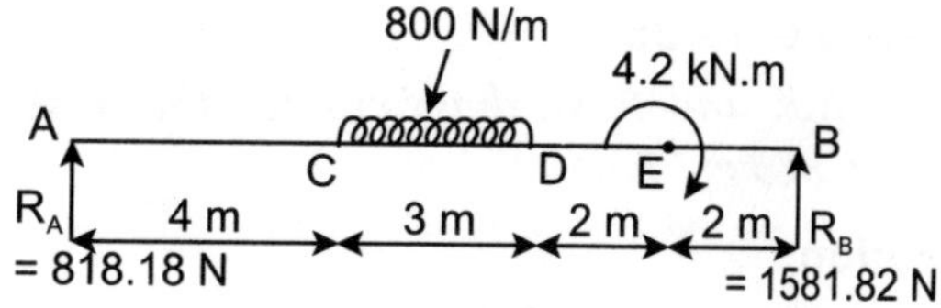

Fig. 13.106

2. *S.F.D.* $\underset{+ve}{\downarrow}$ $\underset{-ve}{\uparrow}$

$$F_B = -1581.82 \text{ N}$$

$$F_C = -1581.82 + 2400$$

$$= 818.18 \text{ N}$$

$$F_E = F_B$$

$$F_D = F_B$$

$$F_A = F_C$$

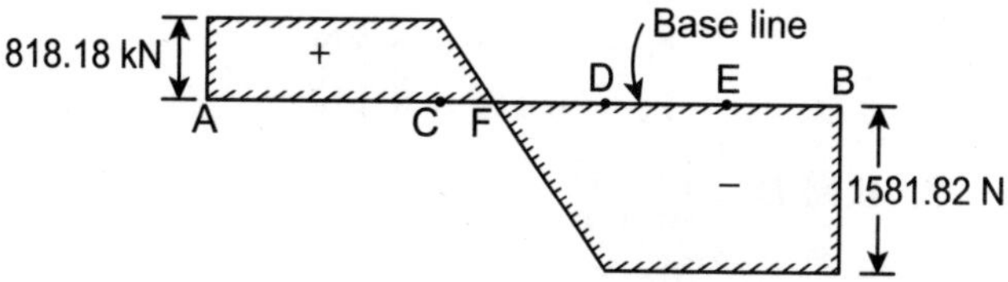

Fig. 13.107: S.F. Diagram

3. *B.M.D.* $\underset{-ve}{\circlearrowleft}$ $\underset{+ve}{\circlearrowright}$

$$M_B = 0$$

$$M_{Er} = +1581.82 \times 2$$

$$= 3163.64 \text{ N.m}$$

$$= 3.16 \text{ kN.m}$$

$$M_E = 3.16 - 4.2 = -1.04 \text{ kN.m}$$

$$M_D = \frac{1581.82}{1000} \times 4 - 4.2$$

$$= 2.13 \text{ kN.m}$$

$$M_C = \frac{1581.82}{1000} \times 7 - 4.2 - \frac{2400}{1000} \times \frac{3}{2}$$

$$= +3.27 \text{ kN.m}$$

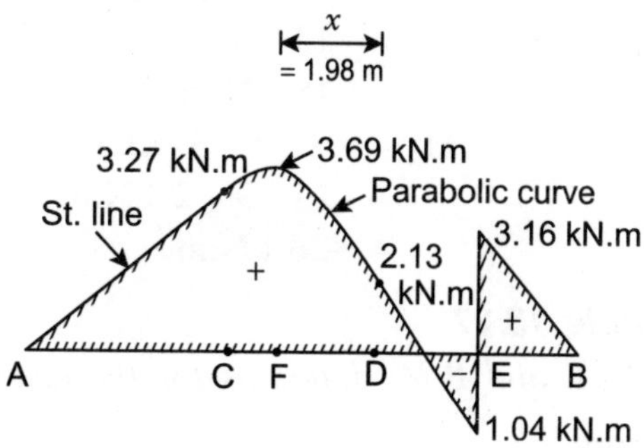

Fig. 13.108: B.M. Diagram

$$F_F = F_x = 0$$

$$-1581.82 + 800 \times x = 0 \Rightarrow x = 1.98 \text{ m}$$

$$M_x = \frac{1581.82}{1000} \times 5.98 - 4.2 - \frac{(800 \times 1.98)}{1000} \times \frac{198}{2}$$

$$= -3.69 \text{ kN.m}$$

$$M_x = -3.69 \text{ kN.m}$$

Example 13.26

Draw S.F. and B.M. diagrams for the beam shown in Fig. 13.109.

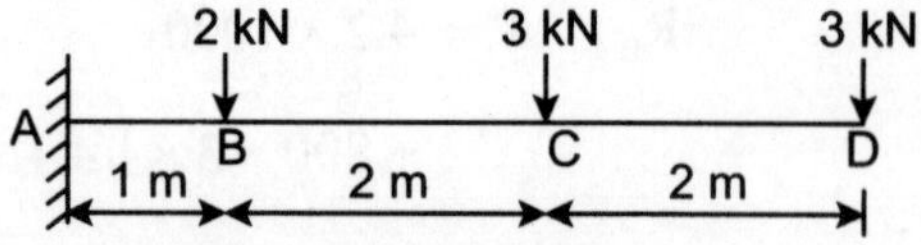

Fig. 13.109

Solution:

1. *S.F.D.* ↓ +ve ↑ −ve

$$F_D = +3 \text{ kN}$$
$$F_C = 3 + 3 = 6 \text{ kN}$$
$$F_B = 6 + 2 = 8 \text{ kN}$$

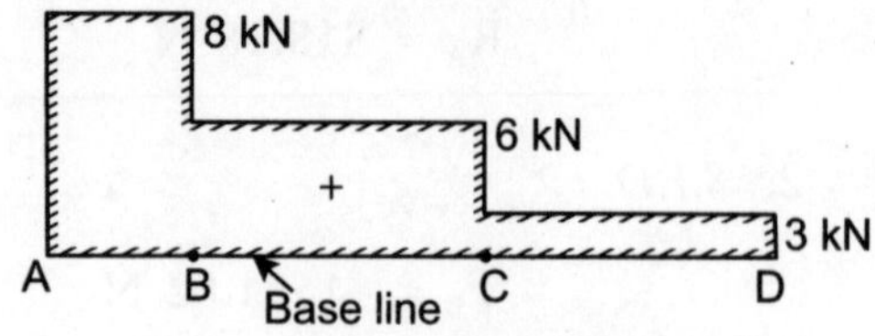

Fig. 13.110: S.F. Diagram

2. *B.M.D.* ↲ −ve ↱ +ve

$$M_D = 0$$
$$M_C = -3 \times 2 = -6 \text{ kN.m}$$
$$F_B = -3 \times 4 - 3 \times 2$$
$$= -12 - 6$$
$$= -18 \text{ kN.m}$$
$$M_A = -3 \times 5 - 3 \times 3 - 2 \times 1$$
$$= -15 - 9 - 2 \text{ kN.m}$$
$$= -26 \text{ kN.m}$$

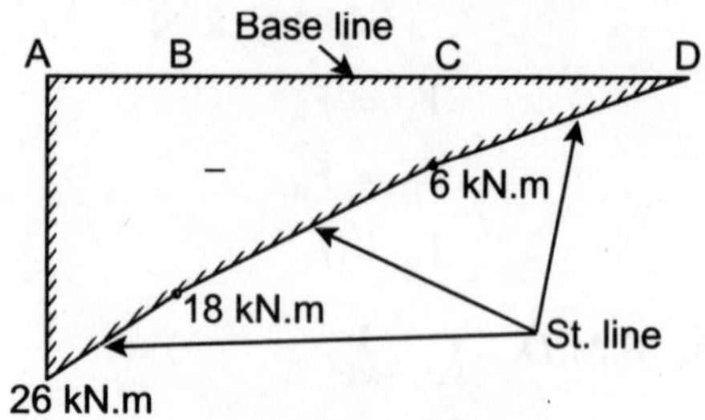

Fig. 13.111: B.M. Diagram

Example 13.27

Draw S.F. and B.M. diagrams for the beam shown in Fig. 13.112.

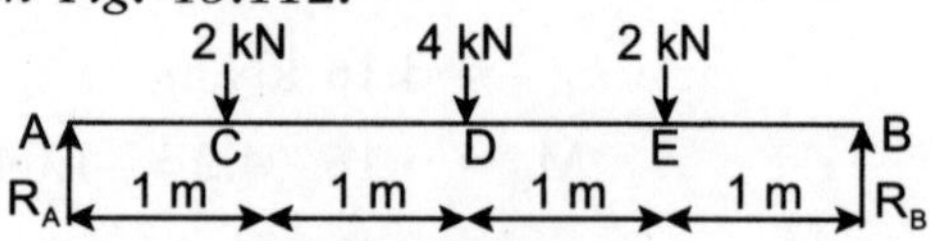

Fig. 13.112

Solution:

1.
$$\Sigma M_A = 0$$
$$R_B \times 4 = 2 \times 3 + 4 \times 2 + 2 \times 1$$
$$R_B = 4 \text{ kN}$$

2. *S.F.D.* ↓ +ve ↑ −ve

$$F_B = -R_B = -4 \text{ kN}$$
$$F_E = -R_B + 2 = -4 + 2 = -2 \text{ kN}$$
$$F_D = -4 + 2 + 4 = +2 \text{ kN}$$
$$F_C = 2 + 2 = 4 \text{ kN}$$

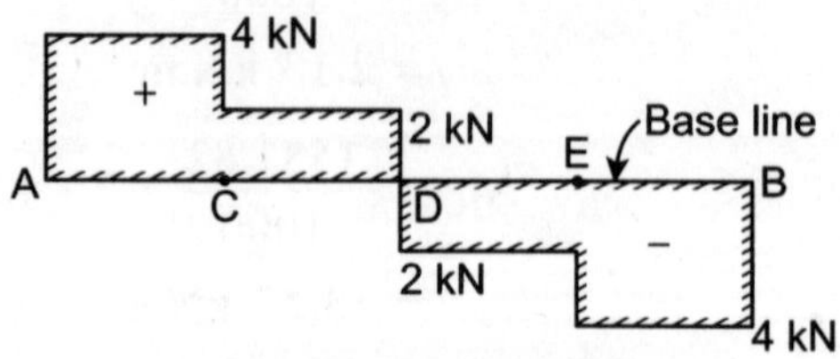

Fig. 13.113: S.F. Diagram

3. *B.M.D.* ↲ −ve ↱ +ve

$$M_B = 0$$
$$M_E = R_B \times 1$$
$$= 4 \times 1 = 4 \text{ kN.m}$$
$$M_D = 4 \times 2 - 2 \times 1$$
$$= 8 - 2 = 6 \text{ kN.m}$$
$$M_C = 4 \times 3 - 2 \times 2 - 4 \times 1$$

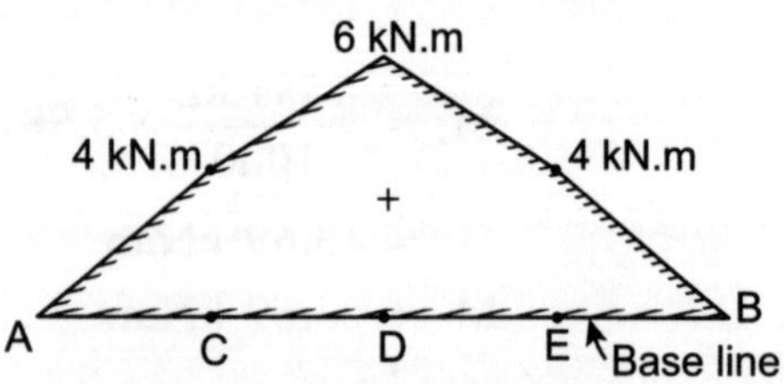

Fig. 13.114: B.M. Diagram

$$= 12 - 4 - 4$$
$$= 4 \text{ kN.m}$$

Example 13.28

Draw S.F. and B.M. diagrams for the beam shown in Fig. 13.115.

Solution:

1. $\Sigma M_A = 0$

$$R_B \times 6 = 1 \times 1 + 2 \times 2 \times \left(2 + \frac{2}{2}\right) + 1 \times 5$$
$$R_B \times 6 = 1 + 12 + 5 = 18$$
$$R_B = 3 \text{ kN}$$

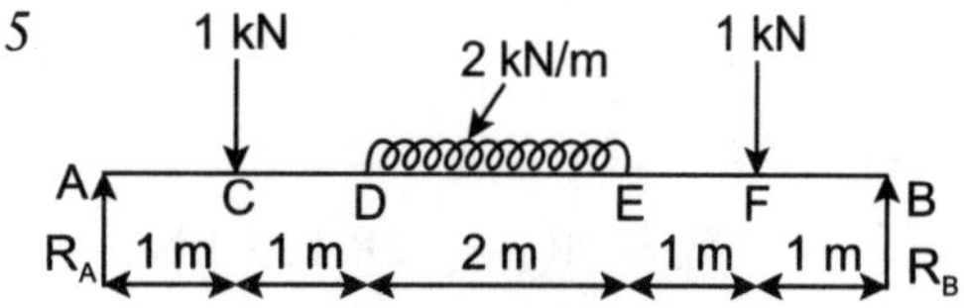

Fig. 13.115

2. *S.F.D.* $\downarrow$ +ve $\uparrow$ −ve

$$F_B = -R_B = -3 \text{ kN}$$
$$F_F = -3 + 1 = -2 \text{ kN}$$
$$F_E = -2 \text{ kN}$$
$$F_D = -2 + 2 \times 2 = +2 \text{ kN}$$
$$F_C = 2 + 1 = 3 \text{ kN}$$

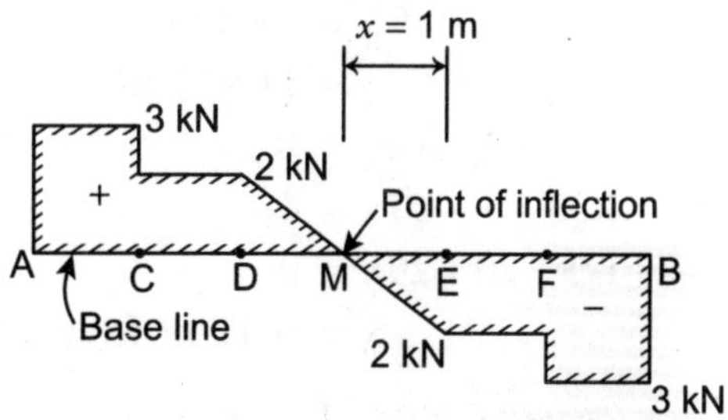

Fig. 13.116: S.F. Diagram

3. *B.M.D.* ↺ −ve ↻ +ve

$$F_x = 0 = F_M$$
$$\Rightarrow -R_B + 1 + 2 \times x = 0$$
$$-3 + 1 + 2x = 0$$
$$2x = 2$$
$$x = 1 \text{ m}$$

Now

$$M_B = 0$$
$$M_F = +R_B \times 1 = 3 \times 1 = 3 \text{ kN.m}$$
$$M_E = 3 \times 2 - 1 \times 1 = 6 - 1 = 5 \text{ kN.m}$$
$$M_M = 3 \times 3 - 1 \times 2 - 2 \times 1 \times \frac{1}{2}$$
$$= 9 - 2 - 1 = 6 \text{ kN.m}$$
$$M_D = 3 \times 4 - 1 \times 3 - 2 \times 2 \times 1$$
$$= 12 - 3 - 4 = 5 \text{ kN.m}$$
$$M_C = 3 \times 5 - 1 \times 4 - 2 \times 2 \times \left(1 + \frac{2}{2}\right)$$
$$= 15 - 4 - 8 = 15 - 12 = 3 \text{ kN.m}$$
$$M_A = 0$$

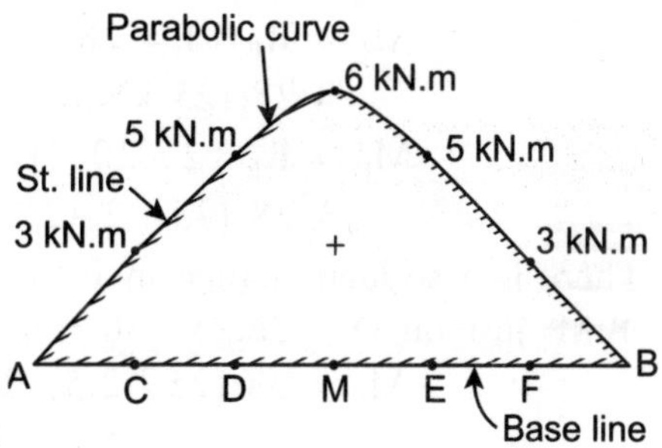

Fig. 13.117: B.M. Diagram

Example 13.29

Draw S.F. and B.M. diagrams for the beam shown in Fig. 13.118.

Solution:

1. $$\Sigma M_A = 0$$

$$R_B \times 4 = 30 + 20 + 1.5 \times \frac{1.5}{2} + 20 \times 3$$

$$R_B = \frac{112.5}{4} = 28.125 \text{ kN}$$

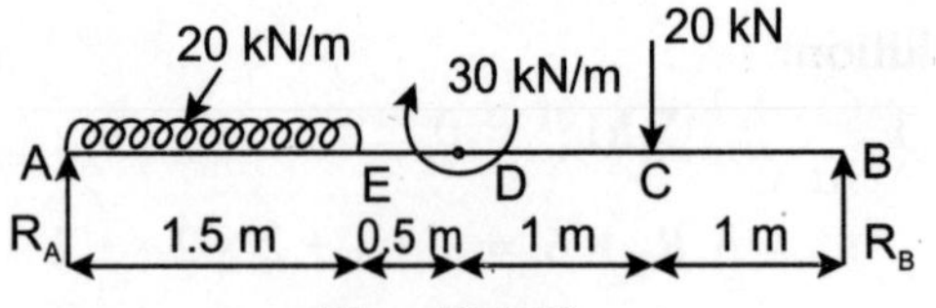

Fig. 13.118

2. *S.F.D.* $\downarrow$ +ve $\uparrow$ –ve

$$F_B = -R_B = -28.125 \text{ kN}$$

$$F_C = -28.125 + 20 = -8.125 \text{ kN}$$

$$F_E = -8.125 \text{ kN}$$

$$F_{Ar} = -8.125 + 20 \times 1.5$$

$$= 21.875 \text{ kN}$$

$$F_M = F_x = 0$$

$$-R_B + 20 + 20\,x = 0$$

$$-28.125 + 20 + 20x = 0$$

$$x = 0.41 \text{ m from E}$$

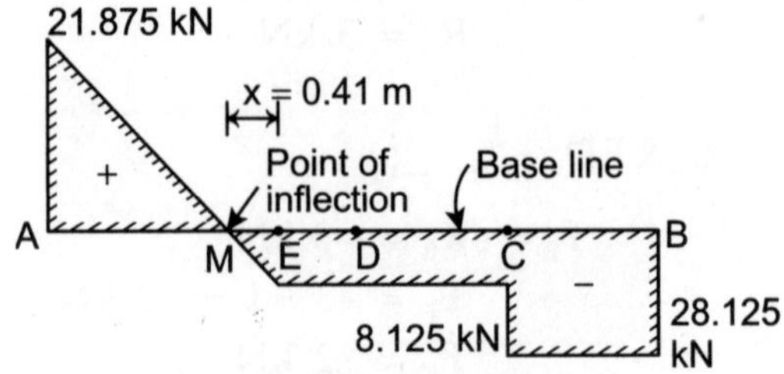

Fig. 13.119: S.F. Diagram

3. *B.M.D.* –ve +ve

$$M_B = 0$$

$$M_C = R_B \times 1 = 28.125 \times 1$$

$$= 28.125 \text{ kN.m}$$

$$M_D = R_B \times 2 - 20 \times 1$$

$$= 28.125 \times 2 - 20 = 36.25 \text{ kN.m}$$

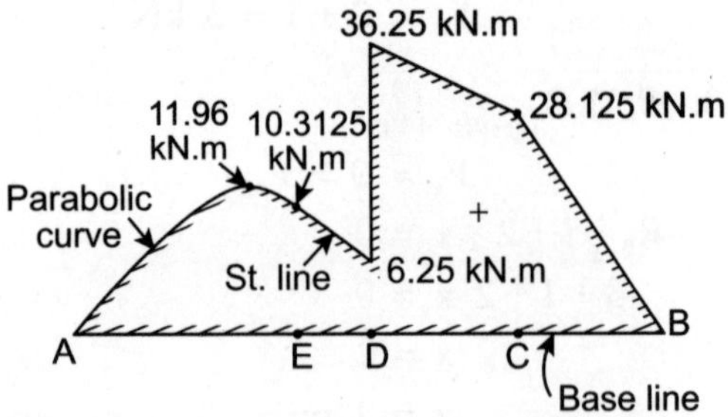

Fig. 13.120: B.M. Diagram

There is a sudden change in B.M. at D due to couple

B.M. just on D = $36.25 - 30 = 6.25$ kN.m

$$M_E = 28.125 \times 2.5 - 20 \times 1.5 - 30 = 10.3125 \text{ kN.m}$$

$$M_M = 28.125 \times (2.5 + 0.41) - 20 \times (1.5 + 0.41) - 30 - 20 \times 0.41 \times \frac{0.41}{2}$$

$$= 81.84375 - 38.2 - 30 - 1.681$$

$$= 11.96275 \text{ kN.m}$$

Example 13.30

Draw S.F. and B.M. diagrams for the beam shown in Fig. 13.121.

Solution:

1. $$R_A + R_B = \frac{\omega \times L}{2}$$

$$\Sigma M_A = 0$$

$$R_B \times L = \frac{\omega L}{2} \times \frac{L}{3}, \quad R_B = \frac{\omega L}{6}$$

$$R_A = \frac{\omega L}{2} - \frac{\omega L}{6} = \frac{2\omega L}{6}$$

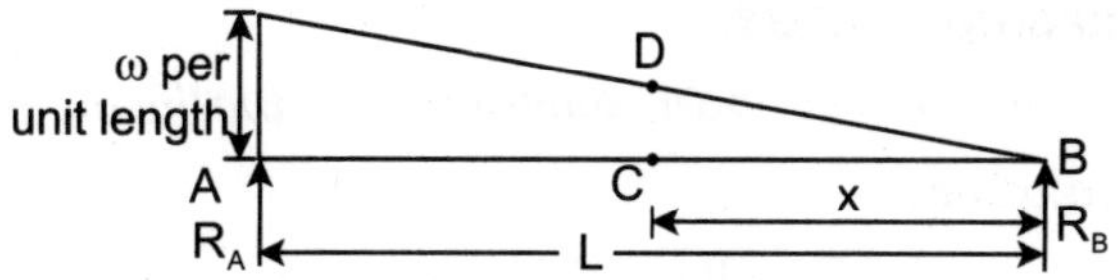

Fig. 13.121

C → Point of inflection

At C

$F_x = 0$ or $F_C = 0$

2. *S.F.D.* $\underset{+ve}{\downarrow}$ $\underset{-ve}{\uparrow}$

$$\frac{\omega}{CD} = \frac{L}{x}$$

$$CD = \left(\frac{\omega}{L} \cdot x\right)$$

$$-R_B + \frac{1}{2} \times x \times CD = 0$$

$$-\frac{\not{\omega} L}{6} + \frac{1}{2} \times x \times \frac{\not{\omega}}{L} \cdot x = 0$$

$$\frac{1}{2} \times \frac{x^2}{L} = \frac{L}{6}$$

$$x = \left(\frac{L}{\sqrt{3}}\right)$$

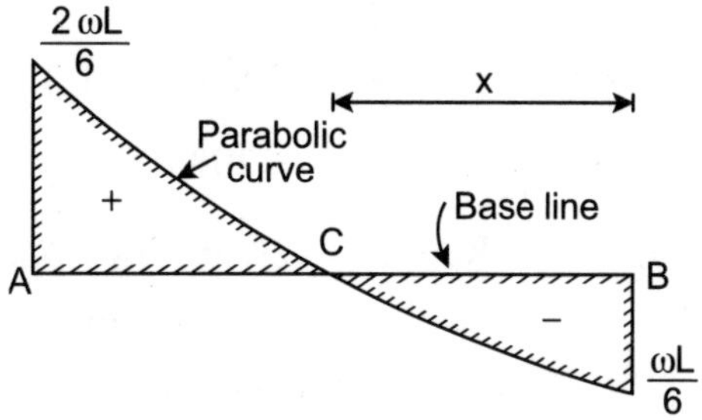

Fig. 13.122: S.F. Diagram

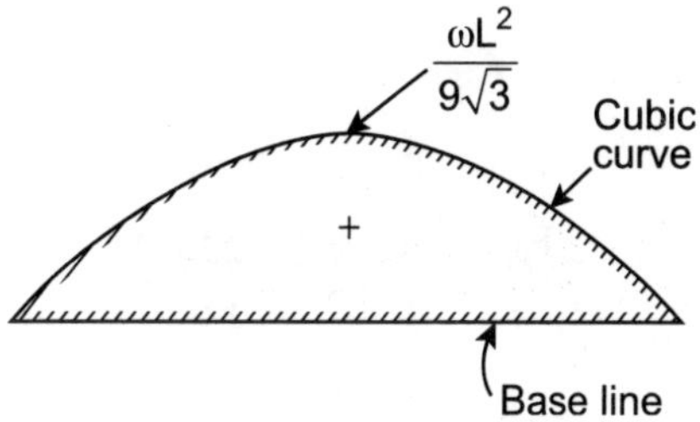

Fig. 13.123: B.M. Diagram

$$M_x = M_C = R_B \times x - \frac{1}{2} \times CD \times x \times \frac{x}{3}$$

$$= \frac{\omega L}{6} \cdot \frac{L}{\sqrt{3}} - \frac{1}{2} \times \frac{\omega}{L} \times x \times \frac{x^2}{3}$$

$$= \frac{\omega L^2}{6\sqrt{3}} - \frac{\omega}{6\not{L}} \times \left(\frac{L^2}{3}\right)\left(\frac{\not{L}}{\sqrt{3}}\right)$$

$$= \frac{\omega L^2}{6\sqrt{3}} - \frac{\omega L^2}{6\sqrt{3} \times 3}$$

$$= \frac{\omega L^2}{6\sqrt{3}} \times \frac{2}{3} = \frac{\omega L^2}{9\sqrt{3}}$$

Example 13.31

Draw S.F. and B.M. diagrams for the beam shown in Fig. 13.124.

Solution:

1. $$R_L + R_R = 200 \times 6 + 1000 + 2000 = 1200 + 3000 = 4200 \text{ N} \quad \ldots (13.19)$$

$$\Sigma M_L = 0$$

$$R_B \times (6+3+7+4) = 2000 \times (6+3+7) + 1000 \times 9 + 200 \times 6 \times \frac{6}{2}$$

$$\Rightarrow \quad R_B \times 20 = 2000 \times 16 + 9000 + 3600 = 32000 + 9000 + 3600 = 44600$$

$$R_R = 2230 \text{ N}$$

$$R_L = 1970 \text{ N}$$

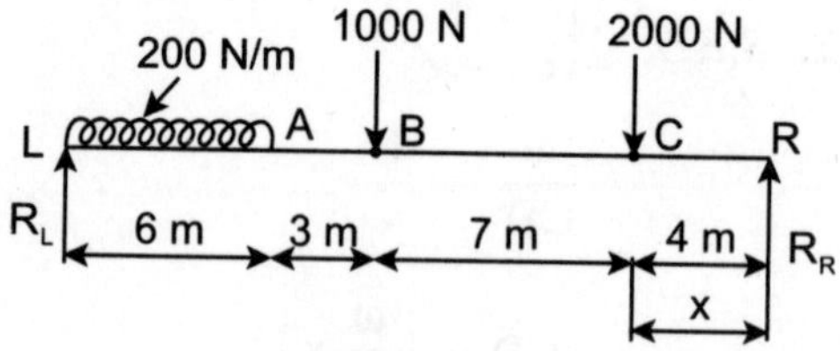

Fig. 13.124

2. *Shear force* $\underset{+ve}{\downarrow}$ $\underset{-ve}{\uparrow}$

$$F_x = -R_R = -2230 \text{ N}$$

$$\therefore \quad F_R = -R_R = -2230 \text{ N}$$

$$F_C = -2230 + 2000 = -230 \text{ N}$$

$$F_B = -230 + 1000 = +770 \text{ N}$$

$$F_A = 770 \text{ N}$$

$$F_L = 770 + 200 \times 6 = 770 + 1200 = 1970 \text{ N}$$

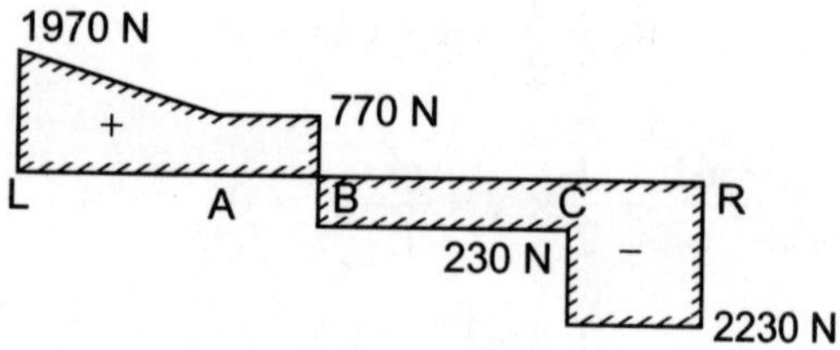

Fig. 13.125: S.F. Diagram

Bending Moment: $M_x = +F_R \times x$

$$M_R = 0$$

$$M_C = F_R \times CR = +2230 \times 4 = 8920 \text{ N.m } (\circlearrowright)$$

$$M_B = F_R \times 11 - 2000 \times 7 = 2230 \times 11 - 14000 = 10530 \text{ N.m}$$

$$F_A = 2230 \times 14 - 2000 \times 10 - 1000 \times 3 = 8220 \text{ N.m}$$

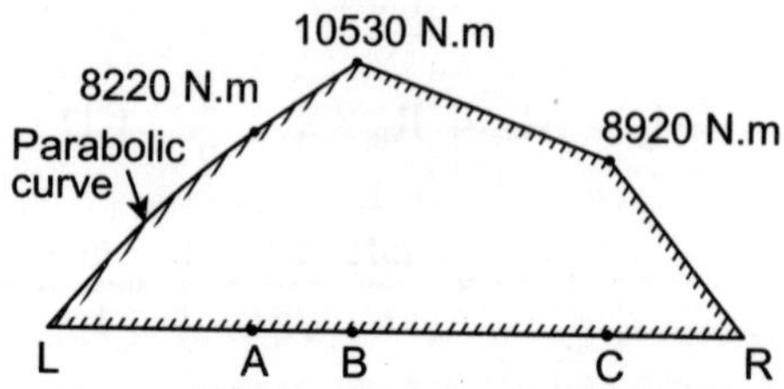

Fig. 13.126: B.M. Diagram

Example 13.32

Draw S.F. and B.M. diagrams for the beam shown in Fig. 13.127.

Solution:

1. *S.F.D.* $\underset{+\text{ve}}{\downarrow}$ $\underset{-\text{ve}}{\uparrow}$

$$F_B = +10 \text{ kN}$$
$$F_C = +10 \text{ kN}$$
$$F_{Ar} = +10 + 2 \times 2$$
$$= 14 \text{ kN}$$

2. *B.M.D.* $\underset{-\text{ve}}{\curvearrowleft}$ $\underset{+\text{ve}}{\curvearrowright}$

$$F_A = 0$$
$$M_B = 0$$
$$M_C = -10 \times 4 = -40 \text{ kN.m}$$
$$M_A = -10 \times 6 - 4 \times \frac{2}{2}$$
$$= -60 - 4$$
$$= -64 \text{ kN.m}$$

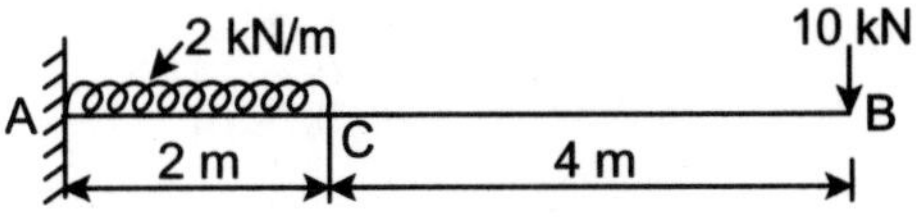

Fig. 13.127

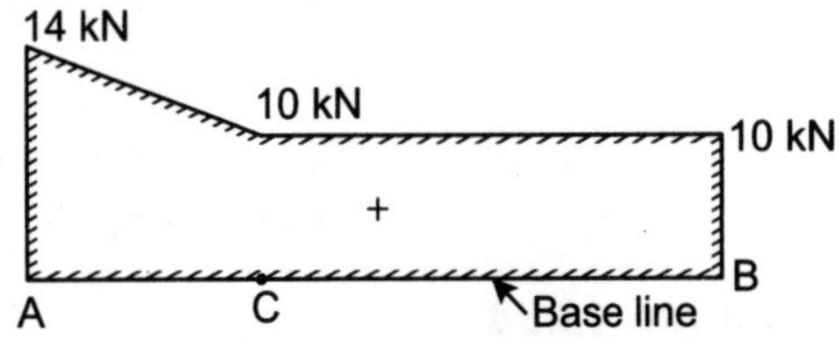

Fig. 13.128: S.F. Diagram

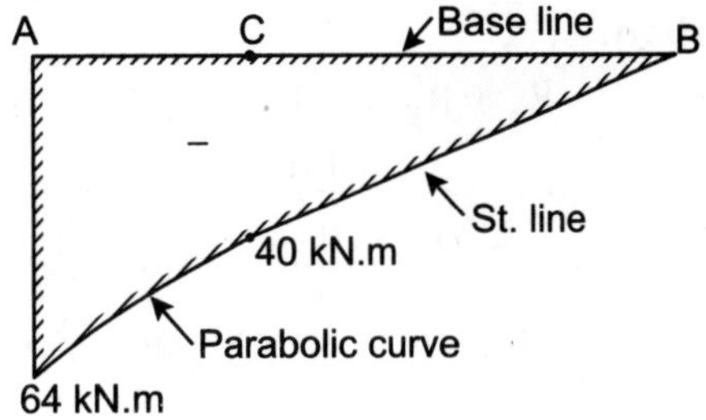

Fig. 13.129: B.M. Diagram

Example 13.33

Draw S.F. and B.M. diagrams for the beam shown in Fig. 13.130.

Solution:

1. *S.F.D.* $\underset{+\text{ve}}{\downarrow}$ $\underset{-\text{ve}}{\uparrow}$

$$F_D = 0$$
$$F_C = 10 \times 2 = 20 \text{ kN}$$
$$F_B = 20 + 20 \text{ Sin}60$$
$$= 37.32 \text{ N}$$
$$F_A = 37.32 \text{ N}$$

2. *B.M.D.* $\underset{-\text{ve}}{\curvearrowleft}$ $\underset{+\text{ve}}{\curvearrowright}$

$$M_D = 0$$
$$M_C = -10 \times 2 \times \frac{2}{2}$$
$$= -20 \text{ kN.m}$$
$$M_B = -10 \times 2 \times \left(2 + \frac{2}{2}\right)$$

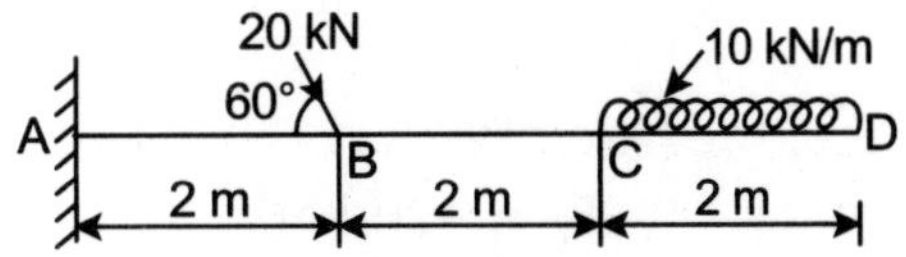

Fig. 13.130

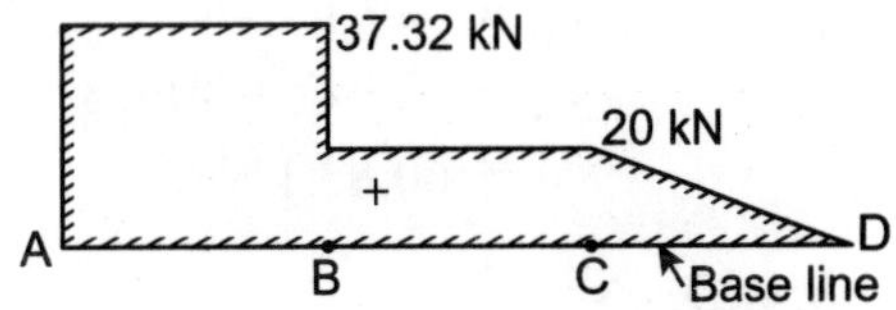

Fig. 13.131: S.F. Diagram

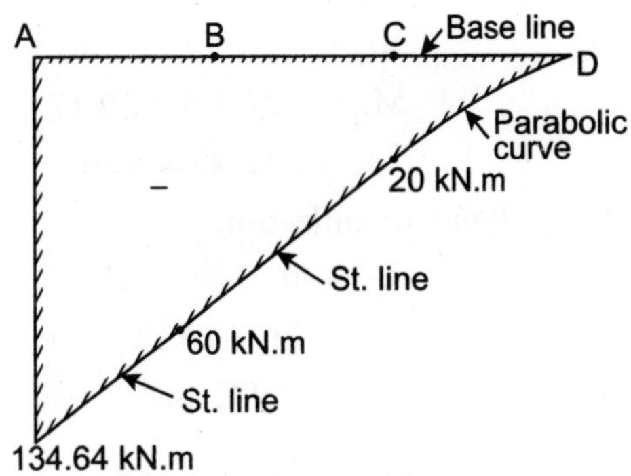

Fig. 13.132: B.M. Diagram

$$= -20 \times 3$$
$$= -60 \text{ kN.m}$$
$$M_A = -10 \times 2 \times \left(4 + \frac{2}{2}\right)$$
$$= -20 \text{ Sin}60 \times 2$$
$$= -20 \times 5 - 40 \text{ Sin}60$$
$$= -134.64 \text{ kN.m}$$

Example 13.34

Draw S.F. and B.M. diagrams for the beam shown in Fig. 13.133.

Solution:

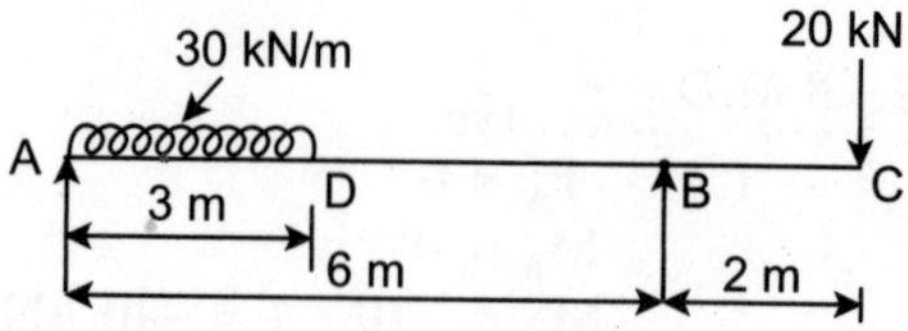

Fig. 13.133

1. $$R_A + R_B = 30 \times 3 + 20 = 90 + 20$$
$$= 110$$
$$\Sigma M_A = 0$$
$$R_B \times 6 = 20 \times 8 + 30 \times 3 \times \frac{3}{2}$$
$$R_B = \frac{160 + 135}{6} = 49.17 \text{ kN}$$

2. *S.F.D.* $\downarrow$ +ve $\uparrow$ –ve

$$F_C = +20 \text{ kN}$$
$$F_B = 20 - 49.17 = -29.17 \text{ kN}$$
$$F_D = -29.17 \text{ kN}$$
$$F_A = -29.17 + 30 \times 3$$
$$= 60.83 \text{ kN}$$

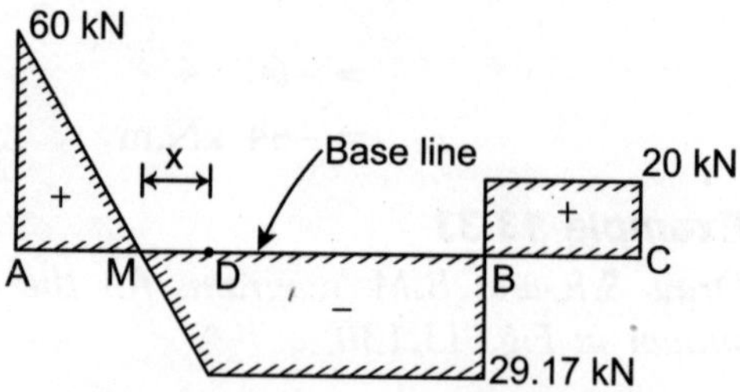

Fig. 13.134: S.F. Diagram

3. *B.M.D.* –ve +ve

$$M_C = 0$$
$$M_B = -20 \times 2 = -40 \text{ kN.m}$$
$$M_D = -20 \times 5 + 29.17 \times 3$$
$$= -12.49 \text{ kN.m}$$

M $\rightarrow$ Point of inflection

$$F_x = 0$$
$$\Rightarrow \quad 20 - 49.17 + 30x = 0$$
$$x = 0.972 \text{ m}$$

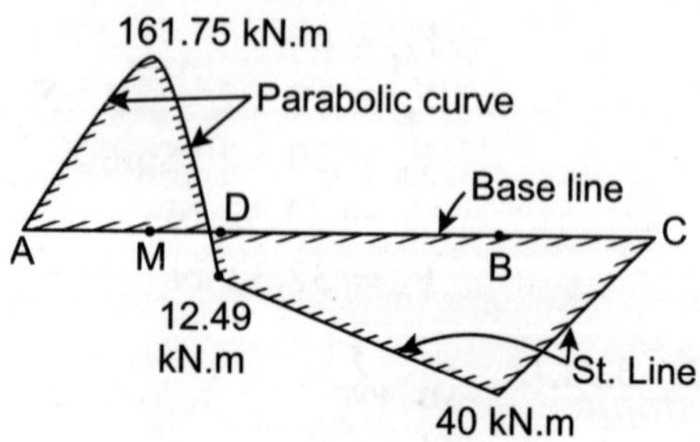

Fig. 13.135: B.M. Diagram

$$M_x = M_M = -20 \times 5.972 + 49.17 \times 3.972 - 30 \times \frac{0.97^2}{2}$$

$$= -19.44 + 195.30 - 14.1135$$
$$= 161.75 \text{ kN.m}$$

Example 13.35

Draw S.F. and B.M. diagrams for the beam shown in Fig. 13.136.

Solution:

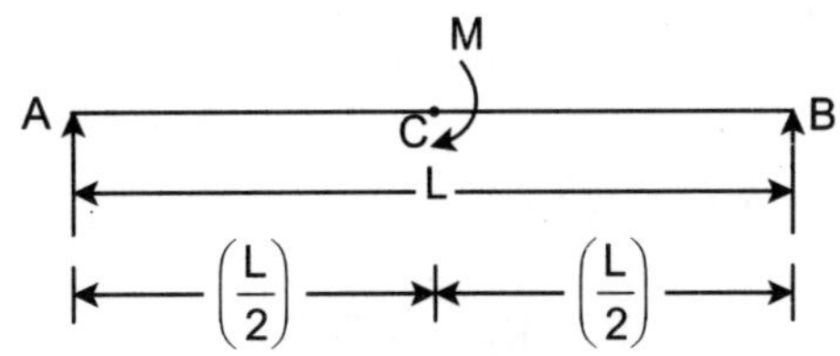

Fig. 13.136

1. $$R_A + R_B = 0$$
$$\Sigma M_A = 0$$
$$R_B \times L = M$$
$$R_B = \left(\frac{M}{L}\right)$$
$$R_A = -R_B = -\left(\frac{M}{L}\right)$$

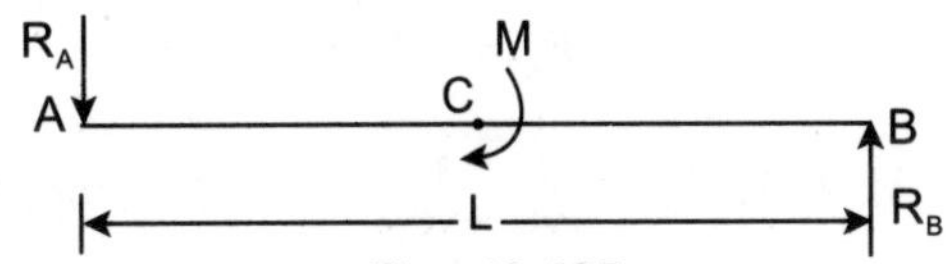

Fig. 13.137

2. *S.F.D.* $\overset{\downarrow}{+ve}$ $\overset{\uparrow}{-ve}$

$$F_B = -R_B = -\left(\frac{M}{L}\right)$$
$$F_A = -\left(\frac{M}{L}\right)$$

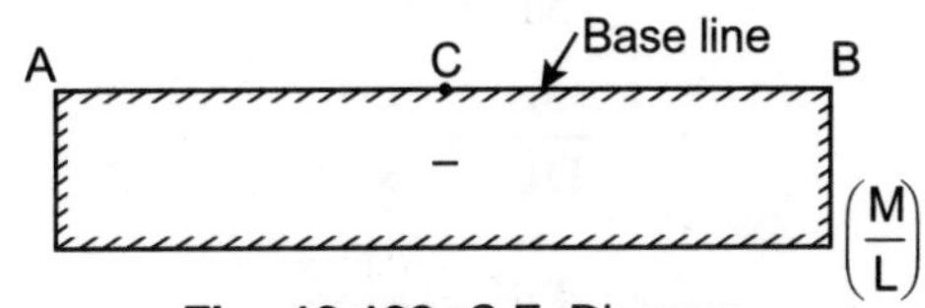

Fig. 13.138: S.F. Diagram

3. *B.M.D.* $\underset{-ve}{\curvearrowleft}$ $\underset{+ve}{\curvearrowright}$

$$M_B = 0$$
$$M_{Cr} = R_B \times \frac{L}{2} = \frac{M}{L} \times \frac{L}{2} = \frac{ML}{2L} = \frac{M}{2}$$
$$M_C = M_{\text{on C}} = \frac{M}{2} - M = -\frac{M}{2}$$
$$M_A = R_B \times L - M$$
$$= \frac{M}{L} \times L - M = 0$$

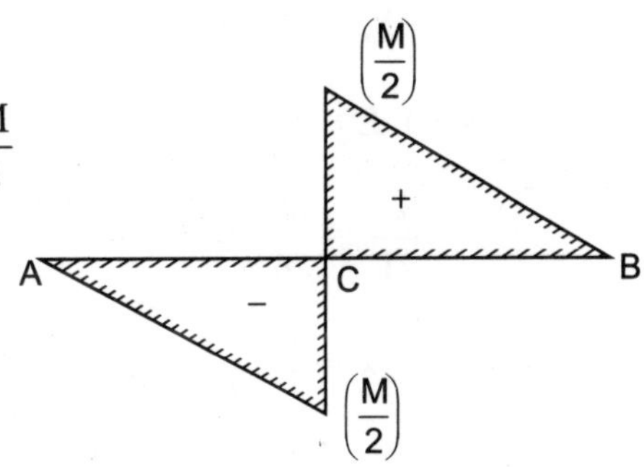

Fig. 13.139: B.M. Diagram

Example 13.36

Draw S.F. and B.M. diagrams for the beam shown in Fig. 13.140.

Solution:

1. $$R_A + R_B = \frac{\omega \cdot L}{2}$$
$$\Sigma M_B = 0$$

$$R_A \times \cancel{L} = \frac{\omega \times L}{2} \times \frac{\cancel{L}}{3}$$

$$R_A = \left(\frac{\omega \cdot L}{6}\right)$$

$$R_B = \left(\frac{2\omega L}{6}\right)$$

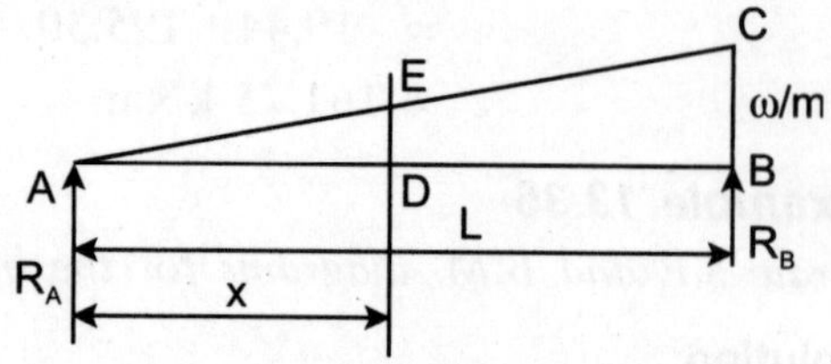

Fig. 13.140

2. *S.F.D.* $\overset{\downarrow}{+ve}$ $\overset{\uparrow}{-ve}$

$$F_B - R_B = -\frac{2\omega L}{6}$$

$$F_A = +\frac{\omega L}{6}$$

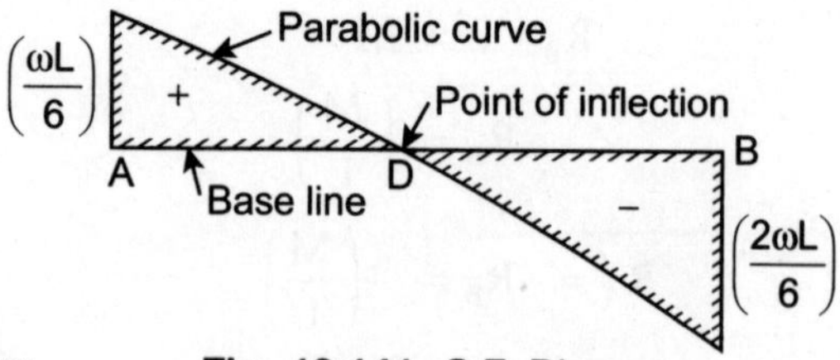

Fig. 13.141: S.F. Diagram

3. *B.M.D.:* $\underset{-ve}{\circlearrowleft}$ $\underset{+ve}{\circlearrowright}$ *for simply supported beam*

$$M_B = 0$$

$$M_A = 0$$

$$\frac{\omega}{DE} = \frac{L}{x}$$

$$DE = \left(\frac{\omega \cdot x}{L}\right)$$

$$F_x = 0$$

$$R_A - \frac{1}{2} x \times DE = 0, \Rightarrow \frac{\omega L}{6} - \frac{x}{2} \times \frac{\omega x}{L} = 0$$

$$\frac{x^2}{2L} = \frac{L}{6} \Rightarrow x^2 = \frac{2L^2}{6} = \frac{L^2}{3}$$

$$x = \left(\frac{L}{\sqrt{3}}\right)$$

$$M_D = +R_A \times x - \frac{DE \times x}{2} \times \frac{x}{3}$$

$$= \frac{\omega L}{6} \cdot x - \frac{\omega \cdot x}{L} \cdot \frac{x^2}{6}$$

$$= \frac{\omega L}{6} \cdot \frac{L}{\sqrt{3}} - \frac{\omega}{6\cancel{L}} \cdot \frac{L^2}{3} \cdot \frac{\cancel{L}}{\sqrt{3}}$$

$$= \frac{\omega L^2}{6\sqrt{3}} - \frac{\omega L^2}{6\sqrt{3}} \cdot \frac{1}{\sqrt{3}} = \frac{\omega L^2}{6\sqrt{3}} \times \frac{2}{3} = \frac{\omega L^2}{9\sqrt{3}}$$

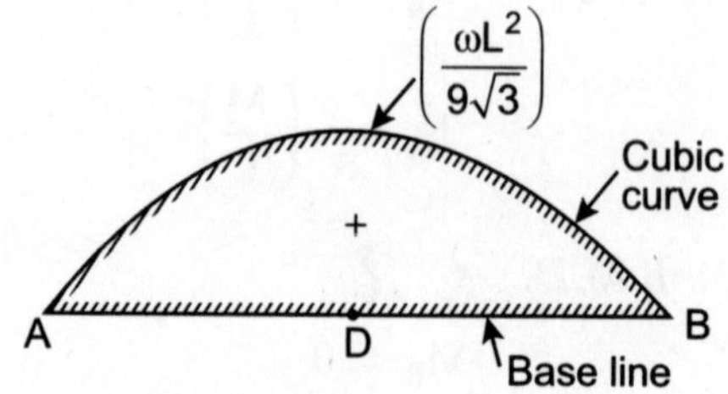

Fig. 13.142: B.M. Diagram

NUMERICAL QUESTIONS

1. A beam AB, 1.2 m long, is simply supported at its ends A and B and carries two concentrated loads one 10 kN at C, the other 15 kN at D. Point C is 0.4 m from A, point D is 1 m from A. Draw the S.F. and B.M. diagrams for the beam inserting principal values.
2. A simply supported beam, with equal overhangs on the two ends, carries a U.D.L. of 500 N/m over whole of its length. If the supported length is 10 m find the overhangs such that (a) the bending moment is zero at the centre and (b) the maximum negative and maximum positive bending moments are equal. Draw B.M. and S.F. diagrams for cases (a) and (b).
3. A cantilever beam AB, 2.5 m long, is rigidly built in at A and carries vertical concentrated load of 8 kN at B and 12 kN at C, 1 m from A. Draw S.F. and B.M. diagrams for the beam inserting principal values.
4. A beam 6 m long overhangs by 1.5 m on the left hand side and by x m on the other side. The beam carries a uniformly distributed load of 1.5 kN/m on whole its length and a concentrated load of 2 kN at the extreme left and of the beam. Find the value of x so that S.F. is zero at the centre. Hence, draw S.F. and B.M. diagrams and indicate the maximum B.M.
5. A beam AB, 5 m long, is simply supported at the end B and at a point C, 1 m from A. It carries vertical loads of 5 kN at A and 20 kN at D, the centre of the span BC. Draw S.F. and B.M. diagrams for the beam intersecting principal values.
6. A beam, 8 m long, is simply supported with overhang equal to a on both sides. The beam carries a uniformly distributed load of 20 kN/m throughout its length in addition to three equal concentrated loads of distances of 0 m, 4 m and 8 m from one end. The sum of concentrated loads is equal to the total U.D.L. over the whole beam. Determine the value of a so that beam is subjected to minimum bending moment. For this condition draw B.M. and S.F. diagrams.
7. A simply supported beam has a span of 4 m and carries a uniformly distributed load of 60 kN/m together with a central concentrated load of 40 kN. Draw the S.F. and B.M. diagrams for the beam and hence determine the maximum B.M. acting on the beam.
8. A beam, 20 m long, is simply supported with overhangs of 2 m at the left side and a m at the right side. The beam carries a concentrated load of 5 w at the extreme left end with uniformly distributed load of w per metre run over whole of the beam. Find the value of a in order that B.M. is zero at the mid-point of the beam. Hence, draw B.M. and S.F. diagrams taking w = 10 kN.
9. A beam ABCDE, with A on the left, is 7 m long and is simply supported at B and E. The lengths of the various portions are AB = 1.5 m, BC = 1.5 m CD = 1 m and DE = 3 m. There is uniformly distributed load of 15 kN/m between B and a point 2 m to the right of B and concentrated loads of 20 kN act at A and D with one of 50 kN at C.

   (a) Draw the S.F. diagrams and hence determine the position from A at which the S.F. is zero.

(b) Determine the value of the B.M. at this point.

(c) Sketch the B.M. diagram approximately to scale, quoting the principal values.

10. A beam, 9 m long, is simply supported at left end and at 6 m from left end. The beam carries a concentrated load of 15 kN at its right end in addition to a total uniformly distributed load of 8 kN on the left 3 m of the beam. Draw S.F. and B.M. diagrams giving maximum S.F. and B.M. Where does the point of contraflexure occur?
11. A beam ABCDE is simply supported at A and D. It carries the following loading: a distributed load of 30 kN/m between A and B; a concentrated load of 20 kN at C; a concentrated load of 10 kN at E; a distributed load of 60 kN/m between D and span AB = 1.5 m, BC = CD = DE = 1 m. Calculate the value of the reactions at A and D and hence draw the S.F. and B.M. diagrams. What are the magnitude and position of the maximum B.M. on the beam?
12. A beam, 8 m long, is simply supported at ends carries a concentrated load of 20 kN at the mid-span along with a uniformly distributed load of 30 kN/m over the left 2 m of the beam. Draw B.M. and S.F. diagrams.

14

Trusses

ENGINEERING STRUCTURES MAY BE CLASSIFIED AS TRUSSES, FRAMES AND MACHINES.

14.1 Trusses

Trusses are designed to support loads and are usually stationary. Trusses consist exclusively of straight members connected at joints located at the ends of each member. Members of a truss are two force members, i.e. members acted upon by two equal and opposite forces directed along the member.

14.2 Frames

Frames are also designed to support loads and are also usually stationary. But frames always contain at least one multiforce member, i.e. a member acted upon by three or more forces, which, in general, are not directed along the member.

14.3 Machines

Machines are designed to transmit and modify forces and are structures containing moving parts. Machines, like frames, always contain at least one multiforce member.

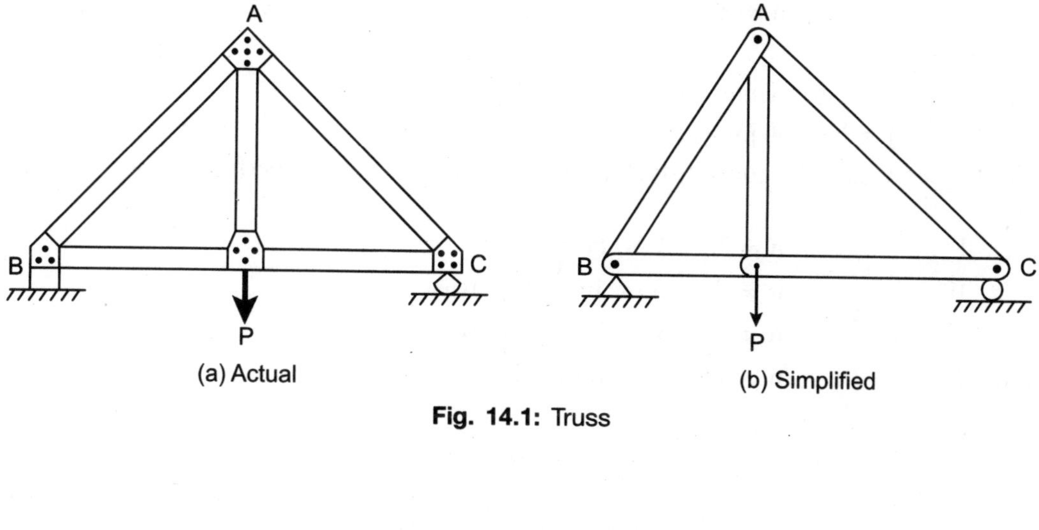

Fig. 14.1: Truss

14.4 Plane Truss

A frame work having members joined at their ends to form a rigid structure is known as a truss. Bridges, roof supports and other such structures are common examples of trusses. Structural members are I-beams, channels, angles, bars and special shapes which are fastened together at their ends by welding, riveting, bolted or pinned joints. When the members of the truss essentially lie in a single plane, the truss is known as plane truss. Plane trusses are designed in pairs with one truss panel placed on each side.

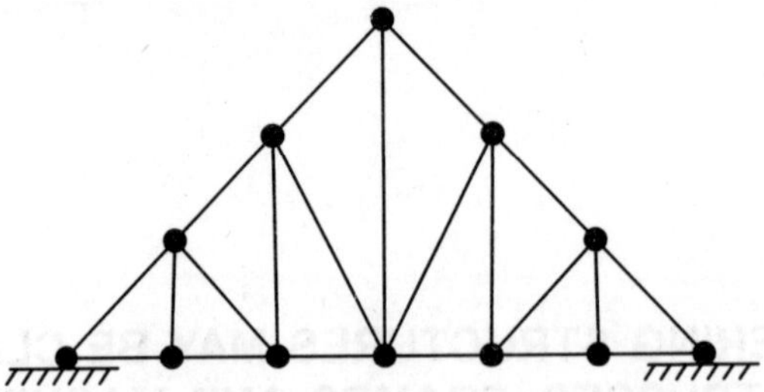

Fig. 14.2: Plane Truss (Roof Truss)

The basic element of a plane truss is the triangle. Three bars joined by pins at their ends, make a rigid frame. The term rigid is used in the sense of non-collapsible and negligible deformation of the members due to induced internal strains.

The structures which are built from a basic triangle, are known as simple trusses. When more members are added to prevent collapse, the truss is statically indeterminate. A statically indeterminate truss cannot be analysed by the equilibrium equations alone. Additional members or supports which are not necessary for maintaining the equilibrium position, are called redundant members.

14.5 Rigid or Perfect Truss

Rigid means non-collapsible when external supports are removed.

The number of members in a perfect truss may be expressed by the relation.

$$n = 2j - 3 \quad \text{.......} \quad (14.1)$$

where

n = No. of members

j = No. of joints

The trusses which do not satisfy Eq. (14.1), are known as imperfect frames or imperfect truss.

i.e. If $n = 2j - 3 \Rightarrow$ Perfect truss

If $n \neq 2j - 3 \Rightarrow$ Imperfect truss

If $n < 2j - 3 \Rightarrow$ Deficient truss (Frame)

and If $n > 2j - 3 \Rightarrow$ Redundant truss

14.6 Assumptions Made in Truss Analysis

1. All the joints are frictionless pin connections.
2. The loads on the truss are taken by the joints only.
3. The members of a truss are straight two force members.
4. The weights of the members are neglected.
5. The axes of all members lie in a single plane.
6. The truss is statically determinate.

14.7 Analysis of Truss

Various methods are

(a). Method of Joints.

(b). Method of Sections.

(c). Graphical Method.

14.7.1 Method of Joints

This method for finding the forces in the members of a simple truss consists of satisfying the conditions of equilibrium for the forces acting on each joint. There are only two independent equilibrium equations. Therefore, we begin the analysis with any joint where at least one known load exists and where not more than two unknown forces are present. In this way, taking one by one joints, forces in all members may be calculated.

Example 14.1

Find the forces in all members of the truss as shown in Fig. 14.3.

Solution:

(1) *Reactions:*

$$R_B + R_C = 10 \;.............\; (14.2)$$

$$\Sigma M_B = 0$$

$$\Rightarrow \quad R_C \times 5 = 10 \times BD$$

$$= 10 \times AB \cos 60$$

$$= 10 \times BC \cos 60 \times \cos 60$$

$$= 10 \times 5 \times \frac{1}{4}$$

$$\therefore \quad R_C = \frac{10 \times 5}{5 \times 4} = \frac{5}{2} = 2.5 \text{ t}$$

$$\text{and} \quad R_B = 10 - 2.5 = 7.5 \text{ t}$$

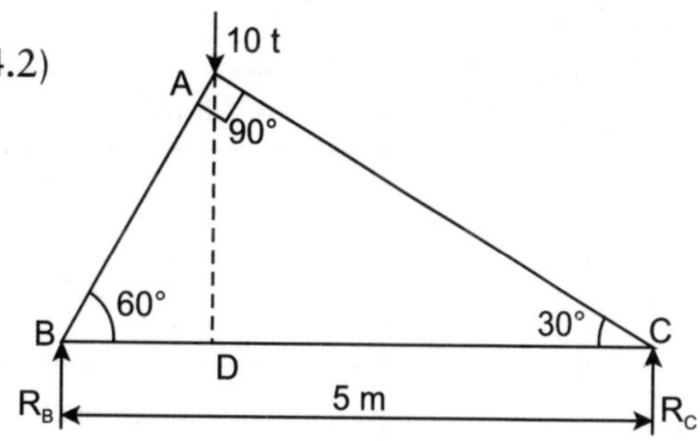

Fig. 14.3

(2) *Using method of joints:*

Considering the equilibrium of Joint B:

$$\Sigma F_x = 0$$

$$\Rightarrow \quad F_{BC} = F_{AB} \cos 60°$$

$$\Rightarrow \quad F_{BC} = \left(\frac{F_{AB}}{2}\right) \quad \ldots\ldots \quad (14.3)$$

and $\quad \Sigma F_y = 0$

$$R_B = F_{AB} \sin 60$$

$$7.5 = F_{AB}\frac{\sqrt{3}}{2}$$

$$\Rightarrow \quad F_{AB} = \frac{7.5\times 2}{\sqrt{3}} = \frac{15}{\sqrt{3}}$$

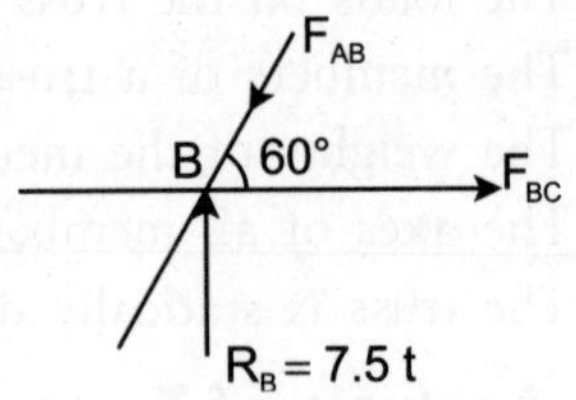

Fig. 14.4

$$\therefore \quad F_{AB} = \frac{15}{\sqrt{3}} \text{ t (Compressive)} \quad \ldots\ldots \quad (14.4)$$

From Eq. (14.3), $F_{BC} = \frac{15}{2\sqrt{3}} = \frac{7.5}{\sqrt{3}}$ t

$$\therefore \quad F_{BC} = \frac{7.5}{\sqrt{3}} \text{ tensile}$$

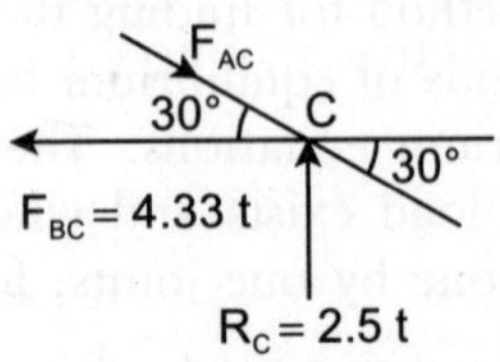

Fig. 14.5

Now, Considering the equilibrium of Joint C:

$$\Sigma F_y = 0$$

$$\Rightarrow \quad F_{AC} \sin 30 = 2.5$$

$$F_{AC} = 2.5 \times 2 = 5 \text{ t}$$

$$F_{AC} = 5 \text{ t (Compressive)}$$

∴

Member	*Force with Nature*
AB	$\frac{15}{\sqrt{3}}$ t (Compressive)
AC	5 t (Compressive)
BC	$\frac{7.5}{\sqrt{3}}$ t (tensile)

Note: Assume any direction of force in the member arbitrarily. If the direction of force in a member is towards the joint then it is compressive as F_{AB} in Fig. 14.1. But if it is away from the joint, then it is tensile as F_{BC} (Fig. 14.4).

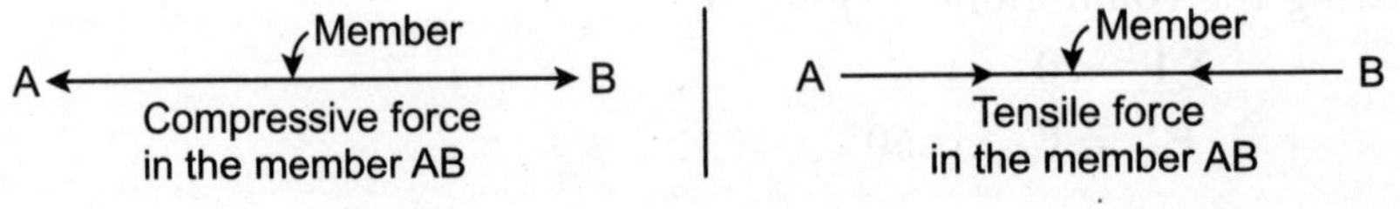

Example 14.2

Calculate the forces in each member of the loaded cantilever truss by the methods of joints.

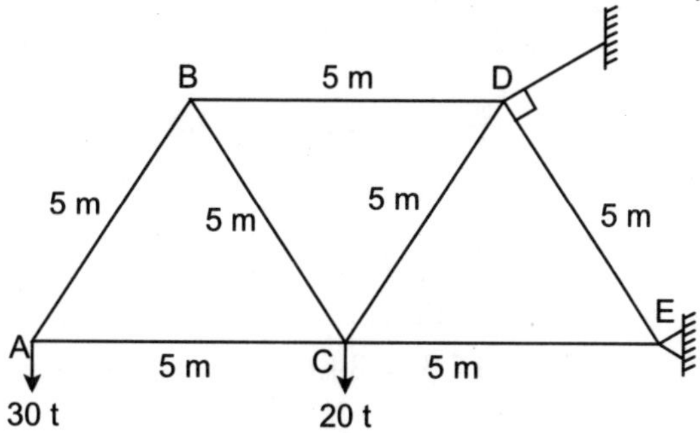

Fig. 14.6

Solution:

1. *Reactions:*

$$\Sigma M_E = 0$$
$$30 \times 10 + 20 \times 5 = T \times 5$$
$$T = 60 + 20 = 80 \text{ t}$$
$$\Sigma F_x = 0$$
$$\Rightarrow \quad R_H = T\cos 30°$$
$$\Rightarrow \quad R_H = 80\cos 30° = 69.28 \text{ t}$$
$$\Sigma F_y = 0$$
$$\Rightarrow \quad R_V + T\sin 30° = 30 + 20$$
$$\Rightarrow \quad R_V = -80 \times \frac{1}{2} + 50 = 10 \text{ t}$$

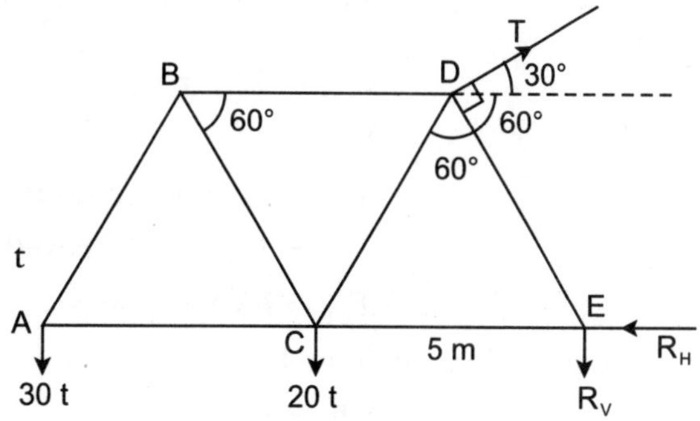

Fig. 14.7

2. Joint A: There should be no question about the correct direction of the forces on Joint A.

$$\Sigma F_y = 0$$
$$\Rightarrow \quad F_{AB}\sin 60° - 30 = 0$$
$$F_{AB} = 30 \times \frac{2}{\sqrt{3}} = \frac{60}{\sqrt{3}} = 34.6 \text{ t (tensile)}$$
$$\therefore \quad F_{AB} = 34.6 \text{ t (tensile)}$$
$$\Sigma F_x = 0$$
$$\Rightarrow \quad F_{AB}\cos 60° = F_{AC}$$
$$\Rightarrow \quad F_{AC} = +34.6 \times \frac{1}{2} = 17.3 \text{ t (Comp.)}$$

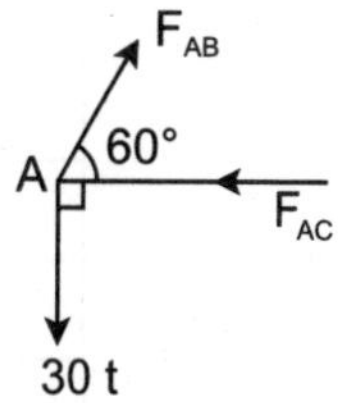

Fig. 14.8

3. Equilibrium of Joint B:

$$\Sigma F = 0$$

$$\Rightarrow \quad F_{BD} = F_{AB}\cos60° + F_{BC}\cos60°$$

$$\Rightarrow \quad F_{BD} = 34.6 \times \frac{1}{2} + F_{BC} \times \frac{1}{2}$$

$$\Rightarrow \quad F_{BD} = 17.3 + \frac{F_{BC}}{2} \quad \ldots\ldots\ldots (14.5)$$

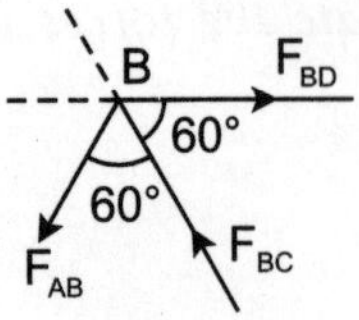

Fig. 14.9

$$\Sigma F_y = 0$$

$$\Rightarrow \quad F_{AB}\sin60 = F_{BC}\sin60° \Rightarrow F_{AB} = F_{BC} = 34.6 \text{ t}$$

$$\therefore \quad F_{BC} = 34.6 \text{ t (Comp.)} \ldots\ldots\ldots\ldots\ldots\ldots\ldots\ldots\ldots\ldots\ldots\ldots (14.6)$$

From Eq. (14.5), $F_{BD} = 17.3 + 17.3 = 34.6 \text{ t} \Rightarrow F_{BD} = 34.6 \text{ t (tensile)}$

4. Equilibrium of Joint C:

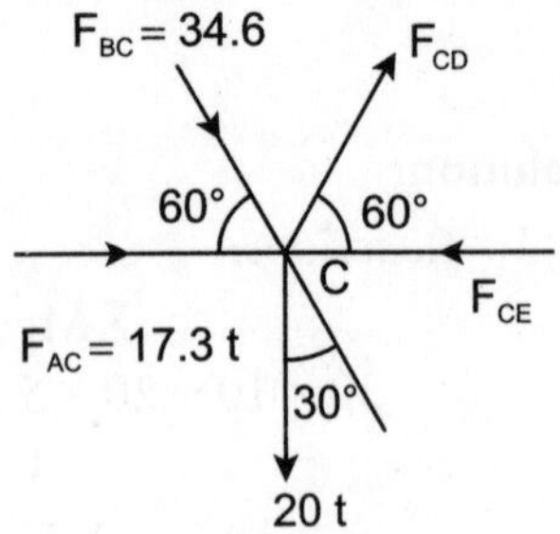

Fig. 14.10

$$\Sigma F_y = 0$$

$$\Rightarrow \quad F_{CD}\sin60 = 20 + F_{BC}\sin60°$$

$$\Rightarrow \quad F_{CD}\sin60 = 20 + 34.6° \times \frac{\sqrt{3}}{2}$$

$$F_{CD} = 57.7 \text{ t (tensile)}$$

$$\Sigma F_x = 0$$

$$\Rightarrow \quad F_{CE} = F_{AC} + F_{CD}\cos60° + F_{BC}\cos60°$$

$$= 17.3 + 57.7\cos60° + 34.6\cos60° = 63.5 \text{ t}$$

$$F_{CE} = 63.5 \text{ t Comp.}$$

5. Equilibrium of Joint E:

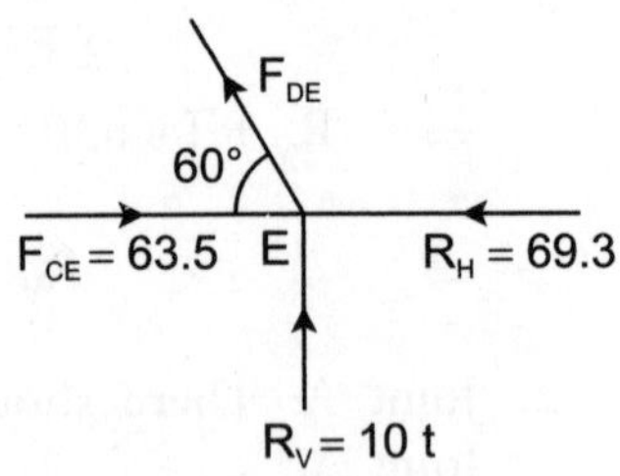

Fig. 14.11

$$\Sigma F_x = 0$$

$$\Rightarrow \quad F_{DE}\cos60° = 63.5 - 69.3$$

$$F_{DE} = -11.6 \text{ t}$$

$$\therefore \quad F_{DE} = +11.6 \text{ t (Comp.)}$$

Finally

Member	*Force with Nature*
AB	34.6 (Tensile)
AC	17.3 t (Comp.)
BC	34.6 (Comp.)
BD	34.6 (Comp.)
CD	57.7 t (Tensile)
CE	63.5 t (Comp.)
DE	11.6 t (Comp.)

Example 14.3

Calculate the force in each member of the truss.

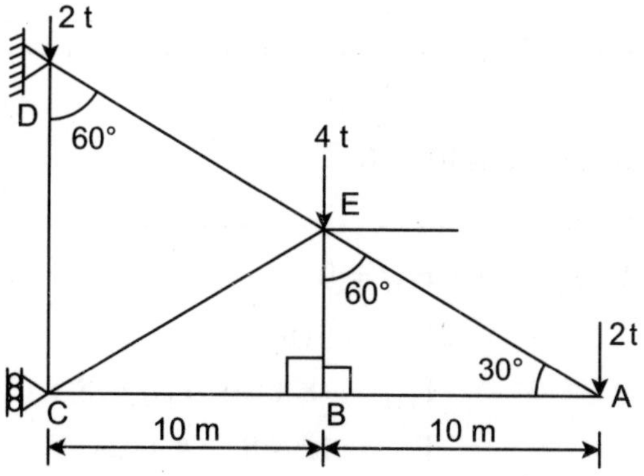

Fig. 14.12

Solution:

In this case we need not to calculate the reactions, R_C and R_D for finding the forces in the members.

We can use method of joints:

1. Equilibrium of joint A:

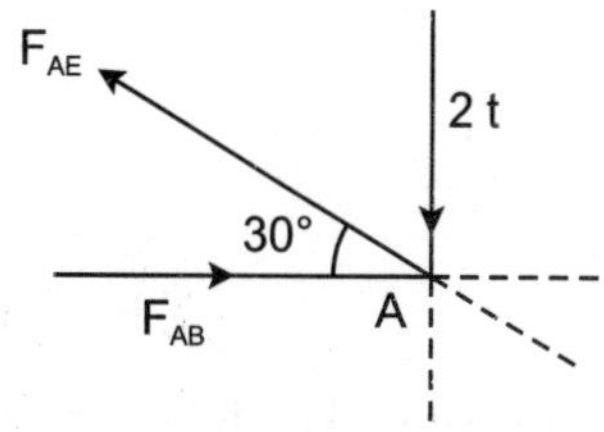

Fig. 14.13

$$\Sigma F_y = 0$$
$$F_{AE} \sin 30 = 2$$
$$F_{AE} = 2 \times 2 = 4 \text{ t}$$
$$F_{AE} = 4 \text{ t (Tensile)}$$
$$\Sigma F_x = 0$$
$$F_{AB} = F_{AE} \cos 30° = 4 \frac{\sqrt{3}}{2} \text{ t}$$
$$F_{AB} = 2\sqrt{3} \text{ t (Comp.)}$$

2. Joint B:

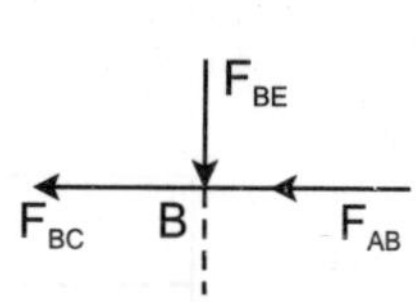

Fig. 14.14

$$\Sigma F_y = 0$$
$$\therefore \quad F_{BE} = 0$$
$$\Sigma F_x = 0$$
$$F_{BC} + F_{AB} = 0$$
$$F_{BC} = -F_{AB} = -2\sqrt{3} \text{ t}$$
$$\therefore \quad F_{BC} = +2\sqrt{3} \text{ t (Comp.)}$$

3. Joint E:

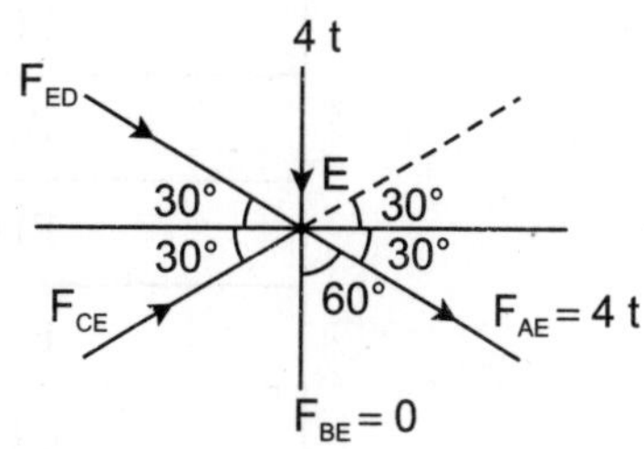

Fig. 14.15

$$\Sigma F_y = 0$$
$$\Rightarrow \quad F_{CE} \sin 30 = 4 + 4 \cos 60° + F_{ED} \cos 60°$$

$$\Rightarrow \quad F_{CE} \times \frac{1}{2} = 4 + 2 + F_{ED} \times \frac{1}{2}$$

$$\Rightarrow \quad F_{CE} = 12 + F_{ED} \quad \text{.......... (14.7)}$$

and $\quad \Sigma F_x = 0$

$$\Rightarrow F_{CE} \cos 30 + 4 \cos 30 + F_{ED} \cos 30 = 0$$

$$\Rightarrow \quad F_{CE} + 4 + F_{ED} = 0 \quad \text{.......... (14.8)}$$

$$\Rightarrow \quad 12 + F_{ED} + 4 + F_{ED} = 0 \quad \text{[From Eq. (14.7)]}$$

$$\Rightarrow \quad 2F_{ED} = -16$$

$$F_{ED} = -8 \text{ t} \Rightarrow F_{ED} = 8 \text{ t (Tensile)}$$

and $\quad F_{CE} = 12 - 8 = 4 \text{ t} \Rightarrow F_{CE} = 4 \text{ t (Comp.)}$

4. Joint C:

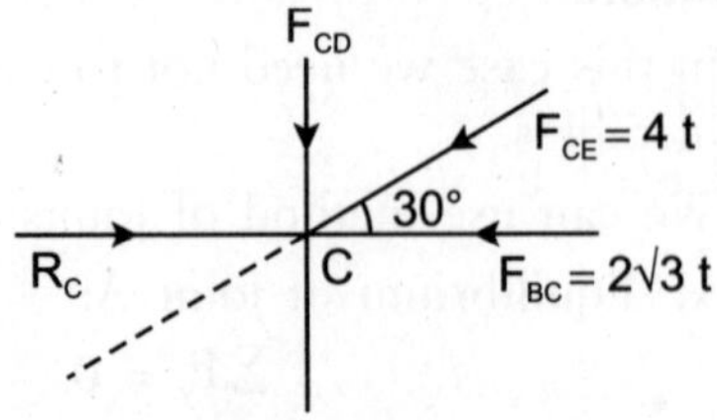

Fig. 14.16

$$\Sigma F_x = 0$$

$$\Rightarrow \quad R_C = 2\sqrt{3} + 4 \cos 30°$$

$$= 2\sqrt{3} + 4 \times \frac{\sqrt{3}}{2}$$

$$R_C = 4\sqrt{3}$$

$$\Sigma F_y = 0$$

$$\Rightarrow F_{CD} + F_{CE} \sin 30° = 0$$

$$\Rightarrow F_{CD} = -4 \sin 30° = -2 \text{ t}$$

$$F_{CD} = 2 \text{ t (Tensile)}$$

Now

Member	*Force with Nature*
AB	$2\sqrt{3}$ t (Comp.)
AE	4 t (Tensile)
BC	$2\sqrt{3}$ t (Comp.)
BE	0
ED	8 t (Tensile)
EC	4 t (Comp.)
CD	2 t (Tensile)

14.7.2 Method of Sections or Methods of Moments

When the forces in all the members of a truss are to be determined, the method of joints is most suitable. However, the forces in only one member or a few members of the truss are to be calculated, the method of section is more suitable.

Procedure:

1. Calculate reactions at the supports.
2. Take a section passing through maximum three members of the truss, including the members in which the forces are to be calculated.
3. This section should divide the truss into two completely separate parts.
4. Either of the two portions of the truss (left or right of the section) is to be used as a free body.
5. Using the equilibrium equations, unknown forces may be calculated.
6. Moments can be taken about any convenient point, which may or may not lie on the section under consideration.

Example 14.4

Calculate the force in the members BC, BD and BE of the truss as shown in Fig. 14.17.

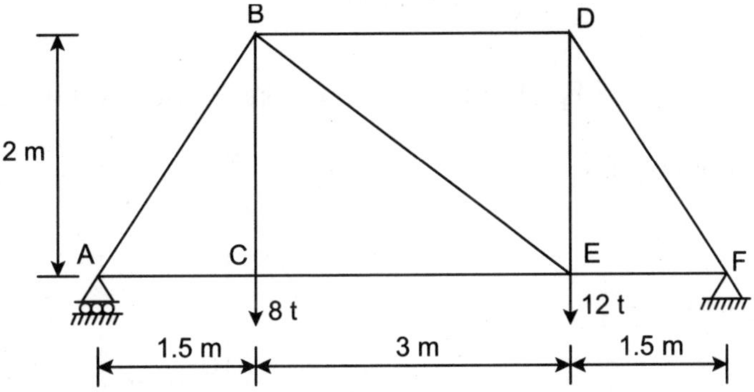

Fig. 14.17

Solution:

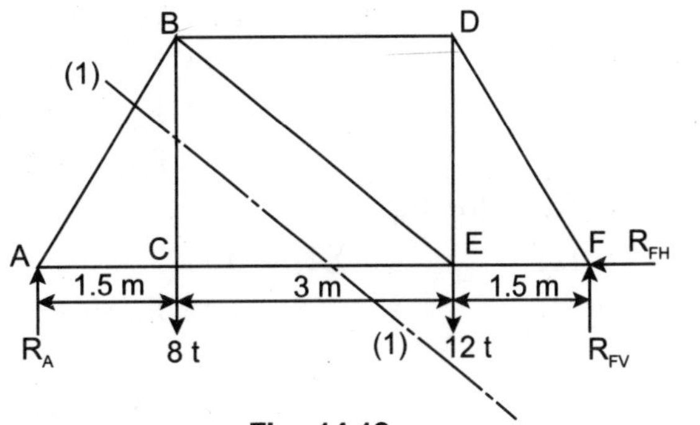

Fig. 14.18

$$F_{BC} = ?,\ F_{BD} = ?,\ F_{BE} = ?$$

1. *Reactions*

$$\Sigma F_x = 0$$

$$\Rightarrow \quad R_{FH} = 0$$

$$\Sigma F_y = 0$$

$$R_A + R_{FV} = 12 + 8$$

or $$R_A + R_{FV} = 20 \ldots\ldots \quad (14.9)$$

$$\Sigma M_A = 0$$

$$R_{FV} \times 6 = 12 \times 4.5 + 8 \times 1.5$$
$$6R_{FV} = 54 + 12 = 66$$
$$R_{FV} = 11 \text{ t}$$
and $$R_A = 20 - 11 = 9 \text{ t}$$

(2) Take a section cutting member BC, BA and CE. Considering equilibrium of left of the section:

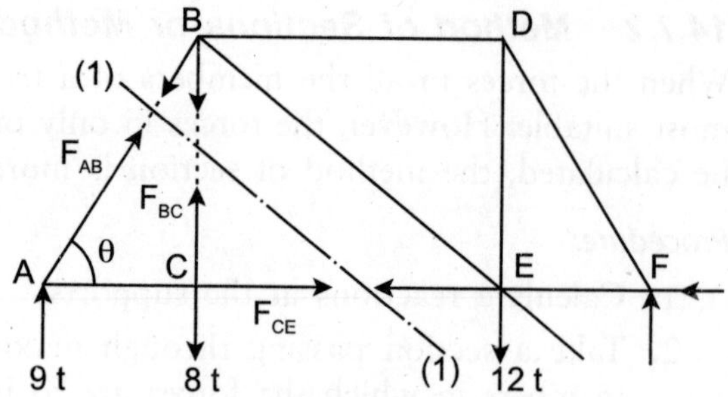

Fig. 14.19

$$\tan\theta = \frac{2}{1.5}$$
$$\theta = 53.13°$$

Equilibrium of left part of the section only:

Now,

From here, we have to find out force in member BC, i.e. F_{BC}. For this, we have to find the suitable point about which moment can be taken. Here, point A is suitable point.

$$\therefore \quad \Sigma M_A = 0 \Rightarrow F_{BC} \times AC = 8 \times AC$$
$$\Rightarrow F_{BC} = \textbf{8 t tensile}$$ **Ans.**

Now,

We have to find F_{BD} and F_{BE}. For this, we can take another section (2)-(2), as shown in Fig. 14.20.

$$F_{BD} = ?$$
$$F_{BE} = ?$$
$$\tan\theta_1 = \frac{2}{3}$$
$$\theta_1 = 33.7°$$

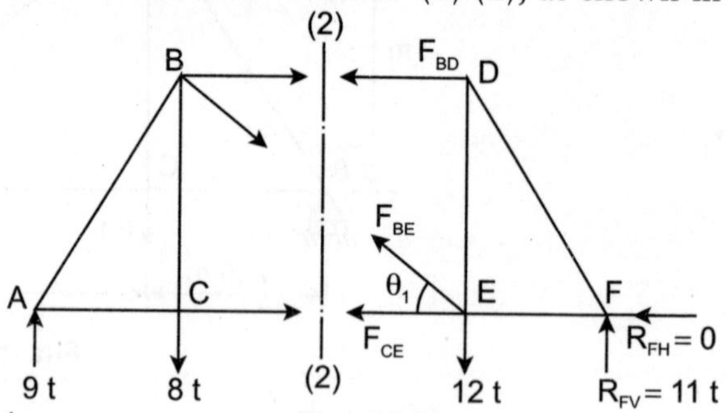

Fig. 14.20

For equilibrium of right part of the section.

$$\Sigma M_E = 0 \Rightarrow F_{BD} \times DE = -R_{FV} \times EF$$
$$\Rightarrow F_{BD} \times 2 = -11 \times 1.5$$
$$\Rightarrow F_{BD} = -8.25 \text{ t}$$
$$\therefore \quad F_{BD} = \textbf{8.25 t (Comp.)}$$ **Ans.**

Now, for F_{BE}

Let $$\Sigma F_y = 0$$ (we are considering right portion only)

$$\Rightarrow F_{BE} \sin\theta + 11 - 12 = 0$$
$$\Rightarrow F_{BE} = \frac{+1}{\text{Sin } 33.7} = 1.8 \text{ t}$$
$$\Rightarrow F_{BE} = \textbf{1.8 t tensile}$$ **Ans.**

or

$$\Sigma M_F = 0$$

$$\Rightarrow F_{BE} \sin\theta \times 1.5 = 12 \times 1.5 + F_{BD} \times 2$$

$$\Rightarrow F_{BE} \sin\theta \times 1.5 = 18 - 8.25 \times 2$$

$\left[\because F_{BD} \text{ is Comp. Hence, -ve sign is used}\right]$

$$\Rightarrow F_{BE} = \frac{1.5}{1.5 \times \text{Sin } 33.7} = 1.8 \text{ t}$$

$\therefore$ $\Rightarrow$ F_{BE} = **1.8 t tensile** **Ans.**

Example 14.5

Determine the stresses in BD, BE and CE of the truss as shown in Fig. 14.21.

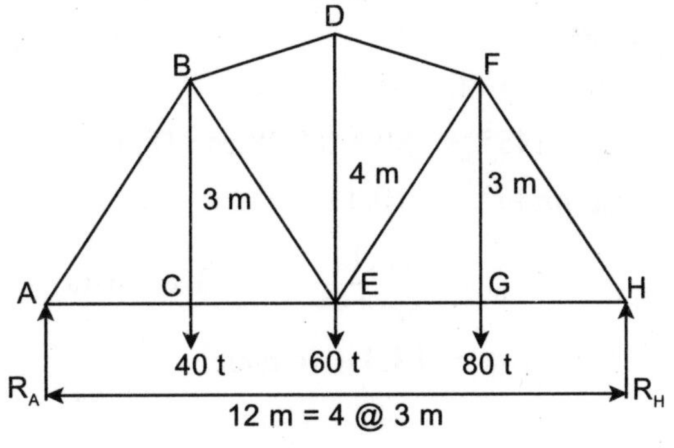

Fig. 14.21

Solution:

$$F_{BD} = ?; F_{BE} = ?; F_{CE} = ?$$

(1) Calculation of Reactions:

$$R_A + R_H = 40 + 60 + 80 = 180$$

$$R_A + R_H = 180 \ldots\ldots\ldots\ldots (14.10)$$

$$\Sigma M_A = 0$$

$$\Rightarrow R_H \times 12 = 80 \times 9 + 60 \times 6 + 40 \times 3$$

$$R_H = (720 + 360 + 120)/12$$

$$R_H = 100 \text{ t}$$

$$R_A = 80 \text{ t}$$

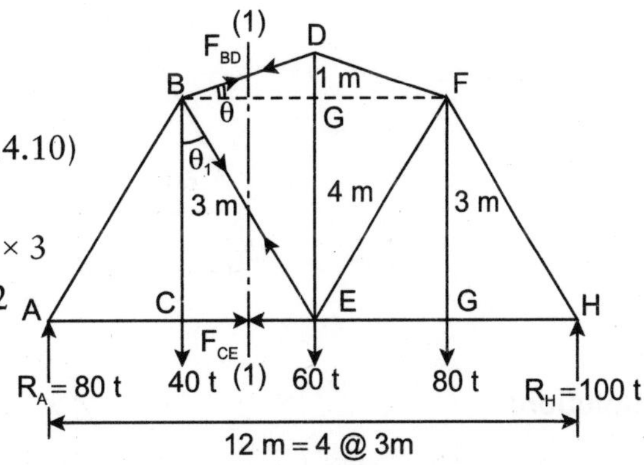

Fig. 14.22

$$\tan\theta = \frac{DG}{BG} = \frac{1}{3} \Rightarrow \theta = 18.43°$$

(2) Taking a section (1)-(1) as shown in the Fig. 14.22. Considering equilibrium of left portion of the section

$$\Sigma M_E = 0 \Rightarrow R_A \times 6 = 40 \times 3 - F_{BD} \times \cos\theta \times EG - F_{BD} \sin\theta \times 3$$

$$\Rightarrow 80 \times 6 = 120 - F_{BD} \times \cos 18.43 \times 3 - F_{BD} \sin 18.43 \times 3$$

$$\Rightarrow 480 = 120 - F_{BD} \times (3.79)$$

$$F_{BD} = \frac{-360}{3.79} \text{ t} = -94.98 \text{ t}$$

∴ $\Rightarrow$ $F_{BD} = -94.98$ **t (Comp.)** **Ans.**

Now

$$M_B = 0 \Rightarrow F_{CE} \times BC = R_A \times AC$$

$$\Rightarrow F_{CE} \times 3 = 80 \times 3$$

$\Rightarrow$ $F_{CE} = 80$ **t (tensile)** **Ans.**

Now

For left portion, $\theta_1 = 45°$

$\Sigma F_x = 0$; F_{BD} is compressive, so –ve sign is used.

$$F_{BE} \sin\theta_1 + F_{BD} \cos\theta + F_{CE} = 0$$

$$F_{BE} \sin 45° - 94.98 \cos 18.43° + 80 = 0$$

$$F_{BE} \sin 45° = -80 + 94.98 \cos 18.43°$$

$$F_{BE} \sin 45° = +10.11$$

or $$F_{BE} = \frac{10.11}{\text{Sin}45°} = 14.3 \text{ t tensile}$$

∴ $F_{BD} = 14.3$ **t (tensile)** **Ans.**

Example 14.6

Calculate the forces in the members AC and AB of the truss loaded as shown the Fig. 14.23.

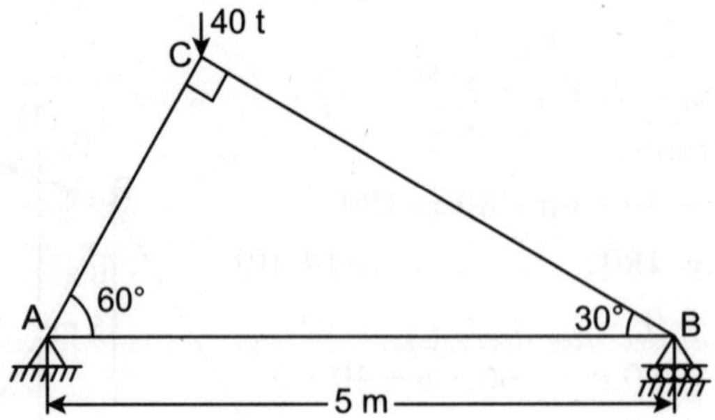

Fig. 14.23

Solution:

$F_{AC} = ?$

$F_{AB} = ?$

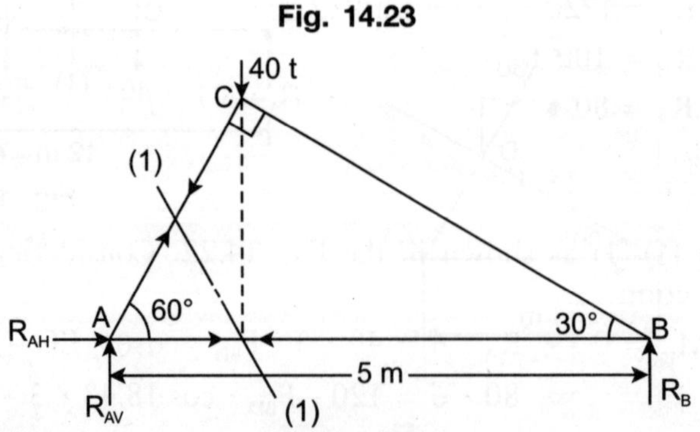

Fig. 14.24

(1) Reactions:

$$\Sigma F_x = 0 \Rightarrow \quad R_{AH} = 0$$

$$\Sigma F_y = 0 \Rightarrow R_{AV} + R_B = 40 \quad \ldots\ldots (14.11)$$

$$\Sigma M_A = 0 \Rightarrow \quad R_B \times 5 = 40 \times AC\cos 60°$$

$$\Rightarrow \quad R_B \times 5 = 40 \times \cos 60°\ AB\cos 60°$$

$$R_B = \frac{40 \times 5}{5} \times \frac{1}{4} = 10 \text{ t}$$

$$R_{AV} = 30 \text{ t}$$

(2) Using method of sections:

Taking section (1)-(1); considering equilibrium of left portion of the section.

$$\Sigma M_C = 0 \qquad \text{(for left portion only)}$$

$$\Rightarrow 30 \times AC\cos 60° = F_{AB}\ AC\sin 60°$$

$$\Rightarrow F_{AB} = 30\cot 60° = 17.32 \text{ t}$$

$\therefore$ F_{AB} = **17.32 t (tensile)** **Ans.**

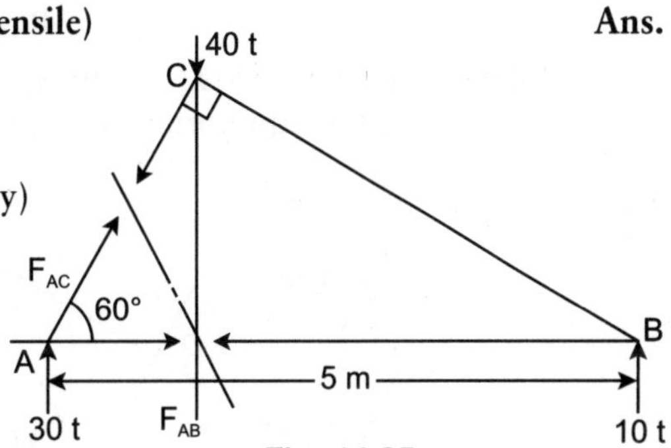

Fig. 14.25

Now

$$\Sigma M_B = 0 \text{ (for left portion only)}$$

$$30 \times 5 + F_{AC} \times \text{Sin}60° \times 5 = 0$$

$$\therefore \quad F_{AC} = \frac{-3}{\sin 60°}$$

$$= -34.64 \text{ t}$$

$\therefore$ F_{AC} = **34.64 t (Comp.)** **Ans.**

Example 14.7

Calculate the axial forces in the members CE, CG and FG of the truss as shown in Fig. 14.26.

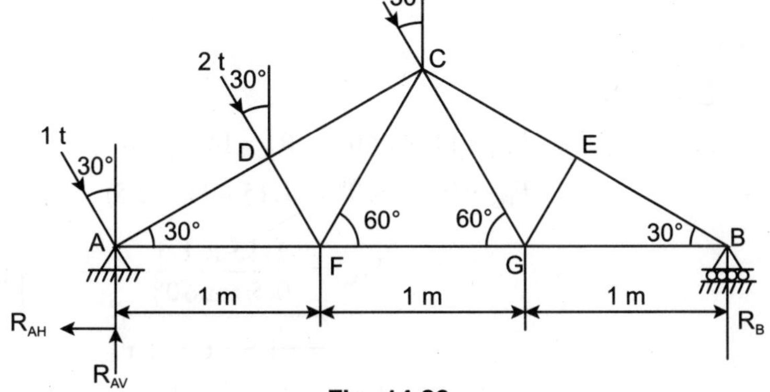

Fig. 14.26

Solution:

$F_{CE} = ?$

$F_{CG} = ?$

$F_{FG} = ?$

(1) Reactions are shown in Fig. 14.26

$$\Sigma F_y = 0 \Rightarrow R_{AV} + R_B = 1\cos 30 + 2\cos 30 + 1\cos 30 = 4\cos 30. \quad (14.12)$$

$$\Sigma F_x = 0 \Rightarrow \quad R_{AH} = 1\sin 30 + 2\sin 30 + 1\sin 30 = 4\sin 30.. \quad (14.13)$$

$$\Sigma M_A = 0 \Rightarrow \quad R_B \times 3 = 1 \times 0 + 2 \times AD + 1 \times AC$$

$$\Rightarrow \quad R_B \times 3 = 2 \times AF\cos 30 + 1 \times AG\cos 30$$

$$R_B \times 3 = (2 \times 1 + 1 \times 2)\cos 30°$$

$$\Rightarrow \quad R_B = \frac{4\cos 30}{3} = 1.15 \text{ t } (\uparrow)$$

$$R_{AV} = 4\cos 30 - 1.15 = 2.31 \text{ t } (\uparrow)$$

$$R_{AH} = 2 \text{ t } (\leftarrow)$$

(2) Taking a section (1)-(1) as shown in Fig. 14.27. The truss is divided into two parts, considering the equilibrium of right portion of the section.

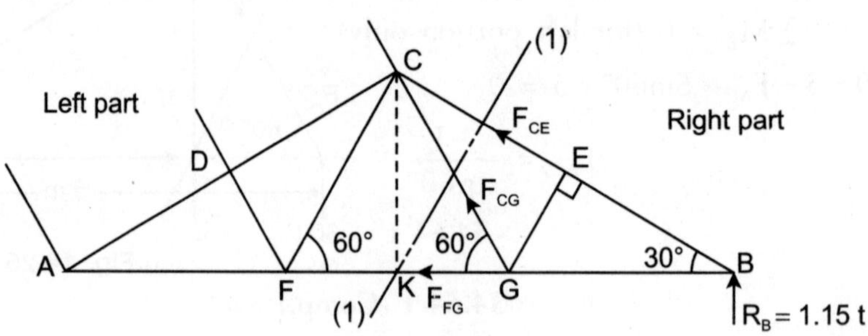

Fig. 14.27

Now

Taking moment about point C

$$\Sigma M_C = 0$$

$$\Rightarrow \quad F_{FG} \times FC\sin 60° = R_B \times BC\sin 30°$$

or $$F_{FG} \times 05\tan 60° = 1.15 \times (1 + 0.5)$$

or $$F_{FG} = \frac{1.15 \times 1.5}{0.5\tan 60°}$$

$$\left[\begin{array}{c} \because \tan 60 = \dfrac{CK}{FK} \\ CK = FK\tan 60° \\ FK = \dfrac{FG}{2} = \dfrac{1}{2}\text{m} \end{array}\right]$$

$$= +1.99 \text{ t} = 2 \text{ t}$$

$$F_{FG} = \mathbf{2 \text{ t (tensile)}}$$ **Ans.**

Now

$$\Sigma M_G = 0$$

$$\Rightarrow R_B \times BG + F_{CE} \times BG \sin 30° = 0$$

$$F_{CE} = \frac{-1.15 \times 1}{1 \times \sin 30°} = -2.3 \text{ t}$$

$\therefore$ $$F_{CE} = \mathbf{+2.3 \ t \ (Comp.)}$$ **Ans.**

Now

For right portion also

$$\Sigma M_B = 0 \Rightarrow F_{CG} \times \sin 60° \times 1 = 0$$

$$\Rightarrow \quad F_{CG} = \mathbf{0}$$ **Ans.**

THEORETICAL AND NUMERICAL QUESTIONS

1. Determine the force in each member of the loaded truss as shown in Fig. 14.28.

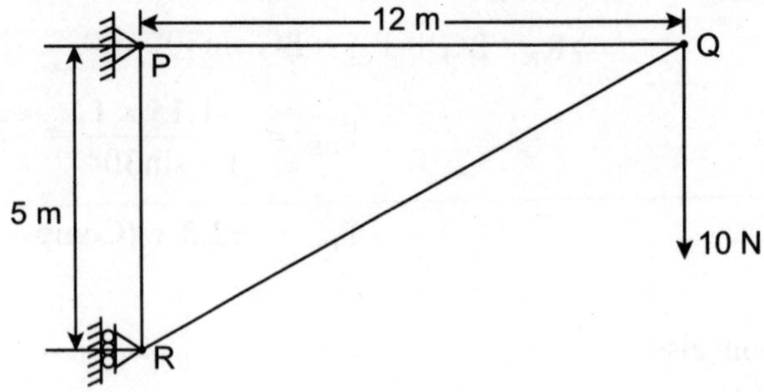

Fig. 14.28

2. Determine the forces in each member of the loaded truss.

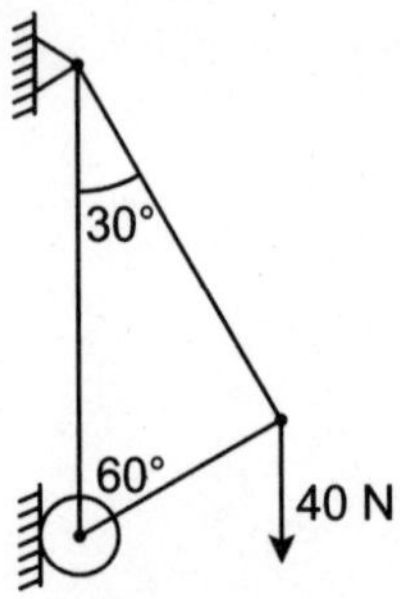

Fig. 14.29

3. Determine the force in each member of the truss.

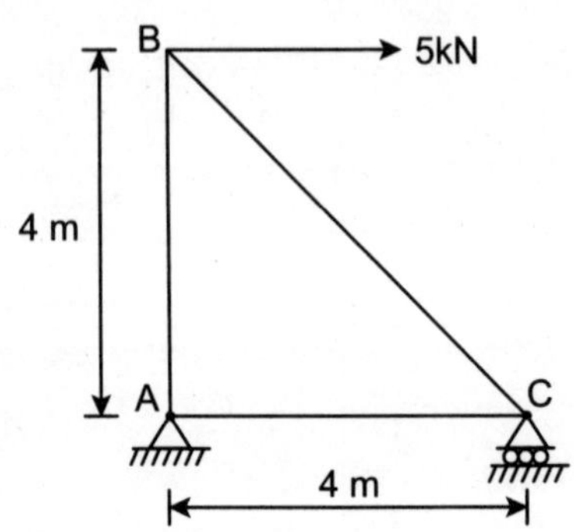

Fig. 14.30

4. When do you prefer the method of sections?
5. Explain the method of joints for analysis of trusses.
6. What do you mean by a simple truss?

7. A crane is shown in Fig. 14.31. The length of member AD is 4 m, all other members are 2 m long. Find the forces in all the members due to a vertical load of 100 t at point E.

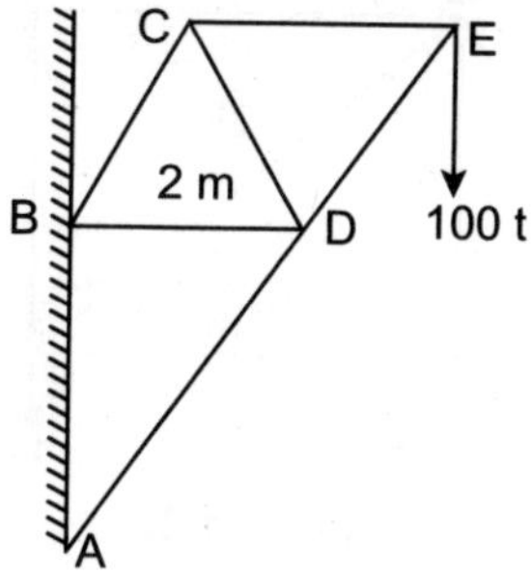

Fig. 14.31

8. Find the forces in the members of the truss as shown in Fig. 14.32.

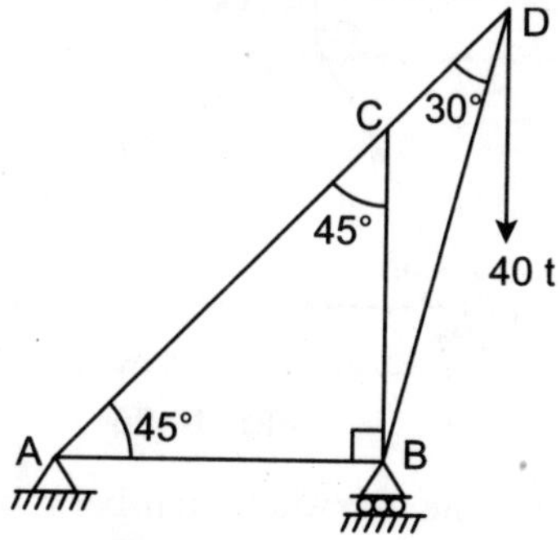

Fig. 14.32

9. Determine by method of sections, the axial force in the members 1, 2 and 3 of the plane truss.

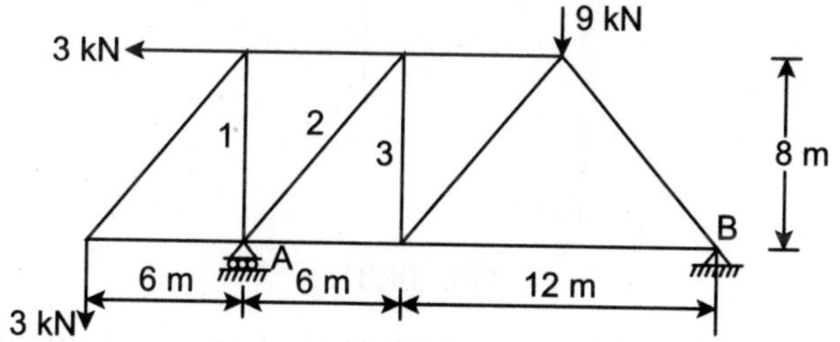

Fig. 14.33

10. Determine the force in each member of the loaded truss. All triangles are isosceles.

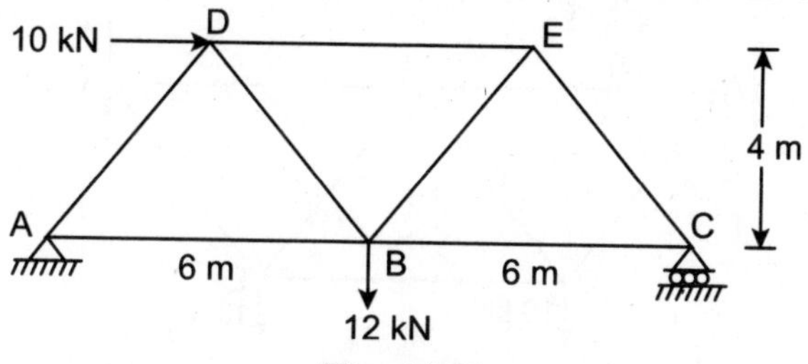

Fig. 14.34

11. Calculate the force in the members BC, BE and EF of the truss as shown in Fig. 14.35.

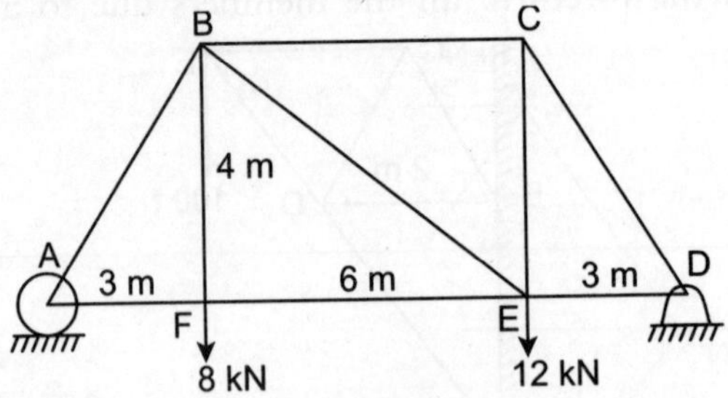

Fig. 14.35

12. Determine the forces in the members AC and AB of a simple triangular truss as shown in Fig. 14.36, use method of sections.

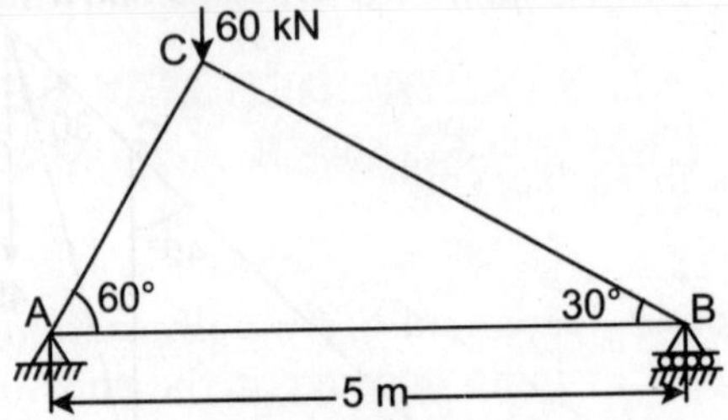

Fig. 14.36

13. Determine the forces in the various members of a pin jointed truss as shown in Fig. 14.37.

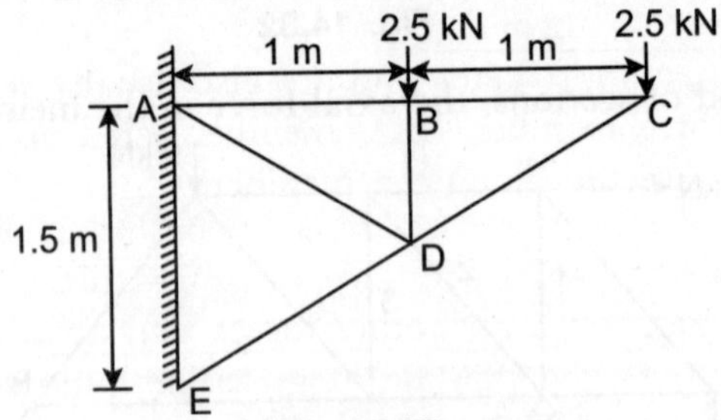

Fig. 14.37

14. The truss as shown in Fig. 14.38, is supported at the wall on the right hand side and by a cable on the left. Determine tension in the cable, the reaction on the wall and forces in each member.

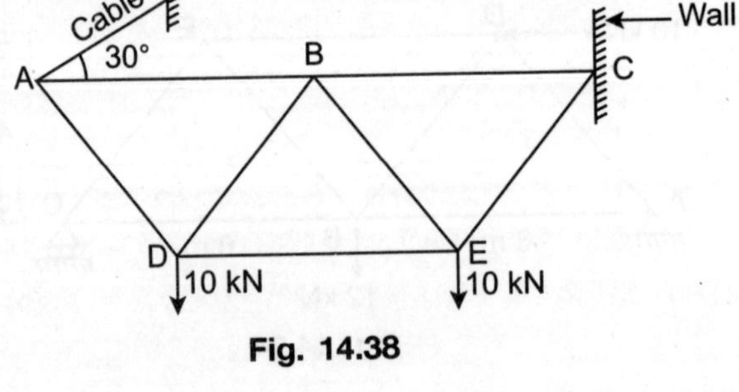

Fig. 14.38

15. A hexagonal truss made of 11 bars of 3 m length each. It is hinged at one end and roller supported at the other end. Find the force in the members CD and GB.

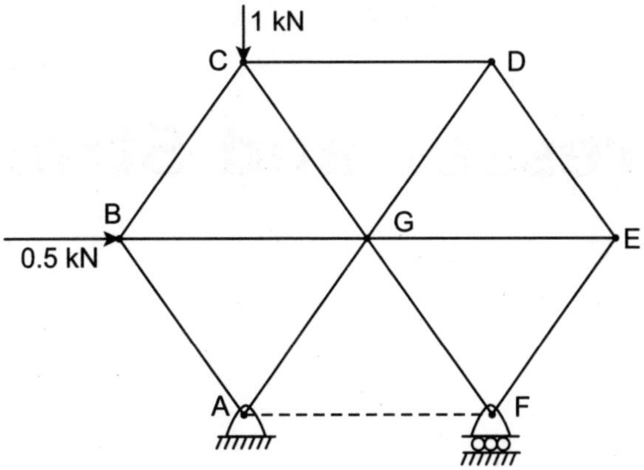

Fig. 14.39

16. Determine the forces in each member of the truss shown in Fig. 14.40.

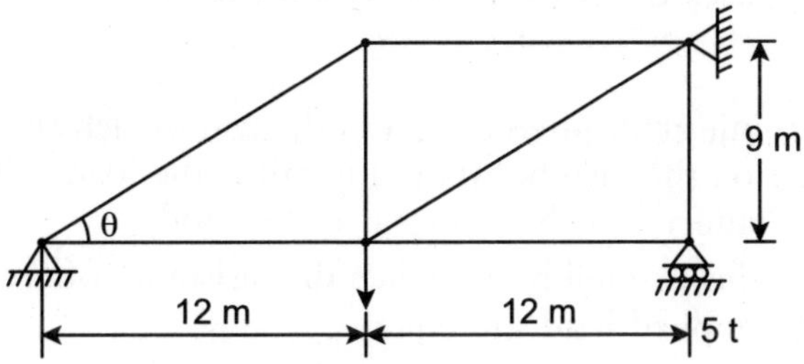

Fig. 14.40

15

Simple Stresses and Strains

15.1 Introduction

When an external force acts on a body, the body tends to undergo some deformation. Due to cohesion between the molecules, the body resists the deformation. This resistance by which the material of the body opposes the deformation is known as strength of material.

15.2 Stress

The resistance force per unit area, offered by a body against deformation is known as stress. The external force acting on the member (body) is called the load. The load is applied on the body while the stress is induced in the material of the body.

A loaded member remains in equilibrium when the resistance offered by the member against the deformation and the applied load are equal.

$$\therefore \qquad \text{Stress } (\sigma) = \frac{\text{Resistance offered by the material (R)}}{\text{Cross-sectional area of the member (A)}}$$

$$\text{or} \qquad (\sigma) = \frac{R}{A} = \frac{P}{A} = \frac{\text{External load (N)}}{\text{X-sectional area (mm}^2\text{)}}$$

Tensile Stress:

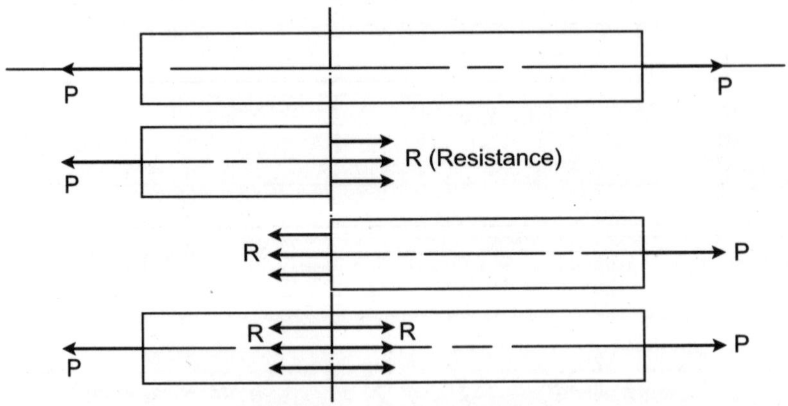

Fig. 15.1: Simple Tension

Tensile stress $(\sigma) = \frac{R}{A} = \frac{P}{A} = \frac{\text{Pull (N)}}{\text{X-sectional area (mm}^2)}$

Compressive Stress:

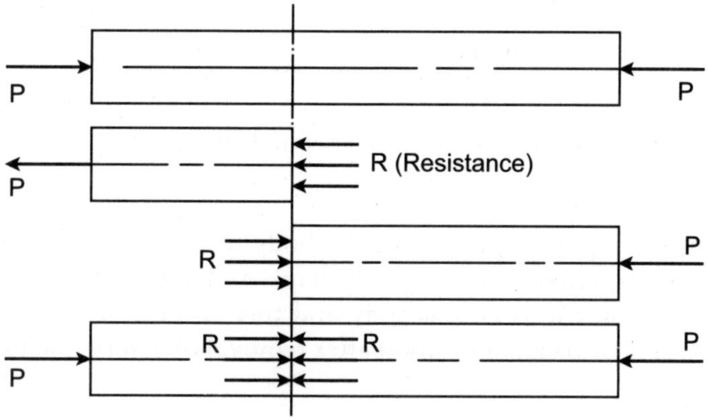

Fig. 15.2: Simple Compression

Compress stress $(\sigma) = \frac{R}{A} = \frac{P}{A} = \frac{\text{Push (N)}}{\text{X-sectional area (mm}^2)}$

15.3 Strain (∈)

When a body is subjected to some external force, there is some change of dimension of the body. The ratio of change of dimension to the original dimension is known as strain.

$$\text{Strain } (\in) = \frac{\text{Change in dimension}}{\text{Original dimension}}$$

Strain is dimensionless.

$$\text{Tensile strain } (\in) = \frac{\text{Increase in length}}{\text{Original length}} = \frac{\delta l}{l}$$

$$\text{Compressive strain } (\in) = \frac{\text{Decrease in length}}{\text{Original length}} = \frac{\delta l}{l}$$

15.4 Shear Stress (τ) and Shear Strain (ϕ)

Let the thickness of block ABCD be 't'.

P = Shear Force

The stress induced in body, when subjected two equal and opposite forces, which are acting tangentially across the resisting section, as a result of which the body tends to shear off across the section, is known as shear stress (τ).

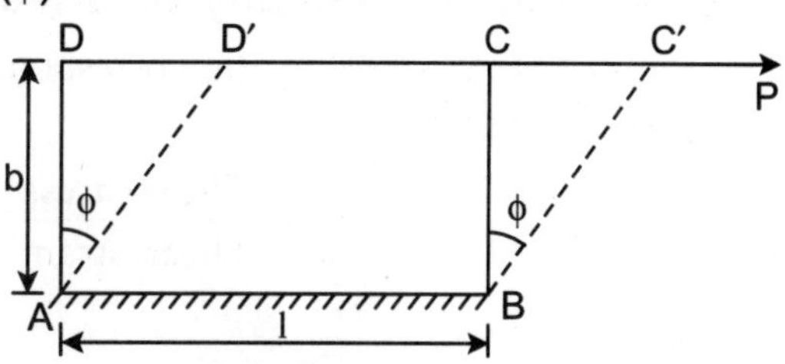

Fig. 15.3

∴ Shear stress

$$\tau = \frac{\text{Shear resistance}}{\text{Sheared area}} = \frac{R}{A} = \frac{P}{l \times t}; \; R = P$$

Shear strain

$$\phi = \frac{\text{Transverse displacement}}{\text{Distance AD}} = \frac{CC' \text{ or } DD'}{t}$$

Shear stress (τ) is tangential to the area over which it acts.

15.5 Elasticity

When an external force is applied on a body, the body tends to deform. If the external force is removed and the body regains its original shape and size (i.e. deformation disappears completely), the body is known as elastic body and this property by virtue of which, certain materials return back to their original position after removal of external load, is called elasticity.

15.6 Elastic Limit

The body will regain its original shape and size (after removal the applied load) only when the deformation caused by the external load, is within a certain limit. Thus, there is a limiting value of force upto and within which, the deformation disappears completely on the removal of the force. The value of stress corresponding to this limiting force, is known as the elastic limit of the material.

But if the material does not regain its original shape and size, the material loses its property of elasticity and there will be residual deformation in the material.

15.7 Hooke's Law

Hooke's law states that within the elastic limit, strain is proportional to stress applied. Stress ∝ strain (within elastic limit)

$$\sigma \propto \epsilon$$

or

$$\sigma = E\epsilon$$

or

where E is a constant and is known as modulus of elasticity.

$$E = \frac{\sigma}{\epsilon} = \frac{\text{Tensile stress}}{\text{Tensile strain}} = \frac{\text{Compressive stress}}{\text{Compressive strain}}$$

15.8 Modulus of Rigidity or Shear Modulus (C or G)

The ratio of shear stress to the corresponding shear strain, within elastic limit, is known as modulus of rigidity.

$$C \text{ or } G = \frac{\text{Shear stress}}{\text{Shear strain}} = \frac{\tau}{\phi}$$

15.9 Factor of Safety (F·S)

$$F{\cdot}s = \frac{\text{Ultimate stress}}{\text{Permissible stress}}$$

$$= \frac{\text{Ultimate stress}}{\text{Working or design stress}}$$

15.10 Stress-Strain Diagram for Ductile Material

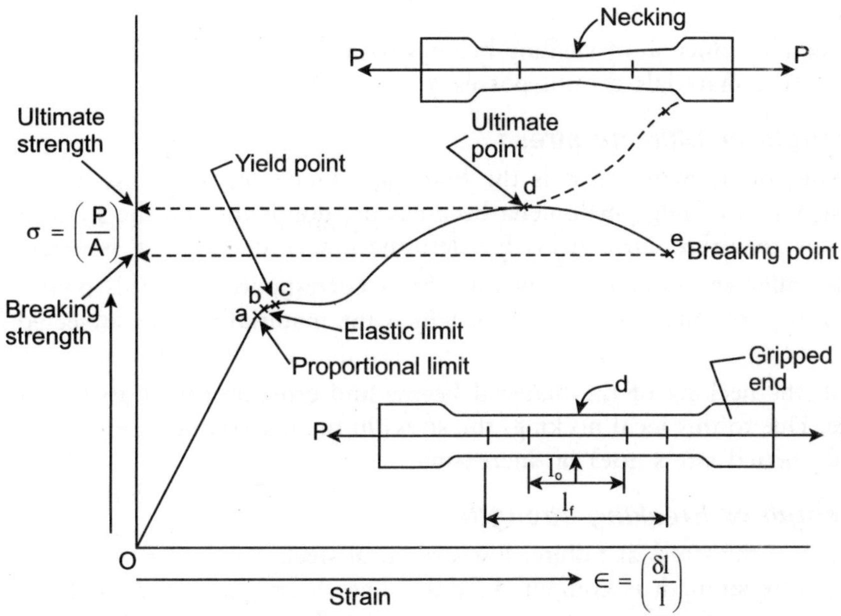

Fig. 15.4: Stress-Strain Diagram for Structural Steel

In tensile test, a specimen is gripped between the jaws of a testing machine. The values of load and elongation in a specified length, called the gauge length, are observed simultaneously. These data are plotted on graph.

Proportional limit (0-a)

From the origin 0 to point 'a' called the proportional limit. Stress is proportional to strain within proportional limit. This proportionality does not extend throughout the diagram, it ends at the proportional limit. Beyond this point, stress is no longer proportional to strain.

Elastic limit

Elastic limit is the stress beyond which the material will not return to its original shape when unloaded but will retain a permanent deformation called permanent set.

The portion of the diagram between 'a' and 'b' is not a straight line but upto point 'b' the material remains elastic, i.e. on removal of load, no permanent deformation is formed and the path is retraced.

The point 'b' is called elastic limit point and the stress corresponding to that is called the elastic limit stress.

In actual practice, the points 'a' and 'b' are so close to each other that it becomes difficult to differentiate between them.

Yield point (C)

The yield point is the point at which there is an appreciable elongation or yielding of material without any corresponding increase of load. Indeed, the load may actually decreases while the yielding occurs.

However, the phenomenon of yielding belongs to structural steel. Other grades of steel and steel alloys or other materials do not posses it.

Ultimate strength or Ultimate stress

Ultimate strength or ultimate stress is the highest ordinate on the stress-strain curve. After yielding, the strain hardening phenomena becomes pre-dominant and the strength of material increases thereby requiring more stress for deformation, until point 'd' is reached.

Point 'd' is called the ultimate point and stress corresponding to this point is called the ultimate stress. It is the maximum stress to which the material can be subjected in a simple tensile test.

At point 'd' the necking of the material begins and cross sectional area starts decreasing at a rapid rate. Due to this local necking, the stress in the material goes on decreasing in spite of the fact that actual stress goes on increasing.

Rupture strength or Breaking strength

Rupture strength is the stress at failure. For structural steel, it is lower than ultimate strength because the rupture strength is computed by dividing the rupture load by the original cross sectional area, which although convenient, is incorrect. The error is caused by a phenomenon known as necking. As failure occurs, the material stretches very rapidly and simultaneously narrows down.

15.11 Stress-Strain Diagram for Brittle Materials

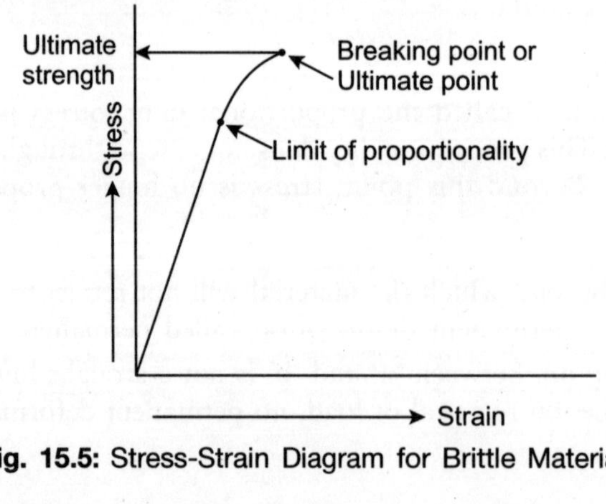

Fig. 15.5: Stress-Strain Diagram for Brittle Materials

Materials which show very small elongation before the fracture are called brittle material such as C.I., concrete and high strength light alloys.

For most brittle materials the permanent elongation (i.e. increases in length) is less than 10%.

15.12 Principle of Superposition

It states that the effect of a set of loads on a body is the same as the sum of the effects caused by each load acting separately. This principle is not valid beyond the yield stress of the materials.

$$\delta l = \delta l_1 + \delta l_2 + \delta l_3 + \ldots.$$

$$\Rightarrow \qquad \frac{P \cdot l}{AE} = \frac{P_1 l_1}{A_1 E_1} + \frac{P_2 l_2}{A_2 E_2} + \frac{P_3 l_3}{A_3 E_3} + \ldots.$$

where P, l, A and E have their usual meanings.

15.13 Analysis of Bars of Varying Sections

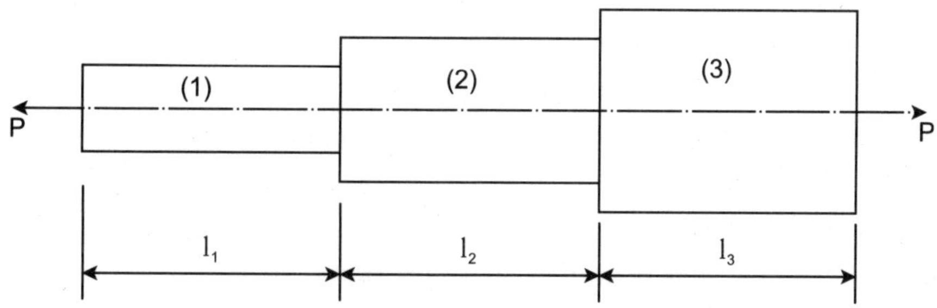

Fig. 15.6: Bar of Varying Sections

The free body diagram (F.B.D.) of individual section is shown in Fig. 15.7.

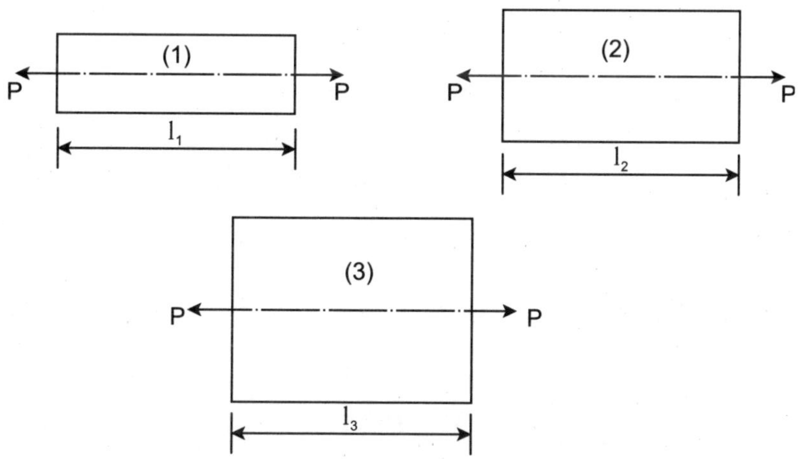

Fig. 15.7: F.B.D. of Individual Sections

$$\sigma_1 = \frac{P}{A_1}, \quad \epsilon_1 = \frac{\sigma_1}{E_1}, \quad \delta l_1 = \frac{Pl_1}{A_1E_1}$$

$$\sigma_2 = \frac{P}{A_2}, \quad \epsilon_2 = \frac{\sigma_2}{E_2}, \quad \delta l_2 = \frac{Pl_2}{A_2E_2}$$

$$\sigma_3 = \frac{P}{A_3}, \quad \epsilon_3 = \frac{\sigma_3}{E_3}, \quad \delta l_3 = \frac{Pl_3}{A_3E_3}$$

Using principle of superposition:

$$\delta l = \delta l_1 + \delta l_2 + \delta l_3 = \frac{P_1l_1}{A_1E_1} + \frac{P_2l_2}{A_2E_2} + \frac{P_3l_3}{A_3E_3}; \; P_1 = P_2 = P_3$$

$$= P\left(\frac{l_1}{A_1E_1} + \frac{l_2}{A_2E_2} + \frac{l_3}{A_3E_3}\right) = P\sum_{i=1}^{n}\frac{l_i}{A_iE_i}$$

$$= \frac{P}{E}\left(\frac{l_1}{A_1} + \frac{l_2}{A_2} + \frac{l_3}{A_3}\right); \; E_1 = E_2 = E_3 = E$$

$$\delta l = \frac{P}{E}\sum_{i=1}^{n}\left(\frac{l_i}{A_i}\right)$$

where: n = number of steps in the bar of varying sections.

Example 15.1

A stepped bar as shown in Fig. 15.8 is subjected to an axially applied compressive load of 35 kN. Find the maximum and minimum stress produced.

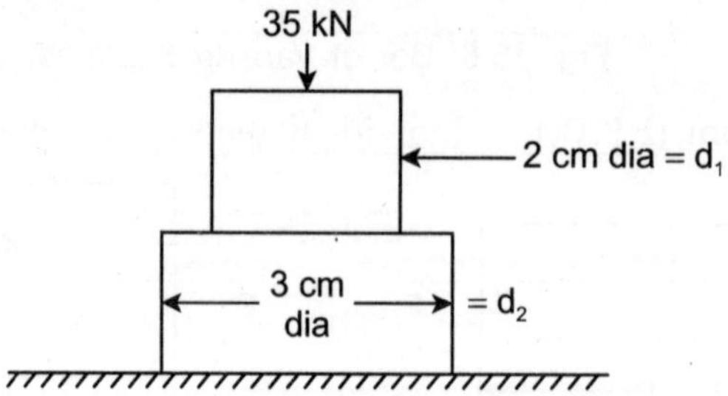

Fig. 15.8

Solution:

$P = 35 \text{ kN} = 35 \times 10^3 \text{ N}$

Let $d_1 = 2 \text{ cm} = 20 \text{ mm}$

$d_2 = 3 \text{ cm} = 30 \text{ mm}$

$$\sigma_{max} = \sigma_1 = \frac{P}{A_1} = \frac{35 \times 10^3}{\frac{\pi}{4} \times d_1^2}$$

$$= \frac{35 \times 10^3}{\frac{\pi}{4} \times (20)^2} = \mathbf{111.41\ N/mm^2}$$ **Ans.**

and
$$\sigma_{min} = \sigma_2 = \frac{P}{A_2} = \frac{35 \times 10^3}{\frac{\pi}{4} \times (d_2)^2}$$

$$= \frac{35 \times 10^3}{\frac{\pi}{4} \times (30)^2} = \mathbf{49.515\ N/mm^2}$$ **Ans.**

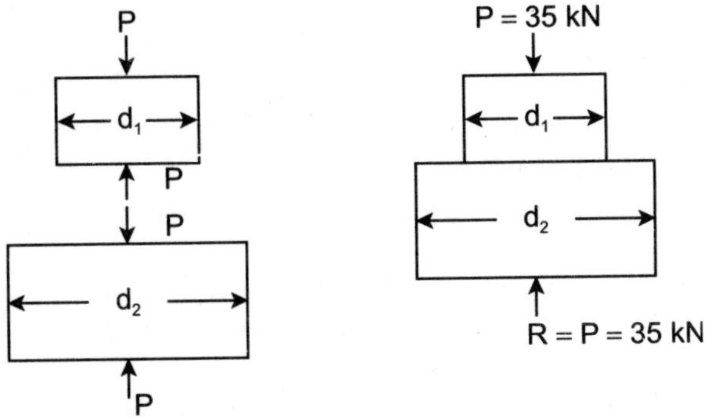

Fig. 15.9: F.B.D. of Individual Parts

Example 15.2

A rod 2 m long, 0.03 m diameter is subjected to an axial tensile load of 30 kN. If the modulus of elasticity for the material of the rod is 2 × 10⁵ N/mm². Calculate (i) Stress, (ii) Strain and (iii) Elongation of rod.

Solution:

$l = 2\ m = 2000\ mm$

$d = 0.03\ m = 30\ mm$

$P = 30\ kN = 30 \times 10^3\ N$

$E = 2 \times 10^5\ N/mm^2$

$\sigma = ?$

$\in = ?$

$\delta l = ?$

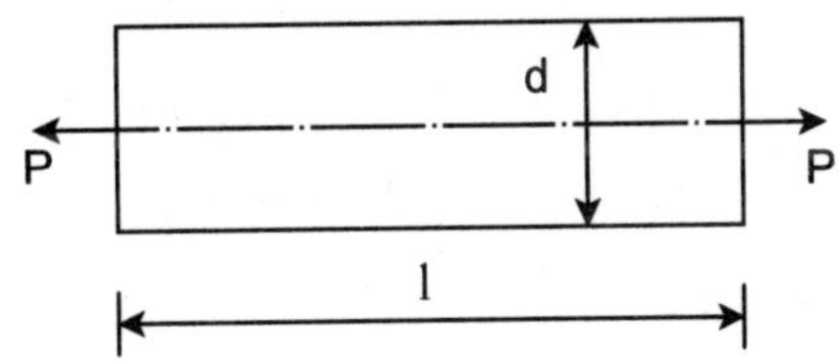

Fig. 15.10

Now

(i)
$$\sigma = \frac{P}{A} = \frac{P}{\frac{\pi}{4}d^2} = \frac{4P}{\pi d^2} = \frac{4 \times 30 \times 10^3}{\pi(30)^2} = \mathbf{42.44\ N/mm^2}$$ **Ans.**

(ii) $$\in = \frac{\sigma}{E} = \frac{42.44}{2 \times 10^5} = \mathbf{2.122 \times 10^{-4}}$$ **Ans.**

(iii) $$\delta l = \in \times l = 2.122 \times 10^{-4} \times 2000 = \mathbf{0.4244\ mm}$$ **Ans.**

Example 15.3

The working stress for a hollow steel column, under axial load of 2.2 × 10³ kN is 120 MPa. The external dia. of column is 250 mm, calculate the internal diameter.

Solution:

$P = 2.2 \times 10^3$ kN $= 2.2 \times 10^6$ N

$\sigma = 120$ MPa $= 120$ N/mm²

$d_o = 250$

$d_i = ?$

The column will be under compressive load as shown in Fig. 15.11.

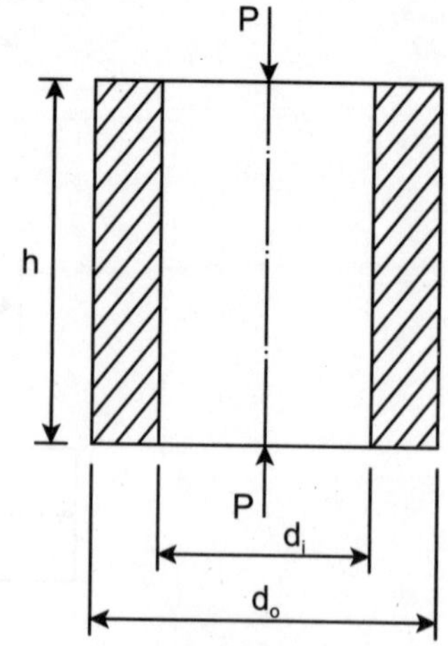

Fig. 15.11

Now

$$\sigma = \frac{P}{A} = \frac{P}{\frac{\pi}{4}\left(d_o^2 - d_i^2\right)} = \frac{4P}{\pi\left(d_o^2 - d_i^2\right)}$$

$$\Rightarrow \quad \left(d_o^2 - d_i^2\right) = \frac{4P}{\pi \cdot \sigma}$$

$$\Rightarrow \quad d_i = \sqrt{d_o^2 - \frac{4P}{\pi \cdot \sigma}}$$

$$= \sqrt{250^2 - \frac{4 \times 2.2 \times 10^6}{\pi \times 120}}$$

$$= \sqrt{250^2 - 2.33 \times 10^4}$$

$$= 197.88 \text{ mm}$$

$$d_i = \mathbf{198\ mm}$$ **Ans.**

Example 15.4

An axial pull of 50 kN is acting on a bar consisting of three sections of length 300 mm, 200 mm and 100 mm and of diameters 20 mm, 40 mm and 60 mm respectively, E = 2 × 10⁵ N/mm². Calculate (i) stress in each section, (ii) total extension of the bar.

Solution:

$P = 50$ kN $= 50 \times 10^3$ N

$l_1 = 300$ mm

$l_2 = 200$ mm

$l_3 = 100$ mm

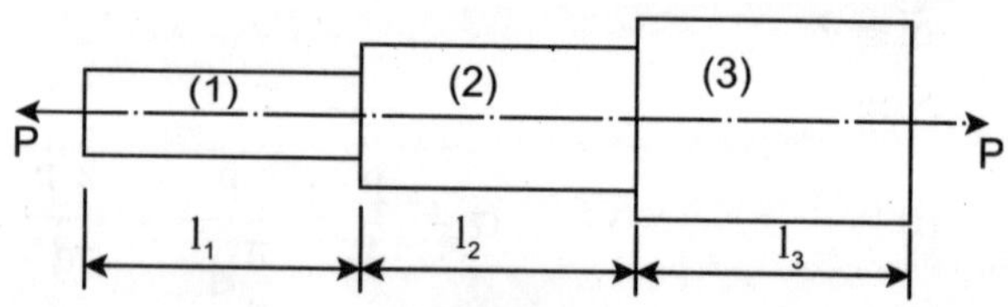

Fig. 15.12

$d_1 = 20$ mm
$d_2 = 40$ mm
$d_3 = 60$ mm
$E = 2 \times 10^5$ N/mm^2

(i) $\sigma_1 = ?$
$\sigma_2 = ?$
$\sigma_3 = ?$
(ii) $\delta l = ?$

Now

(i)
$$\sigma_1 = \frac{P_1}{A_1} = \frac{P}{A_1} = \frac{50 \times 10^3}{\frac{\pi}{4}(20)^2} = \mathbf{159.1\ N/mm^2}$$ **Ans.**

$$\sigma_2 = \frac{P_2}{A_2} = \frac{P}{A_2} = \frac{50 \times 10^3}{\frac{\pi}{4}(40)^2} = \mathbf{39.8\ N/mm^2}$$ **Ans.**

$$\sigma_3 = \frac{P_3}{A_3} = \frac{P}{A_3} = \frac{50 \times 10^3}{\frac{\pi}{4}(60)^2} = \mathbf{17.7\ N/mm^2}$$ **Ans.**

(ii)
$$\delta l = \frac{P}{E}\left(\frac{l_1}{A_1} + \frac{l_2}{A_2} + \frac{l_3}{A_3}\right) = \frac{50 \times 10^3}{2 \times 10^5 \times \frac{\pi}{4}}\left(\frac{l_1}{d_1^2} + \frac{l_2}{d_2^2} + \frac{l_3}{d_3^2}\right)$$

$$\therefore \quad \delta l = \frac{4 \times 50 \times 10^3}{2 \times 10^5 \times \pi}\left(\frac{300}{20^2} + \frac{200}{40^2} + \frac{100}{60^2}\right)$$

$$= \frac{1}{\pi}(67.08 + 0.125 + 0.0277)$$

$$\delta l = \mathbf{21.4\ mm}$$ **Ans.**

Example 15.5

A bar is subjected to a tensile load of 150 kN as shown in Fig. 15.13. If the stress in the middle portion is limited to 140 MPa, determine the diameter and length of the middle portion if the total elongation of the bar is to be 0.2 mm. Take $E = 2 \times 10^5$ N/mm^2.

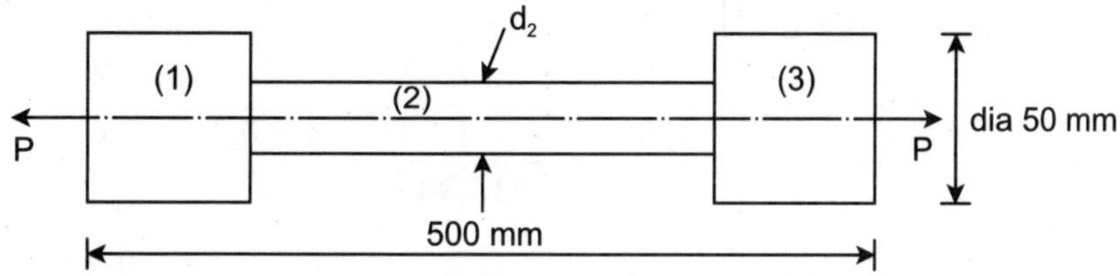

Fig. 15.13

Solution:

$P = 150 \text{ kN} = 150 \times 10^3 \text{ N}$

$\sigma_2 = 140 \text{ MPa} = 140 \text{ N/mm}^2$

$d_2 = ?$

$l_2 = ?$

$\delta l = 0.2 \text{ mm}$

$E = 2 \times 10^5 \text{ N/mm}^2$

$l = l_1 + l_2 + l_3 = 500 \text{ mm}$

$d_1 = d_3 = 50 \text{ mm}$

Now

$$\sigma_2 = \frac{P_2}{A_2} = \frac{P}{A_2} = \frac{150 \times 10^3}{\frac{\pi}{4} d_2^2}$$

$$\Rightarrow \quad d_2 = \sqrt{\frac{150 \times 10^3}{\frac{\pi}{4} \times 140}} = 36.94 \text{ mm}$$

$$\therefore \quad d_2 = \mathbf{36.94 \text{ mm}} \qquad \textbf{Ans.}$$

Now

$$\delta l = \delta l_1 + \delta l_2 + \delta l_3$$

$$\delta l = \frac{P}{E}\left(\frac{l_1}{A_1} + \frac{l_2}{A_2} + \frac{l_3}{A_3}\right)$$

$$\delta l = \frac{4P}{\pi E}\left(\frac{l_1}{d_1^2} + \frac{l_2}{d_2^2} + \frac{l_3}{d_3^2}\right), \; d_1 = d_3$$

$$\Rightarrow \quad 0.2 = \frac{4 \times 150 \times 10^3}{\pi \times 2 \times 10^5}\left(\frac{l_1}{d_1^2} + \frac{l_3}{d_1^2} + \frac{l_2}{d_2^2}\right), \; l_1 + l_3 = (500 - l_2)$$

$$= \frac{3}{\pi}\left(\frac{l_1 + l_3}{d_1^2} + \frac{l_2}{d_2^2}\right)$$

$$0.2 = \frac{3}{\pi}\left(\frac{500 - l_2}{d_1^2} + \frac{l_2}{d_2^2}\right)$$

$$\Rightarrow \quad \frac{500 - l_2}{50^2} + \frac{l_2}{36.94^2} = \frac{\pi \times 0.2}{2}$$

$$\Rightarrow \quad (36.94)^2 \times 500 - (36.94)^2\, l_2 + (50)^2\, l_2 = \frac{\pi \times 0.2 \times (36.94)^2 \times 50^2}{3}$$

$$\Rightarrow \quad 6.82 \times 10^5 - 1364.56\ l_2 + 2500\ l_2 = 7.14 \times 10^5$$

$$\Rightarrow \quad 1135.44\ l_2 = (7.14 \times 10^5 - 6.82 \times 10^5)$$

$$l_2 = \left(\frac{0.32 \times 10^5}{1135.44}\right) = 28.18 \text{ mm}$$

$$\therefore \quad l_2 = \mathbf{28.18 \text{ mm}}$$

Ans.

Example 15.6

A member formed by connecting a steel bar to an aluminium bar is shown in Fig. 15.14. Assuming that the bars are prevented from buckling sideways, determine magnitude of force P, that will cause 0.30 mm decrease in total length, $E_s = 2 \times 10^5$ N/mm² and $E_{al} = 6.5 \times 10^4$ N/mm².

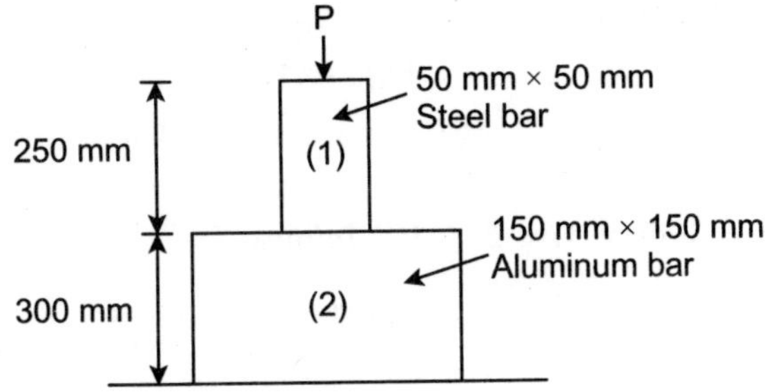

Fig. 15.14

Solution:

$P = ?$

$\delta l = 0.3$

$E_1 = E_s = 2 \times 10^5$ N/mm²

$E_2 = E_a = 6.5 \times 10^4$ N/mm²

$l_1 = 250$ mm

$l_2 = 300$ mm

$A_1 = 50 \times 50 = 2500$ mm²

$A_2 = 150 \times 150 = 22500$ mm²

$$\delta l = \delta l_1 + \delta l_2$$

$$\delta l = P\left(\frac{l_1}{A_1 E_1} + \frac{l_2}{A_2 E_2}\right)$$

$$\Rightarrow \quad 0.3 = P\left(\frac{250}{2500 \times 2 \times 10^5} + \frac{300}{2250 \times 6.5 \times 10^4}\right)$$

$$\Rightarrow \quad 0.3 \times 10^5 = P\left(\frac{250}{2500 \times 2} + \frac{300}{2250 \times 6.5}\right)$$

$$\Rightarrow \quad 0.3 \times 10^5 = P(0.05 + 0.0205)$$

$$\Rightarrow \quad P = 4.25 \times 10^5 \text{ N}$$

$$P = \mathbf{0.42 \text{ mN}}$$

Ans.

Example 15.7

For the bar shown in Fig. 15.15, calculate reaction produce by lower support on the bar. Take E = 200 GN/m². Find also the stresses in the bars.

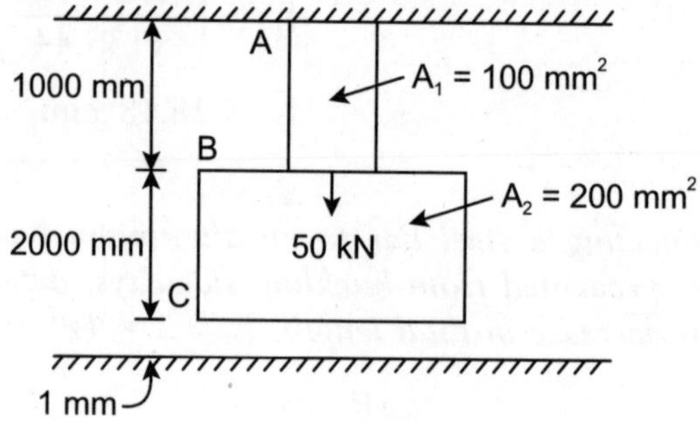

Fig. 15.15

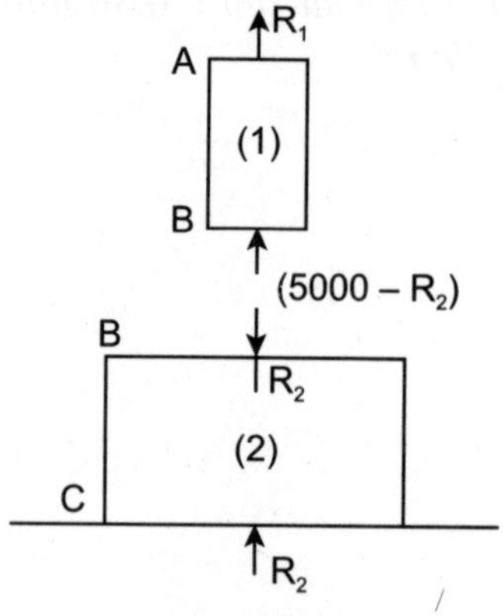

Fig. 15.16

Solution:

1. R_1 = ?, R_2 = ?, δl = 1 mm, E = 2 × 10^5 N/mm²

If the lower bar BC rests on lower support then $R_1 + R_2 = 50000$ N

For bar AB, $R_1 = (50000 - R_2)$, tensile

For bar BC, total force = R_2, compressive.

$$\delta l_1 = \frac{P_1 l_1}{A_1 E_1} = \frac{(50000 - R_2) \times 1000}{100 \times 2 \times 10^5} \text{ mm (extention)}$$

$$\delta l_2 = \frac{P_2 l_2}{A_2 E_2} = \frac{R_2 \times 2000}{200 \times 2 \times 10^5} \text{ mm (contraction)}$$

In order that lower bar rests on lower support,

$$\delta l_1 + \delta l_2 = 1 \text{ mm} \Rightarrow \frac{(50000 - R_2) \times 10^3}{100 \times 2 \times 10^5} - \frac{R_2 \times 2000}{200 \times 2 \times 10^5} = 1$$

$$\Rightarrow \quad (50000 - R_2) \times 2 \times 10^3 - R_2 \times 2000 = 200 \times 2 \times 10^5$$

$$\Rightarrow \quad (50000 - R_2) - R_2 = 2 \times 10^4$$

$$\Rightarrow \quad 2\,R_2 = 50000 - 20000 = 30000$$

R_2 = **15000 N** and R_1 = 50000 – 15000 = **35000 N** **Ans.**

2. Stresses in bars

$$\sigma_1 = \sigma_{AB} = \frac{R_1}{A_1} = \frac{35000}{100} = 350 \text{ N/mm}^2$$ **Ans.**

$$\sigma_2 = \sigma_{BC} = \frac{R_2}{A_2} = \frac{15000}{200} = 75 \text{ N/mm}^2$$ **Ans.**

15.14 Analysis of Bars of Varying Cross Sections Under as Shown in Fig. 15.17.

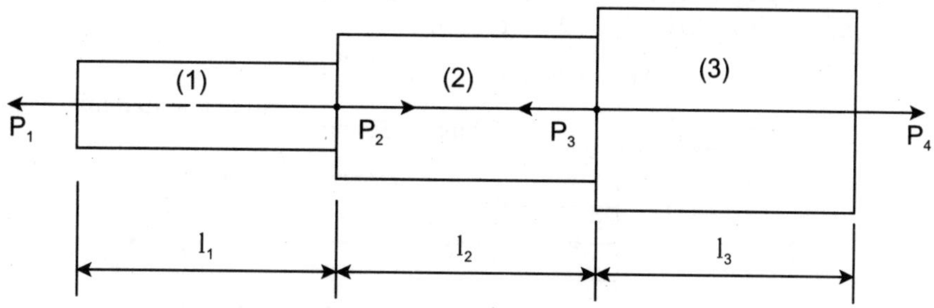

Fig. 15.17: Bar of Varying Cross-section

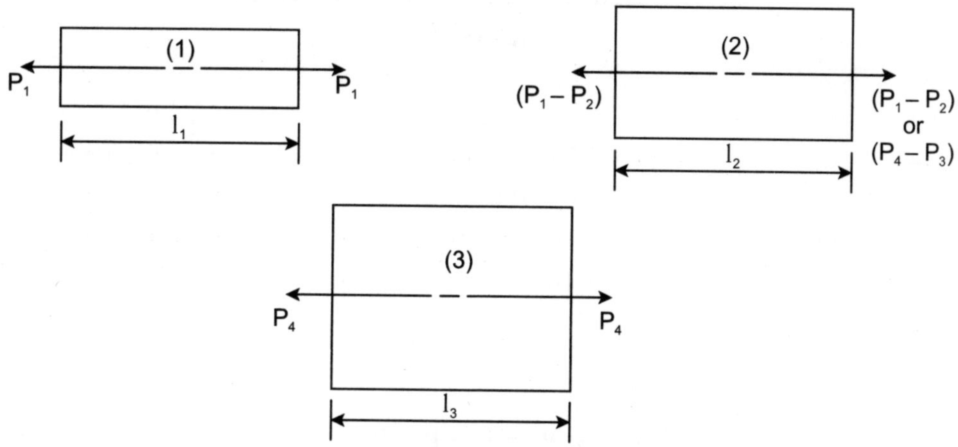

For equilibrium, $P_1 + P_3 = P_2 + P_4$

$\Rightarrow (P_1 - P_2) = (P_4 - P_3)$

Fig. 15.18: F.B.D. of Individual Sections

$$\therefore \quad \delta l_1 = \frac{P_1 l_1}{A_1 E_1}$$

$$\delta l_2 = \frac{(P_1 - P_2) l_2}{A_2 E_2}$$

$$\delta l_3 = \frac{P_4 l_3}{A_3 E_3}$$

If E is same for all components then $E_1 = E_2 = E_3 = E$

$$\therefore \quad \delta l_1 = \frac{P_1 l_1}{A_1 E}, \quad \delta l_2 = \frac{(P_1 - P_2) l_2}{A_2 E}, \quad \delta l_3 = \frac{P_4 l_3}{A_3 E}$$

Example 15.8

A member is subjected to point loads as shown in Fig. 15.19. Calculate the force P_3 necessary for equilibrium if P_1 = 120 kN, P_2 = 200 kN and P_4 = 180 kN. Determine net change in the length of the member also. Take E = 200 GN/m^2.

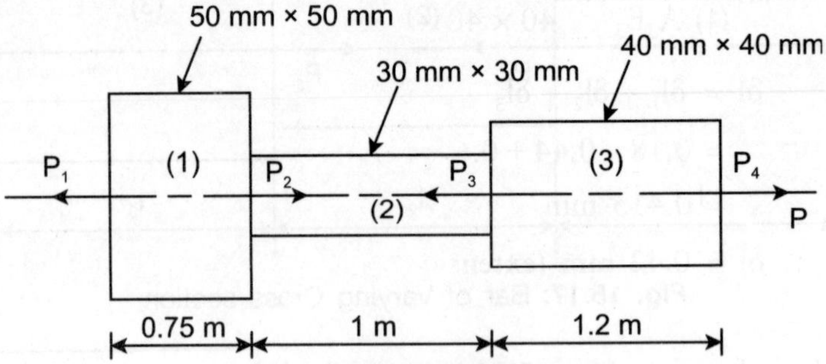

Fig. 15.19

Solution:

P_3 = ?	l_1 = 0.75 m = 750 mm	$A_1 = 50 \times 50$ mm^2
P_1 = 120 kN	l_2 = 1 m = 1000 mm	$A_2 = 30 \times 30$ mm^2
P_2 = 200 kN	l_3 = 1.2 m = 1200 mm	$A_3 = 40 \times 40$ mm^2
P_4 = 180 kN	$E = 2 \times 10^5$ N/mm^2	
δl = ?		

For equilibrium, $\Sigma F_x = 0$

$$P_1 + P_3 = P_2 + P_4 \Rightarrow P_3 = P_2 + P_4 - P_1$$

$\therefore$ $$P_3 = 200 + 180 - 120 = 380 - 120 = \mathbf{260\ kN}$$ **Ans.**

Now, free body diagram of individual sections are as:

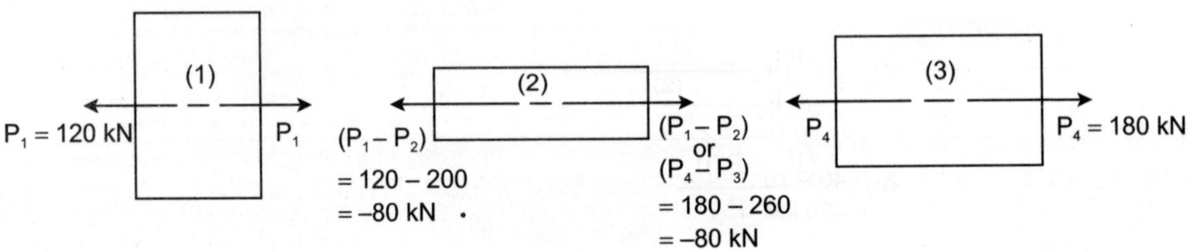

Fig. 15.20

Now

$$\delta l_1 = \frac{P_1 l_1}{A_1 E_1} = \frac{120 \times 10^3 \times 750}{50 \times 50 \times 2 \times 10^5} = \frac{9 \times 10^7}{5 \times 10^8} = 0.18 \text{ mm}$$

$$\delta l_2 = \frac{(P_1 - P_2)l_2}{A_2E_2} = \frac{-80 \times 10^3 \times 1000}{30 \times 30 \times 2 \times 10^5} = -0.44 \text{ mm}$$

$$\delta l_3 = \frac{P_4 l_3}{A_3E_3} = \frac{180 \times 10^3 \times 1200}{40 \times 40 \times 2 \times 10^5} = 0.675 \text{ mm}$$

$\therefore$

$$\delta l = \delta l_1 + \delta l_2 + \delta l_3$$

$$= 0.18 - 0.44 + 0.675$$

$$= 0.415 \text{ mm}$$

$$\delta l = \mathbf{0.42 \text{ mm (extension)}}$$ **Ans.**

Example 15.9

A m.s. bar is loaded as shown in Fig. 15.21. The cross sectional area of the bar is 800 mm². Calculate the change in length of the bar. Take E = 200 GN/m².

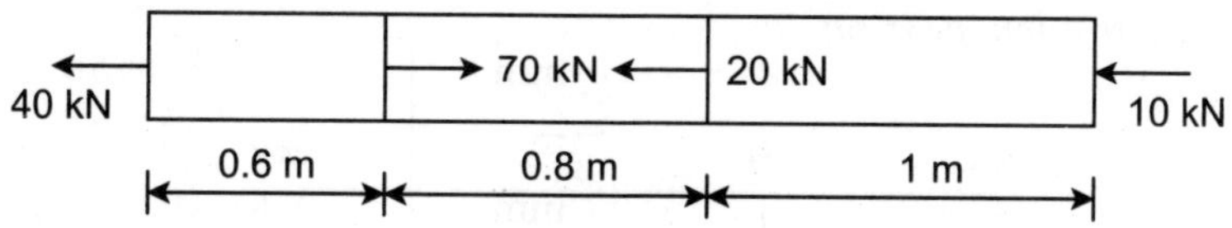

Fig. 15.21

Solution:

$P_1 = 40$ kN	$A_1 = A_2 = A_3 = A = 800 \text{ mm}^2$	$\delta l = ?$
$P_2 = 70$ kN	$l_1 = 0.6 \text{ m} = 600 \text{ mm}$	$E = 2 \text{ GN/m}^2 = \dfrac{200 \times 10^9}{10^6} \text{ N/mm}^2$
$P_3 = 20$ kN	$l_2 = 0.8 \text{ m} = 800 \text{ mm}$	$= 2 \times 10^5 \text{ N/mm}^2$
$P_4 = -10$ kN	$l_3 = 1 \text{ m} = 1000 \text{ mm}$	

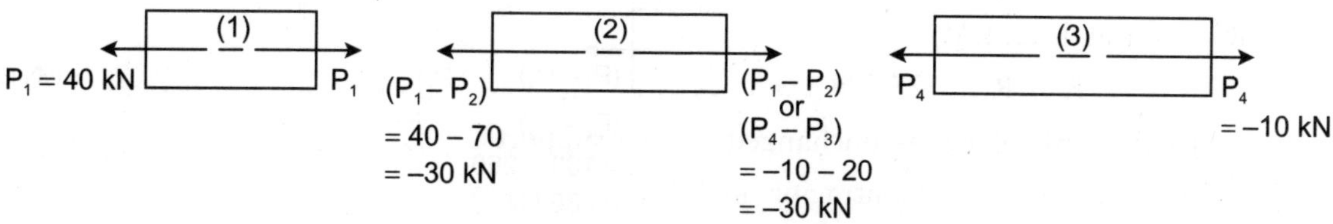

Fig. 15.22: F.B.D. of Individual Sections

Total elongation

$$\delta l = \delta l_1 + \delta l_2 + \delta l_3 = \frac{P_1 l_1}{A_1E_1} + \frac{(P_1 - P_2)l_2}{A_2E_2} + \frac{P_4 l_3}{A_3E_3}$$

$$= \frac{1}{AE}\left[P_1 l_1 + (P_1 - P_2) l_2 + P_4 l_3\right]$$

$$= \frac{1 \times 10^3}{800 \times 2 \times 10^5}[40 \times 600 + (-30) \times 800 + (-10) \times 1000]$$

$$= \frac{1}{160000}\left(24000 - 24000 - 1 \times 10^4\right)$$

$$= -\frac{1}{16} = -0.0625 \text{ mm} = \mathbf{0.0625 \text{ mm (contraction)}}$$ **Ans.**

Example 15.10

A steel bar of cross sectional area 250 mm² held firmly by the end supports and loaded by an axial force of 25 kN as shown in Fig. 15.23. Determine:

(i) Reaction at L and M.

(ii) Extension of the left portion.

E = 200 GN/m²

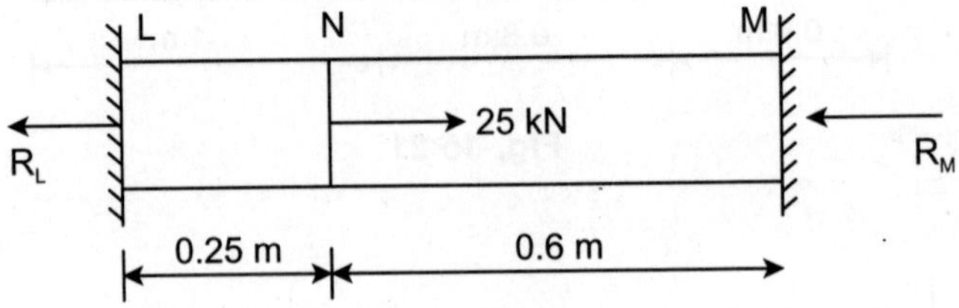

Fig. 15.23

Solution:

$A = 250 \text{ mm}^2$

$$E = 200 \text{ GN/m}^2 = \frac{200 \times 10^9}{10^6} \text{ N/mm}^2 = 2 \times 10^5 \text{ N/mm}^2,$$

(i) Reaction at L and M

$$R_L + R_M = 25 \text{ kN} \qquad (15.1)$$

∵ Total length of bar is unchanged due to supports.

∴ Extension in LN = Contracion in NM.

$$\delta l_1 = \delta l_2$$

$$\Rightarrow \quad \frac{P_1 l_1}{A_1 E_1} = \frac{P_2 l_2}{A_2 E_2}$$

$$\Rightarrow \quad \frac{R_L \times 0.25}{250 \times 200} = \frac{R_M \times 0.6}{250 \times 200}$$

$$\Rightarrow \quad R_L = \frac{0.6 \times R_M}{0.25} = 2.4\ R_M$$

$$\therefore \quad R_L = 2.4\ R_M \quad \ldots\ldots (15.2)$$

From Eqs. (15.1) and (15.2)

we get

$$\left.\begin{aligned} R_M &= \mathbf{7.353\ kN} \\ R_L &= \mathbf{17.647\ kN} \end{aligned}\right]$$ **Ans.**

(ii) Extension of left portion:

$$\delta l_1 = \frac{R_L \times 0.25 \times 1000}{250 \times 2 \times 10^5} \text{mm}$$

$$\delta l_1 \doteq \mathbf{0.0882\ mm}$$ **Ans.**

Example 15.11

A member LMNP is subjected to point loads as shown in Fig. 15.24. Calculate

(i) Force P necessary for equilibrium.

(ii) Total elongation of bar.

Take E = 210 GN/m².

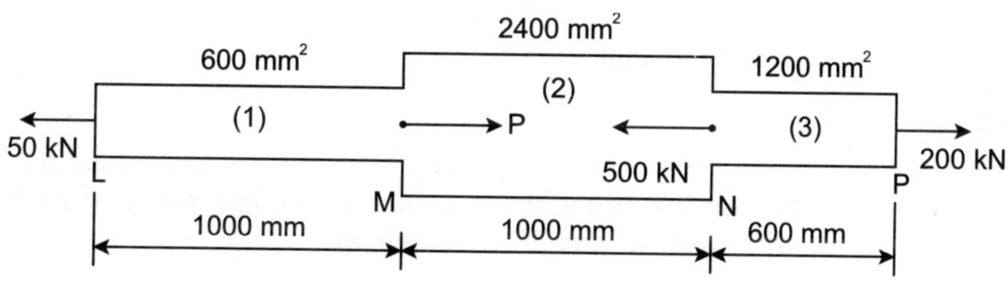

Fig. 15.24

Solution:

1. Force P necessary for equilibrium

$A_1 = 600\ mm^2$

$A_2 = 2400\ mm^2$

$A_3 = 1200\ mm^2$

$$E = \frac{210 \times 10^9}{10^6}\ N/mm^2 = 2.1 \times 10^5\ N/mm^2$$

$$\Sigma F_x = 0$$

$$\Rightarrow \quad 50 + 500 - P - 200 = 0$$

or $\quad 350 - P = 0$

or $\quad P = 350\ kN$

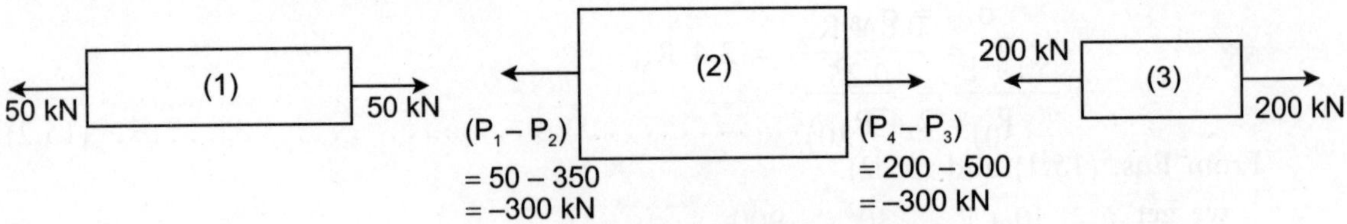

Fig. 15.25: F.B.D. of Individual Sections

Now

$$\delta l_1 = \frac{P_1 l_1}{A_1 E_1} = \frac{50 \times 1000 \times 1000}{600 \times 2.1 \times 10^5} = \frac{5}{6 \times 2.1} = \frac{5}{12.6} \text{ mm}$$

$$\delta l_2 = \frac{P_2 l_2}{A_2 E_2} = \frac{-300 \times 1000 \times 1000}{2400 \times 2.1 \times 10^5} = -\frac{30}{24 \times 2.1} \text{ mm}$$

$$\delta l_3 = \frac{P_3 l_3}{A_3 E_3} = \frac{200 \times 1000 \times 600}{1000 \times 2.1 \times 10^5} = \frac{12}{21} \text{ mm}$$

$\therefore$ Total elongation

$$\delta l = \delta l_1 + \delta l_2 + \delta l_3$$

$$= \left(\frac{5}{12.6} - \frac{30}{24 \times 2.1} + \frac{12}{21}\right) \text{ mm}$$

$$= \mathbf{0.3730 \text{ mm}}$$

Ans.

Example 15.12

Two solid circular rods are welded together as shown in Fig. 15.26. Determine the magnitude of the force P for which the same normal stress occurs at the mid-point of each rod. Also compute the total change in length, if E = 2 × 10⁵ N/mm².

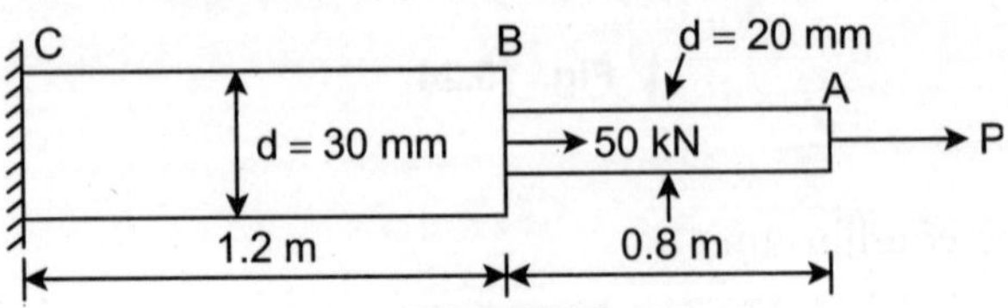

Fig. 15.26

Solution:

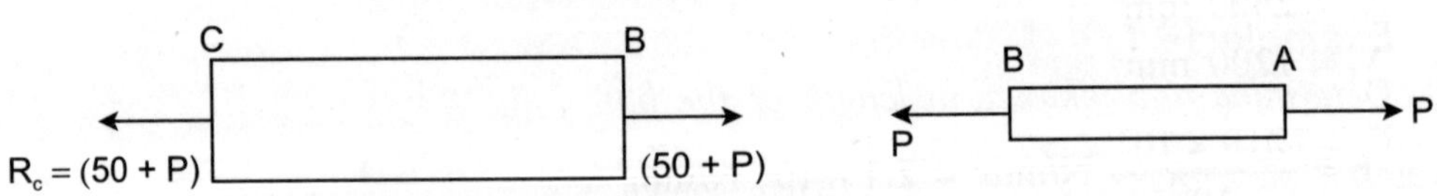

Reaction at C : R_c = (50 + P)

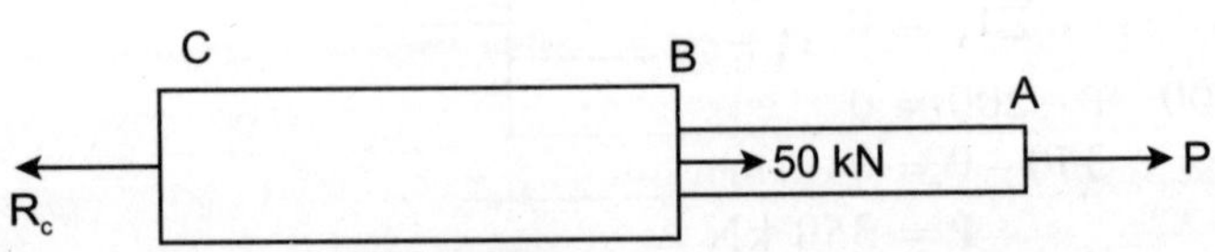

Fig. 15.27

$$\sigma_{CB} = \sigma_{AB}$$

$$\frac{50 + P}{\frac{\pi}{4}(30)^2} = \frac{P}{\frac{\pi}{4}(20)^2}$$

$$\Rightarrow \quad \frac{50 + P}{P} = \frac{30^2}{20^2} = \frac{900}{400} = \frac{9}{4} = 2.25$$

$$\Rightarrow \quad 2.25\ P = 50 + P$$

$$1.25\ P = 50$$

$$\therefore \quad \frac{50}{1.25} = 40 \text{ kN}$$

$$P = \mathbf{40\ kN}$$ **Ans.**

Now, total change in length

$$\delta l = \delta l_1 + \delta l_2$$

$$= \frac{P_1 l_1}{A_1 E} + \frac{P_2 l_2}{A_2 E}$$

$$\Rightarrow \quad = \frac{1}{E}\left(\frac{(50 + P)}{\frac{\pi}{4}(30)^2} \times 1200 + \frac{P}{\frac{\pi}{4}(20)^2} \times 800\right)$$

$$= \frac{1}{2 \times 10^5}\left(\frac{90 \times 1200}{\frac{\pi}{4} \times 900} + \frac{40 \times 800}{\frac{\pi}{4} \times 400}\right) \times 1000$$

$$= \frac{1000}{2 \times 10^5}(152.788 + 101.85916) \text{ mm}$$

$$= \frac{254.64791}{2 \times 10^5} \times 1000$$

$$\delta l = \mathbf{1.273\ mm}$$ **Ans.**

Example 15.13

Determine total change in length of the bar loaded as shown in Fig. 15.28. $E = 2.1 \times 10^5$ N/mm^2.

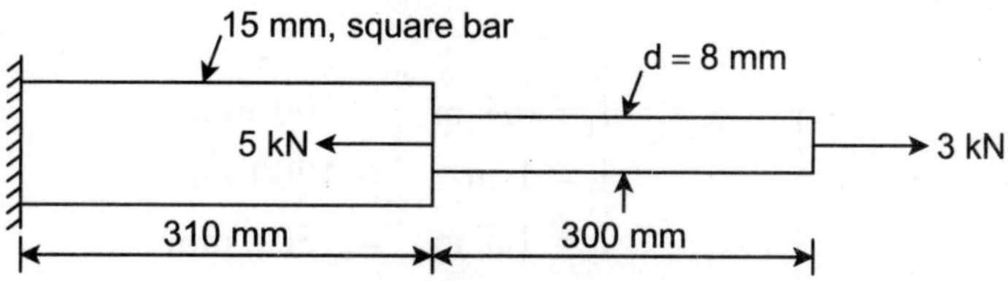

Fig. 15.28

Solution:

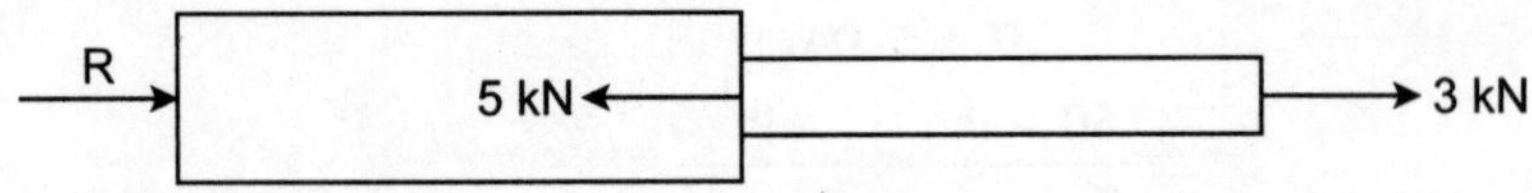

$A_1 = 15 \times 15\ mm^2$

$A_2 = \frac{\pi}{4}(8)^2$

$l_1 = 310\ mm$

$l_1 = 300\ mm$

R + 3 = 5

∴ R = 5 – 3 = 2 kN

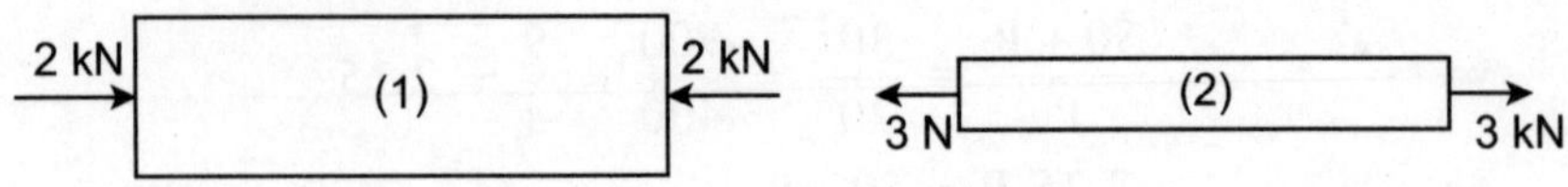

Change in length

Fig. 15.29

$$\delta l = \delta l_1 + \delta l_2$$

$$= \frac{P_1 l_1}{A_1 E} + \frac{P_2 \times l_2}{A_2 E}$$

$$= \frac{1}{E}\left(\frac{P_1 l_1}{A_1} + \frac{P_2 l_2}{A_2}\right)$$

$$= \frac{1}{2.1 \times 10^5}\left(-\frac{2 \times 310}{15 \times 15} + \frac{3 \times 300}{\frac{\pi}{4} \times (8)^2}\right) \times 1000\ mm$$

$$= \frac{1}{2.1 \times 10^5}(-2.76 + 17.90493) \times 100\ mm$$

$= \mathbf{0.0721\ mm}$ **Ans.**

Example 15.14

A bar of cross section 500 mm² is acted upon by forces as shown in Fig. 15.30. Determine the total elongation of the bar. E = 200 GPa.

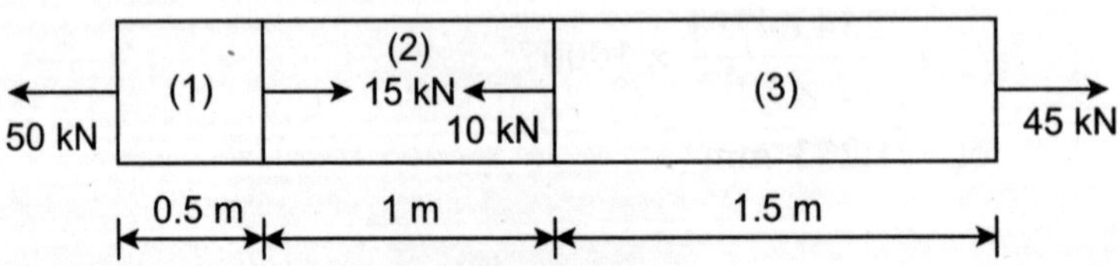

Fig. 15.30

Solution:

$P_1 = 50\ kN$	$l_1 = 0.5\ m = 500\ mm$
$P_2 = 15\ kN$	$l_2 = 1\ m = 1000\ mm$
$P_3 = 10\ kN$	$l_3 = 1.5\ m = 1500\ mm$
$P_4 = 45\ kN$	$E = 200\ GPa = 2 \times 10^5\ N/mm^2$

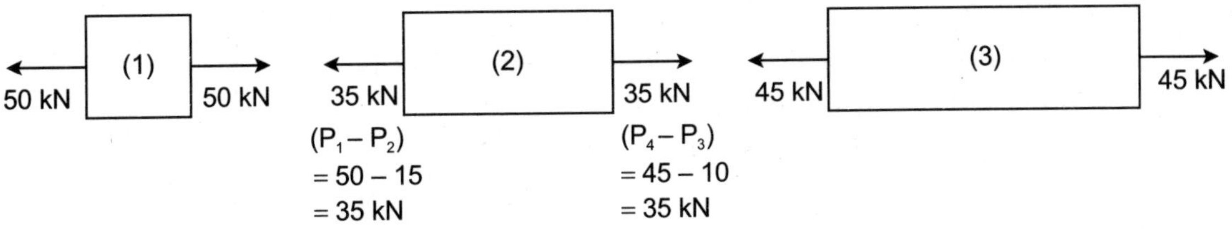

Fig. 15.31

Total change in length

$$\delta l = \delta l_1 + \delta l_2 + \delta l_3$$

$$= \frac{P_1 l_1}{A_1 E_1} + \frac{(P_2 - P_2) l_2}{A_2 E_2} + \frac{P_4 \cdot l_3}{A_3 E_3}$$

$$= \frac{1}{A \cdot E}\left[P_1 l_1 + (P_1 - P_2) l_2 + P_4 l_3\right]$$

$$= \frac{1000}{500 \times 2 \times 10^5}(50 \times 500 + 35 \times 1000 + 45 \times 1500)$$

$$= \frac{\cancel{10^5}}{\cancel{10^5} \times 500 \times 2}(50 \times 5 + 35 \times 10 + 45 \times 15)$$

$$= \frac{1275}{1000} = \mathbf{1.275 \ mm}$$ **Ans.**

Example 15.15

A bar of uniform cross sectional area 100 mm² carries forces in Newtons as shown in Fig. 15.32. Calculate the relative movement of end A with respect to D. $E = 200 \times 10^3$ *N/mm²*.

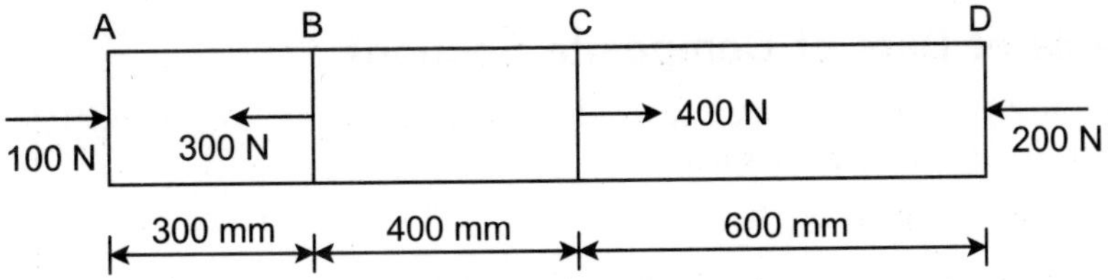

Fig. 15.32

Solution:

$A = 100 \text{ mm}^2$

$\delta l = ?$

$E = 200 \times 10^3 \text{ N/mm}^2 = 2 \times 10^5 \text{ N/mm}^2$

$P_1 = -100$ kN
$P_2 = -300$ kN
$P_3 = -400$ kN
$P_4 = -200$ kN

$\therefore\ P_1 - P_2 = -100 - (-300)$
$= -100 + 300 = 200$ N

and

$P_4 - P_3 = -200 - (-400)$
$= -200 + 400 = 200$ N

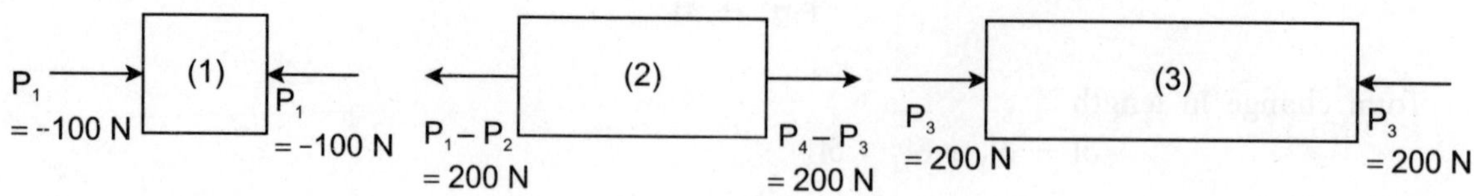

Fig. 15.33

$$\delta l_1 = \frac{P_1 l_1}{A_1 E_1} = \frac{-100 \times 300}{100 \times 2 \times 10^5} = -1.5 \times 10^{-3} \text{ mm}$$

$$\delta l_2 = \frac{(P_1 - P_2) l_2}{A_2 E_2} = \frac{200 \times 400}{100 \times 2 \times 10^5} = 4 \times 10^{-3} \text{ mm}$$

$$\delta l_3 = \frac{P_3 l_3}{A_3 E_3} = \frac{-200 \times 600}{100 \times 2 \times 10^5} = -6 \times 10^{-3} \text{ mm}$$

$\therefore$ Movement of A w.r.t. D

$$\delta l = \delta l_1 + \delta l_2 + \delta l_3$$
$$= -1.5 \times 10^{-3} + 4 \times 10^{-3} - 6 \times 10^{-3}$$
$$= \mathbf{-3.5 \times 10^{-3}} \textbf{ mm}$$ **Ans.**

i.e., the point A and D will come close to each other by 3.5×10^{-3} mm.

15.15 Analysis of Bars of Composite Sections

Note: 1. *Extension or compression in each bar is same, i.e. strain in each bar is same.*

$$\Rightarrow \delta l_1 = \delta l_2 \text{ or } \epsilon_1 = \epsilon_2$$

2. *Total external load on composite bar is equal to the sum of the loads carried by each different material.*

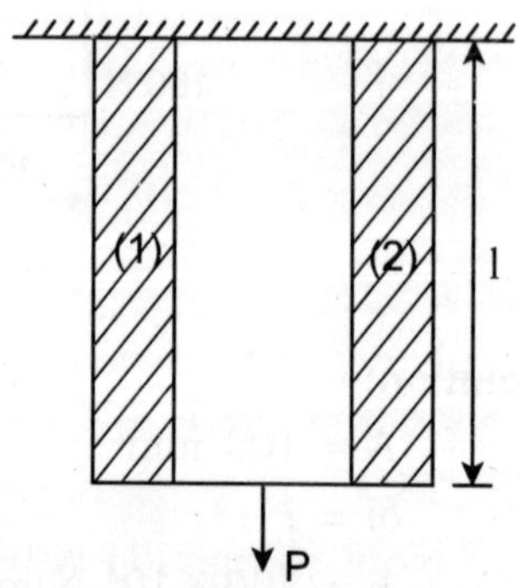

Fig. 15.34

Let

P → total load on composite bar

l → length of different materials

→ length of composite bar

A_1, A_2 → cross sectional areas of bar (1) and (2).
E_1, E_2 → Young's modulus of material 1, and 2.
P_1, P_2 → load shared by bar 1 and 2.
σ_1, σ_2 → stress induced in bar 1 and 2.

Now

$$P_1 + P_2 = P \ldots\ldots\ldots\ldots \quad (15.3)$$

$$\delta l_1 = \delta l_2 \ldots\ldots\ldots\ldots \quad (15.4)$$

$\left| \sigma = \frac{P}{A} \right.$

From (15.4), $\frac{P_1 l_1}{A_1 E_1} = \frac{P_2 l_2}{A_2 E_2}$

From (15.3), $\sigma_1 A_1 + \sigma_2 A_2 = P$

Note: $\frac{E_1}{E_2}$ ⇒ *Modular ratio of first material to second.*

Example 15.16

A beam weighing 450 N is held in a horizontal position by three vertical wires, one attached to one end of the beam, one to the middle of its length. The outer wires are of brass of diameter 1.25 mm and the central wire is of diameter 0.625 mm. If the beam is rigid and wires of the same length and unstressed before the beam is attached, estimate the stress induced in the wires. Take:

$$E_b = 86 \text{ GN/m}^2 \text{ and } E_s = 210 \text{ GN/m}^2$$

Solution:

$$P = 450 \text{ N}$$
$$d_b = 1.25 \text{ mm}$$
$$d_s = 0.625 \text{ mm}$$

$$E_b = \frac{86 \times 10^9}{10^6} \text{ N/mm}^2$$
$$= 0.86 \times 10^5 \text{ N/mm}^2$$

$$E_s = \frac{210 \times 10^9}{10^6} \text{ N/mm}^2$$
$$= 2.1 \times 10^5 \text{ N/mm}^2$$

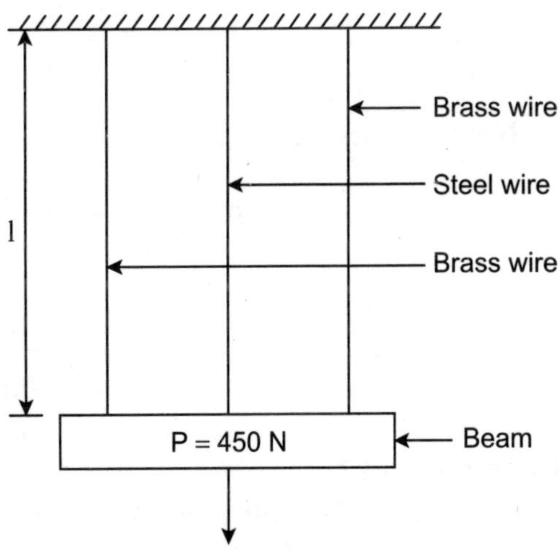

Fig. 15.35

Now, load carried by wires:

$$P_b + P_s + P_b = P$$

$$\Rightarrow \quad 2\,P_b + P_s = 450 \ldots\ldots\ldots\ldots \quad (15.5)$$

Now, elongation will be same

$$\delta l_s = \delta l_b$$

$$\Rightarrow \qquad \epsilon_s = \epsilon_b$$

$$\Rightarrow \qquad \frac{P_s}{A_s \cdot E_s} = \frac{P_b}{A_b \cdot E_b}$$

$$\Rightarrow \qquad P_s = \frac{A_s}{A_b} \cdot \frac{E_s}{E_b} \cdot P_b$$

$$= P_b \times \frac{\frac{\pi}{4}(d_s)^2 \times 210}{\frac{\pi}{4}(d_b)^2 \times 86}$$

$$= P_b \cdot \frac{(d_s)^2}{(d_b)^2} \times \left(\frac{210}{86}\right)$$

$$= \frac{P_b (0.625)^2}{(1.25)^2} \times \frac{210}{86} = 0.61\ P_b$$

$$\therefore \qquad P_s = 0.61\ P_b \qquad \text{(15.6)}$$

From Eqs. (15.5) and (15.6)

$$2\ P_b + 0.61\ P_b = 450$$

$$P_b = 172.4 \text{ kN}$$

and $\quad P_s = 105.2$ kN

Now, stresses induced

$$\sigma_b = \frac{P_b}{A_b} = \frac{172.4}{\frac{\pi}{4}(1.25)^2} = \mathbf{140\ N/mm^2}$$ **Ans.**

$$\sigma_s = \frac{P_s}{A_s} = \frac{105.2}{\frac{\pi}{4}(0.625)^2} = \mathbf{342.9\ N/mm^2}$$ **Ans.**

Example 15.17

A steel rod of 20 mm diameter is enclosed centrally in a hollow copper tube of internal diameter 30 mm and external diameter 40 mm. The composite bar is subjected to an axial pull of 50 kN. Length of each bar is 160 mm. Calculate

(a) stresses in the rod and tube

(b) load carried by each bar

Take $E_s = 2 \times 10^5$ *N/mm*^{2}, $E_c = 1 \times 10^5$ *N/mm*^{2}.

Solution:

$d_s = 20$ mm

$d_i = 30$ mm

$d_o = 40$ mm

$P = 50$ kN $= 50 \times 10^3$ N

$l = 160$ mm

(a) $\sigma_s = ?$; $\sigma_c = ?$ (b) $P_s = ?$; $P_c = ?$

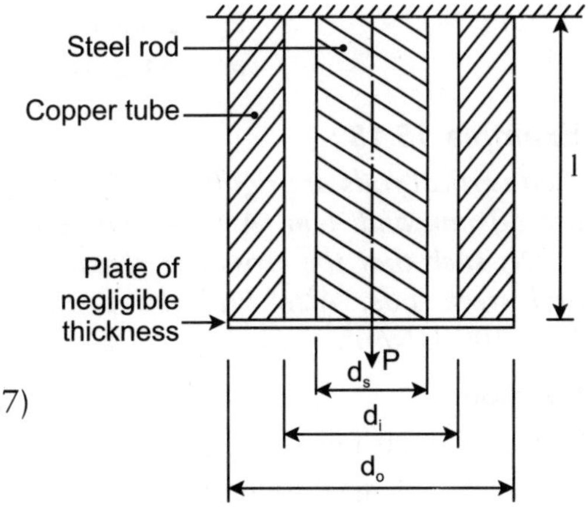

Fig. 15.36

Now

$$P = P_s + P_c \quad \ldots\ldots\ldots (15.7)$$

and

$$\delta l_s = \delta l_c$$

$$\Rightarrow \quad \frac{P_s l_s}{A_s E_s} = \frac{P_c l_c}{A_c E_c}; \quad l_s = l_c \text{ (given)}$$

$$\Rightarrow \quad \frac{\sigma_s}{E_s} = \frac{\sigma_c}{E_c} \quad \ldots\ldots\ldots (15.8)$$

or

$$\sigma_s = \frac{E_s}{E_c} \times \sigma_c = \frac{2 \times 10^5}{1 \times 10^5} \times \sigma_c = 2\,\sigma_c$$

or

$$\sigma_s = 2\,\sigma_c \quad \ldots\ldots\ldots (15.9)$$

$$\Rightarrow \quad \frac{P_s}{A_s} = \frac{2\,P_c}{A_c}$$

or

$$\frac{P_s}{P_c} = \frac{2\,A_s}{A_c} = \frac{2 \times \frac{\pi}{4} d_s^2}{\frac{\pi}{4}\left(d_o^2 - d_i^2\right)} = 2 \times \frac{20^2}{\left(40^2 - 30^2\right)}$$

$$\Rightarrow \quad P_s = 1.14\,P_c \quad \ldots\ldots\ldots (15.10)$$

From Eq. (15.7)

$$P_s + P_c = 50000$$

$$\Rightarrow \quad 1.14\,P_c + P_c = 50000$$

$$P_c = \frac{50000}{2.14} = 23364.5 \text{ N} = 23.4 \text{ kN}$$

$$P_s = 1.14 \times 23.4 = 26635.5 \text{ N} = 26.6 \text{ kN}$$

(a)

$$\sigma_s = \frac{P_s}{A_s} = \frac{26.6 \times 10^3}{\frac{\pi}{4}(20)^2} = \mathbf{84.6\ N/mm^2}$$

$$\sigma_c = \frac{P_c}{A_c} = \frac{23.4 \times 10^3}{\frac{\pi}{4}\left(40^2 - 30^2\right)} = \mathbf{42.6\ N/mm^2}$$

Ans.

(b)
$$\left.\begin{aligned} P_s &= \mathbf{26.6\ kN} \\ P_c &= \mathbf{23.4\ kN} \end{aligned}\right]$$ **Ans.**

Example 15.18

Two vertical rods are rigidly fixed at the top 600 mm apart diameters and lengths of each rod are 30 mm and 4 m. A cross bar is fixed to the rods at the lower ends, carries a load of 6 kN, such that the cross bar remains horizontal even after loading. Find stresses in copper and steel rods. Also find the position of the load on the bar. Take $E_s = 200\ GN/m^2$, $E_c = 100\ GN/m^2$.

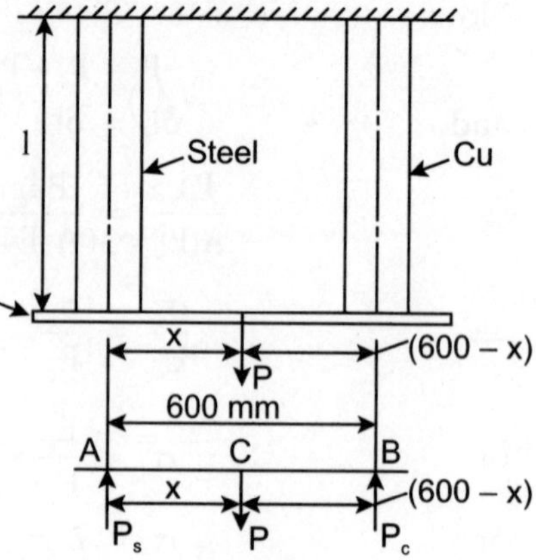

Fig. 15.37

Solution:

$d_s = d_c = 30$ mm

$l_s = l_c = 4$ m $= 4000$ mm

$P = 6$ kN $= 6 \times 10^3$ N

$x = ?$

$E_s = 200\ GN/m^2 = 2 \times 10^5\ N/mm^2$

$E_c = 100\ GN/m^2 = 1 \times 10^5\ N/mm^2$

$\sigma_s = ?$

$\sigma_c = ?$

Now, $\delta l_c = \delta l_s$

$$\Rightarrow \quad \frac{P_c l_c}{A_c E_c} = \frac{P_s l_s}{A_s E_s} \Rightarrow \frac{P_s}{E_s} = \frac{P_c}{E_c}; \; l_s = l_c,\ A_s = A_c$$

$$\Rightarrow \quad P_s = \frac{2 \times 10^5}{1 \times 10^5} P_c \Rightarrow P_s = 2\,P_c \quad \ldots\ldots (15.11)$$

Also $\quad P_s + P_c = 6000$ N $\quad \ldots\ldots (15.12)$

From Eqs. (15.11) and (15.12)

$P_c = 2000$ N

$P_s = 4000$ N

$$\therefore \quad \sigma_s = \frac{P_s}{A_s} = \frac{4000}{\frac{\pi}{4}(20)^2} = \mathbf{12.73\ N/mm^2}$$ **Ans.**

$$\sigma_c = \frac{P_c}{A_c} = \frac{2000}{\frac{\pi}{4}(20)^2} = \mathbf{6.37\ N/mm^2}$$ **Ans.**

Now,

Position of load on the cross bar. Taking moment about steel rod.

$$P_c \times 600 = P \times x$$

$$\Rightarrow \quad x = \frac{2000 \times 600}{6000} = \mathbf{200\ mm}$$ **Ans.**

Example 15.19

A load of 2 MN is applied on a short concrete column 400 × 300 mm. The column is reinforced with four steel bars of 10 mm diameter, one in each corner. Find the stress induced in the concrete and steel. Take $E_c = 1.4 \times 10^4$ N/mm² and $E_s = 2 \times 10^5$ N/mm².

Solution:

$$P = 2 \text{ MN} = 2 \times 10^6 \text{ N}$$

$$\text{Column Area} = 400 \times 300 \text{ mm}^2$$

$$A_s = \text{Area of one steel bar}$$

$$= \frac{\pi}{4}(d_s)^2 = \frac{\pi}{4}(10)^2 = 78.54 \text{ mm}^2$$

$$A_c = \text{Area of concrete}$$

$$= 400 \times 300 - 4 \times 78.54 = 119685.84 \text{ mm}^2$$

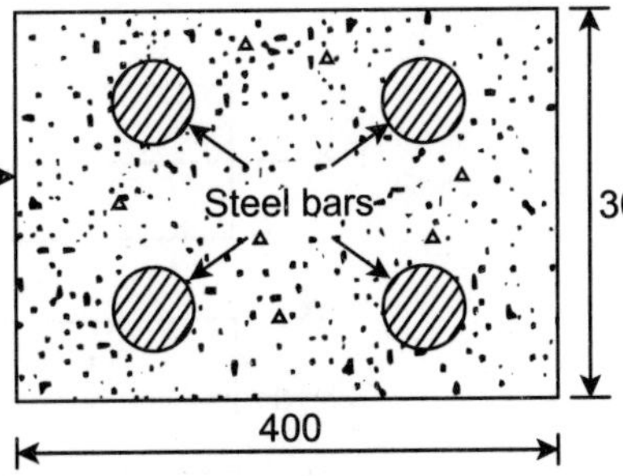

Fig. 15.38

Now

$$\delta l_s = \delta l_c$$

$$\Rightarrow \quad \sigma_s \frac{l_s}{E_s} = \sigma_c \frac{l_c}{E_c} \Rightarrow \frac{\sigma_s}{\sigma_s} = \frac{E_s}{E_c}, \quad l_s = l_c$$

$$\Rightarrow \quad \frac{\sigma_s}{\sigma_c} = \frac{2 \times 10^5}{1.4 \times 10^4} = 14.28 \quad \ldots\ldots (15.13)$$

Also

$$P_s + P_s + P_s + P_s + P_c = P$$

$$\Rightarrow \quad 4\,P_s + P_c = P$$

$$\Rightarrow \quad 4\,\sigma_s A_s + \sigma_c A_c = 2 \times 10^6 \quad \ldots\ldots (15.14)$$

Substituting value of σ_s into Eq. (15.14) from Eq. (15.13)

$$4\,A_s \times 14.28\,\sigma_c + \sigma_c A_c = 2 \times 10^6$$

$$\Rightarrow \quad \sigma_c\,(4 \times 14.28 \times 78.54 + 119685.84) = 2 \times 10^6$$

$$\Rightarrow \quad \sigma_c = \mathbf{16.1\ N/mm^2} \quad \textbf{Ans.}$$

$$\sigma_s = 14.28 \times 16.1 = 229.9 = \mathbf{230\ N/mm^2} \quad \textbf{Ans.}$$

Example 15.20

A steel tie rod 50 mm in diameter and 2.5 m long is subjected to a pull of 100 kN. To what length the rod should be bored centrally so that the total extension will increase by 15 per cent under the same pull, the bore being 25 mm diameter. Take E = 200 GN/m².

Solution:

$$d = 50 \text{ mm}$$

$$l = 2.5 \text{ m} = 2500 \text{ mm}$$

$$P = 100 \text{ kN} = 1 \times 10^5 \text{ N}$$

$d_1 = 25$ mm

$E = 200 \text{ GN/m}^2 = \dfrac{200 \times 10^9}{10^6} \text{ N/mm}^2 = 2 \times 10^5 \text{ N/mm}^2$

$x = ?$

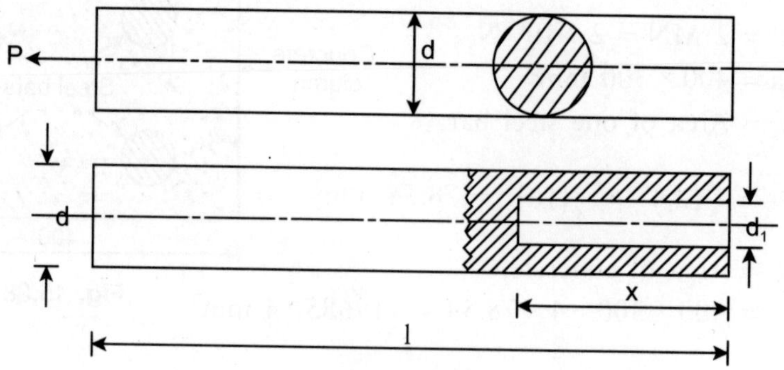

Fig. 15.39

Stress in solid rod

$$\sigma = \frac{P}{A} = \frac{100 \times 1000}{\frac{\pi}{4} \times (50)^2} = 50.93 \text{ N/mm}^2$$

Elongation of solid rod

$$\delta l = \frac{\sigma \times l}{E} = \frac{50.93 \times 2500}{2 \times 10^5}$$

$$\delta l = 0.6366197 \text{ mm}$$

Total elongation in bored rod

$$\delta l_1 = 1.15 \times \delta l$$
$$= 1.15 \times 0.6366197$$
$$= 0.7321127 \text{ mm}$$
$$= 0.732 \text{ mm}$$

Area at reduced section

$$A_1 = \frac{\pi}{4} \times (50^2 - 25^2) = 1472.62 \text{ mm}^2$$

Stress in reduced section

$$\sigma_1 = \frac{P}{A_1} = \frac{1 \times 10^5}{1472.62} = 67.91 \text{ N/mm}^2$$

Elongation of the rod after bored

$$\frac{\sigma(2500 - x)}{2 \times 10^5} + \frac{\sigma_1 \times x}{2 \times 10^5} = 0.732$$

$$\Rightarrow \quad (50.93)(2500 - x) + 67.91 \times x = 0.732 \times 2 \times 10^5$$

$$127325 - 50.93\ x + 67.91\ x = 146400$$

$$16.98\ x = 19075$$

$$x = \frac{19075}{16.98} = 1123.38 \text{ mm}$$

$$x = 1123.4 \text{ mm}$$ **Ans.**

Example 15.21

A concrete column of cross sectional area 400 mm × 400 mm is reinforced by four longitudinal 50 mm diameter round steel bars placed at each corner. If the column carries a compressive load of 300 kN. Determine:

(i) Loads carried

(ii) The compressive stress produced in concrete steel bars. Young's modulus of elasticity is 15 times that of concrete.

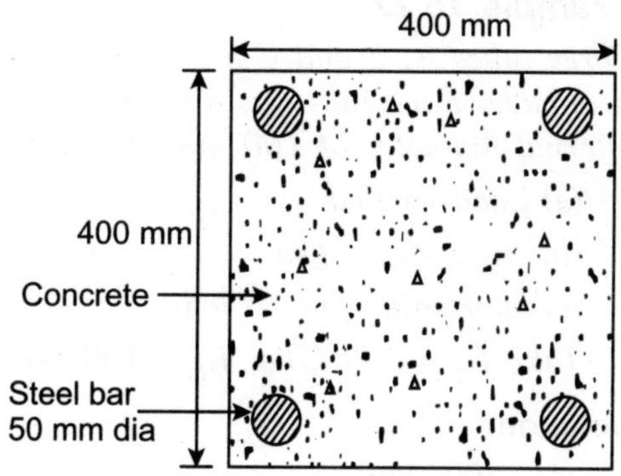

Fig. 15.40

Solution:

Area of concrete column 400×400 mm^2

$$d_s = 50 \text{ mm}$$

$$P = 300 \text{ kN}$$

Area of steel bars

$$A_s = 4 \times \frac{\pi}{4}(d_s)^2 = 4 \times \frac{\pi}{4}(50)^2$$

$$= 7850 \text{ mm}^2$$

Area of concrete

$$A_c = \text{Area of concrete column} - \text{Area of steel bars}$$

$$= (160000 - 7850) \text{ mm}^2$$

$$= 152100 \text{ mm}^2$$

$\because$ Steel bars and concrete column shorten by same amount.

$$\therefore \quad \delta l_s = \delta l_c$$

$$\Rightarrow \quad \epsilon_s = \epsilon_c$$

$$\frac{\sigma_s}{E_s} = \frac{\sigma_c}{E_c}$$

$$\Rightarrow \quad \sigma_s = \sigma_c \cdot \frac{E_s}{E_c} \qquad \Big| \quad E_s = 15\ E_c$$

$$= \sigma_c \cdot 15 \frac{E_c}{E_c}$$

$$\Rightarrow \quad \sigma_s = 15\ \sigma_c \quad \dots\dots \quad (15.15)$$

and $$P_s + P_c = P$$

$\Rightarrow$ $$\sigma_s A_s + \sigma_c A_c = 300 \times 10^3$$

$$15\,\sigma_c + 7850 + \sigma_c \times 152100 = 300 \times 1000$$

$\therefore$ $$\sigma_c = \mathbf{1.11\ N/mm^2}$$

and $$\sigma_s = \mathbf{16.65\ N/mm^2}$$ **Ans.**

and load carried

$$P_s = \sigma_s \times A_s$$

$$= 16.65 \times 7850 = \mathbf{130.7 \times 10^3\ N}$$

and $$P_c = \sigma_c \times A_c = 1.11 \times 152100 = \mathbf{168.9 \times 10^3\ N}$$ **Ans.**

Example 15.22

Three tubes A, B and C are fitting loosely one over the other. Tube 'A' is inside and tube 'C' is outside. Each tube has a thickness of 10 mm and length of 300 mm. Inner tube A has an internal diameter of 100 mm. If an axial thrust of 150 kN is applied, find for each tube

(a) Load carried

(b) Stress developed

(c) Shortening due to load

Take E_A = 200 GPa, E_B = 100 GPa and E_c = 50 GPa.

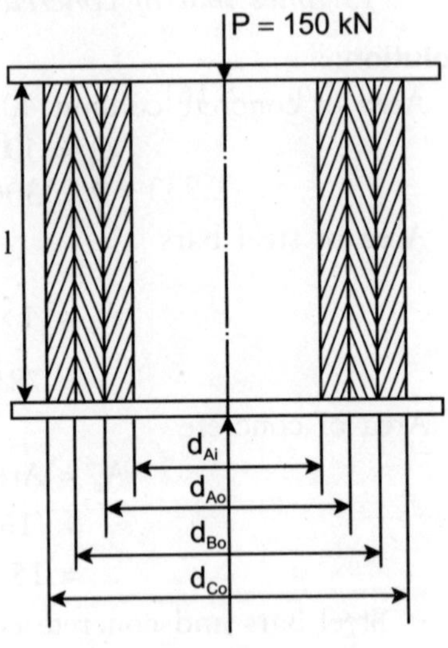

Fig. 15.41

Solution:

l = 300 mm

t = 10 mm

d_{Ai} = 100 mm

d_{Ao} = 120 mm

d_{Bi} = 120 mm

d_{Bo} = 140 mm

d_{Ci} = 140 mm

d_{Co} = 160 mm

P = 150 kN

Now

$$P_A + P_B + P_C = P$$

or $$P_A + P_B + P_C = 150000 \qquad (15.16)$$

and

$$\delta l_A = \delta l_B = \delta l_C$$

$$\frac{P_A \cdot l}{A_A E_A} = \frac{P_B \cdot l}{A_B \cdot E_B} = \frac{P_C \cdot l}{A_C \cdot E_C} \Rightarrow \frac{P_A}{A_A E_A} = \frac{P_B}{A_B E_B} = \frac{P_C}{A_C E_C}$$

$$\frac{P_A}{\frac{\pi}{4}\left(120^2-100^2\right)\times \frac{200}{4}} = \frac{P_B}{\frac{\pi}{4}\left(140^2-120^2\right)\times \frac{100}{2}} = \frac{P_C}{\frac{\pi}{4}\left(160^2-140^2\right)\times 50}$$

$$\Rightarrow \quad \frac{P_A}{4(120^2-100^2)} = \frac{P_B}{2(140^2-120^2)} = \frac{P_C}{(160^2-140^2)}$$

$$\therefore \quad \frac{P_A}{17600} = \frac{P_B}{10400} = \frac{P_C}{6000}$$

or
$$\frac{P_A}{176} = \frac{P_B}{104} = \frac{P_C}{60} \quad \ldots\ldots\ldots\ldots \quad (15.17)$$

$$\therefore \quad P_A = \frac{176}{60}P_C = 2.933\ P_C$$

$$P_B = \frac{104}{60}P_C = 1.733\ P_C$$

From Eq. (15.16)

$$P_A + P_B + P_C = 150000$$

$$\Rightarrow \quad (2.933 + 1.733 + 1)\ P_C = 150000$$

$$\left.\begin{aligned} P_C &= 26470.588\ \text{N} = \mathbf{26.5\ kN} \\ P_B &= 1.733 \times 26.470 = \mathbf{45.8\ kN} \\ P_A &= 150 - (26.5 + 45.8) = \mathbf{77.7\ kN} \end{aligned}\right] \quad \textbf{Ans.}$$

and

$$\left.\begin{aligned} \sigma_A &= \frac{P_A}{A_A} = \frac{77.7\times1000}{\frac{\pi}{4}\left(120^2-100^2\right)} = \mathbf{22.48\ N/mm^2} \\ \sigma_B &= \frac{P_B}{A_B} = \frac{45.8\times1000}{\frac{\pi}{4}\left(140^2-120^2\right)} = \mathbf{11.21\ N/mm^2} \\ \sigma_C &= \frac{P_C}{A_C} = \frac{26.5\times1000}{\frac{\pi}{4}\left(160^2-140^2\right)} = \mathbf{5.62\ N/mm^2} \end{aligned}\right] \quad \textbf{Ans.}$$

Now

$$\epsilon_C = \frac{\sigma_C}{E_C} = \frac{5.62}{50\times10^3} = 1.124\times10^{-4}$$

$$\Rightarrow \quad \delta l_C = l_C \times 1.124\times10^{-4} = 300\times1.124\times10^{-4}$$

$$\therefore \quad \delta l = \delta l_A = \delta l_B = \delta l_C = \mathbf{0.03372\ mm} \quad \textbf{Ans.}$$

Example 15.23

A rigid bar ACDB is hinged at A and supported in a horizontal position by two identical steel wires as shown in Fig. 15.42. A vertical load of 30 kN is applied at B. Find the tensile force T_1 and T_2 induced in these wires by the vertical load.

Solution:

Rigid bar means a bar which will remain straight. For wires (identical)

$A_1 = A_2$, $E_1 = E_2$, $l_1 = l_2$

$$P_B = 30 \text{ kN} = 30 \times 10^3 \text{ N}$$

$$T_1 = ?$$

$$T_2 = ?$$

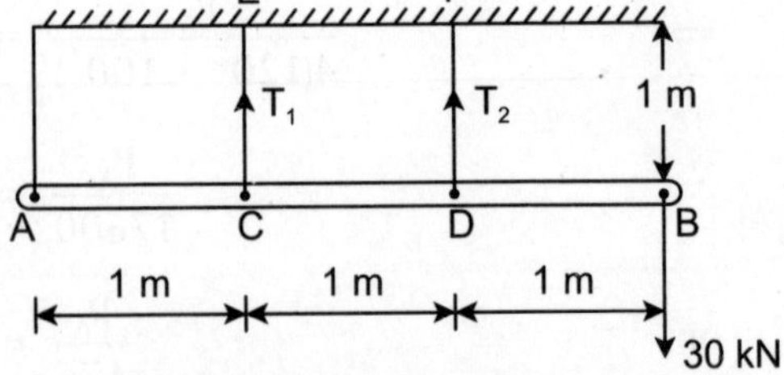

Fig. 15.42(a): Position of rigid bar before load is applied at B.

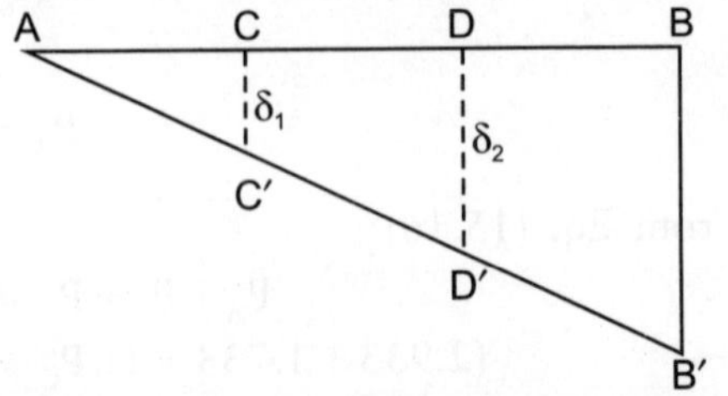

Fig. 15.42(b): Position of rigid bar after load is applied at B.

Since the rigid bar remains straight, hence the extension δ_1 and δ_2 may be given by

$$\frac{\delta_1}{\delta_2} = \frac{AC}{AD} = \frac{1}{2}$$

$$\Rightarrow \quad 2\,\delta_1 = \delta_2 \ldots\ldots\ldots \quad (15.18)$$

Also
$$\delta_1 = \frac{P_1 l_1}{A_1 E_1} = \frac{T_1 l_1}{A_1 E_1}$$

and
$$\delta_2 = \frac{P_2 l_2}{A_2 E_2} = \frac{T_2 l_2}{A_2 E_2}$$

Substituting these values in Eq. (15.18), we get

$$2 \times \frac{T_1 l_1}{A_1 E_1} = \frac{T_2 l_2}{A_2 E_2}$$

For identical wires

$\because \quad A_1 = A_2$

$l_1 = l_2$

$E_1 = E_2$

$$\Rightarrow \quad 2\,T_1 = T_2 \ldots\ldots\ldots \quad (15.19)$$

Now

Taking moments of all the forces about point A.

$$T_1 \times 1 + T_2 \times 2 = 30 \times 3$$

$$T_1 \times 2\ T_2 = 90 \ldots\ldots\ldots\ldots\ldots\ldots\ldots\ldots\ldots\ldots\ldots\ldots \quad (15.20)$$

From Eqs. (15.19) and (15.20)

$$T_1 + 2\,(2\,T_1) = 90$$

$$\Rightarrow \quad 5\,T_1 = 90$$

$$\left.\begin{aligned} T_1 &= \mathbf{18\ kN} \\ T_2 &= \mathbf{36\ kN} \end{aligned}\right]$$

Ans.

and stresses

$$\sigma_1 = \frac{T_1}{A_1}$$

$$\sigma_2 = \frac{T_2}{A_2}$$

Example 15.24

A copper bar 50 mm in diameter is placed within a steel tube 75 mm external diameter and 50 mm internal diameter of exactly the same length. The two pieces are rigidly fixed together by two pins 18 mm in diameter, one at each end passing through the bar and tube. Calculate the stress induced in the copper bar, steel tube and pins, if the temperature of the combination is raised by 50°C. Take $E_s = 210$ GN/m², $E_c = 105$ GN/m², $\alpha_s = 11.5 \times 10^{-6}$/°C, $\alpha_c = 17 \times 10^{-6}$/°C.

Solution:

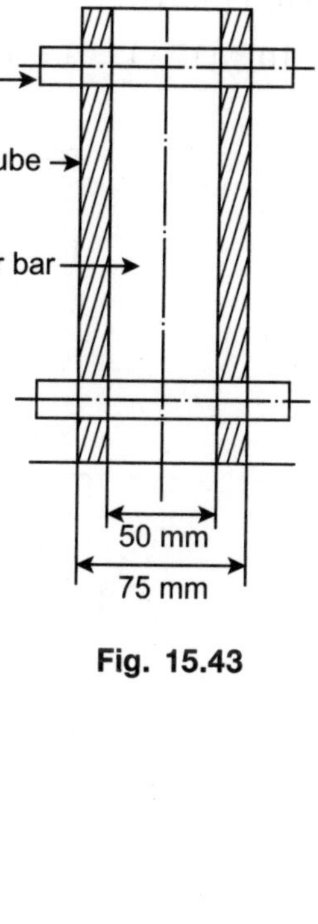

Fig. 15.43

$$d_c = 50 \text{ mm}$$

$$d_{so} = 75 \text{ mm}$$

$$d_{si} = 50 \text{ mm}$$

$$l_c = l_c = l$$

Pin dia., $d_p = 18$ mm

$$\sigma_c = ?$$

$$\sigma_s = ?$$

$$\tau_p = ?$$

$$t = 50°C$$

$$E_s = 2.1 \times 10^5 \text{ N/mm}^2$$

$$E_c = 1.05 \times 10^5 \text{ N/mm}^2$$

$$\alpha_s = 11.5 \times 10^{-6}/°C$$

$$\alpha_c = 17 \times 10^{-6}/°C$$

Now

Actual expansion in copper = Actual expansion in steel.

$$l(\alpha_c)\,t - \delta l_c = l\alpha_s\,t + \delta l_s$$

$$\Rightarrow \quad l\alpha_c t - l\alpha_s t = \delta l_s + \delta l_c$$

or

$$l \cdot t(\alpha_c - \alpha_s) = P \cdot l\left(\frac{1}{A_s E_s} + \frac{1}{A_c E_c}\right)$$

$$\Rightarrow \quad t(\alpha_c - \alpha_s) = P\left(\frac{1}{A_s E_s} + \frac{1}{A_c E_c}\right) \quad \ldots\ldots\ldots (15.21)$$

Now

$$A_s = \frac{\pi}{4}\left(d_{so}^2 - d_{si}^2\right) = \frac{\pi}{4}\left(75^2 - 50^2\right)$$

$$= 2454.3693 \text{ mm}^2$$

$$\therefore \quad \frac{1}{A_s E_s} = \frac{1}{2454.3693 \times 2.1 \times 10^5} = 1.94 \times 10^{-9}$$

and

$$A_c = \frac{\pi}{4} d_c^2 = \frac{\pi}{4}(50)^2 = 1963.4954 \text{ mm}^2$$

$$\therefore \quad \frac{1}{A_c E_c} = \frac{1}{1963.4954 \times 1.05 \times 10^5} = 4.85 \times 10^{-9}$$

From Eq. (15.21)

$$50 \times 10^{-6} (17 - 11.5) = P(1.94 \times 10^{-9} + 4.85 \times 10^{-9})$$

$$P = \frac{50 \times 10^{-6} \times 5.5}{6.79 \times 10^{-9}} = \frac{50 \times 5.5 \times 1000}{6.79}$$

$$P = 40500.736 \text{ N}$$

$$\therefore \quad \sigma_c = \frac{P}{A_c} = \frac{40500.736}{1963.4954} = \mathbf{20.63 \text{ N/mm}^2} \qquad \textbf{Ans.}$$

$$\sigma_s = \frac{P}{A_s} = \frac{40500.736}{2454.3693} = \mathbf{16.50 \text{ N/mm}^2} \qquad \textbf{Ans.}$$

and

$$\tau_{pin} = \frac{P}{2 \times A_p} = \frac{P}{2 \times \frac{\pi}{4}(d_p)^2} \qquad \text{Each pin is in double shear}$$

$$= \frac{40500.736}{2 \times \frac{\pi}{4}(18)^2}$$

$$= \frac{40500.736}{508.93801} = \mathbf{79.58 \text{ N/mm}^2} \qquad \textbf{Ans.}$$

Example 15.25

Two brass rods and one steel rod together support a load as shown in Fig. 15.44. If the stresses in brass and steel are not to exceed 60 N/mm^2 and 120 N/mm^2. Find safe load that can be supported. Take E for steel = 2 × 10^5 N/mm^2 and for brass 1 × 10^5 N/mm^2. The cross sectional area of steel rod is 1500 mm^2 and of each brass rod is 1000 mm^2.

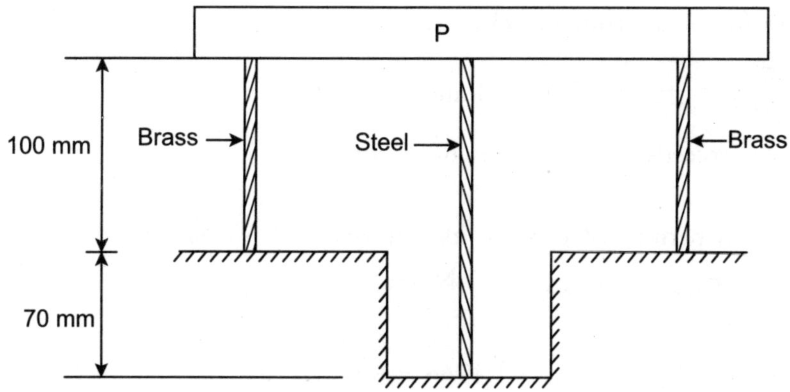

Fig. 15.44

Solution:

$\sigma_{b(max)} = 60 \text{ N/mm}^2$

$\sigma_{s(max)} = 120 \text{ N/mm}^2$

$P_{safe} = ?$

$E_s = 2 \times 10^5 \text{ N/mm}^2$

$E_b = 1 \times 10^5 \text{ N/mm}^2$

$A_s = 1500 \text{ N/mm}^2$

A_b (one rod) $= 1000 \text{ N/mm}^2$

Now

Change in length of Brass = Change in length of steel

$$\delta l_b = \delta l_s$$

$$\sigma_b \cdot \frac{l_b}{E_b} = \sigma_s \cdot \frac{l_s}{E_s}$$

$$\therefore \quad \frac{\sigma_s}{\sigma_b} = \frac{E_s}{E_b} \times \frac{l_b}{l_s}$$

$$= \frac{2 \times 10^5}{1 \times 10^5} \times \frac{100}{170}$$

$$\frac{\sigma_s}{\sigma_b} = \frac{20}{17} = 1.1764 \quad \ldots\ldots (15.22)$$

Now

Suppose steel is permitted to reach its safe stress of 120 N/mm² (i.e. we have assumed

$\sigma_{s(safe)} = \sigma_{s(max)} = 120 \text{ N/mm}^2$

∴ Safe stress for brass from Eq. (15.22) is

$$\sigma_{b(safe)} = \frac{\sigma_s}{1.764} = \frac{120}{1.1764} = 102 \text{ N/mm}^2$$

But this $\sigma_{b(safe)}$ exceeds $\sigma_{b(max)}$ that is 60 N/mm^2.

Now

Suppose, brass is permitted to reach its safe stress of 60 N/mm^2.

i.e. $\sigma_{b(safe)} = \sigma_{b(max)} = 60 \text{ N/mm}^2$

∴ From Eq. (15.22)

$$\sigma_{s(safe)} = \sigma_{b(max)} \times 1.1764 = 60 \times 1.1764$$

$$= 70.6 \text{ N/mm}^2, \text{ which is less than } \sigma_{s(max)}\ 120 \text{ N/mm}^2$$

$$\therefore \quad \sigma_{s(safe)} = 70.6 \text{ N/mm}^2, \quad \sigma_{b(safe)} = 60 \text{ N/mm}^2$$

$$\therefore \quad P = P_b + P_s + P_b = 2\,P_b + P_s = 2\,\sigma_b\,A_b + \sigma_s\,A_s$$

$$= 2 \times 60 \times 1000 + 70.6 \times 1500 = 225900 \text{ N} = 225.9 \text{ kN}$$ **Ans.**

15.16 Analysis of Uniformly Tapering Circular Rod under Axial Pull

Let P = Axial tensile load on the bar
L = Total length of the bar
E = Young's modulus
D_1 = Dia. of larger end
D_2 = Dia. of small end
D_x = Dia. of elementary ring
d_x = Length of elementary ring
x = Distance of ring from left end.

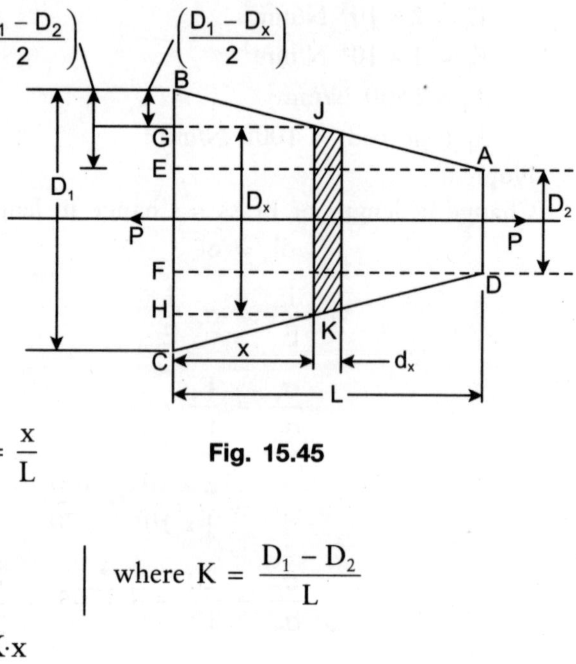

Fig. 15.45

From similar triangles BGJ and BEA,

$$\frac{\frac{D_1 - D_x}{2}}{\frac{D_1 - D_2}{2}} = \frac{x}{L} \Rightarrow \frac{D_1 - D_x}{D_1 - D_2} = \frac{x}{L}$$

or $$D_1 - D_x = \left(\frac{D_1 - D_2}{L}\right)\cdot x \qquad \text{where } K = \frac{D_1 - D_2}{L}$$

$$D_1 - D_x = K\cdot x, \; D_x = D_1 - K\cdot x$$

$$A_x = \frac{\pi}{4}D_x^2 = \frac{\pi}{4}(D_1 - K\cdot x)^2$$

and $$\sigma_x = \frac{P}{A_x} = \frac{P}{\frac{\pi}{4}(D_1 - K\cdot x)^2} = \frac{4\,P}{\pi(D_1 - K\cdot x)^2}$$

$$\epsilon_x = \frac{\sigma_x}{E} = \frac{4\,P}{\pi E(D_1 - K\cdot x)^2}$$

Extension of the small elemental length d_x

$$\delta d_x = \epsilon_x \cdot d_x = \frac{4\,P\cdot d_x}{\pi E(D_1 - K\cdot x)^2}$$

Total extension of the bar

$$\delta l = \int_0^L \delta d_x = \int_0^L \frac{4\,P}{\pi E(D_1 - K\cdot x)^2}\cdot d_x$$

$$= \frac{4\,P}{\pi E}\int_0^L (D_1 - K\cdot x)^{-2}\, d_x = \frac{4\,P}{\pi EK}\left[(D_1 - Kx)^{-1}\right]_0^L$$

$$= \frac{4\,P}{\pi EK}\left(\frac{1}{D_1 - Kx}\right)_0^L$$

$$= \frac{4\,P}{\pi EK}\left(\frac{1}{D_1 - KL} - \frac{1}{D_1}\right)$$

$$= \frac{4\,P}{\pi E\left(\frac{D_1 - D_2}{L}\right)}\cdot\left(\frac{1}{D_1 - \frac{D_1 - D_2}{L}L} - \frac{1}{D_1}\right)$$

$$= \frac{4\,PL}{\pi E(D_1 - D_2)}\cdot\left(\frac{1}{\cancel{D_1} - \cancel{D_1} + D_2} - \frac{1}{D_1}\right)$$

$$= \frac{4\,PL}{\pi E(D_1 - D_2)}\left(\frac{D_1 - D_2}{D_1 D_2}\right)$$

$$\delta l = \frac{4\,PL}{\pi E D_1 D_2}$$

Example 15.26

A tapering bar of circular cross-section of diameter 60 mm at the larger end and 40 mm at the smaller end, is connected to uniform bars of 60 mm diameter at the larger end and 30 mm diameter at the smaller end as shown in Fig. 15.46. The assembly is subjected to point loads *as shown. P_1 = 150 kN, P_2 = 275 kN, P_4 = 100 kN. Determine P_3 for equilibrium and the net change in the length of member. Take E = 200 GPa.*

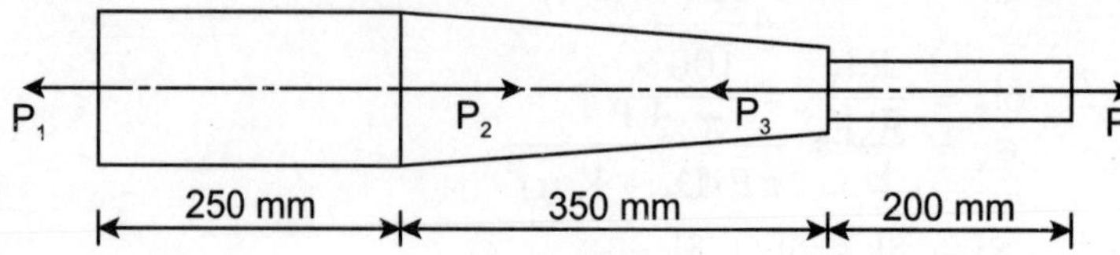

Fig. 15.46

Solution:

l_1 = 250 mm	P_1 = 150 kN
l_2 = 350 mm	P_2 = 275 kN
l_3 = 200 mm	P_3 = ?
d_1 = 60 mm	P_4 = 100 kN
d_2 = 40 mm	
d_3 = 30 mm	

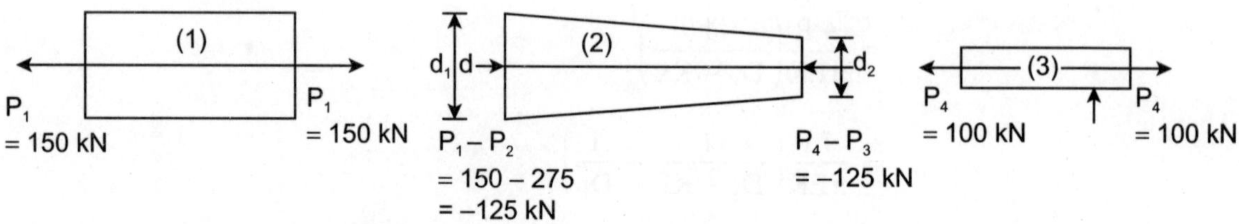

Fig. 15.47: F.B.D. of Individual Members

For equilibrium; $\sum F_x = 0$

$$P_1 + P_3 = P_2 + P_4$$

$$\Rightarrow \quad P_1 - P_2 = P_4 - P_3$$

$$-125 = 100 - P_3$$

$$P_3 = \mathbf{225\ kN} \qquad \textbf{Ans.}$$

Now
$$A_1 = \frac{\pi}{4}d_1^2 = \frac{\pi}{4}(60)^2 = 900\,\pi \text{ mm}^2$$

$$A_3 = \frac{\pi}{4}d_3^2 = \frac{\pi}{4}(30)^2 = 225\,\pi \text{ mm}^2$$

Now
Total elongation

$$\delta l = \delta l_1 + \delta l_2 + \delta l_3$$

$$\delta l_1 = \frac{P_1 l_1}{A_1 E_1} = \frac{150 \times 1000 \times 250}{\frac{\pi}{4}(60)^2 \times 2 \times 10^5} = 0.0663 \text{ mm}$$

$$\delta l_2 = \frac{4\,Pl}{\pi E d_1 d_2} = \frac{4 \times (-125) \times 1000 \times 350}{\pi \times 2 \times 10^5 \times 60 \times 40} = -\,0.1161 \text{ mm}$$

$$\delta l_3 = \frac{P_3 l_3}{A_3 E_3} = \frac{100 \times 1000 \times 200}{\frac{\pi}{4}(30)^2 \times 2 \times 10^5} = 0.14147 \text{ mm}$$

$$\therefore \quad \delta l = \delta l_1 + \delta l_2 + \delta l_3$$

$$= 0.0663 - 0.1161 + 0.14147$$

$$\delta l = \mathbf{0.09167 \text{ mm}}$$

Ans.

15.17 Thermal Stresses

Thermal stresses are the stresses in a body due to change in temperature and the body is not allowed to expand or contract freely. But if the body is allowed to expand or contract freely then no stress will be setup in the body.

Let l = Original length of the body

t = Change in temperature

α = Coefficient of linear expansion

E = Youngs modulus

Thermal strain

$$\in = \frac{\text{Expansion/Contraction, prevented}}{\text{Original length}} = \frac{l\alpha t}{l} = \alpha t$$

If the ends are yielded by an amount δ, then

Actual strain

$$\in = \left(\frac{l\alpha t - \delta}{l}\right)$$

Thermal stress

$$\sigma = \in \times E = \left(\frac{l\alpha t - \delta}{l}\right) E = \alpha t E; \text{ if } \delta = 0$$

load

$$P = \sigma \times A = \in E\,A = \left(\frac{l\alpha t - \delta}{l}\right) EA = \alpha \cdot t \cdot E \cdot A; \text{ if } \delta = 0$$

Example 15.27

A steel rod of 50 mm dia. and 6 mm long is connected to two grips and the rod is maintained at a temperature of 95°C. Determine the stresses and pull exerted when the temperature falls to 30°C, if (a) the ends do not yield; (b) the ends yield by 1.2 mm. Take $E = 2 \times 10^5$ *N/mm²,* $\alpha = 12 \times 10^{-6}$/°C.

Solution:

d = 500 mm	δ = 1.2 mm
l = 6 m = 6000 mm	E = 2×10^5 N/mm²
t_1 = 95°C	$\alpha = 12 \times 10^{-6}$/°C
t_2 = 30°C	$\therefore$ $t = t_1 - t_2 = 95 - 30 = 65$°C
σ = ?	P = ?

(a) When the ends do not yield

$$\sigma = \alpha t E = 12 \times 10^{-6} \times 65 \times 2 \times 10^5 = \mathbf{156\ N/mm^2}$$ **Ans.**

$$P = \sigma \times A = 156 \times \frac{\pi}{4}(50)^2 = 306305\ \text{N} = \mathbf{306.3\ kN}$$ **Ans.**

(b) When δ = 0.12 m = 1.2 mm

$$\sigma = \left(\frac{l\alpha t - \delta}{l}\right) E = \left(\frac{6000 \times 12 \times 10^{-6} \times 65 - 1.2}{6000}\right) \times 2 \times 10^5 = \mathbf{116\ MPa}$$ **Ans.**

$$P = \sigma \times A = 116 \times \frac{\pi}{4}(50)^2 = 227765.5\ \text{N} = \mathbf{227.8\ kN}$$ **Ans.**

15.18 Thermal Stresses in Composite Bar

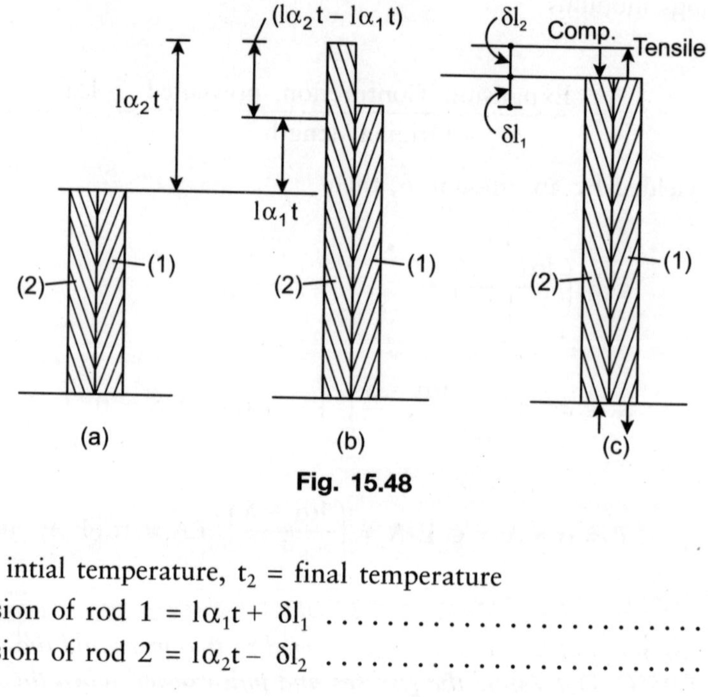

Fig. 15.48

Let,

$\alpha_2 > \alpha_1$, t_1 = intial temperature, t_2 = final temperature

Actual expansion of rod 1 = $l\alpha_1 t + \delta l_1$ .... (15.23)

Actual expansion of rod 2 = $l\alpha_2 t - \delta l_2$ .... (15.24)

We know that

Actual expansion of rod (1) = Actual expansion of rod (2)

$$\therefore \quad l\alpha_1 t + \delta l_1 = l\alpha_2 t - \delta l_2$$

$$\Rightarrow \quad \delta l_1 + \delta l_2 = l\alpha_2 t - l\alpha_1 t \qquad (15.25)$$

Also
$$\delta l_1 = \frac{P_1 l_1}{A_1 E_1} = \frac{Pl}{A_1 E_1} \qquad (15.26)$$

and
$$\delta l_2 = \frac{P_2 l_2}{A_2 E_2} = \frac{Pl}{A_2 E_2} \qquad (15.27)$$

With the help of Eqs. (15.25), (15.26) and (15.27), we will solve the problems.

Example 15.28

A steel rod of 30 mm diameter passes centrally through a copper tube 40 mm internal and 50 mm external dia. The tube is closed at each end by rigid plates of negligible thickness. The nuts are tightened lightly home on the projected parts of the rod. If the temperature of the assembly is raised by 60°C, calculate the stresses developed in copper and steel. Take $E_s = 200$ GN/m^2 and $E_c = 100$ GN/m^2, $\alpha_s = 12 \times 10^{-6}$/°C, $\alpha_c = 18 \times 10^{-6}$/°C.

Solution:

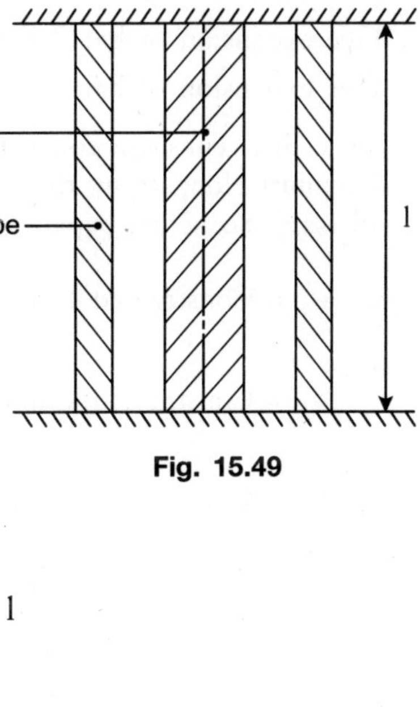

Fig. 15.49

$d_s = 30$ mm

$d_{co} = 50$ mm

$d_{ci} = 40$ mm

$t = 60$°C

$\sigma_s = ?$

$\sigma_c = ?$

$E_s = 200$ GN/m^2 $= 200 \times 10^3 = 2 \times 10^5$ N/mm^2

$E_c = 100$ GN/m^2 $= 1 \times 10^5$ N/mm^2

$\alpha_s = 12 \times 10^{-6}$/°C, $\alpha_c = 18 \times 10^{-6}$/°C

Now, we know that

$$\delta l_s + \delta l_c = l\alpha_c t - l\alpha_s t$$

$$\Rightarrow \quad \frac{P_s l_s}{A_s E_s} + \frac{P_c l_c}{A_c E_c} = lt(\alpha_c - \alpha_s), \; P_s = P_c = P, \; l_s = l_c = l$$

$$\Rightarrow \quad P\left(\frac{1}{A_s E_s} + \frac{1}{A_c E_c}\right) = t(\alpha_c - \alpha_s)$$

$$\Rightarrow \quad P\left(\frac{1}{\frac{\pi}{4}d_s^2 \times 2 \times 10^5} + \frac{1}{\frac{\pi}{4}(d_o^2 - d_i^2) \times 1 \times 10^5}\right) = 60\ (18 - 12) \times 10^{-6}$$

$$\Rightarrow \quad \frac{P}{\frac{\pi}{4} \times 10^5}\left(\frac{1}{2 \times (30)^2} + \frac{1}{1 \times (50^2 - 40^2)}\right) = 60 \times 6 \times 10^{-6}$$

$$\Rightarrow \quad = P(1.6666 \times 10^{-3}) = 28.27$$

$$\Rightarrow \quad P = 16962 \text{ N}$$

$$\therefore \quad \sigma_s = \frac{P}{A_s} = \frac{16962}{\frac{\pi}{4}(30)^2} = 24 \text{ N/mm}^2 \quad \textbf{Ans.}$$

$$\therefore \quad \sigma_c = \frac{P}{A_c} = \frac{16962}{\frac{\pi}{4}(50^2 - 40^2)} = 24 \text{ N/mm}^2 \quad \textbf{Ans.}$$

15.19 Composite System of Equal Lengths Containing More Than Two Components Subjected to Variation of Temperature

Three bars of different materials, each of equal length l, having coefficient of linear expansions α_1, α_2, and α_3.

Free expansion of bar 1 = $l\alpha_1 t$

Free expansion of bar 2 = $l\alpha_2 t$

Free expansion of bar 3 = $l\alpha_3 t$

Since their ends are connected rigidly, so each bar must elongate by the same amount. Say δl (say). So actual expansion of each bar is δl.

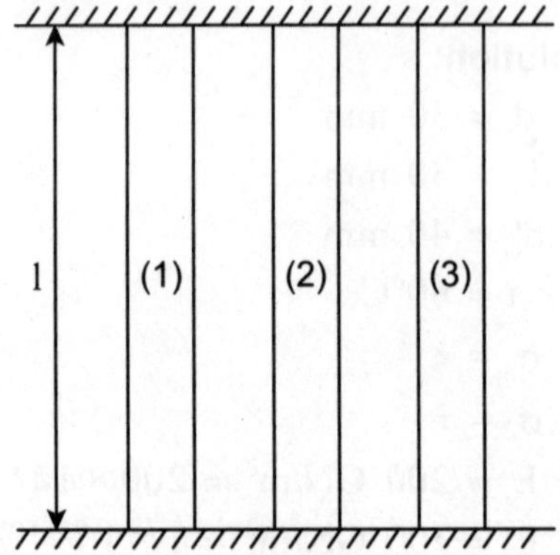

Fig. 15.50

$$\therefore \quad \in_1 = \text{Constrained strain in bar 1} = \left(\frac{\delta l - l\alpha_1 t}{l}\right)$$

$$\in_2 = \text{Constrained strain in bar 2} = \left(\frac{\delta l - l\alpha_2 t}{l}\right)$$

$$\in_3 = \text{Constrained strain in bar 3} = \left(\frac{\delta l - l\alpha_3 t}{l}\right)$$

$\therefore$ Stresses in individual bars are

$$\sigma_1 = \in_1 E_1 = \left(\frac{\delta l - l\alpha_1 t}{l}\right) E_1$$

$$\sigma_2 = \in_2 E_2 = \left(\frac{\delta l - l\alpha_2 t}{l}\right) E_2$$

$$\sigma_3 = \in_3 E_3 = \left(\frac{\delta l - l\alpha_3 t}{l}\right) E_3$$

and forces in each bar:

$$P_1 = \sigma_1 A_1 = \left(\frac{\delta l - l\alpha_1 t}{l}\right) A_1 E_1$$

$$P_2 = \sigma_2 A_2 = \left(\frac{\delta l - l\alpha_2 t}{l}\right) A_2 E_2$$

$$P_3 = \sigma_3 A_3 = \left(\frac{\delta l - l\alpha_3 t}{l}\right) A_3 E_3$$

As composite system is in equilibrium, the total force must be equal to zero.

$$\therefore \quad P_1 + P_2 + P_3 = 0$$

$$\Rightarrow \quad \sigma_1 A_1 + \sigma_2 A_2 + \sigma_3 A_3 = 0$$

$$\Rightarrow \quad \epsilon_1 E_1 A_1 + \epsilon_2 E_2 A_2 + \epsilon_3 E_3 A_3 = 0$$

$$\Rightarrow \quad \left(\frac{\delta l - l\alpha_1 t}{l}\right) E_1 A_1 + \left(\frac{\delta l - l\alpha_2 t}{l}\right) E_2 A_2 + \left(\frac{\delta l - l\alpha_3 t}{l}\right) E_3 A_3 = 0$$

$$\Rightarrow \quad \frac{\delta l}{\cancel{l}}(A_1E_1 + A_2E_2 + A_3E_3) = \frac{lt}{\cancel{l}}(A_1E_1\alpha_1 + A_2E_2\alpha_2 + A_3E_3\alpha_3)$$

$$\delta l = \frac{l \cdot t(A_1E_1\alpha_1 + A_2E_2\alpha_2 + A_3E_3\alpha_3)}{(A_1E_1 + A_2E_2 + A_3E_3)}$$

$$\Rightarrow \quad \delta l = \frac{l \cdot t \cdot \sum_{i=1}^{n} A_i E_i \alpha_i}{\sum_{i=1}^{n} A_i E_i}$$

Note: If a load P is also applied to the composite system in addition to the temperature rise then for equilibrium of the system

$$P_1 + P_2 + P_3 = P$$

$$\Rightarrow \quad \delta l = \frac{lP + l \cdot t \sum_{i=1}^{n} A_i E_i \alpha_i}{\sum_{i=1}^{n} A_i E_i \alpha_i}$$

Example 15.29

A bar of steel and two of copper, each of same area and length, have their ends rigidly connected at a temperature of 20°C. The steel bar lies between the two copper bars, on raising the temperature to 300°C, the length of bar increased by 2 mm. Determine original length and final stresses in each of the bars. Take E_s = 210 GPa, E_c = 100 GPa, $\alpha_s = 12 \times 10^{-6}$/°C, $\alpha_c = 18 \times 10^{-6}$/°C.

Solution:

$$A_1 = A_2 = A_3 = A$$

$$l_1 = l_2 = l_3 = l$$

$t_1 = 20°C$

$t_2 = 300°C$

$\therefore \quad t = 300 - 20 = 280°C$

$\delta l = 2 \text{ mm}$

$l = ?$

$\sigma_1 = ?$

$\sigma_2 = ?$

$E_s = 2.1 \times 10^5 \text{ N/mm}^2$

$E_c = 1 \times 10^5 \text{ N/mm}^2$

$\alpha_s = 1 \times 10^{-6}/°C$

$\alpha_c = 18 \times 10^{-6}/°C$

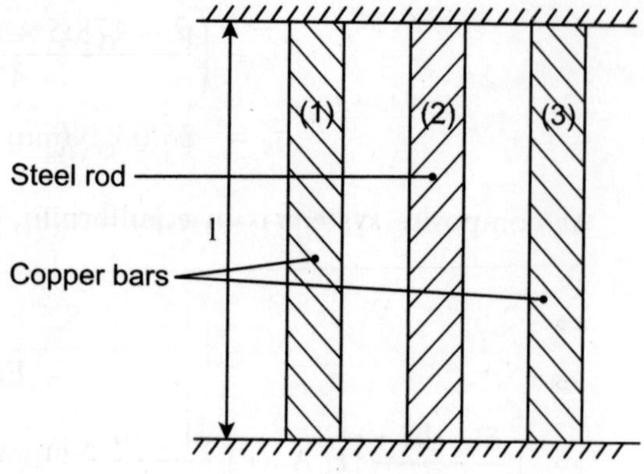

Fig. 15.51

We know that

$$\delta l = \frac{l \cdot t(A_1E_1\alpha_2 + A_2E_2\alpha_2 + A_3E_3\alpha_3)}{(A_1E_1 + A_2E_2 + A_3E_3)}$$

$$= \frac{lt(E_1\alpha_1 + E_2\alpha_2 + E_3\alpha_3)}{(E_1 + E_2 + E_3)}, \quad A_1 = A_2 = A_3$$

$$= \frac{lt(2\,E_1\alpha_1 + E_2\alpha_2)}{(2\,E_1 + E_2)}$$

or
$$\delta l = \frac{l \cdot t(2\,E_c\alpha_c + E_s\alpha_s)}{(2\,E_c + E_s)}$$

$\Rightarrow$
$$2 = \frac{1 \times 280(2 \times 1 \times 10^5 \times 18 \times 10^{-6} + 2.1 \times 10^5 \times 12 \times 10^{-6})}{(2 \times 1 \times 10^5 + 2.1 \times 10^5)}$$

$$= \frac{1 \times 280 \times 10^5 \times 10^{-6}\,(36 + 25.2)}{(10^5 \times 4.1)}$$

$$= \frac{1 \times 280 \times 61.2 \times 10^{-6}}{4.1}$$

$\Rightarrow$
$$l = \frac{4.1 \times 2 \times 10^{-6}}{17136} \text{ mm}$$

$\therefore$ $\quad$ **$l = 478.5$ mm** **Ans.**

and

$$\sigma_c = \sigma_1 = \frac{P_1}{A_1} = \epsilon_1 E_1 = \left(\frac{\delta l - l\alpha_1 t}{l}\right) E_c$$

$$= \left(\frac{2 - 478.5 \times 18 \times 10^{-6} \times 280}{478.5}\right) 1\times10^5$$

$\therefore \quad \sigma_c = -86.03 \text{ N/mm}^2 = 86.03 \text{ N/mm}^2$ (Comp.)

and $\quad \sigma_s = \sigma_2 = \epsilon_2 E_2 = \epsilon_s E_s = \left(\frac{\delta l - l\alpha_2 t}{l}\right) E_s$

$$= \left(\frac{\left(2 - 478.5 \times 12 \times 10^{-6} \times 280\right) \times 2.1 \times 10^5}{478.5}\right)$$

$$= 172.14 \text{ N/mm}^2$$

$\therefore \quad$ **σ_c = 86.03 N/mm² (Comp.)** **Ans.**

σ_s = 172.14 N/mm² (Tensile) **Ans.**

15.20 Elongation of a Bar due to its Own Weight

AB is a bar fixed at end A and hangs freely under its own weight.

l = length of bar

A = Area of cross-section

E = Young's modulus

ρ = Weight per unit volume of the material or density

Consider a small strip of thickness dx at a distance x from lower end.

Weight of bar for a length of x

= Volume of bar upto length x × density

= ρ × A × x | V = A × x, ρ = density

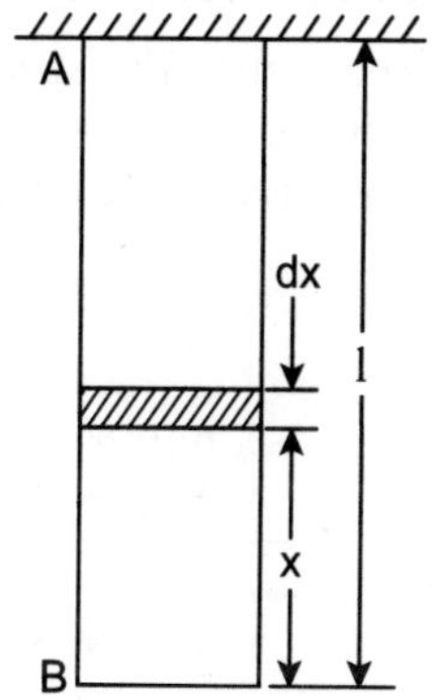

Fig. 15.52

It means that on the strip, a wt. of ρ·A·x is acting in the downward direction. Due to this wt. there will be some increase in length of element. But length of the element is dx.

$$\therefore \quad \text{Sresss on element} = \frac{\text{wt. on element}}{\text{Area of cross section}}$$

$$= \frac{\rho A x}{A} = \rho x$$

The above equation shows that stress due to self weight in a bar is not uniform. It depends on x. The stress increases with increase of x.

i.e. Stress α x

Stress on element = ρ·x

⇒ Stress on element α x

and Strain in element $= \dfrac{\text{Stress}}{E} = \dfrac{\rho x}{E}$

or $\dfrac{\text{Change in length of element } \delta dx}{\text{Original length of element (dx)}} = \dfrac{\rho \cdot x}{E}$

$\Rightarrow$ Elongation of the element $\delta dx = \dfrac{\rho \cdot x \cdot dx}{E}$

$\therefore$ Total elongation of the bar $\delta l = \int_0^l \delta dx = \int_0^l \dfrac{\rho x \cdot dx}{E}$

$$\Rightarrow \quad \delta l = \frac{\rho}{E}\int_0^l x dx = \frac{\rho}{E}\left[\frac{x^2}{2}\right]_0^l = \frac{\rho l^2}{2E}$$

$$\delta l = \frac{\rho l^2}{2E}$$

15.21 Analysis of Bar of Uniform Strength

We know that the stress due to self weight of the bar is not constant but the stress increases with the increase of distance from the lower end. If the self weight is neglected and a bar of uniform section is subjected to an axial load, then the stress in the bar would be uniform.

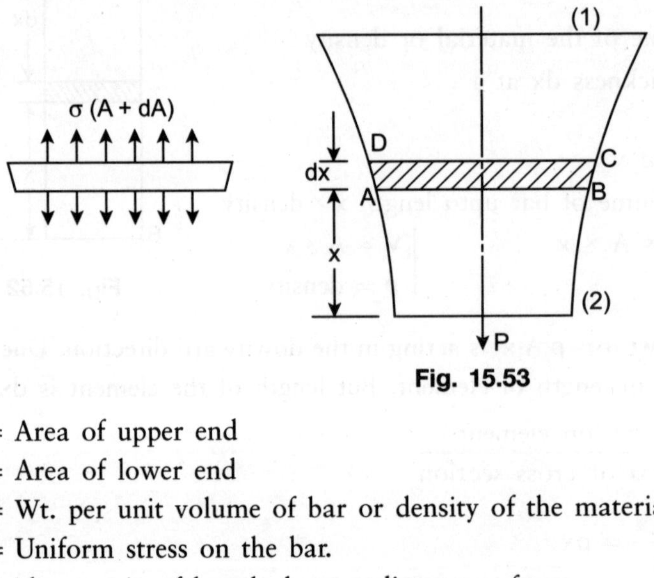

Fig. 15.53

A_1 = Area of upper end

A_2 = Area of lower end

ρ = Wt. per unit volume of bar or density of the material

σ = Uniform stress on the bar.

Consider a strip of length dx at a distance x from the lower end. Let A be the area the strip at section AB and (A + dA) be the area at section DC. Consider equilibrium of strip ABCD. The forces acting on the strip are:

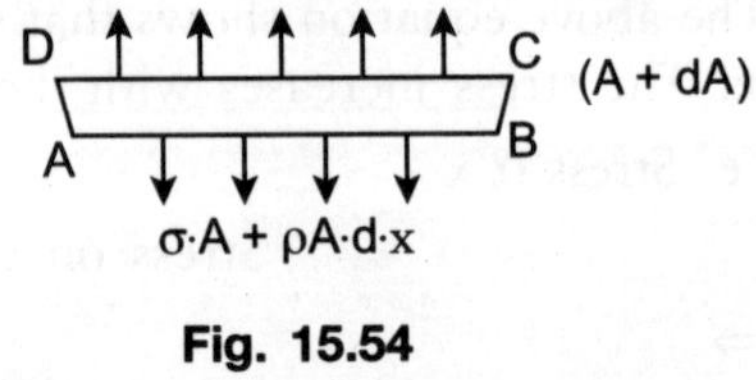

Fig. 15.54

(i) Wt. of strip acting downward and equal to
$\rho \times$ volume of strip. i.e. $\rho \cdot A \cdot dx$.

(ii) Force on section AB due to uniform stress (σ) and is equal to $\sigma \times A(\downarrow)$.

(iii) Force on section CD due to uniform stress (σ) and is equal to $\sigma \cdot (A + dA)$.

Now

Total force acting upwards = Total force acting downwards

$$\Rightarrow \qquad \sigma(A + dA) = \sigma \cdot A + \rho A \cdot dx$$

$$\sigma \cdot A + \sigma \cdot dA = \sigma A + \rho A \cdot dx$$

or

$$\sigma \cdot dA = \rho \cdot A \cdot dx$$

$$\frac{dA}{A} = \frac{\rho}{\sigma} \cdot dx$$

Integrating the above equation

$$\int \frac{dA}{A} = \int \frac{\rho}{\sigma} dx$$

$$\log A = \frac{\rho \cdot x}{\sigma} + C \qquad \ldots\ldots (15.28)$$

where C is the constant of integration.

At $x = 0$, $A = A_2$

$\therefore$ From Eq. (15.28), $\log A_2 = \dfrac{\rho \cdot 0}{\sigma} + C$

$$\Rightarrow \qquad C = \log_e A_2$$

From Eq. (15.28),

$$\log_e A = \frac{\rho}{\sigma} \cdot x + \log_e A_2 = \frac{\rho}{\sigma} \cdot x + \log_e (A_2)$$

$$\Rightarrow \qquad \log_e \left(\frac{A}{A_2} \right) = \frac{\rho}{\sigma} \cdot x$$

$$\Rightarrow \qquad A = A_2 (\rho)^{\rho \cdot \frac{x}{\sigma}} \qquad \ldots\ldots (15.29)$$

The above equation gives the area at a distance x from lower end.

at $x = l$, $A = A_1$

$$\therefore \qquad A_1 = A_2 (e)^{\rho \cdot \frac{x}{\sigma}} \qquad \ldots\ldots (15.30)$$

NUMERICAL QUESTIONS

1. A straight bar 500 mm long is 20 mm in dia. for the first 350 mm length and 10 mm dia. for the remaining length. If the bar is subjected to an axial tensile load of 12 kN, find extension of the bar.
2. A copper rod 20 mm diameter, 1 m length, is heated through 50°C. What is its expansion when free to expand, if the expansion is prevented by gripping it at both ends. Find the stress, its nature and the force applied by the grips when (a) The grips do not yield, (b) One grip yields back by 0.5 mm. Take $\alpha = 18 \times 10^{-6}/°C$, $E = 2 \times 10^5$ N/mm^2.
3. A 1.2 m long copper rod of 60 mm diameter is subjected to an axial tensile load of 50 kN. A hole of 20 mm diameter is to be drilled centrally through it on a length 'x' such that total elongation increases by 20% under same load. Calculate length of bored portion 'x'. Take E = 70 GPa.
4. A copper bar, cross sectional area 1000 mm^2 is loaded as shown in Fig. 15.55. Calculate total elongation of rod.

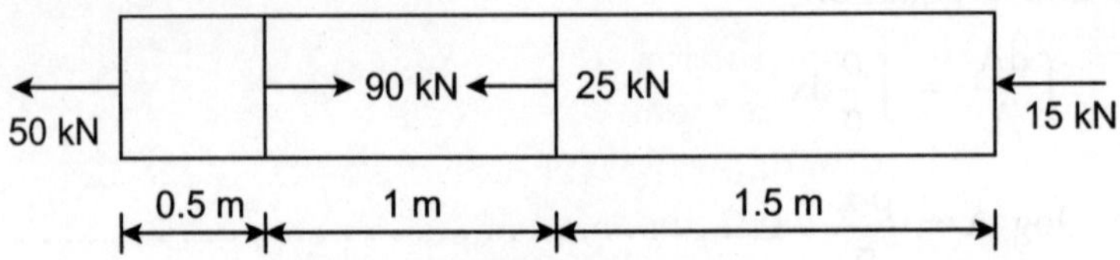

Fig. 15.55

5. Two vertical rods of steel and copper are rigidly fixed with the ceiling at their upper end at 1 m apart. Each rod is 4 m long and 30 mm diameter. A horizontal cross bar connects the lower ends of the rods. Where should a load of 4 kN be placed on the cross bar so that it remains horizontal after being loaded? Take $E_s = 2 \times 10^5$ N/mm^2 and $E_c = 1 \times 10^5$ N/mm^2.

16

Elastic Constants

16.1 Introduction

Engineering materials used in construction of machine and structural components may be isotropic or non-isotropic. Isotropic materials have four elastic constants, which usually do not change under any effect. These four elastic constants are

- Modulus of elasticity or Young's modulus (E)
- Poisson's ratio (μ)
- Modulus of rigidity or shear modulus (C or G)
- Bulk modulus (K).

16.2 Longitudinal Strain ($\in$)

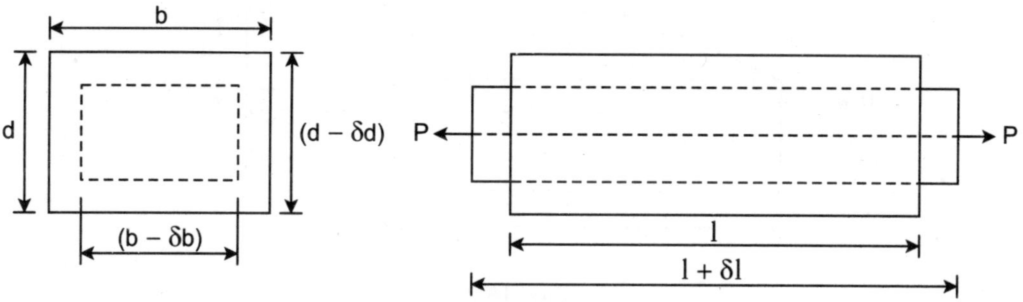

Fig. 16.1

Longitudinal or linear strain may be defined as the deformation of the member per unit length in the direction of applied load.

$$\in = \frac{\delta l}{l}$$

It may be positive or negative depending upon the type of load, i.e. tensile or compressive in nature.

16.2.1 Lateral Strain

The strain at right angles to the applied load direction is called lateral strain

$$\therefore \quad \text{Lateral strain} = \frac{\delta b}{b} \text{ or } \frac{\delta d}{d}$$

If longitudinal strain is tensile then lateral strain will be compressive and *vice-versa.*

16.2.2 Poisson's Ratio (μ)

Within elastic limit, the ratio of lateral strain to longitudinal strain is constant for a material, is denoted by letter μ and called Poisson's ratio.

$$\mu = \frac{\text{Lateral strain}}{\text{Linear strain}} = \frac{\frac{\delta b}{b} \text{ or } \frac{\delta t}{t} \text{ or } \frac{\delta d}{d}}{\frac{\delta l}{l}}$$

The value of μ generally varies from 0.25 to 0.33.

16.2.3 Volumetric Strain (ϵ_v)

The ratio of change in volume to original volume is known as volumetric strain.

$$\epsilon_v = \frac{\delta v}{v} = \frac{\text{Change in volume}}{\text{Original in volume}}$$

*strain has no unit.

16.3 Volumetric Strain of a Rectangular Bar, Subjected to an Axial Load along its Length

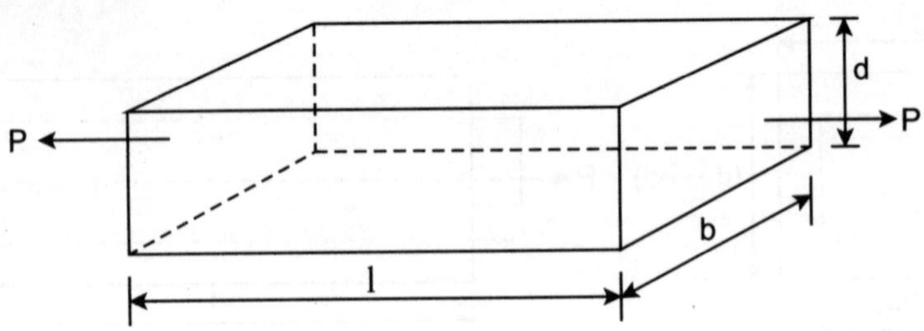

Fig. 16.2

$$\text{Let} \quad V = \text{initial volume} = l \cdot b \cdot t$$

$$V_f = \text{final volume} = (l + \delta l)(b - \delta b)(t - \delta t)$$

$$\delta v = \text{Change in volume} = V_f \sim V$$

$$= (l + \delta l)(b - \delta b)(t - \delta t) - l \cdot b \cdot t$$

$$\epsilon_v = \frac{\delta v}{v} = \frac{(l + \delta l)(b - \delta b)(t - \delta t) - lbt}{l \cdot b \cdot t}$$

$$= \frac{\delta l}{l} - \frac{\delta b}{b} - \frac{\delta t}{t} \text{(neglecting smaller terms)}$$

$$\therefore \quad \epsilon_v = \epsilon - \mu\epsilon - \mu\epsilon$$

$$\epsilon_v = \epsilon(1 - 2\mu) \quad \ldots\ldots \quad (16.1)$$

Equation (16.1) is valid for each type of cross section like square or cylindrical (circular), etc.

16.4 Volumetric Strain ($\in_V$) of a Rectangular Bar Subjected to Three Mutually Perpendicular Forces

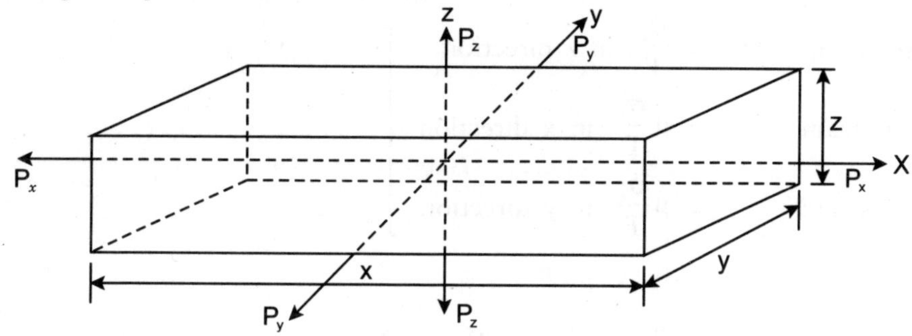

Fig. 16.3

$$V = x \cdot y \cdot z$$

or $$\log v = \log x + \log y + \log z$$

or $$\frac{dv}{v} = \frac{dx}{x} + \frac{dy}{y} + \frac{dz}{z}$$

$$\Rightarrow \quad \epsilon_v = \epsilon_x + \epsilon_y + \epsilon_z \quad \ldots\ldots \quad (16.2)$$

$\epsilon_v \rightarrow$ Volumetric strain $= \frac{\delta v}{v}$

ϵ_x = Net strain in x direction $= \frac{\sigma_x}{E} - \mu\frac{\sigma_y}{E} - \mu\frac{\sigma_z}{E}$

ϵ_y = Net strain in y direction

ϵ_z = Net strain in z direction

Now:

Due to load P_x:

$$\left.\begin{array}{lll} \text{Longitudinal strain} & = \frac{\sigma_x}{E} & \text{in x direction} \\ \text{Lateral strain} & = \mu\frac{\sigma_x}{E} & \text{in y direction} \\ \text{Lateral strain} & = \mu\frac{\sigma_x}{E} & \text{in z direction} \end{array}\right] \quad \ldots\ldots \quad (16.2a)$$

Due to load P_y:

$$\left.\begin{aligned}&\text{Linear strain} = \frac{\sigma_y}{E} \text{ in y direction}\\&\text{Lateral strain} = \mu\frac{\sigma_y}{E} \text{ in x direction}\\&\text{Lateral strain} = \mu\frac{\sigma_y}{E} \text{ in z direction}\end{aligned}\right] \quad \ldots\ldots (16.2b)$$

Similarly, Effect of load P_z:

$$\left.\begin{aligned}&\text{Linear strain} = \frac{\sigma_z}{E} \text{ in z direction}\\&\text{Lateral strain} = \mu\frac{\sigma_z}{E} \text{ in x direction}\\&\text{Lateral strain} = \mu\frac{\sigma_z}{E} \text{ in y direction}\end{aligned}\right] \quad \ldots\ldots (16.2c)$$

Now,

$$\epsilon_x = \frac{\sigma_x}{E} - \mu\frac{\sigma_y}{E} - \mu\frac{\sigma_z}{E}$$

$$\epsilon_y = \frac{\sigma_y}{E} - \mu\frac{\sigma_x}{E} - \mu\frac{\sigma_z}{E}$$

$$\epsilon_z = \frac{\sigma_z}{E} - \mu\frac{\sigma_x}{E} - \mu\frac{\sigma_y}{E}$$

Adding all the strains:

$$\epsilon_x + \epsilon_y + \epsilon_z = \frac{1}{E}(\sigma_x + \sigma_y + \sigma_z) - \frac{2\mu}{E}(\sigma_x + \sigma_y + \sigma_z)$$

or $$\epsilon_x + \epsilon_y + \epsilon_z = \frac{\sigma_x + \sigma_y + \sigma_z}{E}(1 - 2\mu) \quad \ldots\ldots (16.3)$$

From Eqs. (16.2) and (16.3)

$$\epsilon_v = \frac{1}{E}(\sigma_x + \sigma_y + \sigma_z)(1 - 2\mu) \quad \ldots\ldots (16.4)$$

Note: 1. *Here, σ_x, σ_y and σ_z are tensile stresses. If any of the stresses is compressive, it may be regarded as negative and above equation will hold good.*

2. *If ϵ_v is +ve→ Increase in volume and vice-versa.*

3. *Equation (16.4) may be used for a uniaxial, biaxial or triaxial loading.*

Example 16.1

Determine change in length, breadth and thickness of a steel bar which is 6 m long, 50 mm wide and 40 mm thick and is subjected to an axial tensile load of 40 kN in the direction of its length. Take E = 2 × 10⁵ N/mm² and Poisson's ratio = 0.32. Determine volumetric strain and final volume of the bar.

Solution:

$\delta l = ?$	$l = 6 \text{ m} = 6000 \text{ mm}$
$\delta b = ?$	$b = 50 \text{ mm}$
$\delta t = ?$	$t = 40 \text{ mm}$

$P = 40 \text{ kN} = 40 \times 10^3 \text{ N}$

$E = 2 \times 10^5 \text{ N/mm}^2$

$\mu = 0.32$

$\delta v = ?$

$V = ?$

Now
$$\sigma = \frac{P}{A} = \frac{40 \times 10^3}{b \times t} = \frac{40 \times 10^3}{50 \times 40} = 20 \text{ N/mm}^2$$

$$\in = \frac{\sigma}{E} = \frac{20}{2 \times 10^5} = 1 \times 10^{-4}$$

$$\delta l = \in \times l = 1 \times 10^{-4} \times 6000 = \mathbf{0.6 \text{ m}}$$ **Ans.**

$$\mu = \frac{\text{Lateral strain}}{\text{Linear strain}} = \frac{\frac{\delta b}{b} \text{ or } \frac{\delta t}{t}}{\frac{\delta l}{l}}$$

∴ Lateral strain $= 0.32 \times 1 \times 10^{-4} = 0.32 \times 10^{-4}$

∴ $\delta b = b \times \text{lateral strain} = 50 \times 0.32 \times 10^{-4} = \mathbf{1.6 \times 10^{-3} \text{ mm}}$ **Ans.**

$\delta t = t \times \text{lateral strain} = 40 \times 0.32 \times 10^{-4} = \mathbf{1.28 \times 10^{-3} \text{ mm}}$ **Ans.**

$$\begin{aligned} \in_v &= \in(1 - 2\mu) \\ &= 1 \times 10^{-4} (1 - 2 \times 0.32) = 0.36 \times 10^{-4} \end{aligned}$$

$$\begin{aligned} \delta v = V \times \in_v &= lbt \times 0.36 \times 10^{-4} \\ &= 6000 \times 50 \times 40 \times 0.36 \times 10^{-4} \text{ mm}^3 \\ &= 432 \text{ mm}^3 \end{aligned}$$

$$\therefore \quad \begin{aligned} V_f = V + \delta v &= lbt + \delta v \\ &= 6000 \times 50 \times 40 + 432 \\ &= \mathbf{12000432 \text{ mm}^3} \end{aligned}$$ **Ans.**

Example 16.2

Determine the value of Young's modulus and Poisson's ratio of a metallic bar of length 350 mm, breadth 45 mm and thickness 45 mm, when the bar is subjected to an axial compressive load of 500 kN and increase in breadth is 0.03 mm. Calculate volumetric strain also. The decrease in length is 0.75 mm.

Solution:

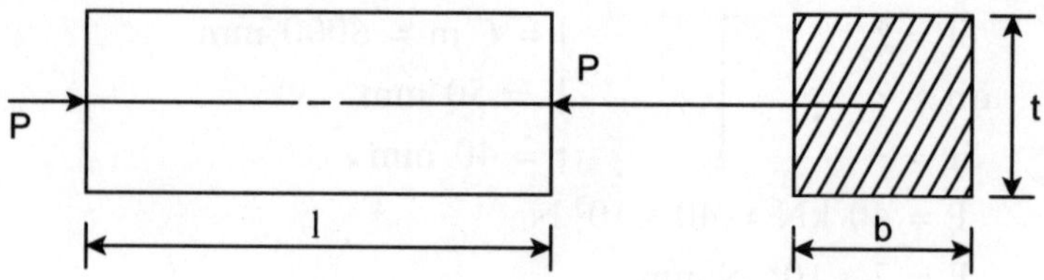

Fig. 16.4

$E = ?$

$\mu = ?$

$l = 350$ mm

$b = 45$ mm

$t = 45$ mm

$P = 500 \text{ kN} = 5 \times 10^5$ N

$\delta b = 0.03$

$\epsilon_v = ?$

Now

$$V = l \cdot b \cdot t = 350 \times 45 \times 45 = 708750 \text{ mm}^3$$

Poisson's Ratio

$$\mu = \frac{\text{Lateral strain}}{\text{Linear strain}} = \frac{\frac{\delta b}{b}}{\frac{\delta l}{l}} = \left(\frac{\frac{0.03}{45}}{\frac{0.75}{350}}\right) = 0.31 \qquad \textbf{Ans.}$$

Young's modulus: $$E = \frac{P \cdot l}{A \cdot \delta l} = \frac{500 \times 10^3 \times 350}{45 \times 45 \times 0.75} = \mathbf{1.15 \times 10^5 \text{ N/mm}^2} \qquad \textbf{Ans.}$$

Volumetric strain $\epsilon_v = \epsilon(1 - 2\mu)$

$$\therefore \quad \epsilon_v = \frac{\delta l}{l}(1 - 2 \times 0.31) = \frac{0.75}{350}(1 - 0.62) = \mathbf{8.14 \times 10^{-3}} \qquad \textbf{Ans.}$$

Example 16.3

A metallic bar 300 mm × 80 mm × 30 mm is subjected to a force of 30 kN, 40 kN and 20 kN (all tensile forces) along x, y and z directions respectively. Calculate the change in volume of block. E = 2 × 10⁵ N/mm² and Poisson's ratio = 0.25.

Solution:

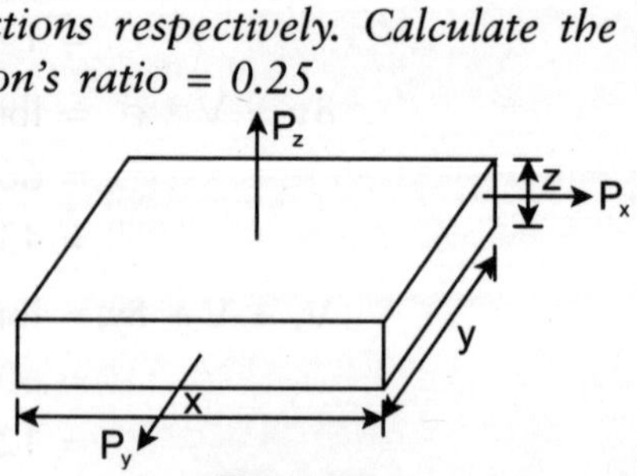

Fig. 16.5

$x = 300$ mm

$y = 80$ mm

$z = 30$ mm

$P_x = 30 \text{ kN} = 30 \times 10^3$ N

$P_y = 40 \text{ kN} = 40 \times 10^3$ N

$P_z = 20 \text{ kN} = 20 \times 10^3 \text{ N}$

$\delta v = ?$

$\mu = 0.25$

Now

$$\sigma_x = \frac{P_x}{A_x} = \frac{P_x}{y \times z} = \frac{30 \times 10^3}{80 \times 30} = 12.5 \text{ N/mm}^2$$

$$\sigma_y = \frac{P_y}{A_y} = \frac{P_y}{x \times z} = \frac{40 \times 10^3}{300 \times 30} = 4.44 \text{ N/mm}^2$$

$$\sigma_z = \frac{P_z}{A_z} = \frac{20 \times 10^3}{300 \times 80} = 0.83 \text{ N/mm}^2$$

We know that

$$\frac{\delta v}{V} = \frac{1}{E}(\sigma_x + \sigma_y + \sigma_z)(1 - 2\mu)$$

$$\therefore \quad \delta v = 300 \times 80 \times 30 \frac{1}{2 \times 10^5}(12.5 + 4.44 + 0.83)(1 - 2 \times 0.25)$$

$$= 31.986 \text{ mm}^3 = \mathbf{32 \text{ mm}^3}$$ **Ans.**

16.5 Bulk Modulus

When a body is subjected to the mutually perpendicular like and equal direct stresses, the ratio of direct stress to the corresponding volumetric strain is constant for a given material when the deformation is within a certain limit. This ratio is known as bulk modulus and is denoted by K.

$$\therefore \quad K = \frac{\text{Direct stress}}{\text{Volumetric strain}} = \frac{\sigma}{\epsilon_V} = \frac{\sigma}{\delta_{V/V}}$$

16.6 Relation in 'K' and 'E'

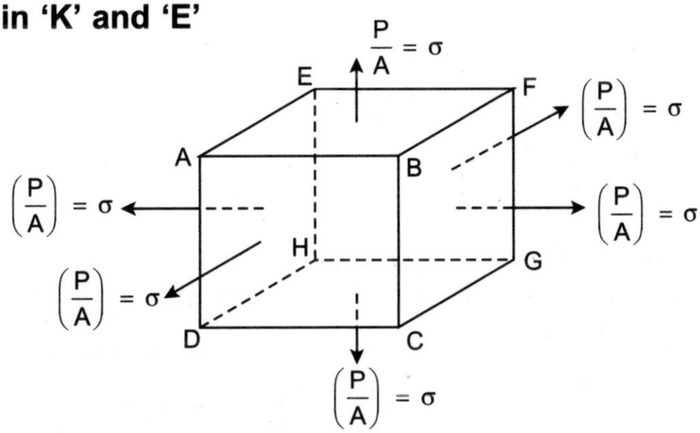

Fig. 16.6

Total strain along side (AB) under the action of three mutually perpendicular stresses.

$$\frac{dl}{l} = \frac{\sigma_x}{E} - \mu\frac{\sigma_y}{E} - \mu\frac{\sigma_z}{E}$$

$$\Rightarrow \quad \frac{dl}{l} = \frac{\sigma}{E} - \mu\frac{\sigma}{E} - \mu\frac{\sigma}{E}, \quad \sigma_x = \sigma_y = \sigma_z = \sigma$$

$$\frac{dl}{l} = \frac{\sigma}{E}(1 - 2\mu) \qquad \text{(16.5)}$$

Original volume of cube

$$V = l^3 \qquad \text{(16.6)}$$

Differentiating Eq. (16.6) w.r.t. dl

$$\frac{dV}{dl} = 3l^2 \qquad \text{(16.7)}$$

Dividing Eqs. (16.7) by (16.6), we get

$$\frac{dV}{V} = \frac{3l^2 \cdot dl}{l^3} = 3\frac{dl}{l}$$

or

$$\frac{dV}{V} = 3\frac{dl}{l} \qquad \text{(16.8)}$$

From Eqs. (16.5) and (16.8),

$$\frac{dV}{V} = 3\frac{\sigma}{E}(1 - 2\mu) \qquad \text{(16.9)}$$

But

$$K = \frac{\sigma}{\frac{dV}{V}} = \frac{\sigma}{\frac{3\sigma}{E}(1 - 2\mu)}$$

$$\Rightarrow \quad K = \frac{E}{3(1 - 2\mu)}$$

$$\Rightarrow \quad E = 3K(1 - 2\mu) \qquad \text{(16.10)}$$

This is the required relation between E and K.

Also

$$E = 2G(1 + \mu) \qquad \text{(16.11)}$$

Example 16.4

A bar 45 mm in diameter is subjected to an axial pull of 50 kN and measured extension on 400 mm gauge length is 0.115 mm. Find Poisson's ratio and values of three modulus. The change in diameter is 0.004 mm.

Solution:

$d = 45$ mm

$P = 50 \text{ kN} = 50 \times 10^3$ N

$\delta\ell = 0.115$ mm

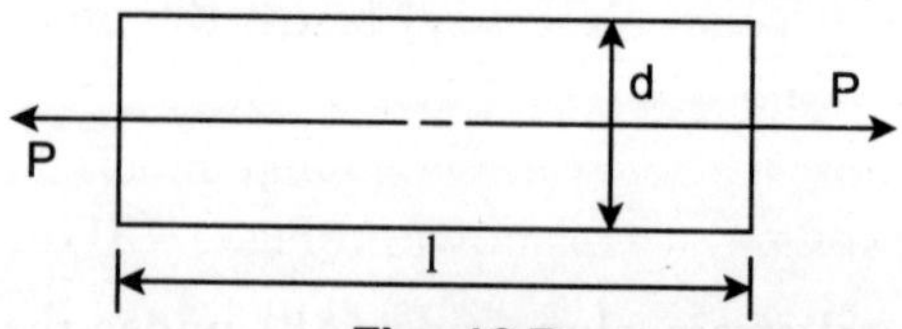

Fig. 16.7

$l = 400$ mm

$\mu = ?$

$E = ?$

$G = ?$

$K = ?$

Now

$$\text{Linear strain } \in = \frac{\delta l}{l} = \frac{0.115}{400} = 2.875 \times 10^{-4}$$

$$\text{Lateral strain} = \frac{\delta d}{d} = \frac{0.004}{45} = 0.88 \times 10^{-4}$$

(i) Poisson's ratio

$$\mu = \frac{\text{Lateral strain}}{\text{Linear strain}} = \frac{\frac{\delta d}{d}}{\frac{\delta l}{l}}$$

or
$$\mu = \frac{\frac{0.004}{45}}{\frac{0.115}{400}} = \frac{0.004 \times 400}{0.115 \times 45} = \mathbf{031} \quad \textbf{Ans.}$$

(ii)
$$E = \frac{\sigma}{\in} = \frac{P \cdot l}{A \cdot \delta l} = \frac{50 \times 10^3 \times 400}{\frac{\pi}{4}(45)^2 \times 0.115} = \mathbf{1.1 \times 10^5\ N/mm^2} \quad \textbf{Ans.}$$

(iii)
$$E = 3\,K(1 - 2\mu)$$
$$1.1 \times 1.0^5 = 3\,K(1 - 2 \times 0.31)$$
$$\Rightarrow \quad K = \mathbf{0.96 \times 10^5\ N/mm^2} \quad \textbf{Ans.}$$

Also
$$E = 2\,G(1 + \mu)$$
$$1.1 \times 10^5 = 2\,G(1 + 0.31)$$
$$G = \mathbf{0.42 \times 10^5\ N/mm^2} \quad \textbf{Ans.}$$

16.7 Principle of Complementary Shear Stresses

It states that a set of shear stresses across a plane is always accompanied by a set of balancing shear stresses (i.e. of the same intensity) across the plane and normal to it.

Proof: ABCD is a rectangular block having a set of shear stresses τ (as shown in Fig. 16.8) on face AB and CD. Thickness of block is t.

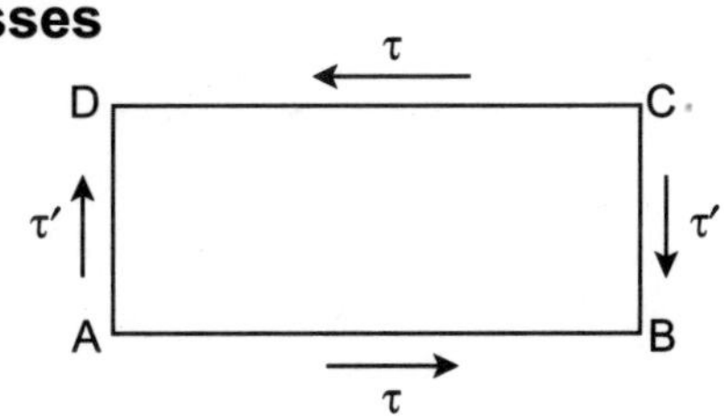

Fig. 16.8

We have to prove that the same stress τ will act on face AD and BC.

Now

$$F_{AB} = \text{Force on face AB} = \tau \times AB \times t = \tau \cdot AB \cdot t$$
$$F_{CD} = \text{Force on face CD} = \tau \cdot CD \cdot t = \tau \cdot AB \cdot t \quad \because AB = CD$$

F_{AB} and F_{CD} are equal and opposite and hence these forces will form a couple.

If the block is in equilibrium there must be an equal and opposite couple.

Let $\tau' \rightarrow$ Shear stress set up on faces AD and CB.

Now
$$F_{AD} = \tau' \times AD \times t$$
$$F_{CB} = \tau' \times CB \times t = \tau' \times AD \times t$$

Taking moment about A

For equilibrium

$$\Sigma M_A = 0 \Rightarrow (\tau \times AB \times t) \times AD = \tau' \times BC \times t \times AB \quad \because BC = AD$$
$$\Rightarrow \tau = \tau' \qquad (16.12)$$

Equation (16.12) proves that a set of shear stresses is always accompanied by a transverse set of shear stresses of the same intensity.

$\tau' \rightarrow$ Complementary shear stress

τ and τ' at right angles together constitute a state of simple shear.

The direction of the shear stresses on the block are either both towards or both away from a corner.

NUMERICAL QUESTIONS

1. A bar of 30 mm diameter is subjected to a pull of 50 kN. The measured extension on the gauge length of 300 mm is 0.10 mm and change in diameter is 0.0040 mm. Calculate Poisson's ratio and the values of the three modulii.
2. A bar of steel 30 cm long, rectangular cross section (25 mm by 50 mm), is subjected to a uniform tensile stress of 180 N/mm^2 along its length. Calculate changes in dimensions. $E = 2 \times 10^5$ N/mm^2, Poisson's ratio = 0.3.
3. A rectangular block 300 mm long × 120 mm wide × 70 mm thick is subjected to axial loads as shown in Fig. 16.9. Calculate (a) Volumetric strain (b) Change in volume of block (c) Bulk modulus for the material. E = 200 GPa and Poisson's ratio = 0.25.

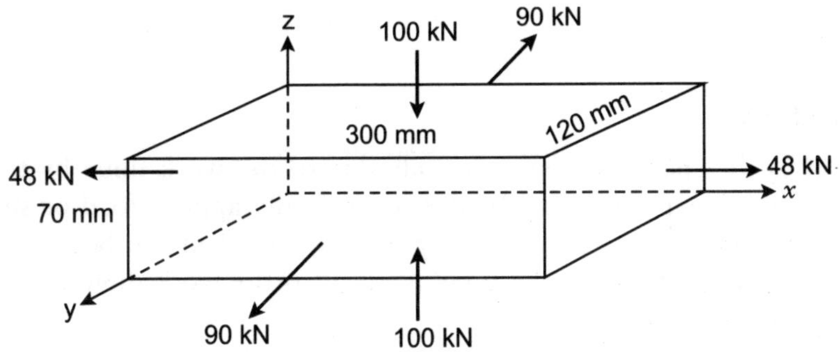

Fig. 16.9

4. A 3 m long circular bar diameter 50 mm is subjected to an axial pull of 1 kN. Observed elongation in length and decrease in diameter are 2 mm and 0.01 mm. Find E and Poisson's ratio.
5. The modulus of rigidity of rod 5 mm × 5 mm is 0.8×10^5 N/mm^2. If the rod is subjected to a pull of 4 kN and lateral dimensions changed to 4.99 × 4.99 mm. Calculate (a) Poisson's ratio (b) Modulus of rigidity.
6. A steel bar 3.5 m long, 40 mm wide and 20 mm thick is subjected to a pull of 30 kN in the direction of its length. Find the change in length breadth and thickness. $E = 2 \times 10^5$ N/mm^2 and Poisson's ratio = 0.35.
7. A vertical circular bar 20 mm in diameter 4 m long carries a pull of 40 kN. Find (i) Elongation (ii) Decrease in diameter (iii) Volumetric strain of $E = 2 \times 10^5$ N/mm^2 and Poisson's ratio = 0.3.
8. A rectangular block 200 mm × 100 mm × 50 mm is subjected to axial loads as follows

   300 kN compressive in the direction of its length.

   200 kN tensile in the direction of its breadth.

   500 kN tensile in the direction of its thickness.

   Find the change in volume. Take $E = 2 \times 10^5$ N/mm^2 and Poisson's ratio = 0.32.

17

Strain Energy

17.1 Introduction

The strain energy is the energy stored in a body due to the work done by the applied load in straining it. The straining effect may be due to gradually applied load or suddenly applied or load with impact. Hence, the strain energy will be stored in the body when the load is applied. The strain energy stored in the body is equal to the work done by the applied load in stretching the body.

17.2 Strain Energy due to Gradually Applied Load

The loading starts from zero and increases gradually till the body is fully loaded.

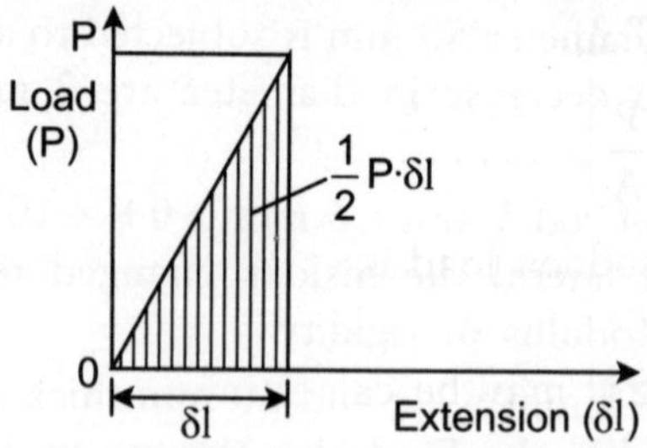

Fig. 17.1: Load-extension Diagram of a Body under Tensile Test upto Elastic Limit

Work done by the load

$$= \text{Average load} \times \text{distance moved (extension)}$$

$$= \left(\frac{0+P}{2}\right) \times \delta l$$

$$= \frac{1}{2} P\,\delta l = \frac{1}{2} \times \sigma \cdot A \times \frac{\sigma \cdot l}{E}$$

$$= \frac{\sigma^2}{2E}(A \times l)$$

$$U = \frac{\sigma^2}{2E} \times \text{Volume}$$

where, P → Gradually applied load; σ → Stress due to gradual load = P/A
U → Strain energy

17.3 Strain Energy due to Suddenly Applied Load

When the load is applied all of a sudden and not stepwise, is called suddenly applied load. This load is constant throughout the process of deformation of the body.

Let

P → Sudden applied load

σ → Stress induced due to sudden load

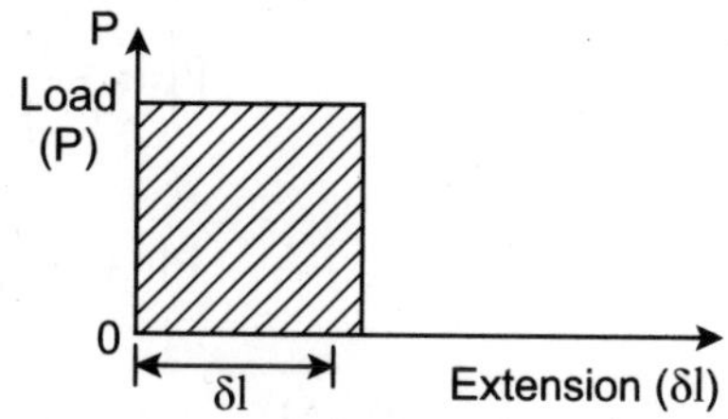

Fig. 17.2

Work done by the load = Sudden load × extension

$$= P \times \delta l$$

$$= P \times \frac{\sigma l}{E} \quad \ldots\ldots (17.1)$$

Maximum strain energy stored in a body

$$U = \frac{\sigma^2}{2E} \times A \times l \quad \ldots\ldots (17.2)$$

Equating Eqs. (17.1) and (17.2),

$$\sigma = 2\left(\frac{P}{A}\right) \quad \ldots\ldots (17.3)$$

i.e. Maximum stress due to sudden load is twice the stress induced when the same load is applied gradually.

After getting σ, the value of U may be calculated from Eq. (17.2) easily.

17.4 Strain Energy due to Impact Load

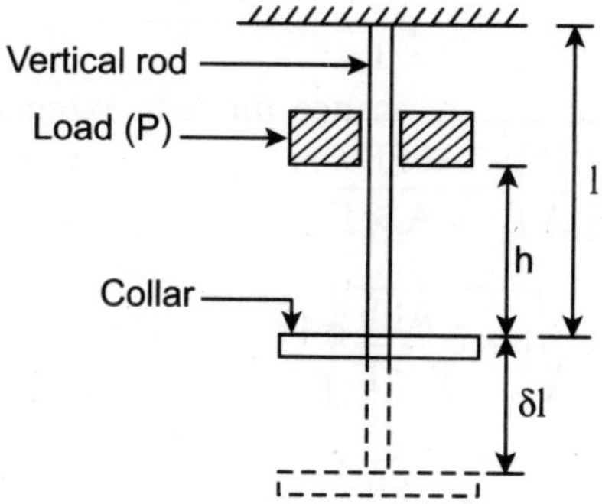

Fig. 17.3

Work done by load = P (h + δl) .... (17.4)

Strain energy stored in rod $= \frac{\sigma^2}{2E} \times V$ .... (17.5)

Equate (17.4) and (17.5)

$$P\,(h + \delta l) = \frac{\sigma^2}{2E}\cdot A\cdot l$$

$$P\left(h + \frac{\sigma\cdot l}{E}\right) = \frac{\sigma^2}{2E}\cdot A\cdot l$$

$$\Rightarrow \quad Ph + P\cdot\frac{\sigma\cdot l}{E} = \frac{\sigma^2}{2E}\cdot A\cdot l$$

$$\Rightarrow \quad \frac{\sigma^2\cdot Al}{2E} - P\cdot\frac{\sigma}{E}\cdot l - Ph = 0$$

$$\Rightarrow \quad \sigma^2 - P\cdot\frac{\sigma}{E}\cdot l\cdot\frac{2E}{Al} - Ph\cdot\frac{2E}{Al} = 0$$

$$\Rightarrow \quad \sigma^2 - \left(\frac{2P}{A}\right)\sigma - Ph\cdot\frac{2E}{Al} = 0$$

$$\Rightarrow \quad \sigma^2 - \left(\frac{2P}{A}\right)\sigma - \frac{2PEh}{Al} = 0$$

This is a quadratic equation in σ,

$$\sigma = \frac{-b \pm \sqrt{b^2 - 4ac}}{2a}$$

$$= \frac{\frac{2P}{A} \pm \sqrt{\left(\frac{2P}{A}\right)^2 - 4\times 1\left(-\frac{2PEh}{A\times l}\right)}}{2\times 1}$$

$$= \frac{P}{A} \pm \sqrt{\left(\frac{P}{A}\right)^2 + \frac{2PEh}{A\times l}}$$

$$\sigma = \frac{P}{A}\left[1 + \sqrt{1 + \frac{2AEh}{P\times l}}\right] \qquad \text{(neglect –ve root)}$$

$$\sigma = \frac{P}{A}\left[1 + \sqrt{1 + \frac{2AEh}{P\times l}}\right] \qquad (17.6)$$

and $$U = \frac{\sigma^2}{2E} \times A \times l$$

where

P → Applied load with impact

σ → Stress induced due to impact load

A → Cross sectional area of the bar

h → height through which load is fall

l → length of rod

E → Young's modulus

After knowing σ, U may be obtained.

Note: If h = 0, then it is suddenly applied load and

$$\sigma = 2\left(\frac{P}{A}\right)$$

which is the case of suddenly applied load.

17.5 Strain Energy in a Body due to Shear Stress

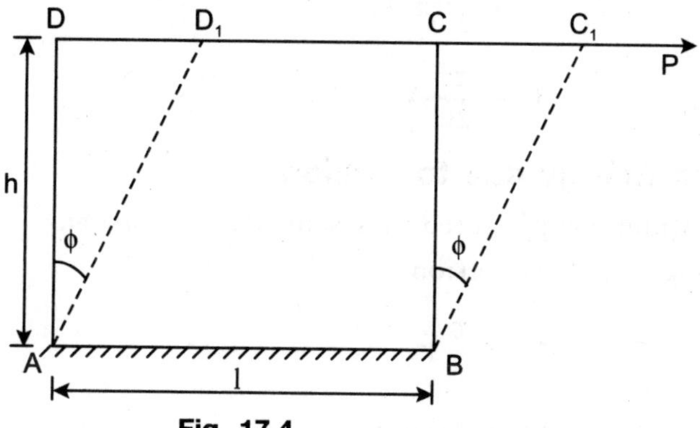

Fig. 17.4

Considering a rectangular block of length l, height h and breadth b.

Bottom face AB is fixed.

Let P → Shear force

τ → Shear stress (or τ)

ϕ → Shear strain

C → Modulus of rigidity,

Now

$$\tau = \frac{\text{Shear force}}{\text{Area}} = \frac{P}{l \times b}$$

$$\therefore \quad P = \tau \cdot l \cdot b$$

and
$$\phi = \frac{CC_1}{CB} \Rightarrow CC_1 = CB \cdot \phi$$

If shear force P is applied gradually then

$$\text{average load} = \frac{0 + P}{2} = \frac{P}{2}$$

$\therefore$ Work done by gradually applied load

$$= \text{Average load} \times \text{distance}$$

$$= \frac{P}{2} \times CC_1$$

$$= \frac{1}{2}(\tau \cdot l \cdot b)(CB \cdot \phi)$$

$$= \frac{1}{2}(\tau \cdot l \cdot b)(h \cdot \phi)$$

$$= \frac{1}{2}\tau \cdot V \cdot \frac{\tau}{C}$$

$$= \frac{1}{2} \cdot \frac{\tau^2}{C} \cdot V$$

| $CB = h$
| $V = l \cdot b \cdot h$
| $C = \dfrac{\tau}{\phi}$
| $\therefore \phi = \dfrac{\tau}{C}$

$$\therefore \quad U = \frac{\tau^2}{2C} \cdot V$$

17.6 Strain Energy due to Torsion

Q. Give the strain energy stored in a shaft due to torsion.

A. Considering a shaft in torsion

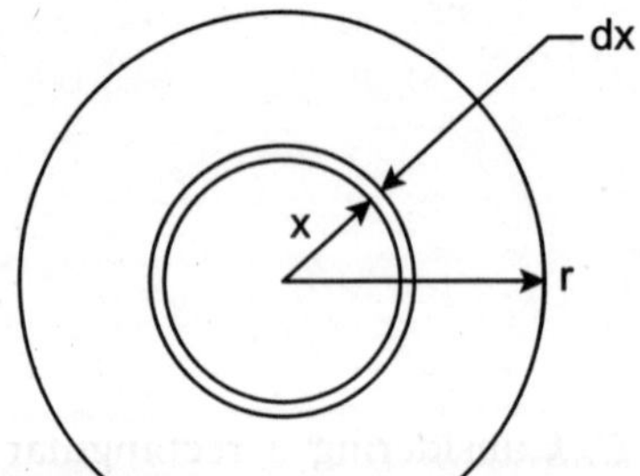

Fig. 17.5

$$\tau_x = \frac{\tau}{r} \cdot x$$

$$dA = 2\pi x \cdot dx$$

$$dV = 2\pi x\, dx \cdot l$$

$$du = \frac{(\text{Shear stress})^2}{2C} \times \text{Volume} = \left(\frac{\tau_x}{2C}\right)^2 \times dV$$

$$= \frac{\left(\frac{\tau}{r} \cdot x\right)^2}{2C} \cdot 2\pi x\, dx \cdot l = \frac{\tau^2 x^2 \cdot 2\pi x\, dx \cdot l}{2C \cdot r^2}$$

$$U = \int_0^r du = \frac{\tau^2 \cdot l}{2Cr^2} \int_0^r dA \cdot x^2 = \frac{\tau^2 \cdot l}{2Cr^2} \cdot J$$

| $dA \cdot x^2 = J$

$$\therefore \qquad U = \frac{\tau^2 \cdot l}{2Cr^2} \cdot J$$

(a) For solid shaft: $J = \frac{\pi}{32} d^4$

$$\therefore \qquad U_s = \frac{\tau^2 \cdot l}{2Cr^2} \cdot \frac{\pi}{32} d^4 = \frac{\tau^2 l}{2Cr^2} \cdot \frac{\pi}{32} (2r)^4$$

$$= \frac{\tau^2}{2C} \cdot \frac{l}{r^2} \cdot \frac{\pi}{32} \cdot 16r^2 \cdot r^2 = \frac{\tau^2}{4C} \cdot \pi r^2 \cdot l$$

$$U_s = \frac{\tau^2}{4C} \times \text{Volume}$$

(b) For hollow shaft:

$$J_H = \frac{\pi}{32}\left(d_o^4 - d_i^4\right)$$

$$\therefore \qquad U_H = \frac{\tau^2 \cdot l}{2Cr^2} \cdot J_H = \frac{\tau^2 \cdot l}{2Cr_o^2} \cdot \frac{\pi}{32}\left(d_o^4 - d_i^4\right)$$

$$= \frac{\tau^2 \cdot l}{2Cr_o^2} \cdot \frac{\pi}{32}\left(16 r_o^4 - 16 r_i^4\right)$$

$$= \frac{\tau^2}{4Cr_o^2} \cdot \pi\left(r_o^2 - r_i^2\right)\left(r_o^4 + r_i^4\right) \cdot l$$

$$= \frac{\tau^2}{4C} \cdot \pi\left(r_o^2 - r_i^2\right) \cdot l \cdot \left(\frac{r_o^2 + r_i^2}{r_o^2}\right)$$

$$U_H = \frac{\tau^2}{4C} \cdot \text{Volume}\left(\frac{d_o^2 + d_i^2}{d_o^2}\right)$$

Example 17.1

Two elastic bars, having the same material and length, one is of circular section of diameter 110 mm and the other square of side 100 mm, absorb the same amount of strain energy delivered by axial forces. Compare the stresses induced in two bars.

Solution:

$E_c = E_s \rightarrow$ Same material

$\rho_c = \rho_s \rightarrow$ Same density

$l_c = l_s \rightarrow$ Same length

$d = 110$ mm

$$a = 100 \text{ mm}$$
$$U_c = U_s$$
$$\frac{\sigma_c}{\sigma_s} = ?$$

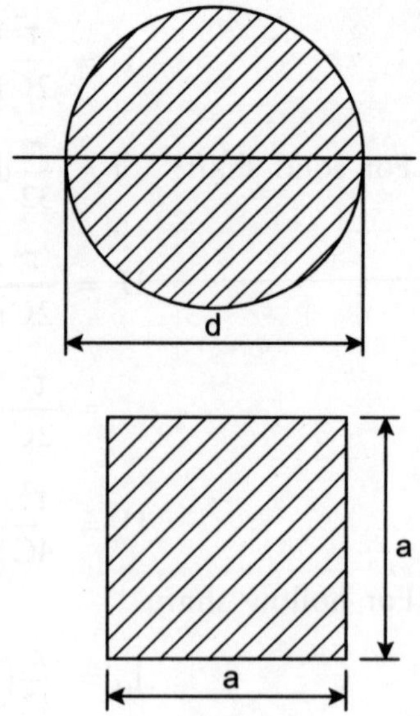

Fig. 17.6

We know that

$$U = \frac{\sigma^2}{2E} \times A \times l$$

$$\therefore \quad U_c = U_s$$

$$\Rightarrow \quad \frac{\sigma_c^2}{2E} \times A_c \times l_c = \frac{\sigma_s^2}{2E} \times A_s \times l_s$$

$$\Rightarrow \quad \frac{\sigma_c}{\sigma_s} = \sqrt{\frac{A_s}{A_c}} = \sqrt{\frac{a^2}{\frac{\pi}{4}d^2}} = \frac{100}{110 \times \sqrt{\frac{\pi}{4}}} = 1.025$$

$$\therefore \quad \frac{\sigma_c}{\sigma_s} = \mathbf{1.025} \qquad \textbf{Ans.}$$

Example 17.2

A tensile load of 50 kN is applied to a square bar of 40 mm side and 5 m long. If E = 2 ×10⁵ N/mm², calculate

(a) Stretch in the rod

(b) Stress in the rod

(c) Strain energy absorbed by the rod

Solution:

Gradually applied load

$$P = 50 \text{ kN} = 50 \times 10^3 \text{ N}$$
$$A = 40 \times 40 \text{ mm}^2$$
$$l = 5 \text{ m} = 5000 \text{ mm}$$
$$E = 2 \times 10^5 \text{ N/mm}^2$$
$$\delta l = ?$$
$$\sigma = ?$$
$$U = ?$$

Now

(a) $$\delta l = \frac{P.l}{AE} = \frac{50 \times 10^3 \times 5000}{40 \times 40 \times 2 \times 10^5} = \mathbf{0.78 \text{ mm}} \qquad \textbf{Ans.}$$

(b) $$\sigma = \frac{P}{A} = \frac{50 \times 10^3}{40 \times 40} = \mathbf{31.25\ N/mm^2}$$ **Ans.**

(c) $$U = \frac{\sigma^2}{2E} \times A \times l$$

$$= \frac{(31.25)^2}{2 \times 2 \times 10^5} \times 40 \times 40 \times 5000$$

$$= \mathbf{19.53\ N.m}$$ **Ans.**

Example 17.3

The maximum stress produced by an axial tensile load in a bar of 1.1 m is 140 MPa. The area of cross sections and lengths are shown in Fig. 17.7. Determine strain energy stared in the bar, if E = 2 × 10⁵ N/mm².

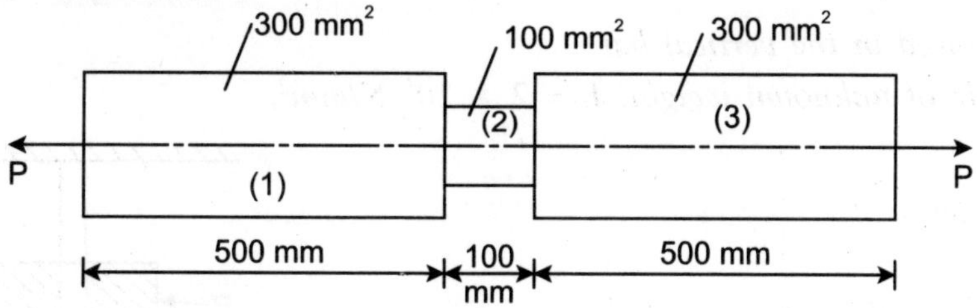

Fig. 17.7

Solution:

$l = 1.1\ m = 1100\ mm^3$ $A_1 = 300\ mm^2$

$E = 2 \times 10^5\ N/mm^2$ $A_2 = 100\ mm^2$

$\sigma_{max} = 140\ N/mm^2 = \sigma_2$ $A_3 = 300\ mm^2$

$U = ?$

$l_1 = l_3 = 500\ mm$

$l_2 = 100\ mm$

Now

$$\sigma_2 = \frac{P}{A_2} \Rightarrow P = \sigma_2 \times A_2 = 140 \times 100\ N$$

$\therefore$ $$P = 14000\ N$$

$\therefore$ $$\sigma_1 = \frac{P}{A_1} = \frac{14000}{300} = 46.7\ N/mm^2$$

$$\sigma_3 = \sigma_1 = 46.7\ N/mm^2$$

Total strain energy

$$U = U_1 + U_2 + U_3 = \frac{1}{2E}\left(\sigma_1^2 V_1 + \sigma_2^2 V_2 + \sigma_3^2 V_3\right)$$

$$= \frac{1}{2E}\left(2\sigma_1^2 V_1 + \sigma_2^2 V_2\right), \quad \sigma_1 = \sigma_3,\ V_1 = V_3$$

$$= \frac{1}{2 \times 2 \times 10^5}\left(2 \times 46.7^2 \times 500 \times 300 + 140^2 \times 100 \times 100\right)$$

$$= 7032.67 \text{ N.mm} = \mathbf{7.032\ N.m}$$ **Ans.**

Example 17.4

The maximum instantaneous extension is 2 mm which is produced by a falling weight (unknown) through a height of 4 cm in a vertical bar of length 3.5 m and of cross sectional area 600 mm². Find

(a) Stress induced in the vertical bar.

(b) Magnitude of unknown weight, E = 2 × 10⁵ N/mm².

Solution:

$\delta l = 2$ mm

$P = ?$

$h = 4$ cm $= 40$ mm

$l = 3.5$ m $= 3500$ mm

$A = 600$ mm²

$E = 2 \times 10^5$ N/mm²

$\sigma = ?$

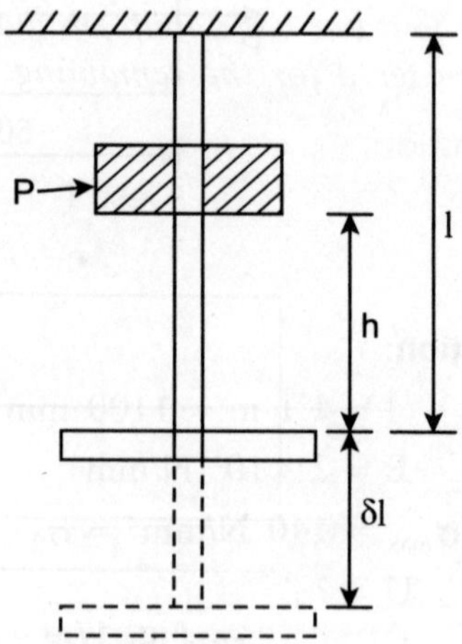

Fig. 17.8

Now

(a) We know that

$$\delta l = \frac{\sigma \cdot l}{E} \Rightarrow \sigma = \frac{\delta l \cdot E}{l}$$

$$\Rightarrow \quad \sigma = \frac{2 \times 2 \times 10^5}{3500} = \mathbf{114.28\ N/mm^2}$$ **Ans.**

(b) Using

$$\sigma = \frac{P}{A}\left(1 + \sqrt{1 + \frac{2AEh}{P \cdot l}}\right)$$

$$140 = \frac{P}{600}\left(1 + \sqrt{1 + \frac{2 \times 600 \times 2 \times 10^5 \times 40}{P \times 3500}}\right)$$

$$8.4 \times 10^4 - P = P\sqrt{1 + \frac{2.74 \times 10^6}{P}}$$

$$\text{or} \quad (8.4 \times 10^4 - P)^2 = P^2\left(1 + \frac{2.74 \times 10^6}{P}\right)$$

$$\Rightarrow \quad P = 68564.57 \text{ N}$$

$$P = \mathbf{68.56 \text{ kN}}$$ **Ans.**

Alternate method:

$$P(h + \delta l) = \frac{\sigma^2}{2E} \times A \times l$$

$$P(40 + 2) = \frac{114.28 \times 114.28 \times 600 \times 3500}{2 \times 2 \times 10^5}$$

$$P = 68564.57 \text{ N}$$

$$P = \mathbf{68.56 \text{ kN}}$$ **Ans.**

Example 17.5

Two bars each of length l and of same material are each subjected to the same axial pull (P). The first bar has a uniform diameter d. The second bar has a diameter d/2 for a length l/2 and diameter d for the remaining length. Compare strain energies of the two bars.

Solution:

Case I

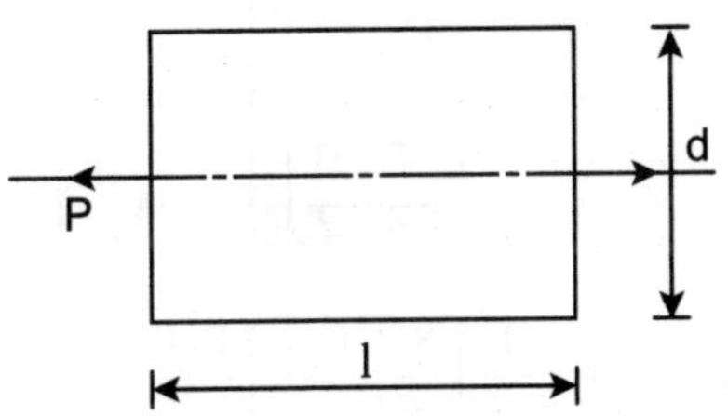

Fig. 17.9

$$A_1 = \frac{\pi}{4}d^2$$

$$V_1 = \frac{\pi}{4}d^2 \times l$$

$$U_1 = \frac{\sigma_1^2}{2E} \times A \times l$$

$$= \left(\frac{P}{A}\right)^2 \times \frac{A \times l}{2E}$$

Case II

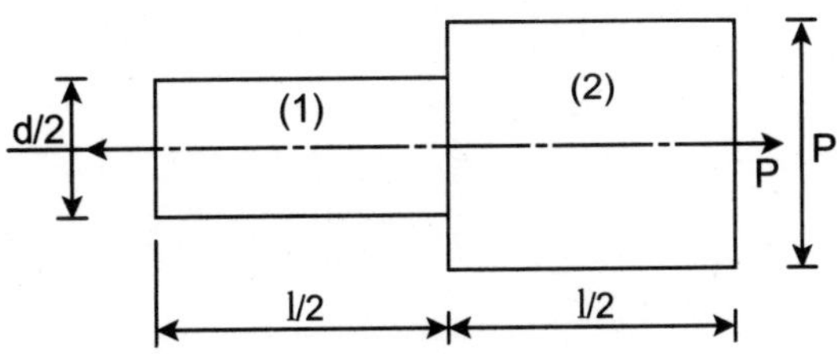

Fig. 17.10

$$A_2' = \frac{\pi}{4}\left(\frac{d}{2}\right)^2 + \frac{\pi}{4}d^2$$

$$= \frac{\pi}{4}\frac{d^2}{4} + \frac{\pi}{4}d^2$$

$$= \frac{\pi}{4}d^2\left(1 + \frac{1}{4}\right)$$

$$= \frac{5}{16}\pi d^2$$

$$= \frac{P^2}{A} \times \frac{l}{2E}$$

$$= \frac{4P^2}{\pi d^2} \frac{l}{2E} = \frac{2P^2 l}{\pi d^2 E}$$

$$V_2' = V_1 + V_2$$

$$= A_1 l_1 + A_2 l_2$$

$$= \frac{\pi}{4}\left(\frac{d}{2}\right)^2 \frac{l}{2} + \frac{\pi}{4} d^2 \times \frac{l}{2}$$

$$= \frac{\pi}{16} d^2 l + \frac{\pi}{8} d^2 l$$

$$= \frac{\pi}{8} d^2 l \left(1 + \frac{1}{2}\right)$$

$$= \frac{3}{2} \times \frac{\pi}{8} d^2 l$$

$$U_2' = U_1 + U_2 = \frac{\sigma_1^2}{2E} V_1 + \frac{\sigma_2^2}{2E} \times V_2$$

$$= \left[\left(\frac{P}{A_1}\right)^2 V_1 + \left(\frac{P}{A_2}\right)^2 V_2\right] \frac{1}{2E}$$

$$= \frac{1}{2E}\left[\frac{P^2}{A_1} l_1 + \frac{P^2}{A_2} l_2\right]$$

$$= \frac{1}{2E}\left[\frac{P^2 \times \left(\frac{l}{2}\right)}{\frac{\pi}{4}\left(\frac{d}{2}\right)^2} + \frac{P^2}{\frac{\pi}{4} d^2} \times l^2\right]$$

$$= \frac{1}{2E}\left[\frac{8P^2 l}{\pi d^2} + \frac{2P^2 l}{\pi d^2}\right]$$

$$= \frac{10P^2 l}{\pi d^2 \times 2E}$$

$$= \frac{5P^2 l}{\pi d^2 E}$$

$$\therefore \quad \frac{U_I}{U_{II}} = \frac{U_1}{U_2'} = \frac{\frac{2P^2 l}{\pi d^2 E}}{\frac{5P^2 l}{\pi d^2 E}} = \frac{2}{5}$$

$$\frac{U_1}{U_2'} = \frac{2}{5}$$ **Ans.**

Example 17.6

A crane chain whose sectional area is 600 mm^2 carries a load of 20 kN. As it is being lowered at a uniform rate of 50 m per minute, the chain gets jammed suddenly at which time the length of chain unwound is 11 m. Calculate the stress induced in the chain due to the sudden stoppage. Neglect the weight of the chain. $E = 2 \times 10^5$ N/mm^2.

Solution:

$$A = 600 \text{ mm}^2$$
$$W = 20 \text{ kN}$$
$$v = 50 \text{ m/min} = \frac{50}{60} \text{ m/sec} = \frac{5}{6} \text{ m/sec}$$
$$E = 2 \times 10^5 \text{ N/mm}^2.$$

Length of chain unwound = 11 m

$$\text{K.E. of crane} = \frac{1}{2} mv^2 = \frac{1}{2}\frac{W}{g}v^2$$

$$= \frac{1}{2} \times \frac{20 \times 10^3 \text{N}}{9.81 \frac{\text{m}}{\text{sec}^2}} \times \left(\frac{5}{6}\right)\frac{\text{m}}{\text{sec}} \times \left(\frac{5000}{6}\right)\frac{\text{mm}}{\text{sec}}$$

$$= 707894.44 \text{ N.mm} \quad \text{.............................} \quad (17.7)$$

and
$$U = \frac{\sigma^2}{2E} \times A \times l \quad \text{.............................} \quad (17.8)$$

Equating Eqs. (17.7) and (17.8),

$$\frac{\sigma^2}{2 \times 2 \times 10^5} \times 600 \times 11000 = 707894.44$$

$$\sigma = \sqrt{\frac{707894.44}{16.5}} = \mathbf{207.13 \ N/mm^2} \qquad \textbf{Ans.}$$

Example 17.7

A rectangular body 600 mm long 120 mm wide and 60 mm thick is subjected to a shear stress of 10 N/mm^2. Calculate the strain energy stored in it. Shear modulus $C = 0.85 \times 10^4$ N/mm^2.

Solution:

$$l = 600 \text{ mm}$$
$$b = 120 \text{ mm}$$
$$t = 60 \text{ mm}$$
$$\tau = 10 \text{ N/mm}^2$$
$$C = 0.85 \times 10^4 \text{ N/mm}^2$$

Strain energy due to shear stress

$$U = \frac{\tau^2}{2C} \times \text{Volume}$$

$$= \frac{\tau^2}{2C} \times b \times t \times l$$

$$= \frac{10 \times 10 \times 120 \times 60 \times 600}{2 \times 0.85 \times 10^4}$$

$$= 25411.76 \text{ N.mm}$$

$$U = \mathbf{25.41 \text{ N.m}}$$ **Ans.**

Example 17.8

The internal and external diameters of a hollow shaft are 300 mm and 600 mm. Calculate maximum strain energy stored in the hollow shaft, if the maximum allowable shear stress is 60 MPa and length of shaft is 6 m. Take C = 0.8 × 10⁴ N/mm².

Solution:

$d_i = 300$ mm

$d_o = 600$ mm

$U = ?$

$\tau = 60$ MPa $= 60$ N/mm^2

$l = 6$ m $= 6000$ mm

$C = 0.84 \times 10^4$ N/mm^2

We know that strain energy stored in a shaft due to torsion is given by

$$U = \frac{\tau^2 \cdot l}{2Cr^2} J$$

$$U_H = \frac{\tau^2 \cdot l}{2Cr_o^2} J_H = \frac{\tau^2 l}{2Cr_o^2} \frac{\pi}{32}(d_o^4 - d_i^4)$$

$$\therefore \quad U_H = \frac{60 \times 60 \times 6000 \times \pi \times \left(600^4 - 300^4\right)}{2 \times 0.85 \times 10^4 \times (300)^2 \times 32}$$

$$= \frac{8.2447 \times 10^{18}}{4.8384 \times 10^{10}} = 1.7 \times 10^8 \text{ N.mm}$$

$$= \mathbf{1.7 \times 10^5 \text{ N.m}}$$ **Ans.**

NUMERICAL QUESTIONS

1. A load of 5 kN attached to the end of a wire is lowered at a uniform velocity of 0.5 m/s. Find the instantaneous stress induced in the wire when its upper end is suddenly jammed. Assume that at the instant of jam the length of wire is 7 m the sectional area of wire is 500 mm^2. Take $E = 2.1 \times 10^5$ N/mm^2.
2. A 1 m long steel rod of rectangular section 80 mm × 40 mm is subjected to an axial pull of 200 kN. Find the strain energy and maximum stress produced in it for the following cases (a) due to gradual load (b) due to sudden application of load (c) when the load falls through a height of 100 mm. Take $E = 2 \times 10^5$ N/mm^2.
3. Two elastic bars of the same material and length, but one of circular cross section of diameter 40 mm and other of square cross section of side 40 mm, absorb the same amount of energy, delivered due to gradually applied axial forces. Calculate the ratio of the stresses induced. Also calculate the ratio of applied forces.
4. A rectangular block of 100 mm^2 base area and 15 mm height is fixed on its bottom and subjected to a shear force of 1 kN on its top surface. Calculate strain energy stored in the block.
5. Prove that the stress induced in a member under suddenly applied load is twice that of gradual loading.
6. A steel bar circular in section 40 mm diameter and 4 m long is subjected to an axial pull of 100 kN. Find strain energy. What will be the strain energy under the above pull if the diameter of the bar is 2.6 cm over one half of its length and 40 mm over the remaining half? Also find strain energy if the bar is 26 mm in diameter throughout its length. E = 210 GPa.
7. A steel bar 1 m long and circular in section diameter 43 mm is subjected to an axial load of 1.5 kN. Find maximum stress induced if
   (a) The load is applied gradually
   (b) The load is applied suddenly
   (c) The load is applied after falling through a height of 6 cm.
   What are the strain energies in above cases. Take E = 200 GN/m^2.

18

Compound Stress and Strains

18.1 Compound Stress

The tensile and compressive stresses act on planes which are normal to the line of action of the applied external forces. The shear stresses are induced on planes parallel to the direction of applied external shear forces. On inclined planes (oblique planes), both normal and shear stresses are induced. The combination of normal and shear stress is called compound stress.

18.2 Principal Stresses and Principal Planes

At any point, within a stressed body, there always exist three mutually perpendicular planes on each of which the resultant stress is a normal stress. These mutually perpendicular planes are called principal planes and the resultant normal stresses acting on principal planes are called principal stresses.

In case of three dimensional problems, one of the principal stress is zero and out of other two, one is major principal stress (σ_1) and other is minor principal stress (σ_2), acting on major and minor principal planes respectively. No shear stress act on the principal planes.

18.3 Principal Strains

Principal strains are the major and minor direct strains in a material subjected to complex stresses. These strains are produced in the direction of the principal stresses.

$$\epsilon_1 = \frac{\sigma_1}{E} - \frac{\mu\sigma_2}{E}$$

$$\epsilon_2 = \frac{\sigma_2}{E} - \frac{\mu\sigma_1}{E}$$

where $\sigma_1, \sigma_2 \rightarrow$ Principal stresses.

$\mu \rightarrow$ Poisson's ratio.

$E \rightarrow$ Modulus of elasticity.

18.4 Stress on an Oblique Plane under Uniaxial Loading

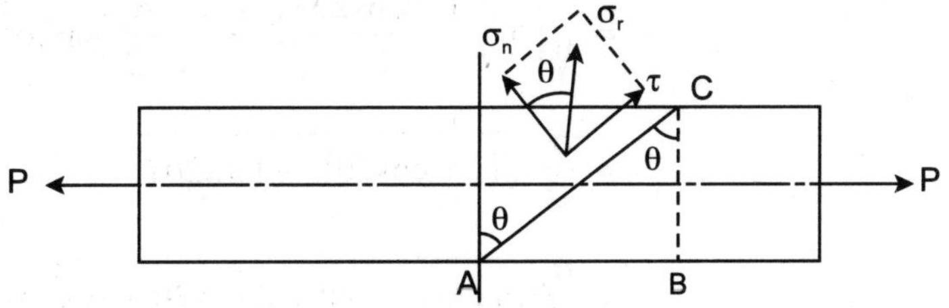

Fig. 18.1

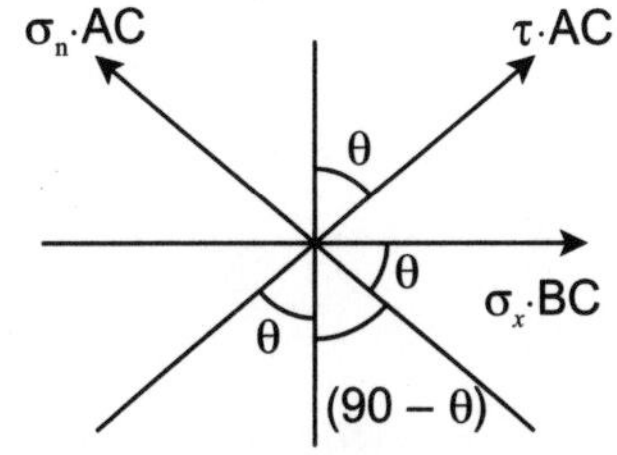

Fig. 18.2

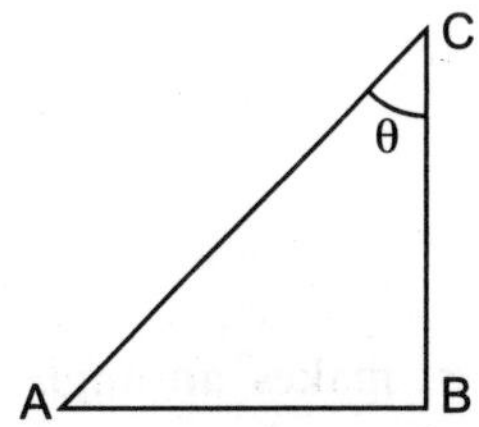

Fig. 18.3

Let us consider a rectangular block which is subjected to a tensile force P along its longitudinal axis. The dimension of the block perpendicular to the plane of paper is assumed to be unity. So that area of cross section, A = BC × 1

$$\sigma_x = \frac{P}{A}$$

Resolving the forces ⊥ to plane AC.

$$\sigma_n \cdot AC \times 1 = \sigma_x \cdot BC \times 1 \cos\theta$$

$$\sigma_n = \sigma_x \frac{BC}{AC} \cdot \cos\theta = \sigma_x \cdot \cos\theta \cdot \cos\theta$$

$$\sigma_n = \sigma_x \cdot \cos^2\theta$$

$$= \sigma_x \left(\frac{1 + \cos 2\theta}{2} \right)$$

$$\cos 2\theta = 2\cos^2\theta - 1$$

$$2\cos^2\theta = 1 + \cos 2\theta$$

$$\cos^2\theta = \left(\frac{1 + \cos 2\theta}{2} \right)$$

If $\theta = 0 \Rightarrow \sigma_n = \sigma_x$

$\theta = 90° \Rightarrow \sigma_n = 0$

Now, resolving the forces parallel to plane AC

$$\tau \cdot AC \times 1 + \sigma_x \cdot BC \times 1 \sin\theta = 0$$

$$\tau = -\sigma_x \frac{BC}{AC} \cdot \sin\theta$$

$$\tau = -\sigma_x \cdot \sin\theta \cos\theta$$

$$\tau = -\frac{\sigma_x}{2} \cdot \sin 2\theta$$

and resultant stress

$$\sigma_r = \sqrt{(\sigma_n)^2 + (\tau)^2}$$

$$= \sqrt{\left\{\sigma_x\left(\frac{1+\cos 2\theta}{2}\right)\right\}^2 + \left(-\frac{\sigma_x}{2}\sin 2\theta\right)^2}$$

$$= \frac{\sigma_x}{2}\sqrt{(1+\cos 2\theta)^2 + (\sin 2\theta)^2}$$

$$= \frac{\sigma_x}{2}\sqrt{\left(1+\cos^2 2\theta + 2\cos 2\theta + \sin^2 2\theta\right)}$$

$$= \frac{\sigma_x}{2}\sqrt{1+1+2\cos 2\theta}$$

$$= \frac{\sigma_x}{2}\sqrt{2(1+\cos 2\theta)}$$

$$= \frac{\sigma_x}{2}\sqrt{2\left(+1+2\cos^2\theta - 1\right)}$$

$$= \frac{\sigma_x}{\not{2}}\cdot\not{2}\cdot\cos\theta$$

$$\sigma_r = \sigma_x\cdot\cos\theta$$

If σ_r makes an angle ϕ with σ_n then

$$\tan\phi = \frac{\tau}{\sigma_n}$$

Example 18.1

Find the diameter of a circular bar which is subjected to an axial tensile load of 100 kN, if the maximum allowable shear stress on any section is 70 MPa.

Solution:

$P = 100$ kN

$= 1 \times 10^5$ N

$A = \frac{\pi}{4}d^2$

$d = ?$

$\tau_{max} = 70$ MPa $= 70$ N/mm^2

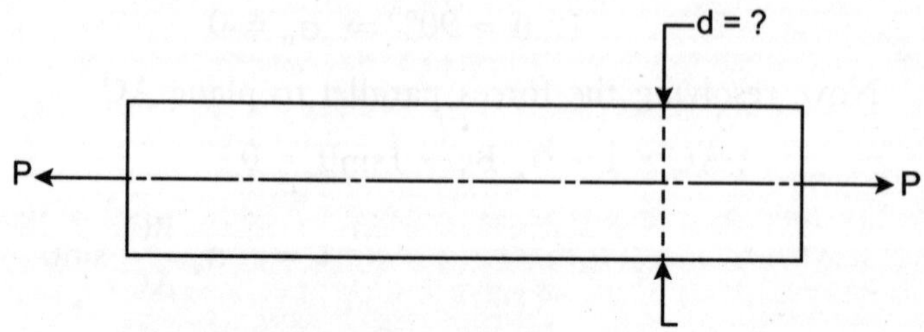

Fig. 18.4

We know that $\tau = -\frac{\sigma_x}{2}2\cos\theta\sin\theta = -\frac{\sigma_x}{2}\sin 2\theta$

For τ_{max}, $\theta = 45°$

$$\therefore \quad \tau_{max} = \frac{\sigma_x}{2}$$

$$\Rightarrow \quad 70 = \frac{\sigma_x}{2}$$

$$\Rightarrow \quad \sigma_x = 140$$

$$\Rightarrow \quad \frac{P}{\frac{\pi}{4}\cdot d^2} = 140 \Rightarrow \frac{4P}{\pi d^2} = 140$$

$$\Rightarrow \quad d = \sqrt{\frac{4p}{\pi \times 140}} = \sqrt{\frac{4 \times 1 \times 10^5}{\pi \times 140}} = 30.15 \text{ mm}$$

$$\therefore \quad d = \mathbf{30.2\ mm}$$ **Ans.**

Example 18.2

A rectangular bar of cross sectional area 1200 mm² is subjected to tensile load P. The permissible normal and shear stresses on an oblique plane inclined at an angle of 60° with the axis of σ_x as shown in Fig. 18.5 are 8 MPa and 4 MPa respectively. Determine safe value of P.

Solution:

$\theta = 90 - 60 = 30°$

$A = 1200 \text{ mm}^2$

$P = ?$

$\sigma_n = 8 \text{ MPa} = 8 \text{ N/mm}^2$

$\tau = 4 \text{ MPa} = 4 \text{ N/mm}^2$

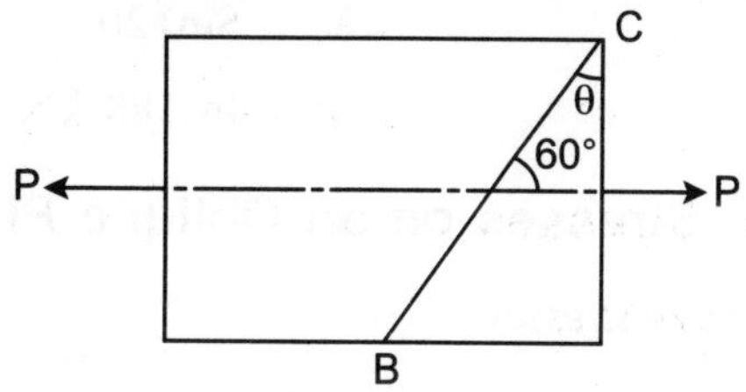

Fig. 18.5

Now

We know that

$$\sigma_n = \sigma_x \cdot \cos^2\theta$$

$$\Rightarrow \quad 8 = \frac{P}{A}\cos^2 30 \Rightarrow P = \frac{8 \times 1200}{\cos^2 30} = 12.8 \text{ kN}$$

and

$$\tau = \frac{\sigma_x}{2}\sin 2\theta$$

$$\Rightarrow \quad 4 = \frac{P}{2A}\sin 60 \Rightarrow P = \frac{4 \times 2 \times 1200}{\sin 60} = 11.08 \text{ kN}$$

$\therefore$ Safe load = minimum load out of two values

$$\therefore \quad P_{safe} = \mathbf{11.08\ kN}$$ **Ans.**

Example 18.3

Two wooden pieces 100 mm × 100 mm in cross section are glued together along line BC as shown in Fig. 18.6. What maximum axial force P can be applied if the allowable shearing stress along BC is 2 MPa.

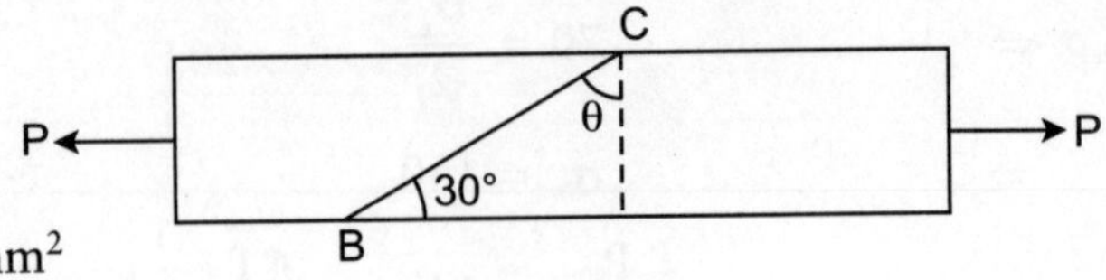

Fig. 18.6

Solution:

$\theta = 90 - 30 = 60°$

$A = 100 \text{ mm} \times 100 \text{ mm} = 1 \times 10^4 \text{ mm}^2$

$P = ?$

$\tau = 2 \text{ MPa} = 2 \text{ N/mm}^2$

We know that

$$\tau = -\frac{\sigma_x}{2}\sin 2\theta$$

$$2 = \frac{\sigma_x}{2}\sin 120 \qquad \text{(ignoring –ve sign)}$$

$$\sigma_x = \frac{4}{\text{Sin}120}$$

$$\Rightarrow \quad \frac{P}{A} = \frac{4}{\text{Sin}120} \Rightarrow P = \frac{4 \times 1 \times 10^4}{\text{Sin}120} = 46188.02 \text{ N}$$

$$\therefore \quad P = 46.188 \text{ kN}$$

Ans.

18.5 Stresses on an Oblique Plane under Biaxial Loading

Case I: Like stresses

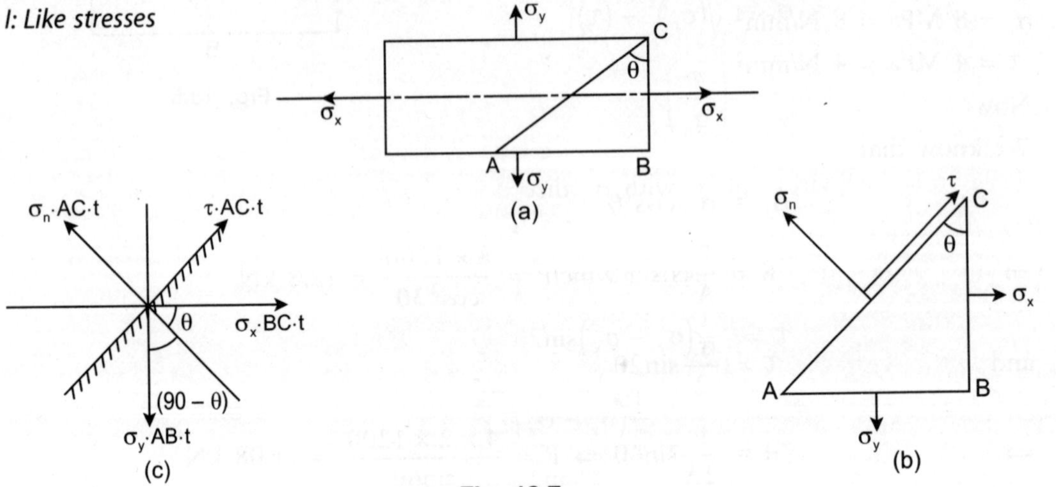

Fig. 18.7

Resolving all the forces perpendicular to plane AC.

$$\sigma_n \cdot AC \cdot t = \sigma_x \cdot BC \cdot t \cdot \cos\theta + \sigma_y \cdot AB \cdot t \cdot \sin\theta$$

$$\Rightarrow \qquad \sigma_n = \sigma_x \frac{BC}{AC}\cos\theta + \sigma_y \cdot \frac{AB}{AC}\sin\theta$$

$$\Rightarrow \qquad \sigma_n = \sigma_x \cos^2\theta + \sigma_y \sin^2\theta \quad \ldots\ldots (18.1)$$

$$= \sigma_x\left(\frac{1+\cos 2\theta}{2}\right) + \sigma_y\left(\frac{1-\cos 2\theta}{2}\right)$$

$$\sigma_n = \frac{1}{2}(\sigma_x + \sigma_y) + \frac{1}{2}(\sigma_x - \sigma_y)\cos 2\theta \quad \ldots\ldots (18.2)$$

Resolving all the forces along the plane AC.

$$\tau \cdot AC \cdot t + \sigma_x \cdot BC \cdot t \cdot \sin\theta = \sigma_y \cdot AB \cdot t \cdot \cos\theta$$

or

$$\tau = \sigma_y \cdot \frac{AB}{AC}\cos\theta - \sigma_x \frac{BC}{AC}\sin\theta$$

$$= (\sigma_y - \sigma_x)\sin\theta\cos\theta$$

$$\tau = \frac{1}{2}(\sigma_y - \sigma_x)\sin 2\theta \quad \ldots\ldots (18.3)$$

For τ_{max} $\theta = 45°$

$$\therefore \qquad \tau_{max} = \frac{1}{2}(\sigma_y - \sigma_x) \quad \ldots\ldots (18.4)$$

and

$$\sigma_r = \sqrt{(\sigma_n)^2 + (\tau)^2}$$

$$\tan\phi = \left(\frac{\tau}{\sigma_n}\right)$$

where ϕ = inclination of σ_r with σ_n direction.

Principal planes:

Principal planes are the planes on which shear stress is zero.

$$\therefore \qquad \tau = \frac{1}{2}(\sigma_y - \sigma_x)\sin 2\theta = 0$$

$$\therefore \qquad \frac{1}{2}(\sigma_y - \sigma_x) \neq 0$$

$$\therefore \qquad \sin 2\theta = 0$$

$$\Rightarrow \qquad 2\theta = 0 \text{ or } 180°$$

$$\Rightarrow \qquad \theta = 0 \text{ or } 90°$$

When $\theta = 0$, $\sigma_n = \sigma_x\cos^2\theta + \sigma_y\sin^2\theta = \sigma_x$

When $\theta = 90$, $\sigma_n = \sigma_x\cos^2\theta + \sigma_y\sin^2\theta = \sigma_y$

Case II: Unlike stresses: Use negative sign with compressive stresses in Eqs. (18.1) to (18.4).

Example 18.4

The principal tensile stresses at a point across two mutually perpendicular planes are 100 MPa and 50 MPa. Find normal, tangential and resultant stress on a plane inclined at 30° to the axis of minor principal stress.

Solution:

$\theta = 30°$

$\sigma_x = 100$ MPa

$\sigma_y = 50$ MPa

$\sigma_n = ?$

$\tau = ?$

$\sigma_r = ?$

$\phi = ?$

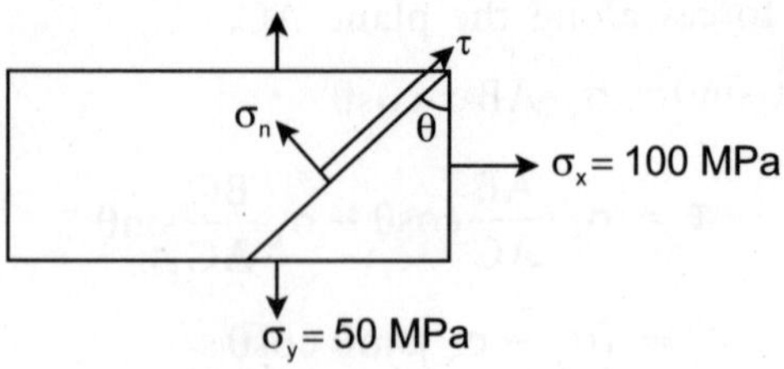

Fig. 18.8

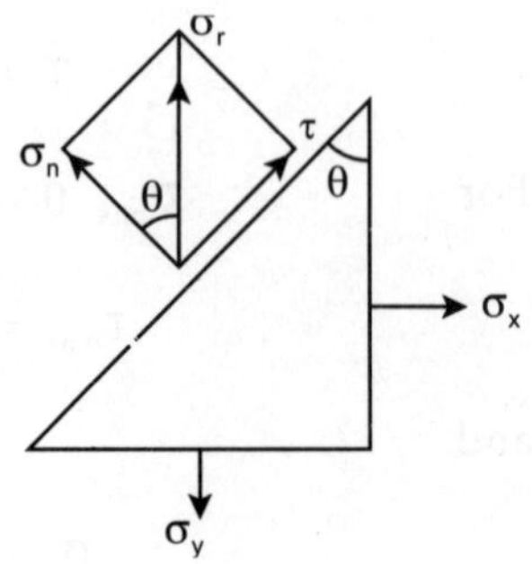

Fig. 18.9

We know that

$$\sigma_n = \sigma_x\cos^2\theta + \sigma_y\sin^2\theta$$

$$= \frac{1}{2}(\sigma_x + \sigma_y) + \frac{1}{2}(\sigma_x - \sigma_y)\cos 2\theta$$

$$= \frac{1}{2}(100 + 50) + \frac{1}{2}(100 - 50)\cos 60$$

$$= 75 + 25 \times \frac{1}{2} = \mathbf{87.5\ MPa} \qquad \textbf{Ans.}$$

and

$$\tau = \frac{1}{2}(\sigma_y - \sigma_x)\sin 2\theta$$

$$= \frac{1}{2}(50 - 100)\text{Sin}60$$

$$= -25\sin 60 = \mathbf{-21.65\ MPa} \qquad \textbf{Ans.}$$

$$\sigma_r = \sqrt{\sigma_n^{\,2} + \tau^2} = \sqrt{(87.5)^2 + (21.65)^2}$$

$$= \mathbf{90.14\ MPa} \qquad \textbf{Ans.}$$

and $$\phi = \tan^{-1}\left(\frac{\tau}{\sigma_n}\right) = \tan^{-1}\left(\frac{-21.65}{87.5}\right) = \mathbf{-13.89°} \qquad \textbf{Ans.}$$

Example 18.5

The principal stresses at a point in a bar are 300 MPa (tensile) and 150 MPa (compressive). Determine resultant stress in magnitude and direction on a plane inclined at 60° to the axis of major principal stress. Also find the maximum intensity of shear stress in the material at the point.

Solution:

$\sigma_x = 300$ MPa

$\sigma_y = -150$ MPa

$\theta = 90 - 60 = 30°$

$\sigma_r = ?$

$\phi = ?$

$\tau_{max} = ?$

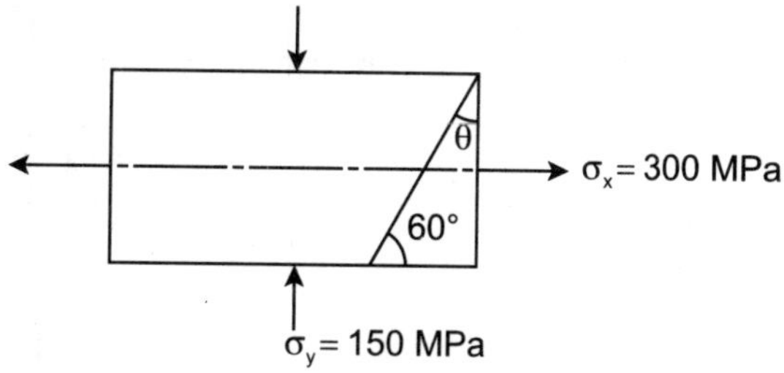

Fig. 18.10

We know that

$$\sigma_n = \frac{1}{2}(\sigma_x + \sigma_y) + \frac{1}{2}(\sigma_x - \sigma_y)\cos 2\theta$$

$$= \frac{1}{2}(300 - 150) + \frac{1}{2}(300 + 150)\cos 60$$

$$= 75 + 225 \times \frac{1}{2}$$

$$= 187.5 \text{ MPa}$$

and

$$\tau = \frac{1}{2}(\sigma_y - \sigma_x)\sin 2\theta = \frac{1}{2}(-150 - 300)\sin 60 = -194.86 \text{ MPa}$$

and

$$\sigma_r = \sqrt{\sigma_n^2 + \tau^2} = \sqrt{(187.5)^2 + (194.86)^2} = \mathbf{270.4 \text{ MPa}} \qquad \textbf{Ans.}$$

$$\phi = \tan^{-1}\left(\frac{\tau}{\sigma_n}\right) = \tan^{-1}\left(\frac{-194.86}{187.5}\right) = \mathbf{-46.1°} \qquad \textbf{Ans.}$$

Also $\tau_{max}\left(\frac{\sigma_x - \sigma_y}{2}\right) = \left(\frac{300 - (-150)}{2}\right) = \mathbf{225 \text{ MPa}}$ **Ans.**

Example 18.6

At a point in a strained material, the principal tensile stresses across two perpendicular planes are 100 MPa and 50 MPa. Find normal, shear and resultant stresses on a plane inclined at 30° with the major principal plane. Determine also obliquity. What will be intensity of stress which acting alone will produce the same maximum strain if Poisson's ratio = 0.25?

Solution:

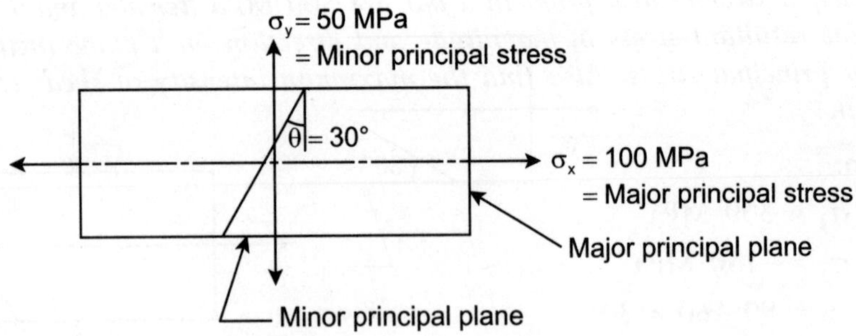

Fig. 18.11

$\sigma_x = 100$ MPa

$\sigma_y = 50$ MPa

$\theta = 30° =$ inclination of oblique plane with major principal plane

$\sigma_r = ?,\ \sigma_n = ?,\ \tau = ?,\ \phi = ?,\ \mu = 0.25$

Now

$$\sigma_n = \frac{1}{2}(\sigma_x + \sigma_y) + \frac{1}{2}(\sigma_x - \sigma_y)\cos 2\theta$$

$$= \frac{1}{2}(100 + 50) + \frac{1}{2}(100 - 50)\cos 60 = \mathbf{87.5\ MPa} \qquad \textbf{Ans.}$$

$$\tau = \frac{1}{2}(\sigma_y - \sigma_x)\sin 2\theta = \frac{1}{2}(50 - 100)\sin 60 = \mathbf{-21.65\ MPa} \qquad \textbf{Ans.}$$

$$\sigma_r = \sqrt{\sigma_n^{\ 2} + \tau^2} = \sqrt{87.5^2 + 21.65^2} = \mathbf{90.11\ MPa} \qquad \textbf{Ans.}$$

$$\phi = \tan^{-1}\left(\frac{\tau}{\sigma_n}\right) = \mathbf{13.89°} \qquad \textbf{Ans.}$$

$$\in_{max} = \frac{\sigma_x}{E} - \mu\frac{\sigma_y}{E} = \frac{100}{E} - 0.25 \times \frac{50}{E} = \frac{87.5}{E} \quad \ldots\ldots\ldots\ldots\ldots \text{(18.5)}$$

Also

$$\in = \frac{\sigma}{E} \quad \ldots\ldots\ldots\ldots\ldots\ldots\ldots\ldots\ldots\ldots \text{(18.6)}$$

Equating (18.5) and (18.6), $\frac{\sigma}{E} = \frac{87.5}{E}$

$\therefore$ $\sigma = \mathbf{87.5\ MPa}$ **Ans.**

Alternate solution:

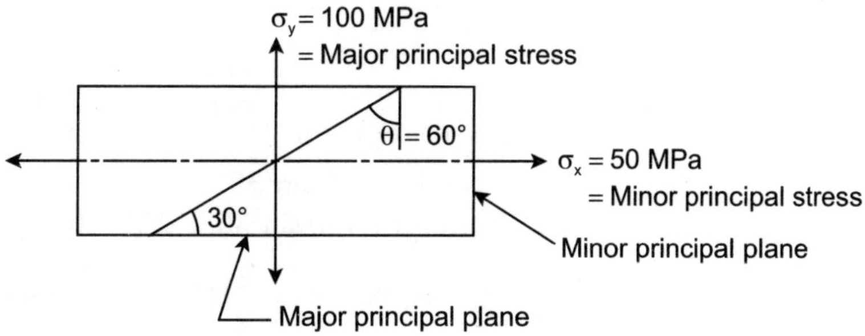

Fig. 18.12

$$\sigma_n = \frac{1}{2}(\sigma_x + \sigma_y) + \frac{1}{2}(\sigma_x - \sigma_y)\cos 2\theta$$

$$= \frac{1}{2}(50 + 100) + \frac{1}{2}(50 - 100)\cos 120$$

$$= 75 + 25\cos 120 = \mathbf{87.5\ MPa}$$ **Ans.**

$$\tau = \frac{1}{2}(\sigma_y - \sigma_x)\sin 2\theta = \frac{1}{2}(100 - 50)\sin 120 = \mathbf{21.65\ MPa}$$ **Ans.**

$$\sigma_r = \sqrt{(\sigma_n)^2 + (\tau)^2} = \sqrt{87.5^2 + 21.65^2} = \mathbf{90.11\ MPa}$$ **Ans.**

$$\phi = \tan^{-1}\left(\frac{\tau}{\sigma_n}\right) = \tan^{-1}\left(\frac{21.65}{87.5}\right) = \mathbf{13.89^\circ}$$ **Ans.**

$$\in_{max} = \frac{\sigma_y}{E} - \mu\frac{\sigma_x}{E} = \frac{100}{E} - 0.25 \times \frac{50}{E} = \frac{87.5}{E} \quad \ldots\ldots\ldots\ldots\ldots \quad (18.7)$$

Also

$$\in = \frac{\sigma}{E} \quad \ldots\ldots\ldots\ldots\ldots\ldots\ldots\ldots\ldots\ldots\ldots \quad (18.8)$$

From Eqs. (18.7) and (18.8),

$$\sigma = 87.5\ \text{MPa}$$ **Ans.**

Example 18.7

At a point in a strained material, the principal stresses are 250 MPa (tensile) and 150 MPa (tensile) at right angles to each other. Determine normal, tangential stresses on a plane inclined at 60° to the 250 MPa stress. Also find the plane on which the resultant stress has maximum obliquity.

Solution:

$$\theta = 90 - 60 = 30^\circ$$

$$\sigma_x = 250\ \text{MPa}$$

$$\sigma_y = 150\ \text{MPa}$$

$$\sigma_n = ?$$

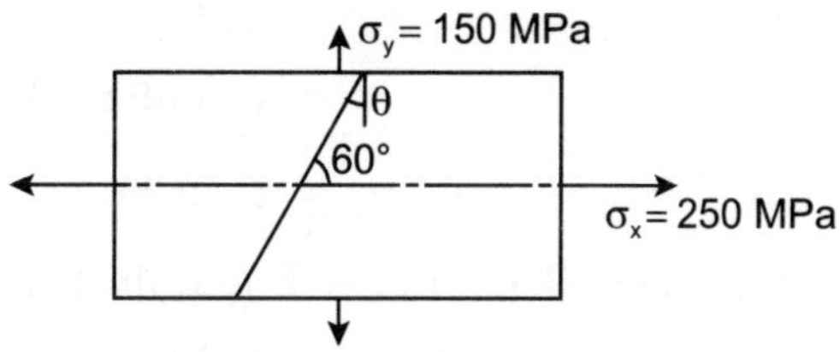

Fig. 18.13

$\tau = ?$

$\phi = ?$

Now

$$\sigma_n = \sigma_x \cos^2\theta + \sigma_y \sin^2\theta$$
$$= 250\cos^2\theta + 150\sin^2 30$$
$$= 250\cos^2 30 + 150\sin^2 30 = \mathbf{225\ MPa} \qquad \textbf{Ans.}$$

$$\tau = \frac{1}{2}(\sigma_y - \sigma_x)\text{Sin}2\theta = \frac{1}{2}(150 - 250)\text{Sin}60 = \mathbf{-43.3\ MPa} \qquad \textbf{Ans.}$$

$$\sigma_r = \sqrt{\sigma_n^{\,2} + \tau^2} = \sqrt{225^2 + 43.3^2} = 229.13 \text{ MPa}$$

$$\phi = \tan^{-1}\left(\frac{\tau}{\sigma_n}\right) = \tan^{-1}\left(\frac{-43.3}{225}\right) = -62.5°$$

For the resultant to have maximum obliquity.

$$\theta = \tan^{-1}\left(\sqrt{\frac{\sigma_y}{\sigma_x}}\right) = \tan^{-1}\left(\sqrt{\frac{150}{250}}\right) = +30.96° \qquad \textbf{Ans.}$$

18.6 Stresses on an Oblique Plane under Shear Stress

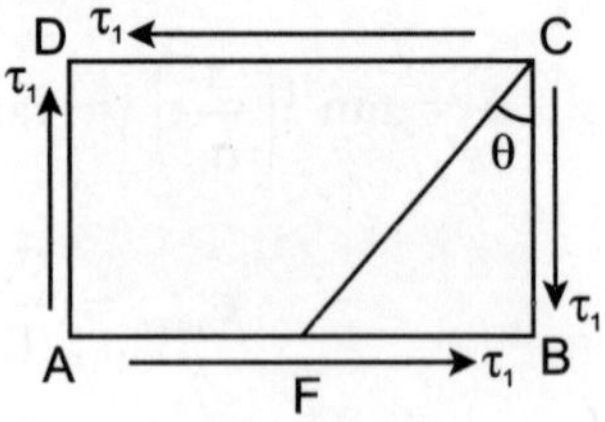

Fig. 18.14

ABCD → rectangular block

T → thickness of block

A → cross sectional area of block

FC → oblique plane

τ_1 = shear stress across face BC and AD.

We know that each pair of shear stress is always accompanied by equal shear stress pair at right angles to it. (Principle of complementary shear stress)

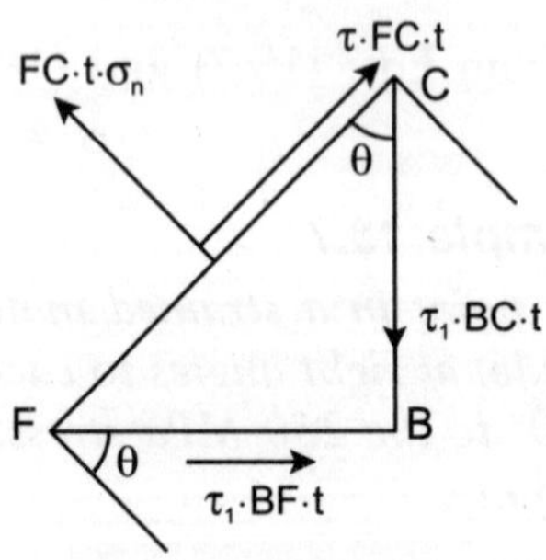

Fig. 18.15

Resolving all the forces ⊥ to oblique plane FC.

$$\sigma_n \cdot FC \cdot t = \tau_1 \cdot BF \cdot t \cdot \cos\theta + \tau_1 \cdot BC \cdot t \cdot \sin\theta$$

$$\Rightarrow \qquad \sigma_n = \tau_1 \cdot \frac{BF}{FC}\cos\theta + \tau_1 \cdot \frac{BC}{FC}\sin\theta$$

$$= \tau_1 \cdot \sin\theta\cos\theta + \tau_1 \cdot \sin\theta\cos\theta$$

$$\Rightarrow \qquad \sigma_n = \tau_1 \cdot \sin 2\theta \qquad \text{(18.9)}$$

Resolving all the forces ∥ (parallel) to plane FC

$$\tau \cdot FC \cdot t = \tau_1 \cdot BC \cdot t \cdot \cos\theta - \tau_1 \cdot BF \cdot t \cdot \sin\theta$$

$$\tau = \tau_1 \cdot \frac{BF}{FC}\cos\theta - \tau_1 \cdot \frac{BC}{FC}\sin\theta$$

$$= \tau_1 \cdot \cos^2\theta - \tau_1 \cdot \sin^2\theta$$

$$\tau = \tau_1 \cdot \cos 2\theta \quad \ldots\ldots\ldots \quad (18.10)$$

18.7 Stresses on an Oblique Plane under Biaxial Loading Accompanied by a Simple Shear Stress

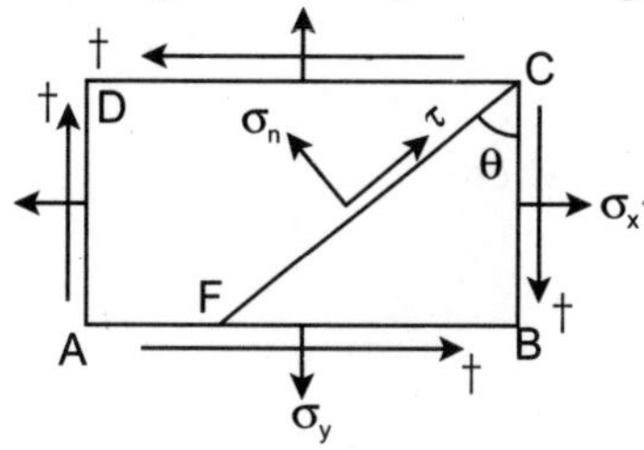

Fig. 18.16

All notations have their usual meanings.

Resolving all forces ⊥ to oblique plane FC.

$$\sigma_n \cdot FC \cdot t = \sigma_x \cdot BC \cdot t \cdot \cos\theta + \dagger \cdot BF \cdot t \cdot \cos\theta + \sigma_y \cdot AB \cdot t \cdot \sin\theta + \dagger \cdot BC \cdot t \cdot \sin\theta$$

$$\Rightarrow \quad \sigma_n = \sigma_x \frac{BC}{FC}\cos\theta + \sigma_y \frac{AB}{FC}\sin\theta + \dagger\frac{BF}{FC}\cos\theta + \dagger\frac{BC}{FC}\sin\theta$$

$$\sigma_n = \sigma_x \cos^2\theta + \sigma_y \sin^2\theta + \dagger\sin 2\theta \quad \ldots (18.11)$$

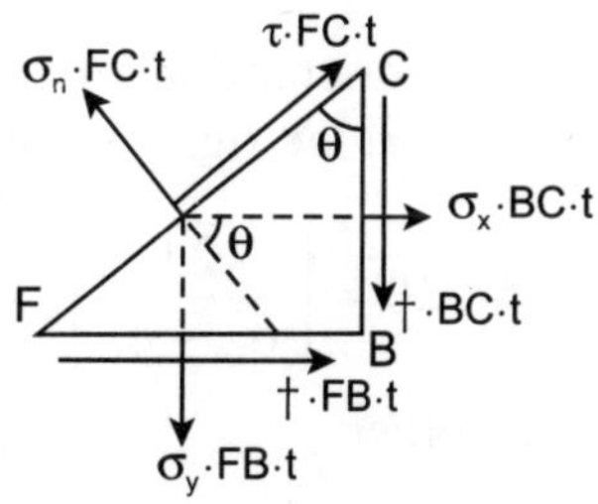

Fig. 18.17

Resolving all forces parallel to plane FC.

$$\tau \cdot FC \cdot t + \sigma_x \cdot BC \cdot t \cdot \sin\theta + \dagger \cdot BF \cdot t \cdot \sin\theta = \dagger \cdot BC \cdot t \cdot \cos\theta + \sigma_y \cdot AB \cdot t \cdot \cos\theta$$

$$\Rightarrow \quad \tau = \frac{1}{2}(\sigma_y - \sigma_x)\sin 2\theta + \dagger\cos 2\theta \quad \ldots\ldots\ldots \quad (18.11)$$

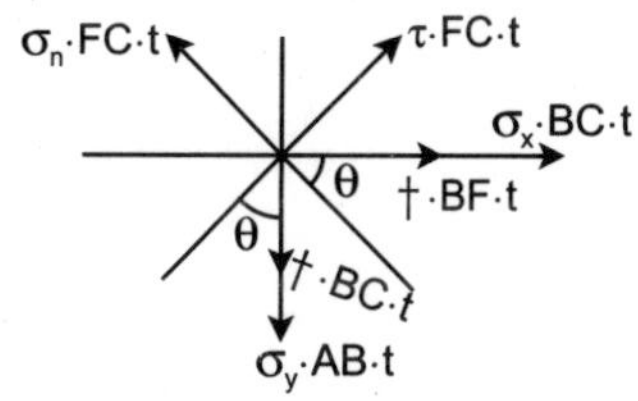

Fig. 18.18

Position of Principal Planes:

For principal planes, $\tau = 0$

$\therefore$ From Eq. (18.12), $\frac{1}{2}(\sigma_x - \sigma_y)\sin 2\theta + \dagger\cos 2\theta = 0$

$$\Rightarrow \quad \tan 2\theta = \left(\frac{2\dagger}{\sigma_x - \sigma_y}\right) \quad \ldots\ldots\ldots \quad (18.12)$$

$\therefore$ Position of principal planes can be find out using Eq. (18.13)

$$\therefore \quad \tan 2\theta = \left(\frac{2\dagger}{\sigma_x - \sigma_y}\right)$$

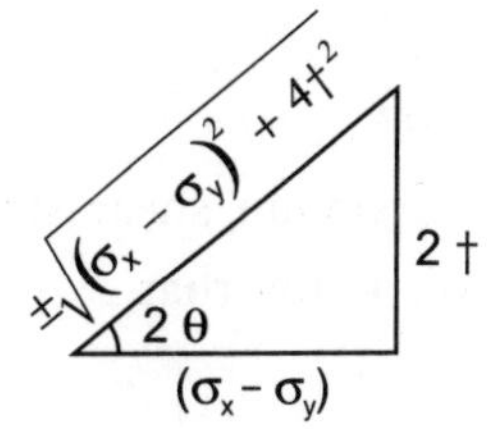

Fig. 18.19

Substituting the value of $\sin 2\theta$ and $\cos 2\theta$ in Eq. (18.11)

$$\sigma_n = \sigma_x \cos^2\theta + \sigma_y \sin^2\theta + \dagger\sin 2\theta$$

or $$\sigma_n = \frac{1}{2}(\sigma_x + \sigma_y) + \frac{1}{2}(\sigma_x - \sigma_y)\cos 2\theta + \dagger \sin 2\theta$$

or $$\sigma_{1,2} = \frac{1}{2}(\sigma_x + \sigma_y) \pm \frac{1}{2}\frac{(\sigma_x - \sigma_y)(\sigma_x - \sigma_y)}{\sqrt{(\sigma_x - \sigma_y)^2 + 4\dagger^2}} \pm \dagger \cdot \frac{2\dagger}{\sqrt{(\sigma_x - \sigma_y)^2 + 4\dagger^2}}$$

$$\sigma_{1,2} = \frac{1}{2}(\sigma_x + \sigma_y) \pm \frac{1}{2}\sqrt{(\sigma_x - \sigma_y)^2 + 4\dagger^2} \quad \text{................} \quad (18.14)$$

where

$$\sigma_1 = \frac{1}{2}(\sigma_x + \sigma_y) + \frac{1}{2}\sqrt{(\sigma_x - \sigma_y)^2 + 4\dagger^2} = \text{Major principal stress}$$

and $$\sigma_2 = \frac{1}{2}(\sigma_x + \sigma_y) - \frac{1}{2}\sqrt{(\sigma_x - \sigma_y)^2 + 4\dagger^2} = \text{Minor principal stress}$$

The orientation of principal planes giving Eq. (18.13). Both minor and major principal planes are at right angles.

$\tan 2\theta = \left(\frac{2\dagger}{\sigma_x - \sigma_y}\right)$; 2θ; and $2\theta_2$ will differ by 180° and θ_1 and θ_2 will differ by 90° with each other.

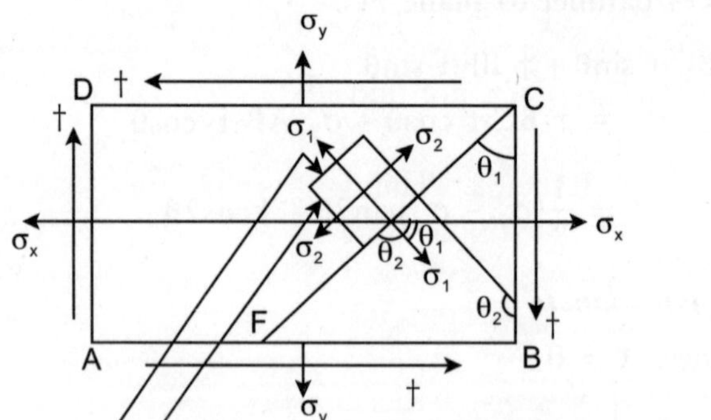

θ_1 and θ_2 are the location of major and minor principal planes as shown in Fig.

Fig. 18.20

Now

Maximum shear stress (τ_{max}):

We know that

$$\tau = \frac{1}{2}(\sigma_y - \sigma_x)\sin 2\theta + \dagger \cos 2\theta \quad \text{......................} \quad (18.15)$$

For τ_{max}, $\frac{d}{d\theta}(\tau) = 0 \Rightarrow \frac{d}{d\theta}\left[\left(\frac{\sigma_y - \sigma_x}{2}\right)\sin 2\theta + \dagger\cos 2\theta\right] = 0$

$$\Rightarrow \quad \tan 2\theta = \frac{\sigma_y - \sigma_x}{2\dagger} \quad \ldots\ldots (18.16)$$

$$\sin 2\theta = \pm\frac{\sigma_y - \sigma_x}{\sqrt{(\sigma_y - \sigma_x)^2 + 4\dagger^2}}$$

$$\cos 2\theta = \pm\frac{2\dagger}{\sqrt{(\sigma_y - \sigma_x)^2 + 4\dagger^2}}$$

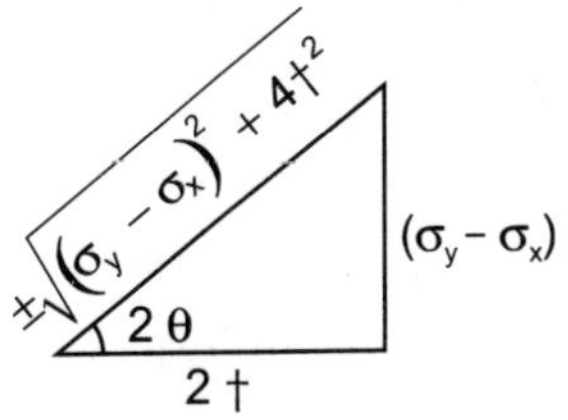

Fig. 18.21

Substituting values of sin2θ, cos2θ in Eq. (18.15),

$$\tau_{max} = \pm\frac{\frac{1}{2}(\sigma_y - \sigma_x)(\sigma_y - \sigma_x)}{\sqrt{(\sigma_y - \sigma_x)^2 + 4\dagger^2}} \pm \frac{\dagger\cdot 2\dagger}{\sqrt{(\sigma_y - \sigma_x)^2 + 4\dagger^2}}$$

$$\tau_{max} = \pm\frac{1}{2}\sqrt{(\sigma_y - \sigma_x)^2 + 4\dagger^2} \quad \ldots\ldots (18.17)$$

$$\tau_{max} = \left(\frac{\sigma_1 - \sigma_2}{2}\right)$$

The planes on which τ_{max} act, are find out by Eq. (18.16), these two values θ_3, θ_4 differ by 90°.

Using the Equation of Principle Plane and (18.16), we can say that principal planes and planes of maximum shear stress will differ by 45°, i.e.

$$\theta_3 = \theta_1 + 45°$$
$$\theta_4 = \theta_2 + 45° = \theta_1 + 135°$$

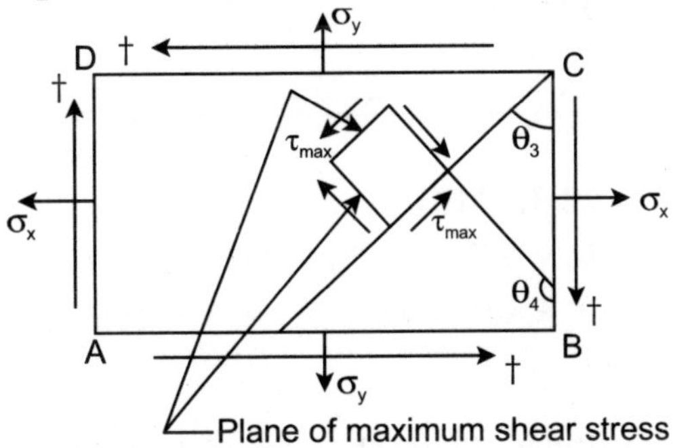

Fig. 18.22

Note: We deduce all relations for tensile stress and shear stress as shown in Fig. 18.21. If compressive stress or the direction of shear stress in opposite direction, then negative sign will be used in all relations.

Example 18.8

In a strained material, at a point, the stresses (mutually perpendicular) are 40 MPa and 20 MPa, both tensile. They are accompanied by a shear stress of 20 MPa. Find:

(i) Principal stresses and their planes.

(ii) Max. shear stress and their planes.

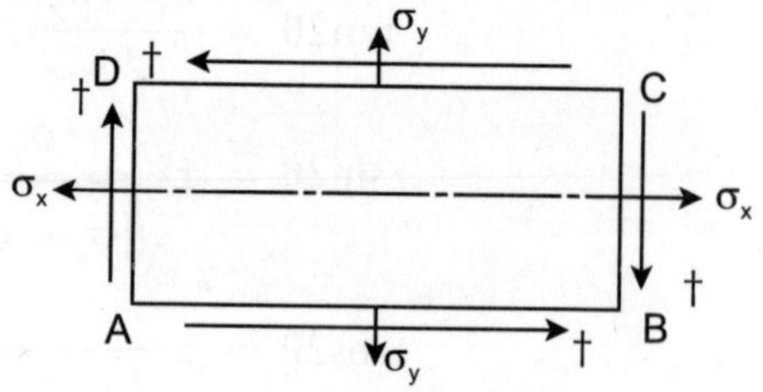

Fig. 18.23

Solution:

$$\theta = 0$$
$$\sigma_x = 40 \text{ MPa}$$
$$\sigma_y = 20 \text{ MPa}$$
$$\dagger = 20 \text{ MPa}$$

(i)
$$\sigma_{1,2} = \frac{1}{2}(\sigma_x + \sigma_y) \pm \frac{1}{2}\sqrt{(\sigma_x - \sigma_y)^2 + 4\dagger^2}$$
$$= \frac{1}{2}(40 + 20) \pm \frac{1}{2}\sqrt{(40 - 20)^2 + 4 \times (20)^2}$$
$$= 30 \pm 22.36$$

$\therefore$
$$\left.\begin{aligned}\sigma_1 &= \mathbf{52.36 \text{ MPa}}\\ \sigma_2 &= \mathbf{7.64 \text{ MPa}}\end{aligned}\right]$$ **Ans.**

$$2\theta = \tan^{-1}\left(\frac{2\dagger}{\sigma_x - \sigma_y}\right) = \tan^{-1}\left(\frac{2 \times 20}{40 - 20}\right)$$
$$= 63.43°, 243.43$$

$\therefore$
$$\left.\begin{aligned}\theta_1 &= \mathbf{31.71°}\\ \theta_2 &= \mathbf{121.71°}\end{aligned}\right]$$ **Ans.**

(ii)
$$\tau_{max} = \frac{\sigma_1 - \sigma_2}{2} = \frac{52.36 - 7.64}{2}$$
$$= \mathbf{22.36 \text{ MPa}}$$ **Ans.**

$$\left.\begin{aligned}\theta_3 &= \theta_1 + 45° = 31.71 + 45° = \mathbf{76.71°}\\ \theta_4 &= \theta_2 + 45° = 121.75 + 45° = \mathbf{166.75°}\end{aligned}\right]$$ **Ans.**

Example 18.9

At a certain point in a strained materials the state of stress is shown in Fig. 18.24. Find: (a) Magnitude and direction of resultant stress on the horizontal plane.

Solution:

$$\sigma_x = 100 \cos 30 \text{ MPa}$$

$\sigma_y = 60$ MPa

$\dagger = 100 \sin 30 = 50$ MPa

(a) Resultant stress on horizontal plane

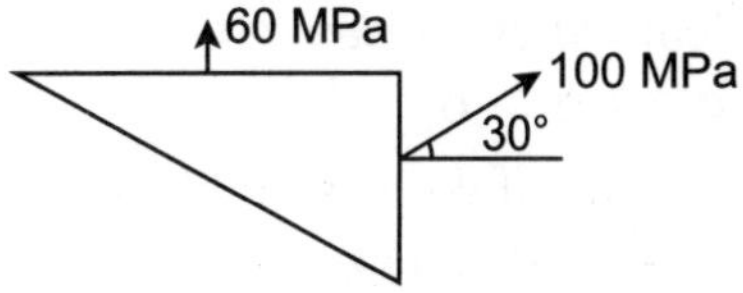

Fig. 18.24

$$\sigma_r = \sqrt{(\sigma_y)^2 + \dagger^2} = \sqrt{60^2 + 50^2}$$

$= 78.1$ MPa **Ans.**

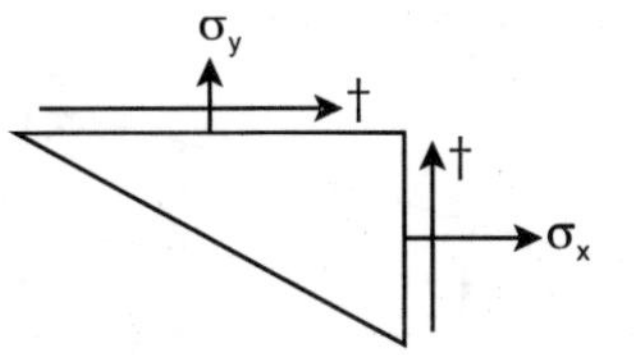

Fig. 18.25

18.8 Mohr's Stress Circle

Case-I: $\sigma_x > \sigma_y$

Scale: Take a suitable scale

$\sigma_x = OA$

$\sigma_y = OB$

$\angle CBD = \theta$

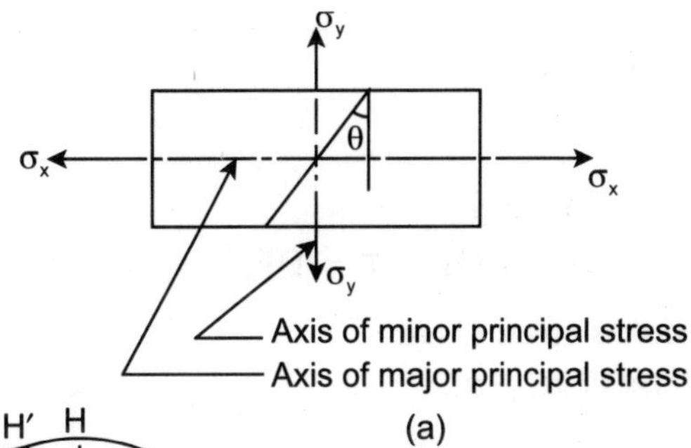

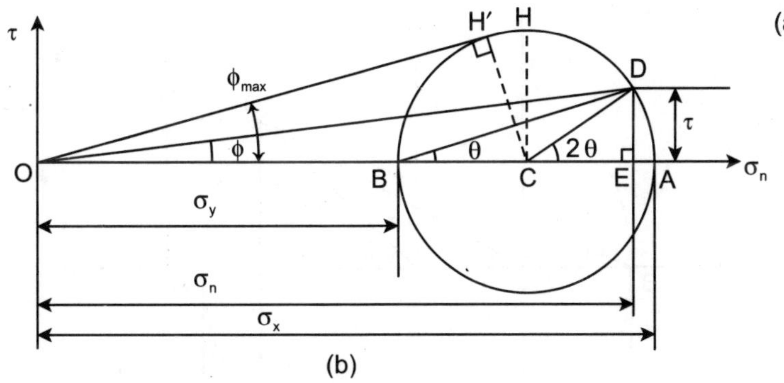

Fig. 18.26

Answer:

$\sigma_n = OE$ $\tau = DE$ $\sigma_r = OD$

$\angle\phi = \angle COD$ $\tau_{max} = CH$ $\angle\phi_{max} = \angle COH'$

Mohr's Stress Circle:
Case-II: $\sigma_y > \sigma_x$

Scale: Take a suitable scale

$$\sigma_x = OA$$
$$\sigma_y = OB$$
$$\angle CBD = (90 - \theta)$$
$$\theta' = (90 - \theta)$$
= Angle with minor principal stress

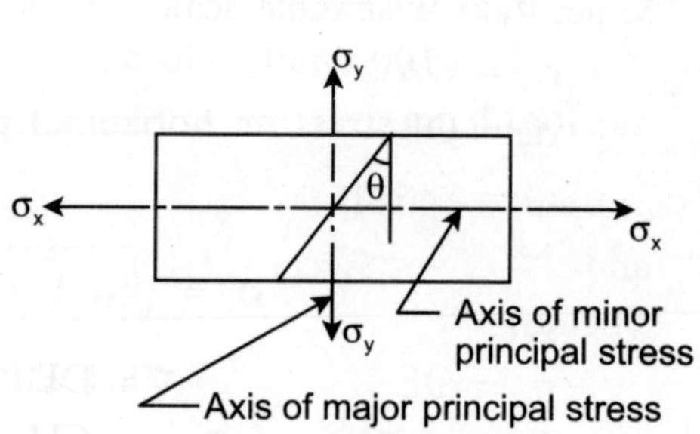

(a)

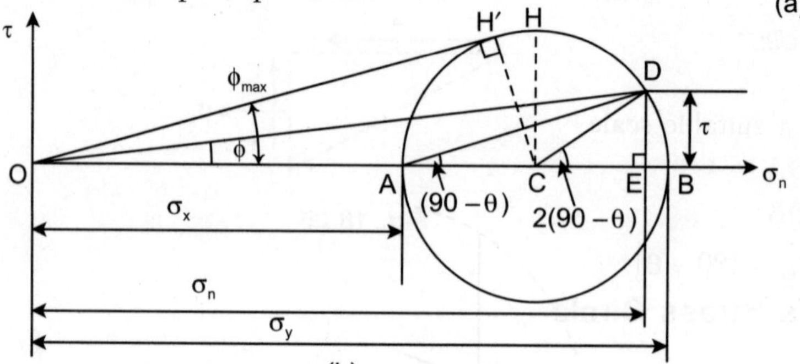

(b)

Fig. 18.27

Answer:

$\sigma_n = OE$; $\tau = DE$; $\sigma_r = OD$; $\angle\phi = \angle COD$; $\tau_{max} = CH$; $\angle\phi_{max} = \angle COH'$

Mohr's Stress Circle:
Case-III: $\sigma_x > \sigma_y$

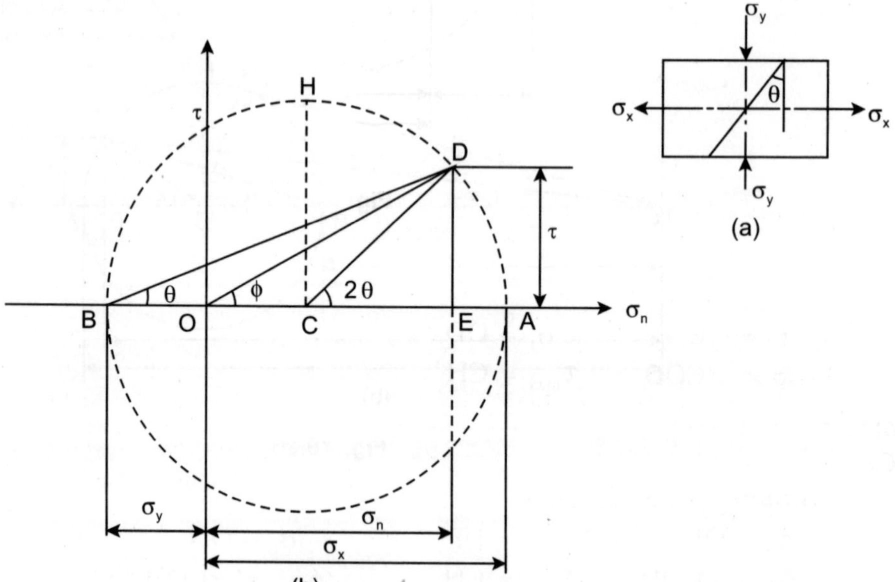

Fig. 18.28

Scale: Take a suitable scale

$\sigma_x = OA$

$\sigma_y = OB$

$\angle\theta = \angle CBD$

and

Answer:

$\sigma_n = OE \qquad \tau = DE \qquad \sigma_r = OD$

$\angle\phi = \angle COD \qquad \tau_{max} = CH$

Mohr's Stress Circle:

Case-IV: $\sigma_y > \sigma_x$

Scale: Take a suitable scale

$\sigma_x = OA$

$\sigma_y = OB$

$\angle CAD = \theta' = (90 - \theta)$

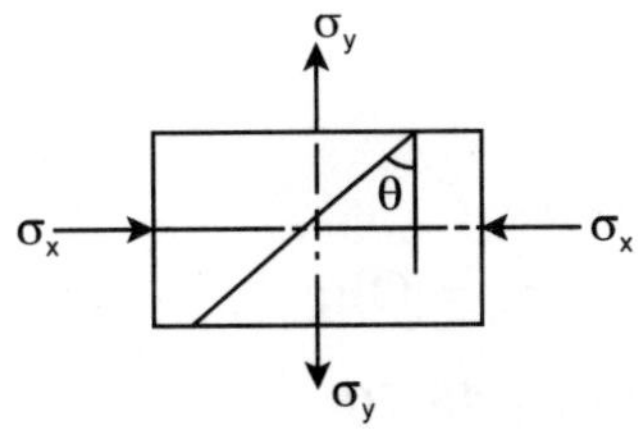

(a)

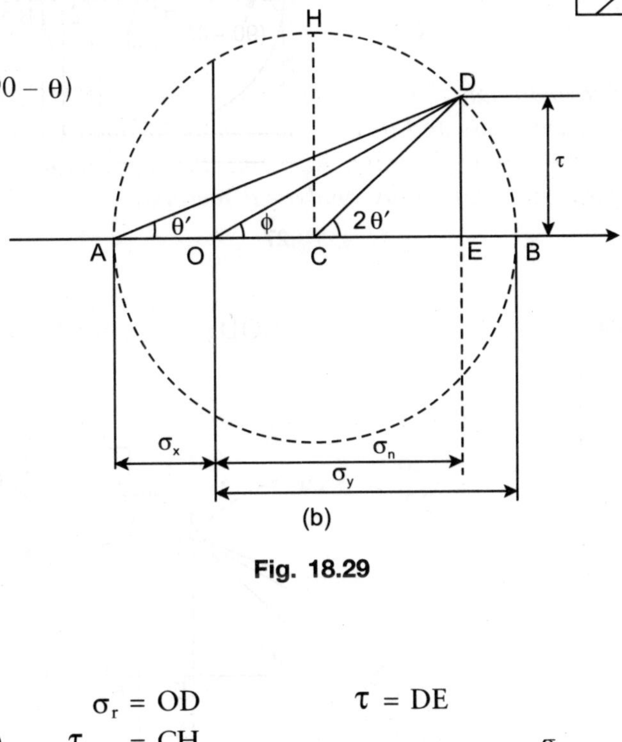

(b)

Fig. 18.29

Answer:

$\sigma_n = OE \qquad \sigma_r = OD \qquad \tau = DE$

$\angle\phi = \angle COD \qquad \tau_{max} = CH$

Mohr's Stress Circle:

Case-V: $\sigma_y > \sigma_x$

Scale: Take a suitable scale

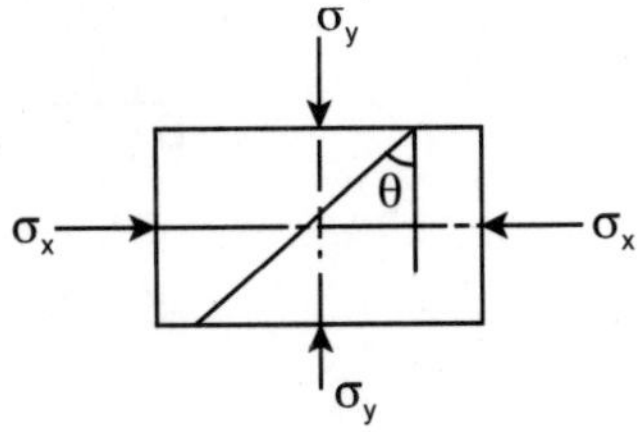

Fig. 18.30 (a)

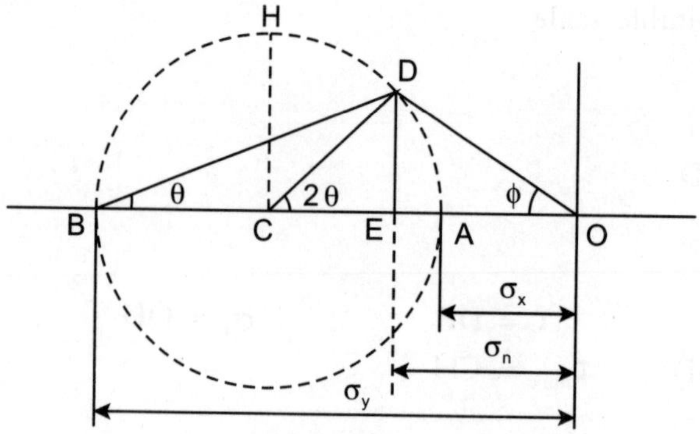

Fig. 18.30 (b)

Answer:

$$\sigma_n = OE; \quad \tau = DE; \quad \sigma_r = OD; \quad \angle\phi = \angle COD; \quad \tau_{max} = CH$$

Example 18.10

At a point in a strained material, the principal stresses are 120 MPa (tensile) and 60 MPa (compressive). Find resultant stress and its direction on an inclined plane, inclined at 30 to the axis of 120 MPa by Mohr's circle diagram. Also find the maximum intensity of shear stress in the material. Compare your results by analytical method.

Solution:

σ_x = 120 MPa

σ_y = –60 MPa

$\angle\theta$ = 90 – 30 = 60°

Scale : 1 cm = 20 MPa

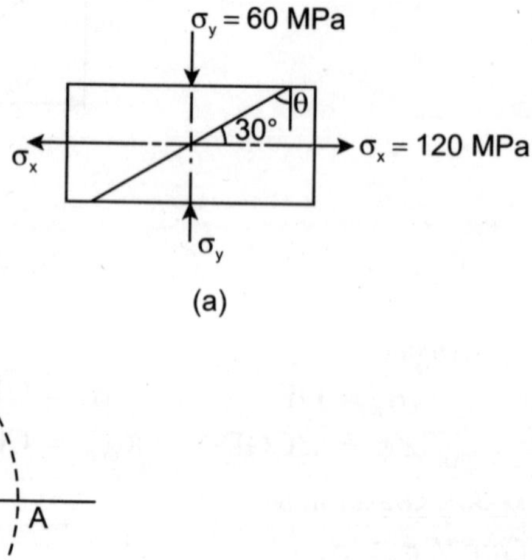

(a)

$$\therefore \quad \sigma_x = OA = \frac{120}{20} = 6 \text{ cm}$$

$$\sigma_y = OB = \frac{60}{20} = 3 \text{ cm}$$

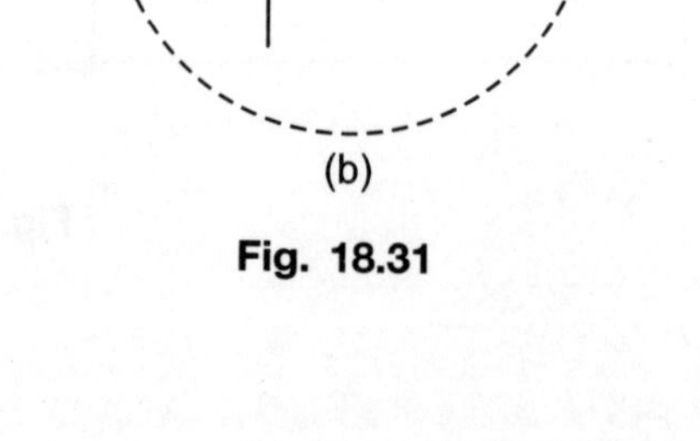

(b)

Fig. 18.31

$$\sigma_n = OE = 0.7 \text{ cm} = 0.7 \times 20 = -14 \text{ MPa}$$

$$\tau = DE = 3.9 \text{ cm} = 3.9 \times 20 = 78 \text{ MPa}$$

$$\sigma_r = OD = 4 \text{ cm} = 4 \times 20 = 80 \text{ MPa}$$

$$\angle\phi = \angle COD = 100°$$

$$\tau_{max} = CH = 4.5 \text{ cm} = 4.5 \times 20 = 90 \text{ MPa}$$

Analytical Method:

$$\sigma_n = \frac{1}{2}(\sigma_x + \sigma_y) + \frac{1}{2}(\sigma_x - \sigma_y)\cos 2\theta$$

$$= \frac{1}{2}(120 - 60) + \frac{1}{2}(120 + 60)\cos 120$$

$$= 30 + 90 \cos 120 = -15 \text{ MPa}$$

$$\tau = \frac{1}{2}(\sigma_y - \sigma_x)\sin 2\theta$$

$$= \frac{1}{2}(-60 - 120)\sin 120$$

$$= -90 \sin 120 = -77.9° \text{ MPa}$$

$$\phi = \tan^{-1}\left(\frac{\tau}{\sigma_n}\right) = \tan^{-1}\left(\frac{-77.9}{15}\right) = -79.1° = 100.9°$$

$$\tau_{max} = \frac{\sigma_x - \sigma_y}{2} = \frac{120 - (-60)}{2} = \frac{180}{2} = 90 \text{ MPa}$$

$$\sigma_r = \sqrt{\sigma_n^2 + \tau^2} = \sqrt{15^2 + 77.9^2} = 79.37° \text{ MPa}$$

Comparison

Parameter	*Graphical Solution*	*Analytical Solution*
σ_n	–14 MPa	–15 MPa
τ	79 MPa	–77.9 MPa
σ_r	80 MPa	79.3 MPa
ϕ	100°	–79.1° or 100.9°
τ_{max}	90 MPa	90 MPa

Example 18.11

The principal tensile stresses at a point in a strained material across two mutually perpendicular planes are 110 MPa and 50 MPa, both tensile. Determine normal, tangential and resultant stresses on a plane inclined at 30 to the axis of minor principal stress. Solve graphically and compare the results with analytical results.

Solution:

$\sigma_x = 110$ MPa

$\sigma_y = 50$ MPa

$\sigma_n = ?$

$\tau = ?$

$\sigma_r = ?$

$\phi = ?$

$\theta = 30°$

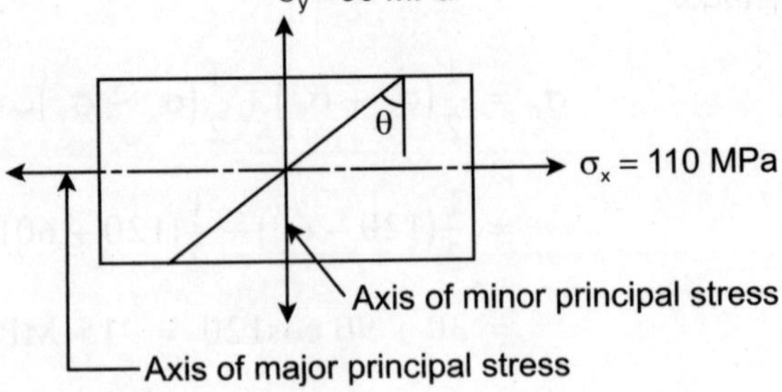

(a)

(1) Mohr's Stress Circle:

Scale: 1 cm = 10 MPa

$$\sigma_x = OA = 11 \text{ cm}$$
$$\sigma_y = OB = 5 \text{ cm}$$

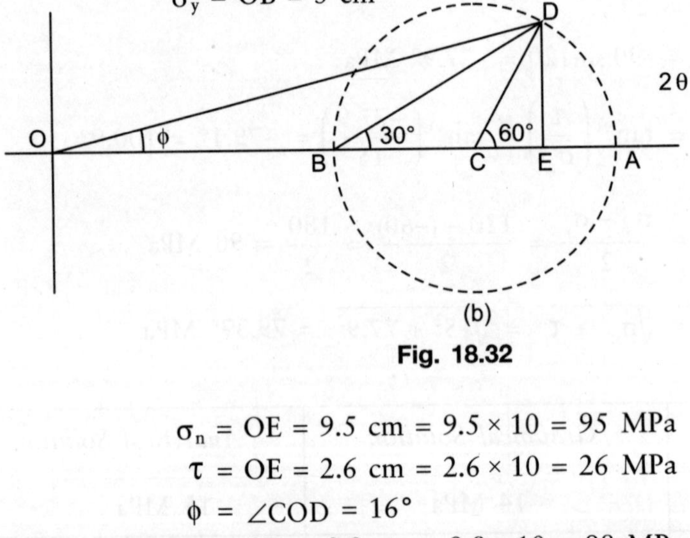

(b)

Fig. 18.32

$$\sigma_n = OE = 9.5 \text{ cm} = 9.5 \times 10 = 95 \text{ MPa}$$
$$\tau = OE = 2.6 \text{ cm} = 2.6 \times 10 = 26 \text{ MPa}$$
$$\phi = \angle COD = 16°$$
$$\sigma_r = OD = 9.8 \text{ cm} = 9.8 \times 10 = 98 \text{ MPa}$$

Analytical Method:

$$\sigma_n = \frac{1}{2}(\sigma_x + \sigma_y) + \frac{1}{2}(\sigma_x - \sigma_y)\cos 2\theta$$
$$= \frac{1}{2}(110 + 50) + \frac{1}{2}(110 - 50)\text{Cos}60$$
$$= 80 + 15 = 95 \text{ MPa}$$

$$\tau = \frac{1}{2}(\sigma_y - \sigma_x)\sin 2\theta$$

$$= \frac{1}{2}(50 - 110)\sin 60 = -25.98 \text{ MPa}$$

$$\sigma_r = \sqrt{\sigma_n^2 + \tau^2} = \sqrt{95^2 + 25.98^2} = 98.48 \text{ MPa}$$

$$\phi = \tan^{-1}\left(\frac{\tau}{\sigma_n}\right) = \tan^{-1}\left(\frac{-25.98}{95}\right) = -15.3°$$

Comparision

Parameter	*Graphical Solution*	*Analytical Solution*
σ_n	95 MPa	95 MPa
τ	26 MPa	–25.98 MPa
σ_r	98 MPa	98.48 MPa
ϕ	16°	–15.3°

Example 18.12

Draw the Mohr's stress circle for direct stresses of 65 MPa (tensile) and 35 MPa (compressive) and estimate the magnitude and direction of the resultant stresses on planes making angles of 20° and 65° with the plane of 65 MPa. Find also normal and tangential stresses on these planes.

Solution:

σ_x = 65 MPa

σ_y = –35 MPa

θ = 20° or 65°

Scale: 1 cm = 10 MPa

$\therefore$ σ_x = OA = 6.5 cm

σ_y = OB = 3.5 cm

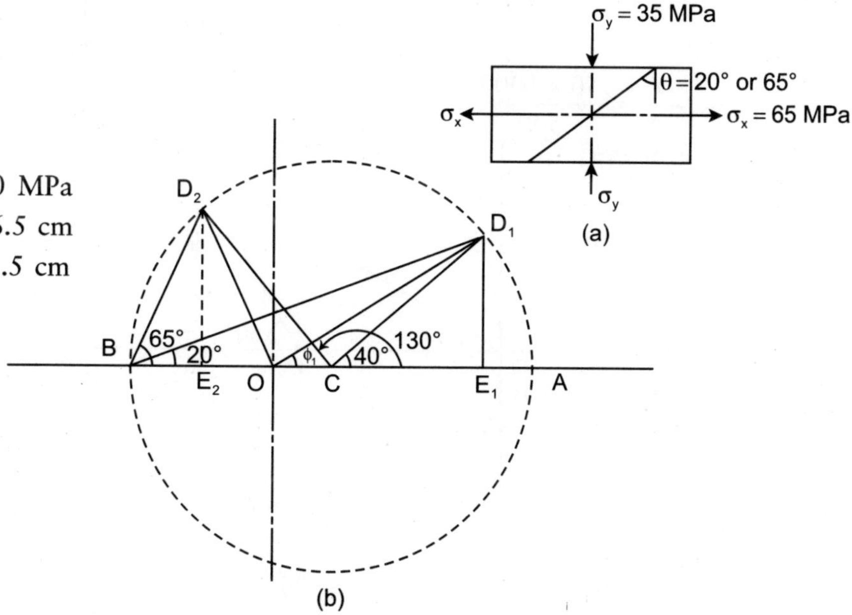

Fig. 18.33

Case-I, θ = 20°

$$\sigma_{n_1} = OE_1 = 5.3 \text{ cm} = 5.3 \times 10 = 53 \text{ MPa}$$
$$\tau_1 = D_1E_1 = 3.3 \text{ cm} = 3.3 \times 10 = 33 \text{ MPa}$$
$$\sigma_{r_1} = OD_1 = 6.3 \text{ cm} = 6.3 \times 10 = 63 \text{ MPa}$$
$$\phi_1 = \angle COD_1 = 31°$$

Case-II, θ = 65°

$$\sigma_{n_2} = OE_2 = -1.8 \text{ cm} = -1.8 \times 10 = 18 \text{ MPa}$$
$$\tau_2 = D_2E_2 = 3.7 \text{ cm} = 3.7 \times 10 = 37 \text{ MPa}$$
$$\sigma_{r_2} = OD_2 = 4.2 \text{ cm} = 4.2 \times 10 = 42 \text{ MPa}$$
$$\phi_2 = \angle COD_2 = \mathbf{117°}$$

Ans.

Example 18.13

A.C.I. block of 500 mm² cross section carries an axial compressive load of 50 kN. Calculate the normal and shear stresses on a plane whose normal is inclined at 30° to the axis of the block. Also find maximum shear stress in the block. Solve using Mohr's circle.

Solution:

$A = 500 \text{ mm}^2$

$P = 50 \text{ kN} = 50 \times 10^3 \text{ N}$

$\sigma_n = ?$

$\tau = ?$

$\sigma_r = ?$

$\tau_{max} = ?$

Now

$$\sigma_x = -\frac{P}{A} = \frac{50 \times 1000}{500}$$
$$= 100 \text{ MPa}$$

Scale: 1 cm = 10 MPa

$$\therefore \quad \sigma_x = OA = \frac{100}{10}$$
$$= 10 \text{ cm}$$
$$\sigma_y = OB = 0$$
$$\theta = 30°$$

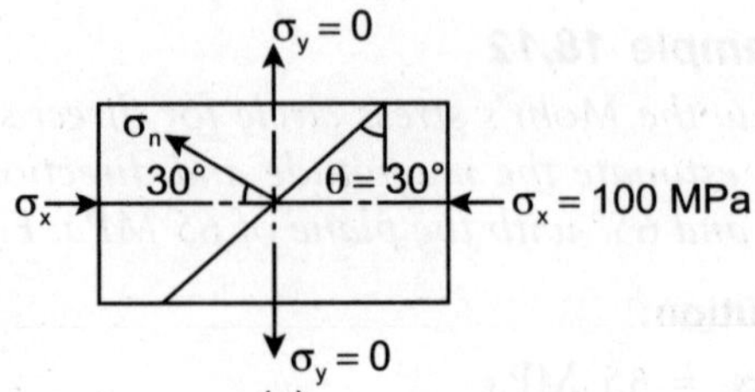

(a)

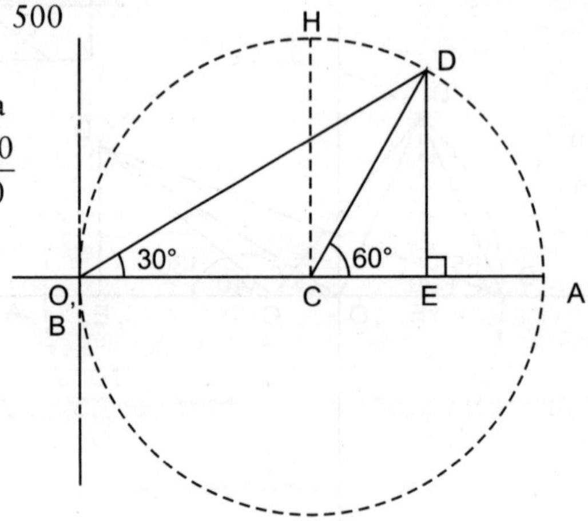

(b)

Fig. 18.34

$$\therefore \qquad \sigma_n = OE = 7.5 \text{ cm} = 7.5 \times 10 = 75 \text{ MPa}$$

$$\tau = OE = 4.5 \text{ cm} = 4.5 \times 10 = 45 \text{ MPa}$$

$$\sigma_r = OD = 8.8 \text{ cm} = 8.8 \times 10 = 88 \text{ MPa}$$

$$\phi = \angle COD = 30°$$

$$\tau_{max} = CH = 5 \text{ cm} = 5 \times 10 = \mathbf{50 \text{ MPa}}$$ **Ans.**

18.9 Mohr's Stress Circle for Complex Cases

Case-I: $\sigma_y > \sigma_x$

Scale: Take a suitable scale

$\sigma_x = OA$

$\sigma_y = OB$

$q = \tau_{xy} = AQ = BP$

$\theta' = (90 - \theta)$

$\angle CBD = \theta$

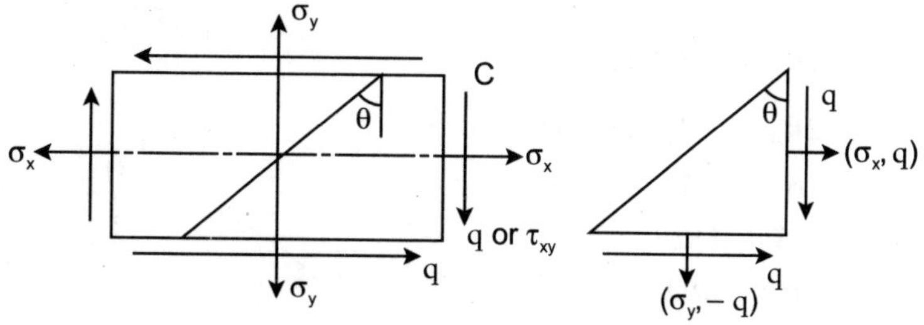

(a)

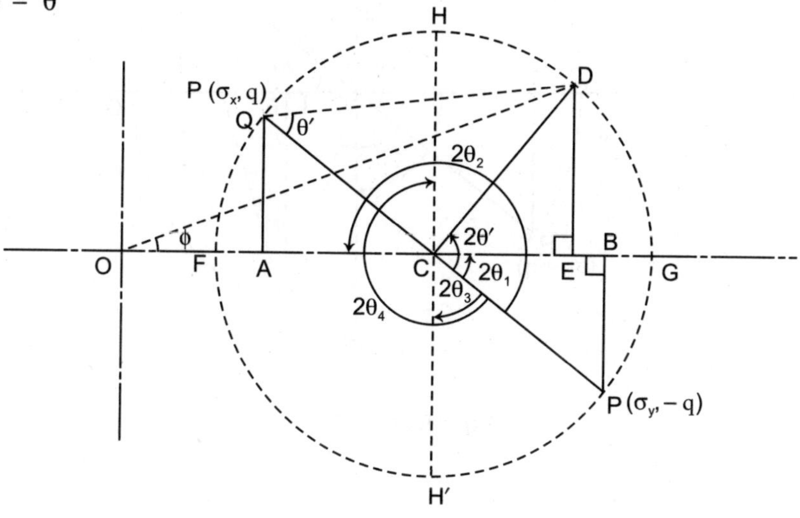

(b)

Fig. 18.35

$\sigma_n = OE$ $\qquad \tau = DE$ $\qquad \sigma_r = OD$

$\phi = \angle COD$ $\qquad \sigma_1 = OG,\ 2\theta_1 = \angle PCD$ $\qquad \sigma_2 = OF,\ 2\theta_2 = \angle PCD + 180°$

$\tau_{max} = CH$ $\qquad 2\theta_3 = \angle PCH'$ $\qquad 2\theta_4 = \angle PCH' + 180°$

Case-II: $\sigma_x > \sigma_y$

$\sigma_x = OA$

$\sigma_y = OB$

$q = AQ = BP$

and

$$\sigma_1 = OG$$
$$\sigma_2 = OF$$
$$2\theta_1 = \angle GCQ$$
$$2\theta_2 = \angle GCQ + 180^\circ$$
$$\tau_{max} = CH$$
$$2\theta_3 = \angle QCH$$
$$2\theta_4 = \angle QCH + 180^\circ$$
$$\sigma_n = OE$$
$$\tau = DE$$
$$\sigma_r = OD$$
$$\phi = \angle COD$$
$$\theta' = (90 - \theta)$$

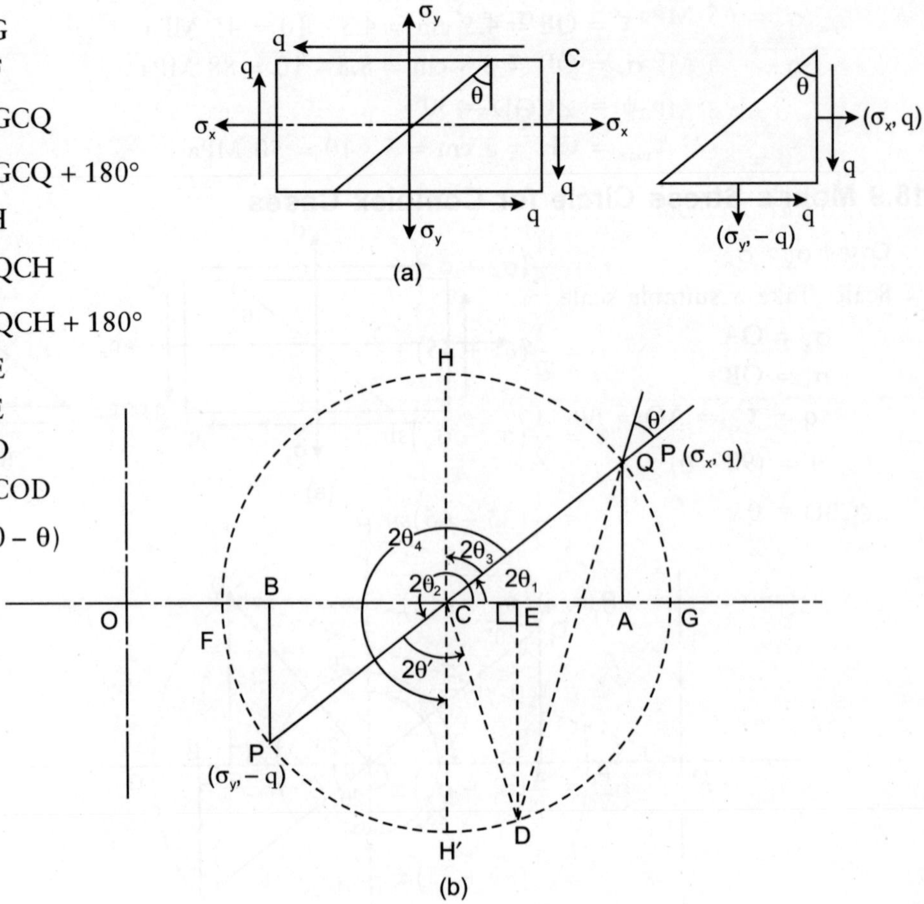

Fig. 18.36

Example 18.14

The state of stress at a point in a strained material is shown in Fig. 18.37. Find normal stress shear, resultant stress, principal stress and their planes, maximum shear stress and planes of maximum shear stress. Give graphical and analytical solution.

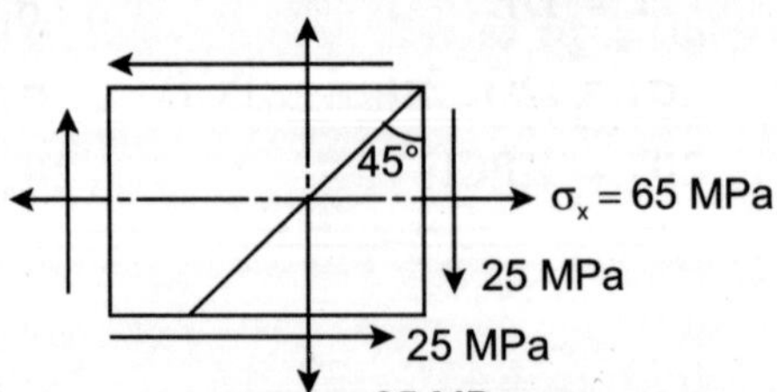

Fig. 18.37 (a)

Solution:

$\sigma_x = 65$ MPa	$\sigma_n = ?$	$\sigma_1 = ?$	$\tau_{max} = ?$
$\sigma_y = 35$ MPa	$\tau = ?$	$\sigma_2 = ?$	$\theta_3 = ?$
$q = 25$ MPa	$\sigma_r = ?$	$\theta_1 = ?$	$\theta_4 = ?$
$\theta = 45°$	$\phi = ?$	$\theta_2 = ?$	

Analytical Method:

$$\sigma_n = \frac{1}{2}(\sigma_x + \sigma_y) + \frac{1}{2}(\sigma_x - \sigma_y)\cos 2\theta + q \sin 2\theta$$

$$= \frac{1}{2}(65 + 35) + \frac{1}{2}(65 - 35)\cos 90 + 25 \sin 90 = \mathbf{75\ MPa}$$ **Ans.**

$$\tau = \frac{1}{2}(\sigma_y - \sigma_x)\sin 2\theta + q \cos 2\theta$$

$$= \frac{1}{2}(35 - 65)\sin 90 + 25 \cos 90 = \mathbf{-15\ MPa}$$ **Ans.**

$$\sigma_r = \sqrt{(\sigma_n)^2 + (\tau)^2} = \sqrt{75^2 + 15^2} = \mathbf{76.5\ MPa}$$ **Ans.**

$$\phi = \tan^{-1}\left(\frac{\tau}{\sigma_n}\right) = \tan^{-1}\left(\frac{-15}{75}\right) = \mathbf{-11.3°}$$ **Ans.**

$$\sigma_n{}^2 = \frac{1}{2}(\sigma_x + \sigma_y) \pm \frac{1}{2}\sqrt{(\sigma_x - \sigma_y)^2 + 4q^2}$$

$$= \frac{1}{2}(65 + 35) \pm \frac{1}{2}\sqrt{(65 - 35)^2 + 4 \times 25^2}$$

$$= 50 \pm 29.15$$

∴ $\sigma_1 = \mathbf{79.15\ MPa}$ **Ans.**

and $\sigma_2 = \mathbf{20.85\ MPa}$ **Ans.**

$$\tan 2\theta = \left(\frac{2q}{\sigma_x - \sigma_y}\right) \Rightarrow 2\theta = \tan^{-1}\left(\frac{2 \times 25}{65 - 35}\right) = 59°, 239°$$

$$\left.\begin{aligned}\theta_1 &= \mathbf{29.5°}\\ \theta_2 &= \mathbf{119.5°}\end{aligned}\right]$$ **Ans.**

$$\tau_{max} = \frac{\sigma_1 - \sigma_2}{2} = \frac{44.15 - (-14.15)}{2} = \mathbf{29.15\ MPa}$$ **Ans.**

$$\left.\begin{aligned}\theta_3 &= \theta_1 + 45° = 29.5 + 45° = \mathbf{74.5°}\\ \theta_4 &= \theta_2 + 45° = 119.5 + 45° = \mathbf{164°}\end{aligned}\right]$$ **Ans.**

Graphical Method:

Scale: 1 cm = 10 MPa

σ_x = OA = 6.5 cm

σ_y = OB = 3.5 cm

q = A = BP = 2.5 cm

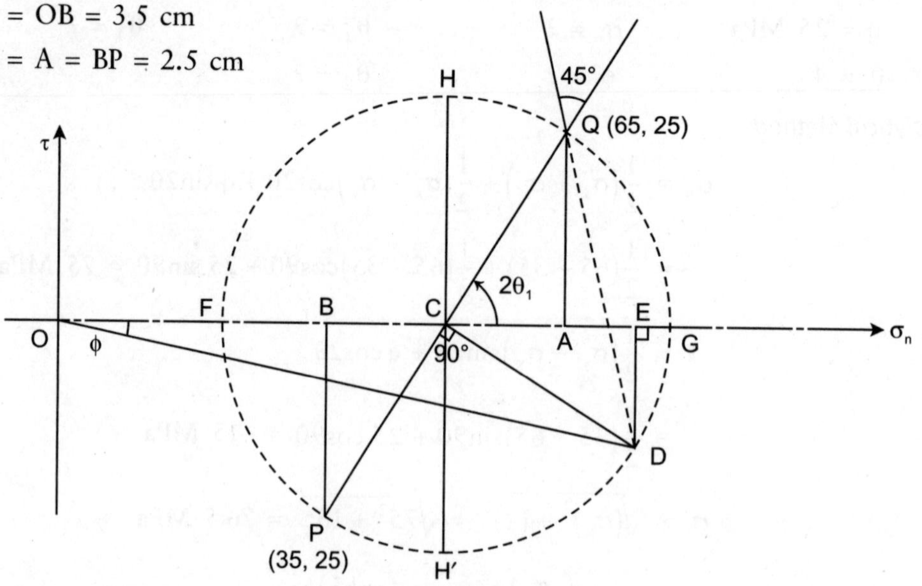

Fig. 18.37 (b)

$$\sigma_n = OE = 7.5 \text{ cm} = 7.5 \times 10 = 75 \text{ MPa}$$ **Ans.**

$$\tau = DE = -1.5 \text{ cm} = -1.5 \times 10 = \mathbf{-15 \text{ MPa}}$$ **Ans.**

$$\sigma_r = OD = 7.7 \text{ cm} = 7.7 \times 10 = \mathbf{77 \text{ MPa}}$$ **Ans.**

$$\angle\phi = \angle COD = \mathbf{-11°}$$ **Ans.**

$$\sigma_1 = OG = 8 \text{ cm} = 8 \times 10 = \mathbf{80 \text{ MPa}}$$ **Ans.**

$$\sigma_2 = OF = 2.1 \text{ cm} = 2.1 \times 10 = \mathbf{21 \text{ MPa}}$$ **Ans.**

$$2\theta_1 = \angle GCQ = 59°$$ **Ans.**

$$\therefore \quad \theta_1 = \frac{59}{2} = \mathbf{29.5°}, \quad \theta_2 = 29.5 + 90° = \mathbf{119.5°}$$ **Ans.**

$$\tau_{max} = CH = 3 \text{ cm} = 3 \times 10 = 30 \text{ MPa}$$

$$\theta_3 = \frac{1}{2}\angle QCH = \frac{1}{2} \times 30° = \frac{1}{2}(180 - 30) = 75°, \quad \theta_4 = 75 + 90 = \mathbf{165°}$$ **Ans.**

Example 18.15

An element in a stressed material has tensile stress of 600 MPa (tensile) and 350 MPa (compressive) acting on two mutually perpendicular planes and equal shear stress of 400 MPa these planes. Find principal stresses and position of principal planes. Find also maximum shearing stress. Solve graphically and compare results with analytical method.

Solution:

$\sigma_x = 600$ MPa

$\sigma_y = -350$ MPa

$q = 400$ MPa

$\sigma_1 = ?$

$\sigma_2 = ?$

$\theta_1, \theta_2 = ?$

$\tau_{max} = ?$

(1) Graphical Solution:

Scale: 1 cm = 100 MPa

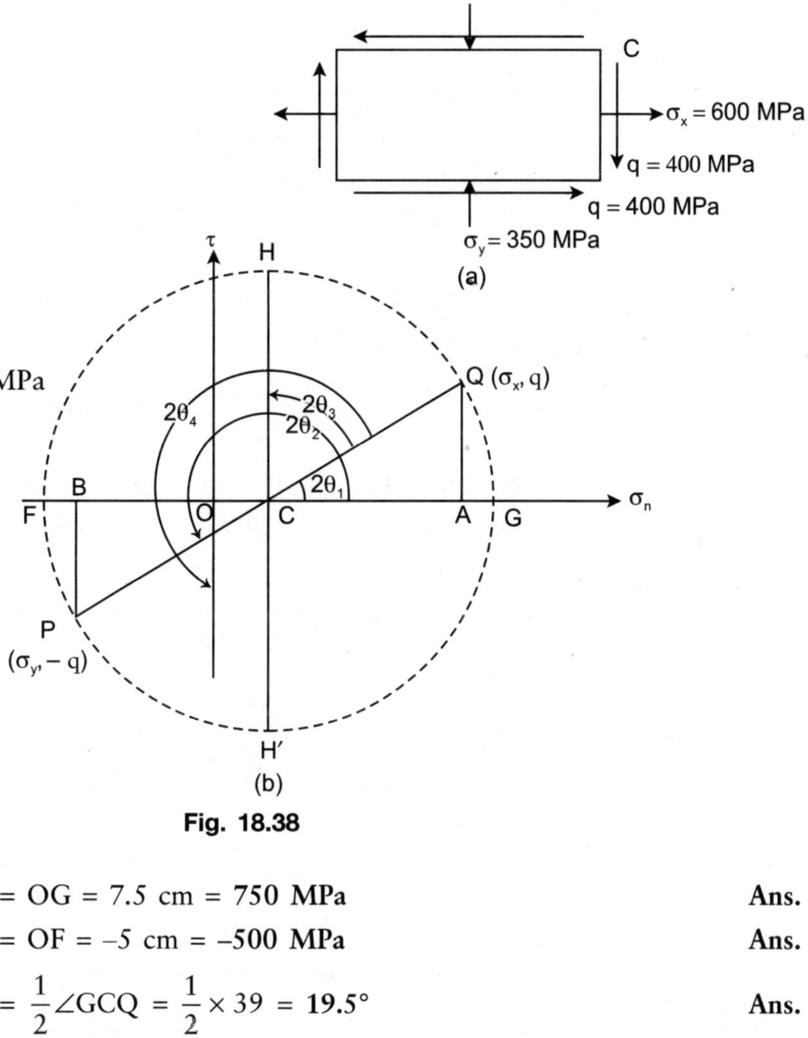

Fig. 18.38

$\sigma_1 = OG = 7.5 \text{ cm} = \mathbf{750 \text{ MPa}}$ **Ans.**

$\sigma_2 = OF = -5 \text{ cm} = \mathbf{-500 \text{ MPa}}$ **Ans.**

$\theta_1 = \frac{1}{2}\angle GCQ = \frac{1}{2} \times 39 = \mathbf{19.5°}$ **Ans.**

$\theta_2 = \theta_1 + 90 = \mathbf{109.5°}$ **Ans.**

$\tau_{max} = CH = 6.2 \text{ cm} = \mathbf{620 \text{ MPa}}$ **Ans.**

$\theta_3 = \frac{1}{2}\angle QCH = \frac{1}{2} \times 48 = 24°$

$\theta_4 = \theta_3 + 90 = 114°$

(2) Analytical Solution:

$$\sigma_{1,2} = \frac{1}{2}(\sigma_x + \sigma_y) \pm \frac{1}{2}\sqrt{(\sigma_x - \sigma_y)^2 + 4q^2}$$

$$= \frac{1}{2}(600 - 350) \pm \frac{1}{2}\sqrt{(600 + 350)^2 + 4 \times 400^2}$$

$$= 125 \pm 620.98$$

$$\therefore \quad \left.\begin{aligned} \sigma_1 &= 125 + 621 = \mathbf{746\ MPa} \\ \sigma_2 &= 125 - 621 = \mathbf{-496\ MPa} \end{aligned}\right] \qquad \textbf{Ans.}$$

$$2\theta = \tan^{-1} \times \left(\frac{2q}{\sigma_x - \sigma_y}\right) = \tan^{-1}\left(\frac{2 \times 400}{600 + 350}\right) = 40.1°, 220.1°$$

$$\left.\begin{aligned} \theta_1 &= \mathbf{20.05°} \\ \theta_2 &= \mathbf{110.05°} \end{aligned}\right] \qquad \textbf{Ans.}$$

$$\tau_{max} = \frac{\sigma_1 - \sigma_2}{2} = \frac{746 + 496}{2} = \mathbf{621\ MPa} \qquad \textbf{Ans.}$$

$$\theta_3 = \theta_1 + 45 = 20.05 + 45 = 65.05° = 90 - 65.05 = 24.95°$$

$$\theta_4 = 24.95 + 90 = 114.95°$$

Comparison

Parameter	*Graphical Solution*	*Analytical Solution*
σ_1	750 MPa	746 MPa
σ_2	–500 MPa	–496 MPa
θ_1	19.5°	20.05°
θ_2	109.5°	110.05°
τ_{max}	620 MPa	621 MPa
θ_3	24°	24.95°
θ_4	114°	114.95°

NUMERICAL QUESTIONS

1. An axial tensile load of 10 kN is applied to a 12 mm diameter bar. Find the maximum shear stress in the bar and the planes on which it acts. Find also the value of normal stresses on these planes.
2. A rectangular block of material is subjected to a shear stress of 30 MPa. Together with its associated complementary shear stress. Determine the magnitude of the stresses on a plane inclined at 30° to the direction of the applied stresses, which may be taken as horizontal.
3. At a point in a strained material the principal tensile stresses across two perpendicular planes are 90 MPa and 45 MPa. Calculate normal, tangential and resultant stresses on a plane inclined at 20° with the major principal plane. Determine also the obliquity.
4. At a point in a strained material, there are two normal tensile stresses of magnitudes 30 MPa and 20 MPa acting on mutually perpendicular planes to each other. There is also a shear stress of 50 MPa acting at that point. Determine principal stresses and their locations. Find also maximum shear stress and planes on which it acts. Solve the problem graphically and compare results with analytical method.
5. Under certain loading conditions in the walls of a cylinder are as follows:
   (a) 80 MPa tensile
   (b) 30 MPa tensile at right angles to (a)
   (c) Shear stresses of 60 MPa on the planes on which the stresses (a) and (b) act, the shear couple acting on planes carrying the 30 MPa stress is clockwise in effect.

   Calculate principal stresses and the planes on which they act. What would be the effect on these results if owing to a change of loading (a) becomes compressive while stresses (b) and (c) remain unchanged?
6. A material is subjected to two mutually perpendicular direct stresses of 100 MPa tensile and 50 MN/m^2 compressive, together with a shear stress of 30 MN/m^2. The shear couple acting on planes carrying 100 MPa stress is clockwise in effect. Calculate:
   (a) The magnitude and nature of principal stresses
   (b) The magnitude of the maximum shear stresses in the plane of the given stress system.
   (c) The direction of the planes on which these stresses act. Confirm your answer by means of a Mohr's stress circle.
7. At a given section a shaft is subjected to a bending stress of 30 MN/m^2 and a shear stress of 50 MN/m^2. Determine:
   (a) The principal stresses.
   (b) The direction of the principal planes.
   (c) The maximum shear stress and the planes on which this acts.
   (d) The tensile stress which acting alone, would produce the same maximum shear stress.

(e) The shear stress which acing alone, would produce the same maximum tensile principal stress.

8. At a point in a piece of elastic material direct stresses of 90 MPa tensile and 60 MPa compressive are applied on mutually perpendicular planes. The planes are also subjected to a shear stress. If the greatest principal stress is limited to 100 MPa tensile, determine:
   (a) Value of shear stress.
   (b) The other principal stress.
   (c) The normal stress on the plane of maximum shear.
   (d) The maximum shear stress.

19

Pure Bending of Beams

19.1 Notations Used

M = Maximum bending moment (N.mm).
I = M.O.I. about neutral axis (mm^4).
σ = Bending stress induced in beam material (N/mm^2).
y = y_{max} = Maximum distance from neutral axis to the outer most layer.
E = Young's modulus (N/mm^2).
R = Radius of curvature (mm).
Z = Section modulus (mm^3).

19.2 Pure Bending or Simple Bending

If a length of beam is subjected to a constant bending moment and no shear force (*i.e.* zero shear force) then the stresses will be setup in that length of the beam due to B.M. only and that length of the beam is said to be in pure bending or simple bending. The stresses setup in that length of beam are known as bending stresses.

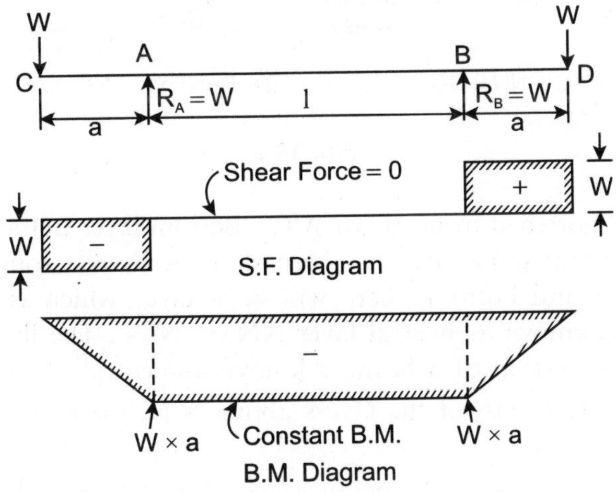

Fig. 19.1

There is no shear force between A and B. But B.M. between A and B is constant, *i.e.* between A and B, the beam is subjected to a constant bending moment only. This condition of the beam between A and B is known as pure bending or simple bending.

19.3 Assumptions Made in Simple Bending Theory

1. Beam material is homogenous and isotropic, *i.e.* Material is same throughout and elastic properties in all directions are equal.
2. The value of Young's modulus (E) is same in tension and compression.
3. The transverse sections, which were plane before bending, remain plane after bending also.
4. The beam is initially straight and all longitudinal filaments bend into circular arcs with a common centre of curvature.
5. The radius of curvature is large compared to the dimensions of the beam cross section.
6. Each layer of beam is free to expand or contract independently of the layer above or below it.

19.4 Theory of Simple Bending

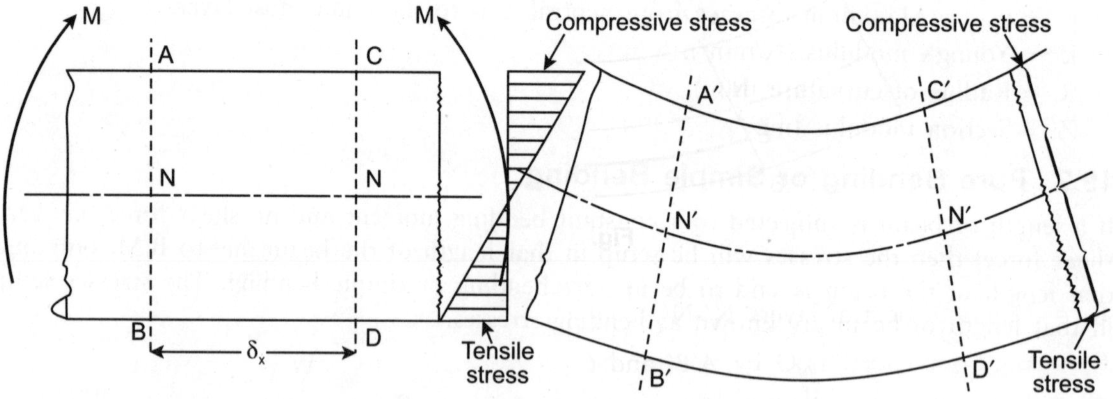

(a) Before Bending— AC = NN = BD (b) After Bending— A′C′ < AC; B′D′ > BD; N′N′ = NN

Fig. 19.2

Top layer has been shortened from AC to A′C′. Bottom layer BD has been elongated from BD to B′D′. It is clear that some layer has been shortened while some layers are elongated. At a level between top and bottom, there will be a layer which is neither shortened nor elongated. This layer is known as neutral layer NN or N′N′. The line of intersection of the neutral layer on a cross section of a beam is known as neutral axis (N.A.).

Due to the decrease in length of the layers above N-N, these layers will be subjected to compressive stresses.

Due to increase in length of layers below N-N, these layers will be subjected to tensile stresses.

The compressive stress will be maximum at the top layer and tensile stress will be maximum at the bottom layer.

Hence, the amount by which a layer increases or decreases in length, depends upon the position of the layer w.r.t. N-N. This theory of bending is known as theory of simple bending.

19.5 Expression for Bending Stress

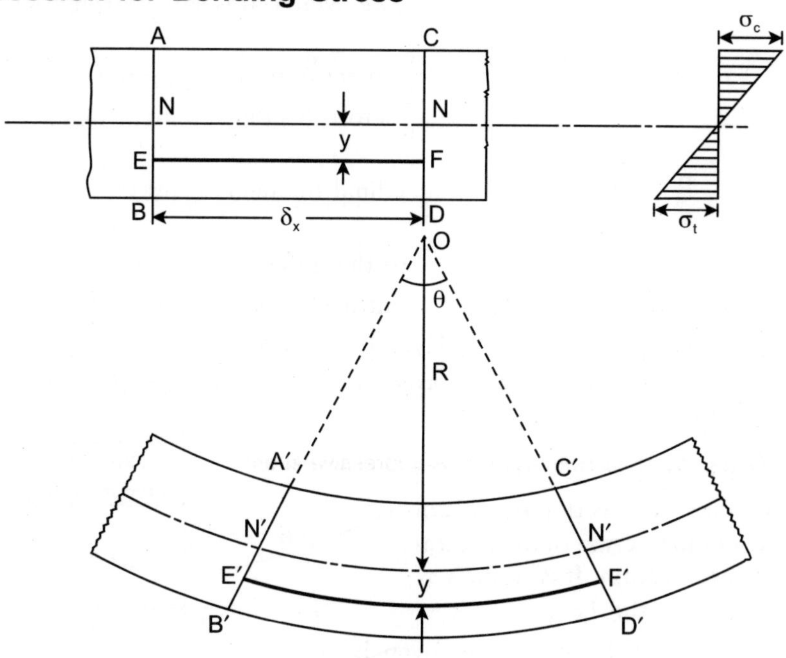

Fig. 19.3

R = Radius of neutral layers N′-N′.

θ = Angle subtended at O by A′B′ and C′D′ produced.

Original length of layers EF = δ_x

Length of neutral layer N-N = δ_x

Also $N'N' = \delta_x$

But $E'F' > EF$

Now

$$N'N' = NN = \delta_x \qquad EF = NN$$

$$N'N' = R \times \theta = \delta_x \qquad NN = N'N' = R\cdot\theta$$

$$E'F' = (R + y) \times \theta \qquad \therefore\ EF = R\cdot\theta$$

$$\delta_{EF} = E'F' - EF = (R + y)\theta - R\theta$$

$$= y\cdot\theta$$

Strain $\in_{EF} = \dfrac{\delta_{EF}}{EF} = \dfrac{y\cdot\theta}{R\cdot\theta} = \dfrac{y}{R}$

$\because$ R is constant.

$\therefore$ Strain $\propto$ distance from neutral axis (y).

Now

$$E = \frac{\text{Stress}}{\text{Strain}} = \frac{\sigma}{\in_{EF}} = \frac{\sigma}{\frac{y}{R}} = \frac{\sigma\cdot R}{y}$$

$$\Rightarrow \quad \frac{\sigma}{y} = \frac{E}{R} \qquad \text{(19.1)}$$

$$\Rightarrow \quad \sigma \propto y$$

$\because$ E, R are constant.

$\therefore$ Strain in any layer $\propto$ distance of layer from N.A.

Note: All layers below N.A. are subjected to tensile stress where as layers above N.A. are subjected to compressive stresses.

19.6 Neutral Axis and Moment of Resistance

Neutral axis of any transverse section of a beam is defined as the line of intersection of the neutral layer with the transverse section. It is written as N.A. There is no stress at the N.A.

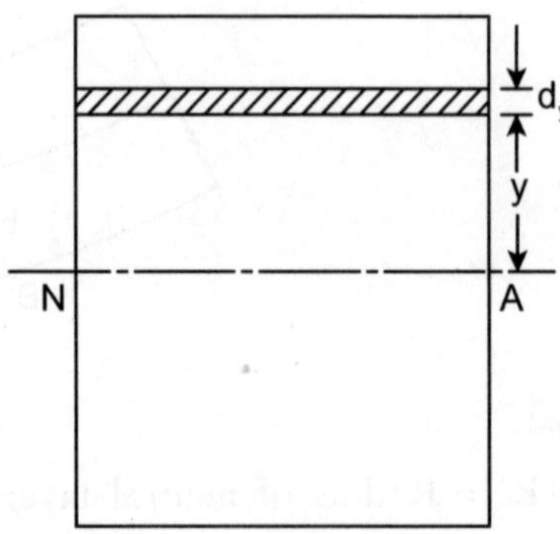

Fig. 19.4: Cross Section of Beam

The stress at a distance y from N.A. is given by

$$\sigma = \frac{E}{R}\cdot y \qquad \left|\ \frac{\sigma}{y} = \frac{E}{R}\right.$$

Let dA = Area of layer

$\therefore$ Force on layer = Stress on layer × Area of layer

$$dF = \sigma \times dA$$

$$= \frac{E}{R}\cdot y\ dA \qquad \text{(19.2)}$$

Total force on the beam section

$$F = \int dF = \int \frac{E}{R}\cdot y\ dA$$

$$= \frac{E}{R}\int y\cdot dA$$

But for 'Pure bending' or 'Simple bending', there is no shear force on the section of the beam (or force is zero).

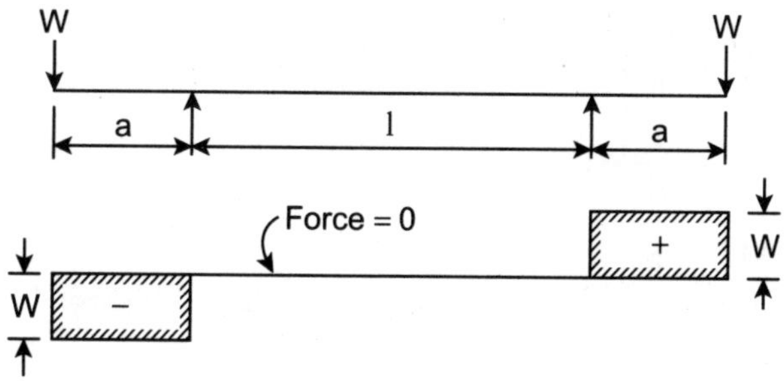

Fig. 19.5: S.F. Diagram

$\therefore$ $$F = 0$$

$\Rightarrow$ $$\frac{E}{R}\int y dA = 0$$

$\Rightarrow$ $$\int y dA = 0 \qquad \left| \because \frac{E}{R} \neq 0 \right.$$

$y \cdot dA$ = Moment of area dA about neutral axis.

$\int y dA$ = Moment of entire area of section about neutral axis.

Also moment of any area about an axis passing through its centroid = 0

Hence, neutral axis coincides with the centroidal axis.

$\therefore$ Centroidal axis of a section gives the position of neutral axis.

19.7 Moment of Resistance

Due to pure bending or simple bending, the layers above the N.A. (neutral axis) are subjected to compressive stresses whereas layers below N.A. are subjected to tensile stresses. Due to these stresses, the force will be acting on the layers. These forces will have moment about the N.A. The total moment of these forces about N.A. for a section is known as moment of resistance of that section.

The force on a layer at a distance y from N.A.

$$dF = \frac{E}{R} y dA \qquad \text{[from Eq. (19.2)]}$$

Moment of this force about N.A.

$$dM = dF \times y$$

$$= \frac{E}{R} y^2 \cdot dA$$

$\therefore$ Total moment of force (or moment of resistance)

$$M = \int dM = \int \frac{E}{R} y^2 dA$$

$$M = \frac{E}{R} y^2 \cdot dA \quad \ldots\ldots\ldots\ldots\ldots\ldots\ldots (19.3)$$

From Eq.(19.3) $\frac{\sigma}{y} = \frac{E}{R}$

$$= \frac{E}{R} \times I$$

$$\Rightarrow \quad \frac{M}{I} = \frac{E}{R} \quad \ldots\ldots\ldots\ldots\ldots\ldots\ldots\ldots\ldots\ldots (19.4)$$

From Eqs. (19.3) and (19.4), $\frac{M}{I} = \frac{\sigma}{y} = \frac{E}{R} \Rightarrow$ Bending equation.

19.8 Bending Equation

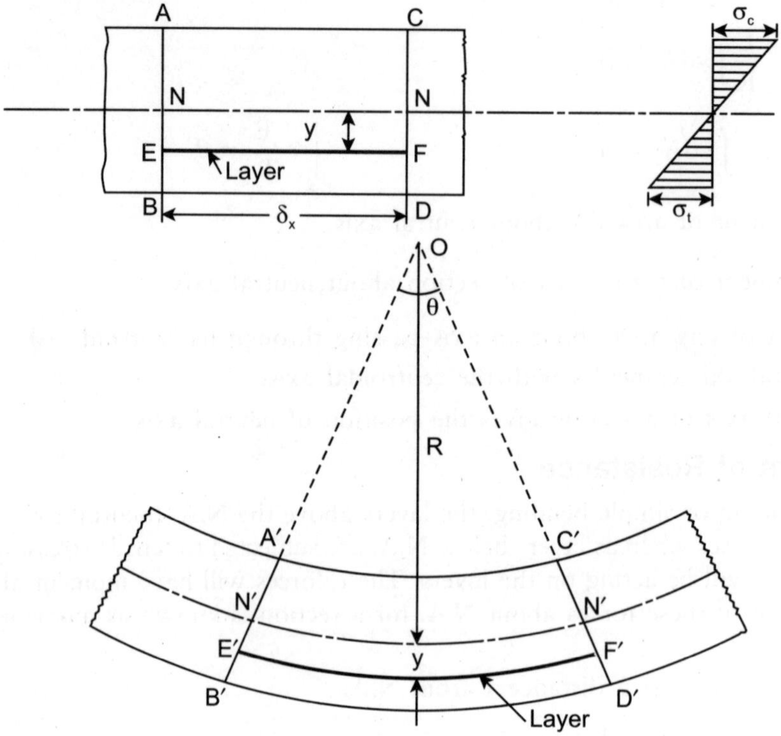

Fig. 19.6

R = Radius of neutal axis N′-N′.

y = Distance of layer under consideration from N.A.

θ = Angle subtended at O by A′B′ and C′D′ produced.

Now

$$N'N' = NN = \delta_x = EF$$

$$EF = N'N' = \delta_x = R \times \theta$$

$$E'F' = (R + y) \times \theta$$

Strain in layer EF

$$\epsilon_{EF} = \frac{\delta_{EF}}{EF} = \frac{E'F' - EF}{EF} = \frac{(R + y)\theta - R\cdot\theta}{R\cdot\theta}$$

$$= \frac{y}{R}$$

and Young's modulus of the beam (E)

$$E = \frac{\text{Stress}}{\text{Strain}} = \frac{\sigma}{\epsilon_{EF}} = \frac{\sigma}{\frac{y}{R}} = \frac{\sigma\cdot R}{y}$$

$$\Rightarrow \qquad \frac{E}{R} = \frac{\sigma}{y} \qquad \ldots\ldots\ldots\ldots \quad (19.5)$$

Now, Force on layer EF

$$dF = \text{Stress on layer} \times \text{Area of layer}$$

$$= \sigma\cdot dA$$

$$= \frac{E}{R}y\cdot dA$$

∴ Moment of this force about N.A.

$$dM = dF \times y = \frac{E}{R}y^2\cdot dA$$

∴ Total moment of force (or moment of resistance)

$$M = \int dM = \frac{E}{R}\int y^2 dA$$

or

$$M = \frac{E}{R}\cdot I \Rightarrow \frac{M}{I} = \frac{E}{R} \qquad \ldots\ldots\ldots\ldots \quad (19.6)$$

From Eqs. (19.5) and (19.6), $\frac{M}{I} = \frac{\sigma}{y} = \frac{E}{R}$ ⇒ Bending equation .... (19.7)

Example 19.1

A steel plate of width 100 mm and thickness 20 mm, is bent into circular are of radius 10 m. Determine the maximum stress induced and bending moment which will produce the maximum stress. Take $E = 2 \times 10^5$ N/mm².

Solution:

$b = 100$ mm

$t = 20$ mm

$R = 10 \text{ m} = 1 \times 10^4$ mm

$\sigma_b = ?$

M = ?

E = 2×10^5 N/mm^2

Now

Bending equation is $\frac{M}{I} = \frac{\sigma_b}{y} = \frac{E}{R}$

$$\sigma_b = \frac{E}{R} \times y = \frac{2 \times 10^5}{R} \times \frac{t}{2} = \frac{2 \times 10^5 \times 20}{1 \times 10^4 \times 2} = \textbf{200 N/mm}^2 \quad \textbf{Ans.}$$

$$M = \frac{E}{R} \times I = \frac{E}{R} \times \frac{bt^3}{12} = \frac{2 \times 10^5 \times 100 \times 20^3}{1 \times 10^4 \times 12}$$

$$= 1.33 \times 10^6 \text{ N.mm}$$

$$M = \textbf{1.33 kN.m} \quad \textbf{Ans.}$$

Example 19.2

Calculate the maximum stress induced in a pipe internal and external diameters are 40 mm and 20 mm respectively and length 6 m. The pipe is supported at its ends and carries a U.D.L. of 10 N/m over the entire span.

Solution:

σ_b = ?

d_o = 40 mm

d_i = 20 mm

l = 6 m = 6000 mm

w = 10 N/m

Bending

Bending equation is $\frac{M}{I} = \frac{\sigma_b}{Y} = \frac{E}{R}$

$$\sigma_b = \frac{M}{I} \times y_{max}$$

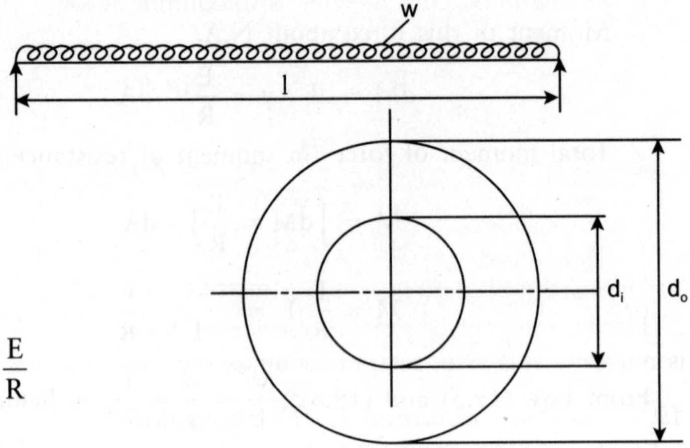

Fig. 19.7

$$M = \frac{wl^2}{8} = \frac{10 \text{ N}}{\text{m}} \times \frac{6 \text{ m}}{8} \times 6000 \text{ mm} = 45000 \text{ N.mm}$$

$$I = \frac{\pi}{64}\left(d_o^4 - d_i^4\right) = \frac{\pi}{64}\left(40^4 - 20^4\right) = 24 \times 10^5 \times \frac{\pi}{64} \text{mm}^4$$

$$= 117809.7 \text{ mm}^4$$

$$y_{max} = \frac{d_o}{2} = \frac{40}{2} = 20 \text{ mm}$$

$$\therefore \quad \sigma_b = \frac{45000 \times 20}{24 \times 10^5 \times \frac{\pi}{64}}$$

$$\sigma_b = 7.64 \text{ N/mm}^2$$ **Ans.**

19.9 Section Modulus or Strength of Section

Section modulus is defined as the ratio of moment of inertia of a section about the neutral axis to the distance of the outermost layer from the neutral axis. It is denoted by symbol Z.

∴ Section modulus

$$Z = \frac{I}{y_{max}}$$

where

I = Moment of inertia about neutral axis.

y_{max} = Distance of outermost layer from N.A.

From bending equation

$$\frac{M}{I} = \frac{\sigma}{Y}$$

σ will be maximum when y is maximum

$$\therefore \quad \frac{M}{I} = \frac{\sigma_{max}}{y_{max}}$$

$$\Rightarrow \quad M = \frac{I}{y_{max}} \cdot \sigma_{max} = Z \cdot \sigma_{max}$$

$$\therefore \quad M = Z \cdot \sigma_{max} \quad \ldots\ldots\ldots (19.8)$$

Here M is maximum bending moment (or moment of resistance offered by the section).

Hence, moment of resistance offered by the section is maximum when section modulus Z is maximum. Hence, section modulus represents the strength of the section.

19.9.1 Section Modulus for Rectangular Section

1. Rectangular Section

$$I = \frac{bd^3}{12}$$

$$y_{max} = \frac{d}{2}$$

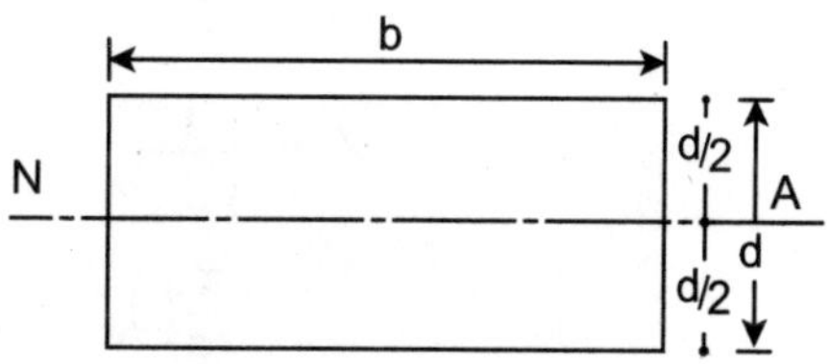

Fig. 19.8

∴ Section modulus

$$Z = \frac{I}{y_{max}} = \frac{bd^3 \times 2}{12 \times d} = \frac{bd^2}{6}$$

$$\therefore \qquad Z = \frac{bd^2}{6}$$

2. Hollow Rectangular Section

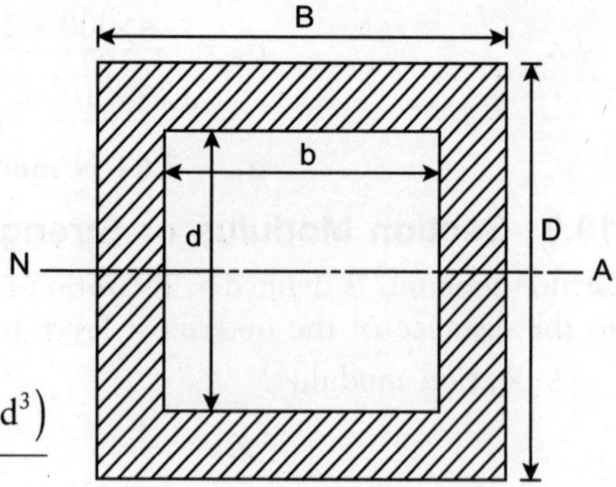

Fig. 19.9

$$I = \left(\frac{BD^3}{12} - \frac{bd^3}{12}\right)$$

$$y_{Max} = \frac{D}{2}$$

$$\therefore \qquad Z = \frac{I}{y_{Max}} = \frac{\frac{1}{12} = \left(BD^3 - bd^3\right)}{\frac{D}{2}}$$

$$Z = \frac{1}{6\,D}\left(BD^3 - bd^3\right)$$

19.9.2 Section Modulus for Circular Section

(3) Circular Section

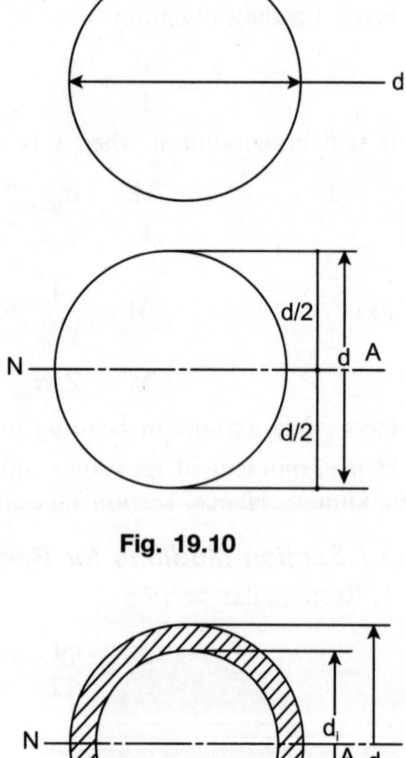

Fig. 19.10

$$I = \frac{\pi}{64}d^4$$

$$y_{max} = \frac{d}{2}$$

$$\therefore \qquad Z = \frac{I}{y_{max}} = \frac{\frac{\pi}{64}d^4}{\frac{d}{2}}$$

$$Z = \frac{\pi}{32}d^3$$

(4) Hollow Circular Section

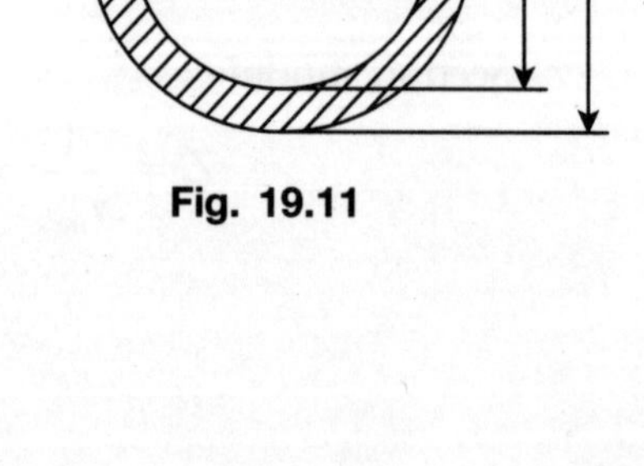

Fig. 19.11

$$I = \frac{\pi}{64}\left(d_o^{\,4} - d_i^{\,4}\right)$$

$$y_{max} = \frac{d_o}{2}$$

$$\therefore \qquad Z = \frac{I}{y_{max}}$$

$$= \frac{\frac{\pi}{64}\left(d_o^{\,4} - d_i^{\,4}\right)}{\frac{d_o}{2}}$$

$$\therefore \qquad Z = \frac{\pi}{32\,d_o}\left(d_o^{\,4} - d_i^{\,4}\right)$$

Example 19.3

A cantilever of length 2 m fails when a load of 2 kN is applied at the free end. If the section of the beam is 4 cm × 6 cm. Find the stress at the failure.

Solution:

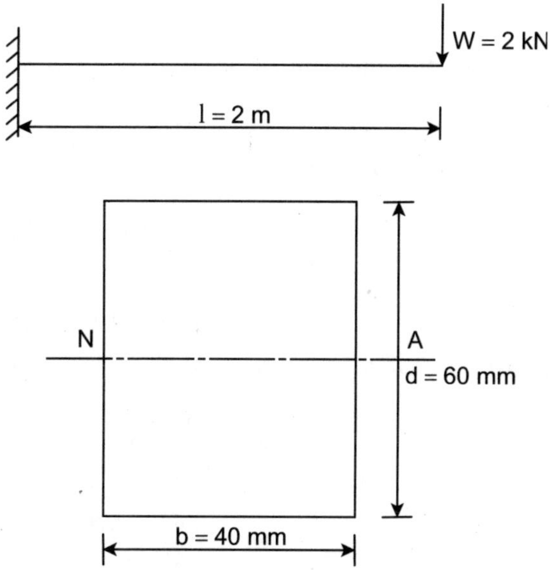

Fig. 19.12

$$l = 2 \text{ m} = 2000 \text{ mm}$$

$$W = 2 \text{ kN} = 2 \times 10^3 \text{ N}$$

$$A = 40 \times 60 \text{ mm}^2$$

$$\sigma = ?$$

$$M = W \times l = 2000 \times 2000$$

$$= 4 \times 10^6 \text{ N.mm}$$

$$I = \frac{bd^3}{12} = \frac{40 \times 60^3}{12}$$

$$= 72 \times 10^4 \text{ mm}^4$$

$$y_{max} = \frac{d}{2} = \frac{60}{2} = 30 \text{ mm}$$

Bending equation is $\frac{M}{I} = \frac{\sigma}{y} = \frac{E}{R}$

Using $\frac{M}{I} = \frac{\sigma}{y}$

$\therefore$ $\sigma_{max} = \frac{M}{I} \times y_{max}$

$$= \frac{4 \times 10^6 \times 30}{72 \times 10}$$

$\therefore$ $\sigma_{max} = \mathbf{166.667 \text{ N/mm}^2}$ **Ans.**

Example 19.4

An I-section girder 200 mm wide by 300 mm deep with flange and web of thickness 20 mm is used as a simply supported beam over a span of 8 m. The girder carries a U.D.L. of 5 kN/m and a concentrated load of 20 kN at mid span. Find (a) The second moment of area of the cross section of the girder (ii) The maximum stress setup.

Solution:

$$B = 200 \text{ mm}$$

$$D = 300 \text{ mm}$$

$$b = 180 \text{ mm}$$

$$d = 260 \text{ mm}$$

$L = 8 \text{ m} = 800 \text{ mm}$

$\omega = 5 \text{ kN/m}$

$W = 20 \text{ kN}$

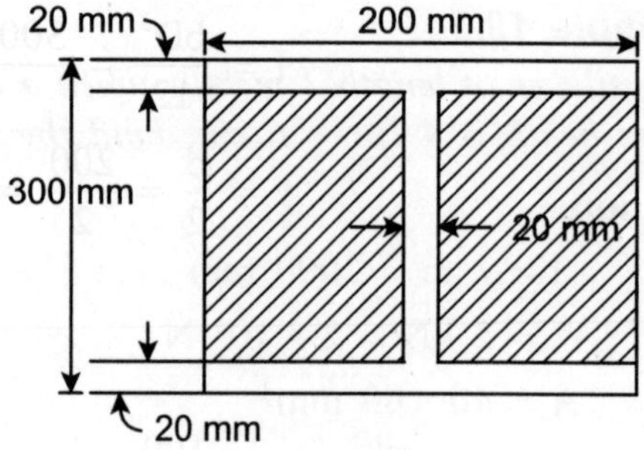

Fig. 19.13

(i) Second moment of area:

$$I = \frac{BD^3}{12} - \frac{bd^3}{12}$$

$$= \left(\frac{200 \times 300^3}{12} - \frac{180 \times 260^3}{12}\right)$$

$$= \mathbf{1.86 \times 10^8 \ mm^4}$$ **Ans.**

(ii) $\sigma_b = ?$

$$\sigma_b = \frac{M}{I} \times y$$

$$M = \frac{\omega l^2}{8} + \frac{Wl}{4} = \left[\frac{5000 \times 8 \times 8}{8} + \frac{20 \times 10^3 \times 8}{4}\right] \text{N.m}$$

$$= 80000 \text{ N.m} = 8 \times 10^7 \text{ N.mm}$$

$$y = \frac{D}{2} = \frac{300}{2} = 150 \text{ mm}$$

$\therefore$ $$\sigma_b = \frac{M}{I} \times y = \frac{8 \times 10^7 \times 150}{1.86 \times 10^8} = \mathbf{64.5 \ N/mm^2}$$ **Ans.**

Example 19.5

A rectangular beam 20 cm deep and 30 cm wide is simply supported over a span of 10 m. What U.D.L. per meter the beam may carry if the bending stress is not to exceed 100 N/mm².

Solution:

$d = 20 \text{ cm} = 200 \text{ mm}$

$b = 20 \text{ cm} = 300 \text{ mm}$

$l = 10 \text{ m} = 10000 \text{ mm}$

$\omega = ?$

$\sigma_b = 100 \text{ N/mm}^2$

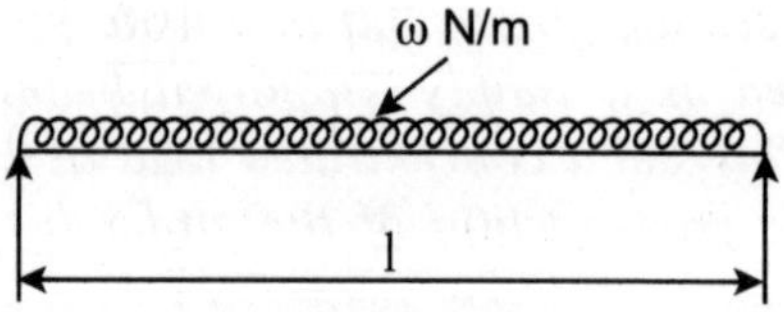

Fig. 19.14

Now

$$M = \frac{\omega l^2}{8}$$

$$I = \frac{bD^3}{12} = \frac{300 \times 200^3}{12} = 2 \times 10^8 \text{ mm}^4$$

$$y = \frac{d}{2} = \frac{200}{2} = 100 \text{ mm}$$

Using $\frac{M}{I} = \frac{\sigma_b}{y}$

$$\Rightarrow \quad \frac{\omega l^2}{8 \times 2 \times 10^8} = \frac{100}{100}$$

$$\Rightarrow \quad \omega \times 10^4 \times 10^4 = 16 \times 10^8$$

$$\Rightarrow \quad \omega = 16 \text{ N/mm}$$

$$\omega = \mathbf{16\ kN/m}$$ **Ans.**

Example 19.6

A beam is simply supported and carries a U.D.L. of 80 kN/m run over the whole span. The section of the beam is rectangular having depth as 400 mm. The maximum stress in the material of beam is 100 N/mm² and I is 8 × 10⁸ mm⁴. Find span of the beam.

Solution:

ω = 80 kN/m = 80 N/mm

d = 400 mm

σ = 100 N/mm^2

I = 8 × 10^8 mm^4

l = ?

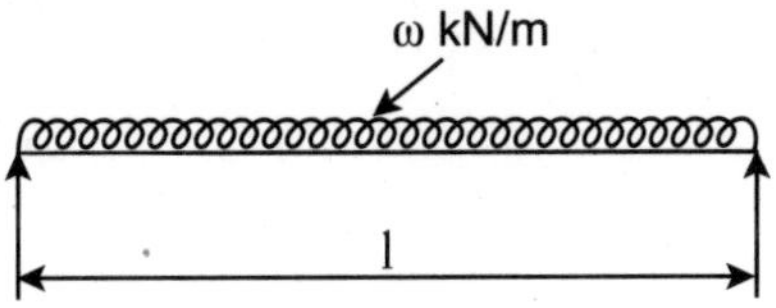

Fig. 19.15

Now

$$M = \frac{\omega l^2}{8}$$

Using $\frac{M}{I} = \frac{\sigma_b}{y}$

$$\Rightarrow \quad \frac{\omega l^2}{8\,I} = \frac{100}{200}$$

$$\frac{80 \times l^2}{8 \times 8 \times 10^8} = \frac{1}{2}$$

$$\Rightarrow \quad l = \left(\frac{64 \times 10^8}{160}\right)^{\frac{1}{2}} = 6324.55 \text{ mm}$$

$$\Rightarrow \quad l = \mathbf{6.32\ mm}$$ **Ans.**

Example 19.7

A wooden beam of rectangular section having a U.D.L. of 30 kN over a span of 4 m, when the beam is simply supported. If depth of beam is twice the breadth and stress in the wood is not to exceed 8 N/mm². Find dimensions of the cross section.

Solution:

$\omega = 30$ kN

$l = 4$ m

$d = 2b$

$\sigma = 8$ N/mm^2

$b = ?$

$d = ?$

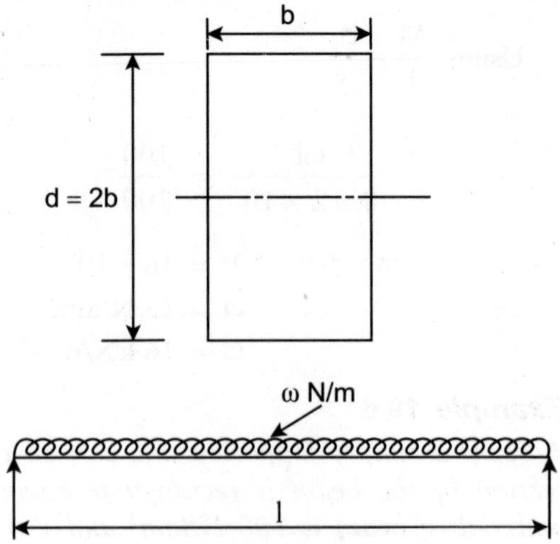

Fig. 19.16

$$M = \frac{\omega l^2}{8} = \frac{\omega l \times l}{8}$$

$$= \frac{\omega l}{8} = \frac{30 \times 4000}{8}$$

$$= 15000 \text{ kN.mm}$$

$$= 15 \times 10^6 \text{ N.mm}$$

$$I = \frac{bd^3}{12} = \frac{b \times (2b)^3}{12} = \frac{8b^4}{12} = \frac{2}{3}b^4$$

$$y = \frac{d}{2} = \frac{2b}{2} = b$$

Using $\frac{M}{I} = \frac{\sigma}{y}$

$$\Rightarrow \quad \frac{15 \times 10^6}{\frac{2}{3}b^4} = \frac{8}{b}$$

$$\Rightarrow \quad \frac{45 \times 10^6}{2b^3} = 8$$

$$\Rightarrow \quad b = \left(\frac{45 \times 10^6}{16}\right)^{\frac{1}{3}} = 141.2 \text{ mm}$$

$\therefore$ **b = 141.2 mm**, **d = 282.4 mm** **Ans.**

Example 19.8

Two circular beams where one is solid of diameter d and other is a hollow of outer dia. d_o and inner dia. d_i, are of same length, same material and of same weight. Find ratio of section modulus of these circular beams.

Solution:

$$\frac{Z_s}{Z_h} = \frac{\left(\frac{I_s}{y_{max}}\right)}{\left(\frac{I_h}{y_{max}}\right)} = \frac{\frac{\frac{\pi}{64}d^4}{\frac{d}{2}}}{\frac{\frac{\pi}{64}\left(d_o^4 - d_i^4\right)}{\frac{d_o}{2}}} = \frac{d^3 \cdot d_o}{\left(d_o^2 + d_i^2\right)\left(d_o^2 - d_i^2\right)}$$

Also

$$W_s = W_h$$

$$\Rightarrow \quad A_s \times l_s \times \rho_s = A_h \times l_h \times \rho_h, \; l_s = l_h, \; \rho_s = \rho_h$$

$$\Rightarrow \quad \frac{\pi}{4}d^2 = \frac{\pi}{4}(d_o^2 - d_i^2)$$

$$\Rightarrow \quad d^2 = (d_o^2 - d_i^2)$$

$$\therefore \quad \frac{Z_s}{Z_h} = \frac{(d_o^2 - d_i^2)d\,d_o}{(d_o^2 + d_i^2)(d_o^2 - d_i^2)} = \frac{d\,d_o}{\left(d_o^2 + d_i^2\right)}$$

$$= \frac{d\,d_o}{d_o^2 + d_o^2 - d^2} = \frac{d\,d_o}{2d_o^2 - d^2}$$

$$\therefore \quad \frac{Z_s}{Z_h} = \frac{\mathbf{d\,d_o}}{\mathbf{2d_o^2 - d^2}}$$ **Ans.**

Example 19.9

A cast iron beam is of I-section as shown in Fig. 19.17. The beam is simply supported on a span of 5 m. If the tensile stress is not to exceed 20 MN/m². Find the safe uniformly load which the beam can carry. Find also the maximum compressive stress.

Solution:

$l = 5$ m $= 5000$ mm

$\sigma_t = 20$ N/mm²

$\omega = ?$

$\sigma_c = ?$

The given section is symmetrical about y axis.

$\therefore \quad \bar{x} = 0$

$\bar{y}$ = distance of C.G. from bottom face.

$\therefore$
$$a_1 = 160 \times 40 = 6400 \text{ mm}^2$$
$$a_2 = 200 \times 20 = 4000 \text{ mm}^2$$
$$a_3 = 80 \times 20 = 1600 \text{ mm}^2$$
$$y_1 = 40/2 = 20 \text{ mm}$$
$$y_2 = 40 + \frac{200}{2} = 140 \text{ mm}$$
$$y_3 = 240 + \frac{20}{2} = 250 \text{ mm}$$

$\therefore$
$$\bar{y} = \frac{a_1y_1 + a_2y_2 + a_3y_3}{a_1 + a_2 + a_3}$$
$$= \frac{6400 \times 20 + 4000 \times 140 + 1600 \times 250}{6400 + 4000 + 1600}$$
$$= \frac{1088\not{000}}{12\not{000}} = \frac{1088}{12} = 90.67 \text{ mm}$$
$$\bar{y} = 90.67 \text{ mm}$$

N.A. lies at a distance of 90.67 mm from bottom face.

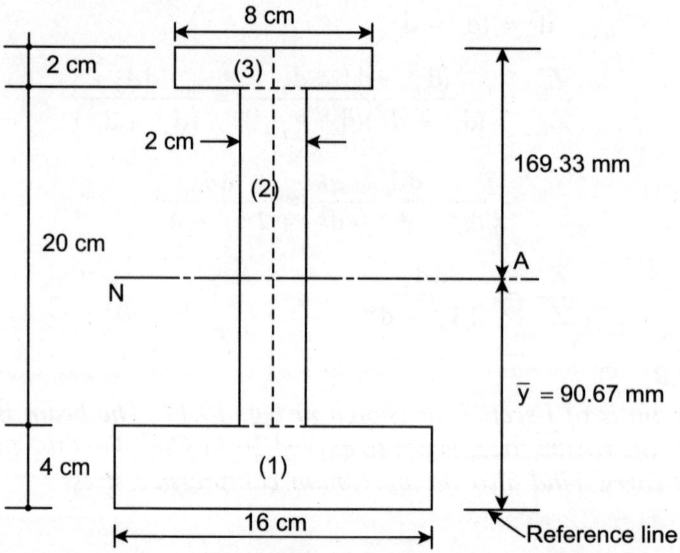

Fig. 19.17

Distance of N.A. from top face
$$= 260 - 90.67 = 169.33 \text{ mm}$$

Now
$$I = I_1 + I_2 + I_3$$
$$I_1 = \frac{b_1d_1^3}{12} + a_1h_1^2, \; h_1 = (\bar{y} - y_1)$$

$$= \frac{160 \times 40^3}{12} + 6400 \times (90.67 - 20)^2$$

$$= 32816526 \text{ mm}^4 = 3.2816 \times 10^7 \text{ mm}^4$$

$$I_2 = \frac{b_2 d_2^{\ 3}}{12} + a_2 h_2^{\ 2}, \; h_2 = (\bar{y} - y_2)$$

$$= \frac{20 \times 200^3}{12} + 4000 \times (140 - 90.67)^2$$

$$= 23067129 \text{ mm}^4 = 2.3067 \times 10^7 \text{ mm}^4$$

$$I_3 = \frac{b_3 d_3^{\ 3}}{12} + a_3 h_3^{\ 2}, \; h_3 = (\bar{y} - y_3)$$

$$= \frac{80 \times 20^3}{12} + 1600 \times (250 - 90.67)^2$$

$$= 40671012 \text{ mm}^4 = 4.0671 \times 10^7 \text{ mm}^4$$

$$I = I_1 + I_2 + I_3$$

$$= (3.2816 + 2.3067 + 4.0671) \times 10^7 \text{ mm}^4$$

$$I = 9.6554 \times 10^7 \text{ mm}^4$$

Now

$$\sigma_t = 20 \text{ N/mm}^2 \text{ (given)}$$

$$y_t = y = 90.67 \text{ mm}$$

$$I = 9.6554 \times 10^7 \text{ mm}^4, \; M = ?$$

Note: For a simply supported beam, tensile stress willl be at the extreme bottom fibre and compressive stress will be at the extreme top fibre.

Using $\frac{M}{I} = \frac{\sigma_t}{y_t}$

$$\Rightarrow \quad \frac{M}{9.6554 \times 10^7} = \frac{20}{90.67}$$

$$\therefore \quad M = 21297893 \text{ N.mm}$$

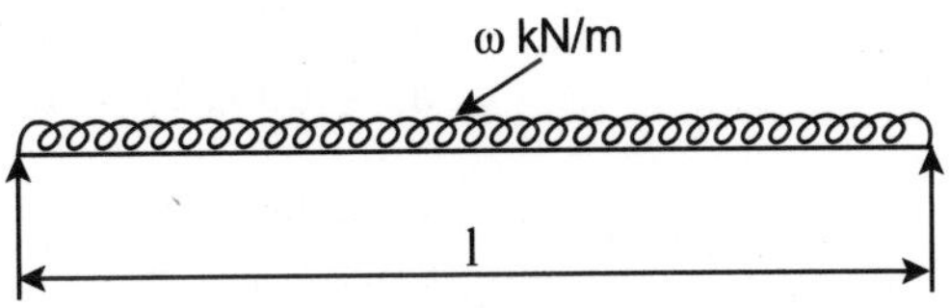

Fig. 19.18

Also $$M = \frac{\omega l^2}{8}$$

$$\therefore \quad \frac{\omega \times l^2}{8} = 21297893$$

$$\omega = \frac{21297893 \times 8}{(5000)^2} = 6.8153 \text{ N/mm}$$

$$\therefore \quad \omega = \mathbf{6.8153 \text{ kN/m}}$$ **Ans.**

(ii) Maximum compressive stress:

$$\sigma_c = ?$$
$$M = 21297893 \text{ N.mm}$$
$$I = 9.6554 \times 10^7 \text{ mm}^4$$
$$y_c = \text{Distance of C.G. from top} = 169.33 \text{ mm}$$

Using $\frac{M}{I} = \frac{\sigma_c}{y_c}$

$$\Rightarrow \quad \frac{21297893}{9.6554 \times 10^7} = \frac{\sigma_c}{169.33}$$

$$\therefore \quad \boldsymbol{\sigma_c = 37.35 \text{ N/mm}^2}$$ **Ans.**

Example 19.10

A cost iron beam is of T-section as shown in Fig. 19.19. The beam is simply supported on a span of 8 m. The beam carries a U.D.L. of 1.5 kN/m length on the entire span. Determine the maximum tensile and maximum compressive stresses.

Solution:

$l = 8 \text{ m} = 8000 \text{ mm}$

$\omega = 1.5 \text{ kN/m} = 1.5 \text{ N/mm}$

$\sigma_t = ?$

$\sigma_c = ?$

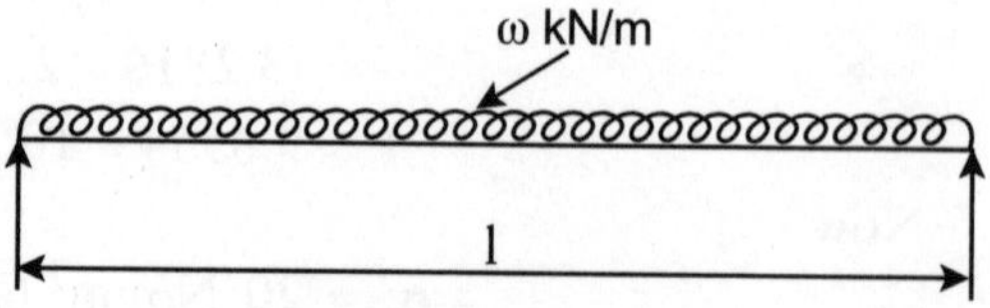

Fig. 19.19

Now

$$M = \frac{\omega l^2}{8} = \frac{1.5 \times (8000)^2}{8} = 12 \times 10^6 \text{ N.mm}$$

∵ The section is sysmmetrical about y-axis.

$$\therefore \quad \bar{x} = 0$$
$$\bar{y} = ?$$

$$\therefore \quad a_1 = 100 \times 20 = 2000 \text{ mm}^2$$
$$a_2 = 80 \times 20 = 1600 \text{ mm}^2$$
$$y_1 = 80 + \frac{20}{2} = 90 \text{ mm}$$
$$y_2 = \frac{80}{2} = 40 \text{ mm}$$

$$\therefore \quad \bar{y} = \frac{a_1 y_1 + a_2 y_2}{a_1 + a_2} = \frac{2000 \times 90 + 1600 \times 140}{2000 + 1600} = 67.78 \text{ mm}$$

For simply supported beam, bottom layer will be subjected to tensile and upper layer will be subjected to compressive stresses.

$$\therefore \quad y_t = \bar{y} = 67.78 \text{ mm}$$

and $\quad y_c = 100 - 67.78 = 32.23 \text{ mm}$

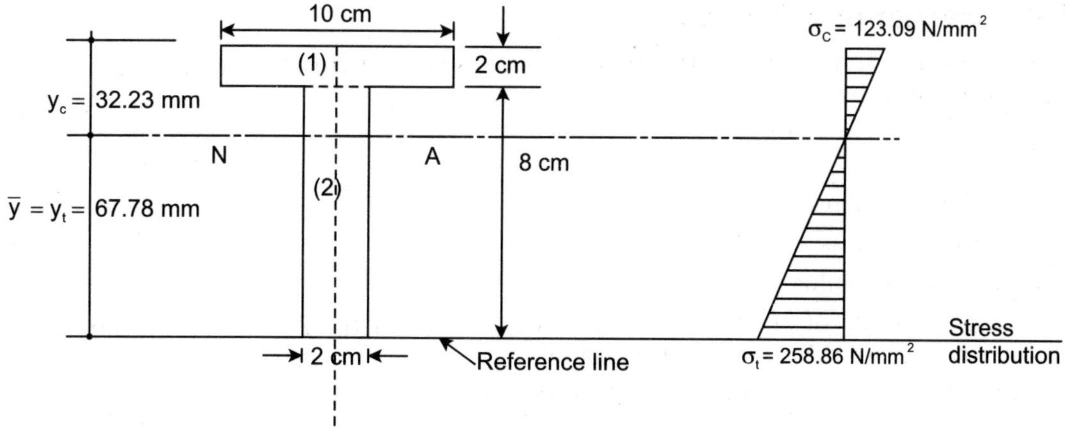

Fig. 19.20

Now $\qquad\qquad\qquad\qquad\qquad\qquad\qquad | \; h_1 = y_1 - \bar{y}$

$$I = I_1 + I_2$$

$$I_1 = \frac{b_1 d_1^3}{12} + a_1 h_1^2 = \frac{100 \times 20^3}{12} + 2000 \times (90 - 67.78)^2$$

$$= 1054123.5 \text{ mm}^4 = 1.054 \times 10^6 \text{ mm}^4$$

$$I_2 = \frac{b_2 d_2^3}{12} + a_2 h_2^2, \; h_2 = (\bar{y} - y_2)$$

$$= \frac{20 \times 80^3}{12} + 1600 \times (67.78 - 40)^2$$

$$= 2088098.8 \text{ mm}^4 = 2.0881 \times 10^6 \text{ mm}^4$$

$$I = I_1 + I_2 = (1.054 + 2.0881) \times 10^6 \text{ mm}^4$$

$$= 3.1421 \times 10^6 \text{ mm}^4$$

Now $\dfrac{M}{I} = \dfrac{\sigma}{y}$

$\therefore$
$$\sigma = \frac{M}{I} \times y$$

(i)
$$\sigma_t = \frac{M}{I} \times y_t = \frac{12 \times 10^6 \times 67.78}{3.1421 \times 10^6} = \mathbf{258.86 \text{ N/mm}^2}$$ **Ans.**

(ii)
$$\sigma_c = \frac{M}{I} \times y_c = \frac{12 \times 10^6 \times 32.23}{3.1421 \times 10^6} = \mathbf{123.09 \text{ N/mm}^2}$$ **Ans.**

19.10 Strength of a Section

The strength of a section means the moment of resistance offered by the section. Moment of resistance is given by:

$$M = \sigma \times Z$$

where

M = Moment of resistance

σ = Bending stress

Z = Section modulus

$$\frac{M}{I} = \frac{\sigma}{y}$$

$$\frac{I}{Y} = Z$$

$$\therefore M = \sigma \times Z$$

For a given value of allowable stress, M depends upon the Z, the section modulus (Z), therefore, represents the strength of a section.

Greater the value of Z, stronger will be the section.

$$\frac{M}{I} = \frac{\sigma}{y} \Rightarrow \sigma = \frac{M}{I} \times y$$

$$\Rightarrow \qquad \sigma \propto y$$

The bending stress at any point in any beam section is proportional to its distance from the neutral axis.

Hence, the maximum tensile and compressive stresses in a beam section are proportional to the distances of the most distant tensile and compressive fibres from neutral axis. Hence, for the purpose of economy and weight reduction the material should be concentrated as much as possible at the greatest distance from the neutral axis. This idea is put into practice, by providing beams of I-section, where the flanges alone with stand almost all the bending stress.

$$\sigma = \frac{M}{I} \times y = \frac{M}{\frac{I}{y}} = \frac{M}{Z}$$

where Z = section modulus.

$$\therefore \qquad \sigma \propto \frac{1}{Z}$$

If Z is small, then σ is more.

Example 19.11

Three beams have the same length, same allowable bending stress and the same bending moment. The cross section of the beams are a square, rectangle with depth twice the width and a circle. Find the ratios of weights of the circular and rectangular beams w.r.t. square beams.

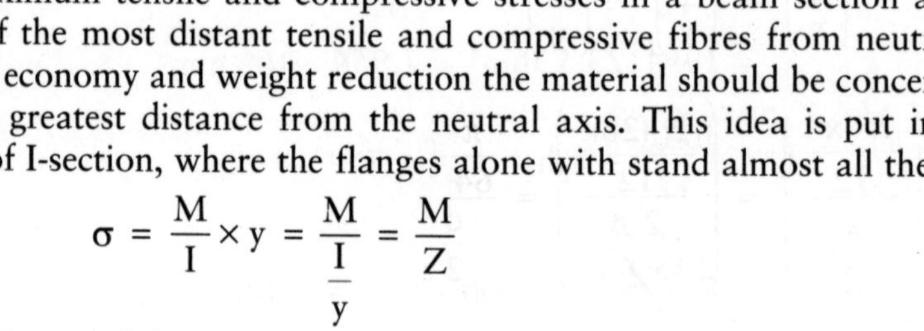

Fig. 19.21

$$\frac{W_c}{W_s} = \frac{V_c \times \rho_{\not{c}}}{V_s \times \rho_{\not{s}}} = \frac{A_c \times l_{\not{c}}}{A_s \times l_{\not{s}}} = \frac{\frac{\pi}{4}d^2}{x^2} = \frac{\pi d^2}{4x^2} \quad \text{(19.9)}$$

$$\frac{W_r}{W_s} = \frac{V_r \times \rho_{\not{r}}}{V_s \times \rho_{\not{s}}} = \frac{A_r \times l_{\not{r}}}{A_s \times l_{\not{s}}} = \frac{b \times 2b}{x^2} = \frac{2b^2}{x^2} \quad \text{(19.10)}$$

Now

$$\frac{M}{I} = \frac{\sigma}{y}$$

$$\Rightarrow \quad \frac{I}{y} = \frac{M}{\sigma}$$

$$\Rightarrow \quad Z = \frac{M}{\sigma}$$

$$\therefore \quad Z_s = Z_r = Z_c$$

$$\Rightarrow \quad \left(\frac{I}{y}\right)_s = \left(\frac{I}{y}\right)_r = \left(\frac{I}{y}\right)_c$$

$$\Rightarrow \quad \left(\frac{\frac{\not{x} \cdot x^3}{12}}{\frac{\not{x}}{2}}\right) = \left(\frac{\frac{\not{b} \cdot (2b)^3}{12}}{\frac{\not{2}\not{b}}{\not{2}}}\right) = \frac{\frac{\pi}{64}d^4}{\frac{d}{2}}$$

$$\Rightarrow \quad \frac{x^3}{6} = \frac{8b^3}{12} = \frac{\pi}{32}d^3$$

$$\Rightarrow \quad \frac{x^3}{6} = \frac{2}{3}b^3 = \frac{\pi}{32}d^3 \quad \text{(19.11)}$$

From Eq. (19.11),

$$x^3 = \frac{6\pi}{32}d^3$$

$$x = \left(\frac{6\pi}{32}\right)^{\frac{1}{3}} d = 0.838\ d \quad \text{(19.12)}$$

and from Eq. (19.11) also;

$$x^3 = \not{6}^2 \times \frac{2}{\not{3}}d^3$$

$$x = \left(4b^3\right)^{\frac{1}{3}} = 1.5874\ b \quad \text{(19.13)}$$

Now from Eq. (19.9)

$$\frac{\text{Wt. of circular}}{\text{Wt. of square}} = \frac{W_c}{W_s} = \frac{\pi d^2}{4x^2} = \frac{\pi d^2}{4(0.838d)^2} = 1.118 \qquad \textbf{Ans.}$$

and from Eq. (19.10)

$$\frac{\text{Wt. of rectangular}}{\text{Wt. of square}} = \frac{W_r}{W_s} = \frac{2b^2}{x^2} = \frac{2b^2}{(1.5874)^2\, b^2} = 0.7937 \qquad \textbf{Ans.}$$

Example 19.12

A beam is of square section of the side 'a'. If the permissible bending stress is 'f', find moment of resistance when the beam section is placed such that (i) two sides are horizontal, (ii) One diagonal is vertical. Find also the ratio of the moments of the resistance of the section in the two positions.

Solution:

Bending stress $\sigma_b = f$

Moment of resistance = M = ?

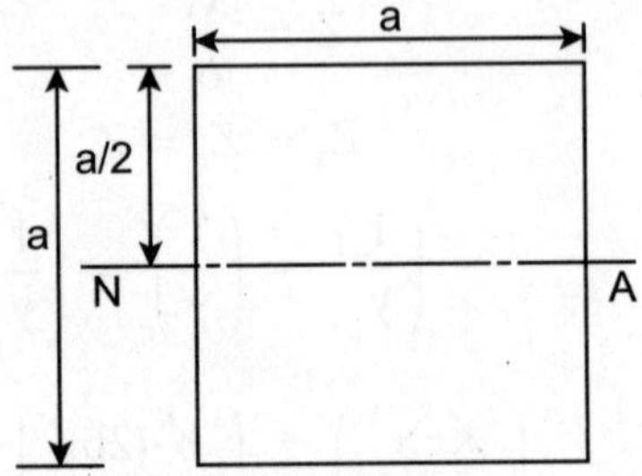

Fig. 19.22 (a)

Case I:

$$\sigma_b = f$$

$$I = \frac{bd^3}{12} = \frac{a \times a^3}{12} = \frac{a^4}{12}$$

$$y = \frac{a}{2}$$

$$M = M_1 = ?$$

Using relation $\dfrac{M}{I} = \dfrac{\sigma_b}{y}$

$$\Rightarrow \quad \frac{M_1}{\frac{a^4}{12}} = \frac{f}{\frac{a}{2}} \Rightarrow \frac{M_1 \times 12}{a^4} = \frac{2f}{a}$$

$$\therefore \quad M_1 = \frac{2fa^3}{12} = f\frac{a^3}{6}$$

$$\therefore \quad M_1 = \left(\frac{fa^3}{6}\right) \qquad \textbf{Ans.}$$

$$h = \sqrt{a^2 - \left(\frac{a\sqrt{2}}{2}\right)^2}$$

$$= \sqrt{a^2 - \frac{2a^2}{4}}$$

$$= \sqrt{a^2 - \frac{a^2}{2}}$$

$$= \sqrt{\frac{a^2}{2}} = \frac{a}{\sqrt{2}}$$

$$= \frac{a\sqrt{2}}{2}$$

Case II:

$$M_1 = M_2 = ?$$

$$\sigma_b = f$$

$$b = \sqrt{a^2 + a^2} = \sqrt{2a^2} = a\sqrt{2}$$

$$h = \frac{b}{2} = \frac{a\sqrt{2}}{2}$$

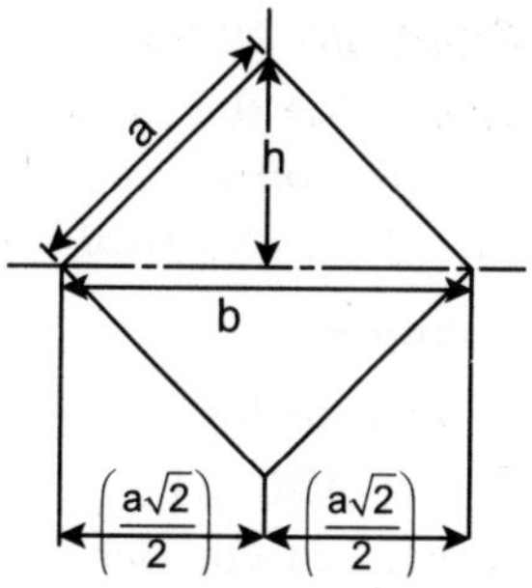

Fig. 19.22 (b)

I = 2 × M.O.I. of a triangle about its base

$$= 2 \times \frac{bh^3}{12}$$

$$= 2 \times \frac{a\sqrt{2} \times \left(\frac{a\sqrt{2}}{2}\right)^3}{12} \qquad \left| \begin{array}{l} b = a\sqrt{2} \\ h = \left(\frac{a\sqrt{2}}{2}\right) \end{array} \right.$$

$$= \frac{a\sqrt{2}}{6} \times \frac{a^3 \times 2\sqrt{2}}{8}$$

$$= \frac{a^4 \times 4}{6 \times 8} = \frac{a^4}{12}$$

$$y = \frac{a\sqrt{2}}{2} = h \qquad \left| \begin{array}{l} h = \sqrt{a^2 - \left(\frac{a\sqrt{2}}{2}\right)^2} \\ \quad = \frac{a\sqrt{2}}{2} \end{array} \right.$$

Using relation $\frac{M}{I} = \frac{\sigma}{y}$

$$\therefore \quad \frac{M_2}{\frac{a^4}{12}} = \frac{f}{\frac{a\sqrt{2}}{2}}$$

$$\Rightarrow \quad \frac{12\,M_2}{a^4} = \frac{2\,f}{a\sqrt{2}}$$

$$\therefore \quad M_2 = \frac{2a^3 f}{12\sqrt{2}} = \frac{a^3 f}{6\sqrt{2}}$$

$$M_2 = \mathbf{\frac{a^3 f}{6\sqrt{2}}}$$ **Ans.**

Ratio of moments of resistance of the section in two positions $= \frac{M_1}{M_2} = \frac{f \cdot \frac{a^3}{6}}{f \cdot \frac{a^3}{6\sqrt{2}}} = \sqrt{2}$

$$\therefore \quad \frac{M_1}{M_2} = \mathbf{1.414}$$ **Ans.**

Example 19.13

Prove that the ratio of depth of width of the strongest beam that can be cut from a circular log of diameter d is 1.414. Calculate the depth and width of the strongest beam that can be cut of a cylindrical log of wood whose diameter is 300 mm.

Solution:

Dia. of log = d

Let ABCD be the strongest rectangular section which can cut out of the cylindrical log.

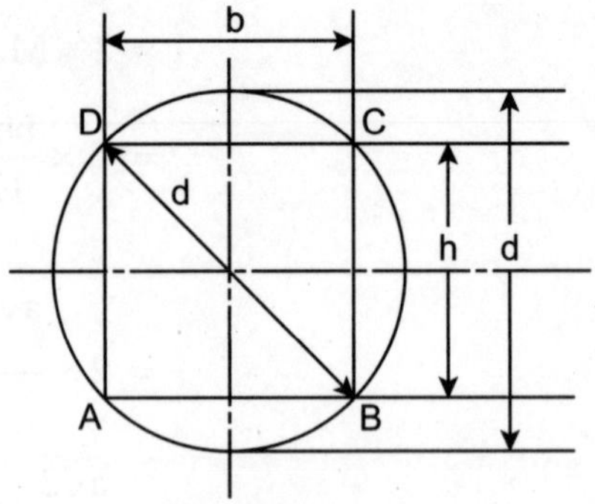

Fig. 19.23

Let

b = Width the strongest section

h = Depth of the strongest section

Now

Section modulus of the rectangular section

$$Z = \frac{I}{y} = \frac{\frac{bh^3}{12}}{\frac{h}{2}} = \frac{b \cdot h^2}{6} \quad \text{.......... (19.14)}$$

and $\qquad b^2 + h^2 = d^2$

$\therefore \qquad h^2 = d^2 - b^2$

$$\therefore \qquad Z = \frac{b(d^2 - b^2)}{6} = \frac{1}{6}(bd^2 - b^3) \quad \text{.......... (19.15)}$$

Now, Ist Part:

For beam to be the strongest, the section modulus (Z) should be maximum,

$\therefore$ For maximum value of Z

$$\frac{dZ}{db} = 0$$

$$\frac{d}{db}\left[\frac{1}{6}(bd^2 - b^3)\right] = 0$$

or $\qquad \frac{1}{6}(d^2 - 3b^2) = 0$

or $\qquad d^2 - 3b^2 = 0$

or $\qquad d^2 = 3b^2 \quad \text{.......... (19.16)}$

also $\qquad d^2 = b^2 + h^2$

$\therefore \qquad b^2 + h^2 = 3b^2$

$\qquad h^2 = 2b^2$

$$\therefore \quad \frac{h}{b} = \sqrt{2} = \mathbf{1.414} \qquad \textbf{Ans.}$$

IInd Part:

$$d = 300 \text{ mm}$$

$$\therefore \quad b^2 + h^2 = (300)^2 = 900$$

$$\therefore \quad b^2 + h^2 = 90000 \qquad (19.17)$$

$$b^2 + 2b^2 = 90000$$

$$3b^2 = 90000$$

$$b^2 = 30000$$

$$b = \mathbf{173.2 \text{ mm}} \qquad \textbf{Ans.}$$

$$\text{and} \quad h = \sqrt{2} \times 173.2 = \mathbf{244.95 \text{ mm}} \qquad \textbf{Ans.}$$

19.11 Application of Bending Equation

The bending equation $\frac{M}{I} = \frac{\sigma}{y} = \frac{E}{R}$ is based upon the theory of pure bending and assumptions taken there upon, which require that the beam should be subjected to constant bending moments unaccompanied by shearing forces, but in actual practice the bending moment varies from point to point along the length of the beam and also the bending moment is accompanied by a shearing force. However, in a large number of practical cases, the B.M. is maximum when the shear force changes sign, *i.e.* crosses the zero shearing force line. In this way, the requirements to simple bending are approximately satisfied at the point of maximum bending moment and therefore it seems justifiable to apply the bending equation at that point only.

NUMERICAL QUESTIONS

1. A uniform T section beam is 10 cm wide and 15 cm deep with a flange thickness of 2.5 cm and a web thickness of 1.2 cm. If the limiting bending stresses for the material of the beam are 80 MPa in compression and 160 MPa in tension. Find maximum U.D.L. that the beam can carry over a simply supported beam span of 5 m.

2. A C.I. test beam 2 cm × 2 cm in section and 1 m long and supported at the ends fails when a central load of 640 N is applied. What uniformly distributed load will break a cantilever of the same material 50 mm wide, 10 cm deep and 2 m long.

3. A rolled steel joist of I section has the following dimensions.

   Flange: 25 cm wide and 2.4 cm thick.

   Web: 1.2 cm thick

   Overall depth: 60 cm

   If this beam carries a U.D.L. of 50 kN/m run on a span of 8 m. Calculate the maximum stress induced due to bending.

4. A rectangular beam 30 cm deep is simply supported over a span of 4 m. What U.D.L. per meter the beam may carry, if the bending stress is not to exceed 120 MPa. Take $I = 8 \times 10^6$ mm^4.

5. A mild steel strap 100 mm wide and 20 mm thick is bent into a circular arc of radius 50 m. Find maximum intensity of stress induced in the strap. Take E for beam = 2×10^6 kg/cm^2.

6. A cantilever beam of length 3 m is carry a U.D.L. of 2 kN/m over its entire span. If the cross section of the beam is circular of diameter 7 cm. Find maximum bending stress induced in the beam.

7. Compare the weights of two equally strong beams of circular sections made of the same material. One beam is of solid circular section and other is of hollow circular section for which $d_i/d_o = 3/5$.

8. A wire of diameter d is wound round a cylinder of diameter D. Find bending stress induced on the cross section of wire. Hence or otherwise find the minimum radius to which a 10 mm diameter circular and of high tensile steel can be bent without undergoing permanent deformation. Take yield stress = 1700 N/mm^2 and E = 2×10^5 N/mm^2. What is the magnitude of bending moment necessary for this.

9. A rectangular section is replaced by an I section of the same area as shown in Fig. 19.24 for a beam of uniform section. Find the ratio of resistance to bending for the

two sections. The material is same and is able to take the same maximum bending stress.

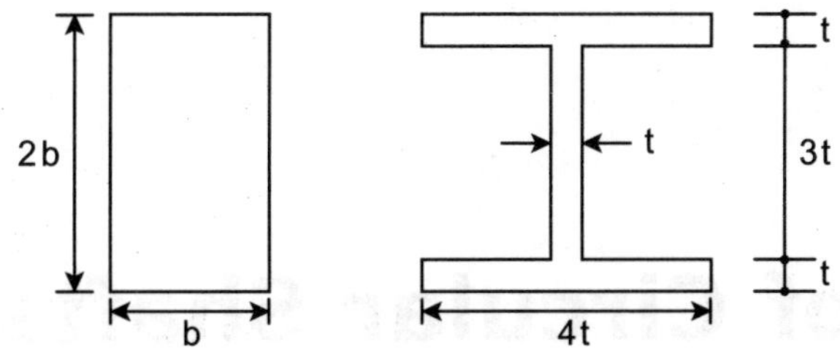

Fig. 19.24

10. What is the least internal radius to which a bar of steel 10 cm wide and 1 cm thick can be bent so that the maximum stress will not exceed 500 MPa? Assume $E = 2 \times 10^5$ N/mm^2.
11. A wooden beam 2 m long is simply supported at its ends and has a cross section 150 mm wide and 600 mm deep. It carries a U.D.L. of 90 kN/m over the entire span. Calculate the bending stress at a point 200 mm above the bottom of the beam and 600 mm from the left support.

20

Torsion of Circular Shafts

20.1 Notations Used

T = Maximum torque or twisting moment (N.mm).

J = Polar moment of inertia (mm^4).

$= \frac{\pi}{32} d^4$ for solid shaft.

$= \frac{\pi}{32}\left(d_o^4 - d_i^4\right)$.... for hollow shaft.

τ = Maximum shear stress (N/mm^2).

r = radius of the shaft (for solid shaft).

r_o = radius of hollow shaft.

C or G = Modulus of rigidity (N/mm^2).

θ = Angle of twist (in radian).

l = length of the shaft (mm).

d_o = Outside diameter of shaft (mm).

d_i = Inside diameter of shaft (mm).

M = Maximum Bending moment (N.mm).

p = Power transmitted (Watt).

N = rpm of the shaft.

T_e = Equivalent torque or twisting moment (N.mm).

M_e = Equivalent bending moment (N.mm).

P = axial load (N).

σ_b = Bending stress (N/mm^2).

$\sigma_{1,2}$ = Principal stresses (N/mm^2).

20.2 Derivation of Torsion Equation $\frac{T}{J} = \frac{\tau}{r} = \frac{C.\theta}{l}$

Assumptions made:

1. The material of the shaft is uniform throughout.
2. The shaft circular in section remains circular after loading.
3. A plane section of shaft normal to its axis before loading remains plane after loading.
4. The twist along the length of the shaft is uniform throughout.
5. The distance between any two normal cross section remains the same after loading.
6. The maximum shear stress induced in the shaft due to loading does not exceed its elastic limit value.

Consider a shaft AB, whose end AD is fixed.

CD is any line on outer surface of the shaft.

After applying a torque T, the line CD gets its new position CD′, as shown in Fig. 20.1.

Distortion in outer surface = DD′ = $r \cdot \theta$.

Shear strain $\phi = \tan\phi = \frac{DD'}{l} = \frac{r \cdot \theta}{l}$

$$\Rightarrow \quad \frac{\tau}{C} = \frac{r \cdot \theta}{l}, \qquad \theta = \frac{\tau}{C}$$

$$\Rightarrow \quad \frac{\tau}{r} = \frac{C \cdot \theta}{l} \qquad \text{(20.1)}$$

For a particular torque T, C, θ and l are constant.

$$\therefore \quad \frac{\tau}{r} = \text{Constant}$$

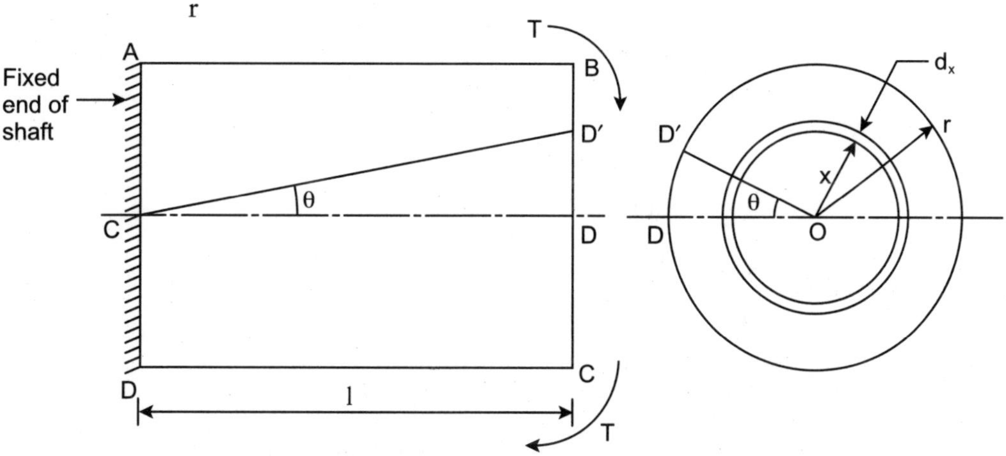

Fig. 20.1

$$\text{or} \quad \frac{\tau}{r} = \frac{\tau_x}{x} = \text{Constant}$$

$$\text{or} \quad \tau \propto r$$

Shear stress is proportional to the radius of the shaft. Considering a small elemental ring of radius x and thickness d_x.

$$\tau_x = \frac{\tau}{r}\cdot x$$

Force on the elemental ring

$$dF = \tau_x \times dA = \frac{\tau}{r}\cdot x \times dA$$

Torque on the elemental ring

$$dT = dF \times x = \frac{\tau}{r}\cdot x^2 \; dA$$

$$T = \int_0^r dT = \frac{\tau}{r}\int_0^r x^2 dA = \frac{\tau}{r}.J$$

$$\Rightarrow \quad \frac{T}{J} = \frac{\tau}{r} \quad \ldots\ldots (20.2)$$

From Eqs. (20.1) and (20.2)

$$\frac{T}{J} = \frac{\tau}{r} = \frac{C\cdot\theta}{l} \quad \ldots\ldots (20.3)$$

This equation is known as torsion formulae.

20.3 Polar Moment of Inertia

The moment of inertia of a plane area w.r.t. an axis perpendicular to the plane of the figure is called polar moment of inertia w.r.t. the point, where the axis intersects the plane. In circular plane, this point is always the centre of the circle:

We know that

$$\frac{\tau}{r} = \frac{C\cdot\theta}{l} \quad \ldots\ldots (20.4)$$

and

$$T = \frac{\pi}{16}\tau d^3 \quad \ldots\ldots (20.5)$$

$$\Rightarrow \quad \tau = \frac{16T}{\pi d^3}$$

From Eq. (20.4)

$$\frac{16T}{\pi d^3 \cdot r} = \frac{C\cdot\theta}{l}$$

$$\Rightarrow \quad \frac{T}{\frac{\pi}{16}d^3\cdot\frac{d}{2}} = \frac{C\cdot\theta}{l}$$

$$\Rightarrow \quad \frac{T}{\frac{\pi}{32}d^4} = \frac{C\theta}{l}$$

$$\Rightarrow \qquad \frac{T}{J} = \frac{C\theta}{l}$$

where $J = \frac{\pi}{32}d^4$, and is known as opolar moment of inertia.

Note: For hollow circular shaft.

$$J = \frac{\pi}{32}\left(d_o^{\,4} - d_i^{\,4}\right)$$

Section Modulus

$$Z = \frac{J}{r} \Rightarrow \text{Torsional section modulus or Polar modulus.}$$

∴ Polar modulus for solid shaft.

$$Z_p = \frac{J}{r} = \frac{\frac{\pi}{32}d^4}{\frac{d}{2}} = \frac{\pi}{16}d^3$$

For hollow circular shaft

$$Z_p = \frac{J}{r_o} = \frac{\frac{\pi}{32}\left(d_o^{\,4} - d_i^{\,4}\right)}{\frac{d_o}{2}}$$

$$= \frac{\pi}{16}d_o^{\,3}\left(1 - K^4\right), \qquad K = d_i/d_o$$

Example 20.1

A solid shaft 100 mm diameter, transmits 75 kW at 200 rpm.

(a) Determine the value of maximum shear stress setup in the shaft and the angle of twist per meter of the shaft length if G = 80 GN/m².

(b) If the shaft were now bored in order to reduce weight to produce a tube of 100 mm outside diameter and 60 mm inside diameter, what torque could be carried if the same maximum shear stress is not to be exceeded. What is the percentage increase in power/weight ratio effected by this modification?

Solution:

(a) $d = 100$ mm

$p = 75 \text{ kW} = 75 \times 10^3$ Watt

$\tau = ?$

$N = 200$ rpm

$\theta = ?$

$l = 1 \text{ m} = 1000$ mm

$G = 80 \text{ GN/m}^2 = 0.8 \times 10^5 \text{ N/mm}^2$

Now

$$p = \frac{2\pi NT}{60}$$

$$\Rightarrow \quad 75 \times 10^3 \times 60 = 2\pi \times 200 \times T$$

$$\Rightarrow \quad T_s = 3580.986 \text{ N.m}$$

$$T_s = 3580.986 \times 10^3 \text{ N.mm}$$

Torsion equation $\frac{T}{J} = \frac{\tau}{r} = \frac{C \cdot \theta}{l}$ .... (20.6)

Using $\frac{T}{J} = \frac{\tau}{r} \Rightarrow T = \frac{\pi}{16}\tau d^3$

or $$\tau = \frac{16T}{\pi d^3} = \frac{16 \times 3580.986 \times 1000}{\pi \times (100)^3}$$

or $$\tau = \mathbf{18.23\ N/mm^2}$$ **Ans.**

Using $\frac{T}{J} = \frac{C\theta}{l} \Rightarrow \theta = \frac{T \times l}{C \times J}$

$$\Rightarrow \quad \theta = \frac{3080.986 \times 1000 \times 1000}{0.8 \times 10^5 \times \frac{\pi}{32} \times (100)^4} = 3.92 \times 10^{-3} \text{ rad.}$$

$$\Rightarrow \quad \theta = \mathbf{0.224°}$$ **Ans.**

(b) $d_o = 100$ mm

$d_i = 60$ mm

$T_h = ?$

$\tau_H = \tau = 18.23$ N/mm^2

Now

$$T_h = \frac{\pi}{16}\tau\, d_o^3\left(1 - K^4\right), \qquad K = \frac{d_i}{d_o} = \frac{60}{100} = \frac{3}{5}$$

$$= \frac{\pi}{16} \times 18.23 \times (100)^3 \left[1 - \left(\frac{3}{5}\right)^4\right] = 3115555 \text{ N.mm}$$

$$\therefore \quad T_h = \mathbf{3115.56\ N.m}$$ **Ans.**

Now

$$W_s = \frac{\pi}{4}d^2 \times l \times \rho g = \frac{\pi}{4} \times \left(\frac{100}{1000}\right)^2 \times 1 \times \rho g = \frac{\pi}{4} \times (0.1)^2 \times \rho g = \frac{\pi}{4} \times 0.01 \times \rho g$$

$$W_h = \frac{\pi}{4}\left(d_o^2 - d_i^2\right) \times 1 \times \rho g = \frac{\pi}{4}\left(0.1^2 - 0.06^2\right) \times 1 \times \rho g = \frac{\pi}{4} \times 6.4 \times 10^{-3} \times \rho g$$

$$\therefore \quad \frac{p_s}{W_s} = \frac{2\pi NT_s}{60 \times \frac{\pi}{4} \times 0.01 \times \rho g} = \frac{2\pi \times 200 \times 3580.986}{60 \times \frac{\pi}{4} \times 0.01 \times \rho g} = \frac{9549296}{\rho g}$$

$$\frac{p_h}{W_h} = \frac{2\pi NT_h}{\frac{\pi}{4} \times 6.4 \times 10^{-3} \times \rho g \times 60} = \frac{2\pi \times 200 \times 3115.56}{\frac{\pi}{4} \times 6.4 \times 10^{-3} \times \rho g \times 60} = \frac{7.7889 \times 10^8}{60 \times \rho g}$$

$$= 1.298 \times 10^7 / \rho g$$

$\therefore$ % increase in power/weight ratio

$$= \frac{\left(\frac{p_h}{W_h} - \frac{p_s}{W_s}\right) \times 100}{\left(\frac{p_s}{W_s}\right)} = \left(\frac{1.298 \times 10^7 - 9549296}{9549296}\right) \times 100$$

$$= 35.94\%$$ **Ans.**

Example 20.2

Determine the dimensions of a hollow shaft with a diameter ratio of 3 : 4 which is to transmit 100 kW at 150 rpm. The maximum shear stress in the shaft is limited to 70 MPa and angle of twist to 3.8° in a length of 4 m. Take G = 80 GN/m².

Solution:

$d_o = ?$

$d_i = ?$

$K = \frac{d_i}{d_o} = \frac{3}{4}$

$p = 100 \text{ kW} = 100 \times 10^3$ Watts

$N = 150$ rpm

$\tau = 70$ MPa

$\theta = 3.8° = \left(3.8 \times \frac{\pi}{180}\right)$ rad $= 0.066$ rad

$l = 4 \text{ m} = 4000$ mm

$G = 80 \text{ GN/m}^2 = 0.8 \times 10^5 \text{ N/mm}^2$

Now

$$p = \frac{2\pi NT}{60} \Rightarrow T = \frac{p \times 60}{2\pi N}$$

$$\therefore \quad T = \frac{1 \times 10^5 \times 60}{2\pi \times 150} = 6366.2 \text{ N.m}$$

Also $$T = \frac{\pi}{16}\tau d_o^3 (1 - K^4)$$

$$\Rightarrow \quad 6366.2 \times 1000 = \frac{\pi}{16} \times 70 \times d_o^3 \left[1 - \left(\frac{3}{4}\right)^4\right]$$

$$\Rightarrow \quad d_o = 87.83 \text{ mm}$$

and $$d_i = 65.87 \text{ mm}$$

Now from angle of twist condition: $\frac{T}{J} = \frac{C \cdot \theta}{l}$

$$J = \frac{T \times l}{C \times \theta} = \frac{6366.2 \times 1000 \times 4000}{0.8 \times 10^5 \times 0.066} = 4799426.2 \text{ mm}^4$$

$$\Rightarrow \quad \frac{\pi}{32} d_o^4 (1 - K^4) = 4799426.2 \Rightarrow d_o = \left[\frac{48886554}{1 - \left(\frac{3}{4}\right)^4}\right]^{\frac{1}{4}}$$

$$\Rightarrow \quad d_o = 91.96 \text{ mm}$$

$$d_i = 68.96 \text{ mm}$$

∴ Safe dimensions are: d_o = **91.96**, d_i = **68.96 mm** **Ans.**

Example 20.3

A steel transmission shaft is 510 mm long and 50 mm external diameter. For part of its length it is bored to a diameter of 25 mm and for the rest to 38 mm diameter.

(a) Find the maximum power that may be transmitted at a speed of 200 rpm, if the shear stress is not to exceed 70 MPa.

(b) If the angle of twist in the length of 25 mm bore is equal to that in the length of 38 mm bore, find the length bored to the latter diameter.

Solution:

l = 5.0 mm

d_o = 50 mm

p = ?

N = 200 rpm

τ = 70 MPa

The shafts are in series and each part is under same torque.

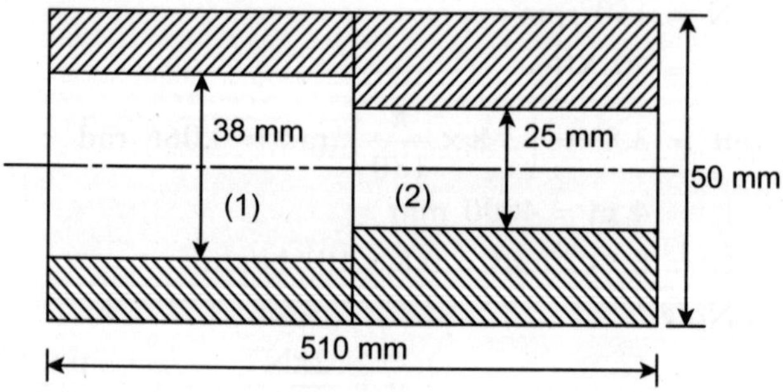

Fig. 20.2

From torsion equation; $\frac{T}{J} = \frac{\tau}{r} \Rightarrow T = \frac{J \times \tau}{r}$ .... (20.7)

(a) Value of $J_1 = \frac{\pi}{32}\left(50^4 - 38^4\right) = 408884.57 \text{ mm}^4$

Value of $J_2 = \frac{\pi}{32}\left(50^4 - 25^4\right) = 575242.8 \text{ mm}^4$

$$\therefore \quad T_1 = \frac{J_1 \times \tau}{r_o} = \frac{408884.57 \times 70}{25} = 1144876.8 \text{ N.mm} = 1144.8 \text{ N.m}$$

$$T_2 = \frac{J_2 \times \tau}{r_o} = \frac{575242.8 \times 70}{25} = 1610679.8 \text{ N.mm} = 1610.6 \text{ N.m}$$

$\therefore$ Safe torque transmitted = Minimum of T_1 and T_2

$\therefore \quad T = T_1 = 1144.8$ N.m

$\therefore$ Maximum power transmitted

$$p = \frac{2\pi NT}{60 \times 1000} \text{kW} = \frac{2\pi \times 200 \times 1144.8}{60 \times 1000} \text{kW} = 23.98 \text{ kW}$$

$= \mathbf{24\ kW}$ **Ans.**

(b) Assuming that $\theta_1 = \theta_2$

$$\Rightarrow \quad \frac{T_1 l_1}{C J_1} = \frac{T_2 l_2}{C J_2}, \quad T_1 = T_2 = T$$

$$\Rightarrow \quad \frac{l_1}{J_1} = \frac{l_2}{J_2} \Rightarrow \frac{l_1}{l_2} = \frac{J_1}{J_2}$$

$$\Rightarrow \quad \frac{l_1}{l_2} = \frac{\frac{\pi}{32}\left(50^4 - 38^4\right)}{\frac{\pi}{32}\left(50^2 - 25^4\right)} = 0.71 \quad \ldots\ldots (20.8)$$

Also $\quad l_1 + l_2 = 510 \ldots\ldots (20.9)$

From Eqs. (20.8) and (20.9),

$$0.71\, l_2 + l_2 = 510$$

$$l_2 = 298.2 \text{ mm}$$

$\therefore \quad l_1 = \mathbf{211.8\ mm}$ **Ans.**

Example 20.4

A solid steel shaft has to transmit 75 kW at 150 rpm. The allowable shear stress is 60 MPa. Find suitable diameter of the shaft, if the maximum torque transmitted on each revolution exceeds the mean by 30%.

Solution:

$p = 75 \text{ kW} = 75 \times 10^3$ Watts

$N = 150$ rpm

$\tau = 60 \text{ MPa} = 60 \text{ N/mm}^2$

$d = ?$

$T_{max} = T = T_{mean} \times 1.3$

$(T = T_{mean} + 0.30\, T_{mean} = 1.3\, T_{mean})$

$$p = \frac{2\pi N\, T_{mean}}{60} \text{ Watts}$$

$$\Rightarrow \quad T_{mean} = \frac{75 \times 10^3 \times 60}{2\pi \times 150} = 4774.6 \text{ N.m}$$

$$\therefore \quad T = 1.3\, T_{mean} = 1.3 \times 4774.6 = 6207 \text{ N.m}$$

Also $\dfrac{T}{J} = \dfrac{\tau}{r} \Rightarrow T = \dfrac{\pi}{16}\tau d^3$

$$\therefore \quad 6207 \times 1000 = \frac{\pi}{16} \times 60 \times d^3$$

$$\Rightarrow \quad d = \left(\frac{6207 \times 1000 \times 16}{\pi \times 60}\right)^{\frac{1}{3}} = 80.76 \text{ mm}$$

$$\Rightarrow \quad d = \mathbf{81\ mm}$$

Ans.

Example 20.5

A solid circular shaft transmits 75 kW at 300 rpm. The twist in the length 2 meter is 1° and shear stress is limited to 50 MPa. Take $C = 1 \times 10^5$ N/mm². Design the shaft.

Solution:

$p = 75 \text{ kW} = 75 \times 10^3$ Watts

$N = 300$ rpm

$l = 2 \text{ m} = 2000$ mm

$\theta = 1°$

$\tau = 50 \text{ MPa} = 50 \text{ N/mm}^2$

$C = 1 \times 10^5 \text{ N/mm}^2$

Now,

$$p = \frac{2\pi NT}{60} \Rightarrow T = \frac{75 \times 1000 \times 60}{2\pi \times 300} = 2387.3 \text{ N.m}$$

Case I: Using $\frac{T}{J} = \frac{\tau}{r}$

$$\Rightarrow \quad T = \frac{\pi}{16}\tau d^3$$

$$\therefore \quad d = \left(\frac{16T}{\pi\,\tau}\right)^{\frac{1}{3}} = \left(\frac{16 \times 2387.3 \times 1000}{\pi \times 50}\right)^{\frac{1}{3}} = 62.4 \text{ mm}$$

$$\therefore \quad d = 62.4 \text{ mm}$$

Case II: Using $\frac{T}{J} = \frac{C \cdot \theta}{l}$

$$\Rightarrow \quad \frac{2387.3 \times 1000}{\frac{\pi}{32}d^4} = \frac{1 \times 10^5 \times 1 \times \frac{\pi}{180}}{2000}$$

$$\Rightarrow \quad \frac{24316838}{d^4} = 0.87266$$

$$\Rightarrow \quad d = 72.65 \text{ mm}$$

The safe value of diameter is the larger value out of two values

$$\therefore \quad d = 72.65 \text{ mm} = \mathbf{73 \text{ mm}}$$ **Ans.**

Example 20.6

The working conditions to be satisfied by a shaft transmitting power are (a) that the shaft must not twist 1° on a length of 20 diameter (b) The shear stress must not exceed 55 MPa. If $C = 0.8 \times 10^5$ N/mm², what is actual working stress and diameter of shaft to transmit 1 MW at 200 rpm?

Solution:

$$\theta = 1° = \frac{\pi}{180} \text{rad}$$

$$l = 20 \text{ d}$$

$$\tau_{max} = 55 \text{ MPa}$$

$$C = 0.8 \times 10^5 \text{ N/mm}^2$$

$$\tau_{actual} = ?$$

$$d = ?$$

$$p = 1 \text{ MW} = 1 \times 10^6 \text{ Watts}$$

$$N = 200 \text{ rpm}$$

Now

Torsion equation is $\frac{T}{J} = \frac{\tau}{r} = \frac{C \cdot \theta}{l}$

(a) Using $\frac{T}{J} = \frac{\tau}{r} \Rightarrow T_{max} = \tau_{max} \times \frac{J}{r}$

$$\therefore \quad T_{max} = \tau_{max} \times \frac{\frac{\pi}{32}d^4}{\frac{d}{2}} = \frac{55}{1} \times \frac{\pi}{32} d^3 \times 2 = 10.8\ d^3$$

$$\therefore \quad T_{max} = 10.8\ d^3$$

(b) Using $\frac{T}{J} = \frac{C \cdot \theta}{l} \Rightarrow T = \frac{C \cdot \theta \times J}{l}$

$$\therefore \quad T_{actual} = \frac{0.8 \times 10^5 \times \pi\, d^4}{20\, d \times 32} \times \frac{\pi}{180} = 6.85\ d^3$$

$$T_{actual} = 6.85\ d^3$$

∴ The strength of the shaft is the minimum torque out of two values:

$\therefore \quad T = 6.85\ d^3$

In fact, $\tau = \frac{r \cdot T}{J}$

$\Rightarrow \quad \tau \propto T \qquad \because$ r and J are constant.

$$\therefore \quad \frac{\tau_{actual}}{\tau_{max}} = \frac{T_{actual}}{T_{max}} = \frac{T_{min}}{T_{max}} = \frac{6.85\ d^3}{10.8\ d^3} = 0.63$$

$$\therefore \quad \tau_{actual} = 55 \times 0.63 = 34.88 \text{ MPa} = 35 \text{ MPa}$$

$\therefore \quad \tau_{actual} = \mathbf{35\ MPa}$ **Ans.**

And now

$$p = \frac{2\pi NT}{60} \text{ Watts}$$

$$\Rightarrow \quad 1 \times 10^6 = \frac{2\pi \times 200 \times T}{60}$$

$$\Rightarrow \quad T = \frac{60 \times 10^6}{2\pi \times 200} = 47746.48 \text{ N.m}$$

$$\Rightarrow \quad 6.85\ d^3 = 47746.48 \times 1000 \text{ N.mm}$$

$d = \mathbf{191\ mm}$ **Ans.**

Example 20.7

Compare the weights of equal lengths of hollow and solid shafts to transmit a given torque for the same maximum shear stress if inside diameter is 3/4 of the outside diameter.

Solution:

$$\frac{W_h}{W_s} = ?$$

$T_h = T_s,\ l_h = l_s,\ \rho_s = \rho_h$

$\tau_h = \tau_s$

$$K = \frac{d_i}{d_o} = \frac{3}{4}$$

Now

$$\frac{W_h}{W_s} = \frac{V_h \times \rho}{V_s \times \rho} = \frac{A_h \times l_h}{A_s \times l_s} = \frac{A_h}{A_s}$$

$$= \frac{\frac{\pi}{4}\left(d_o^2 - d_i^2\right)}{\frac{\pi}{4}d^2} = \frac{d_o^2 - d_i^2}{d^2}$$

$$\frac{W_h}{W_s} = \frac{d^2 - \frac{9}{16}d_o^2}{d^2} = \frac{7}{10}\left(\frac{d_o}{d}\right)^2 \quad \text{.........................} \quad (20.10)$$

We know that $T_h = T_s$

$$\Rightarrow \frac{\pi}{16}\tau_h\, d_o^3\left(1 - K^4\right) = \frac{\pi}{16}\tau_s\, d^3$$

$$\Rightarrow d_o^3\left[1 - \left(\frac{3}{4}\right)^4\right] = d^3$$

$$\Rightarrow \left(\frac{d_o}{d}\right)^3 = 1.4628571$$

$$\Rightarrow \left(\frac{d_o}{d}\right) = 1.135$$

$$\Rightarrow \left(\frac{d_o}{d}\right)^2 = 1.2886 \quad \text{....................................} \quad (20.11)$$

From Eq. (20.10),

$$\frac{W_h}{W_s} = \frac{7}{16} \times 1.2886 = \mathbf{0.56}$$ **Ans.**

Example 20.8

A solid shaft in a rolling mill transmits 50 kW at 2 rps. Determine diameter of shaft if shear stress is not to exceed 50 MPa and angle of twist is limited 6° in a length of 4 m. Take C = 0.83 × 10⁵ N/mm².

Solution:

$p = 50\ kW = 50 \times 10^3$ Watts
$N = 2$ rps $= 120$ rpm
$d = ?$
$\tau = 50$ MPa $= 50\ N/mm^2$

$$\theta = 6° = 6 \times \frac{\pi}{180} \text{rad} = \frac{\pi}{30} \text{rad}$$

$l = 4$ m $= 4000$ mm
$C = 0.83 \times 10^5\ N/mm^2$

Now

$$p = \frac{2\pi NT}{60} = T = \frac{p \times 60}{2\pi N}$$

$$\therefore \quad T = \frac{50 \times 1000 \times 60}{2\pi \times 120} = 3978.87 \text{ N.m}$$

$$\therefore \quad T = 3978.87 \times 1000 \text{ N.mm}$$

$$\text{Using } \frac{T}{J} = \frac{\tau}{r} \Rightarrow d = \left(\frac{16T}{\pi\tau}\right)^{\frac{1}{3}}; \qquad T = \frac{\pi}{16}\tau d^3$$

$$\therefore \quad d = \left(\frac{16 \times 3978.87 \times 1000}{\pi \times 50}\right)^{\frac{1}{3}} = 29.36 \text{ mm}$$

$$\text{Using } \frac{T}{J} = \frac{C \cdot \theta}{l} \Rightarrow \frac{3978.87 \times 1000}{\frac{\pi}{32}d^4} = \frac{0.83 \times 10^5}{4000} \times \frac{\pi}{30}$$

$$\Rightarrow \quad d = (18651473)^{\frac{1}{4}} = 65.71 \text{ mm}$$

∴ Safe diameter will be larger one

$\therefore \quad d = 65.71 =$ **66 mm** **Ans.**

Example 20.9

Calculate the maximum torque transmitted by a shaft (safely) of 300 mm diameter. The permissible angle of twist is 2° in a length of 8 m and shear stress is not to exceed 40 N/mm². Take C = 0.8 × 10⁵ N/mm².

Solution:

$T = ?$
$d = 300$ mm

$\theta = 2° = \dfrac{\pi}{90}$ rad

$l = 8$ m $= 8000$ mm

$\tau = 40$ N/mm^2

$C = 0.8 \times 10^5$ N/mm^2

Torsion equation is $\dfrac{T}{J} = \dfrac{\tau}{r} = \dfrac{C \cdot \theta}{l}$

(i) Using $\dfrac{T}{J} = \dfrac{\tau}{r}$, $\quad T = \dfrac{\pi}{16}\tau d^3$

$$\therefore \quad T = \frac{\pi}{16} \times 40 \times (300)^3 = 2.12 \times 10^8 \text{ N.mm} = 2.12 \times 10^5 \text{ N.m}$$

(ii) Using $\dfrac{T}{J} = \dfrac{C \cdot \theta}{l}$, $\quad T = \dfrac{J \cdot C \cdot \theta}{l}$

$$\therefore \quad T = \frac{\pi}{32} \times \frac{d^4 \times C \times \theta}{l} = \frac{\pi}{32} \times \frac{(300)^4 \times 0.8 \times 10^5}{8000} \times \frac{\pi}{90}$$

$$\therefore \quad T = 2.77 \times 10^8 \text{ N.mm} = 2.77 \times 10^5 \text{ N.m}$$

Now, safe value of the torque is smaller one

$\therefore \quad T_{safe} = T_{min} = \mathbf{2.12 \times 10^5}$ **N.m** **Ans.**

Example 20.10

A hollow shaft 45 cm external diameter and 25 cm internal diameter is subjected to a torque of 400 kN.m. Find the shear stress at the outer and inner surfaces of the shaft. Draw shear stress distribution for the wall of the shaft. Find also the twist in a length of 2.5 m of the shaft. Take C = 8 × 10⁴ N/mm².

Solution:

$d_o = 450$ mm

$d_i = 250$ mm

$T = 400$ kN.m $= 400 \times 10^6$ N.mm

$\tau_o = ?$

$\tau_i = ?$

$\theta = ?$

$l = 2.5$ m $= 2500$ mm

$C = 8 \times 10^4$ N/mm^2

Now $\dfrac{T}{J} = \dfrac{\tau}{r} \Rightarrow \dfrac{T}{J} = \dfrac{\tau_o}{r_o}$ and $\dfrac{T}{J} = \dfrac{\tau_i}{r_i}$

∴ Shear stress at outer surface

$$\tau_o = \frac{T}{J} \times r_o = \frac{400 \times 10^6 \times 225}{\frac{\pi}{32}\left(d_o^{\,4} - d_i^{\,4}\right)}$$

$$= \frac{400 \times 10^6 \times 225}{\frac{\pi}{32}\left(450^4 - 250^4\right)} = \mathbf{24.71\ N/mm^2}$$ **Ans.**

And shear stress at inner surface

$$\tau_i = \frac{T}{J} \times r_i = \frac{400 \times 10^6 \times 125}{\frac{\pi}{32}\left(450^4 - 250^4\right)} = \mathbf{13.73\ N/mm^2}$$ **Ans.**

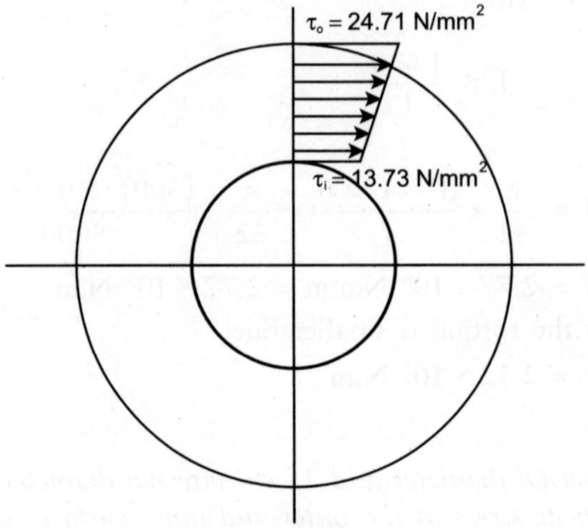

Fig. 20.3

Now, angle of twist (θ):

$$\frac{T}{J} = \frac{C\theta}{l} \Rightarrow \theta = \frac{T \times l}{J \cdot C}$$

$$\therefore \quad \theta = \frac{400 \times 10^6 \times 2500}{8 \times 10^4 \times \frac{\pi}{32}\left(450^4 - 250^4\right)} \text{ rad}$$

$$= \frac{1 \times 10^{12}}{2.91382 \times 10^{14}} = 3.43 \times 10^{-3} \text{ rad}$$

$$\theta = 3.43 \times 10^{-3} \text{ rad}$$

or $$\theta = \mathbf{0.197^\circ}$$ **Ans.**

Example 20.11

The diameter ratio of a hollow shaft is 3 : 5. It is required to transmit 600 kW at 110 rpm. The maximum torque being 12% greater than the mean. If the twist in a length of 3 m is not to exceed 1° and the shearing stress is limited to 60 MN/m². Calculate the minimum external diameter of the shaft satisfying these conditions. Take C = 80 × 10³ MN/m².

Solution:

$$\frac{d_i}{d_o} = \frac{3}{5} = K \text{ (say)}$$

$$p = 600 \text{ kW} = 6 \times 10^5 \text{ Watts}$$

$$N = 110 \text{ rpm}$$

$$T_{max} = 1.12\, T_{mean}$$

$$l = 3 \text{ m} = 3000 \text{ mm}$$

$$\theta = 1° = \frac{\pi}{180} \text{rad}$$

$$\tau = 60 \text{ MN/m}^2 = 60 \text{ N/mm}^2$$

$$d_o = ?$$

$$C = 80 \times 10^3 \text{ MN/m}^2 = 8 \times 10^4 \text{ N/mm}^2$$

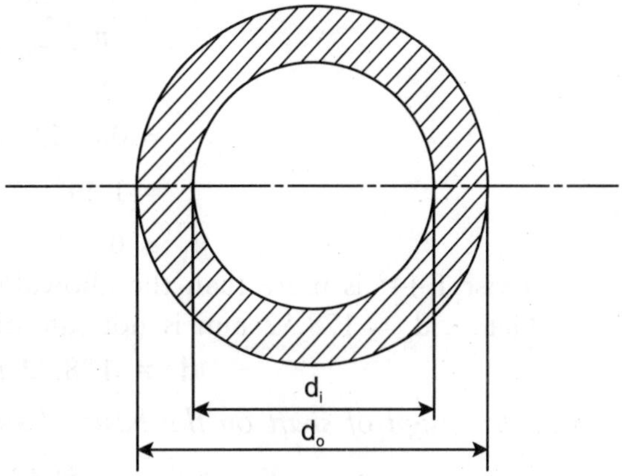

Fig. 20.4

Now

$$p = \frac{2\pi N\, T_{mean}}{60}$$

$$\Rightarrow \quad T_{mean} = \frac{p \times 60}{2\pi N} = \frac{6 \times 10^5 \times 60}{2\pi \times 110} = 52087.072 \text{ N.m}$$

$$\therefore \quad T_{max} = 1.12\, T_{mean} = 1.12 \times 52087.072 = 58337.52 \text{ N.m}$$

Now

Case I: Design of shaft on the basis of strength:

$$\frac{T}{J} = \frac{\tau}{r} \Rightarrow T = \frac{\pi}{16}\tau d_o^3 \left(1 - K^4\right)$$

$$\therefore \quad T_{max} = \frac{\pi}{16}\tau d_o^3 \left(1 - K^4\right)$$

$$\Rightarrow \quad 58337.521 \times 1000 = \frac{\pi}{16} \times 60 \times d_o^3 \left(1 - 0.6^4\right)$$

$$\Rightarrow \quad d_o = \left[\frac{58337.521 \times 1000 \times 16}{\pi \times 60\left(1 - 0.6^4\right)}\right]^{\frac{1}{3}} = \left(\frac{9.334 \times 10^8}{164.06653}\right)^{\frac{1}{3}}$$

$$d_o = 178.52 \text{ mm}$$

Check: For this value of d_o, twist over 3 m length:

$$\theta_1 = \frac{T \times l}{J \times C} = \frac{58337.521 \times 1000 \times 3000}{\frac{\pi}{32}(d_o)^4(1-0.6^4) \times 8 \times 10^4}$$

$$= \frac{58337.521 \times 1000 \times 3000}{\frac{\pi}{32}(178.52)^4(1-0.6^4) \times 8 \times 10^4}$$

$$= 0.0252 \text{ rad}$$

$$= 1.44°$$

$\because \frac{T}{J} = \frac{C\theta}{l}$

$J = \frac{\pi}{32}d_o^4 - d_i^4$

$= \frac{\pi}{32}d_o^4(1-K^4)$

$K = \frac{d_i}{d_o} = \frac{3}{5}$

$= 0.6$

$\because \quad \theta_1 > \theta \quad$ i.e. $1.44° > 1°$

Twist 1.44° is more than the allowable limit

Hence, d_o = 178.52 mm is not safe diameter

$\therefore \quad d \neq 178.52$ mm

Case II: Design of shaft on the basis of stiffness:

$$\therefore \quad \frac{T}{J} = \frac{C\theta}{l} \Rightarrow \frac{58337.521 \times 1000}{\frac{\pi}{32}d_o^4(1-K^4)} = \frac{8 \times \cancel{10^4} \times \pi}{3\cancel{000} \times 18\cancel{0}}$$

$$\Rightarrow \frac{58337.521 \times 1000 \times 32}{\pi\, d_o^4(1-0.6^4)} = \frac{8 \times \pi}{54}$$

$$\frac{6.82698 \times 10^8}{d_o^4} = 0.4654211$$

$$\Rightarrow \quad d_o^4 = \left(\frac{6.82698 \times 10^8}{0.4654211}\right)$$

$$d_o^4 = 1.46684 \times 10^9$$

$$\Rightarrow \quad d_o = (1.46684 \times 10^9)^{\frac{1}{4}} = 195.7 \text{ mm}$$

$$d_o = 195.7 \text{ mm}$$

Check: For d = 195.7 mm, maximum shear stress induced will be

$$T_{max} = \frac{\pi}{16}\tau_2 d_o^3(1-K^4)$$

$$58337.521 \times 1000 = \frac{\pi}{16}\tau_2 \times (195.7)^3(1-0.6^4)$$

$$\tau_2 = 45.54 \text{ N/mm}^2$$

which is less than the allowable shear stress of 60 N/mm².

$\therefore$ Safe value of outer dia.

d = **195.7 mm** **Ans.**

20.4 Strength of Shaft

Strength of shaft means the maximum torque or maximum power the shaft can transmit (T).

20.5 Torsional Rigidity

Torsional rigidity or stiffness of the shaft is defined as the product of modulus of rigidity (C) and polar moment of Inertia (J) of the shaft.

Torsional rigidity can also be defined as the torque required to produce a twist of one radian per unit length of the shaft.

From torsion equation $\frac{T}{J} = \frac{\tau}{r} = \frac{C \cdot \theta}{l}$

Torsional rigidity $= C \times J = \frac{T \times l}{\theta}$

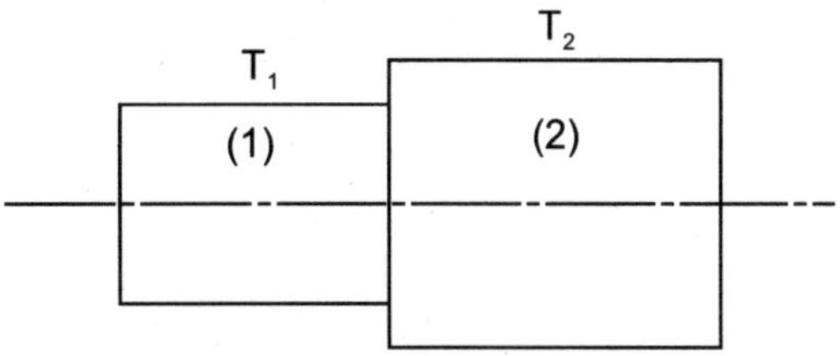

Fig. 20.5: Shafts in Series

20.6 Shaft Connected in Series

Strength of shaft

T = Minimum torque transmitted by a individual section

= Minimum of T_1 and T_2

$\theta = \theta_1 + \theta_2$

20.7 Shaft Connected in Parallel

$T = T_1 + T_2$

$\theta = \theta_1 = \theta_2$

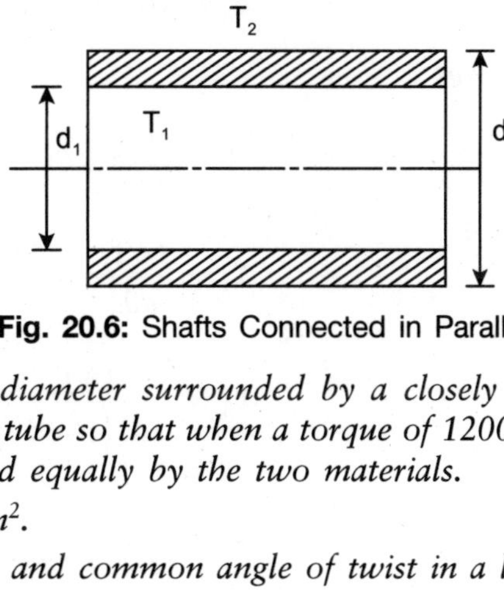

Fig. 20.6: Shafts Connected in Parallel

Example 20.12

A composite shaft consists of steel rod of 80 mm diameter surrounded by a closely fitted tube of aluminium. Calculate outside diameter of the tube so that when a torque of 1200 N.m is applied to the composite shaft, if it will be shared equally by the two materials.

Take $C_s = 0.8 \times 10^5$ *N/mm²*, $C_a = 0.4 \times 10^5$ *N/mm²*.

Find also maximum shear stress in each material and common angle of twist in a length of 4 m.

Solution:

$d_s = 80$ mm

$d_o = ?$

$T = 1200$ N.m

$T_s = T_a = 600$ N.m

$C_s = 0.8 \times 10^5$ N/mm^2

$C_a = 0.4 \times 10^5$ N/mm^2

$\tau_s = ?$

$\tau_a = ?$

$\theta = ?$

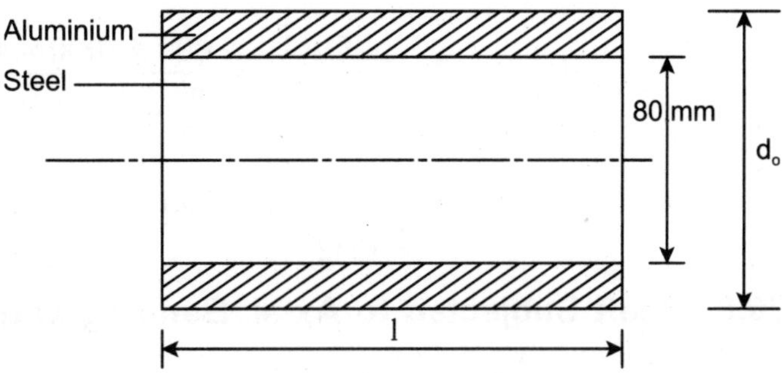

Fig. 20.7

The shafts are connected in parallel

$$T = T_s + T_a \text{ and } \theta = \theta_s = \theta_a$$

From torsion equation $\frac{T}{J} = \frac{\tau}{r} = \frac{C\cdot\theta}{l}$

$$\Rightarrow \quad \theta = \frac{T \times l}{C \times J}$$

$$\theta_s = \theta_a \Rightarrow \frac{T_s \times l_s}{C_s \times J_s} = \frac{T_a \times l_a}{C_a \times J_a}; \qquad T_s = T_a \text{ and } l_s = l_a$$

$$\Rightarrow \quad C_s \cdot J_s = C_a \cdot J_a$$

$$\Rightarrow \quad 0.8 \times 10^5 \times \frac{\pi}{32} d^4 = 0.4 \times 10^5 \times \frac{\pi}{32}\left(d_o^{\,4} - d_i^{\,4}\right)$$

$$\Rightarrow \quad 2 \times (80)^4 = \left(d_o^{\,4} - 80^4\right)$$

$$\Rightarrow \quad d_o = \mathbf{105.3\ mm}$$ **Ans.**

IInd Part

$$T = \frac{\pi}{16} \tau d_o^{\,3} \Rightarrow \tau = \frac{16T}{\pi d^3}$$

$$\therefore \quad \tau_s = \frac{16T_s}{\pi d^3} = \frac{16 \times 600 \times 1000}{\pi (80)^3} = \mathbf{5.96\ N/mm^2}$$ **Ans.**

$$\therefore \quad \tau_a = \frac{16T_a}{\pi d_o^3 \left(1 - K^4\right)} = \frac{16 \times 600 \times 1000}{\pi \times (105.3)^3 \left[1 - \left(\frac{80}{105.3}\right)^4\right]}$$

$$\tau_a = \mathbf{3.92\ N/mm^2}$$ **Ans.**

IIIrd Part, $\theta = ?$

$$\theta = \theta_s = \theta_a = \frac{T_s \times l}{J_s \times C_s} = \frac{600 \times 1000 \times 4000}{\frac{\pi}{32}(80)^4 \times 0.8 \times 10^5}$$

$$\theta = 7.46 \times 10^{-3} \text{ rad}$$
$$= \mathbf{0.42^\circ}$$ **Ans.**

20.8 Shaft Subjected to Axial, Bending and Torsional Stresses

Direct stress $\sigma_o = \sigma_d = \frac{P}{A} = \frac{4P}{\pi d^2}$

Bending stress $\sigma_b = \frac{M}{I} \times y;$ $\frac{M}{I} = \frac{\sigma_b}{y} = \frac{E}{R} \Rightarrow$ Bending equation

$$= \frac{32\,M}{\pi d^3}$$

Shear stress $\tau = \frac{T}{J} \times r;$ $\frac{T}{J} = \frac{\tau}{r} = \frac{C \cdot \theta}{l} \Rightarrow$ Torsion equation

$$= \frac{16\,T}{\pi d^3}$$

Principal stresses are:

$$\sigma_{1,2} = \frac{1}{2}\left(\sigma_x + \sigma_y\right) \pm \frac{1}{2}\sqrt{\left(\sigma_x - \sigma_y\right)^2 + 4q^2}$$

$$= \frac{1}{2}\left(\sigma_o + \sigma_b\right) \pm \frac{1}{2}\sqrt{\left(\sigma_o - \sigma_b\right)^2 + 4\tau^2}$$

$$= \frac{1}{2}\left(\frac{4P}{\pi d^2} + \frac{32M}{\pi d^3}\right) \pm \frac{1}{2}\sqrt{\left(\frac{4P}{\pi d^2} - \frac{32M}{\pi d^3}\right)^2 + 4\left(\frac{16\,T}{\pi d^3}\right)^2}$$

$$\sigma_{1,2} = \frac{16}{\pi d^3}\left[\left(\frac{P \cdot d}{8} + M\right)\right] \pm \frac{1}{2}\sqrt{\left(\frac{P \cdot d}{8} - M\right)^2 + T^2} \quad \ldots\ldots\ldots\ldots (20.12)$$

If P = 0 then

$$\sigma_{1,2} = \frac{16}{\pi d^3}\left(M \pm \sqrt{M^2 + T^2}\right) \quad \ldots\ldots\ldots\ldots (20.13)$$

and maximum shear stress

$$\tau_{max} = \frac{1}{2}\sqrt{\left(\sigma_x - \sigma_y\right)^2 + 4q^2}$$

$$= \frac{1}{2}\sqrt{\left(\sigma_o - \sigma_b\right)^2 + 4\tau^2}$$

$$= \frac{16}{\pi d^3}\sqrt{\left(\frac{P \cdot d}{8} - M\right)^2 + T^2} \quad \ldots\ldots\ldots\ldots (20.14)$$

If P = 0 then

$$\tau_{max} = \frac{16}{\pi d^3}\sqrt{M^2 + T^2} \quad \ldots\ldots\ldots\ldots (20.15)$$

$$\therefore \quad \tan 2\theta = \left(\frac{T}{M}\right)$$

For solid shaft:

$$\sigma_{1,2} = \frac{16}{\pi d^3}\left(M \pm \sqrt{M^2 + T^2}\right)$$

$$\tau_{max} = \frac{16}{\pi d^3}\sqrt{M^2 + T^2}$$

For hollow shaft:

$$\sigma_{1,2} = \frac{16\, d_o}{\pi\left(d_o^4 - d_i^4\right)}\left(M \pm \sqrt{M^2 + T^2}\right)$$

$$\tau_{max} = \frac{16\, d_o}{\pi\left(d_o^4 - d_i^4\right)}\sqrt{M^2 + T^2}$$

$$\sqrt{M^2 + T^2} = T_e = \text{Equivalent twisting moment} = \frac{\pi}{16}\tau d^3$$

$$Me = \frac{1}{2}\left(M + \sqrt{M^2 + T^2}\right) = \frac{\pi}{32}\sigma_b d^3 = \text{Equivalent bending moment.}$$

Example 20.13

A solid steel shaft transmits 1200 kW at 150 rpm, the maximum torque being 50% greater than the mean. The shaft is supported in ball bearings 1.6 m apart with a 8000 kg flywheel midway between bearings. Find shaft diameter if the maximum tensile stress is 70 MN/m².

Solution:

$p = 1200$ kW $= 1200 \times 10^3$ Watts

$N = 150$ rpm

$T = 1.5\ T_{mean}$

$d = ?$

$W = 8000$ kg

$\sigma_1 = 70$ MPa $= 70$ N/mm²

$l = 1.6$ m $= 1600$ mm

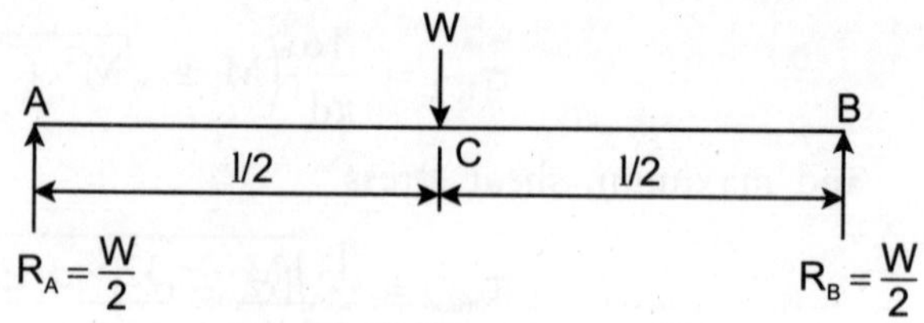

Fig. 20.8

Now

$$p = \frac{2\pi N T_{mean}}{60} \Rightarrow T_{mean} = \frac{1200 \times 10^3 \times 60}{2\pi \times 150}\ \text{N.m}$$

$$T_{mean} = 76394.37\ \text{N.m}$$

$$T = 1.5 \times 76394.37 = 114591.56\ \text{N.m}$$

M = Maximum B.M. on the whole span.

$= M_c$

$$= \frac{W}{2} \times \frac{l}{2} = \frac{W \cdot l}{4} = \frac{80000 \times 9.81 \times 1.6}{4} = 313920\ \text{N.m}$$

We know that

$$\sigma_1 = \frac{16}{\pi d^3}\left(M \pm \sqrt{M^2 + T^2}\right)$$

$$\Rightarrow \quad 70 = \frac{16}{\pi d^3}\left[313920 \times 10^3 \pm \sqrt{\left(313920 \times 10^3\right)^2 + \left(114591.56 \times 10^3\right)^2}\right]$$

$$70 = \frac{16}{\pi d^3}\left[3.139 \times 10^8 + 3.34 \times 10^8\right]$$

$$\Rightarrow \quad d = (47153595)^{\frac{1}{3}} = 361.3 \text{ mm}$$

$$d = \mathbf{362\ mm}$$ **Ans.**

Example 20.14

A shaft is subjected to a bending moment of 500 N.m and a torque 400 N.m. The shaft diameter is 80 mm. Calculate (a) The maximum normal stress on a section perpendicular to the axis. (b) The maximum shear stress on a section perpendicular to the axis. (c) The principal stresses. (d) Maximum shear stress.

Solution:

$M = 500 \text{ N.m} = 5 \times 10^5 \text{ N.mm}$

$T = 400 \text{ N.m} = 4 \times 10^5 \text{ N.mm}$

$d = 80 \text{ mm}$

$\sigma_b = ?$

$\tau = ?$

$\sigma_1 = ?$

$\sigma_2 = ?$

$\tau_{max} = ?$

(a) Bending stress $\sigma_b = \frac{32M}{\pi d^3} = \frac{32 \times 5 \times 10^5}{\pi \times (80)^3} = \mathbf{9.94\ N/mm^2}$ **Ans.**

(b) Shear stress $\tau = \frac{16T}{\pi d^3} = \frac{16 \times 4 \times 10^5}{\pi \times (80)^3} = \mathbf{3.98\ N/mm^2}$ **Ans.**

(c)

$$\sigma_{1,2} = \frac{16}{\pi d^3}\left[M \pm \sqrt{M^2 + T^2}\right]$$

$$= \frac{16}{\pi (80)^3}\left[5 \times 10^5 \pm \sqrt{\left(5 \times 10^5\right) + \left(4 \times 10^5\right)^2}\right]$$

$$= \frac{16}{\pi (80)^3}\left[5 + 10^5 \pm 6.4 \times 10^5\right]$$

$$\therefore \qquad \sigma_1 = \frac{16 \times 10^5}{\pi(80)^3}[5 + 6.4] = \mathbf{11.3\ N/mm^2} \qquad \textbf{Ans.}$$

$$\sigma_2 = \frac{16 \times 10^5}{\pi(80)^3}[5 - 6.4] = \mathbf{-1.4\ N/mm^2} \qquad \textbf{Ans.}$$

$$\text{(d)} \qquad \tau_{max} = \frac{\sigma_1 - \sigma_2}{2} = \frac{11.3 - (-1.4)}{2} = \mathbf{6.4\ N/mm^2} \qquad \textbf{Ans.}$$

Example 20.15

Prove that the stain energy stored in a body due to torsion is given by:

$$U = \frac{q^2}{4C} \times V$$

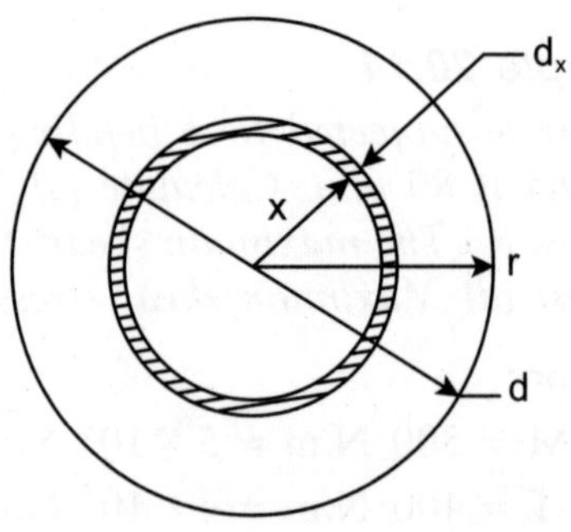

Fig. 20.9

Solution:

Let d — Diameter of shaft

l — Length of shaft

τ or q — Shear stress on surface of shaft

C → Shear modulus

U — Total strain energy

Now

We know that shear stress due to torsion at a radius x from the centre is given by

$$\tau_x = \frac{\tau}{r}\cdot x$$

Area of elementary ring, $dA = 2\pi x\,dx$

Volume of the ring, $dV = dA\cdot l = 2\pi x\,dx\cdot l$

Also, we know that shear strain energy is given by:

$$\text{Shear strain energy} = \frac{(\text{Shear stress})^2}{2\,C} \times \text{Volume}$$

$\therefore$ Shear strain energy in the ring

$$d_u = \frac{\left(\frac{\tau}{r}\cdot x\right)^2 \times 2\pi x\cdot l dx}{2\,C} = \frac{\tau^2\cdot 2\pi x^3\cdot l dx}{2\,C\cdot r^2}$$

$\therefore$ Total strain energy stored in the shaft

$$U = \int_0^r d_u = \int_0^r \frac{\tau^2\cdot 2\pi x^3\cdot l dx}{2C\cdot r^2}$$

$$= \frac{\tau^2 \cdot 2\pi \cdot l dx}{2C \cdot r^2} \cdot \int_0^r x^3 dx$$

$$U = \frac{\tau^2 \cdot l}{2Cr^2} \cdot \int_0^r 2\pi x \cdot dx \cdot x^2$$

$$= \frac{\tau^2 \cdot l}{2Cr^2} \cdot \int_0^r dA \cdot x^2$$

| $dA = 2\pi x dx$

$\int_0^r dA \cdot x^2 = J$

$$U = \frac{\tau^2 \cdot l}{2Cr^2} \cdot J \quad \ldots\ldots\ldots\ldots\ldots\ldots\ldots\ldots\ldots\ldots \quad (20.16)$$

$$= \frac{\tau^2 \cdot l}{2Cr^2} \cdot \frac{\pi}{32}(2r)^4 = \frac{\tau^2 \cdot l}{2Cr^2} \cdot \frac{\pi}{32} 16 \cdot r^4$$

$$= \frac{\tau^2}{4C} \times l \times \pi r^2 = \frac{\tau^2}{4C} \times l \times A$$

For solid shaft

$$U_s = \frac{\tau^2}{4C} \times \text{Volume}$$

Total Strain energy in hollow shaft due to torsion:

We know that total strain energy in a shaft due to torsion

$$U = \frac{\tau^2 \cdot l}{2C r_o^2} \cdot J \qquad \text{| from Eq. (20.16)}$$

$$= \frac{\tau^2 \cdot l}{2C r_o^2} \cdot \frac{\pi}{32}\left(d_o^4 - d_i^4\right)$$

$$= \frac{\tau^2 \cdot l}{2C r_o^2} \cdot \frac{\pi}{32}\left(d_o^2 + d_i^2\right)\left(d_o^2 - d_i^2\right)$$

$$= \frac{\tau^2 \cdot l}{2C\left(\frac{d_o}{2}\right)^2} \cdot \frac{\pi}{32}\left(d_o^2 + d_i^2\right)\left(d_o^2 - d_i^2\right)$$

$$= \frac{\tau^2 \cdot \not{4} l}{2C \cdot d_o^2} \cdot \frac{\pi}{\not{4}}\left(d_o^2 - d_i^2\right) \cdot \left(\frac{d_o^2 + d_i^2}{8}\right)$$

$$= \frac{\tau^2}{4C} \cdot l \frac{\pi}{4}\left(d_o^2 - d_i^2\right) \cdot \left(\frac{d_o^2 + d_i^2}{d_o^2}\right)$$

$$= \frac{\tau^2}{4C} \times V \times \left(\frac{d_o^2 + d_i^2}{d_o^2}\right)$$

For hollow shaft

$$\therefore \quad U_H = \frac{\tau^2}{4C} \times V \times \left(\frac{d_o^2 + d_i^2}{d_o^2} \right)$$

Example 20.16

Determine the maximum strain energy stored in a solid shaft of diameter 100 mm and of length 1.25 m, if the maximum allowable shear stress is 50 MN/m². Take C = 8 × 10⁴ N/mm².

Solution:

$U = ?$

$d = 10 \text{ cm} = 100 \text{ mm}$

$l = 1.25 \text{ m} = 1250 \text{ mm}$

$\tau = 50 \text{ N/mm}^2$

$C = 8 \times 10^4 \text{ N/mm}^2$

We know that strain energy stored in a solid shaft due to torsion

$$U = \frac{\tau^2}{4C} \times \text{Volume}$$

$$\therefore \quad U = \frac{\tau^2}{4C} \times A \times l = \frac{(50)^2}{4 \times 8 \times 10^4} \times \frac{\pi}{4}(100)^2 \times 1250 \text{ N.mm}$$

$$= \frac{50 \times 50 \times \pi \times 1250}{32 \times 4}$$

$$= 76699.04 \text{ N.mm}$$

$$\therefore \quad \mathbf{U = 76.699 \text{ N.m}}$$ **Ans.**

NUMERICAL QUESTIONS

1. A hollow shaft is 50 mm outside diameter and 30 mm internal diameter. An applied torque of 1.6 kN.m is found to produce an angular twist of 0.4°, measured on a length of 0.2 m of the shaft. Calculate the value of the modulus of rigidity. Calculate also the maximum power which could be transmitted by the shaft at 2000 rpm, if the maximum allowable shearing stress is 65 MPa.
2. A solid alloy shaft 50 mm diameter is to be coupled in series with a hollow steel shaft of the same external diameter. Find the internal diameter of the steel shaft if the angle of twist per unit length is to be 75% of that of the alloy shaft.

   Determine the speed at which the shafts are to be driven to transmit 200 kW if the limit of shearing stresses are to be 55 and 80 MPa in the alloy and steel respectively. Take G_{Steel} = 2.2 times Galloy.
3. A hollow steel shaft of 400 mm outer diameter is running at 120 rpm and transmitted 9 MW power. Find the internal diameter and the maximum shear stress induced if the twist over a length of 2 m is observed to be 0.45. Take $G = 0.8 \times 10^5$ N/mm^2.
4. A hollow steel shaft transmits 600 kW at 180 rpm. If the internal and external diameters of the shaft are 125 mm and 200 mm respectively, find the shear stress at the outer and inner radii. Take $G = 0.84 \times 10^5$ N/mm^2.
5. A solid cylindrical shaft 50 mm diameter and 1.5 m long, is passed through the centre of a hollow cylindrical shaft of the same material 1.5 m long, 55 mm and 75 mm inner and outer diameters. The ends of the two shafts are rigidly joined with the shafts concentric. The composite shaft so formed is used to transmit 375 kW at a speed of 600 rpm. Find maximum and minimum stress in the two shafts.
6. A hollow shaft, inter diameter is 40% of the outer diameter, transmits 50 kW at 150 rpm. Find outer diameter of the shaft if shear stress is not to exceed 50 MPa and twist in a length of 3 m should not exceed 1.5°. The maximum torque exceeds the mean by 25% in each revolution. Take $C = 0.9 \times 10^5$ N/mm^2.
7. A hollow shaft is 1 m long and has external diameter 60 mm and has internal diameter 25 mm for a part of length and 30 mm internal diameter for the rest of the length. The maximum shear stress is not to exceed 70 MN/m^2. Calculate the maximum power transmitted by it at a speed of 200 rpm. Assume the twist produced in the two portions of the shafts are equal, find the length of the two portions.
8. A solid steel shaft of 50 mm diameter rotates at 250 rev./min. Find maximum power transmitted by the shaft if the allowable shear stress is not to exceed 60 MN/m^2.
9. Calculate the dimensions of a hollow shaft which transmits 1000 kW at a speed of 500 rpm and maximum torque exceeds the mean by 20% and the greatest intensity of shear stress is limited to 80 MN/m^2. The internal diameter of the shaft is 70% of the external diameter.
10. A hollow shaft is subjected to a torque of 0.25 MN.m. The ratio of inside and outside diameters is 1/3 and shear due to torque is limited to 60 MPa. Find diameters and angle of twist per meter length of the shaft.

11. A circular bar 4 m long, external radius 30 mm is solid over half its length and bored to an internal radius of 15 mm over the other half. A torque 200 N.m is applied at the centre of the shaft, the two ends being fixed. Find maximum shear stress setup in the surface of the shaft and work done by the torque in producing this stress.
12. Calculate the maximum diameter of a solid shaft which transmits 70 kW at 600 rpm if the shear stress is not to exceed 75 MN/m^2. If a bending moment of 300 N.m is now applied to the shaft, find the speed at which the shaft must be driven in order to transmit the same horse power for the same value of maximum shear stress.
13. A solid circular steel shaft is subjected to a bending moment of 10 kN.m and is required to transmit a maximum power of 50 MW at 420 rpm. Assuming the shaft to be simply supported at each end and neglecting the shaft weight, determine the ratio of maximum principal stress to the maximum shear stress induced in the shaft material.
14. A certain section of a shaft of 100 mm diameter, there is a twisting moment of 750 kN.m and a bending moment of 500 kN.m Find the principal stresses induced in the section and specify the plane on which they act.
15. A composite shaft consists of aluminium rod of 40 mm diameter enclosed in a steel tube of 50 mm external diameter and 10 mm thick. The shaft transmits a torque of 800 N.m. Calculate shear stress induced in aluminium and steel if both the shafts have equal lengths and their twist are equal. Take $C_s = 2C_a$.
16. 600 mm and 300 mm are outside and inside diameters of a hollow shaft. Find the maximum strain energy stored in the shaft, if maximum allowable shear stress is 60 MPa and length of shaft is 6 m. Take $C = 0.8 \times 10^5$ N/mm^2.
17. The outside diameter is twice the internal diameter and maximum allowable shear stress is 100 MPa. Find suitable diameter of shaft if it is subjected to a twisting moment (torque) of 5×10^6 N.mm and a bending moment of 3×10^6 mm.
18. A solid shaft of 40 mm diameter and is subjected to a torque of 800 N.m. Find the maximum shearing stress induced in the shaft.

21

Centre of Gravity

21.1 Centre of Gravity

It is a point through which the whole weight of the body acts. It may or may not be located within the body and its position depends upon the shape of the body. It is represented by G.

21.2 Centroid

It is defined as the centre of gravity of a plane figure where its entire area is concentrated. It is also represented by G. The centroid or centre of gravity are at the same point.

For an area A, having three elemental areas a_1, a_2 and a_3.

$\bar{x}$ = distance of centroid of area A from y-axis.

or
$$\bar{x} = \frac{a_1x_1 + a_2x_2 + a_3x_3}{a_1 + a_2 + a_3} = \frac{\sum_{i=1}^{n} a_i x_i}{\sum_{i=1}^{n} a_i}$$

where $A = a_1 + a_2 + a_3$

x_1, x_2, x_3 = Distances of centroids of the elemental areas from y-axis.

Similarly,

$\bar{y}$ = Distance of centroid of area A from x-axis

$$= \frac{a_1y_1 + a_2y_2 + a_3y_3}{a_1 + a_2 + a_3} = \frac{\sum_{i=1}^{n} a_i y_i}{\sum_{i=1}^{n} a_i}$$

where y_1, y_2 and y_3 = Distances of centroids of the elemental areas from x-axis.

$\bar{x}$ and $\bar{y}$ taken together give the position of the centroid of the area A w.r.t. x-y co-ordinate system.

If in place of area, mass is considered, then

$$\bar{x} = \frac{m_1x_1 + m_2x_2 + m_3x_3 + ...}{m_1 + m_2 + m_3 + ...} = \frac{\sum_{i=1}^{n} m_i x_i}{\sum_{i=1}^{n} m_i}$$

and

$$\bar{y} = \frac{m_1y_1 + m_2y_2 + m_3y_3 + ...}{m_1 + m_2 + m_3 + ...} = \frac{\sum_{i=1}^{n} m_i y_i}{\sum_{i=1}^{n} m_i}$$

If the density of the materials are same, then

$$\bar{x} = \frac{V_1x_1 + V_2x_2 + V_3x_3 + ...}{V_1 + V_2 + V_3 + ...} = \frac{\sum_{i=1}^{n} V_i x_i}{\sum_{i=1}^{n} V_i}$$

and

$$\bar{y} = \frac{V_1y_1 + V_2y_2 + V_3y_3 + ...}{V_1 + V_2 + V_3 + ...} = \frac{\sum_{i=1}^{n} V_i y_i}{\sum_{i=1}^{n} V_i}$$

If small area are represented by dA instead of 'a', then

$$\bar{x} = \frac{\int x^* dA}{\int dA} \quad \text{and} \quad \bar{y} = \frac{\int y^* dA}{\int dA}$$

where x^*, y^* = Co-ordinates of C.G. of dA area.

21.3 Centroid of Plane Geometrical Figures

(1) Rectangle:

$$\bar{x} = \frac{b}{2}$$

$$\bar{y} = \frac{h}{2}$$

$$A = b \cdot h$$

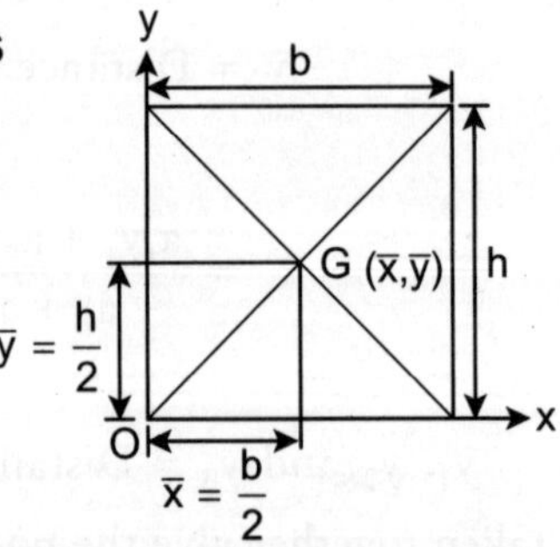

Fig. 21.1

(2) Triangle:

$$\bar{x} = \frac{b}{3}$$

$$\bar{y} = \frac{h}{3}$$

$$A = \frac{b \cdot h}{2}$$

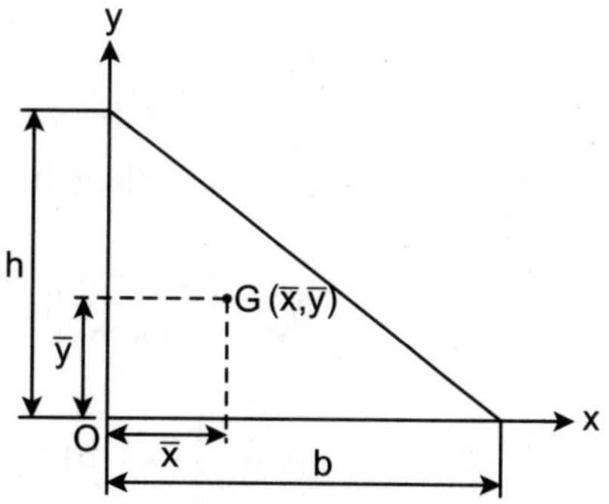

Fig. 21.2

(3) Circle:

$$\bar{x} = \frac{d}{2}$$

$$\bar{y} = \frac{d}{2}$$

$$A = \frac{\pi}{4} d^2$$

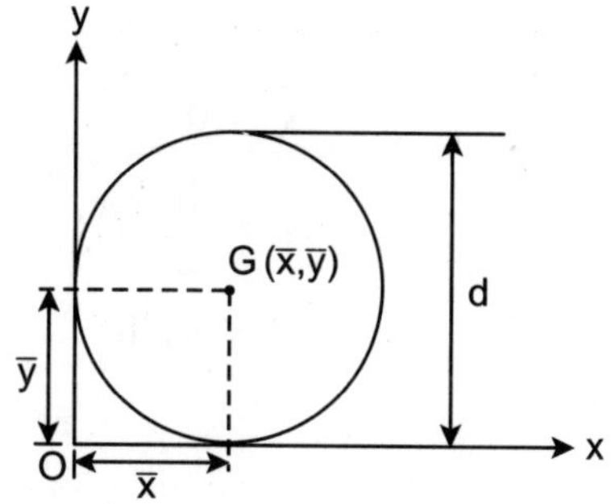

Fig. 21.3

(4) Semi Circle:

$$\bar{x} = \frac{d}{2} = r$$

$$\bar{y} = \frac{4r}{3\pi}$$

$$A = \frac{\pi r^2}{2}$$

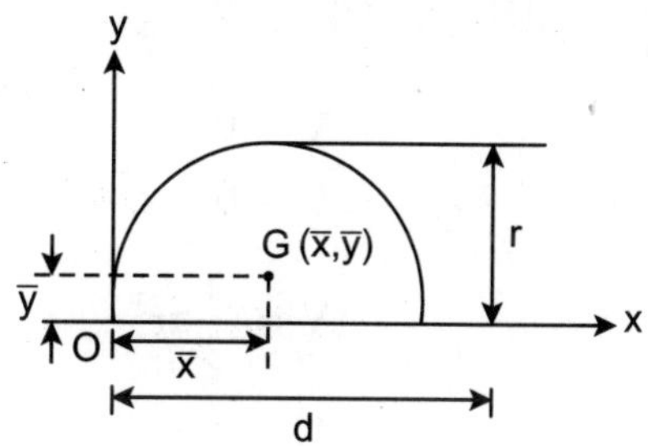

Fig. 21.4

(5) Quadrant of Circle:

$$\bar{x} = \frac{4r}{3\pi}$$

$$\bar{y} = \frac{4r}{3\pi}$$

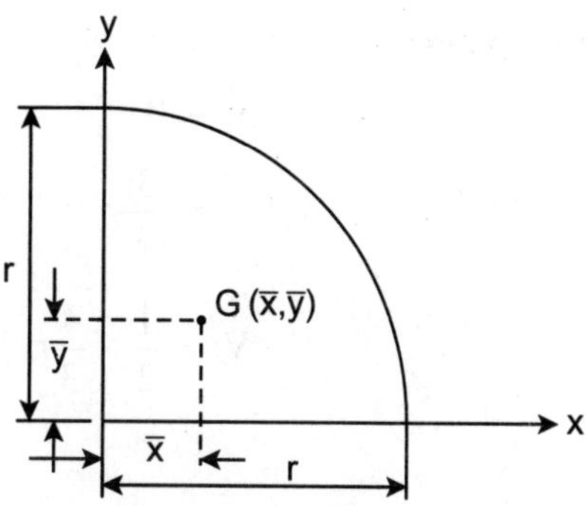

Fig. 21.5

(6) Trapezium:

$$\bar{x} = \frac{a^2 + b^2 + 2ab}{3(a + b)}$$

$$\bar{y} = \left(\frac{2a + b}{a + b}\right)\left(\frac{h}{3}\right)$$

$$A = \frac{1}{2}(a + b)h$$

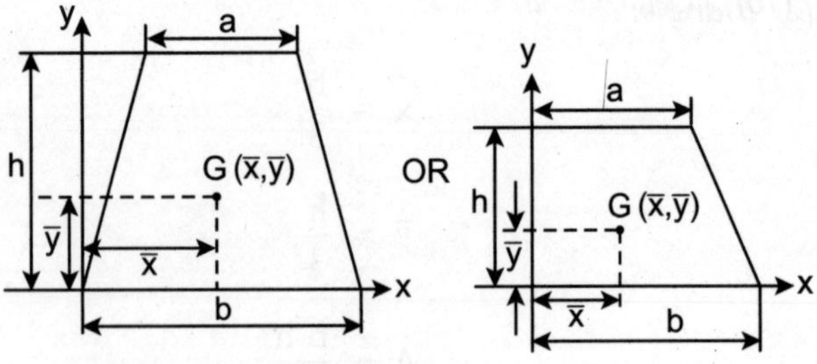

Fig. 21.6

(7) Cylinder:

$$\bar{x} = 0$$

$$\bar{y} = \frac{h}{2}$$

$$V = \pi r^2 h$$

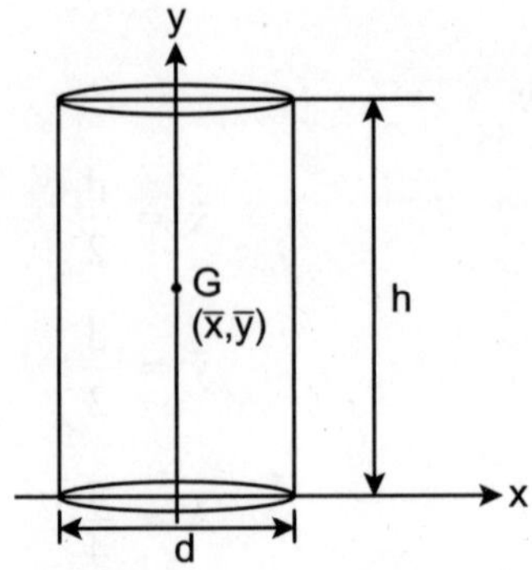

Fig. 21.7

(8) Sphere:

$$\bar{x} = 0$$

$$\bar{y} = 0$$

$$V = \frac{4}{3}\pi r^3$$

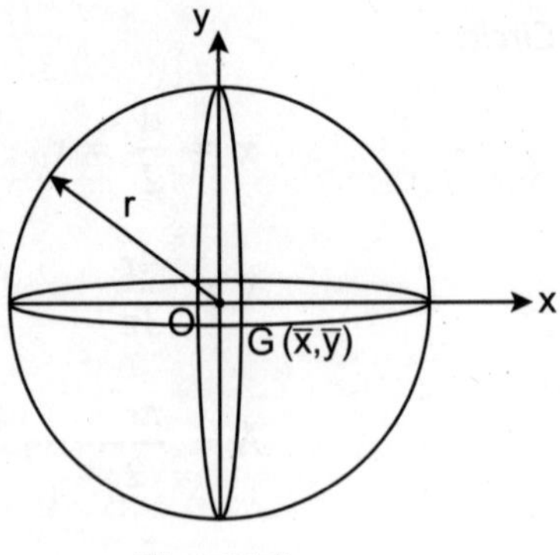

Fig. 21.8

(9) Hemi Sphere:

$$\bar{x} = 0$$

$$\bar{y} = \frac{3r}{8}$$

$$V = \frac{1}{2} \times \frac{4}{3}\pi r^3$$

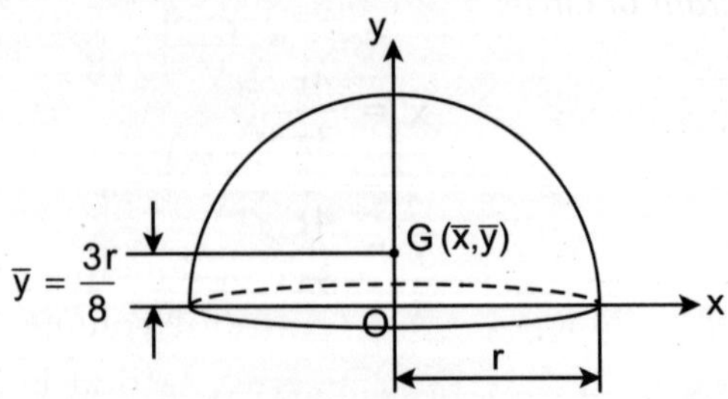

Fig. 21.9

(10) Right Circular Cone:

$$\bar{x} = 0$$

$$\bar{y} = \frac{h}{4}$$

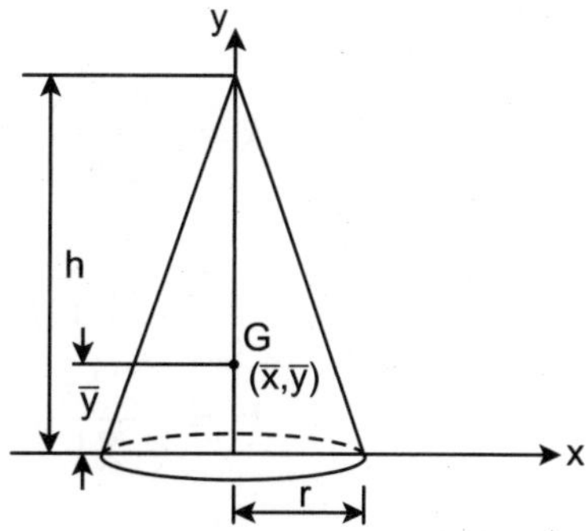

Fig. 21.10

(11) Rod:

$$\bar{x} = \frac{l}{2}$$

$$\bar{y} = \frac{d}{2}$$

$$V = \frac{\pi}{4} d^2 \times l$$

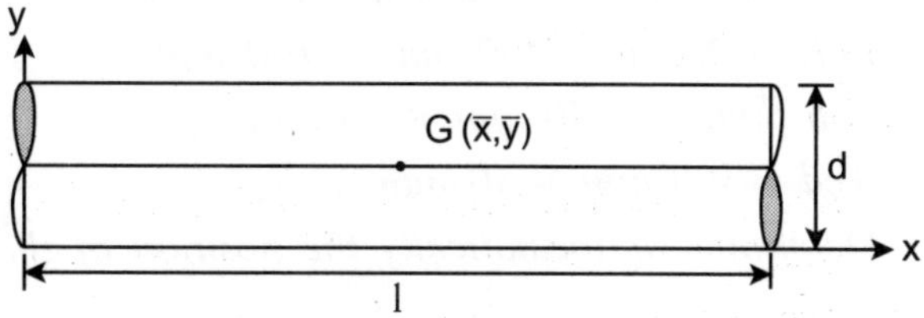

Fig. 21.11

Centre of Gravity (C.G.) of simple solids

$$\bar{x} = \left(\frac{\Sigma W \cdot x}{\Sigma W}\right)$$

$$\bar{y} = \left(\frac{\Sigma W \cdot y}{\Sigma W}\right)$$

$$\bar{z} = \left(\frac{\Sigma W \cdot z}{\Sigma W}\right)$$

If all members (or bodies) are of the same material having same density ρ then

$$W_1 = \rho V_1, \; W_2 = \rho V_2, \; W_3 = \rho V_3$$

$$\therefore \qquad \bar{x} = \frac{\Sigma \rho V x}{\Sigma \rho V} = \frac{\Sigma V \cdot x}{\Sigma V}$$

Similarly,

$$\bar{y} = \left(\frac{\Sigma V \cdot y}{\Sigma V}\right)$$

$$\bar{z} = \left(\frac{\Sigma V \cdot z}{\Sigma V}\right)$$

Thus, if the bodies are made of the same material and of the same density throughout, the C.G. of the bodies is their centre of volume.

If the bodies are of same cross section but perhaps of different lengths then

$$V_1 = al_1, \; V_2 = al_2, \; V_3 = al_3$$

Then

$$\bar{x} = \frac{\sum a \cdot l \cdot x}{\sum a \cdot l} = \left(\frac{\sum l \cdot x}{\sum l}\right)$$

$$\bar{y} = \left(\frac{\sum l \cdot y}{\sum l}\right)$$

$$\bar{z} = \left(\frac{\sum l \cdot z}{\sum l}\right)$$

Example 21.1

An I section has the following dimensions:

Bottom flange = 400 mm × 100 mm

Top flange = 250 mm × 50 mm

Wed = 500 mm × 50 mm

Determine mathematically the position of the centre of gravity of the section.

Solution:

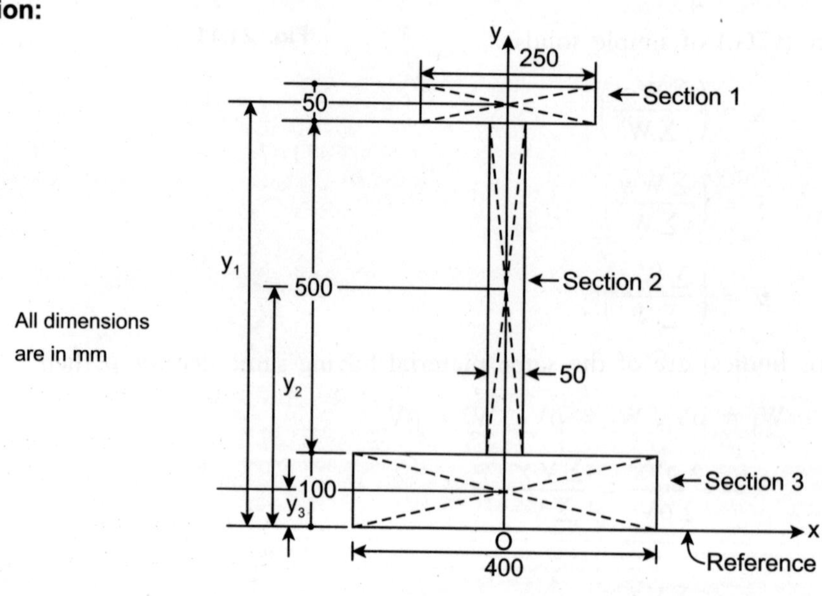

Fig. 21.12

Let co-ordinate of C.G. is $\bar{x}$ and $\bar{y}$ from reference axis Oy and Ox respectively.

Since give section is symmetrical about y–y axis.

So, C.G. will lie on y–y axis and $\bar{x} = 0$

and $a_1 = 250 \times 50 = 12500 \text{ mm}^2$

$a_2 = 500 \times 50 = 25000 \text{ mm}^2$

$a_3 = 400 \times 100 = 40000 \text{ mm}^2$

$$y_1 = 100 + 500 + \frac{50}{2} = 625 \text{ mm}$$

$$y_2 = 100 + \frac{500}{2} = 350 \text{ mm}$$

$$y_3 = \frac{100}{2} = 50 \text{ mm}$$

$$\therefore \quad \bar{y} = \frac{a_1 y_1 + a_2 y_2 + a_3 y_3}{a_1 + a_2 + a_3}$$

$$= \frac{12500 \times 625 + 25000 \times 350 + 40000 \times 50}{12500 + 25000 + 40000}$$

$$= \frac{7812500 + 8750000 + 2 \times 10^6}{77500}$$

$$= \frac{18562500}{77500} = 239.5 \text{ mm}$$

$\therefore \quad \bar{x} = 0$

$\bar{y} =$ **239.5 mm** **Ans.**

Example 21.2

Find the centre of gravity of a channel section 200 × 100 × 30 mm as shown in Fig. 21.13.

Solution

AB = 100 mm

AH = 30 mm

BC = 200 mm

KF = 30 mm

All dimensions are in mm

Ox and Oy are reference axis.

Now

$$a_1 = AB \times AH = 100 \times 30 = 3000 \text{ mm}^2$$

$$a_2 = JK \times KF = (200 - 60) \times 30$$

$$= 140 \times 30 = 4200 \text{ mm}^2$$

$$a_3 = a_1 = 3000 \text{ mm}^2$$

$\because$ The given section is symmetrical about x–x axis.

$\therefore \quad \bar{y} = 0$

and $\quad \bar{x} = \left(\dfrac{a_1 x_1 + a_2 x_2 + a_3 x_3}{a_1 + a_2 + a_3} \right)$

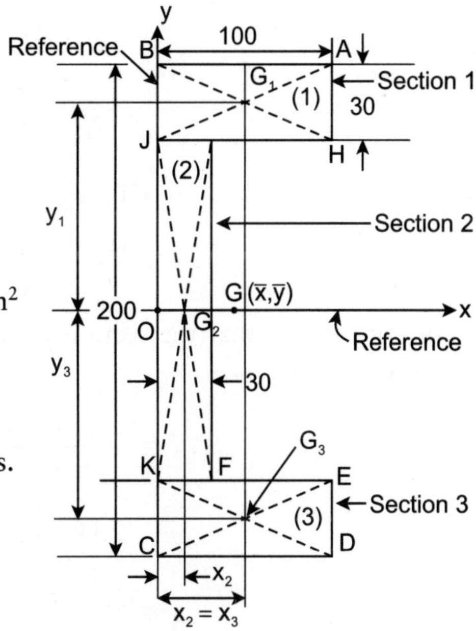

Fig. 21.13

$$= \frac{3000 \times 50 + 4200 \times 15 + 3000 \times 50}{3000 + 4200 + 3000}$$

$$= \frac{15 \times 10^4 + 63000 + 15 \times 10^4}{10200} = \frac{363000}{10200}$$

$$= 35.6 \text{ mm}$$

$\therefore$ $\bar{x} = \mathbf{35.6\ mm}$ **Ans.**

$\bar{y} = 0$

Example 21.3

Find the centre of the gravity of a 100 mm × 150 mm × 30 mm T section as shown in Fig. 21.14.

Solution:

Ox and Oy are reference axis.

$\because$ The given section is symmetrical about y–y axis.

$\therefore$ C.G. will lie on this y–y axis.

Dividing the figure into two sections.

Now

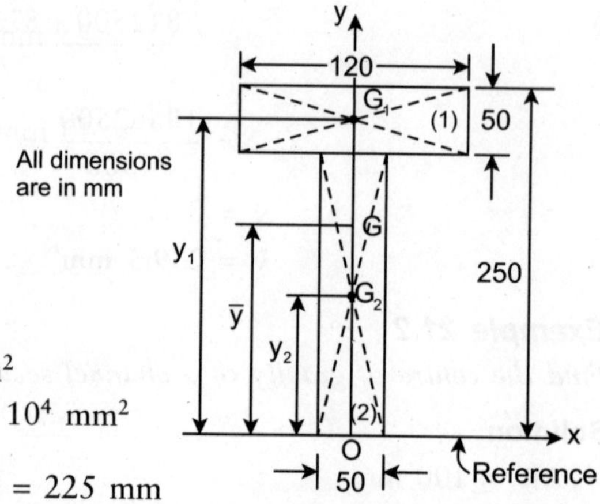

Fig. 21.14

$$a_1 = 120 \times 50 = 6000 \text{ mm}^2$$

$$a_2 = (250 - 50) \times 50 = 1 \times 10^4 \text{ mm}^2$$

$$y_1 = 250 - \frac{50}{2} = 250 - 25 = 225 \text{ mm}$$

$$y_2 = \frac{250 - 50}{2} = \frac{200}{2} = 100 \text{ mm}$$

$$x_1 = 0,\ x_2 = 0$$

$$\bar{x} = \frac{a_1 x_1 + a_2 x_2}{a_1 + a_2} = 0$$

or we can say that the section is symmetrical about y–y axis. Therefore, $\bar{x} = 0$

Now

$$\bar{y} = \frac{a_1 y_1 + a_2 y_2}{a_1 + a_2} = \left(\frac{6 \times 10^3 \times 225 + 1 \times 10^4 \times 100}{6 \times 10^3 + 1 \times 10^4} \right)$$

$$= \frac{235 \times 10^4}{16000} = 146.8 \text{ mm}$$

$\therefore$ $\bar{x} = 0$

$\bar{y} = \mathbf{146.8\ mm}$ **Ans.**

Example 21.4

Find out the centroid of an unequal angle section 200 mm × 80 mm × 50 mm.

Solution:

Ox and Oy are reference axis.

$$a_1 = 50 \times 150 = 7500 \text{ mm}^2$$

$$a_2 = 50 \times 80 = 4000 \text{ mm}^2$$

$$y_1 = 50 + \frac{150}{2} = 125 \text{ mm}$$

$$y_2 = \frac{50}{2} = 25 \text{ mm}$$

$$x_1 = \frac{50}{2} = 25 \text{ mm}$$

$$x_2 = \frac{80}{2} = 40 \text{ mm}$$

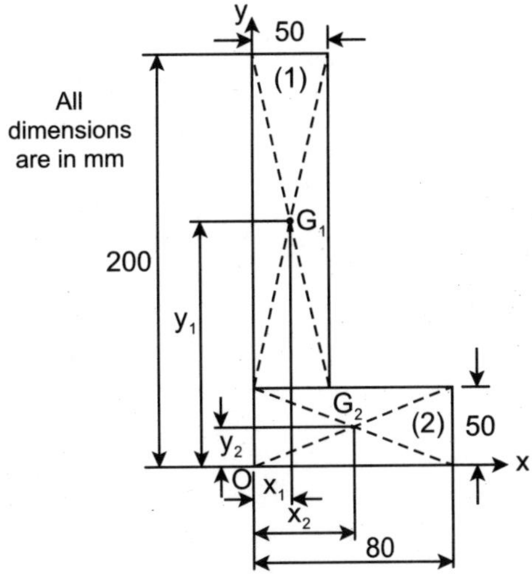

Fig. 21.15

Now

$$\bar{x} = \frac{a_1x_1 + a_2x_2}{a_1 + a_2} = \frac{7500 \times 25 + 4000 \times 40}{7500 + 4000} = \frac{347500}{11500}$$

$$= 30.2 \text{ mm}$$

$$\bar{y} = \frac{a_1x_1 + a_2x_2}{a_1 + a_2} = \frac{7500 \times 125 + 4000 \times 25}{11500} = 90.2 \text{ mm}$$

∴ $\bar{x}$ = **30.2 mm**, $\bar{y}$ = **90.2 mm** **Ans.**

Example 21.5

A uniform lamina is shown in Fig. 21.16. Determine the C.G. of the lamina.

Solution:

$$a_1 = (60 + 50) \times 70 = 7700 \text{ mm}^2$$

$$a_2 = \frac{\pi r^2}{2} = \pi \times \frac{35^2}{2} = 1924.2 \text{ mm}^2$$

$$a_3 = \frac{50 \times 50}{2} = 1250 \text{ mm}^2$$

$$x_1 = 35 + \frac{110}{2} = 90 \text{ mm}$$

$$x_2 = 35 - \frac{4r}{3\pi} = 35 - \frac{4 \times 35}{3\pi} = 20.1 \text{ mm}$$

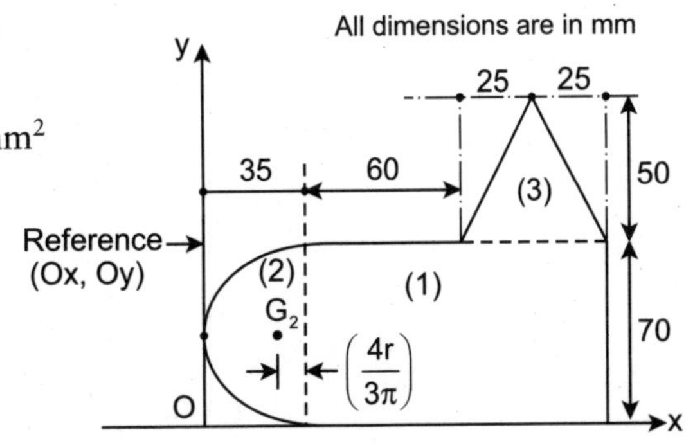

Fig. 21.16

$$x_3 = 35 + 60 + 25 = 120 \text{ mm}$$

$$y_1 = \frac{70}{2} = 35 \text{ mm}$$

$$y_2 = \frac{70}{2} = 35 \text{ mm}$$

$$y_3 = 70 + \frac{50}{3} = 86.7 \text{ mm}$$

Now

$$\bar{x} = \left(\frac{a_1x_1 + a_2x_2 + a_3x_3}{a_1 + a_2 + a_3}\right)$$

$$= \frac{7700 \times 90 + 1924.2 \times 20.1 + 1250 \times 120}{7700 + 1924.2 + 1250}$$

$$= \frac{881676.42}{10874.2} = \mathbf{81.1 \text{ mm}}$$ **Ans.**

$$\bar{y} = \frac{a_1y_1 + a_2y_2 + a_3y_3}{a_1 + a_2 + a_3}$$

$$= \frac{7700 \times 35 + 1924.2 \times 35 + 1250 \times 86.7}{10874.2}$$

$$= \mathbf{40.94 \text{ mm}}$$ **Ans.**

Example 21.6

Determine the co-ordinate of the C.G. of the area OAB shown in Fig. 21.17. If the curve OB represents the equation of a parabola, given by $y = Kx^2$ in which OA = 12 units and AB = 8 units.

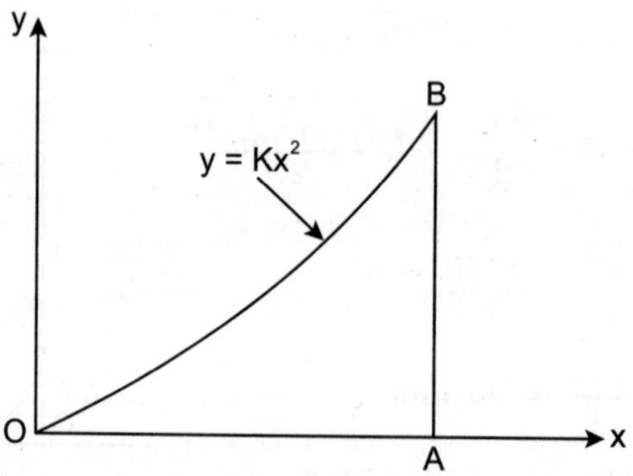

Fig. 21.17

Solution:

Let $\bar{x}$ and $\bar{y}$ are co-ordinates of C.G.

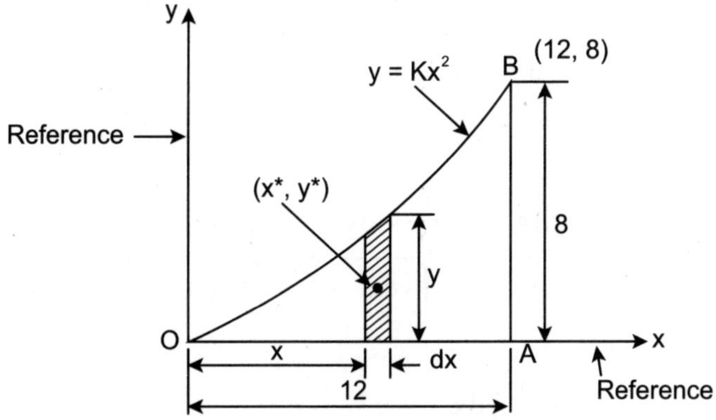

Fig. 21.18

Considering a small strip of height y and width dx.

Co-ordinate of C.G. of small strip are x*, y*.

$$\therefore \quad x^* = x + \frac{dx}{2} = x$$

$$y^* = \frac{y}{2}$$

Neglecting $\frac{dx}{2}$ being small quantity.

Area of small strips, $dA = y \cdot dx$

Co-ordinate of point B are (12, 8)

Point B is lying on curve parabola $y = Kx^2$

Substituting these values of point B in curve.

$$y = Kx^2$$

$$8 = K(12)^2$$

or $$K = \frac{1}{18}$$

$$\therefore \quad \bar{y} = \frac{x^2}{18}$$

or $$x^2 = 18\,y \text{ or } x = 3\sqrt{2y}$$

Now $$\bar{x} = \frac{\int x^* dA}{\int dA} = \frac{\int x \cdot y \cdot dx}{\int y dx} = \frac{\int_0^{12} x \cdot \frac{x^2}{18} dx}{\int_0^{12} \frac{x^2}{18} dx}$$

$$= \frac{\int_0^{12} x^3 dx}{\int_0^{12} x^2 dx} = \frac{\left[\frac{x^4}{4}\right]_0^{12}}{\left[\frac{x^3}{3}\right]_0^{12}} = 9$$

Similarly

$$\bar{y} = \frac{\int y^* dA}{\int dA} = \frac{\int \frac{y}{2} \cdot y \cdot dx}{\int y dx} = \frac{1}{2} \frac{\int y^2 dx}{\int y dx}$$

$$= \frac{1}{2} \frac{\int_0^{12} \frac{x^4}{324} dx}{\int_0^{12} \frac{x^2}{18} dx} = \frac{1}{2} \frac{\left[\frac{x^5}{1620}\right]_0^{12}}{\left[\frac{x^3}{54}\right]_0^{12}} = 2.4$$

$\therefore$ $\left.\begin{array}{l}\bar{x} = 9 \\ \bar{y} = 2.4\end{array}\right]$ **Ans.**

Example 21.7

Determine co-ordinate of C.G. of area OAB as shown in Fig. 21.19.

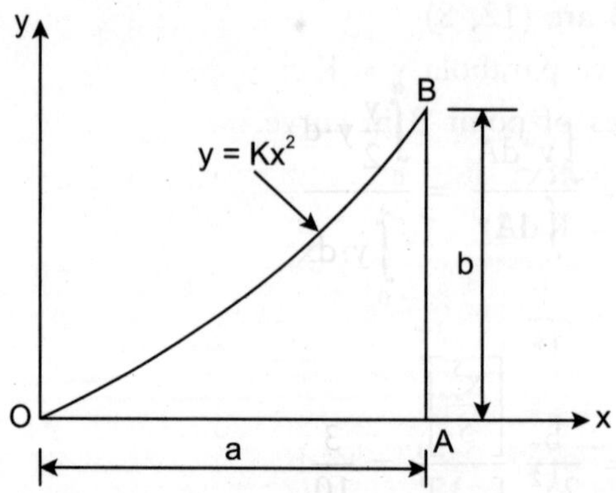

Fig. 21.19

Solution:

Let

$\bar{x}$, $\bar{y}$ are the co-ordinate of C.G. of area OAB

x^*, y^* are co-ordinate of small strip of height y and width dx.

$$\therefore \qquad x^* = x + \frac{dx}{2} = x$$

$$y^* = \frac{y}{2}$$

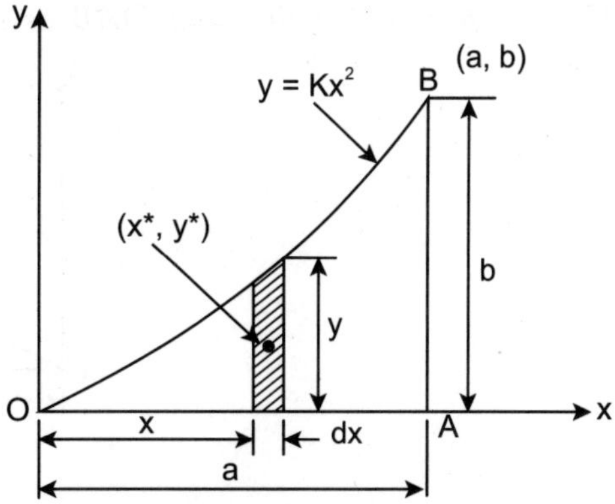

Fig. 21.20

Area of small strip, dA = y dx

Point B lies on parabola $y = Kx^2$

$$\therefore\ K = \left(\frac{b}{a^2}\right), \quad \therefore\ y = \frac{b}{a^2}x^2$$

Now

$$\bar{x} = \frac{\int x^* dA}{\int dA} = \frac{\int_0^a x \cdot y dx}{\int_0^a y dx} = \frac{\int x \cdot \frac{b}{a^2} x^2 dx}{\int_0^a \frac{b}{12} x^2 dx}$$

$$= \frac{\left[\frac{x^4}{4}\right]_0^a}{\left[\frac{x^3}{3}\right]_0^a} = \frac{3}{4}a$$

Similarly

$$\bar{y} = \frac{\int y^* dA}{\int dA} = \frac{\int_0^a \frac{y}{2} y \cdot dx}{\int_0^a y \cdot dx} = \frac{\int_0^a \frac{b^2}{2a^4} x^2 \cdot x^2\ dx}{\int_0^a \frac{b}{a^2} x^2 \cdot dx}$$

$$= \frac{b}{2a^2} \frac{\left[\frac{x^5}{5}\right]_0^a}{\left[\frac{x^3}{3}\right]_0^a} = \frac{3}{10}b$$

$$\therefore \qquad \left.\begin{aligned} \bar{x} &= \frac{3}{4}a \\ \bar{y} &= \frac{3}{10}b \end{aligned}\right]$$

Ans.

Example 21.8

Determine C.G. of the area OAB as shown in Fig. 21.21.

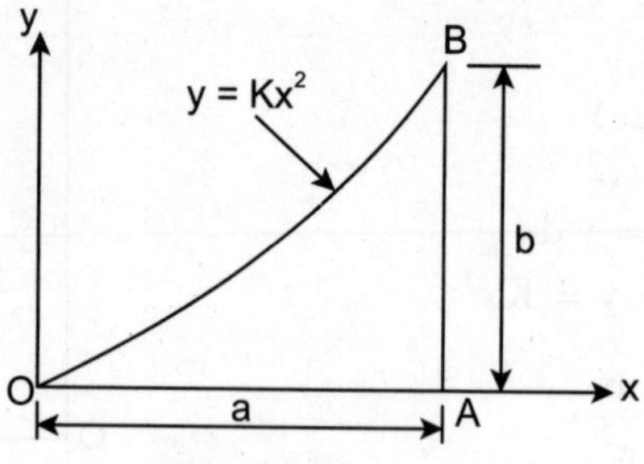

Fig. 21.21

Solution: ***(Alternate Solution)***

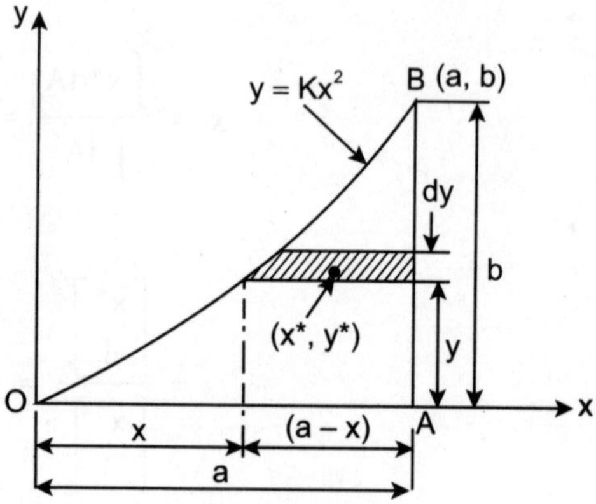

Fig. 21.22

Let $\bar{x}$, $\bar{y}$ are co-ordinates of C.G. of area OAB.

x^*, y^* are co-ordinate of small strip.

Point B will satisfy the curve $y = Kx^2$

$$\therefore \qquad b = a^2 \cdot K$$

$$\therefore \qquad K = \left(\frac{b}{a^2}\right) \quad \text{and} \quad y = \frac{b}{a^2}x^2$$

Considering a horizontal strip of length $(a - x)$ and width dy. Then

$dA = (a - x)dy$

Now

$$x^* = x + \frac{a - x}{2} = \left(\frac{a + x}{2}\right)$$

$$y^* = y + \frac{dy}{2} \equiv y = y$$

We know that

$$\bar{x} = \frac{\int x^* dA}{\int dA} = \frac{\int_0^b \left(\frac{a + x}{2}\right) \cdot (a - x)dy}{\int_0^b (a - x)dy}$$

$$= \frac{1}{2}\frac{\int_0^b (a^2 - x^2)dy}{\int_0^b (a - x)dy} = \frac{1}{2}\frac{\int_0^b \left(a^2 - \frac{a^2}{b}y\right)dy}{\int_0^b \left(a - \frac{a}{\sqrt{b}}\sqrt{y}\right)dy}$$

$$= \frac{1}{2}\frac{\left(a^2y - \frac{a^2}{2b}y^2\right)_0^b}{\left(ay - \frac{a}{\sqrt{b}}\cdot\frac{y^{\frac{3}{2}}}{\frac{3}{2}}\right)_0^b}$$

$$= \frac{1}{2}\frac{\left(a^2b - \frac{a^2}{2b}b^2\right)}{\left(ab - \frac{a}{\sqrt{b}}\cdot\frac{b^{\frac{3}{2}}}{\frac{3}{2}}\right)}$$

$$= \frac{\frac{1}{2}\left(a^2b - \frac{a^2b}{2}\right)}{\left(ab - a\cdot b\cdot\frac{2}{3}\right)} = \frac{1}{2}\frac{\frac{a^2b}{2}}{\frac{a\cdot b}{3}}$$

$\therefore$ $$\bar{x} = \frac{3}{4}a$$

and similarly

$$\bar{y} = \frac{\int y^* dA}{\int dA} = \frac{\int_0^b y(a-x)dy}{\int_0^b (a-x)dy} = \frac{\int_0^b y\left(a - \frac{a}{\sqrt{b}}\cdot\sqrt{y}\right)dy}{\int_0^b \left(a - \frac{a}{\sqrt{b}}\sqrt{y}\right)dy}$$

$$= \frac{\left(\frac{ay^2}{2} - \frac{a}{\sqrt{b}}\cdot\frac{y^{\frac{5}{2}}}{\frac{5}{2}}\right)_0^b}{\left(ay - \frac{a}{\sqrt{b}}\cdot\frac{y^{\frac{3}{2}}}{\frac{3}{2}}\right)_0^b} = \frac{3}{10}b$$

$\therefore$

$$\left.\begin{aligned}\bar{x} &= \left(\frac{3}{4}a\right)\\ \bar{y} &= \left(\frac{3}{10}b\right)\end{aligned}\right]$$

Ans.

Example 21.9

Determine the centroid of the lamina shown in Fig. 21.23.

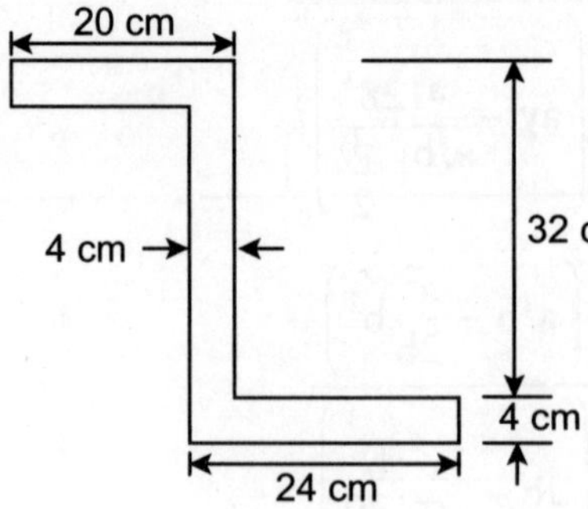

Fig. 21.23

Solution:

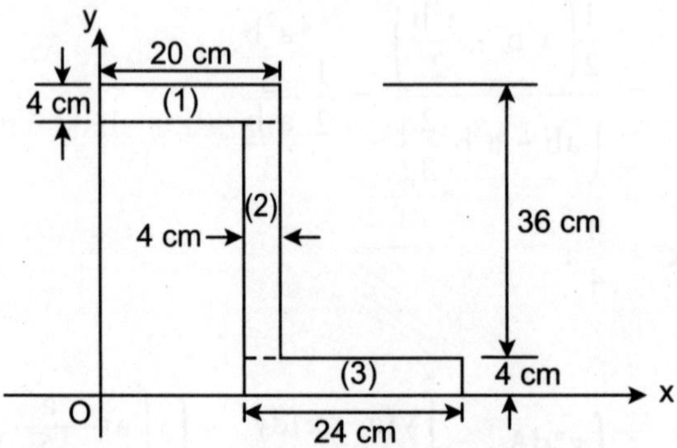

Fig. 21.24

Let $\bar{x}$, $\bar{y}$ → co-ordinates of centroid.

$$a_1 = 20 \times 4 = 80 \text{ cm}^2 \qquad x_1 = \frac{20}{2} = 10 \text{ cm}$$

$$a_2 = 32 \times 4 = 128 \text{ cm}^2 \qquad x_2 = 16 + \frac{4}{2} = 18 \text{ cm}$$

$$a_3 = 24 \times 4 = 96 \text{ cm}^2 \qquad x_3 = 16 + \frac{24}{2} = 28 \text{ cm}$$

and

$$y_1 = 4 + 32 + \frac{4}{2} = 38 \text{ cm}$$

$$y_2 = 4 + \frac{32}{2} = 20 \text{ cm}$$

$$y_3 = \frac{4}{2} = 2 \text{ cm}$$

Now

$$\bar{x} = \frac{a_1x_1 + a_2x_2 + a_3x_3}{a_1 + a_2 + a_3}$$

$$= \frac{80 \times 10 + 128 \times 18 + 96 \times 28}{80 + 128 + 96} = \frac{5792}{304} = 19.1 \text{ cm}$$

and

$$\bar{y} = \frac{a_1y_1 + a_2y_2 + a_3y_3}{a_1 + a_2 + a_3}$$

$$= \frac{80 \times 38 + 128 \times 20 + 96 \times 2}{304} = \frac{5792}{304} = 19.1 \text{ cm}$$

∴ $\bar{x}$ = **19.1 cm**
$\bar{y}$ = **19.1 cm** **Ans.**

Example 21.10

Determine the centroid of the shaded area as shown in Fig. 21.25.

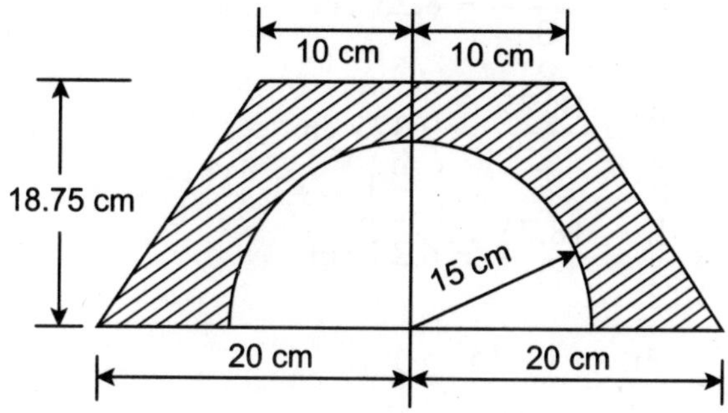

Fig. 21.25

Solution:

Let $\bar{x}$, $\bar{y}$ are co-ordinate of required C.G. Dividing the complete figure into 4 parts

(1) Triangle ABC
(2) Rectangle BCFD
(3) Triangle DEF
(4) Semi circle

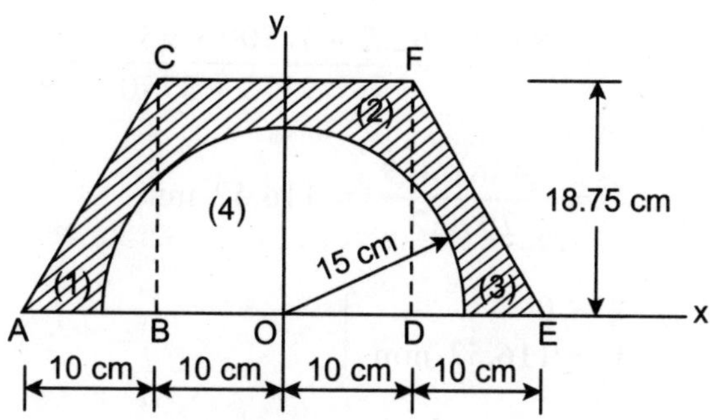

Fig. 21.26

This composite figure is symmetrical about y–y axis.

$$\therefore \quad \bar{x} = 0$$

and

$$\bar{y} = \frac{(a_1y_1 + a_2y_2 + a_3y_3 - a_4y_4)}{(a_1 + a_2 + a_3 - a_4)}$$

Now

$$a_1 = \frac{1}{2} \times 10 \times 18.75 = 93.75 \text{ cm}^2 \text{ (+ve)}$$

$$a_2 = 20 \times 18.75 = 375.00 \text{ cm}^2 \text{ (+ve)}$$

$$a_3 = \frac{1}{2} \times 10 \times 18.75 = 93.75 \text{ cm}^2 \text{ (+ve)}$$

$$a_4 = \frac{\pi r^2}{2} = \frac{\pi \times 15^2}{2} = 353.43 \text{ cm}^2 \text{ (–ve)}$$

$$y_1 = \frac{h}{3} = \frac{18.75}{3} = 6.25 \text{ cm}$$

$$y_2 = \frac{h}{2} = \frac{18.75}{2} = 9.375 \text{ cm}$$

$$y_3 = \frac{h}{3} = \frac{18.75}{3} = 6.25 \text{ cm}$$

$$y_4 = \frac{4r}{3\pi} = \frac{4 \times 15}{3\pi} = 6.37 \text{ cm}$$

Now

$$\bar{y} = \left(\frac{a_1y_1 + a_2y_2 + a_3y_3 - a_4y_4}{a_1 + a_2 + a_3 - a_4}\right)$$

$$= \frac{9375 \times 62.5 + 37500 \times 93.75 + 9375 \times 62.5 - 35343 \times 63.7}{9375 + 37500 + 9375 - 35343}$$

$$= \frac{2436150.9}{2090.7} = 116.52 \text{ mm}$$

$$\therefore \quad \bar{x} = 0, \quad \bar{y} = \mathbf{116.52 \text{ mm}}$$

Ans.

Example 21.11

Where must a circular hole of 1 m radius be punched out of a circular disc of 3 m radius so that the centre of gravity of the remainder be 2 cm from the centre of the disc.

Solution:

The remaining figure is symmetrical about x–x axis.

$$\therefore \quad \bar{y} = 0$$

$$\bar{x} = \frac{a_1x_1 - a_2x_2}{a_1 - a_2}$$

$$a_1 = \pi r^2 = \pi(3)^2 = 9\pi \text{ m}^2 \text{ (+ve)}$$

$$a_2 = \pi r_1^2 = \pi(1)^2 = \pi \text{ m}^2 \text{ (–ve)}$$

$$x_1 = 3 \text{ m}$$

$$x_2 = 3 + C$$

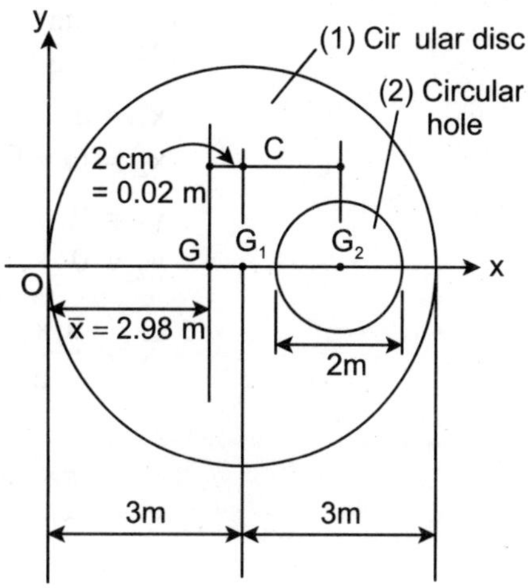

Fig. 21.27

$$\therefore \quad \bar{x} = \frac{a_1x_1 - a_2x_2}{a_1 - a_2}$$

$$= \frac{9\pi \times 3 - \pi \times (3 + C)}{9\pi - \pi}$$

$$= \frac{27\pi - 3\pi - \pi C}{8\pi}$$

$$= \frac{24\pi - \pi C}{8\pi}$$

$$= \frac{24 - C}{8} \quad \ldots\ldots\ldots (21.1)$$

But

$$\bar{x} = (3 - 0.02) \text{ m given from Oy}$$

$$\bar{x} = 2.98 \quad \ldots\ldots\ldots (21.2)$$

From Eqs. (21.1) and (21.2),

$$\frac{24 - C}{8} = 2.98$$

$$C = 0.16 \text{ m}$$

The centre distance (C) between the disc and hole centres should be 0.16 m.

Example 21.12

From a uniform circular disc of radius 'a' is cut of a circular portion of a radius a/2. Find the distance between the centres of the disc and hole if the centre of the mass of the remainder is on the circumference of the hole.

Solution:

Let C is distance between the centres of disc and hole.

$$a_1 = \pi a^2$$

$$a_2 = \frac{\pi a^2}{4}$$

$$x_1 = a$$

$$x_2 = (a + C)$$

$$y_1 = 0$$

$$y_2 = 0$$

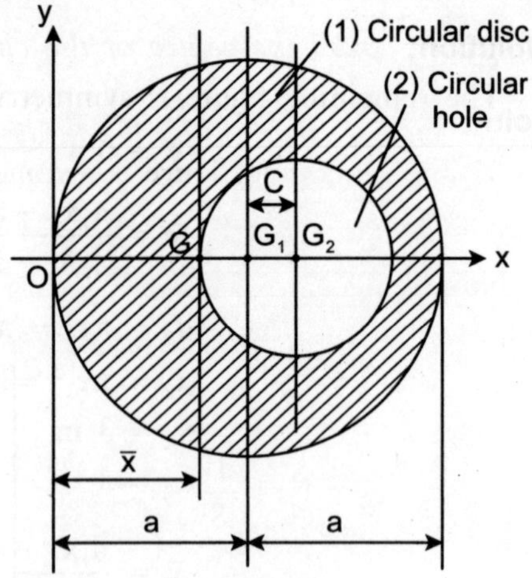

Fig. 21.28

$$\bar{x} = \frac{a_1x_1 - a_2x_2}{a_1 - a_2}$$

$$= \frac{\pi a^2 \cdot a - \frac{\pi a^2}{4}\cdot(a + C)}{\pi a^2 - \frac{\pi a^2}{4}}$$

$$= \frac{\pi a^2\left(a - \frac{a + C}{4}\right)}{\pi a^2\left(1 - \frac{1}{4}\right)}$$

$$\bar{x} = \left(\frac{3a - C}{3}\right) \quad \ldots\ldots\ldots\ldots \quad (21.3)$$

But from figure

$$\bar{x} = a + C - \frac{a}{2} \quad \ldots\ldots\ldots\ldots \quad (21.4)$$

From Eqs. (21.3) and (21.4),

$$a + C - \frac{a}{2} = \left(\frac{3a - C}{3}\right)$$

$$\frac{a}{2} + \frac{2C}{2} = a - \frac{C}{3}$$

$$C + \frac{C}{3} = a - \frac{a}{2}$$

$$\frac{4C}{3} = \frac{a}{2}$$

$$\therefore \quad C = \left(\frac{3a}{8}\right)$$ **Ans.**

Example 21.13

A square hole is punched out of a circular lamina of diameter 'd' with one diagonal of the square coinciding with a radius of the circle. Show that the centre of remainder is at a distance of $\frac{d}{8\pi - 4}$ from the centre of the circle.

Solution:

∵ The remaining figure is symmetrical about x–x axis.

$$\therefore \quad \bar{y} = 0$$

Now

$$a_1 = \frac{\pi}{4}d^2 \qquad\qquad l^2 + l^2 = \left(\frac{d}{2}\right)^2$$

$$a_2 = l^2 = \frac{d^2}{8} \qquad\qquad 2l^2 = \left(\frac{d}{2}\right)^2$$

$$l^2 = \frac{d^2}{8}$$

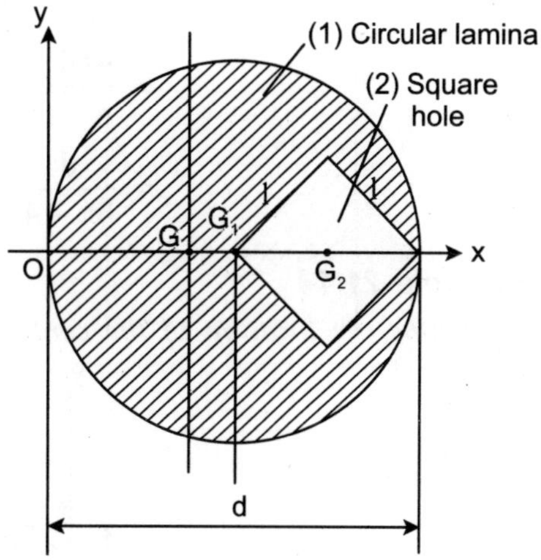

Fig. 21.29

$$x_1 = \frac{d}{2}$$

$$x_2 = \frac{d}{2} + \frac{d}{2} \times \frac{1}{2} = \frac{3d}{4}$$

$$\therefore \quad \bar{x} = \frac{a_1x_1 - a_2x_2}{a_1 - a_2}$$

$$= \left(\frac{\frac{\pi}{4}d^2 \cdot \frac{d}{2} - \frac{d^2}{8} \cdot \frac{3d}{4}}{\frac{\pi}{4}d^2 - \frac{d^2}{8}}\right)$$

$$= \frac{\frac{d^3}{8}\left(\pi - \frac{3}{4}\right)}{d^2\left(\frac{\pi}{4} - \frac{1}{8}\right)}$$

$$= \frac{d}{8}\left(\frac{\frac{4\pi - 3}{4}}{\frac{2\pi - 1}{8}}\right)$$

$$= \frac{d}{4}\left(\frac{4\pi - 3}{2\pi - 1}\right)$$

∴ Centre of remainder from the centre of the circle

$$= \frac{d}{2} - \bar{x}$$

$$= \frac{d}{2} - \frac{d}{4}\left(\frac{4\pi - 3}{2\pi - 1}\right)$$

$$= \frac{2d(2\pi - 1) - d(4\pi - 3)}{4(2\pi - 1)}$$

$$= \frac{4\pi d - 2d - 4\pi d + 3d}{8\pi - 4}$$

$$= \frac{d}{8\pi - 4}$$ **Ans.**

Example 21.14

Determine the location of the centroid of the plane figure shown in Fig. 21.30.

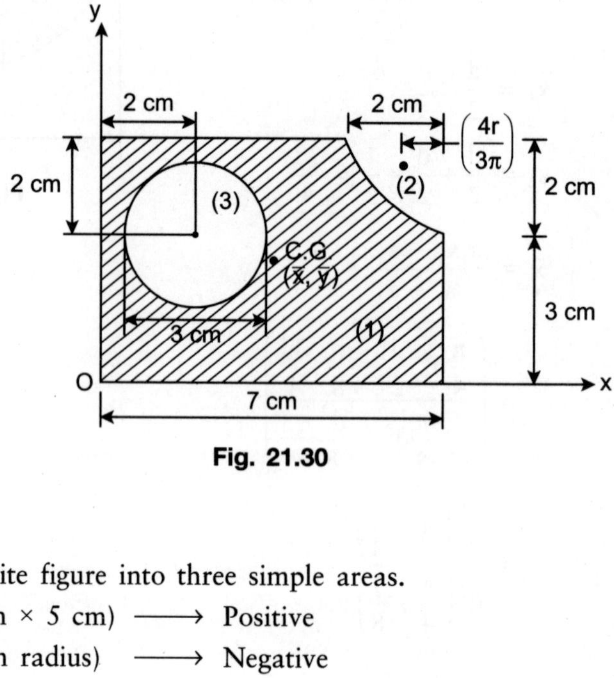

Fig. 21.30

Solution:

Dividing the composite figure into three simple areas.

(1) A rectangle (7 cm × 5 cm) ⟶ Positive

(2) A quadrant (2 cm radius) ⟶ Negative

(3) A circle (3 cm dia.) ⟶ Negative

Now

$$a_1 = 7 \text{ cm} \times 5 \text{ cm} = 35 \text{ cm}^2$$

$$a_2 = \frac{\pi r^2}{4} = \frac{\pi \times 4}{4} = \pi \text{ cm}^2$$

$$a_3 = \pi r^2 = \frac{\pi 9}{4} = 2.25\ \pi\ \text{cm}^2$$

Let C.G. of composite area is $\bar{x}$, $\bar{y}$ from the reference

$$x_1 = \frac{7}{2} = 3.5 \text{ cm}$$

$$x_2 = 7 - \frac{4r}{3\pi} = 7 - \frac{4 \times 2}{3\pi} = 7 - \frac{8}{3\pi} = 6.1512 \text{ cm}$$

$$x_3 = 2 \text{ cm}$$

and

$$y_1 = \frac{5}{2} = 2.5 \text{ cm}$$

$$y_2 = 5 - \frac{4r}{3\pi} = 5 - \frac{4 \times 2}{3\pi} = 5 - \frac{8}{3\pi} = 4.1512 \text{ cm}$$

$$y_3 = 3 \text{ cm}$$

Now

$$\bar{x} = \left(\frac{a_1x_1 - a_2x_2 - a_3x_3}{a_1 - a_2 - a_3}\right)$$

$$= \frac{35 \times 3.5 - \pi \times 6.15 - 2.25\pi \times 2}{35 - \pi - 2.25\pi} = \frac{89.042}{24.7898} = 3.59 \text{ cm}$$

$$\bar{y} = \left(\frac{a_1y_1 - a_2y_2 - a_3y_3}{a_1 - a_2 - a_3}\right)$$

$$= \frac{35 \times 2.5 - \pi \times 4.15 - 2.25\pi \times 3}{24.7898} = \frac{53.26}{24.7898} = 2.15 \text{ cm}$$

$\therefore$ $\bar{x}$ = **3.59 cm**, $\bar{y}$ = **2.15 cm** **Ans.**

Example 21.15

Locate the C.G. of a semi circle of radius 'a' as shown in Fig. 21.31.

Solution:

Let $\bar{x}$, $\bar{y}$ are the co-ordinate of semi circle.

Fig. 21.31 of a semi circle is shown.

Considering a small strip PQ.

Length of elementary strip PQ = 2 × PM

$$= 2\sqrt{(PD)^2 - (DM)^2}$$

$$= 2\sqrt{r^2 - y^2}$$

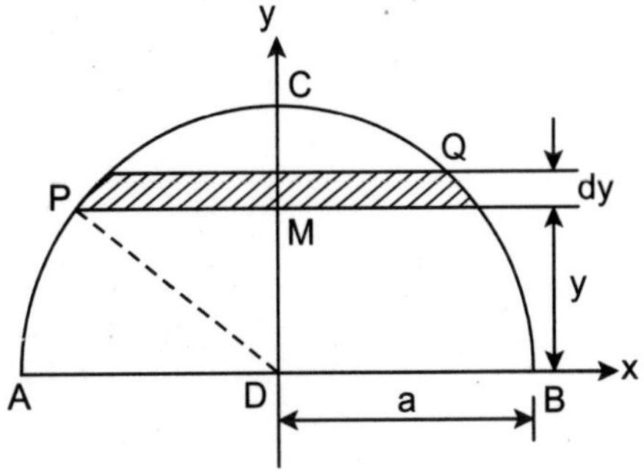

Fig. 21.31

Area of elementary strip

$$dA = PQ \cdot dy = 2\sqrt{r^2 - y^2} \cdot dy = 2\sqrt{a^2 - y^2} \cdot dy$$

Let x*, y* are co-ordinate of C.G. of small strip PQ.

$$x^* = 0$$
$$y^* = y$$

Now

$$\bar{y} = \frac{\int y^* dA}{\int dA} = \frac{\int_0^r y \cdot 2\sqrt{a^2 - y^2} \cdot dy}{\int_0^r 2\sqrt{a^2 - y^2} \cdot dy}$$

$$= \frac{\frac{a^3}{3}}{\frac{\pi a^2}{4}}$$

∴ $$\bar{y} = \frac{4a}{3\pi}$$ **Ans.**

Example 21.16

Locate the C.G. of a solid hemisphere shown in Fig. 21.32.

Solution:

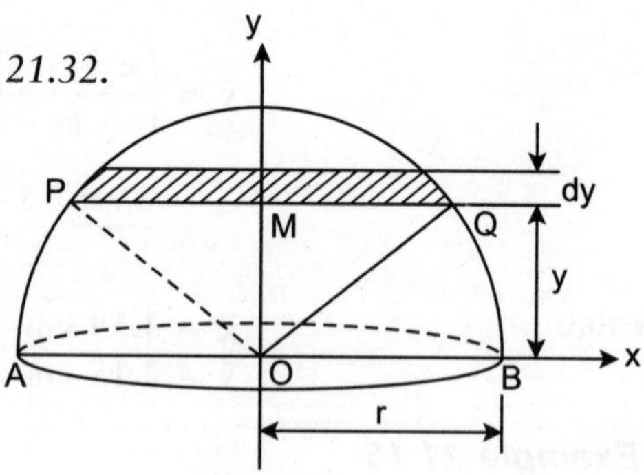

Fig. 21.32

A hemisphere is shown in the Fig. 21.32.

Considering a small element PQ.

M is mid-point of PQ.

$$(PM)^2 = (OP)^2 - (OM)^2 = r^2 - y^2$$

Let

ρ is the density of the material of hemisphere.

$$dW_{PQ} = \text{Volume} \times \text{density}$$
$$= \pi \cdot (PM)^2 \cdot h \cdot \rho$$
$$= \pi\ (r^2 - y^2)\ dy\, \rho$$

$$x^* = 0$$
$$y^* = y$$

Now

$$\bar{y} = \frac{\int y^* \cdot dW}{\int dW} = \frac{\int_0^r y \cdot \pi\left(r^2 - y^2\right) dy \cdot \rho}{\int_0^r \pi\left(r^2 - y^2\right) dy \cdot \rho}$$

$$= \frac{\int_0^r y\left(r^2 - y^2\right)dy}{\int_0^r \left(r^2 - y^2\right)dy} = \frac{\left(\frac{r^2y^2}{2} - \frac{y^4}{4}\right)_0^r}{\left(r^2y - \frac{y^3}{3}\right)_0^r}$$

$$= \frac{\frac{2r^4}{4}}{\frac{2r^3}{3}}$$

$$\therefore \quad \bar{y} = \frac{3r}{8} \qquad \textbf{Ans.}$$

Example 21.17

Locate the centroid of shaded area as shown in Fig. 21.33.

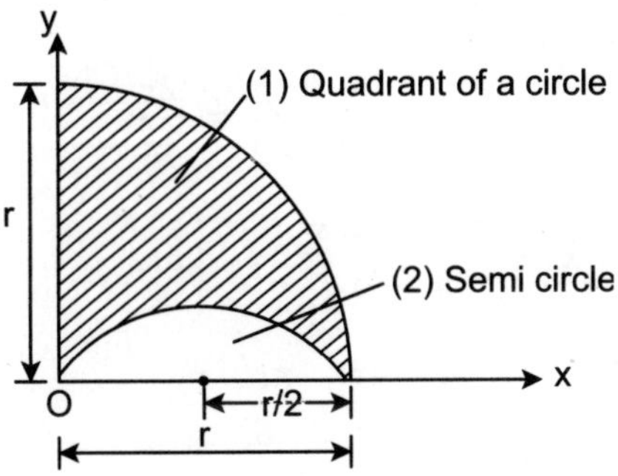

Fig. 21.33

Solution:

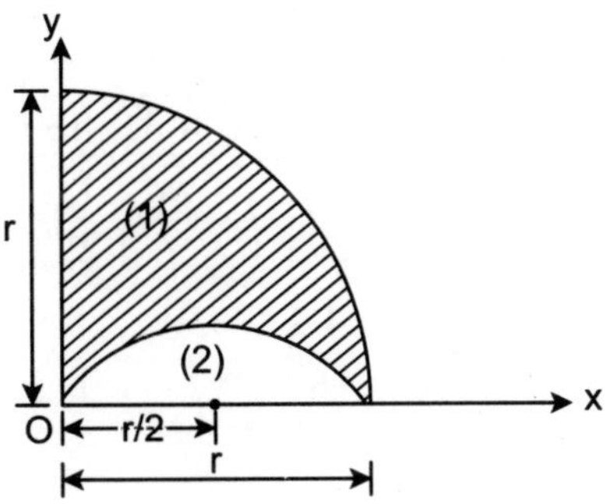

Fig. 21.34

Let $\bar{x}$, $\bar{y}$ are the co-ordinate of centroid of shaded area.

$$\bar{x} = \left(\frac{a_1x_1 - a_2x_2}{a_1 - a_2}\right)$$

$$\bar{y} = \left(\frac{a_1y_1 - a_2y_2}{a_1 - a_2}\right)$$

where $$a_1 = \frac{\pi r^2}{4} = \frac{\pi r^2}{4}$$

$$a_2 = \frac{\pi r_1^2}{2} = \frac{\pi}{2}\left(\frac{r}{2}\right)^2 = \frac{\pi r^2}{8}$$

$$x_1 = \frac{4r}{3\pi} = \frac{4r}{3\pi}$$

$$x_2 = \frac{r_1}{2} = \frac{r}{2}$$

and

$$y_1 = \frac{4r}{3\pi}$$

$$y_2 = \frac{4r_1}{3\pi} = \frac{4}{3\pi}\left(\frac{r}{2}\right) = \frac{2r}{3\pi}$$

∴ $$\bar{x} = \frac{a_1x_1 - a_2x_2}{a_1 - a_2}$$

$$= \frac{\pi \cdot \frac{r^2}{4} \cdot \frac{4r}{3\pi} - \frac{\pi r^2}{8} \cdot \frac{r}{2}}{\frac{\pi r^2}{4} - \frac{\pi r^2}{8}}$$

$$= \frac{\frac{r^3}{3} - \frac{\pi r^3}{16}}{\frac{\pi r^2}{4}\left(1 - \frac{1}{2}\right)} = \frac{r^3\left(\frac{1}{3} - \frac{\pi}{16}\right)}{\frac{\pi r^2}{4}\left(\frac{1}{2}\right)}$$

$$= 8r\left(\frac{1}{3\pi} - \frac{1}{16}\right)$$

and

$$\bar{y} = \left(\frac{a_1y_1 - a_2y_2}{a_1 - a_2}\right)$$

$$= \frac{\frac{\pi r^2}{4} \cdot \frac{4r}{3\pi} - \frac{\pi r^2}{8} \cdot \frac{2r}{3\pi}}{\frac{\pi r^2}{4} - \frac{\pi r^2}{8}}$$

$$\bar{y} = \frac{2r}{\pi}$$

$$\therefore \quad \left.\begin{aligned} \bar{x} &= 8r\left(\frac{1}{3\pi} - \frac{1}{16}\right) \\ \bar{y} &= \frac{2r}{\pi} \end{aligned}\right] \quad \textbf{Ans.}$$

Example 21.18

From a rectangular lamina ABCD 20 cm × 24 cm, a rectangular hole of 6 cm × 8 cm is cut as shown in Fig. 21.35. Find C.G. of the remainder lamina.

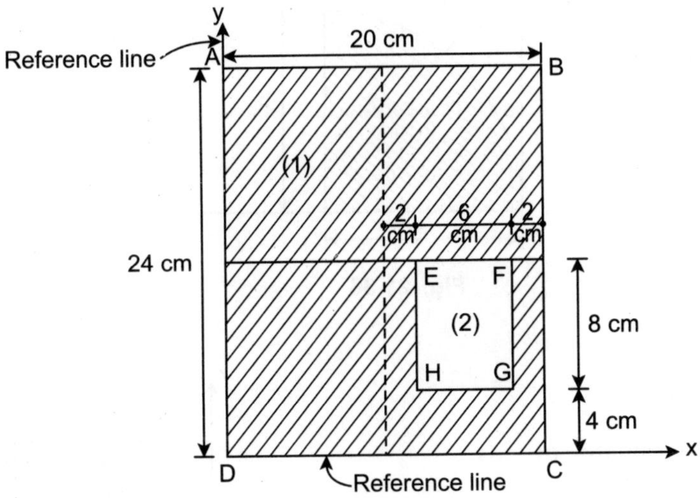

Fig. 21.35

Solution:

Co-ordinates of C.G. are $\bar{x}$ and $\bar{y}$.

Let CD and DA are reference lines.

Now

$$a_1 = AB \times AD = 20 \times 24 = 240 \text{ cm}^2$$

$$a_2 = EF \times EG = 6 \times 8 = 48 \text{ cm}^2$$

$$y_1 = \frac{24}{2} = 12 \text{ cm} \qquad x_1 = \frac{20}{2} = 50 \text{ cm}$$

$$y_2 = 4 + \frac{8}{2} = 8 \text{ cm} \qquad x_2 = 10 + 2 + \frac{6}{2} = 15 \text{ cm}$$

$$\therefore \quad \bar{x} = \frac{a_1x_1 - a_2x_2}{a_1 - a_2} = \frac{240 \times 5 - 48 \times 15}{240 - 48} = \frac{480}{192} = 2.5 \text{ cm}$$

$$\bar{y} = \frac{a_1 y_1 - a_2 y_2}{a_1 - a_2} = \frac{240 \times 12 - 48 \times 18}{240 - 48} = \frac{2496}{192} = 13 \text{ cm}$$

$\therefore$ $\left.\begin{aligned}\bar{x} &= 2.5 \text{ cm}\\ \bar{y} &= 13 \text{ cm}\end{aligned}\right]$ **Ans.**

Example 21.19

Determine the centroid of shaded area shown in Fig. 21.36.

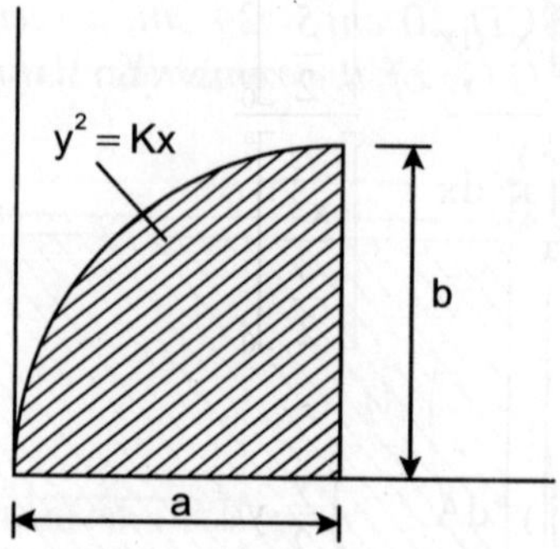

Fig. 21.36

Solution:

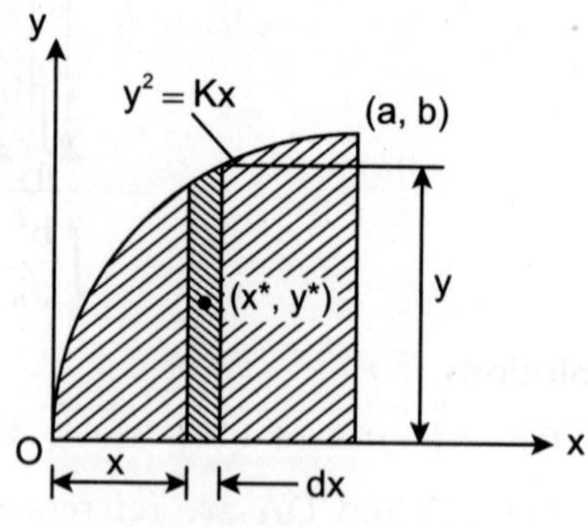

Fig. 21.37

Let $\bar{x}$, $\bar{y}$ are the co-ordinates of C.G. of shaded area.

Considering a small strip of length y and thickness dx,

x*, y* are co-ordinates of C.G. of small strip.

$\therefore$ $$dA = ydx$$

$$x^* = x + \frac{dx}{2} = x \qquad (\because \text{ dx is very small quantity})$$

$$y^* = \frac{y}{2}$$

Now $$y^2 = K \cdot x$$

$$b^2 = K \cdot a$$

$\therefore$ $$K = \left(\frac{b^2}{a}\right) \quad \text{and} \quad y = \frac{b^2}{a} \cdot x$$

Now

$$\bar{x} = \frac{\int x^* dA}{\int dA} = \frac{\int_0^a x \cdot y dx}{\int_0^a y dx} = \frac{\int_0^a x \cdot \frac{b}{\sqrt{a}} \cdot (x)^{\frac{1}{2}} dx}{\int_0^a \frac{b}{\sqrt{a}} \cdot (x)^{\frac{1}{2}} dx}$$

$$= \frac{\int_0^a x^{\frac{3}{2}} dx}{\int_0^a x^{\frac{1}{2}} dx} = \frac{\left[\frac{x^{\frac{5}{2}}}{\frac{5}{2}}\right]_0^a}{\left[\frac{x^{\frac{3}{2}}}{\frac{3}{2}}\right]_0^a} = \frac{\frac{a^{\frac{5}{2}}}{\frac{5}{2}}}{\frac{a^{\frac{3}{2}}}{\frac{3}{2}}} = \frac{3}{5}a$$

Similarly

$$\bar{y} = \frac{\int_0^a y^* dA}{\int_0^a dA} = \frac{\int_0^a \frac{y}{2} \cdot y dx}{\int_0^a y dx}$$

$$= \frac{\frac{1}{2}\int_0^a \frac{b^2}{a} \cdot x \cdot dx}{\int_0^a \frac{b^2}{\sqrt{a}} \sqrt{x}\, dx} = \frac{1}{2} \cdot \frac{\frac{b^2}{a}\left[\frac{x^2}{2}\right]_0^a}{\frac{b}{\sqrt{a}}\left[\frac{x^{\frac{3}{2}}}{\frac{3}{2}}\right]_0^a}$$

$$= \frac{1}{2} \cdot \frac{b^2\sqrt{a}}{a \cdot b}\left(\frac{\frac{a^2}{2}}{\frac{a^{\frac{3}{2}}}{\frac{3}{2}}}\right) = \frac{1}{2} \cdot \frac{b\sqrt{a}}{a} \cdot \frac{a^2}{2} \cdot \frac{3}{2} \cdot \frac{1}{a\sqrt{a}} = \frac{3}{8}b$$

$\therefore$

$$\left.\begin{aligned} \bar{x} &= \frac{3}{5}\mathbf{a} \\ \bar{y} &= \frac{3}{8}\mathbf{b} \end{aligned}\right]$$

Ans.

Example 21.20

A semi circular area is removed from a trapezium. Determine centroid of the remaining area shown in Fig. 21.38.

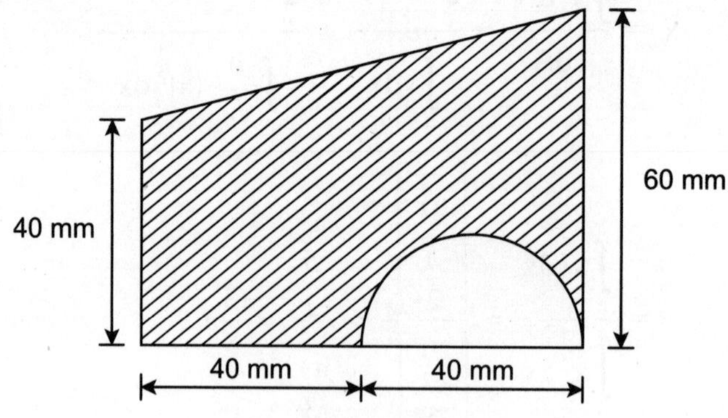

Fig. 21.38

Solution:

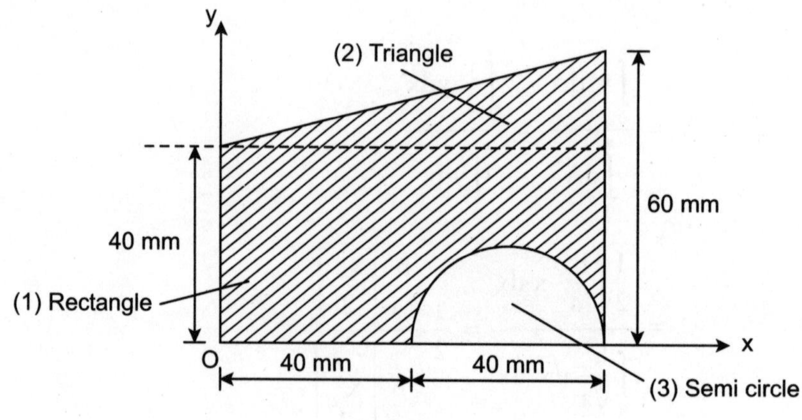

Fig. 21.39

Let $\bar{x}$, $\bar{y}$ are C.G. co-ordinates.

Now

$$a_1 = 40 \times 80 = 3200 \text{ mm}^2 \text{ (+ve)}$$

$$a_2 = \frac{1}{2} \times 20 \times 80 = 800 \text{ mm}^2 \text{ (+ve)}$$

$$a_3 = \frac{\pi r^2}{2} = \frac{\pi}{2} \times 20^2 = 628.3 \text{ mm}^2 \text{ (–ve)}$$

and

$$x_1 = 40 \text{ mm}$$

$$x_2 = 80 \times \frac{2}{3} = 53.33 \text{ mm}$$

$$x_3 = 40 + 20 = 60 \text{ mm}$$

$$y_1 = 20 \text{ mm}$$

$$y_2 = 40 + \frac{20}{3} = 46.67 \text{ mm}$$

$$y_3 = \frac{4r}{3\pi} = \frac{4 \times 20}{3\pi} = 8.49 \text{ mm}$$

$$\therefore \quad \bar{x} = \frac{a_1x_1 + a_2x_2 - a_3x_3}{a_1 + a_2 - a_3}$$

$$= \frac{3200 \times 40 + 800 \times 53.33 - 628.3 \times 60}{3200 + 800 - 628.3}$$

$$= \frac{132966}{3371.7} = 39.44 \text{ mm}$$

Similarly

$$\bar{y} = \frac{a_1y_1 + a_2y_2 - a_3y_3}{a_1 + a_2 - a_3}$$

$$= \frac{3200 \times 20 + 800 \times 46.67 - 628.3 \times 8.49}{3200 + 800 - 628.3}$$

$$= \frac{96001.733}{3371.7} = 28.47 \text{ mm}$$

$$\therefore \quad \left.\begin{aligned} \bar{x} &= \mathbf{39.44 \text{ mm}} \\ \bar{y} &= \mathbf{28.47 \text{ mm}} \end{aligned}\right]$$ **Ans.**

Example 21.21

Locate the C.G. of a solid right circular cone of radius r and height h shown in Fig. 21.40.

Solution:

ABC is a right circular solid cone.

Considering a small strip PQ as shown in Fig. 21.40.

ΔAPM and ΔABD are similar.

$$\frac{y}{r_1} = \frac{h}{r}$$

$$\therefore \quad r_1 = \left(\frac{y \cdot r}{h}\right)$$

Let ω is the density of the material of the cone.

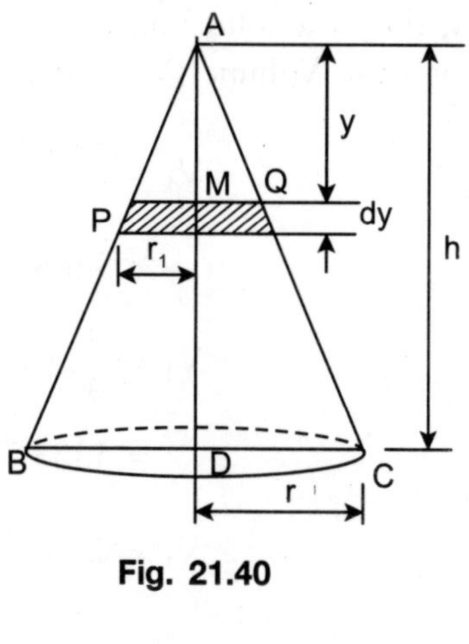

Fig. 21.40

Weight of PQ,

$$W_{PQ} = \pi r^2 h \times \omega = \pi r_1^2 dy \cdot \omega = \text{Volume} \times \text{Density}$$

$$= \frac{\pi\, y^2 r^2}{h^2} \cdot dy \cdot \omega$$

C.G. of PQ from A.

$$\bar{y} = \frac{\Sigma W_{PQ} \cdot y}{\Sigma W_{PQ}} = \frac{\int_0^h \pi y^2 \frac{r^2}{h^2} \cdot dy \cdot \omega \cdot y}{\int_0^h \pi y^2 \frac{r^2}{h^2} \cdot dy \cdot \omega}$$

$$= \frac{\int_0^h y^3 dy}{\int_0^h y^2 dy} = \frac{\frac{h^4}{4}}{\frac{h^3}{3}} = \frac{3}{4} h \text{ from Vertex A}$$

$$= h - \frac{3h}{4} = \frac{h}{4} \text{ from base BC.}$$

Example 21.22

A body consists of a right circular solid cone of height 26 cm and radius 20 cm, placed on a solid hemisphere of radius 20 cm of the same material. Find position of C.G. of the body.

Solution:

Let $\bar{x}$, $\bar{y}$ are the co-ordinates of C.G. of the body.

x, y are the reference axis.

∵ The body is symmetrical about y–y axis.

∴ $\bar{x} = 0$

Now, this is a solid body.

We will use Volume (V) in place of area (a).

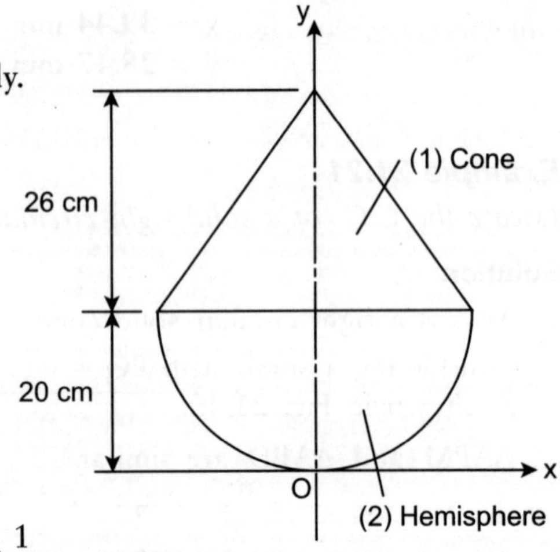

Fig. 21.41

∴ $$V_1 = \frac{\pi r^2 h}{3} = \frac{\pi}{3} \times 20^2 \times 26$$

$$= 3466.7\pi \text{ cm}^3$$

$$V_2 = \frac{4}{3}\pi r^3 \times \frac{1}{2} = \frac{4}{3}\pi \times 20^3 \times \frac{1}{2}$$

$$= 5333.3\pi \text{ cm}^3$$

$$y_1 = 20 + \frac{26}{4} = 26.5 \text{ cm}$$

$$y_2 = 20 - \frac{3r}{8} = 20 - \frac{3 \times 20}{8} = 12.5 \text{ cm}$$

$$\therefore \quad \bar{y} = \frac{V_1 y_1 + V_2 y_2}{V_1 + V_2}$$

$$= \left(\frac{3466.7\pi \times 26.5 + 5333.3\pi \times 12.5}{3466.7\pi + 5333.3\pi} \right)$$

$$= \left(\frac{3466.7 \times 26.5 + 5333.3 \times 12.5}{3466.7 + 5333.3} \right)$$

$$= \frac{158533.8}{8800} = 18 \text{ cm}$$

$$\therefore \quad \left. \begin{aligned} \bar{x} &= \mathbf{0} \\ \bar{y} &= \mathbf{18 \text{ cm}} \end{aligned} \right]$$

Ans.

Example 21.23

A right circular cylinder of 150 mm diameter is joined with a hemisphere of the same diameter face to face. Find the greatest height of the cylinder so that C.G. of the composite section coincides with the plane of joining the two sections. The density of the material of hemisphere is twice that the material of cylinder.

Solution:

Let $\bar{x}, \bar{y} \rightarrow$ co-ordinates of C.G. of the composite body.

$\rho \rightarrow$ density of cylinder material

$\therefore 2\rho \rightarrow$ density of hemisphere material

$\because$ The composite body is symmetrical about y–y axis.

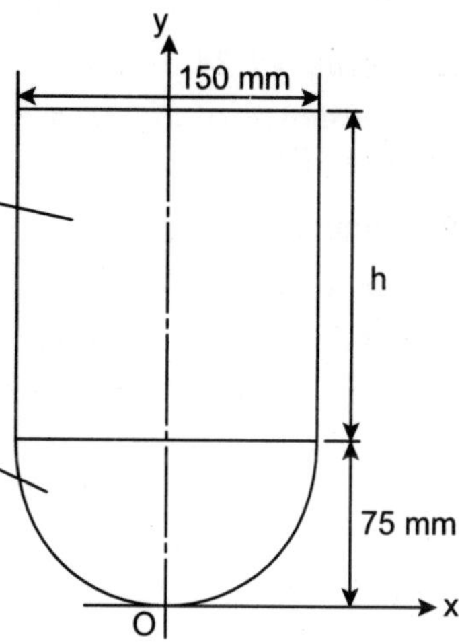

Fig. 21.42

$$\therefore \quad \bar{x} = 0$$

and

$$\bar{y} = \frac{W_1 y_1 + W_2 y_2}{W_1 + W_2} \quad \ldots\ldots\ldots \quad (21.5)$$

$$W_1 = \pi r^2 h \times \rho = \pi \times 75^2 \times h \times \rho = 5625\ \pi h \rho$$

$$W_2 = \frac{4}{3}\pi r^3 \times \frac{1}{2} \times \rho \times 2 = \frac{2}{3}\pi \times 75^3 \times 2\rho = 562500\ \rho{\cdot}\pi$$

Now

$$y_1 = \left(75 + \frac{h}{2} \right) \text{mm}$$

$$y_2 = 75 - \frac{3r}{8} = 75 - \frac{3 \times 75}{8} = 46.875 \text{ mm}$$

$$\bar{y} = 75 \text{ mm (given)}$$

From Eq. (21.5),

$$\bar{y} = \frac{W_1 y_1 + W_2 y_2}{W_1 + W_2}$$

$$\Rightarrow \quad 75 = \frac{5625\ \pi\rho h \times \left(75 + \frac{h}{2}\right) + 562500\ \pi\rho \times 46.875}{5625\ \pi\rho h + 562500\ \pi\rho}$$

$$75 = \frac{5625 \times 75\ h + 2812.5\ h^2 + 26367188}{5625\ h + 562500}$$

$$421875\ h + 42187500 = 421875\ h + 2812.5\ h^2 + 26367188$$

$$\Rightarrow \quad 2812.5\ h^2 = 42187500 - 26367188$$

$$\Rightarrow \quad h = \sqrt{\frac{15820313}{2812.5}}$$

$$\therefore \quad h = 75 \text{ mm}$$ **Ans.**

Example 21.24

A hemisphere of diameter 75 mm is placed on the top of a cylinder, whose diameter is also 75 mm. The height of the cylinder is 175 mm. Find common C.G. of the composite body.

Solution:

Let $\bar{x}$, $\bar{y}$ are the co-ordinate of the C.G. of composite body.

$\because$ Composite body is symmetrical about y–y axis.

$\therefore \quad \bar{x} = 0$

$\bar{y} = ?$

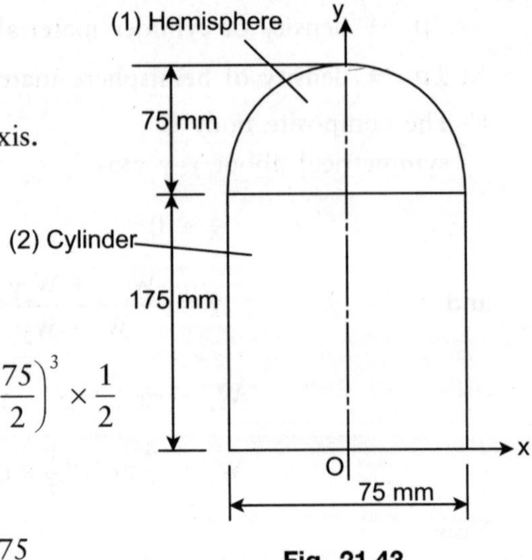

Fig. 21.43

and $$\bar{y} = \frac{V_1 y_1 + V_2 y_2}{V_1 + V_2}$$

Now, $$V_1 = \frac{4}{3}\pi r^3 \times \frac{1}{2} = \frac{4}{3} \times \pi \times \left(\frac{75}{2}\right)^3 \times \frac{1}{2}$$

$$= 35156.25\pi \text{ mm}^3$$

$$V_2 = \pi r^2 h = \pi \times \left(\frac{75}{2}\right)^2 \times 175$$

$$= 246093.75\pi \text{ mm}^3$$

$$y_1 = 175 + \frac{3r}{8} = 175 + \frac{3 \times 75}{8} = 203.125 \text{ mm}$$

$$y_2 = \frac{175}{2} = 87.5 \text{ mm}$$

and

$$\bar{y} = \frac{V_1y_1 + V_2y_2}{V_1 + V_2}$$

$$= \frac{35156.25\pi \times 203.125 + 246093.75\pi \times 87.5}{35156.25\pi + 246093.75\pi}$$

$$= \frac{7141113.3 + 21533203}{281250}$$

$$= \frac{28674316}{281250} = 101.95$$

$\therefore$ $\bar{y} = 101.9$ mm

Hence, $\bar{x} = 0$, $\bar{y} = \mathbf{101.9}$ **mm** **Ans.**

Example 21.25

Determine the C.G. of a homogeneous solid body of revolution as shown in Fig. 21.44.

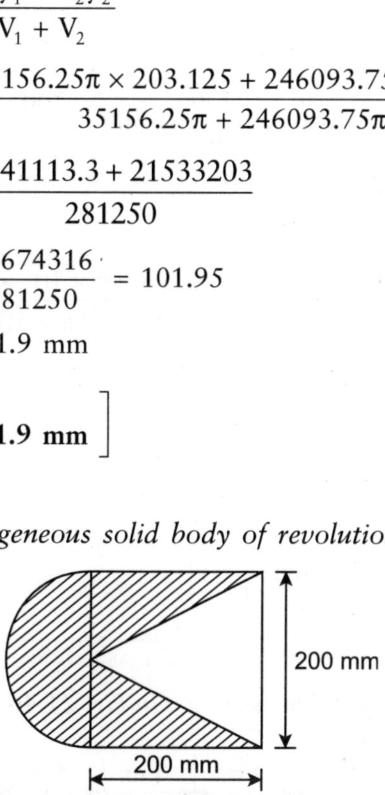

Fig. 21.44

Let $\bar{x}$, $\bar{y}$ are co-ordinates of C.G. of remainder portion.

$\because$ Remainder body is symmetrical about x–x axis.

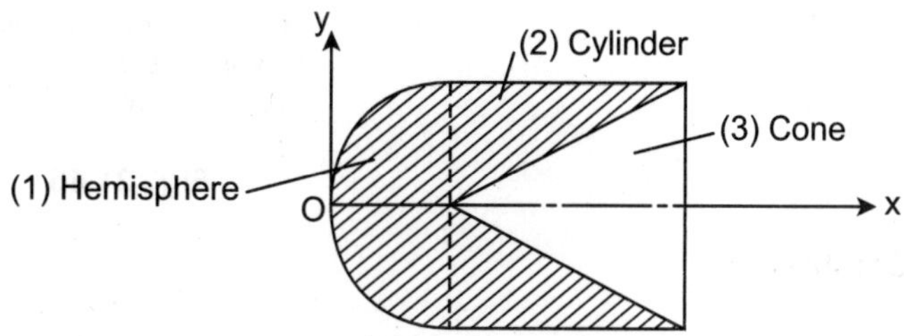

Fig. 21.45

$\therefore$ $\bar{y} = 0$

and

$$\bar{x} = \frac{V_1x_1 + V_2x_2 - V_2x_3}{V_1 + V_2 - V_3}$$

$$V_1 = \frac{2}{3}\pi r^3 = \frac{2}{3}\pi(100)^3 = 0.67 \times 10^6\pi \text{ mm}^3 \text{ (+ve)}$$

$$V_2 = \pi r^2 h = \pi \times 100^2 \times 200 = 2 \times 10^6 \pi \text{ mm}^3 \text{ (+ve)}$$

$$V_3 = \frac{\pi r^2 h}{3} = 0.67 \times 10^6 \pi \text{ mm}^3 \text{ (–ve)}$$

$$x_1 = 100 - \frac{3r}{8} = 100 - \frac{3}{8} \times 100 = 62.5 \text{ mm}$$

$$x_2 = 100 + \frac{200}{2} = 200 \text{ mm}$$

$$x_3 = 100 + 200 - \frac{200}{4} = 300 - \frac{200}{4} = 250 \text{ mm}$$

$$\therefore \quad \bar{x} = \frac{V_1 x_1 + V_2 x_2 - V_2 x_3}{V_1 + V_2 - V_3}$$

$$= \frac{0.67 \times 10^6 \pi \times 62.5 + 2\pi \times 10^6 \times 200 - 0.67\pi \times 10^6 \times 250}{0.67 \times 10^6 \pi + 2\pi \times 10^6 - 0.67 \times 10^6 \pi}$$

$$= \frac{\pi(10^6)[41.875 + 400 - 167.5]}{2\pi \times 10^6}$$

$$= \frac{274.375}{2} = 137.2 \text{ mm}$$

$$\therefore \quad \left.\begin{aligned} \bar{x} &= \mathbf{137.2 \text{ mm}} \\ \bar{y} &= \mathbf{0} \end{aligned}\right]$$ **Ans.**

Example 21.26

Four forces are acting on a straight line as shown in Fig. 21.46. Determine C.G. of these forces.

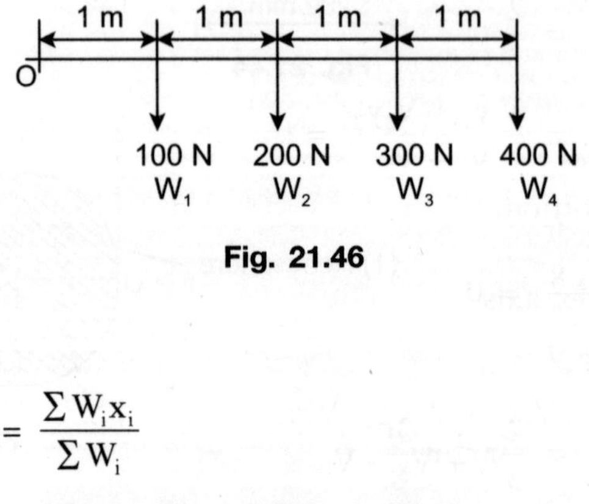

Fig. 21.46

Solution:

$$\bar{x} = \frac{\Sigma W_i x_i}{\Sigma W_i}$$

$$= \frac{W_1 x_1 + W_2 x_2 + W_3 x_3 + W_4 x_4}{W_1 + W_2 + W_3 + W_4}$$

$$\bar{x} = \frac{100 \times 1 + 200 \times 2 + 300 \times 3 + 400 \times 4}{100 + 200 + 300 + 400}$$

$$= \frac{100 + 400 + 900 + 1600}{1000}$$

$$= \frac{3000}{1000} = \mathbf{3\ m}$$ **Ans.**

Example 21.27

A hemisphere and a cone have their bases joined together, the two bases being of the same size. Find the ratio of the height of the cone to the radius of the base, so that their common C.G. may be at the centre of the common base.

Solution:

$$\frac{h}{r} = ?$$

Let $\bar{x}$, $\bar{y}$ are co-ordinates of common C.G.

But common C.G. is given at point G.

i.e. at the common base.

The composite figure is symmetrical about y–y axis.

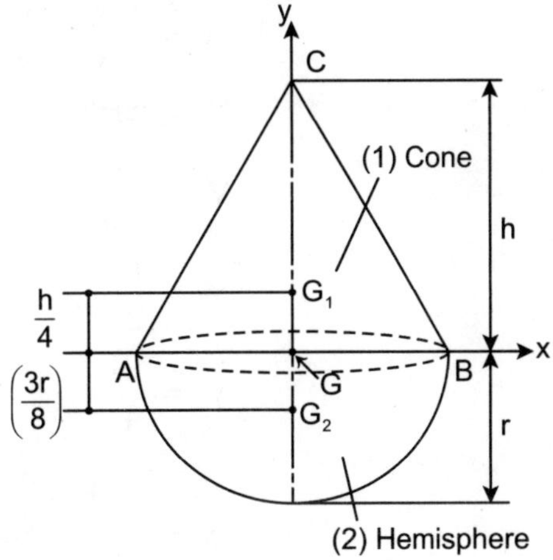

Fig. 21.47

$\therefore$ $$\bar{x} = 0$$

and $$\bar{y} = \frac{V_1 y_1 + V_2 y_2}{V_1 + V_2}$$

$$V_1 = \frac{\pi r^2 h}{3} \qquad y_1 = \frac{h}{4}$$

$$V_2 = \frac{2}{3}\pi r^3 \qquad y_2 = \frac{3r}{8}$$

$\therefore$ $$\bar{y} = \frac{V_1 y_1 + V_2 y_2}{V_1 + V_2} = 0 \text{ (given)}$$

$\therefore$ $$\frac{\frac{\pi r^2 h}{3} \times \frac{h}{4} - \frac{2}{3}\pi r^3 \times \frac{3r}{8}}{\frac{\pi r^2 h}{3} - \frac{2}{3}\pi r^3} = 0$$

or $$\frac{\pi r^2 h}{3} \cdot \frac{h}{4} = \frac{2}{3}\pi r^2 \cdot r \cdot \frac{3r}{8}$$

or $$\frac{h^2}{4} = \frac{3}{4} r^2$$

or $$\frac{h^2}{r^2} = 3$$

$$\Rightarrow \quad \frac{h}{r} = \sqrt{3}$$ **Ans.**

Example 21.28

A solid right circular cylinder has its base scooped out so that the hollow is a right circular cone on the same base and having the same height as the cylinder. Find C.G. of the remainder.

Solution:

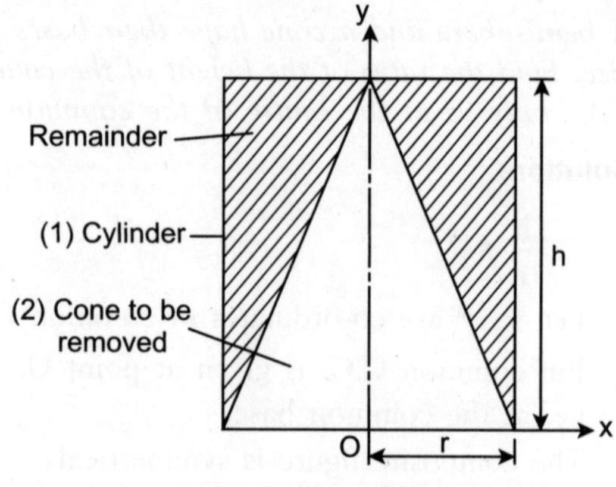

Fig. 21.48

$$\bar{x} = 0$$

$$\bar{y} = \frac{V_1y_1 - V_2y_2}{V_1 - V_2}$$

$$V_1 = \pi r^2 h$$

$$V_2 = \frac{\pi r^2 h}{3}$$

$$y_1 = \frac{h}{2}$$

$$y_2 = \frac{h}{4}$$

$$\therefore \quad \bar{y} = \frac{\pi r^2 h \times \frac{h}{2} - \frac{\pi r^2 h}{3} \times \frac{h}{4}}{\pi r^2 h - \frac{\pi r^2 h}{3}} = \frac{\frac{h}{2} - \frac{h}{12}}{1 - \frac{1}{3}} = \frac{\frac{6h - h}{12}}{\frac{2}{3}} = \frac{5h \times 3}{12 \times 2}$$

$$\bar{y} = \frac{5}{8}h$$ **Ans.**

Example 21.29

The frustum of a solid cone has base diameter 100 mm. The top diameter 50 mm and height 75 mm. Determine C.G. of the solid.

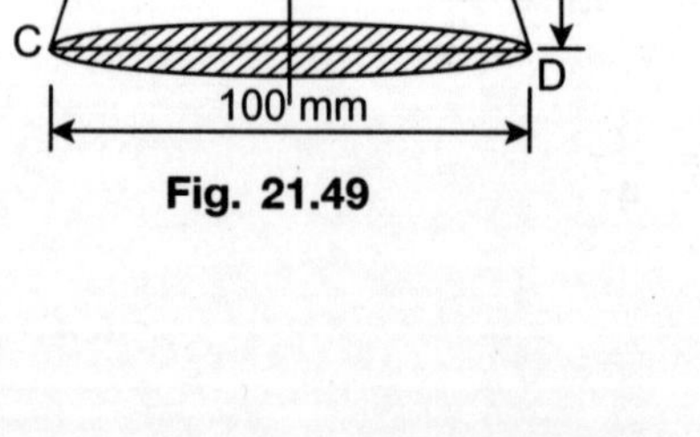

Fig. 21.49

Solution:

From similar triangles

$$\frac{EF}{EH} = \frac{AF}{CH}$$

or
$$\frac{h}{h+75} = \frac{25}{50}$$

$$50\,h = 25\,h + 75 \times 25$$

$\therefore$
$$h = 75 \text{ mm}$$

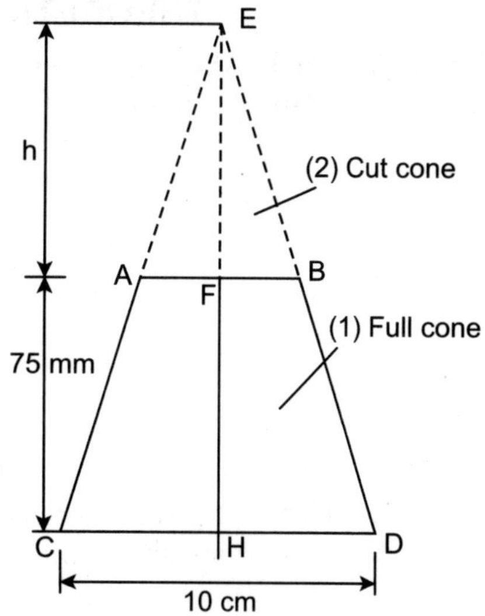

Fig. 21.50

Now

$$V_1 = \frac{\pi r^2 h}{3} = \frac{1}{3}\pi \times (5)^2 \times (7.5 + 7.5)$$

$$= 125\,\pi \text{ cm}^3 \text{ (+ve)}$$

$$V_2 = \frac{\pi r_1^2 h_1}{3} = \frac{1}{3}\pi \times (2.5)^2 (7.5)$$

$$= 15.625\pi \text{ cm}^3 \text{ (–ve)}$$

$$y_1 = \frac{h}{4} = \frac{15}{4} = 3.75 \text{ cm}$$

$$y_2 = \frac{h_1}{4} = 7.5 + \frac{7.5}{4} = 9.375 \text{ cm}$$

$\because$ The frustrum is symmetrical about y–y axis.

$\therefore$
$$\bar{x} = 0$$

and
$$\bar{y} = \frac{V_1 y_1 - V_2 y_2}{V_1 - V_2}$$

$$= \frac{125\pi \times 3.75 - 15.625\pi \times 9.375}{125\pi - 15.625\pi}$$

$$= \frac{322.26\pi}{109.375\pi} = 2.946 \text{ cm}$$

$\therefore$
$$\bar{x} = 0$$
$$\bar{y} = \mathbf{2.946 \text{ cm}}$$

Ans.

THEORETICAL & NUMERICAL QUESTIONS

1. A triangle ABC with sides AB = BC = 80 mm and AC = 40 mm as shown in Fig. 21.51. Calculate the position of its centroid with reference to the axes Ox and Oy.

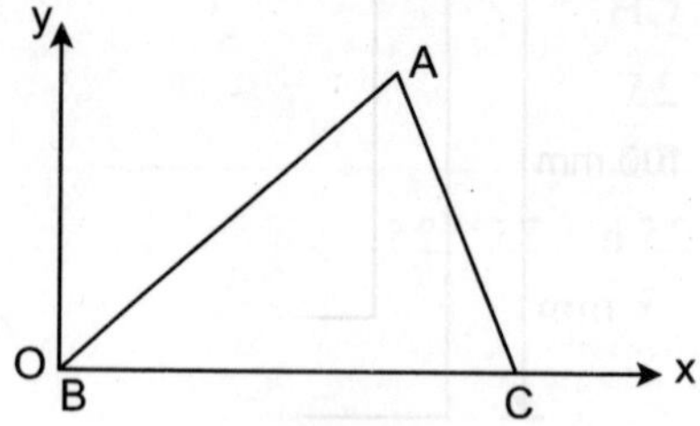

Fig. 21.51

2. Calculate the position of centroid of an unequal channel section as shown in Fig. 21.52. All dimensions are in mm.

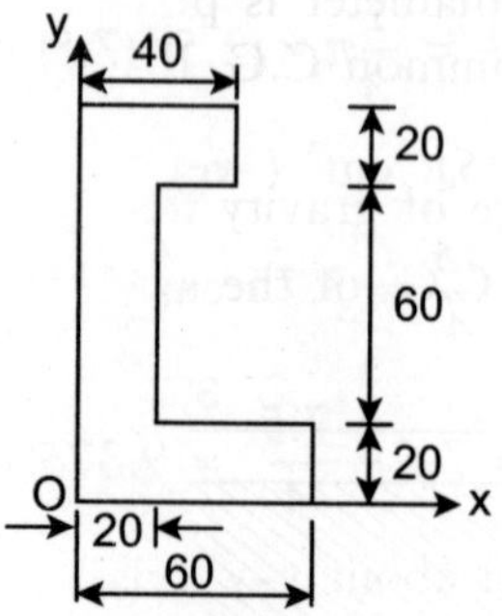

Fig. 21.52

3. A circular disc of radius 120 mm has two equal circular holes punched in it. The centres of holes being at the middle point of two radii at right angles to each other. If the radius of each hole is 20 mm, calculate distance of C.G. of the remainder from the centre.
4. Locate the centroid of a trapezium whose parallel sides are 100 mm and 80 mm and height is 60 mm.
5. Determine the centre of gravity of the area of the circular sector OAB of radius R and central angle α as shown in Fig. 21.53.

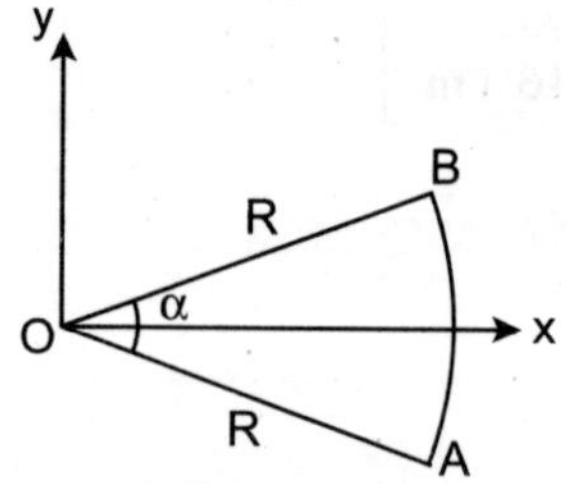

Fig. 21.53

6. Calculate the co-ordinates of the centroid of a L section as shown in Fig. 21.54.

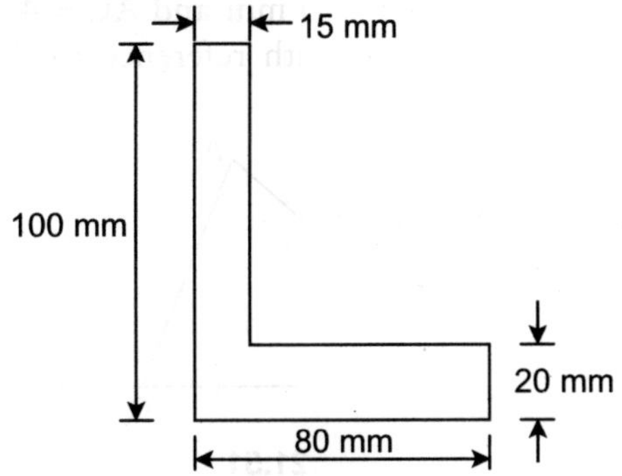

Fig. 21.54

7. A hemisphere of 60 mm diameter is placed on the top of the cylinder having 60 mm diameter. Calculate the common C.G. of the body from the base of the cylinder, if its height is 100 mm.
8. Distinguish between centre of gravity and centroid.
9. Calculate the position of C.G. of the shaded area as shown in Fig. 21.55.

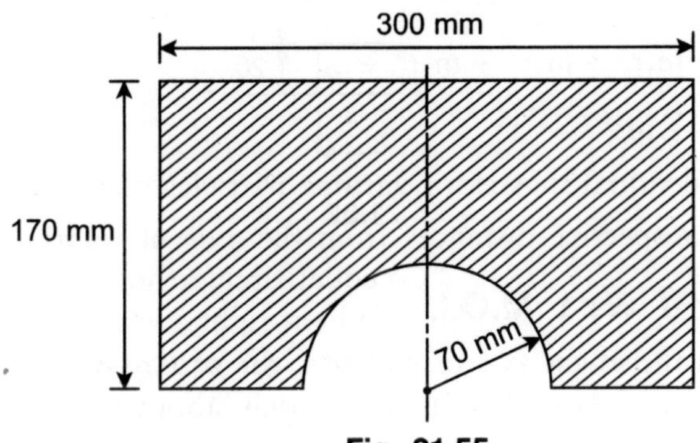

Fig. 21.55

10. Calculate the C.G. of the section if a square hole is cut out from a circular disc of radius 100 mm. The diagonal of the square hole coincides with the radius of the circle.

22

Moment of Inertia

22.1 Introduction

A rotating body about an axis in a reference frame resists any change in its rotational motion. Due to this property, the body is said to possess a moment of inertia or rotational inertia about that axis.

22.2 Mass Moment of Inertia

The mass moment of inertia is defined as

$$I = m_1 r_1^2 + m_2 r_2^2 + m_3 r_3^2 + \ldots$$

$$= \Sigma mr^2$$

where m_1, m_2, m_3, ... → individual masses of various particles consistig the body.

r_1, r_2, r_3, ... → their respective distances from the axis of rotation.

22.3 Radius of Gyration w·r·t· M.O.I.

It is the radial distance from the given axis of rotation, the square of which when multiplied by the total mass of the body, gives the MOI of the body about that axis.

i.e. $$I = MK^2 = \Sigma mr^2$$

$$\Rightarrow \quad K = \sqrt{\frac{I}{M}}, \qquad \text{where } K \rightarrow \text{radius of gyration.}$$

22.4 Area Moment of Inertia

It is also known as second moment of area and is related to the area of the body.

$$I_x = \text{Moment of inertia about } x\text{-axis}$$

$$= \Sigma y^2 dA = \int y^2 dA$$

$$I_y = \text{Moment of inertia about y-axis}$$

$$= \Sigma x^2 dA = \int x^2 dA$$

where x, y → perpendicular distances from y-axis and x-axis respectively.

22.5 Radius of Gyration

It is the distance from a given axis, the square of which when multiplied by the total area of the body, gives second moment of area about that axis.

i.e. $I = AK^2$

$\Rightarrow$ $K = \sqrt{\dfrac{I}{A}}$, where K = Radius of gyration.

For x-axis, $K_x = \sqrt{\dfrac{I_x}{A}}$, K_x = Radius of gyration w.r.t. x-axis.

For y-axis, $K_y = \sqrt{\dfrac{I_y}{A}}$, K_y = Radius of gyration w.r.t. y-axis.

22.6 Moment of Inertia of Standard Sections

S. No.	Shape	Axis	M.O.I. (I)
1.	Rectangle 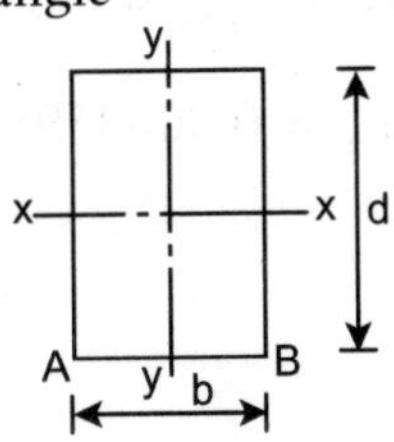 Fig. 22.1	(a) Centroidal axis x–x	$I_{xx} = \dfrac{bd^3}{12}$
		(b) Centroidal axis y–y	$I_{yy} = \dfrac{db^3}{12}$
		(c) A–B	$I_{AB} = \dfrac{bd^3}{12}$
2.	Hollow rectangle 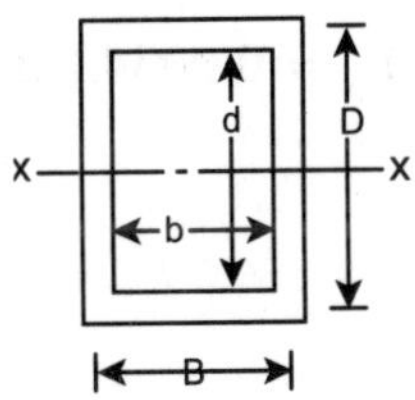 Fig. 22.2	Centroidal axis x–x	$I_{xx} = \left(\dfrac{BD^3}{12} - \dfrac{bd^3}{12}\right)$
		Centroidal axis y–y	$I_{yy} = \left(\dfrac{DB^3}{12} - \dfrac{db^3}{12}\right)$
3.	Triangle 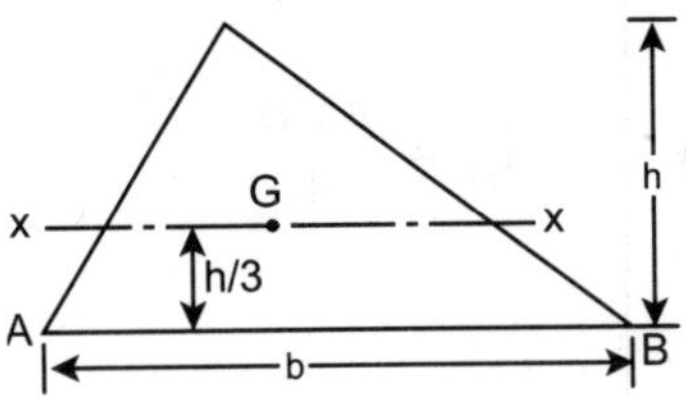 Fig. 22.3	(a) Centroidal axis x–x	$I_{xx} = \dfrac{bh^3}{36}$
		(b) Base AB	$I_{AB} = \dfrac{bh^3}{12}$

4.	Circle 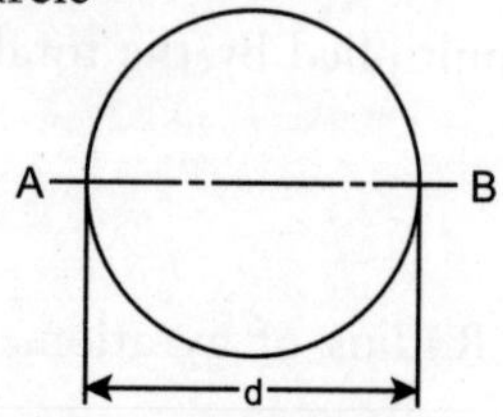 **Fig. 22.4**	Diametral axis	$I = \frac{\pi}{64} d^4 = I_{xx} = I_{yy}$ $I_z = \frac{\pi}{32} d^4$
5.	Hollow Circle 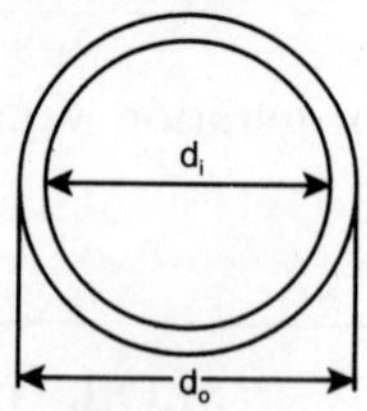 **Fig. 22.5**	Diametral axis	$I = \frac{\pi}{64}\left(d_o^{\,4} - d_i^{\,4}\right)$
6.	Semi Circle 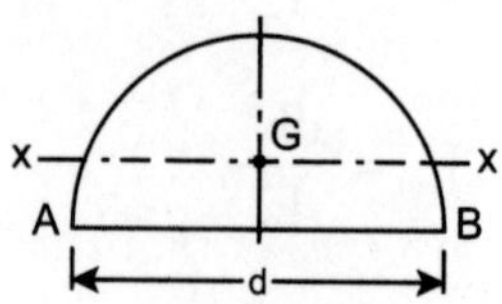 **Fig. 22.6**	(a) A–B (b) Centroidal axis	$I_{AB} = \frac{\pi}{128} d^4$ $I_{xx} = 0.0068598\ d^4$
7.	Quarter of a Circle 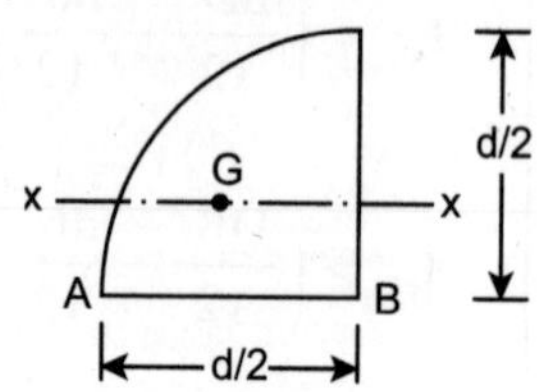 **Fig. 22.7**	(a) A–B (b) Centroidal axis x–x	$I_{AB} = \frac{\pi}{256} d^4$ $I_{xx} = 0.00343\ d^4$
8.	Ellipse 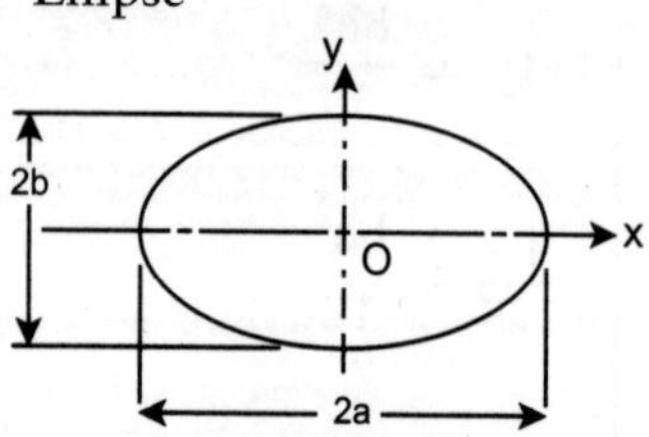 **Fig. 22.8**	(a) Centroidal axis x–x (b) Centroidal axis y–y	$I_{xx} = \frac{\pi a b^3}{4}$ $I_{yy} = \frac{\pi a^3 b}{4}$

9.	Circular Ring $t << r$ 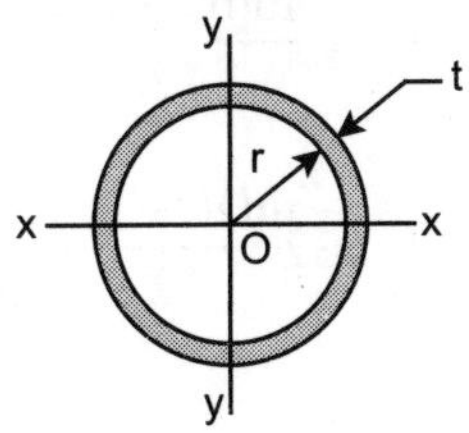 Fig. 22.9	(a) Centroidal axis x–x (b) Centroidal axis y–y	$I_{xx} = I_{yy} = \pi r^3 t$ $= \dfrac{\pi d^3 t}{8}$ $d = 2r$
10.	Circular Sector 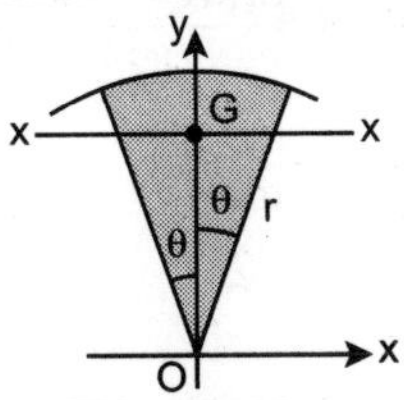 Fig. 22.10	(b) I_{xx} (a) I_{yy}	$I_x = \dfrac{r^4}{4}(\theta + \sin\theta \cos\theta)$ $I_y = \dfrac{r^4}{4}(\theta - \sin\theta \cos\theta)$
11.	Slendor rod	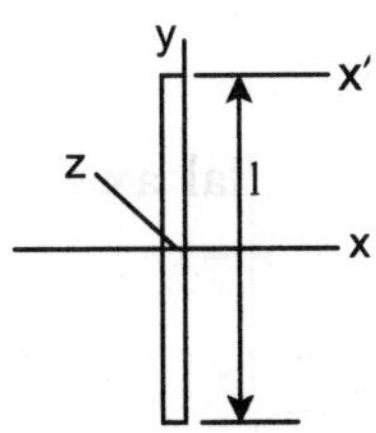 Fig. 22.11	$I_x = \dfrac{ml^2}{12}$ $I_{x'} = \dfrac{ml^2}{3}$ $I_y = 0$ $I_z = I_x = \dfrac{ml^2}{12}$
12.	Thin rectangular plate	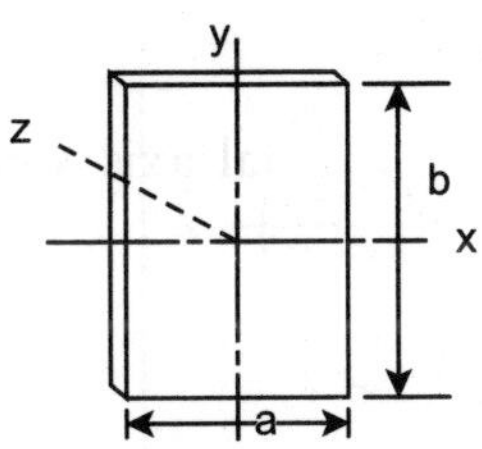 Fig. 22.12	$I_x = \dfrac{mb^2}{12}$ $I_y = \dfrac{ma^2}{12}$ $I_z = \dfrac{m(a^2 + b^2)}{12}$
13.	Thin Disc. or Thin circular ring	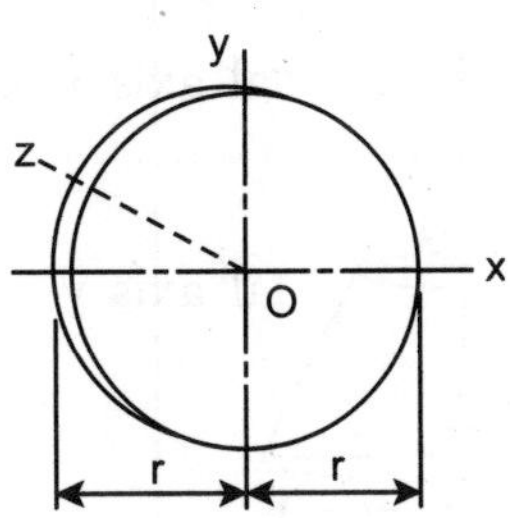 Fig. 22.13	$I_x = I_y = \dfrac{mr^2}{4}$ $I_z = \dfrac{mr^2}{2}$

14. Rectangular Prism

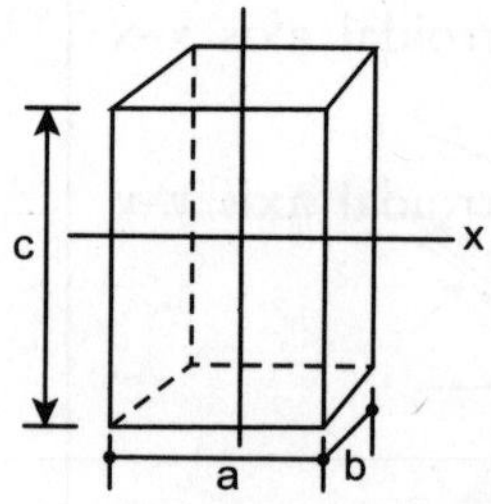

Fig. 22.14

$$I_x = \frac{m(b^2 + c^2)}{12}$$

$$I_z = \frac{m(a^2 + b^2)}{12}$$

15. Circular Solid Cylinder

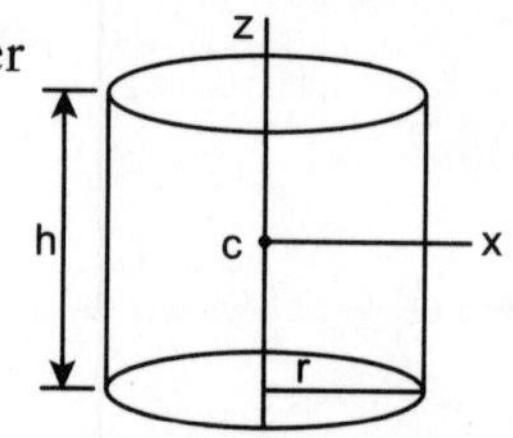

Fig. 22.15

$$I_x = \frac{m(3r^2 + h^2)}{12}$$

$$I_z = \frac{mr^2}{2}$$

16. Cylindrical Shell (hoop)

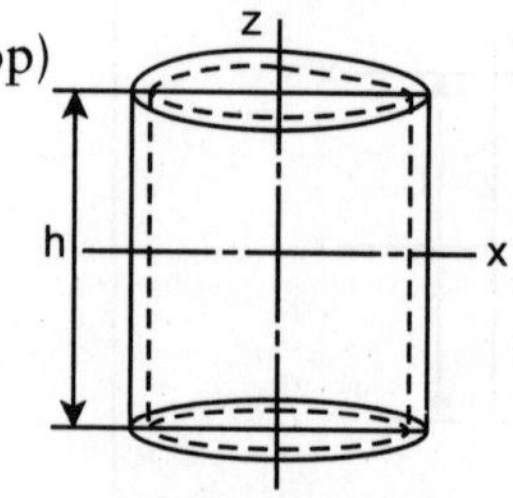

Fig. 22.16

$$I_x = \frac{m}{12}\left(6r^2 + h^2\right)$$

$$I_z = mr^2$$

17. Sphere

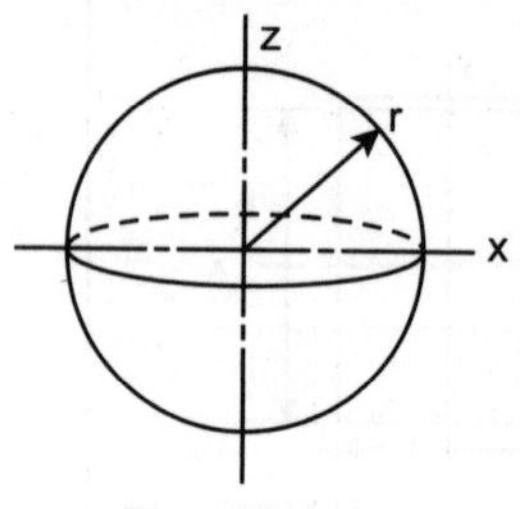

Fig. 22.17

$$I_x = \frac{2}{5}mr^2$$

$$I_z = \frac{2}{5}mr^2$$

18. Cone

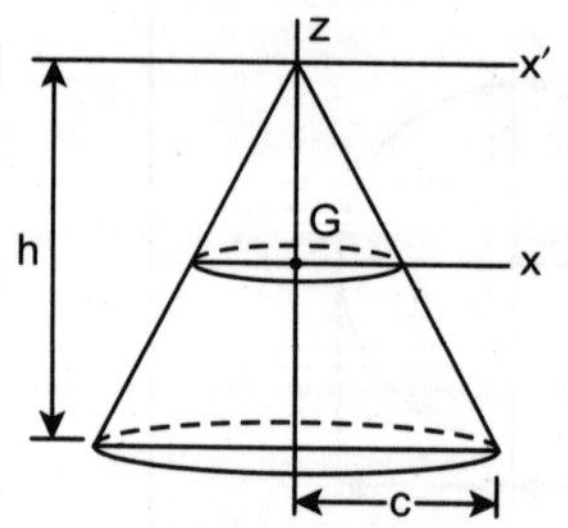

Fig. 22.18

$$I_x = \frac{3}{80}m\left(4r^2 + h^2\right)$$

$$I_{x'} = \frac{3}{5}m\left(\frac{r^2}{4} + h^2\right)$$

$$I_z = \frac{3}{10}mr^2$$

22.7 M.O.I. of Circular Section

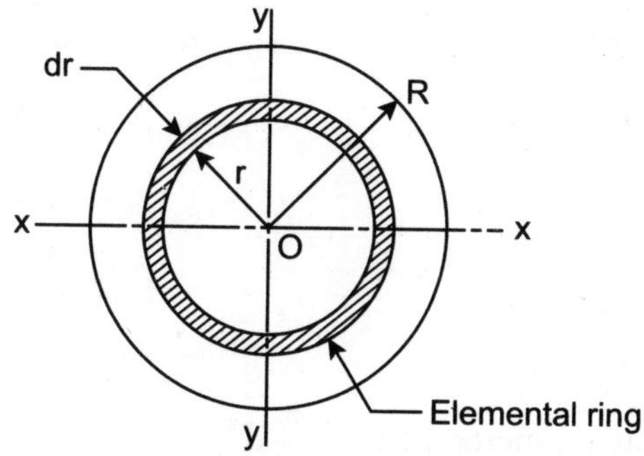

Fig. 22.19

M.O.I. of elementry ring about z–z axis

$$I_{zz} = dA \cdot r^2$$

or $$I_{zz} = 2\pi r dr \cdot r^2$$

or $$I_{zz} = 2\pi r^3 \cdot dr$$

or $$I_{zz} = \int_0^R dA \cdot r^2 = 2\pi \left[\frac{r^4}{4}\right]_0^R = \frac{2\pi}{4}(R^4)$$

$$= \frac{\pi}{2}\left(\frac{D}{2}\right)^4 = \frac{\pi}{32}D^4$$

But from theory of perpendicular axis

$$I_{zz} = I_{xx} + I_{yy}$$

here $$I_{xx} = I_{yy}$$

∴ $$I_{xx} = I_{yy} = \frac{\pi}{64}D^4$$

Notes

1. M.O.I. of a hollow circular

$$I_{xx} = I_{yy} = \frac{\pi}{64}\left(D_o^4 - d_i^4\right)$$

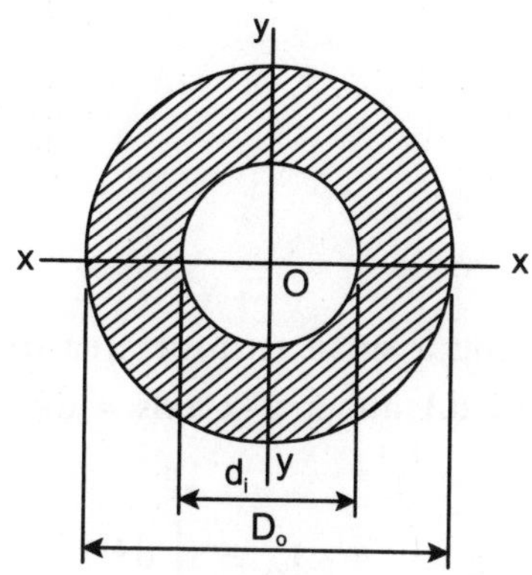

Fig. 22.20

2. M.O.I. of a semi circle:

$$d = 2r$$

$$h = \frac{4r}{3\pi}$$

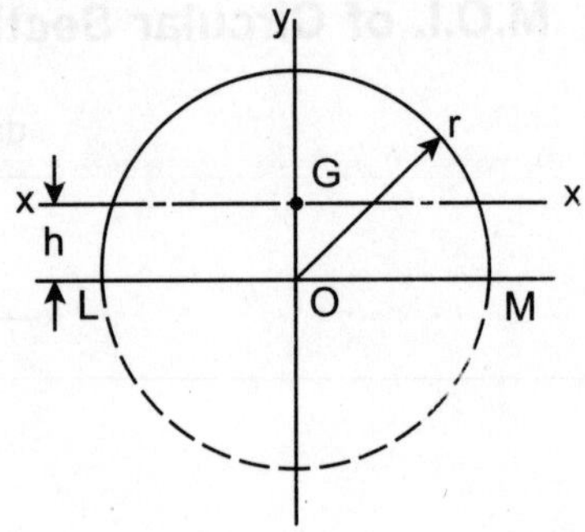

Fig. 22.21

M.O.I. of circle about diameter LM $= \frac{\pi}{64}d^4$

I_{LM} = M.O.I. of semi circle about LM $= \frac{1}{2} \times \frac{\pi}{64}d^4 = \frac{\pi}{128}d^4$

and

$$I_{LM} = I_{xx} + Ah^2 = I_{Gx} = Ah^2$$

$$\therefore \qquad I_{xx} = \frac{\pi}{128}d^4 - \frac{8}{9\pi}\left(\frac{d}{2}\right)^4 = 0.11\ r^4$$

$$I_{yy} = \frac{\pi}{128}d^4$$

22.8 Moment of Inertia of Rectangular Section

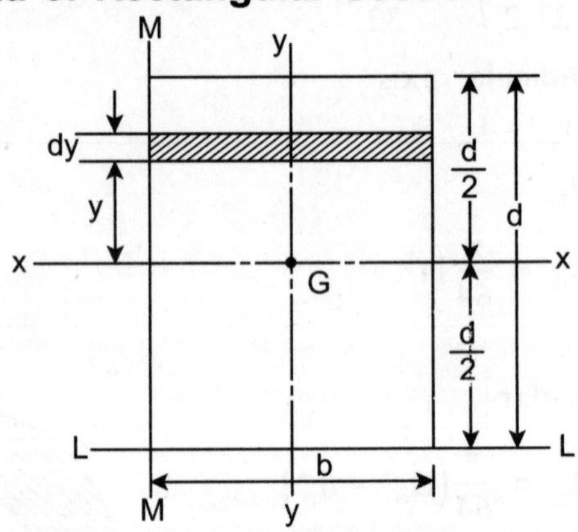

Fig. 22.22

Considering a small strip of area dA as shown in Fig. 22.22.
M.O.I. of dA about x–x-axis $= dA \times y^2$

$$\therefore \qquad I_{xx} = \int_{-\frac{d}{2}}^{+\frac{d}{2}} dA \cdot y^2 = \int_{-\frac{d}{2}}^{+\frac{d}{2}} b \cdot dy \cdot y^2 = b \cdot \int_{-\frac{d}{2}}^{+\frac{d}{2}} y^2 \cdot dy$$

$$= b \cdot \left[\frac{y^3}{3} \right]_{-\frac{d}{2}}^{+\frac{d}{2}} = \frac{b}{3} \left[\left(\frac{d}{2} \right)^3 - \left(-\frac{d}{2} \right)^3 \right]$$

$$I_{xx} = \frac{bd^3}{12}$$

Similarly

$$I_{yy} = \frac{db^3}{12}$$

and

$$I_{LL} = I_G + Ah^2 = I_{xx} + A \cdot h^2$$

$$= \frac{bd^3}{12} + (b \cdot d) \times \left(\frac{d}{2} \right)^2 = \frac{bd^3}{12} + \frac{bd^3}{4}$$

$$I_{LL} = \frac{bd^3}{3}$$

Similarly

$$I_{MM} = \frac{db^3}{3}$$

For hollow rectangular section:

$$I_{xx} = \left(\frac{bd^3}{12} - \frac{b_1 d_1^3}{12} \right)$$

$$I_{yy} = \left(\frac{db^3}{12} - \frac{d_1 b_1^3}{12} \right)$$

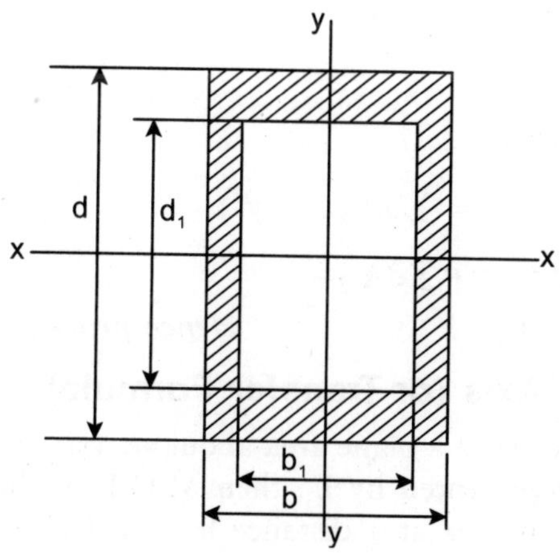

Fig. 22.23

22.9 Theorem of Perpendicular Axis

This theorem states that

$$I_{zz} = I_{xx} + I_{yy}$$

where

I_{xx} = M.O.I. of a plane section about axis x–x.
I_{yy} = M.O.I. of a plane section about y–y axis.
I_{zz} = M.O.I. of a plane section about z–z axis.

Proof:

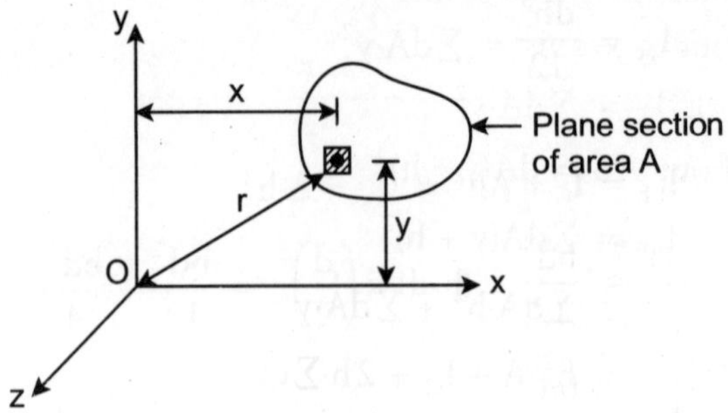

Fig. 22.24

Considering a small area dA as shown in Fig. 22.24.

x = Distance of C.G. of dA from axis Oy.
y = Distance of C.G of dA from axis Ox.
r = Distance of C.G. of dA from axis Oz.

Then $r^2 = x^2 + y^2$

Now

M.O.I. of dA about x–x axis = $dA \cdot y^2$
M.O.I. of dA about y–y axis = $dA \cdot x^2$
M.O.I. of dA about z–z axis = $dA \cdot r^2$

or $I_{xx} = \Sigma dA \cdot y^2$

$I_{yy} = \Sigma dA \cdot x^2$

and $I_{zz} = \Sigma dA \cdot r^2 = \Sigma dA \cdot (x^2 + y^2)$

$= \Sigma dA \cdot x^2 + \Sigma dA \cdot y^2$

$= I_{xx} + I_{yy}$ *Hence proved*

22.10 Theorem of Parallel Axis (or Transfer Formula)

It states that if the moment of inertia of a plane area about an axis in the plane of area through the C.G. of the plane area be represented by I_G, then M.O.I. of the given plane area about a parallel axis AB in the plane of area at a distance h from C.G. of the area is given by

$$I_{AB} = I_G + Ah^2$$

where

$$I_{AB} = \text{M.O.I. of given area about AB.}$$
$$I_G = \text{M.O.I. of given area about C.G.}$$
$$A = \text{Area of section}$$
$$h = \text{Distance between C.G. and axis AB.}$$

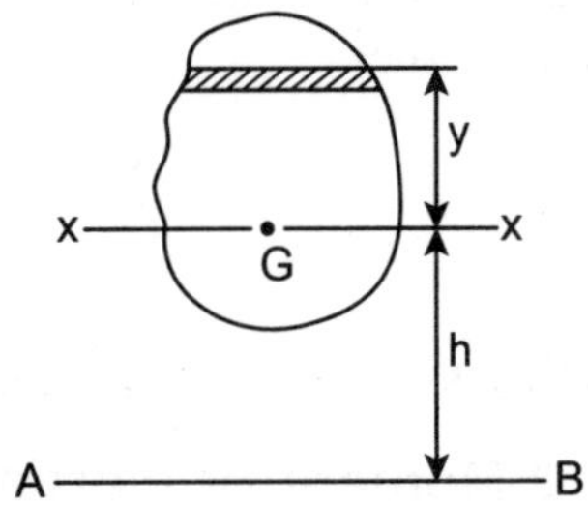

Fig. 22.25

Proof: Considering a small strip as shown in Fig. 22.25.

M.O.I. of 'dA' about x–x axis = $dA \cdot y^2$

M.O.I. of 'A' about x–x axis = $\Sigma dA \cdot y^2$

or I_{xx} or $I_G = \Sigma dA \cdot y^2$

M.O.I. of 'dA' about AB = $dA(y + h)^2$

and
$$I_{AB} = \Sigma dA(y + h)^2$$
$$= \Sigma dA \cdot h^2 + \Sigma dA \cdot y^2 + 2h \cdot \Sigma dA \cdot y$$
$$= h^2 \cdot A + I_G + 2h \cdot \Sigma dA \cdot y$$

But

$dA \cdot y$ = Moment of area 'dA' about x–x axis.

and $\Sigma dA \cdot y$ = Moment of total area about x–x axis.

$= A \times 0 = 0$

$\therefore \quad I_{AB} = Ah^2 + I_G$

or $\quad I_{AB} = I_G + Ah^2$ *Hence proved*

22.11 Radius of Gyration

Radius of gyration of a body (or a given lamina) is defined as the distance from an axis of reference where the whole mass (or area) of a body is assumed to be concentrated so as not to alter the M.O.I. about the given axis.

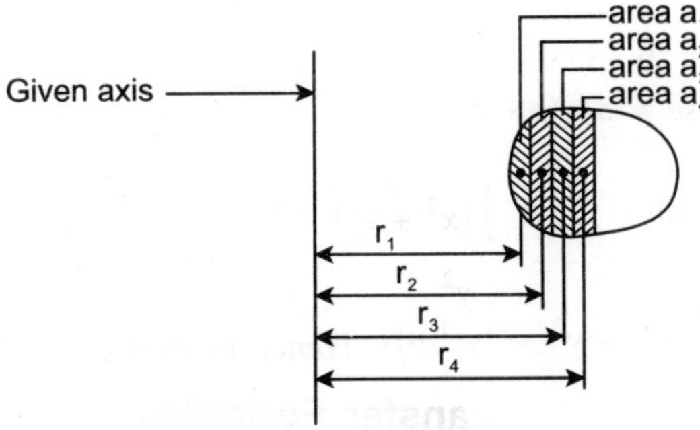

Fig. 22.26

M.O.I. about given axis

$$I = a_1 r_1^2 + a_2 r_2^2 + a_3 r_3^2 + \ldots$$

Let the whole mass (or area) of the body is concentrated at a distance K from the axis of reference, then

$$I = AK^2$$

or $$K = \sqrt{\frac{I}{A}}$$

Then K is known as radius of gyration about the given axis.

22.12 Moment of Inertia of a Triangular Section

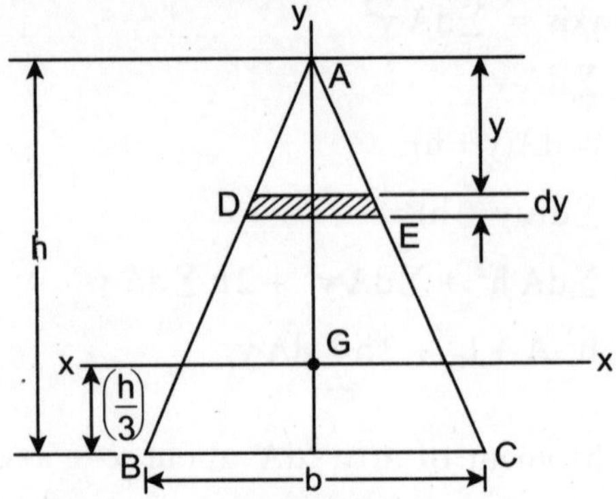

Fig. 22.27

Considering a small strip as shown in Fig. 22.27.

$$dA = DE \cdot dy$$

From similar triangles ADE and ABC.

$$\frac{DE}{BC} = \frac{y}{h} \text{ or } DE = \left(\frac{b \cdot y}{h}\right)$$

$$\therefore \quad dA = \frac{y}{h} \cdot b \cdot dy$$

Distance of strip from base = $(h - y)$

M.O.I. of strip about the base = $dA\,(h - y)^2$

$$\therefore \quad I_{BC} = \int_0^h dA(h-y)^2 = \int_0^h \frac{b \cdot y \cdot (h-y)^2 \cdot dy}{h}$$

$$= \frac{b}{h}\int_0^h (h^2y + y^3 - 2y^2h)dy$$

$$= \frac{b}{h}\left(\frac{h^2 \cdot y^2}{2} + \frac{y^4}{4} - \frac{2y^3}{3}h\right)_0^h$$

$$= \frac{b}{h}\left(\frac{h^4}{2} + \frac{h^4}{4} - \frac{2h^4}{3}\right) = \frac{bh^3}{12}$$

$$\therefore \qquad I_{BC} = \frac{bh^3}{12}$$

Now

M.O.I. of triangular section about an axis passing through C.G. and parallel to base.

$$I_{xx} = ?$$

From parallel axis theorem

$$I_{BC} = I_G + Ah^2$$

or

$$I_{BC} = I_{xx} + Ah^2$$

$$\therefore \qquad \frac{bh^3}{12} = I_{xx} + \left(\frac{b \times h}{2}\right)\left(\frac{h}{3}\right)^2$$

$$\therefore \qquad I_{xx} = I_G = \frac{bh^3}{36}$$

Example 22.1

Determine the moment of inertia of the section about the horizontal and vertical axis passing through the C.G. of the section shown in Fig. 22.28.

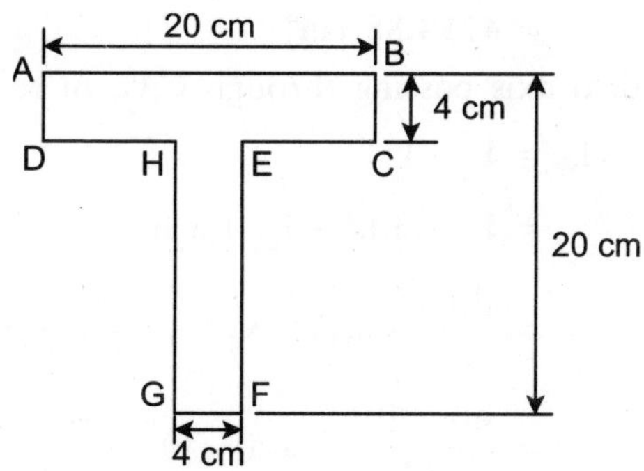

Fig. 22.28

Solution:

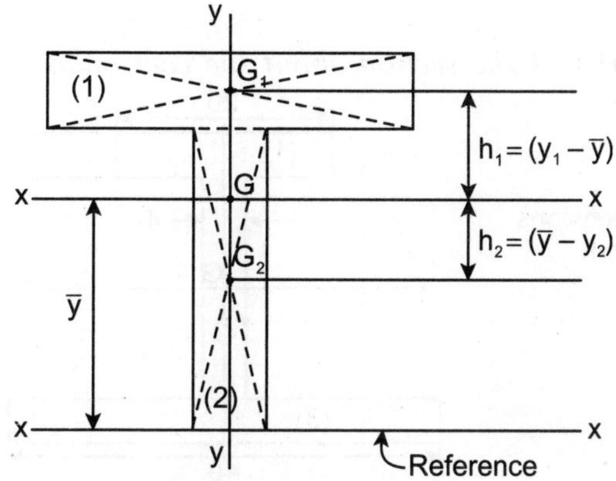

Fig. 22.29

∵ The given section is symmetrical about y–y axis.

$$\therefore \quad \bar{x} = 0$$

$$\bar{y} = \frac{a_1 y_1 + a_2 y_2}{a_1 + a_2} = \frac{12 \times 4 \times 18 + 16 \times 4 \times 8}{48 + 64} = \frac{1376}{112} = 12.3 \text{ cm}$$

M.O.I. about horizontal axis passing through C.G. of the section.

$$I_{xx} = I_{x_1} + I_{x_2}$$

$$= I_{G_1} + a_1 h_1^2 + I_{G_2} + a_2 h_2^2$$

$$I_{G_1} = \frac{b_1 d_1^3}{12} = \frac{20 \times 4^3}{12} = 106.7 \text{ cm}^4$$

$$I_{G_2} = \frac{b_2 d_2^3}{12} = \frac{4 \times 16^3}{12} = 1365.3 \text{ cm}^4$$

$$h_1 = (y_1 - \bar{y}) = (18 - 12.3) = 5.7$$

$$h_2 = (y_2 - \bar{y}) = (8 - 12.3) = -4.3$$

$$\therefore \quad I_{xx} = I_{G_1} + a_1 h_1^2 + I_{G_2} + a_2 h_2^2$$

$$= 106.7 + 12 \times 4 \times (5.7)^2 + 1365.3 + 16 \times 4 \times (4.3)^2$$

$$= \mathbf{4214.88 \text{ cm}^4}$$ **Ans.**

M.O.I. about vertical axis passing through C.G. of section.

$$I_{yy} = I_{y_1} + I_{y_2}$$

$$= I_{G_1} + a_1 h_1^2 + I_{G_2} + a_2 h_2^2$$

$$= \frac{d_1 b_1^3}{12} + a_1(\bar{x} - x_1)^2 + \frac{d_2 b_2^3}{12} + a_2(\bar{x} - x_2)^2$$

$$= \frac{40 \times 20^3}{12} + a_1(0 - 0)^2 + \frac{16 \times 4^3}{12} + a_2(0 - 0)^2 = 26666.7 + 85.3$$

$$= \mathbf{26752 \text{ cm}^4}$$ **Ans.**

Example 22.2

Find moment of inertia of the section about the centroidal axis perpendicular to the web as shown in Fig. 22.30.

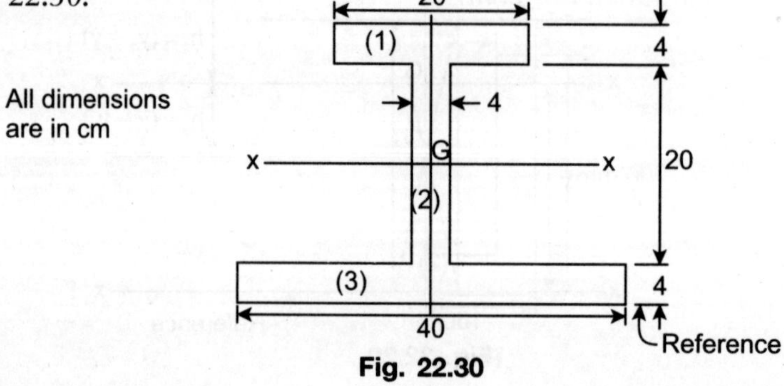

Fig. 22.30

Solution:

$I_{xx} = I_G = ?$

$a_1 = 20 \times 4 = 80 \text{ cm}^2$ $\quad a_2 = 4 \times 20 = 80 \text{ cm}^2$ $\quad a_3 = 40 \times 4 = 160 \text{ cm}^2$

$y_1 = 4 + 20 + \frac{4}{2} = 26 \text{ cm}$ $\quad y_2 = 4 + \frac{20}{2} = 14 \text{ cm}$ $\quad y_3 = \frac{4}{2} = 2 \text{ cm}$

$\because$ The given section is symmetrical about y–y axis.

$\therefore$ $\bar{x} = 0$

$$\bar{y} = \frac{a_1y_1 + a_2y_2 + a_3y_3}{a_1 + a_2 + a_3} = \frac{80 \times 26 + 80 \times 14 + 160 \times 2}{80 + 80 + 160}$$

$$= \frac{3520}{320} = 11 \text{ cm}$$

x–x is the horizontal line passing through the C.G. of the composite member.

$$I_{xx} = I_{x_1} + I_{x_2} + I_{x_3}$$

or $$I_{xx} = I_{G_1} + a_1h_1^2 + I_{G_2} + a_2h_2^2 + I_{G_3} + a_3h_3^2 \quad \dots\dots\dots\dots \quad (22.1)$$

$$I_{G_1} = \frac{b_1d_1^3}{12} = \frac{20 \times 4^3}{12} = 106.7 \text{ cm}$$

$$I_{G_2} = \frac{b_2d_2^3}{12} = \frac{4 \times 20^3}{12} = 2666.7 \text{ cm}$$

$$I_{G_3} = \frac{b_3d_3^3}{12} = \frac{40 \times 4^3}{12} = 213.3 \text{ cm}$$

$$h_1 = (\bar{y} - y_1) = 11 - 26 = -15 \text{ cm}$$

$$h_2 = (\bar{y} - y_2) = 11 - 14 = -3 \text{ cm}$$

$$h_3 = (\bar{y} - y_3) = 11 - 2 = 9 \text{ cm}$$

$\therefore$ From Eq. (22.1),

$$I_{xx} = 106.7 + 80 \times 15^2 + 2666.7 + 80 \times 3^3 + 213.3 + 160 \times 9^2$$

$$= \mathbf{34666.7 \text{ cm}^4}$$ **Ans.**

Example 22.3

Find the moment of inertia about the controidal axis xx and yy of the section shown in Fig. 22.31.

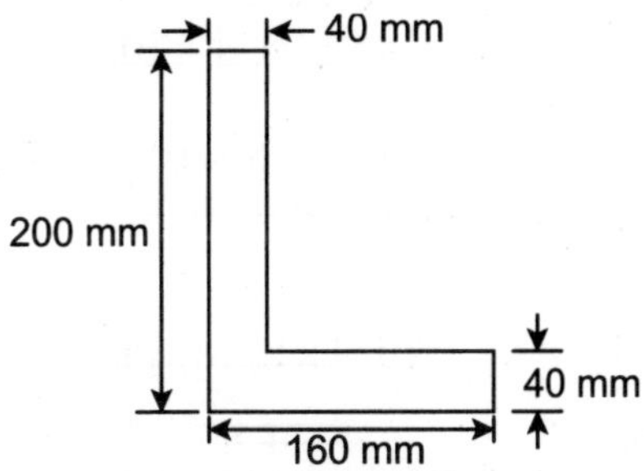

Fig. 22.31

Solution:

$I_{xx} = ?$

$I_{yy} = ?$

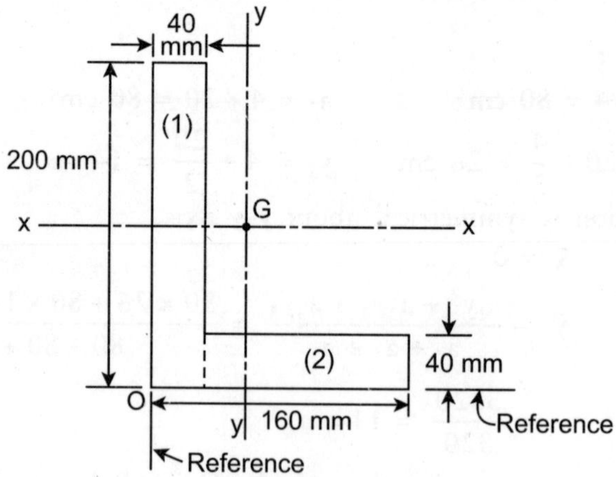

Fig. 22.32

$a_1 = 200 \times 40 = 8000 \text{ mm}^2$ | $x_1 = \frac{40}{2} = 20 \text{ mm}$ | $y_1 = 100 \text{ mm}$

$a_2 = 120 \times 4 = 480 \text{ mm}^2$ | $x_2 = 40 + \frac{140}{2} = 110 \text{ mm}$ | $y_2 = 20 \text{ mm}$

$$\bar{x} = \frac{a_1x_1 + a_2x_2}{a_1 + a_2} = \frac{8000 \times 20 + 480 \times 110}{8000 + 480} = \frac{212800}{8480} = 25.0 \text{ mm}$$

$$\bar{y} = \frac{a_1y_1 + a_2y_2}{a_1 + a_2} = \frac{8000 \times 100 + 480 \times 20}{8480} = 95.5 \text{ mm}$$

Now

$$I_{xx} = I_1 + I_2 = I_{G_1} + a_1h_1^2 + I_{G_2} + a_2h_2^2$$

$$= \frac{b_1d_1^3}{12} + a_1(y_1 - \bar{y})^2 + \frac{b_2d_2^3}{12} + a_2(y_2 - \bar{y})^2$$

$$= \frac{40 \times 200^3}{12} + 8000 \times (95.5 - 100)^2$$

$$+ \frac{140 \times 40^3}{12} + 480(95.5 - 20)^2$$

or

$$I_{xx} = 2.6 \times 10^7 + 16200 + 7.5 \times 10^5 + 2.7 \times 10^6$$

$$= \mathbf{2.96 \times 10^7 \text{ mm}^4}$$ **Ans.**

and

$$I_{yy} = I_1 + I_2 = I_{G_1} + a_1h_1^2 + I_{G_2} + a_2h_2^2$$

$$= \frac{d_1b_1^3}{12} + a_1(\bar{x} - x_1)^2 + \frac{d_2b_2^3}{12} + a_2(\bar{x} - x_2)^2$$

$$= \frac{200 \times 40^3}{12} + 8000(25-20)^2 + \frac{40 \times 140^3}{12} + 480(25-110)^2$$

$$= 1.06 \times 10^6 + 2.0 \times 10^5 + 9.14 \times 10^6 + 3.46 \times 10^6$$

$$= \mathbf{1.39 \times 10^7 \ mm^4}$$ **Ans.**

Example 22.4

Find the moment of inertia about the centroidal axis xx for the lamina as shown in Fig. 22.33.

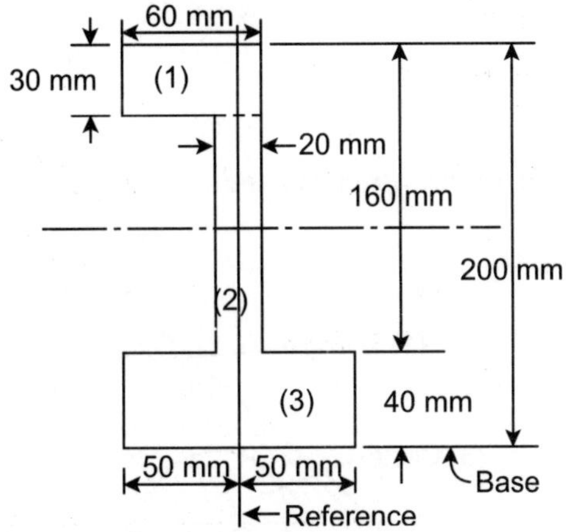

Fig. 22.33

Solution:

$a_1 = 6 \times 3 = 18 \ cm^2$	$y_1 = 17 + 1.5 = 18.5 \ cm$	$x_1 = \frac{6}{2} = 3 \ cm$
$a_2 = 13 \times 2 = 26 \ cm^2$	$y_2 = 4 + \frac{13}{2} = 10.5 \ mm$	$x_2 = 0$
$a_3 = 10 \times 4 = 40 \ cm^2$	$y_3 = \frac{4}{2} = 2 \ mm$	$x_3 = 0$

Now

$$\bar{y} = \frac{a_1 y_1 + a_2 y_2 + a_3 y_3}{a_1 + a_2 + a_3} = \frac{18 \times 18.5 + 26 \times 10.5 + 40 \times 2}{18 + 26 + 40}$$

$$= \frac{686}{84} = 8.17 \ cm$$

Now

$$I_{xx} = I_{x_1} + I_{x_2} + I_{x_3}$$

or

$$I_{xx} = I_{G_1} + a_1 h_1^2 + I_{G_2} + a_2 h_2^2 + I_{G_3} + a_3 h_3^2$$

$\therefore$

$$I_{G_1} = \frac{b_1 d_1^3}{12} = \frac{6 \times 3^3}{12} = 13.5 \ cm^4$$

$$I_{G_2} = \frac{b_2 d_2^3}{12} = \frac{2 \times 13^3}{12} = 366.2 \text{ cm}^4$$

$$I_{G_3} = \frac{b_3 d_3^3}{12} = \frac{10 \times 4^3}{12} = 53.3 \text{ cm}^4$$

$$a_1 h_1^2 = 18 \times (y_1 - \bar{y})^2 = 18(18.5 - 8.17)^2 = 1920.8 \text{ cm}^4$$

$$a_2 h_2^2 = 26 \times (y_2 - \bar{y})^2 = 26(10.5 - 8.17)^2 = 141.15 \text{ cm}^4$$

$$a_3 h_3^2 = 40 \times (y_1 - \bar{y})^2 = 40(8.17 - 2)^2 = 1522.8 \text{ cm}^4$$

$\therefore$ $$I_{xx} = \mathbf{4017.75 \text{ cm}^4}$$ **Ans.**

Example 22.5

Find the moment of inertia of the area shaded in Fig. 22.34, about the axis AB.

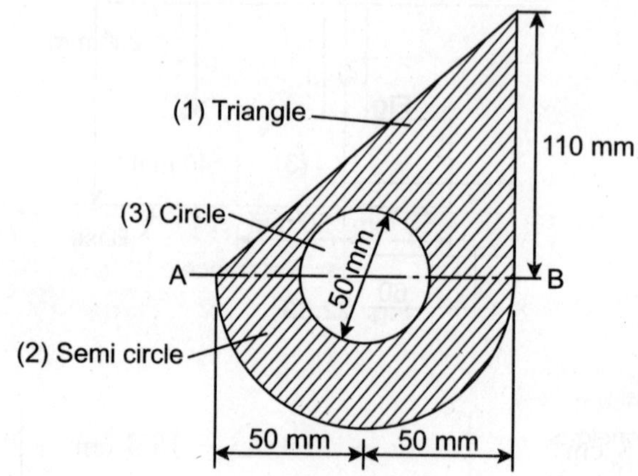

Fig. 22.34

Solution:

$$I_{1(AB)} = \frac{bh^3}{12} = \frac{100 \times 110^3}{12} = 1.1 \times 10^7 \text{ mm}^4$$

$$I_{2(AB)} = \frac{1}{2} \times \frac{\pi}{64} d^4 = \frac{1}{2} \times \frac{\pi}{64} \times (50)^4 = 1.53 \times 10^5 \text{ mm}^4$$

$$I_{3(AB)} = \frac{\pi}{64} d^4 = \frac{\pi}{64} \times (50)^4 = 3.1 \times 10^5 \text{ mm}^4$$

and

$$I_{AB} = I_1 + I_2 - I_3$$
$$= 1.1 \times 10^7 + 1.53 \times 10^5 - 3.1 \times 10^5$$
$$= 1.11 \times 10^7 - 3.1 \times 10^5$$
$$I_{AB} = \mathbf{1.08 \times 10^7 \text{ mm}^4}$$ **Ans.**

Example 22.6

A T-beam is made up of two plates and two angles as shown in Fig. 22.35. Determine the M.O.I. of T-section about an axis passing through the centroid of the section and parallel to the top plate.

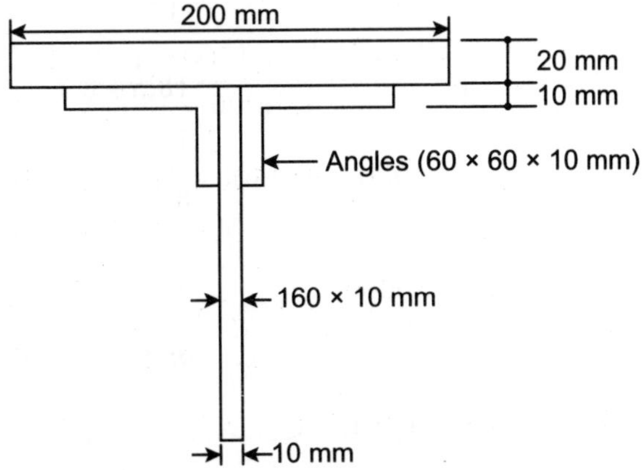

Fig. 22.35

Solution:

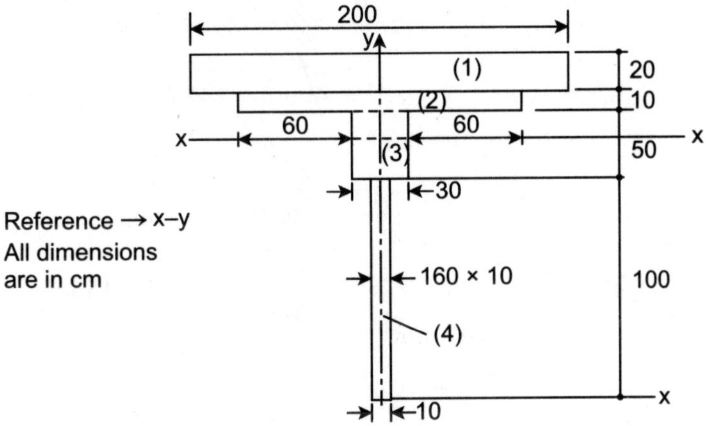

Fig. 22.36

$a_1 = 200 \times 20 = 4000 \text{ mm}^2$	$y_1 = 160 + \frac{20}{2} = 170 \text{ mm}$
$a_2 = 150 \times 10 = 1500 \text{ mm}^2$	$y_2 = 150 + \frac{10}{2} = 155 \text{ mm}$
$a_3 = 30 \times 50 = 1500 \text{ mm}^2$	$y_3 = 100 + \frac{50}{2} = 125 \text{ mm}$
$a_4 = 10 \times 100 = 1000 \text{ mm}^2$	$y_4 = \frac{100}{2} = 50 \text{ mm}$

$\because$ The given section is symmetrical about y–y axis.

$\therefore \qquad \bar{x} = 0$

and

$$\bar{y} = \left(\frac{a_1y_1 + a_2y_2 + a_3y_3 + a_4y_4}{a_1 + a_2 + a_3 + a_4}\right)$$

$$= \left(\frac{4000 \times 170 + 1500 \times 155 + 1500 \times 125 + 1000 \times 50}{4000 + 1500 + 1500 + 1000}\right)$$

$$= \frac{680000 + 232500 + 187500 + 50000}{8000}$$

$$= \frac{1150000}{8000} = 143.75 \text{ mm}$$

Now

$$I_{xx} = I_1 + I_2 + I_3 + I_4$$

$$= I_{G_1} + a_1h_1^2 + I_{G_2} + a_2h_2^2 + I_{G_3} + a_3h_3^2 + I_{G_4} + a_4h_4^2$$

$$I_{G_1} = \frac{b_1d_1^3}{12} = \frac{200 \times 20^3}{12} = 1.33 \times 10^5 \text{ mm}^4$$

$$a_1h_1^2 = 4000 \times (\bar{y} - y_1)^2 = 4000 \times (143.75 - 170)^2$$

$$= 2.76 \times 10^6 \text{ mm}^4$$

$$I_{G_2} = \frac{b_2d_2^3}{12} = \frac{150 \times 10^3}{12} = 1.25 \times 10^4 \text{ mm}^4$$

$$a_2h_2^2 = 1500 \times (\bar{y} - y_2)^2 = 1500 \times (143.75 - 155)^2$$

$$= 1.9 \times 10^5 \text{ mm}^4$$

$$I_{G_3} = \frac{b_3d_3^3}{12} = \frac{30 \times 50^3}{12} = 3.13 \times 10^5 \text{ mm}^4$$

$$a_3h_3^2 = 1500 \times (\bar{y} - y_3)^2 = 1500 \times (143.75 - 125)^2$$

$$= 5.3 \times 10^5 \text{ mm}^4$$

$$I_{G_4} = \frac{b_4d_4^3}{12} = \frac{10 \times 100^3}{12} = 8.3 \times 10^5 \text{ mm}^4$$

$$a_4h_4^2 = 1000 \times (\bar{y} - y_4)^2 = 1000 \times (143.75 - 50)^2$$

$$= 8.8 \times 10^6 \text{ mm}^4$$

$\therefore$

$$I_{xx} = 1.33 \times 10^5 + 2.76 \times 10^6 + 1.25 \times 10^4 + 1.9 \times 10^5 + 3.13 \times 10^5 + 5.3 \times 10^5 + 8.3 \times 10^5 + 8.8 \times 10^6$$

$$= \mathbf{1.35 \times 10^7 \text{ mm}^4}$$

Ans.

Example 22.7

A rectangular hole is made in a triangular section as shown in Fig. 22.37. Determine the moment of inertia of the section about x–x axis passing through its centre of gravity and the base BC.

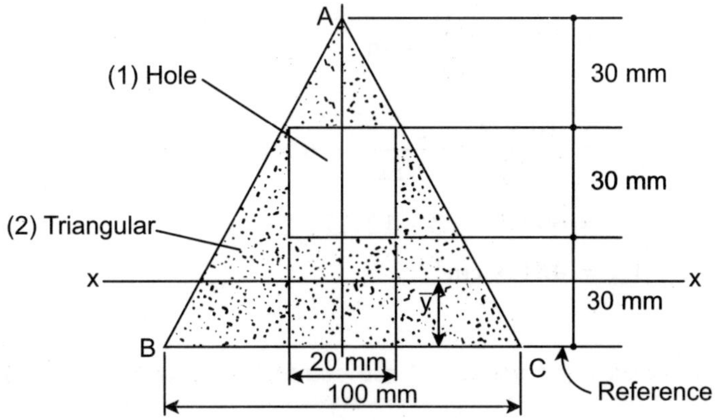

Fig. 22.37

Solution:

Case I

∵ The given section is symmetrical about y–y axis.

∴ C.G. will lie on this axis

$$a_1 = \frac{1}{2} \times 10 \times 9 = 45 \text{ cm}^2$$

$$a_2 = 3 \times 2 = 6 \text{ cm}^2$$

$$y_1 = \frac{h}{3} = 3 \text{ cm}$$

$$y_2 = 3 + \frac{3}{2} = 4.5 \text{ cm}$$

$$\therefore \quad \bar{y} = \frac{a_1 y_1 - a_2 y_2}{a_1 - a_2} = \frac{45 \times 3 - 6 \times 4.5}{45 - 6} = 2.77 \text{ cm} = 2.8 \text{ cm}$$

Now

$$I_{xx} = I_{xx_1} - I_{xx_2}$$

$$= I_{G_1} + a_1 h_1^2 - I_{G_2} - a_2 h_2^2$$

$$= \frac{10 \times 9^3}{36} + 45 \times (3 - 2.8)^2 - \frac{2 \times 3^3}{12} - 6 \times (4.5 - 2.8)^2$$

$$= 202.5 \times 1.8 - 4.5 - 17.34$$

$$I_{xx} = \mathbf{182.5 \text{ mm}^4}$$ **Ans.**

Case II

M.O.I. about base BC:

$$I_{AB} = I_1 - I_2$$

$$= \frac{bh^3}{12} - \frac{bd^3}{12} - ah^2$$

$$= \frac{10 \times 9^3}{12} - \frac{2 \times 3^3}{12} - 6 \times (4.5 - 0)^2$$

$$= 607.5 - 4.5 - 121.5$$

$$I_{AB} = 481.5 \text{ cm}^4$$ **Ans.**

Example 22.8

Find the centroidal moment of inertia of the shaded area as shown in Fig. 22.38.

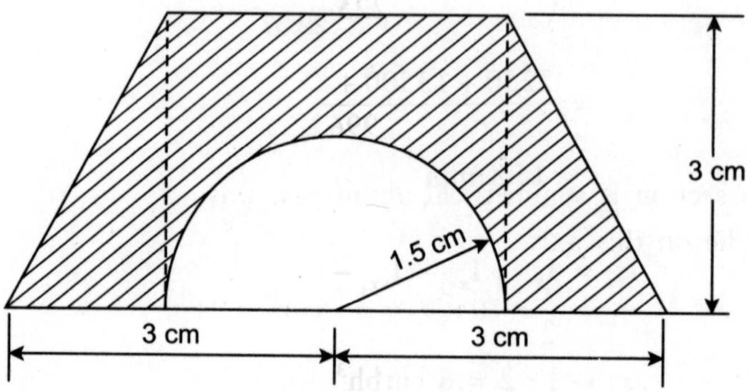

Fig. 22.38

Solution:

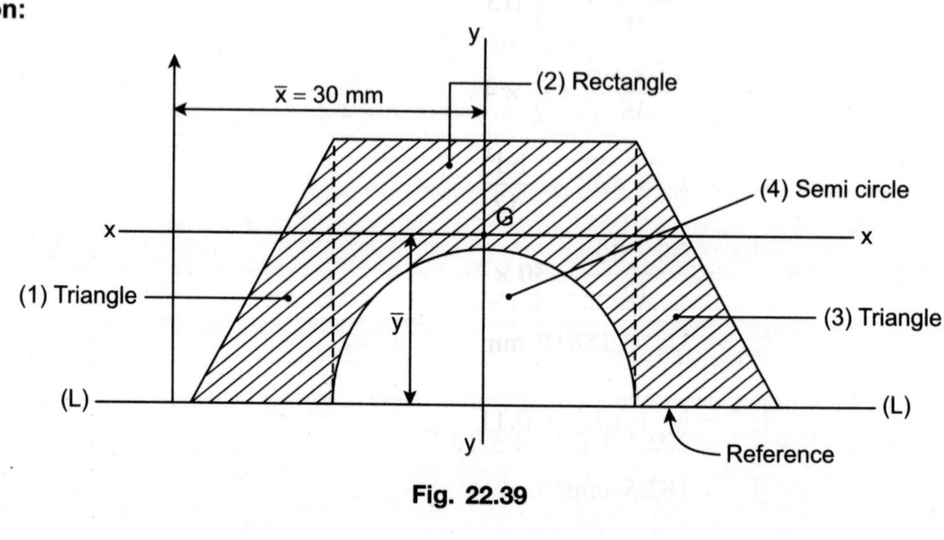

Fig. 22.39

$$a_1 = \frac{15 \times 30}{2} = 225 \text{ mm}^2 \text{ (+ve)} \qquad y_1 = \frac{30}{3} = 10 \text{ mm}$$

$$a_2 = 30 \times 30 = 900 \text{ mm}^2 \text{ (+ve)} \qquad y_2 = \frac{30}{2} = 15 \text{ mm}$$

$$a_3 = \frac{15 \times 30}{2} = 225 \text{ mm}^2 \text{ (+ve)} \qquad y_3 = \frac{30}{3} = 10 \text{ mm}$$

$$a_4 = \frac{\pi \times 15^2}{2} = 353.4 \text{ mm}^2 \text{ (–ve)} \qquad y_4 = \frac{4 \times 15}{3\pi} = 6.37 \text{ mm}$$

and

$$\bar{y} = \frac{a_1 y_1 + a_2 y_2 + a_3 y_3 - a_4 y_4}{a_1 + a_2 + a_3 - a_4}$$

$$= \left(\frac{225 \times 10 + 900 \times 15 + 225 \times 10 - 353.4 \times 6.37}{225 + 900 + 225 - 353.4}\right)$$

$$= \frac{2250 + 13500 + 2250 - 2251.2}{996.6} = \frac{15748.8}{996.6}$$

$$= 15.8 \text{ mm}$$

Now

$$I_{xx} = I_{xx_1} + I_{xx_2} + I_{xx_3} - I_{xx_4}$$

and

$$I_{xx_1} = I_{G_1} + a_1 h_1^2 = \frac{bh^3}{36} + a_1 h_1^2$$

$$= \frac{15 \times 30^3}{36} + \frac{1}{2}(15 \times 30) \times (\bar{y} - y_1)^2$$

$$= \frac{15 \times 30^3}{36} + \frac{1}{2} \times 450 \times (15.8 - 10)^2 = 18819 \text{ mm}^4$$

$$I_{xx_2} = I_{G_2} + a_2 h_2^2 = \frac{bd^3}{12} + a_2(\bar{y} - y_2)^2$$

$$= \frac{30 \times 30^3}{12} + 30 \times 30 \times (15.8 - 15)^2 = 68076 \text{ mm}^4$$

$$I_{xx_3} = I_{xx_1} = 18819 \text{ mm}^4$$

$$I_{xx_4} = I_{G_4} + a_4 h_4^2 = 0.11 r^4 + \frac{\pi r^2}{2} \times (\bar{y} - y_4)^2$$

$$= 0.11 \times (15)^4 + \frac{\pi \times 15^2}{2}\left(15.8 - \frac{4 \times 15}{3\pi}\right)^2$$

$$= 0.11 \times (15)^4 + \frac{\pi \times 15^2}{2}(15.8 - 6.37)^2 = 37023 \text{ mm}^4$$

$\therefore$ $$I_{xx} = 11819 + 68076 + 18819 - 37023$$

$\therefore$ $$I_{xx} = \mathbf{68691\ mm^4}$$ **Ans.**

and

$$I_{yy} = I_{yy_1} + I_{yy_2} + I_{yy_3} - I_{yy_4} \qquad \Big| \; \bar{x} = 30 \text{ mm}$$

$$I_{yy_1} = \frac{30 \times 15^3}{36} + \frac{1}{2} \times 30 \times 15 \times \left(30 - \frac{2}{3} \times 15\right)^2 = 92812.5 \text{ mm}^4$$

$$I_{yy_2} = \frac{30 \times 30^3}{12} = 67500 \text{ mm}^4$$

$$I_{yy_3} = I_{yy_1} = 92812.5 \text{ mm}^4$$

$$I_{yy_4} = \frac{1}{2} \times \frac{\pi}{64} d^4 = \frac{\pi}{128} \times (30)^4 = 19880.4 \text{ mm}^4$$

$\therefore$ $$I_{yy} = 92812.5 + 67500 + 92812.5 - 19880.4$$

$\therefore$ $$I_{yy} = \mathbf{233244.6\ mm^4}$$ **Ans.**

Example 22.9

Find the moment of inertia of the shaded area as shown in Fig. 22.40 about edge AB.

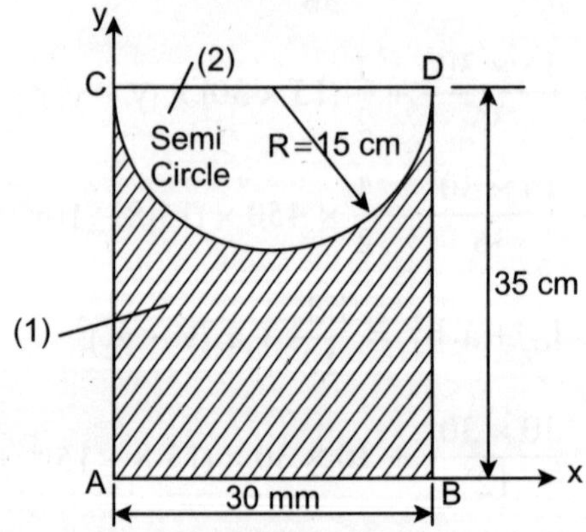

Fig. 22.40

Solution:

Let (1) → Rectangle ABCD, (2) → Semicircle

M.O.I. of shaded portion about AB = ?

$$I_{AB} = ?$$

$$I_{AB} = I_{1(AB)} - I_{2(AB)}$$

$$I_{1(AB)} = I_{G_1} + a_1 h_1^2 = \frac{30 \times 35^3}{12} + 30 \times 35 \times \left(\frac{35}{2} - 0\right)^2$$

$$= 107187.5 + 321562.5 = 428750 \text{ cm}^4$$

$$I_{2(CD)} = \frac{1}{2} \times \frac{\pi}{64} D^4 = \frac{1}{2} \times \frac{\pi}{64}(30)^4 = 19880.4 \text{ cm}^4$$

Also, $$I_{2(CD)} = I_{G_2} + a_2 h_2^2$$

$$\frac{\pi}{128} D^4 = I_{G_2} + \frac{\pi r^2}{2} \times \left(\frac{4r}{3\pi}\right)^2$$

$\Rightarrow$ $$I_{G_2} = \frac{\pi}{128} D^4 - \frac{\pi}{2} \times \left(\frac{D}{2}\right)^2 \times \frac{16}{9\pi^2}\left(\frac{D}{2}\right)^2$$

$$= \frac{\pi}{128} D^4 - \pi \frac{D^2}{4} \times \frac{8}{9\pi^2} \times \frac{D^2}{4}$$

$$= \frac{\pi}{128} D^4 - \frac{1}{18\pi} D^4 = 6.85981 \times D^4 \times 10^{-3}$$

$\therefore$ $$I_{G_2} = 6.85981 \times 10^{-3} \times (30)^4 = 5556.5 \text{ cm}^4$$

Now

$$I_{2(AB)} = I_{G_2} + a_2 h_2'^2 \qquad \because \; h_2' = \left(35 - \frac{4r}{3\pi}\right)$$

$$= 5556.5 + \frac{\pi r^2}{2} \times \left(35 - \frac{4r}{3\pi}\right)^2$$

$$= 5556.5 + \frac{\pi}{2}(15)^2 \times \left(35 - \frac{4 \times 15}{\pi}\right)^2$$

$$= 5556.5 + 89366.2$$

$$= 94922.7 \text{ cm}^4$$

$\therefore$ $$I_{AB} = I_{1(AB)} - I_{2(AB)}$$

$$= 428750 - 94922.7$$

$$I_{AB} = \mathbf{333827.3 \text{ cm}^4}$$ **Ans.**

Example 22.10

Find I_{xx} and I_{yy} of the C.I. cross section beam as shown in Fig. 22.41.

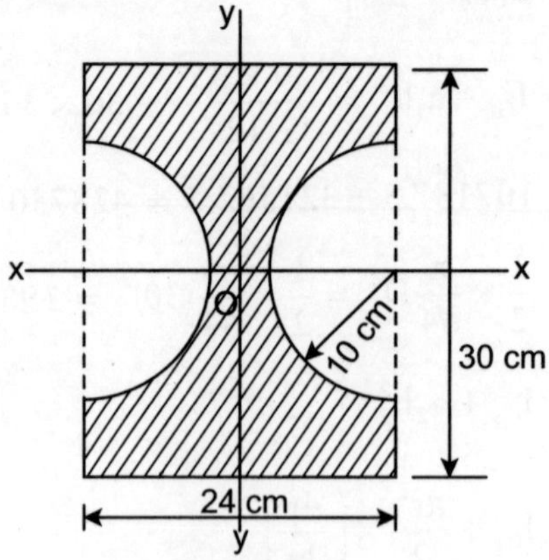

Fig. 22.41

Solution:

$$I_{xx} = ?, \quad I_{yy} = ?$$

Now

$$I_{xx} = I_{xx_1} - I_{xx_2} \times 2$$

$$= \frac{bd^3}{12} - \frac{\pi}{64}D^4 = \frac{24 \times 30^3}{12} - \frac{\pi}{64}(10)^4$$

$$I_{xx} = 54000 - 490.87 = 53509.1 \text{ cm}^4$$

$\therefore$ $\qquad I_{xx} = \mathbf{53509.1 \text{ cm}^4}$ **Ans.**

and

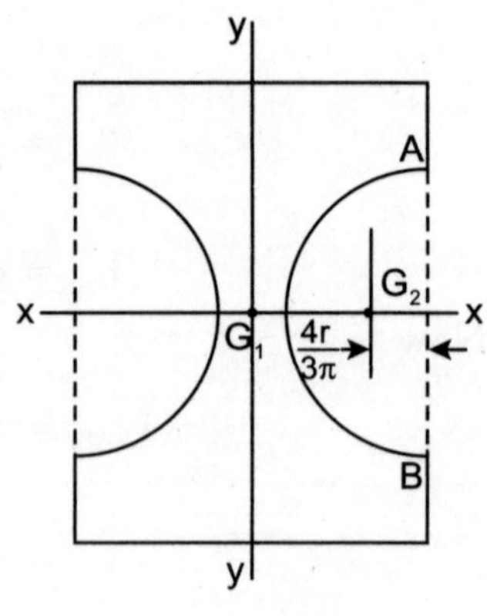

Fig. 22.42

$$I_{yy} = I_{yy_1} - I_{yy_2} \times 2$$

$$I_{yy_1} = \frac{bd^3}{12} = \frac{30 \times 24^3}{12} = 34560 \text{ cm}^4$$

$$I_{AB} = I_{G_2} + a_2 h_2^2$$

$$\frac{1}{2} \times \frac{\pi}{64}D^4 = I_{G_2} + \frac{\pi}{4}D^2 \times \frac{1}{2} \times \left(\frac{4r}{3\pi}\right)^2$$

$$I_{G_2} = \frac{\pi}{128}D^4 - \frac{2}{9\pi} \times \frac{D^4}{4} = 6.85981 \times D^4 \times 10^{-3}$$

$$= 6.85981 \times 10^{-3} \times (20)^4 = 1097.6 \text{ cm}^4$$

Now

$$I_{yy_2} = I_{G_2} + a_2 h_2'^2 = 1097.6 + \frac{\pi}{8} \times 20^2 \times \left(12 - \frac{4r}{3\pi}\right)^2$$

$$= 1097.6 + \frac{\pi}{8} \times 20^2 \times \left(12 - \frac{4 \times 10}{3\pi}\right)^2$$

$$\therefore \quad I_{yy_2} = 1097.6 + 9448.8 = 10546.5 \text{ cm}^4$$

$$\therefore \quad I_{yy} = I_{yy_1} - I_{yy_2} \times 2$$

$$= 34560 - 10546.5 \times 2$$

$$I_{yy} = \mathbf{13467.1 \ cm^4}$$ **Ans.**

Example 22.11

Develop an expression for M.O.I. of area of curve $y = K.x^3$ w.r.t. x and y axes. Area is shown in Fig. 22.43.

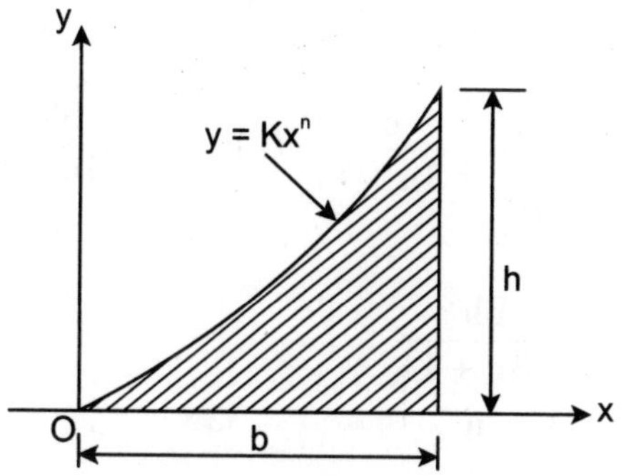

Fig. 22.43

Solution:

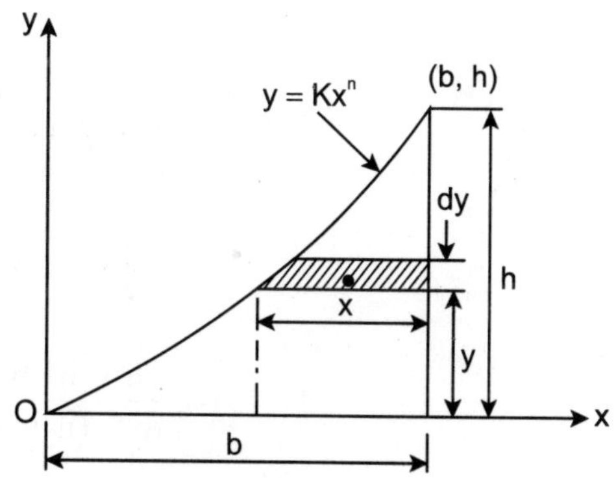

Fig. 22.44

$$y = K \cdot x^n$$

$$\therefore \quad x^n = \left(\frac{y}{K}\right)$$

or

$$x = \left(\frac{y}{K}\right)^{\frac{1}{n}}$$

where x is the length of element.

$$\therefore \quad dA = x \cdot dy$$

$$\therefore \quad I_x = \int_0^h dA \cdot y^2$$

$$= \int_0^h xy^2 dy = \int_0^h y^2 \cdot \left(\frac{y}{K}\right)^{\frac{1}{n}} \cdot dy$$

$$= \frac{1}{(K)^{\frac{1}{n}}} \int_0^h y^{\left(\frac{2n+1}{n}\right)} \cdot dy$$

Also $$K = \frac{y}{x^n} = \frac{h}{b^n}$$

$$\therefore \quad I_x = \frac{1}{(K)^{\frac{1}{n}}} \int_0^h (y)^{\frac{2n+1}{n}} \cdot dy$$

$$= \frac{1}{\left(\frac{h}{b^n}\right)^{\frac{1}{n}}} \cdot \left(\frac{y^{\frac{2n+1}{n}+1}}{\frac{2n+1}{n}+1}\right)_0^h = \frac{b}{(h)^{\frac{1}{n}}} \cdot \left(\frac{y^{\frac{3n+1}{n}}}{\frac{3n+1}{n}}\right)_0^h$$

$$= \frac{1}{(h)^{\frac{1}{n}}} \cdot \left(\frac{n}{3n+1}\right)_0^h (h)^{3+\frac{1}{n}} = \frac{bh^3}{\frac{3n+1}{n}}$$

$$\therefore \quad I_x = \frac{bh^3}{\left(\frac{3n+1}{n}\right)}$$ **Ans.**

Similarly, for I_y,

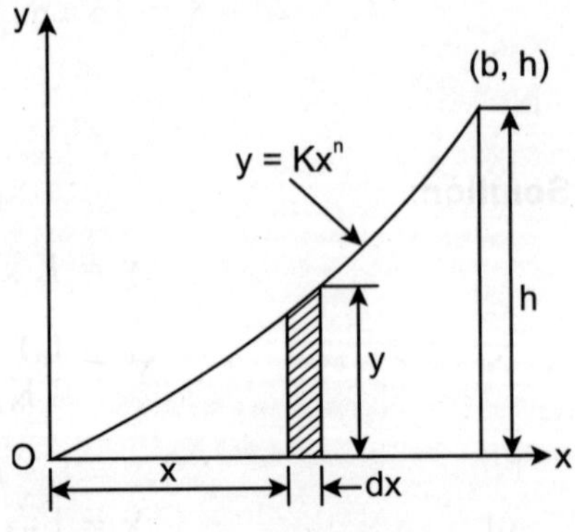

Fig. 22.45

$$I_y = \int_0^b dA \cdot x^2$$

$$= \int_0^b x^2 \cdot y \cdot dx = \int_0^b x^2 \cdot Kx^n$$

$$= K \int_0^b x^{n+2} \cdot dx = K\left(\frac{x^{n+3}}{n+3}\right)_0^b$$

$$= \frac{h}{(b)^n} \cdot \frac{b^n \cdot b^3}{(n+3)} = \frac{b^3 \cdot h}{n+3}$$

$$I_y = \frac{b^3 \cdot h}{n+3}$$ **Ans.**

Example 22.12

From a rectangle of size 16 cm × 24 cm, a hole of 2 cm radius is cut as shown in Fig. 22.46. Determine moment of inertia I_{xx} and I_{yy} about the centroidal axes passing through the centroid of the section.

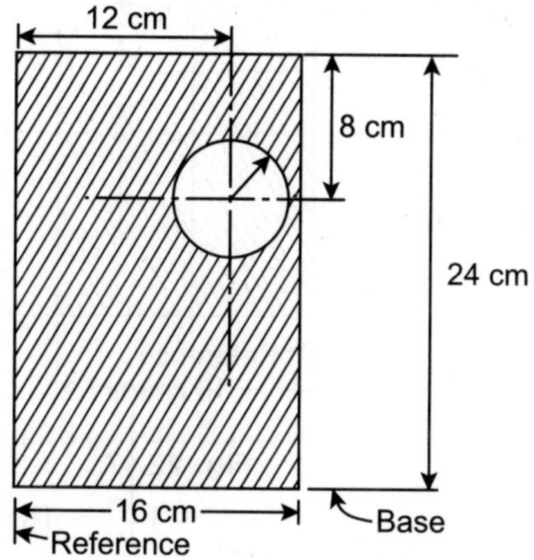

Fig. 22.46

Solution:

$$a_1 = 16 \times 24 = 384 \text{ cm}^2$$
$$a_2 = \pi r^2 = \pi(2)^2 = 12.56 \text{ cm}^2$$
$$y_1 = \frac{24}{2} = 12 \text{ cm} \qquad x_1 = \frac{16}{2} = 8 \text{ cm}$$
$$y_2 = 24 - 8 = 16 \text{ cm} \qquad x_2 = 12 \text{ cm}$$

Now

$$\bar{x} = \frac{a_1x_1 - a_2x_2}{a_1 - a_2} = \frac{384 \times 8 - 12.56 \times 12}{384 - 12.56} = \frac{2921.28}{371.44} = 7.86 \text{ cm}$$

$$\bar{y} = \frac{a_1y_1 - a_2y_2}{a_1 - a_2} = \frac{384 \times 12 - 12.56 \times 16}{371.44} = \frac{4407.04}{371.44} = 11.86 \text{ cm}$$

Now $I_{xx} = I_1 - I_2$ $\qquad \because \; h_1 = y_1 - \bar{y}, \; h_2 = y_2 - \bar{y}$

$$= \frac{bd^3}{12} + a_1h_1^2 - \frac{\pi}{64}d^4 - a_2h_2^2$$

$$= \frac{16 \times 24^3}{12} + 384 \times (12 - 11.86)^2 - \frac{\pi}{64}(2)^4 - 12.56 \times (12 - 16)^2$$

$$= 18432 + 7.52 - 0.78 - 200.96 = 18237.78 \text{ cm}^4$$

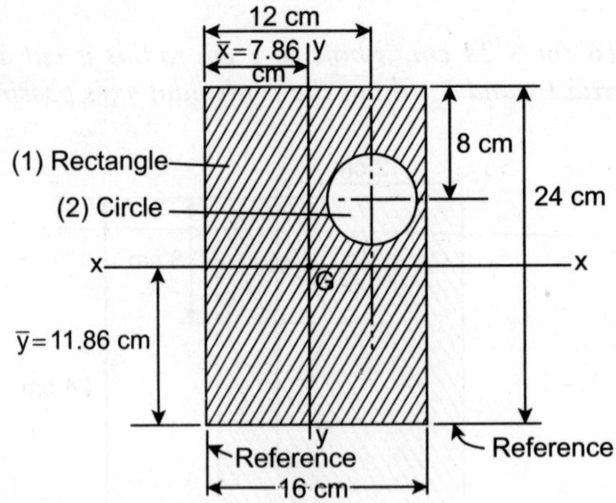

Fig. 22.47

∴ $I_{xx} = 182377.78 \text{ cm}^4$ **Ans.**

Now

$$I_{yy} = I_{y_1} - I_{y_2}$$

$$= \frac{db^3}{12} + a_1h_1^2 - \frac{\pi}{64}d^4 - a_2h_2^2$$

$$= \frac{24 \times 16^3}{12} + 384 \times (\bar{x} - x_1)^2 - \frac{\pi}{64}(2)^4 - 12.56 \times (\bar{x} - x_2)^2$$

$$= 8192 + 384(7.86 - 8)^2\, 8192 - 0.78 - 12.56 \times (7.86 - 12)^2$$

$I_{yy} = 7983.5 \text{ cm}^4$ **Ans.**

Example 22.13

Compute the moment of inertia of the channel section as shown in Fig. 22.48.

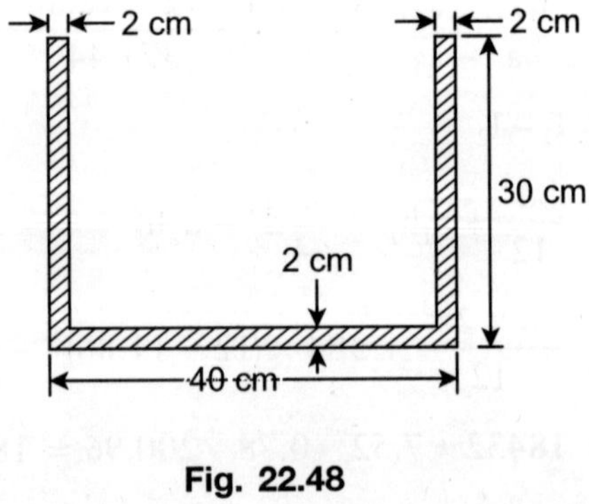

Fig. 22.48

Solution:

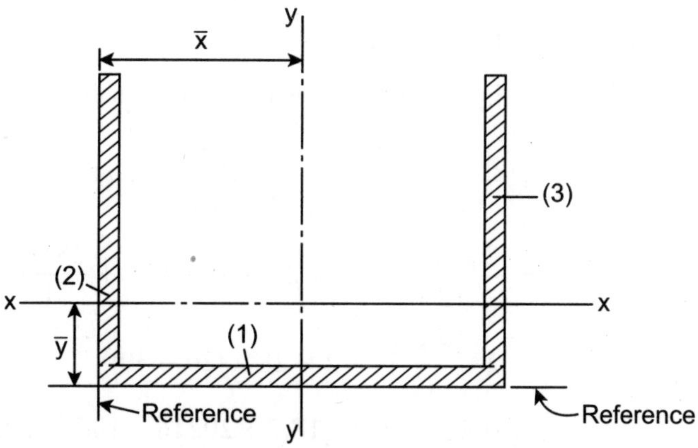

Fig. 22.49

$I_{xx} = ?, \quad I_{yy} = ?$

$a_1 = 40 \times 2 = 80 \text{ cm}^2$	$y_1 = \frac{2}{2} = 1 \text{ cm}$
$a_2 = 28 \times 2 = 56 \text{ cm}^2$	$y_2 = 2 + \frac{28}{2} = 16 \text{ cm}$
$a_3 = 28 \times 2 = 56 \text{ cm}^2$	$y_3 = 16 \text{ cm}$

∵ The section is symmetrical about y–y axis.

∴ C.G. will bie on y–y axis.

∴ $\bar{x} = 20 \text{ cm}$

and $$\bar{y} = \frac{a_1y_1 + a_2y_2 + a_3y_3}{a_1 + a_2 + a_3} = \frac{80 \times 1 + 56 \times 16 + 56 \times 16}{80 + 56 + 56}$$

$$= \frac{1872}{192} = 9.75 \text{ cm}$$

Now

$$I_{xx} = I_{x_1} + I_{x_2} + I_{x_3} = I_{x_1} + 2I_{x_3}$$

$$= I_{G_1} + a_1h_1^2 = 2\left(I_{G_2} + a_2h_2^2\right)$$

$$= \frac{b_1d_1^3}{12} + a_1\left(\bar{y} - y_1\right) + 2\left[\frac{b_2d_2^3}{12} + a_2\left(\bar{y} - y_2\right)^2\right]$$

or $$I_x = \frac{40 \times 2^3}{12} + 40 \times 2 \times (9.75 - 1)^2 + \frac{2 \times 2 \times 28^3}{12} \times (9.75 - 16)^2$$

$$= 26.7 + 6125 + 285833.33 = 291985.03 \text{ cm}^4$$

∴ $I_x = \mathbf{2.9 \times 10^5 \text{ cm}^4}$ **Ans.**

and

$$I_y = I_{y_1} + I_{y_2} + I_{y_3}$$

$$= I_{G_1} + a_1h_1^2 + I_{G_2} + a_2h_2^2 + I_{G_3} + a_3h_3^2$$

$$= \frac{d_1b_1^3}{12} + a_1(\bar{x} - x_1)^2 + \frac{d_2b_2^3}{12} + a_2(\bar{x} - x_1)^2 + \frac{d_3b_3^3}{12} + a_3(\bar{x} - x_3)^2$$

$$= \frac{2 \times 40^3}{12} + 40 \times 2 \times (20 - 20)^2 + \frac{28 \times 2^3}{12} + 2 \times 28 \times (20 - 1)^2$$

$$+ \frac{28 \times 2^3}{12} + 2 \times 28 \times (20 - 39)^2$$

$$= 10666.7 + 0 + 18.7 + 20216 + 18.7 + 20216$$

$$= 51136 \text{ cm}^4$$

$\therefore$ $\mathbf{I_y = 0.51 \times 10^5 \text{ cm}^4}$ **Ans.**

Example 22.14

A compound section is formed by riveting 300 mm × 20 mm flat plates, one on each flange of (ISL 300) 300 mm × 150 mm I-section girder. Find for the compound section:

(i) I_{xx} (ii) I_{yy} (iii) The least radius of gyration.

The properties of I section are as follow:

$I_{xx} = 7332.9 \times 10^4$ mm^4 $I_{yy} = 376.2 \times 10^4$ mm^4 Area $= 48.08 \times 10^2$ mm^2

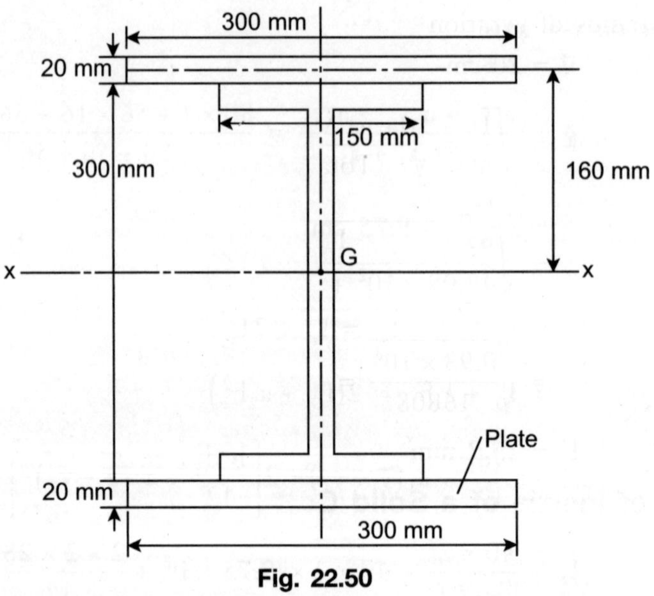

Fig. 22.50

The section is symmetrical about x–x axis and y–y axis.

C.G. of the whole section will lie at G as shown in Fig. 22.50.

$$I_{xx} = I_{xx} \text{ for I-section} + I_{xx} \text{ for two plates}$$

$$= 7332.9 \times 10^4 + 2\left(\frac{bd^3}{12} + ah^2\right)$$

$$= 7332.9 \times 10^4 + 2\left(\frac{300 \times 20^3}{12} + 300 \times 20 \times 160^2\right)$$

$$= 7332.9 \times 10^4 + 3.076 \times 10^8$$

$$I_{xx} = \mathbf{3.8 \times 10^8\ mm^4}$$ **Ans.**

and

$$I_{yy} = I_{yy} \text{ for I-section} + I_{yy} \text{ for two plates}$$

$$= 376.2 \times 10^4 + 2\left(\frac{db^3}{12} + ah^2\right)$$

$$= 376.2 \times 10^4 + 2\left(\frac{20 \times 300^3}{12} + a \times 0\right)$$

$$= 376.2 \times 10^4 + 2\left(\frac{20 \times 300^3}{12} + 0\right)$$

$$I_{yy} = \mathbf{0.93 \times 10^8\ mm^4}$$ **Ans.**

Least value of radius of gyration

$$I = A K^2$$

$$K = \sqrt{\frac{I}{A}} = \sqrt{\frac{\text{Least M.O.I. out of two values}}{\text{Total area of the section}}}$$

$$= \sqrt{\frac{I_{yy}}{48.08 \times 10^2 + 2 \times 300 \times 20}}$$

$$= \sqrt{\frac{0.93 \times 10^8}{16808}} = \sqrt{5578.415}$$

$$K = \mathbf{74.7\ mm}$$ **Ans.**

22.13 Moment of Inertia of a Solid Cone

$$OC = h$$

$$AC = BC = r$$

Considering a thin disc PQ at a distance of x from O and thickness dx.

ΔOPD and ΔOAC are similar

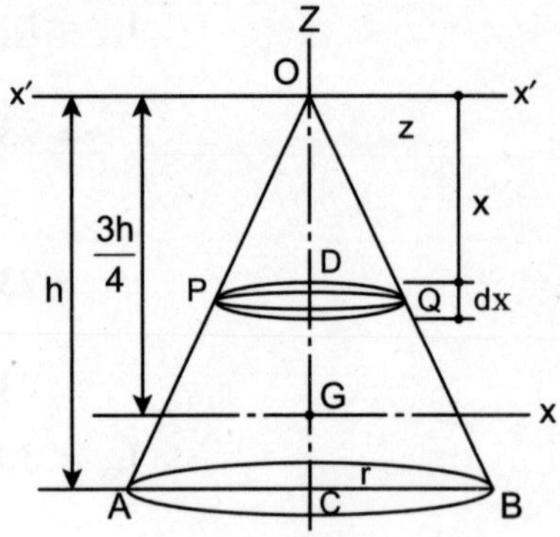

Fig. 22.51

$$\frac{PD}{AC} = \frac{OD}{OC} = \frac{x}{h}$$

$$\Rightarrow \qquad PD = r\cdot\frac{x}{h}$$

Volume of elementary disc

$$dV = \pi r_1^2\cdot dx = \pi(PD)^2\cdot dx = \frac{\pi r^2 x^2}{h^2}dx$$

$$\text{Volume of Cone} = \frac{\pi r^2 h}{3}$$

Let M = Mass of Cone

$$\therefore \text{ Mass per unit volume } = \frac{M}{V} = \frac{M \times 3}{\pi r^2 h} = \frac{3M}{\pi r^2 h} = \rho$$

$\therefore$ Mass of elementary disc = Volume × Density

$$dM = dV \times \rho = \frac{\pi r^2 x^2}{h^2}dx \times \frac{3M}{\pi r^2 h}$$

$$dM = \frac{3Mx^2 dx}{h^3}$$

$$\text{M.O.I. of elementary disc about OC} = \frac{1}{2} m r_1^2$$

$$(dI)_{OC} = \frac{1}{2} \times dM \times PD^2$$

$$= \frac{1}{2} \times \frac{3Mx^2 dx}{h^3} \times \frac{r^2 x^2}{h^2}$$

$$(dI)_{OC} = \frac{3}{2}\,\frac{Mx^4 r^2 dx}{h^5}$$

$\therefore$ Moment of inertia of cone about OC

$$I_{OC} = \int_0^h dI = \int_0^h \frac{3}{2}\,\frac{Mr^2}{h^5}x^4 dx = \frac{3}{10}Mr^2$$

$$I_z = I_{OC} = \frac{3}{10}Mr^2 \qquad \text{.............................} \qquad (22.2)$$

Now, M.O.I. of elementary disc about its dia. PQ.

$$(dI)_{PQ} = \frac{Mr^2}{4} = \frac{1}{4} \times dM \times PD^2 = \frac{dM}{4} \times \frac{r^2 x^2}{h^2}$$

$$= \frac{3Mx^2dx}{4h^3}\cdot\frac{r^2x^2}{h^2} = \frac{3}{4}\frac{Mr^2}{h^5}\times x^4dx$$

$$(I_{x'})_{PQ} = (dI)_{PQ} + M_{PQ}\cdot x^2 \qquad \left|\; \begin{aligned} h &= x \\ M_{PQ} &= dM \end{aligned}\right.$$

$$= \frac{3}{4}\frac{Mr^2x^4dx}{h^5} + dM\cdot x^2$$

$$= \frac{3}{4}\frac{Mr^2x^4dx}{h^5} + \frac{3Mx^2dx}{h^3}\cdot x^2 = \left(\frac{3}{4}\frac{Mr^2}{h^5} + \frac{3M}{h^3}\right)x^4\cdot dx$$

$$I_{x'} = \left(\frac{3}{4}\frac{Mr^2}{h^5} + \frac{3M}{h^3}\right)\int_0^h x^4\cdot dx = \left(\frac{3}{4}\frac{Mr^2}{h^5} + \frac{3M}{h^3}\right)\frac{h^5}{5}$$

$$I_{x'} = \frac{3M}{20}(r^2 + 4h^2) \qquad (22.3)$$

or

$$I_{x'} = \frac{3M}{5}\left(\frac{r^2}{4} + h^2\right) \qquad (22.4)$$

Now

$$(I_G)_{PQ} = (dI)_{PQ} + dM\,h'^2 \qquad \left|\; h' = \left(\frac{3}{4}h - x\right)\right.$$

$$= \frac{3}{4}\frac{Mr^2}{h^5}x^4dx + \frac{3Mx^2dx}{h^3}\cdot\left(\frac{3h}{4} - x\right)^2$$

$$I_{GG} = \int_0^h (I_G)_{PQ}$$

$$I_x = I_{GG} = \frac{3}{4}\frac{Mr^2}{h^5}\int_0^h x^4dx + \frac{3M}{h^3}\int_0^h x^2\left(\frac{3}{4}h - x\right)^2 dx$$

$$= \frac{3}{4}\frac{Mr^2}{h^5}\cdot\frac{h^5}{5} + \frac{3M}{h^3}\left[\frac{3}{16}h^2x^3 + \frac{x^5}{5} - \frac{3}{8}hx^4\right]_0^h$$

$$= \frac{3}{20}Mr^2 + \frac{3M}{h^3}\left[\frac{3}{16}h^5 + \frac{h^5}{5} - \frac{3}{8}h^5\right]$$

$$= \frac{3}{20}Mr^2 + 3Mh^2\left[\frac{15 + 16 - 30}{80}\right]$$

$$= \frac{3}{20}Mr^2 + \frac{3}{80}Mh^2$$

$$I_x = I_{GG} = \frac{3}{20} M\left(r^2 + \frac{h^2}{4}\right) \quad \ldots\ldots (22.5)$$

or

$$I_{GG} = \frac{3}{80} M\left(4r^2 + h^2\right) \quad \ldots\ldots (22.6)$$

Now

$$I_{AB} = I_{GG} + M h'^2 \qquad \Big| \; h' = \text{C.G.} = \frac{h}{4}$$

$$= \frac{3}{20} M\left(r^2 + \frac{h^2}{4}\right) + M\frac{h^2}{16}$$

$$= \frac{3}{20} M r^2 + 80h^2 + \frac{M\cdot h^2}{16}$$

$$= \frac{3}{20} M r^2 + M\cdot h^2\left(\frac{3}{80} + \frac{1}{16}\right)$$

$$I_{AB} = \frac{3}{20} M r^2 + \frac{M h^2}{10}$$

Example 22.15

Determine the M.O.I. of a circular disc about an axis perpendicular the plane of the disc shown in Fig. 22.52.

Solution:

Considering a circular disc of radius r and unit thickness.

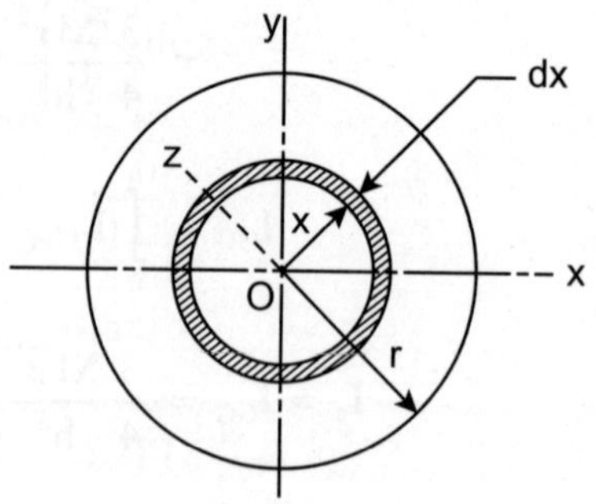

Fig. 22.52

$$I_z = I_O = \int dM\cdot x^2$$

$$dM = 2\pi x\cdot dx\cdot\rho$$

$$\therefore \quad I_z = \int_0^r 2\pi x^3 \rho dx$$

$$= 2\pi\rho\left(\frac{r^4}{4}\right) = \pi r^2\cdot\rho \times \frac{r^2}{2} \qquad \Big| \; M = \pi r^2 \times \rho$$

$$I_z = \frac{M r^2}{2} \quad \ldots\ldots (22.7)$$

For hollow disc of radii r_i and r_o

$$I_z = \int x^2\cdot dM = \int x^2\cdot 2\pi x dx\cdot\rho = \int_{r_i}^{r_o} 2\pi x^3 dx\cdot\rho$$

$$= 2\pi\rho\left[\frac{x^4}{4}\right]_{r_i}^{r_o} = \frac{2\pi\rho}{4}\left(r_o^{\,4} - r_i^{\,4}\right)$$

$$= \frac{\pi\rho}{2}\left(r_o^{\,4} - r_i^{\,4}\right) = \frac{\pi\rho}{2}\left(r_o^{\,2} + r_i^{\,2}\right)\left(r_o^{\,2} - r_i^{\,2}\right)$$

$$I_z = \frac{M\left(r_o^{\,2} - r_i^{\,2}\right)}{2}; \qquad \Big| \; M = \pi\left(r_o^{\,2} - r_i^{\,2}\right)\rho$$

Example 22.16

Determine M.O.I. of a right circular cylinder of radius r and height h w.r.t. geometric axis.

Solution:

$$I_{zz} = \int x^2 dM$$

$$dM = \rho dV = \rho\cdot 2\pi x dx\cdot h$$

$$\therefore \quad I_{zz} = \int_0^r x^2\cdot\rho\cdot 2\pi x dx\cdot h$$

$$= 2\pi\rho h\int_0^r \frac{x^3}{1}dx$$

$$= 2\pi\rho h\left[\frac{x^4}{4}\right]_0^r = 2\pi\rho h\cdot\frac{r^4}{4}$$

$$= \pi\rho h\frac{r^2}{2}\cdot r^2$$

$$= \frac{1}{2}\times(\pi r^2 h\times\rho)r^2$$

$$= \frac{1}{2}M\cdot r^2$$

$$\therefore \quad I_{zz} = \frac{M\cdot r^2}{2}$$

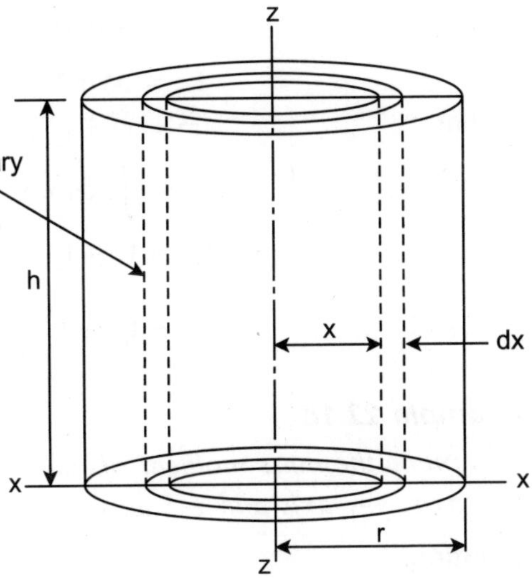

Fig. 22.53

Example 22.17

Determine the mass moment of inertia of a circular ring of radius r.

Solution:

ρ = Mass per unit length of the ring

ds = Elemental length of ring

Oz = Axis passing through C.G. and ⊥ to the plane of the ring

dM = Mass of elemental part

Thickness of ring is unity.

Now

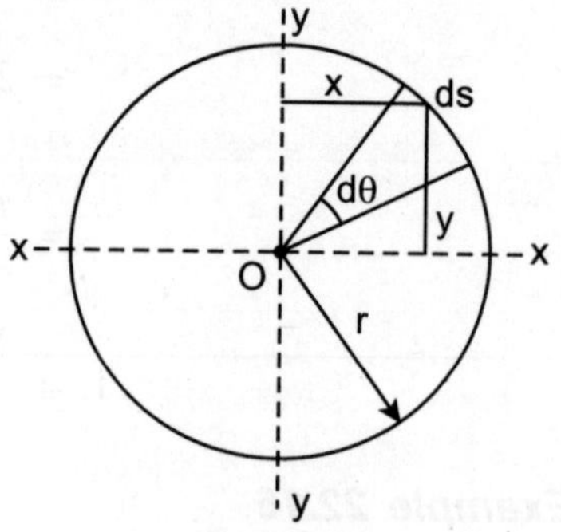

Fig. 22.54

$$dM = \rho ds$$
$$I_x = \rho ds \times y^2$$
$$I_y = \rho ds \times x^2$$
$$I_z = \rho ds \times r^2$$

where $r^2 = x^2 + y^2$

$$\therefore \quad I_{zz} = \int \rho ds \times r^2 = \rho r^2 \int ds = \rho r^2 \times 2\pi r$$
$$= 2\pi r \cdot \rho \cdot r^2 = Mr^2$$

$$\therefore \quad I_{zz} = M \cdot r^2 \qquad | \; 2\pi r \cdot \rho = M$$

but $r^2 = x^2 + y^2$

$$\therefore \quad I_{zz} = \int \rho ds \times x^2 + \int \rho ds \times y^2$$
$$\Rightarrow \quad Mr^2 = I_{yy} + I_{xx}$$
$$\Rightarrow \quad I_{xx} = I_{yy} = \frac{M \cdot r^2}{2}$$

Example 22.18

Determine the mass moment of inertia of a circular lamina of radius r and density ρ about x–x axis, y–y axis and z–z axis.

Solution:

$I_{xx} = ?$

$I_{yy} = ?$

$I_{zz} = ?$

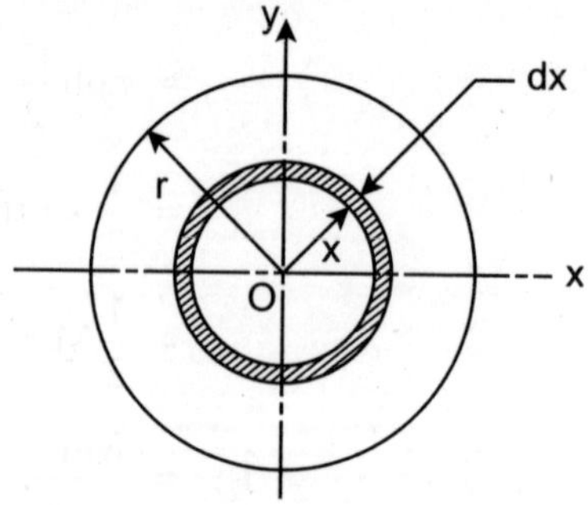

Fig. 22.55

Now

Mass moment of inertia of small ring about x–x axis

$$= \text{Mass} \times \frac{(\text{radius})^2}{2} = 2\pi x \cdot \rho \times \frac{x^2}{2}$$

$$\therefore \quad I_{xx} = \int_0^r 2\pi x\rho \cdot \frac{x^2}{2} = \pi\rho\left[\frac{x^4}{4}\right]_0^r = \pi\rho \cdot \frac{r^4}{4}$$
$$= \pi r^2 \cdot \rho \cdot \frac{r^2}{4} = \frac{M \cdot r^2}{4}$$

$$\therefore \quad I_{xx} = \frac{M \cdot r^2}{4}$$ **Ans.**

Similarly, $$I_{yy} = \frac{M \cdot r^2}{4}$$ **Ans.**

$$I_{zz} = I_{xx} + I_{yy} = \frac{M \cdot r^2}{4} + \frac{M \cdot r^2}{4}$$

$\therefore$ $$I_{zz} = \frac{M \cdot r^2}{2}$$ **Ans.**

22.14 Moment of Inertia of a Uniform Thin Rod

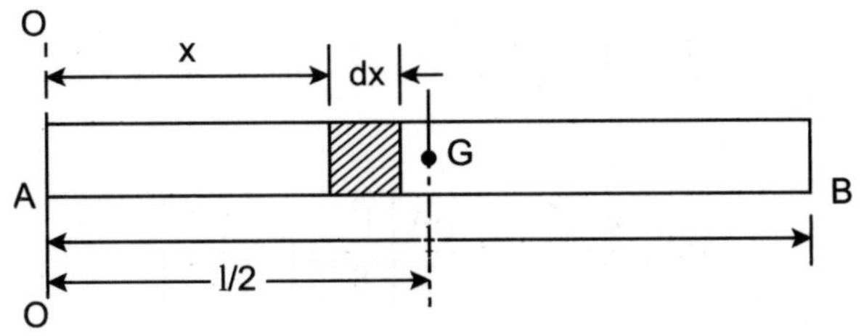

Fig. 22.56

Let

m = Mass per unit length of rod

M = Total mass of the rod = m × l

I_{yy} = ?

Mass of strip = m·dx

$\therefore$ M.O.I. of strip = (Mass of strip) × x^2

$= mx^2dx$

$\therefore$ $$I_{yy} = \int_0^l mx^2dx$$

$$= m\left[\frac{x^3}{3}\right]_0^l$$

$$I_{yy} = \frac{m \cdot l^3}{3} = \frac{m}{l} \cdot \frac{l^3}{3} = \frac{Ml^2}{3} \quad \ldots\ldots (22.8)$$

and $$I_G = I_{yy} - Mh^2$$

$$= \frac{Ml^2}{3} - M\left(\frac{l}{2}\right)^2 = Ml^2\left(\frac{1}{3} - \frac{1}{4}\right)$$

$$I_G = \frac{Ml^2}{12} \quad \ldots\ldots (22.9)$$

Example 22.19

Determine the M.O.I. of a rod of length l.

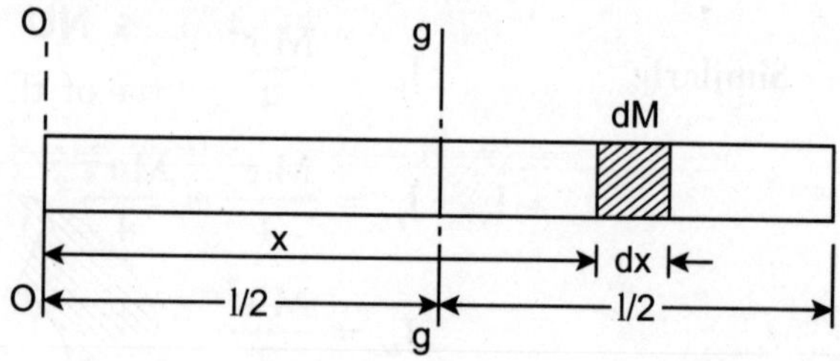

Fig. 22.57

Solution:

$$I_g = \int x^2 dM$$

$$dM = \rho dV = \rho \cdot A \cdot dx$$

$$\therefore \quad I_g = \int_{-\frac{l}{2}}^{+\frac{l}{2}} x^2 \cdot \rho A \cdot dx$$

$$= \rho A \left[\frac{x^3}{3}\right]_{-\frac{l}{2}}^{\frac{l}{2}} = \frac{\rho A}{3}\left[\frac{l^3}{8} - \left(-\frac{l^3}{8}\right)\right]$$

$$= \frac{\rho A}{3} \cdot \frac{2l^2}{8} = \frac{\rho A l^2}{12} = \frac{M \cdot l^2}{12} \qquad | \, M = \rho \cdot A$$

$$I_g = \frac{M \cdot l^2}{12} \quad \text{.................................} \quad (22.10)$$

$$I_O = I_g + M h^2 \qquad h = \frac{l}{2}$$

$$= \frac{Ml^2}{12} + \frac{Ml^2}{4}$$

$$= Ml^2\left(\frac{1+3}{12}\right) = \frac{Ml^2}{3}$$

$$\therefore \quad I_O = \frac{Ml^2}{3} \quad \text{.................................} \quad (22.11)$$

$$= \pi \rho h \frac{r^2}{2} \cdot r^2$$

where M = Total mass of the rod.

THEORITICAL & NUMERICAL QUESTIONS

1. Find the polar moment of inertia of the shaded area as shown in Fig. 22.58.

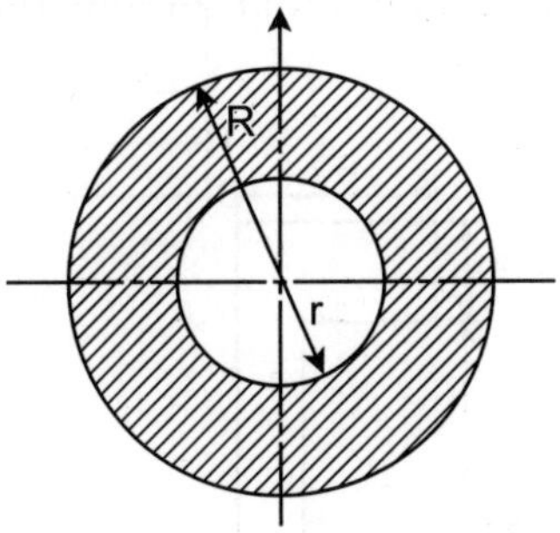

Fig. 22.58

2. Find the M.O.I. of section shown in Fig. 22.59, about AB.

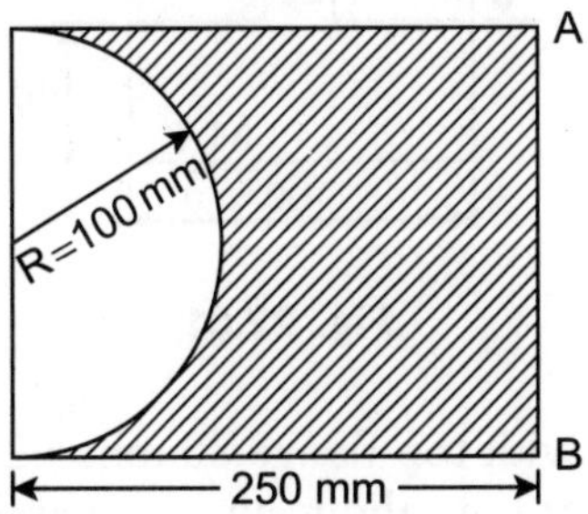

Fig. 22.59

3. Determine the M.O.I. and radius of gyration of a homogeneous solid sphere of mass M and radius r about a diameter.

4. Calculate the M.O.I. of a plane Fig. 22.60 as shown about the base and centroidal axis.

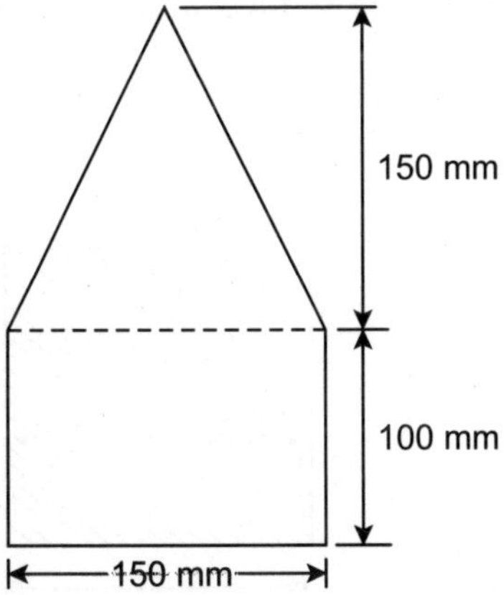

Fig. 22.60

5. The M.O.I. of a rectangular section about x–x and y–y axes passing through C.G. are 270×10^6 mm^4 and 43.2×10^6 mm^4. Find the size of the section.
6. Calculate the M.O.I. of the section about an axis through C.G. and parallel to base as shown in Fig. 22.61.

All diamensions are in mm

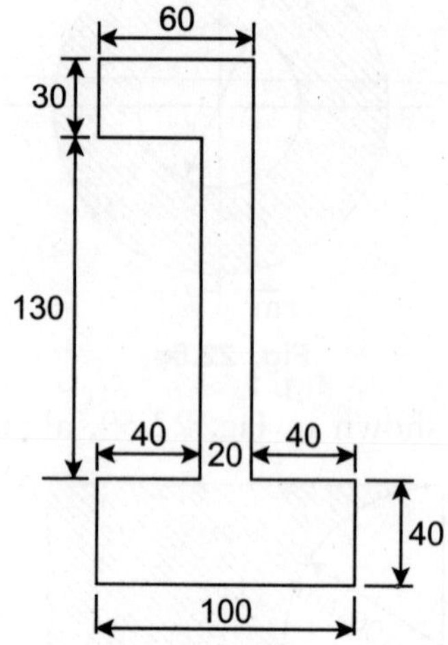

Fig. 22.61

7. Find M.O.I. of an I-section with top flange 80 mm × 20 mm, web 120 mm × 20 mm and bottom flange 160 mm × 20 mm about an axis passing through the C.G. and parallel to the flange.
8. State and prove the theorem of perpendicular axis applied to moment of inertia.
9. Describe the method of finding the M.O.I. of a composite section.
10. Determine the M.O.I. of a circular area about the centroidal axes.
11. Determine the M.O.I. of the shaded area w.r.t. x–axis and y–axis.

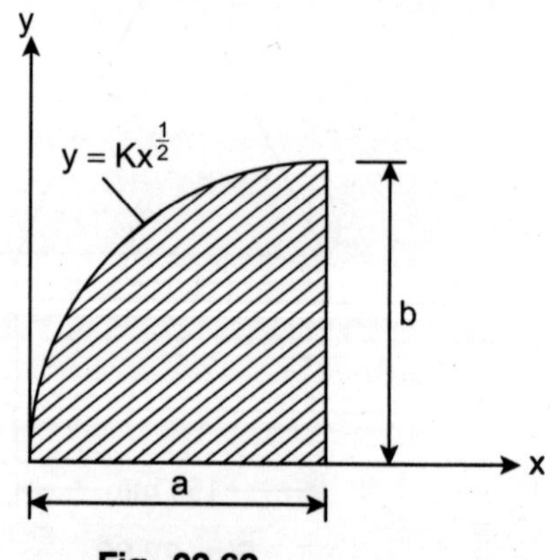

Fig. 22.62

12. Calculate M.O.I. about the edge BC of the parallelogram as shown in Fig. 22.63.

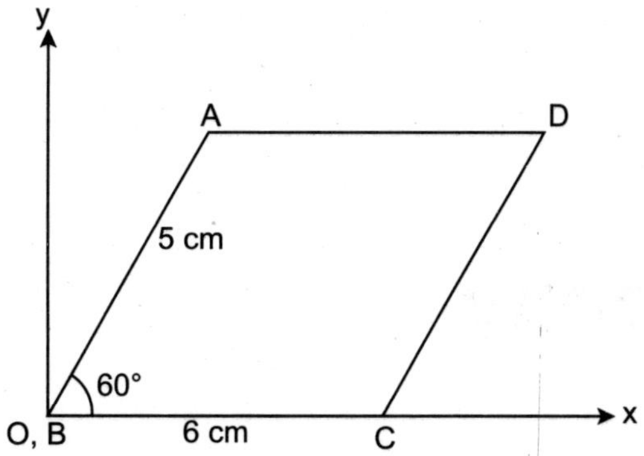

Fig. 22.63

Bibliography

Andrew, Pytel and Singer, F.L., *Strength of Materials*, Fourth Edition, Addison-Wesley, 1999.

Bear, Ferdinand P. and Russell, E., Johnston Jr, *Vector Mechanics for Engineers, Dynamics & Statics*, Third Edition, Tata McGraw-Hill Publishing Company Ltd., Delhi.

Beds, D.S., *Strength of Material*, Khanna Book Publishing Company (P) Ltd., Delhi.

G.J., Van Wylen and R.E., *Fundamentals of Classical Thermodynamics*, John Wiley and Sons Inc., New York.

Hall, N.A. and Ibele, W.E., *Engineering Thermodynamics*, Prentice-Hall Inc., Englewood Cliffs, N.J., 1960.

Hearn, E.J., *Mechanics of Materials*, Vol. I and Vol. II, Third Edition, Butter Worth Heinemann, 2001.

Hibblor, R.C., *Mechanics of Materials*, Macmillan Publishing Company, New York.

Holman, J.P., *Thermodynamics*, Third Edition, McGraw-Hill Book Company, New York, 1988.

Kazimi, S.M.A., *Solid Mechanics*, Tata McGraw-Hill, 1st Edition, New Delhi, 2002.

Meriam, J.L. and Kraige, L.G., *Engineering Mechanics*, Vol. I, Forth Edition, John Willey & Sons Inc., 1998.

Meriam, J.L. and Kraige, L.G., *Engineering Mechanics*, Vol. II, Fourth Edition, John Willey & Sons Inc., 1998.

Mokashi, V.S., *Engineering Mechanics-1*, Tata McGraw-Hill Publishing Company Ltd., New Delhi.

Mokashi, V.S., *Problems and Solutions in Engineering Mechanics, Statics and Dynamics,* Tata McGraw-Hill Publishing Company Ltd., Delhi.

Nag, P.K., *Mechanical Engineering*, Tata McGraw-Hill, Second Edition, New Delhi, 2002.

Palonichamy, M.S. and Nagam, S., *Engineering Mechanics*, Tata McGraw-Hill Publishing Company Ltd., New Delhi, 2002.

Popov, Egor P., *Engineering Mechanics of Solids*, Second Edition, Pearson Education, ASTA, 2003.

Ryder, G.H., *Strength of Materials*, Third Edition, Macmillan India Ltd., 2000.

Shames, Irving H., *Engineering Mechanics, Statics and Dynamics*, Fourth Edition, Prentice-Hall of India Private Ltd., Delhi.

Singh, D.K., *Mechanics of Solids*, Pearson Education Asia, New Delhi, 2002.

Srinath, L.S., *Advanced Mechanics of Solids*, Tata McGraw-Hill Publishing Company Ltd., Delhi, 1999.

Timoshenko, S. and Young, H.D., *Engineering Mechanics*, Fourth Edition, McGraw-Hill Book Company.

Timoshonko, S.P. and Young, D.H., *Elements of Strength of Materials*, Fifth Edition, East-West Press (P) Ltd., 2000.

